Indonesia

a travel survival kit

Joe Cummings
Susan Forsyth
John Noble
Alan Samagalski
Tony Wheeler

Indonesia - a travel survival kit
  2nd edition

Published by
  Lonely Planet Publications
  Head Office: PO Box 617, Hawthorn, Victoria 3122,
  Australia
  US Office: PO Box 2001A, Berkeley, CA 94702, USA

Printed by
  Singapore National Printers Ltd, Singapore

Photographs by
  Alan Samagalski (AS)
  Joost Hoetjes (JH)
  Mary Coverton (MC)
  John Noble (JN)
  Joe Cummings (JC)
  Hugh Finlay (HF)
  Vicki Beale (VB)
  Richard Nebesky (RN)
  Tony Wheeler (TW)
  Front cover: Looking down the terraces, Borobudur, Java – Peter Freeman

Cartoons by
  Tony Jenkins

First Published
  September 1986

This Edition
  January 1990

> **Bali & Lombok**
> The 'nuts and bolts' information about Bali and Lombok in this book is identical to the information in
> *Bali & Lombok – a travel survival kit*.

Although the author and publisher have tried to make the information as accurate as possible, they accept no responsibility for any loss, injury or inconvenience sustained by any person using this book.

National Library of Australia Cataloguing in Publication Data

Wheeler, Tony, 1946 –
  Indonesia, a travel survival kit.

  2nd ed.
  Includes index.
  ISBN 0 86442 044 7.

  1. Indonesia — Description and travel — 1981 Guide-books. I.

915.980438

Alan Samagalski Alan joined LP in 1982 after a long stay on the Indian subcontinent. Before this he worked in the Melbourne University Genetics Department, while baffling audiences at the 'Last Laugh' and 'Comedy Cafe' theatre restaurants. Alan then set off to research our *China* guide, followed by the 1st edition of this book. He has also written guides to *Chile* and *Argentina*, and contributed to several other LP books.

Tony Wheeler was born in England but spent his school years in Pakistan, the West Indies and the USA. He then did an engineering degree in the UK, worked briefly as an automotive engineer, went back to university and did an MBA, then dropped out on the Asian overland trail with his wife Maureen. They've been travelling, writing and publishing guide-books ever since, having set up Lonely Planet Publications in the mid-70s.

John Noble & Susan Forsyth are from Clitheroe (England) and Melbourne (Australia), respectively. John came to LP after a decade of journalism from Clitheroe to Hong Kong; Susan after working in Australian schools went volunteer teaching in Sri Lanka and met John while he was researching LP's Sri Lanka guide. Together they updated half of *Australia* and John co-authored *Mexico*. While writing up Indonesia, they got married and went to live in a a 17th-century farmhouse in North Hampshire.

Joe Cummings has long been involved in South-East Asian studies. He's been a Peace Corps volunteer in Thailand, a translator/interpreter of Thai, a graduate student in Thai language and Asian art history, an East-West Center Scholar, a university lecturer and a bilingual consultant for schools. Joe wrote Lonely Planet's *Thailand* guide and *Thai phrasebook* and helped update LP guides to *Malaysia, Singapore & Brunei*, *Burma* and *South-East Asia on a shoestring*.

Lonely Planet Credits

Editors	Frith Pike
	Peter Turner
Maps	Peter Flavelle
Design, illustrations	Margaret Jung
& cover design	
Typesetting	Ann Jeffree
	Gaylene Miller

Thanks also to Lyn McGaurr for proof reading, to Sharon Wertheim for indexing, to Vicki Beale for design assistance and to Tony Wheeler, Alan Samagalski, John Noble, Roberto Petroni and Richard Nebesky for black & white photographs.

Acknowledgements Susan Forsyth and John Noble would like to thank all the many people who helped them along the way, especially Jonas and Scorpio, Made Nurjana and everyone whose letters helped fill out the picture of these remote regions, notably Miriam Bouverat, Dee Loader-Oliver, Chris Howe, Ralph Carabetta, David Golebiewski and the East Timor pioneers Victor Esbensen, Joakim Boes, Martin Dufty, Stephen Meredith and Horst.

Joe Cummings thanks Doug Glenn, Don Campbell, Michael Ewing, Axel Ridder, Saint Abu, Makmud, Riadi, Rusty & Marjo, Hendy Koesmiadi, Richard Eaton, Kevin & Hanni, Johan & Lina and Jailani for all their assistance along the road. Special thanks to Lynne for her cartographic help and to Allah for sparing Joe's life in the Sunda Straits.

From the authors comes a note of thanks to all those people who sent letters, postcards and other pieces of paper, large and small, telling about their travels through Indonesia and what was going on out there.

A Warning & a Request

Things change – prices go up, schedules change, good places go bad and bad places go bankrupt – nothing stays the same. So if you find things better or worse, recently opened or long since closed, please write and tell us and help make the next edition better!

Your letters will be used to help update future editions and, where possible, important changes will also be included as a Stop Press section in reprints.

All information is greatly appreciated and the best letters will receive a free copy of the next edition, or any other Lonely Planet book of your choice.

This Edition

Following in the footsteps of Ginny Bruce, Mary Covernton and Alan Samagalski, the writer-researchers for the first edition, five experienced LP authors including Alan Samagalski travelled to Indonesia to update the information for this second edition.

Alan went to Sumatra and Sulawesi adding another 20 cm or so to the deepening tourist trenches of Sumatra. He also took a crash course in the pioneer spirit, wading around knee-deep in the mud-clogged goat trails which masquerade as roads through central Sulawesi. As they say in northern Sumatra, *Nala si daed!*. Joe Cummings visited Java and Kalimantan; Susan Forsyth and John Noble spent four months in Nusa Tenggara, Maluku and Irian Jaya – outer provinces which are attracting increasing numbers of travellers these days, while Tony Wheeler returned to Bali and Lombok to research *Bali & Lombok*, accompanied once again by Maureen and their children Tashi and Kieran.

As usual, collective thanks go to our readers who took the time to write to with their suggestions on travel in Indonesia. They include: Marinus Albers (Nl), H Allan, Robert Andechsbeager, Hans-Erik Andersen (Dk), Patrick Andersson, Grant Andrews (NZ), Christian Awuy, Ron Barcikowski (USA),

continued page 891

Contents

Introduction

Like a string of jewels in a coral sea, the 13,000 islands of the Indonesian archipelago stretch almost 5000 km from the Asian mainland into the Pacific Ocean. And like jewels the islands have long represented wealth. A thousand years ago the Chinese sailed as far as Timor to load up cargoes of sandalwood and beeswax; by the 16th century the spice islands of the Moluccas were luring European navigators from the other side of the world in search of cloves, nutmeg and mace, once so rare and expensive that bloody wars were fought for control of their production and trade. The Dutch ruled for almost 350 years, drawing their fortunes from the islands whose rich volcanic soil could produce two crops of rice a year, as well as commercially valuable crops like coffee, sugar, tobacco and teak.

Endowed with a phenomenal array of natural resources and strange cultures, Indonesia became a magnet for every shade of entrepreneur from the west – a stamping ground for proselytising missionaries, unscrupulous traders, wayward adventurers, inspired artists. It has been overrun by Dutch and Japanese armies; surveyed, drilled, dug up and shipped off by foreign mining companies; littered end to end with the 'transmigrants' of Java and Bali; poked and prodded by ethnologists, linguists and anthropologists turning fading cultures into PhD theses.

But one group which Indonesia has never really attracted is the tourist. With the exception of Bali, Torajaland, and the Hindu-Buddhist monuments of Borobudur and Prambanan in Central Java, all of which attract huge numbers of visitors, the islands of western Indonesia are often seen as places to pass through on the way down to Australia or on the way up to the Asian mainland – rather than as destinations in their own right – while the outer islands are considered too expensive to reach or too difficult or time-consuming to travel in. Both views are out-of-date. Travel in some parts of the outer islands can still be tedious, but over the last 10 years things have improved considerably; there are more roads and more buses, more ferry, shipping and air connections between the islands, and the rather neglected tourist industry is being promoted by the government – making it easier to travel than ever before.

Indonesia possesses some of the most remarkable sights in South-East Asia and there are things about this country you will never forget: the flaming red and orange sunsets over the mouth of the Kapuas River in Kalimantan; standing on the summit of Keli Mutu in Flores and gazing at the coloured lakes that fill its volcanic craters; the lumbering leather-skinned dragons of Komodo Island; expatriates in Yogyakarta using an Asian language – *Bahasa Indonesia* – as the common means of communication; the funeral ceremonies of the Torajas in the highlands of Central Sulawesi; the Dani tribesmen of Irian Jaya wearing little else but feathers and penis gourds; the wooden *wayang golek* puppets manipulated into life by the puppet-masters of Yogyakarta; the brilliant coral reefs off Manado on the north coast of Sulawesi.

You can lie on your back on Kuta Beach in Bali and soak up the ultra-violet rays, paddle a canoe down the rivers of Kalimantan, surf at the island of Nias off the coast of Sumatra, trek in the high country of Irian Jaya, catch butterflies the size of your hand in Central Sulawesi, eat your way through a kaleidoscope of fruit from one end of the archipelago to the other, stare down the craters of live volcanoes, learn the art of batik in Yogyakarta or the techniques of kite-making from any Indonesian kid – almost anything you want, Indonesia has got!

Facts about the Country

HISTORY
In the Beginning
It's generally held that the earliest inhabitants of the Indonesian archipelago came from India or Burma, while later migrants, known as 'Malays', came from southern China and Indo-China. This second group is reckoned to have entered the Indonesian archipelago gradually over several thousand years.

Among its phases, it's thought, was what's known as the Dongson Culture, which originated in Vietnam and southern China about 3000 years ago and spread to Indonesia bringing with it techniques of irrigated rice growing, ritual buffalo sacrifice, bronze-casting, the custom of erecting large monumental stones (megaliths) and some of the peculiar *ikat* weaving methods found in pockets of Indonesia today. Some of these practices have survived only in isolated islands or areas which were little touched by later arrivals and cultural currents – such as the Batak areas of Sumatra, Tanatoraja in Sulawesi, parts of Kalimantan and several islands of Nusa Tenggara.

From the 7th century BC – approximately the time of the Dongson arrival – there were well-developed and organised societies in the Indonesian archipelago. The inhabitants knew how to irrigate rice fields, domesticate animals, use copper and bronze, and had some knowledge of sea navigation. There were villages – often permanent ones – where life was linked to the production of rice, the staple crop.

These early Indonesians were animists, believing that all animate and inanimate objects have their own particular life force, *semangat* or soul. Certain people had more semangat than others – such as the tribal and village leaders, and the *shamans* or priests who had magical powers and could control the spirit world. The spirits of the dead had to be honoured

since their semangat could still help the living; there was a belief in the afterlife and weapons and utensils would be left in tombs for use in the next world. Supernatural forces were held responsible for natural events, and evil spirits had to be placated by offerings, rites and ceremonies. In a region where earthquakes, volcanic eruptions and torrential rainstorms are common events, a belief in malevolent spirits is hardly surprising.

Villages, at least in Java, developed into embryonic towns, and by the 1st century AD small kingdoms (little more than collections of villages subservient to petty chieftains) evolved with their own ethnic and tribal religions. The climate of Java, with its hot, even temperature, plentiful rainfall and volcanic soil was ideal for the wet-field method of rice cultivation, known as *sawah* cultivation. The well-organised society it required may explain why the people of Java and Bali developed a more sophisticated civilisation than those of the other islands. The dry field or *ladang* method of rice cultivation is a much simpler form of agriculture and requires no elaborate social structure.

The social and religious duties of the rice-growing communities were gradually refined to form the basis of *adat* or customary law. This traditional law was to persist through waves of imported religious beliefs – Hinduism, Buddhism, Islam and Christianity – and still remains a force in Indonesia today.

The Coming of Hinduism & Buddhism
One of the puzzles of Indonesian history is how the early kingdoms on Sumatra, Java, Kalimantan and Bali were penetrated by Hinduism and Buddhism. The oldest works of Hindu art in Indonesia, statues from the 3rd century AD, come from Sulawesi and Sumatra.

The earliest Hindu inscriptions, in Sanskrit, have been found in West Java and eastern Kalimantan and date from the early 5th century AD.

Several theories regarding the influx of Hinduism and Buddhism have been proposed. Large scale immigration from India is generally ruled out and there is no evidence for the theory that Indian princes, defeated in wars in India, fled to the islands of South-East Asia and established kingdoms on the Indian model. Certainly Indian traders brought Tamil, the language of southern India, but only Brahmins could have brought Sanskrit, the language of religion and philosophy. Some Brahmins may have followed the traders as missionaries – although Hinduism is not a proselytising religion. On the other hand Buddhism *is* a proselytising religion and was carried far from its Indian homeland.

Another theory holds that the early Indonesians were attracted to the cultural life of India in much the same way as the Elizabethan English were to that of Italy. The Indonesian aristocracy may have played an active role in transferring Indian culture to Indonesia by inviting Brahmin priests to their courts. Possibly it was hoped that the new religions could provide occult powers and a mythological sanction for the Indonesian rulers – as had happened in India. This theory fits in well with the mythological and mystical view of history which has persisted since the beginning of recorded Indonesian civilisation. In the Hindu period the kings were seen as incarnations of Vishnu. Even after the arrival of Islam the dynasties traced their lineage on one side back to Mohammed and from there to the prophets and Adam – but on the other side it was traced to the heroes of the *wayang*, the indigenous puppet theatre of Java, and to gods which orthodox Muslims considered pagan. One Sumatran dynasty even claimed descent from Alexander the Great and as late as the second half of the 19th century the rulers of Solo were

boasting of a special alliance with Nyai Lara Kidul, the Goddess of the South Seas, and with Sunan Lawu, the ruler of the spirits on Mt Lawu.

The Development of Early Sea Trade

Foreign traders were attracted by the Indonesian archipelago's unique local products. Foremost were spices which were used as flavourings and also to preserve food (meat in particular). Sumatra was famous for gold, pepper and benzoin (an aromatic gum valued especially by the Chinese) but the real 'Spice Islands' were the tiny specks in the region now known as Maluku (the Moluccas): Ternate and Tidore islands off the coast of Halmahera, Ambon and Banda. These islands grew nutmeg and cloves which could be used for spices and preservatives, in the manufacture of perfumes, and for medicinal purposes. By the 1st century AD Indonesian trade was firmly established with other parts of Asia, including China and India. Indian trade, the more active of the two, linked India, China and Indonesia with Greece and Rome – Ptolemy mentions the islands of Indonesia in his writings as early as 165 AD.

The Early Kingdoms

The Sumatran Hindu-Buddhist kingdom of Srivijaya rose in the 7th century AD and while its power has been romanticised, it nevertheless maintained a substantial international trade – run by Tamils and Chinese. It was the first major Indonesian commercial seapower, able to control much of the trade in South-East Asia by virtue of its control of the Straits of Melaka between Sumatra and the Malay peninsula.

Merchants from Arabia, Persia and India brought goods to the coastal cities to exchange for both local products and goods from China and the spice islands. Silk, porcelain, and Chinese rhubarb (peculiar for its medicinal properties) came from China in return for ivory, tortoise shell, rhinoceros horn, cloves, cardamom and pepper, as well as precious wood like ebony and camphor wood, perfumes, pearls, coral, camphor oil, amber and the dull reddish-white precious stone known as cornelian or chalcedony. Exports to Arabia included aloes for medicinal uses, camphor oil, sandalwood, ebony and sapanwood (from which a red dye is made), ivory, tin and spices. By the 13th century woollen and cotton cloth, as well as iron and rice, were imported to Sumatra.

Meanwhile, on Java, the Buddhist Shailendra and the Hindu Mataram dynasties flourished on the plains of Central Java between the 8th and 10th centuries. While Srivijaya's trade brought it wealth, these land-based states had far greater manpower at their disposal and left magnificent remains, in particular the vast Buddhist monument of Borobudur and the huge Hindu temple complex of Prambanan.

Thus two types of states evolved in Indonesia. The first, typified by Srivijaya, were the mainly Sumatran coastal states – commercially oriented, their wealth

Ground plan of Borobudur

derived from international trade and their cities highly cosmopolitan. In contrast, the inland kingdoms of Java, separated from the sea by volcanoes (like the kingdom of Mataram in the Solo River region), were agrarian cultures, bureaucratic, conservative, with a marked capacity to absorb and transform the Indian influences.

Relief from Borobudur

By the end of the 10th century, the centre of power had moved from Central to East Java where a series of kingdoms held sway until the rise of the Majapahit kingdom. This is the period when Hinduism and Buddhism were syncretised and when Javanese culture began to come into its own, finally spreading its influence to Bali. By the 12th century Srivijaya's power seems to have declined and the empire broke up into smaller kingdoms.

The Hindu Majapahit Kingdom

One of the greatest of Indonesian states and the last important kingdom to remain predominantly Hindu until its extinction was Majapahit. Founded in East Java in 1293, the kingdom had a brief period of conquering glory but in the late 14th century the influence of Majapahit began to decline.

The power of the kingdom was largely due to the rigorous action of one of its early prime ministers, Gajah Mada. Gajah Mada was a royal guard who put down an anti-royalist revolt in the 1320s and then, during the reign of Hayam Wuruk, brought parts of Java and other areas under control. The kingdom has often been portrayed as an Indonesian version of Rome, with its own vast empire, but it is now thought that its power did not extend beyond Java, Bali and the island of Madura. If Gajah Mada did have some control over the other islands he did not govern them like the Romans governed Europe or the Dutch governed Indonesia. Instead it's likely to have been trade which linked these regions and at the Majapahit end this trade was probably a royal monopoly.

Hayam Wuruk's reign is usually referred to as an Indonesian Golden Age, comparable with the Tang Dynasty of China. One account, by the court poet Prapanca, credits the Majapahits with control over much of the coastal regions of Sumatra, Borneo, Sulawesi, Maluku, Sumbawa and Lombok, and also states that the island of Timor sent tribute. The kingdom is said to have maintained regular relations with China, Vietnam, Cambodia, Annam and Siam. However by 1389 (25 years after the death of Gajah Mada) the kingdom was on the decline, and the coastal dependencies in northern Java were in revolt.

The Penetration of Islam

Islam first took hold in North Sumatra, where traders from Gujarat (a western state in India) stopped en route to Maluku and China. Settlements of Arab traders were established in the latter part of the 7th century, and in 1292 Marco Polo noted that the inhabitants of the town of Perlak (present day Aceh) on Sumatra's north tip had been converted to Islam.

The first Muslim inscriptions in Java date back to the 11th century and there may even have been Muslims in the Majapahit court at the zenith of its power in the mid-14th century. But it was not until the 15th and 16th centuries that Indonesian rulers turned to Islam and it became a state religion. It was then superimposed on the mixture of Hinduism and indigenous animist beliefs to produce the peculiar hybrid religion which predominates in much of Indonesia, especially Java, today.

By the time of Majapahit's final collapse at the beginning of the 16th century, many of its old satellite kingdoms had declared themselves independent Muslim states. Much of their wealth was based on their position as trans-shipment points for the growing spice trade with India and China. Islam spread across the archipelago from west to east and followed the trade routes. It appears to have been a peaceful transformation – unlike Arab and Turkish conversions made at the point of the sword. The spread of Islam in Indonesia is often described like some contagious disease, as if it happened simply because it was Islam.

While pockets of the Indonesian population are fundamentalist Muslims, such as the Acehnese in northern Sumatra, the success of Islam was due, on the whole, to its ability to adapt to local customs. The form of Islam followed in much of Indonesia today is not the austere form of the Middle East, but has more in common with Sufism. This is a mystical variant of Islam brought to India from Persia and possibly carried into Indonesia by wandering Sufi holymen and mystics.

The Rise of Melaka & Makassar

By the 15th century the centre of power in the archipelago had moved to the south-west of the Malay peninsula, where the trading kingdom of Melaka (also spelt Malacca) was reaching the height of its power. The rise of Melaka, and of trading cities along the north coast of Java, coincided with the spread of Islam through the archipelago – the Melaka kingdom accepted Islam in the 14th century. Though centred on the peninsula side of the Straits, the Melaka kingdom controlled both sides, based its power and wealth on trade, and gathered the ports of northern Java within its commercial orbit. By the 16th century it was the principal port of the region, possibly one of the biggest in the world.

By the end of the 16th century a seapower had risen in the Indonesian archipelago – the twin principalities of Makassar and Gowa in south-west Sulawesi. These regions had been settled by Malay traders who also sailed to Maluku and beyond. In 1607 when Torres sailed through the strait which now bears his name, he met Makassar Muslims in west New Guinea. Other Makassar fleets visited the north Australian coast for several hundred years, introducing the Aborigines to metal tools, pottery and tobacco.

The Arrival of the Portuguese

When the first Europeans arrived in the Indonesian archipelago they found a varying collection of principalities and kingdoms. These kingdoms were occ-asionally at war with each other, but also linked by the substantial inter-island and international trade over which successive powerful kingdoms – Srivijaya, Majapahit and Melaka – had been able to exert control by virtue of their position or their seapower.

European influence from the 16th to 18th centuries was due to the penetration of individuals and organisations into the complex trading network of the archipelago. Marco Polo and a few early missionary-travellers aside, the first Europeans to visit Indonesia were the Portuguese. Vasco de Gama had led the first European ships round the Cape of Good Hope to Asia in 1498; by 1510 the Portuguese had captured Goa on the west coast of India and then pushed on to South-East Asia. The principal aim of the first Portuguese to arrive in the Indonesian archipelago was the domination of the valuable spice trade in Maluku – the Molucca islands. Under Alfonso d'Albuquerque they captured Melaka in 1511, and the following year arrived in Maluku.

Portuguese control of trade in Indonesia was based on their fortified bases, such as Melaka, and on their supremacy at sea due to the failure of their various foes to form a united front against them. This allowed them to exercise a precarious control of the strategic trading ports that stretched from Maluku to Melaka, Macau, Goa, Mozambique and Angola. From a European point of view the Portuguese were pioneers who opened up the trade routes from Europe to Asia, forerunners of European expansionism. From an Indonesian point of view they were just another group of traders who found their way to the spice islands. The coming of the Portuguese to Indonesia did not represent a fundamental alteration of Indonesian society or trade – even the capture of Melaka did not change anything. The face and the colour of the rulers changed, but local traders took no notice of political boundaries and allegiances if they did not affect trade.

The initial Portuguese successes encouraged other European nations to send ships to the region – notably the English, the Dutch and the Spanish. The latter established themselves at Manila in 1571. By the time these new forces appeared on the horizon, the Portuguese had suffered a military defeat at Ternate and were a spent force. It was the Dutch who would eventually lay the foundations of the Indonesian state we know today.

The Coming of the Dutch

A badly led expedition of four Dutch ships, under the command of Cornelius de Houtman, arrived at Banten in West Java in 1596 after a 14 month voyage in which more than half of the 249 crew died. A Dutch account of Banten at the time gives a lively picture:

There came such a multitude of Javanese and other nations such as Turks, Chinese, Bengali, Arabs, Persians, Gujarati, and others that one could hardly move . . . that each nation took a spot on the ships where they displayed their goods the same as if they were in a market. Of which the Chinese brought of all sorts of silk woven and unwoven, spun and unspun, with beautiful earthenware, with other strange things more. The Javanese brought chickens, eggs, ducks, and many kinds of fruits. Arabs, Moors, Turks, and other nations of people each brought of everything one might imagine.

The Dutch got off to a poor start. They made a bad impression on the Javanese by killing a prince and some of his retainers, concluded a meaningless treaty of friendship with the ruler of Banten and lost one of their ships when attacked by the Javanese north of Surabaya. Nevertheless they returned to Holland with goods that yielded a small profit for their backers. Other independent expeditions followed and met with varying success – some ships were captured by the Spanish and Portuguese. The behaviour of the Dutch was uneven and so was their reception but Dutch trade expanded

quickly. This was partly because regional Indonesian leaders took advantage of the higher prices which the Dutch and Portuguese competition generated.

Then in 1580 Spain, the traditional enemy of Holland, occupied Portugal and this event prompted the Dutch government to take an interest in the Far East. The government amalgamated the competing merchant companies into the United East India Company, or the VOC (Vereenigde Oost-Indische Compagnie). The intention was to create a force to bring military pressure to bear on the Portuguese and the Spanish. Dutch trading ships were replaced by heavily armed fleets with instructions to attack Portuguese bases. By 1605 the Dutch had defeated the Portuguese at Tidore and Ambon and occupied the territory themselves – but it was another 36 years before they captured Melaka.

The Foundation of a Dutch Empire

The founder of the Dutch empire in the Indies was Jan Pieterszoon Coen, an imaginative but ruthless man. Amongst his achievements was the near-total extermination of the indigenous population of the Banda Islands in Maluku. Coen developed a grandiose plan to make his capital in Java the centre of the intra-Asian trade from Japan to Persia, and to develop the spice plantations using Burmese, Madagascan and Chinese labourers.

While the more grandiose plans were rejected he nevertheless acted vigorously in grabbing a monopoly on the spice trade as he had been instructed. An alliance with Ternate in 1607 gave the Dutch control over the source of cloves, and their occupation of Banda from 1609-21 also gave them control of the nutmeg trade. As the Dutch extended their power they forced a reduction in spice production by destroying excess clove and nutmeg plantations, thus ruining the livelihoods of the local inhabitants but keeping European prices and profits high. After capturing Melaka from the Portuguese in 1641 the Dutch became masters of the seas in the region. They not only held a monopoly of the clove and nutmeg trade, they also had a hold on the Indian cloth trade, and on Japanese copper exports. By the middle of the century they had made their capital Batavia, on the island of Java, the centre of trade on a route from Japan to Persia via Ceylon and India. They defeated Makassar in 1667 and secured a monopoly of its trade, and eventually brought the Sumatran ports under their sway. The last of the Portuguese were expelled in 1660 and the English in 1667.

The first effect of Dutch power in the Indies was the disruption of the traditional pattern of trade by their attempts – with some success – to achieve a monopoly of the spice trade at its source. The company's policy at this stage was to keep to its trading posts and avoid expensive territorial conquests. An accord with the Susuhunan (literally 'he to whose feet people must look up') of Mataram, the dominant kingdom in Java, was established. It permitted only Dutch ships, or those with permission from the VOC, to trade with the spice islands and the regions beyond them.

Then, perhaps unintentionally, but in leaps and bounds, the Dutch developed from being one trading company amongst many to the masters of a colonial empire centred on their chief trading port at Batavia. Following a 'divide and rule' strategy the Dutch exploited the conflicts between the Javanese kingdoms and, in 1678, were able to make the ruler of Mataram their vassal and to dominate his successors.

They had already put Banten under their control by helping the ruler's ambitious son to overthrow his father. In 1755 the Dutch split the Mataram kingdom into two, Yogyakarta and Surakarta (Solo). These new states and the five smaller states on Java were only nominally sovereign, in reality they were dominated by the Dutch East India Company. Fighting amongst the princes was halted, and peace was brought to East Java by the forced cessation of invasions and raids from Bali. Thus Java was united – what the native kings had failed to do for centuries had been achieved towards the end of the 18th century by a foreign trading company with an army that totalled only one thousand Europeans and two thousand Asians.

The Decline of the VOC

Despite some dramatic successes, the fortunes of the VOC were on the decline by the middle of the 18th century. The Dutch monopoly of the spice trade was finally broken, after the Dutch-English war of 1780-84, by the Treaty of Paris which permitted free trade in the east. Dutch trade in China was outstripped by European rivals, and in India much of their trade was diverted by the British to Madras. In addition, the emphasis of European trade with the east began to shift from spices to Chinese silk, Japanese copper, coffee, tea and sugar – over which it was impossible to establish a monopoly.

Dutch trading interests gradually contracted more and more around their capital of Batavia. The Batavian government increasingly depended, for its finances, on customs dues and tolls on goods coming into Batavia and taxes from the local Javanese population. Increased smuggling and the illicit private trade carried on by company employees helped to reduce profits. The mounting expense of wars within Java and of administering the additional territory acquired after each new treaty also played a part in the decline.

The VOC turned to the Dutch government at home for support and the subsequent investigation of VOC affairs revealed corruption, bankruptcy and general mismanagement. In 1800 the VOC was formally wound up, its territorial possessions became the property of the Netherlands government and the trading empire was gradually transformed into a colonial empire.

The British Occupation

In 1811, during the Napoleonic Wars when France occupied Holland, the British occupied several Dutch East Indies posts including Java. Control was restored to the Dutch in 1816 and a treaty was signed in 1824 under which the English exchanged their Indonesian settlements (such as Bengkulu in Sumatra) for Dutch holdings in India and the Malay peninsula. While the two European powers may have settled their differences to their own satisfaction, the Indonesians were of another mind. There were a number of wars or disturbances in various parts of the archipelago during the early 19th century, but the most prolonged struggles were the Paderi War in Sumatra (1821-38) and the famous Java War (1825-30) led by Prince Diponegoro. In one sense the Java War was yet another war of succession, but both the Paderi War and the Java War are notable because Islam became the symbol of opposition to the Dutch.

In 1814 Diponegoro, the eldest son of the Sultan of Yogya, had been passed over for the succession to the throne in favour of a younger claimant who had the support of the British. Having bided his time Diponegoro eventually vanished from court and in 1825 launched a guerrilla war against the Dutch. The courts of Yogya and Solo largely remained loyal to the Dutch but many of the Javanese aristocracy supported the rebellion. Diponegoro had received mystical signs that convinced him that he was the divinely appointed future king of Java. News spread among the people that he was the long-prophesied Ratu Adil, the prince who would free them from colonial oppression.

The rebellion finally ended in 1830 when the Dutch tricked Diponegoro into peace negotiations, arrested him and exiled him to Sulawesi. The five year war had cost the lives of 8000 European and 7000 Indonesian soldiers of the Dutch army. At least 200,000 Javanese died, most from famine and disease, and the population of Yogyakarta was reduced by half.

Dutch Exploitation of Indonesia

For 350 years, from the time the first Dutch ships arrived in 1596 to the declaration of independence in 1945, there was little stability in Indonesia. The first Dutch positions in the archipelago were precarious, like the first Portuguese positions. Throughout the 17th century the VOC, with its superior arms and Buginese and Ambonese mercenaries, fought everywhere in the islands. Despite Dutch domination of Java, many areas of the archipelago – including Aceh, Bali, Lombok and Borneo – remained independent.

Fighting continued to flare up in Sumatra and Java, and between 1846 and 1849 expeditions were sent to Bali in the first attempts to subjugate the island. Then there was the violent Banjarmasin War in south-east Borneo during which the Dutch defeated the reigning sultan. The longest and most devastating war was the one in Aceh which had remained independent under British protection (the two had an active trade). In 1871 the Dutch negotiated a new treaty in which the British withdrew objections to a possible Dutch occupation of Aceh. The Dutch declared war on Aceh in 1873. The war lasted for 35 years until the last Aceh guerilla leaders finally surrendered in 1908.

Even into the 20th century Dutch control outside Java was still incomplete. Large-scale Indonesian piracy continued right up until the middle of the 19th century and the Dutch fought a war in Sulawesi against the Buginese. Dutch troops occupied south-west Sulawesi between 1900 and 1910, and Bali in 1906. The 'birds head' of West Irian did not come under Dutch administration until 1919-20. Ironically, just when the Dutch finally got it all together they began to lose it. By the time Bali was occupied the first Indonesian nationalist movements were getting underway.

The determined exploitation of Indonesian resources by the Dutch really only began in 1830. The cost of the Java and the Paderi Wars meant that, despite increased returns from the Dutch system of land tax, Dutch finances were severely strained. When the Dutch lost Belgium in 1830 the home country itself faced bankruptcy and any government investment in the Indies *had* to make quick returns. From here on Dutch economic policy in Indonesia falls into three overlapping periods: the period of the so-called 'Culture' System, the Liberal Period, and the Ethical Period.

The Culture System

A new governor-general, Johannes Van den Bosch, fresh from experiences of the slave labour of the West Indies, was appointed in 1830 to make the East Indies pay their way. He succeeded by introducing a new agricultural policy called the *cultuurstelsel* or Culture System. It was really a system of government-controlled agriculture – or as Indonesian historians refer to it, the *Tanam Paksa* (Compulsory Planting).

Forced labour was not new in Java – the Dutch merely extended the existing system by forcing the peasants to produce particular crops, including coffee, which the Dutch introduced. Instead of land rent, usually assessed at about two-fifths of the value of the crop, the Culture System proposed that a portion of a peasant's land and labour would be put at the government's disposal. On this land a designated crop, suitable for the European market, was to be grown.

In practice things did not work out that way and the system produced fearful hardship. The land required from the peasant was sometimes as much as a third or even a half of his total land. In some cases the new crops demanded more labour than the maximum allowed for, and the government did not bear the losses of a bad harvest. Often the Culture System was applied on top of the land tax rather than replacing it. When the cash crop failed the peasant had no money to buy the rice he would otherwise have planted on his land. In some regions the population starved because the Javanese regents (princes) and their Chinese agents forced the peasants to use almost all their rice land to grow other crops. In the 1840s there was severe famine in some areas because of the encroachments on rice lands.

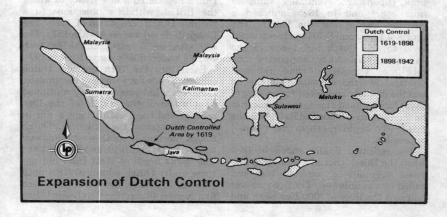

Expansion of Dutch Control

Dutch Control
1619-1898
1898-1942

Malaysia

Malaysia

Sumatra

Kalimantan

Sulawesi

Maluku

Dutch Controlled Area by 1619

Java

The system was never applied to the whole population – by 1845 it involved only about five per cent of the total cleared land, so its impact on the Javanese was very uneven. Amongst the crops grown was indigo (from which the deep blue dye is extracted) which required arduous cultivation, and sugar which took twice the labour required of rice fields. The system was, however, a boon to the Dutch and to the Javanese aristocracy. The profits made Java a self-sufficient colony and saved the Netherlands from bankruptcy. That this gain was made by appropriating all available profits and making the peasants bear all the losses was irrelevant to the Dutch. They believed that the function of a colony was to benefit the coloniser and that the welfare of the indigenous people should not interfere with this.

The Liberal Period

In the 10 years after 1848 efforts were made to correct the worst abuses of the Culture System. The liberals in the Dutch parliament attempted to reform the system, while at the same time retaining the profits and alleviating the conditions of the peasants.

They were committed to reducing government interference in economic enterprises and were therefore opposed to the system of government-controlled agriculture in Indonesia. Their policies advocated opening up the country to private enterprise – in the belief that once the peasant was freed from compulsion, productivity would increase and everyone would be swept to prosperity by the forces of a free economy. But to make the archipelago safe for individual capitalists and to free the Indonesians from oppression were, in fact, two conflicting aims.

From the 1860s onwards, the government abolished monopolies on crops which were no longer profitable anyway. Things moved more slowly for other crops; in 1870 a law was passed by which control of sugar production would be relinquished over a

Javanese Prince

12 year period from 1878 onwards, while the monopoly of the most profitable crop, coffee, was retained right up until 1917.

The 1870 Agrarian Law and other new policies proved profitable for the Dutch but brought further hardships to the Indonesians. Sugar production doubled in 1870-85, new crops like tea and cinchona flourished, and a start was made with rubber which eventually became a valuable export. At the same time oil produced in south Sumatra and Kalimantan became a valuable export, a response to the new industrial demands of the European market.

The exploitation of Indonesian resources was no longer limited to Java but had filtered through to the outer islands. As Dutch commercial interests expanded, so did the need to protect them. More and more territory was taken under direct control of the Dutch government and most of the outer islands came under firm Dutch sovereignty.

The Ethical Policy

At the turn of the century there were two increasingly vocal groups in the Dutch parliament – those who had a humanitarian interest in the welfare of the Indonesian people, and those who wanted to raise the purchasing power of the Indonesians in order to widen the market for consumer goods. The group who aimed at improving the welfare of the Indonesian people approached the task with a strong sense of a moral mission.

New policies were to be implemented, foremost among them being irrigation, transmigration from heavily populated Java to lightly populated islands, and education. There were also plans for improved communications, credit facilities for Indonesians, agricultural advice, flood control, drainage, extension of health programmes, industrialisation and the protection of native industry. Other policies aimed for the decentralisation of authority with greater autonomy for the Indonesian government, as well as greater power to local government units within the archipelago.

There were four main criticisms made against these new policies. As they were actually implemented they improved the lot of the Europeans in Indonesia, not the Indonesians themselves; those programmes which did benefit the Indonesians only reached a small percentage of the population; the programmes were carried out in a paternalistic, benevolent fashion which continued to regard the Indonesians as inferiors; and lastly some of the policies were never implemented at all. Industrialisation was never implemented since it was never seriously envisaged that Indonesia would compete with European industry, and because it was also feared that industrial development would result in the loss of a market for European goods.

Throughout all three periods, the exploitation of Indonesia's wealth contributed to the industrialisation of the Netherlands. Large areas of Java became plantations whose products, cultivated by Javanese peasants and collected by Chinese middlemen, were sold on the overseas markets by European merchants. Before WW II Indonesia supplied most of the world's quinine and pepper, over a third of its rubber, a quarter of its coconut products, and almost a fifth of its tea, sugar, coffee, and oil. Indonesia made Holland one of the major colonial powers.

Indonesian Nationalist Movements

Of all the policies of the Ethical Period, it was the education policies which were to have the least predictable and the most far-reaching effects. The diversification of economic activity and the increasing scope and range of government activity, banks and business houses, meant a growing need for Indonesians with some western education to do the paperwork. As educational opportunities increased and some Indonesians attained higher levels of education, an educated elite developed which became increasingly aware and resentful of European rule.

The first Indonesian nationalist movements of the 20th century had their roots in educational organisations. Initially the nationalist organisations largely concerned the upper and middle class Indonesians whose education and contact with western culture had made them more conscious of their own cultural traditions and critical of the injustices of the colonial system. Then mass movements began to develop, drawing support from the peasants and the urban working class:

The Islamic Association The first truly mass movement was *Sarekat Islam* (Islamic Association) which had its origins in a trading society formed in 1909 to protect Indonesians against Chinese dealers. It quickly became one of the most significant of the early nationalist movements. It was the first movement attempting to bridge the gap between the villagers and the new western-educated elite.

The Indonesian Communist Party Created in 1914

this small Marxist group, later known as the PKI (*Perserikatan Kommunist Indonesia* – the United Indonesian Communists) built up influence in the Islamic Association until a showdown in 1921 forced the Communists out. The Communists organised strikes in urban businesses and in the sugar factories but Communist-led revolts in Java (1926) and Sumatra (1927) were both suppressed by the Dutch. The PKI was effectively destroyed for the rest of the colonial period, its leaders imprisoned or self-exiled to avoid arrest.

The Indonesian Nationalist Party The *Partai Nasional Indonesia* (PNI) was formed (under a different name) in 1927 and advocated an independent Indonesia as its ultimate objective. The party was chaired by and had arisen out of the Bandung Study Group which was formed by Sukarno, who later become the first president of independent Indonesia.

The PNI became the most powerful nationalist organisation. Its early success was partly a result of Sukarno's skill as an orator and his understanding of the common people from whom the party drew and built up its mass support. The Dutch quickly recognised the threat from the PNI, and Sukarno and three other PNI leaders were imprisoned in 1930. The party was outlawed and its membership split into factions.

Other nationalist groups arose. In 1932, Mohammed Hatta and Sutan Sjahrir, who were to become important figures in the nationalist movement, returned from university in Holland and established their own nationalist group. Sukarno was released and then re-arrested in 1933, and Hatta and Sjahrir were arrested in 1934. None of the three leaders were freed until the Japanese invasion of 1942.

As the 1930s progressed, the question of cooperation or non-cooperation with the Dutch in the face of growing European and especially Japanese fascism was raised. While some nationalist leaders attempted to formulate an anti-fascist solidarity pact with the Dutch in return for Indonesian independence, at no time – even after the Nazi occupation of Holland – did the Dutch encourage the Indonesians to believe that their cooperation was needed, nor that their independence aims would be recognised.

The Japanese Invasion & Occupation

The first Japanese landings in Indonesia were in January 1942. The Dutch forces eventually surrendered, and to some extent the Japanese were hailed by the Indonesians as liberators. Sjahrir commented that:

. . .for the average Indonesian the war. . .was simply a struggle in which the Dutch colonial rulers finally would be punished by Providence for the evil, the arrogance and the oppression they had brought to Indonesia.

An ancient prophesy was revived which predicted that Indonesia would be ruled by a white buffalo (interpreted as meaning the Dutch), and then by a yellow chicken (the Japanese) which would stay only for 'a year of corn' before independence was again achieved. The Japanese occupation lasted for 3½ years.

Japanese control was very much dependent on goodwill. Believing the anti-Dutch sentiments of the Indonesians to be stronger than any anti-Japanese sentiments the Japanese were prepared to work with the Indonesian nationalists. Sukarno and Hatta, the best known nationalists, worked above ground and collaborated with the Japanese. Sjahrir led one of the underground groups, amongst whom were people who later became prominent in Indonesian politics.

The period of Japanese occupation was immensely important in the development of the nationalist movement and there is little doubt that the movement grew in strength. The Japanese sponsored mass organisations based on Islam and anti-western sentiments. Sukarno and Hatta were allowed to travel about addressing gatherings of Indonesians, and Sukarno used these occasions to spread nationalist propaganda.

In 1943, the Japanese formed the Volunteer Army of Defenders of the

Fatherland, a home defence corps which Indonesians joined in large numbers. Sukarno and Hatta were allowed to address the recruits and the corps soon became a hotbed of nationalism, later forming the backbone of the Indonesian forces fighting the Dutch after WW II.

The Independence Struggle

In mid-1945, with the tide of war against them, the Japanese set up a committee of Indonesian nationalists entitled the 'Investigating Body for the Preparation of Indonesian Independence'. This committee represented an important point in the history of the nationalist movement because it outlined the geographical limits of a future independent Indonesia.

It also set out the philosophical basis which would underlie the government and social structure of the new state. This was based on a speech Sukarno made on 1 June to the committee announcing the *Pancasila* or 'Five Principles' on which an independent Indonesia would be based: Faith in God, Humanity, Nationalism, Representative Government and Social Justice. As Sukarno put it, it was a synthesis of western democratic ideas, Islam, Marxism and indigenous village customs and traditions of government.

Three plans were drawn up for territorial boundaries and the vote came out strongly in favour of including all the territories of the Netherlands East Indies, plus the territories of North Borneo, Brunei, Sarawak, Portuguese Timor, Malaysia, New Guinea and surrounding islands. Sukarno, according to a book by Hatta, argued for the inclusion of Malaysia in the belief that the interests of Indonesia would not be secure unless both sides of the Straits of Melaka were under her control. Despite majority feeling, the Japanese seemed to have influenced the Indonesians into accepting one of the other plans which claimed only the former territory of the Dutch East Indies.

On 6 August 1945 the Americans dropped the atomic bomb on Hiroshima.

On 9 August the second atomic bomb was dropped on Nagasaki, and the following day Japan surrendered. Japan was no longer in a position to grant or guarantee Indonesian independence, but it still controlled the archipelago. The underground movements were now determined to rise against the Japanese and take over the administration. In the early morning of 16 August a group of students – including Adam Malik, the future foreign minister of the Republic of Indonesia – kidnapped Sukarno, his wife and children, and Hatta, and held them outside Jakarta. The following day Sukarno proclaimed the formation of an independent Indonesia outside his Jakarta home. An Indonesian government of 16 ministers was formed on 31 August, with Sukarno as president and Hatta as vice-president.

In September 1945 the first British and Australian troops landed in Jakarta, and from October onwards began arriving throughout the territories. They had three main tasks – to disarm the Japanese troops and send them back to Japan, rescue Allied prisoners of war, and lastly to hold the Indonesian nationalists down until the Dutch could return to the archipelago and reassert their 'lawful' sovereignty.

Most of the 'British' troops were in fact Indians – the soldiers of one colony being used to help restore colonialism in another – and many deserted to the Indonesian side. Japanese troops were used to recapture towns held by the Indonesians, such as Bandung. Heavy fighting, which lasted for 10 days, broke out in Surabaya between Indonesians and the Indian troops led by British officers.

Against this background of turbulence, attempts were made to begin negotiations between the Dutch and the nationalists but the Dutch failed to recognise that their colonial empire was finished. Hatta said:

The Dutch are graciously permitting us entry into the basement while we have climbed all the way to the top floor and up to the attic. Indonesia today has achieved her own administration as a result of her own efforts. And what earthly reason is there for Indonesia to return to her former status as a colony of a foreign nation which did practically nothing to defend her from the Japanese? The Dutch should not remain under the delusion that they can thwart Indonesia's desire to remain independent.

The last British troops left at the end of November 1946, by which time 55,000 Dutch troops had landed in Java. In Bogor (Java) and in Balikpapan (Kalimantan) Indonesian republican officials were imprisoned. Bombing raids on Palembang and Medan in Sumatra prepared the way for the Dutch occupation of these cities. In southern Sulawesi Captain Westerling was accused of pacifying the region by murdering 40,000 Indonesians in a few weeks. Elsewhere the Dutch were attempting to form puppet states among the more amenable ethnic groups.

The next three years saw a confusing struggle – half diplomatic and half military. Despite major military operations in 1947 and 1948 the nationalists continued to hold out, world opinion swayed heavily against the Dutch and it became obvious that only a concerted and costly campaign could defeat the nationalist forces. The Dutch were finally forced out by international pressure, particularly from the USA which threatened the Dutch with economic sanctions. In December 1949, after negotiations in Holland, the Dutch finally transferred sovereignty over the former Netherlands East Indies to the new Indonesian republic.

Economic Depression & Disunity

The threat of external attacks from the Dutch had helped to keep the nationalists mostly united in the first five years or so after the proclamation of independence. With the Dutch gone the divisions in Indonesian society began to reassert

themselves. Sukarno had tried to hammer out the principles of Indonesian unity in his Pancasila speech of 1945 and while these, as he said, may have been 'the highest common factor and the lowest common multiple of Indonesian thought', the divisive elements in Indonesian society could not be swept away by a single speech. Regional differences in customs (adat), morals, tradition, religion, the impact of Christianity and Marxism, and fears of political domination by the Javanese all contributed to disunity.

In the early years of the republic there were a number of separatist movements which sprang out of the religious and ethnic diversity of the country. These included the militant *Darul Islam* (The Islamic Domain) which proclaimed an Islamic State of Indonesia and waged guerrilla warfare in west Java against the new Indonesian Republic from 1949 to 1962. There was also an attempt by former Ambonese members of the Royal Netherlands Indies Army to establish an independent republic in Maluku, and there were revolts in Minahasa (the northern limb of Sulawesi) and in Sumatra.

Against this background lay divisions in the leadership elite, and the sorry state of the new republic's economy. When the Republic of Indonesia came into being the economy was in tatters following almost 10 years of Japanese occupation and war with the Dutch. The population was increasing and the new government was unable to boost production of foodstuffs and clothing to keep pace with, let alone overtake, this increase in population. Most of the population was illiterate, there were few schools and few teachers. While there was a sufficiently large elite of western-educated Indonesians to fill top levels of government there were insufficient middle-level staff, technicians and people with basic skills such as typing and accountancy. Inflation was chronic, smuggling cost the central government badly needed foreign currency, and many of the plantations had been destroyed during the war. Political parties proliferated and deals between parties for a share of cabinet seats resulted in a rapid turnover of coalition governments. There were 17 cabinets for the period 1945 to 1958. The frequently postponed elections were finally held in 1955 and the PNI – regarded as Sukarno's party – topped the poll. There were also dramatic increases in support for the Communist PKI but no party managed more than a quarter of the votes and short-lived coalitions continued.

Sukarno Takes Over - Guided Democracy

By 1956 President Sukarno was openly criticising parliamentary democracy. Its most serious weakness, he said, was that it was 'based upon inherent conflict' thus running counter to the Indonesian concept of harmony as the natural state of human relationships.

Sukarno sought a system based on the traditional village system of discussion and deliberation upon a problem in an attempt to find common ground and a consensus of opinion under the guidance of the village elders. He argued that the threefold division – Nationalism (*Nasionalisme*), Religion (*Agaman*) and Communism (*Komunisme*) – would be blended into a cooperative government, or what he called a *Nas-A-Kom* government.

In February 1957, at a large meeting of politicians and others, Sukarno proposed a cabinet representing all the political parties of importance (including the PKI). This was his attempt to overcome the impasse in the political system, but it was not an attempt to abolish the parties.

Sukarno then proclaimed 'guided democracy' and brought Indonesia's period of western parliamentary democracy to a close. This was achieved with support from his own party, and with some support from regional and military leaders grown weary of the political merry-go-round in Jakarta.

The Sumatra & Sulawesi Rebellions

As a direct result of Sukarno's actions, rebellions broke out in Sumatra and Sulawesi in 1958. Led by senior military and civilian leaders of the day, these rebellions were partly a reaction against Sukarno's usurpation of power and partly against the growing influence of the Communist Party which was winning increasing favour with Sukarno. The rebellions were also linked to the growing regional hostility to the mismanagement, inefficiency and corruption of the central government. This was intensified by Java's declining share in the export trade, while the foreign earnings of the other islands were used to import rice and consumer goods for Java's increasing population.

The central government, however, effectively smashed the rebellion by mid-1958, though guerrilla activity continued for three years. Rebel leaders were granted amnesty, but the two political parties which they had been connected with were banned and some of the early nationalist leaders were discredited. Sjahrir and others were arrested in 1962.

The defeat of the rebellion was a considerable victory for Sukarno, his supporters and the army, led by General Nasution, which had gained administrative authority throughout the country. The Communist Party had also benefited because they had been a target of criticism by the rebels. Sukarno was now able to exercise enormous personal influence and set about reorganising the political system in order to give himself *real* power.

In 1960 the elected parliament was dissolved and replaced by a parliament appointed by the president. It had no authority over the president and enacted laws subject to his agreement. A new body, the Supreme Advisory Council, with 45 members including the president who appointed the others, was established and became the chief policy-making body. A 'National Front' was set up in September 1960, an organisation intended to 'mobilise the revolutionary forces of the people'. The Front was presided over by the president and became a useful adjunct to the government in organising 'demonstrations' – such as sacking embassies during the period of 'Confrontation' with Malaysia.

Sukarno – Revolution & Nationalism

With his assumption of power, Sukarno set Indonesia on a course of stormy nationalism. During the early 1960s he created a strange language of capital letters: the world was divided between the NEFOS (New Emerging Forces) and the OLDEFOS (Old Established Forces), where the westerners were the NEKOLIM (the Neo-Colonial Imperialists).

His speeches were those of a romantic revolutionary and they held his people spellbound. *Konfrontasi* become a term to juggle with. Malaysia would be confronted, and its protector Britain. The

Sukarno

United States would be confronted, as would the whole western world. The people sometimes called Sukarno *bapak* – father – but he was really *bung*, the daring older brother who carried out the outrageous schemes they wished they could do themselves.

The western world remembers Sukarno's flamboyance and his contradictions. No other Asian leader has so keenly offended the puritan values of the west; abstinence, monogamy and other virtues were conspicuously undervalued by Sukarno. His notorious liking for women and his real and/or alleged sexual exploits were certainly advantageous to him in Indonesia where he was not expected to be the good family man, faithful to his wife in the best traditions of western politics.

He claimed to be a believer in God and also a Marxist – this peculiar blending of contradictory philosophies sprang from the time when he was trying to find common ground against the Dutch. Sukarno set himself up as a conciliator between the nationalist groups because he knew that unity was vital in order to achieve independence. He also made appeals to the emotions and mysticism of the Javanese because these were their characteristics.

Economic Deterioration

What Sukarno could not do was create a viable economic system that would lift Indonesia out of its poverty. Sukarno's corrosive vanity burnt money on a spate of status symbols meant to symbolise the new Indonesian identity. They included the Merdeka (Freedom) Monument, a mosque designed to be the biggest in the world, and a vast sports stadium built with Russian money. Unable to advance beyond revolution to the next stage of rebuilding, with its slow and unspectacular processes, Sukarno's monuments became substitutes for real development.

Another fallen president, Richard Nixon, who visited Indonesia in 1953, presented an image which goes some of the way to explaining one of the main problems with Sukarno:

In no other country we visited was the conspicuous luxury of the ruler in such striking contrast to the poverty and misery of his people. Jakarta was a collection of sweltering huts and hovels. An open sewer ran through the heart of the city, but Sukarno's palace was painted a spotless white and set in the middle of hundreds of acres of exotic gardens. One night we ate off gold plate to the light of a thousand torches while musicians played on the shore of a lake covered with white lotus blossoms and candles floating on small rafts.

A more aggressive stance on foreign affairs also became a characteristic of Sukarno's increased authority. Sukarno believed that Asia had been humiliated by the west and had still not evened the score. He sought recognition of a new state that was once a 'nation of coolies and a coolie amongst nations'. Indonesia was also surrounded, and from Sukarno's view threatened, by the remnants of western imperialism: the British and their new client state of Malaysia; the hated Dutch who continued to occupy West Irian; and the Americans and their military bases in the Philippines.

From this point of view Sukarno's efforts to take over West Irian and his Confrontation with Malaysia – if inadvisable – make some sense. Indonesia walked out of the UN in January 1965 after Malaysia had been admitted to the Security Council.

Under Sukarno, Indonesia turned its attention towards attaining those territories it had claimed in August 1945. First on the agenda was West Irian, still under Dutch rule. An arms agreement with the Soviet Union in 1960 enabled the Indonesians to begin a diplomatic as well as military confrontation with the Dutch over West Irian. It was pressure from the United States on the Dutch that finally led to the Indonesian takeover in 1963.

The same year Indonesia embarked on Confrontation with the new nation of Malaysia, formed from a federation of the Malay peninsula and the states in northern Borneo which bordered on Indonesian Kalimantan. For Indonesia the formation of Malaysia meant the consolidation of British military power on its own doorstep. Sukarno and Indonesian military leaders also suspected that the British and the Americans had aided the separatist rebels in the archipelago. It took three years for the Confrontation to run its course. It tied up 50,000 British, Australian and New Zealand soldiers in military action along the Kalimantan-Malaysia border, but was never really a serious threat to the survival of Malaysia.

The critical effects of Confrontation were economic. The eight-year economic plan announced in 1963 intended to increase revenue from taxes, stabilise consumer prices and strengthen the currency. The plan miscarried, in part due to half-heartedness and corruption on the part of military leaders and administrators but mainly because of the runaway inflation caused by the expenses of Confrontation. Foreign aid dried up because the USA withdrew its aid when Indonesia launched Confrontation.

Without finance the government had to look elsewhere for money. Government subsidies in several areas of the public sector were abolished, leading to massive increases in rail freight and rail, bus and air fares. Similar increases occurred in electricity, tap water, post and telegraph charges. These rises flowed on to the market, with large increases in the price of basic consumer goods like rice, beef, fish, eggs, salt and soap. Salaries were increased in this period but not enough to keep up with the ever mounting prices.

Sukarno, the Army & the Communists

Confrontation also alienated western nations, and Indonesia came to depend more and more on support from the Soviet Union, then increasingly from Communist China. Meanwhile, tensions grew between the Indonesian Army and the PKI

(Communist Party). Though Sukarno often talked as if he held absolute power, his position actually depended on maintaining a balance between the different political powers in Indonesia at the time, primarily between the army and the PKI. Sukarno is often described as the great *dalang* or puppet master, who balanced the forces of the left and right just as competing forces are balanced in the Javanese shadow puppet shows.

The PKI was the third largest communist party in the world, outside the Soviet Union and China. By 1965 it claimed to have three million members, it controlled the biggest trade union organisation in Indonesia (the Central All-Indonesian Workers Organisation) and the largest peasant group (the Indonesian Peasant Front). It also had an influence in the major mass organisation (the National Front). The membership of affiliate organisations of the PKI was said to be 15 to 20 million. Except for the inner cabinet, it penetrated the government apparatus extensively.

It is possible that the successes of the party in the 1955 election suggested to Sukarno that the PKI could be the force that would end centuries of economic oppression of the Indonesian peasant – by feudal lords, the Dutch, the modern upper class, the army, and the superstitions of the people – and to that end he gave the PKI his support.

Guided Democracy under Sukarno was marked by an attempt to give the peasants better social conditions but attempts to give tenant farmers a fairer share of their rice crops and to redistribute land led to more confusion. The PKI often pushed for reforms behind the government's back and encouraged peasants to seize land without waiting for decisions from land reform committees. In 1964 these tactics led to violent clashes in Central and East Java and Bali and the PKI got a reputation as a trouble-maker.

The PKI was dissatisfied with what had been achieved domestically and wanted more control of policy making. It also wanted the workers and peasants armed in self-defence units. The pressure increased in 1965 with growing tension between the PKI and the army. The crunch came with the proposal to arm the Communists. The story goes that after a meeting with Zhou Enlai in Jakarta in April 1965, Sukarno secretly decided to accelerate the progress of the Communist Party. He created a 'fifth force' – an armed militia independent of the four branches of the armed forces (the army, navy, air force and police) and arranged for 100,000 rifles to be brought in secretly from China.

The Slaughter of the Communists

In the early hours of the morning of 1 October 1965, six of the Indonesian Army's top generals were murdered after military rebels raided their houses. They were the Army Commander and Army Minister, Lieutenant-General Ahmad Yani, who had all Indonesian troops under his control and who opposed the establishment of a fifth force, and members of the Army Central High Command.

Three of the generals – Yani, Harjono and Pandjaitan – were shot dead at their homes. Their bodies and the three other generals were taken to the rebel headquarters at Halim air force base outside Jakarta where those still alive were killed. The home of the Defence Minister, General Nasution, was also attacked but he managed to escape. His five-year-old daughter was killed, and his adjutant Lieutenant Tendean (presumably mistaken for Nasution) was taken to Halim where he was shot with the generals.

Other rebel units occupied the national radio station and the telecommunications building on Merdeka Square, and took up positions around the Presidential Palace, yet there appears to have been little or no attempt to coordinate further revolt in the rest of Java, let alone in the rest of the archipelago. Within a few hours of the beginning of the coup, General Suharto, head of the army's Strategic Reserve, was able to mobilise army forces to take counteraction. By the evening of 1 October the coup had clearly failed, but it was not clear who had been involved or what its effects would be.

It has been argued that the coup was primarily an internal army affair, led by younger officers against the older leadership. The official Indonesian view is that it was an attempt by leaders of the PKI to seize power. There are some who think the Communists were entirely to blame for the coup and support the Indonesian Army's assertion that the PKI plotted the coup and used discontented army officers to carry it out. Another view is that military rebels and the PKI took the initiative separately and then became partners. And then there are those who believe that Sukarno himself was behind the coup – and yet another story that Suharto was in the confidence of one of the conspirators. There is also a theory that Suharto himself provoked the coup as a means of clearing out his rivals in the army as well as Sukarno and seizing power himself – advocates of this theory point out that Suharto was not on the rebels' execution list although he was more important than some of those who were killed.

If the Communists *were* behind the attempted coup then for what reason is anybody's guess. They had been fairly successful up until then, gaining mass support and influence in government, and had no apparent reason to risk it all on one badly organised escapade. It's been suggested that they may have reacted to Sukarno's apparently deteriorating health and, fearing a military coup once Sukarno was out of the way, decided to act. Yet there's no way that the Communists, if they were behind the coup, could have fought the army even if the 100,000 guns from China had arrived.

Whatever the PKI's real role in the coup, the effect on its fortunes was devastating. With the defeat of the coup,

a wave of anti-communism swept Indonesia; thousands upon thousands of communists and their sympathisers were slaughtered and more imprisoned. The party and its affiliates were banned, its leaders were killed, imprisoned or went into hiding. Aidit, Chairman of the Party, was eventually shot by government soldiers in November 1965.

Estimates of just how many people were killed vary widely. Adam Malik, the future Foreign Minister under Suharto, said that a 'fair figure' was 160,000; and there are other estimates of 200,000 and 400,000. Army units were organised to kill villagers suspected of being PKI, and anti-Communist civilians were given arms to help with the job. Private grudges were settled and petty landlords seized the opportunity to rid themselves of peasants who, under local PKI leadership, had taken over fields in an attempt to enforce the government's ineffectual land reforms. On top of this, perhaps 250,000 people were arrested and sent to prison camps for allegedly being involved in some way with the coup.

Sukarno's Fall & Suharto's Rise

General Suharto took the lead in putting down the attempted coup with remarkable speed. He took over leadership of the armed forces, ended the Confrontation with Malaysia, and carried on a slow and remarkably patient, but not entirely peaceful, duel with Sukarno.

By mid-October 1965 Suharto was in such a strong position that Sukarno appointed him Commander-in-Chief of the armed forces. Army units, under the command of Colonel Sarwo Edhie, began the massacre of the PKI and their supporters in Central Java. Sukarno was aghast at the killings and into the early part of the following year continued to make public statements in support of the Communists. He sacked General Nasution from his position as Defence Minister and Army Chief of Staff. The army responded by organising violent demonstrations

President Suharto

made up largely of adolescents. One demostration tried to storm the Presidential Palace and another which ransacked the Foreign Ministry.

Sukarno still had dedicated supporters in all the armed forces and it seemed unlikely that he would topple, despite the street riots and the violence in the countryside. Suharto obviously believed it was time to increase the pressure. On 11 March, after troops loyal to Suharto had surrounded the Presidential Palace, Sukarno signed the 11 March Order – a vague document which, while not actually handing over the full powers of government to Suharto, officially allowed Suharto to act on his own initiative rather than on directions from the president.

While always deferring to the name of Sukarno and talking as if he was acting on Sukarno's behalf, Suharto now set the wheels moving for his own outright assumption of power. The PKI was officially banned. Suharto's troops occupied newspaper houses, radio, cable, telex and telephone offices, and the following day again blockaded the Presidential Palace.

Pro-Sukarno officers, men in the armed forces and a number of cabinet ministers were arrested. A new six-man inner cabinet including Suharto and two of his nominees, Adam Malik and Sultan Hamengkubuwono of Yogyakarta, was formed.

Suharto then launched a campaign of intimidation to blunt any grass roots opposition to his steadily increasing power. Thousands of public servants were dismissed as PKI sympathisers, thus putting thousands more in fear of losing their jobs. Suharto intensified his efforts to gain control of the People's Consultative Congress, the body whose function it was to elect the president. The arrest or murder after the abortive coup of 120 of its 609 members had already ensured a certain amount of docility but despite further pressure, Sukarno managed to hang onto the presidency into 1967. In March of that year Congress elected Suharto acting president. On 27 March 1968 it 'elected' him president.

The New Order

Suharto wanted the new regime to at least wear the clothes of democracy, and in 1971 general elections were held. Suharto used the almost defunct *Golkar* party as the spearhead of the army's election campaign. Having appointed his election squad, the old parties were then crippled by being banned, by the disqualification of candidates and by disenfranchising voters. Predictably Golkar swept to power with 236 of the 360 elective seats – the PNI was shattered and won just 20 seats. The new People's Consultative Congress also included 207 Suharto appointments and 276 armed forces officers.

Suharto then enforced the merger of other political parties. The four Muslim parties were merged into the Development Union Party, and the other parties into the Indonesian Democratic Party. Political activity between elections and below the district level – ie, in the villages – was prohibited. Since most people lived in the villages this meant there would be no political activity at all outside of election campaigns. Effectively, it was the end of Indonesian democracy.

Under Suharto Indonesia turned away from its isolationist stance and rejoined the United Nations. It joined in the formation of the Association of South-East Asian Nations (ASEAN), reflecting an acceptance of her immediate neighbours in contrast to Sukarno's Confrontation with Malaysia. It made a determined effort to attract foreign investment. The largest proportion now comes from Japan, which is also Indonesia's biggest trading partner.

While Indonesia consistently views China as the most likely threat to its security, it has taken a conciliatory stance towards China and also to the Soviet Union, aiming for a substantial increase in trade with both those countries. It has established good relations with Vietnam. In 1988 and 1989, Indonesia even played host to talks between Vietnam, the Khmer Rouge and other factions now engaged in power struggles in Kampuchea.

Unfortunately, Indonesia's invasion of East Timor in 1975, not only committed the country to a seemingly interminable war against the Fretilin guerrillas but also strained relations with Australia. This again conjured up the shadow of Confrontation and the image of Indonesia as a potential aggressor. The Indonesians are also continually troubled by the West Irian guerrillas who have never accepted the Indonesian takeover of the province – consequently straining Indonesian relations with neighbouring Papua New Guinea.

Politically, Indonesia is much more stable but this is mainly because the government's authority rests squarely on a foundation of military power. Opposition has either been eliminated or is kept suppressed and muted. The government sees opposition from a number of sources including Muslim extremists (real or imaginary), university students, Communists, racial tension (particularly

anti-Chinese sentiment which could spill over into attacks on the Chinese who run the business enterprises of Suharto and the other generals) and various dissident groups.

The Communist bogeyman has also failed to disappear. In mid-1985 three members of the East Java branch of the PKI, who had been in prison since the 1965 coup, were executed. In late 1986, nine more former members of the PKI were executed in Jakarta; all had been in prison since the time of the coup. At the time of writing a number of other former PKI members are also awaiting possible execution.

On a rather more subtle level of control the newspapers are expected to – and do – practise self-censorship. While stories of corruption, wastage of funds and government ineptitude are frequently run, care is always taken not to point the finger too closely. If imported magazines like *Time* and *Newsweek* have articles that are critical of the government, they are sold in Indonesian shops blacked out and pasted over with a blank sheet of paper. In one way or another the Indonesian government keeps criticism down to a tolerable, non-threatening level.

GEOGRAPHY

The Republic of Indonesia is the world's most expansive archipelago, stretching almost 5000 km from Sabang off the northern tip of Sumatra, to a little beyond Merauke in south-eastern Irian Jaya. It stretches north and south of the equator a total of 1770 km, from the border with Sabah to the small island of Roti off the southern tip of Timor.

The archipelago contains almost 13,700 islands – from specks of rock to huge islands like Sumatra and Borneo – 6000 of which are inhabited. The six main islands are Sumatra, Java, Kalimantan (Indonesian Borneo), Sulawesi and Irian Jaya (the western part of New Guinea). Most of the country is water; the Indonesians refer to their homeland as

Tanah Air Kita which means literally 'Our Earth and Water'. While the total land and sea area of Indonesia is about 2½ times greater than the land area of Australia, the total land area is only 1,900,000 square km or a little larger than Queensland.

Most of these islands are mountainous; in Irian Jaya there are peaks so high they're snow-capped all year round. North-central Kalimantan and much of central Sulawesi are also mountainous, but in most other parts of Indonesia volcanoes dominate the skyline. Running like a backbone down the western coast of Sumatra is a line of extinct and active volcanoes which continues through Java, Bali and Nusa Tenggara and then loops around through the Banda Islands of Maluku to north-eastern Sulawesi. Some of these have erupted with devastating effects – like the massive blow out of Krakatau in 1883 which produced a tidal wave killing 30,000 people, and the 1963 eruption of Gunung Agung on Bali which wasted large areas of the island. To many Balinese the eruption of this sacred mountain was a sign of the wrath of the gods, and in East Java the Tenggerese people still offer a propitiatory sacrifice to the smoking Bromo crater which dominates the local landscape. It is also the ash from these volcanoes that has provided Indonesia with some of the finest, richest and most fertile stretches of land on the planet.

Unlike her large sunburnt neighbour to the south, Indonesia is a country of plentiful rainfall particularly in west Sumatra, north-west Kalimantan, West Java and Irian Jaya. A few areas of Sulawesi and some of the islands closer to Australia – notably Sumba and Timor – are considerably drier but they're exceptions. The high rainfall and the tropical heat make for a very humid climate – but also for a very even one. The highlands of Java and Irian Jaya can get very cold indeed but on the whole most of Indonesia is warm and humid year-round.

Because of this high rainfall and year-round humidity, nearly two-thirds of Indonesia is covered in tropical rainforest – most of it on Sumatra, Kalimantan, Sulawesi and Irian Jaya. Most of the forests of Java disappeared centuries ago as land was cleared for agriculture. Today the rest of Indonesia's rainforest, which is second only to Brazil's in area and makes up 10% of all the rainforest in the world, is disappearing at a rate of at least 5000 square km a year – roughly the area of Bali (some estimates say 15,000 square km). The main culprits are local and foreign timber companies, which carry out little reforestation, and the government which, to say the least, doesn't discourage the companies. Indonesia is the world's largest wood exporter, selling about US$2 billion worth each year, much of it plywood. Other factors are the clearing of forest for agriculture, transmigration settlements and mining.

In 1983 Indonesia was the scene of probably the greatest forest fire ever recorded when 30,000 square km of rainforest were destroyed in the Great Fire of Kalimantan, which lasted nine months. The government blamed shifting 'slash-and-burn' cultivators for this, but outside experts say the fire was triggered by the waste wood and debris left by loggers, which also set off peat and coal fires beneath the ground which burned for months.

Along the east coast of Sumatra, the south coast of Kalimantan, Irian Jaya, and much of the northern coast of Java, there is swampy, low-lying land often covered in mangroves. In many areas the over-clearing of natural growth has led to a continual erosion as topsoil is washed down the rivers by heavy rains, simultaneously wreaking havoc with the Indonesian roads.

The tropical vegetation, the mountainous terrain and the breakup of the country into numerous islands, has always made communication difficult – both between islands and also between different parts of the one island. But it is these factors which have had a marked effect on its history and culture, and also explain some of the peculiarities of the country and its people.

Firstly, Indonesia straddles the equator between the Indian Ocean to the west and the Pacific Ocean to the east. To the north are China and Japan, to the north-west India and beyond that Arabia. Because of this central position the Indonesian islands – particularly Sumatra and Java – and the Malay peninsula have long formed a stopover and staging ground on the sea routes between India and China, a convenient midway point where merchants of the civilised world met and exchanged goods.

Secondly, the regular and even climate (there are some exceptions – in some of the islands east of Java and Bali the seasonal differences are pronounced and even within Java some districts have a sufficiently marked dry season to suffer drought at times) means that a rhythm of life for many Indonesian farmers is based less on the annual fluctuations of the seasons than on the growth pattern of his crops. In areas with heavy rainfall and terraced rice field cultivation there is no set planting season or harvest season, but a continuous flow of activity where at any one time one hillside may demonstrate the whole cycle of rice cultivation, from ploughing to harvesting.

Thirdly, the rugged, mountainous terrain and the fact that the country is made up of many islands has separated groups of people from each other and resulted in an extraordinary differentiation of language and culture across the archipelago. Indonesians are divided – according to one classification – into approximately 300 ethnic groups which speak some 365 languages and dialects.

Politically, Indonesia is divided into 27 provinces for administration by the central government. Java has five provinces – Jakarta Raya, West Java, Central Java, Yogyakarta and East Java.

Sumatra has eight provinces – Aceh, North Sumatra, West Sumatra, Riau, Jambi, Bengkulu, South Sumatra and Lampung. Kalimantan has West, Central, South and East provinces. Sulawesi has North, Central, South and South-Eastern provinces. Other provinces are: Bali, West Nusa Tenggara (Lombok and Sumbawa), East Nusa Tenggara (Sumba, West Timor, Flores, and the Solor and Alor Archipelagos), East Timor, the Moluccas (Maluku) and Irian Jaya.

Java is the hub of Indonesia and its most heavily populated island. The capital of Indonesia, Jakarta, is located on the island's north-western coast. While the Javanese are the dominant group in Indonesian politics and in the military, their control over the other islands is a tenuous one for the reasons already mentioned. The diversity of the archipelago's inhabitants and the breakup of the country into numerous islands helps to fuel separatism – and since the formation of the republic in 1949 the central administration in Jakarta has fought wars against separatists in West Java, Sumatra, Minahasa in northern Sulawesi, West Irian and Maluku.

Indonesia shares borders with Malaysia and Papua New Guinea. Relations with Malaysia were unhappy during the Sukarno era and the period of 'Confrontation' but since then they have very much improved. Trouble with Papua New Guinea results from continuing problems with the OPM (Free West Papua) guerrillas who refuse to recognise Indonesian sovereignty over West Irian and take refuge in Papua New Guinea. East Timor remained a colony of Portugal up until independence but was invaded by Indonesia in 1975.

CLIMATE

Straddling the equator, Indonesia tends to have a fairly even climate all year round. There are no seasons comparable with the four that westerners are familiar with, and you do not get the extremes of winter and summer as you do in Europe or some parts of Asia such as China and northern India.

Indonesians distinguish between a wet season and a dry season. In most parts of Indonesia the wet season falls between October and April, and the dry season between May and September. In some parts you don't really notice the difference – the hot season just seems to be slightly hotter and not quite so wet as the wet season; moreover the rain comes in sudden tropical downpours. In other parts – like Maluku – you really do notice the additional water; it rains almost non-stop and travelling during this period becomes more than difficult.

Because the country lies across the equator, the length of day and night throughout Indonesia remains constant throughout the year, with sunrise at around 6 am and sunset at around 6 pm. It is invariably hot and generally humid during the day and warm during the night. But regardless of where you are, once you get up into the hills and mountains the temperature drops dramatically – in the evenings and during the night it can be bloody cold! Camping out at night atop Mt Rinjani in Lombok, for example, will freeze your arse off. Sleeping out at night on the deck of a small boat or ship can also be bitterly cold, no matter how oppressive the heat may be during the day. You don't exactly need Antarctic survival gear, but bring jeans and some warm clothes. At the other end of the thermometer, an hour's walk along Kuta Beach in the middle of the day will roast you a nice bright red colour – bring a hat, sunglasses, and some sun-block cream.

Java

Across the island the temperature throughout the year averages 22 to 29°C (78 to 85°F) and humidity averages a high 75%, but the north coastal plains are usually hotter (up to 34°C (94°F) during the day in the dry season) and more

oppressively humid than anywhere else. Generally the south coast is a bit cooler than the north coast, and the mountainous regions inland are very much cooler.

The wet season is between October and the end of April. The rain comes as a tropical downpour, falling most afternoons during the wet season and intermittently at other times of the year. The heaviest rains are usually around January/February. Although the climate is generally hot and wet, there are some surprising variations across the island. Large areas of West Java average over 3000 mm (166 inches) of rain a year while East Java, particularly in the lowlands, has a rainfall of only 35 inches and a sufficiently marked dry season to suffer drought from time to time. The dry season in Java is between May and September, and probably the best time to visit the island is June, July and August.

Bali

Here it is much like Java; the dry season is between April and September. The coolest months of the year are generally May, June and July with the average temperature around 28°C (82°F). The rainy season is between October and March but the tropical showers alternate with clear skies and sunshine; the hottest months of the year are generally February and March with the average temperature around 30°C (86°F). Overall, the best time to visit the island is in the dry and cooler months between May and August, with cool evenings and fresh breezes coming in off the sea.

Sumatra

The climate of Sumatra resembles that of Java and is hot and extremely humid. The equator cuts this island into two roughly equal halves, and since the winds of northern Sumatra differ from those of the rest of the archipelago so does the timing of the seasons – though temperatures remain pretty constant year-round. North of the equator the heaviest rainfall is between October and April and the dry season is May to September. South of the equator the heaviest rainfall is December to February, though it will have started raining in September. In Sumatra heavy rains can make bad roads impassable.

Nusa Tenggara

In the islands east of Bali the seasonal differences are more pronounced. The driest months are August and September, and the wettest months are November to February. However the duration of the seasons varies from island to island. The seasons on Lombok are more like those on Bali, with a dry season from April to September and a wet season from October to March. Much the same applies to Sumbawa and Flores. The duration of the dry season increases the closer you get to Australia – the rusty landscape of Sumba and Timor is a sharp contrast to well-vegetated Flores. Timor is also the only island in Indonesia which gets cyclones.

Sulawesi

The wettest months here tend to be from around November/December to March/April but in central and northern Sulawesi the rainfall seems to be a bit more evenly spread throughout the year. In the mountainous regions of central Sulawesi, even in the dry season it may rain by late afternoon – likewise in the northern peninsula. The south-eastern peninsula is the driest part of the island.

Temperatures drop quite considerably going from the lowlands to the mountains. Average temperatures along the coast range from around 26 to 30°C, but in the mountains the average temperature drops by 5°C.

Except in south-western Sulawesi and the Minahasa region of the north (or in odd places where foreign mining companies operate) the wet season turns the mostly unsurfaced roads into excruciatingly frustrating vehicle-bogging mud. It makes travel by road in some parts of the island either impossible or tedious at these times – there's some improvement being made to the roads so check out the current situation when you get there – be prepared to fly, skirt the coast in ships or even do some walking.

Kalimantan

Permanently hot and damp; the wettest period is October to March, and the driest period is July to September. Although the sun predominates between April and September be prepared for heavy tropical downpours during this period.

Maluku (The Moluccas)

Maluku is the big exception to the rules in Indonesia. Whilst the wet season everywhere else is from October to April, in Maluku the wet season is April through to July, and may even carry on to the end of August. Travelling in Maluku during the wet is hardly worth contemplating; the sea is too rough during this time for small boats, so there are fewer inter-island connections. Even when you do get to wherever it is you want to go you'll end up spending most of your time there sheltering in your losmen from the elements. The best time to visit is September to March.

Irian Jaya

Irian Jaya is hot and humid in the coastal regions. In the highlands its warm by day, but can get very cold by night – and the higher you go the colder it gets! August and September in the highlands will be gloomy and misty. In the northern part of Irian Jaya, May to October is the drier season and May is the hottest month. Southern Irian Jaya has a much more well-defined season than the northern part of the island.

Tourist Seasons

Whilst the cool, dry season from April to October is the best time to visit much of Indonesia there are also distinct tourist seasons which alter the picture in some parts. Bali is Australia's favourite Asian getaway and everyone eventually makes the pilgrimage. The Christmas holiday period brings a wave of migratory Australians – and airfares from Australia are also higher at this time. The May and August school holidays also get them flocking in. The European summer holidays bring crowds – July for the Germans, August for the French. The second *big* influx of tourists is into Torajaland in Sulawesi – a French and German destination during the European summer holidays.

GOVERNMENT

Executive power rests with the president, who is head of state and holds office for a period of five years. Officially, highest authority rests with the People's Consultative Congress (MPR) which sits at least once every five years and is responsible for electing the president. The congress is composed of all the members of the House of Representatives (which sits once a year) along with those appointed by the president to represent various groups and regions. Technically, the president is responsible only to the People's Consultative Congress, which elects him and the vice-president. The president appoints ministers to his cabinet and they are responsible only to him.

Party politics, what there is of it, continues under the one 'group' and two-party system devised by Suharto in the early 1970s. This involves the government-run Golkar which is technically not a political party, the Muslim United Development Party (PPP) and the Indonesian Democratic Party (PDI). Distinctions between the parties are deliberately being blurred. The enforced acceptance of the Pancasila philosophy as the sole philosophical base for all political, social and religious organisations is also aimed partly at defusing and partly at suppressing dissent.

Suharto has shown himself to be

remarkably resilient. His rule is certainly not unopposed but he has continually sought to reaffirm his authority and has successfully met any challenges. Being president of Indonesia is like riding a tiger – the succession problem looms closer and closer with each passing year and, unless Suharto dies in the saddle, his real problem is to make sure he doesn't get eaten if he decides to step down.

The Army

The present cabinet contains only a minority of military men but they hold some important ministerial positions. The Defence Minister, General Benny Murdani, for example, is probably the second most powerful man in Indonesia today. Despite its minority in the cabinet, and the fact that Suharto prefers a civilian image in public, the army is where political power in Indonesia rests. Both the political and military philosophy of the Indonesian army positively encourages involvement in politics, and the army hardly regards itself as having usurped power that somehow 'rightfully' belongs to civilians. It was General Nasution who was largely responsible for developing the idea of the army having a social and political as well as a military role.

This idea was taken and developed at the Army Staff & Command School in the late '50s and early '60s (when the then Colonel Suharto was a student there). It was decided that national defence policy was to be based on the army, since the navy and air force would never be strong enough to block an invasion. The army would have to be one that could continue, in the last resort, an indefinite guerrilla struggle. To be successful in such a war the army would have to be accepted and supported by the people.

Therefore to prepare for this eventuality the army would have to be permanently in contact with the people at local level so as to build up and sustain their goodwill. Thus developed the idea and the subsequent implementation of 'Territorial

Management', the establishment of a parallel administration down to village level where resident army personnel could supervise and prod the civil authorities. There is the assumption within the Indonesian army that it *should* play a central role in uniting the nation and guiding its development.

The President

Suharto was born in 1921 and spent his childhood amongst peasants in small villages in Central Java and in Solo, his father ensuring that he got a primary and middle school education. The time he spent from the age of 15 living in the house of a *dukun* appears to have imbued him with a sense of traditional Javanese mysticism which has lasted to this day. He joined the Royal Netherlands Indies Army in 1940 and quickly became a sergeant. He served with the Japanese during the occupation and became an officer in the Japanese-sponsored Volunteer Army of Defenders of the Motherland. He led attacks against the Dutch during the independence struggle after WW II and rose rapidly through the ranks.

In 1962 he was promoted to Major-General by Sukarno and was put in charge of the forces which were set up to take West Irian from the Dutch. In 1961 he became commander of the army's Strategic Reserve (later to be known as KOSTRAD). This was an important posting since the reserve, set up by Nasution, was a well-equipped, highly mobile fighting force directly at the disposal of the General Staff, thus avoiding any argument or even outright opposition from regional commanders.

Just why Suharto took the role of overthrowing Sukarno is unclear –perhaps it was personal ambition, a reaction to the attempted coup, unease at the growing strength of the PKI, a reaction to the deterioration of the economy under Sukarno, or a mixture of all four. Certainly Suharto cut through his opponents with exceptional determination.

The Pancasila Democracy

The present regime calls its rule the Pancasila democracy. Since it was first expounded by Sukarno in 1945 the Pancasila (Five Principles) have remained the philosophical backbone of the Indonesian state. It was meant by Sukarno to provide a broad philosophical base on which a united Indonesian state could be formed. All over Indonesia you'll see the Indonesian coat of arms with its symbolic incorporation of the Pancasila – framed and hung on the walls of government offices and the homes of village heads, emblazoned on the covers of student textbooks, or immortalised on great stone tablets. These principles are:

1. Faith in God – symbolised by the star. It doesn't matter which God – Allah, Vishnu, Buddha or whoever – but all Indonesians must believe in God.

2. Humanity – symbolised by the chain. This represents the unbroken unity of mankind, and Indonesia takes its place amongst this family of nations.

3. Nationalism – symbolised by the head of the buffalo. All ethnic groups in Indonesia must unite.

Pancasila Crest

4. Representative Government – symbolised by the banyan tree. As distinct from the western brand of parliamentary democracy, Sukarno envisaged a form of Indonesian democracy based on the village system of deliberation (*permusyawaratan*) among representatives to achieve consensus (*mufakat*). The western system of 'majority rules' is considered a means by which 51% oppress the other 49%.

5. Social Justice – symbolised by the sprays of rice and cotton. A just and prosperous society that will give adequate supplies of food and clothing for all, the basic requirements of social justice.

While the Pancasila was originally designed as a means of uniting the Indonesians, in practice different political groups have sought to interpret the five principles to serve their own purposes. The attempt by Sukarno to satisfy all religious groups in the archipelago by affirming belief in an unspecified God was not entirely successful since many Muslims insisted that the only valid religion was Islam and the only true God was Allah.

ECONOMY

Indonesia is potentially one of the wealthiest countries in the world since it is endowed with substantial natural resources. The Indonesian government gets something like 60 to 65% of its revenue from oil taxes and 70 to 80% of export earnings comes from oil. Indonesia is the world's eighth largest oil producer and the largest exporter of liquefied natural gas. There are also large reserves of tin, coal, copper and bauxite, substantial cash crops like rubber and copra, and there is now a determined effort to attract the tourist dollar. The problem is utilising these resources effectively; the dependence on oil and natural gas exports makes Indonesia particularly vulnerable to any slump in the world economy, while other raw materials are shipped out of the country by foreign companies with minimal benefit to the local people.

During the Suharto era the Indonesian economy has largely been governed by an alliance of army-leaders and western-educated economists. Rigorous economic measures were taken in the first years of the regime designed to get Indonesia back on its feet after the economic mis-management of the Sukarno years. Sufficiently large cuts were made in government expenditure to balance the budget; the plunge of the rupiah was halted; rice prices were kept temporarily in check by establishing a reserve which reduced speculation; inflation was dramatically reduced; and there was some success in stabilising the price of other basic commodities.

Under Suharto's rule the Planning Body for National Development (*Bappenas*) has implemented a series of Five Year Development Plans designed to rehabilitate and improve the economy. The acronym for these plans is *Pelita*, which also means the lamp which illuminates a wayang performance. While there has been overall improvement, the Indonesian economy over the last 20 years has been racked by incompetence, mismanagement, corruption, and exploitation by the west.

Corruption

There is one seemingly static, permanent feature of the Indonesian economy – corruption. It would be an understatement to say that the army and the economy of Indonesia are closely-knit; military leaders head or are mixed up with an incredible range of business enterprises. The reason for this can partly be found in the 1950s when conventional sources of revenue for the army were so inadequate that other sources had to be found for army leaders to keep their units going. The army was not the only poorly paid institution; civil servants and professional people were taking second jobs and running private businesses to supplement inadequate official pay packets.

In 1957 Dutch assets in Indonesia were seized as part of the government's anti-Dutch nationalisation policy of the time. The seizures were carried out by the army and it left the officers in charge of running factories, trading companies and plantations. Some profits were directed back to their units and in areas with export produce, smuggling flourished. The problem with this sort of system is where philanthropy ends and corruption begins, where bonds of mutual loyalty mean that associates get promoted at the expense of competence, and where the army starts using its muscle – such as martial law powers – to help its profitable business enterprises keep making a profit.

Personal enrichment from holding government office is not something new under Suharto – it was normal under the Dutch rule, the rule of the VOC and during the rule of the Indonesian princes who farmed out monopolies and revenue-collecting agencies to favoured court clients. During the first years of independence one needed friends in key bureaucratic positions and on a small scale this meant cash payments to petty officials. For big business it required an alliance with a minister or senior bureaucrat. When the regime changed in 1965-67 many business fiefdoms also changed – the Mercedes Benz dealership for example passed from a PNI-linked businessman to an army trading company, and when that collapsed it went into the hands of General Ibnu Sutowo who ran the Pertamina oil conglomerate.

While corruption is not a new problem in Indonesia it has certainly been worsened by the political changes since 1965. These changes are the extension of the parallel military administration, and the removal of any counterbalancing political forces. Forces which are needed to keep in check the often united front of

military and civilian administrators, security officials and other local notables.

The Pertamina Debacle

The classic example of corruption and industrial mismanagement under the Suharto government was the near collapse of the oil company *Pertamina* and the industrial empire which grew out of it under the control of Lieutenant-General Ibnu Sutowo (originally appointed to his position by President Sukarno).

The company originated from an oil company under army control which was established in 1957 to develop the north Sumatra oilfields. By 1967 Pertamina had taken over management and control of the nation's oil production. By 1974 Pertamina's interests moved into all sorts of other enterprises: petrochemical production, fertilisers, shipping and real estate, steel manufacture, rice production in Sumatra, even an airline (Pelita).

Sutowo had turned Pertamina into a private financial and industrial complex that was accountable to nobody but himself. In one of the last gasp efforts of what was left of the free press in 1969, Sutowo was accused by the newspaper *Indonesia Raja* of frittering away loans and oil revenue on irrelevant ventures including a mosque at the University of Indonesia, a US$2.5 million sports stadium at Palembang, a travel office and two hotels in Jakarta, and a restaurant in New York. He was also making profits from his position as a director of a Hong Kong insurance company he had set up to insure Pertamina's ships. He sold mining concessions to friends for nominal fees who resold them for huge profits; he collected what amounted to presents from foreigners worth US$60 million; he devised contracts by which Indonesia actually lost money by selling oil through Japanese trading companies. The paper listed the names, prices, and market values of five secondhand tankers which Pertamina was supposed to have bought – on Sutowo's instructions – for more than they were worth, the implication being that someone got a kickback.

Pertamina's schemes were financed by heavy borrowing from overseas and by the early 1970s it had got out of hand. Loans were being repaid with other loans and an enormous debt had accumulated. Finally the Japanese and American banks came to their senses and loans to Pertamina dried up. Pertamina finally crashed in early 1975 and the government had to bail it out. The government took over the responsibility of repaying Pertamina's debts and also determined that in future all borrowing for state enterprises should be through the Bank of Indonesia or the Ministry of Finance. Sutowo was replaced as head of Pertamina in 1976. Pertamina's total debts were estimated at US\$10,500 million – greater than the total 1976-77 national budget and two thirds of the gross domestic product!

Foreign Stakes

The USA and Japan have the biggest economic stakes in Indonesia. Their interests in the archipelago increased significantly between WW I and II although their investments were still well behind the Dutch and British. Japanese and American interests included tin and rubber – they looked to Indonesia as a source of natural rubber, as an alternative supplier to British-controlled Malaya – and they tried to gain a foothold in the Indonesian oil industry. There had been little exploitation of Indonesia's resources before WW II but they remained a factor in US thinking and policy concerning South-East Asia.

With the fall of Sukarno, Suharto made a determined effort to attract foreign aid and investment. Old debts were recognised by the Indonesian government, nationalised estates of former foreign owners were restored, and laws were passed to encourage foreign capital investments. Loans from western nations were provided partly as a lever to obtain licenses to exploit the country's natural wealth. The

west is obviously concerned to protect its interests in Indonesian oil and mineral resources, to maintain Indonesia as a market for its exports, and to support a government which has shown itself amenable to western interests.

The Rural Sector

Although Indonesia produces a range of agricultural products, including exotic introductions from Latin America thanks to the early Spanish and Portuguese settlers, the staple produce remains rice. As you move across the archipelago you also find other staples including maize (corn) and sago in the extreme east.

Rice cultivation in terraced sawah fields has been known for over 2000 years. In sparsely populated areas of Sumatra, Kalimantan and West Java, where the peasants moved from one place to another, a form of shifting cultivation or ladang was developed. In ladang cultivation the jungle is burned off to speed up the normal process of decomposition and enrich the soil in preparation for planting, but the soil quickly loses its fertility.

With the exception of Bali and most of Java, plus a few much smaller patches across the archipelago, the soil is just as poor in Indonesia as it is elsewhere in the tropics. When the top cover of forest is removed the intense heat and heavy rain soon leach the soil of its fertility. As a result settled agriculture is impossible without the continuous addition of soil nutrients.

The difficulties of making any improvement in the rural sector are immense and various schemes introduced in the late '60s and '70s often had poor results due to poor planning, official bungling or corruption. Some schemes, while increasing productivity or improving the lot of the land-owning farmers, completely missed other sectors of the population, such as the landless farm labourers, or actually made them worse off. The introduction of high-yield varieties of rice from 1968 however, has made a great difference.

Tourism

Over the last decade or so, Indonesia has made a big effort to attract tourists and in 1989 the government announced it had passed its target of 1.25 million visitors a year, bringing in more than US$1 billion of foreign exchange – then promptly set a new goal of 2.5 to three million by 1994! It's the up-market foreigners that Indonesia really wants to pull in – specifically those who spend US$75 to US$125 per day for a two-week stay.

Western Europe is still regarded as the steadiest source of longer-staying visitors, followed by the America (many Americans are expatriates living in Asia, such as the US armed forces personnel stationed in the Philippines and Japan). Countries in the region – like Australia, Singapore, Japan and Malaysia – are also important sources of tourists. In Bali the Japanese are the second biggest group of foreign visitors – trooping in behind the Australians who often appear to have co-evolved there with surfboards and motorcycles.

Amongst other ideas aimed at stimulating the tourist trade are campaigns to attract conventions; more hotel rooms in Jakarta and Bali; the new airport in Jakarta; promotion of 'marine tourism' including the great rivers of Sumatra and Kalimantan; even roadside inns along the Trans-Sumatran Highway with a view to developing tours of the island by car. But perhaps the best achievement of the push for more tourists is the two-month tourist pass, which eliminates the need for a visa so long as you enter the country through specific airports or seaports, and makes travel in Indonesia much easier than it ever has been in the past.

Poverty & Prospects for the Future

Government-sponsored and financed irrigation projects, fertiliser subsidies and cheap agricultural credit enabled Indonesia to become self-sufficient in rice production by 1982, and thus reduce its risky dependency on food imports. While this was a significant step forward, attempts to alleviate poverty have met with a mixed bag of successes and failures.

To help assure access to essential goods, both the Sukarno and the Suharto governments have operated a nation-wide system of subsidies and price controls for necessities, including rice, wheat, sugar, cooking kerosene and gasoline. Increasing financial stringency in recent years has forced cutbacks on subsidies. In particular the domestic price of oil has risen, forcing up the price of everything else. Health care has received high priority with considerable expansion in the number of health centres. One sign of general improvement has been a significant drop in the infant mortality rate – from 14% in the early 1970s to 9% today (by comparison the Australian infant mortality rate is 1% and the Japanese is 0.7%). Education also has a high priority and, except for some isolated areas, nearly all children have access to primary school education although there is a shortage of qualified teachers and in rural areas the quality of education doesn't ensure that the majority of children will leave school literate.

New industries have been established and productivity has been greatly increased in older ones. The production of these industries and the employment they offer reaches only a small proportion of the population. The population is still overwhelmingly rural and a large proportion of the population works on small farms. The average Indonesian farm labourer gets by on very little. Typical wages may vary from 500 to 2000 rp a day.

By comparison textile workers and bemo drivers earn about 2500 rp, teachers and government officials average maybe 4000 rp. The rich and the small middle class meanwhile are definitely getting richer and have taken to western consumerism in a big way – as the proliferation of flashy cars in places like Kuta shows.

While rural productivity has increased so has rural unemployment. The introduction of sickles, rotary weeders replacing hand weeding, and even Japanese hand-tractors has reduced the need for farm labour and benefited the larger farmers at the expense of the labourers. Then there's the continuing population increase and the inability of the government to formulate policies to deal with growing unemployment (a failing hardly unique to the Indonesian government).

Since political activity and organisations are now banned at village level (except during the staged elections held every five years) the rural poor – the labourers and those with minimal holdings – are completely unprotected by any sort of legislation, political party, union or other organisation. There may not be any organised resistance but every so often some sporadic outburst of violence is reported in the Indonesian press – such as West Javanese villagers burning down a caustic-soda factory whose acid discharge had poisoned their paddy fields and fishponds; attacks by canoe-fishermen on trawlers intruding into their fishing grounds; wrecking of tractors, and 'night harvests' on the fields of landed farmers.

While Indonesia is economically better off than it was 20 years ago, the lot of the average Indonesian is, arguably, getting harder. In 1988 an estimated 35 million people, one-fifth of the population, were living on less than 450 rp a day. Yet somehow even the poorest of Indonesians show a remarkable resilience and capacity to survive. They sell food, clothing, plastic shoes; sit on the side of the street all day flogging off a few combs or a couple of bunches of bananas; jump on crowded buses to hawk ice blocks, pineapple chunks, or single cigarettes. They sift through garbage, recycle the tobacco from cigarette ends, pedal becaks, shine shoes, mind parked cars, or scratch some of the money from the tourist industry as touts. And if they come home with nothing then their family or neighbours will help them to survive another day.

POPULATION & PEOPLE

Indonesia's national motto is *Bhinneka Tunggal Ika*, an old Javanese phrase meaning 'they are many; they are one' which usually gets translated as 'Unity in Diversity'. The peoples of the archipelago were not 'Indonesian' until 1949 when a line was drawn on the map enclosing a group of islands which housed a remarkably varied collection of people.

Most Indonesians are of Malay stock, descended from peoples who originated in China and Indo-China and spread into Indonesia over several thousand years. The other major grouping is the darker-skinned, fuzzy-haired Melanesians who inhabit much of easternmost Indonesia.

Despite the Malay predominance, the culture and customs of the various islands are often quite different. There are different languages and dialects, different religions, and differences in *adat*, the unwritten village law which regulates the behaviour of everyone in every village in Indonesia. The Indonesian terrain is partly responsible for the incredible diversity; mountains and jungle cut tribes and groups on certain islands off from the outside world – like the Kubu tribe of south Sumatra, thought to be descendants of the original settlers from Sri Lanka. They were barely known to outsiders until guerrillas fighting against the Dutch came into contact with them. Other isolated groups have included the Papuan Dani people of the Balim Valley in Irian Jaya, and the Dayaks – the collective name given to the people who inhabit the interior of Borneo. There are also the Baduis of West Java who withdrew to the highlands as the Islamic religion spread through the island, and have had little contact with outsiders. Other distinctive groups, like the Balinese and Javanese, have had considerable contact with the outside world but nonetheless have managed to maintain their traditional cultures intact.

Population & Overpopulation

Indonesia's total population is around 175 million. Java alone has over 100 million people.

Indonesia's population is growing at a rate of about 1.7% per year. If it continues at that rate it will have almost 200 million people by the turn of the century. By the year 2035 the population will be around 300 million. Overpopulation, however, is largely a Javanese and to some extent a Balinese problem. Java's population was estimated as six million in 1825, 9.5 million in 1850, 18 million in 1875, 28 million in 1900, 36 million in 1925, and 63 million in 1961.

Java and the island of Madura off Java's north coast have a total area of 130,000 square km or about 1½ times the area of Britain. Java's population density is more than 600 people per square km or about twice that of either England or Holland (the two most densely populated countries in Europe) and more than twice that of Japan.

Population Control

Each year perhaps three million people are added to the Indonesian population, most of them in Java. However, there are birth control programmes operating in Indonesia but whether they have had much success is debatable.

After taking power Suharto reversed Sukarno's policies of continued population expansion to provide a work force to develop the outer islands. He set up a National Family Planning Co-ordinating Board which greatly expanded the network of private clinics providing free contraceptive services. Efforts were concentrated on Bali and Java at first and noticeable drops in the birth rate were reported. It was also reported that over 80% of the people who took part in the scheme were the wives of peasants,

'Two Children Is Enough'
Family Planning poster

fishermen and labourers – the poorer end of the scale who normally have the most children.

There has been lesser success in highly traditional areas (like Yogyakarta) and in the more strongly Muslim areas. A major obstacle to change amongst the latter group is the popular belief that Allah will take care of a family's needs no matter how big it grows.

The board's most noticeable propaganda is the 'Happy Family' symbol, a couple with two children, on the five rupiah coin which is the smallest coin in circulation. There has also been a blitz of slogan propaganda; *Kami Keluarga Kecil Yang Bahagia Dan Sejahtera*, for example, means 'We are a small family, which is content and doing fine'. Whether anyone actually takes any notice is hard to say;

personal experience suggests that large families are still the rule in Indonesia.

Transmigration

As well as reducing the birth rate, attempts are also being made to take the pressure off heavily populated areas, particularly Java and Bali, by moving people out to less populated areas like Sumatra, Kalimantan, Irian Jaya and Maluku.

These *transmigrasi* programmes started with Dutch efforts to relieve population pressure in Java in 1905. The Suharto government's first Five Year Plan moved 182,000 out of Java, Bali and Lombok – below target by only 8000 people. The second Five Year Plan aimed to move over a million people in the five years from 1974 – but by 1976 the target figure had to be reduced by half. The third and fourth Five Year Plans (1979-1984 and 1984-89) ambitiously aimed at shifting 500,000 and 750,000 families respectively – more than five million people.

So far, however, the transmigrasi programmes seem to have had little effect on the population burden of Java. The main problem is that insufficient numbers of people can physically be moved to offset the growth in population. Furthermore, transmigration settlements have developed a poor reputation – one of the underlying faults has been the tendency to attempt wet-rice cultivation in unsuitable areas. Settlers have frequently ended up subsistence farmers no better off than they were back in Java, if not because of poor soil and water then because of inadequate support services and isolation from markets.

In addition most government sponsored transmigrants are not experienced farmers; two-thirds of transmigrants are landless peasants, the poorest of the countryside, and another 10% are homeless city dwellers. Up until 1973, the urban poor of Jakarta were often virtually press-ganged into moving out of Java – they turned out to be the least successful transmigrants,

often returning to the towns they came from. The most successful transmigrants are often those who move 'spontaneously' – because they emigrate on their own initiative to the outer islands, and because they can choose where to live. Transmigration is a voluntary programme but as officials strain to meet new targets, there is increasing pressure on people to sign up.

Transmigration also often causes damage to the natural environment through destruction of rainforest, loss of topsoil and degraded water supplies. Tension, even conflict, with the indigenous people in some settled areas is not uncommon.

RELIGION

The early Indonesians were animists and practised ancestor and spirit worship. The social and religious duties of the early agricultural communities that developed in the archipelago were gradually refined to form a code of behaviour which became the basis of *adat*, or customary law. When Hindu-Buddhism spread into the archipelago it was overlaid on this already well developed spiritual culture.

Though Islam was to become the predominant religion of the archipelago it was really only a nominal victory and what we see in ostensibly Islamic Indonesia today is actually Islam deeply rooted in Hindu-Buddhism, adat and animism. Old beliefs carry on and in Java, for example, there are literally hundreds of holy places where spiritual energy is said to be concentrated; amongst them the Sendang Semanggi spring near Yogya, the Gua Sirandil sea-cave near Cilacap, and the misty uplands of the Dieng Plateau – all places where with patient meditation and self-denial the spiritual force may be absorbed. Today a holy stone on Mt Bromo in East Java still receives regular offerings from some Tenggerese villagers as it did when animism was the predominant religion.

As for Christianity, despite the lengthy

colonial era the missionaries have only been successful in converting pockets of the Indonesian population – the Bataks of Sumatra, the Minahasans and Toraja of Sulawesi, some of the Dayaks of Kalimantan, the Florinese, Ambonese and some of the West Irianese. Christian beliefs are also usually bound up with traditional religious beliefs and customs.

There are still a few pockets where animism survives virtually intact, such as in west Sumba and some parts of Irian Jaya.

Hinduism

Outside India, Hindus predominate only in Nepal and Bali. It is one of the oldest extant religions, its roots extending back beyond 1000 BC, in the civilisation which grew up along the Indus River Valley in what is now modern-day Pakistan.

The Hindus believe that underlying a person's body, personality, mind and memories there is something else – it never dies, it is never exhausted, it is without limit of awareness and bliss. What confuses westerners is the vast pantheon of gods found in Hinduism – you can look upon these different gods as representations of the many attributes of an omnipresent god. The symbols and images of Hinduism are meant to introduce the worshipper to what they *represent* – the images should not be mistaken with idolatry, and the multiplicity of them with polytheism. The three main physical representations of the one omnipresent god are Brahma the creator, Vishnu the preserver and Shiva the destroyer.

Central to Hinduism is the belief that we will all go through a series of rebirths or reincarnations – eventual freedom from this cycle depends on your karma – bad actions during your present life result in bad karma and this results in a lower reincarnation. Conversely if your deeds and actions have been good you will be reincarnated on a higher level and you'll be a step closer to eventual freedom from

rebirth. Hinduism specifies four main castes; the highest is the *Brahmin* priest caste, next the *Kshatriyas* who are soldiers and governors, the *Vaisyas* are tradespeople and farmers, and lowest are the *Sudras* who are menial workers and craftspeople. You cannot change your caste – you're born into it and are stuck with it for the rest of that lifetime.

Centuries ago Hinduism pervaded Java and spread to Bali. Today, Hinduism in Bali bears only a vague resemblance to the form practised on the Indian subcontinent. In Indonesia Hinduism survives in a much more tangible form in the remains of great temples like Prambanan near Yogyakarta and those on the Dieng Plateau, and in stories and legends still told in dance and in the wayang puppet performances of both Bali and Java.

These stories are drawn from a number of ancient Hindu texts including the *Bhagavad Gita*, a poem credited to the philosopher-soldier Krishna in which he explains the duties of a warrior to Prince Arjuna. The *Bhagavad Gita* is contained in the *Mahabharata* which tells of a great battle said to have taken place in northern India.

The *Ramayana* is another story and tells of Prince Rama's expedition to rescue his wife, Sita, who had been carried away by the demon prince Rawana. In this epic Rama is aided by the monkey god Hanuman and by an army of monkeys. Rama is regarded as the personification of the ideal man and as an incarnation of the god Vishnu. Vishnu has visited the earth a number of times, the seventh time as Rama, and the eighth time as Krishna.

The gods are also seen depicted in statues and reliefs in the ancient Hindu temples of Java. Often they can be identified by the 'vehicle' upon which they ride; Vishnu's vehicle is the half man-half eagle Garuda, after whom Indonesia's international airline is named. Of all the Hindu gods Shiva, the destroyer, is probably the most powerful and the most worshipped but out of destruction comes creation and so the creative role of Shiva is frequently represented as the lingam – a phallic symbol. Shiva's consort is Parvati by whom he had two children, one of whom is Ganesh the elephant-headed god. Coming back from a long trip Shiva discovered Parvati in her room with a young man and, not pausing to think that their son might have grown up during his absence, lopped his head off! He was then forced by Parvati to bring his son back to life but could only do so by giving him the head of the first living thing he saw – which happened to be an elephant. Ganesh's vehicle is the rat.

Buddhism

Buddhism was founded in India around the 6th century BC by Siddhartha Gautama. He was a prince brought up in luxury, but in his 20s he despaired of ever finding fulfilment on the physical level since the body was inescapably involved with disease, decrepitude and death. Around the age of 30 he made his break from the material world, and plunged off in search of 'enlightenment'. After various unsuccessful stratagems, one evening he sat beneath a banyan tree in deep meditation and achieved enlightenment.

Buddha founded an order of monks and for the next 45 years preached his ideas until his death around 480 BC. To his followers he was known as Sakyamuni. Gautama Buddha is not the only Buddha, but the fourth, and he is not expected to be the last one.

Buddha taught that all life is suffering and that happiness can only be achieved by overcoming this suffering through following the 'eight-fold path' to nirvana, a condition beyond the limits of the mind where one is no longer oppressed by earthly desires. Strictly speaking, Buddhism is more of a philosophy and a code of morality than a religion, since it is not centred on a god. Buddhism appears to retain some of the Hindu concepts, such as the idea of reincarnation and karma.

Hinduism & Buddhism in Indonesia

It remains one of the puzzles of Indonesian history how the ancient kingdoms of the archipelago were penetrated by Hinduism and Buddhism. The evidence of Hindu-Buddhist influence is clear enough in different parts of Indonesia where there are Sanskrit inscriptions dating back to the 5th century AD, and many Hindu and Buddhist shrines and statues have been found in the archipelago. Disentangling the two is difficult since there is usually a blending of Hindu and Buddhist teachings with older religious beliefs. It's been suggested, for instance, that the wayang puppet shows of Java have their roots in primitive Javanese ancestor worship, though the wayang stories that have been passed on are closely linked with later Hindu mythology or with Islam.

The elements of Indian religion and culture which had the greatest influence in Indonesia were those to do with courts and government: the Indian concept of the god-king, the use of Sanskrit as the language of religion and courtly literature and the introduction of Indian mythology. Even the events and people recorded in epics like the Ramayana and the Mahabharata have all been shifted out of India to Java. Various Hindu and Buddhist monuments were built in Java, of which the Buddhist stupa of Borobudur and the Hindu temple complex at Prambanan are the most impressive. The Sumatran-based Srivijaya kingdom, which arose in the 7th century, was the centre of Buddhism in Indonesia.

Bali's establishment as a Hindu enclave dates from the time the Javanese Hindu kingdom of Majapahit, in the face of Islam, virtually evacuated Java to the neighbouring island – taking with them their art, literature and music as well as their religion and rituals. It's a mistake, however, to think that this was purely an exotic seed planted on virgin soil. The

Balinese probably already had strong religious beliefs and an active cultural life and the new influences were simply overlaid on the existing practices – hence the peculiar Balinese variant of Hinduism. The Balinese worship the Hindu trinity of Brahma the creator, Shiva the destroyer and Vishnu the preserver but they also have a supreme god, Sanghyang Widhi. In Bali, unlike in India, the threesome is always alluded to, never seen – a vacant shrine or an empty throne says it all. Secondary Hindu gods, such as Ganesh, may occasionally appear, but there are many other purely Balinese gods, spirits and entities. Other aspects of Balinese Hinduism separate it from Indian Hinduism – like the widow-witch Rangda. She bears a close resemblance to Durga, the terrible side of Shiva's wife Parvati, but the Balinese Barong Dance (in which she appears) certainly isn't part of Indian Hinduism.

Ganesh

Islam

Islam is the most recent and widespread of the Asian religions. The founder of Islam was the Arab prophet Mohammed but he merely transmitted the word of God to his people. To call the religion 'Mohammedanism' is wrong, since it implies that the religion centres around Mohammed and not around God. The proper name of the religion is Islam, derived from the word *salam* which means primarily 'peace', but in a secondary sense 'surrender'. The full connotation is something like 'the peace which comes by surrendering to God'. A person who follows *Islam* is a *Muslim*.

The prophet was born around 570 AD and came to be called Mohammed, which means 'highly praised'. His descent is traditionally traced back to Abraham. There have been other true prophets before Mohammed – among them Moses, Abraham and Jesus – but Mohammed is regarded as the culmination of them and there will be no more prophets.

Mohammed taught that there is one all-powerful, all-pervading God, Allah. 'There is no God but Allah' is the fundamental tenet of the Islamic religion. The initial reaction to Mohammed's message was one of hostility; the uncompromising monotheism conflicted with the pantheism and idolatry of the Arabs. Apart from that, Mohammed's moral teachings conflicted with what he believed was a corrupt and decadent social order, and in a society which was afflicted with class divisions Mohammed preached a universal brotherhood in which all men are equal in the eyes of God. Mohammed and his followers were forced to flee from Mecca to Medina in 622 AD, and there Mohammed built up a political base and an army which eventually defeated Mecca but Mohammed died in 632 AD, two years later.

Mohammed's teachings are collected in the *Koran* (or *Qur'an*), the holy book of Islam, compiled after Mohammed's death. Much of the Koran is devoted to codes of behaviour, and much emphasis is placed on God's mercy to mankind. Mohammed's teachings are heavily influenced by two other religions, Judaism and Christianity, and there are some extraordinary similarities including a belief in a hell and a heaven, a belief in a judgement day, and a creation theory almost identical to the Garden of Eden and myths like Noah's Ark and Aaron's Rod.

Islam hangs on four pegs: God, Creation, Man, and the Day of Judgement. Everything in Islam centres on the fact of God or Allah but the distinctive feature of Islam is the appreciation of the value of the individual. In Hinduism and Buddhism the individual is just a fleeting expression with no permanence or value but the Islamic religion teaches that individuality, as expressed in the human soul, is eternal since once created the soul lives forever. For the Muslim, life on earth is just a forerunner to an eternal future in heaven or hell as appropriate.

Islam is a faith that demands unconditional surrender to the wisdom of Allah. It involves total commitment to a way of life, philosophy and law. Theoretically it is a democratic faith in which devotion is the responsibility of the individual, unrestricted by hierarchy and petty social prerequisites, and concerned with encouraging initiative and independence in the believer. Nor, in theory, is it bound to a particular locale – the faithful can worship in a rice field at home, in a mosque or on a mountain. It is also a fatalistic faith in that everything is rationalised as the will of Allah.

It is a moralistic religion and has its own set of rituals and laws such as worshipping five times a day, recitation of the Koran, almsgiving, and fasting annually during the month of Ramadan. Making the pilgrimage to Mecca is the foremost ambition of every devout Muslim – those who have done this, called *haji* if they are men or *haja* if women, are deeply respected. Other Muslim customs include the scrupulous attention given to cleanliness including ritualistic washing of hands and face. The pig is considered to be unclean and is not kept or eaten by strict Muslims.

Islam also called on its followers to spread the word – if necessary by the sword. In succeeding centuries Islam was to expand over three continents. By the time a century had passed the Arab Muslims had built a huge empire which stretched all the way from Persia to Spain. The Arabs, who first propagated the faith, developed a reputation as being ruthless opponents but reasonable masters so people often found it advisable to surrender to them.

At an early stage Islam suffered a fundamental split that remains to this day. The third Caliph, successor to Mohammed, was murdered and followed by Ali, the prophet's son-in-law, in 656 AD. Ali was assassinated in 661 by the Governor of Syria who set himself up as Caliph in preference to the descendants of Ali. Most Muslims today are *Sunnites*, followers of the succession from the Caliph, while the others are *Shias* or *Shi'ites* who follow the descendants of Ali.

Islam only travelled west for a hundred years before being pushed back at Poitiers in France in 732, but it continued east for centuries. It regenerated the Persian Empire which was then declining from its protracted struggles with Byzantium. In 711, the same year the Arabs landed in Spain, they sent dhows up the Indus River into India. This was more a raid than a full scale invasion but in the 11th century all of north India fell into Muslim hands. From India the faith was carried into South-East Asia by Arab and Indian traders.

Islam in Indonesia

Islam made its first appearance in Indonesia with the establishment of Arabic settlements in the latter part of the 7th century. How it managed to gain a hold over the region is, like the spread of Hindu-Buddhism, a mystery. One theory holds that Islam was introduced through the missionary activity of the Sufis – Muslims who practised forms of mysticism and could thus confront the mystics of the earlier Hindu and animist religions on equal terms. The Sufis were probably more tolerant of adat law which, on a strictly literal interpretation, could have been seen as conflicting with Islamic law.

The state of Pasai in Aceh adopted Islam near the end of the 13th century; the founder of Melaka had accepted the faith in the early part of the 15th century and within 50 years Melaka was renowned as a centre for the teaching of Islam as well as a centre of South-East Asian trade. Possibly the spread of Islam in the next few years was related to the territorial expansion and increasing political influence of Melaka. Trading ships carried the new religion to Java from where it spread to the spice islands of eastern Indonesia via Makassar (now Ujung Pandang) in Sulawesi. Islam caught on in Java in the 16th and 17th centuries and about the same time Aceh developed as a major Islamic power and the religion took root in west and south Sumatra, in Kalimantan and Sulawesi.

By the 15th and 16th centuries, centres for the teaching of Islam along the northern coast of Java may have played an important role in disseminating the new religion, along with previously established centres of Hindu learning which adopted elements of Islam. Javanese tradition holds that the first propagators of Islam in Java were nine holy men, the *wali songo*, who possessed both a deep knowledge of Islamic teaching as well as exceptional supernatural powers. Another theory holds that Islam was adopted by various Javanese princes who sought a supernatural sanction for their rule, and that the common people followed suit in much the same way as Europeans adopted the religions of their kings.

Whatever the reasons for the spread of Islam, today it is the professed religion of 90% of Indonesians and its traditions and rituals affect all aspects of their daily life. Like Hinduism and Buddhism before it, Islam also had to come to terms with older existing traditions and customs.

Indonesian Islam is rather different from the austere form found in the Middle East; customs in Indonesia often differ from those of other Muslim countries. Respect for the dead throughout most of Indonesia is not expressed by wearing veils but in donning traditional dress. Muslim women in Indonesia are allowed more freedom and shown more respect than their counterparts in other Muslim countries. They do not have to wear facial veils, nor are they segregated or considered to be second class citizens. Muslim men in Indonesia are only allowed to marry two women and even then must have the consent of their first wife – Muslims in other parts of the world can have as many as four wives. Throughout Indonesia it is the women who initiate divorce proceedings. The Minangkabau society of Sumatra, for example, is a strongly Muslim group but their adat laws allow matriarchal rule which conflicts strongly with the male supremacy inherent in Islam.

Like other Muslims, Indonesian Muslims practise circumcision. The laws of Islam require that all boys be circumcised and in Indonesia this is usually done somewhere between the ages of six and 11.

One of the most important Islamic festivals is *Ramadan*, a month of fasting prescribed by Islamic law, which falls in the ninth month of the Muslim calendar. It's often preceded by a cleansing ceremony, *Padusan*, to prepare for the coming fast. Traditionally during Ramadan people get up at 4 am to eat and then fast until sunset. During Ramadan many Muslims visit family graves and royal cemeteries, recite extracts from the Koran, sprinkle the graves with holy water and strew them with flowers. Special prayers are said at mosques and at home. The first day of the 10th month of the Muslim calendar is the end of Ramadan. Mass prayers are held in the early morning and these are followed by two days of feasting. Extracts from the Koran are read and religious processions take place; gifts are exchanged and

pardon is asked for past wrong-doings in this time of mutual forgiveness.

Islam not only influences routine daily living but also Indonesian politics. It was with the Diponegoro revolt in the 19th century that Islam first became a rallying point in Indonesia. In the early part of the 20th century Sarekat Islam became the first mass political party, its philosophy derived from Islam and its support from the Muslim population. In post-independence Indonesia it was an Islamic organisation, the Darul Islam, which launched a separatist movement in West Java. Despite the Islamic background of the country and the predominance of Muslims in the government, the government has not followed the trend towards a more fundamentalist Islamic state.

The Mosque A mosque is an enclosure for prayer. The word *masjid* means 'to prostrate oneself in prayer'. Mosques can be differentiated according to function: the *jami masjid* is used for the Friday prayer meetings; the *musalla* is one that is used for prayer meetings but not for Friday prayer meetings; the 'memorial mosque' is for the commemoration of victorious events in Islamic history; and a *mashad* is found in a tomb compound. There are also prayer houses which are used by only one person at a time, not for collective worship – you'll often find larger hotels and airport terminals in Indonesia have a room set aside for this purpose.

The oldest mosques in Indonesia – in Cirebon, Demak and Palembang, for example – have roofs with two, three or five storeys. It is thought that these multi-storeyed roofs were based on Hindu *meru* shrines that you'll still see in Bali. Today's mosques are often built with a high dome over an enclosed prayer hall. Inside there are five main features. The *mihrab* is a niche in a wall marking the direction to Mecca. The *mimbar* is a raised pulpit, often canopied, with a staircase. There is

also a stand to hold the Koran, a screen to provide privacy for important persons praying, and a fountain, pool or water jug for ablutions. Outside the building there is often a *menara* – a minaret, or tower, from which the *muezzin* summons the community to prayer.

Apart from these few items the interior of the mosque is empty. There are no seats and no decorations – if there is any ornamentation at all it will be quotations of verses from the Koran. The congregation sits on the floor.

Friday afternoons are officially decreed as the time for believers to worship and all government offices and many businesses are closed as a result. All over Indonesia you'll hear the call to prayer from the mosques, but the muezzin of Indonesia are now a dying breed – the wailing will usually be performed by a cassette tape.

HOLIDAYS & FESTIVALS

With such a diversity of people in the archipelago there are many local holidays and festivals. On Sumba for example, mock battles and jousting matches harking back to the era of internecine warfare are held in February and March. The Balinese have the *Galungan* festival during which time all the gods, including the supreme deity Sanghyang Widi, come down to earth to join in. In Tanatoraja in central Sulawesi the end of the harvest season is the time for funeral and house-warming ceremonies. In Java *Bersih Desa* takes place at the time of the rice harvest – houses and gardens are cleaned, village roads and paths repaired. This festival was once enacted to remove evil spirits from the village but it's now used to express gratitude to *Dewi Sri* the rice goddess. Since most Indonesians are Muslims, many holidays and festivals are associated with the Islamic religion. Muslim festivals are affected by the lunar calendar and dates move back 10 or 11 days each year, so it's not easy to list what month they will fall in.

Ramadan (Bulan Puasa)

The traditional Muslim month of daily fasting from sunrise to sunset. It's a good time to avoid fervent Muslim areas of Indonesia – you get woken up in your losmen at 3 am in the morning to have a meal before the fasting period begins. Many restaurants shut down during the day leaving you searching the backstreets for a restaurant that's open.

Lebaran (Idul Fitri)

This marks the end of Ramadan, and is a noisy celebration at the end of a month of gastronomic austerity. It's a national public holiday of two days duration.

Other Important Muslim Events

The *Alquran* is a Javanese and Sumatran oriented sacrificial ceremony. *Idul Adha* is a festival commemorating Abraham's willingness to sacrifice his son, Isaac, celebrated with prayers and feasts. *Maulud Nabi Mohammed* (Hari Natal) is the birthday of the Prophet Mohammed. *Isra Miraj Nabi Mohammed* celebrates the ascension of the Prophet. The last three are national public holidays.

Kartini Day

This day falls on 21 April and commemorates the birthday of Raden Ajeng Kartini, who was born in 1879. She was the daughter of the Regent of Jepara in Java and started a school for the daughters of regents aimed at giving them a western-style education. In letters to Dutch friends (which have been published) she poured out her feelings about the burdens and restrictions of Javanese and Islamic customs, and her writings also had a strong nationalist bent to them. She is considered not only an early nationalist but also the first Indonesian women's emancipationist.

Independence Day (Hari Proklamasi Kemerdekaan)

On 17 August 1945 Sukarno proclaimed Indonesian independence in Jakarta, and every year on this day celebrations of the event are held all over the country but particularly in Jakarta where there are parades, a flag-raising ceremony and a reading of the original text of the declaration. It's a national public holiday.

Christmas Day & New Year's Day

These are national public holidays.

A regional *Calendar of Events* is generally available from the appropriate regional tourist office. It lists national holidays, festivals particular to that region and many of the music, dance and theatre performances held throughout the year. There's also an *Indonesia Calendar of Events* booklet which covers holidays and festivals throughout the archipelago. You should be able to pick up a copy from any of the overseas Indonesian Tourist Promotion Offices, or overseas Garuda offices.

LANGUAGE

The 300-plus languages spoken throughout Indonesia, except those of the North Halmahera and most of Irian Jaya, belong to the Malay-Polynesian group. Within this group there are many different regional languages and dialects. There are, in fact, five main language groups in Sumatra alone: Acehnese, Batak, Minangkabau, Lampung and the language spoken along the east coast, originating in southern Sumatra and from which *Bahasa Indonesia* is derived. Sulawesi has at least six distinct language groups and the tiny island of Alor in Nusa Tenggara no less than seven. The languages of the Kalimantan interior form their own distinct sub-family.

Java has three main languages: Sundanese spoken in West Java, Javanese spoken in Central and East Java, and Madurese spoken on the island of Madura (off the north coast of Java) and parts of East Java. The Balinese have their own language. An interesting feature of the

Balinese, Javanese and Sundanese languages is their division into many levels – different words may be used when speaking to an inferior, an equal or a superior. In Javanese, yet another courtly level exists for use when speaking to the sultan. These levels are more than simply the difference between polite or formal usage and everyday speech, for they have different words even for everyday things.

Bahasa Indonesia

Today, the national language of Indonesia is Bahasa Indonesia which is basically the same as Malay. Pure Malay, as spoken by the Malaysians, is confined in Indonesia to Sumatra but it has long been the common language of the Indonesian archipelago, having been the language of inter-island trade for centuries. As spoken, Bahasa Indonesia is close enough to the language spoken on the Malay peninsula for Malay and Indonesian to be mutually intelligible. *Bahasa* simply means 'language' – and so *Bahasa Indonesia* is simply the 'language of Indonesia'.

Javanese, with its 'high' and 'low' forms, was too complicated to become a national language – even if it was used by the main ethnic group of the archipelago. Although educated Indonesians used Dutch as their common language during the colonial era, it was Malay which was taken up by the nationalist movements as a means of mass communication. They used the slogan 'one country, one people, one language' even before national independence was achieved. The use of a single, common language was part of the attempt to achieve unity amongst the diverse peoples of the archipelago.

Indonesian is a language with many foreign words mixed in indicating the long history of contact the archipelago has had with other cultures; Sanskrit words include *angsa* (duck), *gembala* (shepherd) and *kaca* (mirror). The Portuguese left signs of their presence with words like *mentega* (butter), *pesta* (festival), *gereja* (church), *meja* (table) and even the name of the island of *Flores* which is Portuguese for 'flowers'. Indonesian can be a very musical and evocative language, eg the sun is *mata hari* derived from the words for day (*hari*) and eye (*mata*), thus *mata hari* is the 'eye of day'.

Communicating

Bahasa Indonesia is now actively promoted as the national language. Almost anywhere you go in Indonesia people will speak Bahasa Indonesia as well as their own local language. Amongst the older generation, there are still quite a number of Dutch-speaking people. Today, English is the first foreign language and a lot of Indonesians know a few phrases of English but rarely enough to communicate with. In more isolated areas you may find that only younger people and children will know Bahasa Indonesia since they're taught it in school, but that some of the older people don't understand it.

Outside Java and Bali, particularly in places like Nusa Tenggara where there are few tourists, it's essential to know some Indonesian! Learn how to ask for a hotel room, prices, and to order meals. Learn the numbers so you can ask about departure times. Useful phrases are those that begin with 'I go . . .' and 'I want . . .' such as 'I want to buy a bus ticket to Ruteng' or 'I want to go to the Losmen Mutiara'.

Like any language Bahasa Indonesia has its simplified colloquial form and its more developed literate language. For the visitor who wants to pick up just enough to get by, the common language – *pasar* or market Indonesian – is very easy to learn. It's rated as one of the simplest languages in the world as there are no tenses, no genders, and often one word can convey the meaning of the whole sentence. There are often no plurals or it is only necessary to say the word twice. It's an easy language to pronounce with no obscure rules and none of the tonal complications that make some Asian languages difficult – like Thai and Chinese.

You can learn enough Bahasa Indonesia to get by within a month. Once you get deep into the language it's as complicated as any other, but for everyday use it's easy to learn and pronounce. And even if you can't understand much that people say to you, not having to resort to phrase books to communicate your needs is half the battle won.

Apart from the ease of learning a little

Bahasa Indonesia, there's another very good reason for trying to pick up at least a few words and phrases – few people are as delighted with foreigners learning their language as the Indonesians. They don't criticise you if you mangle your pronunciation or tangle your grammar. They make you feel like you're an expert if you know only a handful of words, and bargaining is a lot easier when you do it in their language. And once you know some Bahasa Indonesia you can start picking

up bits and pieces of the regional languages – which can be fun, although you're best off putting your efforts into learning Bahasa Indonesia.

Some of the basics of the language are shown below. For a more comprehensive overview, get Lonely Planet's *Indonesia Phrasebook* by Margit Meinhold. It's set out with a view to teaching the basics of the language, rather than just listing endless phrases.

An English/Indonesian – Indonesian/English dictionary is also very useful. They're sold quite cheaply in Indonesia, and you can also get bilingual dictionaries in French, German, Dutch and Japanese. Western secondary school Indonesian text-books are worth buying before you leave and taking with you.

Get some children's reading books in Indonesia, since they'll be graded from beginner up; Indonesian comic books are also good because the pictures will help you work out the meaning of the words. The Indonesians themselves are enthusiastic and amazingly patient teachers.

Pronunciation

Most sounds are the same as in English although a few vowels and consonants differ. The sounds are nearly the same every time.

a is pronounced like the 'a' in 'father'.

e is like the 'e' in 'bet' when unstressed, as in *besar* (big), and sometimes is hardly pronounced at all, as in the greeting *Selamat*, which sounds like 'slamat' when spoken quickly. When stressed it is like the 'a' in 'may', as in *becak* (rickshaw), pronounced 'baycha'. There is no general rule as to when the 'e' is stressed or unstressed.

i is pronounced like the 'i' sound in 'unique'.

o is similar to the English sound in 'hot'

u is pronounced like the 'u' in 'put'

There are also three vowel combinations, **ai**, **au** and **ua**. The sounds of the individual vowels do not change, but are simply run on by sliding from one to the other;

ai is pronounced like 'i' as in 'line'

au is pronounced like a drawn out 'ow' as in 'cow'

ua at the start of a word is rather like a 'w' sound – such as *uang* which means 'money' and is pronounced like 'wong'.

The pronunciation of consonants is very straightforward. Each is pronounced consistently and most sound like English consonants, except:

c is always pronounced 'ch' as in 'chair'

g is always pronounced hard, as 'g' like in 'garden'

ng is always pronounced like 'ng' in 'singer'

ngg is always pronounced like 'ng' in 'anger'

j is always pronounced like the 'j' in 'join'.

r is pronounced very clearly and distinctly, and is always slightly trilled – achieved by rolling your tongue. For example, 'how are you?' is *apa kabar*, pronounced 'apa kabarrr'

h is always pronounced, except at the end of a word. It is stressed a bit more strongly than in English, as if you were sighing.

k is pronounced like the English 'k' except when it appears at the end of the word – in which case you just stop short of actually saying the 'k'

ny is a single sound like the beginning of 'new', before the 'oo' part of that word.

Stress

There is no strong stress in Indonesian, and nearly all syllables have equal emphasis, but a good approximation is to stress the second to last syllable. The main exception to the rule is the unstressed 'e' in words such as *besar* (big), pronounced be-SARRR.

General Rules

Articles are not used in Indonesian – there's no 'the' or 'a' – nor is the intransitive verb 'to be' used. Thus where we would say 'the room is dirty' in Indonesian it is simply *kamar kotor* – 'room dirty'. To make a word plural in some cases you double it – thus 'child' is *anak*, 'children' *anak anak* – but in many other cases you simply use the same singular form and the context or words such as 'many' (*banyak*) indicate the plurality.

Probably the greatest simplification in Indonesian is that verbs are not conjugated nor are there different forms for past, present and future tenses. Instead words like 'already' (*sudah*), 'yesterday' (*kemarin*), 'will' (*akan*) or 'tomorrow' (*besok*) are used to indicate the tense. *Sudah* is the all purpose past tense indicator; 'I eat' is *saya makan* while 'I have already eaten' is simply *saya sudah makan*.

Except for the adjectives 'all' (*semua*), 'many' (*banyak*) and 'a little' (*sedikit*) adjectives follow the noun. Thus a 'big bus' is *bis besar*.

Pronouns

I	*saya*
you (sing)	*saudara*
he/she/it	*dia/ia*
we	*kita/kami*
you (pl)	*saudara*
they	*mereka*

Pronouns are often dropped when the meaning is clear from the context. This is just as well because more than a dozen words for 'you' are used, depending on the age, status or sex of the person addressed.

Speaking to a older man (especially anyone old enough to be your father) or to show respect for a man of high status, it's common to call them *bapak*, 'father' or simply *pak*. Similarly an older woman is *ibu*, 'mother' or simply *bu*. To use other forms such as *saudara* when talking to someone who is obviously your senior may well cause offence.

Tuan is a respectful term, like 'sir', and is often used to address officials. *Nyonya* is the equivalent for a married woman and *nona* for an unmarried woman. When in doubt, use these forms to avoid causing offence.

You can call someone slightly older or of the same age either *abang* (older brother) or *kakak* (older sister). *Kamu* (or simply *mu*) and *engkau* are only used among friends or to address children.

Saudara is a more formal, less-used word for people of roughly the same age or status whom you do not know well. *Anda* is the egalitarian form designed to overcome the plethora of words for the second person. It is often seen in written Indonesian and is becoming more common in everyday speech.

Greeting & Civilities

good morning	*selamat pagi*
good day	*selamat siang*
good afternoon/ evening	*selamat sore*
good night	*selamat malam*
good night (to someone going to bed)	*selamat tidur*
welcome	*selamat datang*
goodbye (said by the person who is	*selamat tinggal*

leaving to
the person who
is staying)

goodbye   *selamat jalan*
(said by the
person who is
staying to
the person who
is going)

Morning is *pagi* and extends from about 7 to 11 am. *Pagi pagi* is early morning – before 7 am. *Siang* is the middle of the day, around 11 am to 3 pm. *Sore* is the afternoon, around 3 to 7 pm. Night is *malam* and only really starts when it gets dark.

thank you	*terima kasih*
thank you very much	*terima kasih banyak*
please (asking for help)	*tolong*
please open the door	*tolong buka pinta*
please (giving permission)	*silakan*
please come in	*silakan masuk*
sorry	*ma'af*
excuse me	*permisi*
how are you?	*apa kabar?*
I'm fine	*kabar baik*
what is your name?	*siapa nama saudara?*
my name is . . .	*nama saya . . .*
another, one more	*satu lagi*
good, fine, OK	*baik*
nice, good	*bagus*
yes	*ya*
not, no – the negative	*tidak/bukan*

The negative *tidak* is used with verbs, adjectives and adverbs, whilst *bukan* is used with nouns and pronouns.

Questions & Comments

what is this?	*apa ini?*
what is that?	*apa itu?*
how much?	*berapa?*
how much is the price?	*berapa harga?*
how much money?	*berapa uang?*
expensive	*mahal*
how many kilometres?	*berapa kilometer?*
where is?	*di mana ada?*
which way?	*ke mana?*
I don't understand	*saya tidak mengerti*
this/that	*ini/itu*
big/small	*besar/kecil*
finished	*habis*
open/closed	*buka/tutup*

Travelling & Places

I want to go to . . .	*mau pergi ke . . .*
I want to buy one ticket	*saya mau beli satu karcis*
ticket	*karcis*
bus	*bis*
train	*kereta api*
ship	*kapal*
motorcycle	*sepeda motor*
station	*stasiun*
here	*di sini*
stop (verb)	*berhenti*
entry	*masuk*
straight on	*terus*
right	*kanan*
left	*kiri*
fast	*cepat*
slow(ly)	*pelan-pelan*
north	*utara*
south	*selatan*
east	*timur*
west	*barat*
central	*tengah*
town square	*alun-alun*
street	*jalan*
village	*desa*
town	*kota*
bank	*bank*
post office	*kantor pos*
immigration office	*kantor imigrasi*

Hotels & Accommodation

one night	*satu malam*
one person	*satu orang*
sleep	*tidur*
bed	*tempat tidur*
room	*kamar*
bathroom	*kamar mandi*
toilet	*kamar kecil*

General

chemist/drugstore	*apotik*
soap	*sabun*
toilet paper	*kertas WC* (pronounced 'Way Say')
toothpaste	*pasta gigi*
mosquito coil	*ombat nyamuk*
church	*gereja*
cave	*gua*
mountain	*gunung*
forest	*hutan*
bridge	*jembatan*
crater (as in volcano)	*kawah*
garden	*kebun*
sand	*pasir*
island	*pulau*
park	*taman*
lake	*danau*

Numbers

1	*satu*	6	*enam*
2	*dua*	7	*tujuh*
3	*tiga*	8	*delapan*
4	*empat*	9	*sembilan*
5	*lima*	10	*sepuluh*

After the numbers one to ten the 'teens' are *belas*, the 'tens' are *puluh*, the hundreds are *ratus* and the thousands *ribu*. Thus:

11 *sebelas*
12 *duabelas*
13 *tigabelas*

20	*duapuluh*
21	*duapuluh satu*
25	*duapuluh lima*
30	*tigapuluh*
90	*sembilanpuluh*
99	*sembilanpuluh sembilan*
100	*seratus*
200	*duaratus*
250	*duaratus limapuluh*
254	*duaratus limapuluh empat*
888	*delapanratus delapanpuluh delapan*
1000	*seribu*
1050	*seribu limapuluh*

A half is *setengah* which is pronounced 'stenger', so half a kilo is 'stenger kilo'. 'Approximately' is *kira-kira*.

Time

when?	*kapan?*
tomorrow/yesterday	*besok/kemarin*
hour	*jam*
week	*minggu*
month	*bulan*
year	*tahun*
what time?	*jam berapa?*
how many hours?	*berapa jam?*
7 o'clock	*jam tujuh*
five hours	*lima jam*
5 o'clock	*jam lima*

If you ask what time the bus is coming and you're told *jam karet* don't panic, it means 'rubber time', in other words it will come when it comes!

Days of the Week

Monday	*Hari Senin*
Tuesday	*Hari Selasa*
Wednesday	*Hari Rabu*
Thursday	*Hari Kamis*
Friday	*Hari Jumat*
Saturday	*Hari Sabtu*
Sunday	*Hari Minggu*

Facts for the Visitor

VISAS

For many nationalities, a visa is not necessary for entry and a stay of up to two months. This applies to citizens of Japan and most western countries, including Australia, Austria, Belgium, Canada, Denmark, Finland, France, Greece, Iceland, Italy, Luxemburg, the Netherlands, New Zealand, Norway, Spain, Sweden, Switzerland, the United Kingdom, the USA and West Germany.

If you're from one of these countries you'll be issued a tourist pass (which is a stamp in your passport) when you enter Indonesia, and there's no need to obtain a visa beforehand. However, you must have an ongoing ticket and enter and exit through one of the following airports or seaports (remembering that the list of approved gateways often change):

Java
    Soekarno-Hatta Airport & Tanjung Priok seaport of Jakarta
    Tanjung Perak Seaport of Surabaya
    Tanjung Mas Seaport of Semarang
Bali
    Ngurah Rai Airport of Denpasar
    Benoa and Padangbai Seaports of Denpasar
Sumatra
    Polonia Airport & Belawan Seaport of Medan
    Batu Besar Airport & Batu Ampar Seaport of Batam Island in the Riau Archipelago near Singapore
    Simpang Tiga Airport of Pekanbaru
    Tabing Airport of Padang
Kalimantan
    Soepadio Airport of Pontianak
Sulawesi
    Sam Ratulangi Airport of Manado
    Bitung Seaport near Manado
Maluku
    Pattimura Airport & Yos Sudarso Seaport of Ambon

Irian Jaya
    Frans Kaisiepo Airport of Biak
West Timor
    El Tari Airport of Kupang

At some places, Indonesian immigration might waive the onward ticket requirement if you show them you have 'enough' money for two months – A$1000 was the figure quoted by one traveller who entered at Kupang – but without hard-and-fast up-to-date info from other travellers, don't rely on this. If you're not sure where you'll be exiting Indonesia from, try getting a cheap onward ticket such as Medan to Penang. If you don't want to use it, you should usually be able to get a refund but if you can't get a refund, you won't be too much out of pocket.

The tourist pass is valid for two months from the date of entry and is supposedly not extendable. Your passport must be valid for at least a further six months at the time of your arrival in Indonesia. However, apart from money, there's nothing to stop you from going out to, say Singapore, and then re-entering Indonesia for another two month stay – you can do this as often as you want.

If you're not on the list of nationalities who can get the two-month tourist pass, or if you want to enter Indonesia through a place which isn't on the list of designated ports, you will need an Indonesian visa before you enter the country. These can be obtained at Indonesian consulates and embassies abroad and are usually valid for 30 days, though they *might* be difficult to get if you are only visiting Indonesia as a tourist. You'll probably – but not necessarily – be able to extend your initial visa at an immigration office (*kantor imigrasi*) in Indonesia. You also usually need a visa if you are going to *leave* Indonesia through a non-designated port, even though you enter through a designated one – details on the situation in some of these places are given in the relevant town sections of this book.

If you are going to work in Indonesia, you'll probably need a special working visa – see your employer!

CUSTOMS

Customs allow you to bring in a maximum two litres of alcoholic beverages, 200 cigarettes or 50 cigars or 100 grams of tobacco, and a 'reasonable' amount of perfume per adult. Bringing narcotics, arms and ammunition, TV sets, radio/cassette recorders, radio receivers, pornographic objects and publications, printed matter in Chinese characters and Chinese medicines into the country is prohibited. Indonesian customs is by no means the third degree; some entry points might be stricter or more conscientious than others, but probably all they'll do is have you open your bags for a brief rummage around.

MONEY

The unit of currency in Indonesia is the rupiah (rp) – like the lira in Italy there is nothing else. You get coins of 5, 10, 25, 50 and 100 rp. Notes come in 100, 500, 1000, 5000 and 10,000 rp denominations.

There is no restriction on the import or export of foreign currencies in cash, travellers' cheques or any other form – you can take in and take out as much as you like. However, there is a restriction on the movement of Indonesian currency; you're

Australia	A$1	=	1343 rp
USA	US$1	=	1781 rp
UK	£1	=	2779 rp
New Zealand	NZ$1	=	1032 rp
Singapore	S$1	=	907 rp
Switzerland	Fr 1	=	1074 rp
Sweden	Kr 1	=	274 rp
France	Fr 1	=	277 rp
Germany	DM 1	=	906 rp
Canada	C$1	=	1507 rp
Japan	100Y	=	1232 rp

not allowed to take in or take out more than 50,000 rp.

The rupiah does not have a fixed rate against other currencies: in recent years it has tended to fall by about 4% a year against the US dollar.

Changing Money

Changing money in places like Jakarta, Yogya and Kuta where there are large numbers of foreign tourists is generally easy and the exchange rate is usually much the same for cash or travellers' cheques. Places like Kuta and Sanur in Bali have lots of moneychangers as well as the banks and their exchange rates are very similar to, and often better than, bank rates.

Away from the main tourist centres the story is not quite so simple – there are fewer places to change money and travellers' cheques, and some currencies and cheques can't be changed at all, although the situation is much better than it was a few years ago. If you intend travelling extensively around Indonesia then you're better off bringing US dollars – either in cash or in travellers' cheques from a major American company such as American Express, Citicorp or Bank of America.

In major towns and cities it's generally easy to change cash – as long as it's a major currency such as Deutsche marks, US dollars, Australian dollars, pounds sterling, Netherlands florin, French or Swiss francs. Cash can be changed at branches of the Bank Expor Impor Indonesia, and sometimes at branches of the Bank Rakyat Indonesia, Bank Dagang Negara and Bank Negara Indonesia. Slightly more obscure major currencies such as Canadian dollars can be easily changed in Kuta, but even in Jakarta just about the only place you can change the stuff is at the American Express office.

Changing travellers' cheques is usually no problem – so long as you have US dollar travellers' cheques from a major company you can generally change them at the same banks as for cash. Some banks may give better exchange rates than others. Places like Balikpapan, which have large expatriate communities, are easy to change cash and travellers' cheques in, as is Jayapura with its influx of missionaries, expatriates and tourists.

Remote Areas If you're going to really remote places then carry stacks of rupiah because there won't be anywhere to change foreign cash or cheques. Places where you can change cash and travellers' cheques are noted in the relevant sections.

There are two other problems you should be aware of once you get out into the backwoods of Indonesia. First of all it's difficult to change big notes – breaking a 10,000 rp note in an out-of-the-way location can be a major hassle and out in the villages it's damn near impossible.

Secondly, away from the major centres notes tend to stay in circulation much longer and tend to get very tatty – when they get too dog-eared and worn looking they're difficult to spend. Torn notes or

ones held together with adhesive tape won't be accepted by anyone and you should try and avoid having them passed onto you – the only place you'll be able to get rid of them is at the bank.

Credit Cards

These are of limited use. They can be used if you stay in the big hotels; some city shops and restaurants will accept them, as will international airlines. Garuda also takes credit cards for domestic flights and some travel agents will accept them too.

Bargaining

Many everyday purchases in Indonesia require bargaining. This particularly applies to handicrafts, clothes and artwork but can also apply to almost anything you buy in a shop. Restaurant meals, transport and, often, accommodation are generally fixed in price – restaurants usually have their menus and prices posted up on the wall and hotels usually have a price list. Sometimes when

supply exceeds demand hotels may be willing to bend their prices rather than see you go next door. Though transport prices are fixed, *bemos* and colts throughout Indonesia have a well-earned reputation for charging westerners whatever they're willing to pay.

When bargaining, the first step is to establish a starting price. It's usually easiest to ask them their price rather than make an initial offer, unless you know very clearly what you're willing to pay. Just what your initial offer should be depends to a large extent on the item for sale and who is selling it. As a rule of thumb your starting price could be anything from a third to two-thirds of the asking price – assuming that the asking price is not completely crazy. Then with offer and counter offer you move closer to an acceptable price. Don't show too much interest when bargaining, and if you can't get an acceptable price walk away. You will often be called back and offered a lower price.

A few rules apply to good bargaining. First of all it's not a question of life or death where every rupiah you chisel away makes a difference. Don't pass up something you really want that's expensive or unobtainable at home because the seller won't come down a few hundred rupiah more – it is nothing compared to the hundreds of dollars you spent on the airfare! Secondly, when your offer is accepted you have to buy it – don't then decide you don't want it after all. Thirdly, while bargaining may seem to have a competitive element in it, its a mean victory knocking a poor *becak* driver down from 400 to 350 rp for a ride.

Bargaining is sometimes fun – and sometimes not. A lot depends on what you're bargaining for. Sometimes it seems as if people don't want your money if they can't overcharge you. Sometimes they will ask ludicrous prices and will get very upset if you offer a ridiculously low price back, even if you mean it as a joke. This also works in the other direction; there is a

nauseating category of westerner on the Asian trail who will launch into lengthy bitch sessions about being overcharged five cents for an orange.

The locals are usually a good source of information about current prices. If you don't know what the right price for transport is you might try asking another passenger what the regular price (*harga biasa*) is. Then you offer the correct fare. It's not much point doing this when you're buying something in a shop or at a market – onlookers naturally side with their own people, so you don't get past square one.

Don't get hassled by bargaining. Remember that no matter how good you are at it or how inept, there's always going to be someone who is better or will boast about how much cheaper they got something than you did. Don't go around feeling that you're being ripped off all the time – too many people do. In Indonesia you can still buy a lot of stuff cheaper than you would back home.

COSTS

How much it will cost to travel in Indonesia is largely up to the individual and depends on what degree of comfort you desire or what degree of discomfort you're prepared to put up with – and what's cheap to one person may be expensive to another. It also depends on how much travelling you do. But most importantly in Indonesia it's where you go that makes or breaks the budget – some parts of the country cost *much* more to travel through than others.

If you follow the well-beaten tourist track through Bali, Java and Sumatra you'll find Indonesia is one of the cheapest places in South-East Asia (exceptions like Jakarta apart) in which to travel. Travellers' centres like Bali, Yogyakarta and Lake Toba are excellent value for food and accommodation, while Nusa Tenggara is marginally more expensive than Bali but cheap by any standards.

On the other hand, once you get to some of the outer provinces, like Kalimantan,

Maluku, or Irian Jaya, you could be paying five to 10 times as much as you'd pay in Yogyakarta or Kuta Beach for equivalent accommodation. In Yogyakarta you can get some pretty decent accommodation starting at about 1000 rp per night for a single room. But in Ambon, in Maluku, the prices start from around 7000 rp per night and in Jayapura they start from around 10,000 rp per night. The odd cheapies that occasionally pop up in the outer provinces are often permanently full, don't take foreigners or will have gone out of business by the time you get there anyway – you can't rely on them. Food prices don't vary as much as room prices, but in restaurants in eastern Indonesia you still pay more for anything other than basic Indonesian fare.

Travelling expenses also increase once you get into the outer provinces. On Bali, Java, Sumatra and Nusa Tenggara there's very little need to take to the air, while in the interior of Irian Jaya you have no choice but to fly – there is no other way of getting from point A to point B except on foot. Getting between the outer islands you really can't rely on ships; in some places, like Maluku, there may only be one ship a week between any two islands, maybe only one every two or three weeks. If no ship comes along you *must* be prepared to fly. If you're not prepared to fly you'll spend a good deal of your two-month tourist pass just waiting around in port towns. If you fly you have to budget accordingly – air tickets in Indonesia aren't that expensive by western standards, but by the time you've done a few trips you'll find those fares are really mounting up!

To work out how much money you need for an Indonesian trip you really have to decide first where you want to go, and then add up the cost of accommodation and transport. You should keep in mind that in places like Kuta, where living expenses are low, there are more things to buy: massages to be had on the beach, admission charges to discos, copious quantities of alcohol to consume, tours and dance performances in abundance – so you may end up spending as much money as in a place with more expensive accommodation. Try and bring as much money as possible. Before you go out of your way to set new records for austerity, you should remember that travelling is not meant to be some sort of endurance test. If you want to find out how long you can stay away and how little money you can spend doing it, go ahead, but it's not going to earn you any credit in heaven. It is pretentious, and slightly silly, to go overseas in order to spend several months in a permanent state of discomfort.

TIPPING

Tipping is not a normal practice in Indonesia so please don't try to make it one. The expensive hotels slap a 21% service and government tax on top of their bills but there are no additional charges at lower priced establishments. Jakarta taxi drivers seem to expect (demand?) a tip. If you must tip, from 300 to 500 rp would be enough. Airport and hotel porters expect a couple of hundred rupiah per bag – say 200 rp per bag and 400 rp for a suitcase.

TOURIST INFORMATION
Consulates & Embassies

Countries with diplomatic relations with Indonesia will generally have their consular offices in Jakarta, the capital. There are Australian and US representatives in Bali. See the Jakarta and Bali sections for addresses.

Indonesian embassies, consulates and diplomatic offices in foreign countries include:

Australia
Embassy, 8 Darwin Avenue, Yarralumla, Canberra, ACT 2600 (tel (062) 73 3222)
Consulate-General, Piccadilly Court, 3rd Floor, 222 Pitt St, Sydney, NSW 2000 (tel 02 264 2976, 2195, 2323, 2508, 2712)

Consulate, 7 Bennett St, Darwin, NT 0800 (tel (089) 81 9352)

Consulate, 3rd Floor, 52 Albert Rd, South Melbourne, Vic 3205 (tel (03) 690 7811)

Consulate, 133 St George's Terrace, Perth, WA 6000, (tel (09) 321 9821)

Canada

Embassy, 287 Maclaren St, Ottawa, Ontario KIP 6A9 (tel (613) 236-7403 to 5)

Consular offices in Toronto and Vancouver

Denmark

Embassy, Orehoj Alle 12900, Hellerup, Copenhagen (tel (02) 96 72 44)

France

4749 Rue Cortambert 75116, Paris (tel (1) 45030760 or 45041371)

Germany (Federal Republic)

Embassy, 2 Kurt Schumacher Strasse, 5300 Bonn 1

Consular offices in Berlin, Bremen, Dusseldorf, Frankfurt, Hamburg, Hannover, Kiel, Munich and Stuttgart

Hong Kong

Consulate-General, 127-129 Leighton Rd, Causeway Bay, Hong Kong (tel 5 7904421 to 8)

Italy

53 Via Campania, Rome (tel 475 9251)

Malaysia

Embassy, Jalan Pekeliling 233, Kuala Lumpur (tel 421011, 421141, 421228)

Consulate, 37 Northam Rd, Penang (tel 25162, 3, 4, 8)

Consulate, Jalan Sagunting 1, Kota Kinabalu, Sabah (tel 54100, 54245, 55110)

Netherlands

Embassy, 8 Tobias Asserlaan, 2517 KC Den Haag (tel 070-4696/7)

New Zealand

Embassy, 9-11 Fitzherbert Terrace, Thordon, Wellington (tel 736 669)

Norway

Embassy, Inkonitogata 8, Oslo 2 (tel 2 44 19 13)

Papua New Guinea

Embassy, Henao Drive Section 67, Lot 6, Gordon Estate, Boroko, Port Moresby (tel 253116, 253118, 253544)

Philippines

Embassy, 185/187 Salcedo St, Legaspi Village, Makati, Manila (tel 2 85-50-61 to 68, 88-03-01 to 07)

Consular office in Davao

Singapore

Embassy, Wisma Indonesia, 435 Orchard Rd, Singapore 0923 (tel 73 77422)

Sweden

Embassy, Strandvagen 47/V, 11456 Stockholm (tel 08/63 54 70, 74)

Switzerland

Embassy, 51 Elfenauweg, 3006 Bern

Thailand

Embassy, 600-602 Petchburi Rd, Bangkok (tel 252 3135 to 40)

UK

Embassy, 38 Grosvenor Square, London W1X 9AD (tel 01-499 7661)

USA

Embassy, 2020 Massachussetts Ave NW, Washington DC 20036 (tel 202 293-1745)

Consular offices in Chicago, Houston, Honolulu, Los Angeles, New York and San Francisco

Indonesian Tourist Offices

Unlike many other Asian countries, Indonesia has neither an excellent tourist information service pumping out useful brochures, nor well-equipped offices with all the facts at their fingertips.

The Indonesian national tourist organisation, the Directorate General of Tourism (which has its base in Jakarta) maintains tourist offices called *Kanwil Pariwisata* in each province. The regional tourist offices are called DIPARDA or BAPPARDA.

The usefulness of the tourist offices varies greatly from place to place. This happens in Java, where the city tourist offices (sometimes called 'Visitors Information Centres') in Jakarta, Yogya, Solo attract lots of tourists and provide excellent maps and information about the city and its immediate vicinity, while offices in the less-visited areas may have nothing at all – they'll always try to help, but it's pretty hopeless if they don't speak English or you don't speak Indonesian. For more details of local offices read the information sections listed under the main cities. Literature is sometimes not displayed so ask to see what they've got. Sometimes their stocks are severely limited and they can't give anything away – but you could borrow it from them and whip down the road to a shop with a photocopier and get a copy. Useful publications are the *Tourist Map of Indonesia* and the *Calendar of Events* for the whole country.

There are a number of Indonesian Tourist Promotion Offices (ITPO) abroad where you can get some brochures and information about Indonesia. The ITPO headquarters is at the Directorate General of Tourism, Jalan Kramat Raya 81, PO Box 409, Jakarta. There are also offices in San Francisco, Tokyo, Singapore and Frankfurt. Overseas, Garuda Airlines offices are also worth trying for information.

GENERAL INFORMATION
Post
The postal service in Indonesia is generally pretty good and the poste restantes at Indonesian *Kantor Pos* – at least in major travellers' centres like Jakarta, Yogya, Bali, Medan and Lake Toba – are efficiently run. Expected mail always seems to arrive. Have your letters addressed to you with your surname in capitals and underlined, the poste restante, Kantor Pos and city in question. 'Lost' letters may have been misfiled under Christian names so always check under both your names.

Letters and small packets bound for overseas or domestic delivery may be registered for an extra fee at any post office branch. There are also two forms of express service available for mail within Indonesia: blue *kilat* envelopes are for air mail, yellow *kilat khusus* are the equivalent of air mail special delivery. These envelopes, plus aerogrammes, can be bought at all post offices.

Overseas parcels can be posted, insured and registered (*tercatat*), from a main post office but they'll usually want to have

a look at the contents first so there's not much point in making up a nice tidy parcel before you get there. If you're going to Singapore you'll find it's considerably cheaper to post overseas packages and parcels from there than from Indonesia.

Typical charges for sending a 20 gram letter air mail are: to Australia 650 rp, to Europe 800 rp, to USA 1000 rp. The charges for an aerogramme are: to Australia 450 rp, to Europe 525 rp, to USA 650 rp.

Telephones

Public pay phones are a rare sight. Many of the large hotels (certainly those in the big cities) have public pay phones which are more reliable than call boxes on the street – they take 100 rp coins. Hotels will also often be able to put local and trunk calls through for you.

The Telephone & Telegraph Offices (*Kantor Telepon dan Telegrap*) are usually open 24 hours and they are generally very efficient. There is no direct dialling for overseas, but it doesn't take long for calls to be put through by the operator and lines are usually clear.

Charges for a three-minute international call are: to Australia 23,000 rp, to the UK 26,000 rp, to Europe 31,000 rp, to Canada 26,000 rp, to USA 23,000 rp. You can reverse charges.

For long distance calls within Indonesia the country is divided up into zones. For example, if you're ringing from Biak in Irian Jaya Zones I, II and III include the local area around Biak plus Nabire and Manok; Zone IV is the rest of Irian Jaya plus Ambon and Ternate; and Zone V is Java, Sumatra, Sulawesi, Nusa Tenggara and Kalimantan.

There are two types of calls: normal (*biasa*) and immediate (*segera*). The second is a type of express call that gets you through faster than a normal call. Express calls cost twice as much as normal calls. For example, a three-minute biasa call to a Zone V destination would cost about 3500 rp, and a segera call would cost about 7000 rp.

Telegrams

International telegram charges (per word) are: to Australia 500 rp, to Canada and the USA 650 rp, and to Europe 650 rp.

Electricity

Electricity is usually 110 volts 50 cycles AC, but 220 to 240 volts 50 cycles AC is increasingly found – so check first before you plug in a foreign electrical appliance! Power points are for two-pronged plugs. Electricity is usually pretty reliable too – blackouts are few and far between.

In some small towns, or even in parts of larger towns, electricity is still a fairly futuristic thing – you find the odd losmen where lighting is provided with oil lamps. Even where there is electricity you're likely to find the lighting can be very dim. Electricity is expensive, so many losmen have light bulbs of such low wattage that you can almost see the electricity crawling laboriously around the filaments. If you can't get by with just 25 watts then it might be worth carrying a more powerful light bulb with you.

Street lighting can also be a problem – sometimes there's very little, sometimes none at all. Walking down dark, pot-holed streets in some Indonesian cities is like walking through a minefield – as you wonder where to put your feet next. A torch (flashlight) can be very useful.

Time

There are three time zones in Indonesia. Sumatra, Java, West and Central Kalimantan are on Western Indonesian Time which is seven hours ahead of GMT. Bali, Nusa Tenggara, South and East Kalimantan and Sulawesi are on Central Indonesian Time which is eight hours ahead of GMT. Irian Jaya and Maluku are on East Indonesian Time which is nine hours ahead of GMT.

Allowing for variations due to daylight saving, when it is 12 noon in Jakarta it is 1 pm in Ujung Pandang, 2 pm in Jayapura, 5 am in London, 3 pm in Melbourne or Sydney, 12 midnight in

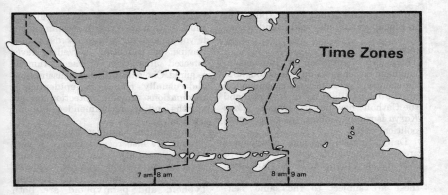

Time Zones

7 am | 8 am   8 am | 9 am

New York and 9 pm the previous day in San Francisco or Los Angeles. Due to a detour in the time zones Singapore is one hour ahead of Sumatra and Java.

Strung out along the equator, Indonesian days and nights are approximately equal in length. Sunrise is around 5 am and sunset is around 5 or 6 pm.

Business Hours

Most government offices are open Monday to Thursday from 8 am to 3 pm, Friday from 8 to 11.30 am, and Saturday from 8 am to 2 pm.

Private business offices have staggered hours; Monday to Friday from 8 am to 4 pm or 9 am to 5 pm, with a lunch break in the middle of the day. Some offices are also open on Saturday mornings until about 12 noon.

Banks are open Monday to Friday, usually from 8 am to 12 noon (sometimes until 2 pm), and on Saturdays usually from 8 to 11 am. Most post offices have similar opening hours. Bank branches in hotels stay open longer hours, and moneychangers in places like Kuta Beach stay open until the evening.

Shops tend to open around 8 am and stay open until around 9 pm. Sunday is a public holiday but some shops and many airline offices open for at least part of the

day. In the big cities, shopping complexes, supermarkets and department stores stay open from 8.30 am to 8 pm every day and often on Sunday.

MEDIA
Foreign

For information on what's happening in Indonesia today (including Indonesian politics, history and culture) take out a subscription to *Inside Indonesia* published in Australia at PO Box 190, Northcote, Vic 3070, Australia. Excellent articles cover everything from powerplays within the army, to the environment, and it discusses issues not raised in the Indonesian media and rarely covered overseas.

The monthly magazine *South*, devoted to Third World issues and news, has occasional articles on Indonesia. It's published by South Publications Ltd, 13th Floor, New Zealand House, 80 Haymarket, London SW1Y 4TS, England.

Western magazines like *Time* and *Newsweek* and the excellent Hong Kong-published *Far Eastern Economic Review* are available in Indonesia, but they're often bizarrely censored with articles unfavourable to the Indonesian government blotted out. The *International Herald-*

Tribune and the *Straits Times*, (published in Singapore) are also sold in Indonesia.

Indonesian

There are a number of Indonesian-language newspapers on sale throughout the country. Two of the leading newspapers are the Jakarta daily *Sinar Harapan* and the Catholic newspaper *Kompas*. *Suara Karya* is run by Golkar, the government political party.

Daily English-language newspapers are the *Indonesian Observer*, the *Jakarta Post* and the *Indonesia Times* (published in Jakarta) and the *Surabaya Post*. While these are subject to the same 'self-censorship' as other Indonesian publications, they do manage to tell you quite a lot about Indonesia – and the rest of the world – in a roundabout way. You can even get English soccer and US baseball and football scores from the *Jakarta Post*! For the official government line there are a number of regular publications issued by the Centre for Strategic and International Studies (CSIS) in Jakarta. You should be able to pick up their publications in the bookshops in major tourist hotels in Jakarta.

One of the main non-government organisations in Indonesia which researches and attempts to influence the Indonesian government to develop alternative social and economic policies is the Institute for Social and Economic Research, Education and Information (LP3ES). This organisation was founded in 1971, mainly by a group of Jakarta intellectuals, many of them western-trained academics. Their monthly journal is called *Prisma* and articles from it are translated and published in an English-language quarterly called *Prisma – The Indonesian Indicator*. You should be able to find it in the bookshops in the larger tourist hotels in Jakarta.

HEALTH

Vaccinations

Very few people will be required to have vaccinations but there are several vaccinations that are certainly recommended. If you're arriving within six days after leaving or transiting a yellow fever infected area then a vaccination is required. Cholera is a disease of insanitation and usually comes in epidemics – vaccinations provide protection for six months and are recommended, but not required.

Vaccinations against typhoid and tetanus are also recommended. A very useful vaccination is TABT which provides protection against typhoid, paratyphoid A and B, and tetanus. Typhoid and paratyphoid are both diseases of insanitation spread by contaminated food. Tetanus is due to a bacillus which usually enters the blood system through a cut, or as the result of a skin puncture by a rusty nail, wire, etc. It is worth being vaccinated against tetanus since there is more risk of contracting the disease in warm climates where cuts take longer to heal.

Polio is also a disease spread by insanitation and is found more frequently in hot climates. A booster every five years is recommended by many doctors.

You should have your vaccinations recorded in the yellow International Health Certificate.

Travel Insurance

A travel insurance policy is a *very* good idea – to protect you against cancellation penalties on advance purchase flights, against medical costs through illness or injury, against theft or loss of possessions, and against the cost of additional air tickets if you get really sick and have to fly home. Read the small print carefully since it's easy to be caught out by exclusions. For example, a travel insurance policy widely used in Australia specifically excludes motorcycle injuries if you don't hold a current Australian motorcycle licence. It's obviously designed to cut out all those people who obtain Balinese licences, but it could also catch people travelling through Australia and then on to Indonesia who hold, say, a British or American licence.

Medical Kit

It is always a good idea to travel with a basic first aid kit. Some of the items which should be included are: Band-Aids, a sterilised gauze bandage, Elastoplast, cotton wool, a thermometer, tweezers, scissors, antibiotic cream and ointment, an antiseptic agent (Dettol or Betadine), burn cream (Caladryl is good for sunburn, minor burns and itchy bites), insect repellent and multi-vitamins.

Don't forget water sterilisation tablets or iodine, anti-malarial tablets, any medication you're already taking, some sort of diarrhoea medication, paracetemol (Panadol) for pain and fever, a course of antibiotics (check with your doctor), and contraceptives if necessary.

Food & Water

Indonesia is hot! It's easy to dehydrate if you don't keep up your fluid intake, which is why it's a good idea to carry a water bottle with you. You are dehydrating if you find you are urinating infrequently or if your urine turns a deep yellow or orange; you may also find yourself getting headaches. Dehydration is a real problem if you go hiking in Indonesia. Hiking is not just a case of putting a pack on your back and taking along some presents for the locals – if you can't find water along the way or can't carry enough with you, then you will soon learn just how hot this place really is!

If you don't want to drink unboiled water, but don't have boiled water available, then you could use water purification tablets. If you don't have either, you have to consider the risks of drinking unboiled water against the risks of dehydrating – the first is possible, the second is definite. Also remember that some water-purifying tablets are not safe for prolonged use. Water is more effectively sterilised by iodine solution than by

tablets, because it kills amoebic cysts – but it's like drinking swimming pool water.

Fruit juices, soft drinks, tea and coffee will not quench your thirst – when it's really hot you need water. Drinking hot tea, however, will make you sweat and cool you down.

When it comes to food, what you eat or don't eat should be a personal decision. Some travellers insist upon avoiding all dairy products, meat, fish, salads and even hot drinks which contain milk or unboiled water. They subsist on bottled drinks, and personally-peeled fruit and vegetables. Some still get the trots. Other travellers sample everything, eat indiscriminately at markets and even drink untreated water without ill effects. However, we don't recommend going that far. Use your best judgement.

Health Precautions

The Indonesian sun is bright and good sunglasses are a must. Sunburn is also a problem (particularly with people just off the plane in Denpasar who can't wait to hit the beach). Bring something to cover your head.

If you're sweating profusely, you're going to lose a lot of salt and that can lead to fatigue and muscle cramps for some people. If necessary you can make it up by putting extra salt in your food (a teaspoon a day is enough), but don't increase your salt intake unless you also increase your water intake.

Take good care of all cuts and scratches. In this climate they take longer to heal and can easily get infected, making them even more difficult to heal. Treat any cut with care; wash it out with sterilised water, preferably with an antiseptic, keep it dry and keep an eye on it – they really can turn into tropical ulcers! It would be worth bringing an antibiotic cream with you. Cuts on your feet and ankles are particularly troublesome – a new pair of sandals can quickly give you a nasty abrasion which can be difficult to heal. Try not to scratch mosquito bites for the same reason – to stop the itching, try rubbing on heaps of Tiger Balm.

You *can* get colds in Indonesia – one of the easiest ways is leaving a fan on at night when you go to sleep – during the night the temperature drops and you wake up feeling cold. Sleeping out on the decks of ships at night, or going up to mountainous areas without warm clothes may also lead to colds – places like the Dieng Plateau in Java, Kintamani in Bali or the Balim Valley in Irian Jaya can be bitterly cold at night. Procold, which is available widely over the counter in Indonesia, is said to be pretty good for colds. Citrus fruits will also help fight off a cold.

Get your teeth checked and any necessary dental work done before you leave home. Always carry a spare pair of glasses or your prescription in case of loss or breakage, and a basic medical kit. As for motor cycle accidents in Indonesia – unless you have some extraordinarily close relationship with God, I suggest you get some decent protective clothing and a helmet, drive carefully and pray. There are more details on things to watch out for in the Getting Around chapter.

Malaria

The parasite that causes this disease is spread by the bite of the anopheles mosquito. The disease has a nasty habit of recurring in later years, even if you're cured at the time, and it can kill you.

There are four different types of malaria, but 95% of all cases are one of two varieties. The most serious of these two types is falciparum malaria, which occurs in Africa, Central and South America, certain Pacific islands, some of the West Indies, and is widespread across Asia – including Indonesia and Papua New Guinea.

The illness develops 10 to 14 days after being bitten by the mosquito and symptoms consist of high fever with alternate shivering and sweating, intense headaches, and usually nausea or vomiting. Without treatment the condition gets worse. It is this variety of malaria which is now showing widespread resistance to one of the major anti-malarial drugs, chloroquine.

Vivax malaria is the other main type and the two rarer types are similar to vivax. Vivax malaria may be severe, but is not dangerous to life. However, the illness will continue and recur, causing chronic ill-health, if not adequately treated.

Malaria is a risk year-round throughout all of Indonesia below 1200 metres. Some areas, like Bali, are low risk and at some times of the year you don't see any mosquitoes at all, but it's wise to take precautions.

It is not (yet) possible to be inoculated against malaria but protection is simple, either a daily or weekly tablet depending on which variety your doctor recommends. The tablets kill the parasites if they get into your bloodstream. You usually have to start taking the tablets about two weeks before entering the malarial zone and continue taking them for several weeks after you've left it. Resistance to one type of anti-malarial drug, chloroquine, has been reported in Indonesia. You may be prescribed two types to be taken simultaneously – chloroquine and maloprim for example – in order to guard against resistance to either one.

If you're travelling with children or if you're pregnant then the story with anti-malarial tablets is more complicated. For a rundown see Lonely Planet's *Travel with Children*. Basically, the story is that some anti-malarials may stay in your system for up to a year after the last dose is taken and may cause birth defects. So if you get pregnant or are planning to get pregnant within 12 months of taking anti-malarials your unborn child could be endangered. With newer drugs there's not much information around on the effects of long-term use. You should try and find out if there is resistance to the drug you are prescribed.

Another precaution is to avoid being bitten in the first place. Some Indonesian hotels (though not many) have mosquito nets. In the evenings when mosquitoes are most active, cover bare skin, particularly the ankles. Use an insect repellent – tiger balm works very well. Mosquito coils are readily available in Indonesia – burn these at night and sleep under a cover. Burning incense also seems to keep them away.

Hepatitis
If any serious disease is likely to afflict you in Indonesia then it will probably be infectious hepatitis (there are several varieties of hepatitis, of differing severity, but infectious hepatitis is the one you're most likely to pick up).

Hepatitis is a disease which affects the liver. It occurs in countries with poor sanitation – of which Indonesia is definitely one. It's spread from person to person via infected food or water, or contaminated cooking and eating utensils. Salads which have been washed in infected water, or fruit which has been handled by an infected person, might carry the disease.

Symptoms appear 15 to 50 days after infection (generally around 25 days) and consist of fever, loss of appetite, nausea, depression, complete lack of energy, and pains around the bottom of your rib cage (the location of the liver). Your skin turns progressively yellow and the whites of your eyes change from white to yellow to orange.

The best way to detect hepatitis is to watch the colour of your urine, which will turn a deep orange no matter how much liquid you drink. If you haven't drunk much liquid and/or you're sweating a lot, don't jump to conclusions since you may just be dehydrated.

The severity of the disease varies; it may last less than two weeks and give you only a few bad days, or it may last for several months and give you a few bad weeks. You could feel depleted of energy for several months after. If you get hepatitis, rest and good food is the only cure; don't use alcohol or tobacco since that only gives your liver more work to do. It's important to keep up your food intake to assist recovery.

Rabies
This is a disease worth guarding against. The rabies virus infects the saliva of the animal and is usually transferred when the rabid animal bites you and the virus passes through the wound into your body. That also means that if you have a scratch, cut or other break in the skin you could catch rabies if an infected animal licked that break in the skin. If you are bitten or licked by a possibly rabid animal you should wash the wound thoroughly (but without scrubbing since this may push the infected saliva deeper into your body) and then start on a 14-day series of injections which will prevent the disease developing. Rabies, once developed, is fatal. New rabies vaccines have been developed which have fewer side effects than the older animal-derived serums and vaccines.

The incubation period for rabies depends on where you're bitten. If on the head, face or neck then it's about 30 days, on the arms 40 days and on the legs 60 days. This allows plenty of time to be given the vaccine and for it to have a beneficial effect. With proper treatment, given quickly after having been bitten, rabies will not develop.

Diarrhoea

Diarrhoea is often due simply to a change of diet or because your digestive system is unused to spicy or oily food (the former being a feature of much Indonesian cooking). A lot depends on what you're used to eating and whether or not you've got an iron gut. If you do get diarrhoea, the first thing to do is wait – it rarely lasts more than a few days. Just make sure that you keep up your fluid intake otherwise you'll dehydrate.

If the diarrhoea persists then the usual treatment is Lomotil tablets – in the west it's a prescription drug, so ask your doctor for a supply. The usual dose is two tablets, three times a day. Lomotil is neither a cure nor a heavy gun; it doesn't cure anything but just slows down the digestive system so that the cramps go away and you don't have to go to the toilet all the time.

Another anti-diarrhoeal medicine which may be useful goes under the name of Diatabs and is available over the counter without prescription in Indonesia – it's mainly charcoal and also contains an antibiotic and a sedative. You take four tablets to start with, followed by two tablets every four hours until you have taken a total of 12 (including the initial four).

If you get a severe bout of diarrhoea, you'll dehydrate – keep up your fluid intake as well as your salt intake. Oral rehydration salts are available at pharmacies. Dissolve these powders in water and drink them – the quantities are specified on the packet – and you not only get your fluid intake but also a charge of energy. One quite common brand is Oralit, described in Indonesian as *bubuk glukosa elektrolit* (glucose electrolyte powder). Fruit juice can aggravate diarrhoea and it's probably best to eat lightly until you've recovered. If the diarrhoea persists for a week or more, it's

probably not simple travellers' diarrhoea and you should see a doctor.

Dysentery

Diarrhoea is very different from dysentery. Dysentery is diarrhoea with blood, pus or fever. Diarrhoea with blood or pus but without fever is usually amoebic dysentery and requires an anti-amoebic drug like metronidazole or flagyl. Diarrhoea with blood or pus and fever is usually bacillary dysentery and requires antibiotics like tetracycline, or a sulpha drug.

Prickly Heat & Fungal Infections

You sweat profusely in Indonesia; the sweat can't evaporate because the air itself is already moist, and before long you'll be dripping in it. Prickly heat is a common problem for people from temperate climates. Small red blisters appear on the skin where your sweat glands have been unable to cope with the amount of sweat you're generating. The problem is exacerbated because the sweat fails to evaporate. To prevent (or cure it), wear clothes which are light and leave an air space between the material and the skin; don't wear synthetic clothing since it can't absorb the sweat; dry well after bathing and use calamine lotion or a zinc-oxide based talcum powder. Anything that makes you sweat more – exercise, tea, coffee, alcohol – only makes the condition worse.

Fungal infections also occur more frequently in this sort of climate – guys sometimes get patches of infection on the inside of the thigh. It itches like hell but is easy to clear up with an anti-fungal cream (bring one with you). Fungal ear infections usually result from swimming or washing in unclean water – Aquaear drops, available over-the-counter in Australia, are a preventative to be used before you enter or wash in the water. Some travellers carry a broad-spectrum antibiotic like Septrim to cure fungal infections. This is not a bad idea, although antibiotics can lower your resistance to other infections. For women, thrush is a not an uncommon side-effect in a humid climate, however, Indonesian doctors usually know how to treat thrush.

Wearing thongs in showers and mandis can protect you against athlete's foot and other fungal infections of the feet.

Worms - Roundworm, Threadworm & Hookworm

In warmer climates where hygiene standards are low there are many forms of worm infestation. Some are spread by infected meat, some by infected fish, some by infected water, and others by faecally infected earth or food.

If you get roundworm, threadworm or hookworm, then try taking Combantrin – also available without prescription over the counter in Indonesia. Children under six months old, nursing mothers and pregnant women should not take it without first consulting a doctor.

Roundworm eggs are usually ingested through vegetables that have been grown using human faeces as manure, and which have not been properly washed; the eggs hatch in the stomach and then the larvae burrow through the intestines, enter the bloodstream and make their way through the liver to the heart, from where they work their way up to the lungs and the windpipe. They are then coughed up, swallowed and deposited in the intestines where they mature and grow up to a length of 20 to 35 centimetres (eight to 14 inches). The most common symptoms of adult roundworm infestation are abdominal discomfort increasing to acute pain due to intestinal blockage.

Threadworm eggs, when swallowed, hatch in the stomach. The worms enter the intestine where they grow and mate; the mature female worms make their way through the bowel to the anus where the depositing of their sticky eggs causes intense itching. One way to diagnose the presence of worms is to stretch a piece of adhesive tape over a flat stick, with the sticky area on the outside, and press it into the area around the anus. If there is an infestation you may be able to see worms and eggs on the tape – the mature worms look like little strands of cotton thread about 1.3 cm (half an inch) long.

Hookworms can be picked up by walking around in bare feet, in soil littered with infected faeces. The eggs hatch in the soil and then the larvae enter the bloodstream by burrowing through the skin, following much the same internal route as the roundworm they reach the intestine and hook onto the lining. By feeding on the host's blood, hookworms can grow up to 1.3 cm (half an inch) long. The most common result of hookworm infestation is anaemia, although they can also do damage to the organs they come into contact with. The best prevention is to wear shoes unless on the beach. Hookworms can also be absorbed by drinking infected water or eating uncooked and unwashed vegetables.

Medical Supplies

If you really need something, take it with you. You shouldn't count on getting what you want in Indonesia, though there are lots of well-stocked pharmacies (*apotiks*) supplying western and Indonesian medicines. Many of the big tourist hotels have drugstores (but they won't fill doctor's prescriptions). Chinese shops often sell Chinese medicines. Often you can buy what you want over the counter, however, sometimes you do need a doctor's prescription.

In each apotik there is an English-language copy of the IIMS (Indonesian Index of Medical Specialities), a guide to pharmaceutical preparations available to doctors in Indonesia. It's updated three times a year and it lists drugs by brand name, generic name, manufacturer's name and therapeutic action. Names of medicines in Indonesia may be different, so if you're after a specific drug it would be worth knowing the scientific name as well as the trade name. The other problem with buying medicines in Indonesia is that the labels are, of course, in Indonesian and you may have trouble figuring out what the appropriate dose is. Drugs may not be of the same strength as in other countries or may have deteriorated due to age or poor storage conditions.

Hospitals, Doctors & Medical Clinics

If you do need a doctor or other medical help your embassy or consulate or a five-star hotel should be able to recommend someone, as should offices of foreign companies in places where large expatriate communities work – Balikpapan for example. In the towns and cities there seems to be a fair supply of doctors and dentists to choose from. In Bahasa Indonesia a doctor is *dokter* and a dentist is *dokter gigi*. In the outback of places like Irian Jaya there are the clinics set up by the missionaries. There are also public hospitals (*rumah sakit*) in the cities and towns.

Hospitals in Jakarta There are a number of group practice clinics in Jakarta. Most expatriates use the Medical Scheme (tel 515597) in the Setiabudi Building, Jalan H Rasuna Said, Kuningan. It's a private practice but they will deal with all emergencies and vaccinations are given to non-members for a small fee. Doctors speak English and Dutch.

The Metropolitan Medical Center (tel 320408) is in the Hotel Wisata, Jalan Thamrin – behind the Hotel Indonesia. Hours at this practice vary so it's best to ring first. Dr Darmiyanti & Associates (tel 346823) is at Jalan Lombok 57, Menteng. Some English is spoken and they have branch practices in a number of major hotels.

Better known hospitals in Jakarta are the Rumah Sakit Dr Cipto Mangunkusumo (tel 344003), Jalan Diponegoro 71 – government public hospital; the Rumah Sakit Pertamina (tel 707214), Jalan Kyai Maja, Kebayoran – private Pertamina hospital; and the St Carolus Hospital (tel 883091), Jalan Salemba Raya 41 – private hospital.

TRAVELLING IN INDONESIA

As in other Asian countries, limited English on the part of the locals means that there's a set of stock questions that everybody asks you. It's hard to know how to react when you're sitting on a bus or boat and someone asks you 'Where are you going?'. Indonesians use this line in much the same way as westerners open with 'How are you?'.

The usual stock questions in Indonesia are: Where are you going? What is your name? How long have you been in Indonesia? Where are you from? Are you married? What is your religion?

The question to be careful of is the one on religion; Indonesians presume that westerners are Christian. If you are an atheist you'll be better off not telling them; in Indonesia the logic is that Communists are atheists, and therefore if you are an atheist you must be a Communist.

The friendliness of the Indonesians does manifest itself in some peculiar ways – sometimes you get people who start following you on the street just to look at you. And there are some people who 'collect' foreigners. Some just have to be friendly regardless of the time or situation, even if it means waking you from your peaceful slumber.

You tend to get stared at in Indonesia, particularly in places like Nusa Tenggara where few white people go. But on the whole the Indonesians stand back and look, rather than gather round you. Those that do come right up to you are usually kids, though some teenagers also do this. Getting stared at is nothing new; almost 500 years ago when the first Portuguese arrived in Melaka the *Malay Annals* recorded that:

the people of Melaka . . . came crowding to see what the Franks (Portuguese) looked like; and they were all astonished and said, 'These are white Bengalis!' Around each Frank there would be a crowd of Malays, some of them twisting his beard, some of them fingering his head, some taking off his hat, some grasping his hand.

The other habit which is altogether ordinary to Indonesians and Asians in general is touching. In overcrowded areas, particularly places like Java, people have learnt how to get along through sheer necessity and the area of empty space Indonesians need around them is much smaller than that necessary for westerners to be comfortable.

The Indonesians are an extraordinarily physical people; they'll balance themselves on your knee as they get into a bemo, or reach out and touch your arm while making a point in conversation, or simply touch you every time they mean to speak to you, or when they want to lead you in a new direction if they're showing you around a house or museum. While touching among members of the same sex is regarded as OK, this sort of casual body contact between people of different sexes is not.

On the debit side, watch out for some of the young guys who hang around bus stations, outside cinemas, and ferry docks with not much else to do except stir foreigners. They'll crack jokes, laugh, and try and pinch your bum. If it happens don't give them their entertainment by chucking a fit. Just leave and come back some other time.

On the whole you'll find the Indonesians (including the army and the police, despite the nasty reputation they've had in the past) an *extraordinarily* hospitable people and very easy to get on with. Lonely Planet's *Bali & Lombok – a Travel Survival Kit* covers most of Bali and Lombok and has a section on surfing in Bali, including some useful information on the peculiar health hazards of that sport. The surfing section was written by Kirk Willcox while editor of *Tracks*, an Australian surfing magazine.

Travel with Children

Travelling anywhere with children requires energy and organisation. The Indonesians are generally very friendly and receptive to children which makes travel that much easier. Of course some areas of Indonesia are hard going, probably too hard for most people to want to tackle with the additional burden of small children. Other areas, eg Bali, are easy. For more information on travelling in Asia with children see LP's *Travel with Children*.

Indonesian Customs

Asians resent being touched on the head – the head is regarded as the seat of the soul and is therefore sacred. In traditional Javanese culture, a lesser person should not have his head above that of a senior person, so you may sometimes see a Javanese duck his head when greeting someone or walk past with a dropped shoulder as a mark of respect.

When handing over or receiving things remember to use the right hand – the left hand is used after you've been to the toilet. Talking to someone else with your hands on the hips is impolite and is considered a sign of contempt, anger or aggressiveness – it's the same stance taken by characters in traditional dance and operas to signal these feelings to the audience. Hand shaking is customary for both men and women on introduction and greeting.

Keeping 'face' is important to Indonesians and they are generally extremely courteous – criticisms are not spoken directly and they will usually agree with what you say rather than offend. They will also prefer to say something rather than appear as if they don't know the answer. They mean well but when you are ask where to go, you may often find yourself being sent off in the wrong direction!

Indonesians will accept any lack of clothing on the part of poor people who cannot afford them; but for westerners thongs, bathing costumes, shorts or strapless tops are considered impolite except perhaps around places like Kuta. Elsewhere you have to look vaguely respectable, particularly if you're visiting a government office! Even T-shirts and shorts are regarded as very casual, although in some areas the locals are starting to get accustomed to seeing travellers dressed this way. While places of worship are open to all, permission should be requested to enter, particularly when ceremonies are in progress, and you should ensure that you're decently dressed.

Indonesians, both men and women, are generally not comfortable being alone – even on a simple errand they are happier having a friend along. Travelling alone is considered an oddity – women travelling alone, even more of an oddity. Nevertheless, as a woman travelling alone or with a female companion, Indonesia can be easier going than some other Asian countries. Lots of western women travel in Indonesia either alone or in pairs – most seem to enjoy the country and its people, most seem to get through the place without any problems, or else suffer only a few minor hassles with the men. There are some things you can do to avoid being harassed; dressing modestly helps a lot.

DANGERS & ANNOYANCES

Having valuables like your passport and/ or travellers' cheques stolen in Indonesia is a problem because it often means a long trek back to Jakarta to get them replaced. There is, however, an Australian consulate and also an American consular agent in Bali. Some travellers' cheque companies also have an office in Bali.

A money belt is the safest way to carry your valuables, particularly when travelling on the crowded buses and on trains. The only problem with money belts, particularly in hot, humid climates, is that they are very uncomfortable to wear! A vest (waistcoat) with two large zip-up pockets inside to keep your valuables in is a good idea. Other people wear small leather pouches with a strap looped around their neck and under their clothes.

One precaution you can take, which will help if you do lose your valuables, is to leave a small stash of money (say US$100) in your hotel room, with a record of the travellers' cheque serial numbers and your passport number; you'll need the money if you've got a long trip to a replacement office. If you get stuck try telephoning your consulate or embassy. It's a sensible precaution to carry more than one type of travellers' cheque with you. Make sure that the company you buy your cheques from has a replacement office in Indonesia. Also ensure that you keep your original receipt of purchase separate from the cheques themselves – without the receipt you may have to wait weeks for replacement and may not even get any at all.

It's a sad fact of travelling life that sometimes it's your fellow travellers who rip you off. If you do stay in dorms (there are a few hotels in Jakarta with dorms catering to foreigners) or share your hotel room with strangers, don't leave valuables like your passport, travellers' cheques, money, health certificates and air tickets lying around.

And remember, something may be of no value to the thief, but to lose it would be a real heartbreak to you – like film. Some losmen have rooms that are locked with a padlock, but it might still be worth bringing your own padlock. Another thing worth making a copy of before you leave home is your address book.

A level of prudence is always good to have but it's not worth getting paranoid. It's all too easy to be suspicious and you may find sometimes that people you thought were trying to con you were only trying to help.

Drugs

In much of Indonesia drugs are utterly unheard of and the closest you get is betel nut. Many villagers chew this mild drug, known as *sirih*, constantly. It's what causes that red stain on what's left of their teeth and gums. The betel nut (*pinang*) is chewed in combination with sirih leaf, *kapor sirih* (powdered lime) and a brown substance called *gambir*.

Bali used to be the place to float around sky-high, but that image has faded considerably. There aren't so many drugs about now and the authorities are much heavier. The Bali drug scene was basically marijuana and mushrooms, but neither are so readily available and it's now unsafe to buy from a local supplier unless you know the person very well. Losmen owners are quick to turn you in as well. There are a number of westerners soaking up the sunshine in the prison at the back end of Legian.

Those who want to go in search of Bali's famed magic mushrooms should remember that their effect is extremely variable. Some people have stratospheric highs, but a lot more suffer deep-down lows. Magic mushrooms are also common in Sumatra, again around the tourist areas.

The most readily available drug in Indonesia is alcohol. In Bali thare are a lot of empty beer bottles and full Australians. Beer, *brem* and *tuak* are available at restaurants in the main centres but in many of the isolated villages, forget it. In places like Tanatoraja in Sulawesi where Muslim strictures do not apply amongst this ostensibly Christian population, you can drink yourself into a happy stupor on endless supplies of tuak, fermented from the sap of a palm tree and brought into town in long bamboo tubes frothing at the top.

FILM & PHOTOGRAPHY

Indonesia is an incredible country to photograph and you can whip through large quantities of film! All brands of film commonly used in the west, such as Kodak, Fuji and Agfa, are available in Indonesia but their cost is usually higher. If you're entering Indonesia from Singapore stock up on film there, it's much cheaper.

Jakarta and Bali are the best places to buy film in Indonesia, with plenty to choose from. Elsewhere, the supply is more variable and many types of film aren't available at all – though you find a good selection in some surprisingly out-of-the-way places like Ampenan in Lombok or Jayapura in Irian Jaya. Outside the main centres, turnover of stock is often slow, so it's best to check the expiry date of the film. The most readily available film will generally be Fujicolor, along with Indonesian-made or some types of Kodak black-and-white film. Kodachrome colour slide film is rare outside the main tourist centres. You can get Polaroid film, movie film and video tape in Jakarta. Camera batteries are readily available from photo shops.

Film Processing

Developing and printing is quite good and much cheaper than in the west. You can get Ektachrome slide film developed in two or three days and colour print film can be done the same day through photographic shops in major towns all across the archipelago. Many of these have machines which churn out prints in 45 minutes, and the quality is usually very good. Kodachrome slides (or other films where the cost of purchase includes the processing cost) need to be sent overseas. Film manufacturers warn that films should be developed as quickly as possible once exposed – although in practice, if put back in their canisters, they seem to last for months without deterioration even in Indonesia's heat and humidity. If you're worried, take a packet of moisture-absorbing silica gel crystals from a photographic shop.

Technical Problems

Shoot early or late. From 10 am to 1 or 2 pm, the sun is uncomfortably hot and high overhead and you're likely to get a bluish washed-out look to your pictures. If you have to shoot at that time of day, a skylight filter will cut the haze. A lens hood will reduce your problems with reflections and direct sunlight on the lens. Beware of the sharp differences between sun and shade – if you can't get reasonably balanced overall light you may have to opt for exposing only one area or the other correctly. Or use a fill-in flash.

Those lush, green rice paddies come up best if back-lit by the sun. For those sunset shots at Kuta, Kalibukbuk or Pontianak, set your exposure on the sky without the sun making an appearance then shoot at the sun. Photography from fast moving trains and buses doesn't work unless you have high-speed film; with low-speed film, window shots tend to get rather blurred. Dust can be a problem – hazy days will make it difficult to get sharp shots. A polarising filter is good for reducing the haze.

Be wary of X-rays at airports, which may fog your film. Some airports have signs warning you that the machine is not safe for film – many do not. Generally speaking X-ray machines only damage high speed film, but if there's any doubt it's wise to keep your film away from the things! Camera batteries are readily available from photographic shops.

People Photos

You get a fantastic run for your money in Indonesia – not only are there 175 million or so portraits to choose from but the variation in ethnic types is phenomenal.

Few people expect payment for their photos – the Balim Valley in Irian Jaya being an odd exception. What Indonesians will go for is a copy of the photo – if you hang around Indonesia long enough, you'll wind up with a pocketful of bits of paper with addresses of people to send their photos to.

There are three basic approaches to photographing people; one is to be polite, ask permission and pose the shot; another is the no-holds-barred and upset-everyone approach; the other is surreptitious, standing half a km away with a metre-long telescopic lens. Some Indonesians will shy

away from having their photo taken and duck for cover, some are timid but only too pleased to be photographed, some are proud and ham it up for the camera, while others won't get out of the way of the bloody lens when you want them to!

Whatever you do, photograph with discretion and courtesy. Not surprisingly many people don't like having a camera lens shoved down their throats – it's always polite to ask first and if they say no then don't take the photo. A gesture, a smile and a nod are all that is often necessary. In some places you may come up against religious barriers to taking photographs – for example of Muslim women in the more devoutly Islamic parts of the archipelago. The taboo might also apply to the minority groups. In Bali, for example, you should not take photographs at public bathing places; just because the Balinese bathe in streams, rivers, lakes or other open places doesn't mean they don't think of them as private places – intruding with your camera is no different to sneaking up to someone's bathroom window and pointing your camera through. Remember, wherever you are in Indonesia, the people are not exotic birds of paradise and the village priest is not a photographic model.

Prohibited Subjects

Be careful of what you photograph in Indonesia – they're touchy about places of military importance and this can include airports (like the one at Malang in Java which is an air-force base but also handles civilian flights), bridges, railway terminals and stations, seaports and any military installations or bases. If in doubt ask.

ACCOMMODATION

Accommodation in Indonesia comes in different grades of price and comfort. At the bottom end of the scale is the *penginapan* which is a simple lodging house, and at the top end are the international standard hotels, particularly in Jakarta and Bali. In some cases there's no difference between the different grades other than the name, but on the whole accommodation can be roughly divided into the following categories.

Penginapan

These are the lowest price on the regular accommodation scale. A penginapan is a lodging house and has very basic facilities – a bare room with a bed, a table, a light bulb, and partitions made of masonite (or some other flimsy material) masquerading as walls.

Losmen

Though the distinction between a losmen and a penginapan often blurs, a losmen is usually slightly more up-market than a penginapan. Places that call themselves losmen may be as basic as a penginapan, they might also double as brothels. Sometimes they're virtually uninhabitable, other times they're places of quiet retreat. What you get really depends on the people who run the place. Often the price of accommodation will include coffee or tea, bananas or sweets for breakfast; sometimes you can pay extra and get three meals per day (a common practice in Banda for example).

Many losmen will be family-run, generally with no more than about 10 or 12 rooms. In Bali they'll often be built around a central compound with an outer wall and separate buildings around an inner garden; outside each room will be a verandah with chairs and a table. Apart from the fact that it's pleasant to be sitting out in the garden in any case, this plan has a second very important benefit – you're out there with other people rather than being locked away inside a room, so you talk, meet people and learn more about wherever you are.

Wisma

This is a guest house or lodge. It's also sometimes called a *pondok* and is a bit more expensive than a losmen. Again there's an overlap, and often the only thing that distinguishes a *wisma* from a losmen is the name.

Hotel

Although a hotel can be cheap and sometimes also dirty, technically the word implies a larger, up-market establishment – though once again there may be little or no difference between a hotel, wisma, losmen or penginapan. At this end of the scale you may well be hit with 10% tax, or even 10% tax and a 10% service charge, on top of the the room price. At the very top end of the price range are the appropriately opulent multi-storey cubby houses built for appropriately opulent people – like the large international-standard hotels you'll find in Sanur (Bali), Jakarta, Yogya, or the odd one planted in a far-flung place such as the Hotel Benakutai in Balikpapan. In these sort of places a double can be up towards US$100 per night!

In Indonesia what you pay depends on where you are; the cost of accommodation varies considerably across the archipelago. If you follow the well-beaten tourist track through Bali to Java and Sumatra you'll find Indonesia one of the cheapest places in South-East Asia (exceptions like Jakarta apart). Travellers' centres like Bali, Yogyakarta and Lake Toba are good value for food and accommodation. Nusa Tenggara is marginally more expensive than Bali, but cheap by any standards. On the other hand, once you get to some of the outer provinces, like Kalimantan, Maluku, or Irian Jaya you could be paying, from five to 10 times as much for equivalent accommodation as you'd pay in Yogyakarta or at Kuta Beach.

Among the odd cheapies that pop up in the outer provinces, some are often permanently booked up with full-time lodgers; others don't take foreigners for one reason or another (often because they don't want to run down to the police station to register you); and some will have gone out of business by the time you get there anyway. If you get into a town and the cheap places mentioned in this book have closed down, or you have no information on cheap places to stay, then ask taxi drivers and becak drivers what's available. Other travellers who have come from where you're heading are also good sources of information.

Often you have to bargain for your room price just as you do for other purchases. After a fairly short time you get a feel for whether a place is likely to come down from the initial asking price. Some losmens routinely ask for more than they expect – you're a mug if you don't haggle a bit. In the end what you should pay really depends on what you think the room is worth, taking into account other prices in the same town.

On the whole it's cheaper if two people travel together and split the cost of the room – the price for a two-person room is nearly always well below the cost of two singles. You rarely get dorm accommodation in Indonesia, although there are a few hotels catering to western budget travellers, notably in Jakarta, that provide dorm beds. Even the cheapest losmen and penginapans tend to be reasonably clean, if spartan, though some stand out as long overdue for demolition. Some places can be abominably noisy with the inevitable television booming in the passageway outside your room or punching up through the floorboards until midnight. Other hotels are just several layers of hot little sweat boxes and slimy bathrooms. Fortunately, those sort of places are pretty much exceptions. The best way to survive some of the more dismal places is to go to Indonesia with a level of saintly tolerance, a good pair of earplugs, or enough money to afford some up-market accommodation now and then and avoid the worst places. Again, it really depends on what you can put up with.

How good a time you have in Indonesia often depends on where you're staying, the friendliness and location of your hotel or losmen. If you want to enjoy yourself or learn something about the country then there's no point incarcerating yourself in the large tourist hotels. If you want to meet the local people and/or other travellers then you've got to stay in the cheap places. So pick your losmen carefully; while some places may not have such comfy beds the people you meet more than make up for it.

Staying With People

In many places in Indonesia you'll often be welcome to stay in the villages. Ask for the village head – the *kepala desa* or *kepala kampung*. They're generally very hospitable and friendly, not only offering you a roof over your head but also meals. Obviously you don't get a room of your own, just a bed. What you pay for this depends on the bargain you reach with the kepala desa. Sometimes he may offer it to you for nothing but more often some payment will be expected: about 2000 or 3000 rp a night as rule-of-thumb. If you intend to stay with a kepala desa it's a good idea to have one or two gifts to offer – cigarettes are popular gifts, as are photographs.

The Police

In places where there's no accommodation available you can often stay in the local police station. Indonesian police and military are actually quite friendly to foreigners.

The Mandi

The word *mandi* simply means to bath or to wash. A mandi is a large water tank beside which you'll find a plastic saucepan. The popularity of the mandi is mainly due to a frequent lack of running water in Indonesia – sometimes the tank is refilled by a hose attached to a hand-pump. Climbing into the mandi is very bad form indeed – it's your water supply and it's also the supply for every other guest that comes after you, so the idea is to keep the water clean. What you're supposed to do is scoop water out of the mandi and pour it over yourself, then soap yourself down and repeat the scooping and showering procedure.

Even when there is running water the mandi remains the traditional form of bathing – bathtubs pop up in some of the more touristy parts, and not-very-good showers make an appearance here and there. Get used to cold water – losmen have nothing else and even in most middle range hotels hot water is a rarity. You're in the tropics though and you soon forget what hot water feels like.

The Toilet
Indonesian toilets are the traditional hole in the ground, footrests on either side, over

'The Mandi' BATHING IN INDONESIA

The Mandi is an Indonesian bathroom. To 'shower' one does not hop into the stone basin, one ladles the generally icy water over oneself... an early morning eye-opener.

which you squat and aim. In some of the tourist areas – like Bali and Rantepao in Tanatoraja – Asian toilets are fading away as more places install western-style showers and western-style toilets. Since there's usually no running water to flush toilets what you do is reach for that plastic saucepan again, scoop water from the mandi and flush it that way. Apart from some places catering to the tourist trade you won't find toilet paper in restaurant toilets – bring your own. Kamar kecil is Bahasa Indonesia for toilet or for the WC say 'way-say'.

FOOD
You'll generally eat well in most parts of Indonesia. While you won't get everything in one place, the variety of food available across the archipelago is stunning. Midyear in Tanatoraja in Sulawesi, when harvest and funeral ceremonies are at their height, is the chance to try pig and buffalo meat barbecued in bamboo tubes, washed down with copious quantities of white and red alcoholic tuak tapped from a palm tree.

Jalan Malioboro in Yogyakarta is the longest restaurant in the world – lined in the evening with innumerable food stalls serving up genuine Yogya food, which you eat while sitting on mats laid out on the footpath. Pontianak and Samarinda in Kalimantan have the biggest river prawns you've probably ever seen in your life – a meal in themselves; Jayapura has the biggest selection of barbecued fish (ikan bakar) in the archipelago; while Ternate in Maluku is piled high with sago biscuits.

The Indonesians are keen snackers and everywhere you'll find lots of street stall snacks such as peanuts in palm sugar, shredded coconut cookies or fried bananas. If you've never got past apples, oranges and bananas then Indonesia is going to change all that with giant nangkas in Jayapura, piles of durians in Pontianak, creamy zurzats sold on the street outside your hotel in Samarinda, and avocados abundant everywhere. With such an exotic selection of fruit, the fruit juices are out of this world.

In some parts of the country such as the eastern provinces, however, there's a lack of food variety. Carrying vitamin pills and milk powder can be a good idea, particularly if you're a vegetarian. On the health score, the same rules apply in Indonesia as in any other country – the cleanliness of a warung or restaurant is a good guide to how hygienic its kitchen is likely to be. Some people like to avoid raw fruit and vegetables that may have been washed in unclean water.

Places to Eat

At the bottom of the barrel in terms of price are the warungs. These are the poor persons' restaurants, and they can be seen everywhere in Indonesia. They're usually just a rough table and bench seats, surrounded by sheets or canvas strung up to act as walls. In Yogya on Jalan Malioboro they're basically food trolleys and you sit on mats laid out on the footpath. Sometimes the food is as drab as the warung looks though frequently it will be some of the best (and cheapest) food in town. A *pasar malam* is a night market and is often a congregation point for warungs.

One step up from the warungs, sometimes in name only, is the *rumah makan* – literally the 'house to eat', often only distinguished from the warung by its fixed position and the addition of solid walls – but many such places call themselves warungs so it's a hazy distinction.

A *restoran* is a restaurant – once again often nothing more than the name distinguishes it from a rumah makan. But in many cases a restoran will be an up-market place, often Chinese run and with a Chinese menu. Chinese food is nearly always more expensive than Indonesian food, but there is usually a more varied menu.

The places you should really avoid if you want proper Indonesian food is anything catering strictly for tourists. That's not to say that the food in these places is bad, nor that they're unpleasant places to eat, it just means you don't get real Indonesian food! The food is not so spicy, it's not so hot, or it's not so sweet, or the 'funny tasting' spices are eliminated to cater for western tastes. And sometimes these places will be unpleasant – large bare rooms stocked with large bare tables, lit by bright neon lights, a television booming away in the corner, and will serve overpriced and boring food. There is no real comparison with an evening meal eaten in the warm outdoors at a warung under the soft glow of a kerosene lamp.

Ordering a Meal

A few basic words and phrases will help make ordering a meal easier.

makan	to eat
minum	to drink
makanan	food
minuman	drink
makan pagi	breakfast
makan siang	lunch
makan malam	dinner
saya mau makan	I want to eat
enak	delicious!
daftar makanan	the menu
rekening	the bill
manis	sweet
pedas	spicy hot
asam manis	sweet and sour
dingin	cold
panas	hot (temperature)
goreng	fried
bakar	barbecued
rebus	boiled

Snacks, Main Courses & Ingredients

Food in Indonesia – particularly meat dishes – is generally Chinese influenced, although there are a number of purely Indonesian dishes. Pork is not widely used since it is regarded by Muslims as unclean, but it sometimes appears in Chinese dishes. Javanese cooking uses fresh spices and a mixture of ingredients, the chilli mellowed by the use of sugar in many dishes. Sumatran cooking, on the other hand, uses a blending of fresh and dry spices to flavour the main ingredient. The types of fresh spices that Indonesians use are known to most westerners only as dried ground powders. There is also some Dutch influence in the use of vegetables from temperate zones in some recipes.

Rice is the basis of the meal with an assortment of side dishes, some hot (with chilli) and spicy, and some just spicy. Many dishes are much like soup, the water being used to moisten the large quantity of rice eaten. Salad is usually served, along with *sambal* (a spicy side dish) and *acar* (pickles). Many dishes are cooked in *santan*, the liquid obtained when grated coconut is squeezed. *Bumbu* is a combination of pounded ingredients used to flavour a dish. Indonesians use every part of a plant, including the leaves of cassavas, papayas, mangoes and beans. Potatoes and other starchy roots are eaten as a snack – either steamed, with salt, and grated coconut added, or thinly sliced and fried. Fresh fruit is used as dessert.

An easy guide to the identification of weird looking food is *A Jakarta Market* by Kaarin Wall, published by the American Women's Association – you should be able to pick up a copy in Jakarta. It's got pictures and descriptions of vegetables, roots and herbs, dry goods, fish, fruit and other foods you'll find in the markets in Jakarta, which are also relevant to the rest of Indonesia. Some of the dishes you're likely to encounter in Indonesia are listed here:

abon – spiced and shredded dried meat often sprinkled over nasi rames or nasi rawon

acar – pickle; cucumber or other vegetables in a mixture of vinegar, salt, sugar and water

apam – delicious pancake filled with nuts and sprinkled with sugar

ayam – chicken; *ayam goreng* is fried chicken

babi – pork. Since most Indonesians are Muslim, pork is generally only to be found in market stalls and restaurants run by Chinese, and in areas where there are non-Muslim populations such as in Bali, Irian Jaya and Tanatoraja.

bakmi – rice-flour noodles, either fried (*bakmi goreng*) or in soup

bakso or *ba'so* – meatball soup

bawang – onion

bubur ayam – Indonesian porridge with chicken. The porridge is generally sweetened and made from rice, black sticky rice or mung beans.

bubur kacang – mung bean porridge cooked in coconut milk

buncis – beans

cap cai – usually pronounced 'chop chai'. This is a mix of fried vegetables, although it sometimes comes with meat as well.

cassava – Known as tapioca to westerners, this is a long, thin, dark brown root which looks something like a shrivelled turnip.

daging babi – pork

daging sapi – beef

daging kambing – goat or mutton

dragonflies – a popular Balinese snack, caught with sticky sticks and then roasted!

emping – powdered and dried *melinjo* nuts, fried as a snack to accompany a main meal

es krim – ice cream. In Indonesia you can get western brands like Flipper's and Peters, and also locally manufactured varieties.

fu yung hai – a sort of sweet & sour omelette

gado-gado – another very popular

Indonesian dish of steamed bean sprouts, various vegetables and a spicy peanut sauce

garam – salt

gula – sugar

gula gula – lollies (sweets, candy)

gulai/gule – thick curried-meat broth with coconut milk

ikan – fish. Understandably there's a wide variety to choose from in Indonesia: *ikan laut* is saltwater fish, *ikan danau* is freshwater fish and *ikan cumi* is squid. *Ikan asam manis* is sweet and sour fish and *ikan bakar* is barbecued fish. If you're buying fresh fish (you can often buy these at a market and get your losmen to cook them up). The gills should be a deep red colour, not brown and the flesh should be firm to touch.

ikan belut – eels. Another Balinese delicacy, kids catch them in the rice paddies at night.

jahe – ginger

kacang – peanuts or beans

kacang hijau – mung bean sprouts. These can be made into a sweet filling for cakes and buns.

kare – curry; as in *kare udang* (prawn curry)

kecap asin – salty soya sauce

kecap manis – sweet soya sauce

keju – cheese

kentang – potatoes; usually the size found in the west and used in various ways including dishes of Dutch origin and as a salad ingredient

kepiting – crab; features in quite a few dishes, mostly of Chinese origin

kodok – frog; plentiful in Bali and caught in the rice paddies at night

kroket – mashed potato cake with minced meat filling

krupuk – is made of shrimp and cassava flour or of fish flakes and rice dough, cut in slices and fried to a crisp

krupuk melinjo (emping) – is made of the seeds of the melinjo fruit (*gnetum-gnemon*), pounded flat, dried and fried to make a crisp chip and served as a snack with a main course

kueh – cake

lemper – sticky rice with a small amount of meat inside, wrapped up and boiled in a banana leaf; a common snack found throughout the country

lombok – chilli. There are various types: *lombok merah* (large, red); *lombok hijau* (large, green) and *lombok rawit* (rather small but deadliest of them all, often packaged with *tahu*, etc).

lontong – rice steamed in a banana leaf

lumpia – spring rolls; small pancake filled with shrimp and bean sprouts and fried

madu – honey. The best Indonesian honey is said to come from Sumbawa Island.

martabak – found on food trolleys all over the archipelago. A martabak is basically a pancake but there are two varieties. The one that seems to be everywhere is the sickeningly sweet version guaranteed to set your dentist's bank account soaring you get back home. But (at least in Java) you can also get a delicious savoury martabak stuffed with meat, egg and vegetables. Some people think the sweet version isn't all that bad.

mentega – butter

mentimun – cucumber

merica – pepper

mie goreng – fried wheat-flour noodles, served sometimes with vegetables, sometimes with meat

mie kuah – noodle soup

mentega – butter

nasi campur – steamed rice topped with a little bit of everything – some vegetables, some meat, a bit of fish, a krupuk or two – a good, usually tasty and filling meal

nasi goreng – This is the most common of

Indonesian dishes; almost like hamburgers are to Americans, meat pies to Australians, fish & chips to the British – popular at any time of day, including breakfast time. Nasi goreng simply means fried (goreng) rice (nasi) – a basic nasi goreng may be little more than fried rice with a few scraps of vegetable to give it some flavour, but sometimes it includes some meat. *Nasi goreng istemewa* (special) usually means nasi goreng with a fried egg on top. The dish can range from the dull and dreary to very good.

nasi gudeg – unripe jackfruit cooked in santan and served up with rice, pieces of chicken and spices

nasi Padang – Padang food, from the Padang region of Sumatra, is popular all over Indonesia. It's usually served cold and consists of the inevitable rice, with a whole variety of side dishes including beef, fish, fried chicken, curried chicken, boiled cabbage, sometimes fish and prawns. The dishes are laid out before you and your final bill is calculated by the number of empty dishes when you've finished eating. Nasi Padang is traditionally eaten with the fingers and it's also traditionally very hot (pedas not panas) – sometimes hot enough to burn your fingers let alone your tongue! It's sometimes wonderful, like the stuff you get up in Balikpapan, and sometimes very dull. It's also one of the more expensive ways to eat in Indonesia and you generally end up spending a couple of thousand rupiah on a meal, although it can be well

nasi pecel – similar to gado-gado with boiled papaya leaves, tapioca, bean sprouts, string beans, fried soybean cake, fresh cucumber, coconut shavings and peanut sauce

nasi putih – white (putih) rice – usually steamed; glutinous rice is mostly used in snacks and cakes

nasi rames – rice with a combination of egg, vegetables, fish or meat

nasi rawon – rice with spicy hot beef soup, fried onions and spicy sauce

nasi uduk – rice boiled in coconut milk or cream

opor ayam – chicken cooked in coconut milk

pete – a huge broad bean, quite spicy, which is often served in the pod

pisang goreng – fried banana fritters; a popular street-side snack

rijstaffel – Dutch for 'rice table'. Indonesian food with a Dutch interpretation, it consists of lots of individual dishes with rice. Rather like a glorified nasi campur or a hot nasi Padang. Bring a big appetite.

roti – bread. The stuff you get in Indonesia is nearly always snow white and sweet.

sago – a starchy, low protein food extracted from a variety of palm tree. Sago is the staple diet of the Maluku islands.

sambal – a hot spicy chilli sauce served as an accompaniment with most meals

sate – One of the best known of Indonesian dishes, sate (satay) are small pieces of various types of meat on a skewer served with a spicy peanut sauce. Street sate-sellers carry their charcoal grills around with them and cook the sate on the spot.

sayur – vegetables

sayur-sayuran – vegetable soup with coconut milk

sop – clear soup with mixed vegetables and meat or chicken

soto – meat and vegetable broth, often a main meal eaten with rice and a side dish of sambal

tahu – soya bean curd; soft bean cake made from soya bean milk. It varies from white and yellow to thin and orange-skinned. It's found as a snack in the food stalls and is sometimes sold with a couple of hot chillies or with a filling of vegetables.

tempe – made of whole soya beans fermented into cake, wrapped in plastic or a banana leaf; rich in vegetable protein, iron and vitamin B. Tempe goreng is pieces of tempe (tempeh) fried with palm sugar and chillies.

telur – egg

ubi – sweet potato; spindle shaped to spherical with a pulpy yellow or brown skin and white to orange flesh

udang – prawns or shrimps

udang karang – lobster

Fruit

It's almost worth making a trip to Indonesia just to sample the tropical fruit – apples and bananas curl and die before the onslaught of nangkas, rambutans, mangosteens, salaks and zurzats.

apel – apple

apokat – Avocados are plentiful and cheap. Try an avocado and ice-cream combo.

belimbing – The 'starfruit' is a cool, crispy, watery tasting fruit – if you cut a slice you'll immediately see where the name comes from.

durian – the most infamous tropical fruit, the durian is a large green fruit with a hard, spiky exterior. Inside are pockets of creamy white fruit. Stories are told of an horrific stench emanating from an opened durian – hotels and airlines often ban them because of their foul odour. Some don't smell so bad – unpleasant yes, but certainly not like holding your nose over an overflowing sewer. It's worth noting that the juice

leaves a permanent stain on your clothing. The durian season is in the later part of the year.

jambu – guava. The crispy, pink-skinned, pear-shaped ones are particularly popular. Others have pale green or white skin. The small seeds should not be eaten. Many Asians like to dip the cut fruit in thick soya sauce with sliced chilli before eating

jeruk – the all-purpose term for citrus fruit. There are a variety available. The main kinds include the huge *jeruk muntis* or *jerunga*, known in the west as the pomelo. It's larger than a grapefruit but has a very thick skin, tastes sweeter, more like an orange and has segments that break apart very easily. Regular oranges are known as *jeruk manis* – sweet jeruk. The small tangerine-like oranges which are often quite green are *jeruk baras*. Lemons are *jeruk nipis*.

kelapa – coconut; as plentiful as you would expect! *Kelapa mudah* means young coconut and you'll often get them straight from the tree. Drink the milk and then scoop out the flesh.

mangga – mango. The mango season is the second half of the year.

manggis – mangosteen. One of the most famous of tropical fruits, this is a small purple-brown fruit. The outer covering cracks open to reveal pure-white

segments with an indescribably fine flavour. Queen Victoria once offered a reward to anyone able to transport a mangosteen back to England while still edible. From November to February is the mangosteen season.

nangka – Also known as jackfruit this is an enormous yellow-green fruit that can weigh over 20 kg. Inside are individual segments of yellow fruit, each containing a roughly egg-shaped seed. The segments are held together by strong white fibres. The fruit is moist and fairly sweet, with a slightly rubbery texture. As each nangka ripens on a tree it may be individually protected in a bag. The skin of a nangka is green when young, yellow when ripe.

the lychee. From November to February is the rambutan season.

salak – Found chiefly in Indonesia, the salak is immediately recognisable by its perfect brown 'snakeskin' covering. Peel it off to reveal segments that, in texture, are like a cross between an apple and a walnut but in taste are quite unique. Each segment contains a large, brown oval-shaped seed. Bali salaks are much nicer than any others.

sawo – brown skinned, looks like a potato and has a honey flavoured flesh

zurzat – Also spelt *sirsat* or *sirsak* and sometimes called white mango, the zurzat is known in the west as custard apple or soursop. The Indonesian variety is one of the best. The warty green skin of the zurzat covers a thirst quenching, soft, white, pulpy interior with a slightly lemonish, tart taste. You can peel it off or slice it into segments. Zurzats are ripe when the skin has begun to lose its fresh green colouring and become darker and spotty. It should then feel slightly squishy rather than firm.

nanas – pineapple

papaya – or paw paw are not that unusual in the west. It's actually a native of South America and was brought to the Philippines by the Spanish, and from there spread to other parts of South-East Asia.

pisang – banana. The range in Indonesia is astonishing, from midgets to specimens well over a foot long. A bunch of bananas, by the way, is *satu sisir pisang*.

rambutan – a bright red fruit covered in soft, hairy spines – the name means hairy. Break it open to reveal a delicious white fruit closely related to

Western Food

Kuta Beach and Jakarta are the two places in Indonesia where western food has grabbed hold. In Kuta you would be forgiven if you thought there was no such thing as Balinese cooking – while the food you get around Kuta is good and cheap, traditional Balinese food has just about dropped out of the picture, and even Indonesian food is succumbing to the onslaught of hamburgers, Australian meat pies and steaks.

Jakarta has a range of culinary delights – from European and Mexican to Indian,

Chinese, Thai, Korean and Japanese. Here you've got places like the Cafe de Paris, Omar Khayyam, Rugantino's and the George & Dragon Pub to name but a few. (There are more details in the Jakarta section.)

Parts of Indonesia where there are large expatriate communities working for foreign firms – Balikpapan for example – are also sources of foreign food.

Kentucky Fried Chicken has soft-landed on Java and built monuments to the colonel's enterprise in Jakarta, Yogya and in Bali, complete with laminex tables.

You can get Peters and Flipper's ice cream in Kuta and various other popular tourist places.

Books

If you want to try cooking Indonesian food when you get home, cookery books are listed in the Book section.

DRINKS

American gastronomic imperialism wraps its tentacles around the archipelago – you will not escape Coca Cola here. In a country where delicious, fresh fruit juices are sold you can still rot your teeth on Coca Cola, 7-Up, Sprite and Fanta. Prices are typically around 200 rp and up for a bottle, and from 500 rp for a can.

There is a saying that while the British built roads in their colonies, the Dutch built breweries. Many of these still exist and, while beer is comparatively expensive (in some places you can get a losmen room for less than the price of a bottle of beer!) it is good. The three popular brands are San Miguel, Anker and Bintang – the latter two are manufactured locally. Bintang is probably the most popular. Some other popular Indonesian drinks, both alcoholic and non-alcoholic, include:

air – water. You usually get a glass of it at the end of a restaurant meal. It should have been boiled (and may not have cooled down since), although some

Indonesians find it hard to understand that westerners want water that has been boiled as opposed to just heated: *air putih* (literally white water) is a phrase that usually brings the right result. *Mendidih duapuluh menit* means 'boil 20 minutes'.

air jeruk –citrus fruit juice. *Jeruk manis* is orange juice and *jeruk sitrun* is lemon juice.

air minum – drinking water

arak – a stage on from brem (distilled rice wine). It's usually home-produced, although even the locally bottled brands look home-produced. It makes quite a good drink mixed with 7-Up or Sprite. Taken in copious quantities it has a similar effect to being hit on the head with an elephant.

Aqua – the most common brand of mineral water. It usually comes in litre bottles and is a good standby if you're dubious about drinking other water, although it's not cheap at 1000 rp plus per bottle.

brem – rice wine; either home-produced or there's the commercially bottled 'Bali Brem'. A bit of an acquired taste, but not bad after a few bottles!

es juice – Although you should be a little careful about ice and water the delicious fruit drinks are irresistible. Just take one or two varieties of tropical fruit, add crushed ice and pass it through a blender. You can make mind-blowing combinations of orange, banana, pineapple, mango, jackfruit, zurzat or whatever else is available.

es buah – more a dessert than a drink; a curious combination of crushed ice, condensed milk, shaved coconut, syrup, jelly and fruit. Sickening say some, wonderful say others.

kopi – coffee. Excellent coffee is grown in Indonesia. It's usually very sweet and served up with the coffee granules floating on top.

lassi – a refreshing yoghurt based drink. Some people regard it as divine; maybe not, but it's one of my favourites.

stroop – cordial

susu – milk; not common in Indonesia although you can get long-life milk in cartons and powdered milk (Dancow is a common brand) in packets. Cans of condensed Indomilk, 'prepared from the rich, creamy milk of Australian cows' according to the label, are also sold in Indonesia and are very sweet. Another common one is Bear Brand canned milk from every third world country's favourite multinational, Nestles (1000 rp a can). Fresh milk (*susu segar*) can be found in Yogya and Solo.

teh – tea; Some people are not enthusiastic about Indonesian tea but if you don't need strong, bend-the-teaspoon-style tea you'll probably find it's quite OK. *Teh tawar* or *teh pahit* is tea without sugar and *teh gula* is tea with sugar.

tuak – an alcoholic drink fermented from the sap tapped from a type of palm tree

BOOKS

Indonesia is not a straightforward country. Its history, economics, politics and culture – and their bizarre interactions – are wide open to interpretation, and different writers come up with astoundingly different interpretations of events. If you read about Java or Bali you'll be suffocated beneath the literature but trying to find out anything about the outer islands is like putting together bits and pieces of a jigsaw.

History & Politics

A good general history that does piece together some of the jigsaw is *A History of Modern Indonesia* (Macmillan, 1981) by M C Ricklefs, Professor of History at Monash University in Melbourne, Australia. It takes you through from 1300 and, while it mainly concerns itself with Java and the Dutch conquest, it does tie in what was happening in the outer islands.

Indonesia – an alternative history (Alternative Publishing Company, Sydney, 1979) by academics Malcolm Caldwell and Ernst Utrecht, is an interesting book. Utrecht was once a member of Indonesia's Supreme Advisory Council which Sukarno set up to advise him on government policy. The book argues that the Dutch were to blame for Indonesia's economic problems today, and criticises the western view of Indonesia only as a cornerstone of defence against Communism and as a lucrative place for investment.

Indonesia (Melbourne University Press, Melbourne, 1964) by Australian journalist Bruce Grant gives background info about the country and takes you through the tumultuous Sukarno years. The book was first published in 1964, with later reprints taking in the events just after the attempted coup of 1965. The biography of the leader and translations of Sukarno's speeches makes for some fascinating reading.

An interesting and very readable account of the Suharto years is *Suharto's Indonesia* (Fontana, 1980) by Australian journalist Hamish McDonald, who worked as a freelance correspondent in Jakarta from 1975 to 1978.

One of the more evocative books on contemporary Indonesia is *The Indonesian Tragedy* (Routledge & Kegan Paul, UK, 1978) by Australian journalist Brian May. Much of the book, as May himself says, 'is a tale of Western-aided despotism' that Indonesia has suffered under Suharto's rule. It also gives a rather more sympathetic account of Sukarno than has generally been afforded.

The best account of the top echelons of the Indonesian government and military is Australian journalist David Jenkin's *Suharto and his Generals: Indonesian Military Politics 1975-1983* (Monograph Series No 64, Cornell Modern Indonesia Project, South East Asia Program, Cornell University, 1984). Jenkins interviewed many of Indonesia's leading generals, including those both in and out of power. The final product is an intriguing and illuminating work.

Travel Books

If you think travel through the outer islands of Indonesia is time-consuming now, then just read Helen & Frank Schreider's *Drums of Tonkin* (published 1965) – they overcame the lack of transport by island-hopping all the way from Java to Timor in a tiny amphibious jeep, defying landslides, oncoming monsoons, hostile (or just over-enthused?) natives and the strange propensity Jakartan soldiers once had to shoot at vehicles making illegal turns.

While the Schrieders only took their pet dog with them, zoologist and TV personality, David Attenborough, left Britain with practically nothing in the 1950s and returned from Indonesia with an orang-utan, a couple of pythons, civets, parrots and assorted other birds and reptiles. The whole saga of the enterprise 'eventually to be dignified by the title expedition' is recounted in his book *Zoo Quest for a Dragon*, recently reprinted as an Oxford in Asia paperback.

Also now in paperback, the highly readable *Unbeaten Tracks in Islands of the Far East* by Anna Forbes (Oxford University Press, Singapore, 1987) was first published in 1887. This Victorian Englishwoman accompanied her naturalist husband for more than a year round parts of Indonesia which even now are hard to reach. *The Malay Archipelago* by another Victorian, the naturalist Alfred Russel Wallace, (reprinted by Oxford University Press, Singapore, 1986) describes six solid years of wanderings, again in incredibly remote parts of Indonesia, in the 1860s. Wallace's name was given to a line between Bali and Lombok which he found marked a transition between Asian and Australasian fauna and flora. This discovery helped him develop the theory of natural selection at a similar time to Charles Darwin, who received more credit. His book is still a fascinating read,

full of titbits about human as well as animal and vegetable life.

Recently two English brothers, Laurence and Lorne Blair, have produced *Ring of Fire*, an expensive but fascinating coffee-table book which recounts 10 years of travel, partly inspired by Wallace, round isolated regions of Indonesia. Watch out for repeats of the television series on which it was based.

Indonesians: Portraits from an Archipelago by Ian Charles Stewart (published 1983 by Concept Media, Singapore) is a photographic essay on Indonesian life and culture which took the Australian photographer/author three years to compile. It's a very large, expensive book but the photographs are very fine.

Robin Hanbury-Tenison's *A Pattern of Peoples* was based on his trip to Indonesia in 1973, visiting minority groups like the Danis of Irian Jaya and the Torajas of Sulawesi. He comments on the effects that tourism and other developments have had on what were, until recently, isolated peoples. Marika Hanbury-Tenison, Robin's wife, travelled with him, and her book *A Slice of Spice* (Hutchinson, London, 1974) is also well worthwhile.

A compilation of some of the intriguing religious, social and mystical customs of the diverse peoples of Indonesia is Lee Khoon Choy's *Indonesia between Myth & Reality* (Federal Publications, Singapore, 1977). It's a journalistic travelogue, derived from short spells in the country as a journalist and politician and his stay as Singapore's Ambassador to Indonesia from 1970 to 1975.

Guide Books

Bill Dalton's *Indonesia Handbook* (Moon Publications, USA, 1988) was for a long time 'the' guide to Indonesia, getting to even the most out-of-the-way locales.

Other Lonely Planet guides covering Indonesia are *South-East Asia on a Shoestring* and *Bali & Lombok – a travel survival kit*.

The Tropical Traveller by John Hatt (Pan Books, London) is a good general introduction to travel in the tropics.

If you intend trekking, camping out, heading off to the great outdoors beyond everything, or are just interested in doing something different then get Christina Dodwell's *An Explorer's Handbook – travel, survival & bush cookery* (Hodder & Stoughton, London).

Phrasebooks

Lonely Planet's *Indonesia Phrasebook* teaches you how to use the basics of this relatively easy language. Also get hold of an English-Indonesian dictionary – they're available quite cheaply in the major cities and are very handy.

Fiction

Christopher Koch's *The Year of Living Dangerously* is an evocative reconstruction of life in Jakarta during the final chaotic months of the Sukarno period and a sympathetic portrayal of the Indonesians and their culture and society. The movie by Australian director Peter Weir conveys a feel for the place that few other movies could ever hope to achieve.

Twilight in Djakarta, a novel by the Indonesian journalist Mochtar Lubis, is an outspoken condemnation of political corruption and one of the most vivid documentations of life in the capital at the beginning of the 1960s, particularly of Jakarta's lower depths – the prostitutes, becak drivers and rural immigrants. Lubis is well known for his forthright views and he was twice imprisoned during the Sukarno regime for his political convictions. The book goes on and off the ban list in Indonesia, but at present the Oxford in Asia paperback (Oxford University Press, Singapore, 1983) is on sale in Indonesia. Two other short books by Lubis, *The Outlaw & Other Stories* (Oxford University Press, Singapore, 1987), and the Indonesian Dilemma (Graham Brash, Singapore, 1983) are also among the best writings by Indonesians in

their own country. The latter is a delicately worded but biting attack on the self interest prevailing in Indonesia's top echelons.

Pramoedya Ananta Toer, a Javanese author, has written four novels about life in colonial Indonesia. The first two – *This Earth of Mankind* and *Child of All Nations* – are available in Penguin paperback. Both novels were best sellers in Indonesia but the Suharto government banned them claiming that, while they might be skilful accounts of the colonial era, they are also subtle Marxist parodies of President Suharto's Indonesia. The author has been in and out of prison ever since he started writing: the Dutch jailed him during the independence struggle; he was briefly detained by the Army in the 1960s, as an anti-Sukarno move, and his history of the Chinese in Indonesia was banned; then in 1965 he was jailed by Suharto's New Order government and exiled to Buru Island for 14 years. In 1988 he was back in Jakarta and the fourth novel of his series, *Rumah Kaca* (Glass House), was published – only to be banned within a few weeks.

Health

The Traveller's Health Guide by Dr Anthony C Turner (Roger Lascelles, London) or *Staying Healthy in Asia* (Volunteers in Asia Publications) are useful guides to staying healthy while travelling, or what to do if you fall ill.

Children, particularly babies and unborn children, present their own peculiar problems when travelling and Lonely Planet's *Travel with Children* by Maureen Wheeler gives a rundown on health precautions to be taken with kids, or if you're pregnant and travelling.

Cooking

Many general books on Asian food include a section on Indonesian cuisine, including *South-East Asia Food* by Rosemary Brissenden (Penguin). *Indonesian Cookery* by David Scott with Surya Winata

(Rider) is a good introduction to Indonesian cooking. *Cooking the Indonesian Way* by Alec Robeau (A H & A W Reed) is another useful introduction to the art and it includes interesting legends and stories from various islands of the archipelago.

MAPS

Until recently it was not at all easy to get good maps of Indonesia outside of Indonesia itself. Even inside, the quality was often poor, but there are now a number of very good maps around.

Maps Available Outside Indonesia

The standard *Bartholomews Asia, South-East* is still not bad, covering Indonesia and the rest of the region. Two much superior maps of parts of Indonesia are *Hildebrand's Travel Map Western Indonesia* which covers Sumatra, Java and Sulawesi, and probably the best – the *Apa Maps Western Indonesia* series which covers Sumatra, Java, Bali, Lombok and Kalimantan.

For real map-freaks, the Operational Navigation Charts (ONCs) prepared by the US and other air forces cover Indonesia in about 10 maps of one by 1½ metres each. They are excellent on coastline, river and altitude detail but weak on roads and towns. There's also the WAC (World Aeronautical Chart) series at four times the scale. They're on sale at top map shops like Stanfords, 12-14 Longacre, London WC2, England, or write to NOAA Distribution Branch (N/CG33), National Ocean Service, Riverdale, MD 20737, USA, or Internationales Landenkartenhaus GMBH, Stockenriedstrasse 40 A, Postfach 80 08 30, D-7000 Stuttgart 80, West Germany.

Maps Available In Indonesia

A useful map of all Indonesia is also published by P T Pembina (tel 813886), Jalan D I Panjaitan 45, Jakarta. They also have very good individual maps of Java, Sumatra, Kalimantan and Sulawesi.

The *Jawa-Bali Kilometer & Tourist Map* published by P T Pembina isn't *absolutely* accurate in fine detail but it's the best general map available for Java.

The Directorate General of Tourism publishes a useful give-away information booklet, the *Indonesia Tourist Map*, which includes maps of Java, Bali, Sumatra and Sulawesi and a good overall map of Indonesia. Maps of major Javanese, Sumatran and Balinese cities are easy enough to come by – ask at the tourist offices or try bookshops, airports and major hotels particularly in Jakarta, Denpasar and Kuta.

In the outer islands the odd good map may pop up but quite often you'll be lucky to come across anything at all or else only fairly simple maps. Hotels often have a good, detailed map of the town or city hanging on the wall of their foyer – if not, go to the local police station and ask to see their map.

WHAT TO BRING

The usual travellers' rule applies; bring as little as possible. It is much better to get something you've left behind than to have to throw things away because you've got too much to carry. If you have to get something it shouldn't be too hard to pick it up in Indonesia – there are many well stocked shops everywhere. The only major problem is getting large-size clothes – in particular shoes.

Luggage

For budget travellers the backpack is still the best single piece of luggage. Adding some thief-deterrent by sewing on a few tabs so you can shut your pack with a padlock is a good idea. On the other hand, packs can be cumbersome and difficult to get on crowded bemos and colts. An excellent innovation is the travel-pack which can be used as either a backpack or a carry bag.

If you're into hiking then you've got heaps of opportunity in Indonesia – like on Lembata Island in Nusa Tenggara, the Balim Valley in Irian Jaya, parts of Flores,

Mamasa in Sulawesi – the possibilities are endless if you really want to get off the beaten track. So a large pack with a frame may come in use.

For most people though, a soft pack, with no frame or with a semi-rigid frame, is much better all round. A large soft zip-bag with a wide shoulder strap is less prone to damage and a bit more thief-proof. Shoulder bags are easier to wield on crowded buses and trains, but they're hard to carry for any distance – so if you've got any walking to do you're better off with a pack. A small day-pack is very useful. Whatever you bring, try and make it small; in some parts of Indonesia colts and bemos are packed to the hilt with passengers and there's next to no space left over to stow baggage.

Clothes

Most of the time it's going to be hot – temperatures are uniformly tropical year-round in Indonesia so short-sleeve shirts or blouses and T-shirts are the order of the day. A light sweater is a good idea for cool evenings.

There are a few exceptions in places like the Balim Valley in Irian Jaya, Kintamani in Bali and the Dieng Plateau in Java where it can get bloody cold in the evenings and at night! You don't need Antarctic survival gear, but long jeans, shoes, and a warm jacket are very necessary. If you travel in passenger trucks with the evening wind blowing on you, or on the decks of ships and small boats at night on the ocean or along rivers, you'll be surprised just how much the temperature drops.

A sleeping bag is really only useful if you intend doing a lot of hiking, camping or sleeping outside. A silk T-shirt or other silk clothes give surprisingly good insulation – silk is also light and will pack small.

The usual standards of Asian decorum and modesty prevail. Bring thongs, shorts, singlets and T-shirts for wandering up and down Jalan Legian at Kuta Beach and some better clothes for elsewhere.

Women are better off dressing modestly wherever you are – revealing tops are just asking for trouble. Higher dress standards particularly apply whenever you're visiting a government office – you see signs up around Kuta showing how you should and should not dress on these occasions.

Dark coloured clothes hide the dirt better. Artificial fibres like rayon and nylon are too hot and sticky in this climate; drip-dry cottons are the best. You need clothes which will dry fairly quickly in the humidity – thicker jeans are a problem in this regard.

You'll also need more protective gear if you're travelling through Indonesia by motorcycle. Bare skin is *not* a good idea if you're planning to fall off – Indonesian bitumen is just as hard as western bitumen and Indonesia is not the place to have accidents. Apart from that, travelling in hilly country by motorcycle can get very cold indeed!

A hat and sunglasses are absolutely essential as the Indonesian sun can be incredibly hot and bright. It could even be worth bringing a light long-sleeve shirt with you in case you get sunburnt (which you probably will, particularly if you leap off the plane in Denpasar and can't wait to hit the beach). A water bottle is also more than a good idea!

A sarong is about the most useful piece of material anyone travelling in Indonesia can have. Not only can you wear it as a sarong, you can also wrap it around you for warmth during the cold night-time hours on the Dieng Plateau; lie on it on the white-sand beach near Singkawang in West Kalimantan; wrap it round your head to counter the pounding sun as the ferry slogs its way from Bali to Lombok; use it as a top sheet, or alternatively as a barrier between yourself and an unhealthy-looking mattress in an unhealthy-looking losmen; pin it up over the window of your hotel room to block the outside lights that burn fiercely all night long; wet it for hand-to-hand combat; and even use it as a towel – if it still seems clean enough.

Toiletries

Things like soap, shampoo, conditioner, toothpaste are all readily available in Indonesia – in many of your favourite western brands too (Lux soap, Sunsilk shampoo, Colgate toothpaste). Toilet paper is also readily available. Bring dental floss and Interdents with you – they're hard to find. Women should bring their own tampons.

Cigarettes & Alcohol

Various brands of western cigarettes and alcohol are available here and there – less so in the areas not frequented by foreigners, and they're expensive.

Camera & Film

For details of what film is available and how much it's going to cost, see the section on Film & Photography.

Books

If you want to read, bring your own books. American and British paperbacks in English are available from the bookshops in some of the larger hotels in the main cities, sometimes from airport shops, but they're expensive and the supply and range is extremely limited. There are second-hand bookshops in well-touristed places like Kuta, Sanur or Ubud in Bali.

Torch

A torch (flashlight) comes in useful for finding your way down dark *gangs*, and around your losmen room in areas where there is still no electricity or it gets turned off in the late evening.

Photos

Stock up on some passport photos – these are readily obtained at photographic shops in Indonesia but they may be cheaper from machines in your own country; a couple of places in Indonesia require permits to visit them (like the interior of Irian Jaya) and you're usually required to provide a couple of photos.

ACTIVITIES

Surfing

Bali has long had a reputation as something of a surfing Mecca, an image created in part by those surfing-travelling films. For details on surfing and what to bring with you (apart from your board) see *Bali & Lombok – a travel survival kit.* Apart from Bali, Nias off the west coast of Sumatra has long had a reputation as Indonesia's second surfing Mecca and I've even met people hunting waves on Sumba Island in Nusa Tenggara.

Windsurfing

Indonesians windsurf the Kapuas River at Pontianak in West Kalimantan, and there's a place at Waiara Beach near Maumere on Flores that rents windsurfers.

Diving

With so many islands and so much coral,

Indonesia presents all sorts of possibilities for diving. In Bali, the coral reefs off Menjangan Island – which lies off the north-west corner of Bali – are a popular diving spot. Tulamben on the north-east coast has a reef with a sheer drop of 800 metres – a second attraction here is the American ship SS *Liberty*, sunk by the Japanese in 1942 and offering fascinating diving at depths between 10 and 40 metres. Further afield there are the brilliant coral reefs around Bunaken Island off Manado in northern Sulawesi, and around the Bandas in the Maluku. In several of these places you can get trips out to the reefs including the use of diving equipment.

Snorkelling

If diving is beyond your budget then try snorkelling. There are plenty of opportunities for snorkelling in Indonesia – around the beautiful coral reefs of Gili Trawangan in Lombok, the Banda Islands and off Manado to name a few places. But if you want to see anything underwater you *have* to have a mask and snorkel. Whilst you can usually buy or rent the gear when you need it, packing your own snorkel and mask is a good idea.

Getting There

There are a number of possible entry points into Indonesia by land or sea. Jakarta remains the principal gateway for entry by air and Bali also has an international airport, but only two international airlines have direct flights to Bali – the Indonesian national airline Garuda and the Australian airline Qantas. There are also international flights to various cities in the outer islands and a couple of possible land and sea entry routes.

There is a variety of discounted ticket possibilities to Indonesia including advance purchase fares or more straightforward discounts on regular fares. When you're looking for bargain fares you have to go to a travel agent rather than directly to the airline which can only sell fares by the book. Always check what conditions and restrictions apply to whatever ticket you intend buying.

ROUND-THE-WORLD TICKETS

If Indonesia is just one stop on a round-the-world trip then consider getting a round-the-world (RTW) ticket. These are just what they say – you have a limited period in which to circumnavigate the globe and you can go anywhere the carrying airlines go, as long as you don't backtrack. Usually the tickets are valid for one year.

One such ticket takes you with Continental/Garuda from Melbourne to London and back via Indonesia and the USA from A$1740 depending on the season of your departure – fares rise to A$2050 in peak season from December to February. Even if you can't get a round-the-world ticket that will take you through Indonesia, you could get one through Singapore (eg one of the combinations offered with Singapore Airlines or Qantas) and then side-trip to Indonesia.

An alternative to RTW tickets marketed by airlines is a ticket put together by enterprising travel agents. London agents offer tickets that fly you round the world with a variety of stopovers from around £800 to £1100. The London-Australia sectors on these tickets can often be with Garuda, permitting stopovers in Jakarta or Denpasar.

FROM AUSTRALIA

You can fly direct to Jakarta and/or Bali (Denpasar) from Sydney, Melbourne, Perth, Darwin and Port Hedland in Western Australia. Only Garuda operate the Darwin and Port Hedland flights, while both Garuda and Qantas operate flights on the other sectors.

Both airlines operate direct Melbourne/Denpasar flights some days of the week, and via Sydney on the other days. Some Garuda flights go Melbourne/Sydney/Denpasar while some go Sydney/Melbourne/Denpasar. Flight time Melbourne/Denpasar is about 5½ to 6½ hours; and Sydney/Denpasar is slightly shorter. For West Australians Bali is almost a local resort. Perth/Denpasar flying time is just 3½ hours, less time than it takes to go from Perth to the east coast of Australia.

There's one very interesting alternative to the Garuda or Qantas flights and that is to take Merpati (tel (089) 41 1030) from Darwin to Kupang on the island of Timor. From Kupang there are regular flights to Bali or you can island-hop through the Nusa Tenggara archipelago to Bali. Natrabu (tel 81 3695), at 12 Westlane Arcade off Smith St Mall, is a Merpati agent in Darwin. You do not need a visa to enter or leave Indonesia through Kupang, but require an onward ticket from Indonesia if you wish to buy a one-way ticket to Kupang. The low season Darwin/Kupang fare is A$164 one-way or A$250 return. From there the Kupang/Bali fare is 96,000 rp, about A$60. So you can get from Darwin to Bali for about A$220 one-way or A$370 return. It is a roundabout route, but it is certainly much cheaper than the direct Garuda flight.

Regular Fares

Economy one-way fares from Sydney or Melbourne are A$1017 to Denpasar or A$1119 to Jakarta and from Perth and Darwin, A$675 to Bali and A$776 to Jakarta.

Advance Purchase Fares

There are two discount fares available between Australia and Bali. Excursion fares are available to anyone, but the other category, accommodation-inclusive fares, is only available in connection with a holiday package. Both fares have a high and a low season.

There is no one-way excursion fare to Bali, but there is a one-way advance purchase fare. This must be purchased 21 days prior to departure and there are cancellation penalties within that period. Fares are seasonal, and advance purchase return fares to Bali range from A$782 to A$1009 from Sydney or Melbourne, less from Perth, Port Hedland or Darwin – ranging from A$591 to A$719. Advance purchase excursion fares must be booked and paid for 21 days prior to departure and once you're in that 21-day period any change in reservations or cancellation of your ticket incurs a penalty equal to 25% of your fare (although insurance is available to guard against this cancellation penalty). The cost depends on whether you're leaving from the east or west coast of Australia and your departure date; the year is divided into 'peak' (from 10 December to 15 January), 'high' (22 November to 9 December) and 'low' (the rest of the year) seasons.

The following table outlines fares from the east and west coasts of Australia to Bali and Jakarta.

one-way	season	Bali	Jakarta
East	peak	A$586	A$690
	high	A$558	A$669
	low	A$483	A$569
West	high	A$351	A$403
	low	A$295	A$339

return	season	Bali	Jakarta
East	peak	A$954	A$1009
	high	A$889	A$944
	low	A$782	A$841
West	high	A$667	A$719
	low	A$591	A$632

At certain times during the peak season, flights to or from Australia are very heavily booked and you must plan well ahead if you want to fly to Indonesia then.

Accommodation-inclusive fares

To get the accommodation-inclusive package fare you have to combine the fare with an accommodation package. Some tour operators and travel agents can arrange tour-inclusive fare and minimal accommodation packages that cost about the same as the cheapest advance purchase fare. As the packages include accommodation they're particularly good bargains on short trips. Cheap children's fares are also available.

Accommodation-inclusive fares for low season departures allow a maximum stay of 45 days; for high season departures the maximum stay is 90 days. Fares can be offered with 'voucher' tours. You buy a package in Australia which includes air fare and hotel accommodation. You're given vouchers which can be used to pay for accommodation at a number of hotels. Sometimes the vouchers can also be used for motorcycle or bicycle rental, even for meals. Usually the vouchers are good for the cheaper losmen and hotels – don't expect three-star accommodation. The real bargain with this set-up is that the total cost on a short trip can actually be lower than the straight excursion fare. The vouchers are just a useful bonus – you don't even have to use them.

For good fares to Indonesia try STA offices in the main cities or the various agents who advertise in the travel pages of the main newspapers.

FROM NEW ZEALAND

Garuda has introduced a weekly service from Auckland to Bali, with some talk of increasing this to two flights a week. The fares from New Zealand to Bali operate on a similar system to the Australian fares, but as this is a relatively new service fares and discounts through travel agents should only get better. Check latest fare developments and discounts with Garuda or shop around a few travel agents for possible deals.

FROM THE UK

Ticket discounting is a long established business in the UK and it's wide open – the various agents advertise their fares and there's nothing under-the-counter about it at all. To find out what is available and where to get it, pick up a copy of the giveaway newspapers *Australasian Express* or *LAW* or the weekly 'what's on' guide *Time Out*. These days, discounted tickets are available all over England, they're not just a London exclusive.

A couple of excellent places to look are Trailfinders (tel 938 3366) at 46 Earls Court Rd, London W8 and STA Travel at 74 Old Brompton Rd, London W7 (tel 581 1022) and at Clifton House, 117 Euston Rd (tel 388 2261).

Garuda is one of the enthusiastic fare discounters in London so it's relatively easy to find cheap fares to Australia with stopovers in Indonesia. It's not, however, such a bargain to go just to Bali or Bali return. A London/Australia ticket with a stopover in Jakarta (and Singapore or Bangkok for that matter) costs around £600, add another £100 to include Bali. London/Denpasar costs around £300 one-way and £580 return.

Another alternative is to fly London/ Singapore for around £250 one-way or £475 return and then make your own way down to Bali by air or sea and land.

FROM EUROPE

Garuda has flight connections between Jakarta and several European cities: Paris, Amsterdam, Zurich, Frankfurt and Rome.

On the continent Amsterdam, Brussels and Antwerp are some of the best places for buying discount air tickets. WATS, de Keyserlei 44, Antwerp, Belgium, has been recommended. Also try the Swiss agents SOF Travel (tel 01 301 3333) in Zurich, and Stohl Travel (tel 022 316560) in Geneva.

FROM THE USA

You can pick up interesting tickets from North American to South-East Asia, particularly from the US west coast. The intense competition between Asian airlines has resulted in ticket discounting operations very similar to the London bucket shops. To find cheap tickets simply scan the travel sections of the Sunday papers for agents – the *New York Times, San Francisco Chronicle-Examiner* and the *Los Angeles Times* are particularly good. The network of student travel offices known as Council Travel is particularly good and there are also Student Travel Network offices which are associated with Student Travel Australia.

From the US west coast you can get to Hong Kong, Bangkok or Singapore for about US$500 to US$750 return and get a flight from there to Bali. Discount tickets for a Hong Kong/Denpasar flight can be bought for around HK$2700 to HK$3000, with return fares around HK$4000. You can also find interesting fares from Hong Kong via Bali to Australia. Singapore/ Denpasar costs around S$400 one-way and S$550 return.

Alternatively Garuda has a Los Angeles/ Honolulu/Biak/Denpasar route which is an extremely interesting back door route into Indonesia and good value at US\$472 one-way or about US\$800 return. Biak is a no-visa entry point so that's no problem.

FROM CANADA

Getting discount tickets in Canada is much the same as in the USA – go to the travel agents and shop around until you find a good deal. Again you'll probably have to fly into Hong Kong or Singapore and carry on from there to Indonesia.

CUTS is Canada's national student bureau and has offices in a number of Canadian cities including Vancouver, Edmonton, Toronto and Ottawa – you don't necessarily have to be a student. There are a number of good agents in Vancouver for cheap tickets, CP-Air are particularly good for fares to Hong Kong.

FROM SINGAPORE & MALAYSIA

There are direct flights from Singapore to Jakarta, Denpasar and several cities in Sumatra. You can also fly from Penang or Kuala Lumpur to Sumatra. There is a regular shipping service between Malaysia and Sumatra. There are daily ferries and some flights between Singapore and the Riau Archipelago, which is the cluster of small Indonesian islands immediately south of Singapore.

In Singapore you can get a Singapore, Jakarta, Yogyakarta, Denpasar ticket for S\$410 one-way or S\$580 return. A straight through ticket from Singapore to Denpasar is S\$380 or S\$500 return. Singapore to Jakarta is S\$175 or S\$240 return.

An air ticket from Singapore to Medan is S\$200 or S\$360 return. For more details of flights from Singapore and Malaysia, and the sea connections between Singapore, Malaysia and Sumatra, see the Sumatra chapter.

Singapore is also a good place to buy a cheap air ticket if you're leaving Indonesia for the west. Cheap air tickets from Singapore are available at *Student Travel* (tel 7345681), Ming Court Hotel, corner Tanglin Rd and Orchard Rd. Another good place is *Sky Centre Air*

Travel (tel 3371033), 2nd floor, 32 Prinsep St, which is just around the corner from Bencoolen St. Other agents advertise in the *Straits Times* classified columns.

Fares from Singapore to the west vary with when you want to fly and who you want to fly with. The cheapest fares are likely to be with various East European or Middle East airlines. There are also cheap fares available on various South-East Asian airlines to other parts of South-East Asia and to the west. Typical discount fares (in Singapore dollars) from Singapore are listed below.

Fares from Singapore to other parts of South-East Asia include: Bangkok S\$170 to S\$210; Manila S\$500 or S\$750 return; Hong Kong S\$550 or S\$750 return.

To the Indian subcontinent there are tickets to: Colombo S\$380; Madras or Bombay S\$520; Kathmandu S\$570 to S\$600.

Fares to Australia or New Zealand include: Sydney or Melbourne from S\$560 to S\$800; Auckland S\$900 or S\$1400 return; Perth or Darwin via Bali and Jakarta S\$600.

Fares to London or other European destinations are from S\$650 with the Eastern European airlines, or from S\$750 with the South-East Asian and western airlines.

Fares to North America are: Vancouver S\$1050; USA west coast S\$850 by the northern (Asian) route with stops; and S\$1600 by the southern (Pacific) routes.

There are always some special multi-stop deals on offer, such as Singapore, Bangkok, Hong Kong, Taipei, Amsterdam for S\$900 with China Airlines. Or Singapore, Bangkok, Hong Kong, Taipei, US west coast for about the same price. You can add Tokyo and Honolulu on that route for a few dollars more.

Between north Borneo (the Malaysian states of Sabah and Sarawak) there is a weekly flight with Merpati between Pontianak and Kuching, and Bouraq flies between Tarakan and Tawau. The usual route into Indonesia from Singapore is

Singapore-Jakarta. There are all sorts of flights on this route with all sorts of fares quoted from around S$175. Singapore-Denpasar costs about S$375.

FROM HONG KONG

There are direct flights between Hong Kong and Jakarta, with connections to Denpasar. Hong Kong is a good place for air fare bargains. Travel agents advertise in the classified sections of the *South China Morning Post* and the *Hong Kong Standard* newspapers but some are definitely more reliable and helpful than others.

One of the more popular places for buying tickets is the Hong Kong Student Travel Bureau (HKSTB) 10th floor, Star House, Tsimshatsui, Kowloon. Another popular place is the Traveller's Hostel, 16th floor, Chungking Mansions, Nathan Rd, Tsimshatsui, Kowloon.

Typical one-way fares from Hong Kong are Jakarta HK$2300, Denpasar around HK$2700 to HK$2900. Better still are the return flights to Jakarta or Denpasar for around HK$3500. You can also find interesting fares from Hong Kong through Indonesia to Australia.

OTHER ENTRY & EXIT POINTS

Jakarta and Denpasar are not the only gateways to Indonesia; there are a number of other entry (and exit) points around the country which are worth considering. Some crossings – like Irian Jaya to PNG, and eastern Malaysia to Kalimantan – are rather tenuous for one reason or another, though they can *sometimes* be done.

Sumatra

From Penang in Malaysia you can fly to Medan in Sumatra; this is one of the cheapest (about US$50) and most popular routes into Indonesia. The long-halted ferry service on this route seems to have resumed.

Alternatively from Singapore you can take a boat to Batam and another to Tanjung Pinang, an Indonesian island a few hours south of Singapore. From Tanjung Pinang you can catch a boat to Pekanbaru or Medan. For more details of these routes – plus other possibilities for getting to or from Sumatra – see the Sumatra chapter.

Irian Jaya

From Papua-New Guinea there is a once-weekly flight between Wewak and Jayapura in Irian Jaya (via Vanimo). Officially, there is no land or sea crossing between Irian Jaya and PNG although it would be easy to do. For more details see the Irian Jaya chapter.

Kalimantan

There are air connections between Indonesian Kalimantan and the eastern Malaysian states of Sabah and Sarawak. Merpati has a regular flight between Pontianak and Kuching, and Bouraq has a regular flight between Tarakan and Tawau. Land crossings between Kalimantan and eastern Malaysia are also possible. There are also some rather ephemeral Bouraq flights between Singapore and Kalimantan. See the Kalimantan chapter for details.

Other Possibilities

From time to time there have been charters between Darwin in Australia and Maluku. Also worth watching out for are international flights from Manado in the northern peninsula of Sulawesi; Manado now has an international airport and the logical step from northern Sulawesi would be to the Philippines.

Yachts

Surprisingly for an island country there are few opportunities to arrive in Indonesia by sea. Apart from cruise ships and private yachts the only really feasible route is the Jakarta-Tanjung Pinang-Singapore service – see the Jakarta section for more details.

With a bit of effort it's still possible to get yacht rides around South-East Asia. Very often yacht owners are travellers too and need another crew member or two; willingness to give it a try is often more important than experience and often all it costs you is the contribution to the food kitty. Where to look – well, anywhere that yachts pass through or in towns with western-style yacht clubs. We've had letters from people who have managed rides from Singapore, Penang, Phuket (in Thailand) and Benoa (in Bali). Other popular yachting places include the main ports in Papua New Guinea and Hong Kong. Every August there is a Darwin to Ambon (capital of the Maluku Islands) yacht race.

TICKETS OUT OF INDONESIA

Cheap, discount air tickets out of Indonesia can be bought from various travel agents in Jakarta and at Kuta Beach on Bali. You can also buy discount tickets in Kuta for departure from Jakarta.

From Bali

There are numerous airline ticket discounters around Kuta and Legian. Typical fares from Denpasar to Asia include Singapore US$150, Bangkok US$250, Hong Kong US$300, Tokyo US$350. From Denpasar to Australia fares are Darwin or Perth US$210, Sydney or Melbourne US$376. Further afield you can fly from Denpasar to the US west coast for US$550 to US$650 or to London for about US$550.

You can also buy tickets in Bali for departure from Jakarta and Singapore to other parts of South-East Asia, as well as to Auckland, Honolulu, the US west coast or London. You can hook up with the UTA trans-Pacific services out of Jakarta with flights to Noumea, Papeete, the US west coast and New York.

From Jakarta

Jakarta is the other place for cheap tickets. Kaliman Travel (tel 330101) in the President Hotel on Jalan Thamrin is a good place for cheap tickets. The staff are very helpful and they offer a discount on some tickets if you pay in cash. Other agents worth checking are Vayatour (tel 336640) next door to Kaliman, and Pacto Ltd (tel 320309) at Jalan Cikini Raya 24.

The agent for STA (Student Travel Australia) is Travair Buana (tel 371479) in the Hotel Sabang on Jalan H A Salim, close to Jalan Jaksa.

To Asian destinations typical fares include Singapore US$125, Bangkok US$250, Calcutta US$400, Kuala Lumpur US$150, Taipei US$450. You can also hook up on the UTA trans-Pacific services out of Jakarta with good fares to the Pacific and to the US west coast. Typical one-way fares to Asian destinations include Bangkok US$314 and Hong Kong US$379, both with Garuda.

Departure Tax

Airport tax on international flights is 9000 rp and on domestic flights is between 500 and 3500 rp depending on the airport.

Getting Around

AIR

Indonesia has a great variety of airlines and aircraft, and an extensive network of flights makes some pretty amazing, isolated corners of the country easily accessible. There are four main airlines – Garuda, Merpati, Bouraq and Mandala – and several smaller ones. Not all domestic airfares are equal – Garuda has the most expensive fares, unless you qualify for the special discounts offered by them on domestic flights if your're flying internationally with Garuda.

Each airline publishes a nationwide timetable – definitely worth picking up if you're going to do a lot of flying. They list flights, fares and addresses of airline offices. The best place to get one of these timetables is from their offices in one of the major cities or tourist destinations, like Jakarta, Yogyakarta or Denpasar.

Don't rely on this book to tell you every flight that's available to or from a given place. There are so many flights – sometimes with two or three airlines covering the same route – that it's impossible to list them all here! All we can give you here is a few of the main flights, or those which are probably most useful to tourists, together with some idea of the fare involved. If you want to fly out of a place always check with the local airline offices about what's available.

Airport tax on domestic flights varies from 500 to 3500 rp and should be included on your ticket. On most flights baggage is limited to 20 kg, sometimes to 10 kg on the smaller planes so check first. Sometimes they charge you excess baggage and sometimes they don't.

Bookings On the more popular routes, try to book as far in advance as possible, especially in the peak tourist season around August when flights can be fully booked two or three weeks in advance. Don't expect to be able to make a booking in advance in one town and then buy your ticket at the departure point.

Always try to reconfirm your flight at least the day before departure. Merpati, for one, is notorious for over-booking and selling tickets without definite bookings.

Fares All airfares quoted in this book are the basic fares. On top of this a 10% tax is charged, as well as insurance and baggage charges (usually no more than 1500 rp).

Garuda The major airline is Garuda, named after the mythical man-bird vehicle of the Hindu god Vishnu. Garuda

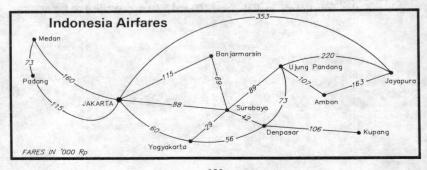

Indonesia Airfares

FARES IN '000 Rp

not only operates Indonesia's international flights but also a wide range of flights right across the country using DC9s, DC10s, F28s and Airbuses. Although the territory covered by their flights is extensive, they usually only operate on major routes and between major cities.

Garuda has discontinued the 'Visit Indonesia Air Pass' which allowed you to fly between a certain number of cities in a limited period of time, but offers cheaper domestic fares to those flying internationally with Garuda.

Merpati This was once an independent airline but was taken over in 1979 by Garuda and is now integrated into Garuda's network. Merpati operates a mind-boggling collection of aircraft, but the intention is they should run services to remote and out-of-the-way locations; they're most useful in some of the outer places like Irian Jaya and Nusa Tenggara. However, their flights often overlap with Garuda's so if you want to save some money check out what they've got available. Merpati also flies Pontianak-Kuching (Malaysia).

Bouraq The network of this privately run airline is nowhere near as extensive as Merpati's or Garuda's, but they have some useful flights in Kalimantan and Sulawesi which are worth investigating, including connections between those two islands and Java. They also have several flights around Nusa Tenggara, connecting with Denpasar and Java. Their fares are the same as Merpati's. Bouraq also flies Pontianak-Singapore and Tarakan-Tawau (Malaysia).

Mandala In this dull jumbo-jet age Mandala's four-engined prop-planes make an interesting change. They serve a couple of main routes connecting Java with various cities in Sumatra, Sulawesi and Maluku, including Ujung Pandang, Ambon, Palembang and Medan. Fares are the same as Merpati's.

Other There are some other possibilities for flying in Indonesia. The mission aircraft which operate in places like Kalimantan, Central Sulawesi and Irian Jaya fly to some really remote parts of the interior of these islands and will take (paying) passengers if they have room. You're most likely to use the flights around Irian Jaya – see that section for details.

Various aircraft and helicopters are used by the foreign mining and oil companies – if you meet the right people in the right place, they like the look of your face, and if they're not yet sick of every self-proclaimed Marco Polo looking for a free ride you never know where you could end up.

Other airlines include *Sempati* and *Bali Air* which is owned by Bouraq and operates charter flights.

ROAD

Once upon a time, getting from point A to point B by road in much of Indonesia involved intermittent days of pure hell jolting over roads constructed of trenches big enough to swallow half a truck. Roads seemed to be built by pushing one truck through the jungle leaving two tyre marks for the rest to follow. In the wet season these long trails of overgrown potholes would turn to rivers of deep, almost impenetrable mud. Other roads would be wrecked by earthquakes and tremors, or washed away in the monsoon. The good news is that in many places things have improved greatly; the bad news is that in many other places the state of the roads hasn't changed a bit.

Basically, areas of political, military and economic importance have got priority on road construction. Java, as the political centre of Indonesia, the most heavily populated island, and the island to which much of the wealth of Indonesia is drawn, has an extensive system of surfaced roads. Bali, also heavily populated and catering to a large tourist trade, is also served by many surfaced roads making transport around the island quick and easy. In Indonesia the further off the beaten track you get the more beaten up the track becomes.

You find some curious roads in the outer islands. In Timor – once neglected by both the Indonesians who controlled the western half and the Portuguese who used to control the east – both sides had abominable roads. Then came the Indonesian invasion of East Timor and the subsequent construction of a road all the way from Kupang in the west to Bacau in the east – plus the construction of new roads in the interior of East Timor by the Indonesian military to help them suppress the Fretilin guerrillas as well as to economically exploit the new province. For many years the only fully surfaced road in Flores ran up the side of the Keli Mutu Volcano – the road was especially built for a vice-presidential visit several years back. The dirt track through Central Sulawesi has been upgraded from a footpath to a cattle path as part of the ongoing piecing together of the Trans-Sulawesi Highway. On the same island, the road from Palopo to Soroako in Central Sulawesi is probably one of the best in Indonesia – built by a foreign mining company to help it ship out the nickel deposits.

Vehicles

You've got a choice of bemos, colts, minibuses, buses and trucks to get you from point A to point B. Sometimes the type of vehicle used is an indication of what's in store on the road ahead. On some roads only small vehicles like colts or bemos are used because they're the only ones light enough to be pushed out of the mud. If trucks are being used then it's probably rough going, but in most cases not a road you'll get bogged on (but don't quote me!). If large buses are plying the route then the road is probably a good one. Whilst that works as a general rule, it's not always the case.

There's generally no shortage of road transport and all you usually have to do is go down to the local colt/bemo/bus/truck station and hop aboard. For short routes on good roads you'll probably find frequent vehicles departing all through the day. For longer routes you'll have to get down to the station early in the morning to get a vehicle; on bad roads there'll be fewer vehicles, so buying a ticket beforehand can be a good idea. In many places the bus companies will have an office from where you can buy a ticket and reserve a seat; there may be shops which act as agents (or own the buses) from where you can buy tickets in advance. Sometimes losmen and hotels will act as agents or will buy a ticket for you and arrange to have the bus pick you up at the losmen – sometimes they will charge a few hundred rupiah for this service but it's sometimes worth it.

Some of the bus companies offer door-to-door service. For a lengthy trip they'll go all around town picking up passengers who have already bought tickets, or searching out additional business. This, of course, can take a considerable amount of time since they won't finally leave until the bus is reasonably full, and you seem to drive around town endlessly in circles. At the end of the trip they'll take each passenger to whatever particular part of town he wants to go to – and again if you're the last one they drop off this can also take a considerable amount of time. With the picking-up round included, a five-hour journey can easily become a seven-hour journey! This system doesn't always apply, particularly in large cities like Yogya, Jakarta, Manado or Balikpapan – in those sort of places the vehicles fill up and leave from one bus station and dump you off at the bus station in the next town.

Regardless of whether you're travelling by bus, truck or whatever, bring as little luggage as possible – there is rarely any room to store anything, even under the seats! A large pack with a frame will be a positive abomination to find a space for –

so if you can travel with a small bag then do so.

Bemos Bemos are the standard transport, used both as local transport around cities and towns and on short inter-city runs. Basically, a bemo is a small pickup truck with a row of seats down each side. Most of them operate a standard route at a standard fare picking up and dropping off people and goods anywhere along the way. Unless you get on at standard starting point A and get off at standard finishing point B you may have to bargain a bit.

Bemo drivers will try to overcharge you – more in some places than others. You can ask other passengers what the *harga biasa* (normal price) should be although they may side with the bemo driver. If you know the fare is 100 rp and they try and charge you 200 rp just hand over the right fare; if they really insist that 200 rp is the correct fare then it most likely is – the fares will have gone up since this book was published so use the prices given as a rough guide only! The other thing to remember is that the difference between 100 rp and 200 rp is only 10 cents – if your budget is so tight that you really feel you have to argue passionately about being overcharged by 10 cents then its time to either go home or walk.

Beware of getting on an empty bemo; you may end up chartering it! One annoying problem you come across time and time again in Indonesia is wandering into the bemo station to search out a bemo going where you want to go, and being told by driver after driver how much it will cost you to charter it! On the other hand, sometimes chartering a bemo is worth considering – between a group of half a dozen people it can work out cheaper than hiring a motorcycle by the day and much cheaper than hiring a car. It can also be much more convenient for some straight-forward point A to point B trips. For example, to travel by regular bemo between Kuta Beach and Sanur Beach in Bali you have to take one bemo into Denpasar, transfer to another bemo station and then take another bemo out. With a bit of bargaining half a dozen people could charter a bemo directly for the same cost; it's faster, more convenient and you get to-the-door service at your destination. Regular bemos carry around 12 people so multiplying the usual fare by 12 should give you a rough idea of what to pay. Smaller bemos are, of course, cheaper than big ones. By the day, from 20,000 to 25,000 rp is probably a good rule of thumb figure to work from in Bali. If you find yourself in the sticks without any wheels you'll either have to try and charter a bemo or bus, camp out or find the kepala desa (head of the village) and ask to be put up for the night.

As with all public transport in Indonesia, the drivers wait until their vehicles are crammed to capacity before they contemplate moving. Often there are people, produce, caged and uncaged birds, stacks of sarongs, laden baskets, even bicycles hanging out the windows and doors and at times it seems you're in danger of being crushed to death or at least asphyxiated. There's no such thing as air-conditioning on any of these vehicles and, more often than not, you won't be able to organise yourself to get a good vantage spot to see much of the countryside along the way. Indonesians don't travel well; many people have amazingly weak stomachs that chuck up last night's gado-gado the first time the vehicle crosses a ripple in the road.

Colts Bemos are gradually being replaced by small minibuses or colts, particularly on inter-city runs. Colts (also known as *opelets*) are small minibuses. They've got their name since they're often Mitsubishi Colts although the word is applied to all minibuses, not just Colts. It's an overlapping term since colts have replaced buses on many transport routes – they're more comfortable and, since they carry fewer passengers, depart more frequently than the big buses. The old pick-up truck bemos also seem to be disappearing, to be replaced by colt-style minibuses. If there's a choice between a bus and a colt the colt will probably be a bit more expensive, but a real bemo-bemo and a colt-bemo will be the same price.

It's blurring the distinction between bemos and colts, but the method of operation and the fares will be the same. In a colt-style bemo you probably get a better view at the expense of less fresh air, and greater difficulty getting on and off. If you're a big person your knees and legs get crushed by the seat in front of you and there's no room to stretch out. Like in bemos, they pack in as many people as possible.

Trucks Trucks operate with rows of bench seats in the tray at the back to sit on. These are used in some of the more distant islands – like in parts of Flores – or sometimes in areas where the roads are bad. If you are on a truck – and that implies a rough road may be in store – it's imperative to try and get a seat in front of the rear axle, otherwise every time the truck hits a pothole you shoot up about two feet and land with a spinal-cord-compressing thud back down on the seat.

Buses As the roads are improved, trucks are gradually being replaced by colts, minibuses or large buses. Buses are more comfortable than trucks, although if there are both trucks and buses on a route then the truck will usually be a bit cheaper. In many parts of Indonesia buses don't usually run at night, however, there are night buses between Bali and Java and with improvements in the roads on the other islands, more and more companies are putting on night services.

HITCH-HIKING
Yes, you can even hitch-hike in Indonesia. You meet a lot of nice people, and enjoying the scenery from the back of a truck is a good experience! The only problem is that it might take a very long time to get anywhere. There aren't many private cars

on the roads (even in Java) and the trucks can be too crowded or moving too fast to stop anyway. You're probably more likely to get short rides on the back of motorcycles.

DRIVING
People in Indonesia drive on the left of the road like in Australia, Japan, Britain and most of South-East Asia. Opportunities for driving yourself are fairly limited in Indonesia unless you bring your own vehicle with you. An exception is in Bali where jeeps and VW safari vehicles can be hired for from 25,000 to 30,000 rp; by asking around, you can hire small minibuses for about half that. There is also self-drive and chauffeur-driven car hire available in Java. See the Bali and Java sections for more details. Punctures are usually repaired at roadside stands known as *tambal ban*. Whatever you do, try not to have an accident – if you do, as a foreigner it's *your* fault.

Petrol Petrol is no longer especially cheap in Indonesia – it's typically between 350 and 400 rp a litre – around US$1.50 a gallon. There are petrol stations around the larger towns but out in the villages it can be difficult to find. If you intend going to out-of-the-way places it may be advisable to take some with you, so long as you can carry it safely. If not, it's available from small wayside shops and hawkers on the streets – look for signs that read *press ban*, or crates of bottles with a sign saying *bensin*. Some of the stuff off the roadside stands is said to be of dubious quality, so it's probably best to refill whenever you see a Pertamina petrol station (*pompa bensin*) – although they're few and far between in some areas.

MOTORCYCLES
Hiring or bringing your own motorcycle would be one of the easiest ways to travel through Indonesia. They've long been a favourite means of getting around Bali but they're also suited to many other parts

of the country – particularly where there are poor, unsurfaced roads on which large vehicles get bogged. In fact, you'll avoid a bone-shattering ride on some of these roads if you can hire a trail-bike! Outside of Java and Bali traffic is generally not heavy until you hit the cities and towns. Ferries and ships between the islands are more regular these days and will transport motorcycles.

Motorcycles definitely have their pluses and minuses: the minus points are danger and distance. Another disadvantage is that on a motorcycle you forsake many opportunities to get to grips with Indonesia. You don't meet people the way you do on a bemo, you don't see life as it's lived, you just rush round keeping your eye on the road. Furthermore motorcycles are an unpleasant intrusion in many places – noisy, distracting, annoying and unwanted. But by the same token, the major plus is the enormous flexibility a motorcycle gives you – allowing you to get to places that people without their own

transport have to walk to, and it saves having to wait endlessly for transport. And if you see something you like you can stop and continue on 10 minutes or 10 hours later. With a bemo you're likely to just shoot straight by – perhaps without even seeing it.

Motorcycles can be hired in Java, and more easily in Bali. Those for hire in Bali are almost all between 90 and 125 cc with 100 cc as the usual size. You really don't need anything bigger – the distances are short and the roads are rarely suitable for going very fast. Anyway what's the hurry? In any case, for long distance travel, a small bike is better if it breaks down or runs out of gas and you have to push – particularly if it breaks down on some of those hilly islands like Flores or Sumbawa where it's a long way between service stations! You also have to load and unload the thing on and off boats and ships – much easier with a small bike.

Rental charges vary with the bike and the period of hire. The longer the hire

period, the lower the rate: the bigger or newer the bike, the higher the rate. Typically in Bali you can expect to pay at least 4000 rp per day. A newish 125 cc in good condition might cost you 6000 rp a day for short periods. It's virtually impossible to hire a bike in Bali and take it to another island. You need to have a licence, but in Bali getting that is as easy as opening a cornflakes packet. See the Bali section for details of how to rent a motorcycle there and how to get a licence.

Motorcycle Safety There is no denying the dangers of bike riding in Indonesia – combined with all the normal hazards of motorcycle riding are narrow roads, unexpected potholes, crazy drivers, buses and trucks which (through size alone) reckon they own the road, children who dart onto the road, bullocks who lumber in, dogs and chickens that run around in circles, and unlit traffic at night. Take it slowly and cautiously around curves to avoid hitting on-coming traffic – this includes very large and heavy buses, buffaloes, herds of stray goats or children. Rocks, boulders and landslides on poor stretches of roads are another hazard. Watch out for animals that are tethered to one side of the road and then wander over to the other side, stretching their ropes across the road at neck height for a motorcyclist.

Roadworks are another hazard – you round a corner and come slap up against a grader, rocks piled into the middle of the road or 44-gallon drums of tar. They rarely, if ever, put up warning signs that there are roadworks in progress. Up in the mountains there are perilous and unprotected drops down sheer cliff faces to the valleys below – it limits your opportunities for swerving round these obstacles!

At home, most people would never dream of hopping on a motorcycle in shorts and thongs and without a crash helmet – but in Bali they take one rudimentary test, stick their bikes in gear and their brains in neutral and charge off. Indonesia is no place to learn how to ride a motorcycle.

BICYCLES

The story on bicycle hire is much the same. Bicycles can be rented in the main centres of Java, Bali and also Lombok, but they're not used very much either by Indonesians or by travellers. A few places like Yogyakarta and the island of Sumba are exceptions, with plenty of bicycles in common use. My advice is to bring your own bicycle with you if you want to get around this way – or be prepared to do some maintenance work on the rusty old hulks you'll find in Indonesia.

The main advantage of cycling is the quality of the experience. You can cover many more km by bemo, bus or motorcycle but you really don't see more. Bicycles also tend to bridge the time gap between the rush of the west and the calm of rural Asia – without the noise of a motorcycle engine you can hear the wind rustling in the rice paddies, or the sound of a gamelan practising as you pass a village in Bali.

The main problems with seeing Indonesia by bicycle are the traffic in Java and the hills everywhere, which make it rather impractical or tough-going to ride all over Indonesia. Bali-by-pushbike has become much more popular in recent years. More people are giving it a try, more places are renting bikes, some people are even bringing their bikes with them. You can usually bring your pushbike with you as baggage and some airlines (like Qantas) may carry it free.

At all the main sights in Java there are bicycle parking areas (usually 50 rp) where an attendant keeps an eye on your bicycle.

RAIL

Train travel in Indonesia is restricted solely to Java and Sumatra – for full details see those sections. Briefly, there is a pretty good railway service running from one end of Java to the other – in the east it connects with the ferry to Bali, and in the west with the ferry to Sumatra. There are a few lines tacked down in Sumatra, but most of that island is reserved for buses. There are no railways on any of the other islands. Trains vary – there are slow, miserable, cheap ones; there are fast, comfortable, expensive ones; and in-between ones. Some major towns like Jakarta and Surabaya have several railway stations so check where you'll be going to and where you have to leave from. Student discounts are available, but they tend to vary too, from about 10% to 25%.

BOAT

Along with the roads the shipping connections between the various islands of the archipelago have also improved greatly over the last few years, particularly in Nusa Tenggara. There are regular ferries connecting Sumatra and Java, Java and Bali, and almost all the islands of Nusa Tenggara – like the thrice-weekly Sumbawa to Flores ferry which drops in at Komodo once a week – see the relevant sections in this book for details. These ferries run either daily or several times a week so there's no longer any need to spend days in sleepy little port towns, reading big thick books, waiting for the elusive piece of driftwood to take you to the next island. Some of these ferries can transport vehicles, all of them will take motorcycles.

Inter-island & Coastal Shipping

Along with the more regular ferry hops, inter-island and coastal shipping has also improved greatly, with more passenger-carrying ships on regular runs. In particular there are two passenger ships commonly used by travellers: the *KM Kambuna* and the *KM Kerinci*. These are two modern German-built passenger liners that only came into service a couple of years ago, and which are run by the national shipping line Pelni (*PT Pelayaran Nasional Indonesia*). Both run to timetables and do regular loops out of Java around

Sulawesi, Kalimantan and Sumatra, stopping at various ports depending on the ship. These destinations include Ujung Pandang and Bitung in Sulawesi, Balikpapan in Kalimantan, and Medan in Sumatra.

The *Kerinci* has a capacity of around 100 people in 1st class, 200 in 2nd, 300 in 3rd, 400 in 4th and 500 in economy. Economy class has replaced 'deck' class. Economy class consists of a long, low platform divided into 10 two-metre by one-metre sections by small plastic pegs. Each section is numbered and assigned with an overhead luggage rack. These are located at the rear of the ship on decks three, four and five (there are nine decks in all). Deck three is near the waterline – it's advisable to request deck five as it's less stuffy and there are fewer vibrations. Lucky you – economy class even comes with a colour TV set and videos each night. The bathrooms have hot and cold water. Four meals are served each day – economy class meals may include rice, fish, vegetables or meat and a hard boiled egg, all served on a plastic dish with a plastic spoon and cup in a tidy cardboard box. Billycans are filled three times a day with hot water and hot tea.

At the other end of the ship 1st class has two single beds in a small air-con room, and the 1st class restaurant has white tablecloths and champagne. Second class consists of a larger room with four bunks each – the rooms divided into male and female rooms. With Superman and James Bond movies on the video, lifeboat drill and perpetual English lessons notwithstanding, it should be a great trip!

The following are the basic routes of the main Pelni passenger ships. Each ship takes about two weeks to 2½ weeks to do a return trip.

KM Lawit Malahayati (Banda Aceh), Lhokseumawe, Belawan (port of Medan), Dumai, Muntok, Tanjung Priok (port of Jakarta), Ketapang, Pontianak.

KM Kerinci Sibolga, Padang, Tanjung Priok, Surabaya, Ujung Pandang, Balikpapan, Pantoloan (port of Palu), Toli Toli, Tarakan.

KM Rinjani Belawan, Tanjung Priok, Surabaya, Ujung Pandang, Bau Bau, Ambon, Sorong.

KM Kambuna Belawan, Tanjung Priok, Surabaya, Ujung Pandang, Balikpapan, Pantoloan, Bitung (port of Manado).

KM Umsini Tanjung Priok, Surabaya, Ujung Pandang, Bitung, Ternate, Sorong, Jayapura.

KM Kelimutu Surabaya, Padang Bai (Bali), Lembar (Lombok), Ujung Pandang, Bima (Sumbawa), Waingapu (Sumba), Ende (Flores), Kupang (west Timor).

Apart from these six, getting a ship is generally a case of hanging around a port until something comes by. Check with the shipping offices, Pelni, the harbour master's office, and anyone else you can think of. Tickets can be bought at shipping offices, although for some ships and in some ports (big ones like Jakarta and Surabaya aside) it may be possible and cheaper to negotiate your fare onboard rather than buy tickets from the office in advance.

Other Pelni ships are far less salubrious than the *Kerinci*. Most of them are filthy with overflowing toilets, poor food, and the decks covered in an intricately lumpy carpet of people and their belongings, often fencing off their own little patch of deck with their cases, bundles and bunches of bananas. If you're travelling deck class then unroll your sleeping bag and make yourself comfortable - a good idea is to take some newspapers with you and lay them out on the floor to cover up the dirt and chicken crap. Deck class in the wet season can be very uncomfortable, cold and wet. The crew have their own cabins and they often rent these out - it's

one way they make some extra money. Bring some food of your own. Here are some readers' comments and recommendations regarding boat travel in Indonesia:

Unless it's really wet I reckon deck class is as good as cabin but get as high in the ship as possible. Privacy and security are major considerations. If you want fresh air in your cabin you get a lot of Indonesian faces too. If you keep your ultra-valuables on you an official will give you somewhere to stick your pack. Cabins get very hot, windows often don't help. Rats and cockroaches do not abound on the higher decks . . .

If you're travelling in a cabin take 1st class - very little more than 2nd class, but you get reasonable food, a private cabin and your own private collection of cockroaches and mice!

Definitely a once-only experience . . .

Another possibility worth trying is getting a passage on one of those magnificent Bugis schooners you see lined up at the Pasar Ikan in Jakarta. They sail between Java, Kalimantan and Sulawesi often going as far as Nusa Tenggara.

Other Boats

There's a whole range of floating tubs used to hop between islands, across rivers, down rivers and over lakes. Just about any sort of vessel can be rented in Indonesia. Fishing boats or other small boats can be chartered to take you to small offshore islands - have them drop you off on an uninhabited island in the morning and come back and get you in the afternoon, or next day. The most common way of getting from Flores to Komodo is to charter a small boat in the fishing village of Labuhanbajo on the western end of Flores.

The *longbot* (longboat) is a long, narrow boat powered by a couple of outboard motors, with bench seats on either side of the hull for passengers to sit on. You find these mainly on the rivers of Kalimantan where they're a common means of transport.

Outrigger canoes powered by an outboard motor are a standard form of transport for some short inter-island hops – like the trip out from Manado in northern Sulawesi to the coral reefs surrounding nearby Bunaken Island. On Lombok these elegant, brilliantly painted fishing boats, looking rather like exotic dragonflies, are used for the short hop from Bangsal harbour to the offshore islands of Gili Air and Gili Trawangan. There are standard fares for standard routes, and you can charter these boats.

Speedboats are not all that common, though they are used on some routes on the rivers of Kalimantan, or for some short inter-island hops in some parts of Indonesia. They are, of course, considerably faster than longbots or river ferries – although also considerably more expensive.

River ferries are commonly found in Kalimantan where the rivers *are* the roads. They're large bulky vessels that carry people and goods up and down the water network.

LOCAL TRANSPORT

Bemos and colts are the usual form of transport around Indonesian towns and cities – most run on standard routes with standard fares. Large buses aren't used much as a means of local transport except in Java, perhaps because most Indonesian towns aren't that big, smaller vehicles suffice. There are a number of other vehicles which are used around towns:

Becaks These are three-wheeler cycle-rickshaws. Unlike the version found in India where the driver sits in front of you, or the Filipino version with the driver at the side, in Indonesia the driver sits at the rear nosing your life ever forwards into the traffic. The Javanese drivers add personal touches to their machines: brightly painted pictures, tinkling bells or whirring metal discs strung across the undercarriage. In Yogyakarta one guy peddled furiously

A becak. (bet-juh)
An armada of pedal powered tasicabs plys the sea of humanity on the Javanese byways

around the streets at night with a tiny flashing light-bulb on the point of his coolie hat! Whilst becaks are now banned from the main streets of large Javanese cities (and plans are underway to get them banned from Jakarta altogether), in just about any town of any size in Java as well as in some other parts of Indonesia (like Ujung Pandang in Sulawesi), they're the most basic form of transport – for people and anything else that has to be shifted.

Bargain your fare *before* you get into the becak! And make sure that if there are two of you that it covers both people – otherwise you'll be in for an argument when you get to your destination. Indonesian becak drivers are hard bargainers – they have to be to survive! But they will usually settle on a reasonable fare – say 200 rp per km, but expect to pay extra for every piece of luggage you stow on-board and every hill that has to be peddled over. Hiring a becak by time or for a round-trip often makes good sense if you're planning to cover a lot of ground in one day, particularly in large places like Yogyakarta or Solo.

Bajaj These are neat little three-wheel

vehicles with a driver at the front, a small motorbike engine below and seats for two passengers behind. They're a common form of local transport in Jakarta, but you don't see them very often elsewhere – I've come across them in Banjarmasin in Kalimantan, and another version with an additional seat next to a driver in Palu in Sulawesi, but otherwise they're rather uncommon.

Dokar Dokars are the jingling, horse-drawn carts found all over Indonesia. The two-wheel carts are usually brightly coloured with decorative motifs and fitted with bells which chime when they're in motion. The small horses or ponies that pull them are often equipped with long tassles attached to their gear. A typical dokar has bench-seating on either side which can comfortably fit three people, four if they're all slim; their owners generally pack in as many people as possible plus bags of rice and other

paraphernalia. It's a picturesque way of getting around if you don't get upset by the ill-treatment of animals – although generally the ponies are looked after pretty well since they mean the difference between starvation and survival. Count on paying about 100 rp per person per km.

In Java you also see the *andong* or *delman* which is a larger horse-drawn wagon designed to carry six people. In some parts of Indonesia like Manado and Gorontalo in northern Sulawesi you also see the *bendi* which is like a small dokar, designed to carry two people.

Other There are various other ways of getting around. In many of the hill resorts in Java you can hire horses. Likewise just about anywhere in Indonesia where horses are raised it's often possible to hire one – possibly the ideal solution to getting over some of that rough terrain and actually enjoying those abominable roads! In Jakarta, bicycles with little seats at the

rear are used as a taxi service – see them near the Pasar Ikan. Guys with motorcycles are permanent fixtures at some large city bus stations around Indonesia – they'll take you to anywhere in town (and probably beyond) for a bargainable price.

Airport Transport There are generally taxis waiting outside the airports – even if the taxi has no meter there will usually be a fixed fare into town and tickets for the journey can be bought from the taxi desk in the airport terminal. From the town to the airport you just have to bargain a fare with the driver. In other towns local buses or bemos may pass within walking distance the the airport; they are considerably cheaper than taking a taxi. In some of the smaller outer islands, like those of Nusa Tenggara, where some of the airports are quite far from the town and have no regular road transport between them, the airlines have taxis or colts to take passengers to the airport. The cost of these airline taxis is *not* included in the ticket so you have to pay extra, but often it's the only reliable way of getting to your flight.

Java

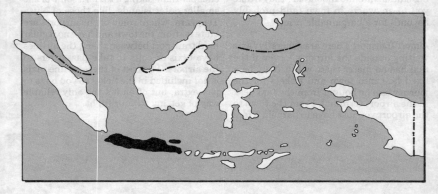

There is a Javanese myth which opens with Semar (the wise clown of the wayang shadow-puppet plays) speaking with a powerful Hindu-Muslim priest, the first of Java's long line of colonisers. The priest asks Semar to tell him the story of Java before there were people on the island. Semar replies that in those days the whole island was covered with primeval forest except for the small patch of rice fields he himself cultivated at the foot of Mt Merbabu, a volcano in central Java, where he lived peacefully tilling the soil for thousands of years.

Then the startled priest, exclaiming that no man could live for so long, demands that Semar tell him what sort of being he actually is. 'In truth,' says Semar, 'I am not a man, I am the guardian spirit – the *danjang* – of Java. I am the oldest spirit of Java, and I am the king and ancestor of all the spirits, and through them of all men.' Then Semar continues in a changed tone: 'I have also a question to ask you. Why are you ruining my country? Why have you come here and driven my children and grandchildren out? The spirits, overcome by your greater spiritual power and religious learning, are

slowly being forced to flee into the craters of the volcanoes or to the depths of the Southern Sea. Why are you doing this?'

The priest replies that he has been ordered by his king, in a country to the west of Java, to fill the island with people, to clear the forests for rice fields, to set up villages and to settle thousands of families here as colonists. Those of the spirits who protect the colonists may continue to live on Java, and Semar will be the spiritual adviser and magical supporter of all the kings and princes to come, the chief danjang of Java.

HISTORY

In this story Javanese history begins with a migration, rather than a creation, myth. Considering the successive movements of people from South-East Asia into the Indonesian archipelago this is hardly surprising. The harmful spirits which inhabited Java were pushed into the mountains and forests or into the ocean and the helpful ones were adopted as protectors and advisers.

The island's exceptional fertility allowed the development of an intensive sawah agriculture which in turn required close cooperation between villages for the maintenance of the irrigation systems. From this first need for local government small kingdoms eventually developed but the first major principality appears to have been that of King Sanjaya's; around the beginning of the 8th century he founded the kingdom of Mataram which controlled much of central Java. Mataram's religion centred on the Hindu god Shiva, and the kingdom built some of the earliest of Java's Hindu temples on the Dieng Plateau.

Sanjaya's Hindu kingdom was followed by a Buddhist interlude under the Shailendra dynasty; it was during this time that Mahayana Buddhism was established in Java and work began (probably around 780 AD) on Borobudur. Either Hinduism continued to exist alongside Buddhism or else there was a Hindu renaissance. In either case the massive Hindu Prambanan complex was built and consecrated around 856 AD. Despite the Hindu resurgence Buddhism continued to flourish.

Mataram eventually fell, possibly as a result of conflict with the Sumatra-based Srivijaya kingdom which invaded Java in the 11th century. Srivijaya, however, also suffered attacks from the Chola kingdom of southern India and Javanese power revived under King Airlangga, a semi-legendary figure who brought much of Java under his control and formed the first royal link between Java and Bali. Airlangga divided his kingdom between his two sons, resulting in the formation of the Kediri and Janggala kingdoms.

In the early 13th century, the commoner Ken Angrok usurped the throne of Singosari (a part of the Janggala kingdom), defeated Kediri and then brought the rest of Janggala under his control. He founded a new kingdom of Singosari which expanded its power during the 13th century. The reign of its last king, Kertanagara, ended when he was murdered around 1292 but his son-in-law, Wijaya, established the Majapahit kingdom, the greatest kingdom of the Hindu-Javanese period. During the 14th century the Majapahit kingdom claimed sovereignty over the entire Indonesian archipelago, although its territorial sovereignty was probably restricted to Java, Madura and Bali.

The Majapahits did something which no previous Javanese kingdom had done: while previous kingdoms had based their power on the control of the rich Javanese agricultural areas, the Majapahits established the first Javanese commercial empire by taking control of Java's main ports and the shipping lanes throughout Indonesia. The memory of Majapahit lives on in Indonesia and the kingdom is sometimes seen as having established a precedent for the present political boundaries of the Indonesian republic.

The Majapahit kingdom began to decline soon after the death of Gajah Mada, the strongman prime minister who had been responsible for its territorial conquests. Various principalities began breaking away from Majapahit rule and adopting Islam. Although the usual view is that Islam in Java originally represented a religious and political force opposed to the Majapahit, there is evidence that Islam was making converts amongst the Majapahit elite even at the height of the kingdom's power. Exactly how or why Islam spread to Java is unknown, but around the 15th and 16th centuries new kingdoms were arising on the island which professed Islam rather than Hinduism.

By the end of the 16th century a Muslim kingdom calling itself Mataram had taken control of central and eastern Java. The last remaining independent principalities, Surabaya and Cirebon, were eventually subjugated leaving only Mataram and Bantam (in West Java) to face the Dutch in the 17th century. The conquest of Java by the Dutch need not be recounted here, but by the end of the 18th century practically all of the island was under Dutch control.

During the Dutch period there were

strong Muslim powers in Java, most notably Mataram. The Javanese were great warriors who continually opposed the Dutch but they were never a united force. If they weren't quarrelling amongst themselves they were at odds with the Sundanese or the Madurese. The last remnants of the Mataram kingdom survived as the principalities of Surakarta (Solo) and Yogyakarta until the foundation of the Indonesian republic. Javanese kings claimed to rule with divine authority and the Dutch helped to preserve the vestiges of a traditional Javanese aristocracy by confirming them as regents, district officers, or sub-district officers in the European administration.

It has been said that Suharto is much more a Javanese king than an 'elected' president, and Indonesia much more a Javanese kingdom than a republic. Admirers of Suharto compare him to the wise kings of the wayang puppet shows, who turn chaos into order and bring prosperity to the kingdom. Critics respond that he rules much more like a Javanese king or sultan with systems of palace-centred patronage, favouritism and officially-sponsored corruption.

There are many sensitive subjects in Indonesia today: Muslim extremists, Communism, racial problems (particularly anti-Chinese sentiment), human rights, East Timor, Irian Jaya, students (seen as potential subversives), the military, and the business enterprises of Suharto, his wife, and the Indonesian military leaders. The ultimate base for Suharto's authority is always the military, which is over-whelmingly Javanese at the top level.

A strong consciousness of ancient religious and mystical thought carries over into modern-day Java and is thought to reach right up to the top Javanese in the Indonesian government. Sukarno identified with Bima, the strong-willed prince of the wayang. Suharto is said to identify strongly with the clown-god Semar, who in the traditional wayang plays often steps in to save the situation when more

refined characters have failed. Suharto is even thought to meditate occasionally in one of the caves on the Dieng Plateau, said to be a dwelling place of the god, in order to revitalise his spiritual energy.

Java plays an extraordinary role in Indonesia today. It is more than simply the geographical centre of Indonesia. Much of Indonesian history was hacked out on Javanese soil. The major battles of the independence movement took place on Java and two of the strongest political parties in the first decade of independence – the Nationalist Party (PNI) and the Communist Party (PKI) – drew their support from the Javanese. To a large extent the rebellions of the Sumatrans, Minahasans and Ambonese in the 1950s and 1960s were rebellions against Javanese domination. Furthermore the Darul Islam rebellion against the new republic broke out in West Java. The abortive Communist coup of 1965 started in Jakarta and some of its most dramatic and disastrous events took place in Java. Arguably the transmigration programme – of dubious benefit to solving the problem of Javanese overpopulation – is really just a systematic Javanese colonisation of the outer islands.

ECONOMY & GEOGRAPHY

Socially Java is an island of contrasts, while geographically it is an island of great and varied beauty. Java provides leadership in politics and trade, an abundant labour force and great potential markets but also, in terms of population pressure, the nation's greatest economic problems. In the late '60s foreign investment went initially to the area surrounding booming Jakarta. Today Java has Indonesia's three largest commercial cities, secondary industries are developing and Java is tapping the hydro-electric and geothermal potential of its rivers and volcanic lakes. Fishing is a major occupation and the many small fishermen are protected by the prohibition of trawlers in coastal waters. The country, however, remains overwhelmingly rural. About 70% of the workforce is engaged in agriculture, but Java's long-established hot-house style of wet-rice cultivation is barely efficient enough to support families on small holdings diminishing in size on over-crowded land.

Java is predominantly a land of mountain peaks and smoking volcanoes (34% of the world's active volcanoes are found in Indonesia), fertile green fields and terraces, but to the north is the flat coastal plain and the sluggish Java Sea. The south coast faces the onslaught of the crashing waves of the Indian Ocean. It's a land of strong contrasts: wealth and squalor; majestic, open country and crowded, filthy cities; quiet, rural scenes and hustling, modern traffic.

Java is a long, narrow island which can be conveniently divided into three sections. In West Java is the capital Jakarta, a city which seems to epitomise all of Indonesia's problems. Tourist attractions like Bandung (the cultural centre of the Sundanese), Cirebon, Pangandaran and the Ujong Kulon National Park are also found in West Java. In Central Java you will find temples and royal cities that tell of the rise and fall of the Hindu, Buddhist and Muslim kingdoms. Here too the old Javanese-Hindu traditions were least altered by the Muslims and outside influences and this region remains the vital centre of Javanese culture. Java is people and lots of them. Wherever you go it's hard to escape the fact that this is one of the most densely populated areas in the world; but there are isolated places where you can find yourself out of sight and sound of other people. There's the huge Dieng Plateau in the beautiful central highlands and, in East Java, the area around the spectacular Mt Bromo volcano is as wild and desolate as you could hope for.

THE JAVANESE

While the inhabitants of the whole island of Java are often referred to as Javanese, it is more correct to distinguish the Javanese proper from other major groups like the Sundanese and Madurese and from minor groups like the Tenggerese and Badui. The Sundanese are concentrated in West Java; the Madurese on the island of Madura off the north coast of Java and on the adjacent coast; the Badui in a pocket in the mountains of West Java; and the Tenggerese are centred on Mt Bromo in East Java. The Javanese proper inhabit the central and eastern parts of the island.

All of them are Malay people – their differences seem to be mainly cultural. The Sundanese and the Madurese retained much less of the Hindu influence than the people of central and eastern Java. The Badui and the Tenggerese are distinguished by their history of resistance to Islam. India has had probably the most profound and enduring influence on religion in Java, yet the Indian poet Rabindranath Tagore, when visiting the country, said: 'I see India everywhere, but I do not recognise it.'

Although the Javanese are nominally Muslim, their religion is a mixture of pre-Hindu animism, Hinduism and Islam. The current division between the *santri* (the devout Muslim) and the *abangan* (the nominal Muslim whose real beliefs stem from older and more accommodating mysticism) reflects the Javanese ability to absorb different beliefs. There is a continuing and very real belief in ghosts and numerous benevolent and malevolent spirits. Graveyards are generally thought to be haunted. When the Solo municipal cemeteries were relocated in 1981 many of the living relatives, before exhuming the bodies, consulted soothsayers to determine if the spirits of the dead were still present in or near the graves. Magical power can be concentrated in amulets and heirlooms (especially the Javanese dagger known as the kris), in parts of the human body like the nails and the hair, and in sacred musical instruments. The traditional medicine man, the *dukun*, is still consulted when illness strikes.

To be Javanese literally means to be civilised; the Javanese ideal is to be polite and refined. Loud displays of emotion and flamboyant behaviour of any kind are considered *kasar* (coarse and rough, bad manners). Reserve is a Javanese trait, and stems from an unwillingness to make anyone else feel uncomfortable or ashamed. It is impolite to point out mistakes, embarrassments, sensitive or negative areas, or to directly criticise authority. Even the Javanese language reinforces this deferral to authority. Like Balinese, Javanese has 'high' and 'low' forms; different words are used when speaking to superiors, elders, equals or inferiors. This underlines differences in status, rank, relative age, and the degree of acquaintance between the two people talking.

While the Javanese developed what is probably the most refined culture in Indonesia, Java, particularly Jakarta, is also home to some of the poorest people in the archipelago. Yet somehow the people continue to find means of survival – they sell food and clothing; sit all day on the streetside selling combs or a few bunches of bananas; or jump on a crowded bus hawking ice-creams, pineapple chunks and single cigarettes. They recycle trash or cigarette ends, pedal becaks, shine shoes, mind parked cars, become prostitutes, beg or tout. And if they return with nothing at the end of the day then their family or neighbours will always help them to survive.

Someone operating a pushcart warung on a street in Jakarta might work 16 hours a day to make 2000 to 3000 rp. In a provincial town a fish carter (delivering basket-loads of fish) might make only 1000 to 3000 rp a day. The cities are less than half of the story; the rest of the population are engaged in agriculture, most of them working tiny rice plots barely sufficient to meet their daily needs. Others seek outside income – like many of the becak drivers who work in the cities –

or sell up their land and then either move to the cities and towns or work as farm labourers. At the other end of the scale is the Indonesian elite who can afford to buy an imported leg of lamb (at around 25,000 rp) or imported grapes (around 20,000 rp a kg) from Jakarta's Sarinah Department Store to serve to their dinner guests in the high-fenced mansions of Jakarta's Pondok Indah district.

CULTURE – WAYANG

Javanese culture is a product of pre-Hindu, Hindu and Islamic influences. The rise of the 16th century Islamic states brought a rich new cultural heritage but the Hindu heritage also managed to continue its influence.

The Javanese shadow-puppet (wayang) theatre has been a major means of preserving the Hindu-Buddhist heritage in Java. The main wayang form is the *wayang kulit*; the word wayang means shadow, and the word *kulit* means leather. Thus the wayang kulit indicates a form of shadow theatre using puppets made of leather. In the wider sense the word wayang refers to all dramatic plays.

Wayang Kulit

The shadow-puppet theatre, in which perforated leather figures are manipulated behind an illuminated cotton screen, is the best known of the wayang forms. The stories are usually based on the Hindu epics, the *Ramayana* and the *Mahabharata*, although other pre-Islamic stories are also performed. In a traditional performance a whole night might be devoted to just one drama (*lakon*) from a legend. A single puppeteer (the dalang) animates the puppets and narrates and chants through the entire night to the accompaniment of the gamelan orchestra.

The real origin of the wayang kulit is unknown. Shadow-puppet theatre is not unique to Java, it can also be found in Turkey, India, China and parts of South-East Asia. Strangely enough, given that the wayang kulit tells stories from pre-

Islamic days, Javanese tradition credits the creation of the wayang to the nine *walis*, the semi-legendary apostles of Islam in Java. Many wayang kulit figures and even whole stories have a specific mystical function; certain stories are performed for the purpose of protecting a rice crop (these incorporate the rice goddess Dewi Sri, the welfare of a village or even individuals).

By the 11th century wayang performances with leather puppets were flourishing in Java and by the end of the 18th century the wayang kulit had developed most of the details of puppet design and performance techniques we see today. The standardisation of the puppet designs is traditionally attributed to King Raden Patah of Demak (an Islamic kingdom on the site of modern-day Semarang) who reigned in the first half of the 16th century.

The puppets are made of leather, water buffalo leather from a young animal being the most favoured material. The outline of the puppet is cut using a thin knife and the fine details, carved out using small chisels and a hammer. When the carving is finished the moveable arms are attached and the puppet is painted. Lines are drawn in and accentuated with black ink which is also used to increase the contrast of the carved holes. The *cempurit*, the stick of horn used to hold the puppet upright, is then attached.

The leaf-shaped *kayon* is meant to represent the 'tree' or 'mountain of life' and is used to end scenes or to symbolise wind, mountains, obstacles, clouds, or the sea. Made of the same flexible hide as the other puppets the kayon might be waved softly behind the cloth screen while a puppet figure is held horizontally – a surprisingly effective way of indicating flight through the cloudy sky. There are a number of symbolic decorations on the kayon including the face in the centre of the tree which symbolises the danger and risk that all people must confront in life.

The characters in wayang are brought to life by the dalang. To call him a puppeteer belittles the extraordinary range of talents he must possess. Sitting cross-legged on a mat before the white screen the dalang might manipulate dozens of figures in the course of a performance.

He recounts events spanning centuries and continents, improvising from the basic plot a complex network of court intrigues, great loves, wars, philosophy, magic, mysticism and comedy. He must be a linguist capable of speaking both the language of his audience and the ancient *kawi* language spoken by the aristocratic characters of his play. He must be a mimic capable of producing a different voice for each of his characters. He must have great physical stamina to sustain a performance which will last from the evening until the early hours of the morning. He must be a musician, able to direct the village's gamelan orchestra which accompanies the performance. He must be versed in history, as well as have a deep understanding of philosophy and religion. He must be a poet capable of creating a warm or terrifying atmosphere, but he must also be a comedian able to introduce some comic relief into his performances. Understandably, the dalang has always been regarded as a very special type of person. Most dalang are men but today there are a number of female dalang in Java.

The dalang directs the gamelan orchestra using a system of cues, often communicating the name of the composition to be played using riddles or puns. The player of the *kendang* (drum) acts as the liaison between the dalang and the other gamelan players, in setting the proper tempo and changes of tempo for each piece, and executing the important signals for ending pieces. The dalang may communicate with the orchestra using signals tapped out with the wooden *cempala* (a mallet) held in his left hand. Or there may be other types of cues, eg one of the clowns in the performance may announce that a singing contest is to be held, then announce the song he intends singing and the gamelan will play that song.

The mass of the audience sits in front of the screen to watch the shadow figures, but some also sit behind the screen with the dalang, to watch the master at work.

Wayang Golek
These three-dimensional wooden puppets have moveable heads and arms and are manipulated in the same way as shadow puppets – but without using a shadow screen. Although wayang golek is found in Central Java it is most popular amongst the Sundanese of West Java. Sometimes a wayang golek puppet is used right at the end of a wayang kulit play to symbolise the transition back from the world of two dimensions to the world of three.

Wayang golek uses the same stories as the wayang kulit, including the *Mahabharata* and *Ramayana*, as well as the stories about the mythical Javanese King Panji and other legendary kings. It also has its own set of stories, for which there is some direct Islamic inspiration. These include the elaborate romances inspired by legends about the Prophet Mohammed's uncle Amir Hamzah.

Wayang Klitik
In East Java the wayang kulit is replaced by the wayang klitik or *keruchil*, a flat wooden puppet carved in low relief; this type of wayang is performed without a shadow screen. The wayang klitik is associated with the Damar Wulan stories which are of particular historical relevance to East Java. The stories relate the adventures of a handsome prince and his rise to become ruler of the Majapahit kingdom.

Wayang Orang
Also known as Wayang Wong, this is a dance drama in which real people dance the part of the wayang characters, imitating the movements and speech of the puppets.

Wayang Topeng
This dance drama is similar to wayang orang but uses masks. The two forms of dance drama were cultivated at varying times in the courts of Central Java. Wayang Topeng is the older of the two and dates back as far the Majapahit kingdom. In more recent times wayang wong was the official court dance-drama, while wayang topeng was also performed outside the walls of the palace. The stylisation of human features seen in the shadow puppets is also seen in the wayang topeng masks; elongation and refinement are the key notes of the noble (halus) characters, while grotesque exaggeration denotes the vulgar (kasar) characters.

THE MAHABHARATA & RAMAYANA
Ancient India, like ancient Greece, produced two great epics. The *Ramayana* describes the adventures of a prince who is banished from his country and wanders for many years in the wilderness while the *Mahabharata* is based on the legends of a great war. The first story is a little reminiscent of the *Odyssey* which relates the adventures of Ulysses as he struggles to return home from Troy; the second has much in common with the *Iliad*.

When Hinduism came to Java so did the *Ramayana* and the *Mahabharata*. The Javanese shifted the locale to Java; Javanese children were given the names of the heroes and by tradition the kings of Java were descendants of the epic heroes.

The Mahabharata
The great war portrayed in the *Mahabharata* is believed to have been fought in northern India around the 13th or 14th century BC. The war became a centre of legends, songs and poems and at some point the vast mass of stories accumulated over the centuries were gathered together into a narrative called the 'Epic of the Bharata Nation (India)' – the *Mahabharata*. Over the following centuries more was added to it until it was seven

times the size of the Iliad and the Odyssey combined!

The central theme of the *Mahabharata* is the power struggle between the Kurava brothers and their cousins the Pandava brothers. Important events along the way include the appearance of Krishna, an incarnation of Lord Vishnu, who becomes the adviser of the Pandava; Prince Arjuna of the Pandavas marries the Princess Drupadi; the Kuravas attempt to kill the Pandavas; and the kingdom is divided in two in an attempt to end the rivalry between the cousins. Finally, after 13 years in exile and hiding, the Pandavas realise there is no alternative but war, the great war of the *Mahabharata*, which is a series of bloody clashes between the cousins.

It is at this time that the Pandava warrior Arjuna becomes despondent at the thought of fighting his own flesh and blood; so Krishna, his charioteer and adviser, explains to him the duties and obligations of the warrior in a song known as the *Bhagavad Gita*. Krishna explains that the soul is indestructible and that whoever dies shall be reborn and so there is no cause to be sad; it is the soldier's duty to fight and he will be accused of cowardice if he runs away.

In the course of the battles many of the great heroes from both sides are slain one by one; many others also lose their lives but in the end the Pandavas are victorious over the Kuravas.

The Ramayana

The *Ramayana*, the story of Prince Rama, is thought to have been written after the *Mahabharata*. Long before Prince Rama was born the gods had determined that his life would be that of a hero – but like all heroic lives it would be full of grave tests. Rama is an incarnation of the god Vishnu, and it will be his destiny to kill the ogre king Rawana (also known as Dasamuka and Dasakhantha).

Due to scheming in the palace Rama, his wife the beautiful Sita, and his brother Laksamana are all exiled to the forest where Sita is abducted by the ogre king. Rama begins his search for Sita, and is joined by the Monkey God Hanuman and the Monkey King Sugriwa. Eventually a full-scale assault is launched on the evil king and Sita is rescued.

Performances & Characters

The *Mahabharata* and the *Ramayana* are the basis of the most important wayang stories, particularly in the wayang kulit, and also appear in Balinese dances, especially the *kecak*. While they often come across like ripping yarns, both are essentially moral tales, which for centuries have played a large part in establishing traditional Javanese values. In the *Mahabharata*, the Kuravas are essentially the forces of greed, evil and destruction, while the Pandavas represent refinement, enlightenment and civilised behaviour.

The division between good and evil is never absolute; the good heroes have bad traits and vice versa. Take, for example, Yudistra, the eldest of the Pandava brothers. His moral integrity is high, but his great fault is his extravagant generosity. Although the forces of good usually triumph over evil, more often than not the victory is an ambivalent one; both sides will suffer grievous loss and though a king may win a righteous war he may lose all his sons in the process. In the *Mahabharata*, when the great battle is over and the Pandavas are victorious, one of their enemies sneaks into the encampment and kills all the Pandava women and children.

Bima Bima is the second-eldest of the Pandavas. He is physically big, burly, aggressive, not afraid to act on what he believes; he can be rough, even using the language of the man of the street to address the gods. He is able to fly and is the most powerful warrior on the battlefield, but he also has infinite kindness and a firm adherence to principle which makes him an heroic figure who can't really be criticised for his faults.

Arjuna Arjuna is the handsome and refined ladies' man, a representative of the noble class, whose eyes look at the ground because it's kasar to stare into people's faces. He can also be fickle and selfish, and that is his weakness. He has one single quality which outweighs his failings; he is halus – a Javanese word which means refined in manner, never speaking ill to offend others, polite and humble, patient, careful, the direct opposite of kasar. Arjuna's charioteer is Krishna, a spiritual adviser but also a cunning and ruthless politician.

Semar A purely Javanese addition to the story is Arjuna's servant, the dwarf clown Semar. An incarnation of a god, Semar is a great source of wisdom and advice to Arjuna – but his body is squat with an enormous posterior, bulging belly, and he sometimes has an uncontrollable disposition for farting. Semar has three sons: Gareng with his mis-shapen arms, crossed eyes, limp and speech impediment; Petruk with his hilarious long nose, enormous smiling mouth, and a general lack of proportion both in physical stature and thinking; and Bagong, the youngest of the three with a voice like he had a mouthful of marbles. Though they are comic figures, they play the important role of interpreting the actions and speech of the heroic figures in the wayang kulit plays. Despite their bumbling nature and gross appearance they are the mouthpieces of truth and wisdom.

Kurava Characters On the Kurava side is Duryudana, a handsome and powerful leader, but too easily influenced by the prevailing circumstances around him and thus often prey to the evil designs of his uncle and adviser, Sangkuni. Karna is the good man on the wrong side, whose loyalty is divided between the Kuravas and the Pandavas. He is actually a Pandava but was brought up a Kurava; adhering to the code of the warrior he stands by his king, as a good Javanese should and, as a result, he dies at the hands of Arjuna.

Ramayana Characters The characters of the *Ramayana* are a little more clear-cut. Like Arjuna, Rama is the epitome of the ideal man – a gentle husband, a noble prince, a kindly king, a brave leader. His wife Sita is the ideal wife who remains totally devoted to her husband. But elements of the *Mahabharata* can also be found in the *Ramayana*; Rawana's warrior brother knows that the king is evil but is bound by the ethics of the *Ksatria* warrior and remains loyal to his brother to the end, consequently dying a horrible death by dismemberment.

Wayang Kulit Performances It's fairly easy to tell the kasar figures from the halus figures. The halus figures tend to be smaller in size and more elegant in proportion; their legs are slender and close together, and their heads are tilted downwards presenting an image of humility and self-effacement. The kasar characters are often enormous, muscular and hairy, their heads upturned. Eye shape and the colour of the figures, particularly on the faces, are of great importance. Red often indicates aggressiveness, greed, impatience, anger or simply a very forthright personality. Black, and often blue, indicates calmness, spiritual awareness and maturity. Gold and yellow are reserved for kings and the highest nobles. White can symbolise purity or virtue, high moral purpose and the like. Hair styles, ornamentation and clothing are all important in identifying a particular puppet.

A traditional wayang kulit performance transmits the desirable values and characteristics of the heroes of the *Ramayana* and *Mahabharata* – inner control, dedication and self-sacrifice – and stresses the importance of refined behaviour over the violent and crude. One's passions, desires, lust and anger must be disciplined; in the *Bhagavad Gita* Krishna tells Arjuna that these cause men to do evil, even against their own will. All is clouded by desire, says Krishna, as a fire by smoke, as a mirror by dirt. The performance portrays the forces upon which all life depends; the meaning and purpose of life; the inconsistencies, weakness and greatness of its epic heroes and, by implication, human society as a whole.

Although the wayang theatre still teaches the traditional Javanese values it's difficult to determine its current direction. Some argue that its ritual function seems to be disappearing and that it's becoming more and more purely a form of entertainment, with much of the mystical aura and traditional philosophy being lost. In the past the skills of the dalang were handed down from father to son, but for years now there have been schools in Java – some more traditional than others – which also teach the techniques. Even puppet design is changing and on TV for 15 minutes each Sunday morning characters from the wayang cackle, sing and shriek about such matters as paying taxes on time, birth control and agricultural development.

THE GAMELAN

The musical instruments of Indonesia can be grouped into four main strata: those from pre-Hindu days, those from the Hindu period from the first centuries AD until about the 15th century, the Islamic period from about the 13th century AD, and the last from the 16th century which is associated with Christian and European influences.

The oldest known instruments in Indonesia are the bronze 'kettle drums' belonging to the Dongson culture which developed in what is now northern Vietnam and spread into the Indonesian archipelago – they are not really drums as they have bronze rather than membrane heads. These instruments have been found in Sumatra, Java, Bali, Kalimantan as well as in other parts of South-East Asia; amongst the most curious examples are those of the island of Alor in Nusa Tenggara.

Other instruments, particularly those made of bamboo (like flutes and reed pipes), are also thought to be very old. By the Hindu period there was a wealth of metallic as well as wooden and bamboo instruments played in Java, and these are depicted on the stone reliefs of Borobudur and Prambanan and other shrines. On Borobudur there are reliefs of drums (waisted, hour-glass, pot and barrel-shaped), two-stringed lutes, harps, flutes, mouth organs, reed pipes, a keyed metallophone (*saron*), xylophone, cymbals and others. Some of these instruments are direct imports from India, whilst others resemble the instruments now used in the Javanese gamelan orchestra.

One interesting and ancient instrument is the *calung*, a Sundanese instrument which is also found in a few places in Java and in southern Thailand. The basic version consists of a set of bamboo tubes, one end of each tube closed off by the natural node of the bamboo, and the other end pared down for part of its length like a goose-quill pen. The instrument is played with one or two sickle-shaped wooden hammers (*panakol*) padded with cotton or rubber. The calung is still commonly found in Java.

The oldest instruments still in use include drums, gongs, various wind instruments and plucked strings. The large Javanese gamelan, whose total complement comprises 60 to 80 instruments, has sets of suspended and horizontal gongs, gong chimes, drums, flutes, bowed and plucked string instruments, metallophones and xylophones.

Gamelan Instruments

The word gamelan is derived from the Javanese word *gamel*, which means a type of hammer, like a blacksmith's hammer. The orchestra is composed almost entirely of percussion instruments so they are played by being struck. Javanese tradition credits a god with the invention of the gamelan orchestra, used to summon

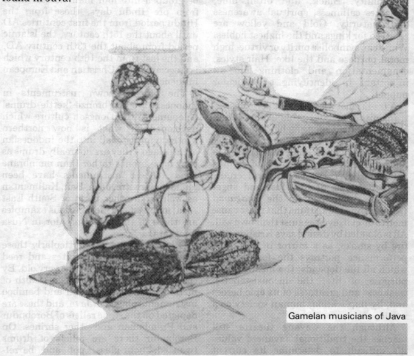

Gamelan musicians of Java

the other gods to his palace at the summit of Mt Lawu, between Solo and Madiun.

There are two types of gamelan styles: a soft style for indoor use and a loud style for outdoor functions, the difference being in the instruments used. Around the 17th century, the two styles were blended to form the modern gamelan. It was mainly because of the different ways in which the two styles were mixed and balanced that variations between the gamelan music found in Bali, Central Java and West Java were created. The *gong*, *kempul*, *kenong*, *ketuk* and *kempyang* belong to both the loud and soft styles. The *saron*, *bonang*, and *kendang* belong to the loud style. The *slentem*, *gender*, *gambang*, *celempung*, *sitar*, *suling* and *rebab* belong to the soft style.

Gong Ageng – or *gong gede* is suspended on a wooden frame. There is at least one such gong in a gamelan orchestra, sometimes more. The gong is made of bronze and is about 90 cm in diameter. It performs the crucial task of marking the end of the largest phrase of a melody.

Kempul – is a small hanging gong, and marks a smaller musical phrase than the big gong.

Kenong – is a small gong laid horizontally on crossed cord and sitting inside a wooden frame.

Ketuk – is a small kenong tuned to a certain pitch, which marks subdivisions of phrases; it is played by the kenong player. The sound of the ketuk is short and dead compared with the clearer, resonant tone of the kenong.

Saron – is the basic instrument-type of the gamelan, a xylophone with bronze bars which are struck with a wooden mallet. There are three types of saron: high, medium and low pitched. The high one is called *saron panerus* or *saron peking* and

is played with a mallet made of buffalo horn rather than wood.

Bonang – consists of a double row of bronze kettles (like small kenongs) resting on a horizontal frame; there are three kinds although the lowest in pitch is no longer used in gamelan orchestras. The bonang is played with two long sticks bound with red cord at the striking end. Although in modern Javanese gamelan the bonang has two rows of bronze kettles, originally it had only one row, as it still does in Bali.

Kendang – the drums are all double-ended and beaten by hand (with the exception of the giant drum, the *bedug* which is beaten with a stick). The drum is an important leading instrument; they are made from the hollowed tree-trunk sections of the jackfruit (nangka) tree with cow or goat skin stretched across the two ends. There are various types of drums but the middle-sized *kendang batangan* or *kendang ciblon* is chiefly used to accompany dance and wayang performances; the drum patterns indicate specific dance movements or movements of the wayang puppets.

Slentem – carries the basic melody in the soft ensemble, as the saron does in the loud ensemble. The slentem consists of thin bronze bars suspended over bamboo resonating chambers; it is struck with a padded disc on the end of a stick.

Gender – is similar to a slentem in structure, but there are more bronze keys and the keys and bamboo chambers are smaller in size. The gender is played with two disc-shaped hammers, smaller than those used for the slentem. The hand acts as a damper, so that each hand must simultaneously hit a note and damp the preceding one.

Gambang – is the only gamelan instrument with bars not made of bronze, but made instead of hard wood and laid over a wooden frame. They are struck with two sticks made of supple buffalo horn, each ending with a small, round, padded disc. Unlike the gender keys the gambang keys do not need to be damped.

Celempung – is a plucked, stringed instrument, looking somewhat like a zither. It has 26 strings arranged in 13 pairs. The strings are stretched over a coffin-shaped resonator which stands on four legs; the strings are plucked with the thumb nails. The sitar is a smaller version of the celempung, with fewer strings and a higher pitch; the body is box-shaped and without legs.

Suling – or flute, is the only wind instrument in the gamelan orchestra. It is made of bamboo and played vertically.

Rebab – is a two-stringed bowed instrument of Arabic origin. It has a wooden body covered with fine, stretched skin. The moveable bridge is made of wood. The bow is made of wood and coarse horsehair tied loosely, not stretched tight like the bows of western instruments. The rebab player sits cross-legged on the floor and stands the rebab in front of him.

In a piece of gamelan music, the gong ageng marks the end of each of the largest phrases of the melody; the saron instruments play the main melody at various ranges of pitches and speeds; and the bonang play their own rippling configurations at a faster speed than the main melody. The gamelan also uses male and female singers – traditionally they make up part of the soft ensemble. The gamelan orchestra does not accompany the singer as western orchestras do; rather the singer in a gamelan is really just another instrument, no more or less important than any of the instruments.

Traditionally, gamelan players learnt to play by ear, beginning on the simpler instruments and moving forward as their repertoire and technique developed. A musician did not use notation when he played, although there are systems of written notation. The palaces at Solo and Yogyakarta had developed their own systems of notation, but in the late 19th century the *kepatihan* system, now used in Java, was developed and numbers were used for the notes (just as western music uses letters). The older notation systems are only found in palace records of older music.

The saron and the slentem are the only instruments which can play exactly what is written down, the notation is just a skeleton of everything that is going on in a performance. The phrase-making instruments – the ketuk, kempul, kenong and gong – give some order and form to these notes, the gong marking the end of the longest musical phrase while the other instruments elaborate on the basic skeleton.

In the loud ensemble the drummer is the leader, the conductor of all the instruments; he controls the tempo, speeds up or slows down the orchestra, signalling the entrance of the elaborating instruments and shifting the emphasis from the loud to the soft ensemble. Apart from signalling changes within one piece of music he also signals a change from one piece of music to another, because usually at least two or three pieces are combined to form a medley. The rebab ornaments the music and its line is closely related to the singing.

A gamelan orchestra always accompanies a wayang performance although the *gamelan wayangan* used for a traditional wayang kulit is much smaller than the usual gamelan seen today. A full size gamelan orchestra has instruments with two different tunings, the *slendro* and the *pelog*. A gamelan wayangan only uses instruments with the slendro tuning. Incidentally, although most gamelan players are men, it is not a strictly male occupation.

ARTS & CRAFTS

Indonesia has produced a range of

performing and visual arts, and apart from the gamelan and the wayang, the ornamented kris (dagger) and the batik technique have reached a particularly high standard on Java.

Kris Some think the Javanese kris – from the word *iris*, to cut – is derived from the bronze daggers produced by the Dongson culture around the 1st century AD. Bas-reliefs of a kris appear in the 14th century Panataran temple-complex in east Java, and the carrying of the kris as a custom in Java was noted in 15th century Chinese records. The kris is still an integral part of men's formal dress on ceremonial and festive occasions. A dalang will wear his kris while giving a wayang performance, and the kris is still part of the uniform of the guards at the palace in Yogyakarta.

The kris is no ordinary knife. It is said to be endowed with supernatural powers; adat law requires that every father furnish his son with a kris upon his reaching manhood, preferably an heirloom kris enabling his son to draw on the powers of his ancestors stored in the sacred weapon. Distinctive features and the number of curves in the blade, and the damascening, are read to indicate good or bad fortune for its owner. Damascening is a technique whereby another metal is hammered onto the blade of the kris to produce a design. The number of curves in the blade also have symbolic meaning; five curves symbolise the five Pandava brothers of the *Mahabharata* epic; three stand for fire, ardour or passion. Although the blade is the most important part of the kris, the hilt and scabbard are also beautifully decorated.

Before the arrival of Islam, Hindu-inspired images were often used to decorate the wooden hilts – the mythological man-bird Garuda was a popular figure. After the spread of Islam such motifs were discouraged, but were often preserved in stylised forms. In any case, the origins and symbolism of the kris lay too deep in Javanese mysticism to be eradicated by the laws of Islam.

Batik Indonesian textiles come in a dazzling variety of fabrics, materials, techniques, colours and motifs. Basically there are three major textile groupings, which roughly parallel three cultural groups within Indonesia – a loose generalisation but a useful one to make.

The first is *ikat*, a form of tie-dyeing patterns onto the threads before weaving them together; this technique is associated with the proto-Malay people of the archipelago such as the various ethnic groups of Nusa Tenggara (see the Nusa Tengarra chapter for more on ikat). Silk weaving and *songket* (where gold or silver threads are woven into the silk cloth) is a technique strongest where Islam has made most impact in places like Aceh in Sumatra and amongst the Malays of coastal Kalimantan. The third group is batik, the alternate waxing and dyeing technique most clearly associated with those parts of central Java where the great Javanese kingdoms were established. It was also taken up in Bali, Madura and in

Batik cloth motif

Jambi in Sumatra, all of which have been subject to considerable Javanese influence.

The technique of applying wax or some other type of dye-resistant substance (like rice-paste) to cloth to produce a design is found in many parts of the world. The Javanese were making batik cloth at least as early as the 12th century but its origins are hard to trace. Some think the skills were brought to Java from India, others that the Javanese developed the technique themselves. The word batik is an old Javanese word meaning 'to dot'.

The development of batik in Indonesia is usually associated with the flowering of the creative arts around the royal courts – it's likely that the use of certain motifs was the preserve of the aristocracy. The rise of Islam in Java probably contributed to the stylisation of batik patterns and the absence of representations of living things from most designs. More recently batik has grown from an art mainly associated with the royal courts, into an important industry with a number of noted production centres.

In the older method of making batik the wax is applied hot to the smooth cloth with the *canting*, a pen-like instrument with a small reservoir holding liquid wax. The design is first traced out onto the prepared cloth and the patterns drawn in wax on the white cloth, or on a cloth previously dyed to the lightest colour required in the finished product. The wax-covered areas will resist colour change when immersed in a dye bath. The waxing and dyeing procedures are continued with increasingly dark shades until the final colours are achieved. Wax is added to protect previously dyed areas or scraped off to expose new areas to the dye. Finally all the wax is scraped off and the cloth boiled to remove all traces of the wax. The wax mixture usually includes beeswax, paraffin, resins and fats mixed in varying proportions. This type of batik is called *batik tulis* or 'written batik', since the patterns are drawn onto the cloth in freehand style.

From the mid-19th century production was speeded up by applying the wax with a metal stamp called a *cap*. The cap technique can usually be identified by the repetition of identical patterns, whereas in the freer composition using the canting even repeated geometric motifs vary slightly. Some batik combines the cap technique with canting work for the fine details. It's worth noting that batik cap is true batik; don't confuse it with screen-printed cloth which completely bypasses the waxing process and is often passed off as batik.

BOOKS

The classic book on Javanese religion, culture and values is *The Religion of Java* by Clifford Gertz, perhaps a rather dated book (it was based on research done in the 1950s), but nevertheless fascinating reading. Also worth reading is *Indonesia: Between Myth & Reality* by Lee Khoon Choy (London: Nile & Mackenzie 1976). Choy was the Singaporean ambassador to Indonesia from 1970 to 1975 and has written a readable journalistic account of the customs, traditions and spirituality of Indonesia. The chapters on Kebatinan and Java's isolated minorities (the Badui and the Tenggerese) are particularly interesting.

The 'Oxford in Asia' paperback series (Oxford University Press) has a number of excellent books including *Javanese Wayang Kulit – An Introduction* by Edward C van Ness and Shita Prawirohardjo (1980); *Javanese Gamelan* by Jennifer Lindsay (1979); and *Borobudur* by Jacques Dumarcay (1978).

An excellent way to become familiar with the *Ramayana* and *Mahabharata* epics is to read the English adaptations written by William Buck. Buck's inspired versions read like fantasy novels and will give you a greater appreciation for these Indian epics. His *Ramayana* and *Mahabharata* are published separately by The New English Library in the UK and by The New American Library in the

US and are available in paperback. They make good train and bus reading.

GETTING THERE & AWAY

You can enter or exit Java at several points. Popular sea routes are from Sumatra to Java, either by the Padang-Jakarta Pelni shipping service or by the short ferry trip from Panjang to Merak in West Java – see the Sumatra chapter for details. At the eastern end of the island, there are regular ferries on the short crossing between Banyuwangi and Gilimanuk on Bali – see the Bali section. Or you can fly or sail between Java and the outer islands like Sulawesi, Kalimantan and Maluku. Many people fly to Jakarta from Singapore or further afield.

Air

Jakarta is Indonesia's busiest entrance point for overseas airlines and, though not in the same class as Singapore, it's a good place to shop around for cheap international air tickets.

Jakarta is also the hub of the domestic airline network. Garuda and Merpati are the main airlines serving the outer islands from Java. Bouraq has services to Bali, Kalimantan, Sulawesi and Ternate (in Maluku). Mandala has services to Sumatra, Sulawesi and Ambon (in Maluku).

Boat

There are, of course, shipping services from other Indonesian islands to Java but there is only one international connection – and even that isn't a real international connection, since it goes to the Indonesian island of Tanjung Pinang near Singapore. This long-running Pelni service has gone through changes recently and seems to have improved.

A new service to Singapore has begun on the *KM Lawit*, which leaves from Jakarta's port of Tanjung Priok every other Wednesday and takes about 36 hours to Tanjung Pinang. Second class fare is 30,000 rp per person in a four-bunk air-con cabin with hot water. The fare

includes three meals a day but savvy travellers bring food to supplement the meagre Indonesian menu. Boiling water is available from a tap in the ship's galley, so instant noodles and coffee/tea are choice items to bring along.

Tanjung Pinang is part of Indonesia and from here you take a 25,000 rp hydrofoil to Batam where you clear Indonesian immigration and go on from there to Singapore. There's an additional 1000 rp port charge at Tanjung Pinang. There's also a slower ferry service between Tanjung Pinang and Singapore which takes five or six hours instead of the faster 2½ hour hydrofoil service.

Take care in Tanjung Pinang coming from Singapore; there are various 'travel agents' in cahoots with losmen owners who will try to ensure that you miss the boat or give up trying to buy a ticket because it's 'full' so that you'll stay in Tanjung Pinang – see the Sumatra section for more details. Also be on watch for pickpockets arriving or departing Tanjung Priok, since they work overtime during the congested stampede to or from the ship. What's it like travelling with Pelni?

Well deck class (*ekonomi*) includes nothing – you have to provide your own sleeping bag, even your own plate and eating utensils if you want to eat the infamous rice-and-a-fish-head food. Toilet facilities are nothing to write home about either. It's a wise idea to bring some food with you and drinks too, since they tend to be expensive on board. One advantage this service does have is the 'nightclub'; anyone is welcome (not just cabin class passengers) and beers are reasonably priced.

If, on the other hand, you fork out for a cabin you can travel in reasonable comfort, especially in the better cabins which are only marginally more expensive than the most basic ones. Four-berth cabins utilise the same lousy toilet facilities as deck class. Cabins tend to be booked out some time ahead, but for deck class you simply turn up and buy your ticket on the boat. Whatever you say about travelling with Pelni lines it's certainly a trip people remember – and usually not in a bad way. 'That Pelni ship, boy what a ride,' they'll say years later. You can be sure nobody is going to say that about flying. If being comfortable is really important to you, you can always stay home.

There are now six different Pelni passenger ships: the *KM Lawit, KM Kerinci, KM Kelimutu, KM Kambuna, KM Rinjani* and *KM Unsini*. All except the Lawit and Kelimutu offer five classes of passage, starting with economy (sometimes called deck class) and moving up to Class IV, Class III, Class II and Class I. The Lawit and Kelimutu only have classes I, II and economy. All six ships have central air-con, although operating efficiency is variable. All have bar/ restaurants, cafeterias, a mini-market, TV/video facilities (Class I cabins come with their own TVs), *musholla* (prayer rooms) and health clinics. Class I sleeps two people to a cabin, Class II four people, Class III six people, Class IV eight people. In Economy there are long sleeping platforms where passengers sleep side by side in rows; in this class a ship may sleep anywhere from 500 on three decks (*Kerinci* and *Kambuna*) to 866 on four decks (*Lawit* and *Kelimutu*). Roughly speaking, you can add 15,000 rp to your fare for every step up you make in terms of ticket class.

From Jakarta there are also a number of private freight-shipping lines operating from the Sunda Kelapa harbour to Tanjung Pinang (and other islands) which will take passengers; fares are generally lower than Pelni's. For details of ships out of Jakarta see the Getting There & Away section of Jakarta.

To Bali
Bali is the one place you can get to by bus or train. The ferry connection across the narrow strait separating Bali from Java is included in the bus or train ticket. You can takes buses from Yogyakarta or, more popularly, Surabaya direct to Denpasar. Or from Surabaya there are tickets available on the *Mutiara Timur* train straight through to Denpasar. The fare –

5900 rp in 2nd class, and 5200 rp in 3rd class – includes the train to Banyuwangi/ Ketapang harbour, and the ferry and bus to Denpasar. There are two trains daily and the trip takes roughly 15 hours.

The express *Bima* and *Mutiara* night trains from Jakarta link up with the morning train from Surabaya to Denpasar and it's possible to buy a ticket to cover the whole Jakarta-Bali trip.

GETTING AROUND
Java is a long, narrow island which can be divided into three sections: West Java, Central Java and East Java. Most travellers going through Java follow the well-worn route from Jakarta to Bogor, Bandung, Yogyakarta, Solo, Surabaya and on to Bali with short diversions or day trips from points along that route. Many only stop at Jakarta and Yogya! There are also a number of major towns along the north coast but, except for Cirebon and Semarang, they attract few visitors.

Air
There's no real need to fly around Java unless you're in a real hurry or have money

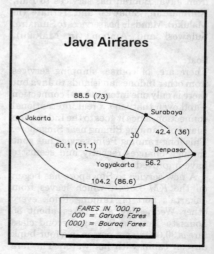

Java Airfares

Jakarta — 88.5 (73) — Surabaya
Surabaya — 42.4 (36) — Denpasar
Jakarta — 60.1 (51.1) — Yogyakarta
30
Yogyakarta — 56.2 — Denpasar
Jakarta — 104.2 (86.6) — Denpasar

FARES IN '000 rp
000 = Garuda Fares
(000) = Bouraq Fares

to burn as there's so much transport at ground level. If you do take to the air you'll get some spectacular views of Java's many mountains and volcanoes.

Within Java, Garuda operates the most extensive service between the major cities, followed by Merpati, then Bouraq and Mandala. Garuda is usually 10% to 20% more expensive than the other domestic airlines, though supposedly more efficient and reliable. Students may be able to get a 25% discount on fares from Garuda or Merpati with student ID, but don't count on it. Flights may be heavily booked so it's worth making reservations in advance. Bookings can be made through most travel agents or at the airline offices.

Bus

Java has to be one of the easiest places in the world to get around by bus. Buses run all over the island, including to places not accessible by train, and just about anywhere you might stand on the roadside is as good as a bus stop. Fares are cheap and, where the buses run a parallel service to the railways, they are sometimes also faster. The main advantage of buses over trains is that buses go so often, and there's rarely a problem getting one.

The big disadvantage of bus travel is that buses are nearly always hot, cramped, crowded and reasonably slow (though unnervingly erratic!) on busy daytime roads. Travelling by night bus (*bis malam*) is more expensive but it's cooler and faster because they're nonstop, although if you're awake it can be fairly bad on your nerves. In some cases there are particularly good reasons for going by day bus (as on the Jakarta to Bandung trip over the Puncak Pass) but generally, if it's a long trip, you're better off taking a night bus or opting for the train.

Various types of buses run many of the same routes and fares differ. Where the fare isn't ticketed or fixed, it's worth checking what the other passengers pay –

colts and opelets are the worst culprits for doubling fares for foreigners. The big public buses are the cheapest and they run local, long distance and some night services.

At most bus stations there will be an information office where you can store things. Major cities are also connected by night buses operated by private bus companies, some of them with air-con deluxe services. They're more expensive but fares often include snacks or a meal stop. Private buses sometimes depart from company offices (usually in the centre of town) and/or from the main bus stations where they may also have a ticket desk. They'll often drop you off wherever you want when you arrive at your destination. Bus touts are paid a small commission by the drivers and they're so keen to bundle you into a bus that they'll often help with baggage too.

Colts and opelets run the shorter local routes and get up the mountains where the big buses can't go. They're a little more expensive than the big public buses but run more frequently (although they will only depart when they're packed to the gunwales, so you can find yourself driving round and round a market-place for an hour or so to collect passengers – which can be very frustrating!). Once they do go they're slightly quicker than big buses, and probably the most dangerous form of public transport! There are also share-taxi services from Jakarta to Bogor, Bandung and a few other destinations.

Theft Baggage is carried inside the buses and, if the bus is very crowded, large rucksacks and bags that are cluttering up the aisle can be shifted to any small space that's available. Theft is sometimes a problem and your bags are most vulnerable on night buses, particularly public buses, when most people (including you) are sleeping – so have your things close at hand.

Once again, travelling light has definite advantages.

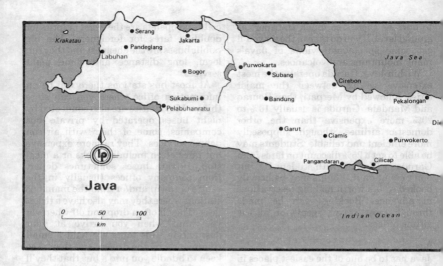

Rail

Java has a pretty good railway service running from one end of the island to the other. In the east (at Ketapang/ Banyuwangi) it connects with the ferry to Bali and in the west (at Merak) it connects with the ferry to Sumatra. The two main lines run between Jakarta and Surabaya and trains between the two cities either take the longer central route via Yogyakarta and Solo or the shorter northern route via Semarang.

One good thing about train stations is that they're centrally located (bus stations generally aren't) and there's nearly always a losmen just around the corner. Travelling by train can be less tiring and more comfortable than by bus, particularly on long hauls. However, there are a number of factors to consider: train services do vary a great deal, schedules do change with reasonable frequency, and although trains nearly always leave on-the-second they nearly always arrive late – sometimes very late. Some cities, Jakarta and Surabaya for example, have several stations and some are more convenient than others, so always check

which station you'll be arriving at or departing from.

Timetables You should be able to pick up a regional timetable at any of the main stations. Ask for a *jadwal perjalanan*; it's a free leaflet and lists major train services throughout Java, local trains and connecting ferry services. A separate *tarif* booklet listing all the fares is also available. The complete timetable and fares booklet, the *buku petunjuk tarif dan jadwal perjalanan*, costs 1200 rp. It's available from Jakarta's Gambir railway station, but it may be more difficult to find elsewhere.

Classes You need to choose your trains for comfort and speed, as well as destination. Trains in Java vary widely – there are expensive 1st and 2nd-class expresses, reasonably cheap and fast 2nd and 3rd-class trains, and slow and uncomfortable all-3rd-class trains. Travel times and fares, even for the same journey in the same class, can vary from train to train. Student discounts, from 10 to 25%, are generally available but not for the

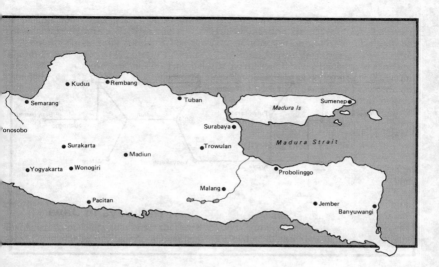

expensive *Bima* and *Mutiara* night expresses.

In 1st class (air-con) and 2nd class (fan-cooled) you have a seat or sleeper assigned to you. At the top end of the scale are the deluxe, air-con night expresses that do the Jakarta-Surabaya run. The *Bima*, which runs via Yogyakarta, has 1st-class two-berth sleepers and 2nd-class three-berth sleepers. The *Mutiara*, which runs via Semarang, has 1st and 2nd-class reclining chairs.

Third-class travel is unreserved, but in the more expensive 2nd and 3rd-class trains even 3rd class is reasonable. The *Express Siang* trains, for example, (which run from Bandung to Surabaya via Yogya and Solo) have fairly comfortable cane seats, and are not as crowded as the all-3rd-class trains.

In all-3rd-class trains, unreserved travel can be a nightmare as they are often hopelessly crowded and there is never much time to get organised before the train leaves. It's slightly easier if there are two of you – one of you can guard your gear while the other battles through the train in search of a seat. These trains – the

Cepats, *Gaya Baru* and *Senja* trains – are also slow and uncomfortable on a long trip.

What you don't want for any length of time is a *langsam* train. They're peak hour commuter trains to the big cities and crammed not only with people but market vegetables, cattle, the lot.

Tickets Buying tickets can be a frustrating and chaotic experience. If the queue is miles long or even if the train is officially booked right out, see the station master (*kepala stasiun*) and plead your case – he may be able to help. Tickets cannot generally be bought from the station before the day of your departure, but tickets for the *Bima* and *Mutiara* trains are available the night before or on the same day before 9 am.

Train tickets can be bought and reservations made from one to three days in advance at some travel agents in main cities. There is a charge for this service which varies depending on the train and class, but it can definitely be worth the money to save the time and the

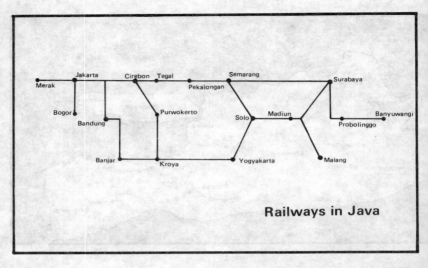

Railways in Java

hassle of fighting the crowds at the stations.

Sector by sector on the main train routes through Java:

Jakarta-Yogyakarta All trains between Jakarta and Yogyakarta pass through Cirebon on the north coast. From Jakarta to Yogyakarta takes from 10 to 12 hours with fares from 4500 rp in 3rd class (*Cepat Solo*), 9500 rp in 2nd (*Senja Ekonomi*).

The fast *Bima Express* costs 17,000 rp or 21,000 rp with sleeping berth, 1st class only. It departs Jakarta (Kota) at 4 pm and arrives in Yogya at 1.15 am then continues on to Surabaya. In the other direction it leaves Surabaya at 4.10 pm, goes through Yogya at 9.10 pm and arrives in Jakarta at 7 am the next day. A better schedule if you don't mind spending the night in a seat recliner is aboard the *Senja Utama*, which leaves Jakarta at 7.20 pm and arrives in Yogya at 5.20 am; it's 10,000 rp 2nd class.

At the other end of the comfort scale is the all-3rd-class *Gaya Baru Malam Selatan*, 5500 rp from Jakarta to Yogya; it also continues from Yogya to Surabaya. In comparison, by bus it costs 6500 rp from Java to Yogyakarta and takes about 14 hours.

Jakarta-Surabaya Trains between Jakarta and Surabaya either take the shorter northern route via Semarang or the longer southern route via Yogyakarta.

The most expensive train is the deluxe *Bima Express*, via Yogya, which departs Jakarta (Kota) at 4 pm and arrives in Surabaya (Gubeng) at 7.40 am. Returning, it leaves Surabaya at 4 pm and arrives Jakarta at 7 am. Fare is 22,500 rp for a seat or 27,000 with sleeper, 1st class only.

The deluxe *Mutiara Utara* takes the northern route from Jakarta (Kota) to Surabaya (Pasar Turi). The 15-hour trip costs 25,000 rp 1st class with sleeper on this very comfortable train.

The cheapest service is the all-3rd-class *Gaya Baru Malam Utara* (also north coast), which goes from Jakarta's Pasar Senen to Surabaya's Pasar Turi and costs 7700 rp. Officially it takes 14 hours but in practice it can take from 22 to 24 hours or longer. The *Gaya Baru Malam Selatan* takes the longer southern route via Yogya.

By comparison, non-air-con buses between Jakarta and Surabaya cost around 10,000 rp (15 hours by night bus).

Yogyakarta-Surabaya There are about half a dozen trains a day between Yogya and Surabaya. It takes from 5½ to 7½ hours and costs from 3800 rp in 3rd class. The deluxe *Bima Express* between Jakarta and Surabaya operates through Yogyakarta. Solo is on the main Yogyakarta to Surabaya route. Buses between Yogya and Surabaya cost around 6000 rp.

Driving

Self-drive car rental is a fairly new thing in Java and only Avis and National Car Rental operate from Jakarta. Rates are very expensive although there are lower weekly or monthly rates. A typical small car might be a Ford Laser, Toyota Corolla or Suzuki Jeep. A medium car could be a Toyota Corona, Mitsubishi Lancer or Renault 18. To hire a car you must have a valid local or international driving licence, and you must be at least 25 years of age to hire an Avis car, or 19 for a National car. Avis is substantially more expensive than National.

National Car Rental (tel 33423-333425), is at Kartika Plaza Hotel, Jalan Thamrin 10, Jakarta. Small cars are 54,000 rp a day, large cars 63,000 rp a day.

Avis (tel 341964, 349206), Jalan Diponegoro 25, Jakarta. Avis are also represented at the Hotel Borobudur (tel 370108 ext 2153), Hotel Sari Pacific (tel 323707 ext 1281) and at Soekarno-Hatta International Airport.

It's also possible to hire chauffeur-driven cars or minibuses quite easily through the car-rental companies and some travel agents and hotels in main cities. Rates vary but it's likely to be around 6000 rp an hour for a minimum of two hours, or a flat rate for a set route.

Blue Bird Transport in Jakarta (tel 333461) offers chauffeur-driven cars starting at 60,000 rp per day for a Toyota Corona, up to 150,000 rp per day for a Mercedes.

Many taxis operate as 'hire cars' too and charge in the same way. Privately it's possible to hire cars and drivers outside of Jakarta for somewhat lower rates – in most cities in Java for about 40,000 rp per day with driver.

If you've got the money there are obvious advantages to having your own transport but driving a car yourself is likely to be fairly hard going. You can get out of Jakarta all right on the Merak Highway to the west and the Jagorawi Highway to the south, but elsewhere roads vary enormously. Java's country roads are generally narrow and busy and drivers are alarmingly unpredictable. City streets too are crowded with fearless becaks, cyclists and pedestrians. Night driving may be faster but unlit becaks, cyclists and bullock carts are the danger!

Petrol It is worth refuelling whenever you see a Pertamina petrol station (pompa bensin) because they're few and far between in some areas and the alternative is buying petrol of dubious quality from drums at roadside stands.

Boat

There are plenty of ferries and boats from Java to the outer islands but there is also a boat trip across the inland sea between Cilacap and Kalipucang on the south coast which is really worth doing. If you're travelling between Central Java and Pangandaran in West Java the boat is an excellent alternative to taking the bus and/or train all the way.

There is a daily boat service to the Pulau Bidadari Island in the Bay of Jakarta, but trips to the small islands off the coast usually involve chartering a fishing boat – an outrigger vessel with sails or a motorised boat – and are dependent on the weather. There are regular daily ferries between Java and Madura, Bali and Sumatra.

Hitching

It's possible but it might take a very long time to get anywhere. There aren't many private cars on the roads and trucks can be crowded or moving too fast to stop. You're probably more likely to get short rides on the back of a motorbike.

Local Transport

All the major towns and cities have a network of local buses and often a variety of vehicles including double-deckers, big city buses and minibuses. And, of course, there is the ubiquitous bemo – a tiny covered pick-up truck with a row of seats down each side – which is designed to carry six small people but there always seems to be room for one more. For all city buses and bemos there is a fixed fare no matter how far you are going, although where there is no ticketing system it's worth checking with other passengers how much the fare is. The buses are fine in some places for getting around, but in cities like Jakarta and Surabaya, bus routes are bewildering and buses, usually overflowing so you may do better sticking to taxis and becaks.

There are metered taxis in Jakarta (although you have to make sure the drivers use the meters) but for every other form of local transport the fare – for passengers and baggage if you've got baggage – has to be agreed beforehand. And agreed clearly or there could be all sorts of hassles at the end of the journey.

Airport Transport Apart from in Jakarta there are no official airline buses to the airports but local city buses sometimes pass within easy walking distance. There are always taxis and, if the taxi has no meter, there is usually a fixed fare from the city to the airport.

Taxis Taxi drivers in Jakarta are a disreputable lot although they *do* have

meters. Elsewhere there are unmetered taxis in most cities, usually to be found around hotels and at airport, train and bus terminals. Many are private 'hire cars'; they charge about 5000 rp an hour for a minimum of two hours within city limits, and out of town charge according to distance.

Becak The becak is basically a three-wheeler bicycle with a seat for two in front of the rider. The becak men, though, put their own personal touch to their carriages and across Java there are superb variations in their brightly painted pictures, tinkling bells or whirring metal discs strung across the undercarriage. They've got a sense of humour too – in Yogya there was one guy who peddled furiously down the streets at night with a tiny flashing lightbulb on the point of his coolie hat! Becaks are now banned from busy main streets in the big cities but in every town of any size in Java they're still the most basic form of transport – for people and anything else that has to be shifted.

Fares must always be agreed beforehand with the becak men. They'll often try to charge far too much although they will usually settle on a reasonable fare – about 300 rp a km. You can expect to pay a few more rp for every piece of baggage you have and every hill that has to be peddled over. Hiring a becak by time or for a round-trip often makes good sense if you're planning to cover a lot of ground in one day, particularly in places like Yogya or Solo.

Bajaj The *bajaj* (pronounced 'ba-jai') is found only in Jakarta and only operates in certain zones of that city. It's a motorised three-wheeler for two people and, as for becaks, fares have to be agreed.

Other In some country towns horse-drawn carts operate. The dokar is a two-wheeled pony cart for two or three people and the andong (sometimes known as a delman) is a larger horse-drawn wagon carrying up to six people.

Horses can be hired around many of the hill resorts and villages, and bicycles and motorcycles can be hired in Solo and Yogya. In Jakarta bicycles are actually used as a taxi service near the old harbour.

Tours

At most places of tourist interest there are city tours and day trips to tourist sights operated by local travel companies, and they can be good value, particularly if you're short of time. The tourist offices should have details but the large hotels are often a good source of information.

Longer trips – to Krakatau or to the Ujong Kulon National Park, for example – can be arranged through a number of tour and travel agents. This might be less of a hassle for you but it's unlikely to be any cheaper than doing it on your own. Some travel agents also operate an overland trip from Bali to Java but if you're being whisked around for about 10 days or so you won't get more than a fleeting glimpse of the country; it's better doing it on your own at a slower pace.

There are numerous travel agents in Jakarta but the following have a good reputation, and also have branches in most tourist cities:

Nitour
    Jalan Majapahit 2, Jakarta (tel 346347)
    Hotel Indonesia, Jakarta
    Also Bandung, Yogya, Surabaya, Banyu-wangi
Pacto
    Jalan Surabaya 8, Jakarta (tel 347457)
    Hotel Borobudur, Jakarta (tel 356952)
    Also Bandung, Yogya, Surabaya
Vayatour
    Jalan Batutulis 38, (tel 380-0202)
    Also Bandung, Yogya, Surabaya

Jakarta

Trying to characterise Jakarta is like being caught in a riptide: you're pulled in one direction by western-style high-rise glass-and-concrete urbanisation and an elite of Indonesian academics and intellectuals, only to find yourself bogged down in the poverty of the kampungs of immigrant peasants who have come into the city in search of work. Jakarta is a city which asks for neither affection nor commitment; other than to scratch out a living peddling things – bodies, political power, diplomacy or becaks – there is no reason to stay here and certainly little reason to actually like the place for itself. Yet this is where the rest of the archipelago gets its marching orders; this is where they decide how many transmigrants will be sent to colonise the outer islands; or which former colony (Malaysia, West Irian, East Timor) gets thumped this year; or which foreign mining company gets to dig up rocks in the middle of the Sulawesi or Kalimantan jungles.

Sukarno had a completely different image of what Jakarta could be. He wanted to transform it into a city of grand structures more in keeping with his conception of Jakarta as a world centre. The 14-storey Jakarta Hotel broke the

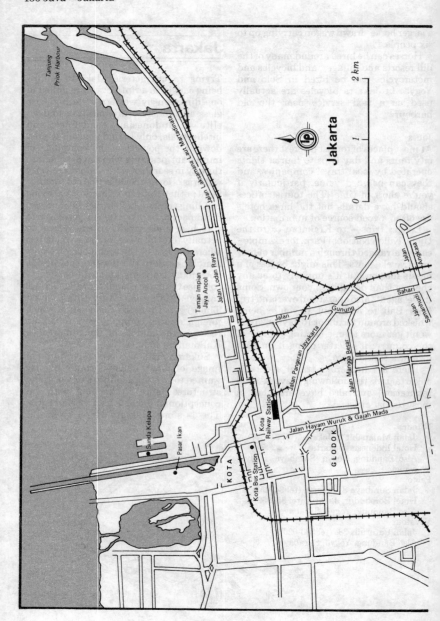

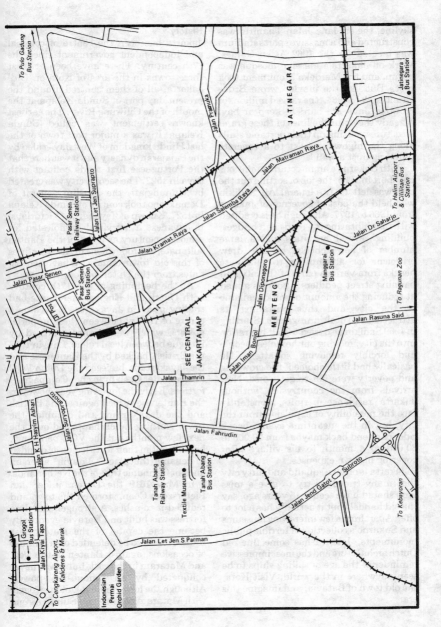

skyline, the six-lane Jalan Thamrin was constructed and a massive sports stadium was erected for the 1962 Asian Games. Work on Jakarta's massive mosque was begun, and the Merdeka Monument took root. 'But like the jungle,' wrote Bruce Grant back in 1964, 'the ragged millions of crowded Java are hard to keep at bay. Already they blur the lines of these grand structures, setting up their portable stalls along the highways, next to a concrete pillar, against a wall.'

With Sukarno's architectural ambitions cut short in 1965, the job of sorting out the city was left to Lt-General Ali Sadikin who held the post of governor of Jakarta from 1966 to 1977. Although he is credited with rehabilitating the roads and bridges, building several hospitals and a large number of new schools, he also drew criticism for attempting to eliminate becaks from various parts of the city and banning street peddlers – policies aimed at reducing the amount of work available in the city and thus curtailing its attraction to rural immigrants. Starting in 1969 Sadikin also tried to halt migration into the city, moving out homeless people and forcibly removing squatters. He basically had little choice if the crowding and poverty were not to get worse. New arrivals from the countryside, without Jakarta residence permits, constantly face the possibility of expulsion from the city, but in the meantime even a becak rider can send back maybe from 20,000 to 30,000 rp a month to his village after covering his own expenses.

Jakarta is often a squalid and dirty city that many travellers try to give a miss (you should have seen it 15 years ago, say the old hands!) but it actually has a lot to offer. Apart from a few interesting museums and Sukarno's collection of terrible public monuments, Jakarta has some fine old Dutch architecture and the most impressive reminder of the age of sailing ships to be seen anywhere in the world. Visit Kota, the old town of Batavia, and imagine this era.

History

Jakarta has been the centre of colonial and independent government since the 17th century. There have been at least three towns in the area of Kota or 'Old' Jakarta, all of them centred around the present day port of Sunda Kelapa at the mouth of the Ciliwung River. The earliest known settlement was called Sunda Kelapa. It was a major port town of the last Hindu kingdom of West Java ruled by the Pajajaran dynasty and it was here that the Portuguese first made contact with Java in 1522. The second city was created by Gunungjati, the Muslim general of Demak who took control of Sunda Kelapa in 1527. Known as Jayakarta, 'Victorious' in Javanese, it survived unmolested for almost a century as a fief of the Banten sultanate, but today none of the structures of this old town remain. What there is, dates from the Dutch period.

At the beginning of the 17th century both Dutch and English merchants had trading posts in Jayakarta. It became a centre of rivalry between these imperial powers, which was further confused by intrigue between local rulers. Late in 1618 the British, backed by the Bantenese and the Jayakartans, besieged the Dutch VOC (Vereenigde Oost-Indische Compagnie) fortress. Early the following year, however, the Bantenese turned against the British and the Jayakartans and occupied the town. Nothing much happened over the next few months but the VOC personnel, holding out in their fortified post, decided to rename the place 'Batavia' after an ancient Germanic tribe of the Netherlands.

In May 1619 the Dutch, under Jan Pieterszoon Coen, stormed the town and reduced it to ashes. A stronger shoreline fortress was built and Batavia eventually became the capital of the Dutch East Indies. It had to be defended on a number of occasions, against Banten in the west and Mataram in the east, but it was never conquered by an Indonesian power. Although the long-running Dutch struggle with Mataram began when Sultan Agung attacked Batavia in 1628, the Javanese suffered enormous losses and finally withdrew after executing their failed commanders. Agung's second siege in 1629 was an even greater debacle, and after this devastating defeat, Batavia was never again threatened by an army of Mataram.

Within the walls of Batavia the prosperous Dutch built tall stuffy houses and pestilential canals on virtual swampland and by the early 18th century Batavia was suffering growing pains. Batavia grew rapidly as Indonesians and especially Chinese were attracted by its commercial prospects but by the early 18th century the growing Chinese population was creating unrest and violence broke out. In October 1740 a general massacre of Chinese took place and a year later Chinese inhabitants were moved to Glodok, outside the city walls. Other Batavians, discouraged by the severe epidemics between 1735 and 1780, moved when they could and the city began to spread far south of the port. The Koningsplein, now Merdeka Square, was finished in 1818; Merdeka Palace in 1879; and Kebayoran Baru was the last residential area to be laid out by the Dutch after WW II.

Dutch colonial rule came to an end when the Japanese occupied Java and the name Jakarta was restored to the city. The republican government of the revolution retreated to Yogyakarta when the Dutch returned after the war but in 1950, when Indonesian independence was finally secured, Jakarta was made the capital of the new republic.

In 1945 Jakarta had a population of 900,000, since then there has been a continual influx of migrants from depressed rural areas and newcomers continue to crowd into the urban slums. Today the population is 6.5 million. Sukarno concentrated on prestigious projects and monumental buildings for Jakarta, and the Suharto government too has met criticism for their seeming neglect of the city's impoverished people. The massive Taman Mini project in particular was widely condemned as a waste of the nation's resources although overall Jakarta is a much better looking place than it was 10 years ago.

Information & Orientation

Jakarta sprawls out in every direction but Sukarno's towering gold-tipped Monas monument in Merdeka Square serves as an excellent landmark for the city. Most areas of interest in Jakarta are to the north and south of the Monas monument although the city stretches 25 km from the docks to the suburb of Kebayoran and covers 590 square km in all.

North of the monument, down Jalan Gajah Mada, is the older part of Jakarta now known as Kota and the adjoining district of Glodok, Jakarta's Chinatown. Kota is the heart of the 17th-century Dutch town of Batavia, around the cobbled square of Taman Fatahillah and the Kali Besar canal. Here you will also find Kota railway station. Further north on the waterfront is the old harbour area of Sunda Kelapa with Makassar schooners, old Dutch warehouses and Pasar Ikan, the fish market. The modern harbour, Tanjung Priok, is several km east along the coast past the Ancol Recreation Park.

The area around Merdeka Square itself is crowded with museums, the Jakarta fair grounds, the Presidential Palace and the great white-domed Istiqlal mosque. Gambir, the main railway station, is on the east side of Monas.

The more modern part of Jakarta is to the south of the Monas monument. Jalan Thamrin, which runs to the west of Monas, is the main north-south street of the new city with most of the big hotels, big banks, airline offices, Sarinah (Jakarta's main department store) and the Hotel Indonesia roundabout at the bottom of it. The Qantas, Cathay Pacific, and Garuda airline offices are at the intersection of Jalan Thamrin and Jalan Kebon Sirih, and a couple of blocks east along Kebon Sirih you'll find Jalan Jaksa, the cheap

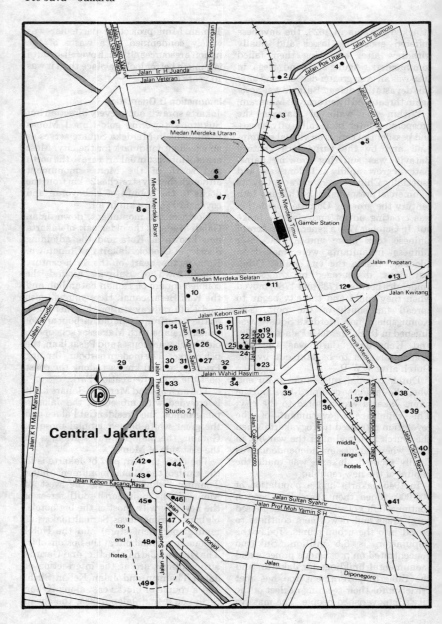

Central Jakarta

1	Presidential Palace
2	Pelni Office
3	Istiqlal Mosque
4	Post Office
5	Borobudur Hotel
6	Entrance To Monas
7	Merdeka Monument (Monas)
8	National Museum
9	Taman Ria Amusement Park
10	Hotel Sabang Metropolitar
11	US Embassy
12	Bumi Hyatt Hotel
13	4848 Taxis
14	Qantas & Thai International
15	Sakura Anpan Bakery
16	Family Homestay
17	Puja Sera 4 Food Centre
18	Senayan Satay House
19	Wisma Delima (Jalan Jaksa)
20	Angies Cafe
21	Bloem Steen & Kresna Homestays
22	Norbeck Hostel
23	Djody Hostel & Hotel
24	Coq Hardi Restaurant & Nicks Cafe
25	Borneo Hostel
26	Natrabu Padang Restaurant
27	Budi Bondo Restaurant
28	Hotel Sari Pacific
29	Wisma ISE Guest House
30	Jakarta Theatre Building & Tourist Office
31	A & W Hamburgers
32	Bali International Hotel
33	Sarinah Department Store
34	Hotel Wisma Indra
35	Media Taxis
36	Immigration Office
37	Hotel Menteng I
38	TIM Cultural Centre
39	Hotel Cikini Sofyan
40	Hotel Menteng II
41	Hotel Marcopolo
42	Australian Embassy
43	Grand Hyatt Hotel
44	President Hotel
45	Hotel Indonesia
46	British Embassy
47	Mandarin Hotel
48	Vic's Viking Restaurant & George & The Dragon Pub
49	Kartika Plaza Hotel

accommodation centre of Jakarta. Sarinah, on the corner of Jalan Thamrin and and Jalan Wahid Hasyim, is another good landmark for this area. The Jakarta Tourist Information Office is opposite the store, across Jalan Wahid Hasyim, and Sarinah is also particularly useful for telling bus drivers where you want to go.

The districts in the southern part of the city include the wealthy enclave of Menteng where the diplomats live and, south-east of Menteng, the residential area of Jatinegara. South-west of Menteng is the new suburban area of Kebayoran Baru with a busy shopping and restaurant centre at Blok M. The Statue of Youth at the end of Jalan Jenderal Sudirman marks the entrance to Kebayoran.

There are suburban bus stations in all the main city districts and several inter-city bus stations – Kalideres in the west, Cililitan in the south and Pulo Gadung in the east. Jakarta's new international airport is called Sukarno-Hatta and it opened in 1985. See the Airport Transport section for details.

Tourist Office The Jakarta Tourist Information Office (tel 344117) is in the Jakarta Theatre building on the corner of Jalan Wahid Hasyim and Jalan Thamrin. They have a good give-away map of Jakarta, and a number of excellent information leaflets on what to see and how to get around the city. Among them *See for Yourself, Places of Interest* and *General Information* are very useful. The tourist office can also help you in finding accommodation. If you're heading for the west coast, you can pick up a 25% discount coupon here for the hostel at the Carita Krakatau Beach Hotel. The office is open from 8.30 am to 3 pm Monday to Thursday; to 11 am Friday and until 1 pm Saturday; closed Sundays.

The headquarters of the Indonesia National Tourist Organisation is the Directorate General of Tourism (tel 359001), at Jalan Kramat Raya 81. They publish travel information for the whole country but nothing is on display so you have to know what you want. Particularly useful are the annual *Calendar of Events* which lists all major festivals and events and the *Indonesia Tourist Map* booklet which includes some good maps and helpful travel information. The *Indonesia Travel Planner*, if you can get them to give you a copy, is a useful compendium of information on hotel accommodation, train and bus travel, and government office addresses. It's open the same hours as the city tourist office from Monday to Friday, but it closes at 2 pm Saturday.

Immigration Office The Directorate General of Immigration is fairly central at Jalan Teuku Umar 1 in Menteng. The office is open from 8 am daily except Sunday and closes at 3 pm Monday to Thursday, 12 noon Friday and 2 pm Saturday.

Travel Agencies For international flights Kaliman Travel (tel 330103) in the President Hotel on Jalan Thamrin is a good place for cheap tickets. The staff are very helpful and they offer a discount on some airline tickets if you pay in cash. The office is open from 8 am to 6 pm Monday to Saturday, 8 am to 2 pm Sunday. Other agents worth checking are Natrabu (tel 331728) Jalan Agus Salim 29A (near Jalan Jaksa) and Pacto Ltd (tel 320309) at Jalan Cikini Raya 24.

The agent for STA (Student Travel Australia) (tel 639-2703) is Indo Shangrila Travel, Jalan Gajah Mada 219G. Any student with an international student card is entitled to their fares, which are usually cheaper than a normal student discount of 25%. Their tickets for non-students are the same or slightly more expensive than Kaliman's. For domestic bucket shops in Jakarta see the following airport section, under Getting There & Away.

Post & Communication The main post office and Jakarta's poste restante are at Jalan Pos Utara 2, opposite the market Pasar Baru off to the north-east of Monas.

The poste restante here is pretty efficient – they give you the whole bundle from your pigeonhole to look through and will willingly give you all the newly arrived mail that hasn't been sorted yet as well. There is a 50 rp charge for each letter from poste restante. It is open from 8 am to 4 pm Monday to Friday and until 1 pm on Saturday. For ordinary stamp sales and postmarking there are always a few windows open from 6 am till 10 pm Monday to Saturday (closed 11 am till 12 noon Friday) and 9 am till 4 pm Sunday. It's a good half-hour walk from the centre of town, or you can take a No 12 bus from Jalan Thamrin. There's also a small post office inside the Sarinah Department Store which is open from 9 am till 2.30 pm Monday to Thursday, 9 am to 12 noon Friday, and 9 am till 12.30 pm Saturday, closed Sunday.

To make international and inter-city phone calls go to the telecom centre opposite the tourist office in the Jakarta Theatre Building. It's open 24 hours and is very efficient. They now have International Direct Dialling, which means cheaper rates. There are some public telephones for local calls in the same building but they're so often in need of repair that you're better off using public phones in the large hotels.

Banks In Jakarta there are major offices of all the Indonesian banks and some overseas banks are also represented. At major banks, or at moneychangers, there's no problem changing foreign money and travellers' cheques, but it's worth shopping around. Bank rates vary slightly and the Indonesian banks may offer a lower rate of exchange than the foreign banks, or the moneychangers. Many of the foreign exchange banks are found on and around Jalan Thamrin and most are open from 8 am to 12 noon Monday to Friday, 8 to 11 am Saturday.

On the Jalan Wahid Hasyim side of the Sarinah Department Store building is a branch of the Bank Dagan Negara

(BDN), which generally has the best exchange rates in Indonesia. There is also a money changer inside Sarinah on the 1st floor that is open longer hours than the BDN but of course exchange rates are not as good. Bank Dagang Negara also has a larger branch on Jalan Kebon Sirih, near the intersection with Jalan Agus Salim.

The American Express headquarters in Jakarta is at Gedung Arthaloka, Jalan Jenderal Sudirman 2 (tel 587409).

Bookshops Books – particularly imported ones – are expensive but if you want to stock up on paperbacks or look for Indonesian books then Jakarta is the best hunting ground. The large illustrated books on Borobudur, for example, that are sold at the temple site itself (published by Djambatan and Intermasa) are about 2000 rp cheaper in Jakarta.

Ayumas at Jalan Kwitang 6, near Pasar Senen, is one of the largest bookshops in Jakarta and has a fair range of English paperbacks and Indonesian books and a good selection of maps and books on Indonesia. Sarinah Department Store also has a fairly good book and map section. Other bookshops include the Toko Buku Gramedia shops at Jalan Gajah Mada 109 and Jalan Melawai IV/13 Blok M, Gunung Agung at Jalan Kwitang 24-25 and Gunung Mulia next door at 22-23. And there are, of course, bookstalls in most of the large hotels where you'll find paperbacks, magazines, foreign and Indonesian newspapers. In fact, probably the best selections of English-language reading in Jakarta, or anywhere in Indonesia for that matter, are available at the Hotel Indonesia and Borobudur Hotel.

Mochtar Lubis' controversial study *Twilight in Jakarta* has gone on and off the ban list in Indonesia but for the moment it's available as an *Oxford in Asia* paperback in the National Museum shop. You'll also find a number of other interesting books on Indonesia here.

Newspapers Three daily English-language newspapers are published in Jakarta – *Indonesian Times, Indonesian Observer* and the *Jakarta Post*. The Post is the best, but all three impose strict self-censorship and the end results are very slim daily issues. The Times seems to be the ruling party's mouthpiece, with headlines like 'Development of Thoughts on Archipelagic Concept Called for'.

Maps If you're planning to stay a long time in Jakarta it could be worth investing in a detailed city map. The *Falk City Map* and the *PT Pembina Guide & Map of Jakarta* cost about 5000 rp.

Film & Photography Jalan Agus Salim, just to the east of and parallel to Jalan Thamrin, is a good place for your photographic supplies. The other good place to look is 'Blok M' near the pasar which lies between Jalan Sultan Hasanuddin and Jalan Melawai in the Kebayoran Baru district in south-west Jakarta.

There are about 15 Kodak-only stores in Jakarta. The distributor and laboratory for Kodak is at Jalan Kwitang 10. Jalan Kwitang lies roughly south-east of the Merdeka Monument; it is an eastwards continuation of Jalan A R Hakim, which is a continuation of Jalan Wahid Hasyim. If you can't find the stuff you want in the stores, then try this place. Nirwana Photo Company, Jalan Krekot Raya 67B is the distributor for Sakuracolor. Modern Photo Film Company, at various addresses in Jakarta, is the Fuji distributor.

Colour prints cost around 125 or 150 rp each at places offering same-day processing. Try Jakarta Foto on Jalan Agus Salim and Globe Photo on Jalan Melawai V 26, Blok M, Kebayoran Baru.

Libraries & Organisations The Ganesha Society, an organisation of volunteer museum workers, holds weekly lectures or films about Indonesia at the Erasmus Huis (tel 772325) on Jalan Rasuna Said, beside the Dutch Embassy in South Jakarta. Admission is around 1000 rp. The National Museum (tel 360976) has their schedule, or ask the Ganesha guides who work there part-time.

The Indonesian/American Cultural Center (Perumpunan Persahabatan Indonesia Amerik) (tel 881241), Jalan Pramuka Kav 30, has exhibits, films and lectures related to Indonesia each week. The Australian Cultural Centre (Pusat Kebudayaan Australia), in the Citibank Building on Jalan Thamrin, has a good library. (It's open from 9 am to 2 pm Monday to Thursday and until 12 noon Friday.) The British Council's Library is open from 9 am to 1 pm and is in the Widjoyo Centre, Jalan Jenderal Sudirman 56. There are also cultural centres from Czechoslovakia, France, Germany, India, Italy and Japan.

National Parks/Nature Reserves Jakarta no longer has a branch office of the PHPA (Perlindungan Hutan dan Pelestarian Alam), the Directorate General of Forest Protection and Nature Conservation. For detailed information on Indonesia's parks and reserves, you'll have to visit the national PHPA headquarters in Bogor, where there is now a special office for National Park and Forestry Tourism. The address is Jalan Ir H Janda 100, Bogor (tel (0251) 21014. Dr Sophie can be contacted at this office and he speaks English.

There is no need to go to the Bogor headquarters for entry permits to national parks and/or reserves. Permits can be acquired directly from local offices located on-site throughout Indonesia.

Airlines Addresses of international airlines that fly to and from Jakarta include:

Air India
Sari Pacific Hotel, Jalan Thamrin 6 (tel 325470)
British Airways
Wisma Metropolitan I, Jalan Jenderal Sudirman, Kav 29-31 (tel 578-2460)

Canadian Pacific
PP Building, Jalan Thamrin 57 (tel 325086)
Cathay Pacific
Borobudur Hotel, 3rd floor, Jalan Lapangan Banteng Selatan (tel 380-6664)
Garuda Indonesian Airways
BDN Building, Jalan Thamrin 5 (tel 334425). Also at Borobudur Hotel (tel 359901) and Hotel Indonesia (tel 310-0568)
Japan Airlines
President Hotel, Jalan Thamrin 59 (tel 322207)
KLM
Hotel Indonesia, Jalan Thamrin (tel 320708)
Lufthansa
Panin Centre Building, Jalan Jenderal Sudirman 1 (tel 710247)
MAS
Hotel Indonesia, Jalan Thamrin (tel 320909)
Pan Am
Borobudur Hotel, Jalan Lapangan Banteng Selatan (tel 361707)
Philippine Airlines
Borobudur Hotel (tel 370108 ext 2310)
Qantas
BDN Building, Jalan Thamrin 5 (tel 325707)
Singapore Airlines
Sahid Jaya Hotel, Jalan Jenderal Sudirman 86 (tel 584021)
Thai Airways International
BDN Building, Jalan Thamrin 5 (tel 325176)
UTA
Jaya Building, Jalan Thamrin (tel 323609)
United Airlines
Borobudur Hotel, Jalan Lapangan Banteng Selatan (tel 361707)

Embassies Addresses of some of the embassies in Jakarta include:

Australia
Jalan Thamrin 15 (tel 323109)
Burma
Jalan H A Salim 109 (tel 340440)
Canada
5th Floor, Wisma Metropolitan I, Jalan Jenderal Sudirman, Kav 29 (tel 510709)
China
represented by the Embassy of Romania, Jalan Teuku Cik Ditiro 42A (tel 349524)
Denmark
Bina Mulia Bldg, 4th floor, Jalan Rasuna Said, Kav 10 (tel 518350)

Finland
  Bina Mulia Bldg, 10th floor, Jalan Rasuna
  Said, Kav 10 (tel 516980)
France
  Jalan Thamrin 20 (tel 332807)
India
  Jalan Rasuna Said 51 (tel 518150)
Iran
  Jalan Cokroaminoto 110 (tel 330623)
Italy
  Jalan Diponegoro 45 (tel 348339)
Japan
  Jalan Thamrin 24 (tel 324308)
Malaysia
  Jalan Imam Bonjol 17 (tel 332170)
Netherlands
  Jalan Rasuna Said, Kav S-3 (tel 511515)
New Zealand
  Jalan Diponegoro 41 (tel 330552)
Norway
  Bina Mulia Bldg, 4th floor, Jalan Rasuna
  Said, Kav 10 (tel 517140)
Pakistan
  Jalan Teuku Umar 50 (tel 350676)
Papua New Guinea
  6th Floor, Panin Bank Centre, Jalan
  Jenderal Sudirman, Kav (tel 711218)
Philippines
  Jalan Imam Bonjol 6-8 (tel 348917)
Poland
  Jalan Diponegoro 65 (tel 320509)
Singapore
  Jalan Proklamasi 23 (tel 347783)
Spain
  Wisma Kosgoro, 12th floor, Jalan Thamrin
  53 (tel 322689)
Sri Lanka
  Jalan Diponegoro 70 (tel 321018)
Sweden
  Jalan Taman Cut Mutiah 12 (tel 333061)
Switzerland
  Jalan Rasuna Said, Blok X/3/2, Kuningan
  (tel 516061)
Thailand
  Jalan Imam Bonjol 74 (tel 343762)
UK
  Jalan Thamrin 75 (tel 330904)
USA
  Jalan Merdeka Selatan 5 (tel 360360)
USSR
  Jalan Thamrin 13 (tel 327007)
West Germany
  Jalan Thamrin 1 (tel 323908)

Other Information The daily *Jakarta Post*

gives a useful run down of what is on, temporary exhibitions and cinema programmes. The swimming pools at Ancol are great but you could also try some of the hotel pools closer at hand. Many of the hotels do open their pools to the public for a small admission – the Hotel Marco Polo is one.

Events The Jakarta Anniversary on 22 June celebrates the establishment of the city by Gunungjati back in 1527 with fireworks, a 'Miss and Mr Jakarta' competition(!), and the Jakarta Fair. The latter is an annual commercial and country-fair event with displays from all over the country and lots of music. It's held on the southern side of Merdeka Square and runs from early June till mid-July.

Old Batavia (Kota)

The old town of Batavia, known as Kota today, at one time contained Coen's massive shoreline fortress, the Kasteel, and was surrounded by a sturdy defensive wall and a moat. In the early 19th century Governor-General Daendels did a good job of demolishing much of the unhealthy city but there is still a Dutch flavour to this old part of town. A few of Batavia's old buildings remain in active use, though others were restored during the 1970s and have become museums. Cleaning up the stinking canals though is a superhuman task.

The centre of old Batavia is the cobblestone square known as Taman Fatahillah. A block west of the square is the Kali Besar, the Great Canal along the Ciliwung River. This was once the high-class residential area of Batavia and on the west bank overlooking the canal are the last of the big private homes dating from the early 18th century. The Toko Merah or Red Shop, now occupied by the Dharma Niaga company, was formerly the home of Governor-General van Imhoff. The north end of the Kali Besar is marked by a small Dutch drawbridge called the Chicken Market Bridge.

There are two booklets about Old Batavia which are worth buying for background information and further detail. They're extracts from the *Historical Sites of Jakarta* by A Heuken and entitled *The City Hall & its Surroundings* and *Gereja Portugis*. The booklets cost 1500 rp from the Jakarta History Museum in Kota, but only 800 rp from the National Museum on Merdeka Square!

Sunda Kelapa

At the old port of Sunda Kelapa you can see more sailing ships, the magnificent Makassar schooners called *pinisi*, than you ever thought existed. This is undoubtedly one of the finest sights in Jakarta. Entry to the docks is only 50 rp but ultra-skinflints can avoid this by cutting through Pasar Ikan (the fish market across the bridge) to the gateway of Luar Batang village on the water's edge. Small boats ferry the local people across from Luar Batang to the docks and there are plenty of boatmen around wanting to take you out on the water. You can spend a good half-hour or so rowing around the schooners, avoiding decapitation by mooring ropes and gangplanks and occasionally having rubbish thrown on you from the ships! If you get out to the Thousand Islands (Pulau Seribu) in the Bay of Jakarta you will probably see Makassar schooners under sail.

The best time to visit Pasar Ikan is around dawn when the day's catch is sold in an intense, colourful scene of busy crowds.

Museum Bahari/Maritime Museum At the entrance to Pasar Ikan, one of the old Dutch East India Company warehouses has been turned into a maritime museum.

A sea-going pinisi at Sunda Kelapa

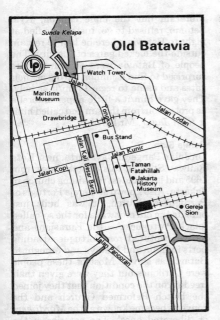

Exhibits are fairly meagre but include large models of boats from various islands and it's worth a short wander. The museum is open from 8 am to 2 pm Tuesday to Thursday, to 11 am Friday, to 1 pm Saturday and until 2 pm Sunday. It's closed on Mondays. Entrance is 150 rp. You can ascend the old watchtower back near the bridge for free; there is a good view over the harbour from the top.

Taman Fatahillah Square

There are three museums located here. Entrance to each is 150 rp and they are open from 9 am daily, except Monday, to 2 pm Tuesday to Thursday, to 11 am Friday, to 1 pm Saturday and until 2 pm Sunday.

Jakarta History Museum On the south side of Taman Fatahillah, the museum is housed in the old City Hall of Batavia, which is probably one of the most solid

reminders of Dutch rule to be found anywhere in Indonesia. This large bell-towered hall, built in 1627 and added to between 1707 and 1710, served the administration of the city. It was also used by the city law courts and its dungeons were the main prison compound of Batavia. In 1830 the Javanese hero, Prince Diponegoro, was imprisoned here for a time on his way into exile in Menado.

Today it contains lots of heavy carved furniture and other memorabilia from the Dutch period and there are sections for the earlier kingdoms that ruled the Jakarta area. Amongst the more interesting exhibits is a series of gloomy portraits of all the Dutch governors-general (which seems to set the mood for this place!), early pictures of Batavia, and models of inscribed stones from the Hindu Tarumanegara kingdom of West Java.

In the courtyard at the back of the building there is a strange memorial stone to one Pieter Erbervelt who was put to death in 1722 for allegedly conspiring to massacre the Dutch inhabitants of Batavia.

Wayang Museum This museum has one of the best collections of wayang puppets in Java and includes puppets not only from Indonesia but China, Malaysia, India and Kampuchea. Among the more interesting items is a very fine chess set of wayang golek figures (Rama and his monkeys versus Rawana and his giants) and a number of wayang kulit puppets used in the Yogyakarta Family Planning Programme. Formerly the Museum of Old Batavia, the building itself was constructed in 1912 on the site of the Dutch Church of Batavia which was demolished by Daendels in 1808. In the downstairs courtyard there are some interesting memorials to the Dutch governors-general once buried here. These include some mention of Jan Pieterszoon Coen, founder of Batavia, who died of cholera in 1629 during the siege by Mataram.

Wayang golek or wayang kulit performances are put on at the museum every Sunday morning between 10 am and 12 noon.

Balai Seni Rupa/Art Museum Built between 1866 and 1870, the Palace of Justice now houses Jakarta's principal art gallery. There's a permanent exhibition of works by Indonesia's most prominent painters, including Raden Saleh and Affandi, and a section for the Chinese ceramic collection of Indonesia's former Vice-President Adam Malik.

Si Jagur-Taman Fatahillah
This huge bronze cannon is one of the most intriguing sights of old Batavia. Its outer surface is adorned with a Latin inscription *Ex me ipsa renata sum* which means 'Out of myself I was reborn' and the cannon tapers at one end into a large clenched fist. In Indonesia the fist is a sexual symbol and for that reason childless women at one time used to visit the cannon. They would offer flowers to their talisman and complete the ritual by sitting on top of the cannon. This must have upset the authorities a great deal for Si Jagur was shifted to a museum for some years to counteract the superstition. Si Jagur is a Portuguese cannon which was brought to Batavia as a trophy of war after the fall of Melaka in 1641 but the Javanese, naturally, have a mystical story to tell.

The legend relates that a King of Sunda had a dream in which he heard the thundering sound of a strange weapon. He ordered his prime minister, Kyai Setomo, to find a similar weapon, threatening him with death if he failed. Kyai Setomo discussed his fateful task with his wife, Nyai Setomi and they both did some meditation. Days passed and the king grew so impatient that he visited Kyai Setomo's home, only to discover that the couple had been transformed into two large cannons! Sultan Agung then heard about the great weapons and ordered them to be brought to his court at Mataram but the male cannon, Kyai Setomo, refused to go. Instead he fled at night to Batavia where he had to remain outside the locked gates of the city. The people of Batavia were of course quite surprised to find a cannon sitting at their gates and came to regard him/it as holy. They gave him/it a little paper umbrella as protection from the sun and called him/it *Kyai Jagur*, Mr Fertility.

Gereja Sion
On Jalan Pangeran Jayakarta, near Kota Railway Station, this church dates from 1695 and is the oldest remaining church in Jakarta. Also known as Gereja Portugis or Portuguese Church, it was built just outside the old city walls for the so-called 'black Portuguese' – the Eurasians and natives captured from Portuguese trading ports in India and Malaya and brought to Batavia as slaves. Most of these people were Catholics but they were given their freedom on the condition that they joined the Dutch Reformed Church and the converts became known as the *Mardijkers* or 'liberated ones'. The exterior of the church is very plain, but inside there are copper chandeliers, the original organ and a baroque pulpit. Although in the year 1790 alone, 2381 people had to be buried in the graveyard here, very few tombs remain. One of the most interesting is the ornate bronze tombstone of Governor-General Zwaardecroon, who died in 1728 and wished to be buried among the 'ordinary' folk.

Glodok
After the Chinese massacre of 1740, the Dutch decided there would be no repetition and all Chinese were prohibited from residing within the town walls, or even from being there after sundown. In 1741 a tract of land just to the south-west of Batavia was allocated as Chinese quarters. The area became Glodok, Jakarta's Chinatown, and the city's flourishing commercial centre. It's now bounded to the east by Jalan Gajah Mada,

a wide road lined with offices, restaurants and modern shopping plazas. But if you walk in from Jalan Pancoran, beside the Glodok Plaza, you'll find a small part of old Glodok still consists of winding lanes, narrow crooked houses with balconies, slanting red-tiled roofs and tiny obscure shops. In between there are numerous eating places, markets, street hawkers and half the city's becak population! It can be a fascinating area to wander around and, just south of Jalan Pancoran, near the Petak Sembilan fish market, you'll find the Chinese Dharma Jaya Temple – one of the most interesting in Jakarta. Built in 1650, it was the chief temple for the Chinese of Batavia and was once known for its casino and Chinese wayang kulit. At present this is the largest Buddhist temple in Jakarta.

If you're walking from Glodok back along Jalan Gajah Mada, it's worth pausing to have a glance at two old Jakarta buildings along this street. The Candra Naya, at No 188, was once the home of the Chinese 'Captain' employed by the Dutch to manage the affairs of Batavia's Chinese community. Since 1946 the building has housed the offices of a social work society but you may be able to have a short wander inside. Further south at No 111, the National Archives building dates from 1760 and was formerly the country-house of Governor-General Reinier de Klerk.

Taman Impian Jaya Ancol

Along the bayfront between Kota and Tanjung Priok, the people's 'Dreamland' is built on land reclaimed in 1962. This huge landscaped recreation park, providing non-stop entertainment, has hotels, nightclubs, theatres and a wide variety of sporting facilities.

Ancol's prime attractions include the Pasar Seni art market (see Things to Buy), its many sidewalk cafes and a gallery where there are often interesting exhibitions of modern Indonesian art and photography. Near Pasar Seni there's an oceanarium (Gelanggang Samudra) and an amazing swimming pool complex, including a wave pool and slide pool (Gelanggang Renang). Jakarta's sports hall for *jai alai*, said to be the 'fastest ball game in the world', is also within the park and matches can be seen at 7 pm every evening. The Ancol beach, so close to the city, is hardly likely to be a pleasant place to swim but you can take a boat from the Marina here for day trips to some of Jakarta's Pulau Seribu islands.

The latest addition to Jaya Ancol is Dunia Fantasi or 'Fantasy Land', a Disneyland type of park that's great for kids. It's open daily, from Monday to Friday from 2 pm to 9 pm, 2 pm to 10 pm Saturday and 10 am to 9 pm Sundays and holidays. The basic entry fee for Fantasy Land is 600 rp from Monday to Friday, 800 rp Saturday, 1200 rp Sundays and holidays, plus additional fees for the five classes of rides ranging from 500 rp to 2000 rp or 4500 rp for an unlimited ride pass.

Basic admission to Ancol is 550 rp Monday to Thursday, 650 rp Friday and Saturday, 700 rp Sundays and holidays. Pasar Seni is open from 9 am to 10 pm daily, the swimming pool complex from 7 am to 9 pm daily. It costs an additional 1500 rp to use the pools from Monday to Thursday, 2000 rp Friday and Saturday, and 2500 rp Sunday and holidays. Admission into the oceanarium is 500 rp Monday to Thursday, 600 rp other days. Children's rates for all Jaya Ancol attractions cost less than half the adult admission. Apart from being more expensive the park can be very crowded on weekends, but on weekdays it's fairly quiet and a great place to escape from the hassles of the city. From the Kota bus station you can get there on a No 64 or 65 bus or a M15 minibus. For more information, call 681511 in Jakarta.

National Monument (Monas)

This 132-metre high column towering over Merdeka Square is both Jakarta's

Monas – National Monument

The monument is open daily from 9 am to 5 pm. It costs 1500 rp (500 rp for students) to go to the top of Monas and queues can be lengthy – tourists on weekends, schoolkids on weekdays. If you want to avoid hanging around it's probably best to go early. There's an additional 300 rp (100 rp for students) entry fee to the museum which, according to one traveller, is 'so atrocious it shouldn't be missed' though another visitor felt it did 'give a fair description of Indonesian history'. Unless you've got nothing better to do, you wouldn't be missing much if you skipped it.

Indonesian National Museum

On the west side of Merdeka Square, the National Museum was built in 1862. It is probably the best museum in Indonesia and one of the best in South-East Asia. Its collection includes a huge ethnic map of Indonesia and an equally big relief map on which you can pick out all those volcanoes you have climbed. It has an enormous collection of cultural objects of the various ethnic groups – costumes, musical instruments, model houses and so on – and numerous fine bronzes from the Hindu-Javanese period and many interesting stone pieces salvaged from Central Javanese and other temples. There's also a superb display of Chinese ceramics dating back to the Han dynasty (300 BC-220 AD) which was almost entirely amassed in Indonesia.

Just outside the museum there is a bronze elephant which was presented by the King of Thailand in 1871, after which the museum building is popularly known as the Gedung Gajah or Elephant House. As in most museums throughout Indonesia, exhibit labels are either absent or in Indonesian only, so unless you're an art historian or can read Bahasa Indonesia you'll occasionally be left guessing.

The museum is open from 8.30 am to 2.30 pm Tuesday to Thursday, to 11 am Friday, to 1.30 pm Saturday, and until 2.30 pm Sunday. It's closed on Mondays.

principal landmark and the most famous architectural extravagance of Sukarno. Commenced in 1961, the monument was not completed until 1975 when it was officially opened by Suharto. Architecturally it is pretty much a phallic symbol topped by a glittering flame symbolising the nation's independence and strength (and, some would argue, Sukarno's virility). It is constructed 'entirely of Italian marbles' according to a tourist brochure and the flame is gilded with 35 kg of gold leaf. In the base of Monas there is a museum with a series of dioramas giving a rundown of Indonesia's history and there is a fine view from the top-yard of the column. Close to the monument's entrance on the square's northern side is a statue of the freedom fighter, Prince Diponegoro, astride his horse. During the annual Jakarta Fair, the entrance shifts to the north-east side of the monument.

The entry fee is 200 rp for adults, 100 rp for children. It's well worth a visit, for here you will find some reminder of almost anywhere you have been in Indonesia. On Tuesdays and Thursdays there are useful guided tours (free) at 9.30 am. Gamelan performances are held every Sunday between 9.30 and 10.30 am. On Sundays the museum also opens its 'treasure' room of gold and silver.

Istiqlal Mosque
On the north-eastern corner of Merdeka Square is Jakarta's principal place of Muslim worship. Recently completed, the modernistic Istiqlal mosque is reputedly the largest in South-East Asia.

All Saints Anglican Church
Due south-east of Merdeka Square, across from the Hyatt Arduta Hotel, this is probably the oldest remaining British institution in Indonesia. The origins of this church date back to the more humble beginnings of the London Missionary Society which constructed a small bamboo chapel here in 1822. The present building was constructed on the same site in 1829 and there are still some interesting old tombstones in its graveyard. The hand-painted windows of the church were taken from the WW II Prisoner of War Camp Chapel in Tanjung Priok.

Other Museums
Jakarta has a number of other museums apart from the excellent National Museum and those in old Batavia. To the north-west of the National Museum is the Taman Prasati Museum or Park of Inscription on Jalan Tanah Abang. This was once called the Kebon Jahe Cemetery and a number of important figures of the colonial era are buried here including Olivia Raffles, wife of British Governor-General Sir Stamford Raffles, who died in 1814. The cemetery is open from 8 am to 3 pm Monday to Thursday, to 11 am Friday, and until 6 pm Saturday. It's closed Sundays and holidays.

The Textile Museum is housed in a Dutch colonial house on Jalan Satsuit Tubun 4, near the Tanah Abang district bus station. It has a large collection of batiks and woven cloth from all over Indonesia, as well as looms and batik-making tools, and it's well worth a visit. This museum is open from 9 am daily, except Monday, until 2 pm Tuesday to Thursday, 11 am Friday, 1 pm Saturday and 3 pm Sunday. Admission is 150 rp.

The Abri Satriamandala Army Museum, on Jalan Gatot Subroto, has an enormous display of weapons and endless dioramas glorifying the Indonesian Armed Forces in their battles for independence. It's open from 9 am to 4 pm daily except Monday and admission is 250 rp.

If you're a stamp collector, you might want to check out the Stamp Museum at Taman Mini. Not only is there a historical exhibition of Indonesian stamps, but also dioramas depicting the designing/printing of stamps, as well as the homey satisfactions of philatelics. The Stamp Museum (Musium Prangko) is open daily from 8 am until 4 pm Monday to Saturday, until 3 pm Sundays and holidays.

Other Sukarno Monuments
Inspired tastelessness best describes the plentiful supply of statues Sukarno left to Jakarta – in the Russian 'heroes of socialism' style. All of them have acquired descriptive nicknames including the gentleman at Kebayoran, holding the flaming dish, who is known as 'the mad waiter'. There's also the Statue of Welcome – Hansel and Gretel – which was built by Sukarno as a symbol of Indonesian friendliness for the 1962 Asian Games held in Jakarta.

Gedung Perintis Kemerdekaan – Jalan Proklamasi
Independence was proclaimed on the site of the former home of Sukarno at Jalan Proklamasi 56 in Menteng and there is a monument to President Sukarno and Vice-President Hatta here.

Taman Ismail Marzuki

On Jalan Cikini Raya, not far from Jalan Jaksa, the TIM (tel 322606) is Jakarta's cultural showcase. There is a performance almost every night and here you might see anything from Balinese dancing to poetry readings, gamelan concerts to overseas jazz groups, an Indonesian PKI film to a New Zealand film festival! The TIM monthly programme is available from the tourist office, the TIM office and major hotels, and events are also listed in the Jakarta Daily Post.

There are also two art galleries within the compound – the Gallery Graphics and the Cipta Art Gallery which exhibit contemporary Indonesian art. Both galleries are open from 9 am to 1 pm and 5 to 9 pm Monday to Saturday. Jakarta's Planetarium is also here but shows are generally given in Indonesian. For information about shows in English you can phone 337530. The whole complex is open from morning till midnight and there are good outdoor cafes here, so it can be a useful place. The No 34 bus from Jalan Thamrin stops nearby.

Zoo

Jakarta's Ragunan Zoo is about 10 km south of the city centre in the Pasar Minggu area. The zoo has komodo dragons, orang-utans and other interesting Indonesian wildlife and it's open daily from 9 am to 6 pm. Admission is 500 rp weekdays, 600 rp weekends and holidays, half for children.

Taman Mini Indonesia Indah

In the south-east of the city, past Cililitan, Taman Mini is another of those 'whole country in one park' collections which every South-East Asian country seems to be acquiring. The idea behind the park was conceived by Mme Tien Suharto in 1971, the families inhabiting the land were cleared out to make way for the project (then estimated to cost the awesome total of US$26 million) and the park was duly opened in 1975.

This 100-hectare park has 27 full-scale traditional houses from the 27 provinces of Indonesia with displays of regional handicrafts and clothing; and a large 'lagoon' where you can row around the islands of the archipelago or take a cable car across for a bird's eye view. There are also museums, theatres, restaurants, an orchid garden and a bird park with a huge walk-in aviary. There's even a mini Borobudur. The 'Indonesia Indah' is a three-dimensional screen show of the Indonesian panorama which takes place at the Keong Mas (Golden Snail) Theatre. In 30 minutes the film packs a lot in but it's special effects all the way – there's no subtlety about it at all! Admission is 1000 rp and there are showings at noon, 2 and 4 pm Monday to Friday, and every hour between 11 am and 5 pm on Saturday and Sunday.

You can walk or drive your own car around Taman Mini. Or you can go by horse and cart or take the mini train service that shuttles around the park dropping people off and picking them up. The park is open from 8 am to 5 pm daily, the houses and Museum Indonesia from 9 am to 4 pm. Admission is 600 rp (children 300 rp, cars 500 rp) and the train service costs an additional 150 rp, horse and cart 300 rp. The park is quite good value and of course Indonesians will tell you that if you see this there's no need to go anywhere else in the country! On Sunday mornings there are free cultural performances in most regional houses from 10 am to 2 pm. For other cultural events here, check the Taman Mini monthly programme which is available from the Tourist Office.

Taman Mini is about 10 km from the centre so you need to allow about 1½ hours to get out there and then about three hours to look round. From Jalan Thamrin you can take a No 408 or a P11 bus to Cililitan and from there a T55 metro-mini to the park entrance. For additional information call 801905 in Jakarta.

Lubang Buaya

There is a memorial to the six generals and the army officer killed here by the Communists in 1965, called Pancasila Cakti, a few km east from Taman Mini. 'Lubang Buaya' means 'Crocodile Hole'.

Other Attractions

Jakarta has a number of gardens specialising in cultivating orchids and the Indonesian Permai Orchid Gardens in Slipi, near the Grogol bus station, is the best place to see them. There are 35,000 square metres of orchids, open from 9 am to 5 pm daily. There's also the Taman Anggrek Ragunan orchid gardens near the zoo.

Taman Buaya Pluit is a crocodile farm with about 500 of the friendly beasts. It's located at Jalan Bandengan Utara 27, to the north-west of Kota. The Pasar Burung, on Jalan Pramuka in Jatinegara, is Jakarta's market for captive birds from all over Indonesia.

The Bharata Theatre is on Jalan Kalilio near the Pasar Senen bus station. There are wayang orang performances from 8.15 pm to midnight every evening, except Monday and Thursday when there are ketoprak (popular comedy) performances. Tickets cost from 1500 rp. Wayang kulit/ golek puppet shows are held outdoors in the Jakarta Fair area every second Saturday of the month during the Jakarta Fair in late June and July. These all-night performances start around 9 pm and admission is usually less than 500 rp.

Tours

Numerous travel agents offer daily tours of Jakarta but they tend to be expensive. Information on many of them is available from the Tourist Office and major hotels. They include Vayatour (tel 380-0202), Nitour (tel 346347) and Setia Tours (tel 639-0008). All tour buses pick up from the major hotels, and tour prices and sights are very similar. A four-hour morning city tour, for example, costs about US$8 and, starting at 9 am, includes the Central Museum, National Monument, Sunda Kelapa and a batik factory or a trip to Taman Mini.

There are also a variety of tours to nearby towns in West Java which basically go to Bogor, the Puncak and Tangkuban Prahu volcano near Bandung. A five-hour tour to the Bogor Botanical Gardens and zoological museum costs US$20 including lunch; to the Puncak US$30. The Setia day tour to Tangkuban Prahu and Ciater hot springs starts at 6.30 am and costs US$60 including a round-trip air ticket with Garuda and lunch.

Places to Stay – bottom end

Jalan Jaksa Area Jakarta's cheap accommodation centre is Jalan Jaksa, a small street centrally located in the newer part of Jakarta and just south of that useful landmark, the Monas Monument. It runs between Jalan Kebon Sirih and Jalan Wahid Hasyim, a few blocks over from Jakarta's main drag – Jalan Thamrin – and about 10 to 15 minutes walk from Gambir railway station.

The Wisma Delima, Jalan Jaksa 5, has been Jakarta's most popular resting place for so long that simply asking for 'Jalan Jaksa' will probably get you here. There are both pros and cons to staying at Wisma Delima. It is small and they've certainly converted every available inch into room space, so rooms are rather cramped and stuffy, but otherwise it's OK and it is the cheapest place on Jalan Jaksa. The Lawalata family who run Wisma Delima remain unfailingly helpful and calm in the face of non-stop demand for space. Despite the pressure, it's a friendly place and a good contact point. The only problem is that it is very often full. There are two dormitories with fans and beds cost 2000 rp (or 1750 rp with a YHA card). Singles cost 4000 rp and there are doubles at 5000/6000 rp. Food, cold drinks and cheap beer are available – good value for Jakarta.

If you don't have any luck here or don't like the place, there is an increasing number of good alternatives springing up along or close to Jalan Jaksa. *Norbeck Hostel* (tel 330392), Jalan Jaksa 14, is very popular of late, probably because of its high visibility and cosy garden in front. They have dorm beds for 6000 rp and rooms at 8000 rp or 11,000 rp with air-con. Food is available.

At No 27 is another old and popular standby, *Djody Hostel*. Beds in dormitories cost 3000 rp, rather airless rooms cost 7000 to 9000 rp. There are open sitting areas at front and back, it's clean and there are good showers and toilets. Mosquitoes can be a problem, but mosquito nets are provided. Like most places on Jalan Jaksa, what it lacks most is ventilation. Further down on the same side of the street at No 35 is the slightly more upscale *Djody Hotel*, with fan-cooled rooms from 8,000 rp and a couple of air-con rooms for 20,000 rp. The staff at both Djody locations are friendly and helpful.

At No 35 on Kebon Sirih Barat Dalam, a small lane running west off Jalan Jaksa, is the *Borneo Hostel* (tel 320095). It has a fan-cooled dormitory with beds at 2000 rp, rooms at 6000 rp and 8000 rp or 10,000 rp for a room with attached shower. Kitchen facilities and a fridge are available. Some people think it 'looks cleaner and not so stuffy' as the Wisma Delima and it's a useful addition to the cheap hotel scene. Others insist that it's unfriendly and expensive. At No 1 on the same lane the *Family Homestay* (tel 335917), formerly Wim Homestay, is a large family home with fairly basic rooms for guests and the couple who run it are very friendly. Singles/doubles cost 3500/5000 rp and cheap breakfasts are available. You can also have the use of the kitchen (but heed the sign barring frogs!), there's a small patio garden and a balcony upstairs.

On Gang 1, Jalan Kebon Sirih Timur Dalam (east off Jalan Jaksa) there are two other popular places. The *Bloem Steen* at No 173 is an attractive bungalow with several rooms. It's often full but is good value with rooms at 5000 and 8000 rp, good

showers and a fine garden terrace. Drinks, breakfast and other meals are available at reasonable prices. Next door, the *Kresna* at No 175 has good, clean doubles with fan for 7000 rp or 9000 rp with bath. Highly recommended by a 'long-term stayer'.

If you walk to the south end of Jalan Jaksa, turn right on Jalan Wahid Hasyim and cross Jalan Thamrin, you'll eventually come to the *Wisma ISE Guest House* (tel 333463) at No 168, right side of the street. It looks plain, but is good value for Jakarta with clean singles/doubles at 5500/8800 rp and you can get breakfast for 1000 rp. The management is very friendly and there's a pleasant balcony/bar on the top floor where you can look out over quite a bit of Jakarta. There are always some Indonesians staying at Wisma ISE since it serves as the Jakarta mess for Telecom workers from Bandung – it's a good place to practise Bahasa Indonesia.

Several readers wrote to recommend *Celebes House*, at Jalan Menteng 35, not far from Jalan Jaksa and within walking distance of Gambir station. Clean and spacious single rooms are 6000 rp, while doubles start at 8000 rp. Reasonably priced meals are available.

For price, the *Bali International Hotel* at Jalan Wahid Hasyim 116, (next to the sleazy Pink Panther disco) might fit into the upper bottom end at 16,000 rp per room, except that conditions here are too atrocious for even the most hardened bottom-end traveller. Don't bother going in – they'll give you a room but you'd be just about the only person spending the night since its primary function is as a business location for the hookers from the Pink Panther.

Places to Stay – middle

There are a number of middle-bracket hotels in the Jalan Jaksa area. The *Hotel Karya* (tel 320484) at Jalan Jaksa 32-34 has rather dismal economy rooms with fan and bathroom for 14,000 rp. Slightly better rooms are available at 18,000/21,000 rp for singles/doubles or 22,000/25,000 rp with air-con and hot water. Rates include a rather basic toast-and-jam breakfast. Also close to Jalan Jaksa, but more expensive, is the *Hotel Wisma Indra* (tel 334556) at Jalan Wahid Hasyim 63. It's a small and spotlessly clean place with attractively decorated rooms. Prices for air-con singles/doubles with attached bath (showers and hot water) start at US$18/22 including breakfast. These rates do not include tax and service charges. The hotel has its own bar and a restaurant with 'continental and oriental' cuisine, and there's a laundry service.

The larger *Sabang Metropolitan Hotel* (tel 373933), Jalan H A Salim 11, is also good value for this price bracket with air-con rooms from US$22 (plus 15% tax and service). The hotel has a not-so-special swimming pool and coffee shop, but the service is fair and it's in a good location. A 15% discount is usually available for the asking.

Moving to the Menteng area, south of Jalan Thamrin and close to the TIM cultural centre, is a small three-hotel chain representing good mid-range value. *Hotel Menteng I* (tel 357635) is at Jalan Gondangdia Lama 28, the *Hotel Menteng II* (tel 325543) is at Jalan Cikini Raya 105 and the *Grand Menteng* (tel 882153) is a bit further south on the next avenue to the east, at Jalan Matraman Raya 21. All three offer air-con rooms with private bathrooms and hot water, piped muzak, coffee shop, bar and swimming pool. The Grand Menteng also has a modest fitness centre. Prices start at US$15 for an economy room and there are standard singles/doubles from US$18/22 (plus 15% tax & service). The *Marcopolo Hotel* (tel 325409), at Jalan T Cik Ditiro 19, has air-con rooms with bathroom at 29,000 rp (hot water in the morning and evening). The hotel has a swimming pool, nightclub, bar and restaurants serving Indonesian, Chinese and European food.

Also in the Menteng area is a family-run losmen recommended by a Dutch reader. *Losmen Luhandydan* (tel 371865),

Jalan Sawo 15, has four double rooms with fan and attached mandi and toilet for 15,000 rp per person including breakfast. The proprietors are friendly and they speak Dutch and English. The house has a pleasant garden and good lunches and dinners are available at 2500 rp each.

Places to Stay – top end

Most of the 'international-class' hotels are in the city centre, on or around the main boulevard of Jalan Thamrin. The *Hotel Indonesia*, built for the Asian Games which Jakarta hosted in 1962, heralded a new era for hotel development in Indonesia – at 14 storeys it was the first 'skyscraper' in the archipelago and it was to be the largest, most modern hotel in South-East Asia. A number of luxury hotels with superb facilities followed, spurred on in part by the boom that brought troupes of business travellers to the capital. The economic recession, however, seems to have put a stop to this frenetic building and perhaps due to lack of competition, prices for Jakarta's luxury hotels are staggeringly steep. Rates quoted below are before a 10% to 15% 'luxury tax' and a 5% to 10% 'service charge'. Special weekend rates are generally for Indonesian residents only but better rates are often available through travel agents. You can also try asking for a discount at the reception desk – this often nets an immediate 10% to 20% discount. Some of the more important hotels include:

Borobudur Intercontinental Hotel (tel 374967) is on Jalan Lapangan Banteng Selatan, between Merdeka Square and Pasar Senen. It is Jakarta's biggest hotel and offers everything from a health club, an olympic-size swimming pool, a jogging track, tennis and squash courts to restaurants and full air-con. Singles cost US$110, doubles US$120 and up.
Hyatt Aryaduta Jakarta (tel 363202) is central at Jalan Prapatan 44/46. Singles/doubles cost from US$100.
Hotel Indonesia (tel 320008) is on the Statue of Welcome roundabout, Jalan Thamrin. Major

renovations in 1985 resulted in renewed splendour and higher rates. It has restaurants, a bar and an olympic-size swimming pool. Singles cost from US$90 and doubles from US$100.

Jakarta Hilton (tel 583051) at Jalan Jenderal Gatot Subroto, on the outskirts of Kebayoran Baru, is the latest luxury hotel. It has large grounds, an attractive shopping bazaar, and is generally considered to have the best facilities and decor. Singles/doubles cost from US$110/125.

Jakarta Mandarin (tel 321307), across from the Hotel Indonesia on Jalan Thamrin, has all the usual luxuries and services, a swimming pool and health centre but no grounds. It rivals the Borobudur Intercontinental for swank. Singles/doubles cost from US$120/130.

President Hotel (tel 320508) is at Jalan Thamrin 59. It's a smaller and rather more old-fashioned looking hotel with no sports facilities. It was recently taken over by the Nikko chain – most of the guests are Japanese businessmen. Singles/doubles cost from US$67/81.

Sahid Jaya Hotel (tel 581220) is at Jalan Jenderal Sudirman 86, midway between Jalan Thamrin and the Hilton. A big hotel with restaurants and a coffee shop, also owned by Nikko. Singles cost from US$85 and doubles from US$95.

Hotel Sari Pacific (tel 323707) is conveniently located about midway down Jalan Thamrin at number 6. It's popular for good service and good food and there's a disco and large swimming pool. Singles cost from US$110, doubles from US$120.

Places to Eat

Jakarta probably has the best selection of restaurants of any major Indonesian city, although a meal in a better class restaurant tends to be expensive. Plenty of street hawkers and night markets cater for cheaper meals.

Jalan Jaksa Area There are plenty of places to eat around the Jalan Jaksa area. Meals at some of Jalan Jaksa's losmen are among the best deals going, but there's also *Angies* at Jalan Jaksa 16. A small cafe with a few tables in the front garden and more inside, it's popular for its cheap western breakfasts and fruit salads. Standard Indonesian dishes are also

cheap, 750 rp for basic nasi or mie goreng.

Nick's Cafe at Jalan Jaksa 16, near Norbeck Hostel, serves good reasonably priced food in a pleasant fan-cooled room. Most dishes are from 1000 to 1500 rp. Further south on Jalan Jaksa on the same side of the street is *Pondok Gorontalo*, which specialises in north Indian dishes and Sulawesi-style *ikan bakar*. The Indian food is good but perhaps a tad over-priced for this area – by the time you've put together a decent meal you'll have spent well over 3000 rp.

There are cheap Indonesian warungs at either end of Jalan Jaksa, but be a little wary about cleanliness if you've just arrived and are not used to the local food standards. The alley between and parallel to Jalan Jaksa and Jalan H A Salim has a number of warungs as well.

Out on Jalan Kebon Sirih, to the north of Jalan Jaksa, there are several eating possibilities. On the corner of Jalan Jaksa and Jalan Kebon Sirih, the *Senayan Satay House* is more expensive than anything on Jalan Jaksa but good value. It has a varied menu including seafood, noodles and particularly good sate. Most dishes cost from 2000 to 3000 rp, it's comfortably air-conditioned and mainly patronised by expats and middle-class Chinese Indonesians.

At Jalan Kebon Sirih 63, back towards Jalan Thamrin, you'll find *Puja Sera 4*, a large hangar-like building set up as a hawkers centre. Choose from a variety of different stalls serving Chinese, Sundanese, Central and East Javanese, and Makassar cuisines, as well as fresh fruit juices and beer. Food here is not dirt cheap but it's not expensive either and this is a good place if you like to sample more than one type of Indonesian cuisine at the same time. More or less across the street from Puja Sera 4 is an air-conditioned north Indian restaurant called *Maharajah* with a medium-priced menu. On the floor above the Maharajah is *Ikan Bakar Kebon Sirih*, which specialises in the very popular Sulawesi dish *ikan bakar khas makassar*, Makassar-style roast fish curry. On the south-east corner of Jalan Kebon Sirih and Jalan H A Salim is *Salero Bagindo*, a popular air-conditioned place with Padang food.

There is a string of restaurants along both sides of Jalan H A Salim, just a block over towards Jalan Thamrin. The shiny *Sakura Anpan*, a Japanese bakery at No 25/27, is a good, reasonably priced place for a quick snack, cold drink or ice cream. The popular *Natrabu Restaurant* specialises in Padang/Minang food or there's the *Budi Bundo* which is cheaper and also good. *Lim Thiam Kie* at No 53 has excellent Chinese food and most dishes average around 2500 rp. Down a little alley next to the A&W is the *Paradiso 2001*, an interesting little vegetarian restaurant with good food and a claim that they're 'a restaurant for men of the future'. Women and children of the future can eat there too.

Jalan H A Salim was once known as Jalan Sabang and is still often called Sabang by locals. Throughout Java, Jalan Sabang is known as the sate capital of Indonesia because there are so many traditional food trolleys (*gerobak makanan* in Indonesian) hawking sate on this street. On a good night you may see as many as a hundred of them and the pungent smoke from their charcoal braziers will fill the street. It's ironic then, that in spite of all the delicious sate ayam cooking away right there at the curb, at least two different fast food chicken places have opened their glass doors on Jalan Salim. Take your pick of *El Pollo Loco* at the corner of Salim and Jalan Wahid Hasyim, or *Kentucky Fried Chicken* next door to Natrabu. Other western-style fast food joints have popped up here: *A&W* (burgers from 1500 to 3000 rp) across from Kentucky Fried and *Kim's Hamburgers* on the other side of A&W.

The *Jakarta Cafeteria*, in the Jakarta Theatre Building with the tourist office, is not bad for a coffee or cold drink while you read all that tourist info you've just picked up. In the same building, but downstairs, there's the small *Restaurant Asri* which is clean, air-conditioned, has crisp white cloths on the tables and good service. It has an Indonesian and western menu including sandwiches, salads (2500 rp) and steak (7000 rp). The *Green Pub* has Mexican food and a happy hour from 3 to 6 pm with half-price drinks. There is also a small take-away place next door with reasonably priced Padang food. *Golden Truly* is a large supermarket with western foods upstairs behind the Jakarta Theatre.

Across the road, the *Sarinah Department Store* has an excellent, if fairly expensive, bakery and snack counter – their *tahu Jakarta* is a tasty snack filled with spiced vegetables for a few hundred rupiah.

The *Indah Kuring*, at Jalan Wahid Hasyim 131A near Wisma ISE, specialises in Javanese and Sundanese seafood. Service is good and it has a nice ambience for Jakarta. Two can eat here for about 7000 rp not including drinks. Opposite Wisma ISE is a similar seafood place called *Seafood Raturia*.

The well-known and very popular *Bakmi Gajah Mada* has a branch in the Studio 21 Theatre complex on Jalan Thamrin. They have an extensive menu of Chinese noodle and rice dishes starting at 2000 rp for an excellent bakmi goreng. If you plan to come for lunch, you may have to wait for a table as it can get very crowded.

Elsewhere Away from the Jalan Jaksa hotel enclave, along Jalan Gajah Mada there are numerous restaurants, bakeries, fast-food and ice cream parlours. The original *Bakmi Gajah Mada* noodle house is at Jalan Gajah Mada 92. If you just want a snack or a cheap drink and somewhere cool to drink it, try the air-conditioned Gajah Mada Plaza shopping centre. There are very good milkshakes, sundaes and superb ice cream flavours (a bit expensive at 1500 rp) at the American *Swensen's*. Chinese eating places abound in Glodok but this area really comes to life at night at which time it's best to get there by taxi.

The Blok M shopping centre in Kebayoran, around the Aldiron Plaza and Kebayoran market, has a wide variety of places to eat. There's a second *Swensen's* branch on Jalan Melawai Raya 16 and, above the ice cream parlour, there's a canteen serving cheap Indonesian 'fast foods'. The modern *Restaurant Melawai*, Jalan Melawai 1/92, is clean and has a wide variety of Indonesian dishes from 1500 rp to 10,000 rp. There's yet another *Bakmi Gajah Mada* noodle house at Jalan Melawai IV/No 25 and the *Ratu Bahari* has good Chinese seafood at reasonable prices. Other places include the English-style *King's Head* pub and *Rugantino's*, Jalan Melawai Raya 28, for good Italian food.

The Markets Lots of stalls set up around the central area of the city, as well as in Old Jakarta. Jalan Kebon Sirih and Jalan Wahid Hasyim have a collection of food stalls but some of them look remarkably dirty. After dark the parking lot behind Sarinah turns into *Selara Nusantara*, a kind of Singapore food centre where you can eat from any stall you choose and take a seat at any one of the tables scattered amongst them. It's fairly tame but there's plenty of choice and it is reasonably cheap – sate 1800 rp, fish 1500 rp, nasi gudeg 1250 rp, fruit juices 750 rp and beer (large bottle) 1800 rp.

If you go west along Jalan Wahid Hasyim from Wisma ISE towards the Tanah Abang bus terminal, you'll come to a good collection of cheap and very popular night warungs.

Jakarta is well known for good seafood and the lively Chinese-seafood night market on *Jalan Pecanongan* is excellent. Prices tend to be a bit higher though – a good meal for two (fish, rice and beer) might cost 5000 rp. Jalan Pecanongan is directly north of the Monas monument, about a three-km walk from Jalan Jaksa. Stalls start setting up here around 5 pm.

During the Jakarta Fair in June and July there are many other stalls operating in Merdeka Square.

There's also the *Pasar Boplo* night market, north of the main post office. *Jalan Mangga Besar*, off Jalan Hayam Wuruk in northern Jakarta, is a good night market area for Chinese, Indian and Padang food. *Pasar Senen* shopping centre, a km east of Merdeka Square, has a wide selection of food stalls – but only during daytime. This is a particularly busy area for pickpockets, so take care.

South of the Hotel Indonesia roundabout, there's a string of interesting stalls including a good Korean barbecue along Jalan Kendal – if you walk south past the massage parlours on Jalan Blora, you turn left (where the transvestites hang out) along Jalan Kendal which runs parallel to the railway line. At Blok M, Kebayoran, the *Pasar Kaget* is a night market run by people from Central and East Java.

More Expensive Restaurants
Many of Jakarta's ritzy hotels, including the *Sari Pacific*, offer a rijstaffel buffet 'special' for around 6500 rp. The President Hotel has a range of restaurants that mostly cater to Japanese tastes for steak and seafood. There's also a good pastry shop here and the views from the *Cocktail Bar* on the 30th floor of the adjacent Nusantara Building are superb.

The *Omar Khayam* (tel 356719) at Jalan Antara 5-7, near the post office, is reputed to have excellent Indian curries and they also do a special all-you-can-eat lunch buffet .

Jakarta has a particularly good selection of Chinese seafood restaurants and some say the *Jun Njan*, Jalan Batu Ceper 69 at the north end of Jalan Pecanongan, has the best seafood in Indonesia. It has a small menu, with most dishes from 4000 to 6000 rp, but we'd recommend it as an excellent place for a splurge. Try the fried squid in oyster sauce or fried prawns in butter sauce. They also have a branch in south Jakarta at Jalan Panglima Polim

Raya 77. The Jun Njan is closed on Mondays.

South along Jalan Thamrin the *Vic's Viking Restaurant*, between Hotel Indonesia and Hotel Kartika Plaza, has an 80-dish smorgasbord (European, Chinese and Indonesian) which costs 6000 rp for all you can eat – traveller opinions are divided as to whether it's really good value or not. It's open from 11 am to 3 pm and 5 to 11 pm. In the same area, the *George & Dragon Pub* on Jalan Teluk Betung has English-style pub food. You can even indulge yourself in sausage & mash there! A couple of doors down, the *Korea House* has good Korean barbecue food.

The historic *Oasis Bar & Restaurant* (tel 327818) on Jalan Raden Saleh 47 is housed in a large, old, Dutch villa and has the feel of an extravagant 1930s Hollywood film set with prices to match – more than a dozen waitresses serve up a traditional rijstaffel (25,000 rp!), while you are serenaded by a group of Batak singers from Sumatra. It's closed on Sundays.

Entertainment
Jakarta's cheapest entertainment is to walk to the *Taman Ria* at Merdeka Square. It's open daily from 5 pm to midnight and admission is 500 rp. The fairground lights up, the merry-go-round turns but few people visit so take your own crowd. There are local pop-bands and singers but it's more lively on Saturdays. The annual Jakarta Fair is held here.

Air Mancur Menari, on the western side of Monas, is the dancing fountain – coloured lamps produce movements, depending on the music, from 7 to 10 pm. There's an image of a naked woman in the flame from the north side.

The bar at the Hotel Indonesia has a happy hour from 6 to 8 pm with half-price drinks and free hors d'oeuvres. The Hyatt has the same with live chamber music from 7 to 9 pm. The *Tavern Pub* at the Hyatt has live music nightly featuring local bands like Galactic Band, The Big Kids and the Syncopators. The *Pitstop* at

the Sari Pacific Hotel is a popular discotheque for locals and visitors alike. The *Jaya Pub* in the Jaya building at Jalan Thamrin 12 has live pub music most nights.

The best cinema house in Jakarta is the relatively new *Studio Twenty-One* on Jalan Thamrin, four buildings south of the Sarinah Department Store. The *Jakarta Theatre* is showing its age and has a visible population of rats.

Things to Buy
Good buys in Jakarta include batik and antiques but probably the most important thing about Jakarta is that you can find things from almost anywhere in Indonesia. If this is your first stop, it's a good place to get an overall view of Indonesian crafts and, if it's your last stop, then it's always a last chance to find something that you missed elsewhere in the country.

A good place to start is the Sarinah Department Store on Jalan Thamrin. The 4th floor of this large building is devoted to batik and another to handicrafts from all over the country. It's a little variable – you might find some areas poorly represented – but items are generally good quality and reasonably priced. The batik floor is divided into different concessions sponsored by the big batik manufacturers like Batik Keris and Batik Danar Hadi. Check the basement for bargains. The Pasar Seni at Ancol Recreation Park is an excellent place to look for regional handicrafts and to see many of them actually being made. Whether it's woodcarvings, paintings, puppets, leather, batik or silver you'll find it all here. The Indonesian Bazaar is another craft market but this is an extension of the Hilton Hotel Shopping Arcade so it's likely to be expensive.

In Menteng, Jalan Surabaya is Jakarta's famous fleamarket. Here you'll find jewellery, batik, oddities like old typewriters and many (sometimes instant) antiques. It attracts a lot of tourists these days but it's worth a visit. Either early morning or late afternoon would probably be best, when they want to make last sales and go home. There are many other shops for antiques and curios along Jalan Kebon Sirih Timur Dalam and Jalan H A Salim, both in the Jalan Jaksa area. The Duta Suara shop on Jalan H A Salim has a good range of Western and Indonesian tapes at around 4000 rp each. Pirate tapes have been available in Indonesia despite the 1 June 1988 law to enforce international music copyright.

Getting There & Away

Jakarta is the main international gateway to Indonesia and for details on arriving from overseas see the introductory Getting There section at the start of the Java chapter. Travel agencies worth trying for discounted airfares on international flights out of Jakarta are listed under the information section.

Jakarta is also a major centre for domestic travel with extensive bus, rail, air and sea connections.

Air International and domestic flights now both operate from the new Sukarno-Hatta International Airport. Airport tax is 9000 rp on international departures, 2000 rp on domestic flights. The domestic tax may already be included in the ticket. Domestic airlines in Jakarta are:

Garuda (tel 334425), BDN Building, Jalan Thamrin 5. Open 8 am to 12.30 pm and 1.30 to 4 pm Monday to Friday; 8 am to 1 pm Saturday; 9 am until 1 pm Sundays and holidays. Garuda also has offices in the Hotel Indonesia and Borobudur Intercontinental Hotel. Garuda flights depart from Jakarta to all the main cities in Java and to places all over the archipelago.

Bouraq (tel 6295150), Jalan Angkasa 1, Kemayoran. Open 8 am to 4 pm daily.

Mandala (tel 368107), Jalan Veteran I No 34. Open 8 am to 4 pm Monday to Friday; 8 am to 1 pm Saturday; 9 am until 1 pm Sunday.

Merpati (tel 413608), Jalan Angkasa 2, Kemayoran. Open 7 am to 4 pm Monday to Friday; 7 am to 2 pm Saturday; 8 am until 1 pm Sundays and holidays.

Sempati (tel 348760), Jalan Merdeka Timur 7, charter their planes out to other companies. Most travel agents can book Sempati including Bhayangkara Travel at Jalan Kebon Sirih 23. Sempati flies to Tanjung Pinang, Pontianak, Kalimantan, and Bangka Island, near Sumatra (daily, 47,600 rp).

There are a number of travel agents in the Pasar Baru district which offer discounted airfares on domestic flights (Merpati and Mandala flights in particular) and for flights to Nusa Tenggara, Sulawesi, Sumatra and Bali you can get as much as 25% discount. The Mitra Kercana Tour & Travel Service (tel 349699, 361366) at Jalan Pintu Air 20A, near the Pelni office, is one.

Bus Jakarta has three major bus stations. They are in the outer suburbs but are linked by city bus to the various district bus stations in central Jakarta. The bus stations are:

Kalideres Buses to the west go from the Kalideres Station which is several km to the north-west of Merdeka Square. Buses to Merak, via Serang, depart roughly every 10 minutes and there are frequent buses to Labuhan and Carita.

Cililitan Buses depart from Cililitan to areas south of Jakarta. Popular buses include Bogor 600 rp (30 to 45 minutes), Puncak, Bandung 2000 rp (4½ hours) and Banjar 3000 rp (nine hours).

Pulo Gadung This is the station for buses to destinations east. Both public and private night buses operate from here. There are frequent services daily to Cirebon.

From Pulo Gadung, some travel times and approximate costs include:

to	time	fare
Cirebon	5 hours	2,700 rp
		3,900 rp*
Semarang	12 hours	5,200 rp
		7,600 rp*
Yogyakarta	12 hours	6,500 rp
		9,500 rp*
		13,500 rp**

Top: Travellers arriving by becak at the Cilacap jetty, Java (TW)
Left: Relief representing a sailing ship, Borobudur, Java (JH)
Right: Bugis schooners at Pasar Ikan, Jakarta, Java (AS)

Top: Sultan's palace, Yogyakarta, Java (JH)
Left: Bird market, Yogyakarta, Java (JH)
Right: Dieng children, Java (JH)

Solo	13 hours	6,300 rp
		9,100 rp*
Surabaya	15½ hours	9,200 rp
(via Solo)		13,300 rp*
		19,200 rp**
Surabaya	14½ hours	8,500 rp
(via Tuban)		12,400 rp*
Malang	18 hours	9,400 rp
		13,600 rp*
Denpasar	25½ hours	15,000 rp
		19,600 rp*
		26,000 rp**

*air-con buses
**deluxe air-con buses with toilet and reclining seats

Bus companies operating to Sumatra are found along Jalan K H Mansyur. The best buses with aircraft seats, toilets, air-con (and video) are Bintang Kejora; next best is ANS. If you buy tickets from the offices, they'll arrange free transport to the Kalideres bus station. Fares include Bukittinggi from 25,000 to 28,000 rp for buses with 2 by 2 seating, 18,000 rp for 2 by 3. Buses with toilets stop less frequently so they're faster.

Taxi There are also inter-city taxis and minibuses to Bandung that will pick you up and drop you off at your hotel. Fares start at 7000 rp per person; they're fast and convenient but taxis will only depart when they have five passengers. Parahiyangan (tel 353434) is at Jalan Wahid Hasyim 13. '4848' is at Jalan Prapatan 34 (tel 348048) and Jalan Kramat Raya 23 (tel 368488).

Rail Jakarta has four major railway stations. Gambir, on the east side of Merdeka Square and most convenient for Jalan Jaksa, handles trains to the south and east, plus most services through to Surabaya via Yogya. Pasar Senen, further east of Gambir, has most services to Surabaya via Semarang. If you're going west to Merak, for Sumatra, then the trains will be from Tanah Abang station which is directly to the west of Jalan

Thamrin. Beware of pickpockets at any of Jakarta's train stations, but particularly at Gambir.

Note that the super deluxe night express trains to Surabaya – the *Bima Express* (via Yogya) and the *Mutiara Utara* (via Semarang) – do not depart from either Gambir or Pasar Senen but from Kota, which is to the north of Merdeka Square in old Jakarta. If you're departing from Kota station you should allow adequate time to wind your way through the rush hour traffic snarls. From Jalan Thamrin you can take a No 70 or P11 bus to Kota station for just 200 or 350 rp. On the return journey, the *Bima* and *Mutiara* trains stop at Gambir and then continue on to Kota.

Tickets for the *Bima* and *Mutiara* can be purchased from the station ticket counter one day before departure. Tickets for other trains can usually only be bought a couple of hours before the train leaves when collection is nearly always chaotic. If queues are hopelessly long or if trains are 'officially full', it's always worth trying the station master for tickets. If you want to be certain of a sleeper or a seat, bookings (with the exception of all-3rd class) can be made at some travel agents for a small charge. Carnation Tours & Travel (tel 344027) at Jalan Menteng Raya 24, on the corner of Jalan Kebon Sirih, handle bookings and the office is open from 8 am to 3 pm Monday to Friday, 8 am to 2 pm Saturday and 9 am to 1 pm Sunday. Bhayangkara Tours & Travel, Jalan Kebon Sirih 23, also handle railway bookings.

From Gambir station trains depart every hour to Bogor and take 1½ hours at a cost of 500 rp in all-3rd class. The *Parahiyangan* is a comfortable express train from Gambir to Bandung. There are six trains daily, the first departing at 5.39 am and arriving three hours later. The fare is 8000 rp in 1st class, 6000 in 2nd. Trains to Merak depart Tanah Abang station at 6 am and 5 pm and take four hours, 1300 rp all-3rd class.

Trains to Yogya take from 10 hours and fares vary from 4500 rp in 3rd class, 9500 rp in 2nd, 17,000 rp in 1st. From Jakarta to Surabaya, an 859-km trip, takes 14 hours; the fares start at 7700 rp in the 3rd class Gaya Baru trains. The *Bima Express* sleeper train, through to Surabaya, is marginally slower (two hours) and cheaper than the *Mutiara Utara*. The Bima costs 22,000 rp in 1st for a reclining chair or 27,000 rp with sleeper. The *Mutiara* is 25,000 in first with reclining seats, no sleeper available.

Boat Pelni has lots of services out of Jakarta. Ships link Jakarta to Tanjung Pinang (from 30,000 rp economy class), Padang (from 23,600 rp economy class), Ujung Pandang (from 36,200 rp economy class), Belawan (from 37,300 rp economy class), Pontianak (28,800 rp economy class) and via Semarang and Surabaya to other destinations in Kalimantan and Sulawesi.

The Pelni ticket office (tel 358398) is at Jalan Pintu Air 1 behind the Istiqlal Mosque. It's open from 8.30 am to 12 noon and 1 to 2 pm Monday to Friday, 8.30 am to 12 noon Saturday.

Cargo Boat The Pelni cargo ship to Pontianak sometimes takes passengers (22,000 to 25,000 rp), but it depends on the cargo carried and there's never a regular service. For details, check with the Pelni office at Tanjung Priok harbour (tel 491014, 493184) but tickets have to be bought from the Pintu Air office.

The best place to get information on non-Pelni cargo boats is the old harbour, Sunda Kelapa. The staff at the harbour master's office (Kantor Syahbandar) are the people to see first. Most of them speak excellent English and they're very helpful. It's also worth going around all the ships at the dock. The Pulau Indah company, for example, has a boat to Tanjung Pinang once a month; it costs 25,000 rp and takes three days. At least one cargo ship a day goes to Pontianak in Kalimantan; the going passenger rate is a bargain at about 17,000 rp. Conditions on board these cargo ships are spartan. Usually you have to sleep on a sheltered deck. Occasionally, there's a small cabin for hire for an additional 5000 to 10,000 rp or so.

Getting Around

Airport Transport In 1985 Jakarta's old central Kemayoran domestic airport and Halim international airport were both superseded by the new Sukarno-Hatta International Airport, 35 km west of the centre. A toll road links the airport to the city and a journey between the two takes 45 minutes to an hour.

There's a Damri airport bus every 30 minutes to Gambir station (near Jalan Jaksa) and four other points in Jakarta. It costs 2000 rp per person. Alternatively a taxi to Jalan Thamrin would cost 16,000 to 18,000 rp by meter including the 2700 rp toll–road charge. Bluebird Taxis give a 50% discount on the toll but add a 2300 rp airport surcharge, so it comes out about the same. You can do it cheaper if you can stop the driver from taking the toll road (2700 rp) but this takes longer. Going to the airport, you can usually negotiate with a driver to take you for a flat 15,000 rp including the toll.

Many hotels have minibus services to the airport for 4000 to 5000 rp. The Sabang Metropolitan Hotel on Jalan H A Salim has a 5000 rp minibus to the airport daily at 1 pm but you must book a day in advance.

Tanjung Priok Harbour Transport The Pelni ships all arrive at (and depart from) Pelabuhan or Dock No 1. It's a distance of two km from the dock – past the Pelni office – to the Tanjung Priok bus station, from where you can take a No 64 bus or pale blue minibus M15 to the Kota city bus terminal. From Kota you can then take a No 70 bus to Jalan Thamrin. The harbour is 20 km from the centre of the city so allow an hour, at least, to get there, particularly on public transport. A taxi should cost around 3500 rp.

Bus In Jakarta everything is at a distance. It's hot and humid and hardly anybody walks – you will need to use some form of transport to get from one place to another. Jakarta has probably the most comprehensive city bus network of any major Indonesian city. Its buses, however, tend to be hopelessly crowded particularly during rush hours. Jakarta's pickpockets are notoriously adept and they're great bag slashers too. So take care.

Around town there are lots of big regular city buses charging a fixed 200 rp fare. The big express 'Patas' buses charge 350 rp and are usually less crowded – well, less so by Jakarta's standards. These services are supplemented by orange toy-sized buses which cost 200 rp and, in a few areas, by pale blue Mikrolet buses which cost 300 rp. You need to be a midget for the latter though.

If you'll be using city buses then a copy of *See for Yourself* (from the Jakarta Tourist Office) will be useful as it contains a fairly comprehensive list of the city bus routes. Sarinah on Jalan Thamrin is a good landmark for Jalan Jaksa and some of the more useful buses that will drop you there include:

408, P11	Cililitan bus station to Jalan Thamrin
59	Pulo Gadung bus station to Jalan Thamrin
16	Kalideres bus station to Jalan Thamrin
70, P1, P11	Kota railway station to Jalan Thamrin
10	Pasar Senen railway Jalan Thamrin
34	Jalan Thamrin to 'TIM' on Jalan Cikini Raya
10, 12, 16	Jalan Thamrin to Blok M, Kebayoran
507	Jalan Kebon Sirih to Pulo Gadung bus station

'P' equals 'Patas', express
10, 12 and 110 go by the post office

Taxi Taxis in Jakarta have real working meters and most drivers use them these days without having to be asked. Jakarta has a large fleet of taxis and it's usually not too difficult to find one. Many residents swear by Bluebird cabs (pale blue) which have a radio call service (325607) and well-maintained cars. Steady Safe (356322) also has a good reputation. There are several other companies with acceptable service; the only one to avoid is President Taxi, which is famous for its surly drivers, poorly-maintained vehicles and refusal to use the meter from bus stations. In 1988, it was reported in the *Jakarta Post* that the government might soon revoke President's business licence.

Flagfall is 600 rp for the first km, then 20 rp each additional 100 metres, and most trips will cost between 2000 and 3500 rp. Tanjung Priok to Jalan Thamrin, for example, should cost around 3000 rp. It's worth carrying plenty of small notes – another favourite game is 'sorry, no change'. It is customary to let the driver keep any change under 100 rp.

Bajaj & Other Bajajs (pronounced ba-jai) are nothing less than Indian auto-rickshaws – orange or green three-wheelers that carry two passengers (three at a squeeze if you're all dwarf-size) and sputter around powered by noisy two-stroke engines. Always agree the price beforehand. Short trips – Jalan Jaksa to the post office for example – will cost between 500 rp and 800 rp and they're good value especially during rush hours. Note that bajajs are not allowed along main streets, such as Jalan Thamrin, so make sure they won't be simply dropping you off at the border.

Jakarta also has some weird and wonderful means of getting around – like the 'Morris' bemos that run mainly down Jalan Gajah Madah and are all old English Morris vans. And near the Pasar Ikan in Kota there are pushbikes with a padded 'kiddy carrier' on the back!

Hire Car If you feel up to driving yourself

around, Jakarta has branches of three major rent-a-car operators. National Car Rental (tel 332849) is in the Kartika Plaza Hotel, Jalan Thamrin 10. Avis Rental Car (tel 349206) is at Jalan Diponegoro 25 and they also have a desk at the Sari Pacific Hotel on Jalan Thamrin. Hertz Car Rental (tel 371208) is at the Mandarin Hotel on Jalan Thamrin.

Becak Becaks (man-powered rickshaws) are a rare sight around Jakarta these days but not so very long ago they were probably the biggest source of employment in the city. Since becaks were first introduced by the Japanese and used for hauling goods within the old city their use has spread all over Java and in the 1960s there were about 400,000 in Jakarta alone.

Over the last 15 years or so, Jakarta's becak men have been pushed back to side-streets by regulations aimed at tidying up the city. Permits for becaks are not renewed once they expire and whole fleets of becaks have been shipped out to country towns. Becaks are banned from the city centre before 10 pm but they survive in the less accessible kampongs and you'll find a surprising number of becaks in areas like Glodok. In fact, it's estimated that there are probably about 24,000 still in the city. They rarely venture on to Jakarta's heavily trafficked streets but late at night the odd solitary becak man can even be seen pedalling down Jakarta's main boulevard, Jalan Thamrin.

AROUND JAKARTA
Pulau Seribu/Thousand Islands
Scattered across the Java Sea to the north of Jakarta are these tropical islands – called Pulau Seribu or Thousand Islands although they are actually only 112 in number. The entire island group has a population of 11,000 and almost half of these people live on just one island, Pulau Kelapa. So far only a few of the islands have been developed as tourist attractions, such as Pulau Bidadari, Pulau Pelangi

and Pulau Putri. Some of the others are privately owned but many of them have no permanent population at all and there are some beautiful beaches and good opportunities for scuba diving or simply exploring.

Jakarta's 'off-shore' islands start only a few km out in the Bay of Jakarta. Best known of these is Pulau Bidadari which has been developed into a locally popular resort. It attracts a few tourists on day trips but it has been a big hit with Jakartans, particularly on weekends when it can be very crowded. The sea around Bidadari is not so clear. From Bidadari you can visit other nearby islands like Pulau Untung Jawa, Pulau Kahyangan, Pulau Kelor (which has the ruins of an old Dutch fort), or Pulau Onrust where the remains of an old shipyard from the 18th century can be explored. Bidadari has bungalow accommodation, a restaurant, bar and small shop. There are camping sites on Pulau Kahyangan and Untung Jawa.

Islands good for swimming and diving include Pulau Damar, Pulau Tikus and Pulau Pari. They're within reasonable day-tripping distance of Jakarta and also reached from the Ancol Marina, but boats have to be chartered. You can also charter boats from Sunda Kelapa harbour – Pulau Panggang for example is a four-hour trip and you can reach other islands from there.

Getting There & Away To get to Bidadari take a boat from the Marina at Ancol. The round trip is 7000 rp and it takes about one hour to get out there. On weekdays a boat departs at 10.30 am, returning at 3 pm. On Saturdays there are departures at 10.30 am and 2 pm but only one service back at 4 pm. On Sundays and holidays boats depart at 8 and 10.30 am, returning from Bidadari at 2 and 4 pm.

Pulau Seribu Paradise
Much further north, among the more unpeopled islands and some of Indonesia's most beautiful coral reefs, four islands

have been developed as Jakarta's tropical paradise. Pulau Putri, Pulau Pelangi, Pulau Perak and Pulau Papa Theo all cater for the affluent traveller although skin diving enthusiasts will find slightly (just) cheaper accommodation and a 'serious dive camp' at the latter island.

On Pulau Putri and Pulau Pelangi there are small native-style huts and larger bungalows with air-conditioning, all overlooking the sea. Pulau Papa Theo dive camp has 10 huts and there are also two lodges for groups of up to 10 people. It's possible to take a hut for one night from US$55 on weekdays/weekends but there are package trips offered which work out more cheaply. Rates include accommodation and three meals but not transport to the islands. Pulau Perak is for day trips from the other three islands, but if you bring camping gear you can spend the night here for a nominal charge.

Scuba diving costs US$15 per dive or $US25 per day, including equipment and guide. Basic scuba instruction leading to a certificate is US$20.

Getting There & Away Transport is either by boat or light aircraft. A daily boat trip from Ancol Marina takes four hours, US$40 round trip. Daily flights connect Jakarta with Pulau Panjang. The flight takes 25 minutes and then there's a 25-minute boat transfer from the air strip on Pulau Panjang to the other islands, for a total round-trip fare of US$120. For further details and bookings contact Pulau Seribu Paradise (tel 515884), Setia Budi Building, Block C1, Jalan H R Rasuna Said, Jakarta.

West Java

The province of West Java has a population of 27.5 million, an area of 46,300 square km and its capital is Bandung. It is historically known as Sunda, the home of the Sundanese people and their culture. West Java is also the region of perhaps the most extreme contrasts. It is here, on the flattest, hottest coastline, that you will find the special territory of Jakarta and all the noise, confusion and squalor of Indonesia's largest city. Yet geographically the rest of the province merges imperceptibly into Central Java. It is predominantly mountainous and agricultural with lush green valleys and high volcanic peaks surrounding its own capital, Bandung, at the core of the region. West Java is also strongly Islamic, yet in the remote Kendeng mountains there is still a small isolated community known as the Baduis who are believed to be descendants of the ancient Sundanese who fled from Islam more than 400 years ago. The name Sunda is of Sanskrit origin and means 'pure' or 'white'.

For travellers, West Java has tended to be a place to whiz through between Jakarta and destinations east but, apart from its historic and cultural centres, West Java offers one of the best beaches in Indonesia at Pangandaran and a fine backwater trip along the coastal lagoons to Central Java. Other major attractions, though remote and isolated, are the famous Krakatau Islands off the west coast and the unique Ujung Kulon National Park in the south-west of the province.

History

Early in its history Sunda, unlike the great land-based Javanese kingdoms, was primarily dependent on overseas trade. It was not only an important spice centre in its own right but also a trans-shipment point for trade with Asia. West Java was the first contact point in Indonesia for the Dutch and earlier it was one of the first regions to come into contact with Indian traders and their culture. Ancient stone inscriptions record an early Hindu influence during the reign of King Purnawarman of Taruma and one of his rock edicts can be seen near Bogor. In the

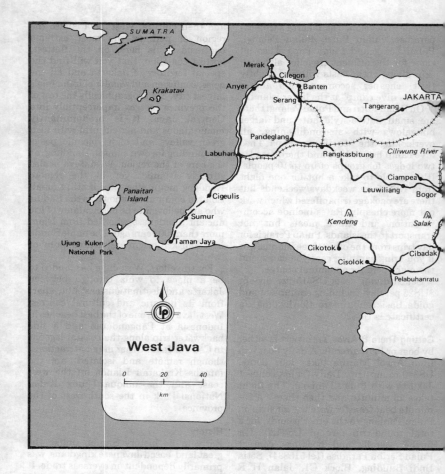

West Java

0   20   40

km

7th century Taruma was destroyed by the powerful Sumatran-based Buddhist kingdom of Srivijaya. Much later Hinduism reasserted itself alongside Buddhism when the Pajajarans ruled the region. They're chiefly remembered for constructing the first trading settlement on the site of Old Batavia when it was called Sunda Kelapa, and for establishing trading relations with the Portuguese.

The first half of the 16th century saw

the military expansion of the Muslim state of Demak and in 1524 Muslim power first made itself felt in West Java. In that year Demak's general, Sunan Gunungjati, took the port of Banten and then Sunda Kelapa. Some time after 1552 he became the first of the kings of Cirebon, which today is the least visited and thus the most surprising of Java's surviving sultanates. Banten, on the other hand, was the maritime capital of the only

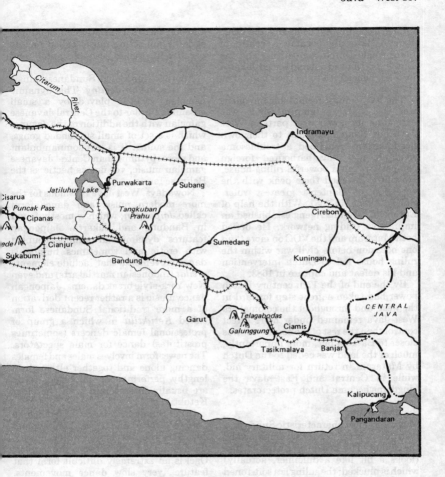

Muslim state to remain independent of the great Javanese power, Mataram, but today it is little more than a small fishing village.

After the fall of Melaka in 1511 Chinese, Arabs and Indians poured into Banten and it became a major trading centre for Muslim merchants who made use of the Sunda Straits to avoid the Portuguese. Gunungjati's successor, Hasanuddin, spread Banten's authority to the pepper-

producing district of Lampung in south Sumatra. His son, Maulana Yusuf, finally conquered the inland Hindu kingdom of Pajajaran in 1579 and so carved out a huge slice of Sunda as Banten's own domain.

Towards the end of the century Banten felt the first impact of a new force – the Europeans. In 1596 the Dutch made their first appearance at Banten, in 1600 the English established an East India Company trading post and two years later the Dutch formed a counterpart company, the VOC. Banten naturally became a centre of fierce Anglo-Dutch competition and the Dutch soon moved out and seized Jakarta instead, henceforth to be their capital as Batavia.

The VOC's most formidable opponent was the Mataram empire which was extending its power over parts of West Java but Banten, so close to their own headquarters, remained a troublesome rival. It not only harboured foreign competitors but a powerful ruling house. Hostilities reached their peak with the accession of Banten's greatest ruler, Sultan Ageng, in 1651. With the help of European captains Ageng established an impressive trading network. He defied both Mataram and the VOC on more than one occasion before civil war within the ruling house led to Dutch intervention and his defeat and capture in 1683.

By the end of the 17th century Dutch power had taken a great step forward in the west, and throughout the colonial era West Java remained under more direct control than the rest of the country. It was closer to Batavia but, more importantly, much of the land was ceded to the Dutch by Mataram in return for military aid, while in Central and East Java the kingdoms became Dutch protectorates.

Sundanese Arts

Music The most characteristic Sundanese instrument is the *kecapi* accompanied by the suling. The kecapi is a type of lute (looks a bit like a dulcimer, actually) which is plucked; the suling is a soft-toned bamboo flute which fades in and out of the long vibrating notes of the kecapi. Another traditional instrument is the *angklung* – a device of bamboo pieces of differing lengths and diameter loosely suspended in a bamboo frame – which is shaken to produce hollow echoing sounds. Originally the angklung was tuned to a five-note scale but it's being revived using western octaves and can be played by a single performer or a large orchestra. In Cirebon there's a variation on Bandung-style kecapi-suling music called *tarling* because it makes use of gui*tar* and su*ling*.

Another traditional Sundanese music form is *gamelan degung*. This dynamic gamelan style is played by a small ensemble similar to the Central Javanese gamelan with the addition of the *degung*, which is a set of small suspended gongs, and the suling. It is less somnambulant and more rhythmic than Central Javanese gamelan music, yet not as hectic as the Balinese forms.

Nowadays, West Java is famous for the more modern music and dance form called *Jaipongan*, which is mostly found in Bandung and Jakarta. Jaipongan features dynamic drumming coupled with erotic and sometimes humorous dance movements that include elements of *silat* (Indonesian martial arts) and even New York-style break dancing. Jaipongan dance/music is a rather recent derivation of a more traditional Sundanese form called *Ketuktilu* in which a group of professional female dancers (sometimes prostitutes) dance for male spectators. The newer form involves males and females dancing alone and together although in lengthy performances Jaipongan songs are usually interspersed with the older Ketuktilu style.

Other Sundanese dance forms include *Longser*, *Joker* and *Ogel*. Longser and Joker are couples dances which involve the passing of a sash between the couples. Ogel is an extremely difficult form that features very slow dance movements. Traditional Ogel is in danger of dying out since few younger performers are patient enough to endure the many years of training required to master the subtle movements.

Wayang The wayang golek puppet play, although it can be seen elsewhere in Java, is traditionally associated with West Java and the Sundanese prefer it to the shadow play. First used in north coast towns for

Muslim propaganda, this type of puppet play was Islamic and a popular, robust parody of the stylised aristocratic wayang kulit play. In the early 19th century a Sundanese prince of Sumedang had a set of wooden puppets made to correspond exactly to the wayang kulit puppets of the Javanese courts. With these he was able to perform the Hindu epics with the traditional splendour of his rivals, but at the same time preserve his regional identity by using puppets long associated with anti-Javanese art. In West Java the stories are still usually based on the Mahabharata and Ramayana legends and the puppets are larger and more vivid than those found in Central Java.

Sundanese Food

Long-standing connections with Sumatra have probably made a significant contribution to West Java's regional cuisine. Padang restaurants abound, particularly in the north-west of the province, but in Bandung you'll find a local variation of Padang food. There is the same emphasis on meat but, while the Sumatrans go for the really hot stuff, Sundanese food is spicy rather than chilli hot. Popular dishes include pepes usus, chicken steamed in bamboo leaf; steamed goldfish; fish flavoured with laos, a spice rather like ginger; and spiced buffalo meat similar to Sumatran rendang. There is often a plate of petei, huge broad beans; tempe, salad and sambal. Soto Bandung is a soup made from tripe – it's another Sundanese speciality of Bandung. In Cirebon, the local speciality is nasi lengko, rice with bean sprouts, tahu, tempe, fried onion, cucumber and peanut sauce.

Things to Buy

In Bandung you can can buy wayang golek puppets and Sundanese musical instruments, including the bamboo angklung. Cirebon is famous for its batik which you'll find in shops and markets in Cirebon and in the villages of Trusmi and Indramayu where the batik is made. Tasikmalaya is a centre for woven bamboo crafts, colourful umbrellas and batik.

In Bandung and Cirebon it's easy to find cassette tapes of kecapi-suling, degung, tarling and Jaipongan music.

JAKARTA TO MERAK

Although most people just head straight through from Jakarta to Merak on their way to (or from) Sumatra there are a couple of places of interest between the two centres and, along this route, you can also branch off and head for the west coast. The west coast's greatest attractions are undoubtedly the Krakatau Islands and Ujung Kulon – both of which require some effort to get to – but the beaches are worth considering if you're feeling in need of a break from the noise and hassle of Jakarta. These places can also be reached using Jakarta as a base.

The Jakarta to Merak road runs through a flat coastal area which is slated for industrial development and it's one of the busiest in Java with a great deal of traffic of all types. Getting out of Jakarta, from Kalideres, used to be agonisingly slow but a 'superhighway' has cut down on travel time a bit.

Serang

This town, 90 km west of Jakarta, is important mainly for its crossroads function. From here you can turn off to Banten, 10 km north of the town on the coast; or turn south and take the inland route via Pandeglang to Labuhan and Carita Beach on the west coast, which in turn is the jumping off point for Krakatau and Ujung Kulon. An interesting alternative route to Carita is to continue on from Serang to Cilegon and take a colt from there along the coastal road.

Serang is a convenient base from which to visit Banten but only very basic accommodation is available and there's no real need to stay here. If you take an early morning bus from Jakarta and a late afternoon bus back (or on to the west coast) you're going to have all the time in the world to fit in a trip to explore Banten's ruins. The bus between Jakarta and Serang takes roughly two hours.

Places to Stay Along Jalan A Yani, which runs from the Ciceri bus station to the town square, there's a collection of rather drab and dismal losmen – OK for a night but not much longer. Near the bus station there's the *Hotel Abadi* with rooms from 4500 rp and further down is the similarly priced *Penginapan Buyis*. The latter is run by friendly people and it's clean enough but bathrooms consist of a toilet, tap and heavy-duty garbage can. Further down still, near the square, the *Hotel Serang* is another possibility.

Banten

Due north of Serang, on the coast, are the few fragments of the great maritime capital of the Banten sultanate where the Dutch and English first landed on Java to secure trade and struggle for economic supremacy. Banten reached its peak during the reign of Sultan Ageng (1651-83) but he unwisely clashed with rising Dutch power in Batavia. In 1680 Ageng declared war on Batavia but, before he could make a move, internal conflict within the royal house led to Dutch intervention on behalf of the ambitious crown prince. Ageng fled from Banten but finally surrendered in 1683 and his defeat marked the real beginning of Dutch territorial expansion in Java. Not only was Banten's independence at an end but their English East India Company rivals were driven out, which effectively destroyed British interests in Java.

The Dutch maintained trading interests in Banten for a time but they did a good job of demolishing the place in the 19th century. At some point too this coastline silted up and Banten became a ghost town, a small dusty fishing village which is really all that Banten is today.

The chief landmark of a prosperous era is the 16th century Masjid Agung mosque which dominates the village, and this is perhaps the most interesting part of a visit to Banten. It's a good example of early Hindu-Islamic architecture, but the mosque's great white lighthouse of a minaret was reputedly designed by a Chinese Muslim and it's quite unlike any other in Java. A narrow staircase spirals up through the thick walls of the minaret to two high balconies and from the top you have a fine view of the coastline.

The mosque also has a small archaeological museum with a very modest collection of old clay pipes and weapons including a few of the long, iron, chained spikes which the 'Debus players' are famous for. Banten has long been a centre for practitioners of the Debus tradition which is supposed to have come from India. They are Islamic ascetics who reputedly engage in masochistic activities such as plunging sharp weapons into their bodies (without drawing blood!), and are able to control pain and fear by the strength of their faith. It's said that in Banten this was originally part of the training of the invincible special soldiers to the court.

Directly across from the mosque is the large grass-covered site of Hasanuddin's fortified palace, the Surosowan, which was wrecked in the bloody civil war during the reign of Sultan Ageng and rebuilt, only to be razed to the ground by the Dutch in 1832.

Other points of interest around the mosque include the massive ruins of Fort Speelwijk to the north-west, which now overlook an expanse of sand-silt marsh although at one time it stood on the sea's edge. The fort was built by the Dutch in 1682 and finally abandoned by Governor-General Daendels at the beginning of the 19th century. Opposite the entrance to the fort there is a Chinese temple, dating from the 18th century, which is still in use. Back along the road to Serang are the huge crumbling walls and archways of the Kaibon palace and near it is the tomb of Maulana Yusuf who died in 1580.

Pulau Dua Bird Sanctuary

Off the coast of Banten, the Pulau Dua island is one of Indonesia's major bird sanctuaries. It has a large resident population – mainly herons, storks and cormorants – but peak time is between March and July when great numbers of migratory birds flock here for the breeding season. At low tide the island may be accessible by land now that the mudflats between it and the mainland have silted up; otherwise it's a half-hour boat ride from the Karanghantu harbour in Banten. A PHPA guard is stationed on the island and there's a watchtower and guest house but if you are planning to stay bring both food and water. For more information you could try the PHPA office in Jakarta.

Getting There & Away Colts depart from the Pasar Lama bus stand (a bemo-ride from the Ciceri bus station) in Serang. The fare is 400 rp and they will drop you right by the mosque.

Cilegon

Cilegon, 20 km north-west of Serang, is almost 100% industrial and dominated by the vast Krakatau Steel plant. This giant enterprise was begun in the early 1960s with Russian aid, partially dismantled when the Russians were expelled after the 1965 coup, and has now been resurrected with foreign aid and backing from Pertamina.

MERAK

Right on the north-western tip of Java, 140 km from Jakarta, Merak is the terminus for ferries shuttling to and from Panjang and Bakauheni on the southern end of Sumatra. It's of little interest otherwise – just an arrival and departure point – and most people shoot straight through.

Places to Stay

If you do have a reason to stay you could try the *Hotel Anda* – singles/doubles with fan and mandi at 4500/6000 rp – or the *Hotel Robinson* next door. They're standard, clean losmen and both are on

Jalan Florida (Pulorida), just across the railway line opposite the bus station. The bus station cafeteria is pretty good.

For those determined to pay more, there's the modern *Merak Beach Hotel* (tel Merak 15) several km out of town on the road to Cilegon. It has small air-con units on the beach, a bar and restaurant; singles/doubles from 26,000/29,000 rp. The hotel is also known as the 'Ramayana'.

Getting There & Away

The bus station and the railway station in Merak are right on the docks and only a hundred metres or so apart.

Bus A bus from Jakarta (Kalideres) to Merak takes about three hours and costs 1300 rp. There are plenty of them, operating almost every five minutes from 3 am to midnight.

Rail From Jakarta trains for Merak depart from the Tanah Abang railway station at 6 am and 5 pm. The fare is 1400 rp all-3rd class and the trip takes about four hours. The day train is faster and links up with the daytime ferry service to Strengsem. Going the other way, trains depart Merak at 6.30 am and 4.30 pm.

Sumatra Ferry The ferry to Strengsem leaves at 11 am and 11 pm from the dock near the train station and takes four to six hours. It costs from 1300 rp in 3rd class to 3750 rp in 1st. Ferries to Bakauhuni depart every hour from the dock near the bus station and the trip takes 1½ hours; it's 750 rp in 3rd class, 1700 rp in 1st.

The Merak to Bakauheni crossing is becoming one of the busiest waterways in Indonesia as more people are encouraged by better roads including the Trans-Sumatra Highway. One disadvantage of this progress is that there can be enormous traffic jams during the holiday seasons, although passenger cars and buses are usually given priority over goods trucks.

DOWN THE WEST COAST

At Cilegon the road branches south to Anyer and runs close to the sea all the way to Labuhan along a flat green coastal strip bordered by long stretches of white sand beach. Here there are masses of coconut palms and banana trees and, along the roadside, piles of old white coral which the villagers collect to make building lime. The area is fairly sparsely populated with small fishing settlements and coconut ports. This is perhaps simply because the land isn't suitable for intensive rice agriculture but it's also said that survivors of the Krakatau eruption, and succeeding generations, believed it to be a place of ill omen and never returned.

From the coast, particularly around Carita, you'll often see a mass of lights strung out across the sea at night. They're the night fishermen, fishing for shrimp, prawns and lobster from platforms called *bagang* – small bamboo huts on stilts firmly embedded in the sea bottom way out from the shore.

Anyer

The Anyer beach, 15km south of Cilegon, is an up-market resort, mainly frequented by the expatriate community working at the Cilegon steel plant. The most interesting story about Anyer is that this was once the biggest Dutch port in the Sunda Strait before being totally destroyed by tidal waves generated by Krakatau. One Dutch freighter is said to have been pushed 100 kilometres inland by the tidal waves. The Anyer lighthouse was built by the Dutch, at the instigation of Queen Wilhelmina, in 1885 after the disaster.

From here you can hire a boat, about 25,000 rp return, to make the 1½ hour trip to explore the deserted island of Sangiang. Surrounded by coral reef, it is seven square km of jungle, mangrove and monkeys. Parts of the island are inhospitably swampy and mosquito-ridden (so be prepared) but on the east coast there are small coves with coloured coral and shells washed up on the shore where you could

possibly camp. The water is fine for swimming and snorkelling but be careful of the tides. To the south of the island are the remains of Japanese fortifications that were built to control the narrow strait between Java and Sumatra during WW II.

Places to Stay The *Anyer Beach Hotel* (tel Jakarta 510322), part of Pertamina's hotel chain, is a modern motel complex with individual beachfront cottages – all with air-con, bathroom and hot and cold running water – costing from 42,350 rp (plus tax & service). The resort has a restaurant and bar, swimming pool and bowling alley.

Karang Bolong

There's another good beach here, six km south of Anyer and 30 km north of Labuhan, where a huge stand of rock forms a natural archway from the land to the sea.

LABUHAN

Besides the coastal road from Anyer, Labuhan can also be reached from Jakarta by taking the more direct inland route through Serang and Pandeglang. The port of Labuhan is really only important as a junction town and this is where you'll find the PHPA office for the Ujung Kulon National Park. Otherwise it's a dreary, dirty little place and the beach is pretty much the local toilet.

Ujung Kulon National Park

Permits If you're planning a trip to Ujung Kulon you must first get a permit and make reservations for accommodation at the Labuhan PHPA office, which is located about two km from the centre of town on the road to Carita. They have maps of the reserve and the PHPA staff will also arrange boat transport to the Ujung Kulon peninsula. The office is open from 7 am to 2 pm Monday to Thursday, to 11 am Friday and until 12 noon Saturday. It's closed on Sunday.

Places to Stay & Eat

You can stay at the very basic *Hotel Citra Ayu* for 6000 rp or *Hotel Caringin* where rooms cost 8000 rp with bath, but with a pleasant hotel so close by at Carita Beach there's not much point in doing so.

CARITA BEACH

There's a German-run beach resort at Carita, seven km north of Labuhan. It has a good white-sand beach and swimming and, about five minutes out by boat, good snorkelling on the reef. Masks, surfboards and windsurfers can be hired from the hotel though most of the equipment is in poor condition.

This is a popular base for visits to the Krakatau Islands and the Ujung Kulon National Park – if you're interested in either, ask to see the hotel's video documentary about the 1883 eruption and its effects on the west coast. Around Carita there are plenty of opportunities to go wandering, along the beach or inland. About two km from Carita across the rice paddies see the village of Sindanglaut ('end of the sea') where the giant *tsunami* wave of 1883 ended. The Curug Gendang waterfall is a six-km hike through the hills and jungle.

Place to Stay & Eat

The *Carita Krakatau Beach Hotel* has simple 'Badui-style' wooden cottages strung out along the beach, a few hostel rooms and a restaurant/bar on a pleasant shaded verandah. It's a very easy-going friendly place and the hostel rooms are good value, basic but clean with big comfortable beds and towels provided. Rooms in the hostel across the road from the beach cost US$3 or US$6 with bath during the week, US$9 on weekends. On the beachfront spacious rooms with mandi cost US$27 during the week, US$45 on weekends. There are also a few more expensive beachfront cottages. If you're coming from Jakarta you can get a Krakatau newsletter from the tourist office that will get you a 25% discount on your first night (10% on weekends). During the low season you may be able to negotiate lower prices.

More upscale lodging is appearing north of the Carita Krakatau Beach Hotel. Just up the beach is the recently built *Desiana Cottages* (tel in Jakarta 593316) where clean, comfortable bungalows with kitchens and dining rooms start at 35,000 rp on weekdays (55,000 weekends). A two-bedroom bungalow with two double beds costs 55,000 rp weekdays (80,000 rp on weekends).

Across the road and north a bit is the *Wisma Wira Carita* (tel Jakarta 341240). It's also rather new, with large clean rooms for 30,000 rp during the week, 40,000 rp weekends.

The restaurant at the Carita Krakatau Beach Hotel is outdoors and serves both Indonesian and western food. Prices are reasonable but not cheap, eg the fish of the day with rice is 4200 rp and a small beer is 1800 rp, but portions are large and the food is pretty good. Noodles/fried rice are 2700/3300 rp. The Desiana and the Wisma Wira Carita both have restaurants but few people seem to eat at either of these hotels. The Wisma Wira Carita restaurant is the cheaper of the two, with fried rice at 2500 rp, a small beer costs 1300 rp.

If you're on a tight budget, head south to the warungs close by on the main road. The one nearest to Carita Krakatau Beach Hotel has good nasi goreng and mie kuah for 750 rp and the local people are delighted to have visitors. There are also a number of local children who tour the beach selling pineapples and bananas and you can always buy basic foods in Labuhan.

The massage women who frequent the beach in front of the Carita Krakatau Beach Hotel will also deliver home-cooked Indonesian meals to guests upon request.

Getting There & Away

Buses depart hourly from the Kalideres station in Jakarta for Labuhan. The trip, through Serang and Pandeglang, takes about three to four hours on a winding road and costs 1700 rp. From Labuhan a colt will take you to Carita Beach (Pantai Carita) for 200 rp. The Carita Beach Hotel is affiliated with the Menteng Hotel (tel 330846) in Jakarta, Jalan Gondangdia Lama 28, which operates a transport service on Friday afternoons for US$10.

Buses from Merak go to Carita via Cilegon in about 2½ hours and cost 1250 rp.

KRAKATAU

The legendary Krakatau lies only 50 km from the West Java coast. Today only a small part of the original volcano remains but when Krakatau blew itself apart in 1883, in one of the world's greatest and most catastrophic eruptions, the effects were recorded far beyond the Sunda Straits and it achieved instant and lasting infamy.

For centuries Krakatau had been a familiar nautical landmark for much of the world's maritime traffic which was funneled through the narrow Sunda Straits. The volcano had been dormant since 1680 and was widely regarded as extinct but from May through to early August in 1883 there were reports from passing ships of moderate activity. By 26 August Krakatau was raging and the explosions became more and more violent. At 10 am on 27 August Krakatau erupted with the biggest bang ever recorded on earth. On the island of Rodriguez, more than 4600 km to the south-west, a police chief reported hearing the booming of 'heavy guns from eastward'; in Alice Springs, 3500 km to the south-east, residents also reported hearing strange explosions from the north-west.

With its cataclysmic explosions, Krakatau sent up a record column of ash to a height of 80 km and threw into the air nearly 20 cubic km of rock. Ash fell on Singapore 840 km to the north and on ships as far away as 6000 km; darkness covered the Sunda Straits from 10 am on the 27th until dawn the next day. Far more destructive were the great ocean waves triggered by the collapse of Krakatau's cones into its empty belly. Giant *tsunamis*, over 40 metres high, swept over the nearby shores of Java and Sumatra and the sea wave's passage was recorded far from Krakatau, reaching Aden in 12 hours over a distance 'travelled by a good steamer in 12 days'. Measureable wave effects were even said to reach the English Channel. Coastal Java and Sumatra were devastated: 165 villages were destroyed and more than 36,000 people were killed.

The following day a telegram sent to Singapore from Batavia (160 km east of

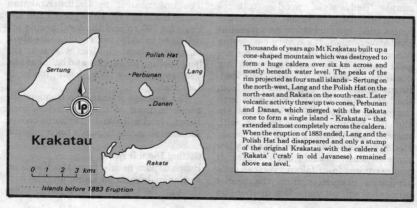

Krakatau

Polish Hat

Sertung

Perbunan

Lang

Danan

0   1   2   3 kms

Rakata

····· Islands before 1883 Eruption

Thousands of years ago Mt Krakatau built up a cone-shaped mountain which was destroyed to form a huge caldera over six km across and mostly beneath water level. The peaks of the rim projected as four small islands – Sertung on the north-west, Lang and the Polish Hat on the north-east and Rakata on the south-east. Later volcanic activity threw up two cones, Perbunan and Danan, which merged with the Rakata cone to form a single island – Krakatau – that extended almost completely across the caldera. When the eruption of 1883 ended, Lang and the Polish Hat had disappeared and only a stump of the original Krakatau with the caldera of 'Rakata' ('crab' in old Javanese) remained above sea level.

2.0 KRAKATOA, EAST OF JAVA. 1969 adventure starring Maximilian Schell and Diane Baker. After the eruption of Krakatoa, a disparate group of survivors search for a treasure-laden sunken ship. With Brian Keith, Rossano Brazzi, Barbara Werle, John Leyton, Sal Mineo, J.D. Cannon, Marc Lawrence. Directed by Bernard Kowalski. R, PGR.

Hollywood relocates Krakatau to the east of Java

Krakatau) reported odd details such as 'fish dizzy and caught with glee by natives'! Three months later the dust thrown into the atmosphere caused such vivid sunsets in the United States that fire engines were being called out to quench the apparent fires, and for three years it continued to circle the earth creating strange and spectacular sunsets.

The astonishing return of life to the devastated islands has been the subject of scientific study ever since. Not a single plant was found on Krakatau a few months after the event; 100 years later – although the islands are virtually bereft of fauna except for snakes, insects, rats, bats and birds – it seems as though the vegetation was never disturbed.

Krakatau basically blew itself to smithereens and died but, roughly where the 1883 eruption began, Anak Krakatau (the 'Child of Krakatau') has been vigorously growing ever since its first appearance in 1928. It has a restless and uncertain temperament, sending out showers of glowing rocks and belching smoke and ashes, but boats can land on the east side and it is possible to climb right up the cinder cones to the caldera. The hike is best made in the early morning when it's cool, which means an over-night trip.

A Guide to Krakatau, by zoologist I W B Thornton, has detailed maps and information and is available at the Carita Krakatau Beach Hotel or from the Krakatau Foundation, PO Box 4507, Jakarta 10001.

Getting There & Away

The Krakatau Islands are about 50 km from the nearest point on Java and getting out there can be a real hassle – during the rainy season there can be strong ocean currents and during July and August there are sometimes strong south-east winds. So the best times of year to visit are April-June and September-October. When weather conditions are fine it's a long one-day trip, four or five hours there and four or five hours back, but having visited Krakatau we'd say it's definitely worth the effort – *if* you can hire a safe boat.

Ship passing through sea choked with corpses in the Krakatau area

It's possible to charter a boat yourself from Labuhan or Carita. The PHPA office in Labuhan or the Carita Krakatau Beach Hotel can arrange a boat for 200,000 rp that can take up to 20 people, or you can haggle with the fishermen on the beach and get a much smaller boat for about 100,000 rp. However, be forewarned that many of these smaller boats used by the fishermen have a history of engine trouble when they get into the strong currents of the Sunda Straits. It's not unusual for a four-hour trip to turn into two or three days drifting at sea. While researching this edition, writer Joe Cummings spent the night on such a boat in high swells along with ten other travellers and reports it was a dire situation. In 1986, two foreigners and their Indonesian crew drifted for nearly three weeks before washing up at Bengkulu, Sumatra. If you do decide to take one of the fishing boats, be sure to take along a food reserve, some water and warm clothes in case you go adrift.

A couple of tour agencies in Jakarta do pinisi (Makassar-style schooner) tours of Ujung Kulon National Park which include visits to the Krakatau Islands: Kalpataru Club (tel 336545), Kartika Plaza Hotel and Krakatau Ujung Kulon Tours & Travel (tel 320251), Wisata International Hotel.

UJUNG KULON NATIONAL PARK

Covering about 420 square km, the Ujung Kulon National Park is on the remote south-western tip of Java, cut off from the rest of the island by a narrow marshy isthmus. Getting there usually involves a long boat ride from the port of Labuhan, roughly midway along the west coast. The best time for visiting Ujung Kulon is the dry season (April to August) when the sea is generally calm and the reserve is not so boggy. Another option is to go by land from Labuhan to Taman Jaya. In Taman Jaya you can hire a guide for a two-day walk down the peninsula.

The main park area is on the peninsula but the park also includes the nearby island of Panaitan and the smaller offshore islands of Peucang and Handeuleum. Much of the peninsula is dense lowland rainforest and a mixture of scrub, grassy plains, swamps, pandanus palms and long stretches of sandy beach on the west and south coasts. Walking trails loop round Mt Payung on the western tip, along the south coast and north to the park headquarters at Taman Jaya.

Ujung Kulon is best known as the last refuge on Java for the once plentiful one-horned rhinoceros. The shy Javan rhino, however, is an extremely rare sight (there are only about 55 in the park at this writing) and you are far more likely to come across less exotic animals including banteng (wild cattle), wild pigs, otters, squirrels, leaf monkeys and gibbons. There are about 300 blue panthers living in the forest, but these, too, are a rare sight. Green turtles nest in some of the bays and Ujung Kulon also has a wide variety of birdlife. On Peucang Island rusa deer, long-tailed macaques and big monitor lizards are common, and there is good snorkelling around coral reefs.

There are a couple of bungalows on Peucang and Handeuleum Islands and many people base themselves at Peucang – 10 minutes and 4000 rp by boat from the far western tip – and make trips to the mainland from there. If you want to visit the peninsula you must hire a PHPA guide for 5000 rp a day plus 5000 rp per meal – which the guide will cook. Plus 1500 rp for insurance – in case they have to transport your injured or lifeless body out of the park, according to the PHPA. Two Australian visitors reported they made a four-day hike from Peucang along the south coast trail to Karangranjang and walked out of the reserve to the PHPA headquarters at Taman Jaya (about 45 km in total); but they also suggested walking around the reserve from Taman Jaya or establishing a base for walks at the Karangranjang PHPA office which is right on the beach. They didn't spot any rhinos!

Places to Stay
On Handeuleum Island there is a PHPA guest house and another two on Peucang Island, with a cook and bedding provided but you must bring your own food. Each bungalow sleeps eight people and small rooms cost 7500 rp, larger rooms 10,000 rp.

Within the park on the peninsula you can camp but there are also huts at regular intervals along the trails. They're basically a roof over your head but along the south coast trail hikers have found a 'good roof' at Citadahan and a good PHPA hut on the beach at Karangranjang. You need to provide bedding and food for yourselves and the PHPA guide, but he cooks. The best place to buy provisions is Labuhan; Taman Jaya is more expensive.

Getting There & Away
You must first get a permit from the PHPA office at Labuhan, so this fishing port on the west coast, about four hours from Jakarta, is the usual jumping off point for park visits. From Labuhan you can charter the PHPA government boat for around 200,000 rp return trip to Peucang Island or Taman Jaya on the mainland; or hire a local fishing boat for about half that but you'll have to bargain hard. As with boat rides to Krakatau, try to make sure you hire a sea-worthy boat. The boat ride to Peucang takes between six and nine hours depending on the weather.

A cheaper alternative is to take a colt for 2500 rp from Labuhan south to Sumur. From Sumur it's possible to get a ride on a motorbike to Taman Jaya for around 5000 rp. In Taman Jaya you can hire a PHPA guide (5000 rp per day) for the 45-km walk across the peninsula, or hire a local boat to Peucang for about 30,000 to 50,000 rp one way. You might also be able to take a colt from Labuhan to Panimbang, the main coconut port on the west coast, charter a local boat to Peucang (25,000 rp

one way) and then walk out through the reserve.

BOGOR
Bogor, 60 km south of Jakarta, is most famous for its botanical gardens. In the days before independence, however, this was probably the most important Dutch hill station, midway between the mountains and the heat-ridden plains. Governor-General van Imhoff is credited with its discovery in 1745. He built a large country estate which he named 'Buitenzorg' ('Without a Care') but it was not until 1811 that it was first used as a country residence by Sir Stamford Raffles, during the British interregnum, and not until many years later that Bogor became the semi-official capital.

Raffles judged it as 'a romantic little village' but Bogor has grown and, other than the gardens, its beauty has somewhat faded. Although the town itself has become more or less a suburb of Jakarta, it makes a good base for nearby mountain walks. Many people visit the gardens from Jakarta or stop off on their way to Bandung and points further east, but Bogor could also be used as a Jakarta base since it only takes 30 minutes by bus between the two. From Bogor you can continue east to Bandung via the Puncak Pass or turn south to Pelabuhanratu on the coast.

Though Bogor stands at a height of only 290 metres it's appreciably cooler than Jakarta, but visitors in the wet season should bear in mind the town's nickname: the 'City of Rain'. Bogor has probably the highest annual rainfall in Java and is credited with a record 322 thunderstorms a year.

Information & Orientation
The bus station, to the south of town, is about 10 minutes walk from the garden entrance. Many of Bogor's losmen and hotels are located in the area near the railway station, roughly two km from the bus station.

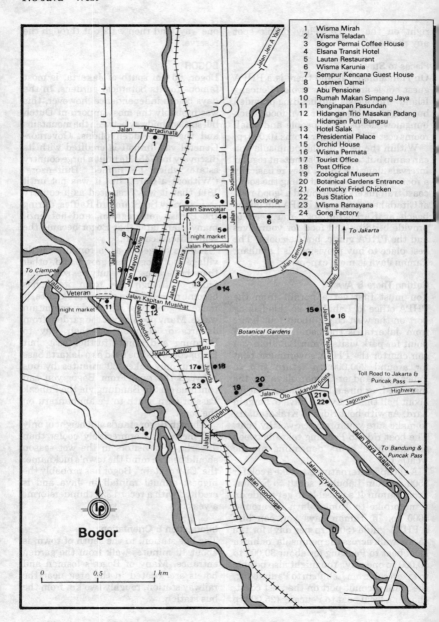

1 Wisma Mirah
2 Wisma Teladan
3 Bogor Permai Coffee House
4 Elsana Transit Hotel
5 Lautan Restaurant
6 Wisma Karunia
7 Sempur Kencana Guest House
8 Losmen Damai
9 Abu Pensione
10 Rumah Makan Simpang Jaya
11 Penginapan Pasundan
12 Hidangan Trio Masakan Padang
   Hidangan Puti Bungsu
13 Hotel Salak
14 Presidential Palace
15 Orchid House
16 Wisma Permata
17 Tourist Office
18 Post Office
19 Zoological Museum
20 Botanical Gardens Entrance
21 Kentucky Fried Chicken
22 Bus Station
23 Wisma Ramayana
24 Gong Factory

Jalan Jen A Yani
Jalan Martadinata
Jalan Merdeka
Jalan Jen Sudirman
footbridge
Jalan Sawojajar
Jalan Pengadilan
night market
Jalan Mayor Oking
Jalan Dewi Sartika
To Ciampea
Jalan Veteran
Jalan Kapitan Muslihat
Jalan Paledan
night market
Jalan X Kantor Batu
Jalan Ir H Juanda
Jalan Empang
Jalan Suryakencana
Jalan Bondongan
Jalan Oto Iskandardinata
Botanical Gardens
To Jakarta
Jalan Sempur
Jalan Gunungede
Jalan Raya Pajajaran
Jalan Raya Pajajaran
Toll Road to Jakarta &
Puncak Pass
Jagorawi Highway
To Bandung &
Puncak Pass

Bogor

0   0.5   1 km

From the tourist office, on the west side of the gardens at Jalan Ir H Juanda 38, a rough map of the town is available. The office is open 8 am to 2 pm Monday to Thursday, 8 am to 6 pm (closed 11 am to 2 pm) Friday, 8 am to 1 pm Saturday. At No 9 on the same street, next to the garden gates, is the headquarters of the PHPA – the official body for administration of all of Indonesia's wildlife reserves and national parks.

The Bogor Regency Tourist Office at Jalan Veteran 2 also has information on things to do in and around Bogor, especially hiking. If you're interested in caving, see Suwesta Wignyakuta at Esta Sports Equipment (tel 0251-21050), at the Muria Plaza shopping centre near the railway station. You can also write in advance to Dr Ko at the Federation of Indonesian Speleological Activities (FINSPAC), PO Box 55, Bogor. Dr Ko can arrange speleological expeditions in the area as well as treks along the Buena Vista Trail outside Bogor.

Kebun Raya – Botanical Gardens

At the heart of Bogor are the huge botanical gardens, known as the Kebun Raya, covering an area of 100 hectares. The gardens were the inspiration of Raffles but they were originally laid out by Professor Reinhardt and assistants from Kew Gardens, and officially opened in 1817. It was from these gardens that various colonial cash crops such as tea, cassava, tobacco and cinchona were developed by early Dutch researchers during the so-called Forced Cultivation Period in the 19th century.

The gardens contain streams and lotus ponds and more than 15,000 species of trees and plants; these include 400 types of magnificent palms and the world's largest flower, the 'Rafflesia', which blooms in October. The garden's orchid houses are reputed to contain more than 3000 orchid varieties but unfortunately appear to be closed for the present. Some mutter that visitors have been pinching precious orchid cuttings. Close to the main entrance of the gardens there is a small monument in memory of Olivia Raffles who died in 1814 and was buried in Batavia.

The gardens are open between 8 am and 4 pm and although they tend to be very crowded on Sundays on other days they are very peaceful and a fine place to escape from the hassles and crowds of Jakarta. The entrance fee is 1100 rp during the week and only 600 rp on Sundays and holidays.

Zoological Museum

Adjacent to the botanical gardens entrance is a good zoological museum with a skeleton of a blue whale and other interesting exhibits and a large library of rare botanical books. It is open from 8 am to 2 pm daily except Friday when it closes at 11 am. The entrance fee is 200 rp.

Presidential Palace

In the north-west corner of the botanical gardens, the summer palace of the president was formerly the official residence of the Dutch governors-general from 1870 to 1942. The present huge mansion is not 'Buitenzorg' though; this was destroyed by an earthquake and a new palace was built on the site a few years later in 1856. In colonial days, deer were raised in the parklands to provide meat for banquets. The Dutch elite would come up from the pesthole of Batavia and many huge, glamorous parties were held here. Following independence, the palace was a much favoured retreat for Sukarno although Suharto has ignored it.

Today the building contains Sukarno's huge art collection of 219 paintings and 156 sculptures (which is reputed to lay great emphasis on the female figure) but the palace is not normally open to the public. The Hotel Salak, opposite the palace, arranges tours for groups of 10 people or you can write directly to the Head of Protocol at the Istana Negara, Jalan Veteran, Jakarta. You need to give at least a week's notice. Through the gates you can see herds of white-spotted deer roaming on the immaculate lawns.

Other Attractions

South of the gardens, on Jalan Batu Tulis and almost opposite the former home of ex-president Sukarno, the 'Batu Tulis' is a small shrine with a stone inscribed by a priest of the region in 1533. A small donation is expected and you have to remove your shoes before entering the shrine. It's said that Sukarno chose this spot for his home because he believed the stone to be a source of mystical power.

One of the few remaining gongsmiths in West Java is Pak Sukarna's at Jalan Pancasan 17 where you can order gongs and other gamelan instruments and see them being made in the workshop. The Gong Foundry is a short walk south from the garden gates down Jalan Empang and west across the river. It consists of two buildings facing each other on both sides of the street; on one, a sign reads 'Gong Factory', on the other, 'Gong Home'. On Jalan Kantor Batu, near the tourist office, the Java carpet works of P P Dobbe & Son make wool rugs in natural colours, and attractive floor and doormats out of coconut fibre and sisal.

Places to Stay – bottom end

Abu Pensione (tel 22893) is one of the new travellers' standbys, located at Jalan Mayor Oking 7, near the train station. It's a friendly, family-run guest house with dorm beds at 3000 rp. Clean, comfortable private rooms are 8000 rp with shared bath, 12,000 rp with attached bath. All room rates (but not the dorm) include a large breakfast of toast with Mama's delicious homemade pineapple jam, eggs, cheese and coffee or tea. Other meals are available and there's a pleasant garden terrace that overlooks the river. The owner, Abu, is a good source of information on do-it-yourself tours around Bogor. To get there from the bus terminal, take a No 3 Daihatsu and get off at the Muria Plaza

shopping centre at the intersection of Jalan Mayor Oking and and Jalan Kapitan Muslihat. Another recommended place is *Homestay Puri Bali* at Jalan Paledang 30, not far from the Kebun Raya. Doubles are 9000 rp and include a large breakfast. And there's the similar *Pensione Firman* next door at No 28.

The *Losmen Damai*, a bit further up Jalan Mayor Oking from Abu Pensione at No 28, is the rock-bottom choice but rooms are pretty drab and grubby. Rates are 3500/6500 rp single/double. Over the railway tracks and the river, the *Penginapan Pasundan* is at Jalan Mantarena 19 close behind Jalan Veteran. It's more expensive but hardly any better – doubles with a bathroom cost 12,500 rp. The *Wisma Teladan* (tel 25327) at Jalan Sawojajar 3A is similarly priced but a little better; rooms starting at 10,000 rp (15,000 rp with bath) are somewhat shabby but at least it has a large grass courtyard.

Near the main gates for the botanical gardens at Jalan Ir H Juanda 44 is *Wisma Ramayana*, where rooms are from 8500 to 16,000 rp. It's convenient to the tourist office, post office and bus terminal, but is often frequented by would-be guides and touts so may not be the best choice for peace and quiet.

Places to Stay – middle

There are two more guest houses across the river to the north of the botanical gardens, a little out of the way but quiet. *Wisma Karunia* (tel 23411), Jalan Sempur 34-37, is a large private home with clean well-kept rooms starting at 11,000 rp for a double with shared bath, 15,000 rp with attached bath. Larger rooms cost 25,000 rp and there is also a large dorm which costs 5000 rp per bed. *Sempur Kencana* (tel 28347) at Jalan Sempur 6 is similar and also has a restaurant. Rooms here are 8000, 12,000 and 15,000 rp. They also have a large double with attached bath for 22,000 rp and a family room with verandah for 35,000 rp. To get to Jalan Sempur from the railway terminal, take a No 7 Daihatsu, or from the bus terminal, a No 8 or 9.

Places to Stay – top end

The *Hotel Salak* (tel 22091), at Jalan Ir H Juanda 8 opposite the palace, is a big colonial hotel with enormous rooms from 15,000 rp without bathroom, from 19,000 rp with bathroom, or 23,000 or 32,000 rp with air-con. It could be quite a nice place to stay if it weren't run-down, decaying and damp. Hordes of lackeys do nothing for the standards in this all but deserted hotel.

At Jalan Sawojajar 36, the *Elsana Transit Hotel* (tel 2252) has doubles with attached bath from 19,000 rp including breakfast and tax. It's nothing special, but the staff is friendly and the rooms fairly well-kept.

Places to Eat

The *Puja Sera Muria* is an open-air hawkers' centre on Jalan Mayor Oking between the Muria Plaza shopping centre and Abu Pensione. It is a good clean place with an assortment of Indonesian and Chinese stalls. The *kwetiaw* here is particularly good, and ice drinks and beer are available. Cheaper food stalls appear at night along Jalan Dewi Sartika and during the day you'll find plenty of food stalls and good fruit at Pasar Bogor, the market close to the garden gates. Behind the bus station is another good area for cheap warung food.

Also in the vicinity of the railway station and Muria Plaza are several Padang restaurants, including *Hidangan Trio Masakan Padang, Hidangan Puti Bungsu* and *Rumah Makan Simpang Jaya*. Next to the Wisma Ramayana is *Fajar*, which specialises in Sundanese food.

The *Bogor Permai Coffee House*, on Jalan Jenderal Sudirman near Jalan Sawojajar, is a large, semi-modern restaurant and bakery where most meals cost from 2500 to 3500 rp. There is also a supermarket here. The nearby *Lautan Restaurant* is similar in menu and price.

Bogor also has a *Kentucky Fried Chicken* south of the garden near the bus terminal.

Getting There & Away

Bus Buses depart every 10 minutes or so from the Cililitan bus station in Jakarta. Take a Jalan Tol bus which goes via the toll expressway and is a fair bit faster (30 minutes) and only marginally more expensive at 600 rp than the buses which go via Cibinong. If you're heading west from Bogor there are buses straight through to Merak, via Jakarta and Serang, for around 1500 rp (four hours). You can also travel by bus between Labuhan on the west coast and Bogor, changing buses in Pandeglang. Buses run frequently between Bogor and Bandung via the Puncak Pass. The fare is 1500 rp and the trip takes three hours.

Colts also depart from the bus station for Cibadak, the turn-off point for Pelabuhanratu. Colts to villages around Bogor, including Ciampea, depart from the stand near the railway station.

Rail Trains operate to and from Jakarta (Gambir) at least every hour between 7.20 am and 6.30 pm – ideal for day trips but avoid the crowded commuter trains in the early morning and late afternoon at all costs. The trip takes about 1½ hours and the fare is 500 rp all-3rd class. Three daily trains operate between Bogor and Sukabumi; they depart Bogor at 6.30 am, 11.30 am and 4.30 pm, and take about two hours. There is no direct railway link to Bandung.

Getting Around

There are lots and lots of bemos for a fixed fare of 100 rp around town for three-wheelers and 150 rp for four-wheelers. They run between the bus station and the main bemo/colt stand near the train station. There are plenty of becaks too, but they're banned from the main street, Jalan Ir H Juanda.

AROUND BOGOR

Purnawarman Stone (Batu Tulis)

From the village of Ciampea, about 18 km north-east of Bogor, you can walk (about two km) through the rice fields to the site of a huge black boulder on which King Purnawarman inscribed his name and footstep around 450 AD. His inscription, in the Palawa script of South India, reads: 'This is the footstep of King Purnawarman of Tarumanegara Kingdom, the great conqueror of the world.'

Another stone inscription of the Taruma kingdom – the Prasati Tugu – can be seen in the National Museum in Jakarta. It refers to the digging of an 11-km-long canal in the Jakarta area during the reign of Purnawarman – which may have been the first of many efforts to solve Jakarta's flooding problem! The canal was dug by Brahmans in only 21 days and for their labours they were rewarded with 1000 cows. The Ciampea boulder lies embedded in the shallow water of the Ciaruteun River, so you have to climb down into the gorge to see it. The inscription is still remarkably clear after more than 1500 years.

Other Attractions

In Ciampea, you can see one of the last remaining Chinese gamelan ensembles at the home of Lu Liang Beng. He needs two to three days advance notice to arrange a performance and can be contacted through Abu Pensione in Bogor. Ciampea can be reached from Bogor by a 300 rp, 20-minute Daihatsu ride.

Several travellers have recommended hiking in the Lokapurna area near Bogor. To get there, take a colt (300 rp) to Cibadak, then another to Pasar Jumbat (500 rp). From Pasar Jumbat it's a 5-km walk to Lokapurna, about 1½ hours. Most people spend the night in Lokapurna so they can get in a full day's hiking the next day. From Lokapurna, you can hike either to the local hot springs (*air panas*), to the

volcano crater of Kawa Ratu, or if you're feeling fit, all the way to Pelabuhanratu on the south coast.

Places to Stay

In Lokapurna, you can stay at *Haji's* for 3000 rp per night. The *Kopo Hostel* at Cisarua, just outside Bogor is good value. See 'Bogor to Bandung'.

PELABUHANRATU

A small fishing town 90 km south of Bogor and roughly 150 km south-west of Bandung, Pelabuhanratu is a popular local seaside resort. Though quiet during the week, it can be crowded at weekends and holidays and – unless you camp out – accommodation is fairly expensive. This is mainly a place for hiking – there are magnificent rocky cliffs along West Java's deserted southern coastline, and deep river gorges and caves. There's also a fine beach but the crashing surf can be treacherous. One or two people are reportedly drowned every year in spite of the warning signs which went up after the Bulgarian Ambassador disappeared here some years ago.

Swimming off most of Java's south coast is dangerous. If you want to go into the realms of legend, Pelabuhanratu ('Harbour of the Queen') actually witnessed the creation of Nyai Lara Kidul, the malevolent Goddess who takes fishermen and swimmers off to her watery kingdom. Locals will tell you not to wear green on the beach or in the water (it's her colour), and in the Samudra Hotel a room is always kept unoccupied for offerings to the Queen of the South Seas. The beach is also the scene for an annual Sea Festival in April during which the fishermen sacrifice a buffalo head to the sea and scatter flowers on the water.

Five km or so west of the Samudra Hotel, at Pantai Karang Hawu there is a towering cliff with caves, rocks and pools which were created by a large lava flow that pushed over the beach. According to legend, it was from the rocks of Karang

Hawu that Nyai Lara Kidul leapt into the mighty ocean to regain her lost beauty and never returned. Farther west, near the fishing village of Cisolok, there are hot springs. Cikotok, about 30 km from the Samudra, is the site of Java's most important gold and silver mines.

Places to Stay – bottom end

Along the four km between Pelabuhanratu's fish market and the big Samudra Beach Hotel, there's a camping place and a number of beach bungalows to rent but rates for the latter are likely to be over 10,000 rp.

The *Bayu Armta* (tel Pelabuhanratu 31 or Bandung 50882) has basic but comfortable bungalows perched on the edge of a cliff. Doubles and triples cost between 10,000 and 20,000 rp. Also known as 'Hoffman's' (after the owner) or the 'Fish Restaurant', this is a popular place and its attached restaurant has a reputation for excellent seafood.

The *Pondok Dewata* (tel Pelabuhanratu 22 or Bandung 772426) has cottages (all air-con) from 25,000 to 50,000 rp, a restaurant and swimming pool. Other bungalows include *Karang Sari* and *Gunung Kutu*.

Places to Stay – top end

A few km west of town, the *Samudra Beach Hotel* (tel Pelabuhanratu 23) is a modern high-rise with several restaurants and a good swimming pool. Rooms rates are high and standards may not be as good as they once were; air-con singles/doubles cost from US$35/45 and suites from US$75, plus 15.5% tax and service.

Getting There & Away

By road or rail from Bogor the route cuts south over the pass between Gunung Salak and Pangrango through valleys and hillsides of rubber and tea plantations and terraced rice fields. You can take a colt or the train from Bogor as far as Cibadak or Sukabumi (20 km further east) and then another colt south to the coast. You can

also hike here in one day from Lokapurna, a village near Cibadak. See Around Bogor for details on how to get to Lokapurna.

From Bandung it's about 4½ hours by bus for around 1400 rp. From Labuhan you can take various buses through the towns of Saketi and Malimping for a total of 2000 rp and seven hours – it's a very scenic and little-travelled route.

BOGOR TO BANDUNG

Puncak Pass

If you take the bus from Bogor to Bandung you cross over this beautiful 1500-metre-high pass on a narrow, winding mountain road which passes through small resort towns and tea plantations. At high altitudes it's cool and often misty but in the early mornings the views across the valleys can be superb. There are some good hikes in this area, especially from Tugu and Cisarua on the Bogor side of the pass or Cibodas and Cipanas on the other side. You can get up to the towns on the pass by taking a colt or any Bandung bus from Bogor.

Cisarua

Ten km from Bogor on the slopes of the Puncak, there are good walks to picnic spots and waterfalls around this small town. On the way up to the Puncak summit you can stop at the huge Gunung Mas tea plantation for a free tour of the tea factory. Then walk on through the plantation to Telaga Warna, a small 'lake of many colours' just below the top of the pass which reflects red, yellow or green with changing daylight. Cut back to the main road nearby and you can flag down a bus or colt as they pass by the *Rindu Alam Restaurant*.

Places to Stay The *Kopo Hostel* (tel 0251-4296) is at Jalan Raya Puncak 557 in Cisarua. Its several bungalows offer a total of 17 rooms and three dormitories in a garden setting. It's excellent value with dorm beds at 2000 rp and rooms from 6000 rp with blankets provided. There are discounts available for IYH cardholders. Coffee, cold drinks and meals are available. They also have maps of walks and information on places of interest in the area. The hostel is open from 7 am to 10 pm and from Bogor it's about 45 minutes by bus or colt (300 rp). Ask for the Cisarua Petrol Station (*Pompa Bensin Cisarua*) and you'll find the hostel right next door.

The *Chalet Bali International* in Cisarua is affiliated with the infamous Bali International in Jakarta and has dorm beds at 3500 rp, singles/doubles at 10,000/12,500 rp.

In Cibulan, the next town on towards the Puncak, the *Hotel Cibulan* is a fairly run-down old-world Dutch hotel but a friendly place. Rooms with a bathroom cost from around 6000 rp and include free admission to the swimming pool opposite. Rates are more expensive on weekends when people from Jakarta flock up here to escape the heat.

Along the main road, in the various towns, there are numerous sate places and restaurants. The Puncak is an excellent place for fruit which is sold along the roadside – pineapples, melons, durian and delicious mangosteens (in season around November, December).

Cibodas

At Cibodas, just over the Puncak Pass, there is a beautiful high-altitude extension of the Bogor botanical gardens surrounded by thick tropical jungle on the slopes of the twin volcanoes Gunung Gede and Pangrango. These 80 hectare gardens were originally planted in 1860. The gardens are five km off the main road from Bogor to Bandung and only a short distance from Cipanas.

Gunung Gede

The Cibodas gardens are also the start of the climb to the 2958-metre peak of volcanically active Gunung Gede. From the top of Gede on a clear day you can see Jakarta, Cirebon and even to Pelabuhan-

ratu on the south coast – well Raffles reported he could! To make the climb you must first get a permit from the PHPA office, located just outside the garden entrance. There is no admission charge and you can pick up free route maps here and useful information on the Gede-Pangrango National Park at the same time. The office is open 8 am to 3 pm Monday to Thursday, to 11.30 am Friday and until 2 pm Saturday. It is closed Sundays and holidays.

Along the trail there are beautiful waterfalls such as Cibeureum Falls (one hour) and another where the falls drop deep into a steaming gorge (another hour). It's a 10-km hike right to the top which takes six to 12 hours there and back so you should start as early as possible and take warm clothes (night temperatures can drop to 5°C). There is a also a steeper trail to the top of Gunung Pangrango (3019 metres) which requires an extra one to two hours. Dense fog is common on the mountain so take extra care when on the steeper trails – hikers have been known to walk off into unseen gorges during foggy conditions. The best time to make the hike is from May to October. Gede is only marginally less rainy than Bogor and the climb isn't recommended during the rainy season. An alternative approach is to climb Gede from the south and take the trail from the PHPA office at Selabintana, seven km north of Sukabumi.

Places to Stay The modern *Pondok Pemuda Cibodas* near the Cibodas PHPA office has dorm beds at 4200 rp and doubles at 8000 rp. It's a friendly comfortable place in a superb location, but by putting small windows under the eaves they've successfully managed to block out the lovely view! In the village, 500 metres down the hill, you can stay with Muhamed Saleh Abdullah (also known as Freddy) for around 1000 rp. There's cheap food at the warungs near the gardens and in the village.

Cipanas

At Cipanas, five km beyond the Cibodas turn off, there is another seldom-used summer presidential palace. Built in 1750, it is an elegant country house in beautiful gardens but, like the Bogor Palace, it is not normally open to the public. In the centre of town, the *Roda Restaurant* is a popular lunch stop. There's good food and from the terrace at the back of the restaurant you have a fine view of the valleys around the Puncak. From Cipanas, Bandung is about two hours away by bus.

BANDUNG

Bandung with its population of 1,500,000 is the capital of West Java and Indonesia's third largest city. Despite its size, it is a fairly unhurried provincial place and lacks the often suffocating overcrowding of Jakarta and Surabaya. At 750 metres above sea level and with a cool and comfortable climate, it's the city to which people from all over Indonesia, and from abroad, go to look for work and higher education. The majority of the population are the native Sundanese of West Java, who not only have a reputation as extroverted, easy-going people compared to the extremely refined Javanese, but also as zealous guardians of their own ancient culture. In contrast, the city itself is relatively new.

Bandung was originally established in the late 19th century as a Dutch garrison town of some 90,000 Sundanese, Chinese and Europeans. It rapidly acquired importance as a commercial and educational centre, renowned in particular for its Institute of Technology. Up until 1962 there was speculation – and hope – that it was to become the capital of the nation, but Bandung's chief claim to fame has been that it was the site for the Afro-Asian conference in 1955. On the industrial front, Bandung has maintained some of its European-created production centres, and its major concerns include textiles, tea and food processing and one of the world's largest quinine factories.

Though in the past Bandung has been described as the 'Paris of Java', due to its many fine parks and gardens, much of the city's former glamour has faded. As far as its general appearance goes, what exists today is a mish-mash of dilapidated colonial and modern buildings. One exception is the Savoy Homann Hotel, a superb example of Art-Deco architecture.

Bandung is an excellent place to visit if you're interested in Sundanese culture; otherwise its main attractions lie in the beautiful countryside around the city. To the north and south there's a wild tangle of high volcanic peaks, including the famous Tangkuban Prahu volcano, and several huge tea plantations. There are some fine walks in the area – one of the best is the river walk from the village of Maribaya to Dago Hill on the outskirts of Bandung.

Information & Orientation

Bandung sprawls out over the northern foothills of a huge plateau surrounded by high mountain ridges. The city is divided into two parts by the railway line which cuts roughly through the centre. The main part of the city lies south of the railway line and is very compact. Bandung's main road, Jalan Asia Afrika, runs through it and the main focal point is the city square (Alun-Alun) which is only about 700 metres from the train station. Along Jalan Asia Afrika are the tourist offices, the post office and most of the banks, airline offices, restaurants and top-range hotels. On the south side of the square the Parahyangan Plaza is a modern shopping complex with bakeries, snack bars and a variety of retail outlets. Jalan Braga, on the north side, is the ritzy central shopping area with several useful bookshops, plenty of souvenir shops and cafes.

The budget hotel area in Bandung lies on either side of the railway station. Across the railway tracks to the north is the residential area studded with tree-lined streets and parks, and bordered on

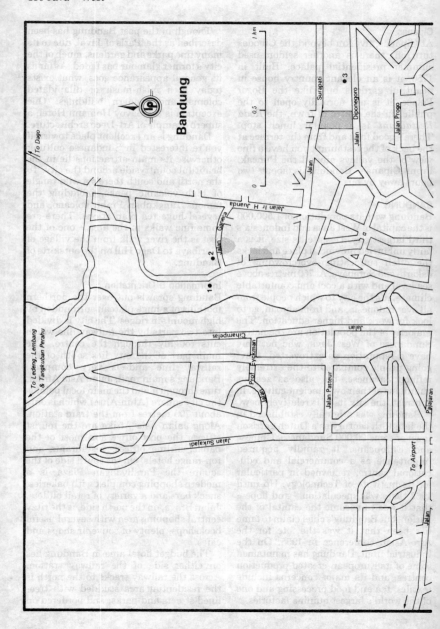

Bandung

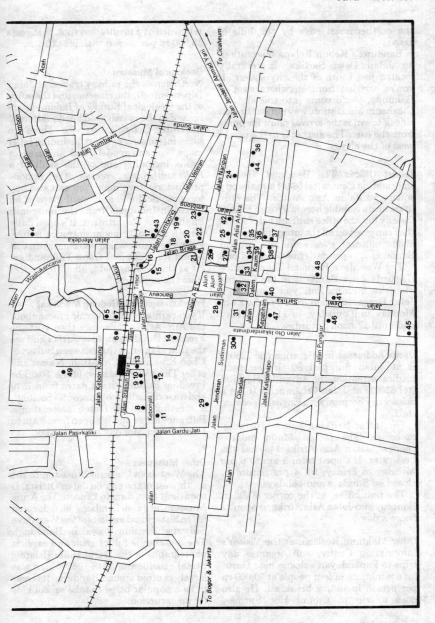

To Cicaheum

Jalan Jenderal Ahmad Yani

Jalan Aceh

Jalan Ambon

Jalan Ambon

Jalan Sunda

Jalan Sumbawa

Jalan Veteran

Jalan Naripan

36
44
24
23
42
35
36
37
20
22
25
34
39
38
48
33
32
40
41
45
46
47
48

Jalan Merkeka

17
18
19
16 Jalan Lembong
15
21
26
27

Jalan Braga

Jalan Asia Afrika

Jalan Kaum

Jalan Dewi

Jalan Sarikah

Jalan Dalem

Jalan Kepatihan

Jalan Oto Iskandardinata

Jalan Pungkur

4

Jalan Wastukencana

Jalan Stasiun Timor

Jalan Sumatera

Jalan A B C

Alun Alun Square

Jalan Bancuy

Jalan Sudirman

Jalan Jenderan

Jalan Cibadak

Jalan Kalipahapo

5
7
28
31
30
29

6
14
12

49
13
9 10
8 11
Kebonjati

Jalan Kebon Kawung

Jalan Stasiun Bara

Jalan Pasirkaliki

Jalan Gardu Jati

To Bogor & Jakarta

the northernmost edge by the hills of Dago.

Bandung's Kebun Kelapa bus station, on Jalan Dewi Sartika, is centrally located just south of the city square. If you're arriving from anywhere west of Bandung, you'll come into this station. Cicaheum bus station, way out on the east side of town, is the arrival point for buses from the east. The airport is to the north-west of the city.

Tourist Offices The Bandung Visitor's Information Centre (tel 5644) is at the city square on Jalan Asia Afrika. The only literature available here is a rough map of the city but the office staff are helpful and they can give you all the latest information about cultural events in and around Bandung. It's open daily from 9 am to 7 pm.

The West Java Regional Tourist office (Diparda Jawa Barat) is in the Gedung Merdeka building but you enter from Jalan Braga. It's open from 8 am to 2 pm Monday to Thursday, to 11 am Friday and until 12 noon Saturday.

Useful Addresses Immigration (tel 72801) is at Jalan Surapati 80. If you need medical attention, the Adventist Hospital (tel 82091) at Jalan Cihampelas 161 is a missionary hospital with English-speaking staff.

For after-banking-hours currency exchange, The *Dwipa Mulia* money-changer, Jalan Asia Afrika 148, has the best rates. It's open from 8 am to 6 pm Monday to Friday, till 4 pm Saturday, closed on Sundays and holidays.

The post office, at the corner of Jalan Banceuy and Jalan Asia Afrika, is open 24 hours a day.

Other Makmun Rustina, at the Visitor's Information Centre, will organise day trips to Papandayan volcano near Garut for a minimum of four people at 30,000 rp per person including breakfast. He also does a trip to Cibuni Hot Springs,

renowned as a meditation spot, that costs 15,000 rp per person with breakfast.

Geological Museum
North across the railway tracks, at Jalan Diponegoro 57, the museum and the office of the Geological Survey of Indonesia are housed in the massive old headquarters of the Dutch Geological Service. There are some interesting exhibits including relief maps, volcano models and an array of fossils including one of the skull of a *Pithecanthropus erectus*, the famous pre-historic Java man. You can also buy topographical and geological maps of all places in Indonesia from the museum's Publications Department. It's open daily from 8 am to 12 noon; entrance is free. From the train station you can take a colt bound for 'Terminal Gang Tilil' and get off at the Gedung Sate, about 50 metres from the museum.

Freedom Building (Gedung Merdeka)
If you're interested in learning more about the Afro-Asian conference then visit the Freedom Building on Asia-Afrika and see the film of the meeting between Sukarno, Chou En-Lai, Ho Chi Minh, Nasser and other Third World leaders of the '50s. The Freedom Building itself dates from 1879 and was originally the 'Concordia Sociteit', a meeting hall of Dutch associations. Entrance is free and it's open from 8 am to 1 pm, closed Monday and Saturday.

Other Museums
The West Java Cultural Museum, to the south-west of the city on Jalan Ottista, is open daily from 8 am to 12 noon. The Army Museum, at Jalan Lembong 38, is devoted to the history and exploits of the West Java Siliwangi division (based in Bandung). The museum is full of grim and explicit photographs of the Darul Islam (Islamic State) rebellion of 1948-1962 which was largely centred around Bandung. It seems to be a popular place to take school kids for an excursion.

1	Zoo
2	ITB
3	Geological Museum
4	Wisma Remaja
5	Hotel Sahara
6	Hotel Guntur
7	Hotel Malabar
8	New Losmen Sakadarna
9	Old Losmen Sakadarna
10	Hotel Melati I
11	Hotel Surabaya
12	Hotel Melati II
13	Warungs & Restaurants
14	Pasar Baru
15	Cafe Corner
16	4848 Taxi Station
17	Hotel Panghegar
18	Braga Permai
19	Army Museum
20	Sumber Hidangan
21	French Bakery
22	Canary Bakery
23	Rasa Bakery
24	Galaya Restaurant
25	Garuda Office
26	Braga Fast Food
27	Gedung Merdeka
28	Main Post Office
29	Tjoen Kie Restaurant
30	Golden Moneychanger
31	Dunkin' Donuts
32	Tourist Office
33	Palaguna Shopping Centre
34	Queen Restaurant
35	Savoy Homann Hotel
36	Dwipa Mulia Moneychanger
37	Hotel Pangang Sari
38	Hotel Mawar
39	Rumah Makan Kartika Jaya
40	Warung Nasi Mang Udju
41	Kebun Kelapa Bus Station
42	Grand Hotel Preanger
43	YPK Theatre
44	Kumala Hotel Panghegar
45	Langen Setra
46	Hotel Brajawijaya
47	Hotel Harapan
48	Hotel Pacific
49	Hotel Nugraha

Institute of Technology/ITB

To the north of town on Jalan Ganeca is the Bandung Institute of Technology, constructed at the beginning of the century. The university has large grounds and gardens and the main campus complex is notable for its Minangkabau style of architecture. You can get there by taking a Dago Honda from the railway station terminus.

Opened in 1920, the ITB was the first Dutch-founded university open to Indonesians. It was here that Sukarno studied civil engineering (1920-1925) and helped to found the Bandung Study Club, members of which formed a political party which grew as the PNI (Indonesian Nationalist Party) with independence as its goal. ITB students have maintained their reputation for outspokenness and political activism and in 1978 they published the *White Book of the 1978 Students Struggle* against alleged corruption in high places. It was banned in Indonesia but later published in the United States. The ITB is the foremost scientific university in the country but it's also reputed to have one of the best fine arts schools, and its art gallery can be visited. Across from the main gate there is a useful canteen in the *Asrama Mahasiswa* (student dorm complex) where many of the students congregate.

Zoo

A few minutes' walk from the ITB, Bandung's zoo on Jalan Taman Sari has Komodo dragons, a wide variety of Indonesian birdlife and lots of open park space. It's open daily from 9 am to 5 pm and admission is 400 rp.

Dago

At the end of Jalan Merdeka, Jalan Haji Juanda climbs up to Dago Hill to the north, overlooking the city. The *Dago Tea House*, set on a projecting bluff, is the best view point – from here you can see the lights of Bandung and it's a fine place for catching the sunset. This is part of the

Pajajaran University Campus and it's a very popular place with students and travellers. Not only is the food good and cheap, but you can also eat out on the garden terrace. The teahouse is open until 11.30 pm.

Dago itself was, and perhaps still is, an expensive residential suburb; it's a pleasant tree-shaded area to walk around. Just behind the teahouse is the Dago waterfall, and about 2½ km to the north there is a huge cliff in which the Gua Pakar Cave was hacked out by the Japanese to store ammunition during the war. The latter is the start (or the end) of the walk between Maribaya and Dago along the River Cikapundung (see 'Around Bandung').

Performances

The wayang golek puppet performances which are held every Saturday night are worth seeing. They are presented in the YPK (Yayasan Pusat Kebudayaan) theatre at Jalan Naripan 7 and tickets cost 1000 to 2000 rp, depending on the reputation of the dalang. It's a lively performance – punctuated by exploding fireworks just to make sure you keep awake – that runs from 9 pm to 5 am, finishing just in time to catch an early morning train out!

You can see Sundanese dance every Wednesday and Saturday at 7 pm at the Panghegar Hotel – admission is free with dinner. Langen Setra is a Jaipongan dance club that features Ketuktilu, Jaipongan, and 'breakpong' (break dancing mixed with Jaipongan), every evening from 9 pm to 2 am. Entry is a steep (for Indonesia) 3000 rp, but it's the real thing. If you join the performers for a dance, 750 rp is added to your bill for each song. There's a bit of ambiguity in the air as to whether the dancers are for hire after hours, but this is in keeping with the original spirit of Jaipongan's progenitor, Kutuktilu, which is traditionally danced by prostitutes. The club is in the Purwa Setra building on Gang Tegalega off Jalan Oto Iskandardinata,

about 700 metres south of Kebun Kelapa bus station.

The ASKI-Bandung (or Kokar-Konservatori Karawitan), also in the southern part of the city at Jalan Buah Batu 212, is a school for traditional Sundanese arts – music, dancing and pencak silat (the art of self defence). It is open to visitors every morning, 8 am to 1 pm, except Sunday. You can get there by bemo from Kebun Kelapa bus station. Take one going to the Buah Batu bus terminal for 150 rp.

Pak Ujo's Bamboo Workshop (*Saung Angklung*) on Jalan Padasuka has angklung performances some afternoons, but it's expensive at 3500 rp and reportedly rather tailored to western tastes. To get there take a city bus towards Cicaheum and ask for 'Saung Angklung' or 'Pak Ujo'.

Some of the large hotels, including the Hotel Panghegar and the Grand Hotel Preanger on Jalan Asia Afrika, also have programmes of Sundanese music and dancing.

Finally, when strolling down Jalan Braga, keep an eye out for local celebrity Braga Stone, a blind kecapi-player. He sometimes plays on the sidewalk when not touring with the Sundanese pop music group 'Rollies'.

Ram fights On the second and fourth Sunday mornings of the month, noisy traditional ram-butting fights (known as *adu dombak*) are held at Cilimus near Ledeng to the north of the city. To the sound of drums, gongs and hand clapping, two rams keep charging at each other with a head-on clash of horns until one of them gets knocked out. If a ram gets dizzy they tweak his testicles and send him back into combat until he's had enough! This sport has been popular in West Java for so long that most villages have their own ram-fight societies and there are organised tournaments to encourage farmers to rear a stronger breed of ram. At village level it's just good fun; at district and provincial level there's wild betting.

Places to Stay – bottom end

Near the railway station and the centre of town on Jalan Kebonjati there are two economical guest houses with similar names. The original *Losmen Sakadarna* (tel 439897) at No 50/7B is a small, quiet place with an upstairs balcony and basic rooms for 4000 rp.

Further down at Jalan Kebonjati 34 is the newer and more spacious *Sakadarna International Travellers Homestay & Restaurant*, run by the outgoing Rusty Muchfree and his Dutch wife Marjo. On the bottom floor is a good restaurant with a full selection of breakfasts – tea or coffee with toast and jam is only 400 rp; other breakfasts start at 1750 rp. On the roof is a pleasant terrace and the whole place is well kept and clean. Dorm beds are 3000 rp, rooms 5000 rp for one person, 7000 rp for two.

The *Surabaya Hotel* (tel 51133), near the Sakadarnas at Jalan Kebonjati 71, is a rambling old colonial building with grubby singles/doubles at 3000/6000 rp. Not recommended unless it's the only thing available. Just north over the railway pass is the *Hotel Malabar* at Jalan Kebun Jukut 3. Small, dingy singles cost 5000 rp including free tea in the morning, or better doubles/triples cost 6000/9000 rp. The lobby is set up as an information centre of sorts, with maps, train schedules, and so on. It's fairly clean if a little dark.

The *Wisma Remaja*, in a lively government youth activities centre at Jalan Merdeka 64, is cheap and popular but sometimes rather crowded. Dormitory beds cost 2500 rp, doubles 4500 rp and there is a small reasonably-priced cafe. It's about a 20-minute walk from the train station or take a Dago minibus and ask for the youth centre, *Gelanggang Generasi Muda Bandung*.

Right in the centre of town, the *Hotel Mawar* at Jalan Pangarang 14 is a short walk from the Kebun Kelapa bus station. Very few westerners stay here but it's quiet and friendly if not the cleanest place in town and has something of a garden. The rooms are 5500/6000 rp including coffee in the morning. The *Pangarang Sari Hotel* nearby at No 3 has slightly better rooms with mandi at 7000/9000 rp including the usual jam sandwich & coffee breakfast.

Places to Stay – middle

Round the corner from the Malabar, the *Hotel Sahara* (tel 51684) at Jalan Oto Iskandardinata 3 has clean, simple rooms around a courtyard for 7500/11,500 rp including breakfast. Rooms with mandi, western toilet and TV cost 17,000/23,000 rp. Also in the vicinity of the railway station is the newly renovated *Hotel Nugraha* (tel 436146) at Jalan H Mesri 11, off Jalan Kebon Kawung. Surrounding a garden with rattan and bamboo furniture are clean rooms that range between 10,000 and 25,000 rp including breakfast. The friendly staff and good service make it good value.

The *Hotel Guntur* (tel 50763) at Jalan Oto Iskandardinata 20, just north of the railway line and near the Malabar, is a very comfortable mid-range hotel. Singles/doubles, with hot water, telephone and TV, start at 21,000/24,000 rp including a substantial breakfast.

Near the Kebun Kelapa bus terminal are three more hotels in this range. Best of the three is *Hotel Harapan* (tel 51212) at Jalan Kepatihan 14-16. Room rates are in the 15,000 to 25,000 rp range, the facilities are nice (hot water during certain morning and evening hours) and it is generally very well maintained. *Hotel Braja Wijaya* (tel 50673), just west of the bus terminal at Jalan Pungkur 28, is a passable Indonesian-style place where doubles start at 15,000 rp including a bread & coffee breakfast. The *Hotel Pacific*, to the east of the terminal on the other side of Jalan Pungkur, is in the same price range, but a bit nicer with quiet, fairly clean rooms, some of which are carpeted.

Straddling the bottom and middle categories are two places with mid-range prices but bottom-end facilities. *Hotel Melati II* (tel 56409) on Jalan Kebonjati near the two Sakadarna losmens, has just adequate rooms for 12,000/22,000 rp. Its older sister, *Hotel Melati I* starts at 8500/11,000 rp but is noisy and poorly kept.

Places to Stay – top end

The *Savoy Homann Hotel* (tel 58091) is conveniently central at Jalan Asia Afrika 112. Once 'the' hotel of Bandung, it is still a stylish old Art Deco building with spacious rooms off a small courtyard garden. Air-con singles/doubles with bathroom cost US$39/49 (plus 21% tax and service charge) or there are 'deluxe' rooms available at US$91. The hotel has a comfortable coffee lounge and restaurant.

The *Hotel Panghegar* (tel 57584) at Jalan Merdeka 2 is Bandung's top hotel. Rooms cost from US$56 and the hotel has all the modern facilities.

A fairly new hotel is the modern *Kumala Panghegar* (tel 51242) at Jalan Asia Afrika 140. Rooms, all air-con, start at 44,000 rp and the hotel has a bar and restaurant.

The *Hotel Trio* (tel 615055) at Jalan Gardujati 55-61 is a very clean, unpretentious, centrally located hotel frequented by Chinese businessmen with rooms in the 40,000 to 50,000 rp range.

Places to Eat

Bandung has some excellent food venues. In the railway station area, the restaurant at *Sakadarna International Travellers Homestay* at Jalan Kebonjati 34 is popular even among travellers who aren't staying there for its reasonably priced (but not cheap) Dutch and Indonesian meals and western-style breakfasts. Directly in front of the railway station, in the area where the bemos stop between the station and Jalan Kebonjati, is a selection of good night warungs and restaurants. Popular places include *Rumah Makan Hadori Satay House*, *Rumah Makan Gahaya Minang*, and *Warung Gizi*. There is also an alley of inexpensive warungs between the Sahara and Malabar Hotels off Jalan Oto Iskandardinata.

Restaurants in the centre of town can be fairly expensive but there is a good, lively night market on Jalan Cikapundung Barat, directly across Asia Afrika from the Visitor's Information Centre. There are stalls for all kinds of food from soto and sate to gado-gado and seafood and probably the number one *martabak manis* in Java. One traveller has recommended trying *roti bakar* – a whole loaf sliced horizontally and spread with peanut butter and condensed milk! Well, he reported it to be 'delicious and filling'. For the cheapest warung food try those up near the river where the becak men eat.

At the *Simpang Raya*, beside the central square to one side of the Tourist Information Centre, you'll find excellent Padang food and have a view of the square. On the mosque side of the square is the similar *Minang Jaya*. Nearby on Asia-Afrika at No 113 the *Galaya Pub & Restaurant* is clean, quiet and pleasant. It's split into two restaurants: one has a western menu and is fairly expensive; the other is a self-service canteen with good Sundanese food at reasonable prices – specialities include soups and steamed goldfish.

On the ground floor of the Palaguna Shopping Centre on the east side of the square is the *Istana Peters* ice cream parlour which features interesting flavours like durian, jackfruit, and zurzat for 650 rp. Upstairs there are other fast food type places – *Home Bakery*, *Hero Fast Food* and *Pioneer Fried Chicken*. Nearby on Jalan Dalem Kaum, there's even a *Dunkin' Donuts* (500 rp each) with what looks like a thousand varieties of donuts.

The *Galaxy Cafeteria* on the top floor of the Galaxy Theatre complex on Jalan

Top: Segara Anakan, Central Java (JC)
Bottom: Riverboat, Segara Anakan, Central Java (JC)

Top: Religious procession, Ubud, Bali (VB)
Left: 'Unspoilt beauty', Candidasa, Bali (RN)
Right: Repairing a retaining wall, Candidasa, Bali (VB)

Kepatihan has probably the cheapest beer in central Bandung. A large bottle of Bintang is only 1500 rp. The Chinese and Indonesian food on the menu is also cheap, and most nights there is live pop music – nothing spectacular but it's free. Out by the Kebun Kelapa bus terminal on Jalan Dewi Sartika is a popular outdoor restaurant called *Taman Parahyangan* where a large bottle of beer is 1400 rp, draught beer 1150 rp.

Bandung also has a number of excellent Chinese restaurants including the popular *Queen* at Jalan Dalem Kaum 79, a block south of the Savoy Homann. The Cantonese *Tjoen Kie* at Jalan Jenderal Sudirman 62 is as good and slightly cheaper; most dishes are around the 3000 rp mark. At Jalan Merdeka 17 the *Rumah Makan Vanda Sari* has good, though pricey, Chinese food.

On Jalan Braga there's a string of fancy coffee shops and bakeries where you can indulge yourself in a sort of east-west food fantasy. The centrepiece of this quasi-European avenue is the *Braga Permai* sidewalk cafe at No 74. Most meals are in the 6000 to 9000 rp range, with simpler dishes like nasi goreng 2750 to 3500 rp, sandwiches 1500 to 2250 rp, plus a variety of cakes and ice creams at 1000 to 2250 rp. Skip the mediocre *Braga Coffee Shop* in front of the Braga Hotel. Across the road is *Braga Fast Food*, a shiny place with reasonable Indonesian and light western meals. On the corner of Jalan Braga and Jalan ABC/Naripan is the *Canary Bakery*, and a little further along are the *Sumber Hidangan* bakery and the *French Bakery*, good places for a snack or light meal – try croissants or Danish pastries or chicken curry puffs.

If you're looking for a minor splurge you could try the restaurant in the *Savoy Homann*; they do a rijstaffel for 10,000 rp.

Sundanese Restaurants Bandung is one of the few places where you can try traditional Sundanese food. In addition to the Galaya Pub, there's also the *Warung Nasi Mang Udju* on Jalan Dewi Sartika, just south of the square. It's a simple place but the food is excellent and you can eat well for about 2000 rp. Try the chicken steamed in bamboo leaf and fish with ginger. The owners speak little English but you simply help yourself from the various dishes on the table and pay for what you eat.

Sakadarna International Travellers Homestay & Restaurant does a modest set dinner in the Sundanese style for 3250 rp. Other well-known and moderately priced Sundanese restaurants are the *Babakan Siliwangi* on Jalan Siliwangi (near the zoo), and the *Ponyo* on Jalan Prof Eykman.

Things to Buy

Wayang golek puppets, both new and old, are good buys. In the centre of town, down a small alley behind Jalan Pangarang 22, there's a small 'cottage industry' run by Pak Ruhiyat at No 78/17B where you can buy puppets and masks and see them being carved. It's an interesting place to visit and the puppets are really very fine, with a range of sizes and priced from 15,000 rp to 50,000 rp. A full set of wayang

Pavement seller – Bandung

golek puppets consists of 81 characters, enough for performances of both the *Ramayana* and the *Mahabharata*. The asking price for a full set is four million rp. Pak Ruhiyat's son, Maman Permana, speaks good English.

The Cupu Manik puppet factory is on Gang Haji Umar, off Jalan Kebon Kewung just north of the train station. On Jalan Arjuna, about one km from the railway station, there is a daily antique market. Jalan Braga is a good shopping street for crafts and antiques. Traditional Sundanese musical instruments can be bought at Pak Ujo's Workshop or the Toko Musik at Gang Suniaraja 3, off Jalan ABC.

A stroll down Jalan Braga for a look at the fancy furniture and fashion boutiques is worthwhile if only to gain insight into the upper-class Indonesian consumer consciousness.

Getting There & Away

Air The domestic airline offices are all centrally located on or near Jalan Asia Afrika but if you want to compare prices and make bookings/reservations you could try the Vista Express Travel Agent in the Savoy Homann Hotel. Mandala Airlines do not operate flights out of Bandung.

Garuda flights to and from Bandung include Jakarta (three flights daily), Yogya, Surabaya (three flights daily), Denpasar and Ujung Pandang (one flight daily). The Garuda office (tel 51497) is at Jalan Asia Afrika 73, opposite the Savoy Homann Hotel. It's open from 8 am to 2 pm Monday to Thursday, to 11 am Friday and until 1 pm Saturday; closed Sundays.

Merpati flights from Bandung include Jakarta, Yogya, Surabaya, Denpasar, Palembang, Tanjung Pinang and Ujung Pandang. The Merpati office (tel 57474), Jalan Veteran 46, is open from 8 am daily to 3 pm Monday to Thursday, to 1 pm Friday, to 2 pm Saturday and until noon Sunday.

Bouraq fly to Jakarta, Yogya, Surabaya,

Banjarmasin and Balikpapan. The Bouraq office (tel 437896) is at Jalan Cihampelas 27. It's open from 8 am daily to 4 pm Monday to Friday, to 2 pm at the weekend.

Bus Buses depart from the Cililitan station in Jakarta every 10 minutes or so for the 4½ hour trip to Bandung, via Bogor and the Puncak Pass. The fare is 2000 rp. Bandung has two bus stations. Go to Kebun Kelapa bus station if you're travelling west and south to places like Bogor, Jakarta, Sukabumi and Pelabuhanratu.

If you're heading east, the Cicaheum bus station's services include those to Cirebon, Banjar and Yogya.

The following information will give you an idea of fares and travel time. Buses run from Bandung to Bogor 1500 rp (3½ hours), Sukabumi 1100 rp (three hours), Pelabuhanratu 1500 rp (four hours), Banjar 1800 rp (five hours), Merak 3200 rp (eight hours) and Cirebon 1500 rp (3½ hours).

Public buses to Yogya cost from 5100 rp and take about 12 hours. There are also daily night buses to Yogya run by private bus companies. Bandung Cepat has buses that go the northern route via Semarang; they leave Jalan Doktor Cipto 5 at 7 pm, arriving in Yogya at 6 pm. Yogya Cepat buses take the southern route via Banjar leaving from Jalan Sunda 4 at 5 pm, arriving at 4 am the following morning. Both companies charge 7500 rp for non-air-con buses, 9500 rp air-con.

Rail There are six daily *Parahyangan* trains between Jakarta and Bandung. From Gambir, Jakarta, trains depart at 5.39 am, 9.49 am, 11.24 am, 1.53 pm, 3.29 pm and 6.50 pm. Going the other way trains depart Bandung at 5 am, 6.15 am, 9.10 am, 10.45 am, 2.50 pm and 6.15 pm. Fares are 6000 rp in 2nd class, 8000 rp in 1st and it's a comfortable, hassle-free train for the 3½ hour trip. Though the train avoids the hills around the Puncak, it cuts east of the huge dam and lake at

Jatiluhur and the views are quite spectacular at times along this route.

There are three daily trains to Yogya. The all-3rd-class *Cepat* departs at 7.40 am, takes 9½ hours and costs 3500 rp.; or there's the faster *Ekspress Siang* at 5.25 am – 5000 rp 2nd class, 3800 rp 3rd class. The *Mutiara Selatan* is a night train that leaves Bandung at 5.30 pm and arrives in Yogya at 1.50 am; 2nd class costs 9000 rp, 1st class 13,500. The same trains continue on to Solo for the same fare, except for the *Cepat* which terminates in Yogya. In the reverse direction the *Cepat* leaves Yogya at 8.10 am, the *Express Siang* at 11.27 am, and the *Mutiara Selatan* at 11.37 pm.

Taxi Apart from the regular buses there are also door-to-door taxi services between Jakarta and Bandung for 8000 rp through *4848* on Jalan Kramat Raya in Jakarta. In Bandung the 4848 Taxi office is located near the railway station. They also have taxis from Bandung to Cirebon (3500 rp), and to Semarang (7500 rp).

Getting Around
Airport Transport Bandung's Husein Sastranegara airport is four km north-west of town, about half an hour away and 4000 rp by taxi.

Bus Bandung has a fairly good city bus service using Indian Tata buses which charge a fixed 150 rp fare, or 200 rp if they are express buses. The most useful service is city bus No 1 to the Cicaheum bus station, which operates between 7 am and about 9 pm. It runs from the west of town right down Asia Afrika and along Jalan Jenderal A Yani to Cicaheum in the east. The Kebun Kelapa bus station is centrally located on Jalan Dewi Sartika, about 10 minutes walk south of the city square.

Bemo, Becak & Taxi Downtown bemos, Hondas and Daihatsus charge a fixed 150 rp fare. For destinations north (including Dago, Lembang and Tangkuban Prahu)

they depart from the terminal outside the railway station. Bemo No 05 runs between the railway station and Kebun Kelapa bus terminal. As in other cities the becaks are being relegated to the back streets and are no longer seen in great number. Taxis can usually be found near the city square on Jalan Asia Afrika; some run on meters now, at about the same rates as in Jakarta and Surabaya.

AROUND BANDUNG
Lembang
On the road to Tangkuban Prahu, 16 km north of Bandung, Lembang is a good place to stop for lunch or a snack. It is renowned for its market and on Jalan Raya Lembang, the main Bandung road, you'll find excellent fruit and cheap avocados at the Pasar Buah Buahan. Along the same street there are a number of good, cheap restaurants. At the market and on the road up to the crater there are stalls selling delicious hot corn on the cob for 50 rp.

Lembang's Planetarium – the Bosscha Astronomical Observatory – can be visited on special request. You have to contact the Director of the Department of Astronomi at ITB, Jalan Ganeca 10.

Places to Stay The *Grand Hotel* (tel 82393), just down the road from the market at Jalan Raya Lembang 288, is an old-fashioned and comfortable place with beautiful gardens, a swimming pool and tennis courts. Rooms, some with a private bathroom, cost from 18,000 rp and the hotel has a bar and restaurant.

Tangkuban Prahu
The 'overturned prahu' volcano crater stands 30 km north of Bandung. Years ago the centre of Tangkuban Prahu collapsed under the weight of built-up ash and, instead of the usual conical volcano shape, it has a flat elongated summit with a huge caldera more than seven km across. There is, of course, a legend to explain this phenomenon. It tells of an estranged

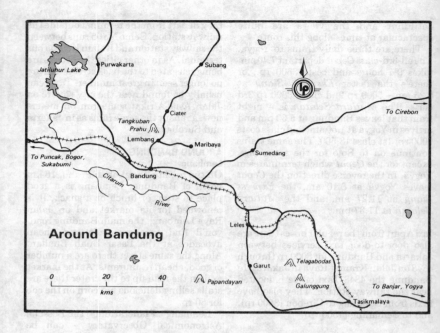

Around Bandung

young prince who returned home and unwittingly fell in love with his own mother. When the Queen discovered the terrible truth of her lover's identity she challenged him to build a dam and a huge boat during a single night before she would agree to marry him. Seeing that the young man was about to complete this impossible task, she called on the gods to bring the sun up early and as the cocks began to crow the boat builder turned his nearly completed boat over in a fit of anger. Tangkuban Prahu still simmers and bubbles, sending up noxious sulphurous fumes; its last serious eruption was in 1969.

Tangkuban Prahu is the only volcano in Java easily accessible by car, so it's very much a tourist attraction. Up at the crater there are car parks and warungs, and enterprising locals run around selling postcards, strange tree-fern souvenirs and soft drinks. You'll find that foreigners are

as much a photographic attraction for snap-happy Indonesian tourists as the volcano itself! All the same, there are plenty of opportunities to walk away from this bedlam of activity. For a start the main crater is actually divided into two parts and you can walk away from the car park around the rim of the first for almost 20 minutes before the second is fully visible. From the top you can also head off across country towards Ciater.

Getting There & Away At 1830 metres, Tangkuban Prahu can be quite cool and around noon the mist starts to roll in through the trees so try to go early. From Bandung's minibus station, take a Subang colt (800 rp) via Lembang to the park entrance, where there is a 400 rp admission charge. At weekends there's a minibus up to the main crater – other days you'll have to hitch or walk. It's four km by road but there is a more interesting, little-used shortcut through the jungle. There's no need for a guide; start up the road and take the first turning on the right. The path leads through the jungle to the Kawah Domas crater, an active open area of bubbling hot geysers, and another steep path with steps cuts up to the main crater.

An alternative is to get dropped off at Jayagiri Hill, just outside Lembang, and from there you can walk up through the forest to the crater (about eight km).

Ciater Hot Springs

Eight km beyond Tangkuban Prahu, Ciater is a pretty little place in the middle of huge tea and clove estates and there are good walks in the area. Opposite the turn off to Ciater is the Ciater Tea Factory (Paberik Teh Ciater). At the end of the

Tangkuban Prahu

road through the village you'll come across the Ciater Hot Springs Resort. The pools are probably the best of all the hot springs around Bandung and if you've been climbing around the volcano on a cool, rainy day there's no better way to get warm. There is a 600 rp admission into the resort area and it costs another 500 rp to use the pool. You can walk to Ciater – about 12 km across country – from the main crater of Tangkuban Prahu, or flag down a colt (200 rp) at the entrance point.

Maribaya Hot Springs

Maribaya, five km east of Lembang, has a thermal spa, landscaped gardens and a thundering waterfall. It's another tourist spot, crowded on Sundays, but worthwhile visiting. You can extend your Tangkuban Prahu trip by walking from the bottom end of the gardens down through a brilliant, deep and wooded river gorge all the way to Dago. There's a good track and if you allow about two to three hours for the walk (six km) you can be at the *Dago Tea House* for sunset. From there it's only a short trip by colt back into Bandung.

Jatiluhur Lake & Dam

The man-made Jatiluhur Lake, 70 km north of Bandung in the hills near Purwakarta, is a popular resort for swimming, boating and water-skiing. The tourist blurb certainly raves about the giant Jatiluhur Dam which stretches 1200 metres across, is 100 metres high, and has created a lake some 80 hectares in surface area! It's part of a hydro-electric generating system supplying Jakarta and West Java and also provides irrigation water for a large area of the province. Jatiluhur is also the site of the country's ITT earth satellite station, opened in 1969. The village was built by the French for their staff when they were building the dam. Purwakarta is the access point either from Jakarta (125 km by rail or road) or from Bandung (by road).

BANDUNG TO PANGANDARAN

Heading south-east from Bandung, the road passes through a scenic and fertile stretch of hilly countryside and volcanic peaks. This is the Bandung-Yogya road as far as Banjar; the Bandung-Yogya railway line passes through Tasikmalaya and Banjar, but not Garut. The district is known as Priangan.

Garut

Fifty-seven km south-east of Bandung, Garut is a small Sundanese town and a centre for orange and tobacco growing. From Garut you can visit the hot springs (*air panas*) at Tarogong, five km to the north of town. Near Leles, about 10 km further north, is the site of one of the few stone Hindu temples found in West Java. Dating from the 8th century, some of its stones were found to have been carved into tombstones for a nearby Islamic cemetery and what little remains of the temple lies on the edge of Cangkuang Lake.

To the east, Gunung Telagabodas (2201 metres) has a bubbling bright-green crater lake alive with sulphur. Off to the south-west, you can climb Gunung Papandayan (2622 metres) for magnificent views of the area. One of the most active and spectacular of Java's volcanoes, Papandayan has only existed since 1772 when a large piece of the mountain exploded sideways in a catastrophe that killed more than 3000 people.

Garut is famed for its *dodol* – a confectionery made of coconut milk, palm sugar and sticky rice rolled into a long brown tube shape. At the bus station hawkers selling tubes of sweet dodol besiege the passing buses and it's sold at many shops around town. The 'Picnic' brand is said to be the best quality.

Places to Stay The *Hotel Nasional*, at Jalan Kenanga 19, is neither very cheap nor reportedly very friendly. You could try the *Hotel Mulia* at No 17 on the same street where rooms are around 5000 rp.

At Tarogong, the choices are better: the *Bratayuda* has rooms from 7500 rp; the *Sari Panas* and *Tarumanegara* are both in the 15,000 to 25,000 rp range.

Tasikmalaya

Sixty km east of Garut, this small town is a centre for rattan crafts. Palm leaf and bamboo are used to make floormats, baskets, trays, straw hats and paper umbrellas. For cheaper rattan visit the village of Rajapolah, 12 km north of town, where many of the weavers work. Tasikmalaya also has a small batik industry.

Gunung Galunggung, 17 km to the north-west, is a volcano which exploded dramatically only a few years ago in 1982. You can get there from Tasikmalaya by motorcycle for 800 rp.

Banjar

Banjar, 42 km east of Tasikmalaya, is the junction point where the Pangandaran road branches from the Bandung-Yogya road and rail route. There are banks in Banjar where you can change money before continuing on to Pangandaran where there are no money changing facilities. See the Getting There & Away section for Pangandaran for details of transport to and from Banjar. If you arrive in Banjar by train it is only five minutes walk to the bus station. There are good warungs at both stations.

PANGANDARAN

Pangandaran is one of Java's finest beaches – but you need to take great care when swimming especially at the west beach. There can be dangerous undertows even though a coral reef has reduced their impact. The Pangandaran Nature Reserve is part of this small fishing town, and the focus for travellers, it lies along the narrow isthmus of a peninsula with broad white-sand beaches that sweep back along the mainland. The large jungle headland of the peninsula teems with wild buffalo, deer and monkeys. Secluded, tree-fringed

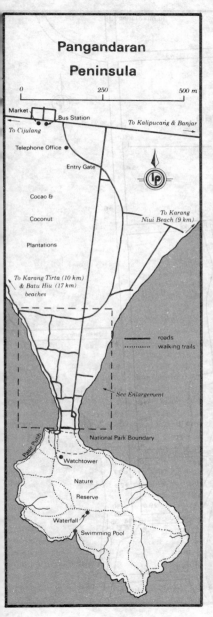

Pangandaran Peninsula

| 0 | 250 | 500 m |

Market
Bus Station
To Cijulang
To Kalipucang & Banjar
Telephone Office
Entry Gate
Cocao &
Coconut
To Karang
Niui Beach (9 km)
Plantations
To Karang Tirta (10 km)
& Batu Hiu (17 km)
beaches

roads
walking trails

See Enlargement

Pasir Putih
National Park Boundary
Watchtower
Nature
Reserve
Waterfall
Swimming Pool

beaches are to be found nearly all the way around the headland, though the best beaches for swimming and snorkelling are on the west side. As if all this isn't enough, Pangandaran is also a place where it's possible to enjoy the unique experience of seeing the sun set and the moon rise over the ocean simultaneously at full moon. And every evening, at dusk, you'll see a mass of fruit bats flying west across the setting sun.

With so much going for it, it's hardly surprising that Pangandaran is a popular local resort. It can be crowded at weekends but during holidays – Christmas and after Ramadan in particular – there can be a floating population literally of thousands on the beaches. At any other time this is an idyllic place to take a break from travelling; the people are exceptionally friendly, there are plenty of cheap places to stay and excellent seafood is available. The locals are mostly fishermen, many of them rowing their boats out to sea from the east beach where you'll nearly always find whole families working together to pull in the nets.

If lazing around the beaches and trekking through the jungle reserve of Pangandaran begins to pall, you can head off east or west to other quieter beaches nearby. About a five-km walk along the west beach there are buffalo at Karang Tirta pond. Further west, surf pounds the beaches at Batu Hui (17 km by colt) and there's also a beach at the fishing village of Batu Keras (40 km). Heading east, about seven km, there is another one at Lembah Putri.

Information

There's a post office here where you can have mail sent poste restante but there is no bank. If you're desperate the Cilacap Restaurant may be prepared to change US dollar travellers' cheques, but below the going rate. Electricity comes on between 6 pm and 6 am, though blackouts are pretty common when it's raining hard.

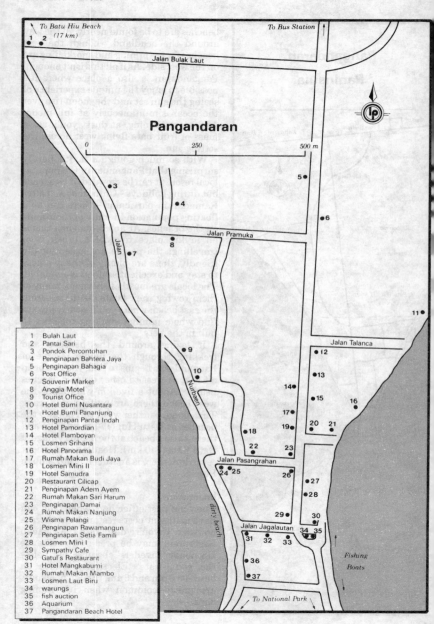

Pangandaran

To Batu Hiu Beach
(17 km)

Jalan Bulak Laut

To Bus Station

0   250   500 m

Jalan Pramuka

Jalan Talanca

Jalan Pasangrahan

Jalan Jagalautan

Fishing
Boats

dirty beach

Nurben

Jalan

To National Park

1   Bulah Laut
2   Pantai Sari
3   Pondok Percontohan
4   Penginapan Bahtera Jaya
5   Penginapan Bahagia
6   Post Office
7   Souvenir Market
8   Anggia Motel
9   Tourist Office
10 Hotel Bumi Nusantara
11 Hotel Bumi Pananjung
12 Penginapan Pantai Indah
13 Hotel Pamordian
14 Hotel Flamboyan
15 Losmen Srihana
16 Hotel Panorama
17 Rumah Makan Budi Jaya
18 Losmen Mini II
19 Hotel Samudra
20 Restaurant Cilicap
21 Penginapan Adem Ayem
22 Rumah Makan Sari Harum
23 Penginapan Damai
24 Rumah Makan Nanjung
25 Wisma Pelangi
26 Penginapan Rawamangun
27 Penginapan Setia Famili
28 Losmen Mini I
29 Sympathy Cafe
30 Gatul's Restaurant
31 Hotel Mangkabumi
32 Rumah Makan Mambo
33 Losmen Laut Biru
34 warungs
35 fish auction
36 Aquarium
37 Pangandaran Beach Hotel

There's a 300 rp admission charge for the beach area, and another 350 rp for the reserve. Maps of the reserve are available from the PHPA office located just inside the east gate.

Places to Stay – bottom end

Most of Pangandaran's cheap losmen are along the main street but they're all squeezed in between the beaches on either side, so no matter where you stay you can hear the sea. A number of them are particularly popular with travellers but they are all good and friendly places, which makes it difficult to recommend one more than another. It's worth having a look around if you're planning to stay for more than a few days; many people do stay, regardless of previous intentions. You could try one of the following:

Hotel Samudra, in its own courtyard with a terrace (and hammock!), has good rooms at 7500 rp and endless free tea. Further down the main street is the friendly *Laut Biru* with a variety of small and large rooms, some with attached mandi – singles from 4000 rp, doubles from 6000 rp, and rooms for three or four people for 7500 rp – plus a large sitting room where you can help yourself to tea and coffee.

Losmen Mini II, between the main road and the west beach, has its own garden and is also good value. It's a small house with a few rooms at 3000/3500 rp. Free tea and coffee are always available. All the above places are particularly good for information – travel, free (well, sometimes) guided walks in the jungle, etc – and they'll often organise barbecue fish suppers.

Losmen Mini I is on the main street, in a small courtyard of palm trees – singles/doubles with private mandi are 5000/6000 rp including breakfast. The somewhat dirty and dilapidated *Adem Ayam*, close to the east beach and near the Cilacap Restaurant, has a few rooms at 3000 rp including breakfast, plus better ones at 7500 rp. If you stay here, try and get an upstairs room

on the balcony with a good view over the sea.

The nearby *Losmen Panorama* is right on the beach and has 8000 rp rooms overlooking the sea. *Pondok Wisata Bulak Laut* on Jalan Pamugaran has nice bungalows for 7500 rp including breakfast. Each bungalow has a living room, open-air bathroom and a bedroom with a large double bed. *Pondok Wisata Pantai Sari* is next door and has bungalows for 7000 rp and a small restaurant with Chinese food.

Slightly more expensive places include the *Anggia Motel* at Jalan Pramuka 15 which has standard doubles at 8000 rp as well as more expensive bungalows. Not far from the Anggia Hotel on Jalan Sumardi is *Hotel Bahtera Jaya*, run by a Dutch woman named Willy. Clean rooms are 7500 rp with fan, mandi, and breakfast.

Places to Stay – top end

The Sunrise Homestay at Jalan Kidang Pananjung 175 on the east beach is a clean, pleasant place with rooms ranging from 10,000 to 15,000 rp per night. For each additional night you stay at the Sunrise, however, there's a price break; eg a 10,000 rp room is only 8,500 per night for two nights or 6,000 rp per night if you stay four or more nights.

In a similar price range are the *Penginapan Pantai Indah* and the government-run *Pondok Peronohan*, both close to the centre of things.

There are a number of bungalows and rather flash hotels along the west beachfront but most are poorly maintained and overpriced. The *Pondok Pelangi* (tel Bandung 81531), opposite the turn-off for Mini I, has comfortable bungalows in an attractive garden each with a mandi, living room and small terrace. A bungalow for four people costs 20,000 rp or 40,000 rp with kitchen facilities.

The most expensive place to stay is the *Hotel Bumi Pananjung* (tel Bandung 84963), right on the east beach behind the post office. There are nine large airy rooms, some with a bathroom and a balcony, and singles are 25,000 rp, doubles and triples 40,000 rp to 60,000 rp (plus 20% tax and service). Rates include a continental buffet breakfast and afternoon tea. It's an impressive Tyrolean-style chalet of timber and thatch with the bedrooms off a gallery that surrounds a large, central sitting area. The owner has obviously been strongly influenced by his visits to Germany!

On the west beach is the equally imposing *Bumi Nusantara*, although the architectural style is more Indonesian. Or there's the *Pangandaran Beach Hotel* on the west Beach near the park entrance. Simple rooms are 12,500 and 15,000 rp.

Places to Eat

Almost all the restaurants and warungs along the main street cater to western tastes – western-style breakfasts (toast, jam, omelettes, porridge, etc), seafood (shrimps, lobster, and fish sometimes with chips), pancakes and a variety of fruit juices and fruit salads. If fresh fish isn't on the menu (fish is generally fried crisp so that it will keep, but it's good) they'll usually cook fresh seafood for you if you order it or buy it yourself at the fish market. There are, of course, plenty of Indonesian dishes too and for as little as 500 rp you can get a big plateful of nasi campur.

They're nearly all good and prices are much the same, eg a breakfast of omelette, toast, tea/coffee is around 800 rp, prawns or lobster around 3000 rp, noodle soup 750 rp. Popular places to try include the group of small, warmly-lit warungs opposite the Laut Biru losmen. The *Sympathy Coffee Shop* is usually packed out; it serves excellent fruit salads, gado-gado (only 500 rp) and 'famous banana porridge'. The *Cilacap Restaurant* at Jalan Kidang Pananjung 187 is slightly more expensive but it probably has the most extensive menu; they always have fresh fish and the food is excellent. Good prawns with garlic for 2000 rp and their

banana pancakes are enough to feed a family. At night (when there is electricity) they make good mixed fruit juices.

At the end of Jalan Pasangrahan on the west beach is *Rumah Makan Nanung* with a pleasant open-air dining area and good food, including excellent barbecued fish for around 3000 rp. Right on the west beachfront there are many late-night warungs which catch the sea breezes. You can get good coffee, pisang goreng and snacks away from the crowds.

In addition to the restaurants, there are a number of local women who do the rounds of the losmen selling fruit and there's a good market on the main road in town. A decent loaf of brown bread and croissants can be bought from the Bumi Pananjung Hotel. Be careful if you're buying seafood at the fish market. Naturally they'll sell you anything you are willing to buy and it hasn't always just been caught. To make sure fish is really fresh an easy check is to look at the gills which should be a good red colour, not brown; the eyes should be bright. Tuna and shark are plentiful.

Beer is usually cold and cheap; *Orang Tua*, probably the most popular drink locally, is cheaper. This is basically a *jamu* (all-purpose medicine) but with a strong alcoholic content and according to the label it will transform the most decrepit old man into Mr Universe. Mixed with coca cola it's not bad at all. There's also a special brand for women called *Kancur* which is supposed to taste a bit like advocaat.

Getting There & Away

Pangandaran lies more or less half-way between Bandung and Yogya or Dieng. Banjar is the turn-off point on the Bandung-Yogya rail and road route. If you're coming from Central Java, an alternative to taking the train and bus all the way is to head for Cilacap and make the very nice backwater trip by boat from there to Kalipucang, 17 km north of Pangandaran. See the paragraph Boat –

The Backwater Trip for details. Note that it can save travelling time to slot in a visit to Dieng between Yogya and Pangandaran.

Bus or Train to Banjar From Cililitan station in Jakarta you can bus directly to Banjar (via Bogor and Bandung). The fare is around 4000 rp. Buses depart every hour until about 11 pm. If you're travelling straight through to Banjar, it's a good idea to take a night bus; they're less crowded and faster (eight to nine hours), but watch your gear on this night run. Bandung to Banjar by bus takes about five hours and costs 1800 rp. Yogya to Banjar takes about nine hours and costs 3000 rp; buses depart every hour until 11 pm.

From Bandung or Yogya you can also approach Banjar by rail – about a five-hour trip from Bandung or six to eight hours from Yogya.

Banjar to Pangandaran The final stretch from Banjar to Pangandaran, by bus or colt, takes two hours and costs about 2000 rp. The colts along this stretch are about the most unscrupulous in Java when it comes to overcharging. Last colts/buses leave around 8 to 9 pm. From the bus stop on the main road you can walk a couple of km or take a becak to the tourist area of Pangandaran.

Express Bus Express buses now run from Pangandaran to Wonosobo (11,000 rp), Bogor (12,500 rp) and Jakarta (14,500).

Taxi The 4848 inter-city taxi company in Bandung has a direct minibus service between Bandung and Pangandaran for 5000 rp that leaves every day at 2 pm, arriving in Pangandaran six to seven hours later.

Boat – The Backwater Trip
The boat ride from Cilacap to Kalipucang is one of the highlights of a trip to Pangandaran. It takes you across the lagoons of 'Segara Anakan' – a stretch of inland sea sheltered by the long island of

Nusakambangan to the south. You'll pass mangrove swamps, a few fishermen in dugout canoes and the boat calls at small fishing villages along the way – clusters of small thatched houses on the water's edge, perched high on stilts off the mud banks. This is the most easy-going trip you can make in Java and it feels an eon away from any of the hassles that Indonesian buses and trains can turn up! The ferry is a small boat – perhaps 10 metres – but there is usually plenty of room and baggage is no problem.

To Kalipucang Boats depart daily from Sleko Harbour (Pelabuhan Lomanis) in Cilacap at 7 am, 8 am, 12 noon and 1 pm. The trip takes roughly four hours and costs 800 rp.

Once you've got to Kalipucang, it's a 500-metre walk to the main road and a half-hour ride by bus or colt to Pangandaran.

To Cilacap From Kalipucang, boats depart at 7.30 am and 8.30 am; also 10.30 am and 12.30 am but these boats will arrive too late for direct connections to Yogya by bus.

Getting Around
Whenever a bus arrives in Pangandaran with foreigners on it, especially express minibuses, the local becak drivers assault the bus in a screaming horde, trying to grab your bags to put in their becaks. There's no need to be alarmed, but keep an eye on your gear; if you don't want a becak, calmly remove it from the becak and walk on. On the other hand, it's over a km from the bus stop to the beach so you may need one. The drivers will ask outrageous rates but you shouldn't have to pay more than 500 rp maximum. Some will go for less, but that means you go to their choice of losmen so they get a commission. You can always walk to another losmen.

You can rent bicycles from Toha, opposite the Rumah Makan Mambo, for 2000 rp per day. They also organise jungle walking tours for 2500 or 3000 rp per person. Some people say it's easy to get

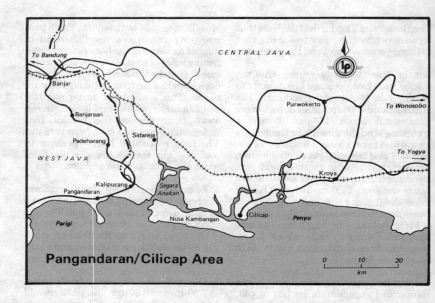

Pangandaran/Cilicap Area

CENTRAL JAVA

To Bandung

Banjar

Banjarsari

Padeharang

Sidareja

WEST JAVA

Kalipucang

Pangandaran

Segara Anakan

Parigi

Nusa Kambangan

Purwokerto

To Wonosobo

To Yogya

Kroya

Cilicap

Penyu

0   10   20
km

lost in the reserve and that a guide is a good idea; others say a guide isn't necessary. If you do go in without a guide, bring along a companion and a good sense of direction.

At Hotel Bahtera Jaya on Jalan Sumardi there's a small travel agency that sells bus tickets, rents bicycles and motorcycles, and also does tours to Nusa Kambangan three times a week for 16,000 rp per person.

CILACAP
Cilacap is actually in Central Java but for convenience it's included here. The only natural harbour on Java's south coast for ocean-going vessels, Cilacap is a fairly big town in a growing industrial area and the only reason travellers would come here is to make the backwater trip to Kalipucang for Pangandaran. Boats depart from the Sleko boat jetty, which is a becak or 150 rp-bemo ride from the bus station or centre of town.

Places to Stay & Eat
If you get into Cilacap in the afternoon, you'll have to stay there overnight as there's no connecting ferry for Kalipucang after 1 pm. *Losmen Tiga*, at Jalan Mayor Sutoyo 61, is a clean, comfortable and friendly place with singles/doubles at 3000/4000 rp – good value if you don't mind being in the centre of town. If you arrive by bus, it can drop you off at the losmen on its way through town to the bus station. Around the corner on Jalan Anggrek is *Losmen Anggrek* with slightly larger rooms for 4000/5000 rp, 7000/8000 rp with fan, or 10,000 rp for 'VIP' rooms.

You can also try the *Losmen Akhmad* where rooms cost 5000 rp or the *Losmen Bahagia* which has rooms with a small mandi at 3000 rp. They're basic and there are lots of mosquitoes, but they're OK for the night. They're both on Jalan Sudirman, a short distance from the Sleko boat jetty.

At the top end is the *Hotel Wijaya Kusuma* (tel 22871), Jalan Jenderal A Yani 12A, on Cilacap's main downtown street.

All rooms have air-con, hot water and color TV; rates start at US$31.

The *Restaurant Perapatan (Sien Hieng)* at Jalan Jenderal A Yani 62, just around the corner from Losmen Tiga, has a fair Chinese menu. Along Jalan Mayor Sutoyo just east of Losmen Tiga are a number of good warungs. One of the best is at No 99 – a small sign over the door reads 'Abdoellah'. You can have whatever's in the cabinet laid over rice for only 100 rp per serving, including tofu curry, spiced tempe, fried fish, with tea included.

Directly across the street from Losmen Tiga is the *Prima Food Centre*, an ambitious restaurant with outdoor tables in front, a fast food room serving burgers and ice cream in the middle, and a *lesehan*-style eating area outdoors in the back. The food in the *lesehan* area is quite good. You serve yourself from a buffet (600 rp per dish) and sit to eat on mats at low tables.

Getting There & Away

Cilacap is 216 km west of Yogya and roughly 150 km south-west of Wonosobo (Dieng). You can get to Cilacap in time for the ferry along the following routes:

Yogya-Cilacap From Yogya you can take the early morning train at 7 am to Kroya for 2200 rp (four to six hours) – and from there take a colt for the hour ride to Cilacap. The bus from Yogya to Cilacap costs 2000 rp and takes about five hours, though you may have to change buses en route at Purworejo. There are also direct buses from Jalan Sosrowijayan in Yogya: the Kartika Travel Agent's minibus departs at 7 am, costs 4000 rp and drops you at the boat jetty around 12 noon. A local bus from Yogya is only 2100 rp but takes seven hours, so you'd most likely have to spend the night in Cilacap.

Going the other way, the early ferries from Kalipucang link up with a door-to-door minibus service from Cilacap. This bus departs from Wijaya Travel in the centre of town, at Jalan Jenderal A Yani 68, at 2 pm. It costs 4000 rp and takes around six hours.

Dieng-Cilacap The trip takes about six hours in total so you need to catch the first colt out of Dieng to Wonosobo. There's no direct bus from Wonosobo early in the morning but you can take a bus to Purwokerto and from there another bus to Cilacap for 1800 rp total fare. With luck you can get to Cilacap in time for the last ferry.

Getting Around

There are plenty of bemos plying the streets of Cilacap for 150 rp per passenger. If you're arriving by ferry from Kalipucang, becak drivers will tell you there are no bemos, but if you walk down the street from the jetty you'll come across a few.

CIREBON

Few people make the trip out to Cirebon but it's an interesting seaport and the seat of an ancient Islamic kingdom with a number of attractions for visitors. Located on the north coast, right on the border with Central Java, the city's history has been influenced by both the Javanese and Sundanese with a bit of Chinese culture thrown in for good measure. A multi-ethnic city, many of the people speak a local dialect blending Sundanese and Javanese, and it has been suggested that the name Cirebon comes from 'Charuban' which is Javanese for 'mixture'.

Cirebon was one of the independent sultanates founded by Sunan Gunungjati of Demak in the early 16th century. Later the powerful kingdoms of Banten and Mataram fought over Cirebon, which declared allegiance to Sultan Agung of Mataram but was finally ceded to the Dutch in 1677. By a further treaty of 1705 Cirebon became a Dutch protectorate, jointly administered by three sultans whose courts at that time rivalled those of Central Java in opulence and splendour. During the Dutch 'culture' system period a flourishing trade in colonial crops attracted many Chinese entrepreneurs,

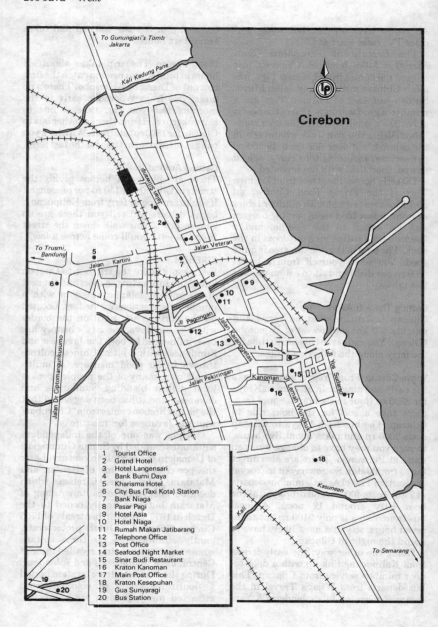

Cirebon

To Gunungjati's Tomb
Jakarta

Kali Kedung Pane

To Trusmi,
Bandung

Jalan Siliwangi

Jalan Veteran

Jalan Kartini

Jalan Dr Ciptomangunkusumo

Jl Pagongan

Jalan Kalijagentes

Jalan Pekiringan

Kanoman

Lemah Wungkuk

Jl Yos Sudarso

Kasunean

Kali

To Semarang

1   Tourist Office
2   Grand Hotel
3   Hotel Langensari
4   Bank Bumi Daya
5   Kharisma Hotel
6   City Bus (Taxi Kota) Station
7   Bank Niaga
8   Pasar Pagi
9   Hotel Asia
10 Hotel Niaga
11 Rumah Makan Jatibarang
12 Telephone Office
13 Post Office
14 Seafood Night Market
15 Sinar Budi Restaurant
16 Kraton Kanoman
17 Main Post Office
18 Kraton Kesepuhan
19 Gua Sunyaragi
20 Bus Station

and the Chinese influence can still be seen in the batik designs for which Cirebon is famous. Two of Cirebon's kratons are open to visitors and, although a bit run down compared to the palaces of Yogya and Solo, they still deserve more recognition.

Though Cirebon has long been a major centre for batik, it is also famous for *Tari Topeng Cirebon*, a type of masked dance peculiar to the Cirebon area, and tarling, a musical tradition reminiscent of Bandung's kecapi-suling music, except that it features guitar, suling (bamboo flute), and voice. The name comes from combining the last syllables of these two instruments (gui-tar plus su-ling).

Cirebon is also important as the major port and fishing harbour between Jakarta and Semarang with the added bonus that there is excellent seafood available. Remember that the north coast, particularly in the dry season, can be a sweltering contrast to the cooler heights inland. Other than that, Cirebon is one of Java's most attractively well-kept cities. It is small enough not to be overwhelming and makes a worthwhile stopover.

Information & Orientation

Jalan Siliwangi is the main boulevard which runs from the train station to the canal by the Pasar Pagi market. Along this road there are banks, restaurants, the bulk of Cirebon's low-budget losmen and the tourist office. The Pasar Pagi here is excellent.

The Regional Tourist Office, Jalan Siliwangi 88 and the Tourist Information Centre on Jalan Pasuketan hand out city maps, but that's about it. If you want literature about the place it's worth hunting around – particularly in Jakarta – for a copy of the guidebook called *Cerbon*, published by Sinar Harapan. It covers the history, arts and traditions of the city.

Cirebon's bus station is some distance to the south-west of town. The main city minibus (taxi-kota) station is on Jalan Gunungsari, a couple of blocks over from Jalan Siliwangi.

Post & Communication There's a post office branch just across the canal on Jalan Karanggetas, but Cirebon's main post office is near the harbour on Jalan Yos Sudarso. The telephone office is on Jalan Pagongan.

Banks The Bank Bumi Daya on Jalan Siliwangi will change travellers' cheques; it's open from 8 am to 2 pm Monday to Friday and to 12 noon Saturday. Bank Niaga on Jalan Siliwangi near the intersection with Jalan Kartini/Veteran, also has a full-service foreign exchange. There is a Bank Dagang Negara on Jalan Kantor near the harbour.

Kraton Kanoman

In the south of the city and approached through the Pasar Kanoman, this palace was constructed in 1681. The courtyards and grounds are sadly neglected and overgrown – goats and roosters wander through the decay and children now fly kites and play here. Under the huge shady banyan trees there are broken walls stuck with antique European plates, some with Dutch reformist scenes from the Bible which seem strangely out of place in a Muslim sultan's palace. There is supposed to be a museum inside the palace and a caretaker with a key but he is not always around.

You may well find the Pasar Kanoman of greater interest. This colourful outdoor market is worth a visit in its own right and amongst the great trays of fruit and vegetables you'll find stacks of brightly painted ceramic piggy-banks in the shapes of animals and the local Cirebon-style spinning top.

Kraton Kesepuhan

A short walk from Kanoman, at the south end of Jalan Lemah Wungkuk, is the Kraton Kesepuhan. The oldest and most well preserved of Cirebon's kratons, it was built in 1527 and its architecture and interior are a curious blend of Sundanese, Javanese, Islamic, Chinese and Dutch styles. Although this is the home of the Sultan of Kesepuhan, part of the building is open to visitors. Inside the palace is a cool pavilion with white-washed walls dotted with blue-and-white Delft tiles, a marble floor and a ceiling hung with glittering French chandeliers.

The museum outbuilding has an interesting, if somewhat run-down, collection of wayang puppets, kris, cannon, Portuguese armour and ancient royal clothes. But the *piece de resistance* of the Sultan's collection is a 17th-century gilded coach with the trunk of an elephant (Hindu), the body and head of a dragon (Chinese-Buddhist) and wings (Islamic)! In the courtyard office you'll find a caretaker who will unlock doors and show you round for a small donation.

On the west side of the playing field, the Masjid Agung with its tiered roof is one of the oldest mosques in Java and similar in style to the Masjid Agung mosque in Banten.

Every Sunday from 10 am to 2 pm in the courtyard there are gamelan and *tari topeng* performances in the traditional Cirebon style.

Kraton Kecirebonan

More of a mansion than a palace, the Kecirebonan was built in 1839 and is occupied by members of the current royal family. Visitors are not usually admitted but the house is worth a quick look for its exterior architecture, a blend of Dutch and Indonesian styles.

Gua Sunyaragi

About four km to the south-west of town, a not-to-be-missed attraction is this bizarre ruined 'cave' – a sort of grotto of rocks, red brick and plaster honeycombed with secret chambers, tiny doors and staircases leading nowhere. It was originally a water palace for a Sultan of Cirebon in the early 18th century and owes its present strange shape to the efforts of a Chinese architect who had a go at it in 1852.

Sunan Gunungjati Tomb

In the royal cemetery, five km north of Cirebon, is the tomb of Sunan Gunungjati who died in 1570. The most revered of Cirebon's kings, Gunungjati was also one of the nine 'walis' who spread Islam throughout Java and his tomb is still one of the holiest places in the country. Although pilgrims are allowed to worship at the doorway, the inner tomb is closed to all but members of the Kraton family who visit on Fridays.

Other Attractions

Cirebon's harbour is always an interesting place to wander around to see the sailing schooners and freighters unload their wares, but it seems that photography is prohibited for 'security reasons'. Along the port area there are several old Dutch East Indies warehouses which were used at a time when opium, tobacco and sugar were shipped out from Cirebon.

Trusmi

Some of Cirebon's finest batik is made in the village of Trusmi, five km to the west of town. You can get there by taking a city bus G4 from the Gunungsari station to Plered and then, from the main road, you walk down a cobbled country lane of whitewashed cottages. At the end of the lane, Ibu Masina's is probably the biggest studio where you can see batik tulis being made. Her showroom has a wide range of colours and designs from 5000 rp or from 15,000 rp for the finer pieces. It's also worth wandering through the lanes to see the work in progress at the many small home workshops in Trusmi and the adjacent village of Kalitengah. Prices are no lower than those in the shops in Cirebon, but there is a wider selection of textiles to choose from and it's an interesting place to visit besides the workshops.

Indramayu

Some say the 'very best' Cirebon batik comes from the small workshops of Pamuan village near Indramayu, 30 km north along the coast. The patterns of the batik are more involved and some of the batik tulis is still coloured with traditional vegetables dyes. For the finest pieces you can expect to pay between 30,000 rp and 40,000 rp, although prices may drop by about 5000 rp. You can get there by taking a colt to Indramayu, and from the colt station it's about a 1½ km walk, or a 300 rp becak-ride, to the village of Pamuan.

Places to Stay – bottom end

There are a number of inexpensive losmen very close to the train station and along Jalan Siliwangi between the train station and the canal. Walking east from the station towards Jalan Siliwangi, the *Palapa Hotel* on the left looks rather grey and dreary but is OK inside. Rooms with a fan are 4500 rp or 6000 rp with a private bathroom; triples are 7500 rp. On the corner of the same street, at Jalan Siliwangi 66, the *Hotel Famili* has adequate rooms starting at 3000 rp for a single without bath, 5000 rp double, 6500 rp triple.

Further south down Jalan Siliwangi is a string of slightly more expensive motel-type hotels beginning with *Hotel Slamet* at No 66 where standard rooms are 10,000 rp with attached bath. For 16,000 rp you can get similar rooms with air-con. Next at No 77 is the *Hotel Cordova*, which is slightly better value with singles/doubles without bath for 5000/7500 rp or air-con double with bath for 12,500 rp. Across from the Grand Hotel further down is *Hotel Langensari* at No 117, a clean place with friendly staff where rooms are 5000 rp without bath, 10,000 rp with bath. The nearby *Hotel Priangan* at No 108 is fairly new and clean with doubles/triples with attached bath for 10,000/13,000 rp. They also have more expensive air-con rooms with hot water.

For atmosphere in this price range, you can't beat *Hotel Asia* (tel 2183) at Jalan Kalibaru Selatan 15, alongside the quiet tree-lined canal near Pasar Pagi. It's about a 15-minute walk or 300 rp by becak from the train station. This is a fine old Dutch-Indonesian inn with a terraced courtyard where you can sit and have breakfast; it's very well kept and the staff are friendly. Basic singles or doubles cost 8000 rp and triples 9600 rp, including breakfast (coffee and jam sandwiches) and a big pot of evening tea. There are also more expensive rooms with private mandi and/or fan.

South along Jalan Siliwangi you can give the *Hotel Baru* at No 163 a miss – it's damp and dingy and the mosquito nets are remarkably grubby. Further down there's a cluster of losmen between the railway tracks and Pasar Pagi including the *Hotel Islam* at Jalan Siliwangi 116, which is nearly as bad as the Baru. The *Hotel Damai* (tel 3045) at No 130 is reasonable at 4000/6000 rp without bath, 7000/10,000 rp with bath. Better value is the *Losmen Semarang* next door at No 132; large, fairly clean rooms here are 3500/7000 rp.

Places to Stay – top end

The *Grand Hotel Cirebon* (tel 2014/5) at Jalan Siliwangi 98, next to the town square, is a pleasantly old-fashioned place with large rooms and a big front verandah. Air-con singles are 15,000 rp including breakfast and there are a variety of larger rooms ranging from 20,000 rp to 65,000 rp for a 'VIP' suite. Chauffeurs (no less) can have a room for 8000 rp. The hotel has a restaurant, coffee shop and a bar (open until midnight).

Hotel Niaga (tel 6018), Jalan Kalibaru Selatan 47, is a newer hotel that is very good value in this price range. Near the older Hotel Asia, it has clean, carpeted single and double rooms with air con, TV, telephone and hot water for 20,000/25,000 rp.

The modern *Cirebon Plaza* (tel 2061) at Jalan R A Kartini 54 has carpeted air-con rooms with TV, hot water, etc from 32,000 rp (including breakfast) to 43,500 rp for VIPs. Chauffeurs' rooms here cost 8500 rp. The hotel has a restaurant and coffee shop.

Next door at Jalan R A Kartini 48 is the newer and flashier *Kharisma Hotel* (tel 2795) with well-appointed rooms at 37,750/39,600 rp. The hotel's satellite dish receives TV broadcasts from Thailand, Malaysia and the US as well as Jakarta, and the water system is solar-heated – it's a very high-tech establishment and the Kharisma takes Visa and MasterCard.

At Jalan R A Kartini 27 is the *Hotel Aurora* (tel 4541) with reasonably-priced air-con rooms for 14,000/19,000 rp with TV and hot water. *Hotel Sidodadi* (tel 2830) at No 74 offers economy fan-cooled rooms from 17,000 rp, air-con rooms from 19,500 rp and air-con rooms with hot water from 32,500 rp.

Places to Eat

Apart from Cirebon's fine seafood, a local speciality to try is nasi lengko, a delicious rice dish with bean sprouts, tahu, tempe, fried onion, cucumber and peanut sauce. One good place for nasi lengko as well as other local and standard Indonesian dishes is *Rumah Makan Jatibarang* on the corner of Jalan Karanggetas and Jalan Kalibaru Selatan. Just south a few doors is the popular ` Kopyor Restaurant* at Jalan Karanggetas 9. It's clean and reasonably priced with meals ranging from 1250 rp to 3000 rp. They also have a nice selection of kerupuk – *kerupuk rambak*, made from dried buffalo skin, *kerupuk bodin*, from sweet potatoes, and others. For decent Chinese food, try the *Hong Kong Restaurant* at No 20 nearby.

At the central market, Pasar Pagi, you'll find a great array of delicious fruits and plenty of food stalls and warungs which stay open till evening. Further along Jalan Karanggetas there are a number of good bakeries where you can also buy ice cream; the *Toko Cermin* at No 22 is a small grocery store with bread, pastries, ice cream and various canned

goods. The *Toko Famili*, near Pasar Pagi, at Jalan Siliwangi 96 is good for all kinds of kerupuk and other baked snacks.

Most of the seafood restaurants are along Jalan Bahagia, towards the junction with Jalan Pasuketan. Of the many along this street, one of the best known is *Maxim's* at No 45-47 which specialises in Chinese, shrimp and crab dishes – 2500 rp for fresh shrimps or 3500 rp fried with delicious oyster sauce.

Cirebon also has a good Chinese seafood night market. Surprisingly prices are similar to the restaurants, eg a meal of grilled fish, rice and tea for two costs about 5500 rp, but there's plenty of it and the food is delicious. The market sets up every evening in the small square at the south end of Jalan Bahagia.

In this same area the *Sinar Budi* restaurant at Jalan Pasuketan 15 has excellent, if slightly expensive, Padang food and good ice juices for around 800 rp.

Near the harbour, the *Moro Seneng Restaurant* is down a small lane at the corner of Jalan Pasuketan and Yos Sudarso. It's worth trying; the menu includes seafood, it's clean and cheap'(dishes start at 750 rp) and you can choose to eat inside or out. Hours are 9 am to 10 pm.

Things to Buy

Cirebon is well known for its distinctive batik which shows a strong Chinese influence in its designs. They include the classical 'cloud and rock' motif, birds and sometimes the white lion of Cirebon royalty. Traditional colours are rich reds and tones of blue.

In town there are a number of shops along Jalan Karanggetas selling batiks from Cirebon, Pekalongan and Solo. Most of them claim to have set prices and start at about 5000 rp for a sarong. *Batik Purnama* on Jalan Karanggetas has a good selection although you'll have to bargain in Bahasa Indonesia. Another place to try is Pasar Balong on Jalan Pekiringan.

There are several cassette shops along

Jalan Pasuketan and Jalan Pekiringan where you can buy tapes of tarling and other Cirebon music. One of the better ones is *Toko Wijaya* at Jalan Pasuketan 57 where you can have 'mie & music', since they also serve noodles.

Getting There & Away

The road and rail route to Cirebon from Jakarta (259 km) follows the flat north coast but it's more interesting to travel up from Bandung (127 km). The trip is by bus only but on a road which covers much more scenic hilly country.

Bus The Cirebon bus station is a 15-minute, 125 rp minibus trip to the south-west part of town. Buses between Jakarta and Cirebon take about five hours and the fare is 2700 rp. Bandung to Cirebon takes about 3½ hours and costs 1500 rp. Semarang (245 km) is about five hours away; from 2500 rp by public bus to 6000 rp by air-con night bus. Yogya (365 km) is about six to seven hours by bus, from 3800 rp.

For express minibuses from Cirebon, the ACC Kopyor 4848 office (tel 4343) is conveniently located in town at Jalan Karanggetas 7, next door to the Kopyor Restaurant. Their minibuses operate to Bandung (3500 rp), Semarang (7500 rp) and Yogya (7500 rp).

Train Cirebon is on both the main northern Jakarta-Semarang-Surabaya railway line and the southern Jakarta-Yogya-Surabaya line, so there are frequent day and evening trains. There are seven daily departures from the Gambir station in Jakarta and trains also depart from Kota and Pasar Senen. Fares vary widely from 3600 rp in all-3rd class to 17,000 rp for a 1st class seat on the *Bima Express* and the trip takes around 3½ hours.

Getting Around

Cirebon's city minibus (taxi kota) service operates from the taxi kota station on Jalan Gunungsari, a couple of blocks west of Jalan Siliwangi. They're labelled G7,

GG, etc and charge a fixed 150 rp fare around town – some even offer 'full music'! The most useful buses are: G7 to the kratons, G4 or GP to Trusmi, G9 or G10 to Gua Sunyaragi, and GG to the Sunan Gunungjati Tomb. City buses, however, have been banned along Jalan Siliwangi between the train station and the Jalan Kartini junction near the mayor's residence so you'll have to take a becak or walk.

There are plenty of becaks ringing through the streets of Cirebon – if they didn't leave Jakarta for Bandung, they surely must have come here. A becak from the train station to Pasar Pagi costs around 400 rp.

Central Java

Central Java has a population of about 27 million, covers an area of 34,503 square km and has its capital at Semarang. It's at the heart of Java and is the most 'Indonesian' part of Indonesia. This was the centre of Java's first great Indianised civilisation and much of the island's early culture. Later, the rise of Islam created powerful sultanates centred around the kratons or courts of Surakarta (Solo) and Yogyakarta. Although the north coast was the early Muslims' first foothold on Java, further inland the new faith was gradually infused with strong Hindu-Buddhist influences and even older indigenous beliefs. The old Javanese traditions and arts, cultivated by the royal courts, are at their most vigorous here. The years of Dutch rule made little impact and even though the Indonesian revolution stripped the sultans of their political powers, the influence of kraton culture still lingers in the minds of many Javanese.

Within the province the Special Territory of Yogyakarta forms an enclave shaped like a triangle with its base on the south coast and its apex at the volcano Mt Merapi. Although the capital of Central Java is

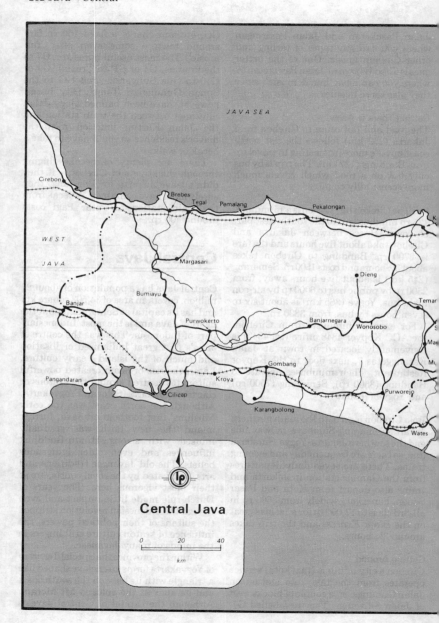

JAVA SEA

WEST JAVA

Cirebon

Brebes
Tegal
Pemalang
Pekalongan
K

Margasari

Dieng

Bumiayu

Banjar

Purwokerto
Banjarnegara
Wonosobo

Temar

Pangandaran

Gombang
Kroya

Mu

Cilacap
Purworejo

Karangbolong

Wates

Central Java

0   20   40
km

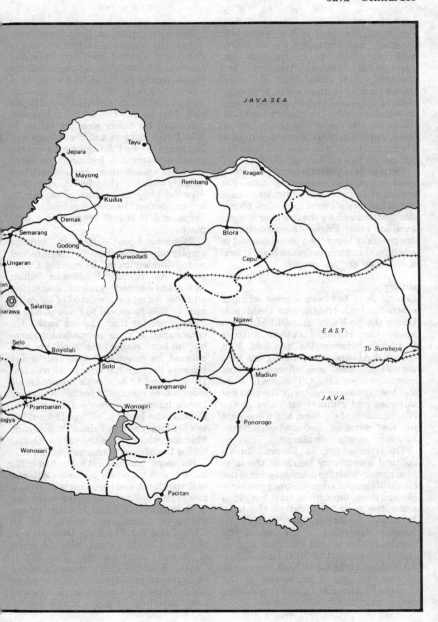

Semarang, the cities of Yogya and Solo (formerly Surakarta) are the emotional and cultural centres, having both been capitals of Javanese kingdoms and frequently rival cities. Most of Central Java's main attractions are in, or close to, these two cities and include the magnificent Borobudur and Prambanan temples. There are also earlier temples in Central Java, particularly the ancient shrines of Dieng, and the province also has some fine hill resorts like Kaliurang.

Despite its population pressure, Central Java is a relaxed, easy-going state. The enclave of Yogyakarta in particular remains one of Indonesia's most important tourist destinations and for the traveller it offers excellent value. Prices of accommodation are generally lower than elsewhere and in addition standards are often higher; food is also good and low priced.

History

Central Java has been a great religious centre for both Hindus and Buddhists. Under the Sailendra and Old Mataram kings the Hindu-Javanese culture flourished between the 8th and 10th centuries AD and it was during this time that Java's most magnificent religious monuments were built. The province has also been the major centre for the political intrigues and cultural activities of the Islamic states of old Java, and it was here too that some of the most significant historical events took place.

The renaissance of Central Java's political ascendancy began in the late-16th century with the disintegration of the Hindu Majapahit empire. Strong maritime Muslim states arose in the north but in the south the most powerful of the later Javanese dynasties had started to develop. According to the legend the founder of this second Mataram empire sought the support of Nyai Laru Kidul, the Goddess of the South Seas, who was to become the special protectress of the House of Mataram and is still very much a part of court and local traditions.

From its capital at Kota Gede, near Yogya, the Mataram empire eventually dominated Central and East Java and Madura. Under Sultan Agung, one of the classic warrior figures of Java's history, it reached its peak. He also sent missions further afield to Palembang, Banjarmasin and Makassar. The only permanent defeats of his career were his failure to take Dutch Batavia and the sultanate of Banten in the west. Sultan Agung was the greatest conqueror in Indonesia, probably since Majapahit times. He not only had military ability but he relied upon a cult of mystical glory and wealth about him to attract loyalty. His tomb is at Imogiri near Yogya and it is still revered as a holy place.

Following Agung's death in 1646 the empire rapidly began to disintegrate and was ultimately to fall to growing Dutch power. Amangkurat I followed Sultan Agung and devoted his reign to destroying all those whom he suspected of opposing him. In 1647 he moved to a new palace at Plered, not far from the old court. He constructed a more permanent palace, built of brick rather than wood, but also ensured its downfall by alienating his subjects through his tyrannical policies. He soon had to cope with revolts on all sides, which eventually led to the start of Dutch intervention in Javanese affairs. Rebellion broke out in 1675 and Plered fell to a predatory raid by Prince Trunojoyo of Madura, who then withdrew to Kediri, taking the Mataram treasury with him.

Following Amangkurat's death in 1677, his son and successor made an alliance with the Dutch and began his reign from a new capital at Kartosuro near present day Solo. In 1678 Dutch and Javanese troops destroyed Trunojoyo's stronghold at Kediri, and the Mataram treasury was plundered by the victors, although some of it was later restored. The Dutch Captain Francois Tack is remembered for being presumptuous enough to sell a piece of royal regalia to Amangkurat II, who was later unwilling to pay up and finally repaid Tack for his effrontery by having him killed at court in 1686.

The Mataram rulers of the 18th century were a uniformly hopeless lot and intrigues and animosities at court erupted into what became known as the First and Second Javanese Wars of Succession. Later the repercussions of the Batavian Chinese massacre in 1740 spilled into Central Java and the fighting lasted almost 17 years. Pakubuwono II unwisely joined those Chinese who escaped slaughter in their siege of Dutch headquarters along the north coast, but was forced to retreat. Madurese intervention on behalf of the Dutch added to the confusion and in 1742 the court of Mataram was once again conquered by Madurese troops. The struggle was finally resolved by the treaty of 1743 by which Pakubuwono II was restored to his battered court but at the cost of enormous concessions to the Dutch.

Kartosuro was now abandoned and in 1745 Pakubuwono II established a new court at Surakarta which is still occupied by his descendants. The new court, however, was no more stable than the old and in 1746 the Third Javanese War of Succession began and continued until 1757. The Dutch, rapidly losing patience, finally adopted a policy of divide and rule – a tactic which was also adopted by the British when they took over control during the five-year interregnum from 1811. By 1757 the former Mataram empire had been split into three rival, self-governing principalities: the realm of Surakarta was partitioned and the Sultanate of Yogyakarta was formed in 1755, and finally a smaller domain was created within Surakarta called Mangkunegara.

The founder of Yogya, Hamengkubuwono I (1755-92), was the most able Mataram ruler since Sultan Agung. During his reign the Sultanate was the predominant military power in Central Java. Yet, within 40 years of his death, his successor had effected the destruction of Javanese independence and the beginning of the truly colonial period of Central Javanese history. The deterioration of Hameng-kubuwono II's relations both with his rivals in Surakarta and with the Dutch was followed by equal hostility towards the British. In 1812 European troops, supported by the sultan's ambitious brother and Mangkunegara, plundered the court of Yogya and Hamengkubuwono was exiled to Penang. He was replaced as sultan by his son and his brother was appointed Prince Paku Alam of a small enclave within the Sultanate.

Java at this time was in a state of flux due to corruption at court, continual European interference and increased hardship among the Javanese villagers. Into this turbulent picture stepped one of the most famous figures of Indonesian history, Prince Diponegoro, to launch the Java War of 1825-30. At the end of the war the Dutch held Yogya responsible and all of its outer districts were annexed. Just to maintain the principle of equality, the outer districts of Surakarta were annexed. Pakubuwono IV was so disturbed by this apparent injustice that he set out for the Indian Ocean to confer with the Goddess of the South Seas but the Dutch, fearing yet more rebellion, brought him back and exiled him to Ambon.

The Java War was the last stand of the Javanese aristocracy. For the rest of the colonial period the courts became ritual establishments and Dutch residents exercised control. With no real room or will for political manoeuvre, they turned their energies to traditional court ceremonies and patronage of literature and the arts. Their cultural prestige among the masses was high and this, combined with their political impotence, possibly explains why the royal elite were not major targets for the nationalist movement which arose in the 20th century. In fact Yogyakarta for a time became the capital of the Republican government and the progressive sultan at that time was so popular that he later served in several government posts. The Sultanate also remained administratively autonomous from Central Java as a Special Territory with the status of a province.

YOGYAKARTA

The city-state of Yogyakarta has a population of about 3 million and covers an area of 3169 square km. It owes its foundation to Prince Mangkubumi when in 1755, following a land dispute with his brother the Susuhunan of Surakarta, the rebel prince returned to the former seat of Mataram and built the kraton of Yogyakarta. He took the title of sultan and adopted the name of Hamengkubuwono, meaning literally 'the universe on the lap of the king', which all his successors have used. He created the most powerful Javanese state since the 17th century but his son was less competent and during the period of British rule the Yogya kraton was sacked, Hamengkubuwono II was exiled and the smaller Paku Alam principality created within the Sultanate.

For the Javanese, Yogya has always been a symbol of resistance to colonial rule. The heart of Prince Diponegoro's Java War (1825-30) was in the Yogya area. More recently Yogya was again the centre of revolutionary forces and became the capital of the Republic from 1946 until independence was achieved in 1949. As the Dutch took control of other Javanese cities, part of the kraton was turned over to the new Gajah Mada University which opened in 1946. Thus, as one of the sultan's advisers observed, in Yogya 'the Revolution could not possibly smash the palace doors, because they were already wide open'.

When the Dutch occupied Yogya in 1948, the patriotic sultan locked himself in the kraton, which became the major link between the city and the guerillas who retreated to the countryside. The Dutch did not dare move against the sultan for fear of arousing the anger of millions of Javanese who looked upon him almost as a god. The sultan let rebels,

including Suharto, use the palace as their headquarters and as a result of this support Yogya has continued as a semi-autonomous territory with the status of sultanate. Under Suharto's government, Sultan Hamengkubuwono IX was Indonesia's vice-president until he stepped down in March 1978. The sultan passed away in October 1988 and in March 1989 Prince Bangkubumi, the eldest of 16 sons, was installed as Sultan Hamengkubuwono X. The coronation involved great pomp and ceremony and included a procession of dwarfs and albinos. The new sultan is a member of the National Assembly and, like his father, is intent on preserving the traditions of Yogya.

Today Yogya is one of the foremost cultural centres of Java and the sultan's walled palace remains the hub of traditional life. The sultan lived here until his death and during the three special Garebeg festivals held each year he led Java's most colourful and grand processions. Palace guards and retainers in traditional court dress and large floats of flower-bedecked *gunungans* of rice all make their way to the mosque west of the kraton to the sound of prayer and the inevitable music of gamelan. These are ceremonies not to be missed if you're anywhere in the area at the time.

Traditional Javanese performing arts can also be seen in various places around Yogya. It is also a major craft centre and one of the best places to shop in Indonesia. Yogya is particularly well known for its fine batik and there are numerous batik workshops selling an incredible range of items, including batik paintings. The contemporary arts are also flourishing and Yogya has given its name to an important school of modern painting, perhaps best personified by the well-known Indonesian impressionist Affandi.

Just south of the city lies Kota Gede, the first capital of Mataram and today a major silverwork centre. The hilltop royal cemetery of Imogiri and the tomb of the famous Sultan Agung are also close by. To the north-east are the ruins of Prambanan while to the north-west is massive and magnificent Borobudur. Once a city of bicycles and pedestrians, Yogya has grown enormously but the pace is still slower than that of other large Indonesian cities. It's one of the most popular cities for travellers in Indonesia and it's easy to see why – apart from its many attractions Yogya is interesting, friendly and easy going with an excellent choice of economical losmen and restaurants.

Information & Orientation

The old, walled kraton of Yogya is situated in the south of the city while the newer parts have spread to the north. Jalan Malioboro, in the centre of the city, is the main street linking the old and new parts of Yogya and the busy main shopping centre. The tourist office is here, there are numerous restaurants and one

long colourful bazaar of bookshops, souvenir shops and sidewalk stalls. Most of the hotels and restaurants frequented by travellers on a tight budget are located just off Malioboro around the railway station. The bus station is some distance south-east from the centre of town.

Yogya's tourist attractions are mainly concentrated in the kraton area of the old city. In the north is the Diponegoro Museum, the Gajah Mada University and, on the east bank of the river, the Yogyakarta Craft Centre and Yogya's best hotel, the Ambarrukmo Palace. The Adisucipto airport is a few km further east of the Ambarrukmo, on the road to Solo.

Note that although Yogyakarta is now spelt with a Y (not Jogjakarta) it's still pronounced with a J. In the 'new' Indonesian spelling system devised in the '60s, the letter 'Y' was chosen to represent

Villagers harvest the ripe heads of grain by hand – Central Java

what is a 'J' sound in English. Asking for Yogya with an English pronunciation will get you blank stares.

Yogya is notorious for pick-pockets and thieves, so take care.

Tourist Office The Tourist Information Centre (tel 2812) is at Jalan Malioboro 16, open 8 am to 8 pm Monday to Saturday. Useful, detailed maps of the city are available, and they can give you all the latest information on cultural performances in and around Yogya. They also have reference maps of city bus routes and lists of train times pinned to various noticeboards.

Post & Communication The main post office with its efficient poste restante, on Jalan Senopati, is open from 8 am to 1 pm Monday to Thursday and Saturday – it closes at 11 am on Fridays. The telephone office is to the north of town on Jalan Suroto.

Bank The Bank Negara, at the junction of Jalan Malioboro and Senopati, has a quick and efficient foreign exchange counter. It's open 8 am to 4 pm Monday to Thursday, 8 to 11 am and 2 to 4 pm Friday and 8 am to 1 pm Saturday.

Other The immigration office is on Jalan Adisucipto, a short distance from the Ambarrukmo Palace Hotel. Hours are 7.30 am to 2 pm Monday to Thursday, 7.30 to 11 am Friday, and 7.30 am to 12.30 pm on Saturday.

You can use the swimming pool at the Mutiara or the Ambarrukmo Palace Hotel (9 am to 6 pm) for 1750 rp a day.

Kraton of Yogya

In the heart of the old city the huge palace of the sultans of Yogya is effectively the centre of a small walled-city within a city. Over 25,000 people live within the greater kraton compound, which contains its own market, shops, batik and silver cottage industries, schools and mosques. A large section of it is still used by the Gajah Mada medical faculty and until fairly recently (from 1949 to 1973) university students were sitting at lectures in the northern courtyards of the palace.

The innermost group of buildings, where the current sultan still lives, were built between 1755 and 1756 although extensions were made over almost 40 years during the long reign of Hamengkubuwono I. European-style touches to the interior were added much later by the sultans of the 1920s, but structurally this is one of the finest examples of Javanese palace architecture providing a series of luxurious halls and spacious courtyards and pavilions. The sense of tradition holds strong in Yogya, and the palace is attended by very dignified and elderly retainers who still wear traditional Javanese dress.

The centre of the kraton is the fabulous reception hall known as the Bangsal Kencana or Golden Pavilion, with its intricately decorated roof and great columns of carved teak. A large part of the kraton is used as a museum with an extensive collection including gifts from European monarchs and gilt copies of the sacred *pusaka* (the heirlooms of the royal family), gamelan instruments, royal carriages and a huge bottle-shaped wooden alarm gong. One of the most interesting rooms contains the royal family tree, old photographs of grand mass weddings and portraits of the former sultans of Yogya.

Other points of interest within the kraton palace include the small European bandstand with stained-glass images of musical instruments. In another part of the kraton there are 'male' and 'female' entrances indicated by giant-sized 'he' and 'she' dragons, although they look pretty much alike!

Outside the kraton, in the centre of the northern square, you'll see two sacred *waringin* or banyan trees where in the days of feudal Java, white-robed petitioners would patiently sit hoping to catch the eye

Cattle market in Yogya

of the king. Entrance to the kraton is from the west gate. It's open from 8.30 am to 1 pm daily, except Friday and Saturday when it closes at 11.30 am. It is closed on national and kraton holidays. Admission is 500 rp which includes an excellent guided tour, although some people have reported that there is a tendency to rush visitors through. Booklets about the palace and excellent postcards of the old sultans are on sale inside. On Mondays and Wednesdays you can see gamelan playing at the pavilion from 10.30 am to 12 noon, and classical dancing on Sunday mornings.

Taman Sari

Just west of the kraton is the Taman Sari or 'Fragrant Garden'. Better known in Yogya as the 'Water Castle', this was once a splendid pleasure park of palaces, pools and waterways for the sultan and his entourage. The architect of this elaborate retreat built between 1758 and 1765 was a Portuguese from Batavia and the story goes that the sultan had him executed to keep his hidden pleasure rooms secret. They were damaged first by Diponegoro's Java War and an earthquake in 1865 helped finish the job. Today most of the Water Castle has tumbled down amidst dusty alleys, small houses and batik galleries. But it's an interesting place of eerie ruins with underground passages and a large mosque at a cool subterranean level which is well worth seeking out. There are often students around who will help out with a guided tour.

Of the remaining fragments, the bathing pools have been restored – not terribly well perhaps, but they give an impression of the ornate architecture and the scale on which things were built here. It was no doubt intended as a cool place for the sultan and ladies of the harem to relax

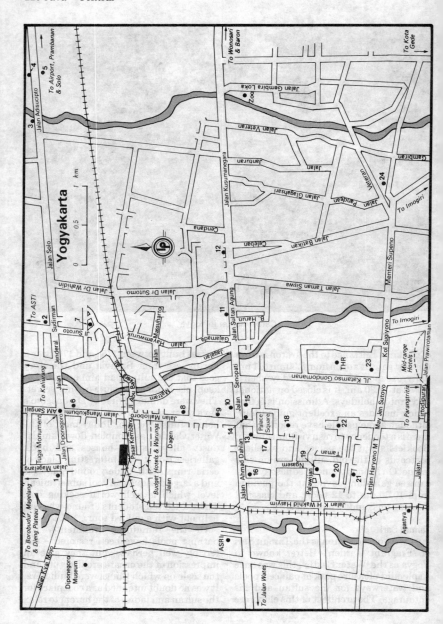

Yogyakarta

1	Bus Stop For Borobudur
2	Army Museum
3	Affandi Museum
4	Ambarrukmo Palace Hotel
5	Yogyakarta Craft Centre
6	Garuda Airways
7	Telephone Exchange Office
8	Pasar Beringharjo
10	Senopati Shopping Centre & Colt Station
11	Paku Alam Kraton
12	Batik Research Centre
13	Sono-Budoyo Museum
14	GPO
15	Taxi Stand
16	Nitour
17	Mesjid Besar Mosque
18	Yogya Kraton
19	Pasar Ngasem Bird Market
20	Taman Sari
21	Batik Galleries
22	Sasono Hinggil
23	Dalem Pujokusuman Theatre
24	Bus Station

in the days when it was surrounded by gardens, and from the tower overlooking the pools the sultan was able to witness what was going on down below. Eating the round and pale-brown fruit of the *kepal* trees growing near the pool is supposed to do wonders for body odour! Entrance to this site costs 200 rp and it's open from 9 am to 4 pm daily.

On the edge of the site the Pasar Ngasem is a colourful bird market crowded with hundreds of budgies, orioles, roosters and singing turtle-doves in ornamental cages. This is a breeding ground though for big red ants (the eggs are sold for bird feed) so beware – they have a mean bite!

Other Palaces

The smaller Paku Alam palace, on Jalan Sultan Agung, is also open to visitors and gamelan concerts are held there about every fifth Sunday. The Ambarrukmo palace, in the grounds of the Ambarrukmo Palace Hotel, was built in the 1890s as a

country house for Hamengkubuwono VII. The pavilion has recently been restored and it's another good example of Javanese palace architecture.

Sono-Budoyo Museum

On the north side of the main square in front of the kraton, the museum is housed in an attractive building constructed in traditional Javanese style. It contains a first-rate collection of Javanese, Madurese and Balinese arts including wayang kulit puppets from China and Bali, a beautiful statue of the Monkey God Hanuman as well as exhibits from the Yogya royal family. Nothing is labelled in English but the museum's keeper speaks English and he may be around to give you a tour. It's open from 8 am to 1.30 pm Monday to Thursday, to 10.30 am Friday, and until 11.30 am at weekends. Entrance is 200 rp.

Sasmitaluka Jenderal Sudirman

The memorial house on Jalan B Harun was the home of General Sudirman, the Commander of the Revolutionary forces whose portrait decorates the older series of Indonesian paper currency. Wasted by tuberculosis, Sudirman reputedly often led his forces from a litter and he died shortly after the siege of Yogya in 1948. The house is open every morning except Monday.

Monumen Diponegoro

This museum was built to honour the Indonesian hero, Prince Diponegoro, leader of the bloody but futile rebellion of 1825-1830. The eldest son of Sultan Hamengkubuwono III, Diponegoro had become thoroughly fed up with the corruption of court life and decided to dedicate himself to more spiritual matters. He is supposed to have received a sign from Nyai Lara Kidul that he was destined to be the man of action to oust the Dutch from Java and, as a religious mystic of royal blood, Diponegoro was an ideal Javanese leader. The bitter five-year war was finally resolved when Diponegoro was cunningly tricked into discussing truce negotiations, captured at Magelang and exiled to Manado on the island of Sulawesi. He was later taken to better quarters in Makassar where he died in 1855 and his grave there is now a shrine.

Most of the Prince's belongings and sacred pusaka are kept in this reconstruction of his Yogya residence which was fired and destroyed by the Dutch in 1825. There's still a hole in the wall which Diponegoro is supposed to have shattered with his bare fists so that he and his supporters could escape. The museum is open 7.30 am to 4 pm daily.

To get to Monumen Diponegoro, about four km from the centre of town, you can take a No 2 bus heading north along Jalan Mataram. A No 1 bus will get you back to Jalan Malioboro.

Other Museums

The Museum Biologi at Jalan Sultan Agung 22 has a collection of stuffed animals and plants from the whole archipelago. It's open in the mornings. The Museum Perjuangan, in the southern part of the city on Jalan Kol Sugiyono, has a small and rather poor collection of photographs documenting the Indonesian Revolution. The large Army Museum, on the corner of Jalan Jenderal Sudirman and Simanjuntak, displays more documents, homemade weapons, uniforms and medical equipment from the revolution years. Records also trace Suharto's rise in the ranks of Yogya's Diponegoro Division.

Performances

All the traditional Javanese arts have their place in Yogya. Classical dancing and gamelan rehearsals in the kraton are mentioned above. Wayang kulit can be seen at several places around Yogya on virtually every night of the week. Most of the centres offer shortened versions for visitors but at Sasono Hinggil, in the south palace square, there are marathon all-night performances every second Saturday starting at 8.30 pm. Tickets cost from 1000 rp. This performance and most others are viewed from the dalang's side of the screen, but if you want to see the 'shadow-play' there are one-hour shows held outdoors at the Yogya Craft Centre from 9.30 pm on Mondays, Wednesdays and Saturdays. Tickets cost 1650 rp. The Arjuna Plaza Hotel, Jalan Mangkubumi 48, also has two-hour wayang kulit shows on Tuesday evenings at 7 pm for 2000 rp.

Wayang golek plays are also performed frequently. The Nitour performance, from 11 am to 1 pm every day except Sunday, has a useful handout explaining the history of the wayang and the *Ramayana* story. They are put on at Jalan Ahmad Dahlan 71, tickets cost 1650 rp. Then on Saturday there are wayang golek performances at the Agastya Art Institute, Jalan Gedongkiwo MD III/237 from 3 to 5 pm, and at the Arjuna Plaza Hotel from 7 to 9 pm. You can also see wayang practice sessions at Agastya daily between 3 and 5 pm. See the information about Hanoman's Forest Pub under the following Places to Eat section as well.

There are evening performances of wayang orang or the 'Ramayana ballet' at theatres and hotels in the city from Monday to Friday. Those at the Dalem Pujokusuman on Jalan Katamso are excellent; they are performed from 8 to 10 pm every Monday, Wednesday and Friday, and admission is 3000 rp. Most Saturday evenings there are *Ramayana* ballet performances for 2000 rp at the old palace pavilion of the Ambarrukmo Hotel; on Monday and Wednesday evenings they're put on at the hotel's Borobudur Restaurant and are free with dinner. Arjuna Plaza Hotel has *Ramayana* performances from 8 to 10 pm every Thursday night for 2000 rp. The People's Park Theatre (THR) has been closed for a while for renovations and the date for reopening is uncertain.

Schools The KONRI (Conservatory of Classical Dance) on Jalan Agus Salim near the kraton, and the ASTI (Academy of Dance) on Jalan Colombo in north Yogya are both open to visitors from 8 am to 2 pm, Monday to Saturday. Bagong Kussudiarja, one of Indonesia's leading dance choreographers, has a school at Jalan Singosaren 9 (off Jalan Wates) where modern and classical dance practice sessions can be seen daily except Friday, 4 to 6 pm. Kussudiarja's main studio is at Padepokan, five km from Yogya, where he runs six-month courses for foreign students.

Ramayana Ballet - Prambanan The *Ramayana Ballet* held at the outdoor theatre in Prambanan, 17 km east of Yogya, is Java's most spectacular dance-drama. Performances are held on the four successive full-moon nights each month of the dry season, from May to October, and you should make time to see a performance if you're here then. The origins of this contemporary version of the Ramayana epic go back to the traditional wayang wong of classical Javanese theatre but far greater emphasis is given to the dancing. With the magnificent floodlit Shiva temple as a backdrop, more than 100 dancers and gamelan musicians take part in a spectacle of monkey armies, giants on stilts, clashing battles and acrobatics. It's a somewhat abbreviated version of the *Ramayana* which unfolds over the four nights – the second in the series is the most spectacular when all the leading characters perform before being killed off in this or later episodes.

Performances last from 7 to 9 pm. Tickets sold through Nitour at Jalan Ahmad Dahlan 71 and other travel agents in Yogya include transport to the theatre but it's cheaper to make your own way to Prambanan. If you do the latter, it is probably wise to be at the theatre to buy tickets about two hours early.

Batik
For a first-hand introduction to batik, the best place to visit would have to be the government-run *Balai Penelitian*

Kerajinan dan Batik (Batik & Handicraft Research Centre) at Jalan Kusumanegara 2. They have an excellent display of batiks found throughout Java plus some unusual batiks from other islands, and they'll give you a detailed guided tour of the processes involved for both hand-painted and cap-printed batik. Some of the batik made there is for sale.

Shops & Workshops Batik in the markets is cheaper than in the stores, but you need to be careful about quality and be prepared to bargain. If you don't know much about batik, a good place to start looking is the Terang Bulan shop on Jalan Malioboro (opposite the Happy Restaurant) which will give you an idea of what you should be paying. There are all kinds of materials and batik lengths (cap and tulis) at fixed, reasonable prices and the quality is reliable. Locally-made lurik homespun is always the cheapest. Other shops in town include Ramayana Batik on Jalan Ahmad Dahlan, specialising in Yogya-style batik and the more expensive Batik Keris (Jalan Mangkubumi) and Danar Hadi showrooms (Jalan Solo), with Solo-style work. The majority of batik workshops and several large showrooms are along Jalan Tirtodipuran and Jalan Prawirotaman to the south of the kraton.

Galleries Many of Yogya's better known artists produce batik paintings as well as paintings in oils. Batik paintings generally start at around 8000 rp but oil paintings are very much more expensive. There are a great number of galleries exhibiting work of varying prices, so look around before you buy.

Top of the scale is probably Amri Yahya's gallery at Jalan Gampingan 67. His dynamic modern batiks range from US$65 to over US$1000 and there are some quite stunning abstract oil paintings on display, nice to look at (if you're not put off by the prominently displayed photos of Imelda Marcos) even if you can't afford them. Amri Yahya also sells clothing of original modern design. The gallery is open from Tuesday to Sunday, from 9 am to 5 pm.

Almost next door to Amri Yahya's, you can visit Yogya's ASRI (Academy of Fine Arts) in the mornings, from Monday to Saturday. Carry on up Jalan Wates (the extension of Jalan Ahmad Dahlan) and you'll come to other galleries with more reasonable prices. Kussudiarja is a student of art as well as dance and his Yoga dance studio off Jalan Wates has a large display of batik and oil paintings.

Kuswadji's, in the north square near the kraton, is another good place for top-quality classical and contemporary batik art. Tulus Warsito has a gallery nearby on Jalan Nyai Dahlan. Bambang Utoro has a gallery to the east of town off Jalan Kusumanegara, the continuation of Jalan Senopati.

Affandi, Indonesia's internationally best-known artist, lives in an unusual tree-house overlooking the river on Jalan Solo and close to the Ambarrukmo Palace Hotel. In the grounds Affandi keeps a museum of his own impressionist works, and paintings by his daughter Kartika and other artists. It's open from 9 am to 4 pm and there's now an entry fee of 200 rp. An interesting film about the artist – *Hungry to Paint: Profile of the Indonesian painter Affandi* – has had occasional showings in Jakarta and it's worth looking out for.

The water palace is the site for most of the cheaper batik galleries. Some of the batik is quite interesting; lots of it is very poor quality and boringly repetitive in theme – endless birds and butterflies and soaring moons over rice paddies, fine if you like that sort of thing but you still need to be prepared to hunt around and be selective if you're buying here. Some batik artists only bother to draw the outline and then have teams of women fill in the intricate details, which certainly enables them to churn out pictures in great numbers! Beware of the teams of touts who follow you around taking you to galleries – Yogya is positively crawling with would-be batik salesmen and they'll inevitably be raking off a commission at your expense. The Astuti Batik Gallery has some good quality surrealist and landscape work.

Batik Courses If you want to have a go at batik yourself there are lots of batik courses and classes in Yogya. Many of the teachers are just self-proclaimed 'experts' out to make some easy rupiah so before investing time and money it's a good idea to ask around among other travellers who may have just completed a course. For beginners, the Lucy Batik Gallery near Superman's is cheap and popular; they'll lead you through the production of your own painting for a nominal fee which is probably the cheapest way to learn basic skills and see how you like it in the first place. Lucy Batik Gallery also run a six-day course, from 8.30 am to 3.30 pm, for 10,000 rp.

The Intensive Batik Course of Hadjir Digdodarmojo seems to get a generally high approval rating although some people have also reported it to be rather mechanical and dull. There are three or five-day courses from 2 to 6 pm daily. It's on the left of the main entrance to the water palace at Taman Kp 3/177.

The Batik Research Centre has recommended Tulus Warsito at Jalan Tirtodipuran 19A. He offers various courses including one-day beginners classes for 5000 rp and three-day courses for 14,000 rp. A three-week course, six days a week 9 am to 3 pm for 70,000 rp, covers theory and practise with chemical dyes and waxing. Wiko Djoan is a young artist who offers a similar variety of curricula and tuition at his batik workshop, Jalan Wates 31.

The most thorough course with the best facilities is likely to be at the Batik Research Centre. They did offer a comprehensive one-month course limited to three students at a time for 284,000 rp per person and are likely to do so again in future.

Curios & Other Crafts Jalan Malioboro is the main antique/curio shop area. There are also a handful of places near the Ambarrukmo Palace Hotel and you can find an interesting variety of antiques at the Jul Shop, Jalan Mangkubumi 29. Toko Tan Jam An on the same street is a silver jewellery shop but if you're visiting Kota Gede you'll find cheaper silver there.

Most of the leather workshops are in the kraton area. Yogya's leatherwork can be excellent value for money but the quality is not always high on closer inspection so look for thick leather, strong stitching and buckles. Kusuman on Jalan Kauman is one good place for leather. Good quality wayang puppets are made at the Mulyo Suhardjo workshop on Jalan Taman Sari and also sold at the Sono-Budoyo museum shop.

Brightly painted children's moneyboxes in the shapes of elephants, roosters and garudas are sold around Yogya, particularly in the bird market near Taman Sari. At Kasongan, the potters' village a few km south-west of Yogya, you can see pots being made.

Along Jalan Malioboro there are a few vendors who create rubber stamps for around 2500 rp apiece. Choose from among the designs in their sample books or have them create an original from your own design. They can usually have the finished stamp for you in 24 hours or less.

Tours

There are various tours from Yogya to the Borobudur and Dieng Plateau temples and around the sights of Yogya. Several travel agencies and hotels can arrange them, including the Hotel Asia-Afrika in the Sosro area. The going low price for a day tour to Borobudur and Dieng is 6500 rp, including admission to the temple sites and snacks. Reliable tour companies include Pacto, Vaya Tour, Natrabu, Tunas Indonesia and Satriavi, all located

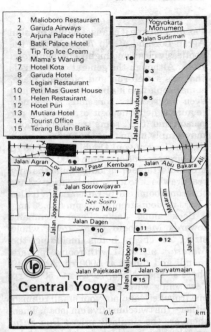

1	Malioboro Restaurant
2	Garuda Airways
3	Arjuna Palace Hotel
4	Batik Palace Hotel
5	Tip Top Ice Cream
6	Mama's Warung
7	Hotel Kota
8	Garuda Hotel
9	Legian Restaurant
10	Peti Mas Guest House
11	Helen Restaurant
12	Hotel Puri
13	Mutiara Hotel
14	Tourist Office
15	Terang Bulan Batik

Central Yogya

at the Ambarukmo Palace Hotel on Jalan Solo (Adisucipto).

Places to Stay – bottom end

Yogya accommodation offers a superb choice of places to stay. Most of the cheap hotels are in the Sosro area, which is bordered on the north and south by Jalan Pasar Kembang, parallel to and immediately south of the railway line, Jalan Sosrowijayan, a block further south, and on the east and west by Jalan Malioboro and Jalan Jogonegara. Connecting Jalan Pasar Kembang and Sosrowijayan and just a couple of doors down from the main street of Yogya (Jalan Malioboro) are two narrow alleyways known as Gang Sosrowijayan I & II. Here you'll find more real cheapies and some of Yogya's most popular eating places. There are more good places to stay in other small gangs in this area.

Jalan Pasar Kembang At the end of Jalan

Pasar Kembang it changes names to Jalan Agran Lor and at No 79 you'll find the spotlessly clean and highly efficient *Hotel Kota*. Although the general consensus is that it's a well-run and pleasant place, some people find it a bit over-officious and even too security conscious. They now require a hefty deposit of 15,000 rp per person and 'full', some travellers report, may simply mean that the owner doesn't like the look of you! Doubles cost 6500 rp and larger rooms cost from 8000 rp. There are comfortable open lounges and the only real drawback to its corner location is that the front rooms can be rather noisy. It also closes its doors from 11.30 pm to 5.30 am.

Back along Jalan Pasar Kembang towards Malioboro there are a whole string of cheap hotels including the *Mataram* at No 61 with rooms (private mandi and toilet) at 5000 rp. At No 49 there's the *Nusantara* at 5000 rp ('swarming with cockroaches,' reported one traveller, 'and not your small rubbish either – the twitching five cm jobs'). Then there are the similarly priced *Dua-Satu* and the *Shinta*, which don't always take foreigners.

The *Asia-Africa* (or 'A-A') at No 25 has a variety of rooms from 7500 rp to more expensive rooms with a private mandi at 10,000 rp and above. It's a good place and there's a garden at the back.

At No 17A the *Ratna* is slightly flashier with rooms from 6000 rp or, with a private mandi and toilet, from 10,000 rp. It's set back from the road and is pleasantly quiet.

Gang Sosrowijayan I This small connecting alley has some very cheap places but make sure your room is secure. Yogya is notorious for theft, including the straight-from-your-room variety. None of the following losmen offers private mandis with their rooms – it's shared bath only. The popular *Losmen Beta* is small, noisy and fairly commercial with singles/doubles at 1500/2500 rp. Nearby on or just off Gang I are *Strowihadi*, only 1500/2000 rp, *Bu Purwo* with bed-size rooms for 1000/1500 rp and the slightly nicer *Losmen Lucy*, 2000/3000 rp.

A bit further along the gang are the *Rama* and *Jogja*, two adjoining losmen with rooms around 3000 rp. The *Lima Losmen* is quite pleasant and located on a tiny alley parallel to Gang I towards Malioboro. Rooms are 1500/2000 rp and there is a good coffee shop next door. On a parallel alley in the opposite direction is *Dewi Homestay*, where fair-sized rooms without bath are 3500 rp and with attached bath are 4500 rp. Those with attached bath and breakfast are 6500 rp.

Gang Sosrowijayan II In the next major alley to the west, the modern *Hotel Bagus* is clean and quiet; it's good value and very popular. It's built around a central courtyard and run by a veritable classroom of children. Singles/doubles with a fan cost 2500/3000 rp. There's free tea three times a day. The *Losmen Setia*, down an alley off Gang II (to the right coming from the train station), is a friendly, quiet place with cheap rooms from 1750 rp. Rooms on the roof for 2500 rp are cooler (they have windows) and are a bit more private than other rooms. Down another little alley to the left is the *Losmen Setia Kawan* which is nothing special for 2500/3000 rp. A better place for the same rates is at the end of the next alley off Gang II. The *Supriyanto Inn* is clean, airy and well-run.

The *Jaya Losmen* is also good with small but clean rooms at 2500 rp and larger rooms with a fan at 3000 rp. It's run by friendly people. The *Gandhi*, in its own garden opposite the Jaya, is a popular place with good rooms at 2500 and 3000 rp. Another in this area, similarly priced and worth trying, is the *Utar Pension Inn*.

Jalan Sosrowijayan Between Gang I and Malioboro, the *Aziatic* is an old Dutch inn with big double beds (no singles) at 4000 rp. It's good value – clean, cool and quiet and very safe. At night the doors are locked and there are stout bars on the windows –

'as secure as Pentridge' wrote one obviously impressed Australian visitor. Pentridge is a major Australian jail! There's a wide central hallway where you can sit and chat and a good restaurant in the back.

Across the road, the *Indonesia* has a nice courtyard, basic rooms for 2000/4000 rp and better rooms with mandis from 6000 rp. Further west on Jalan Sosrowijayan on the same side of the street is *Wisma Gambira* with fair rooms at 4000/5000 rp or 7500 rp with attached mandi. Across the street and down a short alley at Jalan Sosrowijayan 1/192, the *Losmen Wisma Wijaya* has plain but clean singles/doubles at 3000/3500 rp including a small breakfast. The people who run it are reportedly 'very friendly and informative'.

Other Across Malioboro, Jalan Sosrokusuman DN I is a quiet street alongside the Helen Restaurant. The *Hotel Puri* at No 22 is an attractive place built around a small courtyard. It's well kept and very quiet. Singles/doubles cost 4000/5000 rp and there's free tea or coffee in the mornings and evenings. At No 16 the nearby *Hotel Intan* is similarly priced but not quite so nice; the *Prambanan Guest House*, No 18-20, has rooms at 4500/5000 rp or 5500/6000 rp with a mandi. Near the end of Jalan Sosrokusuman toward Jalan Mataram, *Hotel Zamrud* at No 47 is the best on this street; rooms start at 7000 rp for a single including breakfast and cost 12,500 rp for a double with fan and shower.

Places to Stay – middle

Jalan Dagen In the centre of town, the *Peti Mas* (tel 2896) at Jalan Dagen 39 – just off Malioboro – has doubles with bathroom and hot water, fan or air-con from 18,550 rp including morning and evening tea. This clean, well-kept guest house has a laundry service and an attractive garden restaurant. Nearby are the similarly priced *Sri Wibowo* at No 23 and *Blue Safir* at No 34-36. The Blue Safir has air-con rooms with hot water showers and breakfast for 18,000/20,000 rp. There are others: the *Lilik Guest House*, similar to the Peti Mas, and two slightly cheaper places, *Wisma Nendra* and *Sweet Home Hotel*.

Jalan Prawirotaman There are a number of good middle-range places south of the kraton and well away from the centre of town in the area of Jalan Prawirotaman. Most of them are converted houses that are spacious, airy, quiet and have central garden areas. An information desk at the railway station has details on some of them. They often send touts to intercept travellers at the station and you get a free becak ride there – if you don't like the place you only have to say no. Becaks into town from this area cost about 750 rp.

Starting from the west end of Jalan Prawirotaman at Jalan Parangtritis are a couple of semi-flash places with swimming pools, *Wisma Gajah Guest House* (tel 2479) and *Airlangga Guest House* (tel 3344) where air-con rooms cost 20,000 to 22,000 rp single, 23,000 to 26,000 rp double. They also have cheaper non air-con rooms. During the high season these two are often booked by package tour groups. Across the street is the more modest *Borobudur Guest House* (tel 3344) with pleasant fan-cooled rooms for 10,000/12,000 rp. Two doors down from Borobudur at No 7 and very similar in rates and conditions is the *Sriwijaya Guest House* (tel 2387). Across the street at No 4A is the slightly less expensive but nothing special *Putra Jaya Guest House*.

Towards the middle of Jalan Prawirotaman are *Wisma Indah Guest House* (tel 88021) at No 12, the *Sumaryo Guest House* (tel 2852) at No 18A, and the *Duta Guest House* (tel 5219) at No 20. Sumaryo is one of the nicest guest houses in the entire area with a pool, excellent service and a substantial breakfast for 12,000 rp single, 17,000 double. The Wisma Indah and Duta are both in the 10,000 to 15,000 rp range including breakfast; the Duta also has a pool and is often full.

Next door to the Duta at No 22 is the

ever-popular *Rose Guest House* (tel 87991), which has economy singles for 7500 rp and more expensive rooms from 10,000/12,000 rp. Across the road and east a bit with no street number and no telephone is the *Perwita Sari Guest House* (cheapest on the street) with a few rooms without bath for 6500 rp, with bath 7500 rp, and doubles starting at 10,000 rp.

At the east end of Jalan Prawirotaman are three more places, *Prayogo Guest House* (tel 3715), *Galunggung Guest House* (tel 2715), and *Kirana Guest House* (tel 3200). Starting at 15,000 rp, rooms at Prayogo are overpriced for what you get. The Galunggung is slightly better at 12,000 rp and has a large swimming pool located across the street. The Kirana is quite nicely done; doubles are 17,500 rp including breakfast or 22,000 rp with air-con.

The next street south is Jalan Prawirotaman II where the *pasar pagi* is located. There are five guest houses here: the *Muria, Metro, Makuta, Agung* and *Palupi*. The Metro (tel 3982) is the most popular and has a garden area and pool; rooms with breakfast and hot water range from 6000 rp for 'standard' to 23,000 rp for air-con. Agung Guest House is also popular but some travellers have complained that standards are not what they once were. The Palupi Guest House has rooms starting at 8000/10,000 rp.

Around the corner from the west end of Jalan Prawirotaman at Jalan Parangtritis 73 is *Sunarko Guest House* (tel 2047), a cosy little place with fan cooled rooms and private bath starting at 7000/9000 rp. It lacks the interior gardens of places on Jalan Prawirotaman, but the staff tries hard to please.

Other Near the train station, the *Batik Palace Hotel* (tel 2149) at Jalan Pasar Kembang 29 is a small, friendly hotel with a nice garden. Singles/doubles (with bathroom, shower and hot water) are 19,500/24,450 rp including breakfast and afternoon tea; there are more expensive rooms with air-con. A newer branch of the Batik Palace at Jalan Mangkubumi 46 has singles/doubles at 32,600/40,750 rp and a swimming pool. Both hotels have a restaurant and bar.

Places to Stay – top end

Yogya's most prestigious hotel is the grand *Ambarrukmo Palace* (tel 88488), Jalan Adisucipto, which contains the old Ambarrukmo Palace in its grounds. There are singles/doubles for US$60/70 and more expensive suites. The hotel has restaurants, a coffee shop, bar, good shopping arcade, swimming pool and tennis courts.

The *Mutiara Hotel* (tel 3272) is centrally located at Jalan Malioboro 18 near the Tourist Information Centre. The old part of the hotel has air-con singles/doubles from US$25 to US$34 (plus 20% tax and service) and more expensive suites. The new hotel next door is brighter and more expensive with rooms from US$38 to US$44, and has a swimming pool. Other facilities include a restaurant, bar, laundry and free airport transport.

The big Dutch-built *Garuda Hotel* (tel 86353) at Jalan Malioboro 60 is a superb old building that has recently undergone renovations under the new ownership of the Natour Group. It now has a swimming pool, shopping arcade etc. Standard singles/doubles are US$42/50 and suites start at US$88.

Places to Eat

Sosro Area There is as wide a variety of eating places as there are losmen in Yogya. Two of them have earned a permanent niche in the travellers' bottleneck department – everybody seems to pay a visit to either *Mama's* or *Superman's*. They both serve western-style breakfasts (eggs, porridge, french toast, yoghurt, etc) and snacks as well as Indonesian dishes. They have big helpings, the food is generally good and prices are low. If there's a catch to either of these places, it's that they're overwhelmed by

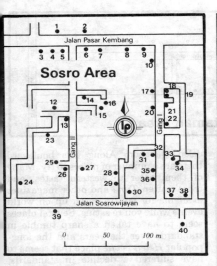

Sosro Area

1	Rumah Makan Padang Surya
2	Mama's
3	Hotel Mendut
4	Losmen Shinta
5	Hotel Cendana
6	Batik Palace Hotel
7	Hotel Asia-Afrika
8	Hotel Ratna
9	Rumah Makan Padang Palito Alam
10	Cheap Warungs
11	Hotel Asia-Afrika
12	Losmen Setia
13	Anna's Restaurant
14	Hotel Bagus
15	Supriyanto Inn
16	Losmen Seita Kawan
17	Losmen Astrowihadi
18	Losmen Lucy
19	Losmen Bu Purwo
20	Losmen Beta
21	Old Superman's Restaurant
22	Bu Sis Restaurant
23	Utar Pension Inn
24	Losmen Wisma Wijaya
25	Heru Jaya Restaurant & Losmen
26	Jaya Losmen
27	Gandhi Losmen
28	Lovina Coffee Shop
29	Dewi Homestay
30	Hotel Rama
31	Eko Restaurant
32	New Supermans's Restaurant
33	Lima Losmen
34	French Grill Restaurant
35	Hotel Jogja Restaurant
36	Hotel Rama
37	Hotel Kartika
38	Hotel Aziatic
39	Wisma Gambira Hotel
40	Hotel Indonesia

westerners and the only local people in sight are the Yogya trendies wasting time at Superman's.

You'll find Superman's on Gang Sosrowijayan I. It's very popular at breakfast time, there's good music and it's a relaxed place to while away a rainy afternoon. Some people say *New Superman's*, a bit further down Gang I, is better. On Jalan Pasar Kembang, beside the railway line, there are a whole host of good warungs but Mama's is definitely number one. Evening time is when it comes into full swing and it's always crowded, since it's about the only place open late at night. The *Pandito Alam* on Jalan Pasar Kembang near Hotel Ratna has fair Padang food.

For delicious spicy food it would be hard to beat the two small warungs just up from Superman's at the station end of Gang I. They are just a couple of tables and benches along the wall, but the food is superb and there's a terrific selection of vegetarian dishes as well as excellent rendang; around 350 rp for a large nasi campur with tea.

Also on Gang I, *Bu Sis Steakhouse* is a small and popular restaurant specialising in, what else, steak. *Eko Restaurant*, down the alley that runs next to New Superman's, serves steak & fries for a remarkable 2000 rp. The *French Grill*, next door to Lima Losmen, offers a similar kind of menu and is quite good.

Over on Gang II, *Anna's* has become just about the most popular restaurant in the area though it is quite an airless little restaurant and closes early. They have a Balinese cook and an interesting and

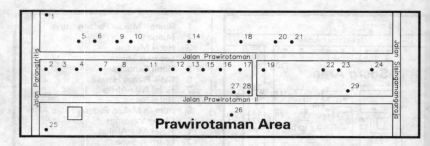

Prawirotaman Area

1	Hotel Sri Timur
2	Warung Java Timur
3	Wisma Gajah
4	Airlangga
5	Borobudur
6	Mario Gallery
7	Putra Jaya
8	Palm House Restaurant
9	Sriwijaya
10	Hanoman's Forest Garden Restaurant
11	Wisma Indah
12	Hunting Art Gallery
13	Sumaryo
14	Griya Bujana
15	Dentist
16	Duta
17	Rose
18	Taxi Stand
19	Artha Gallery
20	French Grill
21	Perwita
22	Prayogo
23	Galunggung
24	Kirana
25	Sunarko
26	Makuta
27	Metro
28	Agung
29	Palup

varied menu, including fruit and cheese jaffles for 250 rp, *kefir* (yoghurt drink) and *arak* (fiery distilled rice brandy). The *Lovina Tavern*, in a cul-de-sac off Jalan Sosrowijayan between Gang I and II, has an outdoor eating area and is popular with local people. It has principally been recommended for its good music and atmosphere; the food is 'reasonable'.

Jalan Malioboro Along this boulevard there are a number of places to try. Many of them cater to western tastes, and there's often *Time* and other magazines available for you to catch up on world events while you're eating. Several places seem to have taken a sharp tumble in standards over the years and the long-popular *Helen* is one place that seems to have suffered a decline in standards, although it still does good business.

The *Shinta*, across from the Helen, is a little more expensive but has some of the best iced juice in Indonesia. Further south, the *Happy* is another long-time survivor that's had its ups and downs over the years.

On the corner of Jalan Malioboro and Perwakilan, the *Legian* is a roof-garden restaurant overlooking the main street. It has western food and ice creams – it's slightly expensive but fairly quiet and free from petrol and diesel fumes, and a good place for a minor splurge. Try the excellent frogs' legs.

Round the corner from the tourist office, in a small cul-de-sac, there are three small warungs, including the *Pak Wongso*, serving good cheap food including good sate for 800 rp and *tahu telur* for 700 rp.

Jalan Malioboro is also a good area for night food stalls serving Yogya's specialities, such as *nasi gudeg* (rice with jackfruit in coconut milk) and *ayam goreng* (fried chicken). At about 9 pm, when the souvenir vendors pack up, a *lesehan* area comes alive along the north end of Malioboro and stays open till early morning. Lesehan is the traditional Yogya style of dining on straw mats; here young Indonesians sit around strumming guitars and playing chess into the wee hours. You take a seat on the mats spread over the pavements and a meal of nasi gudeg plus a glass of hot orange juice costs only 500 to 600 rp. A large bottle of tepid beer is around 1500 rp. The quality really varies from vendor to vendor, so have a look at the food first. There is also a nightly lesehan area within the kraton walls near the two big banyan trees.

North across the railway line, on Jalan Mangkubumi, there are some excellent Padang restaurants including the *Sinar Budi* which make a change from all the pseudo-western travellers' delights found elsewhere in Yogya. The *Tip Top* at Jalan Mangkubumi 28 is good for cakes and delicious ice-cream – from tutti frutti and lychee to durian for 400 rp. On Jalan Jenderal Sudirman the *Holland Bakery* and *Chitty 2 Bang 2* (Chitty Chitty Bang Bang) are next to the President Movie Theatre – their ice cream and cakes are even better, reports a recent visitor.

At Jalan Mangkubumi 105, opposite the Garuda office, the *Malioboro* is a friendly place with an extensive menu of western, Chinese and Indonesian food. Attached is the *Zangrandi Ice Cream Palace*, one of Java's best ice cream places. Hours for both are from 7.30 am to 3 pm and 5 to 10 pm.

Jalan Prawirotaman There are several medium-priced restaurants along this street, but they mostly seem to specialise in slow service and mediocre food for tourists. *Hanoman's Forest Garden Restaurant* is probably the best of this bunch; at least there are wayang golek or wayang kulit shows each night. The *Griya Bujana* is not bad either and is very clean.

The one place worth high recommendations in this area is *Warung Java Timur* at the Jalan Parangtritis intersection. They serve excellent sate, nasi pecel, soto ayam and other Central and East Javanese dishes at very reasonable prices.

Other For a major splurge, the *Floating Restaurant* at the Ambarrukmo Palace is worth considering for a 9500 rp Indonesian buffet meal. The hotel bar is very smart, with cocktails at 3500 rp and free peanuts.

Note that most non-hotel restaurants in Java that are frequented by travellers (Indonesian as well as foreign) follow the custom of handing you a menu with a notepad to write your order on.

Things to Buy

Batik is one of Yogya's major attractions but other popular buys in Yogya include leather, wayang puppets, silver and antiques. And like any good travellers' centre there are plenty of cheap, cotton Bali-style clothes. Jalan Malioboro is one great long colourful bazaar of souvenir shops and stalls and Malioboro's labyrinthine market, Pasar Beringharjo, is always worth a browse. Elsewhere you can visit galleries and workshops and see the crafts being done. There's a fair selection of regional crafts at the government-promoted Yogyakarta Craft Centre, opposite the Ambarrukmo Palace on Jalan Adisucipto. It's a fixed-price place but it will give you an idea of prices and quality even if you buy elsewhere. They have some interesting items which you may not see in the shops.

We've had letters from a number of travellers who were pressured into buying batik 'today, because tomorrow we are taking our best batik to Singapore as part of an ASEAN sponsored exhibition' – don't fall for it.

Getting There & Away

Air The various domestic airlines have regular direct flights to major cities in Java and Bali. Flights to outer islands, and Garuda international flights, are generally routed through Jakarta or Denpasar.

Garuda have several daily direct flights to Jakarta and Denpasar. Other outer island connections are useful for Sumatra and include Medan (two daily), Padang (two daily), Palembang (four daily) and Pekanbaru (daily). To Kalimantan, flights include Pontianak (two daily) and Balikpapan (two daily); to Sulawesi, flights include Ujung Pandang (daily). The Garuda office (tel 4400) is at Jalan Mangkubumi 56, near Jalan Diponegoro. It's open from 7 am to 4 pm Monday to Friday and until 1 pm Saturday; 9 am to 12 noon Sunday. After office hours you can ring 3034 for information.

Merpati operates direct flights to Surabaya daily. Outer island flights – to Bali, Nusa Tenggara islands and Kalimantan – are all routed through Surabaya. Some important connections include Denpasar (five flights a week), Ampenan, Waingapu, Maumere, Banjarmasin, and Balikpapan. Merpati (tel 4272) is at Jalan Jenderal Sudirman 9-11, in the Hotel Merdeka. Open daily 8 am to 3 pm.

Bouraq flies direct to Bandung and Banjarmasin daily. Other flights to Balikpapan, Samarinda, Tarakan and Palu are routed through Banjarmasin, and the daily flight to Jakarta goes through Bandung. The Bouraq office (tel 2143) at Jalan Mataram 60 is open daily 8 am to 5 pm.

Bus Yogya's bus station is four km southeast from the city centre. The city bus stand is just next door (whatever the becak men tell you) and a No 2 bus will drop you on Jalan Mataram, a block over from Malioboro, or on Jalan Parangtritis at the intersection with Jalan Prawirotaman. A No 1 bus will take you to Kota Gede.

Buses operate regularly from here to all the towns in the immediate area: Prambanan 300 rp (500 rp minibus); Parangtritis 450 rp; Muntilan (for Borobudur) 450 rp; Magelang 500 rp; Kaliurang 400 rp (600 rp minibus); Solo 600 rp; Purworejo 600 rp; Ambarawa 750 rp

(2½ hours); Semarang 1200 rp (3½ hours). The bus to Parangtritis can also be caught along Jalan Sisingamangaraja going south near Jalan Prawirotaman. You can catch the Muntilan bus going north along Jalan Magelang near the Yogyakarta Monument. For Kaliurang buses, you should head east on Jalan Kaliurang (which extends east from Jalan Diponegoro).

Buses to Surabaya depart at 8 am, 11 am, 3 pm and 6 pm; they cost 6500 rp and take about eight hours. Note that colts to/from Solo can be waved down as they run up Jalan Mataram, a block over from Malioboro. There is a door-to-door minibus service to Solo from SAA (tel 3238), Jalan Diponegoro 9A, for 1500 rp. The nonstop trip takes one hour.

Night Bus The bus company offices are mainly along Jalan Mangkubumi but it's less hassle to simply check fares and departures with the ticket agents along Jalan Sosrowijayan, near the Hotel Aziatic. They sell tickets for the various bus companies and in some cases run their own services too. Fares from Yogya include Jakarta from 8500 rp (9500 rp air-con); Bandung from 8500 rp (9500 rp air-con); Surabaya 6500 rp (8500 rp air-con); Probolinggo 12,000 rp (16,500 rp air-con); Denpasar around 13,000 rp or 19,500 rp by the super-duper-deluxe bus (which isn't worth it). Early morning buses from Jalan Sosrowijayan to Cilacap (for the ferry to Pangandaran) cost from 3500 rp.

Rail There is only one station in Yogya and it's right in the centre of town. See the introductory Getting Around Java section for details of Jakarta-Yogya and Surabaya-Yogya travel. Solo is on the main Yoga-Surabaya rail route, only about an hour out of Yogya. Three daily trains operate on the Bandung-Banjar-Yogya route. Fares from Bandung to Yogya are 3500 rp (all-3rd class), 13,500 rp 1st class (Mutiara Selatan Night Express). The trip takes from eight to 10 hours.

Getting Around

Airport Transport A taxi to or from Yogya's airport, 10 km to the north-east, is a standard 5500 rp but if you stroll out to the main road, only 200 metres from the terminal, you can get any Solo colt or bus coming by for about 200 rp into Yogya (Yogya's to your left). From Yogya you can catch a colt bound for Solo from Jalan Mataram.

Bus Yogya's city buses – known as 'Bis Kotas' – are bright orange minibuses operating on eight set routes around the city until 6 pm for a flat 150 rp fare. They work circular routes, eg a No 2 bus from the bus station will drop you on Jalan Mataram but the No 1 bus from Jalan Malioboro takes a more direct route to the bus station. The bus for Borobudur runs along Jalan Magelang to the north of the city and a No 5 bus will drop you at the bus stop there. There are route maps for reference in the information centre.

Becak & Andong Becaks cost around 300 rp a km in general and there are plenty of them. If you're touring the batik galleries, for example, it's probably cheapest to negotiate a round-trip or an all-in daily rate. The becak drivers on Jalan Prawirotaman belong to a street union and the standard one-way price to Jalan Malioboro is 750 rp (though they'll ask 1000 rp or more). There are also horse-drawn andongs around town.

Bicycle If you don't want to walk or be pedalled around, Yogya is traffic-free enough to be able to comfortably pedal yourself. Pushbikes can be rented from the Hotel Aziatic and a couple of losmen along Gang I for 1000 rp a day. If you lose a bike or get it stolen it could cost you around US$75, so take care – theft is big business in Yogya. Along Jalan Pasar Kembang you can hire motorcycles for around 7000 rp a day.

Colt Colts leave from the bus station next to the shopping centre on Jalan Senopati for sites around Yogya including Imogiri 250 rp, Parangtritis 450 rp, Kaliurang 600 rp and Prambanan 500 rp.

AROUND YOGYA

Kota Gede

Kota Gede has been famous since the 1930s as the centre of Yogya's silver industry but this quiet old town was the first capital of the Mataram Kingdom founded by Panembahan Senopati in 1582. Senopati is buried in the small mossy graveyard of an old mosque near the town's central market. The sacred tomb is only open Monday mornings and Friday afternoons and visitors must wear conservative dress which basically means hiring a sarong. Other days there is little to see here but a murky mandi, a few goldfish and an ancient three-legged yellow turtle said to be 100 years old and possess magical powers!

The main street of town is lined with busy silver workshops where you're free to wander round and watch the silversmiths at work. Most of the shops have similar stock including hand-beaten bowls, boxes, fine filigree and modern jewellery. Tom's Silver is one of the largest and best-known workshops for high-quality silver. The HS800-925, a bit cheaper than Tom's, has some attractive modern jewellery. You can pick up small filigree pieces here for as little as 2000 rp; a better quality ring might cost 5000 to 6000 rp.

It's only five km to Kota Gede – you can take a Bis Kota (city bus) No 1 or becak or quite easily cycle out there and back in half a day. The road is pretty flat all the way.

Imogiri

Perched on a hilltop, 20 km south of Yogya, Imogiri was built by Sultan Agung in 1645 to serve as his own mausoleum. Imogiri has since been the burial ground for almost all his successors and for prominent members of the royal family, and it is still a holy place. The cemetery

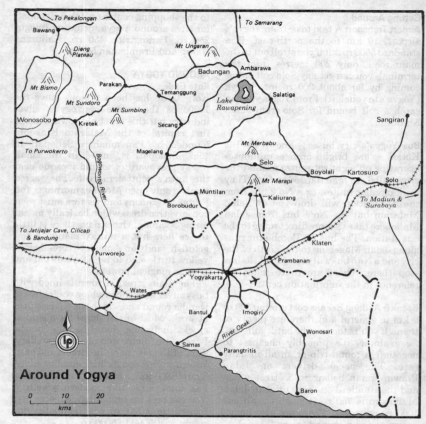

Around Yogya

```
0        10        20
        kms
```

contains three major courtyards – in the central courtyard are the tombs of Sultan Agung and succeeding Mataram kings, to the left are the tombs of the Susuhunans of Solo and to the right those of the Sultans of Yogya. It's an impressive complex, reached by an equally impressive flight of 345 steps but there are plenty of shady trees on the way up! From the top of the stairway there's a walkway circling the whole complex and leading to the real summit of the hill. Here you have a superb view over Yogya to Mt Merapi.

The point of major interest for pilgrims is the tomb of Sultan Agung, a king credited with supernatural powers who has been worshipped as a mystical source of guidance. Legend relates that shortly before Diponegoro's rebellion, the prince's servant was sent to the tomb of Sultan Agung to wait for a sign. This duly appeared in the form of a huge bloodstain on the curtain covering the entrance. The tomb is only open from 10.30 am to 12 noon on Monday and 1.30 to 4 pm on Friday, but there is no objection to visitors attending the praying and chanting sessions then. You have to sign the visitors books and there is a 200 rp entrance charge to the site. For another 150 rp you can hire the traditional Javanese court dress – *kain* and *kebayan* for women and *sarong* for men – and enter the tomb. You must leave your shoes in the changing room and no cameras or bags are allowed in the graveyard – the attendants will guard them for you. Once in the tomb you're expected to kneel twice by the stone sarcophagus as tomb attendants recite prayers and distribute roses and incense to be placed on the coffin. You must pay exactly 500 rp for these materials each time you kneel. The heavy aroma of rose and incense lends an especially mystic atmosphere to the proceedings.

The colt stand in the village is only about 500 metres from the base of the hill. Drinks and snacks are available around the stairway to the cemetery.

Parangtritis

Twenty-seven km south of Yogya, Parangtritis has rough surf and a long sweep of shifting, black sand dunes backed by high, jagged cliffs. It's a place of superstition and, like so many places along the south coast, it is a centre for the worship of Nyai Lara Kidul, the Queen of the South Seas. Legend has it that Senopati, the 16th century Mataram ruler, took her as his wife and thus established the strong tie between the goddess and the royal house of Mataram. Their sacred rendezvous spot is at Parangkusumo, one km down the beach, where the Sultans of Yogya still send offerings every year at Labuhan to appease this consort of kings.

In spite of the fact that the currents and undertows are reputed to be dangerous several travellers have written to say that swimming is quite possible. Perhaps it's seasonal. You can swim very safely though in freshwater pools (the 'Pemandian') at the base of the hill near the village where spring water spills out through high bamboo pipes from the hilltop. The village promenade of warungs and souvenir stalls is nothing to rave about, but this is a quiet, simple place if you want to get away for a while – just avoid weekends and holidays when buses are crowded and the beach is swamped by mobs from Yogya. Parangtritis has 'lovely sand dunes and terrible magic mushrooms,' reported one traveller.

There are trails along the hills above the sea to the west of Parangtritis. A couple of km from town is a cave used for meditation, and some say witchcraft. A narrow trail leads down the cliff face to the cave opening, where a 'caretaker' usually sits. Branches of the cave extend deep into the hillside where would-be mystics sit in contemplation, sometimes for days on end.

Places to Stay Plenty of more or less similar losmen line the main street/promenade down to the beach. Rooms rent for around 2500 rp but facilities are limited (generally there's no electricity) and sometimes a bit unhealthy. *Penginapan Parang Endong*, just beyond the village, is probably the best cheapie. Rooms at 2500 rp are simple (you sleep on mats in some), but clean enough and it has a well-kept freshwater swimming pool.

The *Losmen Widodo* has OK rooms for 7000 rp and 12,500 rp, including breakfast. Its garden courtyard is quite pleasant, bathrooms are clean, and the restaurant's not bad. Nearby is the similar *Agung Hotel & Garden Restaurant* with rooms starting at 7500 rp including breakfast.

Food is cheap in the warungs along the promenade.

Getting There & Away From Yogya it's 450 rp from the main bus station or by colt from the station on Jalan Senopati; it's a bumpy one-hour trip over one of the worst roads in Java! At one time buses went only as far as Kreteg and you had to take a ferry across the river, followed by a long walk or dokar ride to the beach – this may still be the case in the wet season. The last bus back from Parangtritis leaves around 6 pm.

If you're staying in the Jalan Prawirotaman area in Yogya, you can catch the Parangtritis bus (Jatayu line) going south on Jalan Sisingamangaraja, at the east end of Prawirotaman.

Other Beaches

Parangtritis is the best known of the southern beaches. Further afield are the relatively isolated beaches of Baron and Kukup. Baron, inside a sheltered cove with somewhat safer swimming, is 60 km south-east of Yogya via Wonosari; Kukup is a white-sand beach one km east of Baron. Samas is only 25 km south of Yogya but is said to be less attractive than any of the other beaches. There's hot black sand, violent surf and several warungs.

Kaliurang & Mt Merapi

Kaliurang, 25 km north of Yogya, is the nearest hill resort to the city . It stands at 900 metres on the slopes of volcanically active Mt Merapi. Pick a clear, cloudless day during the week when it's quiet and this is a great place to escape from the heat of the plains. There are good bushwalks, waterfalls, two chilly swimming pools and superb views of the smoking, fire-spewing mountain.

Merapi, the 'Fire Mountain', is one of Indonesia's most destructive volcanoes and there are times when the summit is off limits because of dangerous sulphurous fumes. It's a safer and easier climb from Selo, to the north of Merapi (see Around Solo), but many people do climb from Kaliurang. The summit, which often cuts through cloud, is 2911 metres high and the climb from Kaliurang is generally considered the most difficult climb in Central Java.

The trek can take up to 10 hours there and back. The trail up the mountain begins at the car park where colts from Yogya stop. It's a one-hour walk to the observatory (1260 metres) from where you can watch Merapi when it's in action, and some trekkers stop here. To the crater from Kaliurang it's about four hours or all the way to the summit from Kaliurang is

about six hours. If you decide to go for the top, it's a good idea to talk to the owner of the *Vogel* losmen, Christian Awuy, who is friendly, knows the mountain and will advise you how to get up there and down again. He has maps and keeps a log book written up by travellers who've made the great assault. It makes interesting reading and, depending on your level of confidence, will either discourage you from making the climb or convince you to go for it.

Places to Stay & Eat There are a few excellent places to stay in Kaliurang. *Vogel* is the former residence of a Yogya prince and has dorm beds for 1500 rp and rooms starting at 3000 rp. At the back there's a two-storey bungalow with views of Merapi where rooms are 6000 rp and up. The food here is quite good and they even have fresh milk. A number of travellers have written to recommend this place. 'We were dining in candlelight while the rain poured down (as it does every afternoon)', reported one visitor, 'when the staff put on a crackling Bing Crosby record from the '40s – we briefly floated out of Indonesia!'.

Christian Awuy has opened the new *Christian Hostel* nearby in Kaliurang's former town hall where independence negotiations between the Dutch and Indonesians were once held. This large hostel has a 1500 rp dorm, plus very nice rooms for 5000/7000 rp. If you have a IYHF membership card, you can get the 7000 rp rooms for 5000 rp. The Christian Hostel has a great bar & restaurant with a nice view and a large lounge area with dozens of maps, travel guides, novels, newspapers, and 'word of mouth' travel logs.

There are nearly a dozen other places to stay in Kaliurang, including the fair *Hotel Muria* where rooms are 4000 rp. *Losmen Merapi* has adequate rooms at 3500 rp and better rooms for 5000 rp. Other losmen worth trying are *Lestari, Garuda Ngalayang, Corner, Bumi Putra, Gadjah Mada* and *Senoreno*, all with rooms for about 4000 rp.

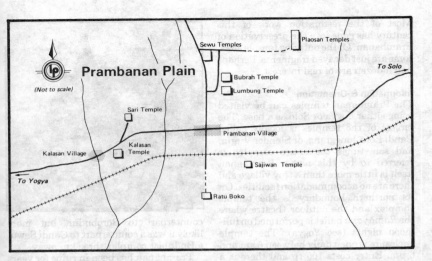

Vogel and Christian Hostel have the most varied menus in Kaliurang, but if you want to get out into the village a bit, try *Restaurant Puas* or *Restaurant Joyo*. The local speciality is *gemblong*, small rounds of pounded sticky rice that are eaten with *tempe bacem*, sweetened soybean cakes.

PRAMBANAN

On the road to Solo, 17 km east of Yogya, the temples at Prambanan village are the cream of what remains of Java's period of Hindu cultural development. These temples not only form the largest Hindu temple complex in Java but the wealth of sculptural detail on the great Shiva temple makes it easily the most outstanding example of Hindu art. As intriguing as the beauty and scale of the Prambanan temples themselves is the fact that this huge complex dedicated to the Hindu god Shiva stands amidst a number of Buddhist temple groups scattered across the Prambanan Plain. And the greatest Buddhist monument of all, Borobudur, lies only 40 km away.

All the temples in the Prambanan area were built between the 8th and 10th centuries AD. Though the origins of the Central Javanese powers during this time are hazy, historians have suggested that two dynasties were established then – the Buddhist Sailendras in the south and the Hindu Sanjayas of Old Mataram in the north. Possibly by the second half of the 9th century these two dynasties were united by the marriage of Rakai Pikatan of Hindu Mataram and the Buddhist Sailendra Princess Pramodhavardhani. This may explain why a number of temples, including the Prambanan and smaller Plaosan group, reveal Shaivite and Buddhist elements in architecture and sculpture. On the other hand, you find this mixture to some degree in India and Nepal, too, so it's hardly a novel idea.

Following this two century long burst of creativity, the Prambanan Plain was abandoned when the Hindu-Javanese kings moved to East Java. In the middle of the 16th century there is said to have been a great earthquake which toppled many of the temples and, in the centuries that followed, their destruction was accelerated by greedy treasure hunters and local people searching for building material.

Most of the restoration work of this century has gone into the preservation of Prambanan. Of the outlying temple sites, some are just decayed fragments. Perhaps half a dozen are of real interest.

Information & Orientation

The Prambanan temples can be visited using either Yogya or Solo as a base. The largest of the temples is locally called Candi Loro Jonggrang, or Slender Virgin, and sometimes the entire complex is referred to by this name. Prambanan itself is little more than a tiny village and there are no accommodation facilities. On its northern boundary is the temple complex and the outdoor theatre where the *Ramayana* ballet is performed on full-moon nights (see Yogya). The temple enclosure is open daily between 6 am and 6 pm. Entry costs 100 rp and there is a 100 rp fee for cameras.

At the temple complex you can buy a copy of *A Short Guide to the Prambanan Complex*, published by the Archaeological Service of Indonesia. It's quite good value and also covers a number of the other temple sites on the Prambanan Plain.

Most of the outlying temples are spread out within a five km radius of Prambanan village. You'll need at least half a day to see them on foot or you can hire a horsecart by the hour in Prambanan. As with any of Java's major tourist attractions, the best time to visit Prambanan is early morning or late in the day when it's quiet. Very few people visit the other sites and the walk through the fields can be as much of a pleasure as the temples themselves.

Prambanan Temple Complex

The huge Prambanan Complex was constructed about the middle of the 9th century – around 50 years later than Borobudur – but remarkably little is known about its early history. It is thought it was built by Rakai Pikatan to commemorate the return of a Hindu dynasty to sole power in Java. Some have even suggested it was intended as a

counterpart to Borobudur, but more likely it was a counterpart to Candi Sewu, a Buddhist complex three km away.

Prambanan has been in ruins for years and although efforts were made in 1885 to clear the site, it was not until 1937 that reconstruction was first attempted. Of the original group the outer compound contains the remains of 244 temples, two of which have been repaired. Eight minor and eight main temples stand in the highest central courtyard. The largest of these, the Shiva temple, has been restored while a few others are still shrouded in scaffolding.

Shiva Mahadeva The temple dedicated to Shiva is not only the largest of the temples, it is also artistically and architecturally the most perfect. The main spire soars 47 metres high and the temple is lavishly carved. The 'medallions' which decorate its base have the characteristic 'Prambanan motif' – small lions in niches flanked by 'trees of heaven' (or *kalpaturas*) and a menagerie of stylised half-human and half-bird heavenly beings (*kinnaras*). The vibrant scenes carved onto the inner wall of the gallery encircling the temple are from the *Ramayana* – they tell how Lord Rama's wife, Sita, is abducted and how Hanuman the Monkey God, and Sugriwa his white monkey general, eventually find and release her. To follow the story ascend the main eastern stairway and go around the temple clockwise. The reliefs break off at the point where the monkey army builds a bridge to the island of Lanka and the end of the tale is found on the smaller Brahma Temple.

In the main chamber at the top of the eastern stairway, the four-armed statue of Shiva, the Destroyer, is notable for the fact that this mightiest of Hindu gods stands on a huge lotus pedestal, a symbol of Buddhism. In the southern cell is the pot-bellied and bearded Agastya, an incarnation of Shiva as divine teacher; in the western cell is a superb image of the elephant-headed Ganesha, Shiva's son; while in the northern cell Durga, Shiva's consort, can be seen killing the demon buffalo. Some people believe that the Durga image is actually an image of Loro Jonggrang, the 'Slender Virgin' who, legend has it, was turned to stone by a giant she refused to marry. She is still the object of pilgrimage for many who believe in her and the name of the cursed princess is often used for the temple group.

Brahma & Vishnu Temples Flanking the large Shiva Temple are these two smaller temples. The Brahma Temple to the south, carved with the final scenes of the *Ramayana*, has a four-headed statue of Brahma, the god of creation. Reliefs on the Vishnu Temple to the north tell the story of Lord Krishna, a hero of the *Mahabharata* epic, while inside is a four-armed image of Vishnu, the preserver.

Nandi Temple This small shrine, facing the Shiva Temple, houses one of Prambanan's finest sculptures – a huge, powerful figure of the bull, Nandi, the vehicle of Shiva.

The shrines to the north and south of Nandi may once have contained Brahma's vehicle, the Swan and Vishnu's sun-bird, the Garuda.

Northern Group
Of the northern group of temples, the Sewu and Plaosan temples are the most

interesting and they are within three km of Prambanan. To start, take the road behind Prambanan and follow signs pointing towards the Lumbung Temple.

Sewu Temples The 'Thousand Temples', dating from around 850 AD, originally consisted of a large central Buddhist temple surrounded by four rings of 240 smaller 'guard' temples. Outside the compound stood four sanctuaries at the points of the compass, of which the Bubrah Temple is the southern one.

All but a few of the minor temples are in various stages of collapse, a great jumble of stone blocks littering the field. Only the shell of the main temple remains but this is interesting for the unusual finely carved niches around the inner gallery, with shapes resembling those found in the Middle East. Once these would have held bronze statues but plundering of the temple went on for many years – some of the statues were melted down and others disappeared into museums and private possession.

Plaosan Temples One or two km east of Sewu, you walk across rice paddies and sugar cane fields to this temple group. Believed to have been built about the same time as the Prambanan temple group by Rakai Pikatan and his Buddhist queen, the Plaosan temples combine both Hindu and Buddhist religious symbols and carvings. Of the original three main temples, once linked by a multitude of small shrines and solid stupas, one has been reconstructed and is notable for its unusual three-part design. It is a two-storied, six-room structure with an imitation storey above and a tiered roof of stupas rising to a single larger one in the centre. Inside the temple there are impressive stone Bodhisattvas on either side of an empty lotus pedestal within the various cells and intricately carved *kala* heads above the many windows. The Buddhas that once sat on the lotus pedestals are now in the National Museum in Jakarta.

Southern Group

Sajiwan Temple Near the village of Sajiwan, about 1½ km south-east of Prambanan, is this very ruined Buddhist temple. Around the base are carvings from the *Jatakas* – episodes of the Buddha's various lives.

Ratu Boko Palace A steep rocky path (opposite the 'Yogya 18 km' signpost) leads up to the main site, two km south of Prambanan village on a small plateau in the Gunung Kidul hills. Ratu Boko, the 'Palace of the Eternal Lord', is believed to have been a huge Hindu palace complex dating from the 9th century. Although little remains apart from a large gateway and a series of bathing places, it is worth the walk. The view from this site across the Prambanan plains is magnificent. On a smaller plateau, a few 100 metres further south, is a large platform of waterspouts and staircases and, below, a group of pools which are still used by the local villagers.

Western Group

There are three temples in this group between Yogya and Prambanan, two of them close to Kalasan village on the main Yogya road. Kalasan and Prambanan village are three km apart, so it is probably easiest to take a colt or bus to cover this stretch.

Kalasan Temple Standing 50 metres off the main road near Kalasan village, this temple is one of the oldest Buddhist temples on the Prambanan Plain. A Sanskrit inscription of 778 AD refers to a temple dedicated to the female Bodhisattva, Tara, though the existing structure appears to have been built around the original one some years later. It has been partially restored during this century and has some fine detailed carvings on its southern side where a huge, ornate kala head glowers over the doorway. At one time it was completely covered in coloured shining stucco, and traces of the hard, stone-like 'diamond plaster' that provided a base for paintwork can still be seen. The bat-infested inner chamber of Kalasan once sheltered a huge bronze image of Buddha or Tara.

Sari Temple About 200 metres north, in the middle of coconut and banana groves, the Sari Temple has the three-part design of the larger Plaosan Temple but is probably slightly older. Some students believe that its 2nd floor may have served as a dormitory for the Buddhist priests who took care of the Kalasan Temple. The sculptured reliefs around the exterior are similar to that of Kalasan but in much better condition.

Sambisari Temple A country lane runs to this isolated temple, about 2½ km north of the '10.2 km Yogya' post on the main road. Sambisari is a Shiva temple and possibly the latest temple at Prambanan to be put up by the Mataram rulers. It was only discovered by a farmer in 1966. Excavated from under ancient layers of protective volcanic ash and dust, it lies almost six metres below the surface of the surrounding fields and is remarkable for its perfectly preserved state. It has some fine decorations and in the niches you can see the stone images of Durga, Ganesh and Agastya.

Getting There & Away

From Yogya it takes only half an hour by road and costs 300 rp by bus (bound for Solo) from the main bus station, or you can catch a Solo colt along Jalan Mataram. Buses from Solo take 1½ hours and cost 450 rp. Prambanan is one of the best places in Java to get to by bicycle as there's a special cycle roadway all the way from Yogyakarta.

BOROBUDUR

From the plain of Kedu, 42 km north-west of Yogya, a small hill rises up out of a pattern of palm trees and fields of rice and sugar cane. It's topped by one of the greatest Buddhist relics of South-East Asia – up there with Cambodia's Angkor Wat and Burma's Pagan – and it ranks as one of Indonesia's most famous attractions. Rulers of the Sailendra dynasty built the colossal pyramid of Borobudur at some time between 750 and 850 AD. Very little else is known about Borobudur's early history but the Sailendras must have recruited a huge workforce, for some 60,000 cubic metres of stone had to be hewn, transported and carved during its construction. According to tradition, the main architect was Gunadharma whose face can be seen in the jagged ridge of the Menoreh mountain range in the background. The name Borobudur is possibly derived from the Sanskrit word 'Vihara Buddha Uhr' which means the 'Buddhist monastery on the hill'.

With the decline of Buddhism and the shift of power to East Java, Borobudur was abandoned soon after completion and for centuries lay forgotten, buried under layers of volcanic ash. It was only in 1815 when Raffles governed Java, that the site was cleared and the sheer magnitude of the builders' imagination and technical skill was revealed. Early in the 20th century the Dutch began to tackle the restoration of Borobudur but over the years the supporting hill had become water logged and the whole immense stone mass started to subside at a variety of angles. A mammoth US$21 million restoration project, begun in 1973, is now more or less complete.

Relief from Borobudur

However, restoration of the mighty temple suffered a set back in 1984 at the hands of both humans and nature – the huge central stupa was damaged when struck by lightning and nine of the smaller stupas were badly damaged by bombs thought to have been planted by Muslim extremists. Not that humans haven't damaged it in the past – in 1896 the Dutch colonial government presented eight cartloads of sculpture to the visiting King of Siam.

Although they are easily forgotten, standing as they do in the shadow of the great Borobudur, there are two smaller structures which form a significant part of the complex. The nearby Mendut and Pawon temples, built about the same time as Borobudur, are aligned east-west and are thought to have been places for purification before entering the main sanctuary.

Information & Orientation
The village of Borobudur itself consists of little more than a crowd of becaks and a handful of warungs and souvenir stalls clustered around the bus station. A park has been built around the monument and there are now several places to stay in the village. There is also a new bus station being built at the base of the hill but at present Borobudur is a two-km walk or becak ride west of the bus stand.

The site is open from 6.15 am to 5.15 pm and admission is 100 rp. On weekends the site can be crowded and noisy, which isn't going to do anything for your appreciation of this contemplative sanctuary – the finest time to see Borobudur and capture something of the spirit of the place would be at dawn or sunset. The first busloads of package tourists usually start arriving at around 10 am. If you're stopping off at Borobudur en route to somewhere else, you can leave your bags in the hut at the entrance to Borobudur where they'll be looked after for a small fee.

Where you enter the site there are a number of useful books on sale about

Borobudur and the Mendut Temple. *Glimpses of Borobudur* and *Chandi Mendut* are small booklets published by the Archaeological Service of Indonesia – they cost 2000 rp each. Both *Borobudur* by Yazir Marzuki and Toeti Heraty, and another version by Jurgen Wickert, can also be worthwhile investments. The former has good illustrations which help in the identification of the symbolic Buddhas that are described. They cost 9000 rp each, although you can bargain with the local people who are selling the same stock just *outside* the gate! They're cheaper still if you buy them in Jakarta.

Waicak The Lord Buddha's birth, enlightenment and his reaching of nirvana are all celebrated on this full moon day. There is a great procession of saffron-robed monks from Mendut to Pawon then Borobudur where candles are lit and flowers strewn about, followed by praying and chanting. Waicak usually falls in May.

Borobudur
Borobudur is a broad, impassive monument, built in the form of a massive symmetrical stupa, literally wrapped around the hill. It stands solidly on its base of 200 square metres and there are six square terraces topped by three circular ones, with four stairways leading up through finely carved gateways to the top. The paintwork is long gone but it's thought that the grey stone of Borobudur was at one time washed with white or golden yellow to catch the sun. Viewed from the air, the whole thing looks like a giant three-dimensional tantric mandala. It has been suggested, in fact, that the Buddhist community that once supported Borobudur were early Vajrayana or Tantric Buddhists who used it as a walk-through mandala.

The entire monument was conceived as a Buddhist vision of the cosmos in stone, starting in the everyday world and spiralling up to nirvana – eternal

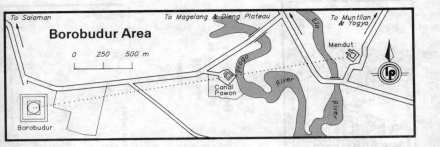

Borobudur Area

0   250   500 m

To Salaman

To Magelang & Dieng Plateau

To Muntilan & Yogya

Mendut

Elo River

Progo River

River

Candi Pawon

Borobudur

nothingness, the Buddhist idea of heaven. Below the base of the monument are a series of reliefs representing a world dominated by passion and desire where the good are rewarded by reincarnation as some higher form of life and the evil are punished by a lowlier reincarnation. Strangely these carvings were covered with stone, possibly to hide them from view, but they are partly visible on the south side. The latest theory is that these covering stones may have been added to keep the base from collapsing.

Starting at the main eastern gateway go around the galleries of the stupa clockwise, as one should around all Buddhist monuments. While Borobudur is impressive for its sheer bulk, it is the close-up sculptural detail which is quite astounding. The pilgrim's walk is about five km in distance. It takes you along narrow corridors past nearly 1500 richly decorated relief panels in which the sculptors have carved a virtual textbook of Buddhist doctrines as well as many aspects of Javanese life a thousand years ago – a continual procession of ships and elephants, musicians and dancing girls, warriors and kings. Over 400 serene-faced Buddhas stare out from open chambers above the galleries while 72 more Buddha images sit only partly visible in latticed stupas on the top three terraces. Reaching in through the stupa to touch the fingers or foot of the Buddha inside is believed to bring good luck. The three circular terraces, which open to the sky and give a

fine view across the valley, represent the world of nothingness. The huge enclosed central stupa, representing nirvana, is symbolically empty.

Candi Pawon

The tiny Pawon temple, about two km east of Borobudur, is similar in design and decoration to Mendut. It is not a stupa, but resembles most Central Javanese temples with a broad base, a central body and pyramidal roof. Pot-bellied dwarves

Buddha from Borobudur

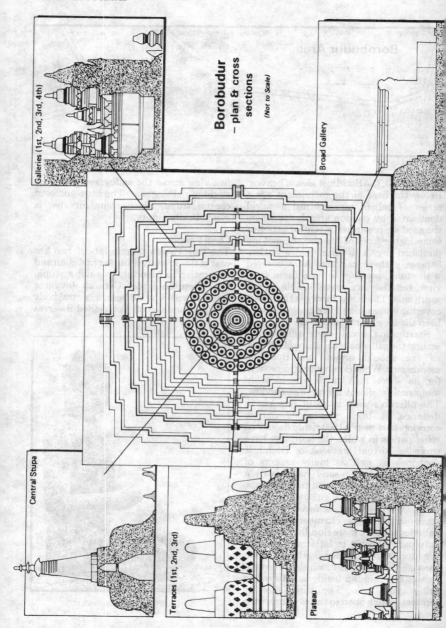

Galleries (1st, 2nd, 3rd, 4th)

Borobudur
– plan & cross sections

(Not to Scale)

Broad Gallery

Central Stupa

Terraces (1st, 2nd, 3rd)

Plateau

pouring riches over the entrance to this temple suggest that it was dedicated to Kuvera, the Buddhist god of fortune.

Mendut

The Mendut Temple is one km east again, back towards Muntilan. It may be small and insignificant compared to its mighty neighbour, Borobudur, but this temple houses the most outstanding statue of any temple in Java that can still be seen in its proper place – a magnificent three-metre-high figure of Buddha, flanked by the Bodhisattvas Lokesvara on the left and Vairapana on the right. The Buddha is also notable for his posture, for instead of the usual lotus position he sits western-style with both feet on the ground.

The Mendut Temple, known as the 'temple in the bamboo grove', was discovered in 1836 and attempts were made by the Dutch to restore it between 1897 and 1904. Although parts of the roof and entrance remain unfinished it is nevertheless a fine temple and the gracefully carved relief panels on its outer walls are among the finest and largest examples of Hindu-Javanese art.

Places to Stay & Eat

There are four losmen located near the monument. The *Losmen Citra Rasa* is the cheapest at 5000 rp for a room with attached mandi. The *Losmen Borobudur* and *Losmen Barokah* both have grotty rooms for 7500 rp. Better is the *Losmen Saraswati*, which offers clean, quiet rooms with mandi for 10,000 rp including breakfast.

To the west of the monument at Jalan Syailendra Raya 8 is the straightforward *Villa Rosita* where doubles with mandi are 10,000 rp.

There are many warungs near the temple and in the village. Look for a sign that says 'Rice Stall 2M' at the temple end of the road from the bus terminal to locate *Mamy's* warung. Here you can enjoy good nasi rames – rice with egg, vegetables, fish and meat for 400 rp.

Getting There & Away

From Yogya it's a 1½ hour, 550 rp trip to Borobudur – by bus to Muntilan and then another to the site. Buses to Muntilan start running at around 5.30 am if you want an early start and stop at Jalan Magelang – see the map of Yogya – to pick up passengers. If you're visiting Mendut and Pawon as well it's a fine walk but you can always use the bus, for 50 rp a go, to hop from one temple to the next. Or hire a becak.

JATIJAJAR CAVE

Situated about 130 km west of Yogya on the main road and rail line to Bandung, Gombang is the junction town from which to visit the Jatijajar Cave. Around the sides of this huge limestone cave are remarkable life-size carved statues of people and animals that relate a legend called *kamandaka*. The cave was discovered by the local people in 1802.

The Jatijajar Cave is 20 km from Gombang towards the coast. Close by is the beach resort of Karang Bolong where the people make a living collecting the nests of sea swallows from the steep cliff-faces above the surf. The nests are collected every three months to be sold to Chinese restaurants at home and abroad.

MAGELANG

Magelang was formerly a Dutch military garrison and it was here that the Javanese hero, Prince Diponegoro, was tricked into captivity in 1829. In the house where he was captured there is a small museum of Diponegoro items but the main collection is in Yogya.

Magelang is 42 km north of Yogya, on the main road to Semarang. Shortly before the town you pass Gunung Tidar which legend credits as the 'Nail of Java', a mountain planted there by the gods to stop Java from shaking.

WONOSOBO

Some people who come to visit the Dieng Plateau use Wonosobo as a base. At 900 metres, in the hills of the central

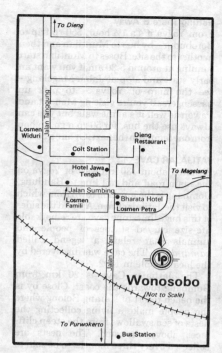

To Dieng

Jalan Tanggung

Losmen
Widuri

Colt Station

Dieng
Restaurant

Hotel Jawa
Tengah

To Magelang

Jalan Sumbing

Losmen
Famili

Bharata Hotel
Losmen Petra

Jalan A Yani

Wonosobo
(Not to Scale)

To Purwokerto

Bus Station

mountain range, Wonosobo has a good
climate and it's a fairly typical country
town with a busy market, quiet streets, a
few horse carts and dilapidated buses. For
most of the year it's not a particularly
interesting place in itself but on national
holidays it comes alive when people from
the surrounding villages gather at Wonosobo
for festivities held in the main square. If
you're here on any of these days you might
see the *kuda kepang* dance from nearby
Temanggung or the local *lengger* dance in
which men dress as women and wear
masks. Virtually the whole town turns out
to watch or take part.

Information
If you want detailed information about
the Dieng Plateau, visit the Dieng
Restaurant on Jalan Kawadenan. Mr Agus

who owns the place used to be a guide for
Dieng and he has quite useful duplicated
handout maps of the area and plenty of
stories and legends to tell. His wife has a
very large photograph album!

There is also an official tourist office at
Jalan Pemuda 2 where you can get a map
of the Dieng Plateau area.

Places to Stay – bottom end
The *Jawa Tengah* (tel 202), on Jalan
A Yani next to the market and colt terminal
for Dieng, is probably the most pleasant
losmen in town for the price. Formerly the
old Railway Guesthouse, it has small,
clean rooms for 4000 rp single or 5000 rp
double, and there are larger rooms for
three or four persons for 7500 rp. The staff
is helpful and there's hot water in the
shared mandi. Rates include a small
breakfast, as do those of all the losmen
mentioned below.

Losmen Petra is also good value with
small singles at 2000 rp and larger rooms
with attached mandi from 3500 rp. It's at
Jalan A Yani 81, between the bus station
and the Jawa Tengah. The *Losmen Famili*
(tel 396) at Jalan Sumbing 6 is clean and
comfortable with singles/doubles at 2500/
5000 rp and larger rooms for three or four.
The TV in the lobby could be an attraction
or a drawback, depending on your taste.
Also on Jalan Sumbing at No 6 is *Losmen
Sindoro*. It has the same rates as the
Losmen Famili and is fairly clean and
comfortable looking, but it also has a
lobby TV.

At Jalan Tanggung 21 is *Losmen
Pendawa Lima*, an adequate little place
with singles for 3000 rp without mandi
and 4000 rp with. Doubles/triples are
6500/7500 rp with bath. The *Losmen
Widuri* on the same street, opposite the
colt terminal, costs 3000/4000 rp for small
dark rooms and the beds are hard – not
recommended.

Places to Stay – top end
Hotel Bharata (tel 522), Jalan A Yani 72,
has clean, good-size rooms starting at

6000 rp without bath, or 15,000/22,000 rp with a hot-water shower and breakfast included.

The Chinese-owned and operated *Losmen Nirwana* (tel 66) at Jalan Tanggung 18 is clean, secure, quiet and friendly. A nicely decorated standard room costs 20,000 rp with hot shower and western toilet, and includes a substantial breakfast of toast, juice, eggs, cheese, and fruit. The main gates are locked at 6 pm, so you have go around to the back to get in after that.

Places to Eat
At the popular *Dieng Restaurant* on Jalan Kawedanan, near the market, you can get very good Indonesian, Chinese and European food served buffet-style. Most dishes cost around 500 rp per portion – try the excellent mushroom sate. The Dieng closes at 9 pm. There's good Chinese food at the *Asia* two doors down but it's more expensive.

Other places to try for cheap food are the friendly little grocery shops next to Losmen Petra. They have good nasi goreng or rames, noodles and gado-gado for around 500 to 600 rp. The *Klenyer* has Indonesian dishes, while the *A-A* is mostly Chinese. They close around 10 pm.

There is also a night market across from the Widuri and Pendawa Lima losmens in the colt station area.

Getting There & Around
The buses which go up to Wonosobo turn down Jalan A Yani (past the Losmen Petra) to the bus station. For any of the losmen or the Dieng colt terminal in the centre of town, tell the driver where you want to get off – otherwise you'll have to walk about a km back up the hill. Horse-carts from the bus station to the centre ask 500 rp. If you arrive by colt they drop you in the centre of town anyway.

Yogya-Wonosobo From Yogya take a bus or colt to Magelang (500 rp, 40 minutes) and from there another colt to Wonosobo. The

fare from Magelang is 700 rp by day, 1000 rp by night and the last colt leaves at 7 pm. Allow plenty of time for this stretch because none of the colts will leave until they're packed to the gunwales – the actual road time is about two hours.

It is possible to see Borobudur on the way from Yogya to Wonosobo but you need to start out early to complete the trip by night, particularly if you plan to continue on to Dieng the same day. Yogya-Muntilan-Borobudur (450 rp) takes 1½ hours. Borobudur-Magelang-Wonosobo (600 rp) takes three hours. Maybe.

Rahayu Travel on Jalan A Yani in Wonosobo has a minibus service to Yogya at 8 am, 10 am, 12 noon, 2 pm and 4 pm for 2000 rp per person.

If you're heading south to Yogya, take a bus to Secang to get back on the main bus route.

Wonosobo-Semarang There are several buses daily to Semarang (via Secang and Ambarawa) which cost 1400 rp and the journey takes about four hours. If you miss these, there are frequent buses and colts to Secang and you're then back on the main Semarang-Yogya bus route.

Wonosobo-Cilacap There are two buses daily to Cilacap at 8.55 and 11.15 am. The journey takes five hours and it costs 1600 rp. If you're heading for Pangandaran in West Java note that these buses are not early enough to connect with the ferries from Cilacap. However there is a much faster minibus going nonstop to Cilacap at 7 am and 2 pm for 6000 rp; the earlier minibus does arrive in time for the ferry to Kalipucang. These minibuses can be arranged by any Wonosobo losmen or hotel.

Alternatively, you can travel between Wonosobo and Cilacap via Purwokerto – the first bus leaves at 5.30 am and there are buses every half hour until late. From Wonosobo to Purwokerto takes three hours and costs 900 rp, Purwokerto to Cilacap takes about three hours and costs 600 rp.

Wonosobo-Dieng Frequent colts leave from the Wonosobo market in the centre of town between 6am and 6pm. The fare is 600 rp (day), 700 rp (night) and it takes 1½ hours uphill and one hour downhill.

DIENG PLATEAU

On the magnificent heights of the Dieng Plateau are some of the oldest Hindu temples in Java. The name Dieng either comes from Di-Hyang which means 'Abode of the Heaven' in Indonesian or Adi-Aeng which is Javanese for 'Beautiful-Amazing'. It is thought that this was once the site of a flourishing temple-city of priests. The temples, built between the 8th and 12th centuries, were dedicated to the Hindu God Shiva; yet the stone stairways for visiting pilgrims (which years ago led up to the sanctuary from the north and the south) were known as the 'Stairs of Buddha'.

With the mysterious depopulation of Central Java this site, like Borobudur, was abandoned and forgotten. When people returned to Dieng around 1830 they found the holy city buried and overgrown. At that time the ruins of 400 temples were reputedly still standing, but in the years that followed, most were destroyed by local people in their quest for building material. The eight temples that remain are characteristic of early Central Javanese architecture – stark in appearance, simple, squat and box-like in structure. Although they're Shiva temples, in more recent times the villagers have named each of them after the heroes and heroines of the *Mahabharata* epic.

The Dieng temples are set in a strange and beautiful landscape within the huge, marshy caldera of a volcano that collapsed long ago. Steep, rugged mountain-sides, cool mineral lakes and the volcanic inferno of steaming craters surround it. One of the best parts of Dieng is the journey there along a narrow, winding and very steep mountain road that follows the swift Serayu River and passes through terraced slopes of vegetable crops and tobacco. The village of Dieng lies on the north side of the plateau and there is an unobtrusive, if rather odd, mushroom factory nearby. Dieng's thermal powers are also being tapped to provide electricity for the area and there is a geothermal plant already in operation not far from the Sikidang crater. The whole region is very obviously volatile for in 1984 there was an earthquake at Sileri and you could feel the tremor at the *Bu Jono Losmen*.

It is quite possible to see all the temples in one day on foot but the superb 'natural' sights around Dieng are scattered over a large area. Although accommodation in Dieng is limited, the plateau has a magical quality about it. In the early morning light the village houses, lacking chimneys, are literally steaming blue smoke through their walls. If you are planning to stay overnight in Wonosobo instead, you need to be at Dieng early, before the mist sets in around noon. At 2000 metres, Dieng alternates between sunshine and rain and you should note that this is one of the few places in Indonesia where there can be morning frost on the ground – the Dieng people call it *bun upas*, or 'poison dew'. Nights can be as cold as an English winter (as low as 4°C) so you will need warm clothing.

The five main temples are clustered together on the central plain. Raised walkways link the temples as most of this land is water-logged, but you can see the remains of ancient underground tunnels which once drained the marshy flatlands. The outlying structures are the Bima Temple, which is probably unique in Java, with its strange sculpted heads like so many spectators looking out of windows; and the Dwarawati Temple on the northern hills with the ruined Parekesit Temple nearby. At the source of the Serayu, the Spring of Youth was once a holy spring, although it's now used by the villagers for more mundane activities such as washing and drinking.

Any number of long walks to quiet, lonely places can be made around Dieng –

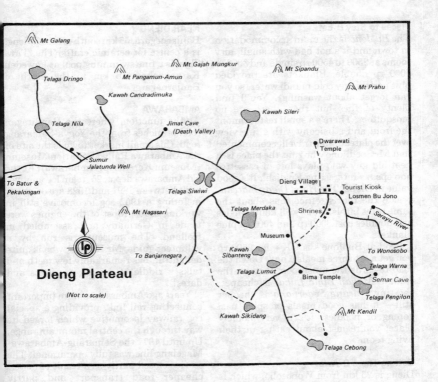

Mt Galang

Telaga Dringo

Mt Pangamun-Amun

Mt Gajah Mungkur

Mt Sipandu

Kawah Candradimuka

Mt Prahu

Telaga Nila

Jimat Cave
(Death Valley)

Kawah Sileri

Dwarawati
Temple

Sumur
Jalatunda Well

To Batur &
Pekalongan

Telaga Siwiwi

Dieng Village

Tourist Kiosk
Losmen Bu Jono

Mt Nagasari

Telaga Merdaka

Shrines

Serayu River

Dieng Plateau

Museum

(Not to scale)

To Banjarnegara

Kawah
Sibanteng

To Wonosobo

Telaga Warna

Telaga Lumut

Bima Temple

Semar Cave

Telaga Pengilon

Kawah Sikidang

Mt Kendil

Telaga Cebong

to the highest village in Java if you're feeling energetic. Close at hand is the beautiful Telaga Warna (the Many-Coloured Lake) and the holy cave of Semar which for years has been used for meditation. Suharto is said to visit the cave occasionally when things get tough; in 1974 he was reportedly accompanied by former Australian Prime Minister Gough Whitlam when he made an unofficial visit to Indonesia. The cave itself is empty and pitch black but the entrance is marked by a huge rock resembling the clown-god Semar himself. Just south past the Bima Temple, the Sikidang Crater with its steaming vents and frantically bubbling mud ponds is a spectacular place to see at sun set.

Information

There's a kiosk at the entrance to the plateau, next to the Bu Jono Losmen, which sells tickets for Dieng for 250 rp (though not everyone buys one) and very vague sketch maps of the area which cost 100 rp. The Tourist Office, almost next door, has similar maps for free and a few leaflets. It's open from 7 am to 6 pm and closes between 12 noon and 1 pm on Fridays.

On the south side of the plateau there's a small site museum containing Hindu statues, including a rather famous image of Shiva sitting astride the shoulders of a seated Nandi (Shiva's bull mount). It's often locked but there's usually someone around who can open it upon request.

Places to Stay & Eat

The *Bu Jono* is the main accommodation in town and it's not bad with small, airy rooms at 2500 to 4500 rp single and 3000 to 5000 rp double. Blankets are provided plus perishingly cold mandi water (so you can forget about washing). You'll find plenty of flies but then there are no mosquitoes. There's a small restaurant at the front and a balcony with a fine view over the plateau. One traveller commented that Mr Soedijono who runs the place is 'a neat old guy who plays lots of cassettes and speaks interesting English'. It's good value in Dieng! The *Hotel Dieng Plateau*, beside the tourist office, has about the same rates but is not as well kept; singles and doubles cost 3000 rp and 4000 rp plus blankets.

Food at Bu Jono's is OK – for 2500 rp you get a set three meals a day. Down the road towards the mushroom factory, the *Rumah Makan Bima Lukar* is cheaper; the tiny *Warung Sederhana* is cheaper still – it has good meals of spicy nasi goreng or noodles. It's a very homely place; you're just about eating in their living room.

Getting There & Away

Dieng is 26 km from Wonosobo, which is the usual access point. Minibuses cost 700 rp up, 600 rp down and the trip takes around an hour. There is also a road between Batur, to the west of Dieng, and Pekalongan on the north coast. If you're feeling fit you can walk out of Dieng and take a colt from Batur to the coast. The bus trip takes about four hours (downhill most of the way but the road surface is broken on long stretches and hair-raisingly steep in places – hence the long journey). Start early from Dieng and you can be in Pekalongan by the afternoon.

There are tour buses direct to Dieng from Yogya for 2500 rp; day tours out of Yogya that include a stop at Borobudur cost 6500 rp and up.

NEAR DIENG

Banjarnegara, 55 km south-west of Dieng, is a centre for ceramic crafts. The 'Tirta Teja' is a fine swimming pool at Paweden Karangbokar, 15 km to the north of Banjarnegara.

AMBARAWA

At the junction, where the Bandungan road branches from the Yogya-Semarang road, this small market town is the site of the Ambarawa Railway Station Museum (Museum Kereta Api Ambarawa). At the old Ambarawa depot, 25 steam locomotives built between 1891 and 1928 are on show, including a 1902 cog locomotive still in working order. Most of the engines were made in Germany and assembled in Holland. The museum is run by a volunteer guide, Mr Rubiya, who is quite delightful, has remarkably few teeth and talks a riddle of gauges, statistics and dates!

Years ago Ambarawa was an important connecting rail link, providing a special cog railway locomotive which forged its way through the central mountain range. Up until 1977 the Semarang-Ambarawa-Magelang line was fully operational. The service closed partly as a result of faster, cheaper road transport and partly because of the destructive activities of Merapi – but it's still possible to charter a train for the 18-km trip from Ambarawa to Bedono on the old cog railway. Indonesian groups do this quite frequently – the railway needs at least one day's notice though a week's advance notice is better. The train can take up to 80 passengers for a total cost of 275,000 rp, which works out to a cost of about US$2 per person! The round-trip journey takes a day and includes a picnic lunch. This special charter trip can be booked through major railway stations such as Yogya or Semarang, in Ambarawa, or through the Central Java Exploitation Office (tel 24500), PJKA, Jalan Thamrin 3, Semarang.

Getting There & Away

By public bus from Semarang to Ambarawa (40 km) takes about one hour, 400 rp; Yogya to Ambarawa (90 km) via Magelang takes 2½ hours, 850 rp. If you're coming from Solo, you may have to change buses at Salatiga or Bawen.

Getting Around

Bandungan/Gedung Songo Colts depart from Pasar Projo (two or three km from the bus station) for the 1/2-hour trip to Bandungan and the Gedung Songo temples.

You can get around Ambarawa by horse and cart; they quote around 300 rp from the bus station to Pasar Projo or the Railway Museum.

GEDUNG SONGO TEMPLES

The site of these nine small Hindu temples is probably the most beautiful of all the temple locations in Java. They are scattered along the tops of the foothills around Mt Ungaran, amongst ravines and gushing hot sulphur springs, and as the clouds sweep down the mountains they are like some ethereal apparition which can suddenly appear out of the shifting mists. From this 1000-metre perch there is also one of the most spectacular views in Java – across the shimmering Rawa Pening lake below to Mt Merbabu and Mt Merapi, smouldering beneath.

'Gedung Songo' means 'nine buildings' in Javanese. Built in the 9th century AD and devoted to Shiva and Vishnu, most of the temples are in good condition but the fifth is in the most complete state of reconstruction. The site is approached from Bandungan, 15 km from Ambarawa, which in turn is on the main Yogya-Semarang road. The temples are about six km from Bandungan and a further three km off the main road. A well-trodden path links the temples and it could take three to six hours to visit all of them on foot – or you can go on horseback. Bandungan and Gedung Songo are very popular with domestic tourists, so if you want peace and solitude try and avoid the weekends.

Places to Stay

The small town of Bandungan, at 980 metres, is a popular hill resort for people from Semarang so there's quite a range of accommodation here. The *Losmen Riani I* has rooms with small mandi for 5000 rp and it's reportedly 'nice but can be noisy'. The *Wisma Kereta Api*, run by the Central Java Railways, has quite comfortable bungalows from 5000 to 10,000 rp and is very popular locally. In its grounds there's a good public swimming pool you can use for 250 rp a day. The modern *Madya Hill View Inn* has rooms with mandi from 4500 rp, including tea and coffee. It has friendly staff and comfortable rooms but the hotel's had problems in the past with invasions of cockroaches. By now they may have done something about it; blankets and piped muzak are provided and there is hot water in the mornings.

There are a number of other places along the road to the Gedung Songo temples including the pleasant *Losmen Pojok Sari* with rooms at 6000 rp. The *Rawa Pening Hotel* (tel 134), about one km out of town, is at the more expensive end of the scale; rooms with attached mandi are 17,500 rp and there are also cottages. The Rawa Pening is a lovely old colonial-style wood bungalow with a front terrace, fine gardens, tennis courts and a restaurant. This is also *the* place to stay for that fantastic view from the temple site but, as you might imagine, it is often full at weekends. The *Amanda Cottage* (tel 145), at the luxurious end of Bandungan's scale, also has a fine view.

Near the junction where the road to Gedung Songo turns off from Bandungan's main street there's an excellent roadside market with fruit and vegetables and there are a number of cheap eating places in the same area. Early in the morning, around 7 am, a flower market gathers here briefly before dispersing to outlying towns and villages.

SOLO (Surakarta or Sala)

On the Yogya-Surabaya road, 65 km north-west of Yogya, the old royal city of Solo lies on the west bank of one of Java's most important rivers – the 'Bengawan Solo'. Formerly known as Surakarta, its founding in 1745 has a mystical past. Following the sacking of the Mataram court at Kartasura in 1742 the Susuhunan, Pakubuwono II, decided to look for a more auspicious site and the transfer of the capital had something to do with voices from the cosmic world. According to legend the king was told to go to the village of Solo because 'it is the place decreed by Allah and it will become a great and prosperous city'.

By the end of the 18th century Solo had already reached the peak of its political importance and the realm of Mataram had crumbled, split by internal conflict into three rivalling courts of which Yogya was one. From then on the ruler of Surakarta and the subsidiary prince of Mangkunegara remained loyal to the Dutch, even at the time of Diponegoro's Java War. During the revolution they fumbled opportunities to play a positive role and with the tide of democracy in the 1940s, the kratons of Solo became mere symbols of ancient Javanese feudalism and aristocracy.

Although Solo's economy once thrived on great sugar, coffee and tobacco estates, smaller businesses such as textile mills have since taken their place and Solo is an excellent source of high quality batik. Solo also competes with Yogya as a centre for Javanese culture, attracting many students and scholars to its academies of music and dance. With a tradition of religious tolerance, Solo has more recently become a major centre of Kebatinan schools, which are popular with westerners interested in spiritualism and meditation.

Solo has two kratons, one even larger and more venerable than Yogya's. It's quite possible to day-trip to Solo from Yogya but it's worth far more than a day, particularly if you were to visit the ancient archaeological site of Sangiran and the mysterious Sukuh Temple, just outside the city.

Information & Orientation

The oldest part of the city is centred around the Surakarta kraton to the east, where the Pasar Klewer, the main batik market, is also located. The Mangkunegara kraton is the centre of Solo. Once you're away from these tranquil palaces Solo can be as busy as any other Javanese city, but it is less congested than its younger sister city, Yogya, and not overwhelmed by tourists. It is perhaps the least westernised of Java's cities and there are corners with narrow walled streets and a strong village-like atmosphere.

Jalan Slamet Riyadi is the main thoroughfare, a broad tree-lined avenue through the centre of Solo. Here the city's double-decker buses run their sedate course from east to west. You will also find the tourist office at one end and most of the banks at the east end, near the Surakarta kraton. Solo's Balapan railway station is in the northern part of the city, about two km from the centre, and the main bus station is just north again. Most hotels, restaurants and craft shops are in the area between Jalan Slamet Riyadi and the railway station. The Adi Sumarmo Airport is eight km north-west of the city centre.

Tourist Office The Solo Tourist Office (tel 6508) at Jalan Slamet Riyadi 235 is one of the best you'll find in the country. They have a useful *Solo Guide Map* and information on cultural events in town and places to visit in the area, including free booklets on Candi Sukuh and Sangiran. It's also worth having a rummage through their bookcase of general leaflets where they keep a good stock of information on the whole country.

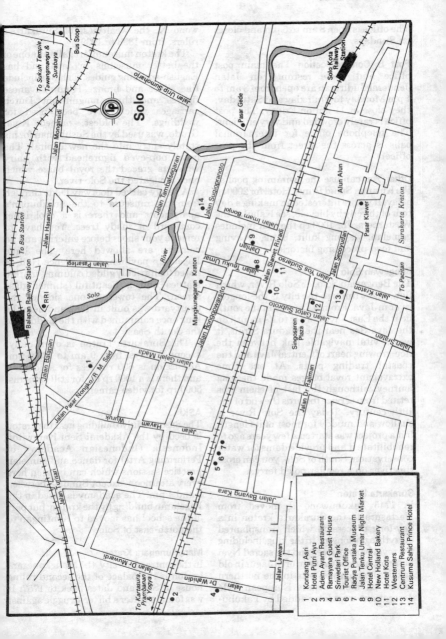

Solo

To Sukuh Temple Tawangmangu & Surabaya

Bus Stop

Jalan Urip Sumoharjo

To Surakarta Kraton

Pasar Gede

Solo Kota Railway Station

To Mongisidi

Alun Alun

Pasar Klewer

Jalan Tambaksegaran

Jalan Sugiopranoto

Jalan Imam Bonjol

14

Jalan Hasanudin

Jalan Pasareleg

To Bus Station

River

Jalan Dahlan

9

8

Jalan Teuku Umar

Jalan Slamet Riyadi

11

Jalan Yos Sudarso

Jalan Seoyudan

To Pacitan

Jalan Kratonan

RRI

Solo

Balapan Railway Station

Mangkunegaran Kraton

Jalan Ronggowarsito

10

13

Singosaren Plaza

12

Jalan Gatot Suboroto

To Solo Kraton

Jalan Sraten

Jalan Gajah Mada

Jalan Pasar Nongko/R. M. Said

1

Jalan Wuruk

Jalan Hayam Wuruk

Jalan Dr. Rajiman

ASRI

To Prambanan & Yogya

Jalan Tursari

3

Jalan Bayang Kara

5 6 7

Jalan Dr. Muwardi

To Kartasura, Prambanan & Yogya

Jalan Dr. Wahidin

2

4

Jalan Lawean

1 Kondang Asri
2 Hotel Putri Ayu
3 Adem Ayam Restaurant
4 Ramayana Guest House
5 Sriwedari Park
6 Tourist Office
7 Radya Pustaka Museum
8 Jalan Tenku Umar Night Market
9 Hotel Central
10 New Holland Bakery
11 Hotel Kota
12 Westerners
13 Centrum Restaurant
14 Kusuma Sahid Prince Hotel

The office is open 8 am to 5 pm and closes on Sundays.

Post & Communication The main post office and poste restante on Jalan Jenderal Sudirman are open from 8 am to 1 pm Monday to Thursday and Saturday; they close at 11 am on Friday. The post office is rarely crowded and very efficient. The telephone office for international calls is across the street from the post office.

Other You can use the swimming pool at the Kusuma Sahid Prince Hotel for 2000 rp a day. If you're interested in making a day tour of the city by bicycle, see Kabul at the Westerners. For 1000 rp the tour includes gamelan, wayang kulit, batik, weaving and food processing factories.

Bengawan Solo

The Bengawan Solo, or Solo River, which flows right through the city is the longest river in Java. From its source in the south near the East Java border to its mouth on the Java Sea near the Madura Strait, it was a vital navigable link between the rice-growing heart of Central Java and the coastal trading ports. At one time extravagant royal barges made the long journey, although the last of them was retired from service towards the end of the 19th century. Today the Solo River is shallow and muddy for most of its length but a project was started a few years ago to rehabilitate it and provide dams for water conservation. South of Solo, you can cross this river on a regular poled ferry.

Surakarta Kraton

In 1745 Pakubuwono II moved from Kartasura to the Surakarta kraton in a day-long procession which transplanted everything belonging to the king, including the royal banyan trees and the sacred Nyai Setomo cannon (the twin of Si Jagur in old Jakarta) which now sits in the northern palace pavilion. Ornate European-style decorations were later added by Pakubu-

wono X, the wealthiest of Surakarta's rulers, from 1893 to 1939.

The kraton museum/art gallery is one of the better museums in Java and has English-speaking guides. Exhibits include fine silver and bronze Hindu-Javanese figures and three magnificent Dutch carriages which have been used for weddings. The oldest, named Kiya Grudo, was used by the Susuhunan for his stately entry into the new capital. The giant pop-eyed figurehead with hairy whiskers graced the royal barge which once navigated the Solo river.

A heavy carved doorway leads through from the museum to the Susuhunan's apartments and there is a cool inner courtyard of shady trees. You have to remove your shoes before entering and no cameras are allowed here. The large Pagelaran pavilion, or Audience Hall, is noted for its richly gilded columns, marble statues and a beautiful stained-glass screen. The tower to one side of the courtyard was built in 1782 and here the king once communed with the Goddess of the South Seas.

The Surakarta kraton is open daily except Fridays, from 9 am to 12.30 pm. Admission is 600 rp (less for students), and there is a 1000 rp fee for still cameras, 5000 rp for video cameras.

ASKI

The Sasono Mulyo building near the kraton is used by the Akademi Seni Karawiton Indonesia (Indonesian Academy of Performing Arts) for dance and gamelan practice sessions which can be seen here every afternoon, except Sunday, between 2 and 4 pm. The academy is based in the Pagelaran building by the kraton, but part of the school has moved to Kentingan to the north-east of Solo.

Mangkunegara Kraton

In the centre of the city, the Mangkunegara kraton is the palace of the second ruling house of Solo and dates back to 1757. It was founded after a bitter struggle against the Susuhunan of Surakarta launched by Raden Mas Said, a member of the Surakarta aristocracy, and an ancestor of Mme Tien Suharto. The Prince and Princess of Mangkunegara still live at the back of the palace.

The centre of the palace compound is the pavilion, bordered on its northern side by the Dalem or main Ceremonial Hall which forms the palace museum. The pavilion has been added to over the centuries and it is probably the largest ever constructed in the country. Its high rounded ceiling was painted in 1937 and it is intricately decorated with a central flame surrounded by eight figures of the Javanese zodiac, each in its own mystical colour. In Javanese philosophy yellow signifies a preventative against sleepiness, blue against disease, black against hunger, green against desire, white against lust, rose against fear, red against evil and purple against wicked thoughts! On the south-west side of the pavilion is one of the kraton's oldest sets of gamelan known as 'Kyai Kanyut Mesem' which translates as 'Drifting in Smiles'.

The museum here is a real delight. Most of the exhibits are the personal collection of Mangkunegara VII. Amongst the items are gold-plated dresses for the royal Srimpi and Bedoyo dances, jewellery and a few oddities including huge Buddhist rings and a bizarre gold genital cover for a queen. There's also a magnificent collection of masks from various areas in Indonesia, a series of royal portraits and a library collection of classical literary works by the Mangkunegara princes.

The palace is open daily except Sunday and entry is 500 rp (less for students). Hours are 9 am to 12.30 pm, except Friday when it closes at 11.30 am. On Wednesday mornings there are dance practice sessions at the pavilion from 10 am and on Saturday mornings there is gamelan. Wayang kulit puppets, most of them made by the the kraton's dalang, can be bought at the shop inside the palace. Prices are fixed but the puppets are

generally of very fine quality and reasonably priced. You'll also find a few beautiful, though expensive, wayang beber scrolls.

Radya Pustaka Museum

This small museum, next to the tourist office on Jalan Slamet Riyadi, has good displays of gamelan instruments, jewelled kris, wayang puppets from Thailand as well as Indonesia, a small collection of wayang beber scrolls and another hairy muppet figurehead from a royal barge. It's open daily from 8 am to 12.15 pm, except Monday when it's closed all day and Friday when it closes at 11 am. Entrance is 100 rp.

Meditation

In Solo there are a number of contemporary mystical groups, of different philosophies and religions, teaching the practice of *kebatinan* (or Javanese spiritualism) which has been recognised as one of the official religions of Indonesia. See the introductory section on religions of Java for more information. A few schools in Solo have large followings of westerners and most gatherings are generally held informally at private homes.

The Majapahit Pancasila, founded by Hardjanta Pradjapangarsa, is a school for studying Hinduism which is popular among westerners. Hardjanta gives lectures in English and the *Kundalini* yoga method of meditation is practised by his pupils. He lives in a shophouse on Jalan Sidikoro, a lane behind the Surakarta Kraton, and you can visit for short or long term study. Pak Suwondo, on Gang 1 Jalan Kratonan, teaches the traditional theory and practise of Javanese meditation. Or you can simply drop by for the evening group meditation sessions at the home of Ananda Suyono, a Javanese 'New Age' eclectic, who lives at Jalan Ronggowarsito 60.

Performances

Wayang orang performances of the

Ramayana can be seen at the Sriwedari Amusement Park, Jalan Slamet Riyadi, from 8 pm to midnight Monday to Saturday and every Sunday morning. The Sriwedari theatre boasts one of the most famous wayang orang troupes in Java but it's had mixed reports from travellers – some say that 'the costumes are stunning', others that it's 'a washout, nobody seems to go'. Still, the seats are cheap; the cheapest are 350 rp and only 500 rp for quite good ones. It's a small, pleasant park and if you want to just wander round and eat at the cheap warungs the entrance fee is 150 rp. On some Saturday nights there may be wayang kulit instead of wayang orang.

At the Kusuma Sahid Prince Hotel, gamelan performances are held in the lobby every evening from 6 pm and there are also wayang orang dance–drama shows.

Various cultural performances are also held at the local broadcasting station of Radio Republik Indonesia. The RRI performances (which are very popular and often excellent) can be a laugh a minute. Note all the action going on in the broadcasting/lighting room right on stage – the technicians have a habit of leaving the curtains open, blissfully unaware of their audience. Or perhaps this is the modern equivalent of watching the dalang behind the screen in wayang kulit! RRI has wayang kulit shows on the third Saturday night of every month from 8 pm till around 4 am, and on the first Tuesday evening of the month there is wayang orang from 8 pm to midnight.

The tourist office has details of other cultural events around Solo. Wayang kulit shows are occasionally performed by the famous dalang, Anom Suroto, at Jalan Notodiningran 100 – you can count on a show there every Malam Rabu Legi, a certain Tuesday evening occurring regularly in the Javanese calendar. Anom also occasionally performs at the Sriwedari Amusement Park.

Other Attractions

The Balekambang Sports Centre on Jalan Jenderal Ahmad on the north-west edge of town has a public swimming pool and a roller disco. There is a government-sanctioned and regulated red-light district along Jalan Prof Dr Supomo.

Places to Stay – bottom end

There are two main areas for cheap hotels in Solo: in the centre of town within one block's walk of Jalan Slamet Riyadi; or along Jalan Raden Mas Said (Pasar Nongko), about five minutes from the train station which in turn is close to the bus station.

You're unlikely to find better value in Solo than the popular *Pak Mawardi's Homestay* (tel 3106) at Kemlayan Kidul 11, a small alley between Jalan Gatot Subroto and Jalan Yos Sudarso, parallel to Jalan Secoyudan. The alley's west entrance is opposite the Singosaren Plaza on Jalan Gatot Subroto. The house is tucked away in a kampung, which makes it wonderfully quiet – but also difficult to find! If you're lost, try asking for the 'Westerners', its other name, although only if you're in the immediate neighbourhood will people know what you're talking about.

The rooms here are clean and airy, set in a pleasant courtyard with tables and chairs; and the family who run the place are friendly and helpful without being overpowering. There are singles at 3500 rp, doubles at 4500 rp, extra beds cost 1000 rp, and there are a couple of spacious 'private rooms' (not adjoining others) for 7000 rp. You can help yourself to free tea and cold drinking water from the kitchen and coffee and soft drinks are available. A good breakfast (egg, toast, fruit salad and coffee) costs 1500 rp. They also rent bicycles for 1000 rp a day. It's easily one of the best budget hotels in Java, about 500 rp by becak from the train station.

Hotel Kota (tel 2841), Jalan Slamet Riyadi 113, still seems to be reasonably popular despite higher prices and reports of a slide in standards. It's a double-storey place built around a large open courtyard and rooms cost from 4000 rp, or from 8000 rp with mandi.

Close by on Jalan Ahmad Dahlan there are a number of places in the same price range including the open and airy *Hotel Central* at No 32. It's a fairly clean and pleasant place in the old 'grand' style with some fine Art Deco woodwork. All rooms are 3500 rp (shared bath only) and you get coffee in the morning and tea in the afternoon. Street rooms can be a bit noisy but you have a great view of the town, the sunset and Merapi volcano. On this same street you'll also find the lesser *Islam*, *Moro Seneng* and *Hotel Keprabon*. The *Losmen Timur*, down a small alley alongside the Hotel Central, has been popular with budget travellers probably because of the price. Singles cost 2500 rp but it's pretty dismal; fine if you don't mind dingy, not-so-clean rooms, although the staff are friendly enough.

At Jalan Imam Bonjol 44, a block over, the *Hotel Mawar Melati* (tel 6434) has adequate rooms from 7500 rp including tea twice a day; rooms with bathroom and fan start at 10,000 rp.

Near the railway station there are several places on Jalan R M Said. The *Wismantara* at No 3 has rooms at 5000 rp around a somewhat gloomy courtyard. The *Kondang Asri* at No 86 has singles at 3000 rp with friendly people, good music (even if it is too loud sometimes) and free tea (sometimes).

The *Hotel Putri Sari* (tel 5317) at Jalan Slamet Riyadi 334B is good value at the high bottom end; doubles are 5000 rp without bath, 9000 rp with bath, or 14,000 rp for a 'deluxe' room with TV, fan, soap and towels.

Places to Stay – middle

Many of the hotels in this bracket are strung out along or just off Jalan Slamet Riyadi, west of the town centre. Becaks from the bus terminal or railway station to this area should be 300-400 rp. Several

readers have recommended the well-maintained *Hotel Putri Ayu* (tel 6154), Jalan Slamet Riyadi 293, where all the rooms have their own mandis. Rooms with fan, single or double, cost 12,500 rp including breakfast; with air-con they are 17,500 rp.

The *Ramayana Guest House* (tel 2814), also in this part of town at Jalan Dr Wahidin 15, is an attractive house with a guest wing around a garden. It has a choice of large comfortable rooms with fan or air-con, all with their own mandi. Rooms here start at 13,500 rp with fan and 22,000 rp with air-con. Rates include breakfast, afternoon snack and tea. There's a restaurant and the staff are friendly.

Probably the best value in this category is the recently refurbished *Hotel Dana* (tel 3891), Jalan Slamet Riyadi 386. The clean and peaceful grounds surround a spacious, tile floor lobby in the main building; a unique wood-and-hide chandelier hangs from a high ceiling supported by gracefully carved wooden columns. Behind the main building, well off the street, is the guest building which features sitting areas both inside and outside the rooms. Rates are 7500 rp without bath, 10,000 rp with attached bath, or 13,000 rp with bath and fan. There are also air-con rooms for 20,000 rp or 27,500 for larger 'deluxe' rooms.

Another good mid-range hotel is the newish *Wisata Indah* (tel 3783), Jalan Slamet Riyadi 173. Rooms here are clean, nicely decorated, and feature comfortable beds for 20,000 rp with attached shower and breakfast, or 25,000 rp with air-con.

Places to Stay – top end

The *Kusuma Sahid Prince Hotel* (tel 6356), Jalan Sugiyopranoto 22, has been designed around a former Solonese palace. It's a grand place set in beautiful grounds with a swimming pool. Other facilities include a coffee shop serving Indonesian and western meals, a bar, shopping arcade, Javanese herb shop, massage and laundry services! Singles/ doubles range from US\$14/17 to US\$37/43, bungalows start at US\$50, and there are three 'royal' suites with rates 'upon request'.

The *Hotel Cakra* (tel 5847), centrally located at Jalan Slamet Riyadi 171, has a variety of air-con rooms and cottages. Singles/doubles range from 24,900/24,990 rp to 51,500/57,000 rp including breakfast; cottages start at 59,100 rp.

Places to Eat

There are countless warungs and restaurants in Solo, including several serving excellent Chinese food. For the cheapest food listen for the weird and distinctive sounds which are the trademarks of the roaming street hawkers. The bread man sings (or screeches) a high-pitched 'Tee'; 'ding ding ding' is the bakso man; 'tic tock' is mie; a wooden buffalo bell advertises sate; and a shrieking kettle-on-the-boil sound is the *kue putu* man. Kue putu are coconut cakes which are pushed into small bamboo tubes to cook over a steam box and then served hot sprinkled with coconut and sugar.

One of the best eating places in Solo is undoubtedly the night market along Jalan Teuku Umar. Here you'll find tents for susu segar or fresh milk, also known as *minuman sehat* (healthy drink) – hot or cold milk with optional egg and honey – and a wide assortment of tasty snacks. Many of the warungs serve nasi gudeg from Yogya and also *nasi liwet*, a delicious Solonese speciality of rice with spiced chicken and creamy coconut sauce for 400 rp. On the sidewalks nearby another local food speciality to try is *srabi* – small coconut/rice puddings served up on a light crispy pancake with banana, chocolate or jackfruit on top. Best when they're piping hot. The tourist office says that this night market may move to the front of the Radya Pustaka Museum in the near future, so if you can't find it at Jalan Teuku Umar, check there.

Another good night market is at Pasar Lagi. Jalan Yos Sudarso is the street for sate warungs. Pasar Gede near the intersection of Jalan Urip Sumoharjo Jalan Sugiopranoto has lots of cheap fruit.

The *New Holland Restaurant & Bakery*, near the Hotel Kota at Jalan Slamet Riyadi 135, is clean, quiet and a good place for breakfast or a break from Indonesian food. Downstairs is the coffee shop and bakery with delicious savoury martabak rolls for 400 rp, good coffee, cold drinks and ice cream. The restaurant upstairs has western food as well as a varied Indonesian menu. Further west on Jalan Slamet Riyadi, next door to the Hotel Dana at No 232, is the clean and reasonably priced *Restaurant Dani Sari Rosa*. Open from 6 am till midnight, it has all the standard rice and noodle dishes, plus good ayam goreng. The *Restaurant Rosana*, next door to the Hotel Wisata Indah at No 173, has a good, inexpensive Indonesian buffet with clearly marked prices.

A number of decent Chinese places along Jalan Slamet Riyadi include the *Jakarta* close to the centre, the *Orient* further out at 341 and the *Adem Ayam* at 296. The Adem Ayam is split into two restaurants, one serving Chinese food and the other Javanese – locals often recommend the Adem Ayam but a few travellers have found it disappointing.

The *Centrum* at Jalan Kratonan 151, just south of the main street towards the kraton, offers very good Chinese food. It's a small restaurant with a good atmosphere, an enormously varied menu and you really get your money's worth. It's very popular and always busy, so to be sure of a meal it's best to go early; the doors are usually closed around 8 pm.

In the vicinity of the Hotel Central on Jalan Ahmad Dahlan are *Rumah Makan Laris* and *Warung Makan Sari Rejeki*, both small, clean places with inexpensive Chinese and Indonesian food.

The *Taman Sari* at Jalan Gatot Subroto 63 has good helpings of noodles and excellent ice juices. On the same street, look out for the *Bu Mari* warung which has miniature chairs around a low table on the sidewalk – great nasi gudeg and chicken curry with rice and sambal for only 1000 rp.

Along Jalan Diponegoro, near the entrance to Pasar Triwindu, there's a row of warungs for cheap meals, snacks and iced fruit juices. The *Rumah Makan Hijau* has good gado-gado and soto Madura.

The *Malibu Restaurant*, next door to the Hotel Kota on Jalan Slamet Riyadi, serves delicious roast chicken (*ayam bakar*) as well as various rice and noodle dishes at fairly reasonable prices in an indoor-outdoor pub atmosphere. A large bottle of cold beer is 1800 rp, further discounted by 15% between 1 and 6 pm. For not-so-cheap western food in air-con comfort, try the *Sasmaya Pub & Restaurant* on Jalan Dr Rajiman or the *Dynasty Pub & Restaurant* on Jalan Honggowongso.

Things to Buy

Solo is a batik centre rivalling Yogya but with a totally individual style. Many people find it better value than Yogya for batik and other crafts and curios, quite possibly because it attracts far fewer tourists.

Batik At Pasar Klewer, a two-storey 'Hanging Market' near the Susuhunan's palace, there are hundreds of stalls selling traditional fabrics, mainly batik and *lurik*. Bargaining is obligatory here and if you're buying used cap batik look it over carefully for holes!

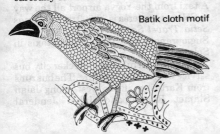
Batik cloth motif

For more sophisticated work, there are numerous shops around town – most of them are marked on the Solo guide map. Batik Semar is one good place for modern cotton and beautiful silk batiks and in the mornings (weekdays only) you can see the batik being made. The Danar Hadi showroom has a good range of batik fabrics and ready-made clothes, and attractive tie-dye cottons for around 5500 rp.

You can take batik courses in Solo but most people do this in Yogya where courses tend to be cheaper.

Curios Pasar Triwindu on Jalan Diponegoro is Solo's flea market. All kinds of bric-a-brac plus a few genuine antiques are sold here – old buttons and buckles, china dogs and fine porcelain, puppets, batik tulis pens, oil lamps, bottles and bell jars – but if you're looking for bargains you have to sift carefully through the rubbish and be prepared to bargain hard. Old batik 'cap' stamps are worth looking out for – they tend to be much cheaper here than in Yogya (about 3000 to 5000 rp) but check that they're not damaged.

Toko Bedoyo Srimpi, Jalan Ronggowarsito 116, is the place for dancers' costumes and theatrical supplies where you'll find all those gold gilt headdresses, painted armbands and so on that you've always wanted. They also sell masks and wayang kulit puppets.

Jalan Secoyudan is the goldsmiths' street. Sundays and holidays in particular, there's sometimes an early morning market for handmade toys from villages around Solo in front of the Rudya Pustaka Museum.

Getting There & Away

Air Only Garuda fly to and from Solo. There are daily flights to Jakarta (60,100 rp) and Surabaya (26,700 rp). The only inter-island flight is to Ujung Pandang (121,200 rp, daily).

The Garuda office (tel 6846) is in the Kusuma Sahid Prince Hotel, Jalan Slamet Riyadi 113, and is open 7 am to 3 pm

Monday to Friday, 7 am to 1 pm Saturday and 9 am to 12 noon Sunday and holidays.

Bus The main bus station (Gilingan) is about three km north of the centre of town, 500 rp by becak. Travelling to or from the west – Semarang, Prambanan and Yogya for example – you can save a few rupiah by taking the city double-decker (150 rp) to the bus station west of town at Kartasura.

Going West There are frequent buses to Prambanan for 500 rp (1½ hours) and Yogya for 700 rp (two hours). Papsa Kasatriyan operates a door-to-door minibus service to Yogya for 1500 rp from their office opposite the Batik Keris shop.

Going North Buses include to Boyolali for 400 rp (one hour), Salatiga for 600 rp (1½ hours) and Semarang for 1100 rp (2½ hours).

Going East Buses include to Wonogiri for 400 rp (one hour) – this is the bus to take if you're heading for Pacitan beach in East Java. There are also buses to Blitar for 3000 rp (six hours) and Surabaya for around 4000 rp (six hours). To Malang buses leave frequently in the morning between 7 and 9 am; the trip takes about nine hours and the fare is 4200 rp.

Night Bus Many of the night bus companies, for Malang and Surabaya, are along Jalan Urip Sumoharjo. Agung Express operate night buses to Malang and Surabaya for 7250 rp including a meal. The Jawah Indah bus to Surabaya costs 7000 rp including a meal. Most buses depart between 9.30 pm and 10.30 pm. You can also buy bus tickets for Malang and Surabaya at the Adem Ayam Restaurant and catch the bus from there which may be more convenient. To Malang fares start at 6000 rp, Surabaya at 7000 rp.

The long haul from Solo to Bandung takes 12 hours so you're really best off opting for a night express train. If you do plan to take the bus, however, one of the best and cheapest companies is Bhayangkara Express at Jalan Jenderal Sudirman 22-24. Their bus to Bandung costs 6000 rp or 7000 rp air-con. They also operate a night bus to Jakarta which costs 5500 rp or 8000 rp air-con.

Rail From the Balapan railway station, it's around 500 rp by becak into the centre. Solo is on the main Jakarta-Yogya-Surabaya train route so there are frequent day trains and there are night trains. The most comfortable way to get to Jakarta is to take the fast *Bima Express*; it departs Solo at 8.09 pm, arrives Jakarta Kota at 7 am and the fare is 18,000 rp 1st class seat or 22,000 with a sleeping berth. Coming the other way it leaves Jakarta Kota at 4 pm and arrives in Solo at 2.50 am in the middle of the night.

Trains from Solo to Surabaya take five hours, with fares from 4200 rp in the all-3rd-class *GBM Selatan* to 21,000 rp in 1st class sleeper on the fast *Bima Express*.

From Bandung there are two trains daily to Solo, the *Express Siang* at 5.25 am (3800 rp 3rd class, 5000 rp 2nd) and the *Mutiara Selatan* at 5.30 pm (9000 rp 2nd class, 13,500 rp 1st). From Solo, these trains depart at 10 am and 10.08 pm, arriving in Bandung at 10.10 pm and 7.35 am respectively.

Yogya is only an hour and 20 minutes away on the *Express Siang* and costs 3800 rp 3rd class, 5000 rp 2nd class.

Getting Around
There are plenty of becaks all over town and there are taxis, but they're unmetered. A taxi to or from the Adi Sumarmo airport eight km west of town will cost 6000 rp. A taxi from the Yogya airport all the way to Solo or vice versa is 23,500 rp. *Hayumas Setia Travel Service* (tel 0271) at Jalan Sugiopranoto 22 arranges these taxis in Solo.

There's a useful double-decker city bus service with a flat 150 rp fare. The bus runs from Kartasura in the west, along Jalan Slamet Riyadi and Jalan Jenderal

Sudirman to Palur in the east. Bicycles can be hired from Pak Mawardi's Homestay (the Westerners) for 1000 rp a day.

The main colt stand is on the opposite side to the Pasar Klewer market, for destinations south of Solo, including Gua Tabuhan and Pacitan (see East Java). The taxi stand is on Jalan Kratonan in the same area.

AROUND SOLO

Sangiran

Fifteen km north of Solo, Sangiran is an important archaeological excavation site where the fossil skull of prehistoric 'Java Man' (*pithecanthropus erectus*) was unearthed by a Dutch professor in 1936. There is a small site museum with a couple of skulls, various pig and hippopotamus teeth and fossil exhibits including some amazing 'mammoth' bones and tusks. Large quantities of bones are simply bundled together in plastic bags, possibly because there are plans to shift to a new museum at Sangiran by late 1985. Archaeologists are still finding things in the area and if you wander up the road past the museum a bit and have a look in some of the exposed banks you may find shells or fossil bones and crabs.

The museum is open daily, except Sunday, from 9 am to 4 pm. Admission is 300 rp. At the museum you can buy a copy of the booklet *Sangiran* for 500 rp, but booklets are available for free at the Solo tourist office. To get there, take a bus or colt from the Solo bus station. It will drop you at Kalioso and from there you have to walk about three km to the museum.

Sukuh Temple

One of Java's most mysterious and striking temples, the Sukuh Temple stands 900 metres high on the slopes of Mt Lawu, 36 km east of Solo. In form it is a large truncated pyramid of rough-hewn stone with a curious Inca look and, while the sculpture is carved in the 'wayang style' found particularly in East Java, the figures are crude, squat and distorted.

The temple is hardly as wildly erotic as it is sometimes made out to be but there are fairly explicit and humorous representations of a stone penis or two and the elements of a fertility cult are quite plain.

Built in the 15th century during the declining years of Majapahit, Sukuh seems to have nothing whatsoever to do with other Javanese Hindu and Buddhist temples and the origins of its builders and the temple's strange sculptural style remains a mystery. It is the most recent Hindu-Buddhist temple in the region, yet it seems to mark a reappearance of the pre-Hindu animism and magic that existed 1500 years before. It's a quiet, isolated place (although the ubiquitous visitors' book may make a brief appearance!) with a strange and potent atmosphere.

At the gateway before the temple there is a large stone *lingam* and *yoni*. Flowers are still often scattered over it and there's a story that the symbol was mainly used by villagers to determine whether a wife had been faithful or a wife-to-be was still a virgin. The woman had to wear a sarong and stride across the lingam – if the sarong tore her infidelity was proven. Other interesting cult objects stand further in amongst the trees, including a tall-standing monument depicting Bima, the *Mahabharata* warrior hero, with Narada, the messenger of the gods, in a stylised womb followed by Bima dropping through at his birth. In the top courtyard three enormous flat-backed turtles stand like sacrificial altars.

From the site the views are superb, to the west and north across terrace fields and mountains. About a one hour climb beyond Sukuh is the less interesting Ceta Temple (1470 metres). Built about the same time, this temple is similarly terraced and carved with Bima figures but is in poor condition.

Getting There & Away From Solo, take the city double-decker to Tertomoyo, then a bus bound for Tawangmangu as far as

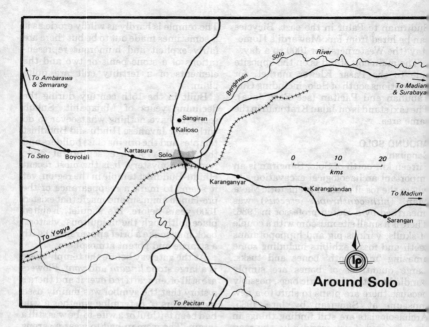

Around Solo

Karangpandan for 300 rp. Finally from Karangpandan catch a minibus to Sukuh for 250 rp. The trip takes about 1½ hours in total. On market days the minibus stops right beside the temple but most days it's a couple of km hike uphill from the bus stop to the site. There is a 100 rp admission charge to the site.

Tawangmangu

Trekkers can make an interesting 2½ walk from Sukuh Temple along a well-worn cobbled path to Tawangmangu, a pretty hill resort on the other side of Mt Lawu. Or you can get there by bus from Solo via Karangpandan which is just as fine a trip along a switchback road through magnificent tightly terraced hills. At Tawangmangu there is Grojogan Sewu, a 100-metre high waterfall and favourite playground for monkeys. It's reached by a long flight of steps down a hillside from the village and you can swim in the very

chilly pool at the bottom. Nobody else uses it.

An interesting alternative to back tracking to Solo is to take a colt to Sarangan, 15 km from Tawangmangu on the mountain road to Madiun, a picturesque hill town with losmen and hotels clustered at the edge of a crater lake.

Places to Stay In Tawangmangu the *Pak Amat Losmen* is quite pleasant and has its own garden. The rooms, from 6000 rp, are individual little houses with mandi and verandah. The *Losmen Pondok Garuda* has a choice of rooms with and without mandi from 6000 rp. There's a mosque right next door, but it has a fine location and the front rooms opening onto the garden offer a superb view over the valley. About one km up from the bus station, the *Hotel Lawu* at Jalan Lawu 20 has double rooms at around 10,000 rp,

There's good food in the warungs further up the hill.

Mt Merapi from Selo

On the northern slopes of volatile Mt Merapi, 50 km from Solo, it is roughly a four-hour trek from Selo to the summit of the volcano (2911 metres) – and this is a safer and easier climb than from Kaliurang to the south. See 'Around Yogya'. However, you shouldn't try to hike around the side of the peak from Selo to see the crater, as this is a very dangerous climb. From the Kaliurang side you can hike to both crater and summit if you're in good shape.

From Solo, take a Semarang bus to Boyolali and from there a colt to Selo. If you want food for the climb it's worth stocking up at Boyolali which is also the milk centre of Java.

Guides can be hired at either of the two losmens in Selo for 2500 rp per person with a minimum of four people.

Places to Stay The Agung Guest House of Yogya has a branch in Selo called *Agung Merapi* where dorm beds are 3500 rp, rooms 6000 rp. About 150 metres east is a small unmarked losmen where beds are 1500 rp per person or 2000 rp with a nasi goreng breakfast. Also in Selo, some people bed down in the central market in sleeping bags – you need to leave Selo at 3 am to make the summit by dawn.

SEMARANG

The capital city of the province of Central Java, the north coast port of Semarang is a strong contrast to the royal cities of Solo and Yogyakarta. Under the Dutch it became a busy trading and administrative centre and great numbers of Chinese traders joined the Muslim entrepreneurs of the north coast. Even in the depressed 1950s great wealth flowed through the city; sugar and other agricultural produce going out, industrial raw materials and finished goods coming in.

Today, Semarang is the only port open to large ships on the central coast; recently deep-water berthing facilities were completed so that ocean-going vessels no longer have to anchor out in the mouth of the Kali Baru River.

More a commercial centre than a city for tourists, Semarang's main point of interest is the famous Chinese Gedung Batu Temple. This little-visited city can also be a good starting point for trips along the north coast or south to the central mountains. It can be a pleasant place to stop over for a night or two, for it seems less crowded and more relaxed than its large size and population (just over one million) would indicate.

Information & Orientation

Semarang is split into two parts. 'Old' Semarang is on the coastal plain, sandwiched between the two Banjir Canals, while the new town has spread away to the southern hills of Candi. An important 'hub' in the old town is the Pasar Johar market on the roundabout at the top of Jalan Pemuda. In this area you'll find the main Tawang railway station, the taxi and colt stations, the main post office and the telephone office. Three main roads radiate out from the roundabout to the southern boundary of the old town – they are Jalan Pemuda, Jalan Imam Bonjol and Jalan Gajah Mada. The airport is off to the west of the city. The Gedung Batu Temple is on the western outskirts of the city across the Banjir Canal 'Barat'.

Candi is the wealthy residential area of Semarang where many of the more expensive hotels are located. From these hills there is an excellent view over the city.

Tourist Offices The Semarang City Tourist Office is in the old amusement park, Tegal Wareng, at Jalan Sriwijaya 29. It's open 8 am to 2 pm Monday to Thursday, to 11 am on Friday and until 1 pm on Saturday.

There's also a good Central Java Tourist Office at Jalan Pemuda 171.

Though information is not always on display, lots of maps and brochures on the province including a regional *Calendar of Events* are available if you ask for them. It's open the same hours as the city tourist office but closes an hour earlier from Monday to Thursday and on Saturday.

Other Information Banks along Jalan Pemuda include Bank Indonesia, Niaga and the Overseas Express Bank. The Bank Bumi Daya on Jalan Kepodang, near the Pelni Office, will change A$ and US$ travellers' cheques. Semarang's main post office is behind the Metro building on the roundabout at the top of Jalan Pemuda and the telephone office is right next door.

The immigration office is on Jalan Siliwangi in Krapyak. The Merbabu at Jalan Pandanaran 108-110, near Simpang Lima, is probably the best bookshop in Semarang for maps and books.

The best hospital in town is R S Saint Elizabeth (tel 315345) on Jalan Kawi in the Candi district. They're used to treating foreigners here and this is always the first choice of the sizeable Semarang ex-pat community.

Warning Visitors should note that Semarang seems to have a spotty power generation system! During the rainy season, there are occasional black outs and virtually every hotel, restaurant or shop has a standby supply of kerosene lamps for those moments when the entire city is plunged into darkness. The national energy department is currently establishing a new system that will link all major cities in Java and Bali and supposedly improve the situation.

Ambarawa Railway If you're interested in organising a group journey on the old cog railway from Ambarawa (40 km from Semarang), it can be arranged with the Central Java Exploitation Office (Exploitasi Jawa Tengah) (tel 24500), PJKA, Jalan Thamrin 3, Semarang.

Gedung Batu/Sam Po Kong Temple

This well-known Chinese temple stands five km south-west of the centre of town, on the west bank of the Banjir Canal 'Barat'. It was built to commemorate Admiral Cheng Ho, the famous Muslim eunuch of the Ming dynasty who led a Chinese fleet on seven expeditions to Java and other parts of South-East and West Asia in the early 15th century. Cheng Ho has since become a saint known as Sam Po Kong and is particularly revered in Melaka, Malaysia. He first arrived in Java in 1405 at a time when the Hindu influence of Majapahit was on the wane. Cheng Ho was possibly the earliest Muslim of prominence and status to have visited Java, and it's possible that Cheng Ho laid the foundation for the spread of Islam in the country. It's also possible that the Sam Po Temple began life as a mosque. An Indonesian book, the *Tuanko Rao*, recounts that the Chinese Muslim communities in Java disintegrated after the death of Cheng Ho in 1434 and the mosque was then turned into a temple to worship Sam Po and his aides. Though contrary to orthodox principles of Islam, it's interesting that the temple attendants appear to be Muslim and the temple is used by Javanese Muslims and Buddhists alike.

In shape, the temple complex resembles any other Chinese Buddhist or Taoist temple with pagoda-type curved eaves and tall red pillars; but the main hall is built around an inner chamber in the form of a huge cave flanked by two great dragons. Hence the temple's popular name *Gedung Batu* which means 'stone building'. Inside the cave is the idol of Sam Po Kong. Here worshippers seek their fortunes by diligently shaking containers of bamboo sticks until one pops out and can be exchanged for a fortune script (or *chiam-si*). The shrine is open to visitors and anyone is welcome to have their fortune told, if you can get someone to translate the Chinese script.

Other points of interest in the complex

include a smaller temple next to the main hall which houses an ancient rusty anchor from one of Cheng Ho's ships. It's said that the place where the anchor stands was actually where a ship had anchored and it has become a sacred *pusaka* which people believe to hold magical powers. There is also a picture of the famous Chinese sage, Confucius, and a plaque honouring the hundreds of unknown sailors who died during the voyages to Java. The anchor chains can be seen hanging in the trees in front of the temple.

To get to Gedung Batu, you can take a Daihatsu from the city's terminal Baru to Karang Ayu and another from there to the temple.

Around Town

Semarang has just enough relics of bygone days to make the old town quite an interesting place to wander round. Behind the Poncol railway station on Jalan Imam Bonjol there is the ruin of an old Dutch East India Company fort while around the Tawang railway station there are numerous bulky Dutch warehouses. Just south of Tawang, on Jalan Let Jenderal Suprapto, is the Gereja Blenduk Church which was built by the Dutch in 1753 and is still functioning. It has a huge copper-clad dome and inside there is a baroque organ which is now little more than a facade as a modern organ was installed some years ago.

For a complete change you could then plunge into the narrow streets of Semarang's old Chinatown, to the south of this Christian Church, and seek out the brightly painted Tay Kak Sie Temple. This Chinese temple complex dates from 1772 and is on Gang Lombok, a small alley off Jalan Pekojan.

Around the Simpang Lima square there are more modern buildings including the large two-storey Mesjid Baiturrakhman mosque. The Tuga Muda, at the southern end of Jalan Pemuda, is a candle-shaped monument commemorating Semarang's

five-day battle against the Japanese in October 1945. Nearby is an impressive European-style building, formerly Dutch offices and later headquarters of the Japanese forces, known to the Javanese as Lawang Sewu – '1000 doors'.

Other Attractions

Semarang is known for its two large *jamu* manufacturers – Jamu Jago and Jamu Nyonya Meneer. By phoning Budi Satyo on 285533 you can visit the Jamu Jago factory on Jalan Setia Budi where herbal medicines are made. You come across their jamus all over Java – their adverts use a squad of dwarves! Jamu Nyonya Meneer (tel 285732) has a jamu museum that's open Monday to Friday from 10 am to 3.30 pm. It's at their factory at Jalan Raya Kaligawe Km 4 (about 45 minutes away on a Kudus-bound bus). They will also give tours of their factory upon request. One traveller reported trying a Jamu Sekhot which 'according to the packet increases health and vitality in men, curing impotence and bringing you to a happy family' but 'unfortunately', he went on to say, 'it didn't help and tasted like shit'!

Every evening there are wayang orang performances at the long-established *Ngesti Pandowo Theatre* at Jalan Pemuda 116. Performances start at 7 pm and tickets cost from 500 to 1000 rp for the best seats. *Radio Republik Indonesia* on Jalan A Yani puts on wayang kulit shows at least once a month.

The Semarang harbour is worth a look to see the pinisi and other traditional ocean-going vessels, but no photography is allowed. Or you could take a city bus out to Candi and have a drink at the Sky Garden Hotel or the even higher Gombel Indah Restaurant. From here you have a fine view over the city and the hazy silhouettes of huge merchant ships can be seen anchored out at sea. To get there take a city bus down Jalan Pemuda bound for Jatingaleh and ask for Gombel Hill, which is just past the Sky Garden.

Festivals Semarang's *Dugderan* Festival marks the beginning of the Muslim fasting month. Its highlight is the great bazaar in front of the city's Grand Mosque in the Pasar Johar area and at Pasar Ya'ik where street vendors gather for several days and nights and a special talisman in the form of a rhinoceros with a duck's egg on its back is sold. The festival's name is taken from the sound of the big mosque drum being beaten combined with the der-r-r of firecrackers. It ends when the drum is beaten to announce the start of the fast, next dawn.

The *Jaran Sam Po* in July is one of the biggest annual Chinese ceremonies in Java during which a colourful procession, including brightly decorated horses and a 'Liong' Chinese dragon, makes its way from the Tay Kak Sie Temple to Gedung Batu. Nowadays the Chinese are forbidden to do the entire route on foot, so trucks and cars are used until the last 50 metres or so to Gedung Batu.

Throughout the month of August, the *Semarang Fair* is held on Jalan Sriwijaya near the old zoo every evening after 5 pm. Exhibits from around Central Java, food stalls and various forms of entertainment are featured.

Places to Stay – bottom end

The losmen in Semarang don't have a great reputation – many say they're 'full' to avoid taking in foreigners and, when you can get a room, conditions are not the best. Most places are in the centre of town near Pasar Johar and the old bus terminal, now a shopping centre. The *Losmen Jaya* at Jalan M T Haryono 85-87 has adequate rooms with fan from 4775 rp including breakfast, to 7500 rp with mandi. The *Losmen Agung*, in the same area at Jalan Petolongan 32-34, is a colonial relic with doubles at 3500 rp. It's had mixed reports – some think that the reasonably clean rooms are good value, but one traveller has written that it is 'appalling, rat-infested, dirty and noisy'!?

A slightly better losmen in this area is the *Djelita* at Jalan M T Haryono 34-38 with fairly clean economy singles for 3500 rp as well as more expensive rooms with bath and fan.

Other cheap hotels are scattered along or just off Jalan Imam Bonjol. This road is very busy with traffic so try and get a room away from the street if you stay here. Ten minutes or so walk from the Tawang railway station (300 rp by becak), there's the *Losmen Singapore* at Jalan Imam Bonjol 12. It has good singles/doubles at 4000/6000 rp including breakfast. The *Hotel Oewa-Asia* (tel 22547), near the Singapore at Jalan Kol Sugiono 12, spans the lower to middle bracket. This is an old colonial hotel so you can expect creaky floors and antiquated plumbing but it's comfortable and reasonably well maintained. Simple, clean rooms cost 6500 rp including breakfast. Rooms with fan and mandi start at 8000 rp and there are also air-con rooms in a modern extension for 14,000 rp. It's in a good central location, near Pasar Johar and the post office, and the friendly staff do their utmost to please.

Further down near the Poncol railway station, the *Losmen Ardjuna* at No 51 is fairly comfortable and friendly; rooms at 5000 rp include breakfast. *Losmen Rahayu* (tel 22532) at No 35 has rooms with fan at 6000 rp including breakfast. Rooms with mandi cost 8000 rp and there are some air-con rooms for 22,000 rp.

Much further out on Imam Bonjol at No 144 is the *Bali* (tel 21974) which has clean if somewhat overpriced rooms starting at 12,000 rp with an exhaust fan and air-con rooms for about twice that. Becak drivers may want to steer you to the Bali so they can claim an outrageous fare. Better value is *Green Guest House* (tel 312787) at Jalan Kesambi 7 in the pleasant Candi district. Clean air-con singles/doubles are 13,500/20,000 rp including breakfast. This is a favourite temporary quarters for ex-pats moving in or out of Semarang.

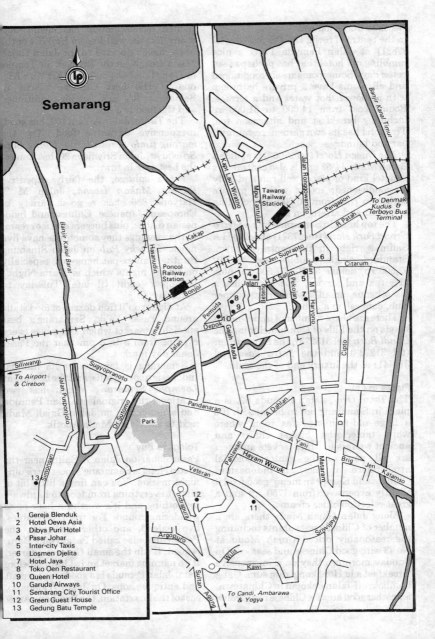

Semarang

Tawang Railway Station

To Demak
Kudus &
Terboyo Bus
Terminal

Poncol
Railway
Station

Park

To Airport
& Cirebon

To Candi, Ambarawa
& Yogya

1 Gereja Blenduk
2 Hotel Oewa Asia
3 Dibya Puri Hotel
4 Pasar Johar
5 Inter-city Taxis
6 Losmen Djelita
7 Hotel Jaya
8 Toko Oen Restaurant
9 Queen Hotel
10 Garuda Airways
11 Semarang City Tourist Office
12 Green Guest House
13 Gedung Batu Temple

Places to Stay – top end

In the centre of town, the *Dibya Puri* (tel 27821) at Jalan Pemuda 11 is a nice rambling old hotel that has perhaps seen better days. Some rooms are air-conditioned and all rooms have a private bathroom with a shower, hot water and a terrace. Rooms cost from 14,000 to 51,000 rp including breakfast and afternoon tea. The hotel has its own garden, restaurant, bar and laundry service.

The *Queen Hotel* (tel 27063) is at Jalan Gajah Mada 44-52 and is also central. It's a motel kind of place, well run and fully air-conditioned; rooms with a private bathroom cost from 20,000 rp including breakfast and afternoon tea.

The top hotel in Semarang is the *Metro Grand Park Hotel* (tel 27371) at Jalan H A Salim 2, right in the centre of town. Standard singles/doubles are 45,000/52,500 rp, deluxe 52,500/57,500 rp, plus 21% tax and service. The Metro has a discotheque, small supermarket, supper club, coffeeshop and bar.

There are also a number of upper-notch hotels on the hills of Candi including the *Candi Baru* (tel 315272), the *Sky Garden* (tel 312733) and the *Patra Jasa* (tel 314441) at the luxury end of the scale.

Places to Eat

The *Toko 'Oen'*, Jalan Pemuda 52, is a place in Semarang not to be missed. It's a large old-fashioned tea room where white tablecloths, basket chairs and ancient waiters in white jackets and *peci* are all part of the genteel colonial atmosphere. It has an Indonesian, Chinese and European menu, good food if slightly expensive (from 1750 rp) and a great selection of ice creams.

Along Jalan Gajah Mada there are a number of Chinese restaurants including the reasonably priced *Gajah Mada* at No 43 with good Chinese and seafood. On Sunday mornings they do a inexpensive 'breakfast a la Hongkong' dim sum. Gang Lombok, off Jalan Pekojan in Chinatown, is another good area for Chinese restaurants though reconstruction has meant that many, like the well-known *Hap Kie* or the *Soen*, have relocated to the Jalan Gajah Mada area. Near the Tay Kak Sie Temple on Gang Lombok you'll find *Kit Wan Kie*, one of the best Chinese places in Semarang; it's ugly but air-conditioned and the food is good.

The *Timlo*, Jalan A Yani 182, has good, inexpensive Javanese food. Try the *lontong timlo* or *nasi timlo*. *Istana Sate Sriwijaya*, Jalan Sriwijaya 20, has some of the best sate in town.

For a splurge, the fairly expensive *Rumah Makan Istana*, Jalan M T Haryono 836, has a good variety of European, Japanese, Chinese and Indonesian dishes, plus burgers and ice cream. In the evenings they sometimes have live music. *Ritzeky Pub* on Jalan Sinabung Buntu, is an ex-pat hang-out, especially on Friday nights which is 'Darts Night'. It's open 'eight til late' Tuesday to Saturday.

At night you'll find dozens of food stalls around Pasar Ya'ik, Semarang's best speciality market which assembles every evening from 5 to 8 pm near the Pasar Johar day market.

Semarang is famous for its lumpia, Indonesian spring rolls, and the best are at *Loempia Semarang* which has two locations, the original on Jalan Pemuda and a newer one on Jalan Gajah Mada next to the Gajah Mada Apotik.

Things to Buy

Pasar Johar on Jalan A Salim near the Metro Hotel is Semarang's most intriguing night market. You can find a little bit of almost everything from food to hardware to clothing and it's worth an hour or so wandering round. For fresh vegetables, live seafood, and other foodstuffs, the Pasar Cina, also called Pasar Gang Baru, is good. It's in the small Chinese quarter. It's a morning market and at its best before 7 am. Jalan Pemuda is a good area for craft and antique shops. On Jalan Widoharjo, east of the bus station, the Pandjang Art &

Gift Shop has a good display of Javanese crafts including silver, Jepara wood carvings and wayang puppets.

Getting There & Away

Air Garuda (tel 20178) is at Jalan Gajah Mada 11. It's open from 8 am to 4 pm Monday to Friday, 8 am to 1 pm Saturday and 9 am to 12 noon Sunday. Garuda has direct flights between Semarang and Jakarta (55,500 rp, seven flights daily), Surabaya (33,400 rp, two daily), Denpasar (74,100 rp, two daily), as well as two daily connecting flights to Pontianak and Ujung Pandang.

Merpati (tel 23027) at Jalan Gajah Mada 58B is open 8 am to 2 pm Monday to Thursday, to 11 am Friday, to 2 pm Saturday, closed Sundays. Their daily flights to Jakarta are 45,000 rp; to Bandung 47,600 rp, Pangakalan Bun 65,100 and Ketapang 91,400.

Bouraq (tel 23065) at Jalan Gajah Mada 61A is open daily 8 am to 4 pm. They have daily direct flights from Semarang to Jakarta (45,000 rp) and Banjarmasin (81,700 rp).

Mandala (tel 285319) at Jalan Pemuda 40 is open daily 8 am to 4 pm with daily direct flights to Jakarta (45,000 rp).

Both Merpati and Mandala provide free transport between Semarang and the airport.

Bus Semarang's Terboyo bus station is located a bit far from the city centre on Jalan Kaligawe, on the way to Kudus and Surabaya. It's a large bustling station, but fairly well organised. Most ticket-agent offices for night and express buses are here, but for express minibuses go to the old bus terminal area, on the corner of Jalan H A Salim and Jalan M T Haryono near Pasar Johar.

Going South There are frequent services to Yogya for 1300 rp public bus (3½ hours) or 2750 rp express minibus, and Solo 1100 rp (2½ hours) or 1500 rp air-con Patas (express) bus. Buses to Wonosobo for Dieng leave early in the morning and cost 1400 rp (four hours).

Going East Kudus, via Demak, costs 500 rp (one hour). Night buses to Surabaya start at 7000 rp (4300 rp public bus) and take eight hours.

Going West Pekalongan 1100 rp (four hours) and Cirebon 2500 rp (six hours). Taxi 4848 express minibuses between Cirebon and Semarang are 7500 rp; there are three per day from Rajawali Express (tel 288812), Jalan Dr Cipto 96 in Semarang. Fares to Jakarta start at 5500 rp by public bus or around 12,000 rp by private express bus, but it's a long nine-hour haul and buses arrive at ungodly hours at the remote Pulo Gadung station. You're better off taking the train.

Rail Semarang is on the main Jakarta-Cirebon-Surabaya train route and there are frequent services operating to and from these cities. Tawang is the main railway station in Semarang.

Trains between Jakarta and Semarang take about seven hours and cost from 4000 rp on the all-3rd-class *Cepat* to 22,000 rp on the all-1st-class *Mutiara Utara*. Third class fares are 2300 rp on the *Cepat* between Semarang and Cirebon, and 4200 rp on the *GBM Utara* between Semarang and Surabaya. Oddly enough, fares on the Semarang-Cirebon and Semarang-Surabaya legs of the *Mutiara Utara* are exactly the same as from Jakarta to Semarang – 22,000 rp. However, Jakarta to Surabaya with a stopover in Semarang is only 25,000 rp 1st class.

Trains between Semarang and Pekalongan take four hours (same as the bus) and cost only 900 rp 3rd class.

Boat The Pelni Office (tel 20488) is at Jalan Tantular 25 near the Tawang railway station. It's open 8 am to 4 pm Monday to Friday and to 1 pm Saturday. Jakarta and Surabaya are the usual ports for catching ships to the outer islands but there is one biweekly passenger ship, Pelni's *KM Kelimutu*, that originates in

Semarang and sails to Banjarmasin, Padang Bai, Lembar, Ujung Pandang, Bima, Waingapu, Ende and Kupang. There are also occasional cargo boats from Semarang to Banjarmasin which take passengers for around 20,000 rp – enquire in the harbour area.

Getting Around
Airport Transport Ahmad Yani airport is eight km to the west of town and 4000 rp by taxi. Transport can easily be arranged through the Dibya Puri and Metro Hotels or by calling Taxi 515 (tel 312515) or Indra Kelana Taxi (tel 22590).

Becak, Taxi, Bus Semarang has becaks, taxis and a big city bus service, supplemented by orange Daihatsu minivans. City buses charge a fixed 150 rp fare and depart from the main Terboyo bus station. The most useful service is the bus that runs south along Jalan Pemuda to Jalan Dr Sutomo and Jalan Sultan Agung to Candi. Daihatsus are 125 rp and start out from Terminal Baru – on Jalan H A Salim, behind the Pasar Johar – and operate to Karangayu, Tegal Wareng and Candi.

A becak from Tawang railway station or the bus station to the Oewa Asia Hotel will cost about 300 rp. You shouldn't pay more than 500 rp for any becak ride in town, though the drivers here will ask much more, especially at night. Becaks aren't allowed along Jalan Pemuda or Jalan Gajah Mada.

There are a limited number of taxis around town, mostly used by guests of large hotels like the Metro. They are unmetered so bargaining is usually required.

AROUND SEMARANG
The north-east of Central Java is a region of people noted for their extreme orthodoxy. During the 15th and 16th centuries this was the home of nine shrewd, capable Muslims who have been immortalised as the *Wali Songo* or 'Nine Saints' to whom the establishment of Islam in Java is credited. With the exception of Suan Gunungjati in Cirebon, the tombs of the *walis* all lie between Semarang and Surabaya and are important pilgrimage points for devout Muslims. A number of these places lie on the road to Surabaya and can also be visited using Semarang as a base.

Kudus lies roughly on the border of land which is the product of gradual soil erosion and is known as the Mt Muria Peninsula – at the beginning of the colonial era it was an island. In this region there are many houses of purely local design, often with interesting scroll-shaped decorations along the roof tops.

Demak
Twenty five km east of Semarang on the road to Surabaya, Demak was once the capital of the first Islamic state on Java and the most important state during the early 16th century. At the time this was a good seaport but silting of the coast has now left Demak several km inland. Ancient Javanese chronicles traditionally picture Demak as Majapahit's direct successor and even suggest that Raden Patah, the first 'Sultan' of Demak and the Muslim hero who defeated the Majapahit empire, was of Chinese origin. Named Jin Bun, he may have been the son of Majapahit's last king by a Chinese princess, Putri Cina, who had been sent away from court before her son was born. In 1474 Jin Bun is supposed to have visited Cheng Ho's mosque in Semarang only to find that it had been converted into a temple for idol worship. Three years later he led a 1000-strong Islamic army against the Hindu Majapahits and vowed that, if his revolt was successful, he would make the non-Muslim Chinese conform to Islamic rule in Demak.

The Mesjid Agung mosque dominates the village of Demak and is one of Indonesia's most important places of pilgrimage for Muslims. It's so holy that seven pilgrimages to it are said to be the equivalent of a pilgrimage to Mecca. It is the earliest mosque known on Java, founded jointly by the 'wali songo' in 1478, and it combines Javanese-Hindu and Islamic elements in its architecture. Constructed entirely of wood it has four main pillars, called the *soko guru*, in the central hall which are said to have been made by four of the saints – one of them, erected by Sunan Kalijagga, is made of chips of wood glued together. This early mosque has been deteriorating over the centuries but it's still much in use and is now being restored.

The mausoleum of Sunan Kalijagga is at Kadilangu, two km south of Demak.

PEKALONGAN
On the road and rail route between Semarang (100 km away) and Cirebon, Pekalongan is another major centre for batik and is often called 'Kota Batik' or Batik City. It's a small town which few travellers visit so it's surprising how rapidly street peddlers descend upon you, casually waving batik from the doorways of hotels and restaurants. There are also a number of shops along Jalan Hayam Wuruk in the centre of town. B L Pekalongan, perhaps the best shop and the most expensive, is at Jalan Mansyur 87. Others include the Kencana Souvenir Shop at Gang Podosugih I No 3, Jalan Mansyur.

There are batiks in Pekalongan which you won't easily find elsewhere in Java and if you're really interested you can visit the batik village of Kedungwuni, nine km south of town. At Oey Soe Tjoen's small workshop here intricate and colourful batik tulis is still produced. You can see it being made every day of the week except Fridays.

Pekalongan also has a Batik Museum, near the fruit market on Jalan Pasar Ratu. It's open from 9 am to 1.30 pm and closed on Sundays.

In late August or early September, on Kliwon Friday of the Javanese calendar, Sedekah Laut is celebrated at Wonokerto Kulon on the coast. Miniature boats laden with offerings of buffalo heads, flowers, cookies and farm implements are floated into the sea. There are also cultural performances and boat-racing.

Places to Stay
There are three budget losmen directly opposite the train station on Jalan Gajah Mada. The best of these is probably the *Hotel Gajah Mada* (tel 41185) at No 11A which has basic but clean rooms at 4500 rp or 6000 rp with mandi. The *Losmen Ramayana*, behind the Ramayana 'Billyard Room' at Jalan Gajah Mada 9 and *Losmen Damai* at No 7 are similarly priced.

The *Hotel Istana* (tel 61581) is near the train station at Jalan Gajah Mada 23. Singles/doubles with fan cost from 12,000/13,000 rp and there are more expensive rooms with air-con. Rates include breakfast and they have a swimming pool. In the centre of town, the *Hotel Hayam Wuruk* (tel 41823) at Jalan Hayam Wuruk 152-158 has a variety of rooms ranging in price from 8000 rp to 17,500 rp for singles; and from 10,500 rp to around 20,000 rp for doubles including breakfast. The *Nirwana Hotel* (tel 41691), Jalan Dr Wahidin 11, is similar in price to the Istana and also has a pool; deluxe air-con singles/doubles are 35,0000/42,000 rp including breakfast and afternoon tea.

Places to Eat
Rumah Makan Saiyo, near the train station, has reasonable Padang food. The *Buana Restaurant*, at Jalan Mansyur 5, is a moderately priced seafood restaurant. In town, the *Purima* on Jalan Hayam Wuruk has unusual decor – mirrors, pink doilies and plastic greenery – loud music, a cheap restaurant, bakery and good ice-cream sodas. At the *Pekalongan Remaja*, Jalan Dr Cipto 20, good and reasonably cheap Chinese food is available. The *Es Teler 77* at No 66 has a good selection of cold ice juices and a cool shady garden. There are good mangoes and

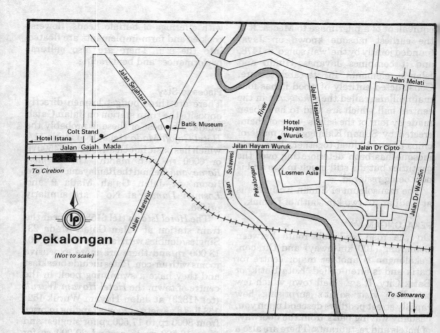

Pekalongan
(Not to scale)

avocados at the Pasar Ratu and plenty of food stalls in this area at night.

Getting There & Away

Pekalongan is on the main Jakarta-Semarang-Surabaya road and rail route. There is also a road linking Pekalongan and the Dieng Plateau.

Pekalongan's bus station is a fair distance east from the centre of town, 150 rp by colt or 400 rp by becak. If you're arriving by bus from Cirebon you can get dropped off on the way through town. Similarly, you can catch a bus to Semarang or Cirebon from outside the Hotel Gajah Mada. From Cirebon to Pekalongan takes about four hours and costs 1600 rp. The bus from Semarang takes about two hours and costs 1100 rp.

Getting Around

Colts to villages around Pekalongan depart from the stand behind the

Pertamina petrol station on Jalan Hayam Wuruk near the train station.

TEGAL

Halfway between Pekalongan and Cirebon, this north coast town is a centre for ochreware pottery. The best place to buy pottery and local handicrafts is at roadside stalls about 10 km south of Tegal.

KUDUS

Founded by the Muslim saint, Sunan Kudus, this was something of an Islamic holy city and like Demak it is still an important place of pilgrimage. Its name comes from the Arabic al-Quds which means holy and it is the only place in Java which permanently acquired an Arabic name. The people of Kudus are noted for their extreme orthodoxy and the old part of the town is strongly Muslim in feeling. Yet, strangely, some old Hindu customs prevail and there is still a tradition that cows may not be slaughtered within the town. History and religion aside, Kudus is a prosperous town and a major centre of Java's kretek cigarette industry.

Old Town

West of the river on the road to Jepara, Kauman, the oldest part of town, can be an interesting place to wander around. Its streets are narrow and winding, stark white and almost Middle Eastern in atmosphere, crowded with little boys in sarong and topi and women in full orthodox Muslim dress. Some of the buildings are colourful 'adat' (traditional) houses with ornately carved wooden fronts.

In the centre of the old town, the Al-Manar (or Al-Aqsa) Mosque was constructed in 1549 by Sunan Kudus. The mosque is notable for its name which is like the mosque of Jerusalem and, like so many of Java's early mosques, it displays elements of Islamic and Hindu-Javanese design such as the Old Javanese carved split doorways. In fact it was probably built on the site of a Hindu-Javanese temple and is particularly famous for its tall red-brick minaret or *Kudus Menara* which may have originally been the watchtower of that temple. Leaving your shoes at the bottom, you can climb up the wooden ladder inside the tower and from the top there is a fine view over the town.

In the courtyards behind the mosque is the imposing tomb of Sunan Kudus which is now a shrine. His mausoleum of finely carved stone is hung with a curtain of lace. The narrow doorway, draped with heavy gold-embroidered curtains, leads through to an inner chamber and the grave.

Kretek Factories

One of those distinctive 'aromas' of Indonesia is the sweet spicy smell, almost like incense, of clove-flavoured cigarettes. The kretek was invented in Kudus by a man who claimed they relieved his asthma. Today the addiction to kretek is almost nationwide. So high is the consumption of cloves for smoking that Indonesia, traditionally a supplier of cloves in world markets, has become a substantial net importer from centres like Zanzibar and Madagascar.

In Kudus more than 100 businesses account for roughly a quarter of Indonesia's annual production of kretek cigarettes. Although in the last few years modern tools and methods have been brought to various economic enterprises, there has been official protection of labour-intensive techniques in the kretek industry. Huge numbers of people are employed. They are mostly young women engaged in hand-rolling cigarettes on simple wooden forms, and the process is quite an interesting one to see. The most convenient business to visit is the Chinese-owned Djarum company which started in 1952 and is now the biggest producer in Kudus. Their head office is a rather incongruous modern block on Jalan A Yani. Factory tours are free.

...1000 women were employed in one large room, full of the clacking noise of the wooden rolling machines. The women work in pairs with one rolling the cigarettes and the other snipping ends. They work an eight to 10-hour day: one roller gets 350 rp per 1000 cigarettes; 500 rp per 1000 after the first batch of 3000 cigarettes. Maximum production was cited as 6000 to 8000 cigarettes. The tobacco is locally grown but the cloves come all the way from Madagascar.

Places to Stay

The *Hotel Notasari* (tel 21245), Jalan Kepodang 12, is within reasonable walking distance of the bus station. Comfortable rooms with mandi start at 12,000 rp including breakfast (coffee, bread & eggs or nasi goreng); air-con rooms start at double that price. It's well kept, there's a quiet courtyard and restaurant and the staff are friendly.

The central *Losmen Slamet*, Jalan Jenderal Sudirman 63, has spartan rooms at 6850 rp. It's just OK – some rooms are better than others. The *Hotel Duta*

Wisata (tel 22694) is at Jalan Barongan 194, to the north of town. It's a bit out of the way but it's a nice place, in a quiet residential area, with rooms from 8600 rp including breakfast (coffee, bread & eggs). A becak from this area into the centre of town costs about 400 rp.

Places to Eat

Local specialities to try include *soto Kudus*, chicken soup, and *jenang Kudus*, which is a sweet made of glutinous rice, brown sugar and coconut. The *Rumah Makan Hijau*, near the bus station at Jalan A Yani 1, is cheap and good for Indonesian food and super-cool fruit juices. It's closed on Fridays. There are also night food stalls at the Pasar Bitingan near the bus station.

The *Hotel Notasari* restaurant is reasonably priced for the big helpings you get. The *Garuda* at Jalan Jenderal Sudirman 1 has Indonesian, Chinese and western food.

Getting There & Away

Kudus is on the main Semarang-Surabaya road. From Semarang to Kudus is 55 km, a one-hour bus trip costing 500 rp. Surabaya is 286 km away. Kembang Express (tel 282) at Jalan A Yani 90 has night express buses to Surabaya and Jakarta. Public buses to Solo cost 1800 rp and the trip takes two hours.

Colts to villages around Kudus depart from the bus station and include Jepara 400 rp, Rembang 500 rp and Mantingan 700 rp.

AROUND KUDUS
Mayong

Raden Ajeng Kartini (1879-1904) was born in Mayong, 12 km north-west of Kudus on the road to Jepara. She was the daughter of the Regent of Jepara and was allowed, against Indonesian custom, to attend the Dutch school in Jepara along with her brothers. As a result of her education, Kartini questioned both the burden of

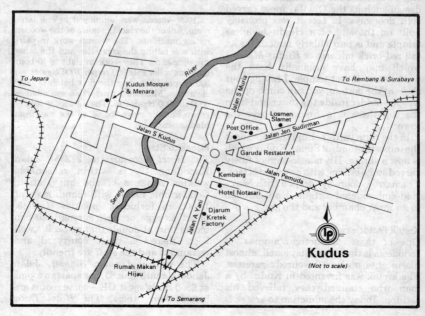

Kudus
(Not to scale)

To Jepara
To Rembang & Surabaya
To Semarang
River
Serang
Kudus Mosque & Menara
Jalan S Muria
Jalan S Kudus
Post Office
Losmen Slamet
Jalan Jen Sudirman
Garuda Restaurant
Kembang
Jalan Pemuda
Hotel Notasari
Jalan A Yani
Djarum Kretek Factory
Rumah Makan Hijau

Javanese etiquette and the polygamy permitted under Islamic law. In letters to Dutch friends she criticised colonial behaviour and vocalised an 'ever growing longing for freedom and independence, a longing to stand alone'.

Kartini married the Regent of Remban, himself a supporter of progressive social policies, and they opened a school in Remang for the daughters of regents. In 1904 Kartini died shortly after the birth of her son. Perhaps the first modern Indonesian writer, Kartini's letters were published in the original Dutch in 1911, entitled *Through Darkness to Light*; the English edition is available in a Norton paperback.

At Mayong there is a monument to Kartini. Jepara and Rembang are other important points where ceremonies are held on 21 April to celebrate Kartini Day.

Jepara

Jepara, only 35 km north-west of Kudus, is famed as the centre for the best traditional woodcarvers in Java. Intricately carved wooden chests, tables, wall panels, jewellery boxes, picture frames and the like are most often carved from teak. They usually follow a similar pattern to the ornate floral designs of batik although wall panels often depict scenes from Javanese legends. Fine chess sets are sometimes carved out of ebony. The road into Jepara passes workshops stacked high with furniture so you get a fair idea of places to visit as you arrive. Tirto Samodro, eight km from town, is a white-sand beach.

Jepara is a small, peaceful country town but it has had a colourful history. An important port in the 16th century, it had both English and Dutch factories by the early 1600s and was involved in a violent dispute between the VOC and Sultan Agung of Mataram. After Dutchmen reputedly compared Agung to a dog and relieved themselves on Jepara's mosque, hostilities finally erupted in 1618 when the Gujarati who governed Jepara for

Agung attacked the VOC trading post. The Dutch retaliated by burning Javanese ships and much of the town, and in 1619 Jan Pieterszoon Coen paused on his way to the conquest of Batavia to burn Jepara yet again and with it the English East India Company's post. The VOC headquarters for the central north coast were then established at Jepara.

Places to Stay The *Meno Jaya Inn* (tel 143) at Jalan Diponegoro 40B has rooms from 3500 rp to 9950 rp. It's friendly and the owner, Mr Teopilus Hadiprasetya, speaks good English. He runs a wood-carving shop at the front of the losmen and without a doubt he'll proudly show you the thank you letter from Prince Charles and Lady Di for a carved plaque he sent them as a wedding present!

Other places include the *Hotel Terminal* right by the bus station where rooms with fan cost from 3500 rp, with air-con 15,000 rp. The *Losmen Asia* at Jalan Kartini 32 has rooms for 3650 rp.

Rembang

There is a good beach for swimming (Pantai Kartini) at Rembang, a small fishing town 59 km east of Kudus. In the Rembang Regency Office building is the Kartini Museum.

Mantingan

The memorial tomb of Kartini stands in the grounds of the old mosque at Mantingan, 20 km south of Rembang on the road to Blora and 8 km from Jepara. The tomb of Ratu Kalinyamat is also located here. She was the great warrior-queen of Jepara who twice laid siege to Portugal's Melaka stronghold in the latter part of the 16th century. Neither campaign was successful but she scared the Portuguese witless. The mosque was restored some years ago and the tomb has some interesting Hindu-style embellishments, particularly medallions.

East Java

The province of East Java, or Jawa Timur, officially includes the island of Madura off the north-west coast. With that island it has a total population of 29.2 million and an area of 47,922 square km. The majority of its population are Javanese, but many Madurese farmers and fishermen live in East Java. They are familiar faces, particularly around Surabaya, the capital of the province. In the Bromo area there is a small population of Hindu Tenggerese.

Geographically much of the province is flatter than the rest of Java. In the north-west is lowland with deltas along the rivers Brantas and Bengawan Solo, and km upon km of rice-growing plain. But the rest of East Java is mountainous and hilly, containing the huge Tengger massif and even Java's highest mountain. This region offers a raw, natural beauty and some magnificent scenery.

Major attractions for the visitor include the magnificent Mt Bromo, still one of Java's most active volcanoes. Then there's a host of other mountains, pleasant walks and fine hill towns like Malang. In the north-east corner of the province there is also the important Baluran National Park, the most accessible of Java's wildlife reserves. Finally, although East Java is closely related culturally to Central Java, the Madurese are best known for their rugged sport called *kerapan sapi*, the famous bull races which take place on the island during August and September.

East Java's hazy past comes into focus with its political and cultural ascendancy in the 10th century AD, and the reign of Airlangga. Before claiming the throne in 1019 AD he had spent many years as a hermit, devoting time to accumulating wisdom through fasting and meditation. Significantly, it was during his reign that the ancient Hindu poem of Arjuna's temptation, the *Arjuna Wiwaha*, was first translated into Old Javanese and it is still one of the most popular of the wayang stories. Under Airlangga's government, eastern Java became united and powerful but shortly before his death he divided his kingdom between his two sons. There was Janggala to the east of the River Brantas and Kediri to the west, and a third kingdom – Singosari – joined in the struggle for the ascendancy.

In 1049 the Kediri dynasty rose to power and continued its rule through to 1222. Kediri is best remembered today for the famous prophecy attributed to its soothsayer King Joyoboyo. He made the prediction that the 'white buffalo' (the Dutch) would come to rule Java until supplanted by the 'yellow chicken' (the Japanese) who would remain for only the lifetime of the maize plant after which the *Ratu Adil*, the Just Prince, would take power and usher in a golden age. This prophecy was revived during the Japanese occupation of the Dutch East Indies in WW II and sustained Indonesian hopes during the hard years that followed.

In 1222 the Singosari kingdom came to power and gradually superseded Kediri under the leadership of the usurper Ken Angrok. He was a violent man who took the throne by murdering the former ruler of Singosari and then marrying his wife. Legend relates that Ken Angrok first tried out his murder weapon on its maker who then cursed it with his dying breath, predicting that seven kings should die by the sword. The curse was fulfilled – the rule of Singosari lasted a mere 70 years, but under its kings the Javanese culture nevertheless flourished. East Java inherited some of its most striking temples from that era and the Singosaris also pioneered a new sculptural style that owed little or nothing to original Indian traditions. Shaivism and Buddhism also evolved into a new religion called Shiva-Buddhism and even today there are many followers in Java and Bali.

Kertanegara (1262-92) was the last of the Singosari kings and a skilful diplomat who sought alliance with other Indonesian rulers in the face of the threat from another great power. In 1292 the Mongol ruler, Kublai Khan, demanded that homage be paid to China. Kertanegara, however, foolishly humiliated the Great Khan by having the nose and ears of the Mongol envoy cut off and sent back to China. This effrontery precipitated the launching of a Mongol invasion of Java but by the time they arrived Kertanegara had already been killed in a civil war. The new king, Wijaya, defeated the Mongols but the barbaric invasion left such a bitter taste that for nearly a hundred years relations between China and Java were at a standstill.

Wijaya was also the founder of the Majapahit empire, the most famous of the early Javanese kingdoms. With a capital at Trowulan the Majapahits ruled from 1294 to 1478 and during the reign of Hayam Wuruk carried their power overseas with raids into Bali and an expedition against Palembang in Sumatra. Majapahit also claimed trading relations with Cambodia, Siam, Burma and Vietnam, and sent missions to China. Hayam Wuruk died in 1389 and the Majapahit empire rapidly disintegrated. By the end of the 15th century, Islamic power was growing on the north coast and less than a century later there were raids into East Java by Muslims carrying both the Koran and the sword. Many Hindu-Buddhists fled eastwards to Bali, but in the mountain ranges around Mt Bromo the Tenggerese people trace their history back to Majapahit and still practise their own religion – a variety of Hinduism that includes many proto-Javanese elements. During the 17th century the region finally fell to the rulers of Mataram in Central Java.

Today Surabaya, the provincial capital and second largest city in Indonesia, is a vital centre for trade and manufacturing but East Java is still a region of agriculture and small villages. In marked contrast to the practically-always-wet western end of Java, East Java has a monsoonal climate and a real dry season from April to November.

Temples

Although East Java does not have any monuments that approach the awe-inspiring scale of Borobudur and Prambanan, it does have several small but interesting ones. Around Malang there are several Singosari temples and near Blitar there is the large Panataran complex. All these temples exhibit a strikingly different sculptural style in which figures were exuberantly carved in a two-dimensional wayang kulit form. At Trowulan there are ruins from the great Majapahit empire. Overall, the innovative East Javan temple style is an obvious prototype for later Balinese sculpture/architecture.

The decorative imagination of the East Javanese sculptors also found expression in richly ornamented items cast in bronze and more costly metals. A great variety of ritual objects, weapons and other utensils have been preserved and many can be seen in Jakarta's National Museum.

MALANG

Malang is one of Java's finest and most attractive hill towns. On the banks of the River Brantas, it was established by the Dutch around the end of the 18th century when coffee was first grown as a colonial cash crop in this area. In more recent years, local farmers have been growing tobacco; cigarette factories and the army have set themselves up here. It's a cool, clean place with a well planned square and the central area of town is studded with parks, tree-lined streets and old Dutch architecture.

The main attractions for travellers are the Singosari temples a few km north-east of Malang but the city, apart from being a good base for many points of interest in East Java, is also worth a day or two's visit for its own sake. Unlike many Javanese towns which are planned on a grid

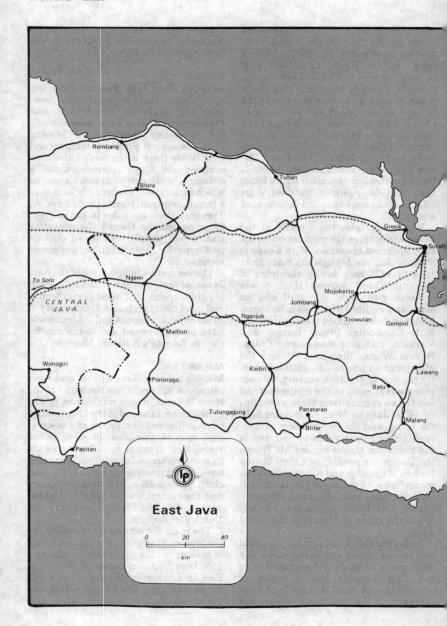

East Java

0   20   40

km

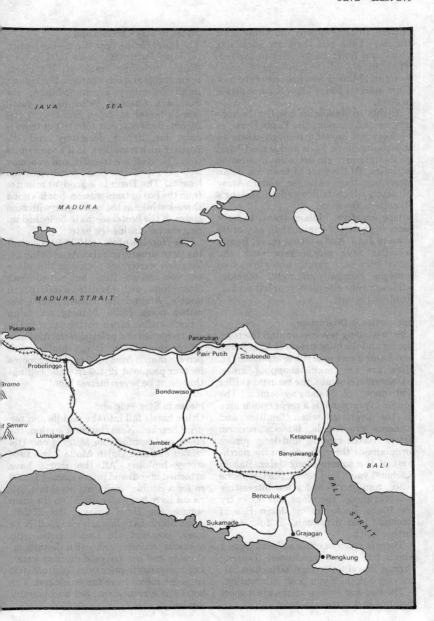

pattern, this one sweeps and winds along the river bank and there are surprising views and quiet backwaters to explore. The living is good, the atmosphere is easy-going and Malang also has one of the best night markets you're likely to come across in Java.

'Sights' in Malang are few, but the huge new central market, the Pasar Besar, is always worth browsing through – there's a superb jumble of foods and second-hand goods and you might find some interesting antiques. To the west of town, on Jalan Besar Ijen, there's also the modern Army Museum which is devoted to Malang's Brawijaya Division.

One negative: Malang seems to have more beggars per capita than any other town in Java. And a recent report from a traveller says pickpockets work the crowd-trick here: a group closes in on you, someone bumps your right, shoulder while someone else picks your left pocket. Strollers beware!

Information & Orientation

Life in Malang revolves around the town square and the busy streets of Agus Salim and Pasar Besar near the central market. Here are the main shopping areas, restaurants, cinemas, the main post office and many of Malang's losmen. The square in particular is a very popular area in the evenings when families and students promenade, buskers perform before riveted crowds, and long queues form outside the cinemas. To the north-west of the square along Jalan Basuki Rachmat you'll find banks, the telephone office, restaurants and a few interesting souvenir shops. For maps and books try the Riang Bookshop on Jalan Basuki Rachmat near the square, or Toko Atlas further north.

There is a tourist office at Jalan Tugu 1 which has a few brochures; Tanjung Permai Travel, Jalan Basuki Rachmat 41, are very helpful if you need information.

The bus and train stations are a short distance east across the river.

Places to Stay – bottom end

The *Hotel Helios*, opposite the bus station on Jalan Pattimura, costs 7000 rp for a double including breakfast. It's clean, comfortable and has a garden. If you don't mind dormitory accommodation, the Surabaya *Bamboe Denn* has a small branch-hostel at Jalan Semeru 35 (tel 24859). Beds cost just 1500 rp but there is only one 10-bed dormitory and it's popular with travellers, so it's sometimes full. The staff are friendly and you may well get roped into English conversation lessons! The Denn is a good 10 minutes from the bus or train station, but it's not a three-km hike as the becak men will often claim. If the hostel seems to be locked up ring the bell inside the gate.

The *Hotel Santosa* (tel 23889) is just off the town square, at Jalan Agus Salim 24. Very few westerners patronise this place but you can get basic but not-so-clean clean rooms, with mandi from 7600 rp for a double. Around the corner, there's the rather noisy *Hotel Malang* on Jalan Zainul Arifin. Much better value is the old-fashioned and palatial *Hotel Malinda* on the same street. It has doubles with private mandi from 9100 rp, larger rooms for four people at 12,400 rp – and ceilings that must be seven metres high!

Places to Stay – top end

Other hotels fall into the middle and top price bracket. Near the train station, the clean and comfortable *Hotel Aloha* (tel 26950) at Jalan Gajah Mada 7 is a two-storey building. All the rooms have attached mandi and prices start at 15,000 rp for a double, including breakfast. All rooms have hot water. Right on the town square, the *Hotel Pelangi* (tel 27456), Jalan Merdeka Selatan, is also good. It's a large, pleasant old Dutch hotel with spacious rooms - all with bathroom, showers and hot and cold running water. Doubles range in price from 7500 to 20,000 rp; some rooms have fan or air-con. The hotel has a restaurant, bar and laundry service.

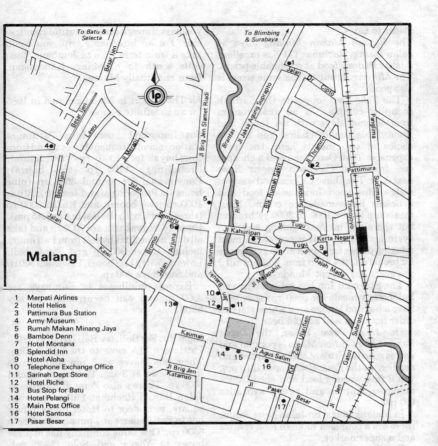

Malang

1 Merpati Airlines
2 Hotel Helios
3 Pattimura Bus Station
4 Army Museum
5 Rumah Makan Minang Jaya
6 Bamboe Denn
7 Hotel Montana
8 Splendid Inn
9 Hotel Aloha
10 Telephone Exchange Office
11 Sarinah Dept Store
12 Hotel Riche
13 Bus Stop for Batu
14 Hotel Pelangi
15 Main Post Office
16 Hotel Santosa
17 Pasar Besar

Also on the town square, near the Sarinah Department Store and Toko Oen Restaurant, is *Hotel Riche* (tel 24560) at Jalan Basuki Rachmat 1. It's a rambling old place with good-sized rooms starting at 11,500 rp including breakfast, 15,000 rp with attached mandi.

At Jalan Kahuripan 8, between the bus station and the river, are Malang's top digs, the *Montana Hotel*. Standard rooms here are 32,000 rp complete with air-con, hot water, satellite TV, telephone and breakfast. For 45,000 rp you get a larger

room and your own refrigerator. They accept payment by Visa/MasterCard.

For the colonial feel, there's the smaller *Splendid Inn* (tel 23860) where all the expats connected with the local tobacco plantations tend to stay. It's an old Dutch house with quite luxuriously furnished rooms, a lounge and small restaurant area, at Jalan Mohopahit 2-4 just off the Jalan Tugu circle. Singles/doubles, all with hot water showers and colour TV, start at 24,000/31,000 rp including breakfast and afternoon tea.

Places to Eat

The *Rumah Makan Minang Jaya* at Jalan Basuki Rachmat 111 has excellent quality Padang food at reasonable prices. The *Minang Agung* on the same street is also good.

The *Toko Oen*, opposite the Sarinah shopping complex, is an anachronism from colonial days with tea tables and comfortable basket chairs. You have a choice of two menus here: the more expensive Toko Oen menu and a cheaper one from the *Cafeteria Aneka Rasa* next door. They have Chinese and western dishes plus good Indonesian food and delicious home-made ice cream. Most meals are in the 1000 to 3000 rp bracket but there are mie/nasi goreng and soto ayam for 850 rp. This is one of the most relaxing places for a meal and a good place for breakfast; it's open from 8.30 am till 9 pm every day except Monday.

The Splendid Inn has set western and Indonesian meals for 3500 rp; they also have a bar and lounge area where you can order liquor as well as cold beer.

On Jalan Pasar Besar, the *Depot Pangsit Mie Gadjah Mada* is popular and serves good bowlfuls of cheap won-ton and noodles. At the Pasar Besar, open till 8 pm, you'll find warung food and good fruit – mangoes, apples and cheap avocados (50 rp).

In Malang Plaza, on Jalan Agus Salim, there are a couple of modern food centres and a supermarket.

Finally there's the *Pasar Senggol* night market – a bustling crowd of hawkers and warmly-lit warungs strung out along Jalan Majapahit and across the Brantas river. The Warung Sederhana here has excellent gado-gado for 350 rp and *tahu telur*, a bean-curd omelette with beansprouts, cucumber and peanut sauce.

Getting There & Away

Malang can be approached from a number of directions. Taking the back route, between Yogya and Banyuwangi, you pass through some beautiful countryside. For an interesting trip, you could take a train from Solo to Jombang, then colts south to Blimbing, Kandangan, Batu and finally Malang.

Air The airport in Malang closed in 1985 for an indefinite period.

Bus Important buses from Pattimura station include frequent buses to and from Surabaya for 1000 rp (2½ hours); Probolinggo 1100 rp (two hours); Banyuwangi for around 3500 rp (nine hours via Probolinggo and Jember); Blitar 1000 rp (two hours); and Kediri 2000 rp (three hours, with the last bus at 3.45 pm). Buses to Yogyakarta are 7000 rp and take all day. Some fares by colt from Pattimura include Blitar 900 rp and Purwodadi/Lawang 500 rp (1/2 hour); Pasuruan 500 rp and Surabaya 900 rp.

Express minibuses to Surabaya are 3500 rp and can be arranged by any hotel.

Night Bus For Bali, try Bali Indah at Jalan Pattimura 11A close to the bus station. Their bus leaves at 6 pm and arrives in Denpasar at 3 am. The fare is around 8000 rp. There's also Pemudi Express at Jalan Basuki Rachmat 1 near the town square, next door to Hotel Riche. Their bus to Bali departs at 7 pm and the fare is 8500 rp. This same company has express buses to Yogya and Solo (7500 rp), Banyuwangi (7500 rp), and Bandung (17,500 rp). Rosalie Indah and several other agents along Jalan Agus Salim across from Malang Plaza shopping complex run express buses to Yogya (7500 rp), Probolinggo (3500 rp), and Surabaya (3000 rp).

Rail There are nine services daily between Malang and Surabaya. The trip takes about three hours and the fare is 3800 rp 3rd class, 5000 2nd. Trains also run between Malang and Blitar for 1000 rp in all-3rd class. There are six trains to Blitar daily between 7 am and 6 pm.

Trains from points west such as Solo and Yogya are all-3rd class and very slow – bus is a much better choice on these routes.

Getting Around

Around Malang there are becaks and bemos. The biggest bemo station is on Jalan Pasar Besar, in front of the market, and they run around town for a fixed fare of 150 rp. A becak between the Pattimura bus station and the town square will cost around 500 rp – it's an up-and-down hilly stretch and you'll find that most passengers get out and walk the ascents. Apart from that, the best way to see Malang is to walk.

Local Colts A bemo-ride to the north of town, Blimbing is the focal point for colts to the temples around Malang. Other colt stations are at the Pattimura bus station, on Jalan Julius Usman and Jalan Halmahera.

AROUND MALANG
Singosari Temples

A good day trip is a rough circle north from Blimbing colt station in Malang to the Singosari Temple, backtrack to Blimbing for a colt east to the Jago Temple at Tumpang, and from there south-east to the Kidal Temple. Finally you can circle back south to Malang via Tajinan. All you need is a pocketful of change for a total fare of about 2000 rp.

Candi Singosari Right in Singosari village, 12 km north of Malang, this temple stands 500 metres off the main Malang-Surabaya road. One of the last monuments erected by the Singosari dynasty, it was built around 1300 AD in honour of Hindu and Buddhist priests who died with King Kertanegara in the bloody war against the Kingdom of Kediri. The main structure of the temple was completed but, for some reason, the sculptors never finished their task. Only the top part has any ornamentation and the kala heads have been left strangely stark with smooth bulging cheeks and pop eyes. Of the statues that once inhabited the temple's chambers only Agastya, the Shaivite teacher, remains – the others disappeared long ago to museums in Holland.

About 200 metres beyond the temple are two enormous figures of *dwarapalas* (believed to be guardians against evil spirits) wearing clusters of skulls and twisted serpents. These may have been part of the original gates to the headquarters of the Singosari kingdom. There is a 200 rp entry fee to the temple area, plus another 200 rp fee to view the dwarapalas.

Tumpang Along a small road (18 km) near the market in Tumpang, the Jago (or Jajaghu) Temple was built in 1268 AD and is thought to be a memorial to another Singosari king, Vishnuvardhana. The temple is in fairly poor condition but it still has some interesting decorative carving – in the two-dimensional wayang kulit style typical of East Java – which tell tales from the stories of the *Jataka* and *Mahabharata*. The caretaker described it as a Buddhist temple, yet there are Javanese-Hindu statues scattered around the garden including a six-armed death-dealing goddess and a lingam, the symbol of Shiva's virility and male potency.

Kidal The Kidal Temple, a small gem and perhaps the finest example of East Javanese art, is 24 km east of Malang. Built around 1260 AD to honour King Anushapati of Singosari, it is tapering and slender with portraits of Garuda on three sides; bold, glowering kala heads and medallions of the *haruna* symbol. Two *kala makara* (dragons) guard the steps – like at the kraton steps in Yogya, one is male and the other female.

Batu & Selecta

If you feel like a day or two's outing, then take a bus to Batu, a smaller hill town on

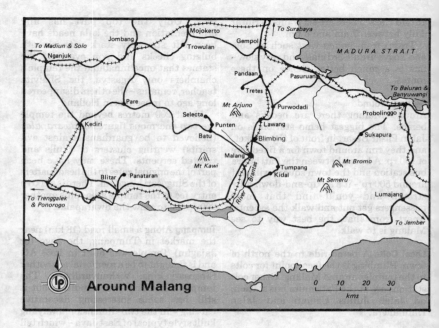

Around Malang

the slopes of Mount Arjuna and 15 km north-west of Malang. There are a few basic losmen in Batu such as the *Losmen Kawi* on Jalan Panglima Sudirman, a friendly place with rooms for 4000 rp. There is a good night market on Jalan Agus Salim near the town square. Three km from Batu there are well-known hot springs at Songgoriti.

Selecta, smaller still, is only five km further up the mountain from Batu. From this hill resort there are superb views over the surrounding volcanoes. There are good walks and you can visit the tiny mountain village of Sumber Brantas high above Selecta at the source of the Brantas River. The 'Senkaling Pemandian' swimming pool has a superb setting in landscaped gardens and is really worth the trip from Malang. It costs 600 rp to have a swim and there is a fine terrace restaurant overlooking the pool. The Pemandian is open daily from 6 am to 6 pm.

Places to Stay There are a couple of upper-notch hotels in Selecta such as the *Hotel Selecta* where rooms with a bathroom start at 16,820 rp (including free use of the swimming pool). More expensive rooms, from 19,000 rp, include three meals. In Punten, half-way between Batu and Selecta, the *Palem Punten* has rooms at 6500 rp. Other places include the similarly-priced *Losmen Garuda* and the *Losmen Mustikasari*.

Wendit

This is another hill resort, nine km east of Malang, with a pool, forests and a troupe of monkeys. At the end of Ramadan, Wendit is the site of a festival called *Lebaran Kupatan*. The celebrations last 11 days, and on the seventh day thousands of people jump into the pool in the belief that they will be blessed with eternal youth.

Mt Kawi

Near the village of Wonosari on Mt Kawi, 40 km west of Malang, is the tomb of a great Muslim sage, Mbah Jugo, who died in 1871. It has, surprisingly, become a Mecca for non-Muslim Chinese and attracts a regular stream of pilgrims who attend daily prayer sessions which are held at 6 am, 11 am and 7 pm. Inside the sanctified property there's a warning sign forbidding 'painting, writing on walls, use of radio or tape recorders, photographs – and *explosives*'.

Lawang

At Lawang, a hill town 18 km from Malang on the road to Surabaya, you can visit the *Hotel Niagara*. Dating from the turn of the century, this grand five-storey Art-Nouveau mansion was designed by a Brazilian architect for a wealthy Chinese gentleman but the family sold their inheritance in the early 1960s. There is lots of beautiful old furniture, some of it quite unusual, painted wall tiles, terrazzo floors and stained-glass lights. From the rooftop there is a magnificent view of Mt Arjuno. The hotel even has a story about three female ghosts who haunt one of the rooms.

The inmates of the Sumber Porong Mental Institution in Lawang give free musical performances every Wednesday and Saturday morning at 9 am.

Purwodadi

A few km north of Lawang, the Kebun Raya Purwodadi are big dry-climate botanical gardens with a high waterfall.

PANATARAN

The Hindu temples at Panataran are the largest remaining Majapahit sanctuaries and perhaps the finest examples of East Javanese architecture and sculpture. Construction was actually begun around 1200 AD during the Singosari dynasty but the temple complex took some 250 years to complete and most of the important surviving structures date from the great years of Majapahit during the 1300s. The arrangement of the three gradually rising courtyards and the beautiful detailed reliefs and sculptures of Panataran are similar to many temples found in Bali.

Around the base of the first level platform, which would once have been a meeting place, the comic-strip carvings tell the story of a test between the fat meat-eating Bubukshah and the thin vegetarian Gagang Aking.

Farther on is the small 'Dated Temple', so called because of the date 1291 (1369 AD) carved over the entrance. On the next level there are colossal serpents snaking endlessly around the 'Naga Temple' which once housed valuable sacred objects.

At the rear stands the 'Mother Temple' – or at least part of it for the top of the temple has been reconstructed alongside its three-tiered base. Followed anti-clockwise, panels around the base depict stories from the *Ramayana* with Hanuman's secret mission to Rawana's palace on Sri Lanka to find Sita; a drama of battles, flames and giants, Hanuman flying across the trees and monkeys building bridges across the seas. The more realistic people of the Krishna stories on the second tier of the base show an interesting transition from almost two-dimensional representation to three-dimensional figures.

Nearby there is a small royal mandi with a frieze of lizards, bulls and dragons around its walls.

Getting There & Away

Panataran is 10 km from Blitar, which is the most convenient place to use as a base. It is possible to see the Panataran temples comfortably in a day from Malang – and possibly from Surabaya – so long as you're prepared to hire a motorbike or dokar in Blitar to take you there and back. Colts from Blitar generally only run as far as Nglegok village, three km short of Panataran. You could also hire a minibus from any of Malang's hotels to Panataran and back – figure on about 30,000 rp for the day.

BLITAR

Blitar is the usual base from which to visit Panataran. It's quite a pleasant country town to stay in overnight, and is also of interest as the site of President Sukarno's grave.

There are no official moneychangers in Blitar, but if, you're in a pinch the Hotel Sri Lestari will change travellers' cheques at 20 rp below the Bank Indonesia's rate.

Makam Bung Karno (Sentul)

At Sentul, a few km outside Blitar on the road to Panataran, an elaborate monument now covers the spot where former President Sukarno was buried in 1970. Sukarno is looked on by many as the 'father of his country', though he was only reinstated as a national hero in 1978 by the present regime. The leader of Indonesia from 1949 to 1965, he had been worshipped by the people –almost as a god – but by 1970 he was little more than a figurehead, suspected of having had ties with the attempted Communist coup of 1965 and discarded by the army. His last two years were spent under house arrest, in isolation in Bogor and Jakarta.

Sukarno was given a state funeral but, despite family requests that he be buried at his home in Bogor, the hero of Indonesian independence was buried as far as possible from Jakarta in an unmarked grave next to his mother in Blitar. It was only in 1978 that the lavish million-dollar monument was built over the grave and opened to Indonesian pilgrims.

Places to Stay

Blitar is a small compact town and there are a few losmen within 10 minutes' walk of the bus station. The *Hotel Sri Lestari* (tel 81766), Jalan Merdeka 173, is definitely the best of them. It's a well-kept colonial house and you can get rooms for 3000 rp facing a pretty garden and pond (plus an orchestra of frogs that can make enough noise to waken the dead!). In the main building, standard rooms are 4250 to 5500 rp, larger rooms for three or four people cost 8000 rp and doubles with attached mandi cost 15,000 rp. There are also more expensive rooms with hot and cold running water. In spite of vocal frogs the hotel is excellent value. All room rates include breakfast, there is also a bar and good tasty meals are available in the family kitchen (nasi rawon or nasi campur for 850 rp). The woman who runs the place is friendly and can arrange transport to Panataran (car or motorcycle) for reasonable fees.

The *Penginapan Aman*, Jalan Merdeka 130, has rooms at from 2000 to 6000 rp There's also the *Penginapan Harjuna*, in a small lane off Jalan Anggrek which in turn runs off Jalan Merdeka. Rooms cost a rock-bottom 1500 rp. It's adequate, but we're loath to recommend it – somehow we didn't feel welcome in this area. There are a couple of other losmen on this lane which won't take foreigners.

Places to Eat

Overall, the Sri Lestari kitchen is your best bet in Blitar, but *Rumah Makar Jaya* and *Ramayana*, both on Jalan Merdeka, are worth trying for Chinese food.

Getting There & Away

From Malang to Blitar is 80 km and it takes about two hours by bus for 800 rp There are also several trains operating daily between Malang and Blitar. From Surabaya to Blitar, via Malang, is close or four hours by bus and the fare is 1500 rp.

From Solo to Blitar is 370 km. Four early morning buses from Blitar to Solo via Kediri, depart on the hour between 4 and 8 am and take about six hours. The fare is 3000 rp. The Timbul Jaya Co also have two express minibus services from Solo for 4500 rp leaving the bus station at 8 and 9 am. Even with a stop for lunch, this trip takes only five hours (they drive fast enough to scare you witless) and the minibus drops you right in the centre of town, so it can be a useful service.

Getting Around

Panataran & Sentul If you're not staying at the Sri Lestari Hotel, you can hire a motorcycle (with rider) near the bus station. It's likely to cost 2000 rp round-trip to Panataran and you can stop off en route at Sentul. Dokars also hang about near the bus and train stations and they're another possibility. Alternatively you can take a colt (or an antique '47 Dodge – there are a few of them around) from the bus station as far as Nglegok village for 600 rp. Panataran is another three km along the main road and it's probably simplest to walk. Colts occasionally go all the way to Panataran, but don't make the return trip very often.

PACITAN

On the south coast near the provincial border, Pacitan is a quiet beach, one of the finest in East Java. The village of Pacitan is three km from a large bay enclosed by the rocky outcrops of rugged cliffs. The beach here is beautiful and deserted apart from a few outriggers, but the best place to swim is at small, secluded cove on the south-western side of the bay. Up on a hill above the cove there is a *pasanggrahan*, a kind of lodge, and a public swimming pool. On the road out there from Pacitan (seven km) you pass a strangely misplaced classical Greek temple, inscribed with the words *Gegaan maar niet vergeten*, 'Gone but not forgotten'. About five km beyond the pasanggrahan there's a picnic spot from where you have probably the best view of the coastline.

Other beaches accessible from Pacitan are Watu Karung (22 km) and Latiroco Lorok (41 km). Just beyond Punung village, 30 km east of Pacitan, the Gua Tabuhan or 'Musical Cave' is a huge limestone cavern which is said to have been a refuge for the 19th-century guerilla leader Prince Diponegoro. Here you can listen to an excellent 'orchestral' performance, played by striking rocks against stalactites, each in perfect pitch and echoing pure gamelan melodies. You have to hire a guide and a lamp for perhaps 500 rp and the concert lasts about 10 minutes, it's 2000 rp for six tunes. Bargaining is obligatory! This is also agate country and there are lots of people at the cave selling very reasonably priced polished stones and rings.

Places to Stay & Eat

There are a number of losmen in Pacitan strung out along Jalan Yani, the main street between the bus station and the road to the beach. One traveller has recommended the *Losmen Remaja* on Jalan Yani which costs 2000/4000 rp. Other places to stay include the *Losmen Sidomulyo* and *Wisma Wijaya* near the bus station, and the cheaper *Rahayu*. The prices of these places range between 1600 and 4000 rp. The *Hotel Bali Queen* is more up-market with doubles at 6000 rp.

For food, there are plenty of warungs, especially round the bus stand. The *Depot Makan Pujabar*, a block behind Jalan Yani, has excellent food; gado-gado for

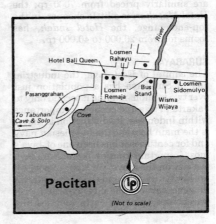

Pacitan

(Not to scale)

350 rp, nasi campur and fish for 500 rp, nasi goreng for 600 rp and fruit juices for 300 rp. There's good music and maps of the area here.

If you want to stay near the sea at the *pasanggrahan*, ask at the 'kabupaten' office in Pacitan. The cottage only has two bedrooms and it's often full, particularly on weekends. There are warungs nearby or you could take your own food.

Getting There & Around

Pacitan can be approached from Solo, via Wonogiri, or from Ponorogo which is just south of Madiun. From Solo it is almost a four-hour bus journey and the fare is 1400 rp. From Pacitan to Ponorogo takes about four hours and the fare is 800 rp; from Ponorogo to Surabaya, via Madiun, is a five-hour bus journey for 1950 rp. Or you might head from Ponorogo or Madiun to Blitar and Malang. Buses to Solo pass the junction point where the road from Pacitan meets the final short track to the beach, so you can use these buses if you don't want to walk or take a becak.

MADIUN

North of Ponorogo, on the Solo-Surabaya road, there's a group of cheap hotels clustered on the Surabaya side of town. The *Hotel Madiun* and *Hotel Sarangan* are similarly priced from 7000 rp; the *Hotel Matahari* is a little cheaper. In the top-end range, the *Hotel Indah*, has rooms for from 20,000 to 40,000 rp.

SURABAYA

The capital of East Java, the industrial city of Surabaya has a population just over two million, making it second only to Jakarta in size and economic importance within Indonesia. Its distinction is that it is the main base for the Indonesian navy and for centuries it has been one of Java's most important trading ports. Surabaya is a city on the move, yet signs of poverty are always in sight and the narrow streets in some parts of the city, crowded with warehouses, bullock carts and jostling becaks, contrast strongly with the modern buildings and shopping centres making an appearance on the city skyline. For most people this is just a short stop between Central Java and Bali or you also might be visiting Madura. For some travellers, this is also an important focal point for shipping to Kalimantan and Sulawesi but otherwise it's a hot and dusty, crowded city with precious little to see. People who do find Surabaya interesting, and to be fair quite a few people do, generally enjoy the real Indonesian atmosphere of the place.

Information & Orientation

Surabaya is spread out over a considerable area, but the tourist office, most of the restaurants and banks are all on, or very near to, Jalan Pemuda which runs through the centre of the city from Gubeng railway station to the Jalan Tanjungan Shopping Centre. Most of the budget hotels are also in this area, though few of them can really be recommended as good places to stay.

Tanjung Perak harbour is several km north of Jalan Pemuda. The main bus station, Joyoboyo, and Surabaya's zoo are several km south. Surabaya has two other main railway stations aside from Gubeng – the Kota railway station to the north of Jalan Pemuda and Pasar Turi to the north-west.

Tourist Office The East Java Regional Tourist Office is at Jalan Pemuda 118. The staff are helpful and they have maps, some information on places to visit in the province and a regional calendar of events. They'll also be able to tell you where and when Madura's bull races are being held. If you're interested in seeing a Reyog performance make enquiries here; they say it's possible to hire a whole group of performers for 125,000 rp! The office is open from 7 am to 2 pm Monday to Thursday, until 11 am Friday and 1 pm Saturday.

Banks The Bank Niaga on Jalan Tunjungan will change American and Australian travellers' cheques. The Bank BNI on Jalan Pemuda also has money changing facilities.

Post & Communication A branch post office on Jalan Pemuda, roughly opposite the Mitra cinema, is open from 8 am to 2 pm Monday to Thursday, until 11 am Friday, and 12 noon Saturday. Surabaya's main post office and poste restante, on Jalan Kebon Rojo, is a good half-hour walk from Jalan Pemuda so you will need to take a bemo or city bus to get there. The telephone office is on Jalan Margoyoso near its junction with Jalan Pemuda.

Immigration The immigration office (tel 45496) is at Jalan Jenderal S Parman 58A. It's a half-hour ride from Jalan Pemuda on an 'Aloha' bus (250 rp).

Note There have been a couple of reports from people who have been befriended in Surabaya, have then been given drugged coffee and woken up later to find their valuables gone. Take care.

Things to See
If you do have to hang around for a while, waiting for a ship to Sulawesi for example, there are a few things to do. The Bamboe Denn Transito Inn offers a morning walking tour of the city.

Surabaya Zoo
On Jalan Diponegoro, near the Joyoboyo bus station, the Surabaya zoo (Kebun Binatang) is reputed to be the largest zoo in South-East Asia. It specialises in nocturnal animals, exotic birds and fish. The animals look just as bored as they do in any other zoo, but the park is quite well laid-out with large open enclosures and it has a great collection of pelicans and lively otters, plus a couple of rather dazed-looking Komodo dragons.

The zoo is open from 7 am to 6 pm. Entry costs 600 rp and another 250 rp for the aquarium (which is worth it) or the nocturama. This park is popular with local people and outside there are warungs and a permanent gaggle of vendors selling drinks, and peanuts for the monkeys. The zoo is about an hour's walk from Jalan Pemuda or a short ride, by city bus No 2 or bemo V, from Jalan Panglima Sudirman.

MPU Tantular Museum
Across the road from the zoo, this small archaeological museum is open from 8 am to 1 pm Tuesday to Thursday, to 10 am Friday, to 12 noon Saturday and until 2 pm Sunday. It's closed on Mondays.

THR People's Amusement Park
On the east side of town, but close to the centre, the THR is Surabaya's amusement centre after dark. The Taman Remaja (500 rp entrance), on one side, features carnival rides and sometimes live pop bands. Taman Hiburan Rakyat on the other side (100 rp entrance) has a couple of theatres giving nightly performances (from 8 pm) of wayang orang and srimulat (East Javanese comedy). There are plenty of cheap warungs, but it's all a bit sad and gloomy – nobody seems to bother going anymore. The sidewalks outside are more lively with a bizarre collection of street hawkers and some excellent snacks.

East Java Ballet Festival – Pandaan
The East Java ballet festival takes place on the first and third Saturday nights of the months from May until October at the Candra Wilwatikta amphitheatre in Pandaan, 40 km south on the road to Tretes.

The festival season includes performances of a one-night version of the *Ramayana* but a large part of the programme consists of dances based on East Java's indigenous tales. It takes about one hour to get to Pandaan; you travel by bus from Joyoboyo (500 rp) and then by colt (200 rp) to the theatre.

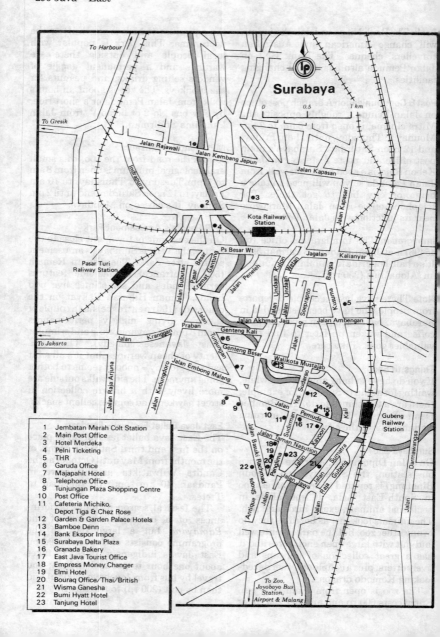

To Harbour

To Gresik

Surabaya

0   0.5   1 km

Jalan Rajawali

Jalan Kembang Jepun

Jalan Kapasan

Jalan Kapasari

Kota Railway Station

Ps Besar Wt

Pasar Turi Railway Station

Kramat Gantung

Pasar Besar

Jalan Buburan

Jalan Peneleh

Jalan Undaan Kulon

Jalan Undaan Wetan

Jagalan

Kalianyar

Bangsa

Kusuma

Jalan Akhmad Jais

Jalan Ambengan

Jalan Soeprapto

Jalan Ag

To Jakarta

Jalan   Kranggan

Praban

Genteng Kali

Genteng Besar

Jalan Embong Malang

Jalan Kedungdoro

Jalan Raja Arjuna

Jalan Tunjungan

Walikota Mustajab

Jalan Mas

Yos Sudarso

Jalan Pemuda

Jalan Taman Nasution

Jalan Sudirman

Jalan Panglima Sudirman

Kaloon

Gubeng Railway Station

Jalan Kali

Jalan Sumatra

Jalan Gubeng

Jalan Raya Guboeng

Jalan Darmawangsa

Jalan Bauki Rachmad

Antique   Stops

Jalan Jawa

To Zoo,
Joyoboyo Bus
Station,
Airport & Malang

1   Jembatan Merah Colt Station
2   Main Post Office
3   Hotel Merdeka
4   Pelni Ticketing
5   THR
6   Garuda Office
7   Majapahit Hotel
8   Telephone Office
9   Tunjungan Plaza Shopping Centre
10 Post Office
11 Cafeteria Michiko,
     Depot Tiga & Chez Rose
12 Garden & Garden Palace Hotels
13 Bamboe Denn
14 Bank Ekspor Impor
15 Surabaya Delta Plaza
16 Granada Bakery
17 East Java Tourist Office
18 Empress Money Changer
19 Elmi Hotel
20 Bouraq Office/Thai/British
21 Wisma Ganesha
22 Bumi Hyatt Hotel
23 Tanjung Hotel

Other Attractions

One of the most interesting places in Surabaya to wander round is the harbour. It's both busy and decrepit, filled with a variety of vessels ranging from brightly painted schooners to aging warships and small craft shuttling back and forth to the island of Madura. On Jalan Pemuda, across from the governor's residence, is the statue of Joko Dolog which dates from 1289 and commemorates King Kartanagara of Singosari. It's known as the 'fat boy'. When you've had enough of Surabaya's heat and dust, you can cool off in the Garden Hotel swimming pool or try the Simpang Lima pool.

There is a French Cultural Centre (tel 68639) at the French Consulate, at Jalan Darmokali 10-12, and a Goethe Institute (tel 40368) at Jalan Taman Ade Irma Suryani Nasution 15.

Places to Stay – bottom end

If you're staying in this busy port town – and many people do at least overnight here between Yogya and Bali – there's really only one very cheap place. The *Bamboe Denn Transito Inn* (tel 40333) when on Jalan Pemuda became a Surabaya institution, always packed out with travellers. Now it's got a new name, *Bamboe Denn Yeugd Herberg* and has moved to Jalan Ketabang Kali 6A, a 20-minute walk from Gubeng railway station. From the station, go along Jalan Pemuda, turn right into Jalan Yos Sudarso (an extension of Jalan Panglima Sudirman) then after the bridge, turn left (near the house of the naval commander-in-chief) into Jalan Ketabang Kali. A room here costs 5000 rp and dorm beds cost 2500 rp. It's clean and friendly and you can get lots of travel information (everything you ever wanted to know about Bromo and more!). There's a dining room and a cafeteria which is open 24 hours. You will be welcomed with pineapple. Safe-keeping facilities and comfortable sitting rooms are also provided.

The Denn is close to bus routes, a supermarket and a bank. You may well get roped into a little English conversation with Indonesian students at the language school also run from this youth hostel. If becak drivers haven't heard of the Denn, ask for the *Transito* (part of its former name).

Other cheap hotels in the Gubeng railway station area tend to be fairly dismal. The *Hotel Gubeng* at Jalan Sumatra 18, only 100 metres from Gubeng station, is good but not too cheap. Rooms with fan cost 12,000 rp including breakfast. Further down Jalan Sumatra from the Hotel Gubeng you'll find *Wisma Ganesha* at 34A – believe the number, there's no sign. It has a choice of rooms without mandi from 5000 rp including breakfast, 7000 rp for the better rooms with mandi that are round a small garden at the back. *Hotel Kayoon* round the corner on Jalan Kayoon is dirty and none too quiet; at 6000 rp per room this should be a last choice.

There are a few hotels close to the Kota railway station, but some of the cheaper places in this area won't take foreigners as they then have to fill in forms for the police which is a nuisance (this is true of a number of towns in Java). A reader has recommended *Losmen Ganefo* (tel 311169) at Jalan Kapasan 169-171, where 'large, clean rooms' start at 6000 rp. There's also the *Hotel Paviljoen* (tel 43449), an old colonial house at Jalan Genteng Besar 94 with four-poster beds in rooms from 8000 rp.

Places to Stay – top end

The *Garden Hotel* (tel 470001) is central at Jalan Pemuda 21. It has three restaurants (one on the rooftop overlooking the city – with a choice of Chinese, Indonesian and western food), banking and travel facilities, swimming pool and sauna. All the rooms have air-con, with bathroom and hot and cold water, and cost US$39 single and US$43 double. These rates include an all-you-can-eat buffet breakfast including mie/nasi goreng, omelettes, pancakes, croissants, fruit and juices/coffee/tea.

Just behind the Garden Hotel and attached by an interior hall, the 250-room *Garden Palace Hotel* (tel 479250) at Jalan Yos Sudarso 11 is one of Surabaya's top tourist-class hotels. Singles/doubles from US$55/58. There are three restaurants and a pub with live jazz music; the Cathay Pacific Airlines office is located here.

At the modern *Elmi Hotel* (tel 471571), Jalan Panglima Sudirman 42-44, singles/doubles cost from 53,600/63,000 rp and the hotel has a restaurant, bar, disco, fitness centre and swimming pool. Across the street is the economical *Tanjung Hotel* (tel 44031) at No 43-45. Air-con rooms with satellite TV, hot-water showers, and telephone start at 26,620/31,460 rp, tax and breakfast included. It's good value.

At Jalan Tunjungan 65 the older *Majapahit Hotel* has charm and a surprisingly fine garden; it was designed in 1910 by the Dutch architect Sarkies. Singles/doubles cost from US$28/33.

On the outskirts of the city on the road to the airport, the modern *Hotel Mirama* (tel 69501), Jalan Raya Darmo 68-76, is convenient for passengers in transit. Singles/doubles (all with air-con) start at US$60/65 and there's a swimming pool.

Note that all hotels in this category except the Tanjung have a 21% service charge and government tax on top of the room charge.

Places to Eat

Food here seems painfully expensive compared to that in Bali or Yogya but it can be quite good. There are some good places like *Depot Tiga*, a grocery shop on Jalan Sudirman next to the cinema. One visitor raved that their 'es buah susu surpassed all es campurs and for that matter all other taste treats in South-East Asia'! On the same street, but a few doors down, there's the cheap and popular *Cafeteria Michiko*, which features 'Turkey yoghurt'. The *Chez Rose* next door to the Michiko is much more expensive, but a good place for a splurge if you want a break from Indonesian food. They do a great

lunchtime buffet; the eat-all-you-can and lie-down-to-recover variety. The Chinese *Yun Ding Songmie Restaurant* further down on Jalan Panglima Sudirman is worth checking out.

Back on Jalan Pemuda, the *Warung Kosgoro* has a limited Indonesian menu, but good, cheap food. Across the road is *Kantin Webb* where they serve a few simple Indonesian dishes.

The *Granada Modern Bakery* on the corner of Jalan Pemuda and Jalan Panglima Sudirman is a good place for breakfast buns and cakes. Just around the corner on Jalan Yos Sudarso, you can have an expensive ice cream at the *Zangrandi Ice Cream Palace* and watch the wealthy Surabayans roll up in their Mercedes and Volvos. Or try the *Garden Restaurant* at Jalan Pemuda 3 for delicious Turin Italian ice cream for only 300 rp.

At the Surabaya Delta Plaza there are two Pizza Huts (check out the squid pizza), a Dairy Queen, a Church's Texas Fried Chicken, a Japanese fast food place and various bakeries. There is also a food centre serving moderately priced Chinese and Indonesian dishes (near the Pizza Hut on the ground floor) and a Hero supermarket.

For really cheap eating you can go to the stalls around the Gubeng Station, near the THR or off Jalan Tunjungan. There is a good hawkers' centre open at night near the flower market on Jalan Kayoon and on Jalan Pandegiling.

Nightlife

Surabayans are big on discos. Popular places include the *Top Ten* in Tunjungan Plaza, *Blue Sixteen Bar & Nightclub* at Jalan Pemuda 10, and *Tifa*, on the ground floor of the Hyatt Bumi on Jalan Basuki Rachmad.

Things to Buy

Surabaya has no particular crafts of its own, but the city is a good hunting ground for antiques. At the junction of Jalan Basuki Rachmad and Jalan Urip Sumoharjo, there are a number of small shops where you'll find good quality antiques - with prices to match. The Sampurna at No 144 has an interesting collection. Surabaya also has something of a reputation as a free port, but it's nothing like Singapore. Tunjungan Shopping Centre was the hunting ground for electrical goods and cheap music cassettes, but it seems to be on its way to closing down completely. The new Surabaya Delta Plaza shopping centre on Jalan Pemuda is very flash and Indonesians claim it's the largest shopping centre in South-East Asia (a title also claimed by the Subang Jaya shopping complex outside Kuala Lumpur, Malaysia).

Getting There & Away

Air Surabaya is an important hub for domestic flights. Garuda flights depart from Surabaya to most major Indonesian centres. Some important connections include Jakarta (88,500 rp, 11 flights daily); Denpasar (42,400 rp, three daily); Palembang (144,900 rp, five daily); Banjarmasin (68,800 rp, two daily); and Ujung Pandang (98,700 rp, two daily). Garuda has a special night fare to Jakarta for 75,600 rp. The Garuda office (tel 470640), at Jalan Tunjungan 29, is open from 7.30 am to 4 pm Monday to Friday, until 1 pm Saturday and from 9 am to 12 noon Sunday.

Bouraq, Mandala, and Merpati all have cheaper domestic fares than Garuda, but since only Garuda is allowed to operate jets (to stifle competition), non-Garuda flights generally take a bit longer.

Bouraq operate flights from Surabaya to Jakarta (73,000 rp), Bandung (58,700 rp), Denpasar (36,000 rp), Banjarmasin (58,500 rp), Balikpapan (92,700 rp), Samarinda (101,000 rp) and Ternate (205,200 rp). Bouraq (tel 42383) at Jalan Panglima Sudirman 70 is open from 7 am to 9 pm daily.

Mandala operate flights to Jakarta (73,000 rp), Ujung Pandang (83,800 rp), Ambon (163,800 rp) and Manado (166,300 rp). Mandala (tel 66861) at Jalan Raya Darmo 109 is open from 8 am to 4 pm Monday to Friday, to 1 pm Saturday and from 9 am to 12 noon Sunday.

Garuda's subsidiary Merpati (tel 40773) flies to Ujung Pandang, Sumbawa and Ternate with a rate structure similar to Bouraq's. Merpati is at Jalan Urip Sumoharjo 68 and is open from 8 am to 4 pm Monday to Saturday and until 1 pm Sunday.

Bus Most buses operate from Surabaya's main Joyoboyo bus station, which is on the southern edge of the city. If you're heading for the north coast, then buses and colts depart from the Jembatan Merah station which is to the north of Kota railway station.

Going East There are frequent buses to Probolinggo 1150 rp (2½ hours). Buses to Banyuwangi are 3100 rp (10 hours) via Situbondo or 3500 rp via Jember (11 hours). There are also buses to Jember (2050 rp), Pasir Putih (2000 rp) and Situbondo (2500 rp).

Going South There are buses to Pandaan for 500 rp. From Pandaan you have to continue by colt (300 rp) to Tretes. There are frequent buses to Malang, via Purwodadi and Lawang, 1000 rp (2½ hours). Hotels in Surabaya can also arrange express minibuses to Malang for 3500 rp.

Going West There are frequent buses to Trowulan, via Mojokerto, 600 rp (1½ hours); to Solo, via Madiun, 3500 rp (6½ hours); for Yogya, 4000 rp (eight hours), buses depart between 6 and 9 am.

Going North Buses and colts (from Jembatan Merah) include Gresik 300 rp, Tuban 1500 rp, Kudus 1800 rp and Semarang 5000 rp.

Madura Buses depart every hour from Joyoboyo to major towns on Madura. From Surabaya to Kamal is 750 rp (one hour); to Pamekasan 2000 rp (two/three hours) and to Sumenep 3000 rp (four hours). Fares include the ferry.

Night Bus Most night buses depart from the Bratang bus terminal (to the east of Joyoboyo) between 5 and 9 pm. There are a number of private stands for night buses on Jalan Basuki Rachmad but take care – they are very keen on overcharging. Bali Indah is about the cheapest and fares include a snack and stop-over meal. Their main ticket office is inconveniently located at Jalan Wonocolo 8, about 6 km from the city centre. To Denpasar their fare is 10,000 rp and the trip takes around 16 hours. The best night bus service to Denpasar is reputed to be Jawa Indah, who charge 20,000 rp for the 'deluxe bus' trip. Elteha has also been recommended for night buses to Denpasar (10,000 to 14,000 rp depending on the bus) and they have offices at the Joyoboyo bus terminal (open from 8 am to 5 pm).

To Solo, Yogya, Kudus or Semarang, night bus fares are around 8000 rp. It's a long 859 km trip to Jakarta by bus – for 14,400 rp regular air-con or up to 20,000 rp deluxe –but you're really better off taking the train.

To get to the Bratang terminal use Bemo 'N' (200 rp per person) from the Gubeng railway station area.

Rail Surabaya has three main train stations. Gubeng station has trains to Jakarta via Solo and Yogyakarta, plus trains east to Banyuwangi and south to Malang and Blitar. Pasar Turi railway station handles services to Jakarta via Semarang. Note that some trains arriving at Gubeng continue on to Kota. Gubeng is much more convenient for the Bamboe Denn and other central places than either Kota or Pasar Turi.

See the introductory Getting Around section for Java for details on Jakarta-Surabaya and Yogyakarta-Surabaya by rail. Apart from services to the main cities, there are several trains operating from Surabaya to Malang. There are nine services daily by the *Tumapel* train between Kota or Gubeng station and Malang; the first departs Gubeng at 7.36 am

and the last service departs at 6.33 pm. The trip takes about two hours each way and the fare is 1200 rp in all-3rd class. Some of these trains continue on from Malang to Blitar which is a five-hour trip and costs 1700 rp.

Mutiara Timur trains depart from Gubeng station at 10 am and 10 pm for Banyuwangi and the ferry to Bali. The trip takes seven hours to Banyuwangi. The fare is 2800 rp in 3rd class and 3500 rp in 2nd. Through to Denpasar, the trip takes 15 hours; the fare is 5200 rp in 3rd class and 5900 rp in 2nd, including the ferry to Bali and a bus to Denpasar. At Gubeng station, they will usually claim they can't sell 2nd class tickets to Banyuwangi – if this is the case, simply purchase a 3rd class ticket and once you're on the train take a 2nd class seat and pay the conductor the difference. But check the information board in the terminal first to make sure that the train you're taking has 2nd class cars.

Boat Surabaya is a travellers' centre for ships to Kalimantan and Sulawesi in particular; Pelni operates regular services to both these islands and to Sumatra. Tickets for both passenger services and Pelni cargo ships must be bought at the Pelni ticketing office (tel 21041/21694) at Jalan Pahlawan 20. Catch a Bemo M on Jalan Pemuda near the Warung Kosgoro. The office is open from 9 am to 1.30 pm Monday to Friday and 8 am to 1 pm Saturday. Tickets can be bought up to 10 days before departure. The front ticket counter can be hopelessly chaotic. If you can't get through to the surly staff in front, go around to the office at the back where the staff are more helpful.

The Pelni passenger services follow.

KM Kambuna This boat sails every other Thursday at 2 pm from Surabaya, to the west one week and to the east the following week. The route east is Tanjung Priok-Surabaya-Ujung Pandang-Balikpapan-Pantaloan-Bitung. From

Bitung the ship turns west for the reverse route. The journey takes 28 hours to Ujung Pandang and two days to Balikpapan. To the west, the journey to Tanjung Priok takes 24 hours and to Belawan it's about three days.

KM Kelimutu The route east is Semarang-Banjarmasin-Surabaya-Padang Bai-Lembar-Ujung Pandang-Bima-Waingapu-Ende-Kupang. From Kupang the Kelimutu follows the same route in reverse. The ship leaves Surabaya for Padang Bai (Bali) every two weeks at 3 pm Tuesday afternoons, docking at Padang Bai 22 hours later. Arrival in Ujung Padang is 1½ days later. Going north-west to Banjarmasin, it leaves every other Friday morning, arriving in Banjarmasin in 23 hours.

KM Umsini This boat sails east every other Friday at 2 pm from Surabaya-Ujung Pandang-Bitung-Ternate-Sorong-Jayapura and then the reverse. It takes 28 hours to Ujung Pandang, three days to reach Ternate and a week to Jayapura.

KM Rinjani Leaving every other Thursday at 2 pm, the KM Rinjani sails Surabaya-Ujung Pandang-Bau-Bau-Ambon-Sorong and then returns. It's 2½ days to Ambon.

KM Kerinci This boat leaves every other Tuesday at 2 pm going east from Surabaya-Ujung Pandang-Balikpapan-Pantaloan-Toli-Toli-Tarakan before turning

around. It's two days to Balikpapan, three days to Pantaloan, 3½ days to Toli-Toli and four days to Tarakan.

Fares Fares are the same for all five ships, except for the KM Kelimutu which has no Kelas (Class) III or IV (see the table).

Cargo Ship There are at least 15 cargo ships a day sailing from Surabaya to the outer islands. For fares and departure dates, you really have to get down to the harbour and ask around at the shipping company offices. For information about Pelni cargo ships see Mr Rifai or Captain Abu at the Tanjung Perak office (tel 293347). For information about non-Pelni ships, go to the ground floor of the harbour master's office at Kalimas Baru 194, Tanjung Perak. Each morning they get a list of every ship leaving that day and some, if already confirmed, for the following day.

For Banjarmasin, try P T Sumber Kalimas Agung on Jalan Kalimas Baru; the KM Eska sails every week and the journey takes about 18 hours for around 25,000 rp. PT Meratus Shipping Co (tel 293096) at Jalan Alun-Alun, Tanjung Perak has a weekly cargo ship (KM Meratus) to Ujung Pandang.

Pinisi In the nearby port town of Gresik, you may be able to hitch a ride on a pinisi, the traditional Makassar schooner (also sometimes called Bugis – actually these

Kelas:	I	II	III	IV	Ekonomi
Ambon	131,100	96,900	74,000	57,800	43,500 rp
Balikpapan	79,600	59,600	46,200	37,700	28,800 rp
Banjarmasin	57,900	55,400	–	–	24,700 rp
Bitung	166,800	122,600	93,500	75,100	56,300 rp
Ende	126,000	92,100	–	–	48,100 rp
Padang Bai	36,500	27,500	–	–	16,000 rp
Tarakan	104,300	80,700	61,800	49,600	40,900 rp
Tg Priok	45,200	34,700	27,160	21,300	17,300 rp
Ujung Pandang	65,200	48,800	37,700	30,300	22,500 rp
Banjarmasin	58,100	45,900	–	–	24,600 rp
Belawan	147,600	108,300	82,800	65,900	51,400 rp

boats are built in East Java and South Kalimantan as well as in Sulawesi, home of the Bugis), with a little persistence. Strictly speaking, pinisi crews transporting cargo are forbidden to take passengers to other islands, but money rules the day here.

PT Wisata Bahari Mas Permai (tel 291633) does 'East Java Pinisi Traditional Cruises' at reasonable (for cruises) rates. They have a 10-day cruise to Madura, Bali, and Lombok for US$650 per person, a 17-day cruise to Bali, Lombok, Sumbawa, Komodo, and Flores for US$950 and a 31-day cruise to Bali, Sumbawa, Komodo, Flores, Solor, Alor, Wetar, Tanimbar, Banda, Ambon, Bau-Bau, and Ujung Pandang for US$1700. Rates include transport to and from and accommodation on the pinisi, three meals a day and guided tours; all cruises end with a night in a mountain resort in Trawas, near Mojokerto. The 17-day cruise includes air transport between Ende and Surabaya and the 31-day cruise includes passage on Pelni's *KM Rinjani* from Ambon to Surabaya. Wisata Bahari is at Jalan Tanjung Priok 11 Blok H, Tanjung Perak, not far from the harbour. There is a minimum of 15 people needed for a confirmed departure.

Getting Around

There are taxis, becaks and hordes of bemos around town which are useful for local transport. A taxi to or from the Juanda airport (15 km) will cost about 7000 rp.

Surabaya also has big city buses which charge a fixed 150 rp fare and basically run north-south. Useful buses include the No 1 bus from Jalan Basuki Rachmad to Tanjung Perak harbour, and the No 2 bus from Jalan Panglima Sudirman to the zoo and Joyoboyo bus station.

Becaks aren't allowed on the main streets of Surabaya, but in neighbourhoods where they are, expect to pay about 300 rp per km.

Most taxis in Surabaya run on meters

with similar rates to Jakarta's: 500 rp for flagfall, 25 rp each quarter kilometre.

Bemos Bemos are labelled A, B or K etc and they run all over town for a fixed 200 rp fare. The biggest bemo stations are Wonokromo station (near Joyoboyo bus station) and Jembatan Merah station. Some useful bemos and the routes they take are:

Bemo M	Joyoboyo – via Gubeng railway station, the post office, Pelni and Kota railway station – to Jembatan Merah
Bemo V	Joyoboyo – via the Zoo and Jalan Pemuda – to THR
Bemo D	Joyoboyo – via Pasar Turi railway station – to Jembatan Merah
Bemo N	Jembatan Merah – via Gubeng station – to Bratang.

AROUND SURABAYA
Gresik

On the road to Semarang, 25 km from Semarang, this port was once a major centre for international trade and a major centre of Islam in the 15th century. Close by, at Giri, is the tomb of the first Sunan Giri who is regarded as one of the greatest of the nine *wali songo*. He was the founder of a line of spiritual lords of Giri which lasted until it was overwhelmed by Mataram in 1680. According to some traditions Sunan Giri is said to have played a leading role in the conquest of Majapahit and to have ruled Java for 40 days after its fall – to purify the country of pre-Islamic influences.

Gresik has a colourful pinisi harbour that is probably the last fully traditional one in Java – everything is carried on board by hand and there are no fixed departure schedules.

Tretes

This hill town, standing at 800 metres on the slopes of mounts Arjuno and Welirang, is renowned for its cool climate and beautiful views. Tretes also has an intriguing reputation as a red light district. If you have to kill time in Surabaya, it can be a pleasant enough place to escape to but there's not a great deal to do. The Katek Boko and Putuh Truno waterfalls are nearby and there are a number of interesting walks around the town including the trek to the Lalilijiwo Plateau and Mt Arjuno (3339 metres).

Tretes is 55 km south of Surabaya. On the way you pass through Pandaan, the site for the East Java Ballet Festival which takes place over the dry season (see Surabaya). The Jawi Temple here is an early 14th century Hindu temple, basically a Shaivite structure although some time later a Buddhist stupa was added on top. There are the remains of other old temples scattered over the slopes of Mt Penanggunan to the west. The Belahan bathing place on Penanggunan, perhaps a 10 km hike from Tretes, was the home of the Airlangga-as-Vishnu statue now in the Mojokerto Museum.

Places to Stay & Eat If you're planning to stay here, the best bet is to look for a room in a private home. Take a cottage if you plan to stay long – there are plenty available if you ask around. Prigen, a bit lower down, is cheaper than Tretes. Typical of hotel accommodation is the *Tanjung Plaza* with rooms at US$38. *Tretes Bungalow Park & Motel* is probably the cheapest place with rooms from 8000 rp including breakfast.

There are some good, reasonably priced places to eat around the fruit market and shopping centre, near the police station.

MADURA ISLAND

Madura is a large and rugged island, about 160 km long by 30 km wide, and separated from Surabaya on the East Java coast by a narrow channel. It is especially famous for its bull races, the kerapan sapi, but also has a few interesting historical sites, some fine beaches and beautiful scenery. It is a place that is almost completely undiscovered by tourists.

The people of Madura are familiar faces in East Java, particularly in Surabaya where many have gone to look for work. Since independence, the island has been governed as part of the province of East Java but Madura has had a long tradition of involvement with its larger neighbour and with the Dutch. The Dutch were not interested because of the island itself, which was initially of little economic importance, but rather because of the crucial role the Madurese played in Javanese dynastic politics.

In 1624 the island was conquered by Sultan Agung of Mataram and its government united under one Madurese princely line, the Cakraningrats. Until the middle of the 18th century the Cakraningrat family fiercely opposed Central Javanese rule and harassed Mataram, often conquering large parts of the kingdom. Prince Raden Trunojoyo even managed to carry off the royal treasury of Mataram in 1677 and it was restored only after the Dutch intervened and stormed Trunojoyo's stronghold at Kediri. In 1705 the Dutch secured control of the eastern half of Madura following the conflict of the First Javanese War of Succession between Amangkurat III and his uncle, Pangeran Puger. Dutch recognition of Puger was largely influenced by Cakraningrat II, the lord of West Madura. He probably supported Puger's claims simply because he hoped a new war in Central Java would give the Madurese a chance to interfere but, while Amangkurat was arrested and exiled to Ceylon, Puger took the title of Pakubuwono I and concluded a treaty with the Dutch which, along with large concessions in Java, granted them East Madura.

The Cakraningrats fared little better by agreeing to help the Dutch put down the rebellion in Central Java that broke out after the Chinese massacre in 1740. Although Cakraningrat IV attempted to contest the issue, a treaty was eventually signed in 1743 in which Pakubuwono II ceded full sovereignty of Madura to the

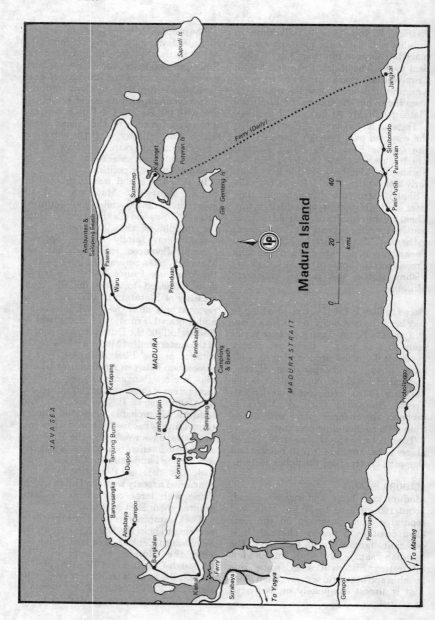

Dutch. Cakraningrat fled to Banjarmasin and took refuge on an English ship but was robbed, betrayed by the Sultan and finally captured by the Dutch and exiled to the Cape of Good Hope. Under the Dutch, Madura continued as four states, each with its own *bupati* or lord mayor. Madura was initially important as a major source of colonial troops but in the second half of the 19th century it acquired greater economic value as the main supplier of salt to Dutch-governed areas of the archipelago where salt was a profitable monopoly of the colonial government.

The southern side of the island, facing Java, is shallow beach and cultivated lowland while the northern coast alternates between rocky cliffs and beaches of great rolling sand dunes, the best of which is at Salopeng. At the extreme east there is tidal marsh and vast tracts of salt around Kalianget. The interior of this flat and somewhat arid island is riddled with limestone slopes and is either rocky or sandy, so agriculture is limited. There are goat farms, tobacco estates, some orchards and extensive stands of coconut palms but the main industry of Madura would have to be cattle, followed by salt and fishing.

Kerapan Sapi – Bull Races

As the Madurese tell it, the tradition of bull races began long ago when plough-teams were raced against each other across the arid fields; this pastime was encouraged by an early king of Sumenep, Panembahan Sumolo. Today, when stud bull breeding is big business in Madura, the Kerapan Sapi is as much an incentive for the Madurese to breed good stock as simply a popular form of entertainment and sport. Only bulls of a certain standard can be entered for important races and the Madurese keep their young bulls in superb condition dosing them with an assortment of medicinal herbs, honey, beer and raw eggs.

Traditional races are put on annually between mid-August and October in bull-racing stadiums all over Madura. The first races in August are small village events, then in late August and September contests are held at district and regency level until the cream of bulls fight it out for the big prize at the grand final in Pamekasan, the island's capital.

This is, of course, the biggest and most colourful festival. As many as 100 bulls, wearing fancy halters and yokes of gilt, ribbons and flowers, are paraded through town and around the open field of the stadium to a loud fanfare of drums, flutes and gongs. For each race two pairs of bulls, stripped of their finery, are matched against each other with their 'jockeys' perched behind on wooden sleds. Gamelan is played to excite the bulls and then, after being given a generous tot of arak, they're released and charge flat out down the track – just as often plunging right into the seething crowds of spectators! The race is over in a flash – the best time recorded so far is nine seconds over the 100 metres which is faster than man's world track record. After the elimination heats the victorious bulls are proudly trotted home to be used at stud.

The regency centres where major bull-racing events are held are Bangkalan, Pamekasan and Sumenep. The East Java Tourist Office in Surabaya will have details of where and when races are held; dates are also listed in the *East Java Calendar of Events*. For the grand final, entry to the stadium costs only 300 rp or, if you want a seat, you can pay from 1500 to 3000 rp. PT Orient Express Tours (tel 43315, Surabaya) operate a tourist bus to the Madura Grand Final in September from Surabaya. The bus collects from major hotels and the day trip costs 30,000 rp per person.

Bangkalan

This is the next town north of Kamal along the coast and one of the primary locations for the annual bull races. There is also a small museum of Madurese history and culture in a building on the grounds of the Bupati's home. The

Museum Cakraningrat is open from 8 am to 2 pm Monday to Saturday, except Friday when it closes at 11 am.

Air Mata

Near Arosbaya, 27 km north of Kamal, the tombs of the Cakraningrat royalty are at the Air Mata cemetery which is superbly situated on the edge of a small ravine overlooking a river valley. The ornately carved *gunungan* headstone on the grave of Ratu Ibu, consort of Cakraningrat I, is the most impressive and is on the highest terrace. The turn off to Air Mata is shortly before Arasbaya and from the coast road it's a four km walk inland. Air Mata means 'Tears'.

Tanjung Bumi

Tanjung Bumi is a village on the north-west coast of Madura, about 60 km from Kamal. It's primarily a fishing village but is also the island headquarters for the manufacture of traditional Madurese batik and Madurese prahus. On the outskirts is what may be Madura's most beautiful beach, Pantai Siring Kemuning.

Places to Stay

There's no official place to stay in either Air Mata or Tanjung Bumi, but you can camp on the beach near Tanjung Bumi with the permission of the kepala desa. In Bangkalan there are several possibilities.

The *Losmen Purnama*, Jalan Kartini 19 in Bangkalan, has basic rooms starting at 6000 rp. Nearby are several small restaurants – the *Citra Rasa* is decent.

The rather new *Cakra Ningrat Hotel* (tel 388), at Jalan Kahaji Muhammed Khalil 113, on the main road through Bangkalan has air-con singles/doubles with TV and hot water for 30,000/40,000 rp, or fan-cooled economy rooms for 10,000/15,000 rp. The furnishings are traditional Madurese – very elegant.

Pamekasan

On the southern side, 100 km east of Kamal, the capital of Madura is a quiet

and pleasant enough town but during August and September each year it comes alive with the festivities of the Kerapan Sapi Grand Final. From this town you can visit a natural fire resource, known locally as 'Api Alam'. Legend tells that the fire comes from the mouth of a giant that was sentenced by the gods.

Camplong (15 km west) is the nearest beach to Pamekasan and it's safe for swimming, though the Pertamina storage tanks nearby do nothing for its visual appeal. However, it is a breezy oasis from the interior of Madura, which can be quite hot. Strung out along this coastline are small fishing villages where twin-outrigger dugout canoes are used and the prahus carry huge, triangular striped sails. Local people are friendly but travellers are a rare sight so you can expect to be the centre of interested mobs of children, if not the whole village!

Places to Stay & Eat In the centre of town, 200 rp by becak from the bus station, the *Hotel Garuda* (tel 81589) at Jalan Masigit 1 has doubles at 4000 rp. Large rooms with mandi are 9000 rp. Around the corner, the *Hotel Trunojoyo* (tel 81181), down a small alley off Jalan Trunojoyo, is clean and quiet. Rooms cost from 4400 rp including breakfast; rooms with air-con and mandi cost 14,000 rp. *Losmen Bahagia*, further up Jalan Trunojoyo, is basic but adequate and the family who run it are friendly. Singles/doubles cost 2500/3000 rp including breakfast.

The *Hotel Purnama* (tel 81375) is conveniently near the bus terminal at Jalan Ponorogo 10A. It's clean and friendly; the regular rooms have attached mandi and are good value at 7,000 rp. Air-con rooms have nothing going for them except air conditioning, so they're a bit overpriced at 23,000 rp.

The Garuda and Trunojoyo hotels both have attached restaurants. The small restaurant next to Losmen Bahagia does cheap and tasty Chinese food. On the traffic circle in the middle of town is the clean, green *Lezat* with outdoor tables arranged cafe-style. They have good food, including local specialties like *soto madura*.

Pamekasan to Sumenep

To see something of the island, it's interesting to take a colt from Pamekasan inland through tobacco country to Waru, another to Pasean, then along the north coast to Salopeng beach and back down to Sumenep. Taking the south coast road from Pamekasan, there is a colourful market at Prenduan with everything from fruit, batik and bright children's toys to painted bird cages, goats and the village barber.

Sumenep

At the eastern end of the island, Sumenep is Madura's most interesting town to visit. It is centred around the kraton, mosque and markets; many of the attractive old houses are examples of typical Madurese architecture, constructed with an unlikely frontage of thick, white Roman-style columns under overhanging red-tiled roofs.

Near the main square of this small, quiet, easy-going town are a few losmen and restaurants, along with the post office (there are no banks with money changing facilities). The main bus station is on the southern edge of town and buses to Surabaya, via Pamekasan and Kamal, operate from here. The bus stand for colts to the north coast is near the Giling bull-race stadium on the northern side. Sumenep is reputed to breed champion bulls and most Saturday mornings practice bull races can be seen at the stadium.

The kraton and its *taman sari*, pleasure garden, is worth visiting. It was built in the 18th century by Panembahan Sumolo, son of Queen Raden Ayu Tirtonegoro and her spouse Bendoro Saud, who was a commoner but a descendant of Muslim scholars. The architect is thought to have been the grandson of one of the first Chinese to settle in Sumenep after the Chinese massacre in Batavia. The kraton is occupied by the present bupati of Sumenep but part of the building is a small museum with an interesting collection of royal possessions including Madurese furniture, stone sculptures and *binggels*, the heavy silver anklets worn by Madurese women. Opposite the kraton, the royal carriage house contains the throne of Queen Tirtonegoro and a superb Chinese-style bed reputedly 300 years old.

Sumenep's 18th century Masjid Jamik mosque is notable for its three-tiered Meru-style roof, Chinese porcelain tiles and ceramics. Sumenep also has a Chinese temple.

The tombs of the royal family are at the Asta Tinggi cemetery, which looks out over the town from a peaceful hilltop one km away. The main royal tombs are interesting and decorated with carved and painted panels, two depicting dragons which are said to represent the colonial invasion of Sumenep. One of the small pavilions in the outer courtyard still bears the mark of an assassin's sword when an unsuccessful attempt was made to murder Bendoro Saud.

Near Sumenep Salopeng, near the village of Ambunten 20 km north of Sumenep, has a beautiful beach with strong waves, rolling sand dunes and coconut groves. Here you may see men fishing in the shallower water with large cantilevered hand nets which are rarely seen elsewhere in Java.

Lombeng beach, 30 km north-east, is said to be even more beautiful and remote. You can get out there by colt from Sumenep but there's no road all the way to the village. The local people ride their bicycles along the sands.

Places to Stay & Eat *Losmen Wijaya I* and *Wijaya II* (tel 21532), near the main bus station, are clean and well-run and both have small restaurants. Doubles with common mandi start at 5500 rp including

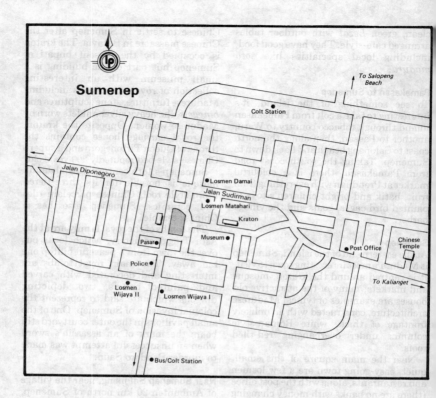

Sumenep

To Salopeng Beach

Colt Station

Jalan Diponegoro

Losmen Damai

Jalan Sudirman

Losmen Matahari

Kraton

Museum

Pasar

Police

Losmen Wijaya II

Losmen Wijaya I

Post Office

Chinese Temple

To Kalianget

Bus/Colt Station

morning coffee and there are more expensive rooms with private mandi and fan or air-con. Alternatively there's the *Losmen Damai* where rooms cost 3500 rp or the similarly priced *Losmen Matahari*, both on Jalan Sudirman.

Decent restaurants to try around town include the *Mawar* at Jalan Diponegoro 105 and *Rumah Makan 17 Agustus* at Jalan Sudirman 34. There are good day and night markets in the area around the mosque.

Getting There & Away
From Surabaya ferries sail to Kamal, the port town on the western tip of Madura, from where you can catch colts to other

towns on the island. It's a half hour trip by ferry and they cost just 250 rp, operating about every 10 minutes until late at night. Buses go directly from Surabaya's Joyoboyo station via the ferry as far as Pamekasan, Sumenep, and Kalianget but if you're already based in the centre of town it's just as easy, and probably quicker, to take a city bus to the ferry terminus at Tanjung Perak, take the ferry across to Kamal, and then take local buses around the island.

Another possibility, if you're coming from Bali say, is to take a ferry from Jangkar (near Situbondo) to Kalianget on the eastern tip of Madura. This trip takes about four hours and a ferry departs daily from Jangkar around 12 noon. To Jangkar the ferry departs from Kalianget at 7 am. Tickets are 2,250 rp.

Pintu Laut Express, across from the Wijaya I, Sumenep, operates a daily collect-and-drop minibus service between Sumenep and Surabaya which costs 4000 rp. It departs Sumenep at 4 am to catch the 7 am ferry from Kamal. Any of the losmen in Sumenep should be able to make arrangements for the minibus service.

Getting Around

Becaks exist in the main towns and colts go just about everywhere on the island. From Kamal to Bangkalan takes 1/2 hour; from Kamal to Pamekasan is a two to three hour ride by bus. Allow plenty of time if you're travelling along the north coast; the roads are rough and colts only run short distances between the villages. There are hardly any private cars on the island but then this is a place where you're more than likely to get offered a ride on a motorcycle – or even a bicycle!

TROWULAN

Trowulan was once the capital of the largest Hindu empire in Indonesian history. Founded by a Singosari prince, Wijaya, in 1294 it reached the height of its power under Hayam Wuruk (1350-89) who was guided by his powerful prime minister, Gajah Mada. During his time Majapahit claimed control over, or at least received tribute from, most of today's Indonesia and even parts of the Malay peninsula. The capital was a grand affair, the kraton forming a miniature city within the city and surrounded by great fortified walls and watchtowers.

Its wealth was based both on the fertile rice-growing plains of Java and on control of the spice trade. The religion was a hybrid of Hinduism with Shiva, Vishnu and Brahma being worshipped though, as in the earlier Javanese kingdoms, Buddhism was also prominent. It seems Muslims too were tolerated and Koranic burial inscriptions, found on the site, suggest that there were Javanese Muslims within the royal court even in the 14th century when this Hindu-Buddhist state was at the very height of its glory. The empire came to a sudden end in 1478 when the city fell to the north coast power of Demak and the Majapahit elite fled to Bali, thus opening up Java for conquest by the Muslims.

The Majapahit ruins are scattered over a large area – along the winding lanes of the small village of Trowulan and across great fields planted out with tobacco and other crops. Some of the ruins are quite superb in their shattered grandeur and this is a fine place to simply walk around and explore. It's possible to get round the sites in one day on foot if you start early, but hiring a becak makes life a lot easier.

On the main road from Surabaya to Solo, the Trowulan Museum houses some superb examples of sculpture collected locally. There's also a large table-top map here of the sites in the area. Some of the most interesting sites include the Kolam Segaram (a vast Majapahit swimming pool); the gateway of Bajang Ratu with its strikingly sculptured kala heads; the Tikus Temple (the Queen's bath) and the recently restored Siti Inggil Temple with the impressive tomb of Wijaya (people still come to meditate here and in the early evening it has quite a strange spiritual atmosphere). The Pendopo Agung is an open-air pavilion recently built by the Indonesian Army. Two km south of the pavilion, the Troloyo cemetery is the site of the oldest Muslim graves found on Java, the earliest is from 1376 AD.

Information

The Trowulan Museum is open from 7 am to 2 pm Tuesday to Thursday, to 11 am Friday, to 12.30 pm Saturday and until 2 pm on Sunday. It's closed Mondays. If you're en route to somewhere else, you can leave your gear safely at the museum

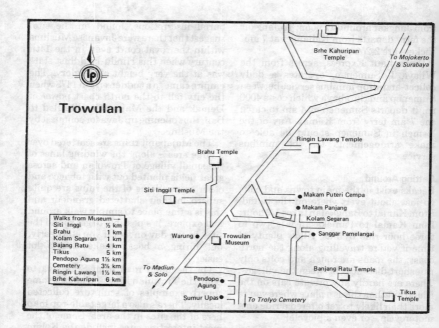

Trowulan

Walks from Museum →
Siti Inggi	½ km
Brahu	1 km
Kolam Segaran	1 km
Bajang Ratu	4 km
Tikus	5 km
Pendopo Agung	1½ km
Cemetery	3½ km
Ringin Lawang	1½ km
Brhe Kahuripan	6 km

Brhe Kahuripan Temple

To Mojokerto & Surabaya

Ringin Lawang Temple

Brahu Temple

Siti Inggil Temple

Makam Puteri Cempa

Makam Panjang

Kolam Segaran

Warung

Trowulan Museum

Sanggar Pamelangai

To Madiun & Solo

Pendopo Agung

Sumur Upas

To Trolyo Cemetery

Banjang Ratu Temple

Tikus Temple

office. Entry is 150 rp. There is nowhere to stay in Trowulan but there's a useful restaurant opposite the museum where you can get a cheap meal.

Getting There & Away
Trowulan is 60 km west of Surabaya which is the place many people use as a base, and only 10 km from Mojokerto which is an alternative if you want to stay near the ruins. From the Joyoboyo bus station in Surabaya it's a one-hour trip, via Mojokerto, to Trowulan and buses will drop you right in front of the museum. The bus fare is 600 rp. At the museum it's quite easy to hire a becak to get you around the sites, perhaps 5000 rp for a four-hour round trip but you have to bargain hard.

When you're leaving Trowulan there's no problem flagging a bus down on the road from Surabaya to Solo. There are scores of buses going in either direction

and from Trowulan it's 1000 rp on to Madiun towards Solo. If you're heading east to Probolinggo or south to Malang, you can take a bus or colt as far as Gempol and continue on from there by public bus which is cheaper. For Malang, an interesting alternative to backtracking through Mojokerto to Gempol is to travel by colt via Jombang and the hill town of Batu.

MOJOKERTO
Like Surabaya, Mojokerto can be a useful base from which to visit the Majapahit ruins at Trowulan. On the banks of the Brantas River, this is quite an attractive town with an old quarter of winding alleys, canals and old houses from the Dutch era. Mojokerto also has a small archaeological museum of its own, with various Majapahit stone carvings and a splendid statue of Kediri's King Airlangga-as-Vishnu astride a huge

Garuda. The Museum Purbakala is in the centre of town on Jalan A Yani, and open the same hours and days as the Trowulan museum.

Places to Stay

Opposite the bus station, the *Hotel Nagamas* has singles/doubles with mandi at 3850/5500 rp including breakfast and more expensive rooms with fan and hot water.

The *Wisma Tenera* is on Jalan Hos Cokroaminoto, roughly halfway between the bus station and the centre of town. There are good singles/doubles here at 7500 rp including breakfast, or with mandi at 10,000 rp. Most of the other losmen are located in the centre of town, about 3½ km from the bus station so you would definitely need to take a becak. They include *Losmen Merdeka*, Jalan Pamuji 73, with rooms at 7700 rp including breakfast. The old *Penginapan Barat* is along a quiet canal on Jalan Kradenan, just off Jalan Majapahit. It has reasonable rooms at 3000/5000 rp, plenty of mosquitoes and goldfish in the mandi - well, what more could you ask for?

Places to Eat

One of the best places to eat in Mojokerto is the *Depot Murni* at Jalan Majapahit 72. It's run by very friendly people and they serve excellent Indonesian food; most meals cost around 1000 rp. There are also plenty of warungs at night around the market, Pasar Kliwon, on the same street. The *Rumah Makan Surya* next to the Alun-Alun also has good reports.

Getting There & Away

Buses along the road from Surabaya to Madiun all pass through Mojokerto. If you stop off here for the night en route to Trowulan, you can pick up a colt going that way from the road running parallel to Jalan Majapahit (behind Pasar Kliwon) in the centre of town rather than heading back out to the bus station. The fare between Surabaya and Mojokerto is 550 rp.

PROBOLINGGO

Probolinggo is basically important as the transport centre for people visiting Mt Bromo. There's nothing special about Probolinggo but it can also be a useful midpoint on the Surabaya to Banyuwangi coastal road. The last colt to Mt Bromo leaves around 7 pm, after that you'll have to charter a colt for about 10,000 rp or stay overnight in Probolinggo.

Places to Stay

There are hotels and some cheap restaurants along the main street, Jalan P Sudirman, all within a 10-minute walk west of the bus station. The *Hotel Bromo Permai II* (tel 21510), opposite the bus station, is a source of copious but not always reliable information on Bromo and transport for Bali. It's a sister location of the Bromo Permai I up at the Mt Bromo crater in Cemoro Lawang and together these two hotels would like to get all the rupiah you spend between Probolinggo and the crater. The hotel itself is comfortable enough and a reasonably priced place to stay; dorm beds are 2100 rp, single/doubles with fan and mandi are 3500/5500 rp.

At the west end of Jalan P Sudirman at the crossroads with Jalan Suroyo, you'll find the imposing *Hotel Victoria* (tel 21040). It has quite comfortable rooms at 3000 rp and rooms with mandi and fan from 12,500 rp. There are also rooms with air-con. Tea on arrival and breakfast are included.

The *Hotel Kemayoran*, almost opposite the Victoria, is cheap but cheerless and grubby. *Hotel Ratna* (21597) further up at No 94 is a good place. Economy rooms are 3500 rp including breakfast; doubles with mandi and fan start at 7500 rp.

The main post office and most of the banks and government buildings are on Jalan Suroyo. Here at No 16, just around the corner from Jalan P Sudirman, you'll find perhaps Probolinggo's most pleasant place to stay, the *Hotel Tampiarto Plaza* (tel 21280). Economy singles/doubles are

3500/4000 rp, 5500 rp with mandi, or 8000/12,000 rp with fan and hot water. There are also rooms with air-con starting at 25,000 rp.

Places to Eat

The *Warung Sudi Mampir*, near the bus station at No 206-208, has good meals for around 750 to 1000 rp. The nearby *King Restaurant* has mostly Chinese and seafood; it's slightly pricey but good. *Restaurant Malang*, Jalan P Sudirman 104 near the Hotel Victoria, is also a bit expensive but there's a wide range of items on the menu and the food is good – most meals cost around 1000 to 2000 rp. For ice cream and iced juice try the *Sumber Hidup* garden cafe near the Hotel Ratna – they also have good sate. You'll find plenty of small restaurants and 'depots' at the night market around Pasar Gotong Royong near the colt station.

Getting There & Away

Bus Probolinggo is a 1150 rp bus ride from the Joyoboyo bus station in Surabaya. There are several departures an hour and the trip takes about 2½ hours. Malang is only two hours away by bus and the fare is 1200 rp.

Coming from Bali it's 8000 rp (9500 rp for an air-con bus) to Probolinggo from Denpasar; an evening bus departing around 7.30 to 8.30 pm will get you there at about 4 am. The bus from Banyuwangi, via Situbondo, costs 2400 rp and takes about five hours.

To Denpasar, a night bus leaves Probolinggo every hour between 6 and 11 pm. It takes eight hours and the fare is 9500 rp. To Yogya, night buses start running at 11 pm; it's an eight hour ride for around 8500 rp. Cheap, slow day buses cost only 4000 rp.

Rail The train station is about three km from the bus station, two km if you cut along the railway tracks. From Surabaya to Probolinggo (two trains a day) the fare is 3000 rp 2nd class, 2500 rp 3rd class; from Probolinggo to Banyuwangi (two trains a day) the fare is the same, plus 2400 rp through to Denpasar, but it's quicker to take a bus. A train to Yogya (one train per day departing at 7.30 am) is 3800 rp 3rd class but it's a long, slow trip.

Getting Around

Bromo The colt station in Probolinggo is only 300 metres or so west of the bus station (away from the railway line). There are frequent colts between 7 am and 7 pm from Probolinggo as far as Ngadisari via Sukapura. The fare is 1000 rp and the trip to Ngadisari takes 1½ to two hours uphill (less on the way down). From Probolinggo to Ngadisari is 45 km; from Ngadisari to Bromo is three steep km on foot. There are bemos that do the short run from Ngadisari to Cemoro Lawang (the village at the edge of the crater) for 1000 rp per person.

Don't believe the staff at Hotel Bromo Permai II in Probolinggo if they tell you their private colt is the only one going to Bromo – it costs twice as much as the public colts. And it stops for passengers along the way, just like the public colts! They may also tell you their colt goes all the way to Cemoro Lawang (which would save you the steep walk or a 1000 rp); this is also a lie.

MT BROMO

This powerful volcano is one of the most spectacular sights in Java. Bromo rises up in a desolate landscape – a vast sea of lava sand that stretches 10 km across, surrounded by craggy peaks – and it has a strange end-of-the-world feeling particularly at sunrise. Like Mt Batur on Bali, Bromo is a crater within a crater – one of four mountains that have emerged within the caldera of the ancient Tengger volcano. Legend has it that the great Tengger crater was dug out with just half a coconut shell by an ogre smitten with love for a princess. When the king saw that the ogre might fulfil the task he had set, which was to be completed in a single night, he

A lone rider crosses Mt Bromo's Sea of Sand

Brahma worshipped on the volcanic mountain of Bromo (Bromö in fact is the Javanese pronunciation of 'Brahma'). Each year, in January or February, Bromo is the site for the Kesada (Kesodo) festival with a colourful procession of Tenggerese who come to throw offerings into the crater at sunrise to pacify the god of the volcano.

Probolinggo Approach

Most people turn off at Probolinggo, to the north of Bromo, and plan to be on the rim of the crater for sunrise. From Probolinggo you have to get up the mountain to Ngadisari, sign the visitor's book at the police office and pay your 1000 rp. (If you're planning a day trip, note that the police aren't prepared to look after bags.) You can stay in Ngadisari or climb the last steep three km on foot to the hotel at Cemoro Lawang on the rim of the Tengger crater.

From Cemoro Lawang it's another three km down the crater wall and across the Sand Sea to Bromo. Sunrise is about 5 am, so if you're staying in Ngadisari you'll have to leave around 3 am, from Cemoro Lawang at 4 am. There's no real need for a guide or horses, although if you want to ride across to Bromo it costs about 5000 rp return from Ngadisari. It's cold and windy in the early morning so you'll need warm gear and take a torch (flashlight) – the descent on the path to the Sand Sea can be a bit dodgy in the dark. Once you're on the sand, white painted rocks mark the trail straight across to Bromo (about halfway they fork right to the Penanjakan Viewpoint) and by the time you've crossed the plain and started to climb up Bromo (246 steps, one traveller reported) it should be fairly light. The view from the top, of the sun sailing up over the outer crater, and that first glimpse into the steaming depths of Bromo is quite fantastic.

From Cemoro Lawang trekkers can take an interesting walk across the Sand Sea to Ngadas (eight km) on the southern

ordered his servants to pound rice and the cocks started to crow thinking dawn had broken. The coconut which the ogre flung away became Mt Batok and the trench became the Sand Sea – and the ogre died of exhaustion.

Bromo is also a centre for the Tenggerese – farmers who cultivate market vegetables on the steep mountain slopes and are found only on the high ranges of the Tengger-Semeru massif. They are a people whose history can be traced back to the rule of the Hindu-Majapahit Empire when followers of rim of the Tengger crater. Along the road from Ngadas you can eventually flag down a colt to Malang, via Gubug Klakah and Tumpang. It entails at least six or seven hours walking, so you'd need to start early in order to get to Malang by evening.

Ngadas Approach

If you want to avoid the Probolinggo to Mt Bromo shakedown, you can trek into the Tengger crater from Ngadas to the southwest of Mt Bromo. This is definitely a trek for those willing and able to rough it a bit. The reward is spectacular mountain scenery and not having to deal with the Bromo hustlers until after you've experienced Bromo.

You can start this route either from Malang or Surabaya – either way you must get to Blimbing, just north of Malang. From Blimbing it's a short bemo ride east to Tumpang; in Tumpang get another bemo to the town of Gubug Klakah. From Gubug Klakah it's a full-day 13-km walk to the village of Ngadas which is 2 km south-west of the crater rim – you may be able to catch a ride along the way and shorten the journey. You can spend the night with the villagers of Ngadas and explore Mt Bromo and the Tengger crater the next day. It's about a three-hour walk (8 km) across the crater to Cemoro Lawang, where you can get a bemo down to Probolinggo – or do the entire route in reverse.

There is a PHPA office in Ngadas that has good information and maps of the Bromo-Semeru area.

From Gubug Klakah you also have the option of trekking to Mt Semeru, the tallest mountain in Java. See the Nature Reserves in East Java section.

Whichever route you take, the ideal time to visit Bromo to be sure of a blood-red sunrise would be during the dry season, April to November. In the wet season the dawn and the clouds are likely to arrive simultaneously so an early rise may not be worth the effort – you might as well stroll across later when it's warmer. At any time of year it's cold on these mountains; from June to September night temperatures can get down to around 2 to 5°C, while from October to May minimums range from 10 to 15°C.

Places to Stay

In Ngadisari there are plenty of villagers who will offer you a room for the night, although the quality varies a lot and security is usually minimal. Prices vary from around 2500 rp; less for really basic rooms (kapok beds) and much higher if you arrive too late to hunt around. There are a couple of warungs and a small restaurant near the police office.

Up at Cemoro Lawang, right on the rim of the Tengger crater, the *Hotel Bromo Permai* is much more expensive than its sister hotel in Probolinggo. But staying here does save an hour or so of pre-dawn walking. Even at 2500 rp (2100 rp with a YHA card), the dorm is poor value as it's dingy and the toilets are sometimes clogged. Rooms are even more preposterous for what you get, from 10,000 rp to 33,750 rp for a double with mandi. The restaurant is expensive and of questionable quality, and we can't say much about the service either. Why would you stay here? Your only alternative is in one of the village houses below. The PHPA office in Cemoro Lawang sometimes has space to put people up for around 4000 rp per night.

Getting There & Away

Probolinggo, 42 km away, is the departure point for colts as far as Ngadisari. The trip takes 1½ hours and the fare is 1000 rp. For Ngadas, catch a bemo from Blimbing to Tumpang, then another to Gubug Klakah – this should take two hours at most and total fare is 650 rp. From Gubug Klakah it's walk or hitch.

If you read any of the literature turned out by the Indonesian Tourist Office, you'll probably come across some delightful Indonesian-English turns of phrase. Here's a lyrical example:

Bromo should be the choice for only there, on the crater rim with the sea of sand stretching below as far as the eyes can see on one's left and the ghostly grumble mixed with dense lumps of smoke crumple up from the inner pitfall on one's right, and on the height of 2,383 metres above sea level would one see how lustrous the aurora of the sun, in mixing colours of white, pale yellow, yellowish red turning red appears from behind the hills quite in front, to brighten the atmosphere to daylight, does one feel oneself to be like one grain of small green pea amidst a vessel of sand – you'll be aware of the Greatness of the Creator of men!

PASIR PUTIH

Roughly half way between Probolinggo and Banyuwangi, on the north coast road, this is East Java's most popular seaside resort but Pasir Putih (which means 'white sand') is a misnomer – the sand is more grey-black than white! There are lots of picturesque outrigger boats, there's swimming and there are boats to hire but – compared to Lovina Beach only a few hours away on Bali – it's really no big deal. It's a useful stopover point, but go during the week if you want the beach to yourself. Pasir Putih is mobbed on weekends with sun 'n sand worshippers from Surabaya.

Places to Stay

There are a number of losmen, restaurants, fruit and souvenir stalls all jammed in between the highway and the beach. The *Pasir Putih Inn* has its own garden and is probably the nicest of them, though their rooms (with mandi) are somewhat overpriced for what you get at 7000 rp. More expensive rooms, from 8400 rp, are good and have a terrace.

Hotel Sidho Muncul has clean, airy rooms on the beachfront at 6000 rp and larger rooms for three from 15,000 rp. *Hotel Bhayangkara Beach* is the cheapest of all with rooms facing the highway: some small and stuffy ones cost 5000 rp; better rooms (with mandi) facing the beach start at 7500 rp. Also decent is the *Mutiara Beach Hotel*, which has rooms with mandi for 7500 rp.

SITUBONDO

Only a short distance on the Banyuwangi side of Pasir Putih, Situbondo is a reasonably large town with several places to stay. The *Hotel Asia*, near the bus station, is on the main road and is quite pleasant. The *Losmen Asita* is near the railway station or there's the *Hotel Situbondo*.

KALIKLATAK

At Kaliklatak, 20 km north of Banyuwangi, you can go on tours of large coffee, cocoa, rubber, and clove plantations. Accommodation is available at the *Wisata Irdjen Guesthouse* (tel 323 in Kaliklatak, 41896 in Banyuwangi), but is likely to be expensive. Tours and accommodation must be booked in advance – many travel agencies in Bali as well as Surabaya can make the arrangements, or call Wisata Irdjen directly.

BANYUWANGI

Although there are no particular attractions to drag you there, schedules or just the urge to be somewhere different might take you to Banyuwangi, the ferry departure point for Bali. The actual ferry terminus for Bali is a few km north of town at Ketapang.

The old Banyuwangi railway station has been closed down and replaced by a new one in Ketapang, just a couple of hundred metres from the ferry terminus. This means more people will probably be travelling straight through without stopping in Banyuwangi. If you choose to spend a night or two here, you'll find the town fairly pleasant if not particularly attractive.

Banyuwangi has its own music/dance style that has been likened to Sundanese Jaipongan. It's called Gandrung Banyuwangi and can be seen at weddings and during holiday periods. In the nearby villages of Bakungan and Oleh Sari you can see *Seblang*, a trance dance performed in propitiation of certain spirits by female *dukuns* who pass the gift of trance from mother to daughter. On Satu Suro, the

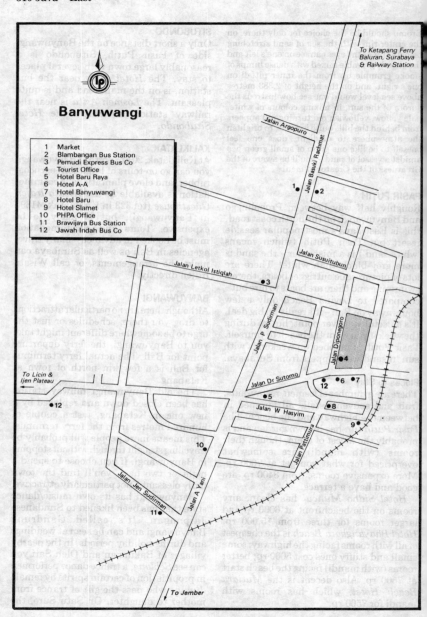

To Ketapang Ferry
Baluran, Surabaya
& Railway Station

Banyuwangi

1 Market
2 Blambangan Bus Station
3 Pemudi Express Bus Co
4 Tourist Office
5 Hotel Baru Raya
6 Hotel A-A
7 Hotel Banyuwangi
8 Hotel Baru
9 Hotel Slamet
10 PHPA Office
11 Brawijaya Bus Station
12 Jawah Indah Bus Co

Jalan Argopuro

Jalan Basuki Rachmat

Jalan Susuitubun

Jalan Letkol Istiqlah

Jalan P Sudirman

Jalan Diponegoro

Jalan Dr Sutomo

Jalan W Hasyim

Jalan Pattimura

To Licin &
Ijen Plateau

Jalan Jen Sudirman

Jalan A Yani

To Jember

first day of the Javanese calendar, a ceremony called Petik Laut is performed at the seaside in Muncar to give thanks to the sea spirits for good harvests.

Information & Orientation

There are three bus stations in Banyuwangi, the main one is Blambangan to the north of town on the road to Ketapang. Blambangan and Ketapang are quite some distance from each other so you will need to take a bemo from one to the other.

Banyuwangi's Tourist Office is on the town square at Jalan Diponegoro 2. A map of Banyuwangi and a leaflet on places of interest in the area is available if you ask for it; they have little else but they speak English and they're very helpful if you drop in. It's open 7 am to 2 pm Monday to Thursday, to 12 noon Friday and until 1 pm Saturday. Opposite the tourist office you'll find the post office and telephone office. Next to these offices in the grounds of a school there's another tourist information centre run by an enterprising junior guide, open from 3 pm to 9 pm. There's a bank nearby on Jalan Dr Sutomo.

Wildlife Parks/Nature Reserves

If you're coming from Bali and planning a visit to Baluran National Park (37 km from Banyuwangi) or the Ijen Plateau (about 18 km from Banyuwangi) you can get information from the Baluran National Park Office (tel 41119) at Jalan A Yani 108, Banyuwangi (tel 41119). There is a PHPA office at the entrance to Baluran in the village of Wonorejo, but you can book accommodation in advance through the main Banyuwangi office if you want to be sure of a bed for the night. A rough map of Baluran is available here and staff are very helpful. The office is open from 7 am to 2 pm Monday to Thursday, to 11 am Friday, to 1 pm Saturday and until 2 pm Sunday.

Places to Stay – bottom end

The *Hotel Baru* (tel 21369), Jalan Pattimura 82-84, is one of Banyuwangi's most popular places to stay for budget travellers. It's clean, well run and friendly, and there are big airy rooms. Singles/doubles cost 2000/3000 rp including breakfast; rooms with mandi and fan start at 3500/4000 rp. There's also the *Hotel Berlin Barat* nearby which is similarly priced. *Hotel Slamet*, next to the old railway station, charges 4500/5000 rp.

In the centre of town, the *Hotel Baru Raya* at Jalan Dr Sutomo 26 is not bad for cheap rooms at 1000/2000 rp or 1500/2500 rp with mandi. *Hotel Asia-Afrika* on Jalan Dr Sutomo near the tourist office has grubby rooms for 3500 rp.

The *Hotel Anda* at Jalan Basuki Rachmad 36, near the Blambangan bus station, is adequate and has rooms at 4000 rp.

Places to Stay – top end

The best hotel in the area is the *Manyar Hotel* (tel 41741) on the road between Ketapang and Banyuwangi. Rooms (all air-con with hot water) range from US$10 to US$33, and there are more expensive suites. There's a laundry service available and the hotel has a bar and restaurant.

In Banyuwangi there are a couple of places with comfortable air-con rooms which cover the cheap and more expensive brackets. The *Wisma Blambangan* (tel 21598), Jalan Dr Wahidin 4, has non air-con singles/doubles from 15,000 rp including breakfast and air-con rooms at 22,000 rp. *Hotel Banyuwangi* (tel 41178) on the same street at No 10 is similar, a little more expensive but rates include breakfast, lunch and dinner.

Out by the Ketapang ferry harbour, about the only place to stay is the overpriced *Hotel Banyuwangi Beach*. All rooms have air-con and cost 22,500 but conditions are not on a par with this rate. Other places will surely open up in this area eventually.

Places to Eat

Jalan Pattimura is a good street for

warungs and night stalls with delicious *air jahe* (ginger tea) and snacks – *dadak djagung* (egg & sweetcorn patties), *ketan* (sticky rice topped with coconut) and fried banana. Across from the Hotel Baru, the *Depot Baru* is an excellent family-run place with good *nasi pecel istimewa* for 500 rp. The *Depot Surya* around the corner on Jalan W Hasyim is also quite good and inexpensive. *Rumah Makan Ria* at Jalan P Sudirman 107 has good Chinese food from 2000 to 3000 rp per dish.

Getting There & Away

See the Getting there & Away section for Surabaya for details of Banyuwangi to Surabaya transport by road and rail.

Bus There are two main bus stations in Banyuwangi.

Blambangan is the most important bus station, north of town on the road to the Bali ferry port at Ketapang. Buses operating from here to Surabaya take the coastal route via Ketapang Ferry, Baluran National Park and Probolinggo. Fares include to Baluran 500 rp (half an hour); Pasir Putih 700 rp (two hours); Probolinggo 2400 rp via Situbondo (four hours). Colts include to Ketapang Ferry 300 rp; Kaliklatak coffee plantation 600 rp and Baluran 600 rp.

Blambangan is also where you get the local Lin colts, which cost 150 rp per person. Take a Lin 2 to get to the centre of Banyuwangi near the Alun-Alun and Hotel Baru. If you're heading for the Ijen Plateau Nature Reserve, you can take a Lin 3 colt from Blambangan to Sasak Perot and then an intercity colt as far as Licin for 500 rp.

On the southern edge of town, buses from the Brawijaya bus station to Surabaya take the inland route via Jember. The bus to Jember costs 1500 rp (two hours) and this is the bus to take if you're heading for Sukamade Beach in the Meru Betiri Reserve. Colts from Brawijaya operate to villages south of Banyuwangi.

Jawah Indah Express have a night bus to Surabaya for 5000 rp including a food stop in Pasir Putih. It departs from Blambangan bus station at 9.15 pm and arrives in Surabaya at 3.30 am. If you want to be sure of a seat, you can buy tickets 1½ hours before departure from their office at Jalan Dr Sutomo 86.

If you're heading for Malang, Pemudi Express near the mosque at Jalan Kapten Ilyas 6 operates a night bus for 7000 rp. The ticket office opens at 6 pm and the bus departs from there at 10 pm, arriving in Malang at the crack of dawn.

Bali Ferry Ferries from Ketapang, eight km north of town, depart every hour round the clock for Gilimanuk on Bali. You can book from Surabaya right through to Denpasar including the ferry. See the Bali section for more details.

Getting Around

Banyuwangi has a squadron of bemos running between the various colt and bus stations; they're marked Lin 1, 2, 3 and charge a fixed 150 rp fare around town.

Useful bemos include Lin 1 between Ketapang Ferry and the Blambangan and Brawijaya bus stations. Lin 2 between Blambangan (past the train station) and Brawijaya bus station. Lin 3 between Blambangan (past the tourist office) and Sasak Perot, where you get colts to Licin and then on to the Ijen Plateau.

NATURE RESERVES IN EAST JAVA

Baluran National Park, on the extreme north-eastern tip of the province, is the most accessible of Java's large wildlife sanctuaries – the other being the relatively more remote Ujung Kulon National Park in West Java. Six areas in East Java have also been designated 'Nature Reserves'; three on the south coast and the others in the volcanic mountain regions inland. The latter three areas offer limited wildlife but magnificent scenery and are likely to appeal to those interested in trekking.

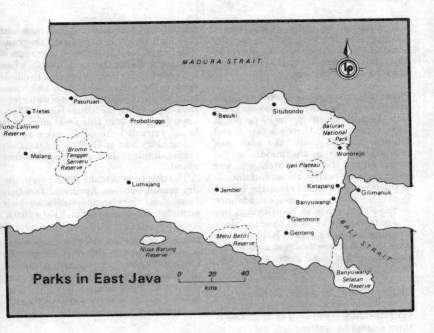

Parks in East Java

MADURA STRAIT

Pasuruan
Tretes
uno-Lalijiwo
Reserve
Probolinggo
Besuki
Situbondo
Baluran
National
Park
Bromo
Tenger
Semeru
Reserve
Malang
Wonorejo
Ijen Plateau
Lumajang
Jember
Ketapang
Gilimanuk
Banyuwangi
Glenmore
Genteng
Nusa Barung
Reserve
Meru Betiri
Reserve
BALI STRAIT
Banyuwangi
Selatan
Reserve

0   20   40
kms

Guest house accommodation is available at Baluran but facilities in the nature reserves are basic if they exist at all. In some cases you need to be relatively self-sufficient and equipped with provisions and, sometimes, cold-weather gear.

Baluran National Park

On the north-east corner of Java, Baluran National Park covers an area of 250 square km. The park lands surround the solitary hump of Mt Baluran (1247 metres) and contain a mixture of monsoon forest and, on the north side, surprisingly extensive dry savannah grassland threaded by stony-bedded streams. The main attractions are the herds of feral water buffalo, banteng (wild cattle), rusa deer (barking deer), monkeys, and the wild pigs, leopards and civet cats which live in the upland forest. Birds include the green junglefowl, peacocks, bee-eaters, king-fishers and owls.

It's possible to make arrangements with the PHPA staff at the park entrance for a jeep to take you to some of the more remote parts of the savannah, but you will have to negotiate a price. Even around Bekol, where the main guest house is located, you can see deer and water buffalo, usually in the early morning or late afternoon so you should stay here for the night. Banteng are sighted less often – they only come down to the savannah in the dry season and are being displaced by the large numbers of buffalo which apparently breed more efficiently.

The main service area for Baluran is the village of Wonorejo, on the main coast road between Surabaya and Banyuwangi, where food supplies can be bought – the PHPA office is just inside the park entrance. Baluran is open daily from 7 am to 5 pm and if you're not staying overnight, baggage can be left safely at the PHPA office.

Baluran can be visited at any time of the year but the best time is the dry season, between June and November. The best time of day is in the very early morning or late evening.

Places to Stay Accommodation is available at two places. The *Bekol Guesthouse*, 12 km into the park, sleeps up to 10 people at 2500 rp per person; there's a mandi and kitchen but you must take your own provisions. It is in the middle of the savannah and there is a watchtower and water reservoir nearby. *Bama Guesthouse* is three km east of Bekol on the beach. Bookings for both can be made in advance at the PHPA office in Banyuwangi but you're more than likely to have the place to yourself. If you arrive at Baluran after dark there is a free camping area at the entrance and a small guest house (also free) available for a temporary stay.

Getting There & Away Surabaya to Banyuwangi buses, taking the coast road via Probolinggo, will stop at Wonorejo if there's anyone getting off. If you're leaving the park, buses are easily flagged down. From Banyuwangi (or Ketapang ferry, if you're coming from Bali) it's only a 1/2 hour journey which costs 500 rp. Coming from the west, Baluran is 3½ hours from Probolinggo/Mt Bromo and the bus costs around 1500 rp.

Ijen Plateau

The Ijen Plateau, part of a reserve area which stretches north-east to Baluran, was at one time a huge active crater complex 134 square km in area. Today Ijen is dormant, not dead, and the landscape is dominated by the volcanic cones of Ijen (2400 metres) and Merapi (2800 metres) on the north-eastern edge of the plateau and Raung (3332 metres) on the south-west corner. Coffee plantations cover much of the western part of the plateau where there are a few settlements.

This is not an outstanding area for wildlife, but the Ijen Crater has a magnificent turquoise sulphur lake and this high region is completely unspoilt. The Ijen crater lake is almost surrounded by sheer walls but the north-west face has crumbled and it may be possible to climb down to the 'safety-valve' dam which was built here to regulate the flow of water into the Banyu Pahit, the 'Bitter River'. There are a few people in this area: sulphur is being extracted from the lake and a vulcanology post at Ungkup-Ungkup, on the south side of the crater, is staffed year round.

The best time to make the hike is in the dry season between April and October. Note that night temperatures at high altitudes can drop to around 10 to 16°C.

Places to Stay A *Forestry Office Guesthouse* is available at the village of Jampit. At Ungkup-Ungkup, a former resthouse provides shelter but little else; it's run-down and there are no facilities. The sulphur quarry workers may cook for you, but you must take provisions.

Getting There & Away You can approach the Ijen Crater from Banyuwangi by bus to Licin (15 km) and then on foot to Ungkup-Ungkup (six hours) and the crater rim (one hour). It can also be reached from Bondowoso or Wonosari to the west, by bus from either point to Jampit via Gempol. The trek across the plateau between Jampit and Ungkup-Ungkup takes about five hours.

Banyuwangi Selatan Reserve

Also known as 'Blambangan', this reserve occupies the whole of the remote Purwo peninsula at the south-eastern tip of Java. This is perhaps the last area in Indonesia where the fast-dwindling species of Indonesian wild dog (*ajak*, a subspecies of the Indian dhole) still exists in any numbers. The reserve is also noted for its turtle-nesting beaches which, sadly, are often raided by Balinese turtle hunters. There are jungle fowl, leaf monkeys, muncaks, rusa deer, leopards and wild pigs.

Surfers from Bali have 'discovered' Grajagan Bay and there is a small surfing camp at Plengkung which has apparently had official permission to build bamboo bungalows – actually tree-houses. Facilities are likely to be limited though and you should take your own provisions. You can book ahead of time at travel agencies in Surabaya (Orient Express) or Bali (Bhayangkara Travel).

Getting There & Away You can get to Blambangan by bus from Banyuwangi to Benculuk; colt from Benculuk to Grajagan, and then by fishing boat across the Grajagan Bay (2½ hours) to Plengkung.

Meru Betiri Reserve

Covering 500 square km, the Meru Betiri Reserve is on the south coast just south of the Jember district. The major attraction here is the protected Sukamade 'Turtle Beach', a three km sand strip where five species of turtle come ashore to lay their eggs. In the mountain forests there are wild pigs, muncaks, squirrels, civets and jungle cats, and some leopards; the silvered-leaf monkey and long-tailed macaque are common. Meru Betiri is also known as the home of the almost extinct Javan Tiger (*hariman macam jawa*) but you'd be very lucky to see one. An intensive study in 1978 revealed that there were between three and five tigers; in 1981 a 'fairly reliable' sighting was reported. The reserve contains pockets of rainforest and the area is unusually wet much of the year. The best time to visit would be the dry season, from April to October.

Places to Stay There are two possibilities at Sukamade village. The *Wisma Sukamade* hotel has rooms at 5000 rp and accommodation is also available at the *Sukamade Baru Estate* (about 30 beds), which is a large plantation of coffee, rubber and coconut palms and it may be possible to hire a jeep and driver here. There is also a *PHPA Guesthouse* at Rajegwesin village, about two hours from Sukamade beach, which sleeps four to six people with food available by arrangement.

Getting There & Away Sukamade can be reached by bus from Genteng or Glenmore, both on the Jember to Banyuwangi road. From Genteng to Sukamade is 70 km (about three hours); From Glenmore to Sukamade is 100 km and the best access point if you're coming from the west.

Mt Semeru

Part of the huge Bromo-Tengger massif, Mt Semeru is the highest mountain in Java at 3680 metres. Also known as 'Mahameru', the 'Great Mountain', it has been looked on by Hindus since time immemorial as the most sacred mountain of all and father of Mt Agung on Bali.

The trek to the peak commences from Rano Pani, a small village on a lake at 2200 metres, accessible by bus and colt from Malang via Tumpang, Gubug Klakah and Ngadas. It's also possible to cross the Tengger Sand Sea from Mt Bromo (12 km) and then ascend to Rano Pani (another 12 km). From Rano Pani the path trails up through open grasslands and woods, across the 2800 metre pass of Mt Ayek-Ayek, and drops steeply to the beautiful Rano Kumbolo crater lake (2400 metres). From Rano Pani to Kumbolo is about 10 km. To the top of Semeru and back it's a hard day's climb and you need to be well equipped and prepared for camping overnight. At Rano Pani there is a small PHPA resthouse – free but no bedding or food provided. The best time to make the climb is May to October.

Mt Arjuno-Lalijiwo Reserve

This reserve includes the dormant volcano Arjuno (3339 metres), the semi-active Mt Welirang (3156 metres) and the Lalijiwo Plateau on the north slopes of Arjuno. From the hill resort of Tretes, 55 km south of Surabaya, there is a track used by people collecting sulphur which leads to the summit of Arjuno. It's a stiff four-hour climb from Tretes to the plateau and another two hours to the saddle between the mountains. To the summit and back would be a long day's climb. Arjuno has meadows and, on the higher slopes, there are forests where deer and wild pigs are common. There are hotels in Tretes (but they're expensive – see 'Around Surabaya'). On the Laliliwijo Plateau, there's a shelter used by the sulphur gatherers but you would have to take camping gear and food – water is no problem.

Bali

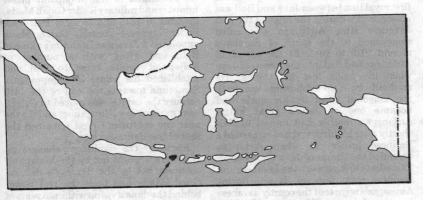

For many westerners, Bali doesn't extend beyond the tourist leaflet: idyllic tropical beaches, lush green forests and happy islanders who work and play in childlike innocence. This vision of paradise has been turned into a commodity for the tens of thousands of western tourists who flood into Bali's Kuta Beach every year, who see nothing but Kuta Beach, and go away leaving the sand scarred end to end with motorcycle tracks.

In actual fact the tourist trade is only a peripheral thing; away from the commercial traps of the southern beaches you can still find Bali's soul, towards the mountains where it has always been. It is there you *will* find rice paddies tripping down hillsides like giant steps, holy mountains reaching up through the clouds and dense tropical jungle. And it's there you'll discover the extraordinary resilience of the Balinese people and their culture.

HISTORY
An old manuscript, the *Catur Yoga*, tells of the formation of the world and places Bali in the centre of the universe, as an island resting on the back of a turtle floating in an ocean, beneath a canopy of 'perfumed sky, beautiful and full of rare flowers'. Another story tells of a great Javanese priest drawing his finger across the isthmus which joined Bali to Java and cutting the island free. At one time Bali was indeed connected to Java – the strait separating the two islands is just three km wide and no more than 60 metres deep.

The earliest written records found in Bali are stone inscriptions, dating from around the 9th century AD, by which time the foundations of the Balinese society of today had already been laid. Rice was grown with the help of a complex irrigation system probably very like the one in use now; metalwork and stone and woodcarving were developing; and a political system of regional princedoms had arisen, later presided over by a king when the first Balinese dynasties evolved. Before then little is known of the island – a few stone tools are the only traces of the earliest inhabitants, though certainly by the onset of the metal age around 300 BC the island was well-populated and an orderly village life had developed. It was during the first half of the 11th century that Hindu Java began to spread its influence into Bali and from then much of

Balinese history is inseparable from events on Java.

It was during the 11th century that the first royal link between Java and Bali was established – during the reign of the east Javanese King Airlangga who ruled somewhere to the south of Surabaya around 1019 to 1042. At the age of 16 Airlangga had fled into the forests of Java when his uncle lost his throne. He gradually built up a following, won back the kingdom ruled by his uncle and became one of Java's great kings. Airlangga's mother had moved to Bali shortly after his birth and had remarried a Balinese prince, so when Airlangga ascended the throne of Java there was an immediate link between the Javanese and Balinese royal families. It was during Airlangga's reign that the courtly Javanese language known as *Kawi* came into use amongst the royalty of Bali and the rock-cut memorials at Gunung Kawi, near Tampaksiring, provide a clear architectural link between Bali and 11th century Java.

After Airlangga's death Bali was ruled by the descendants of his mother and retained semi-independent status for two centuries until Kertanagara became king of Java's Singasari dynasty. The last and most powerful prince of that dynasty, he conquered Bali in 1284, but was murdered eight years later. Although his kingdom broke up, his son later founded the powerful Majapahit dynasty in Java and Kertanagara's conquest of the island began a turbulent period in Balinese history – for the next 200 years the indigenous rulers of Bali were in constant conflict with the Javanese for control of the island.

With Java in turmoil after the collapse of the Singasari dynasty however, Bali was able to regain its independence for a while and the Pejeng Dynasty, centred near modern day Ubud rose to power. The last king of the dynasty, the legendary Dalem Bedulu – said to have had the head of a pig and the powers of a magician –

refused to recognise Majapahit supremacy. Consequently the Javanese armies, under the command of the Majapahit prime minister and military leader Gajah Mada, invaded in 1343 and brought Bali back under Javanese control. Gajah Mada appointed a Javanese Brahmin as king of Bali, and along with a number of Majapahit nobles came to Bali and established his palace at Samprangan. Sometime towards the end of the 14th century the capital was moved to Gelgel, near modern day Klungkung, and for the next two centuries Gelgel remained the seat of the Balinese kings.

Ironically the significant changes on Bali were wrought not by the Majapahit conquest but by the dynasty's demise. Gajah Mada had been the real power behind the dynasty, and within 25 years of his death, in 1364, the Majapahit kingdom was on the decline. As Islam spread into Java, luring converts amongst the newly independent princes, the kingdom fell apart and many of its intelligentsia, artisans, dancers, musicians, scholars and priests retreated to Bali. Among them was the priest Nirartha who is credited with developing many of the complexities of Balinese religion. The final great exodus to Bali took place in 1478. As the Majapahit kingdom collapsed into disputing sultanates the Gelgel dynasty in Bali, under Dalem Batur Enggong, gained strength and extended its power eastwards to Lombok and even crossed the strait to the western end of Java.

So the curious mixture of position and events accounted not only for Bali's relative isolation from the rest of Indonesian history and religion but also for the amazing vitality of its culture. The island's extraordinary fertility had already encouraged the development of a highly active arts and culture, and the injection of creative energy from Java sparked off a level of activity which has hardly faltered to this day.

The first Europeans to set foot on Bali

were Dutch seaman led by Cornelius Houtman in 1597. At that time the Balinese aristocracy was enjoying unprecedented prosperity and the Balinese king, who befriended Houtman, is said to have had 200 wives, a chariot pulled by two white buffaloes, and a retinue of 50 dwarves whose bodies had been bent to resemble kris handles! Setting a tradition which has prevailed to the present day some of his crew fell in love with the island and refused to leave when Houtman set sail.

Despite Houtman's other blunders around the archipelago, this first meeting with the Balinese seems to have gone gloriously well. Although the Dutch returned to Bali, they were primarily interested in profit not culture and since Bali offered little of the former it escaped the attentions of the Dutch East India Company which decided to plunder Java and the spice islands of Maluku instead. But, as with so many other places, the seeds of eventual conquest were sown through that first 'innocent' contact with Europeans.

In 1710 the Balinese king shifted from Gelgel to Klungkung, thereby becoming the raja of Klungkung, considered by the Balinese ruling class to be the highest position of authority. But many of the local rulers – descendents of Majapahit nobles who had been given land to rule as dependencies of Gelgel – were gradually breaking away from Gelgel authority and the Dutch, now interested in control, used the local discontent to divide and conquer.

The first military confrontation with the Dutch was in 1846 when the Dutch used Balinese salvage claims over shipwrecks as a pretext to land military forces in north Bali. In 1882 the northern states of Buleleng and Jembrana were placed under the direct administration of the Netherlands East Indies government. With northern Bali under Dutch control, the south was not going to last long and, once again, it was disputes over the ransacking of wrecked ships that gave the Dutch the excuse they needed to move in. A Chinese ship was wrecked and 'looted' off Sanur in 1904 – the owners held the Dutch government responsible but the Dutch government demanded that the raja of Badung (Denpasar) pay damages and punish the culprits. Those demands were rejected and two years later the Dutch used the incident as an excuse to land a force of several thousand soldiers at Sanur. The first battles were fought on the beach and along the road to Denpasar, and within four days the Dutch had reached the outskirts of the town.

On 20 September 1906 the Dutch mounted a naval bombardment on Denpasar and then commenced their final assault. The three princes of Badung realised that they were outnumbered and outgunned and that defeat was inevitable. Surrender and exile was, however, an even worse alternative and they decided to take the honourable path of *puputan* or a suicidal fight to the death. First the palaces were burnt then, dressed in their finest jewellery and waving golden krises, the raja led the royalty and priests out to face the Dutch.

The Dutch begged the Balinese to surrender rather than make their hopeless stand but their pleas went unheard and wave after wave of the Balinese nobility marched forward to be gunned down by the Dutch. In all, 4000 Balinese were massacred in a single day outside the Denpasar and Pemecutan palaces. Some days later the Dutch marched to Tabanan, west of Badung, taking the raja of Tabanan prisoner but he too committed suicide rather than face the disgrace of exile. The kingdoms of Karangasem and Gianyar had already capitulated to the Dutch, and the raja of Klungkung obliged the Dutch by carrying out his own bloody *puputan*. With this last obstacle disposed of, all of Bali came under Dutch control.

In just a few days the Dutch had wiped out the power of the island's aristocracy, but little changed for the ordinary people in the villages. There were different faces to pay the taxes to, but traditional Balinese culture and society remained almost entirely intact and, suprisingly, for the next three decades the island underwent a cultural renaissance. While the remaining princes were deprived of their political powers they retained much of their importance as patrons of the arts. On top of that some far-sighted Dutch officials encouraged Balinese artistic aspirations and together with a new found international interest sparked off an artistic revival. By the 1930s western artists like Walter Spies and Rudolf Bonnet had started painting in Bali and their influence gave Balinese art a shot in the arm. For the elite circle of world travellers and minor celebrities who lived in Ubud and Sanur in the 1920s and '30s, Bali became the isle at the end of the rainbow.

Sadly, the second half of the 20th century has been much less kind and the island has undergone three great convulsions in the past 30 years. The huge eruption of Gunung Agung in 1963 killed thousands, devastated vast areas of the island and forced many Balinese to accept transmigration to other parts of Indonesia. Only two years later, in the wake of the attempted communist coup, Bali became the scene of some of the bloodiest anti-Communist killings in Indonesia, perhaps inflamed by some mystical desire to purge the land of evil, but equally likely from motives of revenge. The killings were probably no more brutal than elsewhere in Indonesia, but they certainly conflicted with the stereotyped image of the gentle Balinese.

While the Balinese may have survived Dutch control, the anti-Communist bloodbath and intermittent lava flows it's debatable whether they'll survive the tourist boom which stated in the 1970s. This is potentially more tragic than any of the other convulsions since it threatens the survival of a remarkable culture, the very feature which makes the island so

interesting. While you can hardly expect the Balinese to set themselves up as a living museum you can't help but wonder in what direction their island is heading.

THE BALINESE

Something like 2½ million people are crammed into this tiny island. The Balinese have their own clearly defined social strata, resembling the Indian Hindu caste system, although there are no untouchables. Nor is there an intricate division of labour based on caste and, except for the Brahmana priesthood, a

Balinese thrashing rice stalks in the field

particular title does not entail an exclusive right to a given occupation.

They do, however, speak a language which reflects their caste, a tiered system where (like the Javanese) at each level their choice of words is governed by the social relationship between the two people having a conversation. Low Balinese is used between intimates, equals and when talking to inferiors. Middle Balinese is used when speaking about superiors, or when addressing superiors or strangers, mainly when one wishes to be very polite but doesn't want to emphasise caste differences. High Balinese is used when talking to superiors. While it sounds remarkably complex the difference between each of the languages is only in the words used. High Balinese includes its own additional vocabulary of about 600 words, essentially connected with the person and bodily actions.

Balinese Society

Balinese society is an intensely communal one; the organisation of villages, the cultivation of farmlands and even the creative arts are communal efforts – a person belongs to their family, clan, caste and the village as a whole. Religion permeates all aspects of life so each stage of existence from soon after conception until after the final cremation is marked by ceremonies and rituals. In fact the first ceremony of life takes place at the third month of pregnancy when a series of offerings is made at home and at the village river or spring to ensure the wellbeing of the baby. When the child reaches puberty his teeth are filed to produce an aesthetically pleasing straight line – crooked fangs are, after all, reminiscent of the ghastly grimaces of witches and demons.

Balinese women are not cloistered away and social life in Bali is relatively free and easy although the roles of the sexes are fairly well delineated with certain tasks to be handled by women, while others are reserved for men. For instance the running of the household is very much the women's task, while artistic skills are almost totally a male preserve.

Balinese society is held together by a sense of collective responsibility. The notion of spiritual uncleanliness (*sebel*) is one of the central pillars of Balinese religion; contact with death, menstruation, physical deformity, sexual intercourse, insanity and sexual perversion can all be sources of spiritual uncleanliness under certain circumstances. To enter a temple during menstruation, for instance, is a kind of irreverence, an insult to the gods, and their displeasure falls not just on the transgressor, but on the community as a whole. This collective responsibility produces considerable pressure on the individual to conform to traditional values and customs.

Village Organisation

One of the important elements of village government is the *subak*. Each individual rice field is known as a *sawah* and each farmer who owns even one sawah must be a member of his local subak. The rice paddies must have a steady supply of water and it is the job of the subak to ensure that the water supply gets to everybody. It's said that the head of the local subak will often be the farmer whose rice paddies are at the bottom of the hill for he will make quite certain that the water gets all the way down to his fields, passing through everybody else's on the way!

Each village is subdivided into *banjars* which each adult joins when he marries. It is the banjar which organises village festivals, marriage ceremonies and even cremations. Throughout the island you'll see the open-sided meeting places known as *bale banjars* – they're nearly as common a sight as temples. They serve a multitude of purposes from a local meeting place to a storage room for the banjar's musical equipment and dance costumes. Gamelan orchestras are organised at the banjar level and a glance in a bale banjar at any time might reveal a gamelan practice, a meeting going on, food for a feast being prepared, even a group of men simply getting their roosters together to raise their anger in preparation for the next round of cockfights.

Households

Despite the strong communal nature of Balinese society, their traditional houses are designed to divide the family from the outside world. Traditional houses (many of which can be seen in Ubud) are like houses in ancient Rome, they look inward and are surrounded by a high wall.

The Balinese hold that what goes on in their own households is the concern only of those directly involved and the walls maintain that privacy. Inside there will be a garden and a separate small building for each household function. There will be one building for cooking, one for washing and the toilet, and separate ones to sleep in. There will also be a family temple in one corner of the compound which is usually entered through a gateway backed by a small wall known as the *aling aling*. It serves a practical and a spiritual purpose – both preventing passers-by from seeing in and stopping evil spirits from entering. Evil spirits cannot easily turn corners so the aling aling stops them from simply scooting straight in through the gate.

ECONOMY

Bali's economy is basically agrarian. The vast majority of Balinese are peasants working in the fields. Coffee, copra and cattle are major agricultural exports, while most of the rice grown goes to feed the island's own teeming population. Unlike most island people, the Balinese are not great seafarers and actually shun the sea believing it to be the abode of demons and evil spirits. This is reflected in the very small size of the Balinese fishing industry, although there are many fishing villages and fish provides a useful part of the Balinese diet. The people also keep domestic animals; cows are kept to plough the fields; pigs to clean up refuse and to be spit-roasted at feasts; chickens and ducks for food; cocks as fighting birds; monkeys to ward off evil spirits and apart from the mongrels you usually see in Bali, some dogs are kept and looked after as pets.

Rice, grown on wet paddies, is the staple food of the Balinese and the intricate organisation necessary for growing rice is a major factor in the strength of Balinese village life. The Balinese grow two crops per year, and they do it so well they are possibly the best rice growers in the world. Since the rice terraces are often situated high above the rivers and streams, the water has to be tapped at a considerable distance upstream from the fields and then led over the irregular terrain to the fields. This is done using a system of dams, sluices, canals, tunnels and aqueducts built by the people who own the land on which the water is to be used.

The process of rice growing starts with the bare, dry and harvested fields. The remaining rice stalks are burnt off and the field is then liberally soaked then repeatedly ploughed. Nowadays this may be done with a Japanese cultivator, but more often it will still be done with two bullocks or cows pulling a wooden plough. Once the field is reduced to the required muddy consistency, a small corner is walled off and the seedling rice is planted. The rice is grown up to a reasonable size here then dug up and replanted, shoot by shoot, in the larger field. Once this is done, the walls of the fields have to be kept in working order and the fields have to be weeded, but otherwise there is little work until the harvest. Planting the rice is strictly a male occupation, but everybody takes part in harvesting it.

GEOGRAPHY

Bali is a tiny, extremely fertile and dramatically mountainous island. It has an area of 5620 square km, is only 140 km by 80 km and is just 8° south of the equator. Bali's central mountain chain, which runs east-west the whole length of the island, includes several peaks over 2000 metres and many active volcanoes including the 'mother' mountain Gunung Agung (3142 metres). Bali's volcanic nature has contributed to its exceptional fertility and the high mountains provide the dependable rainfall which irrigates the island's complex and beautiful rice terraces.

South and north of the central range are Bali's fertile agricultural lands. The southern region is a wide, gently sloping area where most of Bali's abundant crops of rice are grown. The northern coastal strip is narrower, rising more rapidly into the foothills. Here the main export crops of coffee and copra are produced, along with some rice, vegetables and cattle raising. Bali also has its arid regions, like the lightly populated western mountain region and its northern slopes, said to be the last home of the Balinese tiger. The eastern and north-eastern slopes of Gunung Agung are also dry and in the south the Bukit Peninsula and the island of Nusa Penida get little rain and have only limited agriculture. The Bali Strait, between Bali and Java, is only 60 metres deep at it's narrowest point, while to the east the Lombok Strait is one of the deepest stretches of water in the archipelago.

RELIGION

The Balinese are nominally Hindus but Balinese Hinduism is half a world away from that of India. When the Majapahits evacuated to Bali they took with them their religion and its rituals as well as their art, literature, music and culture. It's a mistake, however, to think that this was purely an exotic seed planted on virgin soil. The Balinese already had strong religious beliefs and an active cultural life; the new influences were simply overlaid on existing practices – hence the peculiar Balinese interpretation of Hinduism.

The Balinese worship the same gods as the Hindus of India – the trinity of Brahma, Shiva and Vishnu – but they also have a supreme god, Sanghyang Widhi. Unlike in India, the trinity is always alluded to, never seen – a vacant shrine or empty throne tells all. Nor is Sanghyang Widi often worshipped, though villagers may pray to him when they have settled new land and are about about to build a new village; his image appears at the top of many temple shrines and on magic amulets. Other Hindu gods such as Ganesh, Shiva's elephant-headed son, may occasionally appear, but a great many purely Balinese gods, spirits and entities have far more everyday reality.

The Balinese believe that spirits are everywhere, an indication that animism is the basis behind much of their religion. In the Balinese world good spirits dwell in the mountains and bring prosperity to the people while giants and demons lurk beneath the sea and bad spirits haunt the woods and desolate beaches. The people live between these two opposites and their rituals strive to maintain this middle ground. Offerings are carefully put out every morning to pay homage to the good spirits and nonchalantly placed on the ground to placate the bad ones. You can't get away from religion in Bali, there are temples in every village, shrines in every field and offerings being made at every corner. While it enforces a high degree of conformity it is not, however, a fatalistic religion – the bad spirits can be placated or driven out and if you follow the rules, you won't offend the gods and the good spirits.

Funerals

Religion in Bali has two overwhelming features – it's absolutely everywhere and it's good fun. Even a funeral is an amazing, colourful, noisy and exciting event – a stark contrast to the solemn ceremony practised in the west.

A Balinese funeral is a happy occasion since it represents the destruction of the

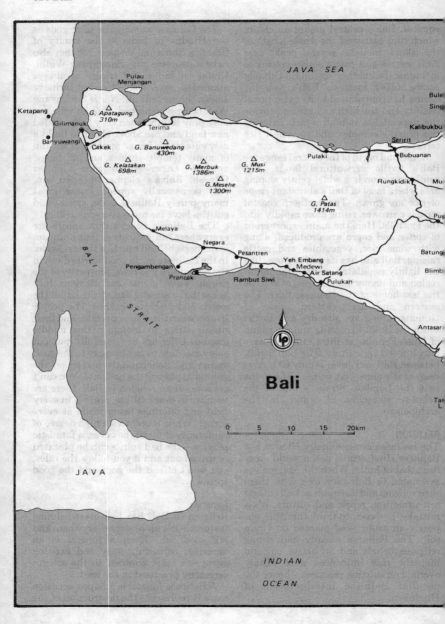

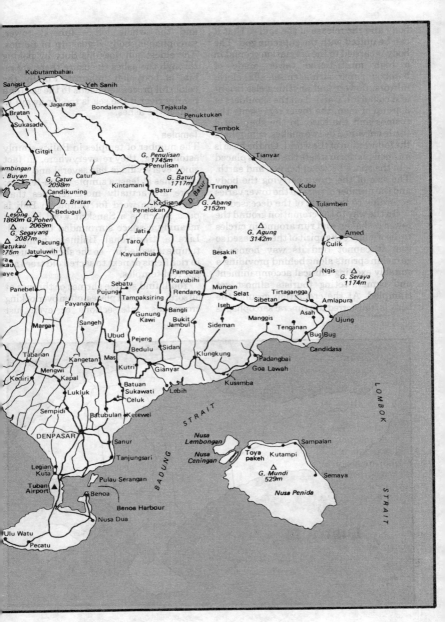

body and the release of the soul so that it can be united with the supreme god. The body is carried to the cremation ground in a high multi-tiered tower made of bamboo, paper, string, tinsel, silk, cloth, mirrors, flowers and anything else bright and colourful. Carried on the shoulders of a group of men, the tower represents the cosmos and the base, in the shape of a turtle entwined by two snakes, symbolises the foundation of the world. On the base is an open platform where the body is placed – in the space between heaven and earth. The size of the group carrying the body and the number of tiers on the tower varies according to the caste of the deceased.

On the way to the cremation ground the tower is shaken and run around in circles to disorientate the spirit of the deceased so that it cannot find its way home. A gamelan sprints along behind providing a suitably exciting musical accompaniment and camera-toting tourists almost get trampled. At the cremation ground the body is transferred to a funeral sarcophagus

and the whole lot – funeral tower, sarcophagus, body – goes up in flames. The eldest son does his duty by poking through the ashes to ensure there are no bits of body left unburnt. Finally the colourful procession heads to the sea (or a nearby river if the sea is too far away) to scatter the ashes.

Temples

The number of temples in Bali is simply astonishing, they're everywhere, in fact since every village has several and every home has at least a simple house-temple; there are actually more temples than homes. The word for temple in Bali is *pura* which is a Sanskrit word literally meaning a space surrounded by a wall. Like a traditional Balinese home, a temple is walled in – so the shrines you see in rice fields or next to sacred old trees are not real temples.

You'll find simple shrines or thrones at all sorts of unusual places, often overlooking crossroads, intersections or even just

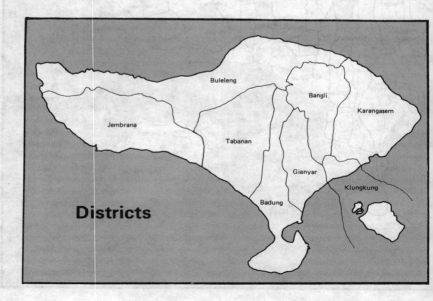

Districts

dangerous curves in the road. They're there to protect passers-by or perhaps to give the gods a ringside view of the accidents. Like in so much of Balinese religion the temples, although nominally Hindu, owe much to the pre-Majapahit era with temples aligned either towards the mountains (kaja), the sea (kelod) or the sunrise (kangin).

There are three basic temple types which almost every village will have. The most important is the pura puseh or 'temple of origin' which is dedicated to the village founders and is located at the kaja end of the village. In the middle of the village is the pura desa for the spirits which protect the village community in its day-to-day life. At the kelod end of the village is the pura dalem or temple of the dead. The graveyard is also located here and the temple will often include representations of Durga, the terrible incarnation of Shiva's wife. The destructive powers of Shiva are also honoured here.

Apart from these three basic temple types others include the temples dedicated to the spirits of irrigated agriculture. Families worship their ancestors in family temples, clans in clan temples and the whole village in the pura puseh. Certain special temples in Bali are of such importance that they are deemed to be owned by the whole island rather than by individual villages. These 'world sanctuaries' include Pura Besakih on the slopes of Gunung Agung.

Architecture Balinese temples usually consist of a series of courtyards entered from the sea side. In a large temple the outer gateway will generally be a candi bentar, modelled on the old Hindu temples of Java. These gateways resemble a tower cut in halves and moved apart, hence the name 'split gate'. The first courtyard is used for less important ceremonies, preparing food, holding meetings and will have a number of open-sided shelters. There will also be a kulkul (alarm drum) tower in this outer courtyard and perhaps a banyan or frangipani tree.

The innermost and holiest courtyard (small temples may have just two courts) is entered by another candi-like gateway except here there is a passage through the middle of it which symbolises the holy mountain through which you must pass to enter the inner court. This gateway will be flanked by statues of guardian figures or by small protective shrines.

In the inner court there will usually be two rows of shrines: the most important on the mountain side and the lesser on the sunrise side. These shrines vary in number and design from temple to temple, although there are detailed rules to cover all of them. In the major temples the shrines will include multi-roofed pagodas known as meru. The word comes from Mahameru, the Hindu holy mountain. The number of roofs are, apart from some rare exceptions, always odd and the holiest meru will have 11 roofs. The meru are roofed with long-lasting black sugar-palm. The inner court may also contain simple little thrones for local and less important gods to use.

Behaviour There are a couple of rules for visiting temples. Except on rare occasions anyone can enter, anytime; there's nothing like the attitude found in some temples in India where non-Hindus are firmly barred from entry. Nor do you have to go barefoot like in many Buddhist shrines, but you are expected to be politely dressed. You should always wear a temple scarf – a sash tied loosely around your waist. Many of the larger, more touristed temples rent them out for 50 or 100 rp. You can also buy one yourself for 500 rp or less. You'll soon recoup the cost if you visit a few temples and it's a nice thing to have when visiting temples where sashes are not available for rent.

Priests should be shown some respect, particularly at festivals. They're the most important people and should, therefore, be on the highest plane. Don't put yourself higher than them by climbing up on a wall to take photographs. There will usually be a sign outside temple entrances asking you to be well dressed, to wear a temple scarf, be respectful and also requesting that women not enter the temple during their periods. Once upon a time the little lakeside temple at Bedugul had the quaintest 'no entry' sign in Bali. It simply announced that 'It is forbidden to enter women during menstruation'.

Nearly every temple (or other site of interest to tourists) will levy an entry charge or ask for a donation from foreigners – any non-Balinese is a foreigner. Usually this is around 100 rp – occasionally less, occasionally more. If there is no fixed charge and a donation is requested then 100 rp is sufficient. Ignore the donation book figures indicating that people have paid thousands – zeros are easy to add on afterwards.

Festivals For much of the year Balinese temples are deserted, empty spaces. But on holy days, the deities and ancestral spirits descend from heaven to visit their devotees and the temples come alive with days of frenetic activity and nights of drama and dance. Temple festivals come at least once a Balinese year of 210 days. Since most villages have at least three temples that means you're assured of at least five or six annual festivals in every village. The full moon periods around the end of September to early October or early to mid-April are often the time for important festivals. One such festival is the *Galungan* which takes place throughout the island. During this 10-day period all the gods, including the supreme deity Sanghyang Widi, come down to earth for the festivities.

Temple festivals are as much a social occasion as a religious one. Cockfights (where two cocks fight with sharp barbs attached to their legs) are a regular part of temple ceremonies: a combination of excitement, sport and gambling. They also provide a blood sacrifice to dissuade

evil spirits from interfering with the religious ceremonies that follow. While the men are slaughtering their prized pets, the women are bringing beautifully arranged offerings of foods, fruit and flowers artfully piled in huge pyramids which they carry on their heads, to the temple. Outside, warungs offer food for sale, stalls are set up to sell toys, trinkets and batik and there are sideshows with card games, gambling, buskers, medicine-men, music and dancing, while the gamelan orchestra plays on in the outer courtyard.

Inside, the *pemangkus* (temple priests) are suggesting to the gods that they should come down and enjoy the goings on. The small thrones in the temple shrines are symbolic seats for the gods to occupy during festivals though sometimes small images called *pratimas* are placed in the thrones to represent them. At some festivals the images and thrones of the deities are taken out of the temple and ceremonially carried down to the sea (or to a suitable expanse of water) for a ceremonial bath. Inside the temple the proceedings take on a more formal, mystical tone as the pemangkus continue to chant their songs of praise before shrines clouded by smoking incense. The women dance the stately *pendet*, in itself an offering to the gods through the beauty of their motions.

During the course of these rituals it's quite common for people to fall into a trance and during this time they're believed to have been possessed by a deity. The trance is taken as a religious experience, a form of communication with the gods and spirits, and certain men and women in every village – like the head *pemangku* – serve the deities as established trance mediums. Through such a medium a request is made to the gods or advice is given. If a person goes into a trance and speaks during the ceremony it is taken as a good sign, a divine gesture to the people that their prayers and offerings have been accepted. When the message is passed on

of the craftsmen was something that was produced for a specific purpose or function; something made today which deteriorated tomorrow, wore out the next day and was thrown away the day after.

It's a different story today with hundreds, even thousands, of galleries and craft shops in every possible crevice a tourist might trip into. You can't turn around without falling over another technicolour Garuda statue, and in the galleries there are so many paintings that the walls can't accommodate them all and they're stacked in piles on the floor. While much of Balinese art is churned out quickly for people who want a cheap souvenir, buried beneath the reproductions of reproductions there's still quite a lot of beautiful work to be found – if you dig deep enough.

Of course some works of art are not so ephemeral, nor even orientated towards the tourist trade. An example is the sacred kris, a knife which is thought to contain

to the priest the person in trance is awoken with prayers and sprinklings of holy water.

As dawn approaches, the entertainment and ceremonies wind down and the women dance a final pendet, a farewell to the deities. The pemangkus politely suggest to the gods that it's time they made their way back to heaven, and the people make their own weary way back to their homes.

ARTS & CRAFTS

The Balinese have no words for 'art' and 'artist' since traditionally art has never been regarded as something to be treasured for its own sake. Prior to the tourist invasion art was just something you did – you painted or carved as a part of everyday life and what you produced went into temples or palaces or was used for festivals. While the painter or carver was a respected person, he was not considered a member of some special elite; there was no cult of the artist as there is in the west, the artists' work was not signed and there were no galleries or craft shops. The work

great spiritual force and thus requires great care in handling, use and even in making. The *wayang kulit* shadow puppet figures (also seen in Java) cut from buffalo hide, are also magical items since the plays enact the eternal battle between good and evil. The Balinese weave a variety of complex fabrics for ceremonial and other important uses, including *songket* cloth which is silk cloth with gold or silver threads woven into it. Even more impressive is the 'double ikat' cloth – where the pattern is dyed onto the lengthwise and crosswise threads before the threads are woven together – produced only in the east Bali village of Tenganan.

It's the everyday, disposable crafts which are probably most surprising in Bali. Even the simplest activities are carried out with care, precision and artistic flair. Just glance at those little offering trays thrown down on the ground for the demons every morning – each one a throwaway work of art. Look at the temple offerings, the artistically stacked pyramids of fruit or other beautifully decorated foods. Look for the *lamaks*, long woven palm-leaf strips used as decorations, the stylised female figures known as *cili*, and the intricately carved coconut-shell wall-hangings. At funerals you'll be amazed at the care and energy that goes into constructing huge funeral towers and exotic sarcophagi, all of which goes up in flames.

Architecture & Sculpture

Of all the Balinese arts it's said that architecture and sculpture have been the least affected by western influence and the tourist boom – nobody's taking temples home and your average stone statue doesn't roll up and stuff in your bag too easily. Architecture and sculpture are inextricably bound together – you don't just put up a temple gateway, you carve every square cm of it and put a diminishing series of demon faces above it as protection. Even then it's not finished

without a couple of stone statues to act as guardians.

Like the other arts, sculpture and architecture have traditionally served the religious life of Bali. Balinese houses, though often attractive places, have never been lavished with the architectural attention that is given to temples and palaces, although some of the new tourist hotels (like the Nusa Dua Beach Hotel) are making use of traditional styles.

It's the temples that are the showcase of Balinese sculpture and architecture. They are designed to set rules and formulas with sculpture serving as an adjunct, a finishing touch to these design guidelines. In small or less important temples, the sculpture may be limited or even non-existent, while in other temples – particularly some of the exuberantly detailed temples of north Bali – the sculpture may be almost overwhelming in its detail and intricacy.

Door guardians, of legendary figures like Arjuna or other protectors, flank the steps to the gateway. Similar figures are also often seen at both ends of bridges. Above the main entrance to a temple Kala's monstrous face often peers out, sometimes a number of times – his hands reach out beside his head to catch any evil spirits foolish enough to try to sneak in. The ancient swastika symbol indicates good fortune and prosperity. Other carved panels may show scenes of sensuous love-making, and nowadays even bicycles, automobile breakdowns, beer parties or aeroplanes. The front of a *pura dalem*, temple of the dead, will often feature images of the witch Rangda and sculptured panels may show the horrors that await evil-doers in the after life.

Painting

The art form probably most influenced both by western ideas and demand is painting. Prior to the arrival of a number of western artists after WW I painting was – like other Balinese art – primarily for temple and palace decoration. The

influence of these artists not only expanded it beyond these limited horizons, it also introduced new subject matters and, perhaps most important of all, gave the artists new materials to work with. Until these new arrivals, Balinese painting was strictly limited to three basic kinds: *langse*, *iders-iders* and calendars. Langse are large rectangular hangings used as decoration or curtains in palaces or temples. Iders-iders are scroll paintings hung along the eaves of temples. The calendars were usually astrological calendars showing auspicious days of each month.

Most of the paintings were narratives with mythological themes, illustrating stories from Hindu epics and literature – rather like a cartoon strip with a series of panels each telling a segment of the story. These paintings were always executed in the *wayang* style, the flat two-dimensional style imitative of the *wayang kulit* (shadow puppet) shows, the figures invariably shown in three-quarter view. Even the colours artists could use were strictly limited to a set list of shades (red, blue, brown, yellow and a light ochre for flesh).

In these narratives the same characters appeared in several different scenes, each depicting an episode from the story. The individual scenes were usually bordered by mountains, flames or ornamental walls. The deities, princes and heroes were identified by their opulent clothing, jewellery, elaborate head-dresses and their graceful postures and gestures; and the devils and giants by their bulging eyes, canine teeth, bulbous noses and bulky bodies. Klungkung is still a centre for the traditional wayang style of painting and the painted ceiling of the Hall of Justice in Klungkung is a fine example. Astrological calendars also remain a popular subject.

Under the influence of Walter Spies and Rudolf Bonnet, who settled in Bali in the 1930s, Balinese artists started painting single scenes instead of narrative tales and using scenes from everyday life rather

than romantic legends as their themes. More importantly, they started painting pictures purely as pictures – not as something to cover a space in a palace or temple. The idea of a painting being something you could do by itself (and for which there might be a market!) was wholly new.

In one way, however, the style remained unchanged – Balinese paintings are packed full; every spare millimetre is filled in. A Balinese forest is branches and leaves reaching out to fill every tiny space and inhabited by a whole zoo of creatures. Idyllic rural scenes or energetic festival scenes were the order of the day for many of the new artists. Others painted engagingly stylised animals and fish. You can see fine examples of these new styles at the Puri Lukisan museum and the Museum Neka in Ubud – and of course you can find them in all the galleries and art shops.

This new artistic enthusiasm was interrupted by WW II and by the political turmoil of the 1950s and 1960s. The new styles degenerated into stale copies of the few original spirits. In Ubud, however, another new style grew up – with particular encouragement from the Dutch painter Aries Smit. His 'young artists', as they were known (they weren't necessarily always young), picked up where those of the 1930s had left off, painting Balinese rural scenes in brilliant technicolour.

Woodcarving

Like painting, woodcarving has also changed from being something done simply for decoration or other purposes in temples and palaces to something created for its own sake. It was originally used for functional objects such as carved doors or columns, figures with a protective or symbolic nature like Garudas or demons, or minor functional carvings like decorative bottle stoppers. As with Balinese painting, it was the same demand from outside which inspired new subjects and styles and some of the same western artists who provided the stimulus.

As with the new painting styles, Ubud was a centre for the revolution in woodcarving. Some carvers started producing highly stylised and elongated figures, leaving the wood in its natural state rather than painting it, as was the traditional practice. Others carved delightful animal figures, some totally realistic and others wonderful caricatures; while other artists carved whole tree trunks into ghostly, intertwined 'totem poles' or curiously exaggerated and distorted figures.

MUSIC, DANCE & DRAMA

Music, dance and drama are all closely related in Bali – in fact drama and dance are really synonymous. While some dances are more drama and less dance, and others more dance and less drama, they can basically all be lumped in together. Just like the painter or the sculptor, a dancer is almost always an ordinary person who dances in the evening or in his or her own spare time. You learn dancing by doing it and long hours may be spent practising, usually by carefully following the movements of an expert.

There's little of the soaring leaps of western ballet or the smooth flowing movements often found in western dance. Balinese dance tends to be precise, jerky, shifting and jumpy. In fact it's remarkably like the Balinese gamelan music which accompanies most dances, with its abrupt shifts of tempo, its dramatic changes between silence and crashing noise. There's also virtually no contact in Balinese dancing, with each dancer moving completely independently. To the expert every movement of wrist, hand and fingers has importance, even facial expressions are carefully choreographed to convey the character of the dance.

There are dances where the story is as important as the dancing, like the *Kechak*. And dances like the *Barong* where the forces of magic, both good and evil, clash. Nor is Balinese dance a static activity. Old dances fade out and new dances or new developments of old dances still take place. For example the *Oleg Tambulilingan* was developed in the 1950s as a solo female dance, but later a male part was added and the dance now mimics the flirtations of two *tambulilingan* or bumblebees.

The Balinese like a blend of seriousness and slapstick and their dances show this. Basically the dances are simply straight-

Balinese Dancer

forward ripping yarns – like vaudeville shows where you cheer on the goodies and cringe back from the stage when the baddies appear. Some dances have a comic element with clowns who counterbalance the staid, noble characters. The clowns often have to put across the story to the audience, since the noble characters may use the classical Javanese *Kawi* language while the clowns (usually servants of the noble characters) converse in everyday Balinese.

It's not hard to find dances – they're taking place all the time, all over the island and are usually open to anyone. Dances are a regular part of almost every temple festival and Bali has no shortage of these. There are also dances virtually every night at all the tourist centres; admission is usually costs from 1000 to 3000 rp for foreigners. Many of the shows put on for tourists offer a smorgasbord of Balinese dances with a little *Topeng*, a taste of *Legong* and some *Baris* to round it off. If you see one disappointing performance of a particular dance then look around for another venue as the quality and the level of drama varies. Some of the more common dances are:

Kechak Probably the best known of the many Balinese dances the Kechak is also unusual because it doesn't have a gamelan accompaniment. Instead the background is provided by a chanting 'choir' of men who provide the 'chak-a-chak-a-chak' noise which distinguishes the dance. Originally this chanting group was known as the Kechak and they were part of a Sanghyang trance dance. Then in the 1930s the modern Kechak developed in Bona, a village near Gianyar, where the dance is still held regularly.

The Kechak tells the tale of the *Ramayana* (see the Java section for a rundown of the story) and the quest of Prince Rama to rescue his wife Sita after she had been kidnapped by Rawana, the King of Lanka. Rama is accompanied to Lanka by Sugriwa the king of the monkeys, with his monkey army. Throughout the Kechak dance the circle of men, all bare chested and wearing checked cloth around their waists, provide a non-stop accompaniment, rising to a crescendo as they play the monkey army and fight it out with Rawana and his cronies. The chanting is accompanied by the movements of the 'monkey army' whose members sway back and forth, raise their hands in unison, flutter their fingers and lean left and right, all with an eerily exciting co-ordination.

Barong & Rangda Like the Kechak the Barong & Rangda or kris dance is a battle between good and evil. Barongs can take various forms but in this dance he takes the form of the *Barong Keket*, the most holy of the Barongs. The Barong Keket is a strange creature, half shaggy dog, half lion and is played by two men in much the same way as a circus clown-horse. His opponent is the witch Rangda.

The Barong personifies good and protects the village from the witch Rangda, but he's also a mischievious and fun loving creature. He flounces into the temple courtyard, snaps his jaws at the gamelan, dances around and enjoys the acclaim of his supporters – a group of men with krises. Then Rangda makes her appearance, her long tongue lolling, her pendulous breasts wobbling, human entrails draped around her neck, fangs protruding from her mouth and sabre-like fingernails clawing the air.

Now the Barong is no longer the clown, but the protector. The two duel with their magical powers and the Barong's supporters draw their krises and rush in to attack the witch. Rangda puts them in a trance and the men try to stab themselves, but the Barong also has great magical powers and casts a spell which stops the krises from harming the men. This is the most dramatic part of the dance – as the gamelan rings crazily the men rush back and forth, waving their krises around, all but foaming at the mouth, sometimes even rolling on the ground in a desperate attempt to stab themselves. Finally Rangda retires defeated and good has won again. Good must always triumph over evil on Bali, and no matter how many times the spectators have seen the performance nor how well they know the outcome, the battle itself remains all important.

The end of the dance still leaves a large group of entranced Barong supporters to be brought back to the real world. This is usually done by sprinkling them with holy water, sanctified by dipping the Barong's beard in it. Performing the Barong and Rangda dance – with all that powerful magic – is an operation not to be taken lightly. Extensive ceremonies must be gone through to begin with, a temple priest must be on hand to end the dancers' trance, and at the end a chicken has to be sacrificed to propitiate the evil spirits.

Legong This is the most graceful of Balinese dances and to sophisticated Balinese connoisseurs of dancing the one of most interest. A *Legong*, as a Legong dancer is always known, is a young girl – often as young as eight or nine years and rarely older than her early teens. Such importance is attached to the dance that even in old age a classic dancer will be remembered as a 'great Legong' even though her brief period of fame may have been 50 years ago.

There are various forms of the Legong but the *Legong Kraton*, or Legong of the palace, is the one most usually performed. Peliatan's famous dance troupe, which visitors to Ubud often get a chance to see, is particularly noted for its Legong. A performance involves just three dancers –the two Legongs and their 'attendant' known as the *condong*. The Legongs are identically dressed in tightly bound gold brocade, so tightly are they encased that it's something of a mystery how they manage to move with such agility and speed. Their faces are elaborately made

up, their eyebrows plucked and repainted and their hair decorated with frangipanis.

It's a very stylised and symbolic dance – if you didn't know the story it would be impossible to tell what was going on. The dance relates how a king takes a maiden, Rangkesari, captive. When Rangkesari's brother comes to release her he begs the king to let her free rather than go to war. The king refuses and on his way to the battle meets a bird bringing ill omens. He ignores the bird and continues on to meet Rangkesari's brother who kills him. The dance, however, only relates the lead-up to the battle and ends with the bird's appearance. When the king leaves the stage he is going to the battle that will end in his death.

The dance starts with the condong dancing an introduction. The condong departs as the Legongs come on. The Legongs dance solo, in close identical formation, and even in mirror image when they dance a nose to nose love scene. They relate the king's sad departure from his queen, Rangkesari's request that he release her and the king's departure for the battle. Finally the condong reappears with tiny golden wings as the bird of ill fortune and the dance comes to an end.

Baris The warrior dance known as the *Baris* is a male equivalent of the Legong in which femininity and grace gives way to the energetic, warlike martial spirit. A solo dance, the Baris dancer has to convey the thoughts and emotions of a warrior preparing for action and then meeting an enemy in battle. The dancer has to show his changing moods not only through his dancing, but also through facial expression. Chivalry, pride, anger, prowess and finally some regret (well war is hell, even in Bali) all have to be there. It's said that the Baris is one of the most complex of the Balinese dances requiring a dancer of great energy, skill and ability.

Ramayana Dance The *Ramayana* is a

familiar tale in Bali but the dance has been a relatively recent addition to the Balinese repertoire. It tells much the same story of Rama and Sita as told in the Kechak but without the monkey ensemble and with a normal gamelan orchestra accompaniment. It's also embellished with many improvisations and comic additions. Rawana may be played as a classic bad guy, the monkey god Hanuman can be a comic clown, and camera-wielding tourists amongst the spectators may come in for some imitative ribbing.

Kebyar This is a male solo dance like the Baris, but with greater emphasis on the performer's individual abilities. Development of the modern kebyar is credited in large part to the famous pre-war dancer Mario. There are various forms of the dance including the seated *Kebyar Duduk* where the 'dance' is done from the seated position and movements of the hands, arms and torso plus, of course, facial expressions, are all important. In the *Kebyar Trompong* the dancer actually joins the gamelan and plays an instrument called the *trompong* while still dancing.

Janger Both Covarrubias and Hickman in their between-the-wars books on Bali comment on this strange new, almost un-Balinese, dance which suddenly popped up in the 1920s and '30s. Today it has become part of the standard repertoire and no longer looks so unusual. It has similarities to several other dances including the *Sanghyang* where the relaxed chanting of the women is contrasted with the violent chak-a-chak-a-chak of the men. In the Janger dance, formations of 12 girls and 12 young men do a sitting dance where the gentle swaying and chanting of the girls is contrasted with the violently choreographed movements and loud shouts of the men.

Topeng The word *Topeng* means 'pressed against the face', as with a mask. This is a mask dance where the dancers have to imitate the character their mask indicates they are playing. The *Topeng Tua*, for example, is a classic solo dance where the mask is that of an old man and requires the performer to dance like a creaky old gentleman. In other dances there may be a small troupe who dance various characters and types. A full collection of Topeng masks may number 30 or 40.

Another mask dance is the *Jauk*, but this is strictly a solo performance. The dancer plays an evil demon, his mask an eerie face with bulging eyes and fixed smile, long wavering fingernails complete the demonic look. Mask dances require great expertise because the dancer is not able to convey the character's thoughts and meanings through his facial expressions, so the character of the unpleasant, frenetic, fast-moving demon has to be conveyed entirely through the dance.

Pendet This is an everyday dance of the temples, a small procedure gone through before making temple offerings which doesn't require arduous training and practice. You may often see the Pendet being danced by women bringing offerings to a temple for a festival, but it is also sometimes danced as an introduction and a closing for other dance performances.

Sanghyang Dances The *Sanghyang* trance dances originally developed as a means of driving out evil spirits from a village. The Sanghyang is a divine spirit which temporarily inhabits an entranced dancer.

The *Sanghyang Dedari* is performed by two young girls who dance a dream-like version of the Legong. The dancers are said to be untrained in the intricate pattern of the dance and, furthermore, they dance in perfect harmony but with their eyes firmly shut. A female choir and a male Kechak choir provide a background chant but when the chant stops the dancers slump to the ground in a faint. Two women bring them round and at the inish a priest blesses them with holy water and brings them out of the trance. The modern Kechak dance developed from the Sanghyan.

In the *Sanghyang Jaran* a boy in a trance dances round and through a fire of coconut husks riding a coconut-palm hobby horse – it's labelled the 'fire dance' for the benefit of tourists. Once again the priest must be on hand to break the trance at the close of the dance.

The Gamelan

As in Sumatra and Java, Balinese music is based around the gamelan orchestra – for more details see the Java section. The whole gamelan orchestra is known as a *gong* – an old fashioned *gong gede* or a more modern *gong kebyar*. There are even more ancient forms of the gamelan such as the *gong selunding*, still occasionally played in Bali Aga villages like Tenganan.

Though the instruments used are much the same, Balinese gamelan is very different from the form you'll hear in Java. The Yogyakarta style, for example, is the most reserved, formal and probably the gentlest and most 'refined' of gamelans – while Balinese gamelan often sounds like everyone going for it full pelt. Perhaps a more telling point is that Javanese gamelan music is rarely heard except at special performances, whereas in Bali you seem to hear gamelans playing all the time everywhere you go.

BOOKS & BOOKSHOPS

There are a number of older books on Bali, but the most interesting is *Island of Bali* (Oxford Paperback) by Mexican artist Miguel Covarrubias. First published in 1937, it is still available as an Oxford in Asia paperback and despite the tourist boom much of Bali is still exactly as Covarrubias describes it. Although it's fairly expensive (25,000 to 30,000 rp in Bali) it's a good investment as few people have come to grips with the island as well as Covarrubias.

Colin McPhee's *A House in Bali* is a lyrical account of a musician's lengthy stay in Bali to study gamelan music. *The Last Paradise* by Hickman Powell and *A Tale from Bali* by Vicki Baum also date from that heady period in the 1930s when so many westerners 'discovered' Bali. All three are available as Oxford Paperbacks. K'Tut Tantri's *Revolt in Paradise* (available in an Indonesian paperback) again starts in the '30s but this western woman who took a Balinese name remained in Indonesia through the war and during part of the subsequent struggle for independence from the Dutch.

Our Hotel in Bali by Louis G Koke (January Books) tells of the original Kuta Beach Hotel which was established by Americans Robert and Louis Koke during the '30s and run by them until WW II spread to the Pacific. Although the book was written during the war it was not published until 1987. From the same publisher comes New Zealander Hugh Mabbett's *The Balinese*, an interesting collection of anecdotes, observations and impressions, and *In Praise of Kuta*, a sympathetic account of that much maligned beach resort.

For a rundown on Balinese arts and culture look for the huge and expensive, *The Art & Culture of Bali* by Urs Ramseyer (Oxford University Press). From the same publisher comes *Dance & Drama In Bali* by Beryl de Zoete and Walter Spies. Originally published back in 1938, this book draws from Walter Spies' deep appreciation and understanding of Bali's arts and culture. An economical and handy introduction to Balinese painting is *Different Styles of Painting in Bali* published by the Neka Gallery in Ubud – it covers the various schools of painting and also has short biographies of well known artists, including many of the foreign artists who have worked in Bali. *Balinese Paintings* by A A M Djelantik (Oxford University Press) is a concise and handy overview of the field.

The Krishna Bookshop on the Legian

Rd in Kuta and the Family Bookshop on Jalan Tanjung Sari in Sanur have a wide selection of English-language books, particularly on Indonesia. You will also find small, but interesting collections of books on Bali and Indonesia at the Bali Foto Centre in Kuta, Murni's Warung in Ubud and the Neka Gallery in Ubud. There are numerous second-hand bookshops around Kuta, Legian and Sanur which might have the odd interesting book on Bali.

GETTING THERE & AWAY

Bali is connected by regular ferries to Java in the west and the island of Lombok in the east, and by air to many other parts of Indonesia and overseas.

Air
Overseas There are direct flights with Garuda and Qantas between Denpasar and Australia. Garuda also has direct connections to Europe and an interesting service from Los Angeles/Honolulu/Denpasar. See the introductory Getting There chapter of this book for fares and more details.

If you're flying out of Bali reconfirm your bookings at least 72 hours before departure. There are Garuda offices in Denpasar, Kuta and Sanur. Qantas has an office in Sanur.

Indonesia Garuda, Merpati and Bouraq all have flights to and from Denpasar. Garuda has offices in Kuta and Sanur, all three have offices in Denpasar. There are frequent connections to Denpasar from Surabaya, Yogyakarta and Jakarta in Java. Flights also operate from Denpasar to Mataram in Lombok (just half an hour for 20,000 rp) and to other centres in the islands of Nusa Tenggara. Bali is also a popular jumping-off point for Ujung Pandang in Sulawesi. The Denpasar-Ujung Pandang flight is cheaper than equivalent flights from Java.

Denpasar Airport The Ngurah Rai Airport is just beyond Kuta Beach. The airport has a hotel-booking counter, although it only covers the more expensive places. There's also a tourist information counter with some useful brochures and helpful staff, a left-luggage room and a fairly quick and efficient money change desk. If you come in on an uncrowded or obscure international flight, you're likely to find it all closed up!

Outside is a taxi counter where you pay for your taxi in advance. Fares from the airport are:

Kuta Beach	3200 rp
Legian	5000 rp
Oberoi Hotel	7500 rp
Denpasar	6800 rp
Sanur Beach	8700 rp
Nusa Dua	9000 rp

Alternatively, if you turn right out of the arrival building and start walking the couple of hundred metres to the airport gates you may find taxi drivers descending upon you independently and they can then be negotiated down to slightly lower rates. Cheaper still, outside the gates you'll be able to pick up a bemo to Kuta for 250 rp or to Denpasar for 400 rp. You can take a taxi straight to Ubud from the airport for from 15,000 to 20,000 rp or go to bemo corner in Ubud and charter a bemo for from 12,000 to 15,000 rp.

On departure there's a duty-free shop and a row of souvenir shops at the airport – they only accept foreign currency. The departure lounge cafeteria takes rupiah, but it's much more expensive than the shop outside. You can change excess rupiah back into hard currency at the bank counter by the check-in desks. There's a 9000 rp departure tax on international flights. Domestic flights have a 2000 rp departure tax, but it's usually included in your ticket price.

Bus
You can get bus tickets through to Java which include the short Bali-Java ferry

rip and sometimes a meal at a rest stop along the way. Generally you have to book a day in advance and air-con and non-air-con buses are available. Typical fares are Surabaya from 9000 to 12,000 rp or Yogyakarta from 13,000 to 20,000 rp.

You're assigned a seat number when booking so make your own choice from the seating chart. Avoid the front rows – the night-bus drivers are maniacs and you don't want to be the first to find out about the accident! In fact the night buses now make the Denpasar to Surabaya trip so quickly that an early evening departure is liable to drop you in Surabaya at an absurdly early pre-dawn hour.

The route takes you from Denpasar to Gilimanuk, then by ferry to Ketapang, then by bus on to Surabaya or beyond. It's also possible to do it in stages – a local bus to Gilimanuk, take the ferry across, then another bus on the Java side. The straight-through buses will drop you in Probolinggo if you want to climb Mt Bromo. Although bus departures and arrivals are generally in Denpasar you can also buy tickets from agents at Kuta Beach. There's also a north coast bus service between Singaraja and Surabaya.

Bus-Rail

There's a connecting bus service to trains from Banyuwangi in Java, tickets are available from the railways office in Denpasar or from agents in Kuta. Combined tickets cover the bus to Gilimanuk, the ferry crossing to Java, bus from Ketapang to the station in Banyuwangi and the train from there.

Boat

Java Ferry A ferry shuttles back and forth across the narrow strait from Gilimanuk on the Bali side to Ketapang, the port for Banyuwangi on the Java side. The 15-minute ferry crossing costs 400 rp per person, 200 rp for a bicycle, 875 rp for a car and 4300 to 6200 rp for a car. Ketapang is several km from Banyuwangi but there are regular buses between the port and

town and most bus services depart directly from the ferry terminal.

Lombok Ferry There's a twice daily ferry service at around 9 or 10 am and 1 or 2 pm from the small port of Padangbai, east of Denpasar. The ferry office in Padangbai is by the pier but get there well before departure as the ferry is sometimes completely full. First class tickets are 5000 rp, Ekonomi is 3500 rp. Children are about half price. You can also take bikes, motorcycles and jeeps along with you – 750 rp for a bike, 4000 rp for a motorcycle, 38,500 rp for a jeep, 49,000 rp for a car. The ferry docks at Lembar, south of Mataram-Ampenan, in Lombok.

Food, soft drinks, coffee, tea and cigarettes are available on board from the small bars in both 1st and Ekonomi classes or from the numerous hawkers who hang around the wharf until the ferry leaves. The trip takes a minimum of 4½ hours, often up to seven, and the afternoon ferry is often slower than the morning one. From Lembar it's easy to reach Ampenan-Mataram, Lombok's main town, the same day.

Other Boats Bali's main shipping harbour is Benoa Harbour, just south of Denpasar. There's a Pelni office (tel 4387) at Jalan Pelabuhan, Benoa and the Pelni ship *Kelimutu* comes through Padangbai on its regular service between Semarang (Java) and Kupang (Timor). See the Getting Around chapter for more details. Foreign yachts moor at Benoa, check the notice boards around Kuta to see if anyone is looking for crew or simply hire a boat at Benoa Harbour to paddle you around the yachts and ask.

GETTING AROUND

Bali is a small island with good roads and regular transport. Denpasar is the transport hub of Bali and has several bemo stations for the various destinations – see the Denpasar section for details. Bemos in Bali follow the usual rules for the rest of Indonesia, but beware of the *harga turis* or special tourist price, which is becoming far too prevalent.

Once you've got out of the southern Bali traffic tangle, the roads are remarkably uncrowded. Traffic is heavy from Denpasar south to Kuta and Sanur, east about as far as Klungkung and west as far as Tabanan. Over the rest of the island it's not trouble at all and mostly it's very light. If you've got your own motorcycle, bicycle or vehicle finding your way around is easy – roads are well signposted and maps are readily available. Off the main routes, roads often get very potholed but most roads are surfaced.

Beware of pickpockets on bemos – on common tourist routes like Denpasar to Kuta Beach they've become notorious. While someone engages you in a friendly conversation, his accomplice is cleaning you out, often using a painting, parcel or similar cover to hide the activity. Sometimes half the bemo will be in on the game, so the odds will really be stacked against you. A lot of unfortunate visitors have suffered from these people so take care, particularly on those heavily used tourist routes.

Motorcycles

Motorcycles are a favourite way of getting around Bali but also a controversial one. Bali is no place to learn how to ride a motorcycle – every year a number of visitors go home in a box.

Motorcycles for hire in Bali are almost all between 90 and 125 cc with 100 cc as the usual size. You really don't need anything bigger – the distances are short and the roads are rarely suitable for going very fast. Anyway what's the hurry? Rental charges vary with the bike, the period of hire and demand. The longer the hire period the lower the rate, the bigger or newer the bike the higher the rate. Typically you can expect to pay from around 5000 to 8000 rp a day, but rates are always lower for longer periods.

The majority of the bikes will be rented out by individual owners, probably to raise some money to help pay for the bike. There are a few places around Kuta which seem to specialise in bike hire but generally it's just travel agents, restaurants, losmen or shops with a sign out saying 'motorcycle for hire'. You can ask around but guys will often approach you along Jalan Legian near bemo corner. Kuta and Sanur are the main bike-hire places but you'll have no trouble finding a motorcycle to rent in Ubud or Singaraja. Check the bike over before riding off – there are some poorly maintained, rotten old clunkers around.

There's a scattering of petrol stations around Bali but they often seem to be out of petrol, out of electricity or out on a holiday. In that case look for the little roadside fuel shops where you fill up with a plastic jug and a funnel.

Licences If you've got an international driving permit *endorsed for motorcycles* you've got no problems. If you haven't then you've got to get a local licence, which is straightforward and easy but time consuming. Your bike owner will take you in to Denpasar where you'll probably find 50 or so other bike renters lined up for their licence. You're fingerprinted, photographed, given a written test (to which you are told the answers in advance) and then comes the hard part. After a friendly send off from the police examiner, who wishes you luck and dispenses the cheerful news that if you fail you can always try again, off you go. Ride once round a circle clockwise, once round anti-clockwise, a slalom through a row of tin cans, don't put your feet down and don't fall off or bump into anything else. Eventually everyone passes and is judged fit to be unleashed on Bali's roads. It costs 11,000 rp and the whole process takes about four hours.

Registration & Insurance Apart from your licence you must also carry the bike's registration paper with you – make sure the bike's owner gives it to you before you ride off. Insurance is a bit of a mystery in Bali – some renters seem to insist on it, others don't. The agents obviously make money from the insurance too because it's usually quite expensive. Read the small print on your own travel insurance policy – you may find you're covered if you fall off only if you have a proper motorcycle licence, not a Balinese one.

Cars

You can also rent cars in Bali. They're often small Suzuki jeeps or open VW safari vehicles, but these days you may find anything from regular cars to bemo-style minibuses. Typical costs are around 30,000 rp a day including insurance and unlimited km. As with motorcycles, just look around Kuta or Sanur for 'car for rent' signs. An alternative to hiring a car is to hire a bemo by the day: including a driver and fuel the cost is probably much the same as for renting a car.

Bicycles

Seeing Bali by pushbike has become much more popular in recent years: more people are giving it a try, more places are renting bikes, some people are even bringing their bikes with them. Airlines will generally fly your bike as part of your baggage weight allowance or even free.

At first glance, Bali with its high mountains, narrow bumpy roads, tropical heat and frequent rain showers does not seem like a place for a bicycle tour. However, far from being an obstacle, the mountains can be turned into allies. With the judicious help of two short bemo trips to scale the central mountains you can accomplish a beautiful, mostly level or downhill 200-km circle trip of Bali. Though the roads are narrow, once you're out of the congested southern region traffic is relatively light. The bumpy roads are no great problem if you invest in a good, padded seat. Since a large part of the trip is level or downhill, the tropical heat problem literally turns into a breeze

and the many roadside foodstalls make it remarkably easy to duck out of a passing rain shower.

There is no lack of bicycles for rent in Bali. The challenge is finding one that works! Rental choices run from one-speed clunkers with terrible seats to one-speed clunkers with terrible seats, no reflectors, bell, lights or brakes. There are numerous bike rental shops in Kuta and Legian. It's also possible to rent bikes in Ubud and sometimes in Sanur. Start bargaining from around 2000 rp per day. Rates by the week or longer period are, of course, cheaper. Proper 10-speed bicycles are beginning to become quite common in Bali.

Bicycles are used extensively by the Balinese themselves and even the smallest village has some semblance of a bike shop. Some shops will allow you to borrow tools to work on your own bike. If you're not used to working on bicycles ask the repairman to repair it for you. Labour charges are very low for tyre puncture repairs in particular. The best shops for any extensive repairs are in Denpasar.

For touring it is absolutely essential that your bike be in good repair. Check that the bike has brakes that work; wheels that don't wobble; tyres that aren't bald or soft; spokes that aren't broken; a bell, light and back reflector; a good soft seat, adjusted to suit your height and a carrier pack. Many bikes are equipped with a claw-like key lock which guards against theft, though a much sturdier steel cable lock may be a worthwhile purchase. Get the bike oiled by the rental shop, check to see the nuts are tightened securely, especially those to the seat, brake cables and brakes which tend to vibrate loose.

With all that done one possible bicycle trip around Bali is the 200-km loop out of Kuta and back. This route is designed to take in the greatest number of points of interest with the minimum use of motorised transport and the maximum amount of level or downhill roads. For convenience the tour is divided into six days of actual riding in a clockwise direction which takes advantage of evening stops where there are convenient losmen. The minimum daily distance is about 20 km, the maximum is 53 km – but 20 to 30 km of this latter number will probably be covered by bemo. With a couple of side-trips and a few stops in villages in-between this could easily become a two-week trip.

Day 1 – Kuta to Bedugul (53 km) The first 37 km is by bicycle, the rest by bemo. Estimated riding time seven hours. On a good bicycle the uphill section is quite manageable.

Day 2 – Bedugul to Singaraja (21 km) Estimated riding time three hours, downhill most of the way.

Day 3 – Singaraja to Penelokan (44 km) The 24 km up to Penulisan is a long hard slog, don't try it unless you've got a good bike, you're very fit and you have lots of drinking water. The first 10 km and the final 10 km are fine.

Day 4 – Penelokan to Klungkung (31 km excluding Besakih) Estimated riding time four hours.

Day 5 – Klungkung to Denpasar (31 km) Estimated riding time six hours. This road has heavy traffic.

Day 6 – Denpasar to Kuta If you go via Sanur and Benoa this is a 24 km ride and estimated riding time is five hours. Again there are some stretches of heavy traffic on this run.

Tours

Tours can be a good way of seeing a lot of things in a short space of time. There are numerous day and evening excursions operating out of Kuta – look along Jalan Legian and Jalan Pantai Kuta near bemo corner for the travel agents who organise them. An excursion to Bona village to see the Kechak Dance, Sanghyang Dedari and Sanghyang Jaran (Fire) Dance is a pretty nifty way of spending an evening. Other tours vary in quality; some are nothing more than shop-crawls, carting

you from one warehouse to another so check the itinerary carefully!

South Bali

The southern part of Bali, south of the capital Denpasar, is the tourist end of the island. The overwhelming mass of visitors to Bali is concentrated down here. All the higher priced package tour hotels are found in this area and many visitors only get out on day-trips. Some never leave it at all.

The Balinese have always looked towards the mountains and away from the sea – even their temples are aligned in the *kaja* direction (towards the mountains) and away from the inauspicious *kelod* direction (towards the sea). So Sanur and Kuta, the small fishing villages that were to become Bali's major international resorts were not notable places prior to the arrival of mass tourism. Today they're artificial enclaves, not really part of Bali at all. Of course the residents have made the most of their new found opportunities, particularly the people of Kuta where an enormous number of small, locally run losmen and restaurants have sprung up, but many of the Balinese who work at Kuta and Sanur are from other parts of the island. The Indonesian government is determined that the rest of Bali should remain as unspoilt as possible so all future large scale development will be confined to this southern region, particularly the newer tourist enclave at Nusa Dua.

Together with Singaraja in the north the southern region has been most influenced from outside Bali. Even some of Bali's earliest legends relate to this area. The first European to make his mark in the south was Mads Lange, a Danish copra trader who set up at Kuta about 1830. He had some success in persuading local rajahs to unite against the Dutch encroachments from the north but he also made enemies and was poisoned later in

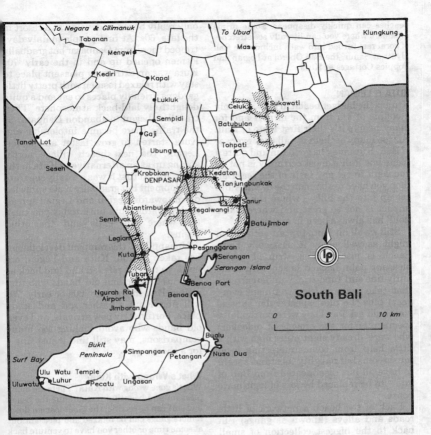

South Bali

0   5   10 km

the century and buried at Kuta. The Dutch takeover of the south finally took place at Sanur in 1906. The Balinese fell back before them all the way from Sanur to Denpasar and there the three princes of the kingdom of Badung made a suicidal last stand, a *puputan* which wiped out the old kingdoms of the south. When the Japanese left Indonesia after WW II the Dutch again returned to Bali at Sanur.

Sanur was an early home for visiting western artists and is still an artistic centre and famed for its gamelan orchestras. The courtly arja opera and wayang kulit shadow puppets are also popular at Sanur and now a positive mania for flying gigantic kites has swept the region.

An unfortunate side effect of the building explosion in the south has been massive destruction of the coral reefs. Coral makes an excellent building material both ground down to make lime and as actual building blocks. The blocks are very attractive and since the coral grows a little after it has been removed from the water the coral actually locks itself together. But as more and more coral is removed there will be less and less fish and the unprotected beaches can quickly disappear. Some prime offenders where you can literally see stretches of coral reef turned into walls include the Bali Hyatt at Sanur, the Bali Oberoi at Legian and Poppies Cottages at Kuta.

KUTA & LEGIAN

Kuta is the budget beach in Bali. It's only a couple of km from the airport and for many people it's their first taste of Bali. For too many of them it's all they ever see of Bali. Kuta may be good fun and quite a scene but Bali it most certainly is not. If you want to get any taste of the real Bali then you have to abandon the beaches and get up into the hills – where the tourist impact is not so great and where Bali's 'soul' has always been in any case.

Still we all hit Kuta to start with so you might as well enjoy it. Basically Kuta Beach is just that, a strip of pretty pleasant palm-backed beach with some fairly fine surf (and tricky undercurrents that take away a few swimmers every year) plus the most spectacular sunsets you could ask for. They were particularly spectacular for the crowds of onlookers who were already eight miles high with a little help from some interesting local mushrooms but naughty substances seem to have all but disappeared from Bali of late – to be replaced by lots of legitimate booze.

Back of the beach a network of little roads and alleys (known as gangs) run back to the biggest collection of small hotels (known as losmen), restaurants, bars, food stalls (known as warungs) and shops you could possibly imagine. It has been estimated there are over 200 different places to stay at Kuta and Legian and more are still being opened. Kuta is a totally self-contained scene and with so many places to work your way through it's hardly surprising that so many people get stuck there semi-permanently.

Although the original Kuta Beach Hotel was operating in the 1930s and its modern namesake opened in 1959 Kuta only really began to develop as a resort in the late '60s. At first people mainly day-tripped there from Denpasar but gradually losmen opened up and in the early '70s Kuta was an extremely pleasant place to stay with relaxed losmen with pretty little gardens, friendly places to eat and a quite delightfully laid-back atmosphere. Then travellers began to abandon Denpasar as the traffic there became intolerable and Kuta started to grow faster and faster. Legian, the next beach village north, sprang up as an alternative to Kuta in the early '70s. At first it was a totally separate development but gradually Kuta sprawled down towards Legian and Legian spread back towards Kuta until today you can't tell where one ends and the other begins.

Unhappily all this rampant development has taken its toll. Kuta and Legian are nowhere near as relaxed and laid back as they used to be and old hands who first visited Bali in the late '60s or early '70s will find Kuta a rather sad and seedy place. Fortunately new arrivals, and even old hands who avoid making too many comparisons, may still find it just fine – for a short stay.

What's Wrong with Kuta?

What's gone wrong with Kuta? There are many pleasant and beautiful restaurants, the beach and surf can be terrific, the quiet losmen down remote gangs can be relaxed and pleasant but at some time or other you have to venture back on to the Legian road and the traffic down this main street is horrific. The constant stream of sellers importuning you to buy, buy, buy can be a little wearing too but the main problem is planning and people. There's too little of one and too many of the other.

Too little isn't the word for Kuta's planning – there's none at all. Anybody seems to have been able to build almost anything anywhere. The result is that many losmen are only accessible down narrow gangs – which is no problem except that people insist on using these footpaths for motorcycle races and even try to squeeze cars and trucks down them. The Legian road is a typical narrow island road, wide enough for one vehicle or perhaps one and a half at a squeeze yet it carries a near continuous flow of buses, bemos, taxis, cars, trucks and motorcycles. Recently they've finally realised that it simply cannot operate as a two way road but the solution has been to build a new road virtually on the beach. And the Legian road remains a noisy, confused, evil smelling, frustrating cacophony.

As if that weren't enough there are no parking restrictions along the roads, not even around bemo corner in Kuta where every evening at sunset time there's an unbelievable and quite unnecessary traffic jam. And what are they doing about it? Nothing, just cramming more hotels in anywhere they can.

As for the people, well 15 years ago Kuta was one of the great overland travel stops. One of the three Ks – Kabul in Afghanistan, Kathmandu in Nepal and Kuta. But travellers don't come to Kuta anymore, it's strictly a beach resort for people who want surf and sand, cheap food and plenty of beer. Where you used to get peacefully stoned freaks gazing at the sunset you now have numerous bars where loud-mouthed drunks get ripped every afternoon, clamber clumsily on to their motorcycles and mercifully fall off at the first corner. Fortunately these folk are usually kept right there in Kuta – it's a whole different visitor population up in Ubud.

And on the Beach

Legian beach early in the morning – grey rain clouds even though it's the dry season – the mountains rise up mistily in the background – surfers out after an early break, they're all congregated in the area posted as 'dangerous' – about 20 people are desperately trying to push a minibus out of the sand before the rising tide gets it – already the surf licks at the point where it got stuck and as they heave it up the beach the sand gets softer – motorcycles buzz up and down the beach, some idiots actually riding through the surf, nothing like saltwater for corrosion – joggers pass by – rich Javanese wade, fully dressed, thigh deep into the water – the inevitable anjings run around in packs.

Information & Orientation

You can visit Bali and never have to leave Kuta. There are hotels, restaurants, travel agents, banks, moneychangers, a post office, markets, motorcycle and car rental places, doctors; in fact you name it

and Kuta has it. Kuta and Legian, once separate little villages, are now just the names for different sections of one long and continuous beach. They merge together. An important Kuta landmark is 'bemo corner', the intersection of Kuta Beach Rd (Jalan Pantai Kuta) and the Legian road (Jalan Legian).

On the corner of Jalan Bakung Sari and the airport road the large building has tourist information counters for Bali and also for several other regions of Indonesia. The Bali counter has some brochures and copies of a Bali tourist newspaper.

If you develop a real interest in Kuta read Hugh Mabbett's *In Praise of Kuta* (January Books, Wellington, New Zealand, 1987). It's widely available in Bali and recounts Kuta's early history and its frenetic modern development. If you want to learn more about Kuta's local entrepreneurs, the development of surfing or what happens if you get caught with drugs then this fascinating book has the goods.

Post There's a post office near the cinema and night market, off the airport road. It's small, efficient and has a poste restante service (50 rp per letter). The post office is open Monday to Thursday 8 am to 2 pm, Friday 8 to 11 am and Saturday 8 am to 12.30 pm. There is also a postal agent on the Legian road, about half a km along from bemo corner. If you want mail sent there have it addressed to 'Kuta Postal Agent, Jalan Legian, Kuta'. These Kuta post offices (or the one in Ubud) are much more convenient than the main Denpasar post office. The information office on the corner of Jalan Airport and Jalan Bakung Sari also has a small post office counter, which is open longer hours than the main post office and is more convenient.

Banks There's a bank on the Legian road but for most people the numerous moneychangers are faster, more efficient, open longer hours and give just as good a rate. If you need a real bank for some

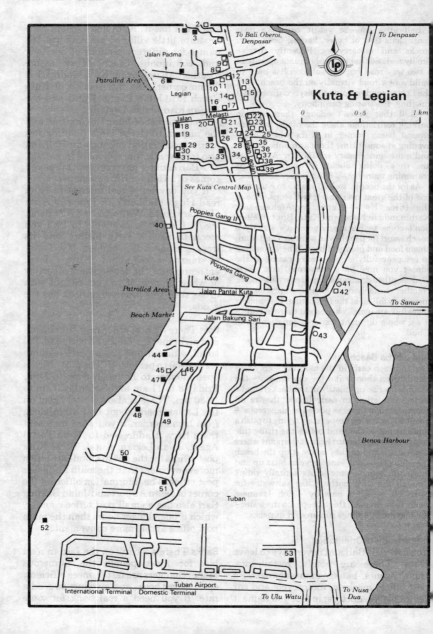

To Bali Oberoi,
Denpasar

To Denpasar

Jalan Padma

Patrolled Area

Legian

Jalan

Jalan Melasti

Kuta & Legian

0   0·5   1 km

See Kuta Central Map

Poppies Gang II

Poppies Gang

Kuta

Jalan Pantai Kuta

Patrolled Area

Beach Market

Jalan Bakung Sari

To Sanur

Benwa Harbour

Tuban

Tuban Airport

International Terminal   Domestic Terminal

To Ulu Watu

To Nusa
Dua

■ HOTELS & LOSMEN
1 Kuta Palace Hotel
3 Orchid Garden Cottages, Sawasdee
  Thai Cuisine & Sari Yasa Inn
6 Bali Mandira Cottages
7 Legian Village Hotel
10 Legian Beach Bungalows
16 Legian Beach Hotel
18 Bali Intan Cottages
19 Bruna Beach Inn
26 Legian Mas Beach Inn
29 Bruna Beach Inn
31 Bali Anggrek Inn
32 Camplung Mas Bungalows
33 Sayang Beach Lodging
44 Kartika Plaza Hotel
46 Bali Rani Hotel
47 Sanika Beach Hotel
48 Raya Beach Cottages
49 Bali Bagus Cottages
50 Rama Beach Cottages
51 Mandara Cottages
52 Pertamina Cottages
53 Puri Nusantara Hotel

□ RESTAURANTS, BARS & DISCOS
2 Topi Kopi French &
  Yamcha Restaurants, The Club
4 Restaurant Glory
5 Warung Kopi
8 Restaurant Happy &
  Bobbie's Bar & Restaurant

9 Lobis Restaurant
11 Norman's Garden Restaurant
12 Sari Restaurant
13 Ned's Place
14 Do Drop Inn
15 Goa Indian Restaurant
17 Bali Too Restaurant
20 Legian Garden Restaurant
21 Orchid Garden Restaurant
22 Kayu Api
23 Made's Restaurant
24 Swiss Restaurant
25 Rivoli Disco
27 Yudit Bakery
28 Il Pirata Pizzeria
30 Southern Cross Restaurant
35 Monte Carlo Bar
36 Depot Viva
37 Pink Panther Club
38 Bali Billabong Restaurant
39 Mastapa Gardens
40 Batu Karang Restaurant
42 Supermarket &
  Kentucky Fried Chicken
45 Godfrey's Bar & Restaurant

○ OFFICES, SHOPS, ETC
34 Krishna Bookshop
41 Petrol Station
43 Market

complicated money transfer or other bank-like activity you should head for the big bank offices in Denpasar.

A number of the moneychangers have safety deposit boxes where you can leave airline tickets or other valuables and not have to worry about them during your stay in Bali.

Airlines & Travel Agents If you're flying Garuda there's a small Garuda office (tel 24764) where you can make reservations or reconfirmations in the Kuta Beach Hotel at the beach end of Jalan Pantai Kuta. The office sometimes gets hopelessly crowded so it's an idea to arrive before opening time or during the lunch break

and be at the head of the queue. It's open Monday to Friday from 9 am to 12 noon and from 1 to 4 pm. Saturday and Sunday it opens 9 am to 1 pm.

The Bali Qantas office is at the Bali Beach Hotel at Sanur where there is also another Garuda office. The myriad Kuta travel agents will offer to make reconfirmations for you but there's a charge and some agents are said to be less than scrupulous about actually reconfirming.

There are countless tours organised from Kuta which can be booked through the agents. Typical prices for a day trip are around US$7 to US$15. Tours further afield – to places like Lombok, Komodo or Sulawesi – are also offered. They also rent cars, motorcycles and bicycles, sell bus and train tickets to Java and perform other travel agent services.

Theft & Security Kuta developed a bad reputation for theft and rip-offs in the late '70s. Perhaps things have quietened down a bit or perhaps people have just become used to it. Thefts usually take place either on the beach or from losmen rooms. You should always keep your room securely locked as it's quite easy for somebody to just wander into your losmen during the day.

It's equally necessary at night, more than a few people have woken up to find their valuables have disappeared from under their nose. Losmen rooms are not always a safe place to leave money, airline tickets or other valuables. There have also been a number of muggings at Kuta, beware of those dark, lonely gangs (alleys) at night. Take care but don't worry unduly, Kuta is not New York. You'd probably have to spend a lot of dark nights stumbling down a lot of dark gangs before you finally ran into somebody you'd prefer not to! Most people who lose things at Kuta are idiots who leave things on the beach while they're in the water.

Beach Safety Yes, Kuta Beach does have its dangers. Every year there are at least a half dozen drownings, often of visitors from other Asian countries who are not good swimmers. There is now a Kuta Lifesaving Club at the end of Kuta Beach Rd. Drownings peaked at 18 in 1980, since then it's varied from five to 13 each year so take care in the water especially when the surf is running. There are patrolled areas at Kuta and Legian.

Kuta Beach is much more likely to cost you money than your life, however. First of all it's going to cost 100 rp (50 rp children) just to set foot on the beach. The whole beach is now fenced off and you're charged admission. Secondly there are more sellers on the beach than swimmers – you're constantly importuned to buy anything from a cold drink to a massage or a hair beading job. What can cost you a whole lot more money is to leave things on the sand while you're in the water. Believe it or not this is how a lot of people lose their passports in Bali each year!

Places to Stay

It has been estimated that there are 200 to 300 places to stay at Kuta and Legian

Balinese boys fishing

And they're still building more. Surprisingly though it's far from crowded apart from in the heart of Kuta or around Jalan Padma-Jalan Melasti in Legian. Even there you only have to walk a couple of steps back from the main street to find palm trees and open fields. Go back on the other side of the Legian road and there's more open space than anything else.

Once upon a time it was very easy to sum up the accommodation story at Kuta. There were a sprinkling of flashier establishments but everything else was alike as peas in a pod. They all offered much the same standards – spartan little double rooms and a pleasant verandah area outside looking on to a central garden. 'Breakfast' was often thrown in, usually consisting of tea and bananas or black rice pudding. Tea was generally available on call at any time of the day.

These standard losmen were alike in one other way, they all charged the same standard price. Back in the early '70s (when you got 400 rp to the dollar) they were 400 rp for a double. With time and successive devaluations they crept up to 600 rp, then 750 rp, then 1500 rp and now they're at all sorts of prices from around 4000 to 10,000 rp.

There are still 'standard' losmen around but now there are countless places at all sorts of different standards and also at all sorts of different prices. Even many of the old bottom-bracket losmen have added attached bathrooms, often with showers instead of mandis, or other modern conveniences. Back in the days of the standard losmen you could always be fairly certain they'd be attractive, relaxing places no matter what else. Unfortunately that is no longer always true. There are lots of places at Kuta today which have obviously been thrown together as quickly and cheaply as possible to try and turn over as many rupiah with as little effort as they can manage.

What to look for in a losmen? You can start with that well known advice from real estate agents – location, location, location. Many places are close to busy roads where the traffic noise and exhaust fumes can make you think you're in the centre of some busy western city. On the other hand there are also places so isolated that getting to the restaurants for a meal is a major trek. Where do you want to be – close to the action or away in the peace and quiet? It's often possible to find a good combination of both factors – a place far enough off the main roads to be quiet but close enough so that getting to the shops and restaurants is no problem.

Then you can look at what the rooms are like and how pleasant and generally well kept the losmen is. My ideal losmen would be fairly small and as much like a traditional Balinese home as possible. That is, it should be enclosed by an outer wall and built around a central courtyard-garden. It should be an attractive and peaceful place to sit around and read or talk. It should be clean and well kept. And it should be friendly. If they're offering breakfast then find out what it will be. Most important of all remember that there are lots more losmen – if you find you don't like your first choice it's very easy to move somewhere else.

When you first arrive at the airport in Kuta you're liable to be pounced upon by the Kuta hotel touts. They're sometimes local kids out to make a little commission from a losmen owner. Other times they may be the people who actually run the losmen, simply in need of some more business. If you've not got a specific losmen in mind they can often be a good way to find a room – you haven't got to hunt around finding a place with rooms free, if necessary you'll have help carrying your gear and you may even get free transport from the airport. If you don't like the place they take you to you can always say no immediately or just take it for a night while you look elsewhere. I've gone along with a tout at Kuta on many occasions and never found myself at a place which I didn't like. If you just wander around the laneways there'll always be people asking 'want room?' – so you'll have no trouble finding a place.

Places to Stay – bottom end

You can still find basic losmen at around 5000 rp for a double but the prices at Kuta are no longer as cheap as for losmen elsewhere in Bali. In fact compared with some of the very pleasant places up at the Singaraja beaches they're really poor value. Down at this bottom end of the scale the losmen will be pretty basic, no attached bathrooms, little else apart from the beds in the rooms. There's no reason, however, that they shouldn't be attractive and well kept even at the very bottom of the range. As you move up the scale you get attached bathrooms, western-style toilets, better furnishings and a generally less spartan atmosphere. The prices are likely to be higher closer in to the centre of Kuta compared to further out. Prices for these 'better' bottom-end places could be in the 7500 to 12,500 rp range.

A popular place in the middle of the bottom end range is the long running *Lasi Erawati's*, further down Poppies Gang towards the beach from Poppies itself. It's just far enough out from the centre to be reasonably quiet (although too many motorcycles buzz by). Rooms here cost 5000 and 10,000 rp and Fat Yogi's is a popular place to eat.

A little further down the gang is the *Kubuku Inn* with just four bungalows at 12,000 to 16,000 rp. Just north of Poppies Gang is *Kempu Taman Ayu*, a pleasant and helpful little losmen with rooms with bathrooms for 9000 rp.

Many of Kuta's original losmen can be found along Jalan Pantai Kuta, or Jalan Bakung Sari, such as the *Yulia Beach Inn* down towards the beach end of Jalan Pantai Kuta. Rooms there start from US$3 without bathroom, US$4 to US$8 with bathroom, on up to US$20 for a bungalow with air-con. The *Pendawa Inn* is five minutes from the centre but quiet and good value. Also a little out from the

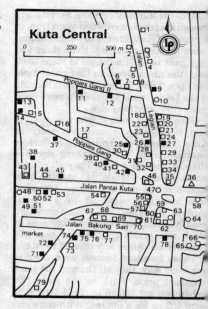

Kuta Central

centre the *Cempaka Losmen* is a low priced but pleasant friendly place, down the lane towards the second lot of Poppies Cottages.

In Legian the *Legian Mas Inn* is in a quiet area off the main streets. Right in the middle of things there are a string of places around Jalan Padma including the long running *Three Sisters*, not bad at 4000 to 7000 rp. *Suri Wathi Beach House* on Jalan Padma is a pleasant and quiet losmen. Basically, however, the best way to find losmen around Kuta and Legian is simply to wander around and look in a few. There are countless places to try, something is bound to suit.

Places to Stay – middle

Kuta also has plenty of middle range hotels, from around US$20 to US$40 a night. They include the very beautiful *Poppies Cottages*, just across from Poppies Restaurant on Poppies Gang.

■ HOTELS & LOSMEN		24	Blue Pub
6	Cempaka Losmen	28	Aleang's
9	Puri Rama Cottages	29	Intan Restaurant
11	Poppies Cottages II	30	TJs
12	Barong Cottages	31	Poppies
13	Kuta Seaview Cottages	32	Perama
14	Maharani Bungalows	33	Eldorado Coffee Shop
25	Kempu Taman Ayu	34	Widya Restaurant
26	Sari Yasa Samudra Bungalows	35	Quick Snack Bar
27	Aquarius Beach Inn	39	Kempu Cafe
37	Kubuku Inn	41	Fat Yogi's Restaurant
38	Yasa Samudra Bungalows	43	Made's Juice Shop
40	Rumah Penginapan Walon	44	Melasti Restaurant
42	Poppies Cottages	46	Made's Warung
45	Budi Beach Inn	50	Green House Restaurant
49	Kuta Beach Hotel	53	Suci Restaurant
51	Kuta Cottages	54	Lenny's
52	Yulia Beach Inn	55	Bali Sunrise &
71	Karthi Inn		Daruma Japanese Restaurants
72	Melasti Beach Bungalows	56	Bali Indah, Wayan's & Dayu II
74	Ramayana Seaside Cottages	57	Bagus Pub
75	Kuta Beach Club	59	Pub 41
76	Agung Beach Bungalows	60	Casablanca
78	Losmen Dharma Yudha	61	Serrina Japanese Restaurant
79	Puspa Ayu Beach Bungalows	62	Gantino Baru Padang Restaurant
		67	Dayu I
□ RESTAURANTS, BARS & DISCOS		68	Bamboo Indah
1	Adam Beer Garden	69	Santai (Lucky) Restaurant
2	Angin Laut Restaurant	70	The Pub
3	Fatty Restaurant	73	Yan's Restaurant
4	Norm's Bar	77	Supermarket &
5	Lenny Garden Restaurant		Carolina Fried Chicken
7	Twice Restaurant		
8	Sari Club	O	OFFICES, SHOPS, ETC
15	Aleang's Coffee Shop	10	Kuta Postal Agent
16	Tree House Restaurant	47	Bemo Corner
17	Warung Transformer	48	Kuta Lifesaving Club
18	Wantilan Restaurant	58	Bali Foto Centre
19	The Spotlight Disco	63	Tourist Offices
20	Peanuts Disco, Koala Blu Pub &	64	Police Station
	other bars	65	Post Office
21	Indah Sari Seafood	66	Cinema
22	Mini Restaurant	△	
23	Prawita Garden Restaurant	36	Temple

The pretty little individual bungalows are dotted around a beautiful garden and even the bathrooms have their own small internal garden. They're very centrally located yet so secluded you can easily forget that noisy Kuta is all around you and there's an equally beautiful swimming pool. This is definitely one of the most attractive hotels in Bali, quite an achievement in a place with so many beautiful hotels. Rooms cost US$36/37. There's also a second Poppies Cottages, along from Kuta towards Legian. Rooms here are US$20/21.

Near the beach market, the *Melasti Beach Bungalows* (tel 51860) on Jalan Kartika has rooms with attached bathroom and fan from US$25, with air-con from US$30. There's a swimming pool, bar and restaurant. In the same vicinity on Jalan Bakung Sari, the *Hotel Kuta Cottages* (tel 51101) has rooms in the same price category, starting from around US$20 and going up to US$40. Again there's a swimming pool.

Along Jalan Legian, the road to Legian, there's the *Puri Rama Cottages* (tel 51591) with a swimming pool and air-con cottages for US$26 to US$32. Also on the Legian road you'll find the similarly priced *Sri Kandi Bungalows*.

The beachfront *Yasa Samudra Bungalows* (tel 51305) has singles/doubles at 15,000/18,000 rp with fan or 22,000/25,000 rp with air-con plus larger family units at 35,000 rp. There's a swimming pool but it's kind of featureless. Right by the beach, between Kuta and Legian, the *Bali Anggrek Inn* (tel 51265) has individual cottages at US$35/40 and a swimming pool.

There are many other middle bracket hotels at Kuta and Legian like the much cheaper *Bruna Beach Inn*, close to the beach about 100 metres on the Kuta side of Jalan Melasti, in Legian. This is a larger than average small hotel with simple losmen-style rooms from US$10 and some pleasant bungalow-style rooms, complete with verandah and bathroom. Or there's the *Matahari Bungalows* (tel 51616) between Kuta and Legian with rooms from US$8/10 up to US$20/25, all including breakfast. The *Rama Gardens Cottages* at the beach end of Jalan Padma are more expensive. They're related to the *Ramayana Seaside Cottages* in the heart of Kuta.

Places to Stay – top end

Kuta isn't like Sanur where nearly all the hotels are bunched at the upper end of the price range. There are, however, a number of places in this category. They include the *Kuta Beach Hotel*, the original hotel at Kuta and right in the centre of things at the beach end of Jalan Pantai Kuta. Two other upper bracket Kuta hotels are at opposite ends of the strip. The very flash *Pertamina Cottages* are right down at the airport end of the beach, not the best bit of Kuta Beach. Way beyond Legian is the *Bali Oberoi* – a nicer beach but relatively isolated.

Other more expensive places include the beachfront *Kartika Plaza Hotel*, the *Kuta Beach Club* from US$40 and the *Kuta Seaview Hotel* (also beachfront). Up towards Legian there's the *Bali Intan Cottages* on the beach with a pool and 'motel-style' rooms and individual cottages. In Legian there's the beachfront *Legian Beach Hotel* at the beach end of Jalan Melasti, a popular hotel with rooms at a wide range of prices. The *Bali Mandira Cottages* is at the beach end of Jalan Padma. Further north along the beach is the *Kuta Palace Hotel* and the *Nusa di Nusa*, quiet lower priced bungalows with a swimming pool and bar right on the beach.

There's a 15.5% tax and service charge on top of the room price at these top end places. The vast majority of people staying at them will be on package tours so the regular room rates are really artificial.

Bali Intan Cottages (tel 51770) Jalan Melasti Legian, PO 1002, Denpasar, 122 rooms, air-con swimming pool, US$40 to US$60.

Bali Mandira Cottages (tel 51381) Jalan Padma, Legian, 96 rooms, air-con, swimming pool, US$35 to US$50.

Hotel Bali Oberoi (tel 51061) Box 351 Denpasar, directly on the beach beyond Legian, 75 rooms, bungalow-style, air-con swimming pool, US$80 to US$160, plus villa rooms.

Kartika Plaza (tel 51067) PO Box 84, Denpasar, right on the beach, close to the centre of Kuta, 120 cottages, air-con, swimming pool, from US$41.

Kuta Beach Hotel (tel 51361) PO Box 393, Denpasar on the beach in the centre of Kuta, 32 rooms, air-con, swimming pool US$50 to US$65.

Top: Snorkelling at the reef off Lovina Beach, Bali (TW)
Bottom: A Buddha and other statuary at Kapal, the 'garden gnome centre of Bali' (TW)

Top: Rice paddy terraces near Tirtagangga, Bali (TW)
Left: Small rice paddy shrine, Bali (TW)
Right: Planting rice shoots, near Pulukan, Bali (TW)

Legian Beach Hotel (tel 51711) Jalan Melasti, Legian, PO Box 308, Denpasar, close to the beach, 118 bungalows, air-con, swimming pool, US$25 to US$51.

Pertamina Cottages (tel 23061) PO Box 121, Denpasar, on the beach at the airport end of Kuta, 178 rooms, air-con, swimming pool, US$84 to US$90.

Santika Beach Hotel (tel 51267) PO Box 1008, Denpasar, air-con, swimming pool, US$49 to US$80.

Sea View Cottage-Kuta (tel 23991) Jalan Pantai, PO Box 36, air-con, swimming pool, US$40 to US$45.

Places to Eat

There are countless places to eat around Kuta, they range from tiny hawker's carts to fancy restaurants, cheap warungs to bars and pubs, steak houses to juice bars. Like so much else about Kuta most of the food here is not Balinese or even Indonesian – you could stay in Kuta for a month, eat in a different place every meal and never ever have to confront so much as a humble nasi goreng. In Kuta the food is pseudo-western top to bottom although it's always going through some sort of current craze. A couple of years back it was Mexican food, more recently it seems to have been the discovery of pizzas. The cheapest food around Kuta or Legian? Try the night market near the post office and cinema.

Around Kuta With so many places to try the following is just a sparse over-view, a mere handful of places to consider, starting with one of Kuta's most popular upper bracket eating places the still delightful *Poppies*. Situated on Poppies Gang, close to the heart of things but just far enough off the main streets to be calm and quiet, Poppies has a beautiful romantic garden and an extensive menu. It's also squeaky clean, ideal for those who worry about their fragile digestive systems. These days, with so many surprisingly fancy restaurants around Poppies doesn't even seem that expensive. Most meals are 4000 to 6000 rp, desserts

1000 to 2000 rp, a big beer costs 2500 rp, a glass of wine slightly less. Although the food is very straightforward (they do a great hamburger) it's also really very good so Poppies is likely to remain a long term survivor.

A few steps beyond Poppies is *TJ's*, the place in Kuta for Mexican food. Somehow Mexico seems a long way from Bali (well it is!) but they do surprisingly good Mexican food here and its popularity is well deserved. Main courses are generally 4000 to 6000 rp.

Further down Poppies Gang towards the beach there are several popular new places for light meals. *Fat Yogi's* used to be the restaurant for Lasi Erawati's and is still an excellent place for a light meal or breakfast. Their croissants are superb and they also turn out pizzas from their genuine wood-fired pizza oven for 3500 to 5500 rp! Other restaurants down the gang towards the beach include the pleasant *Tree House Restaurant*.

There are plenty of other possibilities around Kuta; particularly along Jalan Pantai Kuta, Jalan Bakung Sari and right along the Legian road. Starting from bemo corner there's the antiseptic looking *Quick Snack Bar* right on the corner – a good place for a snack or breakfast, good yoghurt.

Going down Jalan Pantai Kuta (Kuta Beach Rd) there's the long running *Made's Warung*. This simple open-front place has been going since the early '70s so it's as much a long term survivor as Poppies. This is probably the place in Kuta for people watching and is a popular hangout for the leading lights of the Kuta rag trade. The food is simple, straightforward but well prepared and there's always somebody strange to watch from first thing in the morning to way late at night.

Further down towards the beach is *Lenny's*, popular for its seafood, and newer restaurants like the *Green House* or the *Suci Restaurant* plus other familiar names like *Made's Juice Shop*.

Along Jalan Buni Sari, which connects Jalan Pantai Kuta at bemo corner with Jalan Bakung Sari, there's a number of long running and popular eating places. In the well liked and crowded *Bali Indah* you can see the food being prepared in their kitchen – 'something not every place would be proud to do'. A couple of doors down there's *Wayan's* and then *Dayu II*, both have been going nearly as long as Kuta has been a travellers' centre.

On this same stretch of road you'll also find some of Kuta's most popular bars, something that certainly didn't exist in the Kuta of 15 years ago. Back then alcohol was definitely not the drug of choice! *The Pub* is the flashiest, cleanest and most expensive of these bars. Across the road is the Japanese *Serrina Restaurant*. Just round the corner on Jalan Bakung Sari there's the *Gantino Baru*, a nasi Padang specialist.

Along the Legian Road There are lots more possibilities down the Legian road. Most of the time the Legian road is an almost continuous traffic jam and a table near the road can mean you have to shout to be heard. Popular places along the Legian road from Bemo Corner include *Aleangs*, where the yoghurt is still pretty good – try the yoghurt, muesli and honey. Next door, however, *Perama's* is just a shadow of the place it once was.

The *Depot Mini Restaurant* is not very 'mini' at all. It's a big, open, basic and busy place serving straightforward food at low prices. A little further along there are several restaurants set back from the road, so they're relatively quiet. The *Wantilan* and *Lenny's Garden Restaurant* are attractive places with lush gardens, good food and, like many Kuta restaurants these days, Australian wine by the glass at quite affordable prices. Like the other Lenny's this one is good for seafood. Between them is the popular *Sari Club*.

Getting down towards Legian you'll find *Il Pirata* which does pretty good pizzas and even has a generator to cope with the odd blackout. Across the road is *Depot Viva*, an open-roofed place which has surprisingly good Indonesian and Chinese food despite its bare, basic and grubby appearance. The prices are pleasantly basic too. *Yudit's* is a bakery with nice looking bread. A little further along is the *Swiss Restaurant*, ideal for homesick German-speakers although the food is not at all bad if you'd like a change from rice and noodles. Next door is *Made's Restaurant* – good steaks and banana fritters.

Around Legian Down Jalan Melasti the *Legian Garden* does a pretty fair 'rijstaffel' although it's really just a glorified nasi campur. The *Orchid Garden* on Jalan Melasti is very pleasant and the food is delicious – try the whole lobster in onion-butter sauce.

The *Do Drop Inn*, between Jalan Melasti and Jalan Padma, is one of Legian's longest running places; ditto for the *Agung Juice Park* a little further up the road. On the corner of Jalan Padma is *Restaurant Happy* and nearby is *Bobbies* which is also popular.

Dining Out in Kuta

The trouble with Kuta restaurants is that half of them are solid performers like *Poppies* or *Made's Warung* who've been there seemingly for ever and never look any different. The other half are in a constant state of flux, opening, closing, becoming popular and fading away.

So one Kuta night we go in search of new taste treats down Jalan Legian. Yes *Aleang's* and *Perama* look the same as ever, but are pale shadows of their mid-70s peak. *Depot Mini* is doing great business but the *Wantilan, Prawita* and *Lenny's* look very nice but very empty. Further down towards Legian the *Goa Indian Restaurant* is new and from the crowds they must be doing something right so we give it a try.

After being told half the items on the menu aren't available we eventually order. And wait. And then wait some more. After an hour I become suspicious and take a wander around. Nobody in this restaurant is eating anything!

Eventually a chicken curry, a teaspoonful of raita and two miniature chappatis appear. The vegetable curry has run out we're told and, believe it or not, they've run out of rice! We have found the first restaurant in the entire archipelago of Indonesia to actually run out of rice.

Paying the bill (1500 rp for food, 10,000 rp for all the wine we drank while waiting) we rush hungrily across the road to *Il Pirata* for a pizza but five minutes later the tape deck gives a cautionary hiccup and the power fails. This doesn't deter Il Pirata, however, they have what must be the only generator on the entire Legian Rd so the lights are soon back on and the tape running again. You can't hear it over the generator but never mind.

Twenty-two minutes after we stepped through the door (we're timing it by now) Il Pirata delivers not just the pizza we ordered but two of them! Curiously although they're both ostensibly the same one tastes much better than the other so we eat the better one, leave the other, pay for both and dive out into the darkness of Legian Rd to hold fruitless discussions with the hordes of bemo jockeys and eventually walk home.

Entertainment

Kuta is a good place to get a suntan, definitely a good place to get pissed, and supposedly a good place to get laid. The beach caters for the first, the numerous bars and discos cater for the second and provide hope for the third.

The nightspots are scattered around Kuta and Legian, many along Jalan Legian. Discos go through strange fads – five nights a week you need a crowbar to clear a space on the dance floor but come back three months later and there's not a lustworthy body in sight. One year you can't even find enough space to park your motorcycle outside – come back next year and there's enough room to dump an elephant. So if the places listed here turn out to be ever so dull and dreary and you don't get laid – don't blame us.

There also seems to have been a long overdue movement to clean up some of the wilder drunken excesses of Kuta. The pub crawls, where bus loads of increasingly noisy and drunken revellers were hauled from one venue to another, have been cut back considerably. Plus many pubs and discos have been closed down and others concentrated into a sort of 'combat zone' on the Legian road. There everybody can get as drunk as they like without bothering other people.

The centre piece of the Jalan Legian entertainment complex is the large *Peanuts* disco – it's rather like an Australian barnyard-pub-venue; which might be why it caught on so quickly. Admission is usually around 3500 rp which includes a couple of drinks. There's a series of open bars flanking the entrance road into Peanuts. These places kick off earlier than the main disco, and continue even after it's in full flight. For some reason *Koala Blu* is (or was) the far and away favourite. Koala Blu T-shirts seem to pop up all over Asia. *Cock n Bull* also attracts some sort of crowds but some of the other bars can be all but empty. After midnight it's quite a scene with music blasting out from every bar, hordes of people, mostly upright but some decidedly horizontal, and out in the parking lot lines of bemos and dokars waiting to haul the semi-conscious back to their hotels.

Other places include *The Spotlight Disco* on Legian Rd or the *Rivoli Disco* which claims to be 'for serious night lifers'. *Kayu Api's*, at the junction of Jalan Legian and Jalan Melasti, has gone through various role changes in its night life.

Bars & Pubs There are numerous regular pubs around Kuta and Legian like the *Bali Aussie*, the *Bali Billabong*, *Norm's Bar* and *Norman's Garden*. If you can hack it (or even believe it) Wednesday night at the *Casablanca* on Jalan Buni Sari is 'Aussie Party Night' with Aussie beer, Aussie people, drinking contests and other events you'd rather not hear about including ladies' arm wrestling contests, cheese and vegemite sandwich eating contests and other scenes of typical Australian depravity.

Also on Jalan Buni Sari is the *Pub Bagus*, the Buni Sari dancing place, and *The Pub,* one of Kuta's original bars. It's still very popular.

At the opposite end of the price (and decor) scale take the little alley beside Made's to Poppies' Gang. Opposite the *Warung Santai* a large and very relaxed Balinese guy ladles rice wine out of a large container, people sit around, guitars are strummed and it's generally a very peaceful and pleasant scene.

Things to Buy

Parts of Kuta are now almost solid shops, in fact they seem to be squeezing out the restaurants and other businesses and over the years they've become steadily flashier and more sophisticated. Lots of the cheaper shops are now crowded together in 'art markets' like the one at the bottom of Jalan Bakung Sari. Popular Kuta buys include painted to order surfing pictures (they'll even paint you into the hero-size waves). You can find all the Balinese arts and crafts from every part of the island. They range from wood carvings to paintings or those delightful wind chimes which you hear all over Bali.

Clothes are another good Kuta buy, there are lots of clothes shops around Kuta and the prices are more than reasonable. You'll probably see the same items later on from Berkeley to Double Bay at 10 times the cost.

Recently there was a clamp down on the pirate cassette tape business, but they have now reopened, selling the same tapes with 'only for sale in Indonesia' printed on the covers.

With so many things to buy around Kuta it's very easy to be stampeded into buying things you don't really want during your first days. In fact you need real endurance not to succumb to something, there are so many people trying to sell to you. There are also countless masseurs operating along the beach – they'll quickly prove you have dozens of muscles you never knew existed for a couple of thousand rp.

Getting There & Away

The official taxi fare between the airport and Kuta is 3500 rp. Bemos from Kuta are 250 rp to the airport or 350 rp to Denpasar. There are no direct bemos to Sanur from Kuta, you have to go in to Denpasar, change from the Tegal to Kereneng bemo station and take another bemo out to Sanur. There are some Sanur bound bemos which come round via the Tegal station. Between a few people it would be little more expensive to charter a bemo.

There are almost always lots of bemos around bemo corner if you want to charter one – to Ulu Watu, the airport, Ubud or wherever. With haggling, a chartered bemo to Sanur costs about 5000 rp, or 12,000 rp to Ubud. To reach most places by regular public bemos you have to go into Denpasar and change.

Getting Around

Bemos shuttle along the Legian road but most of them would rather charter than take you as a regular passenger so beware. There are also lots of places around Kuta and Legian hiring bicycles, motorcycles, jeeps and anything else with wheels you might like to lay your hands on. See the introductory Getting Around section for details. Also there are countless places operating tours around Bali or selling tickets to places further afield in Indonesia or overseas.

Kuta Banjars

Despite all the excesses Kuta is still a village, a place where little offerings are put out in front of house entrances and at tricky gang junctions. It's this part of Kuta which makes it so much more interesting than the antiseptic Nusa Dua.

The banjars are amongst the most visible evidence of Kuta's thriving village life. A banjar is rather like a small town council and the bale banjars are a meeting place, a place for discussions, meetings, ceremonies, dancing or gamelan practice. If you hear a gamelan ringing out over Kuta some quiet evening it's probably a banjar practise session and nobody will mind if you wander in to watch and listen.

Most banjars are little more than an open pavilion or courtyard but they're easy to spot by the warning drum tower and Kuta banjars, with lots of tourist generated rupiah, can afford some pretty fancy warning towers. Check out the one at Banjar Pande Mas next to Made's Warung on Kuta Beach Rd. Or the one at Banjar Buni Kuta next to the Pub. Best of all is the superb new multi-storey tower at Banjar Tegal Kuta, further down the lane from Banjar Buni Kuta.

SANUR

Sanur Beach is the alternative to Kuta for those coming to Bali for sea, sand and sun. The new resort of Nusa Dua is intended to be an alternative to Sanur. Although Sanur is principally the locale for the Hyatts and the like it does have some more reasonably priced accommodation, although not down to the lower Kuta levels. It's got a pleasant beach and the Sanur reef makes for more sheltered water – no big surf here.

What Sanur doesn't have, thank the gods, is the Kuta noise, confusion and pollution. You're not in constant risk of being mown down by motorcycle maniacs, the traffic isn't horrendous and you're not constantly badgered to buy things – badgered yes, but not constantly.

Information

Sanur has travel agents, moneychangers and other facilities just like Kuta. There's a Sanur post office although, of course, you can also have mail addressed to the large hotels. The Denpasar main post office is in a sort of mid-position between Denpasar and Sanur.

Qantas has its Bali office at the Bali Beach Hotel, and it's open Monday to Friday from 8 am to 4 pm, Saturday from 8 am to 2 pm or you can call the airport on 51472. You will also find a Garuda office here although it's not terribly efficient. It's open Monday to Friday from 7.30 am to 4.30 pm and on Saturday, Sunday from 1 to 5 pm. Singapore Airlines, Cathay Pacific, Thai International and Malaysian Airlines agents are also in the Bali Beach Hotel.

There's an Australian consulate (tel 25997) at Jalan Raya Sanur 146; that's actually between Sanur and Denpasar on the back road. The office is open Monday to Friday from 8 am to 2 pm and also will look after British, Canadian and New Zealand citizens although they may still have to go to Jakarta if they need a new passport. The consulates' main problem is people who run out of money – usually through having it stolen. They also warn of the heavy narcotics penalties in Bali and seem to do a lot of marriages – Australian-Indonesian and Australian-Australian.

Around Sanur

There's plenty of opportunity for wandering around Sanur, along the beach or through the rice paddies. The rice farmers of Sanur are said to grow some of the finest rice in Bali. The beach at Sanur is always full of interesting sights such as the colourful prahus known as *jukungs* ready to take you for a quick trip out to the reef. At low tide you can walk across the sand and coral to this sheltering reef. Villagers collect coral here to make building lime.

Beyond the Hotel Sanur at Belanjong there's a stone pillar with an inscription recounting military victories of over 1000 years ago. Tanjung Sari with its coral pyramid was once a lonely temple by the beach.

Museum Le Mayeur

Sanur was one of the places in Bali favoured by western artists during their pre-war discovery of the island. It was still a quiet fishing village at that time but few traces of that Sanur of 50 years ago remain. The exception is the former home of the Belgian artist Le Mayeur who lived here from 1932 to 1958. It must have been a delightful place then, a peaceful and

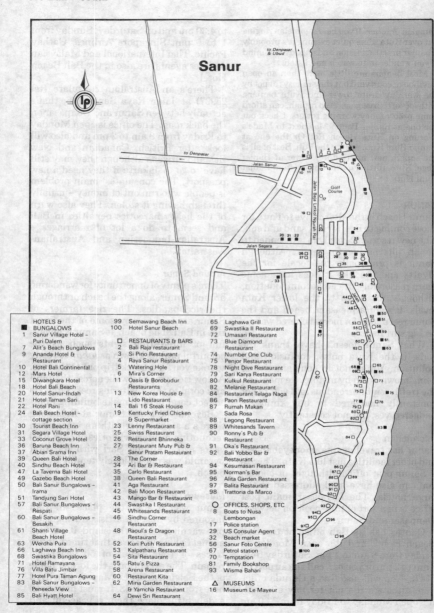

Sanur

to Denpasar & Ubud

to Denpasar

Jalan Sanur

Jalan Baja Lehod Ngurah Ra

Golf Course

Jalan Segara

Tanjung Sari

HOTELS & BUNGALOWS	99 Semawang Beach Inn	65 Laghawa Grill
■	100 Hotel Sanur Beach	69 Swastika II Restaurant
1 Sanur Village Hotel – Puri Dalem		72 Umasari Restaurant
7 Alit's Beach Bungalows	□ RESTAURANTS & BARS	73 Blue Diamond Restaurant
9 Ananda Hotel & Restaurant	2 Bali Raja restaurant	74 Number One Club
10 Hotel Bali Continental	3 Si Pino Restaurant	75 Penjor Restaurant
12 Mars Hotel	4 Raya Sanur Restaurant	78 Night Dive Restaurant
15 Diwangkara Hotel	5 Watering Hole	79 Sari Karya Restaurant
18 Hotel Bali Beach	6 Mira's Corner	80 Kulkul Restaurant
20 Hotel Sanur-Indah	11 Oasis & Borobudur Restaurants	82 Melanie Restaurant
21 Hotel Taman Sari	13 New Korea House & Lido Restaurant	84 Restaurant Telaga Naga
22 Hotel Rani	14 Bali 16 Steak House	86 Paon Restaurant
24 Bali Beach Hotel – cottage section	19 Kentucky Fried Chicken & Supermarket	87 Rumah Makan Sada Rosa
30 Tourist Beach Inn	23 Lenny Restaurant	88 Legong Restaurant
31 Segara Village Hotel	25 Swiss Restaurant	89 Whitesands Tavern
33 Coconut Grove Hotel	26 Restaurant Bhinneka	90 Ronny's Pub & Restaurant
36 Baruna Beach Inn	27 Restaurant Muty Pub & Sanur Pratam Restaurant	91 Oka's Restaurant
37 Abian Srama Hotel	28 The Corner	92 Bali Yobbo Bar & Restaurant
39 Queen Bali Hotel	34 Ari Bar & Restaurant	94 Kesumasari Restaurant
40 Sindhu Beach Hotel	35 Carlo Restaurant	95 Norman's Bar
47 La Taverna Bali Hotel	38 Queen Bali Restaurant	96 Alita Garden Restaurant
49 Gazebo Beach Hotel	41 Aga Restaurant	97 Balita Restaurant
50 Bali Sanur Bungalows – Irama	42 Bali Moon Restaurant	98 Trattoria da Marco
51 Tandjung Sari Hotel	43 Mango Bar & Restaurant	
57 Bali Sanur Bungalows – Respati	44 Swastika I Restaurant	○ OFFICES, SHOPS, ETC
60 Bali Sanur Bungalows – Besakih	45 Whitesands Restaurant	8 Boats to Nusa Lembongan
61 Shanti Village Beach Hotel	46 Sindhu Corner Restaurant	17 Police station
63 Werdha Pura	48 Raoul's & Dragon Restaurant	29 US Consular Agent
66 Laghawa Beach Inn	52 Kuri Putih Restaurant	32 Beach market
68 Swastika Bungalows	53 Kalpatharu Restaurant	56 Sanur Foto Centre
71 Hotel Ramayana	54 Sita Restaurant	67 Petrol station
76 Villa Batu Jimbar	55 Ratu's Pizza	70 Temptation
77 Hotel Pura Taman Agung	58 Arena Restaurant	81 Family Bookshop
83 Bali Sanur Bungalows – Peneeda View	60 Restaurant Kita	93 Wisma Bahari
85 Bali Hyatt Hotel	62 Mina Garden Restaurant & Yamcha Restaurant	△ MUSEUMS
	64 Dewi Sri Restaurant	16 Museum Le Mayeur

elegant home right by the beach. Today it's squeezed between the Bali Beach Hotel and the Diwangkara Beach Hotel but still maintained by his widow Ni Polok, once a renowned and beautiful Legong dancer. The home displays paintings by Le Mayeur but is also an interesting example of architecture in its own right. Notice the beautifully carved window shutters which recount the story of Rama and Sita from the *Ramayana*.

Admission is 200 rp (children 100 rp) and it's open 8 am to 2 pm Sunday, Tuesday, Wednesday and Thursday, 8 to 11 am Friday and 8 am to 12.30 pm Saturday.

Kites

Asian children don't enjoy the same variety and quantity of toys that children in the west commonly have but they certainly do fly kites. Almost anywhere in Asia the sky is likely to be full of kites of all sizes and types. Bali is no exception – you'll see children flying kites in towns and villages and even in the middle of the rice paddies. At Sanur, however, kite-flying is not just child's play. Here the local banjars compete in kite-flying competitions where size seems to be a major factor.

Their kites are enormous, traffic is halted when they're carried down the road, it takes half a dozen men to launch them, two men to carry the drum of heavy nylon cord and a sturdy tree is needed to tie the kite to once it's up and flying. They're up to 10 metres long and the cord tensioning the main cross piece (itself a hefty length of bamboo) makes a low 'whoop-whoop-whoop' noise as they fly. Not unexpectedly they're a danger to aircraft – one of these monsters could bring a 747 down – and they've had to restrict kite flying on the airport approaches, particularly across Serangan Island.

Places to Stay

There are no dirt-cheap Kuta-style places around Sanur although there are a handful of medium-price places, a few of them as good or better value than equivalent places at Kuta. Principally, however, Sanur is the high price resort, the place for 'international standard' hotels where the majority of Bali's package tours go. At these upper bracket hotels there will be a 15.5% service charge. The prices quoted here don't include this additional charge

Places to Stay – middle

At the northern end of Sanur Beach the *Ananda Hotel* (tel 8327) is behind the restaurant of the same name, right by the beach. It's a neat and clean little place with rooms at 15,000/20,000 rp. There are rooms at 15,000 to 25,000 rp at the *Watering Hole*, opposite the Bali Beach Hotel entrance.

In the same price bracket the *Hotel Pura Taman Agung* on Jalan Tanjung Sari is another pleasant place with a pretty garden and well kept rooms with wide verandahs.

On the same side of the road is the *Hotel Ramayana* (tel 8429) with rooms from US$15 to US$25. A little north and on the beach side of the road is the *Werdha Pura*, a government run 'beach cottage prototype'. Further along the road the *Abian Srama Inn* (tel 8415) has rooms from US$12 to US$35.

On Jalan Segara, right next to the Segara Village Hotel and pleasantly close to the beach, the *Tourist Beach Inn* is one of the most economical places at Sanur – straightforward but quite reasonable rooms are 10,000/15,000 rp for singles/doubles including breakfast.

Mrs S Harsojo (PO Box 223, Denpasar) has charming bungalows on the beach at Sanur for US$12 a night including breakfast if you book for a week. The entrance is from Respati Bungalows and it's near the Tandjung Sari's part of the beach. *Swastika Bungalows* near the two Swastika Garden Restaurants has pleasant bungalows around a swimming pool.

On the Jalan Sanur crossroads at the

northern end of Sanur the *Mars Hotel* is about a five or 10 minute walk from the beach while across the other side of the crossroads there's the *Hotel Bali Continental* on the Denpasar road.

Other middle bracket places include the *Laghawa Beach Inn*. Finally on Jalan Segara, but across the main road, there are three lower-priced places side by side – the *Hotel Sanur-Indah, Hotel Taman Sari* and the *Hotel Rani*. Rooms are small and simple.

Places to Stay – top end

Sanur's first 'big' hotel and still one of the biggest is the massive *Hotel Bali Beach* from the Sukarno era of the mid-60s. Today it's very out of place in Bali, a Miami Beach-style rectangular block squarely facing the beach. It's got all the usual facilities from bars, restaurants and a nightclub to swimming pools, tennis courts and even an adjacent golf course. The poolside snack bar here is quite reasonably priced. Adjoining the hotel is the newer cottage section.

Almost all the more expensive hotels are on the beachfront. Immediately north of the Bali Beach and adjacent to the Museum Le Mayeur is the slightly secluded *Diwangkara Beach Hotel*. Across the road north again are the cottages of *Alit's Beach Bungalows*. Going south from the Bali Beach you come first to the *Segara Village Hotel* by the beach – it's a more expensive place with motel-style rooms and nicer double-storey cottages in a pleasant garden area. There's a children's playground here. Then there's the *Sindhu Beach Hotel* and *La Taverna Bali Hotel*, both right on the beach. There's also the smaller *Gazebo Beach Cottages* group here with air-conditioned cottages in a lush garden.

There are several groups of *Bali Sanur Bungalows* at Sanur, continuing south you come to the 'Irama', 'Besakih' and 'Peneeda View' bungalows. The 'Puri Dalem' group of bungalows on Jalan

Sanur are one of the few top-end places not actually on the beach or close to it.

In between the Irama and the Besakih bungalows is the *Tandjung Sari Hotel*, the name means 'cape of flowers' and they spell Tanjung in the old way. Some of the bungalows in this pleasantly relaxed and fairly expensive place are interesting two-storey buildings.

Then it's the *Bali Hyatt*, one of the biggest hotels along Sanur and an interesting contrast with the Bali Beach of 10 years earlier. The lesson had been learnt in the '60s and a regulation was passed that no hotel could be 'taller than a palm tree'. The Hyatt blends in remarkably well with its sloping balconies overflowing with tropical vegetation. Look for the interesting pottery tiles used as decorations on various walls. There's also Sanur's flashiest and most popular disco here. Right down at the southern end of the beach is the big *Hotel Sanur Beach*.

Alit's Beach Bungalows (tel 8560, 8567) PO Box 102, Denpasar, right on the beach, 98 bungalows, air-con, swimming pool, US$35 to US$40.

Hotel Bali Beach (tel 8511) PO Box 275, Denpasar, right on the beach, 605 rooms, air-con, swimming pools, US$55 to US$75 plus suites, some with kitchenettes.

Bali Hyatt (tel 8271-8277) PO Box 392, Denpasar, right on the beach, 387 rooms, air-con, swimming pool, US$70 to US$120 plus suites.

Bali Sanur Bungalows (tel 8421, 8422) PO Box 198, Denpasar, right on the beach, 160 rooms, air-con, swimming pool, US$40 to US$50.

Beach Hotel Diwangkara (tel 8577, 8591) PO Box 120, Denpasar, right on the beach, 36 rooms, air-con, swimming pool, US$25 to US$38.

La Taverna Bali Hotel (tel 8497) PO Box 40, Denpasar, right on the beach, 34 rooms, air-con, swimming pool, US$50 to US$60.

Hotel Sanur Beach (tel 8011), PO Box 279, Denpasar, right on the beach, 320 rooms plus 26 bungalows, air-con, swimming pool, US$70 to US$75.

Hotel Segara Village (tel 8407, 8408, 8231) PO Box 91, Denpasar, on the beach, 110 bungalows, air-con, swimming pools, from US$85.

Sindhu Beach Hotel (tel 28351) PO Box 181, Denpasar, right on the beach, 50 bungalow rooms, air-con, swimming pool, US$40 to US$50.

Tandjung Sari Hotel (tel 8441), PO Box 25, Denpasar, right on the beach, 25 bungalows, air-con, swimming pool, US$70 to US$80.

Welcome to
tandjung
sari
cape
of
flowers

Places to Eat

All the top end hotels have their own restaurants, snack bars, coffee bars and bars of course – generally with top end prices too! The food at Sanur is basically western – there's even Bali's centre for homesick pasta lovers, *Trattoria da Marco* down at the southern end of the beach road. You'll also find a number of quite reasonably priced places, very much from the Kuta restaurant mould. Just south of the Bali Beach Hotel there's the slightly more expensive beachfront *Sanur Beach Market*.

For seafood *Lenny's* and the *Kulkul Restaurant* are worth trying. *Kesumasari*, on the beach south of the Bali Hyatt, has good and commendably fresh food. If you continue down towards the south end of the Sanur hotel strip, beyond the Hyatt, there are a number of reasonably priced small restaurants and bars.

On the corner of Jalan Segara and the main road the *Restaurant Bhinneka* has a buffet of over 30 different dishes for 4000 rp.

Things to Buy

There are lots of shops scattered around Sanur, just like at Kuta. Temptation, near the Hotel Ramayana, is particularly

interesting with a curious collection of 'artyfacts'.

Getting There & Away

Taxi fare between the airport and Sanur is 9000 rp. A new 'superhighway' runs from the Denpasar-Batubulan road to Sanur and on past Benoa, Kuta, the airport and out to Nusa Dua. It makes transport along this route much faster.

There are two different Denpasar-Sanur bemos operating from the Kereneng bemo station in Denpasar. Coming from Sanur the blue ones go past Kereneng and around the south of town past Tegal (the Kuta station) and then around the north of town through Kereneng. The green bemos *sometimes* go around town but may just go straight to the station. The fare is 300 rp.

To get from Kuta to Sanur you have to go into Denpasar and then out again. It's much faster and, between a few people, not that much more expensive to charter a bemo for a Kuta to Sanur trip.

Getting Around

Small bemos shuttle up and down the beach road in Sanur at a cost of 100 rp. There are numerous places around Sanur renting out cars, motorcycles and bicycles from 1500 rp a day. Tunas Tours & Travel, in the Hotel Bali Beach Arcade, rents mountain bikes for US$7.50 a day and also runs bicycle tours of Bali.

SERANGAN ISLAND

Very close to the shore, south of Sanur and close to the mouth of Benoa Harbour, is Serangan, the turtle island. At low tide you can actually walk across to the island. Turtles are captured and fattened here in pens before being sold for village feasts. The island has an important temple, Pura Sakenan, noted for its unusual shrines known as *candi*. Twice a year major temple festivals are held here, attracting great crowds of devotees. The giant puppet figures known as *Barong Landung* are brought across to the island for these festivals.

Day trips to Serangan have become popular with the travel agents at Kuta and Sanur but Serangan has a very strong tourist trap air and is not terribly popular with visitors. You're constantly hassled to spend, spend, spend. In fact you get pounced on as soon as the prahu beaches and you're followed, cajoled, pleaded with and abused until you leave.

Getting There & Away

Like Kuta, Serangan has been affected by tourism – badly. It's not a place to waste time or money on but if you do decide to take a look you can either get there on an organised tour or charter a prahu yourself. Beware of rip-offs if you decide to charter, they may start at 25,000 rp but you can eventually knock a boat (big enough for a half-dozen people) down to around 10,000 rp. Charters are available from Suwan, a small mangrove inlet through a rubbish dump. Serangan Island is hard work from start to finish.

JIMBARAN BAY

Just beyond the airport, south of Kuta, Jimbaran Bay is a relatively new development with air-conditioned bungalows at the *Pansea Bali*. There's a bar and restaurant on the beach.

BENOA

The wide but shallow bay off the end of the runway is one of Bali's main ports. It's also the main harbour for visiting yachts and there's nearly always a few overseas vessels moored here. If you're looking for a yacht berth to some place far away you may find notes on various notice boards around Kuta (try Poppies for example) but you might have equally good luck by simply getting a prahu here to paddle you out to the yachts to ask.

Benoa is actually in two parts. The harbour, Benoa Harbour, is on the north side, directly connected with Denpasar. It consists of little more than a wharf and a

variety of port offices. Benoa village, where you might see turtles brought in from Serangan, is on the south side of the bay. To get there you have to take the highway to Nusa Dua and then the smaller road along the coast from there. Boats also shuttle back and forth between Benoa Harbour and the Benoa fishing village.

The village of Benoa has become much cleaner and more affluent looking in recent years and it's something of an activities centre for Nusa Dua. If you want to go windsurfing, para-sailing, scuba diving or indulge in various other water sports, this is the place.

Places to Stay & Eat

Chez Agung Pension/Homestay is a new development with pleasant doubles with bathroom for 16,000 rp. There are several restaurants in Benoa like the *Dalang Sea View Restaurant*, the *Entari Restaurant*, the *Jeladi Suta Restaurant* or the *Rai Seafood Restaurant*.

NUSA DUA

Nusa Dua, 'two islands', is the new Balinese beach resort – the planned resort area where the mistakes of Kuta won't be repeated! The two islands are actually small raised headlands, connected to the mainland by sand-spits. Nusa Dua is south of Kuta and Sanur and the airport, on the sparsely populated Bukit Peninsula.

The beach here is very pleasant and there is often good surf. The development of Nusa Dua was dogged by interminable delays and this is really a place for people who want to get away from Bali. There is no outside development permitted within the compound so you have a km or so walk if you want to get even so much as a coke at non-international-hotel prices. Or a bemo to the rest of Bali.

Places to Stay & Eat

The Nusa Dua hotels all have swimming pools, a variety of restaurants and bars,

entertainment and sports facilities and various other international hotel mod cons.

The *Nusa Dua Beach Hotel* (tel 71210) is a huge (450 rooms) and very upper bracket hotel with all the luxuries you could expect and prices from around US$70 to US$90 for standard rooms, plus 15.5% service and tax. It's attractively designed using much Balinese architecture and statuary but then how seriously can you take a hotel that promotes itself as being the place where Ronald Reagan stayed when he came to Bali? He probably stayed in the US$1200 a night Nusa Dua Suite.

South of the Nusa Dua Beach Hotel is the 500 room *Hotel Bali Sol* (tel 71510) with regular rooms at US$78 to US$84 and suites at US$138. South again is the *Putri Bali Hotel* (tel 71020, 71420) which has 425 rooms at US$70 to US$88 plus suites, cottages and so on. Just inland from the Putri Bali is the smaller *Hotel Club Bualu* (tel 71310). There are just 50 rooms at this hotel with prices from US$55 to US$70.

Finally at the north end of the Nusa Dua resort area is the *Club Méditerranée Bali* which is strictly an inclusive tour operation.

The hotels offer a wide variety of restaurants but there's not a great deal of choice apart from the hotels since it's a long walk to get out of the resort area. There are some other eating places in the 'amenity core' area but you can't just stroll outside to other restaurants, as you can at Sanur.

Getting There & Away

Taxi fare from the airport is 9500 rp. A bemo from Denpasar costs 500 rp to Bualu, the village outside the Nusa Dua compound. You've got about a km walk from there to the hotels. The bemo service operates on demand but there's usually one about every hour, avoid being pressured into chartering a bemo. There's a hotel bus service to Kuta for 5000 rp return or to Sanur or Denpasar for 8000 rp return. You can easily charter a whole bemo between Kuta and Nusa Dua for around 5000 rp.

ULU WATU

The southern peninsula is known as Bukit, 'hill' in Indonesian. It was known to the Dutch as Tafelhoek. If you follow the road from Kuta around the end of the airport runway it bucks and bounces right down to the end of the peninsula at Ulu Watu. There are plenty of potholes. At times the road climbs quite high, reaching 200 metres, and there are fine views back over the airport, Kuta and southern Bali. Along the roadside you'll notice numerous limestone quarries with large blocks of stone being cut out by hand. Many of the buildings in this area of Bali are constructed of these blocks. This is a dry, relatively sparsely inhabited area – a contrast to the lush rice-growing area which seems to commence immediately north of the airport.

At the southern tip, where the land ends in sheer cliffs which drop precipitously into the clear blue sea, perches the temple of Pura Luhur Ulu Watu. And perches is certainly the word for it – it hangs right over the abyss. The temple has a resident horde of monkeys and is entered through an unusual arched gateway flanked by statues of Ganesh. It's one of several important temples to the spirits of the sea to be found along the south coast of Bali. Others include Tanah Lot and Rambut Siwi.

Ulu Watu, along with the other well known temples of the south – Pura Sakenan on Serangan Island, Pura Petitenget at Krobokan and the temple at Tanah Lot – is associated with Nirartha, the Javanese priest credited with introducing many of the elements of the Balinese religion to the island. He retreated to Ulu Watu for his final days.

Ulu Watu has another claim to fame. It's a Balinese surfing Mecca, made famous through several classic surfing films and a popular locale for the surfers who flock to Bali from all over the world, but particularly from Australia. Just before the Ulu Watu car park a large sign indicates the way to the Suluban Surf Beach, Pantai Suluban. It's two km down a narrow footpath, OK for motorcycles but nothing more. Take care on a motorcycle, the path is narrow, some of the corners are blind and there have been some nasty accidents. From a motorcycle park at the end of the track you continue on foot down to the beach, which is overlooked by a series of warungs catering to the keen surfers who flock here. A letter from a hungry surfer raved on about the *Warung Indra* for three pages!

Denpasar

Fifteen years ago, which seems to be a throw-away cliche for too many things about Bali, Denpasar was a pleasant, quiet little town. Today it's a noisy confusion of motorcycles, a polluted disaster area of bemos and buses; not at all a pleasant place to stay. Still, it's the capital of Bali and does have an interesting museum, an art centre and

lots of shops. The city has a population of around 200,000. Denpasar means 'next to the market' and the city is sometimes referred to as Badung.

Information & Orientation
The main street of Denpasar is Jalan Gajah Mada, a crowded continuous traffic jam even though it is now one-way. This is the main shopping street of Denpasar but the market, Pasar Badung, is on the outskirts of town. There is also a shopping centre beside the river.

Tourist Office The Badung tourist office is on Jalan Surapati, just past the roundabout and across the road from the Bali Museum. They've got a useful calendar of festivals and events in Bali and a pretty good map. The office is open Monday to Thursday from 7 am to 2 pm, Friday 7 to 11 am, Saturday 7 am to 12.30 pm.

Banks All the major Indonesian banks have their main Bali offices in Denpasar, principally along Jalan Gajah Mada. The Bank Ekspor-Impor Indonesia, which isn't on that main street, is probably the best for transfers from overseas.

Post The Denpasar main post office with poste restante is very inconveniently situated, sort of half-way between Denpasar and Sanur by the back route. Avoid getting mail sent to you here, the offices in Kuta or Ubud are much more convenient.

Immigration The Immigration Office (tel 2439) is at Jalan Panjaitan 4, Sanglah – in the south of Denpasar and just around the corner from the main post office. It's open Monday to Thursday 7 am to 2 pm, Friday 7 to 11 am and Saturday 7 am to 12.30 pm. If you are in the rare circumstances these days of having to make visa changes, get there on a Sanglah bemo and make sure you're prettied up in your best.

PHPA The *Direktorat Perlindungan*

Hutan dan Pelestarian Alam (Directorate for Forest Protection and Nature Conservation) is responsible for managing Indonesia's nature reserves and national parks. There's an office just south of Denpasar – take a Benoa-bound bemo from Denpasar and get off at the corner of Jalan Suwung. The PHPA is 400 metres along Jalan Suwung, on the left.

Around Town

If you wander down Gajah Mada, past all the shops and restaurants, you come to the towering Guru statue at the intersection with Jalan Veteran. The four-faced, eight-armed statue is of the god Guru, Lord of the Four Directions. He keeps a close eye on the traffic swirling around him.

Beside the intersection is the large Puputan Square, commemorating the heroic but suicidal stand the rajahs of Badung made against the invading Dutch in 1906.

At the junction of Jalan Hasannudin and Jalan Imam Bonjol (the Kuta road) is the Puri Pemecutan, the rebuilt remains of a palace destroyed during the 1906 invasion.

Bali Museum

The museum consists of an attractive series of separate buildings and pavilions. They include examples of the architecture of both the palace (puri) and temple (pura). There is a split gateway (*candi bentar*) and an alarm drum (kulkul) tower from a temple together with an elevated lookout, as a prince might have used to look out across his lands. The large building in the second courtyard with its wide verandah is like the palace pavilions of the Karangasem kingdom where rajahs would hold audiences. Various other palace building styles from Tabanan and Singaraja are also seen in this courtyard.

Exhibits include both modern and older paintings, arts and crafts, tools and various items of everyday use. Note the fine wood and cane carrying cases for taking your fighting cock to the event. The cultural exhibits include a diorama of a Balinese wedding. Then there are superb stone sculptures, krises, wayang kulit figures and an excellent exhibit of dance costumes and masks including a sinister Rangda figure, a healthy looking Barong and towering Barong Landung figures.

The museum was originally founded by the Dutch in 1932. Admission to the museum is 200 rp for adults, 100 rp for children. The museum is open on Tuesday, Wednesday and Thursday from 8 am to 2 pm, Friday from 8 to 11 am, Saturday from 8 am to 12.30 pm and Sunday from 8 am to 2 pm. It's closed on Mondays.

Pura Jagatnatha

Adjacent to the museum is the state temple Pura Jagatnatha. This relatively new temple is dedicated to the supreme god, Sanghyang Widi and his shrine, the padmasana, is made of white coral. The padmasana (throne, symbolic of heaven) tops the cosmic turtle and the naga serpents which symbolise the foundation of the world.

Art Centres

Abiankapas, the large arts complex on the eastern side of town has an exhibit of modern painting and wood carving together with a dancing stage and other facilities. Dances are held regularly and temporary exhibits are held along with the permanent one. It's open 8 am to 5 pm from Tuesday to Sunday.

A little further out at Tohpati, just beyond the Sanur turn-off from the Batubulan road, is the government handicrafts and art centre Sanggraha Kriya Asta. This large shop has an excellent collection of most types of Balinese crafts. It's a fixed price shop and the items are usually of good quality so it's a good place to look around to get an idea of what's available, what sort of quality to expect and at what prices. It's open Tuesday to Saturday from 8 am to 4.30 pm and Sunday from 8 am to 4 pm. It's

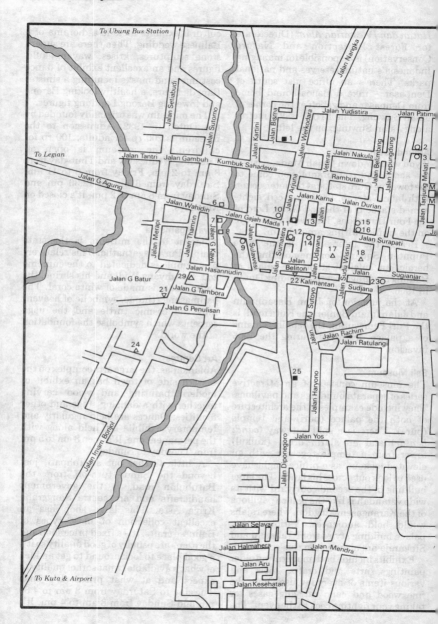

To Ubung Bus Station

Jalan Nangka

Jalan Setiabudi

Jalan Sutomo

Jalan Kartini

Jalan Bisma

Jalan Werkodara

Jalan Yudistira

Jalan Patim

Jalan Berimbing

Jalan Kepungdung

Jalan Nakula

Veteran

Jalan Tanjung Melati

To Legian

Jalan G Agung

Jalan Tantri

Jalan Gambuh

Kumbuk Sahadewa

Rambutan

Jalan Arjuna

Jalan Karna

Jalan Durian

Jalan Wahidin

Jalan Gajah Mada

Jalan Surapati

Jalan Merapi

Jalan Thamrin

Jalan G Kawi

Jalan G Kawi

Jalan Sumatera

Jalan Sulawesi

Jalan Sudi Wisnu

Jalan Udayana

Jalan Hasannudin

Beliton

Jalan G Batur

Jalan G Tambora

Jalan Kalimantan

Sudjana

Sugianjar

Jalan G Penulisan

Jalan MJ Sutoyo

Jalan Rachim

Jalan Ratulangi

Jalan Imam Bonjol

Jalan Haryono

Jalan Diponegoro

Jalan Yos

To Kuta & Airport

Jalan Selayar

Jalan Halmahera

Jalan Mendra

Jalan Aru

Jalan Kesehatan

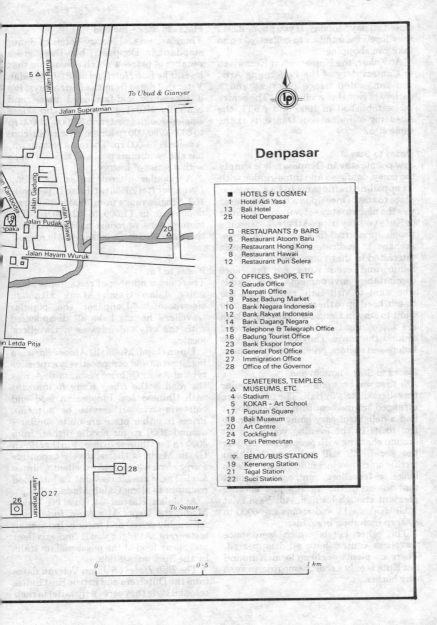

Denpasar

■ HOTELS & LOSMEN
1 Hotel Adi Yasa
13 Bali Hotel
25 Hotel Denpasar

□ RESTAURANTS & BARS
6 Restaurant Atoom Baru
7 Restaurant Hong Kong
8 Restaurant Hawaii
12 Restaurant Puri Selera

○ OFFICES, SHOPS, ETC
2 Garuda Office
3 Merpati Office
9 Pasar Badung Market
10 Bank Negara Indonesia
12 Bank Rakyat Indonesia
14 Bank Dagang Negara
15 Telephone & Telegraph Office
16 Badung Tourist Office
23 Bank Ekspor Impor
26 General Post Office
27 Immigration Office
28 Office of the Governor

△ CEMETERIES, TEMPLES,
 MUSEUMS, ETC
4 Stadium
5 KOKAR – Art School
17 Puputan Square
18 Bali Museum
20 Art Centre
24 Cockfights
29 Puri Pemecutan

▽ BEMO/BUS STATIONS
19 Kereneng Station
21 Tegal Station
22 Suci Station

To Ubud & Gianyar

Jalan Supratman

Jalan Ratna

Jalan Gadung

Jalan Kamboja

Jalan Palawa

Jalan Pudak

Jalan Hayam Wuruk

Jalan Letda Pitja

Jalan Panjaitan

To Sanur

0   0·5   1 km

closed all day Monday. If you phone 22942 they'll send a minibus to collect you and take you shopping!

At Kokar, the Konservatori Kerawitan or Conservatory of the Performing Arts, you can watch dance practices and a variety of gamelan orchestras. The centre was established in 1960 and ASTI, the Academy of Indonesian Dance, is at the same site.

Places to Stay

Few people stay in Denpasar. It is simply too noisy, confused and fume-ridden with its appalling traffic jams to be a pleasant place to stay. Once upon a time Denpasar was the place to stay – if you went to Sanur or Kuta you day tripped there. Later some people preferred to stay in the town, perhaps to indicate that they weren't interested in that vulgar beach life. Now Sanur and even Kuta are far more comfortable environments and people who want to visit Bali, rather than the beach, head up to the mountains. If you do want to stay in Denpasar, however, there are something like 100 hotels scattered around the town. They cater mainly to Indonesian visitors, principally on business.

Places to Stay – bottom end

Adi Yasa was once one of the most popular travellers' hotels in Bali. The rooms were arranged around beautiful gardens and it had a delightful easy-going and friendly feel to it. In the evening you could sit around chatting with people from all over the world. It's still well kept but that terrific spirit has just faded away – it's no longer a travellers' centre and without that magic in the air it's just another pleasant enough losmen. Adi Yasa is at Jalan Nakula 11 and rooms are 6000 to 8000 rp including breakfast.

The other hotels which were once travellers' centres have all disappeared. There are plenty of cheap losmen around but Kuta is only a short bemo ride away so why bother.

Places to Stay – top end

There are no real luxury hotels of Sanur standard in Denpasar, but there are a number of places a notch down from that level. The *Bali Hotel* (tel 25681-5) at Jalan Veteran 3 dates from the Dutch days. It's a pleasantly old-fashioned place and centrally situated. Including breakfast singles/doubles cost from 36,000/44,000 rp to 53,000/60,000 rp for rooms with air-con. A suite is 78,000 rp. There's a restaurant, bar and swimming pool and this is a place with a sense of history.

A popular alternative is the *Hotel Denpasar* (tel 26336) at Jalan Diponegoro 103. Singles range from 7500 to 25,000 rp, doubles from 11,500 to 32,500 rp. The more expensive rooms have air-con and there are also some cottage-style rooms.

Places to Eat

There are a number of restaurants along noisy Jalan Gajah Mada although elsewhere in Denpasar the popular travellers' haunts have all disappeared with the city's demise as a travellers' locale.

Up on Gajah Mada the *Atoom Baru* is a big, spartan and comparatively expensive typical Asian Chinese restaurant. Across the road is the *Hong Kong Restaurant* with Chinese and Indonesian food and cafeteria-style self-service or a menu. Prices in either place are quite similar – around 2000 rp for noodle dishes, from 3000 rp for Chinese dishes. Further down Gajah Mada is the relatively expensive *Puri Selera* which does excellent Chinese food. There are also several Padang food restaurants along Gajah Mada.

At Jalan Kartini 34, just off Gajah Mada, the Depot Mie *Nusa Indah* is a reasonably priced and friendly Indonesian restaurant. At night you'll find excellent and cheap food at the pasar malam stalls by the Suci bus station.

The *Bali Hotel* on Jalan Veteran dates from the Dutch era and in true East Indies colonial style they serve a rijstaffel in their old fashioned dining room. It costs 5500 rp and the service is friendly and efficient.

Entertainment

Dances in and around Denpasar are mainly for tourists only – there are regular performances at the art centre and a Barong dance every morning in nearby Batubulan. Wayang kulit performances can be seen a couple of times a week at the Pemecutan. Near the Kuta bemo station, cockfights used to be held regularly. Officially they're now banned but in practice they probably continue as before.

Things to Buy

Denpasar has no particular crafts of its own although there are numerous 'factories' around town churning out the mass produced handicrafts. Countless craft shops line Jalan Gajah Mada. You can also find an extremely good selection of Balinese crafts just out of town at the Sanggraha Kriya Asta government art centre on the road to Batubulan. It's a fixed price place and an excellent starting point to get an idea of prices and quality, even if you buy elsewhere. They often have articles which you simply may not see anywhere else.

Getting There & Away

Denpasar is the travel centre of Bali – here you'll find buses, colts and minibuses for all corners of the island. Also there are buses for Java, boat tickets, trains tickets and the Garuda, Merpati and Bouraq airline offices here.

See the introductory Getting There & Away section for details of transport between Bali and Java, and Bali and Lombok.

Air Garuda (tel 27825, 22788, 22028) has its office at Jalan Melati 61, near the Kereneng bus station. The office is open Monday to Friday 7.30 am to 4.30 pm, Saturday and Sunday 9 am to 1 pm.

Merpati (tel 22864, 25841) is right next door at Jalan Melati 57. Their hours are Monday to Friday 7 am to 4 pm, Saturday 7 am to 1 pm, Sunday 9 am to 1 pm. Merpati flights are particularly good for the islands of Nusa Tenggara and they have lots of flights to Lombok.

Bouraq (tel 24656) is at Jalan Sudirman 19A. Their fares are the same as Merpati's and they have flights to destinations in Java and Nusa Tenggara.

Bus & Bemo Stations The usual route for land travel to or from Bali is Denpasar-Surabaya by day or night bus. There are a number of bus companies for this run, you find them mainly around the Suci bus station or along Jalan Hasannudin. If you're staying in Kuta, however, there's no need to trek into Denpasar for tickets as there are numerous agents at Kuta.

For travel within Bali, Denpasar has four bus and/or bemo stations so in many cases you'll have to transfer from one station to another if you're making a trip through Denpasar. If, for example, you were travelling from Kuta to Ubud you'd arrive in Denpasar at the Tegal bemo station, transfer to the Kereneng station and take a bemo from there to Ubud. Squadrons of little three-wheeler bemos shuttle back and forth between the various stations and also to various points in the town. The Jalan Thamrin end of Jalan Gajah Mada, for example, is a stop for the transfer bemos. You'll find the transfer bemos lined up for the various destinations at each of the stations.

Fares vary from around 150 to 300 rp between the stations. You can also charter bemos or even those little three-wheelers (cheaper of course) from the various stations. You could, for example, arrive from Surabaya at Ubung or Suci and charter a mini-bemo straight to Kuta rather than bothering with transferring to Tegal and then taking a bemo to Kuta. Between a few of you it might even be cheaper.

Further afield fares vary with the type of bus you take, the smaller minibuses are more expensive than the larger old buses.

The stations and some of their destinations and fares are:

Tegal – south of the centre on the Kuta road. The station for the southern peninsula.

Kuta	300 rp
Legian	400 rp
Airport	400 rp
Nusa Dua	500 rp

Ubung – north of the centre on the Gilimanuk road. This is the station for the north and west of Bali and it is also the main station for buses to Surabaya, Yogyakarta and other destinations in Java. To get to Tanah Lot take a Kediri bemo and another from there for 150 rp.

Kediri	450 rp
Mengwi	400 rp
Negara	1000-1500 rp
Gilimanuk	1500-2000 rp
Bedugul	1000 rp
Singaraja	1500 rp
Lovina Beach	2000 rp

Kereneng – east of the centre, off the Ubud road. This is the station for the east and central area of Bali.

Sanur	300 rp
Ubud	600 rp
Gianyar	500 rp
Tampaksiring	800 rp
Klungkung	800 rp
Bangli	800 rp
Padangbai	1250 rp
Candidasa	1300 rp
Amlapura	1600 rp
Kintamani	1200 rp

Suci – south of the centre is mainly just the bemo stop for Benoa (300 rp) but the offices of many of the Surabaya bus lines and agents for shipping lines are also here. Benoa bemos also leave from the Sanglah Market.

Wangaya – for bemos to Sangeh (450 rp).

Train There are no railways on Bali but there is a railway office where you can get tickets to Surabaya or other centres in Java. This includes a bus ride to Gilimanuk and the ferry across to Banyuwangi in Java from where you take the train.

Boat The usual boat route out of Bali (not counting the short Bali to Java ferry which is included in bus ticket prices) is Padangbai to Lombok. Usually you get tickets for that daily ferry at Padangbai. There's a Pelni agent and other shipping agents at the Suci bus station if you wish to enquire about boat transport further afield.

Getting Around

Small three-wheeler bemos shuttle back and forth between the various Denpasar bus stations and Jalan Gajah Mada. The set fares vary from 150 rp to 300 rp – Tegal to Ubung 300 rp, Ubung to Kereneng 300 rp, Kereneng to Suci 150 rp, Kereneng to Tegal 150 rp. You can also charter these tiny bemos, they'll even buzz you out to Kuta Beach, or you can find taxis. Agree about all prices before getting on board because there are no meters.

Despite the traffic, dokars (horse carts) are still very popular around Denpasar, again agree on prices before departing. Note that dokars are not permitted to go down Jalan Gajah Mada.

Ubud

In the hills north of Denpasar, Ubud is the calm and peaceful cultural centre of Bali. It has undergone tremendous development in the past few years but, unlike at Kuta, this development hasn't ruined Ubud. It has managed to stay relaxed and beautiful, a place where the evenings are quiet and you can really tell you're in Bali. It's worth remembering that electricity only arrived in Ubud in the mid-70s. There's an amazing amount to do in and around Ubud so don't plan to do it in a day trip. You need at least a few days to properly appreciate it and Ubud is one of those places where days can quickly become weeks and weeks become months.

Information

Ubud has a pleasant little post office with poste restante – the letters are just sitting in a box on the counter, you sort through them yourself. There's the usual varied selection of bicycle and motorcycle hire places and a number of shops selling most items you might require. There's no bank but Ubud has a number of money changers and as a result the exchange rates are little worse than those at Sanur or Kuta. The telephone office is on the main road before you reach the post office turn-off from the centre of Ubud.

The Book Shop is a book exchange place on the Monkey Forest Rd or you can find small but excellent selections of new books on Bali at Murni's Warung or the Museum Neka.

Most importantly Ubud has a very friendly and helpful tourist office on the main street. Ubud's survival has been largely due to local efforts. Bina Wisata, the Ubud tourist office is a local venture, not a government one. It was set up in an effort to defend the village from the tourist onslaught – not by opposing tourism but by providing a service aimed at informing and generating a respect amongst visitors for Balinese culture and customs. The British-based magazine *Newz Internationalist* recounted some of the problems that faced the village:

The locals cursed the tourists, for they disturbed ceremonies and dressed impolitely. Guide books had told their readers about the family events, airlines had promoted Bali with all of its glamorous ceremonies, photographers had made public exhibitions out of private occasions. All of this without asking permission. Foreigners were attracted. They came to Ubud full of expectations. They entered any private house as though the religious ceremonies there were tourist attractions. Conflict after conflict developed, anger mounted.

Boards were put on the gates or walls to warn tourists that the ceremony inside was a private event. 'No Tourist, Please,' 'For Guest Only,' 'This is a Religious Event,' 'Entrance is Forbidden,' 'Only for the Family Members.' It was really ugly to see religious offerings and decorations at a compound entrance disturbed by these emergency boards written in a foreign language. Tempers rose further when a group of tourists were ordered to leave a temple because they were disturbing the praying parishioners. The tourists blamed their guide for not informing them. The guide accused the locals of being unfriendly and uncooperative. The villagers chased the guide away.

In 1981, with the problems of the village so acute, a move was made to revive Ubud's former beauty by extensive tree-planting. Then the tourist office was established – its publications even included an English-language newspaper, probably the first such paper to be produced by a village in Indonesia. In many ways they have been very successful although it takes time for the message to get through – an article in the now defunct Australian newspaper *National Times* summed up the problem:

Some greenhorn visitors frequently think the tourist is a king who can do no wrong, possessing an unlimited right to see anything he or she wants to see and to grab as much as possible with as little expense as possible. 'Do you sell tickets for a wedding tour?' 'I want to see a cremation today.' 'Can you give me a good price?' 'How much do you charge to see a tooth filing ceremony?'. . . . I know the Balinese do not cry. But I do. I cry when visitors think that Bali is a huge open stage on which any local activity is exhibited to collect money. . . .

Museum Puri Lukisan

On the main street of Ubud the Museum Puri Lukisan, Museum of Fine Arts, was established in the mid-50s and displays fine examples of modern Balinese art. It was in Ubud that the modern Balinese art

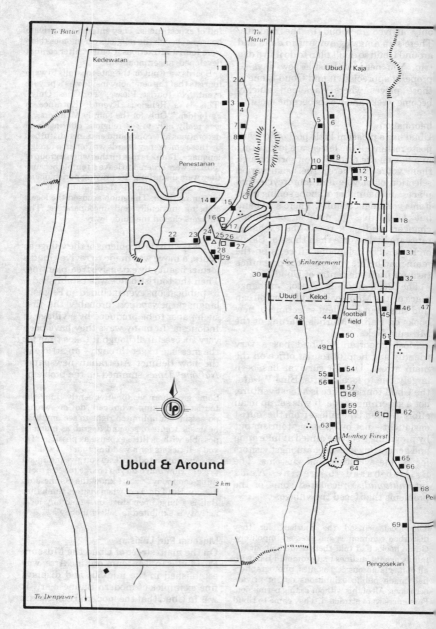

Ubud & Around

0   1   2 km

To Batur

To Batur

Kedewatan

Ubud Kaja

Penestanan

Campuhan

See Enlargement

Ubud Kelod

football field

Monkey Forest

To Denpasar

Pengosekan

Peli

1
2
3
4
5
6
7
8
9
10
11
12
13
14
15
16
17
18
22
23
24
25
26
27
28
29
30
31
32
43
44
45
46
47
49
50
51
54
55
56
57
58
59
60
61
62
63
64
65
66
68
69

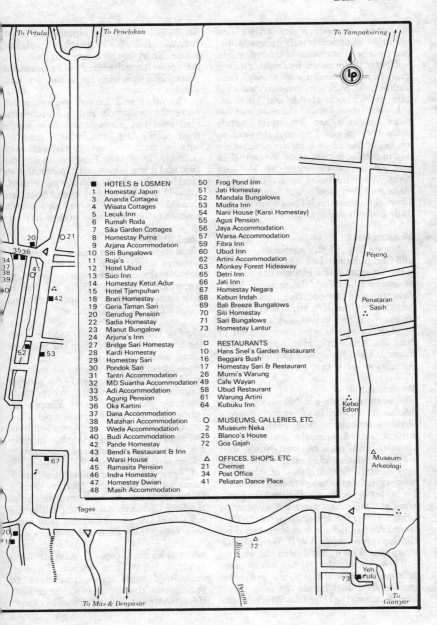

To Petulu
To Penelokan
To Tampaksiring

Pejeng

Penataran
Sasih

Kebo
Edon

Museum
Arkeologi

Teges

River
Petanu

72

Yeh
Pulu

73

To Mas & Denpasar
To Gianyar

	HOTELS & LOSMEN	50	Frog Pond Inn
1	Homestay Japun	51	Jati Homestay
3	Ananda Cottages	52	Mandala Bungalows
4	Wisata Cottages	53	Mudita Inn
5	Lecuk Inn	54	Nani House (Karsi Homestay)
6	Rumah Roda	55	Agus Pension
7	Sika Garden Cottages	56	Jaya Accommodation
8	Homestay Purna	57	Warsa Accommodation
9	Arjana Accommodation	59	Fibra Inn
10	Siti Bungalows	60	Ubud Inn
11	Roja's	62	Artini Accommodation
12	Hotel Ubud	63	Monkey Forest Hideaway
13	Suci Inn	65	Detri Inn
14	Homestay Ketut Adur	66	Jati Inn
15	Hotel Tjampuhan	67	Homestay Negara
18	Brati Homestay	68	Kebun Indah
19	Geria Taman Sari	69	Bali Breeze Bungalows
20	Gerudug Pension	70	Siti Homestay
22	Sadia Homestay	71	Sari Bungalows
23	Manut Bungalow	73	Homestay Lantur
24	Arjuna's Inn		
27	Bridge Sari Homestay	□	RESTAURANTS
28	Kardi Homestay	10	Hans Snel's Garden Restaurant
29	Homestay Sari	16	Beggars Bush
30	Pondok Sari	17	Homestay Sari & Restaurant
31	Tantri Accommodation	26	Murni's Warung
32	MD Suartha Accommodation	49	Cafe Wayan
33	Adi Accommodation	58	Ubud Restaurant
35	Agung Pension	61	Warung Artini
36	Oka Kartini	64	Kubuku Inn
37	Dana Accommodation		
38	Matahari Accommodation	○	MUSEUMS, GALLERIES, ETC
39	Weda Accommodation	2	Museum Neka
40	Budi Accommodation	25	Blanco's House
42	Pande Homestay	72	Goa Gajah
43	Bendi's Restaurant & Inn		
44	Warsi House	△	OFFICES, SHOPS, ETC
45	Ramasita Pension	21	Chemist
46	Indra Homestay	34	Post Office
47	Homestay Dwiari	41	Peliatan Dance Place
48	Masih Accommodation		

movement started, where artists first began to abandon purely religious and court scenes for scenes of everyday life. You enter the museum by crossing a river gully beside the road and wander from building to building through beautiful gardens with pools, statues and fountains.

It's a relatively small museum and has some excellent art but unfortunately these days the buildings and the gardens are beginning to look rather tired, worn and in need of rejuvenation. Nevertheless this gallery, along with the Museum Neka, is worth looking around before you make any decisions about buying art in Ubud. The museum is open 8 am to 4 pm daily and admission is 200 rp.

Museum Neka

Continue beyond the suspension bridge and Campuhan and a km or so up the road is the Museum Neka. Housed in a number of separate buildings the museum has a diverse and interesting collection, principally of modern art. It also includes an excellent and varied display of works by western artists who have resided in Bali like Arie Smit, Han Snel, Antonio Blanco, Theo Meier and Donald Friend. Admission is 200 rp.

Western Artists

The western artists who 'discovered' Bali and its art between the wars encouraged a massive artistic revival. Prior to their arrival 'art' was purely something for temples and palaces, immovable and rigid in its ideals and format. Walter Spies and Rudolf Bonnet, two of the first western artists to change these attitudes – for better or worse – both lived for some time at Campuhan, near the suspension bridge. Bonnet, a Dutchman, was in Bali from 1928 to 1958 and was imprisoned by the Japanese during WW II. Walter Spies disappeared on a ship during the war.

These original artists have been followed by many others right down to the present day. Just beside the suspension bridge, across the river from Murni's, the driveway leads up to Filipino-born artist Antonio Blanco's superbly theatrical house. Entry to the house and gallery is 200 rp, well worthwhile as it's a beautiful place. His speciality is erotic art and illustrated poetry.

The other well known western artist currently resident in Bali is Dutch-born Han Snel but many others have made their mark. Arie Smit, who is credited with inspiring the 'young artist' school of painting, lived near Penestanan around 1960 and it was his painting instruction to local boys that sparked off the movement. Swiss Theo Meier and the Australian Donald Friend are other well-known western artists who have worked in Bali

Ubud Walks

Ubud is a place for leisurely strolls – wanders through the rice paddies, lazy rambles through the forests, walks to surrounding villages. There are lots of interesting places in the area, including Ubud's famous monkey forest.

Monkey Forest Walks Just wander down the Monkey Forest Rd from the centre of Ubud and you'll arrive in a small but dense forest. It's inhabited by a handsome band of monkeys ever ready for passing tourists who just might have peanuts available for a hand-out. There's an interesting old pura dalem, temple of the dead, in the forest. You can walk to Peliatan from Ubud via the monkey forest, more interesting and quieter than following the main road.

If you turn right down the track immediately after the Monkey Forest Hideaway there's a pool down the gorge on the left. Continue down the path to the left where there's a beautiful swimming hole. Often there's no-one there.

Walks to Nearby Villages Popular strolls to neighbouring villages include Peliatan with its famous dance troupe or to Penestanan, the 'village of young artists'. If you continue through the monkey forest you'll come to Nyuhkuning, a small village noted for its woodcarvers. Or follow the road down to Pengosekan, south of Peliatan, another village with many painters.

In the late afternoon take the path to Petulu, off the Tampaksiring road, where towards sunset every day you can enjoy the spectacular sight of thousands of herons arriving home. Take the trail up beside the river on the Ubud side of Murni's to the beautiful Hill of Campuhan. Or walk to the lovely river Sungai Ayung near the village of Sayan.

Pejeng Walk If you take the road out of Ubud and continue straight on past the *apotik* (pharmacy) at the T-junction there's a wonderful trail that leads through typical Balinese country to the superb gorge of the river that runs by Goa Gajah. Following the trail beyond the river eventually brings you out at Pejeng, a very fine walk. From there you can take a bemo back to Ubud.

Bentuyung Walk Just walk straight north (uphill) from the bemo crossroads through Sambahan and Sakti to Bentuyung. Take the path to the right through the fields and wade across the shallow river. You can continue to Tegal Lantang and Taman or loop back via Junjungan to Kutuh and back to the main road near Peliatan. You can also cross from Junjungan to Petulu to see the herons. This complete loop is about eight km and it's a beautiful walk.

Around Town It's equally interesting just wandering around right in the heart of town. Look around the market in the early morning, it's across the road from the old puri in the centre of town. Or sip a coffee in the *Lotus Cafe* and gaze across the lotus-filled pond a little further up the road.

There are often dances in Ubud - at the Puri Ubud or the Peliatan dance place which is at the turn-off one down from the post office road. Ubud is a great place to study dancing or almost anything to do with Bali. You're likely to meet many travellers here on a long-term visit, studying something about Bali.

If you're wandering the streets of Ubud sometime look for the little black signs by each gateway. They detail the name of the occupant, his occupation and other vital details - like the number of LK (laki means boys), PR (prempuan means girls) and JML (jumlah means total). In one early morning stroll the biggest I saw were $8 + 6 = 14$ and $7 + 8 = 15$! Few families seem to have less than five or six children.

Places to Stay

Ubud used to have only a handful of accommodation possibilities but there has been quite a boom in new places opening. They are mainly at the cheaper end of the price scale - prices in Ubud generally start lower than in Kuta and stay lower most of the way up. There are only a few 'top end' places and they're really more medium priced in comparison to the real upper bracket hotels of Sanur or Kuta. You'll find places fairly widely scattered around Ubud - there are places along the main road and on the roads leading off it. In particular the Monkey Forest Rd has become a real centre for new places to stay with more places still under construction all the way down to the forest.

There are also lots of places in surrounding villages like Peliatan or Penestanan or simply scattered around the rice paddies. If you are in a remote losmen - and they can be very relaxing, peaceful places to stay - it's probably wise to have a torch (flashlight) with you if you want to avoid actually falling in to the rice paddies on some starry, starry night. Since Ubud is full of artists and dancers you can often find a losmen run by someone involved with the arts - where you can pick up some of the guidelines of Bali's art.

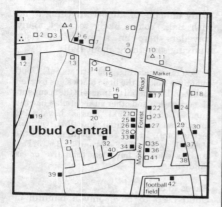

HOTELS, LOSMEN, ETC
1 Cecak Inn
5 Mumbul Inn
6 Puri Saraswati
12 Mawar Homestay
17 Happy Inn
19 Pondok Indah
20 Suarsena House
22 Canderi's
24 Wayan Karya
25 Alit's House
26 Puri Muwa
27 Badra Accommodation
29 Wena Homestay
30 Shena Homestay
32 Okawati's
33 Dewa House
34 Igna Accommodation
36 Ibu Rai
37 Agung's
38 Yoga Pension
39 Nick's Place
40 Sari Nadi
42 Surawan House

□ **RESTAURANTS**
2 Griya Barbecue
3 Rumah Makan Cacik
7 Lotus Cafe
8 Rumah Makan Kartika
11 Restaurant Puri Pusaka
13 Menara Restaurant
15 Ary's Warung
16 Sati's Warung
18 Nomad Restaurant
21 Ayu's Kitchen
23 Harry Chew's Restoran
31 Okawati's Warung
35 Restaurant Dennis
41 Lilies Restaurant

MUSEUMS, GALLERIES,
△ **PALACES, ETC**
4 Museum Puri Lukasan
10 Puri Ubud

○ **OFFICES, SHOPS, ETC**
9 Cinema
14 Tourist Office (Bina Wisata)
28 Book Shop

Places to Stay – bottom end

Ubud has a huge choice of places to stay so what follows is really just a sample. There are many other excellent places apart from those mentioned. Cheaper losmen in Ubud generally start around 6000 rp for simple doubles with attached mandi and go up to around 15,000 rp for the flashiest bottom-end places.

In Ubud There are lots of places in the bottom end price bracket down the Monkey Forest Rd including, close to the top of the road, one of Ubud's really long runners – *Canderi's*. It's a fairly straight-forward losmen-style place with rooms at 5000/7000 rp. Canderi's has been going almost as long as travellers have been staying in Ubud.

There are lots of other places along the Monkey Forest Rd, like *Igna Accommodation, Ibu Rai's* or *Sari Nadi*, just round the corner towards the rice paddies with rooms including attached mandi for 6000 rp. A little further down the Monkey Forest Rd is *Warsi's House*, a good friendly place to stay with excellent food. The similarly priced *Karyawan Losmen* is also good and they do great breakfasts, reported one happy visitor.

Continuing down the road towards the monkey forest other places include the *Bendi Inn*, a standard, well kept losmen with rooms at 6000 and 7000 rp. Or there's the very clean and well kept *Frog Pond Inn* with rooms at 5000/8000 rp including an excellent and very filling breakfast. A sign in the entrance area suggests that if there's nobody around you should just find a vacant room and make yourself at home. *Nani's House* is another place which has been recommended. There are rooms from 4000 rp or upstairs rooms at 8000 rp, good for watching the ducks splashing in the rice paddies at sunset.

Right at the bottom, almost in the forest, is the secluded and pleasant *Monkey Forest Hideaway*. The rooms cost from 12,000 to 15,000 rp and some of them, with balconies looking out over the rice paddies and monkey forest, are quite romantic.

Back up at the main road, down the road opposite the Monkey Forest Rd, the *Suci Inn* is across from the banyan tree. This is a straightforward losmen-style place with simple rooms with bathroom at 6000 rp including black rice pudding for breakfast. The rooms all have small

verandah areas looking out on to the central garden and it's a friendly, relaxed place pleasantly quiet yet very central. There are some better rooms at the back at 7500 rp and Ketut, the manager, also has three 12,500 rp rooms at his parent's house further up the road. He's talking of opening a small losmen of his own which, if it eventuates, might be called *Ketut's Place*.

Next door to the Suci Inn is the old *Hotel Ubud*, one of Ubud's oldest places; for many years it was called the 'Hotel Oboed', the Dutch spelling indicating its age.

There are a number of places along the main road through Ubud – like the long running *Geria Taman Sari*, a bit above the road on the left-hand side as you come in from Denpasar. The *Agung Pension* is fairly new, clean and friendly. Or on the post office road there's the reasonably priced *Budi Losmen*, good breakfasts too. *M D Suartha's Losmen* is also excellent value.

Around Ubud There are lots of places around Ubud, either in neighbouring villages or just out in the rice paddies. Cross the suspension bridge by Murni's, for example, and take the steep path uphill by Blanco's house. There you'll find a pretty little group of homestays including the appealing *Kardi* in the rice paddies – secluded and quiet yet really no distance from the road.

In this same area, right behind and above Antonio Blanco's house, is the attractive *Arjuna's Inn*, run by the artist's daughter. The rooms are small but have attached mandi and toilet and cost 6000 to 8000 rp with breakfast. There are more places further up into the rice paddies around Penestanan, or down almost any road into the rice paddies on the south side of the road through Ubud.

You'll find quite a few other places out of Ubud on the Peliatan road. At the junction where the road bends sharp left to Denpasar you'll see a sign for the *Sari*

Homestay, just 100 metres or so off the road. It has become somewhat run down over the years but it's still a pretty and popular little place right by the rice paddies and at 2500/3500 rp for singles/doubles the prices are hard to beat. The *Siti Homestay* is a new place with a beautiful garden, charming owners and big breakfasts all for around 4000 rp.

Take the back road from Peliatan to Ubud and you'll pass the *Bali Breeze* with rooms at 12,000 rp or the pleasant *Jati Inn*, two-storey rooms with great views across the rice paddies. Turn down towards the Monkey Forest from this road and you reach *Artini Accommodation* a friendly place with a beautiful garden.

Places along the main road from Peliatan towards Ubud include the pleasant *Mudita Inn* with its shady garden, 'and lovely porridge!' reported one guest. Or there are places still further out from Ubud, like the pleasant little *Homestay Lantur* right where the road ends and you start out through the rice paddies from Bedulu to Yeh Pulu.

Places to Stay – middle

A short distance down the Monkey Forest Rd and off to the right you'll find *Okawati's Homestay*, a very pleasant and clean place right on the rice paddies with doubles at 20,000 to 26,000 rp. The rooms are a definite notch above average with bathrooms, fans, bedside lights and other little luxuries.

A bit further down, almost at the monkey forest, is the popular *Ubud Inn* with rooms at US$20 and double-storey rooms at US$22 including breakfast. The rooms are brick with carved wood and thatched roofs and they're quite cool, each with a private bathroom. The double-storey rooms have two beds downstairs and two more upstairs and an upstairs verandah ideal for gazing out over the rice paddies. They do excellent Balinese food here if you give them some warning.

On the main road near the Puri Lukisan Museum, the *Mumbul Inn* has rooms at 8000/12,000 rp – self-contained bungalows and close to the centre of Ubud. Some distance out of town, opposite the Museum Neka, *Ananda Cottages* are very calm, relaxed and pretty with rooms at 20,000/25,000 rp including breakfast or big two-storey rooms for 35,000 rp.

Places to Stay – top end

Just up beyond the suspension bridge is the *Hotel Tjampuhan* (or Campuhan if you use the modern spelling). This long-established hotel is beautifully situated overlooking the river and temple. The rooms are individual bungalows in a wonderful garden and cost US$20/30 including breakfast. It's not a hotel for those in search of all the western comforts and modern conveniences although the hotel, owned by a Balinese prince, even has a spring-fed swimming pool on the edge of a cliff. The pool was built by artist Walter Spies back in the '30s. He actually lived for a time in one of the bungalows here. The hotel had become somewhat run down but seems to be going through some renovations.

On the Ubud side of the bridge *Murni's Bungalows* are near the well known Murni's Warung, one of Ubud's most popular restaurants, perched high above the Campuhan River. Follow the river north to *Ulun Ubud* with beautiful bungalows clinging precariously to the steep sides of the ravine. There's a swimming pool here.

Artist Han Snel's luxurious *Siti Bungalows* are well-equipped individual cottages with all mod cons in a beautiful garden for US$35 to US$40. They're pleasantly quiet, back off the main road, but right in the middle of town.

On the main road the pleasant and well kept *Puri Saraswati*, by the palace of that name, has rooms at US$25/30 or bungalows at US$12/15 including breakfast.

The *Hotel Puri Saren Agung*, near the bemo stop in the centre of Ubud, is part of the home of the late head of Ubud's royal family. The bungalows each have a private courtyard and displays of Balinese antiques.

There are some interesting places to try outside Ubud. A visitor wrote to recommend the *Kupu Kupu Barong Bungalows* in Kedewatan, past the Neka Museum, north of Ubud. Six two-storey bungalows perch on the edge of a ravine, each with bedrooms upstairs and downstairs and superb open-air bathrooms, some even with spa baths. There are wonderful views down to the river from the verandah along the front of each bungalow. They're not cheap!

Taman Harum in nearby Mas has also been recommended. Some of the elegant individual bungalows are two-storey with balconies overlooking the rice paddies and there's also a swimming pool. The food, however, did not get such a high rating.

Dogs – if there's one thing wrong with Bali that's what it has to be, those horrible, mangy, flea-bitten, grovelling, dirty, noisy, disgusting *anjings* – that's the Indonesian word for dog, in Balinese a dog is *asu* in high Balinese, *cicing* in low. Or, if you prefer, asu when you're referring to dogs in a good way, cicing in a bad. Dogs are rarely referred to as asu !

Just why does Bali have so many dogs? Well they're scavengers, garbage clearers, and they're simply accepted as part of the picture. It's widely, and probably correctly, thought that demons inhabit them, which is why you often see them gobbling down the offerings put out for the bad spirits. A popular theory is that they were created simply to keep things in balance – with everything so beautiful and picturesque the dogs are put there to provide a contrast. Ubud, incidentally, is particularly well endowed with anjings; terrible, apocalyptic dogs that howl all night long like it's the end of the world.

Places to Eat

In the past Ubud was very restricted in the restaurant department but now you've got a wide choice, some really interesting places and quite probably the best food to be found in Bali.

Happily some of Ubud's 'original' institutions are still going strong. *Okawati's*, a long term favourite, is just off the Monkey Forest Rd and still a pleasant, friendly and economical place to eat. There are no surprises here but for 1000 rp you can have a good mee goreng (fried noodles) or excellent pancakes. Actually on the Monkey Forest Rd, just down from the market, *Canderi's* is another long-running institution which travellers from the early '70s will remember well, although it now has a new restaurant area.

There's plenty of other places to choose along the Monkey Forest Rd. Starting from the main road end you could sample *Harry Chew's* a basic but very popular warung. The food can be rather variable but it always seems to be crowded and the owner is quite a character. A little further down *Lilies* is a new and interesting place with a menu featuring dishes like ayam jeruk (lemon chicken) for 3000 rp or Balinese-style nasi campur for 2000 rp. And a tendency to run out of things!

Further down the Monkey Forest Rd it's an idea to bring a light at night as it can get very dark. *Cafe Wayan* is another relatively new place with some really delicious food including curry ayam (curried chicken) at 3400 rp, saffron chicken at 3500 rp, special dishes like smoked duck or rijstaffel at around 10,000 rp and a famous coconut pie for 1000 rp. Even further down the road you come to the *Ubud Restaurant*, a quiet and peaceful place looking out over the rice paddies. The food here is very well prepared and includes some Balinese dishes – try the coconut satay which is really more than enough for one. They have fine pancakes too.

You'll find a number of good places to eat along the main road of Ubud including one of Ubud's best restaurants, *Murni's*, right down by the suspension bridge. The food here is excellent, the setting is beautiful, there are some interesting arts and crafts on sale and also a small but very good selection of books on Bali. All in all it's well worth the higher prices – satay for

2500 rp served in a personal charcoal holder, a fantastic nasi campur for 1800 rp, even a pretty good burger for 1800 rp. Their cakes are simply superb. Murni's is closed on Wednesdays.

Closer to the centre the *Lotus Cafe* is a relaxed place for a light lunch or a snack any time. It's not cheap but it is very good – their cheesecake at 1500 rp is a real taste treat. They do good Indonesian food from 2000 rp and a variety of western dishes including pastas from 3000 to 5000 rp. It's closed on Mondays. Ubud is something of an international jet setters haven and Murni's and the Lotus are where they're likely to be.

Other places on the main road include the *Puri Pusaka*, opposite the market with a lengthy menu of Indonesian and Balinese specialities. The *Roof Garden Restaurant* has somewhat westernised food and also provides accommodation.

Han Snel's Garden Restaurant, back off the main road, is not cheap by Balinese standards but a great place to eat. A complete meal for two will cost about 20,000 rp – good food, copious quantities, a beautiful setting (frogs croak in the background) and impeccable service. Their 4000 rp 'mini-rijstaffel' is superb. It's closed on Sundays.

There are plenty of other places. Almost in the centre on the main road is *Ary's Warung* with great gado-gado. Round the corner is *Rumah Makan Kartika*. Further down the main road is the *Nomad Restaurant* or back towards the river is the *Griya Barbecue*. Above the bridge, across the river from Murni's, *Beggar's Bush* has a pleasant bar with draught Bintang beer. It's the local Hash House Harriers meeting point. There are also places along the Peliatan road and, of course, countless warungs.

Finding real Balinese food in Bali is often far from easy but Ketut Suartana, the young man who runs the small *Suci Inn*, offers his guests, and others who care to drop by and enquire, an opportunity to sample real Balinese food at its best. He regularly takes groups of visitors back to his parents' home, further up the road from the Suci Inn, and puts on a Balinese feast for 7000 rp per person. You can contact Ketut either through the Suci Inn or the Suci Store, further up the road in front of his parent's house.

A typical meal would include duck or Balinese satay, which is a minced and spiced meat wrapped around a wide stick and quite different from the usual Indonesian satay. A variety of vegetables will include several that we normally think of as fruits – like papaya, nangkur (jackfruit) and blimbing. *Paku* is a form of fern and *ketela potton* is tapioca leaves, both prepared as tasty vegetables. Red onions known as *anyang* and cucumber known as *ketimun* will also feature. Then there will be gado-gado and mee goreng, both prepared in Balinese style, and a special Balinese dish of duck livers cooked in banana leaves and coconut. Of course there will be krupuks (prawn crackers) and rice. To drink there will be *brem* (Bali rice wine) and you'll finish up with Balinese coffee, peanuts and bananas.

The dining area is decorated with palm-leaf decorations, again as for a Balinese feast and a gamelan player tinkles away in the background. It's fun, delicious and a rare chance to sample real Balinese food but it's also a great opportunity to learn more about Bali and its customs as Ketut talks about his house, his family and answers all sorts of questions about life in Bali.

The Balinese use a flag to keep their ducks in a row, all the way to the market

Things to Buy

Ubud has a wide variety of shops and the inevitable art galleries. It's also worth investigating smaller places or places further out from the centre. As elsewhere in Bali so much is completely standard that it's a real pleasure when you find the odd really different or interesting piece of work. Murni's, down by the river, always seems to have something unusual – pretty cushion covers, carved and painted mirror frames, strange pottery.

Small shops by the market on the Monkey Forest Rd or further down that road often have good wood carvings, particularly masks. M Nama, on the Peliatan corner, also has lots of interesting wood carvings. There are some other good wood carving places along the road from here to Goa Gajah. At Goa Gajah there is a host of stalls selling leatherwork. You'll find good places for paintings along the main road through Ubud or beyond the bridge towards the Museum Neka. The main problem with Ubud is there are simply so many places and it is difficult to find items that rise above the average standard.

Getting There & Away

Bemos from Denpasar to Ubud are 600 rp. The bemos in Ubud start from beside the cinema in the middle of town. Bemos from Kuta can be chartered for 15,000 rp straight off, 12,000 rp with a bit of bargaining.

If you want to go further afield from Ubud you'll have to go down to Gianyar or even back to Denpasar to catch a bus since Ubud is off the main routes to towns in the mountains, to the east and to the north coast. If you're staying in Ubud and have gone to Denpasar or Kuta for the day remember that the last bemo back will probably leave Denpasar's Kereneng station around 4 pm. If you miss it you'll either have to charter one or stay overnight somewhere, which could prove expensive.

Getting Around

To the places around Ubud you can generally count on paying 100 to 250 rp by bemo. Count on about 25 rp a km with a 100 rp minimum. There are a number of places in Ubud where you can hire bicycles (2000 rp a day) or motorcycles or cars.

One traveller's final memory of Ubud:

. . . walking back from a late night festival in Mas along a road surrounded by croaking or squeaking frogs and crickets and lit by glimpses of fireflies. Magic.

DENPASAR TO UBUD

The route from Denpasar to Ubud is

heavily trafficked and lined with craft shops and galleries. This is the tourist shopping centre of Bali but there are also alternative, quieter routes between the two towns.

Batubulan

Soon after leaving Denpasar the roadsides are lined with outlets for the Batubulan craft – stone sculpture. This is where those temple gate guardians – seen all over Bali – come from. You'll also find them guarding bridges or making more mundane appearances in restaurants and hotels. The sculpting is often done by quite young boys and you're welcome to watch them chipping away at big blocks of stone. The stone they use is surprisingly soft and even more surprisingly light. If you've travelled to Bali fairly light it's quite feasible to fly home with a demonic stone character in your baggage!

Not surprisingly the temples around Batubulan are noted for their fine stone sculptures. Pura Puseh, just a couple of hundred metres from the road, is worth a visit. There is also a Barong dance, popular with tourists, held in Batubulan every day.

Celuk

Travelling on from Batubulan to Celuk takes you from stone to filigree for Celuk is the silverwork centre of Bali. The craft shops that line the road here are dedicated to jewellery. Other centres for silverwork in Bali include Kamasan near Klungkung and Kuta.

Batuan & Sukawati

Further on, before the turn-off to Mas and Ubud, are the villages of Batuan and Sukawati. Sukawati is a centre for the manufacture of those noisy wind chimes you see all over the island. Batuan is a noted painting centre.

Mas

Mas means 'gold' but it's wood carving which is the craft here. The great priest Nirartha once lived here and Pura Taman Pule is said to be built on the site of his home. Again the road through Mas is almost solidly lined with craft shops and you are welcome to drop in and see the carvers at work, as well as inspecting the myriad items for sale.

Blahbatuh

Although the most direct route to Ubud is to turn off the main road at Sakah and head north through Mas, you can continue on a few km to the turn-off to Blahbatuh and go via Kutri and Bedulu before turning off again for Ubud. In Blahbatuh the Pura Gaduh has a metre-high stone head said to be a portrait of Kebo Iwa, the legendary strongman and last king of the Bedulu kingdom (see Bedulu). Gajah Mada, the Majapahit strongman, realised that he could not conquer Bedulu, Bali's strongest kingdom, while Kebo Iwa was there so he lured him away to Java (with promises of women and song) and had him killed.

The stone head is thought to be very old, possibly predating Javanese influence in Bali, but the temple is a reconstruction of an earlier temple destroyed in the great earthquake of 1917.

Kutri

Just beyond Blahbatuh you can climb the hill from Pura Bukit Dharma and find a hill-top shrine with a stone statue of Durga thought to date from the 11th century and showing strong Indian influences. Between here and Klungkung the road crosses a series of deep gorges, the bridges rising high above the valleys below.

AROUND UBUD

The Pejeng region encompasses many of the most ancient monuments and relics in Bali, some of them well known and very much on the beaten track, others relatively unknown and little visited.

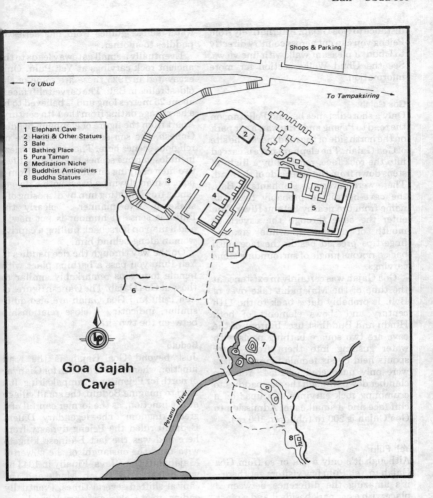

Shops & Parking

To Ubud

To Tampaksiring

1 Elephant Cave
2 Hariti & Other Statues
3 Bale
4 Bathing Place
5 Pura Taman
6 Meditation Niche
7 Buddhist Antiquities
8 Buddha Statues

Goa Gajah Cave

Petanu River

Getting There & Away

You can reach the places around Ubud by bemo and on foot. If you're planning to see a lot of them it's a good idea to go straight up to Tampaksiring to start with, then any walking you have to do is back downhill. It's only a km or two downhill from Tirta Empul at Tampaksiring to

Gunung Kawi, and you can follow the path beside the river and come out right in Gunung Kawi.

From there you can take bemos back down to Pejeng, Bedulu, Goa Gajah and on to Ubud. Pejeng to the Bedulu turn-off is only about a km and from there it's a half km or so to Yeh Pulu and a similar distance to Goa Gajah. Alternatively from Pejeng you can cut across country directly to Ubud, a pleasant walk with fine views. See the Ubud Walks section for more information.

Goa Gajah

Only a short distance beyond Peliatan, on the road to Pejeng and Gianyar, a car park on the north side of the road marks the site of Goa Gajah. The elephant cave is carved into the rock face, reached by a flight of steps down from the other side of the road. There were never any elephants in Bali, the cave-hermitage probably takes its name from the nearby Petanu River. You enter the cave through the cavernous mouth of a demon, while gigantic fingertips pressed beside the face push back a riotous jungle of surrounding stone carvings.

Goa Gajah was certainly in existence at the time of the Majapahit take over of Bali. It probably dates back to the 11th century and shows elements of both Hindu and Buddhist use. In front of the cave are two square bathing pools with water gushing into them from water spouts held by six female figures. These were only uncovered in 1954. You can clamber down through the rice paddies to crumbling rock carvings of stupas on a cliff face and a small cave. Admission to Goa Gajah is 200 rp (children 100 rp).

Yeh Pulu

Although it's only a km or so from Goa Gajah to Yeh Pulu few visitors get there – it's amazing the difference between a place with a car park beside it and a place you have to walk to through the rice paddies! It's quite easy to find your way there. At the end of the road there's a sign which points to the path that follows the small cliff face most of the way. It's as picturesque as any tramp through the paddies in Bali – there are ups and downs, small streams gurgling by and Heath Robinson bamboo contraptions channelling

water across gullies from one series o paddies to another.

Eventually a small gateway leads to the ancient rock carvings at Yeh Pulu. Only excavated in 1925 these are some of the oldest relics in Bali. The carved cliff face i about 25 metres long and is believed to be a hermitage dating from the 14th century Apart from the figure of elephant-headed Ganesh, the son of Shiva, there are no religious scenes here. The energetic frieze includes various scenes of everyday life – two men carrying an animal slung from a pole, a man slaying a beast with a dagger (and a frog imitating him by disposing of a snake in like manner – clearly the Balinese sense of humour is not new!) and a man on horseback pulling a captive woman along behind him.

On the way through the rice paddies to Yeh Pulu you pass a bathing place with female fountains remarkably similar to those at Goa Gajah. The Ganesh figures of Yeh Pulu and Goa Gajah are also quite similar, indicating a close relationship between the two sites.

Bedulu

Just beyond Goa Gajah is the road junction where you turn south for Gianyar or north for Pejeng and Tampaksiring. It's hard to imagine Bedulu, the small village at the junction, as the former capital of a great kingdom. The legendary Dalem Bedaulu ruled the Pejeng dynasty from here and was the last Balinese king to withstand the onslaught of the powerful Majapahits from Java. Finally in 1343 he was defeated by Gajah Mada and the capital shifted several times, eventually ending up at Gelgel and then Klungkung.

A legend relates how Bedaulu possessed magical powers which even allowed him to have his head chopped off and then replaced. Performing this unique party trick one day the servant entrusted with lopping off his head and then replacing it unfortunately dropped it in a river and to his horror watched it float away. Looking around in panic for a replacement he

Top: Muli River, Palembang, Sumatra (TW)
Left: Dokar, Sumatra (MC)
Right: Samosir ferry, Prapat, Sumatra (TW)

Top: Memorial, Brastagi, Sumatra (TW)
Bottom: Clocktower, Bukittinggi, Sumatra (TW)

grabbed a pig, cut its head off and popped it upon the king's shoulders. Thereafter the king was forced to sit on a high throne and forbid his subjects to look up at him.

Pejeng

Up the road to Tampaksiring from the Bedulu junction you soon come to Pejeng and its famous temple. There are a couple of places of interest between the Bedulu junction and there. First on your right is the Museum Arkeologi. Then a little further along on your left is the temple of Pura Kebo Edan, the Crazy Buffalo Temple, with it's nearly four-metre-high statue of Bima, liberally endowed with no less than six penises! Other interesting temples in the Pejeng area include the Pura Puser ing Jagat or Navel of the World temple and the monastery of Goa Garba.

As you enter Pejeng itself the temple of Pura Penataran Sasih, once the state temple of the Kingdom of Pejeng, is on your right. In the inner courtyard, high up in a pavilion where you really cannot see it very well, is the huge bronze drum known as the 'Moon of Pejeng'. It is believed to be over 1000 years older than the Kingdom of Pejeng itself, a relic from the Bronze Age in Indonesia. The hourglass-shaped drum is over three metres long, the largest single piece cast drum in the world.

A Balinese legend relates how the drum came to earth as a fallen moon, landing in a tree and shining so brightly that it prevented a band of thieves from going about their unlawful purpose. One of the thieves decided to put the light out by urinating on it but the moon exploded, killed the foolhardy thief and fell to earth as a drum – with a crack across its base as a result of the fall.

Gunung Kawi

Continuing up the road to Tampaksiring you pass through pleasant rice land along a steady upward climb which continues all the way to the rim of the crater at Penelokan. In the small town of Tampaksiring a sign points off the road to the right to Gunung Kawi. From the end of the access road a steep stone stairway leads down to the river, at one point making a cutting through an embankment of solid rock. There, in the bottom of this lush green valley with beautiful rice terraces climbing up the hillsides, is one of Bali's oldest, and certainly largest, ancient monuments.

Gunung Kawi consists of 10 rock-cut *candis*, memorials cut out of the rock face in imitation of normally constructed monuments – in a similar fashion to the great rock-cut temples of Ajanta and Ellora in India. The *candis* are believed to be memorials to members of the Balinese royalty of the 11th century but little is known for certain. The *candis* stand in seven-metre-high sheltered niches cut into the sheer rock cliff faces. There are four on the west side of the river which you come to first. You cross the river on a bridge to a further group of five on the east side. A solitary *candi* stands further down the valley to the south, reached by a trek through the rice paddies.

Legends relate that the whole group of memorials were carved out of the rock faces in one hard working night by the mighty fingernails of Kebo Iwa. Each of the sets of memorials has a group of monks' cells associated with it, including one on the east side with the only 'no shoes, sandals, boots may be worn' sign I've ever seen in Bali. There are other similar groups of *candis* and monks' cells within the area of Bali encompassed by the ancient Kingdom of Pejeng – but none of them so grand or on so large a scale.

Tampaksiring – Tirta Empul

Continuing through the actual town of Tampaksiring the road branches, the left fork running up to the grand palace once used by Sukarno while the right fork goes to the temple at Tirta Empul and continues up to Penelokan. You can look back along the valley and see Gunung Kawi from this road, just before you turn into Tirta Empul. The holy springs at Tirta Empul are believed to have magical powers so the temple here is an important one.

Each year an inscribed stone is brought from a nearby village to be ceremonially washed in the spring. The inscription on the stone has been deciphered and indicates that the springs were founded in 962 AD. The actual springs bubble up into a large, crystal-clear tank within the temple and gush out through waterspouts into a bathing pool. According to legend the springs were created by the god Indra who pierced the earth to tap the 'elixir of immortality', amerta. Despite its antiquity the temple is glossy and gleamingly new – it was totally restored in the late '60s.

The springs of Tirta Empul are a source of the Pakrisan River, which rushes by Gunung Kawi only a km or so away. Between Tirta Empul and Gunung Kawi is the temple of Pura Mengening where you can see a candi similar in design, but free-standing, to the candis of Gunung Kawi. There is a spring at this temple which also feeds into the Pakrisan. Overlooking Tirta Empul is the Sukarno palace, a grandiose structure built in 1954 on the site of a Dutch rest-house.

The car park outside Tirta Empul is surrounded by the usual unholy confusion of souvenir and craft shops. Chess sets and bone carving are popular crafts here. There is an admission charge to Tirta Empul and you have to wear a temple scarf.

Places to Stay & Eat Tampaksiring is an easy day trip from Ubud or even Bangli but it is possible to stay here. In the village itself there's the small Homestay Gusty and the Homestay Tampaksiring.

Apart from the usual selection of warungs there's also the expensive Tampaksiring Restaurant for tourist parties, some distance below the village.

UBUD TO BATUR

The usual road from Ubud to Batur is through Tampaksiring but there are other lesser roads up the gentle mountain slope. If you go out of Ubud to the road junction but turn away from Peliatan, towards Petulu, this road will bring you out on the crater rim just beyond Penelokan towards Batur. It's a surfaced road all the way except for a few km near the top where it's cobbled and fairly rough. Along this road you'll see a number of woodcarvers producing all those beautiful painted ducks, birds, frogs, Garudas and tropical fruit. Tegalalang and the nearby village of Jati, just off the road, are noted woodcarving centres. Further up, other specialists carve stools and there are a couple of places which carve whole tree trunks into whimsical figures.

Another route from Ubud to Batur can be followed by taking the road through Campuhan and Saggingan and then turning up the hill, instead of down towards Denpasar, at Kedewatan. On this route you pass through Payangan, the only place in Bali where lychees are grown. It's possible to get bemos some distance up the road on both these routes but at the very top finding public transport can be difficult. The roads, once quite rough, are not bad now.

Of course you could walk up to Batur from Ubud too. If you take the path from near the temple down by the suspension bridge and followed it steadily uphill you'd pass through unspoilt villages like Bangkiang Sidem, Keliki and Sebali. They'd make a nice walk in themselves and from Sebali you can cut across to Tegalalang and get a bemo back to Ubud. And if you keep walking? Well it's 30 km to Batur, uphill all the way.

East Bali

The eastern end of Bali is dominated by mighty Gunung Agung, the 'navel of the world' and Bali's mother mountain. Towering 3140 metres high Agung has not always been a kind mother – witness the disastrous 1963 eruption. Today Agung is again a quiet though dominating mountain and the mother temple Pura Besakih, perched high on the slopes of the volcano, attracts a steady stream of devotees. . . .and tourists.

The east has a number of places of great interest. Here you'll find Klungkung, former capital of one of Bali's great kingdoms. From here the road runs close to the coast past interesting fishing villages like Kusamba, the bat infested cave temple of Goa Lawah, the beautiful small port of Padangbai, the pretty little Bali Aga village of Tenganan, the popular beach centre of Candidasa, and finally reaches Amlapura, another former capital.

At Amlapura you can about turn and retrace your route or take an alternative route higher up the slopes of Agung to Rendang. From Rendang you can turn north to Besakih, south to Klungkung or continue west on a pretty but lesser-used route to Bangli. As a third alternative you can continue right round the coast from Amlapura to Singaraja in the north. See the north Bali section for more details on this lightly populated coastal route.

The 1963 Eruption

The most disastrous volcanic eruption in Bali this century took place in 1963 when Agung blew its top in no uncertain manner and at a time of considerable prophetic importance; 8 March 1963 was the culmination of *Eka Desa Rudra*, the greatest of all Balinese sacrifices and an event which only takes place every 100 Balinese years. The sacrifices had not been made 100 years previously so it was now 115 of our years since the last *Eka Desa Rudra*. Naturally the temple at Besakih was a focal point for the festival but Agung was already acting strangely as preparations were made in late February. Agung had been dormant since 1843 but by the time the sacrifices commenced the mountain was belching smoke and ash, glowing and rumbling ominously.

On 17 March 1963 it exploded in a catastrophic eruption that killed more than 1000 people and destroyed entire villages. Streams of lava and hot volcanic mud poured right down to the sea at several places in the south-east of the island, completely covering roads and isolating the whole eastern end of the island for some time thereafter. The entire island was covered in ash and crops were wiped out everywhere. Torrential rainfall that followed the eruptions compounded the damage as boiling hot ash and boulders known as *lahar* were swept down the mountain side, wreaking havoc on many villages like Subagen, just outside Amlapura and Selat, further along the road towards Rendang. All Bali suffered a drastic food shortage and many Balinese, whose rice land was completely ruined, had to be resettled in Sulawesi.

Although Besakih itself is high on the slopes of Agung, only about six km from the very crater, it suffered little damage from the eruption. Volcanic dust and gravel flattened timber and bamboo buildings around the temple complex but the stone structures came through

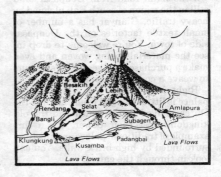

unscathed. The inhabitants of the villages of Sorga and Lebih, also high up on Agung's slopes, were all but wiped out. Most of the people killed at the time of the eruption were burnt and suffocated by searing clouds of hot gas that rushed down the volcano slopes. Agung erupted again on 16 May, with serious loss of life but not on the same scale as the March eruption.

The Balinese take signs and portents seriously – that such a terrible event should happen as they were making a most important sacrifice to the gods was not taken lightly. The interrupted series of sacrifices were finally recommenced 16 years later in 1979.

Getting There & Away
Buses for the east of Bali generally depart from the Kereneng bus station in Denpasar. Fares include Klungkung 800 rp, Padangbai 1250 rp, Amlapura 1600 rp and Bangli 800 rp. To get to Besakih take a bus or colt to Klungkung and another colt from there for 500 rp. Klungkung to Amlapura costs about 700 or 800 rp, then from Amlapura to Singaraja buses cost 1800 rp. From Culik, a little beyond Tirtagangga, to Kubutambahan, it's 1500 rp and takes about 3½ hours. Bemos run locally from Amlapura including some going to Tirtagangga.

GIANYAR
On the main road from Denpasar, and still in the region of south Bali plagued by heavy traffic, Gianyar has a number of small textile factories on the Denpasar side of town. You're welcome to drop in, see the materials being woven and even make a purchase. It takes about six hours to weave a complete sarong.

Right in the centre of town the old palace is little changed from the time the Dutch arrived in the south and the old kingdoms lost their power. It's a fine example of traditional palace architecture, surrounded by high brick walls. You can look in through the gates.

SIDAN
Continuing beyond Gianyar you come to the turn-off to Bangli at Sidan, just a few km out of town. Go up the road less than a km from the junction and at a sharp bend you'll find the Sidan Pura Dalem, a good example of a temple of the dead. Note the sculptures of Durga with children by the gate, and the separate walled in enclosure in the front-left corner of the temple – this is dedicated to Merajapati, the guardian spirit of the dead. If you continue up this road to Bangli there's another interesting Pura Dalem at Penunggekan, just before you reach Bangli. See the Bangli section for more details.

BONA
The village of Bona, on the back road between Gianyar and Blahbatuh, is credited with being the modern home of the Kechak dance. Kechak and other dances are held here every week and they're easy to visit from Ubud – tickets inclusive of transport from Ubud are around 4000 rp. Bona is also a basket-weaving centre.

KLUNGKUNG
Klungkung was once the centre of Bali's most important kingdom and a great artistic and cultural focal point. The Gelgel Dynasty, which was the most powerful kingdom in Bali, held power for about 300 years, until the arrival of the Dutch. It was here that the Klungkung school of painting, with its characters all presented in side-profile wayang kulit style, was developed. Today Klungkung-style paintings are still produced but a few km outside Klungkung in Kamasan.

Klungkung is a major bus and colt crossroads – from here you can find transport up to Besakih or further east to Padangbai, Candidasa and Amlapura. A new bridge crosses the river beyond Klungkung and until its construction in 1985 there were often lengthy traffic jams.

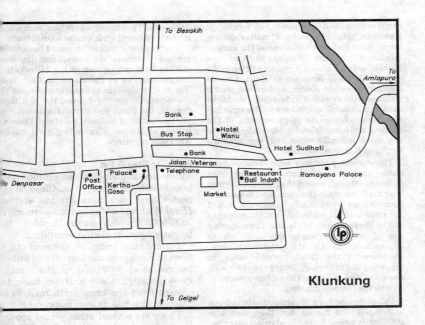

To Besakih

To Amlapura

Bank

Hotel Wisnu

Bus Stop

Bank

Jalan Veteran

Hotel Sudihati

To Denpasar

Post Office

Palace

Kertha Gosa

Telephone

Restaurant Bali Indah

Ramayana Palace

Market

Klungkung

To Gelgel

Kertha Gosa

Right beside the road as you reach the centre of town from Denpasar stands the Kertha Gosa or Hall of Justice. Surrounded by a moat this open pavilion is a superb example of Klungkung architecture and the roof is completely painted inside with fine paintings in the Klungkung style. The paintings, done on asbestos sheeting, were installed in the 1940s, replacing cloth paintings which had deteriorated.

This was effectively the 'supreme court' of the Klungkung kingdom, where disputes and cases which could not be settled at the village level would eventually be brought. The defendant would be brought before the three priests who acted as judges and his gaze could wander to the ceiling where wrongdoers were tortured by demons while the innocent enjoyed the pleasures of Balinese heaven. The capital of the kingdom was shifted to Klungkung from nearby Gelgel in the early 1700s and

the Kertha Gosa was probably constructed around the end of that century.

Palace

Adjoining the Kertha Gosa is the palace with its beautiful Bale Kambang or Floating Pavilion. Its ceiling is also painted in Klungkung style, having been repainted in 1945. Around the Kertha Gosa and the Bale Kambang note the statues of top-hatted European figures, an amusing departure from the normal statues of entrance guardians. Admission to the palace and Kertha Gosa is 200 rp (children 100 rp).

Kamasan Paintings

The village of Kamasan, a few km outside of Klungkung, has long been a bastion of traditional painting – the origins of which can be traced back at least 500 years. Highly conventionalised, the symbolism of equating right and left with good and evil, as in the wayang puppet shows, is evident in the compositions and placement of figures in Kamasan paintings. Subject matter derives largely from Balinese variations of the ancient Hindu epics, the Ramayana and the Mahabharata. *Kakawins*, poems written in the archaic Javanese language of Kawi, provide another important source, as does indigenous Balinese folklore with it's pre-Hindu/Buddhist beliefs in demonic spirit forces. The style has also been adapted to large versions of the zodiacal and lunar calendar, especially the 210-day *wuku* calendar which still regulates the timing of Balinese festivals.

The earliest paintings were done on bark cloth, said to have been imported from Sulawesi – though a coarse handspun cloth and later machine-made cloth was used as support. Kamasan art is essentially linear – the skill of the artist was judged by his draughtsmanship and by the sensitivity of his line. The colouring was of secondary importance and left to apprentices, usually the artist's children. Members of the family would assist in preparing the colours, stiffening the cloth with rice paste and polishing the surface smooth to receive the fine ink drawing.

Paintings were hung as ceremonial backdrops in temples and houses and they were also sufficiently prized by the local rulers that they were acceptable gifts to rival royal households. Whilst they were traditionally patronised by the ruling class, paintings also helped fulfill the important function of imparting ethical values and customs – *adat* – to the ordinary people, in much the same way as traditional dance and wayang puppetry. In fact, it is from the wayang tradition that Kamasan painting takes its essential characteristics – the stylisation of human figures, their symbolic gestures, the treatment of divine and heroic characters as refined and evil ones as vulgar and crude, and the primary function of narrating a moral tale.

It's worth noting that there are striking similarities between Kamasan paintings and a now almost totally abandoned form of wayang theatre, the *wayang beber*. The slender horizontal format of Balinese paintings almost certainly derives from the *wayang bebe*, which is a large handscroll, held vertically and unrolled and expounded upon by the puppet-master, accompanied by the gamelan orchestra The wayang beber was still being performed during the Dutch occupation, but a performance now is very rare, although craftsmen in East

Java are still producing scenes from such scro in the traditional style for the tourist trade.

The wayang style can be traced back to 9 century Javanese sculpture, and its mo mature form can be seen at the 14th-centu temple complex at Panataran in East Jav The relief sculptures at Panataran display t characteristic wayang figures, the rich flor designs, the flame-and-mountain motifs – vital elements of Balinese painting. There's gallery at Banjar Siku selling good quali Kamasan paintings.

Places to Stay & Eat

There are a couple of accommodatio possibilities in Klungkung. Close to th centre, just back from the bus statio *Hotel Wishnu* has fairly average rooms 3000/6000 rp for singles/doubles. It brighter upstairs than downstairs.

Towards the bridge on the road out town to Amlapura the *Ramayana Palac* has rooms at 4000/6000 rp. It's a muc more pleasant place and set back fa enough from the busy main road to quiet. It also has its own restaurant.

There are several other places aroun town to eat including the Chines *Restaurant Bali Indah*.

Things to Buy

There are a number of good shops alon Jalan Veteran in Klungkung sellin Klungkung-style paintings and som interesting antiques. Klungkung is also good place for buying temple umbrellas several shops sell them.

KUSAMBA

Beyond Klungkung the road crosses lav flows from the '63 eruption of Agung and now much overgrown. The road come back to the coast at the fishing village Kusamba. Turn off the main road and g down to the beach to see the lines colourful fishing prahus lined up on th beach. Fishing is normally done at nigh and the 'eyes' on the front of the boats hel them to see through the darkness. You ca charter a boat out to Nusa Penida, clearl visible opposite Kusamba. Regular trip re made out to the island carrying supplies so you can try to get on one of these cargo prahus. The crossing takes several hours.

Just beyond Kusamba you can see the hatched roofs of salt-panning huts along the beach. Saltwater-saturated sand from the beach is dried out around these huts and then further processed inside the huts. You can see the same process being carried out beside the Kuta-Sanur road.

GOA LAWAH

The road continues to run close to the coast beyond Kusamba and after a few km you come to the Bat Cave, Goa Lawah. A cave in the cliff face here is packed, rammed, jammed full of bats. There must be untold thousands of the squeaking, flapping creatures, tumbling and crawling over one another and occasionally launching out of the cave only to zip straight back in as they realise it's still daytime. The cave is, of course, part of a temple and is said to lead all the way to Besakih but it's unlikely anybody would be too enthusiastic about investigating! Entry to the bat cave temple is 200 rp (100 rp children) and it costs another 150 rp to park in the car park.

PADANGBAI

Padangbai is the port for the ferry service between Bali and Lombok. Along with Benoa it's the principal shipping port in the south of the island. Padangbai is a couple of km off the main road, a scruffy little town situated on a perfect little bay, one of the very few sheltered harbours in Bali. It's very picturesque with a long sweep of sand where colourful outrigger fishing boats are drawn up on the beach.

Padangbai can be an interesting place to spend a day or so if you don't want to simply arrive in the morning and depart straight for Lombok. If you walk round to the right from the wharf and follow the trail up the hill it leads to an idyllic little

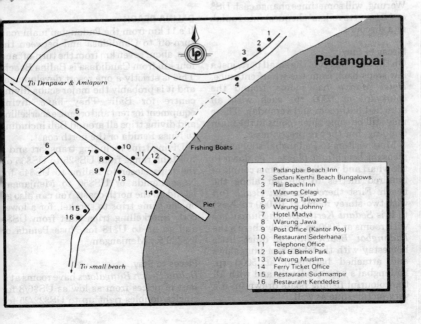

To Denpasar & Amlapura

To small beach

Fishing Boats

Pier

Padangbai

1 Padangbai Beach Inn
2 Sedani Kerthi Beach Bungalows
3 Rai Beach Inn
4 Warung Celagi
5 Warung Taliwang
6 Warung Johnny
7 Hotel Madya
8 Warung Jawa
9 Post Office (Kantor Pos)
10 Restaurant Sederhana
11 Telephone Office
12 Bus & Bemo Park
13 Warung Muslim
14 Ferry Ticket Office
15 Restaurant Sudimampir
16 Restaurant Kendedes

beach on the exposed coast outside the bay.

The coral reefs around Pulau Kambing, off Padangbai, offer excellent diving possibilities. Gili Toapekong, with a series of coral heads at the top of the drop off, is apparently the best site. The currents here are strong and unpredictable and there are also sharks – it's recommended for experienced divers only.

Cruise ships visiting Bali usually use Padangbai but have to anchor offshore outside the harbour as only small ships can actually enter the bay.

Information

There are no banks or moneychangers in Padangbai so whether you're planning to stay here or continuing on to Lombok make sure you've changed enough money before you get here. Otherwise you may have to backtrack to Klungkung to the nearest bank or continue to Candidasa to find a moneychanger. Johnny, at Johnny's Warung, will sometimes change cash US$ or A$ (not travellers' cheques) into rupiah at a discount.

Places to Stay

On the main street of the small port, just a few steps back from the wharf entrance, *Hotel Madya* has rooms around the courtyard at 6000 rp, each with an attached bathroom and verandah. There may still be some older rooms in the main building, but they're pretty basic.

Most visitors to Padangbai stay at the pleasant beachfront places – go down to the wharf and you'll find them a couple of hundred metres to the left along the beach. First there's the *Rai Beach Inn* with two-storey rooms at 10,000 rp. Next to it is *Sedani Kerthi Beach Bungalows* with rooms at 5000 rp. Finally there's the *Padangbai Beach Inn*, a quiet little homestay with thatched roof bungalows and attached bathroom at 5000 rp. Padangbai's beach is lovely and with all the colourful fishing boats drawn up it's very picturesque as well.

Places to Eat

Padangbai has a number of restaurant including the *Rumah Makan Candra* a the Hotel Madya. A major road widenin project demolished all the places on th northern side of the road so it remains t be seen if restaurants there will re-ope *Johnny's Warung, Warung Jawa* and th *Warung Muslim* are other small place On the beach near the cluster of losmen i the *Warung Celagi*.

Getting There & Away

See the introductory information on th ferry service between Bali and Lombok fo details on the daily ferry from Padangba The ticket office is down by the pier. Buse meet the ferry and go straight t Denpasar. There are also connection from Padangbai right through to Surabay (13,000 rp) and Yogyakarta (17,500 rp) i Java. Padangbai is a couple of km off th main Klungkung-Amlapura road, 54 kr from Denpasar.

BALINA BEACH

It's 11 km from the Padangbai main roa turn-off to Candidasa and between th two, about seven km from the turn-off an four km from Candidasa is Balina Beach This is strictly a one resort developmen and it is probably the major scuba divin centre for Bali. They have divin equipment for rent and organise snorkellin and diving trips all around Bali includin to Nusa Penida or the north coast.

Diving trips including transport and full tank range from US$25 to US$35 o the trips closer to Balina to US$45 fo Nusa Penida or US$50 to Menjangar Island on the north coast. You can also g on the same trips to snorkel, for a lowe cost. Snorkelling trips start from US$ and go up to U$18 for Nusa Penida o US$20 for Menjangan.

Places to Stay

Balina Beach Bungalows have rooms at a host of prices from as low as US$6/8 fo singles/doubles right up to US$22/25 fo he fanciest rooms with balcony or US$35 or a large family unit. All prices include breakfast. This is a large, attractive new development.

TENGANAN

Continuing from Padangbai the road enters a beautiful stretch where the hills clamber up inland while glimpses of fine beaches can be seen below. At the turn-off to Tenganan a little posse of motorcycle riders wait by the junction, ready to ferry you up to Tenganan for 200 or 300 rp. There's also a walking path there from Candidasa but the trail is sometimes hard to follow.

Tenganan is a Bali Aga village, a centre of the original Balinese prior to the Majapahit arrival. Unlike that other well known Bali Aga centre, Trunyan, this is a friendly place and also much more interesting. Tenganan is a walled village and consists basically of two rows of identical houses stretching up the gentle slope of the hill. They face each other across a grassy central area where the village public buildings are located. The Bali Aga are reputed to be exceptionally conservative and resistant to change but even here the modern age has not been totally held at bay. A small forest of television aerials sprout from those oh-so-traditional houses! The most striking feature of Tenganan, however, is its exceptional neatness – it all looks spick and span and neat as can be and the hills behind provide a beautiful backdrop.

Tenganan is full of strange customs, festivals and practices. Double ikat cloth, known as *gringsing*, is still woven here – where the pattern to be produced is dyed on the individual threads, both warp (lengthwise) and weft (crosswise), *before* the cloth is woven. This is the only place in Indonesia where the double ikat technique is practised, all other ikat produced in the archipelago is single ikat where only the warp or weft, never both, is dyed.

A magical cloth known as *kamben gringsing* is also woven here – a person

wearing it is said to be protected against black magic! A peculiar old-fashioned version of the gamelan known as the *gamelan selunding* is still played here and girls dance an equally forgotten dance known as the *Rejang*. At the *Usaba sambah* festival once a year around June or July men fight with their fists wrapped in sharp-edged pandanus leaves – similar events occur on the island of Sumba, far to the east in Nusa Tenggara. At this same festival small man-powered ferris wheels are brought out and the village girls are ceremonially twirled round. There are other Bali Aga villages in the vicinity including Asak where the even more ancient *gamelan gambang* is played.

If you walk right up through the village to the road off to the right you'll see a sign pointing to the home of I Made Muditadnana who produces lontar palm books – the traditional Balinese palm-leaf books. He's a friendly man and well worth visiting but if you're thinking of buying one of his books check the prices at the village handicraft shops first!

There's a delightful legend about how the villagers of Tenganan came to acquire their land. It's a story that in slightly different forms pops up in various places in Indonesia. The Tenganan version relates how Dalem Bedaulu (the king with a pig's head – see the Bedulu section for details) lost a valuable horse and offered to reward the villagers of Tenganan who had found its carcass. They asked that they be given the land where the horse was found – that is all the area where the dead horse could be smelt. The king sent a man with a keen nose who set off with the village chief and walked an enormous distance without ever managing to get away from the foul odour. Eventually accepting that enough was enough the official headed off back to Bedulu, scratching his head. Once out of sight the village chief pulled a large hunk of dead horse out from under his clothes.

CANDIDASA

Less than a km beyond the turn-off to Tenganan and about 13 km before Amlapura the road runs right down to the coast at Candidasa. In 1983 it was just a quiet little fishing village but two years later a dozen losmen and half a dozen restaurants had sprung up and this was suddenly *the* new beach place in Bali. Fortunately it's still a quiet, relaxed little resort, this isn't Kuta.

Beyond Candidasa the road spirals up to the Pura Gamang pass from where there are fine views down to the coast.

Information

Homestay Kelapa Mas has a book exchange. At night dance performances are often put on at the Pandan Harum dance place. Candidasa has shops, moneychangers and other facilities.

The Beach & the Sea

The beach is great, when the tide's out. When the tide's in it almost completely disappears and you have to take refuge up on the bank behind the beach. Unfortunately the villagers have been attempting to preserve their suddenly valuable strip of beach by building ugly concrete walls against the sea. The most probable result will just be an acceleration of the usual erosion. Still, the water's fine, sheltered, relatively calm and great for children. If

you swim out a couple of hundred metre to where the waves break there's goo coral and lots of colourful fish.

Just beside the road, at the lagoo there's a temple built up the hillside. Th fishing village, just beyond the lagoon, ha colourful fishing prahus drawn up on th beach. In the early morning you can watc them coasting in after a night's fishin Outriggers regularly appear at Candidas beach to take snorkellers out to the re and the nearby islets.

If you follow the beach round fror Candidasa towards Amlapura a tra: climbs up over the headland with fir views over the rocky islets off the coast From the headland you can see tha although they look as if they're in straight line, from Candidasa beach it' actually one cluster of the smaller one plus the solitary larger island isolated of to the east. There's good diving aroun these islands.

Looking back inland there's no sign a all of the village below or the road – just ar unbroken sweep of palm trees. If it's clea Agung rises majestically behind the rang of coastal hills. Round the headland there's a long sweep of beach – as wide

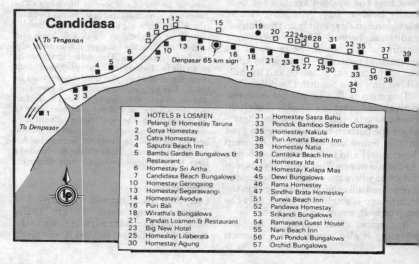

Candidasa

To Tenganan

Denpasar 65 km sign

To Denpasar

	HOTELS & LOSMEN	
1	Pelangi & Homestay Taruna	
2	Gotya Homestay	
3	Catra Homestay	
4	Saputra Beach Inn	
5	Bambu Garden Bungalows & Restaurant	
6	Homestay Sri Artha	
7	Candidasa Beach Bungalows	
10	Homestay Geringsing	
13	Homestay Segarawangi	
14	Homestay Ayodya	
16	Puri Bali	
18	Wiratha's Bungalows	
21	Pandan Losmen & Restaurant	
23	Big New Hotel	
25	Homestay Lilaberata	
30	Homestay Agung	

31	Homestay Sasra Bahu
33	Pondok Bamboo Seaside Cottages
35	Homestay Nakula
36	Puri Amarta Beach Inn
38	Homestay Natia
39	Cantiloka Beach Inn
41	Homestay Ida
42	Homestay Kelapa Mas
45	Dewi Bungalows
46	Rama Homestay
47	Sindhu Brata Homestay
51	Purwa Beach Inn
52	Pandawa Homestay
53	Srikandi Bungalows
54	Ramayana Guest House
55	Nani Beach Inn
56	Puri Pondok Bungalows
57	Orchid Bungalows

lack and shadeless as Candidasa is
arrow, white and shady.

laces to Stay

'andidasa's losmen are mainly out of the
ame mould – simple rooms with attached
athroom and a small verandah area out
ront. They start from the Tenganan turn-
ff and extend right through the tourist
art of the village to the original fishing
illage, hidden in the palm trees where the
oad turns away from the coast. Typical
rices are from 6000 rp for basic doubles
ut as at Kuta or Ubud there are so many
laces to choose from the best advice is
imply to wander around and have a look
t a few rooms.

Starting at the Denpasar side the
Candidasa Beach Bungalows are pleasant
f a little tightly packed together and cost
rather expensive 30,000 rp. Next to it
Iomestay Geringsing has rooms at 10,000
r at Wiratha's Bungalows pleasant
ooms with attached mandi are 6000 rp. In
etween them Puri Bali's 12,000 rp rooms
re good value, they're simple but clean
nd well kept.

The Pandan Losmen has simple solid
ooms at 22,000 rp. Homestay Lilaberata

is a rock bottom place but quite popular
with rooms at 5000, 6000 and 10,000 rp and
a discount for longer stays. A big new hotel
was built in 1988 between these two.

Pondok Bamboo Seaside Cottages has
doubles at 26,000 rp and a beachfront
restaurant. Puri Amarta Beach Inn has
6000 rp rooms plus larger ones with a small
attic-type room above – ideal for families.
The larger rooms are 15,000 and 20,000 rp.

Homestay Ida, close to the lagoon,
definitely doesn't fit the usual pattern,
with pleasantly airy bamboo cottages
dotted around a grassy coconut plantation.
Smaller rooms are 15,000 or 18,000 rp, the
larger rooms with mezzanine level are
35,000 rp, all including breakfast. Next
door is the Homestay Kelapa Mas and
then the small lagoon.

There are plenty of small losmen
beyond the lagoon. These include Dewi

Candidasa

MAP / LEGEND

To Amlapura

48 49 50
44
51 56 57
45 Fishing Village 55
46 53 54
47 52

ESTAURANTS
asa Garden Restaurant
lade's Restaurant
andidasa Restaurant
afe Sayang
J's Restaurant
yu Seaside Restaurant
usti Restaurant & Pub
amplung Restaurant
unjung Restaurant
Varung Chandra
epot Sumber Rasa
lawaii Restaurant
andawa Restaurant
ropical Bar
ondok Bamboo Restaurant

37   Murni Restaurant
40   Sri Jati Restaurant
43   Warung Rasmini
44   Lila Arnawa Stage Restaurant
48   Budi's Restaurant
49   Pizzeria Candi Agung
50   Ngandi Restaurant

●   OTHER
19   Pandun Harum dance place

Bungalows, Rama Homestay and the Sindhu Brata Homestay, three fairly standard losmen right beside the lagoon. Several more can be found further along the beach.

Places to Eat

Restaurants are dotted along the road although curiously there are not a great number right on the beach. The fish is usually good at Candidasa. The *Hawaii Restaurant* has good food at reasonable prices and the *Camplung Restaurant* is popular, particularly for breakfast. *Warung Chandra* and *Depot Sumber Rasa* are both straightforward places with simple menus and low prices attracting a steady stream of customers.

There are some places on the beach like the *Pondok Bamboo's* with fairly standard food including quite good sandwiches. *Ayu Seaside Restaurant* seems to have its ups and downs, definitely down when I tried it.

Puri Amarta has quite good food, they have a restaurant by the road and a second, open area down by the beach. There are plenty of other possibilities like the *Gusti Restaurant & Pub*, *Murni's Restaurant* and *TJs*. The *Arung Restaurant* has excellent food. Down towards the lagoon the *Sri Jati Restaurant* has good straightforward Indonesian food.

Beyond the lagoon and the temple, towards Amlapura, there's *Budi's*, the *Pizzeria Candi Agung* and the *Ngandi Restaurant* on the inland side of the road, the *Lila Arnawa Stage Restaurant* on the coast side.

Getting There & Away

Candidasa is on the main route between Amlapura and Denpasar so any bus or bemo coming by will get you somewhere!

AMLAPURA

The main town at this end of Bali and capital of the Karangasem regency this is also the 'end of the road' travelling east. A road continues from Amlapura down to the coast at Ujung and beyond but

basically at Amlapura you chang directions, turn north and then ben round west to follow the coast to Singaraj on the north coast. This road is now i much better condition than it was in th '70s and the route to Singaraja is n problem at all.

The kingdom of Karangasem brok away from the Gelgel kingdom in the lat 17th century and a century later ha become the most powerful kingdom i Bali. Amlapura used to be known a Karangasem, the same as the regency bu it was changed after the '63 eruption c Agung in an attempt to get rid of an influences which might provoke a simila eruption!

Palace

The palace, Puri Agung Karangasem, i an imposing reminder of Karangasem' period as a kingdom although it actuall dates from the 20th century. Take a loo at the three-tiered gate and the beautifu sculptured panels on the outside of th main building, which is known as the Bal London because of the British Royal Cres on the furniture. Because Karangasem co operated with the Dutch during thei take-over of the island the rajah o Karangasem was able to retain his ol power, at least for a while.

Ujung

A few km beyond Amlapura, on the road down to the sea, is the Ujung Water Palace, an extensive, picturesque and crumbling complex. It has been crumbling away for some time but a great deal more damage has been done to it since the mid '70s. The last king of the Kingdom of Karangasem, Anak Agung Anglurah, was obsessed with moats, pools, canals and fountains and he completed this grand palace in 1921. You can wander around the pleasant park, admire the view from the pavilion higher up the hill above the rice paddies or continue a little further down the road to the fishing village at the coast.

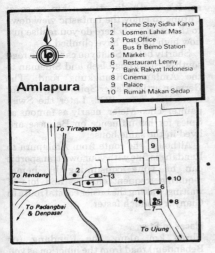

1	Home Stay Sidha Karya
2	Losmen Lahar Mas
3	Post Office
4	Bus & Bemo Station
5	Market
6	Restaurant Lenny
7	Bank Rakyat Indonesia
8	Cinema
9	Palace
10	Rumah Makan Sedap

Amlapura

To Tirtagangga

To Rendang

To Padangbai & Denpasar

To Ujung

Places to Stay

Amlapura has a few places to stay but most travellers prefer to stay out of town, either in Tirtagangga or at Homestay Lila, a short distance down the road towards Rendang. If you do want to stay in Amlapura there are two options only a few steps apart and another just out of town.

On your left, just as you enter town, the *Lahar Mas Inn* has rooms with bath at 5000/6000 rp including breakfast – bread, an egg and coffee. They're around a large common room area and quite comfortable. The Lahar Mas backs on to the rice paddies and visitors report that it's a pleasant place with friendly people.

On the other side of the road a short distance in towards the centre, *Homestay Sidha Karya* was the original losmen in Amlapura but most visitors deserted it as soon as the Tirtagangga water-palace inn opened. Rooms here are 3000/4000 rp, again including breakfast. A third possibility is the *Losmen Kembang Ramaja*, just out of Amlapura on the Rendang road.

Places to Eat

There's the usual collection of rumah makans and warungs around the bus station plus the *Restaurant Lenny* and the *Rumah Makan Sedap* on the main street. Amlapura tends to shut down early so don't leave your evening meal until too late.

Getting There & Away

Although Amlapura is the 'end of the road' for bus services from Denpasar, you can continue round the coast all the way to Singaraja in the north.

TIRTAGANGGA

Amlapura's water-loving rajah, having constructed his masterpiece at Ujung, later had another go at Tirtagangga. This water palace, built around 1947, was damaged in the 1963 eruption of Agung and during the political events that wracked Indonesia around the same time. Nevertheless it's still a place of beauty and solitude and a reminder of the power the old Balinese rajahs once had. There's a swimming pool here as well as the ornamental ponds. Entrance to the water palace is 200 rp (children 100 rp) and another 500 rp (children 200 rp) to use the fine swimming pool (300 rp for the lower one, children 100 rp).

The rice terraces around Tirtagangga are reputed to be some of the most beautiful in Bali. They sweep out from Tirtagangga almost like a sea surrounding an island. A few km beyond here, on the road round the east coast to Singaraja, there are more dramatically beautiful terraces.

Places to Stay & Eat

Right by the water palace is the peaceful *Losmen Dhangin Taman Inn* with rooms at 3000, 4000, 5000 and 10,000 rp. Breakfast is included. The most expensive rooms are large and have an enclosed sitting area. You can sit in the courtyard, gazing across the rice paddies and the water palace while doves coo in the background. The losmen owner here is very amusing and the food is not bad although the warung nearest the losmen also does excellent food.

Actually within the palace compound the *Tirta Ayu Homestay* has pleasant individual bungalows at 7000, 8000 and 10,000 rp. Alternatively you can continue 300 metres beyond the water palace and climb the steep steps to the *Kusuma Jaya Inn*. The 'Homestay on the Hill' has a fine view over the rice paddies and rooms at 3000/6000 rp including breakfast and tea. Other meals are also available and they have information about local walks.

Across the road from the palace the *Rijasa Homestay* is a small and simple place with rooms at 2500/3000 rp or 3000/4000 rp, all including breakfast and tea. There's another losmen here, the *Taman Sari Inn*, but it is closed down at present.

Getting There & Away

Tirtagangga is about five or six km from the Amlapura turn-off on the road that runs around the eastern end of Bali. Bemos from Amlapura cost 200 rp. Buses continue around this way to Singaraja. See the section on the east coast under North Bali.

AMLAPURA TO RENDANG

The Amlapura-Rendang road branches off from the Amlapura-Denpasar road just a km or two out of Amlapura. The road gradually climbs up into the foothills of Gunung Agung, running through some pretty countryside. It's a quiet, less travelled route than the relatively busy Amlapura-Denpasar road – very busy between Klungkung and Denpasar. At Rendang you meet the Klungkung-Besakih road close to the junction for the very pretty minor road across to Bangli.

The road runs through Bebandem, with a busy market every three days, Sibetan and Selat to Rendang. Sibetan and Rendang are both well known for the salaks grown there. If you've not tried this delicious fruit with its curious 'snakeskin' covering then this may be the time to do

so. It's worth diverting a km or so at Putung to enjoy the fantastic view down to the coast, only here do you realise just how high up you have climbed.

Shortly before Selat you can take a road south-west through Iseh and Sideman to the Amlapura-Klungkung road. The German artist Walter Spies lived here for some time from 1932. Later the Swiss painter Theo Meier, nearly as famous as Spies for his influence on Balinese art, lived in the same house.

Although the route from Amlapura to Rendang is fine with your own transport it can be time consuming by bemo, requiring frequent changes and lots of waiting. Taking the busier coastal route to Gianyar is much faster.

Places to Stay

Three km along the Rendang (or Bebandem) road from the junction as you leave Amlapura, *Homestay Lila* is a very pretty little place just off the road but right in the rice paddies. It's quiet and well away from everything, an ideal place to relax. The individual bungalows have bathrooms and a verandah out front, but no electricity. Singles/doubles cost 3000/5000 rp including breakfast – there's no where else to eat around here but the homestay also does other meals. It's a half-hour walk from here to Bukit Kusambi.

Further along towards Rendang, 11 km beyond Bebandem, you can turn off the road a km or so to the superbly situated *Putung Bungalows*. On the edge of a ridge they look out over the coast far, far below. You can see large ships anchored off Padangbai and across to Nusa Penida. They have two-storey bungalows, with a bathroom and small sitting area downstairs and also 'losmen class' rooms. Prices are from 8000 rp and there's also a restaurant in the complex.

BANGLI

Half-way up the slope to Penelokan the town of Bangli, once the capital of a kingdom, is said to have the best climate in Bali. It also has a very fine temple and quite a pleasant place to stay. Bangli is a convenient place to visit Besakih from, so it's quite a good base for exploring this area.

Pura Kehen

At the top end of the town Pura Kehen, the state temple of the Bangli kingdom, is terraced up the hillside. A great flight of steps leads up to the temple entrance and the first courtyard, with its huge banyan tree, has colourful Chinese porcelain plates set into the walls as decoration. Unfortunately most of them are now damaged. The inner courtyard has an 11-roof meru and a shrine with thrones for the three figures of the Hindu trinity – Brahma, Shiva and Vishnu. This is one of the finest temples in Bali. There's a large arts centre just round the corner from the Pura Kehen.

Bukit Demulih

If you take the Tampaksiring road out of Bangli about three km, the hill of Bukit Demulih is just off the road to the left (south side). There's a sign pointing to it or local children will direct you. You can make the short climb to the top where there's a small temple and from there you can look back over Bangli. Or walk along the ridge line to the end of the hill where all of south Bali spreads out below. You can see the long sweep of Sanur Beach with the Bali Beach Hotel, a minuscule rectangular box, far away.

Pura Dalem Penunggekan

Just below Bangli, right beside the road down to Gianyar, there's an interesting temple of the dead, the Pura Dalem Penunggekan. Along the front the reliefs illustrate particularly vivid scenes of wrong-doers getting their just deserts in the afterlife. In one panel a demon rapes a woman while other demons simultaneously stab and castrate a man. Elsewhere in the same panel demons gouge out eyes and a particularly toothy demon takes a bite out

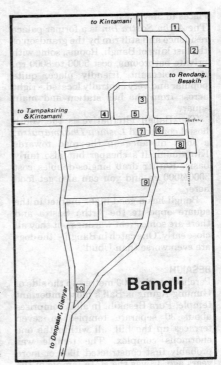

1	Pura Kehen
2	Art Centre
3	Losmen Dharmaputra
4	Post Office
5	Cinema
6	Artha Sastra Inn
7	Bus Stop
8	Market
9	Telephone Office
10	Pura Dalem Penunggekan

of some ne'er-do-well. On an adjoining panel unfortunate sinners are hung by their heels from a tree branch and roasted over a fire.

Places to Stay & Eat

The *Artha Sastra Inn* is a former palace residence and still run by the grandson of the last king of Bangli. Rooms, some with private bathrooms, cost 5000 to 8000 rp. It's a pleasant, friendly place, quite popular and very centrally located – right across from the bus station and main square.

The Bangli alternative is the youth hostel connected *Losmen Dharmaputra*, a short distance up the road towards Kintamani. It's cheaper but also fairly basic. Rather drab singles/doubles cost 3000/4000 rp and you can also get food here.

Bangli has a good night market in the square opposite the Artha Sastra and there are some great warungs but they all close early. One catch in Bangli – 'the dogs are even worse than Ubud'.

BESAKIH

Perched nearly 1000 metres up the side of Gunung Agung is Bali's most important temple, Pura Besakih. In all it comprises about 30 separate temples in seven terraces up the hill, all within the one enormous complex. The temple was probably first constructed 1000 or more years ago. It was the state temple of the powerful Gelgel and Klungkung kingdoms 500 years ago and today is the 'mother temple' of all Bali. Every regency in Bali has its own shrine or temple at Besakih and just about every Balinese god you care to name is also honoured. Apart from its size and majestic location Besakih is also probably the best kept temple you'll see on the island. This is not a temple simply built and then left to slowly decay.

Besakih is the Balinese mother temple and also the mother of Balinese financial efforts. You pay to park, pay to enter, pay to rent a scarf and then have to brave the usual large collection of souvenir sellers. After which it's quite possible you'll find the inner courtyards are all closed to visitors!

The temple is definitely impressive, but you do not need a guide to see it. So if someone latches on to you and begins to tell you about the temple, let them know quickly if you don't want their services. If you don't they will expect to paid at the end, and whatever you do give them is certainly not going to be enough – they have no qualms about asking for more.

Places to Stay

About five km below Besakih the *Arca Valley Inn* has rooms and a restaurant. It's prettily situated in a valley by a bend in the road. This could be a good place to stay if you wanted to climb Gunung Agung from Besakih and would like to make an early morning start. There is also a losmen close to the temple entrance.

Getting There & Away

The usual route to Besakih is by bus or bemo to Klungkung from where there are regular bemos up the hill to the temple for 500 rp.

If you go up to Besakih with your own wheels take the left fork about a km before the temple. There may be a 'No Entry' sign on the left fork, ignore it. This brings you to a car park close to the entrance. The right fork ends about a half km from the temple – leaving you with a long walk up the entrance road or a little hassling with the motorcycle gang who'll offer to ferry you up there. Extortionate first price – 1000 rp. You can't take your own bike up the entrance road.

The 'guardhouse' on the right fork is a bit of a scam as well, here they'll try and get you to sign a visitor's book where you'll find that lots of previous foreign guests have dispensed little donations, like 50,000 rp! Taking the left road not only brings you out closer to the temple it also bypasses the souvenir sellers and the 'donation' collectors.

GUNUNG AGUNG

If you want to climb Gunung Agung from Besakih you must leave no later than 6.30 am, it's a pretty tough climb. It's easy to get lost on the lower trails so hire a guide, which can cost anything from 10,000 to 20,000 rp depending on the size of your party, plus a few thousand as a tip. Take plenty of food and water, an umbrella, raingear, a warm woollen sweater and a torch (flashlight) with extra batteries – just in case you don't get back down by nightfall. An Agung climber's account of the ascent:

We were approached by a young man named Gede who told us that he could take us up Gunung Agung the next day. He took us to a losmen near the temple entrance for the night. It would be unwise to attempt Agung without a guide, as there are numerous trails leading in all directions in the early stages of the climb. In the later stages there are a few choices, some of them less dangerous, some more time consuming. In general the guides have all been to the top on a number of occasions. They are all particularly strong and will carry your daypack for you.

The cost of a guide depends on how many are going to climb and on how hard you bargain. We met a New Zealander who had bargained for about one hour to get the price down to 10,000 rp plus water and lunch. In effect that meant 12,000. Two of us paid 12,000 plus lunch between us although we also gave Gede a well earned tip at the end of the day. We also met another party of three on their way down. They had started climbing at 1 am and given up at 7 am, only an hour or two from the top. Their guide had cost them 22,000 rp.

Our daypack contained three litres of water, three packs of Marie biscuits, half a dozen bananas and a few fistfuls of boiled sweets as we set out from our losmen at 5.15 am. It was cold so we were glad of our woollen sweaters. After walking through the temple we hit upon a very narrow path. It was very dark and humid here and we would have been lost without our torches (flashlights). Our guide was setting a roaring pace, so it wasn't long before our sweaters became a burden. Gradually the path steepened and it became lighter. The vegetation was very thick and we would often lose sight of our guide as he surged ahead. Eventually it became so steep in this jungle that we had to grab onto roots or branches to pull ourselves up the track.

After about three hours of oppressive humidity there was a rather sudden change in terrain. The vegetation all but disappeared and we found ourselves at the base of a slope made entirely of small fragments of volcanic rock. Perseverance saw us struggle successfully through this slippery avalanche scenario to a point where we had to haul ourselves up onto a ledge above the slope. Briefly the ground levelled out for the first time in around three hours – a great relief! This was where we met the vanquished trio who had started out at 1 am. To come so far and then to turn back must have been very painful I'm sure. I found it hard to imagine that the climb could become more difficult, yet our guide assured us that 'most' people turned back somewhere between our present position and the top.

A 10 minute rest was followed by a new phase in the ascent. The next hour was spent scrambling up a slope which appeared to have no end. There was no path to follow, it was just a matter of clawing your way from one rock to the next. There was only one way to go – up. Looking back down the 'hill' only bought fear to my heart as I became convinced I would fall off the mountain into oblivion. The ground was made of an apparently sturdy lichen covered rock which unfortunately was not as sturdy as it looked. On many occasions during that hour I would grab a rock only to find it crumble in my hand. It's important to be alert on this section which is probably the steepest part of the climb.

Finally the summit was in view – or so we thought. It was with an incredible sense of frustration that we reached the top of the lichen field. It was no longer as steep, but the way had become very narrow. This was the beginning of the summit ridge which was no wider than two metres and in some places less than a metre across. It took about half an hour to the top, from both sides of the ridge the mountain dropped away alarmingly steeply. The wind was particularly strong up here and we began to notice the altitude, needing to catch our breath every five minutes or so. With the thought of plunging off the mountain into infinity ever present, we pressed on.

There was only room for one person to stand on the actual summit. From Besakih we had climbed some 2200 vertical metres to an altitude of around 3150 metres (10,300 feet). One step in any direction would take you to a lower point, either along the ridge or over the edge. The wind was positively biting but the view was breathtaking. It was also brief. We reached the summit at around 10 am, looked at the view for no more than a few seconds when the clouds rolled in. An icy dew formed on our arms and legs. Our guide showed us his thermometer. It read 3°C! There was nowhere to hide from the cold and the wind, so we headed off along the ridge toward the crater some 10 to 15 minutes away.

I peered nervously over the edge into the gaping abyss. There appeared to be no bottom. My nose, ears and hands were stinging and I wanted desperately to get off the summit ridge and out of the cold. This was a frighteningly hostile place.

We arrived back in Bekasih at 3 pm after some four hours of slipping and sliding our way down Agung. Our knees were quite visibly swollen and distinctly painful. Our arms and legs were covered in small cuts and abrasions and we were covered from head to toe in grime. We felt decidedly like heroes returned from battle and indeed we were given a heroes' welcome by everyone we passed on our way through the temple. To an inexperienced mountaineer like myself this had been an epic climb. I number it among the great experiences of my life and I wouldn't do it again if you paid me.

Mark Balla

South-West Bali

Most of the places regularly visited in the south-west of Bali, like Sangeh or Tanah Lot, are easy day trips from Denpasar. The rest of the west tends to be a region travellers zip through on their way to or from Java. In the latter half of the last century this was an area of warring kingdoms but with the Dutch takeover the princes' lands were re-distributed amongst the general population. With this bounty of rich agricultural land the region around Tabanan quickly became one of the wealthiest parts of Bali.

Further west there are two spectacular roads up into the hills and across to the north coast but still further west the rugged hills are sparsely populated and the agricultural potential limited due to the low rainfall. This is the area where periodic rumours tell of the continued existence of the Balinese tiger. Along the south coast there are long stretches of wide black-sand beach and rolling surf. Countless little roads run down to the coast from the main road, which runs close to the coast but never actually on it.

Getting There & Away
Buses to the west of Bali generally go from the Ubung station in the north of Denpasar. It's around 2500 rp to Gilimanuk, 400 rp to Mengwi.

SEMPIDI, LUKLUK & KAPAL
Kapal is the garden gnome and temple curlicue centre of Bali. If you're building a new temple and need a balustrade for a stairway, a capping for a wall, a curlicue for the top of a roof, or simply any of the countless standard architectural motifs then the numerous shops which line the road through Kapal will probably have what you need. Or if you want some garden ornamentation, from a comic book deer to a brightly painted Buddha then again you've come to the right place.

Lukluk's Pura Dalem and Sempidi's three desa temples are all worth inspecting but Kapal's Pura Sadat is the most important temple in the area. Although it was restored after WW II, following its destruction in an earthquake earlier this century, this is a very ancient temple, possibly dating all the way back to the 12th century.

TANAH LOT
The spectacularly placed temple of Tanah Lot is possibly the best known and most photographed in Bali. It's almost certainly the most touristed – the crowds here are phenomenal, the gauntlet of souvenir hawkers to be run is appalling and the commercial hype is terrible. Signs direct you to the best place for photographs and even where to catch the sunset. In fact sunset time has definite overtones of Australia's Ayers Rock with the faithful lined up, cameras at the ready, for the hallowed moment.

It's easy to see why it's such an

attraction because Tanah Lot's setting is fantastic. It's perched on a little rocky islet, connected to the shore at low tide but cut off as the tide rolls in. It looks superb whether it's delicately lit by the dawn light or starkly outlined at sunset.

It's also an important temple – one of the venerated sea temples respected in similar fashion to the great mountain temples. Like the equally spectacularly situated Ulu Watu, at the southern end of the island, Tanah Lot is closely associated with the legendary priest Nirartha. It's said that Nirartha passed by here and, impressed with the tiny island's superb setting, suggested to local villagers that this would be a good place to construct a temple. Entry to the temple is 200 rp.

Getting There & Away

Tanah Lot is reached by turning off the Denpasar-Gilimanuk road at Kediri and taking the road straight down to the coast. You can reach it by bemo but if you're going with your own wheels this would be a good place for which to make a very early

start – and miss the tourist jam. If you go out by bemo note that there is no regular service, and come sunset time when all the visitors flock back you may find the car park quickly empties and you only have a choice of chartering or walking.

MENGWI

The huge state temple of Pura Taman Ayun, surrounded by a wide moat, was the main temple of the kingdom which ruled from here until 1891. The kingdom split off from the Gelgel dynasty, centred near Klungkung in east Bali. The temple was originally built in 1634 and extensively renovated in 1937. It's a very large, spacious temple and its elegant moat gives it a very fine appearance. The first courtyard is a large, open grassy expanse while the inner courtyard has a multitude of shrines and merus.

In a beautiful setting across the moat from the temple is a rather lost looking art centre. Built in the early '70s it became an almost instant white elephant and today seems forgotten and neglected and is

The best-known temple in Bali – Tanah Lot

already beginning to take on the ageless look of all Balinese architecture. There's also a small museum here and the Mandala Wisata, *Water Palace Restaurant*, overlooking the moat, is not a bad place for lunch.

BLAYU

In Blayu, a small village between Mengwi and Marga, traditional songket sarongs are woven with intricate gold threads. These are for ceremonial use at festivals, not for everyday wear.

MARGA

Near Mengwi stands a peculiar memorial to Lt Colonel I Gusti Ngurah Rai who in 1946 led his men in a futile defence against numerically superior and better armed Dutch forces. The Dutch were trying to recover Bali after the departure of the Japanese. They even called in air support but the Balinese refused to surrender and in an outcome similar to the *puputans* of 40 years before all 94 of his men were killed. Denpasar's airport is named Ngurah Rai in his memory.

SANGEH

North of Denpasar stands the monkey forest of Bukit Sari. It is featured, so the Balinese say, in the *Ramayana*. To kill the evil Rawana, king of Lanka, Hanuman had to crush him between two halves of Mahameru, the holy mountain. Rawana, who could not be destroyed on the earth or in the air, would thus be squeezed between the two. On his way to performing this task Hanuman dropped a piece of the mountain here, complete with a band of monkeys. Of course this sort of legend isn't unique, Hanuman dropped chunks of landscape all over the place!

There's a unique grove of nutmeg trees in the monkey forest and a temple, Pura Bukit Sari, with an interesting old Garuda statue. Plus, of course, there are lots of monkeys. They're very worldly monkeys, very aware of what visiting tourists have probably bought from the local vendors – peanuts. Take care, they'll jump all over you if you've got a pocketful of peanuts and don't dispense them fast enough. The Sangeh monkeys have also been known to steal tourists hats, sunglasses and even, as they run away, their thongs!

There are also plenty of Balinese jumping on you, clamouring to sell you anything from a sarong to a carved wooden flute. This place is geared to tourists.

Getting There & Away

You can reach Sangeh from Denpasar, bemos run directly there, but there is also a road across from Mengwi and from Ubud

TABANAN

Tabanan is in the heart of the south Bali rice-belt, the most fertile and prosperous rice-growing area in the island. It's also a great centre for dancing and gamelan playing. The renowned dancer of the pre-war period, Mario, who perfected the Kebyar dance and is featured in Covarrubias' classic guide to Bali, was from Tabanan.

AROUND TABANAN

Near Tabanan is Kediri, where Pasar Hewan is one of Bali's busiest markets for cattle and other animals. A little beyond Tabanan a road turns down to the coast through Krambitan, a village noted for its beautiful old buildings and also its interest in ancient Javanese and Balinese literature.

About 10 km south of Tabanan is the village of Pejaten, which is a centre for the production of traditional pottery including elaborate, ornamental rooftiles. Recently they have started to make porcelain clay objects for purely decorative use. They can be seen in the Pejaten Ceramics Workshop.

TABANAN TO NEGARA

There's some beautiful scenery but little tourist development along this stretch of coast, the road running for 74 km from Tabanan to Negara.

Lalang-Linggah

The *Balian Beach Club* overlooks the Balian River and is surrounded by coconut plantations. There are bunk beds for 4000 rp plus bungalows at 6000/10,000 rp or a pavilion for 15,000 rp. To get there from Denpasar take any Negara or Gilimanuk bus and ask to stop at Lalang-Linggah, by the 49.6 km post.

Rambut Siwi

Between Air Satang and Yeh Embang a short diversion off the main road leads to the beautiful coastal temple of Pura Luhur at Rambut Siwi. Picturesquely situated on a clifftop overlooking a long, wide stretch of beach this superb temple with its numerous shady frangipani trees is one of the important coastal temples of south Bali.

Before you reach Rambut Siwi, at 22.5 km before Negara, a large sign announces the Medewi Surfing Point. Beyond Rambut Siwi, just seven km before Negara, there's the Delod Brawah Beach, two km off the main road, which is reputed to be good for windsurfing.

NEGARA

The capital of the Jembrana regency, Negara comes alive each year when the bullock races take place between July and October. The normally docile creatures, pulling tiny chariots, charge down a two-km stretch of road. Their riders often stand on top of these chariots forcing them on. This is still Bali, however, so it's not necessarily first past the post which wins. Style also plays a part and points are awarded for the most elegant runner!

Places to Stay & Eat

On Jalan Ngurah Rai, the main street, just on the Denpasar side of the centre, *Hotel Ana* is a standard losmen with rooms from around 3000 rp. Just down from it is the *Losmen & Restaurant Wirapada* (tel 161) at Jalan Ngurah Rai 107 which is more expensive.

The Denpasar-Gilimanuk road actually

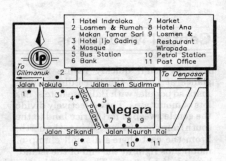

1	Hotel Indraloka	7	Market
2	Losmen & Rumah	8	Hotel Ana
	Makan Taman Sari	9	Losmen &
3	Hotel Ijo Gading		Restaurant
4	Mosque		Wirapada
5	Bus Station	10	Petrol Station
6	Bank	11	Post Office

bypasses the town centre. There are several accommodation possibilities along this road including, on the Gilimanuk side of town, the *Hotel Indraloka* at Jalan Nakula 13-15. The friendly *Losmen & Rumah Makan Taman Sari* at Jalan Nakula 18 has rooms at 4000 rp. Or there's the *Hotel Ijo Gading* at Jalan Nakula 5.

GILIMANUK

Right at the western end of the island Gilimanuk is the terminus where ferries shuttle back and forth across the narrow strait to Java. It's of little interest apart from this, just an arrival and departure point.

Gilimanuk is actually off the main road around the island. About a km on the Denpasar side from the junction there's a curious new temple like a pagoda with a spiral stairway around the outside. For more information on the north coast route to Gilimanuk see the North Bali section.

Places to Stay

Most people simply zip straight through Gilimanuk but if you do have a reason to stay there are several places along Jalan Raya, the main road into the port. They're all about a km from the ferry dock. First there's the *Homestay Putra Sesasan* at No 1, then a *Rumah Makan Padang* and *Homestay Kartika Candra*. At No 24 there's the *Homestay Gili Sari* and at No 12 the *Homestay Surya*.

Central Mountains

Bali, as you'll quickly realise from a glance at one of the three-dimensional maps so popular with Balinese hotels, has lots of mountains. They effectively divide the gentle sweep of fertile rice land to the south from the narrower strip to the north. From the east there's a small clump of mountains right at the end of the island, beyond Amlapura. Then there's the mighty volcano Gunung Agung, the island's mother mountain. North of Agung rises the great crater of Batur with its lake and smaller volcano inside. Finally another series of mountains marches off to the west, a region sparsely inhabited and little visited.

The popular round trip to the north coast takes you up across the mountains on one route and back on the other thus covering most of the mountain region. It's often said the Balinese look away from the sea and towards the mountains; how the mountains are the abode of the gods and the sea is the home of demons and monsters. It's true enough but in reality the Balinese look towards them rather than actually live on them. The true Balinese heartland is the gentle, fertile rising land sweeping up to the mountains. The villages up in the mountains are strange, often chilly and cloudy places.

PENELOKAN

The roads up to Batur from Bangli and from Tampaksiring meet just before they finally reach the crater rim at Penelokan. This is an incredibly spectacular place, the age old crater rim is quite narrow and the road runs right along it with superb views down into the crater to Lake Batur and Mt Batur. Penelokan appropriately means 'the place to look'. In many places you can see down the other side as well and at the far end of the crater road, at Penulisan, you can look back into the crater or turn the other way and see the

north Bali coast spread out at your feet, far below.

At Penelokan, from where the road runs down into the crater to Kedisan, the views are particularly spectacular. This a popular place to stay for those intending to tour the lake or climb the mountain. Unfortunately Penelokan also has a reputation as a bit of a money grubbing place where you're constantly importuned to buy things and where you need to keep an eye on your motorcycle or other gear. It can get surprisingly chilly up here so come prepared. Clouds often roll in over the crater, sometimes getting hung up along the rim and making all the crater rim towns cold and miserable places to be. The Balinese here look very different to those from the warm lowlands.

Places to Stay

There are several places to stay in Penelokan, a couple of them teetering right on the edge of the crater with tremendous views. If hotels could sell their views these places would be five-star. As it is they're just standard little losmen charging standard little prices. Take care though, the Penelokan business attitude carries over to the losmen and they'll charge whatever they reckon the market will bear.

First of the Penelokan places if you arrive from the south is the newer *Caldera Batur* with rooms at 15,000 rp. A little further along the *Lakeview Homestay* clings to the crater rim and has standard rooms at 5000 rp and also more comfortable bungalow-style rooms complete with bathroom for rather more money. The standard rooms are impossibly small – if the beds weren't so tiny and narrow they wouldn't be able to get two in a room. Ah, but the view, the view...

Continuing a little further, past the road down to Kedisan inside the crater, you come to *Losmen Gunawan* – almost an exact duplicate of the Lakeview. Again the view is terrific, the rooms are tiny (they cost 6000 rp) and the bungalow-style rooms are rather better at 10,000 rp and up. A little further along the expensive *Danau Batur Restaurant* may have rooms available at the back of the building. No crater view though.

Places to Eat

Almost everywhere in Bali where there's a major tourist attraction there will also be a major restaurant, somewhere you can pour the tour group into for lunch before it's back to the bus for the afternoon activities. Along the road between Penelokan and Kintamani there is quite a crowd of them, all with fine views over the crater and Mt Batur. They generally do buffet-style lunches at prices suitable for international tourist standards. The restaurants, from Penelokan to Kintamani, include the *Batur Garden*, the *Danau Batur*, the *Puri Selera*, the *Puri Aninditha* and the *Kintamani Restaurant*. Lunch costs from around 7500 to 10,000 rp. The Kintamani Restaurant is the most expensive and possibly the best.

Of course there are also cheap warungs along the main road like the *Warung Makan Ani Asih* or the *Warung Makan Sederhana* The Penelokan losmen also have reasonably priced places to eat.

Getting There & Around

To get to Penelokan you'll probably have to take a bemo first from Denpasar to Gianyar or Bangli and another from there up the mountain. From Ubud go first to Gianyar. Bemos shuttle back and forth regularly between Penelokan and Kintamani (200 rp) and down to the lakeside at Kedisan (300 rp).

From Penelokan you can hike around the crater rim to Gunung Abang (2152 metres), the high point of the outer rim. Or you can follow the road which starts out around the crater rim then drops down to Rendang, joining the Rendang-Besakih road at Menanga. If it's clear there are fine views of Gunung Agung along this route.

The two main routes up the mountain to Penelokan are through Gianyar and Tampaksiring, meeting just before you get to Penelokan. There are, however, several lesser routes, OK for motorcycles but with very little public transport. See the Ubud section for details. The country off to the west of Batur is remote and not visited much.

BATUR & KINTAMANI

Batur and Kintamani virtually run together, it's impossible to tell where one ends and the other begins but the village of Batur used to be down in the crater. Batur had a violent eruption in 1917 which killed thousands and destroyed over 60,000 homes and 2000 temples. Although the village of Batur was wiped out the lava flow stopped at the entrance to the villagers' temple. Taking this as a good omen they rebuilt their village only for Batur to erupt again in 1926 and this time the lava flow covered all but the loftiest temple shrine. The shrine was moved up to the crater rim and placed in the new temple Pura Ulun Danu, where its construction commenced in 1927 and still continues. Mt Batur is the second most important mountain in mountain-conscious Bali, only Agung outranks it, so the temple here is of considerable importance.

Kintamani is a long spread out town, just one main street right along the rim. It's often cold and grey and Kintamani is far from the most attractive place in Bali. This is, however, a major centre for growing oranges and you'll often see them on sale. Kintamani is famed for its large and colourful market, held every three days. Like most markets throughout Bali it starts and ends early – by 11 am it's all over. The high rainfall and cool climate up here makes this a very productive fruit and vegetable growing area. Kintamani is also another place challenging for the hard fought title of 'miserable howling dog capital of Bali'.

Places to Stay & Eat

There are a number of losmen along the

A scenic view of Mt Batur & Gunung Agung

main street of this volcano-rim town but they don't have the spectacular setting of the Penelokan places and most of them are pretty drab and dismal. There's not much incentive for staying here longer than you need to.

Starting from the Penelokan end of town there's *Losmen Superman's* with rooms with bathroom at 4000 rp. It's OK, nothing special but survivable.

If you continue in to town, past the Batur temple, you come to *Losmen Batur Sari* – very drab and plain, with rooms at 5000 rp. A little further along is the *Losmen Lingga Giri* which is also very drab and plain but also very cheap at around 2500 rp for a tiny room. The beds and blankets 'are designed for midgets and there's a warming open fire in the evenings – which no longer adequately compensates for the rather run down and grubby surrounding'. The food is, however, quite good so this is the popular gathering place in the evenings.

Almost next door is the *Hotel (ex-Losmen) Miranda*. Rooms here cost from 2000 to 5000 rp, the most expensive have attached bathrooms. It's a bit better than the general run of Kintamani accommodation and has good food and an open fire at night. Made Senter who runs it also acts as a mountain guide.

Continuing along the road, beyond the main 'centre' of Kintamani, if this strung out little town can be spoken of as having such a thing, you come to *Losmen Kencana*. It's rather brighter and airier than the other places, quite pleasant in fact. Next to it is the *Losmen Sasaka*.

Finally a bit further along again a sign points off the road to the *Hotel Puri Astini* – it says 200 metres but it's probably more like four times that distance. Rooms with attached bathrooms are 10,000 to 20,000 rp including breakfast. That's a big price jump since the last edition although the somewhat remote location, OK if you've got your own wheels, is compensated for by the crater-rim position and the fine sunset views. *Wisma Ardi* is next door to the Puri Astini.

Getting There & Away

From the south coast you get up to Penelokan by bus or bemo then take a bemo to Kintamani for 200 rp. Buses run between Kintamani and Singaraja on the north coast.

PENULISAN

The road continues along the crater rim beyond Kintamani, gradually climbing higher and higher. Sometimes if you come up from the south you'll find yourself ascending through the clouds around Penelokan and Kintamani then coming out above them as you approach Penulisan. There are more fine views down over the crater, this time looking across the land to the north of Mt Batur. Sometimes you can even see Rinjani in Lombok.

At a bend in the road at Penulisan a steep flight of steps leads to Bali's highest temple, Pura Tegeh Koripan at 1745 metres. Inside the highest courtyard there are rows of old statues and fragments of sculptures in the open bales. Some of

them date back as far as the 11th century. The views from this hilltop temple are superb, looking to the north you can see down over the rice terraces clear to the Singaraja coast.

Towering over the temple, however, is a shrine to a new and powerful god – Bali's television repeater mast!

LAKE BATUR & MT BATUR

The crater rim from Penelokan through Batur and Kintamani to Penulisan offers superb views. However the real thrill is the descent into the massive outer crater, a trip across Lake Batur and an ascent of Mt Batur.

Kedisan

A winding road hairpins down from Penelokan to Kedisan on the shore of the lake. From there you can take a boat

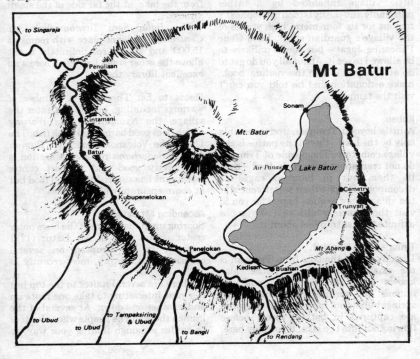

across the surprisingly large and very deep lake to Trunyan, and to the hot springs at Tirtha. From Kedisan or Tirtha you can climb to the summit of Mt Batur in just a couple of hours.

Places to Stay There are several losmen in Kedisan including the new *Segara Homestay* just on the Toyah Bungkah side of the junction. Rooms cost 12,000 rp.

Trunyan

On the shore of Lake Batur the village of Trunyan is squeezed tightly between the lake and the outer crater rim. This is a Bali Aga village, inhabited by remnants of the original Balinese, the people who pre-date the Majapahit arrival. Unlike the other well known Bali Aga village, Tenganan, this is not an interesting and friendly place. Trunyan is just a scruffy little village inhabited by a rather unfriendly and pushy bunch of people. It's famous for its four-metre high statue of the village's guardian spirit, Ratu Gede Pancering Jagat – but you're unlikely to be allowed to see it. About all you do get to do at Trunyan is sign the visitors' book, make a donation and be told you can't visit the temple.

Kuban

A little beyond Trunyan, and accessible only by the lake – there is no path – is the village cemetery. The people of Trunyan do not cremate or bury their dead – they lie them out in bamboo cages to decompose. Despite their secretiveness in the village they're quite happy for you to visit the cemetery although it's got a definite tourist trap feel about it.

Tirtha – Toyah Bungkah

Directly across the lake from Trunyan is the small settlement of Tirtha, also known as Toyah Bungkah, with its famous hot springs *(air panas)*. The springs bubble out in a couple of spots and are captured in bathing pools before flowing out into the lake. If you stay here,

perhaps to climb Mt Batur in the early morning, you can join half the village for a sunset bath – women at one end, men at the other. The water is soothingly hot, ideal for aching muscles after you've climbed the volcano.

Places to Stay There are a number of places to stay in Tirtha Just as you come into the village there's the *Under the Volcano Homestay* with rooms at 4000, 5000, 10,000 and 15,000 rp. The rooms are standard value for money and it's quite a pleasant place with a popular restaurant.

Across the road is the small and basic *Siki Inn* with rooms at 3000/5000 rp. Other cheaper losmen are the *Losmen Tirta Yatra* right by the lake or also on the lakeside, above the hot springs, *Losmen Amertha* with rooms at 5000/6000 rp. *Kardi's Mountain View Losmen* is back from the lake, at the far side of the small village.

The *Balai Seni Toyabungkah Art Centre* is a pleasant place with rooms at 15,000 and 20,000 rp, definitely a cut above the other small losmen. There's an excellent library there.

Places to Eat There are a number of warungs including, just as you enter the village, the *Nyoman Pangus Warung* which does good barbecued fresh fish. The Under the Volcano Homestay's *Rumah Makan Sederhana* restaurant section is also pretty good and the art centre restaurant has surprisingly good food but at commensurately higher prices.

Ascending Mt Batur

Soaring up in the centre of the huge outer crater is the cone of Mt Batur (1717 metres). It has erupted on several occasions this century, most recently in 1963.

There are several routes to the top but it's most interesting to take one route up and another one down. At several of the losmen there will be people who volunteer as guides although finding your way up

Mt Batur by yourself is no problem at all – there are plenty of paths and the way to the top is clear as day. Two popular guides are Made from the hot springs or flute-playing Gede (he's quite a character) from Kintamani.

The shortest and most direct route is probably from the hot springs. Just take a straight line and head right up the mountain, it gets pretty steep towards the top. The most popular route is probably from Kedisan – it's quite a beaten track and there are even a number of refreshment stops along the way. If there are no local children running them they will be operated on the honour system – leave your money in the jar and help yourself to the pause that refreshes! This is quite an interesting route, winding across the lava flows to the west of Mt Batur and climbing across the smaller cone, created by the most recent eruption. A third possibility is to ascend from Kintamani, first descending the outer crater rim and then climbing up the inner cone.

It's possible to walk right around the rim of Mt Batur, or even descend into the crater and up the other side. Wisps of steam issuing from fissures in the rock and the surprising warmth of many stretches of the thinly crusted ground indicate that things are still happening down below. A possible round trip could be to climb Mt Batur from the hot springs, follow the rim round to the other side or cut across through the crater, then descend on the regular route back to Kedisan. Climbing up, spending a reasonable time on the top and then strolling back down can all be done in an easy four or five hours.

Down to the East Coast

The rough old jeep track across the lava field has been surfaced not only to the hot springs but beyond to Sonam and right to the very edge of the outer crater. From the temple at the crater edge you can climb to the top of the crater rim in just 15 minutes and from there you can see the east coast,

only about five km away. It's an easy downhill stroll to the coast road.

Getting Around

Getting across the lake was at one time Bali's great rip-off. After negotiating a sky-high price your boatmen would then want to renegotiate half-way across. Meanwhile your motorcycle was being stripped back at Kedisan. It got so bad that the government took over and everything is now at set prices. At Kedisan, where the boats depart from, there is a boat office, car park and the usual assortment of rumah makans and warungs. Your motorcycle will be safe here!

Standard prices vary with the route you want to take – there are charges for the charter of a whole boat or per person. A boat will carry about 12 people. If you can't get a group together then try tagging on to one of the many Indonesian tourist groups. Charter prices are in the 7000 to 9000 rp range, for 9000 rp you can make the whole lake circuit Kedisan-Trunyan-Kuban-Tirtha-Kedisan. Per person costs range from 875 to 2000 rp.

If you want to do it on the cheap don't consider the alternative of hiring a dugout canoe and paddling yourself. For a start the lake is much bigger than it looks from the shore. More important it can quickly get very choppy if a wind blows up – in those conditions the middle of the lake can be a very dangerous place. A better alternative is to walk, the road continues from Kedisan to Buahan and from there you just follow the good footpath around the lakeside to Trunyan, an easy hour or two's walk. From Trunyan you should be able to negotiate a cheaper fare to the cemetery and hot springs. You can walk from there back across the lava field to Kedisan, it's about four km along a surfaced road. Or why not spend the night at the *air panas*, climb Mt Batur in the morning and descend from there back to Kedisan?

BEDUGUL

The serenely calm Lake Bratan is on the road from Denpasar to Singaraja. You can also reach Singaraja from Denpasar via Penelokan and Kintamani but the Bedugul route is faster. The climb to Bedugul is like the one to Penelokan, you gradually leave the rice terraces behind and ascend into the cool, damp mountain country. Gunung Bratan, overlooking the lake, is 2020 metres high.

At Candikuning, on the shores of the lake, with one courtyard actually isolated on a tiny island right in the lake, is the temple of Ulu Danu. This temple is dedicated to Dewi Danu the goddess of the waters. It has classical thatched-roof merus and an adjoining Buddhist stupa. Admission is 200 rp (children 100 rp). There are several places to stay near the lake and this can be an excellent base for walking trips into the surrounding hills. If you descend from Bedugul to Lake Buyan you can make a fine walk around the southern lakeside of Buyan and over the saddle to the adjoining, smaller Lake Tamblingan and from there to Munduk. It takes about two to three hours from Lake Buyan to Munduk and from there

you can take the road back to the starting point or continue to Seririt on the north coast. The road around the north side of the lake is now sealed and makes an interesting descent from Munduk through picturesque villages to the coast.

Near Bedugul the market of Bukit Mungsu is noted for its wild orchids. The orchid plantation near here is being developed as a botanical garden. The road beyond Bedugul descends past an expensive golf course, opened in the mid-70s, and Lake Buyan. There's a beautiful waterfall near the road at Gitgit.

It's possible to hire a prahu for 2500 rp an hour (but we got the same rate for a half day) and paddle across Lake Bratan from the lakeside just below the Lila Graha to some caves which the Japanese used during WW II. You can also walk there in about an hour. From there a very well marked path ascends to the top of Gunung Catur. It takes about two hours for the climb up and an hour back down, the final bit is steep and you should take some water but it is well worth the effort. There is an old temple on the summit with lots of monkeys.

Anne Whybourne & Peter Clarke, Australia

Places to Stay & Eat

There are now several places to stay dotted along the road up to Bedugul from the Denpasar side as well as a number of places around the lake. There's a 200 rp entry charge to the lakeside at the Denpasar end of the lake. Here you'll find the *Bedugul Hotel* with rooms at 15,000, 20,000 and 25,000 rp. On the main road just by the turn-off is the *Hadi Raharjo*, a

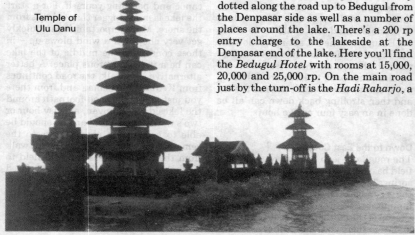

Temple of
Ulu Danu

airly basic and straightforward losmen
with rooms at 6000 rp.

Continuing north the road climbs
higher up the hillside to the turn off for the
new and expensive *Bukit Mungsu Indah
Hotel*. Rooms here cost from US$25 to
US$40. The road then turns the corner
and drops down towards the lake, passing
the turn-off to the *Lila Graha*, which is
also expensive at 30,000 rp. They do have
not showers though!

In Candikuning you can eat at the
Restaurant Pelangi, the *Rumah Makan
Mini Bali* or others in the same area.

Just north of Bedugul is the *Bali
Handara Country Club*, situated at
Bedugul's lush green golf course.

MT BATUKAU

West of the Mengwi-Bedugul-Singaraja
road rises 2093 metre Mt Batukau, the
'coconut-shell mountain'. This is the third
of Bali's three major mountains and the
holy peak of the west end of the island.

Pura Luhur

On the slopes of the mountain Pura Luhur
was the state temple when Tabanan was
an independent kingdom. The temple has
a seven-roof meru to Maha Dewa, Mt
Batukau's guardian spirit, as well as
shrines for the three mountain lakes
Bratan, Tamblingan and Buyan.

There are several routes to Pura Luhur
but none of them are particularly high
class roads – it's a remote temple. You can
reach the temple by following the road up
to Penebel from Tabanan. Or turn off the
Mengwi-Bedugul road at Baturiti near
the 'Denpasar 40 km' sign and follow the
convoluted route to Penebel. Wongaya
Gede is the nearest village to the forest-
surrounded and often damp and misty
temple.

Jatuluih

Also perched on the slopes of Gunung
Batukau, but closer to Bedugul and the
Mengwi-Bedugul road, is the small
village of Jatuluih, whose name means

'truly marvellous'. The view truly is, it
takes in a huge chunk of south Bali.

ROUTES THROUGH PULUKAN

Although the routes through Kintamani
and Bedugul are the two most popular
roads over the mountains, between the
south and north coast there are two other
routes. One starts from Pulukan, the
other from Antosari, both on the Denpasar-
Gilimanuk road, and they meet at
Pupuan before dropping down to Seririt,
to the west of Singaraja. They're
interesting and little used alternatives to
the regular routes.

The Pulukan-Pupuan road climbs
steeply up from the coast with fine views
back down to the sea. The route runs
through spice-growing country and you'll
often see spices laid out on mats by the
road to dry – the smell of cloves rises up to
meet you. At one point the narrow and
winding road actually runs right through
an enormous banyan tree which bridges
the road. Further on the road spirals down
to Pupuan through some of the most
beautiful rice terraces on the island.

North Bali

The north of Bali, the regency known as
Buleleng, makes an interesting contrast
with the south of the island. For a start it's
physically separated from the south by
the central mountains and that short
distance, only a few hours by bus, keeps
the tourist hordes at bay. Along the coast
near Singaraja there's a string of popular
beaches with a varied collection of places
to stay and eat but it's nothing like the
hassle and confusion of Kuta, and
nowhere near the expense of Sanur. Most
visitors to the north are attracted by the
peaceful beaches but there are also a
number of other features worth visiting.

The north has been open to influence
from the west far longer than the south of
Bali. While the Dutch had established full

control of north Bali by 1848-49, it was not until the beginning of this century that they extended their power to the south. Having first encountered Balinese troops in Java in the 18th century, the Dutch were the main purchasers of Balinese slaves – many of whom served in the East Indies Company armies. The Dutch did not become directly involved with internal affairs of the island, as they had in Java, although in 1816 they made several unsuccessful attempts to persuade the Balinese to accept their authority. Various Balinese kings continued to provide the Dutch with soldiers but in the 1840s disputes over the looting (salvaging?) of shipwrecks, together with fears that other European powers might establish themselves in Bali, prompted the Dutch to make treaties with several of the Balinese rajahs. The treaties proved ineffective, the plundering continued and in 1844 disputes arose with the rajah of Buleleng over the ratification of agreements.

In 1845 the rajahs of Buleleng and Karangasem formed an alliance, possibly to conquer other Balinese states but equally possibly to resist the Dutch. In any case the Dutch attacked Buleleng and Karangasem in 1846, 1848 and 1849, and in the third attempt they finally took control of the north. The western regency of Jembrana came under Dutch control in 1853, the rajah of Gianyar surrendered his territory in 1900 but it was not until 1906 that they finally subdued the south. The last confrontation was in 1908 when Klungkung rebelled – unsuccessfully.

From the time of their first northern conquests the Dutch interfered more and more in Balinese affairs. It was here that Balinese women first covered their breasts – on orders from the Dutch to 'protect the morals of Dutch soldiers'.

SINGARAJA

For years Singaraja was the usual arrival point for visitors to Bali. All those pre-war travel books start at Singaraja because at that time land transport through Java

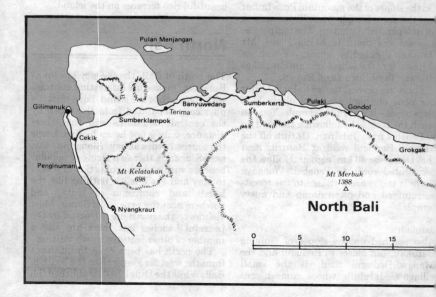

North Bali

Pulan Menjangan

Gilimanuk
Cekik
Penginuman
Nyangkraut

Banyuwedang
Terima
Sumberklampok
Mt Kelatakan 698

Sumberkerta
Pulaki
Gondol
Grokgak
Mt Merbuk 1388

0 5 10 15

as slow and circuitous and there was certainly no busy airport near Denpasar. Singaraja is hardly used as a harbour anymore due to lack of protection from bad weather. Shipping for the north coast now generally uses the new port at Celukanbawang where you might be lucky enough to find a Bugis schooner willing to take you to Surabaya, or further afield. The cruise ships that include Bali in their itinerary use Padangbai, in the south, as their entry point.

The centre of Dutch power, throughout their rule in Bali, was Singaraja and it remained the administrative centre for the Nusa Tenggara islands (Bali through to Timor) until 1953. With a population of around 15,000 it's still a busy little town although a long way behind Denpasar in the cosmopolitan metropolis stakes. It has some pleasant tree-lined streets and dokars are still an everyday means of transport. The 'suburb' of Beratan to the south of Singaraja is the silverwork centre of north Bali.

Singaraja is still a major educational and cultural centre. The Gedong Kirtya, an historical library in the town, contains a magnificent collection of around 3000 old Balinese manuscripts inscribed on lontar palm. These lontar books include literature, mythology, history and religious works including some of the oldest written work on the island in the form of inscribed metal plates known as *prasastis*.

Places to Stay

There are plenty of places to stay and eat in Singaraja but few people bother – the attractions of the beaches, only 10 km away, are too great. If you do want to stay here then the *Hotel Sentral* or the *Hotel Cendrawasih*, next to each other on the Gilimanuk side of the centre, are fairly cheap at 4000/5500 rp.

Other low priced central hotels include the *Hotel Merta Yadnja*, right on the main intersection so it's likely to be very noisy, and the *Hotel Ratna* at Jalan Imam Bonjol 33, also on a noisy street.

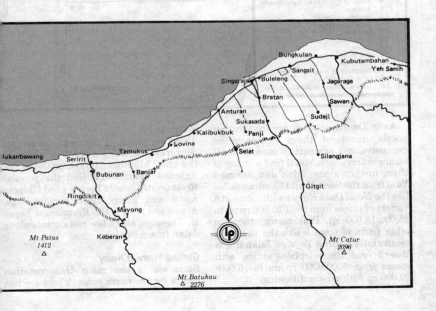

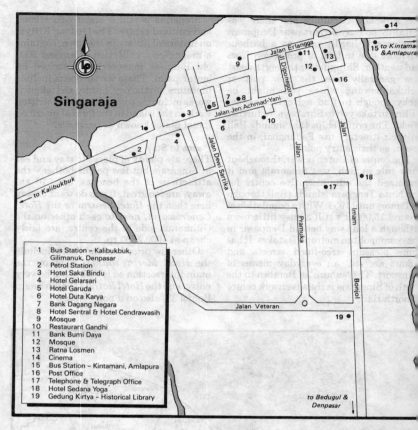

Singaraja

1. Bus Station – Kalibukbuk, Gilimanuk, Denpasar
2. Petrol Station
3. Hotel Saka Bindu
4. Hotel Gelarsari
5. Hotel Garuda
6. Hotel Duta Karya
7. Bank Dagang Negara
8. Hotel Sentral & Hotel Cendrawasih
9. Mosque
10. Restaurant Gandhi
11. Bank Bumi Daya
12. Mosque
13. Ratna Losmen
14. Cinema
15. Bus Station – Kintamani, Amlapura
16. Post Office
17. Telephone & Telegraph Office
18. Hotel Sedana Yoga
19. Gedung Kirtya – Historical Library

As in Denpasar there are many other hotels, most of them rather more expensive and principally used by local business travellers. You'll find a string of them further along Jalan Jen Achmad Yani from the Sentral and Cendrawasih – like the *Hotel Duta Karya* with rooms at a variety of prices from 8500/10,000 rp up to 15,000/18,000 rp. Plus many others in other parts of town – like the neat and clean *Hotel Sedana Yoga* on Jalan Imam Bonjol near the telephone office with rooms from 5000/8000 rp up to 15,000/20,000 rp with air-conditioning.

Places to Eat

There are plenty of places to eat around Singaraja including a batch of places in the small Mumbul Market, on Jalan Jen Achmad Yani. You'll find the popular *Restaurant Gandhi* here, a good Chinese menu and glossy clean surroundings. Across the road is the *Restaurant Segar II*. There are also a few restaurants along Jalan Imam Bonjol.

Getting There & Away

Singaraja is the main transportation centre for the north coast. There are bus stations on the east and west side of the town for travel in the various directions. To Denpasar minibuses leave about every half hour from 6 am to 4 pm, the fare is around 1500 rp and they go via Bedugul. Some other typical fares around Bali from or to Singaraja are Amlapura 1200 rp, Gilimanuk from 1000 rp (takes two hours), Kintamani and Bedugul also cost from around 1000 rp depending on the vehicle. Buses to Amlapura run around the coast now that the road is so much improved.

There are also direct buses to or from Surabaya which saves going down to Denpasar. You'll find a number of ticket offices near the junction of Jalan Jen Achmad Yani and Jalan Diponegoro but you can also arrange tickets from the Lovina Beach places. There aren't direct buses to Yogyakarta but it is possible to arrange to connect with a direct Denpasar-Yogyakarta bus in Gilimanuk.

SINGARAJA BEACHES

To the west of Singaraja is a whole string of popular beaches – Happy Beach, Lovina Beach, Kalibukbuk. They developed as a resort much later than Sanur and Kuta and their development has been a lot slower – which is just fine as this area is relaxed and unhassled. The continuous string of shops which seem to line Sanur and, to an even greater extent, Kuta simply does not exist here. Nor are you endlessly hassled on the beaches to buy things, have a massage or do anything more than simply laze there.

The beaches here are black sand, not the white stuff you find at Sanur or Kuta. Nor is there any surf, a reef keeps it almost flat calm most of the time. Generally the water is very clear and the reef is terrific for snorkelling. It's not the best coral you'll ever find but it's certainly not bad and getting out to it is very easy. In many places you can simply swim out from the beach, elsewhere a prahu will take you out there and they should know the best places for diving. All the hotels seem to

have their own boats or access to one or you can simply ask in the various fishing villages. There always seems to be someone ready to cater to snorkelling enthusiasts and the standard price is about 3000 rp per person.

This is a wonderful place to introduce children to snorkelling. Out on the reef the water is calm, clear and relatively shallow and even beginner swimmers can easily have a good look around and have the prahu outrigger to hang on to for security. My son Kieran can boast that he first went diving on a coral reef at the age of four.

The beach also provides plenty of local entertainment with goats and ducks making a morning and evening promenade along the sand. The sunsets along here are every bit as spectacular as Kuta and there's quite a programme of entertainment around sunset time. As the sky reddens the bats come out to play and then the lights of the fishing boats appear as bright dots right across the horizon. Earlier in the afternoon, at fishing villages like Anturan, you can see the outriggers being prepared for the night's fishing. It's quite a process bringing out all the kerosene lamps and rigging them up around the boat.

Information

There are a couple of good bookshops beside the Badai Restaurant at Kalibukbuk.

Places to Stay

The Singaraja beach strip hasn't had the explosion of accommodation construction which you find at Kuta-Legian or even Ubud but there certainly are far more places than a few years ago and more are gradually being added. Unlike Kuta it's not a compact cluster of losmen, here they are strung out along the beach for several km. The first place is soon after the six km marker, the last at nearly 14 km. You might find one place, then nothing for a half km or so, then a small cluster of places.

Singaraja to Anturan As with almost

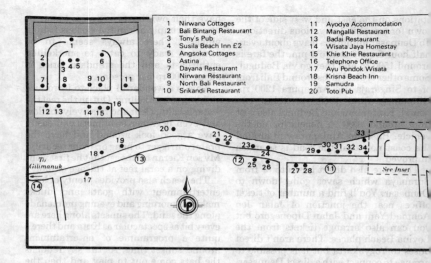

1	Nirwana Cottages	11	Ayodya Accommodation
2	Bali Bintang Restaurant	12	Mangalla Restaurant
3	Tony's Pub	13	Badai Restaurant
4	Susila Beach Inn £2	14	Wisata Jaya Homestay
5	Angsoka Cottages	15	Khie Khie Restaurant
6	Astina	16	Telephone Office
7	Dayana Restaurant	17	Ayu Pondok Wisata
8	Nirwana Restaurant	18	Krisna Beach Inn
9	North Bali Restaurant	19	Samudra
10	Srikandi Restaurant	20	Toto Pub

anywhere in Bali these days prices are very variable with season and demand. Starting from the Singaraja end the first place is the somewhat higher priced *Baruna Beach Cottages*. There are individual cottages and rooms in a larger two-storey block. All have bathrooms and including breakfast costs range from around 12,000 to 15,000 rp. It's quite nice and has a bar/restaurant on the beach but is not the best value to be found.

Next up is the *Suci Jati Reef*, also higher priced, a series of cottage complexes right in the rice paddies close to the beach. They're quite comfortable with double rooms with those bathroom-gardens at around 5000 to 10,000 rp. The reef off the beach here is reputed to be the best along the Singaraja beach strip.

Anturan Continuing along the road you come to the turn-off at the scruffy little fishing village of Anturan, where there is a small cluster of lower-priced places and lots of local colour. Closest to the village is *Mandhara Cottages*, a neat little complex at 6000/10,000 rp for singles/doubles with bathrooms. Further round the beach is

Simon's Seaside Cottages which was rebuilt and renovated after becoming somewhat run down.

Next door again is the very neat and clean little *Homestay Agung* complex. There are rooms from 5000 up to 7500 rp, the more expensive rooms are interesting 'two-storey' places with double bunk beds. The food at Agung can be quite good. *Homestay Sri* is a newer place on this same bit of beach. It's very plain but rooms with attached mandi are just 3000/4000 rp.

Anturan to Kalibukbuk Pressing on from Anturan you pass the *Hotel Perama* up on the main road and then come to the *Lila Cita* down from the turn-off, a simple but very friendly and popular place. Everyone who stays here seems to like it. Rooms are 6000/7500 rp or 7500/10,000 rp with mandi and you could hardly get any closer to the beach. Made, who runs it, is a pleasant guy with family up at Tirtha (the hot springs) at Lake Batur.

Continue along the road to the next turn-off where you'll find the *Kalibukbuk Beach Inn* right down by the beach.

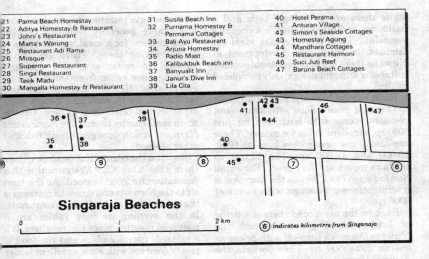

Singaraja Beaches

0   1   2 km

⑥ indicates kilometres from Singaraja

Rooms with bath are 10,000 rp, very plain but they have nice verandahs and it's quite a pleasant place to stay. Back a bit from the beach is the *Banyualit Inn* with rooms at 12,500 rp and the new *Janur's Dive Inn* with rooms at 6000 and 7000 rp.

Kalibukbuk A little beyond the 10 km marker you come in to the village of Kalibukbuk itself. Here you'll find *Ayodya Accommodation*, a traditional but truly delightful place. It's a beautiful, spacious, wonderfully furnished old Balinese house – clean, friendly and extremely well run. The rooms cost 3000 and 4000 rp, but are generally bare and functional, but you sit outside and take your meals there. In the evening, with the bamboo gamelan tinkling in the background, you can really appreciate one traveller's description of Ayodya as 'Gothama's stately home – taking in guests'. Unfortunately Ayodya has one drawback – it's right by the road and in recent years the traffic on this road has increased so much as to make the noise a real problem. It's particularly bad after dark as in Indonesia so much of the long-

distance traffic runs at night when there are fewer obstacles on the road – less children, animals, bicycles and bemos stopping at every opportunity.

Across the road from Ayodya is the small *Wisata Jaya Homestay* and a little further along on the same side as Ayodya there's *Srikandi*. Down by the beach – just follow the track almost beside Ayodya – is *Astina*, a newer development owned by the Ayodya people. Gardens surround the cottages here which cost 6000, 8000 and 12,000 rp.

Right next to Astina on the beach is *Nirwana*; on the road the turn-off is just beyond the 11 km marker. This is the biggest development at Lovina Beach and deservedly so as it's well placed and very well run. They have a variety of rooms starting with basic rooms at 3000/4000 rp and 8000/12,000 rp plus some even nicer ones at 10,000/12,000 rp in a new development beside Astina. Then there are three double-storey cottages which are quite delightful and cost US$16/18. They have a bedroom upstairs with a double bed and are surrounded on all sides by screened windows, without glass. Downstairs there are two single beds and a bathroom and outside there's a spacious verandah. These cottages are ideal for families. In the newer development at Nirwana there are four new double-storey cottages of different design, only completed in 1988.

Right behind Nirwana are the *Angsoka Cottages*, a small place with simple but pleasant rooms with bathroom for just 6000 rp, excellent value for money. There are also some new rooms here at 9000, 10,000 and 12,000 rp. The 12,000 rp upstairs rooms are very good. The small *Susila Beach Inn 2*, beside the Angsoka, is a straightforward losmen with rooms at 4000 rp.

Back on the main road there is a string of lower priced places beyond the Nirwana/Angsoka turn-off with prices as low as 2500/3500 rp. They include the *Arjuna Homestay, Permana Cottages, Purnama Homestay* and *Susila Beach Inn* which are all grouped together in one little clump by the road. Some of the places here extend through to the beach so you can get away from the road noise. There is also the *Mangalla Homestay* with rooms at 3000/4000 rp and up. Next up is *Tasik Madu* which was the original place along the Singaraja beach strip but in recent years became rather run down and then closed up completely.

Beyond Kalibukbuk Continuing further along there's a group of bungalows at the *Aditya Homestay*, some of them right on the beach and costing from 10,000/12,000 rp. Finally there's the *Parma Beach Homestay* with rooms from 5000 rp, the *Samudra Inn,* surprisingly expensive at 25,000 and 30,000 rp, and the *Krisna Beach Inn* 3000 rp or 4500 rp with bathroom, midway between the 13 and 14 km marker from Singaraja. In all the Singaraja beach strip extends seven km from just after the six km marker.

Places to Eat

Most of the places to stay along the beach strip also have restaurants and snack bars and you're generally welcome to visit other losmens for a meal, you don't have to be staying there. There are also a handful of restaurants and warungs. Starting once again from the Singaraja end the small *Homestay Agung* has a good reputation for its food and people from other losmen often drop in here. On the main road nearby there's the *Restaurant Harmoni* which does great fresh fish and other seafood.

Right on the edge of Kalibukbuk village there's the *Khie Khie Restaurant* with a reputation for good seafood. At the turn off to the Nirwana and Angsoka cottages is the extremely popular *Badai Restaurant*. In the evening its long tables are a convivial meeting place for travellers. It's a relaxed, friendly place and the food is pretty good too with some excellent 'order a day in advance' dishes like fish curry, duck (6000 rp for two) or Hidangan Jawa (like a rijstaffel) for 4000 rp for two. The Badai also has a useful bulletin board.

The open double-storey Nirwana Restaurant across the road is closed down but at *Nirwana Cottages* the restaurant area overlooking the beach is very popular. On the road down to the beach there's also the *Bali Bintang Restaurant* on one side and *Tony's Pub* on the other. The Bintang is good, relatively cheap and happy to tackle food not featured on the menu.

Back at the main road you'll find the *Mangalla Restaurant* next to the Badai and *Jacky's Pub* across the road. Next to it the *Dayana Restaurant* has good seafood at reasonable prices. Then there's the *Bali Ayu Restaurant* with good food and regular Balinese dance performances. Further along you come to the *Singa Restaurant* and the *Superman Restaurant* followed by a couple of small warungs – the popular *Marta's Warung* and then *Johni's Restaurant* with an extensive menu and pretty reasonable food. The *Aditya Restaurant* also has dance performances.

Getting There & Away

To get to the Singaraja beaches from the south of Bali you first have to get to Singaraja, then take a bemo out from here. The regular bemo fare from Singaraja to Kalibukbuk in the middle of the beach strip is 250 rp. See the Singaraja section for details of buses.

There are buses direct between Surabaya and Singaraja and if you're coming in from Surabaya you can get off along the beaches rather than have to backtrack from Singaraja. You can also be picked up here and save going in to Singaraja to start with. The Mangalla Restaurant is one place where you can get tickets and arrange to be collected. Night buses to Surabaya cost 9500 rp, through to Yogyakarta 13,000 rp.

AROUND SINGARAJA – WEST

There are numerous places of interest around Singaraja both to the east and the west. Heading west you'll find several places worth a visit between the Kalibukbuk beach strip and the junction town of Seririt.

Waterfalls

At the village of Labuanhaji, only just beyond the end of the Singaraja beach strip, there's a sign to the Singsing Air Terjun – Daybreak Waterfalls – about a half km off the road. It's about 200 metres through the fields, along a concrete path, to the first falls which cascade down the hill into a deep pool. Balinese kids will leap from a tree high up the hill side into the deep water – for a fee.

You can clamber further up the hill side to the higher Singsing Dua falls. Again they cascade into a deep pool – which is much deeper in the wet season of course. You can swim in either pool.

Buddhist Monastery & Hot Springs

About a half km beyond Banjar Tega (which is about two steeply uphill km off the main coast road) is Bali's only Buddhist monastery. It's indeed vaguely Buddhist-looking with its bright orange roof and Buddha statues but overall it's very Balinese with the same decorative carvings and door guardians. From the walls you can see the sea, beyond the rice paddies far below. The road continues past the monastery, winding further up into the hills.

The hot springs, air panas, are only a short distance from the monastery. If you head back down to Banjar Tega, turn left in the centre and cut across to Banjar. It's then only a very short distance uphill again before you see the 'air panas one km' sign. Follow the dirt trail to the inevitable motorcycle park and on down to the lukewarm baths by the riverside. The water pours into the bath and overflows into the river. Bring your swimming gear if you want to try them, there's a small changing enclosure.

Getting There & Away The monastery (wihara) and the air panas are both signposted from the road. If you've not got your own transport it's probably easiest to first continue beyond the Banjar Tega turn-off to the Banjar turn-off (around the 18 km marker) where there are horse carts that can take you up to the air panas path. Then you can walk across to the monastery and back down to the main road afterwards.

SERIRIT TO GILIMANUK

Seririt is little more than a junction town for the roads that run south over the mountains to Pulukan or Bajera, on the way to Denpasar. On to Gilimanuk, the ferry port for Java, the road runs either close to or right by the coast and there are a few places of interest.

Seririt

Seririt has a reasonable selection of shops, though not as good as Singaraja, but if you're staying at the beaches and need something unobtainable at the local shops this might be a place to try. You can stay here in the Losmen Singarasari but with the pleasant Singaraja beach hotels so close there's little reason to do so.

Celukanbawang

Celukanbawang is now the main port for the north coast of Bali, and it has a large wharf. You may see the odd Bugis schooner here.

Pulaki

Pulaki is famous for its coastal monkey temple which has been rebuilt. The village of Pulaki seems to be entirely devoted to grape growing, the whole village is almost roofed over with grapevines. For some reason grape growing has become popular at several locations on the north coast in recent years. They'll be making wine next! There are several hot springs close to the road on this route, one is a km or so beyond Pulaki and a half km off the road, and another one further on.

Terima

This national park in the north-west corner of Bali includes Pulau Menjangan, an unspoilt and uninhabited island with excellent diving around it. There's a 500 rp entry charge to the park, payable to the PHPA Kantor. At Lalang, 16 km from Gilimanuk, there's a dock for boats to the island. A motor prahu costs 25,000 rp for four hours, 5000 rp for each additional hour. There are also coral formations close to the mainland and since this area of Bali is lightly populated, and now protected in the national park, the variety of both fish and coral is amazing. Day trips can be arranged to the island by the various diving centres.

The outcrop of land between Terima and Gilimanuk is also protected and a 25 km walking track skirts the coast. It's a hot walk so take plenty of liquids.

Places to Stay At the 13 km marker before Gilimanuk there's a place to stay at Teluk Terima where *P T Margarana Accommodation* is just off the road. It's clean

and has good showers and rooms for 6000 rp plus a small restaurant area. Otherwis there are just some basic warungs with chicken and rice, drinks and some snacks

AROUND SINGARAJA – EAST

There are a number of places of interes close to the coast road between Singaraj and the turn-off to Kintamani, including some of north Bali's best known temples The north coast sandstone used in templ construction is very soft and easily carvee and this has allowed local sculptors to giv a free rein to their imagination, to an eve greater extent than in the south. You'l find some delightfully whimsical scene carved into a number of the temples here Overall the exuberant, even baroque style of the north makes temples in the south appear almost restrained in contrast

Although the basic architecture of th temples is similar north or south there ar some important differences. Whereas the inner courtyard of southern temple usually houses a number of the multi roofed meru towers together with othe structures, in the north everything will be grouped on a single pedestal. On the pedestal you'll usually find houses for the deities to use on their earthly visits an also for storing important religious relics Also there will probably be a padmasana or 'throne' for the sun god.

Sangsit

Only a few km beyond Singaraja you'l find an excellent example of the north's colourful architectural style at Pura Bej at Sangsit. This is a subak temple dedicated to the spirits which look afte irrigated rice fields, about a half km off the main road on the coast side. The sculptured panels along the front wall se the tone with their Disneyland demons and amazing nagas (snakes).

It's just the same on the inside, with a variety of sculptures covering every available space. Like many other northern temples the inner courtyard is spacious and grassy, shaded by a frangipani tree.

Continue beyond Sangsit to Bungkulan where there is another fine temple with an interesting kulkul drum.

Jagaraga

Only a couple of km off the main road as you enter the small village of Jagaraga there's a temple to the left of the road. This small and otherwise unprepossessing temple has a number of delightful sculptured panels along its front wall both inside and out. On the outer wall look for a vintage car driving sedately past, a steamer at sea and even an aerial dogfight between early aircraft. Jagaraga is also famous for its legong troupe, said to be the best in the north of Bali. It was the capture of the local rajah's stronghold at Jagaraga that marked the arrival of Dutch power in Bali in 1849. A few km further along on the right hand side look for another small temple with ornate carvings of a whole variety of fish and fishermen.

Sawan

Sawan, several km further inland, is the centre in the north of Bali for the manufacture of gamelan gongs and complete gamelan instruments. You can see the gongs being cast and the intricately carved gamelan frames being made. It's very much a local cottage industry and they don't get many visitors so they're usually pleased to see you and show you around.

Kubutambahan

Only a km or so beyond the Kintamani turn-off at Kubutambahan, is the Pura Maduwe Karang temple, beside the coast side of the road. Like Pura Beji at Sangsit it's dedicated to agricultural spirits, but this one looks after unirrigated land. The temple is usually kept locked but ask in the shop opposite, they'll have the key.

This is one of the best temples in the north and particularly noted for its sculptured panels, including the famous bicycle panel with a gentleman riding a bicycle with flower petals for wheels. It's on the base of the main plinth in the inner enclosure but there are other panels worth

The famous bicycle panel from the Pura Maduwe Karang Temple

inspecting in this peaceful and pleasant temple.

YEH SANIH

Only about 15 km east of Singaraja this is a popular local spot where freshwater springs are channelled into a very pleasant swimming pool before flowing into the sea. It's right by the sea and the small centre is very attractively laid out with pleasant gardens, a restaurant and a couple of places to stay. It's well worth a visit and admission to the springs and pool is 150 rp (children 100 rp). On the hill overlooking the springs is the Pura Taman Manik Mas temple.

Places to Stay & Eat

There are a couple of places to stay right by the springs. In fact the *Bungalow Puri Sanih* is actually in the springs complex. It's got a very pretty garden and doubles at 8000, 10,000 and 15,000 rp – the most expensive rooms are little two-storey bungalows. Just beyond the springs is the *Yeh Sanih Seaside Cottages* with very pleasant rooms at 20,000/25,000 rp.

The Puri Sanih also has a restaurant looking out over the springs and the gardens. There are a number of warungs across the road from the springs.

YEH SANIH TO AMLAPURA

Beyond Yeh Sanih the road runs close to the north-east coast, although rarely right beside it, to Culik where it turns inland towards the south-east coast. It climbs over a small range of hills then drops down to Tirtagangga and Amlapura. This used to be a rough route but with improvements it's now no problem at all. There are a number of villages along the way but this part of Bali is relatively dry and you see none of the usual rice paddies until just before Tirtagangga – and there you'll see some of the most spectacular rice terraces in Bali. Not far beyond Yeh Sanih you can turn inland to the interesting village of Sembiran; a little further on at Tejakula

there's a famous horse bath; and there's a good beach near Culik.

The main feature of this route is the superb view of Gunung Agung. Along this coast Bali's mightiest mountain descends right down to the sea and its slopes beckon enticingly to climbers. The road crosses a great number of dry riverbeds, most of them too wide to be easily bridged and, in the dry season at least, showing no sign of water. They're probably similar to many rivers in Australia, running briefly during the heavy rains of the wet season but remaining dry for the rest of the year.

Tulamben

The American ship SS *Liberty*, sunk by the Japanese in 1942, lies just off the beach at Tulamben. You can snorkel over it, only 50 metres off-shore. The beach here is pebbles rather than sand but the water is clear and the snorkelling good. In June and July there's good windsurfing. The recently constructed losmen makes this an interesting place to pause on your way around the east coast. It's a long way from anywhere on this barren coast.

Places to Stay & Eat

Until recently there was no place to stay anywhere along the east coast from Yeh Sanih until you reached Tirtagangga. Now there's the *Paradise Palm Beach Cottages* at Tulamben and Bali being Bali more places will no doubt spring up along the coast. Rooms in this cheerful little losmen right on the beach cost 10,000/15,000 rp with breakfast. There's electricity at night.

Nusa Penida

Clearly visible from Sanur, Padangbai, Candidasa or anywhere else along the south-east coast the rocky island of Nusa Penida is beginning to attract increasing numbers of visitors for its seclusion, surf and snorkelling. The island has a

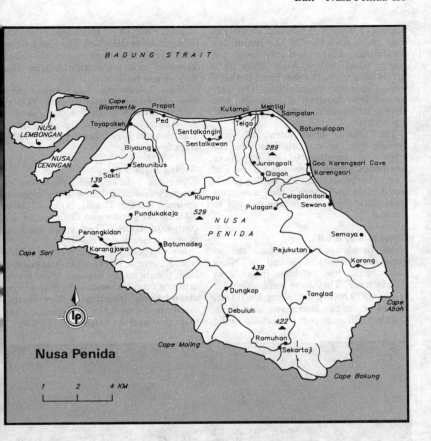

Nusa Penida

population of around 40,000 and was once used as a place of banishment for criminals and other undesirables from the Kingdom of Klungkung. It's still part of the regency of Klungkung. Nusa Penida is also the legendary home of the demon Jero Gede Macaling who inspired the Barong Landung dance.

The island has some interesting temples including Pura Ped near Toyapakeh and Pura Batukuning near Sewana. There is also a huge limestone cave, Goa Karangsari, about a km from Sewana. The mountain village of Tanglad in the south-east with

its throne for the sun-god Surya is also interesting. Salak, a village on the south coast, is spectacularly situated on a cliff top high above the sea.

Rice terraces on the island are all faced with stone and at some villages a unique ikat cloth is woven. When making an animal offering to propitiate evil spirits a certain type of chicken raised on the island is supposed to be particularly efficacious. Nusa Penida is also the sole home for Rothchild's Mynah, one of the world's rarest birds.

On some approaches to Denpasar

airport or from Bali-Lombok flights you may get a good view of the island. It's surprisingly hilly, especially along the south coast where high cliffs falls precipitously into the sea. From the air it looks completely uninhabited. The ferry to and from Lombok also passes quite close to it but you'd need binoculars to get a good look.

The tourist development at Nusa Penida has, so far, all been on the adjoining smaller island of Nusa Lembongan where there are a variety of losmen to choose from. The surfing here is world class and there's also some fine snorkelling. Prahus will take you out to the reef.

Places to Stay & Eat

Nusa Lembongan Bungalows are at Jungutbatu on the island of Nusa Lembongan, just offshore from Nusa Penida itself. They have singles/doubles at 15,000/19,500 rp including breakfast. You can book the bungalows from Kuta and they will arrange transport out to the island. *Wayan's Restaurant* at the Bungalows is definitely *the* place to eat with excellent food at reasonable prices, however the popularity means that service can be slow.

Nusa Lembongan has various other cheaper losmen from around 3000 rp including the *Mainski Inn*, but *Johnny's Losmen* on the left end of the beach, one of the pioneers here, seems to have fallen from favour.

Getting There & Away

There are twin-engined prahus out to Nusa Penida from Sanur every morning around 7 to 9 am. The fare is about 7000 to 8000 rp per person and the trip takes a couple of hours. They come back at various times during the day.

It's also possible to reach Nusa Penida from Kusamba, on the south-east coast of Bali. Boats make regular trips across bringing supplies because the island is dry and relatively uncultivated. The crossing takes about two hours. Sampalan is the main port and the usual arrival point.

Sumatra

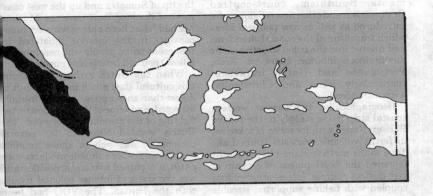

Indonesia's 'new frontier', Sumatra has an extraordinary wealth of natural resources, people and cultures. Compared to Java it is relatively under populated and underdeveloped, but during Dutch rule this island provided the world with an enormous quantity of everything from oil and rubber to pepper and coffee. With its seemingly inexhaustible resources Sumatra continues to prop up the Indonesian economy today. Its oil wells and rubber plantations are set against a background of peoples which could drive an ethnologist delirious. These range from former Batak head-hunters and cannibals, to the matrilineal Muslim Minangkabau and to the almost-fundamentalist Islamic Acehnese. The diversity of cultures on this island may well be unmatched in the archipelago.

That's not the only attraction. There is also wild jungle country in the south, the peculiar architecture of the Minangkabau and Batak people, orang-utan and elusive Sumatran tigers lurking in the forests, massive rivers like muddy facsimiles of the Amazon, perfect cone-shaped volcanoes, and the Bukit Barisan or

'marching mountains', which do just that right down to the west coast.

HISTORY

The reasons for the remarkable diversity of cultures on Sumatra and its outlying islands are numerous, but certainly the geography and the way this has influenced contacts between its inhabitants as well as those with foreigners has been of great importance. Sumatra's northern tip faces the west, while much of the island's eastern shore borders the Straits of Melaka – a natural gateway to the South China Sea through which shipping makes its way from India to Java and China.

Trade, controlled initially by Hindu merchants, favoured the development of coastal Hindu city-states. The kingdom of Srivijaya which arose in the second half of the 7th century with its capital on or near the site of modern day Palembang was the most famous, and one of the most important in South-East Asia. Unlike the more insular Javanese kingdoms of the time, Srivijaya always looked outwards towards the sea and trading routes, but since it built no huge monuments like

427

Prambanan or Borobudur, there are few traces left of its existence today.

With foreign trade came other developments. Buddhism, court-centred Brahmanism and other new religions were introduced as well as new political ideas which transformed the coastal chiefdoms and filtered into the tribal societies of the mountainous interior. Later on, Arab, Portuguese and Dutch influences (particularly Islam and Christianity) were introduced.

Geographically, the narrow western coastal strip rising steeply to the rugged Barisan Range with its series of lakes set in fertile volcanic plateaus (from Lake Toba in the north to Ranau in the south) favoured the development of a chain of very distinct cultures. Intensive agriculture coupled with fishing supported sizeable groups of tribal people strong enough to resist conversion to cultural ideas coming up from the lowlands. The outlying islands of Nias, Mentawei, and Enggano also resisted foreign culture until quite recent times because of their remote location.

Srivijaya's control of the Melaka straits continued for seven centuries before it was ended by a Javanese Majapahit attack in 1377. It is said that a Srivijaya prince, Parameswara, fled to the Malay Peninsula, made his way to a tiny port-settlement called Melaka and proceeded to develop it into a major international port, shifting the centre of power in the region from Sumatra to the Malay Peninsula.

About the same time, but for obscure reasons, Islam became an important force in Sumatra. Islamic communities are known to have existed in northern Sumatra since at least the 13th century (Marco Polo mentions finding Muslims here when he visited Sumatra in 1292 on his way home from China) and after the decline of Srivijaya many Islamic trading kingdoms operated on Sumatra, although none enjoyed the wide-reaching power that Srivijaya had possessed. By the early 16th century, most of the kings of the

Sumatran coastal states from Aceh at the far north to Palembang in the south were Muslim. South of Palembang and around the tip of Sumatra and up the west coast most of the kingdoms were not Muslim nor had Islam been able to win very many converts in the interior inhabited by numerous tribal people who continued to follow their old beliefs and customs.

When the Dutch arrived they found this cultural stew much more difficult to digest than they appear to have initially expected, and some of the most protracted fighting of the colonial era followed. The Dutch wanted Sumatra for several reasons: it was rich in spices (mainly pepper) and other valuable products such as tin, it occupied a strategic position and was the scene of intense colonial rivalry with the British. The VOC had been active for a long time in Sumatra, but after its demise and the short period of British rule in Indonesia during the Napoleonic Wars, the Dutch had to rebuild their influence virtually from nothing.

Palembang suffered its first attack from the Dutch in 1818, but was not finally subdued until 1849. Dutch involvement with Jambi began anew in 1833 but it was not until 1907 that guerrilla resistance in the interior was stifled. In the west coast Minangkabau districts, Dutch expansionism clashed head on with the first major Islamic revival movement of Indonesia – known as the 'Padri' movement because its leaders had made their pilgrimage to Mecca via the Acehnese port of Pedir. A civil war erupted between the Islamic reformists and the supporters of traditional or *adat* law. Sensing the opportunity, the Dutch backed the latter entering the 'Padri Wars' in 1821, but it was not until 1838 that they subdued all the Minangkabau territories.

To establish their authority over the island of Nias the Dutch needed three military expeditions – in 1847, 1855 and 1863. A treaty with the British in 1824 resulted in those interlopers clearing out

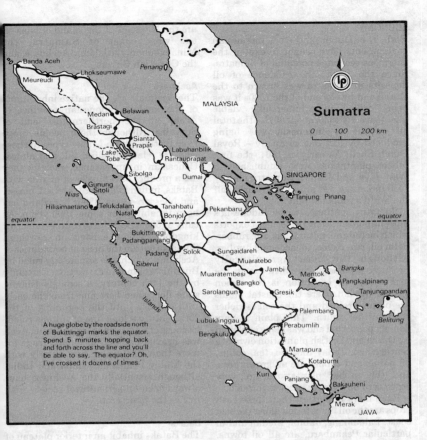

A huge globe by the roadside north of Bukittinggi marks the equator. Spend 5 minutes hopping back and forth across the line and you'll be able to say, 'The equator? Oh, I've crossed it dozens of times.'

of their settlement at Bengkulu in return for the Dutch leaving Melaka and their settlements in India. Treaties and alliances brought other areas of Sumatra under Dutch rule, and a war with the Bataks in 1872 ended in victory for the Dutch, although the Batak resistance was not wiped out until 1895.

The war with the Acehnese, however, was the bloodiest in Sumatra and probably in the whole archipelago. The last of the Acehnese sultans, Tuanku Muhamat Dawot, surrendered to the Dutch in 1903 after a war of more than 30 years – yet even then unrest continued and the Dutch were forced to keep a military government in the area until 1918. It is certainly significant that the Dutch did not try to return to Aceh after WW II. From 1945 until Indonesian independence was gained in 1949, Aceh was ruled chiefly by Daud Beureueh, the leader of an Islamic modernist movement. The region was in rebellion from 1953 until 1961 when it became a province of Indonesia. Even today it retains a sort of semi-autonomous status within the republic.

ECONOMY

Both the Dutch and the Indonesian governments have sought to exploit the enormous economic potential of Sumatra. Since the 1860s, the existence of oil deposits in Sumatra was known to the Dutch and by the end of the 1880s it was being drilled in commercially viable quantities. By 1930, about 85% of the total oil output of Indonesia was being produced by just one company – Royal Dutch Shell. As early as 1864, the first rubber plantations were established in West Java and eastern Sumatra and by 1930 Indonesia was producing nearly half the world's rubber supply.

Sumatra continues to be Indonesia's most important island in terms of exports which include oil, natural gas, tin, rubber, palm oil, tea, coffee, tobacco and lumber. Although the most agriculturally productive areas of Sumatra are in the highlands, one exception is the region around Medan. Here the coastal plains are better drained and the soil is richer than further south. This plain is very densely populated and was being exploited by Dutch and British plantation owners a century ago. Today tobacco, tea, coffee, oil palms and rubber are all grown here, and the rubber plantations are very obvious to any visitor passing through.

Even more important than these cash crops are the oil fields found along the east coast. Palembang, Jambi, Medan and in particular Pekanbaru, are all oil towns. Indonesia is still a major oil exporter and three-quarters of its oil production comes from this region of Sumatra.

PEOPLE

Sumatra is the second most populous island of the archipelago, although its population density is minuscule compared to that of Bali or Java. It's also a major target of the transmigration programme. The 30 million people of the island are some of the most fascinating in the archipelago and can be divided into about 10 major groups of which the best known are the Niassans of the island of Nias off the west coast of Sumatra, the Minangkabau, the Islamic Acehnese, and the Christian Bataks.

Acehnese

The Acehnese are the native inhabitants of the modern Indonesian province of Aceh, at the northernmost end of Sumatra. Although these people range from distinct proto-Malay types to those who are relatively slim, tall and almost Caucasian in appearance, racially they are a product of centuries of mixing with Bataks, Indians, Javanese, Arabs, Chinese, and Niassan slaves. Their homeland has been inhabited for some 1500 years. As early as 500 AD, Chinese sources refer to a kingdom which existed in northern Sumatra within the present boundaries of Aceh, but which was apparently ruled by Buddhists of Indian extraction. Certainly by the 14th century, a strongly Islamic state flourished here and from the early 16th century until the beginning of the 20th century a long line of sultans ruled. Because of its geographical position, Aceh was heavily engaged in foreign trade for more than 1000 years, particularly with the Malay Peninsula, China and India, although essentially the Acehnese have always been an agricultural society with rice as the main crop.

Bataks

The Bataks inhabit an interior plateau of north-central Sumatra, surrounded by mountain peaks and centred on Lake Toba. There is cultural, linguistic and physical evidence of early Hindu contact (such as their Indian-derived script, either incised on bamboo or written on bark leaves and bound in book form). In the past century there has been widespread conversion to Christianity as well as substantial conversion to Islam.

Despite these influences and being surrounded on all sides by Islamic peoples, the Batak lived a way of life which developed largely in isolation.

Their bloody feuds and guerrilla attacks on each other's villages gained them an apparently well-earned reputation for ferocity. They also practised ritual cannibalism in which a token piece of flesh – of a slain enemy or of one judged guilty of a major violation of adat – was eaten. The heads and hands of war captives were sometimes preserved as trophies.

According to Batak tradition, all Bataks are descendants of Si Radja Batak, a hero-ancestor of supernatural parentage born on a holy mountain next to Lake Toba. Through him the Batak received their sacred adat laws. A long period of relative isolation was ended in the 19th century, first by the spread of Islam from the Minangkabau in the north and later, beginning about 1860, by the rapid spread of Protestant Christianity through the efforts of missionaries. Western education furthered by missionaries and by the Dutch colonial government gained ground rapidly, particularly amongst the Toba Bataks (those living around Lake Toba).

Minangkabau

The Minangkabau are Muslims whose traditional homeland is the highlands of west-central Sumatra from where they have spread out into all of western Sumatra and parts of other Sumatran provinces. They are also called *Orang Padang* (Padang people) after their provincial capital. Not much is known about the Minangkabau before the arrival of the Dutch, although archaeological remains of human settlement in the area date at least as far back as the 12th century. Portuguese records suggest there was a lively trade between western Sumatra and Melaka, and that the Minangkabau were bringing pepper to both eastern and western Sumatran ports as early as the beginning of the 17th century. Acehnese suzerainty in the early 17th century led to increased Islamic influence which culminated in the Padri

War of 1803 to 1837. That resulted in the entry of the Dutch into the highlands in support of the adat rulers. Dutch forts in time became towns and many Minangkabaus came to live urban lives and develop as an educated class of Indonesians. Many were active in the Indonesian independence movement – Mohammad Hatta, vice-president under Sukarno for a time, was the most famous of these.

Niassans

The Niassans, the native people of the large island of Nias off the west coast of Sumatra, have long captured the imagination of ethnologists and anthropologists with their monumental use of stone and wood, and their complex social and religious organisation. The importance of head-hunting and human sacrifice in days gone by, as well as their physical features, suggest a mixed descent with some relationship to the Bataks of Sumatra, the Naga people of the Indian province Assam, and even the aboriginal people of Taiwan.

Other Peoples

Along the east coast and particularly in the scattered islands of the Riau Archipelago are the nomadic *Orang Laut* (sea people or sea gypsies). Also seafarers, but more settled, are the coastal Malays who gave their name to the common language of modern Malaysia and Indonesia.

GEOGRAPHY

Stretching nearly 2000 km from end to end, Sumatra is one of the largest islands in the world. For most of its length the Bukit Barisan form a backbone down the island, dropping steeply to the sea on the west coast but sloping gently down on the east. This eastern region is a low-lying swampland, much of it bordering on the shallow Straits of Melaka and comprising a third of the island. It's poorly drained (much of it covered in mangrove swamps) and traversed by wide, meandering rivers.

The river towns of the eastern side of the island include Jambi and Pekanbaru, but the main population is concentrated along the highlands closer to the mountains and towards the west side of the island. Many of the peaks are around 2500 metres high but some are over 3000 metres. The mountains include nearly 100 volcanoes, 15 of them still active.

Off the west coast are a string of islands geologically older than the rest of Sumatra. They are isolated not only geographically but also culturally as the people living here have developed quite separately from those on Sumatra and still follow some ancient customs.

Large areas of the Sumatran rainforest have been cleared for agricultural use, but great stretches of jungle remain, where orang-utan and elephants can still be seen. One place where orang-utan may be found is the Bukit Lawang sanctuary in northern Sumatra. Almost as famous as the orang-utans is Sumatra's amazing flower, the *Rafflesia*, named after Sir Stamford Raffles, founder of Singapore, who was also a noted botanist. The Rafflesia has orange petals spreading up to a metre in diameter.

GETTING THERE

You can approach Sumatra from a number of directions and by a number of means. The most conventional route is to fly from Penang to Medan (or take the ship from Penang to Belawan, the port of Medan), travel through the island on the buses, then either take the ship from Padang to Jakarta or continue right down through Palembang to Panjang and take the ferry across from Panjang to Merak in Java.

There are also regular flights to Medan from Kuala Lumpur. Another easy way of getting there is to fly from Singapore to Medan or Pekanbaru.

A more unusual approach is to travel by boat from Singapore to Batam where you clear customs, and from there to Tanjung Pinang. From Tanjung Pinang, boats depart daily for Pekanbaru.

There are also flights from Batam and Tanjung Pinang to cities in mainland Sumatra including Medan, Pekanbaru and Palembang.

From Malaysia

Air MAS (Malaysian Air Service) has a daily flight from Penang to Medan. This is a popular way for visitors approaching Indonesia from the northern hemisphere to enter Sumatra. As many of Sumatra's attractions are easily accessible from Medan, it's an easy and logical starting point. (The fare from Penang to Medan is US$48.) This is also a popular exit point and a relatively cheap way of satisfying the 'ticket out' requirement of Indonesian visas. Garuda and MAS have daily flights from Kuala Lumpur to Medan for US$72.

Rafflesia – its petals spread up to a metre in diameter making it the world's largest parasitic bloom

There is also an irregular charter service between Pekanbaru and Melaka.

Boat from Penang The ferry *Gadis Langkasuka* operates between Penang and the Medan port of Belawan. It operates about two times a week and takes 15 hours. The one-way fare is M$45, and M$55 for an air-con sleeping berth in a two or four bed cabin. This price includes M$5 (about 3500 rp) for a tourist bus from Belawan to Medan, although there are cheaper public buses between these places. These cost 250 rp plus 150 rp port entrance charge, but coming from Malaysia you are charged M$5 with no option to decline which caused some complaints.

From Belawan the fare is about 38,000 rp for a seat, including administrative charges, port fees, insurance, etc. A sleeping berth is about 49,000 rp. The tourist bus from Medan to Belawan is an extra 2000 rp, although cheaper local buses are available.

In Medan the ticket office for the ferry is PT Eka Sukma Wista Tour & Travel Service at Jalan Brigadir Jenderal Katamso 62A, near the Maimoon Palace. In Penang the operator is Sanren Delta Marine (tel 04-379833) and their office is right beside the tourist office on Jalan Tun Syed Sheh Barakbah.

Boat from Melaka & Kuala Lumpur There's also a twice weekly ferry from Melaka to Dumai. From Dumai you can take a bus to Pekanbaru and Bukittinggi. The ferry crossing takes just two hours and the fare is M$70. Unfortunately, Dumai is not a recognised 'no visa' entry or exit point to Indonesia, although some visitors have managed to leave this way without a proper visa. Coming in, however, you must have an Indonesian visa. There are occasional ships between Port Kelang, the port of Kuala Lumpur, and Dumai.

From Singapore

Air Garuda has a number of flights from Singapore to several cities in Sumatra. These include daily flights to Medan, Padang, and Palembang, and four days a week to Pekanbaru.

Pekanbaru itself is not much of a draw card, but Bukittinggi, one of Sumatra's most appealing hill towns, is easily accessible from Pekanbaru and the bus trip between the two is quite beautiful.

Boat There are regular hydrofoils between Singapore to the islands of Batam and Bintan in the Riau Archipelago, just off mainland Sumatra. From Tanjung Pinang, the chief centre on Bintan Island, you can catch a ferry to Pekanbaru.

Hydrofoils to Batam and Bintan islands depart from Singapore's Finger Pier (tel 3360528) on Prince Edward Rd. They pause at Sekupang on Batam Island, where you clear customs. The fare from Singapore to Batam is S$20. The fare from Singapore to Tanjung Pinang is S$46 via Sekupang, and S$65 direct. Singapore to Sekupang takes half an hour, and after clearing customs it's another two hours from there to Tanjung Pinang.

You can, if you like, disembark at Sekupang on Batam Island. From there you take a bus (500 rp) or taxi to Nagoya, the main centre. From Nagoya there are taxis to Kabil (2000), where regular ferries (1700 rp) depart all through the day for Tanjung Uban on the west coast of Bintan Island. From Tanjung Uban there are regular buses and taxis to Tanjung Pinang.

From Tanjung Pinang There are usually two or three ferries a week from Tanjung Pinang to Pekanbaru. The trip takes at least 36 hours – but that's being optimistic – a far more realistic estimate is somewhere between 40 and 50 hours. Fares start from 12,500 rp.

The ferries are typical Indonesian boats with cramped conditions and abysmal food, but it's a great journey upriver. It's a good idea to take food and drink with you since two meals of boiled rice garnished with a bit of dry salted fish and a dollop of chilli sauce washed down with lukewarm, brackish water is all your ticket includes. All is not lost if you forget or don't have the time to stock up because the boat stops at various river villages along the way and flotillas of salespeople circle around hawking soft drinks, peanuts and fruit.

Travel in Sumatra can often be a memorable experience, and far more amusing in retrospect than it is at the time. The ferry ride between Pekanbaru and Tanjung Pinang is a bit like the novel *Heart of Darkness*. If you've seen the movie *Apocalypse Now* and recall the journey upriver in search of Kurtz you'll have a good idea of what it's like – but at least no one's shooting at you. The trip takes you across the Straits of Melaka, through a vast malarial swamp via the wide, brown and greasy Siak River lined with grotesquely twisted mangroves past small villages and logging camps, lit by fireflies and kerosene lamps.

There are a few things you should know about the boat. Firstly, a 'cabin' does not constitute a private room with a lockable door and a bed. It's a wooden platform constructed on stilts about a metre from the deck. Each cabin is indicated by a number at one end and is separated from the next by painted lines on either side, or perhaps low wooden dividers. However, if you get a cabin you should consider yourself lucky as the rest of the passengers have to squeeze themselves into a foetal position to find enough space on the deck to sleep. With a bit of nimble footwork, you can avoid stepping on bunches of bananas, bags of pineapples, packets of nuts, baskets of beans or other fruit and vegetables that are festooned along the top of the boat, or on a prone body.

The din of the boat's engine is deafening but it seems like the hush of a monastery once the music begins - your ears will take days to adjust. To add to the discomfort, they seem to have a very limited selection of tapes to play. But whatever the decibel level and however dubious their taste in music, at 5 o'clock the faithful – usually women – turn to Mecca and chant their prayers.

The two toilets at the prow of the boat are occupied for the entire trip so you must be prepared to spend hours balanced precariously with legs crossed waiting your turn. Though cramped and grotty, they're not as sordid as many toilets you'll be forced to use in Sumatra as their design is a simple, but effective, hole in the planks and you can see straight down to the river below. Watch where you put your feet as some people's aim is well off the mark.

The musky smell of clove cigarettes eventually becomes heavy and cloying and when it rains it will be your turn to pray. Pray that the wooden shutters or canvas blinds, the main protection from the elements, have not rotted away entirely and that they can be yanked across or let down. Otherwise you can add sodden bedding to your discomfort. Lastly, you will have to accept that you are likely to be the only westerner on board and will be harried with the usual 'What is your name? Where are you from? Where are you going? Can I practise my English?' questions until you are heartily sick of it.

There are also other ways of reaching mainland Sumatra from the Riau Islands. Garuda have a number of flights from Batu Besar (on Batam Island) including daily flights to Pekanbaru. Merpati and two small airlines called SMAC and Sempati have flights from Tanjung Pinang to various destinations, including Pekanbaru. For more details see the Riau Archipelago section in this book.

From Java
Air Garuda has flights from Jakarta to all sorts of places in Sumatra including Banda Aceh (daily 210,000 rp), Bengkulu (daily 76,000 rp), Jambi (twice daily), Medan (four times daily 160,000 rp), Padang (three times daily 115,000 rp), Palembang and Pekanbaru (twice daily 210,000 rp).

Pelni Ships Pelni has four ships which operate between Jakarta and various ports in Sumatra, each on a regular two-weekly schedule. For more details of ships and routes see the Getting Around chapter.

The most popular ship with foreigners is Pelni's *KM Kerinci* which runs between Sibolga, Padang and Tanjung Priok, the port of Jakarta. The *Kerinci* is modern with air-con, hot-water showers and variety of accommodation to choose from. It departs from Jakarta on alternate Fridays at 1 pm and arrives at Padang the following day at 4 pm. Pelni's *KM Kambuna* and *KM Rinjani* also operate between Sumatra and Java.

Merak to Panjang Ferry Ferries shuttle between Merak at the western end of Java and Panjang at the eastern end of Sumatra. In Merak, the ferries depart from the dock near the train station. The trip costs from 1500 to 5000 rp and takes about six hours, but if you catch the night boat it may take longer since these often wait until daybreak before docking.

In Panjang, on the Sumatran side, there are two ferry terminals. The railway ferry is in town, while the car ferry docks at Strengsen, about five km east. You can get to Merak from Jakarta by train or bus. Buses depart frequently (about every 10 minutes) from the Grogol Bus Station, and take 3½ hours. Trains leave from Tanah Abang train station. The morning train is faster and connects with the daytime ferry service. Ferries to Bakauheni, the easternmost tip of Sumatra, depart hourly from the dock near the bus station in Merak. The crossing takes 1½ hours.

GETTING AROUND

To explore Sumatra for the first time and see some of its out-of-the-way attractions you need three things: time (all of the two-month visa), the patience of Job, and the endurance of a marathon runner. If you really want to get off the beaten track you could easily outstay your Indonesian welcome. If you take the well worn travellers trail – Medan, Brastagi, Bukit Lawang, Prapat, Lake Toba, Nias Island, Bukittinggi, Padang and then on to Java – you need about a month to do it quickly and more time to have a reasonably decent look around.

To get some satisfaction from travelling in Sumatra, it's worth taking time out to

think about what you're hoping to do or see. If you're more interested in the culture, history or people of the region then you've got problems.

If you don't speak Indonesian then huge areas of Sumatra will effectively be closed to you. If you fall into the tourist trench, you tend to end up spending most of your time with other westerners and your trip will be self-defeating. Often your impressions of the island and people will be filtered through touts or other people who attach themselves to the tourist trade.

These problems are not so different from some other parts of Indonesia, but they seem to be much more acute in Sumatra. This is probably because of the sheer number of westerners travelling along a fairly defined trail. The northern part of the island is no longer the adventure it has often been made out to be.

Climatic Considerations

Sumatra is a large island – 1760 km long, around 450 km at its widest point, 288,000 square km in area – and you can get around by bus, aircraft and ferry in some of the more isolated areas. Apart from distance it's also important to take weather into account. The equator splits Sumatra into neat halves and the monsoons in the north and south occur at different times of the year. North of the equator the wet season starts in October and can go through to April and the dry season lasts from May until September. In the south the rains start in October but the worst months are between December and February. As it's very difficult to get around Sumatra in the wet (it takes a lot longer and occasionally transport stops functioning altogether) you should aim to visit during the dry season, sometime between May and September.

Air

Of course it's possible to fly around Sumatra and save a lot of time. Garuda fly to all the main centres. Merpati has

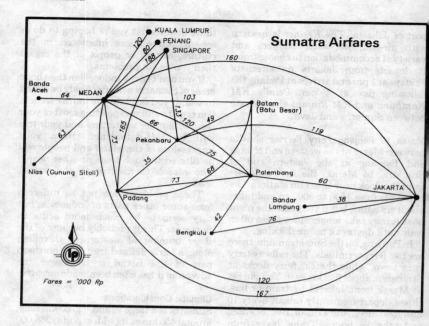

Sumatra Airfares

KUALA LUMPUR
PENANG
SINGAPORE

Banda Aceh

MEDAN

Nias (Gunung Sitoli)

Pekanbaru

Padang

Batam (Batu Besar)

Palembang

JAKARTA

Bandar Lampung

Bengkulu

120 80 188 160 64 103 63 165 73 66 133 120 49 119 35 75 73 68 60 42 38 76 120 167

Fares = '000 Rp

flights to out-of-the-way spots that Garuda doesn't offer. You should also check what Mandala has to offer since they often fly the same routes as Garuda and Merpati but on different days, at different times and for different prices. Since most of the interesting attractions are in northern Sumatra, many people skip the southern half and fly from Jakarta to Padang. For airfares around Sumatra and to adjacent areas, see the Airfare chart in this chapter.

Bus

The most popular and economical method of travel is by bus. Wherever you go in Sumatra, the roads take you through country full of contrasts and changing moods – exotic, lush, romantic, wild, poetic and ugly. Between Palembang and Padang the road (just a dirt track until a few years ago) cuts through magnificent jungle. At that time, when the road wasn't

completely impassable, passengers and driver spent most of the trip winching the bus out of wheel-high muddy bogs.

Things have looked up since the bad old days – or good old days – of the '60s and early '70s when enterprising visitors started coming to Sumatra. Today the bridges destroyed during the Sumatran rebellion of 1958 have been rebuilt, most of the roads are sealed and the Trans-Sumatran Highway has made a huge improvement to speed and pleasure. Even the southern stretch from Panjang to Padang is now a fine road. Minibuses and modern Mercedes buses have been introduced, although it's unlikely that Mercedes ever imagined their vehicles could contain so many seats!

Like on the Sumatran buses of days gone by, the seats are still hard and far too small for average-sized westerners. The drivers are still madmen sustained and kept awake by prodigious quantities of fiery Padang food. Rivers are still muddy, wide, and winding, and too many bridges still get washed away. You can still get stranded for hours or even days on end in the middle of nowhere if you travel during heavy rains. The accounts that follow may give you some glimmer of what sort of things to expect riding on Sumatra's buses.

I must say I've been astounded by the ease of my bus travel through Sumatra. . .The buses are not particularly comfortable but nowhere near as bad as the bemos and colts elsewhere in Indonesia – and it's always been possible to pay extra for an air-conditioned bus with fairly comfortable seats on longer journeys. . .Having said that, I must confess to spending one of the most uncomfortable nights of my life on the bus from Bukittingi to Prapat, but only because I got lumbered with a seat right at the back. The back seats were only half the width and depth of all the others, and to matters worse there was a step in front of my seat which wasn't as wide as my feet are long. In front of that was a wooden bench. . .which left barely enough space for an Indonesian to sit in comfort, let alone someone with my exceptionally long legs! I was feeling distinctly queasy from being flung about as we went tearing around the mountain bends, and I had the added pleasure of being sandwiched between a woman vomiting into a bag on my left, and a fat sleazy Indonesian man with wandering hands on my right! On the bright side, the journey took only 11½ hours. . .against a scheduled time of 13 hours and the local's scathing estimate of 20 hours.

Another bus trip, this time from Jakarta to Bukittingi also had its pros and cons:

The scheduled journey time (from Jakarta to Bukittingi) was 36 hours but it actually took only 32 hours. The journey was certainly comfortable, but what a farce! The driver decided to switch the lights on just as everyone had dozed off, then shortly after the lights were off again we had music blaring out full blast. That went on all night – music and lights alternately – and finished with a grand finale of 90 minutes of mosque music from 4.30 am until 6 am! Unbelievable!

Sure, travel is slow and arduous but you never have to get out and push, etc. But if you want to experience some hard travelling, do Tapaktuan to Sidikalang. . .Three river crossings, mile after mile of pot-holed unsurfaced road, virgin jungle, little villages – it's wild and remote. Eleven hours for 230 km.

The truth is, that often you do have to get out and push. However, on the whole, if you travel in the dry season and confine yourself to the main tourist route in the north, then you won't have these problems. Outside these areas, you should not expect to be able to cover the entire island by bus if you're pressed for time. Avoid seats at the rear where the bouncing is multiplied. The following will give you an idea of what particular sections of roads are like in Sumatra:

Java to Palembang You can take a bus straight from Jakarta to Palembang (17,000 rp), Jambi (19,000 rp) or Padang (20,000 rp) crossing the Sunda Straits between Java and Sumatra by ferry. Jakarta to Palembang takes about 20 hours by bus and there are frequent departures. ANS is probably the best of the various Sumatran bus companies.

An alternative to the bus is the train, which involves the longer ferry crossing from Merak to Panjang. Coming from Panjang by train you can take a break by getting off at Parembulih. Parembulih is between Panjang and Palembang, where the line branches off to Lubuklinggau. The train carries on to Palembang, two hours away, then turns around and comes back to Parembulih before continuing on to Lubuklinggau. From Lubuklinggau you can continue by bus to Bengkulu (where there are sometimes ships to Padang) or Padang.

Palembang to Padang The trip from Palembang to Padang takes about 24 hours if the going is easy. It takes *jam karet* or rubber time during the wet season. Fares are around 15,000 rp or

17,500 rp with air-con. The section of road between Padang and Lubuklinggau (at the end of the railway line northwards) runs along the eastern side of the mountains and is now one of the best and most scenic in Sumatra.

Bengkulu to Lubuklinggau The Bengkulu to Lubuklinggau road is fairly good but slow going. It's surfaced but has some potholes.

Padang/Bukittingi to Prapat Most people make one or more stops on this sector, either at Bukittinggi and/or Sibolga. The roads are paved and travel is now much more reliable than it was several years ago. It can still be difficult in the wet season if bridges or sections of the road get washed out. From Bukittinggi to Prapat there is a special tourist minibus which makes the trip in from 12 to 13 hours.

Padang to Bukittinggi The road between Padang and Bukittinggi is excellent and travelling this scenic sector is no trouble at all.

Prapat to Medan Buses between Prapat, which is the departure point for Samosir Island and Lake Toba, and Medan operate very frequently and take about four hours. Buses also operate frequently between Medan and Brastagi and take two hours. The trip on from Brastagi to Prapat involves changes at Kabanjahe and Pematang Siantar, and usually takes all day.

Medan to Banda Aceh The Medan to Banda Aceh road is a good, surfaced road. The bus trip takes about 14 hours, mainly because of prolonged stops along the way. There are frequent departures in either direction.

Rail
The only regular train service in Sumatra is between Panjang and Palembang in the south. The old steam trains between

Padang and Bukittinggi no longer operate.

Boat
Sumatra's rivers are also major transport highways which team with a motley but colourful collection of multifarious, multi-purpose vessels – rowing boats, rotten boats, speedboats, outriggers, ferries, junks and large cargo vessels. Boats are usually available for hire and will take you almost anywhere it's possible to go.

If you want a break from travelling by bus then catching a boat is a good way of seeing another side of Sumatra. There are also some places in Sumatra which you can't get to any other way – islands which don't have an airstrip, or river villages not connected by road.

Palembang and Jambi are important towns for river transport. There are also boats out to neighbouring islands. These include the ferries from Sibolga to Nias, from Padang to Siberut, from Banda Aceh to Pulau Weh, from Tanjung Pinang to Pekanbaru and those which link the islands of the Riau Archipelago. There is limited coastal shipping, like that between Padang and Bengkulu.

Local Transport
The usual Indonesian forms of transport

Samosir Ferry, Prapat

(bemos, becaks and dokars) are available for getting around towns and cities in Sumatra. The base rate for a bemo is still 100 rp and the minimum fare by becak is 200 rp. The more modern *ojeks* (motorcycle-becaks) cost 300 rp minimum; the three-wheel bicycle type is less. Dokars also have a minimum 300 rp fare.

Hang back and watch what the locals pay if you are not certain of the fare, can't understand what they are telling you or just don't want to be ripped off. Also ask other travellers the correct price.

Riau

Riau consists of four mainland districts – Kampar, Bengkalis, Upper Indragiri and Lower Indragiri – stretching along the eastern seaboard of Sumatra and its myriad islands. The main capital of this province rich with oil, tin and bauxite deposits is Pekanbaru, but the islands have their own capital at Tanjung Pinang. It was not until 1958, that Riau was separated from West Sumatra and became a province in its own right. Its history has all the right ingredients for a best-selling blockbuster: the high seas, pirates, violence, the conflict of nations, greed and romance.

Before air travel, the quickest route between India and China was through the Straits of Melaka which gave eastern Sumatra a strategic importance as well as subjecting it to diverse cultural influences. The first people known to have migrated to its shores were hunter-gatherers who arrived between 600 and 2000 BC and left hardly anything behind except their dead and piles of shells.

After the 16th century, Riau became the centre of the Malay civilisation which managed to cling on to it until the 18th century, despite constant attacks from pirates and the opportunistic Portuguese, Dutch and English. The Portuguese and Dutch struggled for control over the strait with the Dutch eventually gaining the upper hand.

Mainland Riau (then known as Siak) finally became a Dutch colony in 1745 when the Sultan of Johore surrendered his claim to the Dutch East India Company. The Dutch were more interested in ridding the seas of pirates so their fleet could trade without losses and danger than in governing or developing the region, and so they left Riau alone.

Only a small percentage of mainland Riau's rainforest has been cleared for oil development; most of the country is still covered in thick jungle and mangrove swamps. Several animistic and nomadic tribes, including the Sakai, Kubu and Jambisals, still live in the jungle, mostly around Dumai where the Pertamina refinery has been established.

PEKANBARU

Pekanbaru, the capital of the Riau Province, lies 160 km upstream on the Siak River. A sprawling city built with oil money, its sleazy port area contrasts sharply with the galaxy of public buildings at the other end of town. In fact, the further away from the port you go the better Pekanbaru gets. If you came in from the other end it's rather like arriving in a Sumatran version of Canberra or Brazilia. Yet, take two steps off the main street and you're almost back in the jungle again. For most visitors, Pekanbaru is really just a transit town on the way to or from Singapore via Tanjung Pinang and Batam.

Oil was discovered in this area by American engineers just before WW II, but it was the Japanese who drilled the first well at Rumbai. The main fields, not far from Pekanbaru, are connected by pipeline to refineries at Dumai because ocean-going tankers cannot enter the heavily silted Siak River.

Rumbai, just north of Pekanbaru, is the base for Caltex Pacific Indonesia, jointly owned by Standard Oil of California and

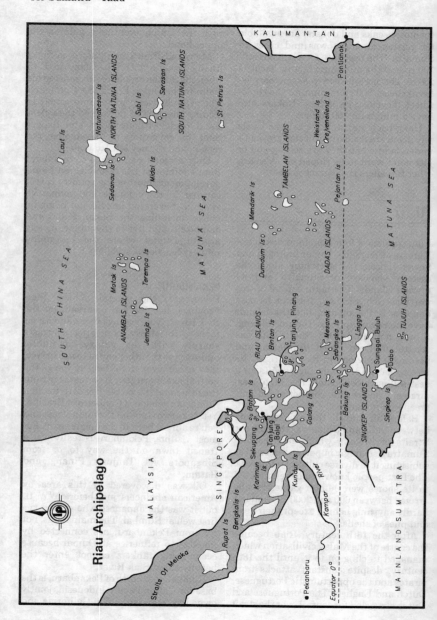

Riau Archipelago

Texaco. A resort-like complex with manicured lawns, it's a world away from downtown Pekanbaru. If you go to Rumbai, it's worth checking with the Caltex public relations office to see whether you can get hold of a visitor's pass which will allow you to use the club facilities.

Pekanbaru is surrounded by a wilderness of dense rainforest and mangrove swamps. The nearby jungle is crisscrossed by pipelines and dotted with oil wells. The creatures lurking in the jungle include the hairy Sumatran rhinoceros, tigers, bears, tapirs and elephants (the latter occasionally storm through villages). Some of these animals can be seen early in the morning along the roads.

Information

The main street of Pekanbaru is Jalan Jenderal Sudirman. Practically everything in the way of banks, hotels and offices is spread out along it or on adjoining streets. The port of Pekanbaru is on the Siak River, at the end of Jalan Saleh Abbas. The main bus station is at the other end of town on Jalan Nangka, and the airport is further out in the same direction.

Tourist Office There is no tourist office as such, but the local government department in the Governor's Office on Jalan Jenderal Sudirman is responsible for handling tourism in Riau Province.

Bank The Bank Negara Indonesia 1946 is at Jalan Jenderal Sudirman 119. The Bank Rakyat Indonesia is at Jalan Jenderal Sudirman 268. You cannot change money at the airport. The *Kirana* moneychanger at Jalan Cokroaminoto 17, near the corner with Jalan Jenderal Sudirman, will change US, Malay and Singapore cash, but will only change US dollar travellers' cheques.

Post & Telephone The telephone office is at Jalan Jenderal Sudirman 199. The telegram & telex office is at Jalan

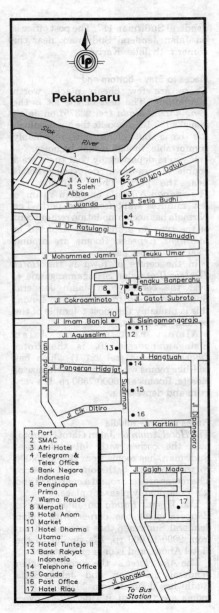

Pekanbaru

1 Port
2 SMAC
3 Afri Hotel
4 Telegram & Telex Office
5 Bank Negara Indonesia
6 Penginapan Prima
7 Wisma Rauda
8 Merpati
9 Hotel Anom
10 Market
11 Hotel Dharma Utama
12 Hotel Tunteja II
13 Bank Rakyat Indonesia
14 Telephone Office
15 Garuda
16 Post Office
17 Hotel Riau

Jenderal Sudirman 117. The post office is on Jalan Jenderal Sudirman, near the corner with Jalan Kartini.

Places to Stay – bottom end

There are few cheap places worth mentioning. The best of the lot is the *Penginapan Linda* (tel 22375) on Jalan Nangka 133-135, opposite the bus terminal. It's basic but clean and reasonably comfortable, though it may be noisy.

If you're departing by boat there are a couple of run-down, depressing hotels near the port. These include the *Penginapan Nirmala* on Jalan Yatim, a few minutes walk from the port. The Nirmala has accommodation reminiscent of the type so prominently depicted in *Midnight Express*. Rooms are around 2500/5000 rp per person.

In the centre of town is the *Hotel Tunteja II* at Jalan Sisingamangaraja 4, near the corner with Jalan Jenderal Sudirman. Apart from the Hotel Linda, this is probably the most tolerable of the bottom end hotels.

Almost next door, at Jalan Sisingamangaraja 10, is the *Hotel Dharma Utama* (tel 22171) which has cell-like rooms with bathrooms the size of closets. Rooms are 6000/7500 rp. It's very grim and depressing.

Places to Stay – middle

The *Hotel Anom* on Jalan Gatot Subroto, near the corner with Jalan Jenderal Sudirman, has rooms from 12,000/15,000 rp with private bathroom and air-con. The rooms are set around a courtyard and it's a reasonably pleasant place.

The *Wisma Rauda* on Jalan Tengku Banpera, near the corner with Jalan Jenderal Sudirman, has rooms with fan from 9000/12,000 rp. It's similar to the Hotel Anom, and is on a quiet street.

The *Afri Hotel* at the corner of Jalan Jenderal Sudirman and Jalan Setia Budhi has doubles from 20,000 rp. The rooms are OK but it's definitely over-

priced, and you may get a lot of street noise.

Places to Stay – top end

The *Riau Hotel* (tel 22986) at Jalan Diponegoro 26 has rooms from 18,000 rp. It's a fine, quiet hotel in the government area of town.

Places to Eat

There are innumerable cheap places to eat along Jalan Jenderal Sudirman, particularly in the evening around the market. For something different try the *France Modern Bakery* at Jalan Jenderal Sudirman 119, for a fine selection of cakes and pastries.

Getting There & Away

Air Garuda (tel 21026) is at Jalan Jenderal Sudirman 207. Merpati (tel 23558) is on Jalan Cokroaminoto, near the corner with Jalan Jenderal Sudirman. SMAC (tel 21421) is at Jalan Jenderal Sudirman 25.

Garuda has daily flights from Pekanbaru to Singapore, Batam, Medan and Jakarta. There are flights three or four days a week to Padang and Palembang. SMAC has flights four days a week from Pekanbaru to Tanjung Pinang.

The airport is 12 km from town. A taxi costs 7000 rp.

Bus Few people hang around in Pekanbaru. Most people take a boat to Tanjung Pinang the day they arrive or get a bus to Bukittinggi. There are daily buses to Bukittingi. The trip takes about six hours and the fare is 3000 rp.

Boat Buy tickets for the ferry to Tanjung Pinang from CV Effi (tel 25730) at Jalan Saleh Abbas 4, which leads to the entrance to the harbour. There are boats to Tanjung Pinang two or three days a week, and the trip takes two days and two nights. Fares range from 12,500 rp to 17,000 rp.

DUMAI

On the coast 158 km from Pekanbaru, Dumai is the port for the ferry service to Melaka in Malaysia. Dumai is strictly a one-street town and once you arrive the only thing to do is catch the ferry to Melaka or the bus to Pekanbaru.

RIAU ARCHIPELAGO

Scattered across the South China Sea like confetti are the islands of the Riau Archipelago. There are more than 3000 islands (many uninhabited) curving south-east from Sumatra to Kalimantan and north to Malaysia, dotted over 170,000 square km of sea.

They can be divided roughly into two groups: one bunched close to the coast of Sumatra, the second nearer to Singapore and the administrative district of Riau (Kabupaten Kepulauan Riau). The main islands in the first group consist of Bengkalis, Rupat, Padang, Tebingtinggi, Rangsang, Lalang, Mendol, Penyalai, Serapung, Muda, Kijang, Pucung and Katemun. The second can be broken down into seven sub-groups: the Karimun islands, the Riau islands (after which the archipelago is named) the Lingga-Singkep, the Tambelan, Anambas, North Natuna and South Natuna.

Tanjung Pinang on Bintan Island is the main centre in the archipelago. There are regular boats from Singapore. You can island hop through the archipelago, but it takes time.

History

The early history of the Riau Archipelago suggests a wave of migration from southern India. Around 1000 AD, Bintan Island emerged as a separate kingdom which was enlarged by a propitious marriage to the son of a king of Palembang. A capital was built in Temasik (now Singapore) and the principality was renamed Bintan Temasik Singapura. By 1500, the kingdom of Melaka had conquered the Riau islands of Kundur, Jemaja, Bunguran, Tambelan,

Lingga and Bintan. Later still, the archipelago came under the control of Raja Hang Tuah for whom a street in Tanjung Pinang is named.

The Portuguese held power in Riau for a brief period following their conquest of Melaka. From 1530 to the end of the 18th century, the archipelago was the pivot of Malay civilisation with the main centres at Penyenget and Lingga. In 1685, Sultan Mahmud Syah II was coerced into signing a cooperative agreement with the Dutch, which greatly diminished his authority. Throughout the next centuries, the Dutch gradually reduced the authority of the rajas. On the death of the raja in 1784, they assumed control of the archipelago.

Opposition to the Dutch did not really re-emerge until the early 1900s when the Rusydiah Club was formed by the last Sultan of Riau-Lingga. This was ostensibly a cultural and literary organisation, but later assisted in the struggle for Indonesian independence.

People

Most of the inhabitants of the islands are of pure Malay stock, but there are several indigenous groups like the Orang Laut of the Natuna islands, the Akit tribes of Bengkalis, the Mantang peoples of Penuba and Kelumu islands and the Baruk people of Sunggai Buluh, Singkep.

Bintan has the largest population of these islands, comprising various ethnic groups – Malay, Batak, Minangkabau and a comparatively large Chinese community. It is also physically the biggest of the Riau islands, being three times the area of neighbouring Singapore. The population is about 90% Islamic.

Architecture

The traditional architecture of the Riau islands is called Rumah Lipat Kijang, meaning hairpin, derived from the shape of the roof. The style is undergoing a revival at present and most new public buildings are being constructed in this manner.

Houses are usually adorned with carvings of flowers, birds and bees. Often there are wings on each corner, said to symbolise the capacity to adapt. Four pillars have much the same meaning: the capacity to live in the four corners of the universe. The flowers are supposed to convey a message of prosperity and happiness from owner to visitor, the birds symbolise the one true God and the bees symbolise the desire for mutual understanding.

Festivals
The main local celebration in the Riau is the Festival of the Sea, held on Pulau Sarasan during the second month of the Islamic calendar. The islanders hang packets of sticky rice on trees near the beach, then cut logs from the forest which they cart down to the beach, load into canoes and drop into deep water to appease the gods of the ocean and for protection from drowning. Apart from this, they uphold the principal festivals of the Islamic calendar.

TANJUNG PINANG
Almost within spitting distance of Singapore is Batam, an official entry point to Indonesia and a convenient gateway to or from Singapore. Further on is Bintan where the biggest town in the archipelago, Tanjung Pinang, is situated. This is where most visitors stop over, although the majority of people only hang around for 24 hours or so waiting for boat connections. Tanjung Pinang is a good base for exploring other islands in the group and has a few interesting sights of its own. There is a constant stream of boats and sampans sailing between the islands and upriver. There's an old section of the town that juts out over the sea on stilts.

Tanjung Pinang has an aura of prosperity and growth. It seems to be sprouting new buildings, both public and private, like shoots in a rice paddy. In its own way it's a rather cosmopolitan town.

Information
Post The post office is on Jalan Merdeka, not far from the harbour.

Bank The Bank Dagang Negara on Jalan Teuku Umar, changes foreign cash and travellers' cheques. The Oriki Money Changer on Jalan Merdeka changes foreign cash but not travellers' cheques.

Things to See
Tanjung Pinang is a good place to stroll around. For a peaceful hour or two, wander down to the old harbour of Pejantan II. There is a Chinese temple in town and another, across the harbour by sampan, in Senggarang. Or you could charter a sampan to take you up the Snake River (Sungai Ular) through the mangroves to see the Chinese Temple with its arrestingly gory murals of the trials and tortures of hell. Nearby you can see the ruins of old Sea Dayak villages.

Riau Kandil Museum
A short distance from the city centre by bemo or ojek is the Riau Kandil Museum which has a mish-mash treasure trove of artefacts from the days of the Sultanates and the Dutch, including old guns, ceramics, charts, antique brassware and other memorabilia. Follow Jalan Ketapang out of town to the museum. It's on the right-hand side just past the junction of Jalan Bakar Batu (an extension of Jalan Ketapang) and Jalan Kemboja.

Places to Stay – bottom end
The term losmen is not widely used in these parts, so look for the sign 'penginapan' for budget accommodation. Most bottom-end accommodation in Tanjung Pinang is clean and generally agreeable.

It's possible to stay with local families for between 1500 to 2000 rp per person. People with rooms, or space, to rent will

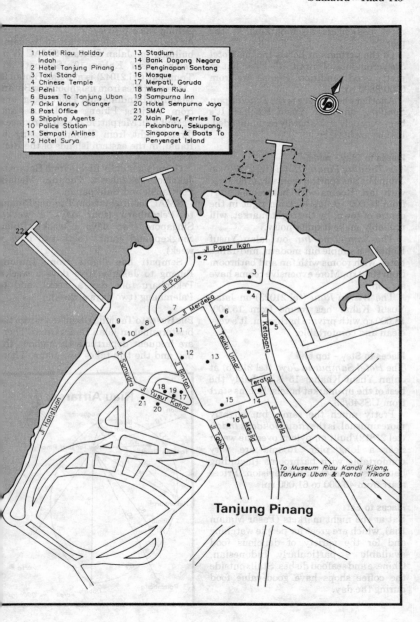

1 Hotel Riau Holiday Indah
2 Hotel Tanjung Pinang
3 Taxi Stand
4 Chinese Temple
5 Pelni
6 Buses To Tanjung Uban
7 Oriki Money Changer
8 Post Office
9 Shipping Agents
10 Police Station
11 Sempati Airlines
12 Hotel Surya
13 Stadium
14 Bank Dagang Negara
15 Penginapan Sontang
16 Mosque
17 Merpati, Garuda
18 Wisma Riau
19 Sampurna Inn
20 Hotel Sempurna Jaya
21 SMAC
22 Main Pier, Ferries To Pekanbaru, Sekupang, Singapore & Boats To Penyenget Island

Jl Pasar Ikan
Jl Pos
Jl Merdeka
Jl Ketapang
Jl Teuku Umar
Jl Samudra
Jl Bintan
Jl Teratai
Jl Gereja
Jl Yusuf Kahar
Jl Hangtuan
Jl Mesjid
Jl Tabib

To Museum Riau Kandil Kijang,
Tanjung Uban & Pantai Trikora

Tanjung Pinang

meet passengers disembarking at the pier.

Of the permanent hotels try the *Hotel Surya* on Jalan Bintan; it's basic but in pretty good condition. Rooms are from 6600/8800 rp.

Another cheap place is the *Penginapan Sondang* on Jalan Yusuf Khahar. It's bare, very ugly and is hardly recommended. Rooms are 7000 rp.

Places to Stay – middle

The *Tanjung Pinang Hotel* (tel 21236) on Jalan Pos has spartan rooms from 8000 rp, with fan. Rooms with bathrooms start from 16,000 rp. It's location right in the centre of town, by the night market, will probably make it quite noisy.

The *Sampurna Inn* on Jalan Yusuf Kahar is a simple but modern, mid-range hotel, with rooms with fan and bathroom from 9900 rp. More expensive rooms have air-con.

The *Wisma Riau* (tel 21023) on Jalan Yusuf Kahar has rooms from 15,000/18,000 rp with private bathroom. It's very clean and comfortable.

Places to Stay – top end

The *Hotel Sampurna Jaya* (tel 21555) at Jalan Yusuf Khahar 15 is probably the best of the up-market hotels. Rooms start from US$46/53.

Pretty much the same, but slightly more unusual, is the *Riau Holidays Indah* (tel 21812) built on pylons over the water near a long pier. Rooms are very comfortable with bathrooms (including bathtubs), carpet and television. Prices start from 46,000 to 61,000 rp.

Places to Eat

Eat at the night markets (Pasar Malam Ria), which are great for people watching and for the variety of delicious food available – particularly Indonesian, Chinese and seafood dishes. Stalls outside the coffee shops have good-value food during the day.

Getting There & Away

Air Garuda and Merpati are in the same building on Jalan Bintan. SMAC is at Jalan Yusuf Kahar 19. Sempati Air Transport (tel 21042) is at Jalan Bintan 9

Merpati flies from neighbouring Batam Island to Bandung and Palembang, and from Tanjung Pinang to Jakarta and Pekanbaru. Merpati may also introduce a direct flight from Tanjung Pinang to Ranai, in the eastern islands of the Riau Archipelago.

Garuda has daily flights from Batam to Jakarta, Pekanbaru, Padang, Medan, Pontianak and Balikpapan.

SMAC has flights from Tanjung Pinang to Pekanbaru (four days a week), Singapore (two days a week), Pulau Singkep and Jambi (both two days a week).

Sempati has flights from Tanjung Pinang to Jakarta (five days a week), Pekanbaru (one day a week), and to Palembang (two days a week).

Bus Buses to Tanjung Uban leave from the bus terminal on Jalan Teuku Umar. There are frequent departures throughout the day and the trip takes two hours. There

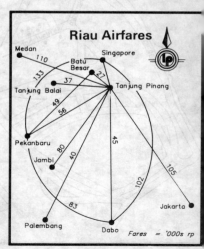

Riau Airfares

Medan — 110 — Batu Besar
133 — 37 — 27
Tanjung Balai — — Singapore
49 — — Tanjung Pinang
56 — 45
Pekanbaru
80 — 105
Jambi — 40
102
83 — Jakarta
Palembang — Dabo

Fares = '000s rp

are also shared taxis on this route. From Tanjung Uban there are regular ferries to Kabil on neighbouring Batam Island. The ferry hop takes 45 minutes.

Local Boats The best way, often the only one, to island hop or travel upriver is by boat.

Boats – including rowboats, sampans, ferries and medium sized ships – of varying degrees of speed and comfort operate around the islands. Tickets for all these boats can be bought from the offices at the entrance to the harbour.

Ferries to Kabil on Batam Island leave from Tanjung Uban which is two hours by bus or taxi from Tanjung Pinang. There are regular departures throughout the day. The crossing takes half an hour and costs 2000 rp.

There are ferries at least two days a week from Tanjung Pinang to Tanjung Balai. You can buy tickets from PT Ayodhia on Jalan Pelabuhan in Tanjung Balai, and from PT Netra at the port in Tanjung Pinang. The fare is 9800 rp.

Pelni Ships Pelni (tel 21513) is at Jalan Ketapang 8. Pelni's *KM Lawit* leaves once every two weeks from the port of Kijang for Dumai, Belawan and Tanjung Priok (the port of Jakarta). Fares from Tanjung Pinang to Tanjung Priok are: economy 30,000 rp; 2nd class 64,000 rp; 1st class 81,000 rp.

To get to Kijang take a shared taxi from Jalan Merdeka in Tanjung Pinang. It's a half-hour ride and the fare is 1500 rp per person.

Pelni ships to the eastern Riau Islands leave about once every 10 days, and do a 10-day round-trip out of Tanjung Pinang stopping off at various ports.

Hydrofoils to Batam & Singapore From Tanjung Pinang there are hydrofoils to Singapore via Sekupang on Batam Island.

Several companies run the hydrofoils and there are a couple of departures daily for both Sekupang and Singapore. In Tanjung Pinang there are ticket offices at PT Pellok Bintan Baruna Sakti at Jalan Samudra 1, the Toko Osaka at Jalan Merdeka 43, or PT Pulau Intan Sari at Jalan Merdeka 77. The fare from Tanjung Pinang to Sekupang is 18,000 rp. Tanjung Pinang to Singapore is 30,000 rp.

In Singapore, the hydrofoils depart from Finger Pier. Tickets can be bought at the offices here.

Pekanbaru Boats Boats depart from Monday to Saturday from Tanjung Pinang for Pekanbaru, up the Siak River. Fares start from 12,500 rp. Tickets are sold on the quay and the trip can take up to 50 hours. From Pekanbaru it's only a few hours by bus to Bukittinggi.

Boats to Singkep Island There are ferries two or three days a week from Tanjung Pinang to Dabo on Singkep Island. The fare is 10,000 rp. The ferries are the same as those used on the Tanjung Pinang to Pekanbaru run, with hard wooden bunks divided off by low slats of timber. The ferry stops briefly at Galang Island. The trip from Tanjung Pinang to Pulau Singkep takes between eight and 12 hours before docking at Sunggai Buluh, where you take a bus to Dabo, the main town on the other side of the island. This takes two hours and costs 2000 rp.

Getting Around

Airport Transport Kijang airport is on the south-eastern tip of Bintan Island about 17 km from Tanjung Pinang. A taxi will cost you 5000 rp, or you can take an ojek for 1500 to 2000 rp.

Around the Island The only bus services in Tanjung Pinang operate to Tanjung Uban. The main method of transport is the ojek – public motorcycle. You can distinguish them from privately owned motorbikes by the small yellow reflector on the front left hand side. The fare is 100 rp around town, 200 rp for short trips or 1000 to 1500 rp an hour for longer trips. There are also bemos; the standard fare is 200 rp.

Tours There are a couple of tour operators in Tanjung Pinang. Try PT Riau Holidays in the Hotel Riau Holidays Indah.

BINTAN ISLAND

Bintan Island, like Batam, is a rough island. Apart from some large rubber plantations it appears curiously un-cultivated, and what small farms there are seem to support barely more than subsistence agriculture. On the other hand, there are some fine opportunities for diving and snorkelling most of the year except from November to March when the monsoon is blowing.

Beaches

There are several beautiful white-sand beaches lapped by sapphire seas here. The best of them are Berakit, Teluk Dalam and Pantai Trikora, but they're on the east coast and there's no public transport there. The beaches are probably a bit overrated, but if you come on a quiet day you probably won't be disappointed. Huge egrets take-off from boulders by the shore and glide across the water. Mapor and several other small palm-covered islands with white sand beaches can be seen from Berakit Beach.

Pantai Trikora This beach is a narrow strip of white sand around a little half-moon bay, and is being developed as a resort for the Singapore Chinese. There is now a moderately-sized hotel called the *Pantai Trikora Country Club* overlooking it. The hotel is made up of timber bungalows on stilts. Rooms are S$45/50 and slightly more expensive on weekends. It's a pleasant enough place, but Trikora is no longer the deserted beach it once was.

It is possible to charter a taxi or an ojek to the beaches. There is a good, surfaced road leading from Tanjung Pinang at least

as far as Pantai Trikora, 20 km away. The trip takes 45 minutes.

Gunung Bintan Besar

You can climb Gunung Bintan Besar (348 metres) in about two hours. It's a fair way out of Tanjung Pinang by road or boat.

Pantai Dwi Kora

About a 20-minute drive from Tanjung Uban, on the west coast of Bintan, is a beach called Pantai Dwi Kora. It's a long strip of white, palm-fringed sand facing Batam Island, and a fine place for a swim with clear, calm sea – although it's very crowded on weekends.

Pulau Bayan

Just off Tanjung Pinang is a lump of rock called Pulau Bayan. Once a dry dock and repair yard, it has now been cleared of scrap metal to make way for the construction of a massive boating marina with hotel, swimming pool, helipad and other facilities for wealthy Singapore Chinese (all within sight of the Indonesian shanties).

Nearby Islands

You can make excursions to other islands like Pulau Penyenget or Pulau Mapor. At Pulau Terkulai the lighthouse keeper lives in solitary splendour and to get there you have to charter a boat.

PENYENGET ISLAND

This tiny island, less than 2½ square km in area (you could walk around it in an hour or two), was once capital of the Riau rajas. It is believed to have been given to the ruling raja as a wedding present in 1805. It seems the Riau rajas finally moved house from Daik (on Lingga Island) to Penyenget around 1900. A bit of fossicking around the jungle reveals ruins, graveyards and other reminders of the past all over the island. Penyenget, incidentally, is said to take its name from a certain type of bee which was in the habit of stinging pirates whenever they landed on the island.

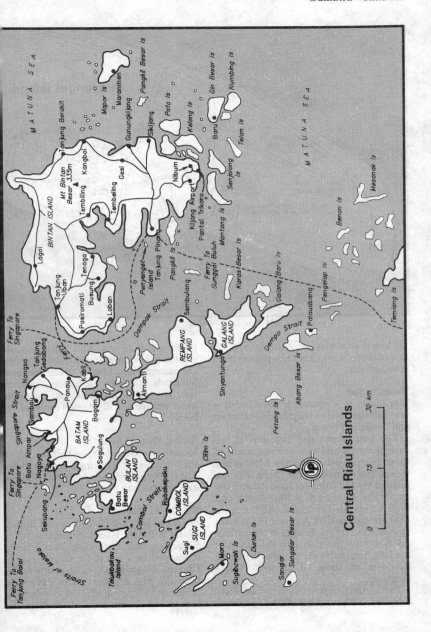

Central Riau Islands

0   15   30 km

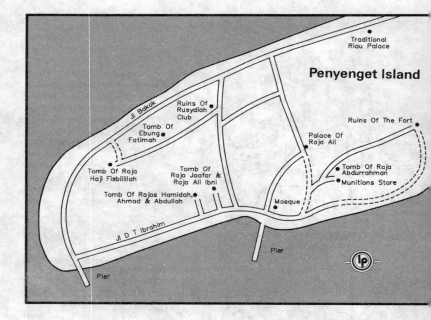

History does not record if this interesting line of defence ever kept the pirates from coming back.

Things to See

The island is a charming place, with a very different feel to neighbouring Bintan and Tanjung Pinang.

The map shows the locations of the various tombs and monuments, many of them dilapidated or in ruins. Most of the village houses are by the shore, but the ruins of the old palace of Raja Ali and the tombs and graveyards of Raja Jaafar and Raja Ali are further inland. All the main sites are sign-posted. A poster in the local mosque depicts the lineage of the former rulers, but for the most part the names of the long dead rajas are as meaningless to outsiders as those of ancient Hittite kings.

Particularly impressive is the sulphur-coloured mosque with its forest of domes, pillars and minarets – a bit like an Islamic version of the Disneyland Castle. Within the mosque is a library which contains hundreds of tomes on history, culture law, languages and religions, including hand-written and illustrated copies of the Koran.

Getting There & Away

Motorboats depart from halfway along the main pier at Tanjung Pinang and the cost is 300 rp per person each way. You can also charter one.

BATAM ISLAND

Squashed between Singapore and Bintan Island is Batam Island. Almost as big as Singapore itself, Batam is gradually being developed as a resort for the Singapore Chinese. Nagoya is the main centre and is basically just a collection of cavernous hotels and shopping edifices, overlooking Indonesian shanty huts. Aside from the shanties, it's startlingly reminiscent of the Special Economic Zones like Shenzhen and Gongbei in China, which are built from the stumps up. Some of the best roads in Indonesia crisscross the island.

Information

Bank In Nagoya, the Bank Rakyat Indonesia will change Singapore and US dollars. The Bank Dagang Negara, opposite, will change some travellers' cheques. Both are on Jalan Sekupang.

Places to Stay

Batam has several massive hotels. Typical are the *Batam View Hotel* at Nongsa Beach on the northern coast, a beach resort for Singapore Chinese. Nagoya has several large hotels including the *Batam Jaya Hotel* (tel 58707) on Jalan Raja Ali Haji and the *Holiday Hotel* (tel 58616) on Jalan Imam Bonjol. Both are in the centre of town and rooms start from 28,000 rp. The Holiday Hotel is more agreeable than the cavernous Batam Jaya Hotel.

Getting There & Away

Air The airport is at Batu Besar. For details of flights see the Tanjung Pinang section.

Boat There are regular hydrofoils from Singapore to Sekupang. The fare is 17,500 rp.

From Kabil, on the other side of the island, there are regular ferries to Tanjung Uban on Bintan Island, from where you can get buses and taxis to Tanjung Pinang. The ferry crossing takes 45 minutes and costs 2000 rp.

There is a ferry service between Tanjung Balai, Batu Ampar (on Batam Island) and Singapore. There are daily departures in both directions six days a week. The ticket office is at the ferry terminal in Batu Ampar.

Getting Around

There is a local bus from Sekupang (the 'Metro Bus' leaving from outside the ferry terminal) to Nagoya. There are shared taxis from Nagoya to Kabil.

Otherwise getting around Batam seems to be a bit of a problem. Unless you can find a shared taxi, you may have to rent one to get to places like Nongsa. A taxi from Sekupang to Nagoya is 7500 rp, to Nongsa 18,000 rp, Batu Ampar 9000 rp, and to Kabil 10,000 rp. Taxis from Nagoya are: to Kabil 5000 rp, Nongsa 12,000 rp and Batu Ampar 1500 rp.

There is a taxi counter and a moneychanger in the Sekupang Ferry Terminal. The large hotels also have taxi counters, or you can hail a taxi on the street.

SINGKEP ISLAND

Singkep Island is the headquarters of the Riau Tin and Timah mining companies and is the third largest island in the archipelago. It has a large Chinese population. Few outsiders visit here, although it's a handy stopover point on the Singapore, Tanjung Pinang, Singkep, Pangkalpinang, Palembang run and has most of the services of a much larger place.

The main town, Dabo, is shaded by lush trees and gardens and is clustered around a central park. Nearby, on the road to Sunggai Buluh, a big mosque dominates the skyline. Dabo is set in the middle of a huge, half-moon beach of white sand, which is perhaps as big as Bali's Kuta Beach.

Information

Bank Dagang Negara on Jalan Penuba will change cash and travellers' cheques. The post office is on Jalan Pahlawan. The telephone office is about three km out of town on the road to Sunggai Buluh.

Things to See

In Dabo the fish and vegetable markets near the harbour are interesting to wander around and are among the best places in town to buy fresh, cheap food. Jalan Pasar

Lingga & Singkep Islands

0   10   20 km

(Map labels: Benan Is, Mesanak Is, Teban, MATUNA SEA, Sebangka Is, Limas, Cempah, Tananmaroh, Airklubi, Ferry To Tanjung Pinang, Lingga Is, Limau, Pebanduk, Kelume, Sambau, Tanjung Dua, Daik, Tengkis, Penuba, Sunggai Buluh, Cukas, Lanjut, Pasirkuning, Maroktua, Singkep Is, Dabo, Labu)

Lamar is a good browsing and shopping area. The small port of Sunggai Buluh is on the north coast 36 km from Dabo. You can get there by bus for 2000 rp. From there you can charter boats to Penuba Island.

Places to Stay & Eat

There are a couple of places to stay in Dabo. The *Penginapan Sri Indah* at Jalan Perusahaan 10 costs 10,000 rp with private bathroom. It's a very simple but clean and agreeable hotel.

The *Penginapan Garupa Singkep* on Jalan Pasar Lama is similar, with rooms from 5000/7000 rp, and rooms from 12,000/14,000 rp with air-con and private bathroom.

The salubrious *Wisma Singkep* is a fine hotel situated in a quiet spot above the town. Rooms are 20,000/40,000 rp. Eat at

the markets behind Penginapan Sri Indah or try any of the warungs on Jalan Pasar Lama and Jalan Merdeka. Eating places pop up all over the place at night.

Getting There & Away

Air SMAC (tel 73) is on Jalan Pemandian. They have flights from Singkep to Tanjung Pinang and Singapore (two days a week), and Pekanbaru (four days a week). The airport is five km from Dabo on Jalan Pahlawan.

Boat There are daily boats from Dabo to Daik, on Lingga Island. Departure time depends on the tide and it's a three-hour trip. The fare is 1000 rp. The 'ferries' are just small motorboats and it's definitely not a trip to contemplate in rough weather.

The *KM Hentry*, a fairly new ship built of teak, operates between Dabo and Tanjung Pinang thrice weekly. The trip takes 11 hours, crosses the equator and passes several islands.

There are ferries from Sunggai Buluh to Tanjung Pinang about two days a week. There is a regular ferry between Singkep and Jambi, departing once a week. Several shops in Dabo act as ticket agents.

There are regular boats between Singkep and Bangka Island run by Riau Tin. You have to register first at the Riau Tin office. There are departures two days a week and the boat pulls into Belinyu on Bangka Island.

PENUBA ISLAND

Penuba is an idyllic place to relax as it is completely unspoilt and the people are friendly. It's fine for doing nothing but swimming, walking and reading. The main settlement on this island is the village of the same name, which is tucked into a small bay on the south-east coast. Only a 10-minute walk from here, around the point, are several sandy beaches. In the centre of the village is the Attaqwa Mosque. On the northern coast is the

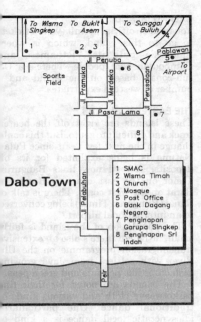

Dabo Town

1 SMAC
2 Wisma Timah
3 Church
4 Mosque
5 Post Office
6 Bank Dagang Negara
7 Penginapan Garupa Singkep
8 Penginapan Sri Indah

village of Tanjung Dua with more fine beaches.

Places to Stay & Eat

A house next to the Attaqwa Mosque is now used as a guest house for foreign visitors. It's very basic, and rooms are 3000 rp. Ask around for the caretaker. There are several small warungs along Jalan Merdeka, the main street.

Getting There & Away

To get to Penuba from Singkep you have to rent a motorboat from Sunggai Buluh. The trip takes about half an hour and you'll be dropped off at Penuba village.

LINGGA ISLAND

Not much remains of the glory that was once Lingga except a few neglected and forgotten ruins. The arrival point is Daik, which is hidden one km up a grey-brown river. It has that all-enveloping atmosphere

of tropical seediness and oppressive humidity that pervades many of Somerset Maugham's stories. Daik is pretty much a single street, some cargo wharves and about a dozen Chinese shops, with dirt roads and tracks branching out to the Malay villages around the island.

Things to See

The main site of historical interest is the ruins of the old palace of Raja Suleiman, the last raja of Lingga-Riau. To one side of the palace are the foundation stones of a building which is said to have been the living quarters of the raja's extensive harem. Otherwise there's not much left of the palace; a few staircases, the foundations of the floor, pavilions and halls. In the jungle you find overgrown bathing pools and squat toilets. The ruins are a two-hour walk from Daik, but you'll need someone to guide you through the maze of overgrown forest paths. Along the same trail is the tomb of Raja Muhammed Jusuf, who reigned from 1859-99.

A half-hour walk from Daik is the Makam Bukit Cenckeh (Cenckeh Hill Cemetery). Situated here are the graves of Raja Abdul Rakhman (who ruled from 1812-1831) and Raja Muhammad (who

Cow tethered near Lingga

ruled from 1832-1841). Like the palace, there is not much left of the tombs, which are slowly crumbling into rubble. On the outskirts of Daik is the Mesjid Sultan Lingga, in the grounds of which is the tomb of Raja Makmud I, who ruled in the early 19th century.

Inland is Gunung Daik, its three peaks looking like a crown. It's possible to scale the two outer peaks but the central one is said to have never been climbed because it's too steep and too dangerous. If you've got some equipment you can walk across the island camping along the way, but get explicit directions before you start out. There are a number of Malay villages on the island (look at the map in the police station in Daik) and it would be possible to walk to them, though you would need quite a lot of time.

Places to Stay & Eat
There is one hotel in Daik, on the main street just near the ferry dock. It's a simple but clean hotel, and a reasonably agreeable place to stay so long as you don't expect too much of the bathrooms. Rooms are 5000 rp. You must report to the police as soon as you arrive. There are a few small warungs on the main street, but there's not much variation in the food.

Getting There & Away
There are daily boats from Daik to Dabo on Singkep Island. The fare is 1000 rp and the trip takes three hours. There are occasional boats direct between Tanjung Pinang and Daik. You might be able to get a ride on a cargo boat from Pekanbaru or Jambi. Around the island you have to walk to most places as there are only two vehicles in use, one of them a truck of 1945 vintage.

KARIMUN ISLAND
The main centre is the port of Tanjung Balai. There is a regular ferry service between Tanjung Pinang and Karimun. SMAC flies from Karimun to Dabo on Singkep Island, and to Pekanbaru.

GALANG ISLAND
You need an official permit (yellow ticket to go to this island, which is wher Indonesia puts its Vietnamese an Cambodian boat people. There's a U sub-consul based on the island and number of western expatriates.

THE EASTERN ISLANDS
These islands are right off the beate track and difficult to get to. But this coul change in the next few years since Pula Natuna is being exploited for its oi deposits. A road now links Bangurun Timor on the east coast to Bunguran Barat on the west coast. There is talk o Ranai (Bunguran Timor) being converte to an international airport.

The population of the island is fairl small, although there's also an extensiv transmigration programme on the Ul River with settlers from Java growin cash crops like peanuts and green peas.

The islands are noted for their fin basketweave cloth and various kinds o traditional dance. One particularl idiosyncratic local dance is a kind o *Thousand & One Arabian Nights* saga incorporating episodes from Riau-Lingga history. Dancers from Sedanau Islan often perform at the national danc contest held in Jakarta each year.

Lampung

Lampung was made a province in 1964 The provincial capital Bandar Lampung is really two cities – Tanjungkarang an the port of Telukbetung – and looks acros the Sunda Strait to Krakatau and Java.

When Krakatau erupted in 1883 Telukbetung and Tanjungkarang wer blanketed in ash and thousands of house and hectares of crops were destroyed Most of Lampung is very flat and it highest mountains – Gunung Pesagi Tanggamas, Seminung, Sekincau and Raya – are all dormant volcanoes.

Historically, the Lampungese forged close cultural and trading links with West Java soon after they began exporting their black pepper crops to Banten. However by 1684, the Dutch East India Company had acquired a monopoly on Lampung pepper and after the fall of the kingdom of Banten in 1808 the Lampungese found themselves subjects of the Dutch.

The cultural links with Java became even closer when the Dutch instituted transmigration schemes between the two regions in an effort to find a solution to Java's over-population. The Javanese brought with them the gamelan and wayang. They also successfully introduced sawah rice cultivation and other innovative agricultural techniques to Lampung. Coffee, cloves and rubber are also grown as cash crops.

PANJANG & BAKAUHUNI

The major significance of Lampung for travellers is that the ports of Panjang and Bakauhuni, which are important entry or exit points between Java and Sumatra, are here. Both ferry terminals are on the east coast and Bakauhuni is on Sumatra's easternmost tip.

Places to Stay

Most people who arrive at Panjang or Bakauhuni take the train from Tanjungkarang and continue straight on to Palembang. If they hang around it's usually for one night only. Most of the losmen are lousy value, but in Panjang try the *Losmen Kastari*.

Getting There & Away

Bus From Panjang you can travel by bus or train to Palembang. You can also get buses from Strengsen, which is the other ferry terminal. Buses go all the way to Bukittinggi or even Medan although most people will prefer to travel sector by sector. ANS is probably the best of the various Sumatran bus companies.

Rail Passenger trains no longer operate in Sumatra except in the south. It's possible to take a train from Panjang to Palembang, continue to Lubuklinggau and catch a bus from there to Bengkulu or Padang.

Trains run twice a day between Panjang and Palembang and the trip takes about 10 hours. The better of the two trains on this route is the Srivijaya Express. The fare on the Srivijaya is 6500 rp in 2nd class and 3000 rp in 3rd. Fares on the other train, the Rajabasa, are about half that.

South Sumatra

The province of South Sumatra stretches from Lubuklinggau in the Barisan foothills in the west to the islands of Bangka and Belitung in the east. All roads, rivers and the railway all lead to Palembang, the provincial capital.

PALEMBANG

Built along the River Musi and only 80 km upstream from the sea, Palembang was forced into the 20th century rather abruptly because of its strategic position. When Sumatra's oil fields were discovered and opened early in the century, Palembang quickly became the main export outlet for south Sumatra. Over a third of Indonesia's total revenue comes from this province. Today Palembang, the second largest city in Sumatra with 650,000 inhabitants, is a heavily industrialised city – it also has tin mines – and is a rather dull place to visit.

A thousand years ago, Palembang was the centre of the highly developed civilisation of Srivijaya. When the Chinese scholar I Tsing was in Palembang in 672 he recorded that a thousand monks, scholars and pilgrims were studying and translating Sanskrit. Few relics from this period remain – no sculpture, monuments or architecture of note – nor is there much of interest from the early 18th century when Palembang was an Islamic kingdom. Most of the buildings of the latter era were

Getting around Palembang

destroyed in battles with the Dutch, the last of which occurred in 1811.

Coming into Palembang from the south you pass plantations of rubber, coffee, pepper and pineapples. In complete contrast are the smokestacks of the Sunggai Gerong refinery and the petrochemical complex at Plaju, which give the landscape a spuriously futuristic look, particularly at night.

Information & Orientation

The city is split in half by the Musi River and sprawls along both banks. The two halves are connected by the Ampera Bridge, only built in the mid-'60s. A hodgepodge of wooden houses on stilts crowd both banks, but the south side known as Ulu is where the majority of people live. The 'better half', Ilir, is on the north bank where you'll find most of the government offices, shops, hotels and the wealthy residential districts. Jalan Jenderal Sudirman is the main street of Palembang, running right on to the bridge.

Tourist Office The tourist office (tel 28450) is at the Museum Sultan Machmud Badaruddin II. You can also get a lot of information and maps from the South Sumatra Regional Government Tourist Office (tel 24981) at Jalan Bay Salim 200.

Post The post office is close to the river and the Grand Mosque.

Bank The Bank Bumi Daya is on Jalan Sudirman. The Bank Ekspor Impor is on Jalan Rustam Effendy. Dhrama Perdana at Jalan Kol Atmo 446 is a moneychanger.

Museums

The Rumah Bari, right in the centre of the Palembang on the street of the same name, has Srivijayan antiquities. The best of the sculptures come from Tegurwangi, on the Pasemah Plateau near Lahat. Outside stands a trumpeting elephant, an evil-looking temple guardian and a serene Buddha. Inside, displayed in red and gold Palembang chests, are wooden sculptures from Kayuagung, a

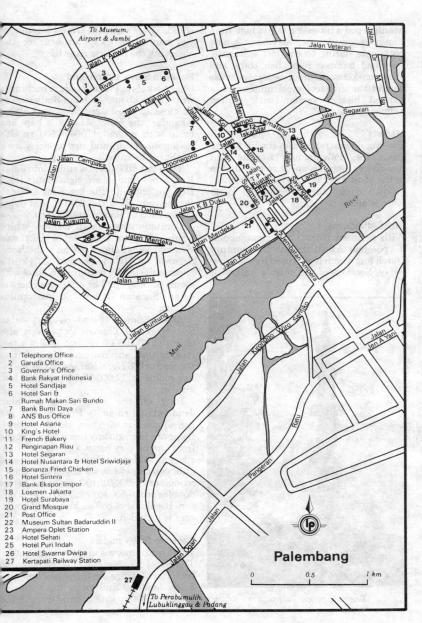

To Museum,
Airport & Jambi

1   Telephone Office
2   Garuda Office
3   Governor's Office
4   Bank Rakyat Indonesia
5   Hotel Sandjaja
6   Hotel Sari &
    Rumah Makan Sari Bundo
7   Bank Bumi Daya
8   ANS Bus Office
9   Hotel Asiana
10 King's Hotel
11 French Bakery
12 Penginapan Riau
13 Hotel Segaran
14 Hotel Nusantara & Hotel Sriwidjaja
15 Bonanza Fried Chicken
16 Hotel Sintera
17 Bank Ekspor Impor
18 Losmen Jakarta
19 Hotel Surabaya
20 Grand Mosque
21 Post Office
22 Museum Sultan Badaruddin II
23 Ampera Oplet Station
24 Hotel Sehati
25 Hotel Puri Indah
26 Hotel Swarna Dwipa
27 Kertapati Railway Station

Palembang

0   0.5   1 km

To Perabumulih,
Lubuklinggau & Padang

headless god a bit over a metre high from Candi Gedeng, lamps, weavings, Chinese pots, oars dating to the last sultanate, inscribed bamboo rods, fish traps and other basketware. In a separate house behind the archaeological museum is a natural history section with stuffed animal displays.

Markets

Two km downstream from the bridge the Pasar Ilir, Palembang's frenetic and fascinating market, spills colourfully on to the Musi's banks with food, household goods and clothing. The smaller Pasar Kuto is also interesting.

Other Attractions

With permission from the commander, it's possible to visit the late 18th century Dutch fort which is still used by the army today. Sections of the outside walls still

Grand Mosque, Palembang

stand. There's also the Grand Mosque, o you can while away an hour or tw observing the frenetic river life.

Places to Stay – bottom end

Cheap hotels in Palembang are nothing t write home about. At Jalan Sudirman 4 E, close to the intersection with Jala Iskandar, the *Hotel Asiana* is bare an basic with rooms at 5000/7500 rp. It reasonably clean and not as noisy as i might be, because it's high up.

Turn left off Jalan Iskandar into Jala Kol Atmo and then right into Jala Dempo, opposite the big King's Hotel *Penginapan Riau* (tel 22011) is at Jala Dempo 409 C. Rooms are 6500 rp.

Continue along Jalan Dempo, whic bends back to cross Jalan Iskandar Where it joins Jalan Segaran is the *Hote Segaran* at Jalan Segaran 207C. It' another decidedly bottom-end hotel wit rooms at 5000 rp. The street numbers o Jalan Segaran follow no discernibl pattern.

Almost down at the river at Jala Sayangan 769 *Losmen Jakarta* is als cheap at 4000/8000 rp, but this is a rea rock bottom, survival-only place. Acros the road at 669 *Hotel Surabaya* (tel 26874 has rooms at 12,000/17,500 rp with fan air-con.

Back on the main road, at Jala Jenderal Sudirman 38, *Hotel Sintera* is big, square box with very variable rooms Some are tiny, gloomy boxes which at th front can be very noisy. Others are large spacious and quite clean and comfortabl although somewhat shabby. The cheape rooms are 9900/12,100 rp, the bette doubles are 16,500 rp or 22,000 rp with air con. Breakfast of coffee, bread and boile eggs is included.

Places to Stay – middle

There are numerous middle-range hotels The *Hotel Sriwidjaja* (tel 24193) at Jala Iskandar 31/488, close to the junction wit Jalan Jenderal Sudirman, has rooms a 9900 to 15,400 rp with fan and from 18,15 to 33,000 rp with air-con. The price includes breakfast.

The *Hotel Nusantara* (tel 23306) at Jalan Iskandar 17, in the same little alley off the main road, has rooms at 12,500/20,000 rp with fan/air-con.

The *Sari Hotel* at Jalan Jenderal Sudirman 1301, on the corner with Jalan Kapten A Rivai, has rooms starting from economy singles at 12,500 rp, through to regular singles/doubles at 17,000/20,000 rp and more expensive rooms, all including breakfast.

The expensive *Hotel Swarna Dwipa* is some distance west of the centre and there are two more middle-range hotels, the *Puri Indah* and the *Sehati*, close by.

Places to Eat

At night Jalan Sajangan, parallel to Jalan Jenderal Sudirman, is crowded with Chinese food stands and sate places. This is a great area where you can eat some excellent food. Round the corner on Jalan Rustam Effendy, there are fruit stalls and stands selling pisang goreng (fried bananas) and other snacks.

On Jalan Iskandar, near Jalan Jenderal Sudirman there is a cluster of places including *Yohan Bakery & Fried Chicken* and the *Warna Warni* ice cream parlour next door. There are a number of bakeries around the centre which also do mie (noodle) dishes and other simple meals. You'll find them along Jalan Jenderal Sudirman or try the *French Bakery* at Jalan Kol Atmo 481B, opposite King's Hotel.

Nasi Padang restaurants can be found all over town. The *Rumah Makan Sari Bundo* on the corner of Sudirman and Jalan Kapitan Rivai is good, but more expensive. Finally *Bonanza Fried Chicken* is Palembang's closest approach to a western fast food joint. It's at Jalan Kol Atmo 425, upstairs in the 'Yuppies Centre'!

Getting There & Away

Few westerners stop in Palembang as it's off the Trans-Sumatran Highway. You can skip past it on the direct Jakarta to Padang buses, or fly or take the direct Jakarta to Padang ship.

Air Garuda (tel 21604) is on Jalan Kapten A Rivai. Merpati (tel 21604) is nearby in the Sandjaja Hotel on Jalan Kapten A Rivai. Bouraq (tel 20410) is at Jalan Dr Sutomo 11.

Talang Betutu airport is 12 km north of town and a taxi costs a standard 6000 rp from the airport. The road runs right by the front of the terminal and you can get into town on a Talang Betutu-Ampera oplet for 300 rp.

Train The Kertapati railway station is on the south side of the river, eight km from the town centre.

Bus The bus company ANS is at Jalan Iskandar 903 C just off Jalan Jenderal Sudirman. Other bus companies are in the same area. There are frequent departures for Jakarta. The 20 hour trip costs 15,000 rp or 22,500 rp with air-con. ANS have a daily bus to Padang, which takes 24 hours and costs 15,000 rp or 17,500 rp with air-con. There are also buses from Palembang to Jambi.

Boat It's also possible to travel to or from Palembang by riverboat. Three times a week there are ferries to Bangalincur. It's a slow, soporific trip departing Palembang in the afternoon and arriving at Bangalincur at dawn the next day. The river cuts through dense jungle, noisy with the chatter of monkeys, past basking crocodiles and villages of river houses on stilts. At dusk, giant fruit bats swoop about in big mobs. When you arrive there is an oplet waiting at the wharf to take you to Jambi.

Getting Around

Oplets around town cost a standard 100 rp. Most routes start or finish at Amerapa, the oplet stop at the northern end of the Ampera Bridge. Take a Kertapati oplet for the railway station or a Km 5 oplet for the Jambi buses and the nearby museum.

AROUND PALEMBANG

Take a sampan for 100 rp across the Musi, then catch an oplet to Kayuagung, a small village on the banks of the Komering, where the women in the Kedaton district make superb pottery using a unique method. The pots, mostly cooking and household utensils like jugs and rice dishes, are fired under a kiln of brushwood in the open air.

The arts building has pictures of local life that include a bride and groom in traditional costume, *pencak silat* fighting, flora and fauna and the battle against the Dutch. Gold and red Palembang cabinets are still made in this village which is also known for its sago cakes and krupuks.

Once a year, usually on August 17 Proclamation Day, a *jalur* race is held by the people of Rantau Kuantan in the district of Inderagiri Hulu. A jalur is a canoe 25 to 30 metres long, a metre wide, and rowed by 40 to 60 men – it's a bit like a Chinese dragon boat.

An important historical site in Riau Province is the Temple of Muara Takua, an ancient Hindu temple now in ruins.

Jambi

On the east coast of Sumatra, facing the Straits of Melaka, Jambi was made a province in 1957 and now has a population of 1½ million.

Because of its geographical situation Jambi has long been a melting pot for different ethnic groups. The population of present-day Jambi is comprised of Chinese, Arabs, Japanese, Malaysians, Pakistanis, Javanese, Minangkabaus, Sudanese, Bataks and the earliest inhabitants of Jambi, the Kubus, who were among the first wave of Malays to migrate to Sumatra, predating the Bataks.

Almost 85% of the existing Kubus, originally nomadic forest dwellers, now live in one area in the jungle fringing Jambi, but they were once scattered far and wide. Only a few of them managed to find sanctuary in the rainforest. Resettlement programmes enforced by the Indonesian Government because of overpopulation in Java have subjected the people to diseases like measles and tuberculosis, which have decimated their numbers.

Historically, Jambi was a dependency of Java's Majapahit empire from 1294 to 1520 before coming under the sway of the Minangkabaus of West Sumatra. In 1616 the East India Company opened an office in Jambi and the Dutch quickly formed a successful alliance with Sultan Muhammad Nakhruddin to protect their ships and cargoes from pirates.

The Dutch negotiated a trade monopoly with Nakhruddin and successive sultans. The predominant export was pepper, which was grown in such abundance in Jambi that it could provide Melaka, Johore, Pattani and Gris with most of their supplies and China with a large percentage of its pepper stocks. In 1901, the Dutch moved their headquarters to Palembang and were not able to retain effective control in Jambi from then on.

JAMBI

Jambi, capital of the province of the same name, is on the banks of Sumatra's longest river, the Batanghari, about 155 km from the coast.

Places to Stay

The cheaper places are generally drab and unpleasant. The more expensive places show no improvement in quality for the extra cost. Try the *Mustika* on the Padang and Palembang side of town, or the *Mutiara* which is slightly closer to the town centre. In the centre itself the *Sumateri* and the *Jelita* are cheaper, but very unfriendly. *Hotel Makmar* at Jalan

Cut Nyak Dien 14 is altogether more pleasant, but also more expensive.

Places to Eat
Of course you'll be eating Padang food. Try the restaurants on Jalan Wahidin and Jalan Thamrin. There are also lots of stalls selling slices of chilled fruit, particularly delicious pineapple.

Getting There & Away
Like Palembang, the Trans-Sumatran Highway does not run through Jambi. Garuda flies to Jambi regularly, connecting directly with Jakarta and to other centres via Palembang. There are buses from Palembang to Jambi, and from Jambi you can continue on to Padang.

Bengkulu

A rather isolated province, particularly during the rainy season when land transport often breaks down completely, Bengkulu (Bencoolen) has particular historical significance for the Indonesians, Dutch and the British.

The British moved into Bengkulu in 1685, three years after they had been kicked out of Banten in Java. From the word go things did not go well for them as disease and outbreaks of malaria decimated the British colony. Pepper was an obvious natural resource to exploit. The first factory was started by Ralph Ord who didn't survive long enough to enjoy success as he was poisoned in 1687.

Involvement in internal Sumatran wars, corruption within the colony, and the destruction of British settlements by the French fleet in 1760 all took their toll. When Sir Stamford Raffles arrived in 1818 the colony was still not a going concern.

BENGKULU
Bengkulu was Raffles' foot in the door to Indonesia but this British attempt to displace the Dutch was half-hearted and never very successful. The British actually established themselves here in 1685 and Raffles arrived in 1818. In 1824, Bengkulu was traded for Melaka on the Malay coast and the British and Dutch now stared at each other across the Melaka Straits. There are still some reminders of the British presence in Bengkulu but overall the town is of very little interest and like Palembang and Jambi, getting there requires a detour from the Trans-Sumatran Highway.

Raffles was anxious to establish a British trading base in Sumatra and Bengkulu was a foot in the door. His Fort Marlborough (Benteng Malioboro) is still there, but British influence in Bengkulu ceased in 1824 when they exchanged it for the Malay port of Melaka. In the short time he was there, Raffles made the pepper market profitable and started cash crops in coffee, nutmeg and sugar cane.

Bengkulu became a separate province from South Sumatra in 1968. It covers an area of 17,858 square km and is split into the city of Bengkulu with a population of 55,000, North Bengkulu, South Bengkulu and the mountainous Rejang Lebong. About ¾ of the Kerinci National Park, which is named after the 3800-metre Gunung Kerinci, lies in this province. It's wild, rugged country extending for 345 km along the spine of Sumatra, Bukit Barisan.

Information & Orientation
Although Bengkulu is right by the sea, it only really touches it near Fort Marlborough. Otherwise the town is set back from the coast. Jalan Suprapto and the nearby Pasar Minggu Besar are the modern town centre, separated from the old town area around Fort Marlborough by the long, straight Jalan Jenderal Ahmad Yani. The coast is surprisingly quiet and rural only a km or so from the centre.

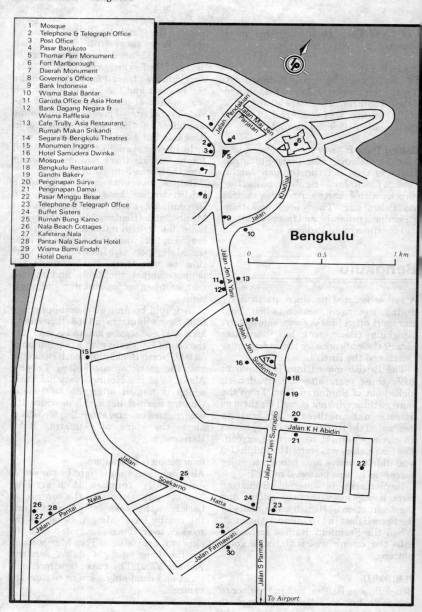

1   Mosque
2   Telephone & Telegraph Office
3   Post Office
4   Pasar Barukoto
5   Thomar Parr Monument
6   Fort Marlborough
7   Daerah Monument
8   Governor's Office
9   Bank Indonesia
10 Wisma Balai Bantar
11 Garuda Office & Asia Hotel
12 Bank Dagang Negara &
    Wisma Rafflesia
13 Cafe Trully, Asia Restaurant,
    Rumah Makan Srikandi
14 Segara & Bengkulu Theatres
15 Monumen Inggris
16 Hotel Samudera Dwinka
17 Mosque
18 Bengkulu Restaurant
19 Gandhi Bakery
20 Penginapan Surya
21 Penginapan Damai
22 Pasar Minggu Besar
23 Telephone & Telegraph Office
24 Buffet Sisters
25 Rumah Bung Karno
26 Nala Beach Cottages
27 Kafeteria Nala
28 Pantai Nala Samudra Hotel
29 Wisma Bumi Endah
30 Hotel Dena

Bengkulu

0   0.5   1 km

To Airport

Fort Marlborough

Raffles' fort, Benteng Marlborough, was originally built between 1714 and 1719. It was restored in 1983 and reopened to the public in 1984 after a long period of use by the army. There are a few small and uninteresting exhibits about the restoration, together with a pile of cannon-balls and a couple of old British gravestones. Admission is 100 rp. Bengkulu has a few other British reminders, including the Thomas Parr monument in front of the Pasar Barukoto and a couple of 'Monumen Inggris'. The one near the beach is to Captain Robert Hamilton who died in 1793, 'in command of the troops'.

Sukarno's House

Sukarno was exiled to Bengkulu by the Dutch from 1938 until the Japanese arrived here in 1941. Through the '30s he had a grand tour of Indonesia at Dutch expense. At his house you can see a few faded photos, the wardrobe where his clothes used to hang and even Bung's trusty bicycle, which like any real Indonesian bicycle has brakes that don't work. His house is closed on Mondays, open other days from 8 am to 2 pm except on Fridays when it closes at 11 am and on Saturdays when it closes at 12 noon.

Other Attractions

Pantai Panjang (the Bengkulu beach) is long, grey, wide, featureless and decidedly unattractive. The Bengkulu Museum Negeri is south of the centre at Jalan Pembangunan P D Harapan and is open the same hours as the Rumah Bung Karno. Dendam Taksuda is a reserve area four km south of the town.

Places to Stay – bottom end

Like in other towns in south Sumatra, the cheap hotels are no great bargains.

Penginapan Surya (tel 31341) at Jalan Abidin 26 is just off Jalan Suprapto. It's a rock-bottom place with rooms at 3500, 4000 and 6000 rp. Right across the road at 18 is Penginapan Damia (tel 32912) with slightly better rooms with mandi at 5000 rp.

Wisma Rafflesia (tel 31650) at Jalan Jenderal Ahmad Yani 924, half way between the town centre and Fort Marlborough is another basic survival place with rooms at 6000 rp.

Places to Stay – middle

Wisma Bumi Endah (tel 31665) at Jalan Fatmawati 29 is much better and still conveniently close to the centre. It's quiet, quite pleasant and rooms are small but clean. Single/double rooms cost 7500/12,500 rp or 17,500 rp with air-con.

Places to Stay – top end

There are a number of middle-range hotels, some of them quite pleasant. Nala Beach Cottages (tel 31855) at Jalan Pantai Nala 133 is right by the beach, below the expensive Pantai Nala Samudra Hotel which is Bengkulu's number one hotel. The individual cottages are good value at 18,500/22,500 rp. It's quiet and relaxed here and more than a kilometre from the centre.

Wisma Balai Buntar (tel 31254) is at Jalan Khadijal 122, near the fort. Rooms at this quiet and pleasant guest house are 18,500 to 22,000 rp. Close to the centre at Jalan Sudirman 245 Hotel Samudera Dwinka (tel 31604) is big, clean, well kept and virtually deserted. Rooms are 15,000 to 20,000 rp with fan, 30,000 rp with air-con. There are other middle-range hotels around, like the Dena Hotel and the Asia Hotel.

Places to Eat

There are a number of restaurants along Jalan Suprapto in the centre including the neat little Buffet Sisters with the usual mie and nasi menu. The Bengkulu Restorant is similar or you can try the Gandhi Bakery with its amazing selection of ice creams.

Half way along Jalan Jenderal Ahmad Yani, between the centre and the fort, there is a small cluster of restaurants opposite the Garuda office and Hotel Asia. They include *Cafe Trully*, the seafood specialist *Asia Restaurant* and the *Rumah Makan Srikandi*.

Overlooking the beach, at the corner right next to the Nala Beach Cottages and the Pantai Nala Samudra Hotel, the *Kafeteria Nala* is a good place for a cold beer. You can look out to sea and wonder what brought you to Bengkulu in the first place!

Getting There & Away
Air Garuda (tel 21416) is at Jalan Ahmad Yani 922 B. There are direct flights with Garuda to Jakarta (76,400 rp) and to Palembang (42,400 rp).

Bus Terminal Panorama, the long distance bus terminal, is several km south of the centre (100 rp by oplet). Buses run to Lubuklinggau, the junction town 110 km away on the Trans-Sumatra Highway, for 3000 rp. Other fares include Curup (half way to Lubuklinggau) for 1500 rp, Palembang 7500 rp and Padang 10,500 rp. Long distance bus operators also have offices in the town centre, like Bengkulu Indah at Jalan Suprapto 5.

Boat The harbour below Fort Marlborough is just for small boats and fishing boats; the main harbour is 15 or so km south, beyond the airport. Sometimes you can get ships going to Padang.

Getting Around
Airport Transport The airport is 14 km south of town and the standard taxi fare is 5000 rp. You can walk 100 metres out to the road from where you should be able to get a bemo or bus into Bengkulu.

Local Transport There are countless tiny *mikrolets* shuttling around town at a standard fare of 100 rp. These operate out as far as eight km, but make sure any vehicle that picks you up from there doesn't decide it's a chartered taxi.

PASEMAH HIGHLANDS
The most important group of megalithic monuments remaining at their original site in Sumatra is concentrated at Tegurwangi, near Lahat on the Pasemah Plateau. There are two distinct styles of sculpture. The older, more primitive style features figures squatting with hands on knees or arms folded over chests; the second is more sophisticated and has single statues as well as groups.

The sculptures in this group are dynamic, powerful and passionate studies of men, women, children and animals. They include several sculptures of men riding buffaloes or elephants, groups of people standing next to elephants and buffaloes, two men battling with a snake, a man struggling with an elephant lying on its back, and a couple of tigers – one guarding the head of a human being between its paws. The sculptures have expressive facial features and are thought to date from the late Bronze Age. Their makers have used the natural curve of the rocks to create a three-dimensional effect, though all the sculptures are in bas-relief.

A couple of stone graves at Tanjungara, also in the Pasemah Highlands, contain fragments of paintings in broad bands of black, yellow, red, white and grey on the inner walls, in the same style as the sculptures. Two are scenes of a warrior and a buffalo, the third is a man with an elephant.

KERINCI
Kerinci is a mountain-valley accessible by bus from either Jambi or Padang – the road from Padang is more beautiful and also much better. It's a rich, green area with two very dominating features: Gunung Kerinci, at 3800 metres the highest mountain in Indonesia outside Irian Jaya, and Danau (lake) Kerinci, at the other end of the valley. Sungai Penuh is the largest town with some 200 small villages in the area. Its matrilineal social

structure is similar to that found in West Sumatra.

Things to See

In Sungai Penuh there is a large, pagoda-style mosque which is said to be over 400 years old. It has large carved beams and old Dutch tiles but you need permission to go inside. Dusun Sungai Tetung is nationally renowned for its basket weaving. All over the area there are stone carvings which have not really been carefully investigated. Locals have a legend of a great kingdom here long ago. The carvings are very different from those of the Majapahit or Srivijaya areas. It's easy to find a cheap guide for day-trips from Sungai Penuh.

Tours around the lake are good – start at Jujun or Keluru (20 km from Sungai Penuh and half a km apart) and make sure to ask to see Batu Gong. About 40 km out of Sungai Penuh on the way to Gunung Kerinci, there is a tea plantation called Kayo Aro worth going to see if you've never been over one before. There are hot springs nearby where it's too hot to swim in the main pool, but you can get a private room with a hot mandi. Watch out for tigers, there are said to be many still around.

Places to Stay & Eat

In Sungai Penuh the *Mata Hari Losmen* is cheap and clean. One of the best restaurants in Sungai Penuh is the *Minang Soto*, which has good Padang food and is cheap and clean. Try *dending batokok*, which is strips of beef smoked and grilled over a fire, and a speciality of the region.

ENGGANO ISLAND

Enggano Island was isolated for so long and so little was known about it that only about a hundred years ago some Sumatrans believed it was inhabited entirely by women. Apparently, these women managed to procreate miraculously through the kind auspices of the wind or by eating certain fruit.

Enggano is a tiny island of just 680 square km, about 100 km off the coast of Bengkulu. It's featured on a map of Asia drawn in 1593 and the name, Enggano, is Portuguese for deceit or disappointment, which suggests that the Portuguese were the first Europeans to discover it. It wasn't until three years later that Dutch navigators record coming across it.

The original inhabitants are believed to be native Sumatrans who fled from the mainland when the Malays migrated there. The present-day inhabitants live by cultivating rice, coffee, pepper, cloves and copra. Wild pigs, cattle and buffalo are abundant.

There are five villages on the island, including Banjar Sari on the north coast, Meok on the west, Kaana and Kahayupu in the east and Malakoni, the harbour. The island is relatively flat (the highest point is Bua Bua which rises to 250 metres) and the coastline's swampy. It's worth visiting if you are a keen anthropologist and/or a real adventurer with plenty of time.

Getting There & Around

The only way to get to Enggano is by boat from Bengkulu (a very irregular service) which docks at Malakoni. The villages are connected by tracks originally made by the Japanese and not very well-maintained since. Once you're there, the only way of getting around is to walk.

West Sumatra

The province of West Sumatra is like a vast and magnificent nature reserve, dominated by volcanoes, with jungles, waterfalls, canyons and lakes. This is the homeland of the Minangkabau, one of Indonesia's most interesting and influential ethnic groups who make up 95% of the province's population of 3½ million.

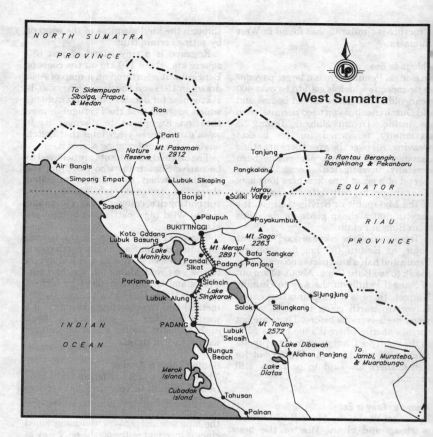

West Sumatra

Padang is the province capital, the other major cities are Payakumbuh, Bukittinggi, Padang Panjang, Solok and Sawahlunto. There are four large lakes in West Sumatra – Singkarak near Solok, Maninjau near Bukittinggi, and Diatas and Dibawah east of Padang.

The fascinating Mentawai Archipelago also falls into the province of West Sumatra. Only recently emerged from the stone age, the inhabitants of these islands are quite different from the people of mainland Sumatra.

The economy, though predominantly based on agriculture (coffee, rice, coconuts and cattle), is strengthened by industries like coal mining.

History

Legend has granted the Minangkabau descent from none other than that tyrannical Macedonian, Alexander the Great. It is said that the original Minangkabau ancestors arrived in Sumatra under the leadership of King Maharjo Dirajo (youngest son of Alexander) or more commonly known in Indonesia as Iskandar Zulkarnair. It is said that the new immigrants settled in the Padang Panjang region, and gradually spread out over western Sumatra.

History suggests that, in fact, the Minangkabau arrived in Indonesia some time between 1000 and 2000 BC. The early Malayu kingdom, which later extended to include what is now West Sumatra, was established by Hindu colonists in the seventh century and became a power in the 12th century following the demise of the Srivijaya empire. It is thought to have been founded by a prince of the Javanese Majapahit empire, and was listed as a dependent of Java in the year 1365. At its zenith, between the 14th and 15th centuries, it stretched right across central Sumatra and included Padang, Jambi, Bengkulu and other cities.

In the 14th century, Islam began to penetrate the area setting up small Muslim states ruled by sultans. They gradually pushed the Minangkabau kingdom further and further inland until by the early 17th century, when the Europeans arrived, it had all but disintegrated. At that time it consisted of little more than a few small-time rajas ruling over minuscule village-states headed by a Palembang-based ruler who was effectively a figurehead.

It continued to survive in this form until the early 19th century when the Padri rebellion, instigated by a group of Muslim fanatics known as the 'men of Pedir', erupted. It was called the Padri rebellion because the Muslim hajis who started it returned to Sumatra via Pedir after their pilgrimage to Mecca. Determined to force the Minang people to follow the strict Islamic law to the letter, the Padri resorted to killing and enslaving anyone who resisted them. The Minangkabau leaders were not prepared to relinquish their power without a fight and defended their rights to follow the traditional system of matriarchy, indulge in gambling and drinking, and practise other pre-Islamic customs. The bitter struggle lasted from 1820 to 1837 but, backed by

the Dutch army and by non-Muslim Bataks, the adat leaders finally overcame the Padri strongholds. Today a curious mix of traditional beliefs and Islam is practised in West Sumatra.

People

For centuries, the West Sumatrans have built their houses with roofs shaped like buffalo horns and called themselves and their land Minangkabau. They have a long literary tradition which includes many popular and imaginative legends about their origins. One of their more flamboyant claims is that they are directly descended from Alexander the Great. There are several theories on the derivation of the name Minangkabau, but the West Sumatrans prefer a colourful 'David & Goliath' version that also demonstrates their shrewd diplomacy and wit:

About 600 years ago one of the kings of Java, who had ambitions of taking over West Sumatra, made the mistake of sending a messenger to advise the people of his intentions and ordering them to surrender. The West Sumatrans, being neither gullible nor stupid, were not prepared to give up without a fight. So as a way of avoiding bloodshed they proposed a bullfight between a Javanese and a Sumatran bull.

When the time came the West Sumatrans dispatched a tiny calf to fight the enormous Javanese bull – a ruse which came as a surprise to both the bull and the onlookers. The calf, which appeared helpless, charged straight for the bull and began to press its nose along the bull's belly searching for milk. Soon after the bull let out a bellow of pain and took to his heels with blood pouring from its stomach and the calf in hot pursuit. When the bull finally dropped dead, the people of West Sumatra were heard to shout, 'minangkabau, minangkabau!' which literally means 'the buffalo wins, the buffalo wins!'

It seems that the owners of the calf separated it from its mother several days before the fight. Half-starved and with sharp metal spears attached to its horns, they sent the calf into the arena. Believing the Javanese bull to be its mother the calf rushed to assuage its hunger and ripped the belly of the bull to shreds.

A far more prosaic explanation is that it is a combination of two words *minanga*, a river in that region, and *kerbau*, meaning buffalo. Or that it comes from the archaic expression *pinang kabhu* meaning original home, Minangkabau being the cradle of the Malay civilisation.

The Minangkabaus are known by their compatriots as the 'gypsies of Indonesia'; they are adaptable, intelligent people and one of the most economically successful ethnic groups in the country. Though staunchly Muslim, the Minangkabau society is still matriarchal and matrilineal. According to Minangkabau adat, a man neither gains possession of a woman by marriage nor a woman a man. Men have no rights over their wives other than to expect them to remain faithful. The eldest living female is the matriarch and has the most power in the household which can number as many as 70 people descended from one ancestral mother, under the same roof. She is deferred to in all matters of family politics.

Every Minangkabau belongs to his or her mother's clan. At the lowest level of the clan is the *sapariouk* which consists of those matri-related kin who eat together. These include the mother, grandchildren and son-in-law. The name comes from the word *periouk* which means rice pot. A number of genealogically related *sapariouk* make up a lineage or *sapayuang*. The word *payung* means umbrella. Children born of a female member of the lineage will, by right of birth, be members of that lineage. Ancestral property is passed down this female line, rather than down the male line.

Property, though worked collectively, belongs to the female line, being inherited by the daughters in the family. All progeny from a marriage are regarded as part of the mother's family group and the father has no say in family affairs. The most important male member of the household is the mother's eldest brother, who replaces the father in being responsible for the children's education and offers them economic advice as they grow older. He also discusses and advises them on their prospective marriages.

Flora & Fauna

Tigers, rhinoceroses, sun bears, elephants and various species of monkey and deer are all native to West Sumatra. Of particular interest in the Mentawai Islands is a rare species of black and yellow monkey, the *siamang kerdil*, usually called *simpai mentawai* by the locals. Their numbers are small and they are strictly protected. There is also diverse birdlife.

The Rafflesia grows in West Sumatra. Some specimens measure as much as a metre across and weigh over seven kg. The flower of the Rafflesia is a gaudy red and white and it gives off a putrid smell which attracts numerous flies and insects. It blooms every year between August and November and can be seen in the small village of Palupuh, 16 km north of Bukittinggi. This province is also famous for its many species of orchids.

Arts & Craft

West Sumatra has a reputation for exquisite, hand-loomed songket cloth and fine embroidery. The development of textile art in West Sumatra was influenced by various countries, but the strongest impact came from Muslim traders when Islam became powerful in the region. One of the many commodities introduced to Sumatra by Muslim traders following the fall of the Hindu Majapahit empire and the emergence of the kingdom of Mataram was the high quality gold and silver threads interwoven through songket cloth.

Today, synthetic substitutes have replaced real silver and gold, but the designs – usually elaborate floral motifs and geometric patterns – are purely Islamic in inspiration. One of the most popular designs, used in both weaving and embroidery, incorporates stylised flowers and mountains in an ornate pattern known as *Gunung Batuah* or magic mountain.

There are various weaving centres in West Sumatra, but the main one is at Silungkang, a small village on the Agam Plateau near the coal mining town of Sawahlunto, which specialises in vividly-coloured silk songket sarongs and scarves. Often the weavings take up to three months to complete. An easily accessible centre is Pandai Sikat, near Padang Panjang on the main road between Padang and Bukittinggi, which is also known for its intricate and decorative woodcarvings.

Another highly developed art form found in West Sumatra is silverwork. Silversmiths are particularly skilled in creating filigree jewellery as fine as spider webs. Kota Gedang near Bukittinggi is the place to go if you're interested.

Dance & Music

The Minangs perform various dances, including the *tari payung* or umbrella dance which is a welcome dance about a young man's love for his girlfriend, and the *tari lilin* or candle dance. The *tari lilin* is performed by a group of young girls who manage by some miracle of physical coordination to rhythmically juggle and balance china saucers, which have lighted candles attached to them, and simultaneously click castanets.

Randai & Pencak Silat The most popular of the Minang dances is the *randai*, a unique dance-drama performed at weddings, harvest festivals and other celebrations. The steps and movements for the randai developed from the pencak silat. The latter is a self-defence dance learned by every Minang boy at the particular stage of puberty when they are considered too old to remain in their mother's house and too young to move into another woman's. It is the custom for Minang youths to spend some time in a *surau* (prayer house) where they are taught, among other things, how to look after themselves. This

includes the pencak silat, a dance with various styles. The one most often performed is the *mudo*, a mock battle which leads the two protagonists to the brink of violence before it is concluded. It is a dramatic dance involving skilled technique, fancy footwork and deliberate pauses which follow each movement and serve to heighten the tension.

The most aggressive and dangerous style of pencak silat originated in the Painan district of West Sumatra. The steps for the *harimau-silat* imitate a tiger stalking and killing its prey. With their bodies as close to the ground as possible, the two fighters circle around menacingly, springing at each other from time to time.

The randai combines the movements of pencak silat with literature, sport, song and drama. Every village in West Sumatra has at least one randai group of 20 performers. Both the female and male roles are played by men wearing traditional *gelambuk* trousers and black dress. The traditional version tells the story of a woman so wilful and wicked that she is driven out of her village before she brings complete disaster on the community. The drama, backed by gamelan music, starts when the actors stand up. Keeping the formation of the circle and adhering faithfully to the pencak silat movements, they begin to sing and dance. Each new scene is indicated when the actors sit down and the characters who have leading roles move to the centre of the circle and begin their performance. The seated actors fulfil three separate functions: they are a living set, they respond to the action centre-stage, and are a prose chorus.

The percussion instruments used to accompany most of the dances are similar to those of the Javanese gamelan and are collectively called the *telempong* in West Sumatra. Two other instruments frequently played are the *puput* and *salung*, both primitive kinds of flute which are usually made out of bamboo, reed or rice stalks.

Festivals

Tabut At the historic seaside town of Pariaman, 36 km north of Padang, the colourful Islamic festival of Tabut is held once a year. It is celebrated in the month of Muharam (the first month of the Islamic lunar calendar) to honour the martyrdom of Mohammed's grandson, Hussein, who was killed in the Kerbala War defending the Muslim faith. Central to the festival is the *bouraq*, a winged horse-like creature with the head of a woman, which is believed to have descended to earth to collect the souls of the dead heroes and take them to heaven.

All the nearby villages construct effigies of bouraqs which they paint in vibrant reds, blues, greens and yellows and adorn with gold necklaces and other paraphernalia. The effigies are carried through the streets with much merriment, dancing and music and are finally tossed into the sea. Spectators and participants then dive into the water themselves and grab whatever remains of the bouraqs, the most valued memento being the gold necklace. When two bouraqs cross paths during the procession a mock fight ensues. Each group praises its own bouraq, belittling and insulting the other at the same time. So popular has this festival become, that people come from all over Indonesia to witness or take part in it. Admission to the area is by donation.

Other West Sumatran towns also celebrate Tabut, but usually on public holidays, such as Independence Day or Hero Day.

Activities

Horse Racing Horse racing is held at Padang, Padang Panjang, Bukittinggi, Payakumbuh and Batu Sangkar throughout the year. It's a vivid, noisy spectacle, nothing like the horse racing of western countries. The horses are ridden bareback and the jockeys are dressed in the traditional costume of the region or village they come from. The aim is to gain prestige for the district where the horse is bred and raised.

Bullfights Bullfighting, known locally as *adu sapi*, is a popular entertainment, unique to West Sumatra. Bullfights are held regularly at three villages between Padang and Bukittinggi: Kota Tinggi, Kota Baru and Kota Lawas. The best places to see one are Kota Baru, which is closer to Bukittinggi than Padang, where they are held every Tuesday afternoon starting at around 5 pm, or Kota Lawas at about the same time.

The afternoon usually kicks off with a meeting of the village elders who discuss matters of communal interest. This is occasionally followed by a demonstration of the martial arts dance, pencak silat, and then the bullfight begins. West Sumatran bullfighting has no resemblance to the Spanish kind – there is no bloodshed (unless by accident) and the bulls, often water buffaloes or *kerbau*, don't get hurt. The original intention was to help develop cattle breeding in the region, but of no less importance is the fact that it gives the men an opportunity to get together to have a good time and to try to make some easy money betting.

Two bulls of roughly the same size and weight are let loose to chase each other round an open field with their owners or attendants goading them on. Once the fight starts it continues until the losing bull tires and runs out of the ring pursued by the winner. Part of the battle is concerned with the animals' strength in pushing each other with locked horns, while another aspect is their skill in breaking away from each other.

The fun for foreigners is in watching the locals make their bets and in seeing them crowd into the ring to urge their favourite on. Occasionally, they get too close for comfort to the tip of the bulls' horns and have to run like crazy with the bulls hot on their heels.

It's an interesting insight into local culture, and well worth going to see. If you want a good vantage spot, far enough away from the stampeding participants to be safe but close to the action, get there early. Catch a bus or a bemo from Bukittinggi to Kota Baru for 200 rp. Give yourself time to check out the Tuesday market which has a small, but good selection of embroidered scarves and sarongs interwoven with gold threads. Follow the crowd down the steps (there are lots of them and they are quite daunting on the way back) and along a path through an exquisite terraced rice paddies until you arrive at the arena.

Other Activities Kite flying is a popular pastime among adults and children. West Sumatrans make huge, colourful kites and many villages hold competitions throughout the year to see whose kite can fly the highest.

In the village of Limbuku, Payakumbuh (the only place in Sumatra where it occurs) they hold a novel duck race with ducks trained to fly a course! It is also customary for the young village girls to attend the race dressed in traditional costume with the idea of attracting a suitor.

Food

West Sumatra is renowned for its hot, spicy food known throughout Indonesia as Padang or Minang cooking. Basic ingredients are beef, mutton, fish, eggs and vegetables with lots of fiery red chillies tempered with turmeric and thick coconut milk. The most famous of the Padang dishes is rendang, chunks of beef or water buffalo cooked for days in coconut milk until the sauce is sludgy thick and the meat is black. In some places rendang is so hot you'd swear you'd received third degree burns to the throat – at least temporarily. Be cautious! Other dishes include eggs dusted in red chillies (*telor balado*), fish (*ikan balado*) and a mutton stew (*gulai kambing*).

There are no menus in a Padang restaurant. Dishes are placed on the table in small bowls – sometimes there could be as many as 10 different kinds of food to sample – with a big bowl of plain rice. You are not obliged to try them all and you

only pay for what you eat. Specialties of the restaurant are often displayed in the front window so you can take a look at what you're going to eat before entering and go somewhere else if you don't like what you see. Don't be overly concerned about the odd fly cruising around the food on display, you'll starve if you try to find a restaurant without flies. Fresh fruit, usually pineapple and bananas, is offered for dessert.

PADANG

Padang is a flat, sprawling city (the name means plain) which looks out across the Indian Ocean and has the Bukit Barisan as a backdrop. It is not only the capital of West Sumatra, but also the biggest seaport along the west coast, Sumatra's third largest city and the province's centre of business and government. For travellers from Java, the port of Teluk Bayur is a major entry and exit point for Sumatra.

Though not particularly inspiring itself, Padang has some fine palm-fringed beaches nearby, the mountains a few hours away and the unique Mentawai Archipelago for the adventurous to explore. The road between Padang and Solok takes you through some of the most picturesque scenery in Sumatra, past exquisite examples of high-peaked Minangkabau houses and lush green carpets of terraced rice paddies. The final descent into Padang from Solok offers spectacular sweeping views along the coastline.

Information & Orientation

Padang is easy to find your way around and the central area is quite compact. Jalan Mohammed Yamin, from the bus terminal corner at Jalan Pemuda to Jalan Azizcham, is the main street of town. The main bus terminal and the oplet terminal are both very centrally located across from the market.

Tourist Office The tourist office (tel 28231) is at Jalan Khatib Sulaiman and is open 8 am to 2 pm Monday to Thursday and

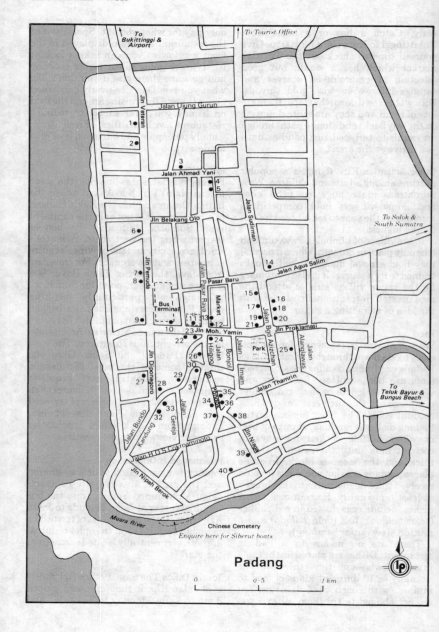

To Bukittinggi & Airport

To Tourist Office

Jln Veteran

Jalan Ujung Gurun

Jalan Ahmad Yani

Jalan Sudirman

Jln Belakang Olo

To Solok & South Sumatra

Jln Pemuda

Jalan Agus Salim

Jalan Pasar Raya

Pasar Baru

Market

Bus Terminal

Jln Moh. Yamin

Jalan Bgd Azizchan

Jln Proklamasi

Jalan Alanglawas

Jalan Hiligoo

Jalan Bonjol

Park

Jln Diponegoro

Jalan Imam

Jln Pondok

Jalan Thamrin

To Teluk Bayur & Bungus Beach

Jalan Bundo

Jalan Kandung

Jalan Gereja

Jalan H.O.S Cokroaminoto

Jln Niaga

Jln Nipah Berok

Muara River

Chinese Cemetery
Enquire here for Siberut boats.

Padang

0   0·5   1 km

1	Telephone Office
2	New Hotel Tiga Tiga
3	Sari Wangi Restaurant
4	Taman Sari Restaurant
5	Tanpa Nama Restaurant
6	Merpati Office
7	Old Tiga Tiga Hotel
8	Cendrawasih Hotel
9	Hang Tuah Hotel
10	Restoran Kubang
11	Oplet Station
12	Taxi Stand
13	Roda Baru Restaurant
14	Garuda Office
15	Bank Dagang Negara
16	Bank Rakyat Indonesia
17	Wisma Femina
18	Hotel Padang
19	Post Office
20	Simpang Raya Restaurant
21	Police
22	Simpang Raya Restaurant
23	Mosque
24	Bank Ekspor Impor
25	Sriwijaya Hotel
26	Machudum's Hotel
27	Art Centre
28	Museum
29	Mariani Hotel
30	Bank Negara Indonesia
31	Pangeran's Hotel
32	New Kartika Hotel
33	Hotel Muara
34	Octavia Restaurant
35	New Kings Restaurant
36	Chan's Restaurant
37	Pagi Sore Restaurant
38	Phoenix Restaurant
39	Aromey Bakery
40	Chinese Temple

Saturday, 8 to 11 am on Friday. It's a fair way out of the city centre. Take an oplet going up Jalan Sudirman and tell them where you're going or look for a 269 mikrolet at the oplet station. The staff are very helpful and several can speak fairly good English. Make sure you make the effort to go to the tourist office if you plan to visit the Mentawai Archipelago. They have lots of information on the islands and

can help you to organise the necessary visitor's permit.

Post & Telephone The post office is at Jalan Azizchan 7, near the junction with Jalan Mohammed Yamin. The Perumtel telephone office is at Jalan Veteran 47.

Bank Bank Negara Indonesia 46 at Jalan Dobi 1 changes foreign cash and travellers' cheques. Moneychangers include C V Eka Jasa Utama at Jalan Niaga 241.

Things to See
Padang itself does not have much to offer apart from Padang food, although in the harbour you can see the rusting remains of Dutch ships, sunk by the Japanese during WW II.

Museums
In the centre of town just down the road from the bus station is the new museum on Jalan Diponegoro, built in the Minang-kabau tradition with two rice barns out front. It has a small but excellent collection of antiques and other objects of historical and cultural interest from all over West Sumatra, and a particularly good textile room. Next to it is the Cultural Centre where local, regional, national, traditional and modern music and dances are performed regularly. They also hold poetry readings, stage plays and hold exhibitions of paintings and carvings. The museum is open daily except Monday, from 9 am to 6 pm. Admission is 200 rp.

Air Manis
Four km south of Padang is the fishing village Air Manis, which literally means Sweet Water. Take a bemo to Muaro, then hire a *prahu* across the river and walk up to the Chinese cemetery which overlooks the town. A km walk will take you to the fishing village of Air Manis and at low tide you can wade out to a small island or take a sampan to a larger one. According to

local mythology, the rock at the end of the beach is all that remains of Malin Kundang (a man who was transformed into stone when he rejected his mother after making a fortune) and his boat. Climb the hill beyond Air Manis for a good view of the port of Teluk Bayur. You can walk to Teluk Bayur, take a look around the harbour and from there get an oplet into the city centre.

Beaches
Bungus, 22 km south of Padang, is a good beach, palm-fringed and postcard-pretty. Oplets run there and you can hire a prahu and paddle out to a nearby island. The last oplet back to Padang leaves at dusk. Other good beaches are Pasir Putih, only seven km from Padang, and Taman Nirwana, 12 km out. To get to Pasir Putih take an oplet or bus to the university at Air Tawar. There are some interesting fishing villages north along the beach.

Islands
There are four islands: Pulaus Pisang Besar, Sikoai, Padang and Bintangur (all within easy reach of Padang and not too expensive to get to) where you can indulge in the life of a lotus-eater. All four offer good skin-diving and snorkelling opportunities, lots of fish and coconut palms. Although it's not difficult to catch your own dinner, take food with you. There are camping grounds on each island and fresh water is available.

The closest island is Pulau Pisang Besar (Big Banana Island), which is only 15 minutes from Muara River Harbour. Hire a sampan with an outboard motor from there. The others are between one and two hours from Teluk Bayur. You can arrange to be dropped off and picked up at a stipulated time a few days later. Ask the harbour master who to approach to take you out to whichever island you choose. It's best to organise a few people to go on this trip. A sampan to carry up to eight passengers with reasonable comfort will cost about 25,000 rp to charter.

Contact the Tourist Information Centre for more information if you are interested in staying on one of these islands.

Festivals
Every year on 17 August, Padang holds a carnival and a huge and colourful boat race on the Batanghari River to commemorate Independence Day. On 5 October the Islamic festival of Tabut commemorates the martyrdom of Mohammed's grandson, Hussein.

Places to Stay – bottom end
Hotel Tiga Tiga (tel 22633) is opposite the bus station at Jalan Pemuda 31. It's still a pretty bare, basic place but mosquito proofing has improved over the years, rooms are clean and plain at 3500 rp per person. The mandis and toilets are OK. In front there are some newer rooms with attached bathroom at 15,000/20,000 rp with fan/air-con.

The *Cendrawasih* (tel 22894) at Jalan Pemuda 27 has rooms at 4000/8000 rp or with attached bathroom at 7000/10,000 rp.

The *Hang Tuah Hotel* (tel 26556) is at Jalan Pemuda 1, right at the corner with Jalan Yaman, and is a modern hotel with rooms with bathroom at 8800 to 13,000 rp with fan, 12,500 to 18,000 rp with air-con. There's a second *Tiga Tiga* (tel 22173) further out at Jalan Veteran 33; rooms in this newer hotel are 13,500/15,000 rp.

The *Hotel Sriwijaya* (tel 23577) at Jalan Alanglawas has singles/doubles at 4000/6000 rp. It's a quiet, small street although not far from the centre and the rooms are simple but each have a little porch area.

Wisma Femina (tel 21950) at Jalan Azizcham 15 has simple rooms with mandis and fan or air-con for 9200/11,500 rp or 14,000/16,000 rp.

Places to Stay – middle
Right across the road from the Wisma Femina is the *Hotel Padang* (tel 22563) at 28, with a large garden area and a variety of rooms starting from simple doubles

with fan at 9500 rp. Better rooms with bathroom and a pleasant little porch out front are 13,500 rp with fan, 20,000 rp with air-con.

Machudum's Hotel (tel 22333) is central, at Jalan Hiligoo 45. It's a big, slightly shabby hotel with a variety of rooms starting from economy singles at 7500 rp, transit rooms at 10,000 rp and then larger rooms, all with air-con, from 16,000 to 28,000 rp.

Places to Stay – top end
More expensive hotels include the *Hotel Mariani International* (tel 25466) at Jalan Bundo Kandung 35.

The *Muara Hotel* (tel 25600) at Jalan Gereja 34 is Padang's number one establishment, complete with swimming pool and rooms at 35,000 to 70,000 rp.

At the springs (Air Manis) near Padang you can stay at cheerful Mr Chili-Chili's, and yes his food is hot!

Places to Eat
Some of the well known Padang food specialists include the *Roda Baru*, upstairs at Jalan Pasar Raya 6, in the market buildings. There are several branches of the *Simpang Raya* nasi Padang chain in Padang. One is at Jalan Mohammed Yamin 125, across from the oplet stand, another larger one is at Jalan Azizcham 24, opposite the post office. *Pagi Sore* ('Morning Evening') is down towards the end of Jalan Pondok at No 143.

There are also some Chinese-Indonesian restaurants, particularly along Jalan Pondok and Jalan Niaga. *Restaurant Octavia* at Jalan Pondok 137 is a simple little place with the standard nasi goreng, mie goreng menu. Across the road is *Chan's* at 94 with live music at night, the *Ri & Ri* at 86A and the *New King's*. Further down at Jalan Niaga 136 is the *Phoenix*, all larger and more expensive.

Towards the end of Jalan Niaga is the *Aromey Bakery* with good baked goods. Or try the *Restoran Kubang* at Jalan Mohammed Yamin 138 near the bus terminal. They really turn out the martabaks here and it's a busy scene with tables set up across the pavement and lots of obviously satisfied customers.

There are lots of small snack stalls operating around the mikrolet/oplet station in the morning. Or at the opposite extreme there are several big restaurants like the *Sari Wangi, Taman Sari* and *Tanpa Nama* along Jalan Ahmad Yani north of the centre.

Getting There & Away
Air Garuda, Mandala and Merpati all have flights to and from Padang. You can arrive in Indonesia at Padang since Garuda connect it with Singapore.

Garuda (tel 23823) is at Jalan Sudirman 2. Merpati (tel 27908) is at Jalan Pemuda 45A. Mandala (tel 21979) is at Jalan Pemuda 29A.

Garuda has flights from Padang to many other parts of Indonesia. Within Sumatra there are daily flights from Padang to Banda Aceh, Medan, Palembang and Pekanbaru. There are daily flights from Padang to Jakarta, Denpasar, Ujung Pandang and many other places.

Mandala has daily flights from Padang to Jakarta. Merpati has flights about once a week from Padang to Sirebut Island.

Rail The railway line from Padang to Bukittinggi used to be quite an attraction for railway enthusiasts, but now it's only used as far as Padang Panjang and only for freight trains. You can see some old steam engines permanently parked at Padang Panjang, the line beyond here is spectacular, crossing and recrossing the road, but derelict and overgrown.

Bus The Padang bus terminal is conveniently central and there are frequent departures for buses north and south.

There are frequent buses to Bukittinggi. The trip costs 1100 rp and takes about 2½ hours along a good road with wonderful scenery. If you arrive in Padang by air there's no need to go into town as the main road with buses bound for Bukittinggi is only 100 metres from the terminal.

From the city terminal there are buses to: Jambi (6000 rp, 12 hours), Palembang (15,000 rp or 17,500 rp with air-con, takes 24 hours), Pekanbaru (5000 rp), Prapat (12,000 rp), and Jakarta (20,000 rp or 30,000 rp with air-con).

You can also take long-distance taxis from Padang. Check with Natrabu at Jalan Pemuda 29B.

Boat The Pelni ship *Kerinci* operates a regular Jakarta-Padang-Sibolga service. Jakarta to Padang takes about 27 hours and costs from 27,000 to 68,000 rp. The Pelni office (tel 22109) is on Jalan Tanjung Priok, Teluk Bayur.

There are occasional ships from Padang to Bengkulu and Nias Island and a regular shipping service from Padang to Siberut Island.

Getting Around

Airport Transport Padang's Tabing airport is nine km north of the centre on the Bukittinggi road. The standard taxi fare into town is 5000 rp, but you can walk 100 metres out to the road and catch an oplet for 100 rp, or head straight north to Bukittinggi.

Local Transport There are numerous oplets and mikrolets around town. The standard fare is 100 rp to 150 rp. There's a taxi stand beside the market building on Jalan Mohammed Yamin.

PADANG TO BUKITTINGI

The 90-km drive north from Padang to Bukittinggi is lyrically beautiful with its pastiche of rice paddies, Minangkabau houses, glimpses of the sea and views of the towering Singgalang and Merapi volcanoes – each almost 3000 metres high. Merapi last erupted in 1926. Along this route is the Lembah Anai Nature Reserve, renowned for its waterfalls, wild orchids and the giant Rafflesia flowers. Lake Singarak, which is bigger than Lake Maninjau and with fewer tourists, is nearby.

PADANG PANJANG

Padang Panjang is the main town the Padang to Bukittingi road passes through. It's interesting for its conservatorium of Minangkabau culture, dance and music – the ASKI. This is the best place to get accurate information on live dance and theatre performances. It has a fine collection of musical instruments which includes Minangkabau and Javanese gamelan outfits. There are also excellent costume displays, which are particularly interesting for the bridal jewellery and ornaments like the headdress, necklace and the deceptively light bracelet called *galang-gadang*.

Getting There & Away

Padang Panjang is a good afternoon or morning trip from either Padang or Bukittingi. There are regular buses between Bukittinggi, Padang and Padang Panjang. Passenger trains no longer run between Padang and Bukittinggi but there is still an ancient steam train that hauls coal up and down the line. Try hitching; a good short trip can be made between Kota Baru and Padang Panjang.

BUKITTINGGI

This cool, easy-going mountain town (about 900 metres above sea level) is one of the most popular tourist destinations in Sumatra. It's often called Kota Jam Gadang, the Big Ben Town, because of the clock tower that overlooks the large market square. Bukittinggi is known locally as Tri Arga, after the three majestic mountains that encircle it – Merapi, Singgalang and Sago. A Dutch stronghold during the Padri rebellion (1821-1837), Bukittinggi is today the cultural and educational centre of the Minangkabau people.

Information & Orientation

The centre of town is compact and the

usty iron roofs make it look remarkably like hill-station towns in India. Like them the different levels of streets connected by steps makes it a bit confusing initially.

Tourist Office The tourist office is beside the market car park, overlooked by the clock tower. They have a few leaflets, maps and brochures on West Sumatra and they are open from Monday to Thursday from 8 am to 2 pm, Friday from 8 to 11 am, and Saturday from 8 am to 12.30 pm.

Post & Telephone The post office is on Jalan Jenderal Sudirman 75. The telephone office is at Jalan Jenderal Sudirman 2.

Bank You can also change money at the Toko Eka on Jalan Minangkabau, in the central market. There's a Bank Negara Indonesia in the Pasar Atas (market) building.

Market

Bukittinggi's large and colourful market is crammed with stalls of fruit and vegetables, clothing and crafts. Market days are Wednesdays and Saturdays.

Museum & Zoo

On a hill top site right in the centre of town is Taman Bundokanduag, a museum and zoo. The museum, which was built in 1934 by the Dutch 'Controleur' of the district, is a superb example of Minangkabau architecture with its two rice barns (added in 1956) out front. It is the oldest museum in the province and has a good collection of Minangkabau historical and cultural exhibits. The zoo is disgusting – the best thing you could do for its inmates would be to shoot them.

Fort de Kock

Except for the defence moat and a few cannons, not much remains of Bukittinggi's old Fort de Kock, built during the Padri Wars (1821-1837) by the Dutch. It provides fine views over the town and surrounding countryside from its hill top position.

Outside Bukittingi market

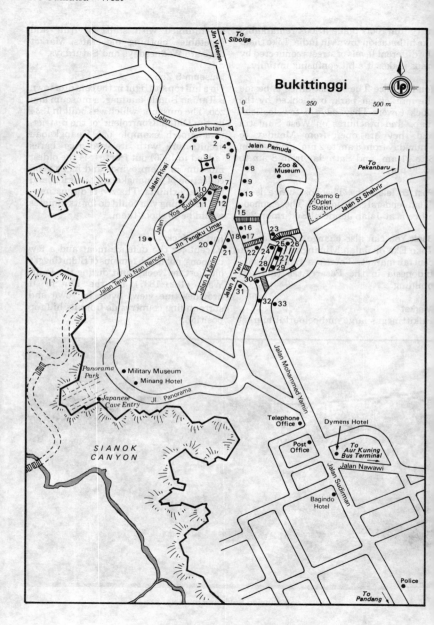

Bukittinggi

0   250   500 m

To Sibolga

Jln Veteran

Jalan Kesehatan

Jalan Pemuda

To Pekanbaru

Zoo & Museum

Jalan Rivai

Jalan St Shahrir

Bemo & Oplet Station

Jalan Yos Sudarso

Jln Tengku Umar

Jalan A Karim

Jalan A Yani

Jalan Tengku Nan Renceh

Panorama Park

Military Museum

Minang Hotel

Japanese Cave Entry

Jl Panorama

SIANOK CANYON

Jalan Mohammed Yamin

Telephone Office

Dymens Hotel

To Aur Kuning Bus Terminal

Post Office

Jalan Nawawi

Jalan Sudirman

Bagindo Hotel

Police

To Pandang

1	Denai Hotel
2	Lima's Hotel
3	Fort de Kock
4	Murni's Hotel
5	Nirwana Hotel
6	Family Restaurant
7	Hotel Yany
8	Three Tables Coffee House
9	Singgalang Hotel
10	Benteng Hotel
11	Suwarni Hotel
12	Grand Hotel
13	Golden Leaf Restaurant
14	Mountain Veiw Hotel
15	Wisma Tiga Bali
16	Gangga Hotel
17	Mona Lisa Restaurant
18	Singgalang Restaurant
19	Wisma Bukittinggi
20	Surya Hotel
21	New American Restaurant
22	Mosque
23	Gloria Cinema
24	Simpang Raya Restaurant
25	Roda Group Restaurant
26	Pasar Wisata
27	Pasar Atas
28	Simpang Raya Restaurant
29	Bank Negara Indonesia
30	Tourist Office
31	Clocktower
32	Jogja Hotel
33	Hotel Antokan

Panorama Park & Japanese Caves

Panorama Park, on the southern edge of the town, overlooks the deep Sianok Canyon that cuts right into Bukittinggi. In the park is the entry to the extensive grid of caves which the Japanese tunnelled out during WW II. Many of the tunnels look out from the cliff faces over the canyon. Entry to the caves or *Lobang Jepang* is 250 rp. At the entrance there's a bas-relief showing the Japanese herding the helpless Indonesians inside.

Military Museum

Next to the Minang Hotel and overlooking Panorama Park is the Military Museum, which mainly houses a collection of faded photographs from the independence war against the Dutch. Of particular interest are photos of the bodies of the five Indonesian generals murdered at the time of the supposed Communist-led attempted coup of 1965, plus war souvenirs and photos from Indonesia's war against the Fretlin guerrillas in East Timor.

Places to Stay – bottom end

Bukittinggi's cheap hotels are a pretty plain, dull and charmless lot although they're certainly cheap. Most of them are concentrated along Jalan Ahmad Yani, right in the centre of town. *Murni's* at 115 has plain, but clean singles/doubles at 1500/3000 rp and a nice sitting area upstairs. *Nirwana's* (tel 21292) is right next door at 113. The *Singgalang Hotel* (tel 21576) at 130 is also plain and basic with rooms at 2000/3000 rp.

The *Hotel Tiga Balai* (tel 21824) at Jalan Ahmad Yani 100 is a rock-bottom rabbit warren with musty rooms for 3000 rp. The closet-size mandis are definitely in need of an overhaul. The only reason for staying here – and quite a few people do – is that it's cheap.

The *Hotel Yany* (tel 22740) at Jalan Ahmad Yani 101 seems to be an old colonial building gone to rack and ruin. Shabby, box-like rooms at the rear are 4000 rp. At the front are some bright, airy dorms for 2000 rp per person. Or try a big, homely double room for 25,000 rp.

The *Grand Hotel* (tel 2133) at Jalan Ahmad Yani 99 is recommended. It has some dingy ground-floor rooms for 5000 rp, but there are some better upstairs rooms for 7500 rp. Some of the rooms have no windows, but for the most part this is a clean, agreeable and fairly quiet hotel. Of all the low budget hotels in Bukittingi, this is probably the best kept.

Places to Stay – middle

Probably the best of the bottom and middle-range hotels is the *Wisma Bukittingi* (tel

22900) at Jalan Yos Sudarso 1A. This is an old, well-kept Dutch house, with single and double rooms from 5000 to 10,000 rp. It's on a quiet street above the main part of town, a few minutes walk from the fort.

The *Gangga Hotel* (tel 22967) at Jalan Yos Sudarso 70 costs 2000/2500 rp for basic rooms, while better rooms are 4000 rp or 5000 rp with shower. A few steps off Jalan Jenderal Ahmad Yani at Jalan Tengku Umar 7 the *Surya Hotel* (tel 22587) has rooms at 5000/6500 rp or with attached bathroom at 7000/8500 rp.

There are several places on the way up to Fort de Kock. The *Mountain View Guest House* (tel 21621) at Jalan Yos Sudarso 3 is a pleasant place with rooms at 7500 rp with mandi. Further up the road, next to the Benteng Hotel, is the quiet *Suwarni's* with dorm beds or rooms at 6000 rp.

Places to Stay – top end

There are some other places at lower and higher levels. *Hotel Jogja* (tel 21142) is directly below the market and clock tower at Jalan Mohammed Yamin 17. There are straightforward rooms upstairs for 3500 rp per person (poor value for two people) and downstairs rooms with mandi for 10,000/15,000 rp and deluxe rooms for 17,500/22,500 rp. (Jalan Yamin is also known as Jalan Perintis Kemerdekaan.)

The *Benteng Hotel* (tel 21115) at Jalan Benteng 1, the road leading up to what remains of the old fort, is favoured by many people and has good views of the town. It has rooms from 21,000/23,000 rp.

After the Benteng, other middle-range hotels are somewhat overshadowed but *Lima's Hotel* (tel 22641 & 22763) at Jalan Kesehatan 34 has rooms at 9000/10,000 rp or with bathroom at 15,000/17,500 rp and 25,000/27,500 rp. It's modern, but the rooms are rather cramped.

Dymen's Hotel (tel 21015) at Jalan Nawawi 3 has rooms for 24,000/28,000 rp. It's a very fine hotel and is definitely recommended.

The *Denai Hotel & Cottage* (tel 21524)

at Jalan Dr Rivai 26 has rooms from 34,000/39,000 rp. It's a very commodious hotel, with very comfortable rooms as well as several cottages in traditional Minangkabau style.

Places to Eat

In amongst the cheap hotels along Jalan Ahmad Yani are two very popular restaurants with menus which feature all those familiar travellers' specials from fruit salad to banana pancakes. The *Coffee House* at 103 is smaller and has a pleasant outdoor area overlooking the street. The newer *Three Tables Coffee House* at 142 is a bit bigger (there are more than three tables) and equally popular.

Further down at Jalan Ahmad Yani 58 is the *Mona Lisa*, a tiny place with a Chinese-influenced menu. Just off that street, at Jalan Tengku Umar 14, is the big *New American Restaurant*. The *Asean Restaurant* is hidden away next door at 12A and has good Chinese food.

Padang food is important in Bukittinggi and the *Roda Group Restaurant* in the Pasar Atas market building has good food. Directly across from it is *Kedai Kopi Sianok* where you can sample the local sweet *sarikaya* (custard on top of bread or rice) which tastes better than it sounds.

In the Pasar Wisata building, right next to the Pasar Atas building, there are more restaurants and warungs including a branch of the *Simpang Raya* nasi Padang restaurants at each end of the block. Up on the Fort de Kock hill, right at the top of the road, the *Family Restaurant* (or Famili) also does pretty good Padang food.

A number of places in Bukittinggi, including the western-oriented coffee houses, do the local speciality *dadhi campur*, a tasty mixture of oats, coconut, avocado, banana, molasses and buffalo yoghurt.

Things to Buy

Bukittingi is one of the more pleasing parts of Indonesia to accumulate handicrafts and souvenirs, for the most part attractive and in good taste. There are a number of antique, souvenir and curio shops around. Try Kerajinan at Jalan Ahmad Yani 44, and Aladdin at Jalan Jenderal Ahmad Yani 14. There are more around the market area.

There are a couple of Minangkabau artefacts that you can pick up as souvenirs in the shops around Bukittingi. *Salapah panjang*, or long boxes, are brass boxes used for storing lime and tobacco. *Salapah padusi* are silver boxes used for storing betel nut and lime (although, of course, the silver is not always real).

Another form of Minangkabau weaving, though one you're probably not likely to find any examples of, uses a technique called 'needle weaving'. In this process, certain threads of the cloth are physically removed and the remaining ones stitched together to form patterns. These patterns may include identifiable motifs such as people, crabs, insects, dogs or horses. Traditionally, such cloth is used to cover the *carano* – a brass sireh stand with receptacles for different ingredients (betel nut, tobacco, lime) – which is used for ceremonial occasions.

Songket cloth is distinguished by the silver and gold threads which are woven into the fabric. Although it would be possible to get cloth with genuine silver and gold thread, all the stuff you commonly see for sale around Bukittingi uses imitation silver and gold thread imported from India. However, even cloth using imitation thread is moderately expensive because of the amount of time and work involved in weaving it.

Songket cloth is made in the Tanah Datar region in the villages of Pandai Sikat and Tanjung Sungayang. Also worth trying is Sungayang, near Batu Sangkar. Pandai Sikat is easy to get to from Bukittingi. Take a bemo for 200 rp from the main bus station and get off at the Pandai Sikat turnoff (half an hour down the road towards Padang Panjang). From there it's half an hour's walk to the village. Pandai Sikat has many workshops making songket cloth as well as the finely carved furniture for which this village is also known.

In the region of Lima Puluh Kota, near the border with Riau Province, traditional weaving is done in several villages. Commercial weaving is done in Kubang, 13 km from the town of Payakumbuh. Ceremonial cloth is produced at Silungkang. Other weaving villages in this area include Balai Cacang, Kota Nan Ampek, and Muaro.

The Minangkabau are also noted for their fine embroidery work. Villages which specialise in this are Kota Gadang, Ampek Angkek, Naras, Lubuk Begalung, Kota Nan Ampek and Sunguyang.

Getting There & Away
Bus The Aur Kuning bus station is some distance from the town centre but you can get there easily on the local oplets.

Padang is only about 2½ hours south of Bukittinggi. The road north to Sibolga and Prapat has improved considerably over the years; regular buses make the trip to Prapat in 15 hours, although heavy rain can still cause big problems. A special tourist bus operates irregularly to Prapat. It costs 12,500 rp and takes 12 to 13 hours.

ANS have an office (tel 22626) on Jalan Pemuda and another office (tel 21679) at the terminal.

Typical bus fares from Bukittingi are: to Sibolga 5500 rp, Prapat 8000 rp, Medan 9000 rp or 15,000 rp with an air-con bus, Padang 1000 rp, Pekanbaru 3500 rp, Jakarta 23,000 rp or 32,000 rp with an air-con bus.

Train The old steam trains on this route no longer carry passengers but railway enthusiasts may be able to organise a ride on the freight trains.

Getting Around
The main bemo, dokkar and oplet station is in the middle of town. From here you

catch one of these to the Air Kuning bus station (Bukittinggi's main station just on the outskirts of town). Oplets around town cost a flat 100 rp.

Tours It's easy to get tours of the area. Ask around in the coffee shops, restaurants and hotels along Jalan Ahmad Yani. They organise tours of the local area, usually on Tuesdays and Saturdays when the bullfighting takes place. A great deal depends on the guide you get. There are a few good guides who are informative and knowledgeable, but others can only provide some basic translation. If you take these tours for what they really are – a quick way of getting a glimpse of a lot of places all at once – and then go back for a better look at the places you found interesting, then they're worthwhile. Sometimes they take you to places like blacksmithing homesteads and sugar cane crushing works that you wouldn't have known existed unless someone showed you.

AROUND BUKITTINGGI
Kota Gadang
There is a path through the Sianok Canyon to the other side and on to the village of Kota Gadang. Turn left at the bottom of the road just before the canyon and keep going. Don't cross the bridge there.

Kota Gadang is noted for its silverwork, which, though exquisite, is limited in range. It is about 12 km from Bukittinggi.

Pandai Sikat
There are several other villages around Bukittinggi which are still producing traditional crafts. One of the more interesting is Pandai Sikat, 13 km away from Bukittinggi, a centre for weaving and wood carving.

Ngalau Kamanga
Ngalau Kamanga, 15 km east of

Bukittinggi, was the scene of active resistance against the Dutch in the 19th and early 20th centuries. The story goes that the villagers used a 1500-metre long local cave as a hide-out from the Dutch conducting effective guerrilla attacks in the surrounding country from this base. The cave is dripping with stalactites and stalagmites and has a small, clear lake.

Kota Baru
Bullfights are held every Tuesday afternoon around 5 pm in the village of Kota Baru. The fight is known as adu sapi and involves two water buffaloes of roughly the same size and weight locking horns under the watchful eyes of their respective owners. Most of the fun is in watching the locals make their bets. Once the fight starts it continues until one of the bulls breaks away and runs out of the ring – which usually results in two bulls chasing each other around and the on-lookers running in every direction.

Batu Sangkar

About 45 km south-east of Bukittinggi, turning off the Padang Panjang to Solok road, is the village of Batu Sangkar. Turn off the road towards the village of Pagaruyang (four km distance) and you'll see many Minangkabau houses. Along the roadside are stone tablets inscribed in Sanskrit.

Rafflesia Sanctuary

There is a Rafflesia sanctuary about 15 km north of Batu Sangha, a sign at the village of Batang Palupuh indicates the path. The Rafflesia bloom between August and December. Further north on the way to Sibolga, a large globe stands in a rice paddy beside the road, indicating the position of the equator. Up this way there's horse racing on Sundays, definitely not the Grand National or the Melbourne Cup, but lots of fun.

Lake Maninjau

About 30 km south-west of the town is Lawang Top and directly below it, Lake Maninjau. The final descent to the lake involves covering 12 km with four-score hairpin bends – it's quite a terrifying trip.

You can take a bus there direct from Bukittinggi or get off at Matur, climb to Lawang for the view and then walk down to the lake, which takes a couple of hours if you're fit and much longer if you're not. If you miss the last bus you either have to charter a bemo back, which could be expensive, or spend the night there.

Lake Maninjau is warmer than Toba and is an extremely beautiful crater lake. You can zip around it by speedboat or water scooter if you wish. The lake walk, with tea stops at the top and bottom of the hill, is well worth doing. The fewer people in your group the more wildlife you'll see.

Mount Merapi

Mount Merapi can be climbed. To get there take a bus towards Padang Panjang and get off at the Koto Baru turnoff. From Koto Baru it's a one hour climb to the forestry station and then another four hours to the top. Merapi is reportedly off-limits to climbers because it's still active and said to be dangerous. Enquire in Bukittingi.

Harau Valley

To get to the Harau Valley, first take a bus to Payakumbuh. Then take a bemo across town to the market. From here you get another bemo to Harau Valley or to Sari Lamak (from here it's a five km walk to the valley). The valley is more of a canyon, with a waterfall cascading down one side. On Sundays it's very crowded with Indonesian day-trippers, although this may be the only day you can get transport the whole way out there. You can walk to Harau village which is three km up the valley.

Other Attractions

Other attractions include Sungai Tarab where you can see coffeemills worked by waterwheel. Pagaruyang has a reconstruction of a massive Minangkabau king's house. Nearby is Lima Kaum where there are a number of stones carved with ancient Sanskrit writing. The village of Balimbing is noted for its fine Minangkabau traditional houses. The village of Kota Gadang is noted for its silverwork. On Wednesday and Saturday mornings there are displays of traditional Minangkabau self-defence at Ujung Bukit. Traditional Minangkabau dance performances are held at the Bukittingi museum on Wednesdays, Saturdays and Sundays.

The Mentawai Islands

Not far off the west coast of mainland Sumatra, in the Indian Ocean, are the islands of the Mentawai Archipelago. The four islands in the group – Siberut, Sipora, North and South Pagai – are almost entirely surrounded by coral reefs. The

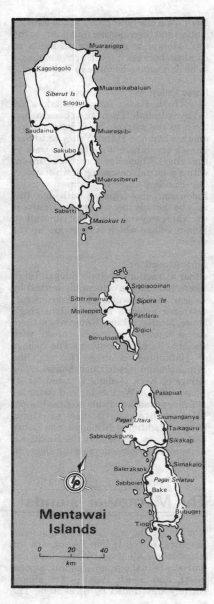

Mentawai Islands

0   20   40
km

largest is Siberut. Over 30,000 people live on the islands, the majority of them on Siberut. The nearest major port is Padang's Teluk Bayur, which is only 150 km away from Siberut.

History

Very little is known about the origins of the Mentawaians but it is assumed that they emigrated from Sumatra to Nias and made their way to Siberut from there. They remained isolated and undisturbed by other cultures until late in the 19th century, when the Dutch permitted Protestant missionaries to attempt to convert them to Christianity.

There are several references to the islands before the 19th century. In 1621, it appears that Siberut was the only island inhabited. The Mentawaians are also mentioned in a scientific paper presented in 1799 by the Englishman John Crisp. Sir Stamford Raffles appears to have been particularly impressed by the Mentawaians and their culture. In one of the many reports he wrote urging the British government to compete with the Dutch in colonising Indonesia he says:

Formerly, I intended to write a book to prove that the Niassans were the most contented people on earth. Now I have to acknowledge the fact that the people of the Mentawai Islands are even more admirable and probably much less spoiled than we.

In 1864 the Mentawai Archipelago was nominally made a Dutch colony, but it was not until 1901, at the time of the Russo-Japanese war, that the Dutch placed a garrison on the islands to prevent another foreign power using them as a naval base.

People

Although the distance between mainland Sumatra and the Mentawai Islands is not great, strong winds, unpredictable seas and coral reefs made navigation to the islands difficult in earlier centuries. The result was that the inhabitants of the

Mentawaians had very little contact with the outside world and remained one of the purest indigenous Indonesian societies until early in the 20th century when the missionaries arrived.

Before then they had their own language, their own adat and their own religion. They were skilled in boat building, but had not developed any kind of handicraft nor cultivated rice. Religious taboos, which prevented them from tending the fields consistently, could account in part for their unwillingness to grow rice.

Physically, the Mentawaians are slim and agile. Traditional clothing consists of a loin cloth made from the bark of the breadfruit tree for men and a bark skirt for women. They decorate themselves with tattoos which cover part of their faces and most of their bodies and wear bands of red-coloured rattan, beads and imported brass rings on their arms, fingers and toes. Both men and women often thread flowers through their long hair.

Culture & Society

Villages are built along river banks and consist of one or more communal houses (*uma*) surrounded by single-storey family houses (*lalep*). A number of families (between five and 10) live in the same building. Bachelors and widows have their own living quarters, known as *rusuk*, which are identical to the family longhouse except that they have no altar. Traditionally all the houses stand on wooden piles and are designed without windows. Each village is surrounded by a log wall to contain the livestock.

Large villages are divided into sections, each with its own uma and each section is referred to as the uma. Although it is essentially a patriarchal society, it is organised on egalitarian principles. There are no inherited titles or positions, and no subordinate roles. It is the uma, not the village itself, which becomes the pivot of social, political and religious life in Mentawai society. It is here that discussions affecting the community take place. Everyone – men, women and children – takes part in major decisions, including choosing a *rimata* (the person who leads religious affairs and is the community's spokesperson to the outside world), building an uma, clearing forests, or laying out a banana plantation.

On such occasions the people of the uma carry out a religious festival known as *punen*. This usually involves ritual sacrifices of both pigs and chickens and, depending on the importance of the occasion, can last for months on end and sometimes years. All kinds of everyday jobs and activities become taboo; work in the fields is stopped and strangers are denied access to the uma – its isolation being marked by a cordon of palm leaves and flowers.

Religion

Apart from taking a few minor precautions to protect the Mentawai Islands from being taken over by any other imperialist nations, the Dutch showed very little interest in them.

It was the missionaries who had the most influence on the people, creating fundamental changes in their culture. The first permanent mission was set up in 1901 in North Pagai by a German missionary, August Lett. Eight years later, Lett was murdered by the local people but the mission survived and by 1916 there had been 11 baptisms recorded. There are now more than 80 Protestant churches throughout the islands. Over half the population claims to be Protestant, 16% to be Catholic, 13% Muslim, while the rest have no official religion.

It was over 50 years after the advent of the Protestant missionaries before the Catholics moved into the islands to vie for converts. They opened a mission in south Siberut which combined a church, a school and a clinic. Free medicines and clothes were given to any islander who became a Catholic and by 1969 there were almost 3000 converts. The Islamic influence began to make inroads once government officials were regularly appointed from Padang during the Dutch era. To complicate religious matters further, the eclectic Baha'i faith was introduced in 1955.

The native Sibulungan religion was a form of animism, involving the worship of nature spirits and a belief in the existence of ghosts as well as the soul. The chief nature spirits are those in the sky, sea, jungle and earth. There are also two river spirits: Ina Oinan (mother of rivers) is beneficent while Kameinan (father's sister) is regarded as being evil. Aside from these nature spirits all inanimate objects have spirits or *kina* which give them life. There is no hierarchy among the spirits, although the sky spirits are considered the most influential, nor do they have any particular gender, but like human beings there's a mixture of men, women and children.

As with all religions in Indonesia, the worship of the soul is of the utmost importance, being vital to good health and longevity. The soul is believed to depart the body at various times during life before its ultimate escape at death. Sickness, for example, is the result of the temporary absence of the soul from the body, while dreams also signify that the soul is on 'vacation'. When the soul leaves the body at death it is transformed into a ghost (*sanitu*). Mentawaians try to avoid these ghosts, whom they suspect of malevolently attempting to rob the living of their souls. To protect themselves from such an awful fate, they place fetish sticks at every entrance to the village. This tactic is fool proof, provided no-one has committed a ritual sin or broken a taboo.

Agriculture

Taros and bananas are the staple crops of both the Pagai islands and Sipora, while on Siberut sago is also cultivated. Traditionally, the women own the taro fields and are responsible for planting and maintaining them. The taros are planted under water in loose, marshy earth and it takes a year before they can be eaten. The banana plantations belong to the men – some are worked by one or two families, others by an entire uma. The Mentawaians also grow cassava, sweet potatoes and other crops. Their diet is supplemented by hunting and fishing.

SIBERUT

In the past, only a few adventurous foreigners have visited Siberut, but it's now becoming increasingly popular as people seek out areas relatively untouched by tourism. Although Siberut is being promoted as a tourist destination, the deluge is not likely to happen overnight. There is no public transport, no losmen or restaurants. However, the government's resettlement policy and the activities of timber felling companies have already created enormous changes in the living conditions of the local people and in the flora and fauna.

Information

Before going to this island you must get a visitor's permit from the Police Station (tel 110), Jalan Prof M Yamin, Padang. While they are likely to tell you the permit is not strictly necessary it is possible that you won't be allowed to explore the interior of the island if you don't have one. There is no official charge for the permit.

Money Siberut is not, by shoestring budget standards, a cheap place to visit. Take plenty of cash as there are no banks on the island. You cannot change foreign cash or travellers' cheques there. In Muarasiberut cash is the everyday currency, but in most other villages the people may prefer food, tobacco and tools. The biggest expense on the island is the cost of getting around. You also have to pay off the police, which will probably be around 5000 rp per day. You also need to take food supplies – rice and sugar – a stock of cigarettes and other goods like tools and medicines for presents and bartering. A visit to an off-the-beaten-track village, including the boat fare to the island, fees for the local guide, accommodation, food and presents for the villagers, costs about 500,000 rp for two people for a three-week visit.

Things to See

Despite recent changes to the island, about two-thirds of the island is still covered with tropical rainforest. It's also surrounded by magnificent coral reefs teeming with fish. The two main towns on Siberut are Muarasikabaluan in the north and Muarasiberut (where the boat docks) at the southern tip of the east coast. There is no public transport on the island and so you either have to walk between the villages, or hire boats to take you along the coast.

From Muarasiberut only four villages are accessible by foot: Sakelot (one km), Mailepet (four km), Muntei (within six km) and Pasakiat (about seven km). Of these four villages, Sakelot is the most interesting because it is the oldest and has retained its traditional houses. The others are new – part of the government's resettlement policy of moving the people out of the jungle and setting them up in villages along the coastal strip.

One of the quickest and easiest villages to get to is Tiop, which takes two hours by boat along a narrow branch of jungle river. A more adventurous, but still comparatively easy trip is to Rokdok. The people live in small, traditional houses and someone has taught the village children to sing Silent Night in Bahasa Indonesia to travellers – a rather eerie experience. It takes between five and six hours there and back by boat. Two more remote villages are Sakudai and Madobak. The journey to Sakudai takes two days – one day by boat and the other trekking through the jungle. The trip to Madobak takes six hours by boat.

Places to Stay & Eat

There are no losmen, no restaurants or warungs. You can stay at missionary buildings, schools or with private families, but don't expect any comforts. Accommodation is usually on the floor and costs around 1000 rp per person a night.

Getting There & Away

Air Enquire at Merpati about flights from Padang to Rokor Mentawai on Siberut Island. There is usually one flight per week for about 20,000 rp.

Boat If you're going by government boat from Padang to Siberut then plan on staying on the island for a minimum of two weeks. Government boats leave Teluk Bayur (the port of Padang) for Siberut about every two weeks. The fare is around 4000 rp per person. Check with the tourist office in Padang for information, and with the harbour master at Teluk Bayur for shipping departures and schedules.

Other options include chartering private boats from Padang or Nias. Small boats are available for charter but are not advised as the sea and winds are rough and unpredictable in this region – the journey is not only likely to be uncomfortable, but could also be dangerous. If you only intend chartering the boat one way, you will have to pay the return passage if it goes back empty.

Tours Many people adopt the easy option, which is to join an organised tour to the island. These can be booked in Bukittingi, at several travel agencies and last roughly nine to 10 days. You leave Bukittingi by bus for Padang, and then take the overnight boat to Muarasiberut. From Muarasiberut, you take a small boat to Madobag village, which takes seven hours. From here you begin trekking to the villages of Butui, Ugai and several other destinations before returning to Padang. The charge is around US$100 per person, but you may have to pay more because of the extra expenses once you're on the island.

North Sumatra

The province of North Sumatra covers an area of 70,787 square km, stretching from Aceh in the north to West Sumatra in the south and from the Indian Ocean in the west to the Melaka Straits in the east. It has a population of over eight million and is divided into 11 *kabupatens* (regencies) and six *kotamadyas* (municipalities).

There are five main ethnic groups in North Sumatra: the Coastal Malays, who live along the Melaka Straits; the Karonese, Simalungun, Dairi and Toba Batak groups in the highlands around Lake Toba and Samosir Island; the Pesisirs (Central Tapanuli) along the Indian Ocean coastline; the Mandailings and Angkolas (South Tapanuli) in the south and the people from Nias Island. These ethnic groups all have their own dialects, religious beliefs and traditional customs, arts and cultures, which in turn are overlaid by the dominant influences of Islam and the national language, Bahasa Indonesia.

North Sumatra produces more than 30% of Indonesia's exports and handles about 60% of them. Fine tobacco is grown around Medan and oil, palm-oil, tea, and rubber are also produced in large quantities and exported from the port of Belawan, about 26 km away.

MEDAN

Medan is the capital of North Sumatra and the third largest city in Indonesia. The city has had a chequered history and has witnessed various wars. From end of the 16th century through to the early 17th century it was a battlefield in the power struggle between the two kingdoms of Aceh and Deli and during the 19th century it was involved in the Sunggal War against the Dutch.

The name is said to have been derived from the Portuguese word Medina, dating

its first use in Sumatra from the beginning of the 16th century. In Indonesian the word 'medan' literally means field or arena and it was on the fertile swamp at the junction of the Deli and Babura rivers, near the present Jalan Putri Hijau, that

1	Bohorok & Banda Aceh Bus Station
2	Medan Fair
3	Dell Plaza Shopping Centre
4	Taman Budaya
5	PT Indosat
6	Deli Dharama Hotel
7	Bank Negara Indonesia
8	Post Office
9	Railway Station
10	Central Bus Station
11	Central Market
12	Indian Restaurant
13	Westin Fried Chicken
14	Indian Temple
15	Dirga Surya Hotel
16	Army Museum
17	Irama Hotel
18	Hotel Danau Toba International, MAS
19	Tourist Office
20	Tip Top Restaurant
21	Bank Dagang Negara
22	Chinese Food Street
23	Brastagi Bus Station
24	Tapian Nabaru Hotel
25	Hotel Polonia
26	Pelni Office
27	Garuda Office
28	Sigura Gura
29	Rumah Makan Gembira
30	Rumah Makan Famali
31	Merpati Office
32	Dhaksina Hotel & Garuda Plaza Hotel
33	Sumatra Hotel & Garuda Hotel
34	Inda Taxi & Penanag Ferry Office
35	Malmoon Castle
36	Great Mosque
37	Padang Bus Station & Melati Hotel
38	Prapat Bus Station
39	Wisma Sibayak
40	Polonia Airport
41	Medan Zoo

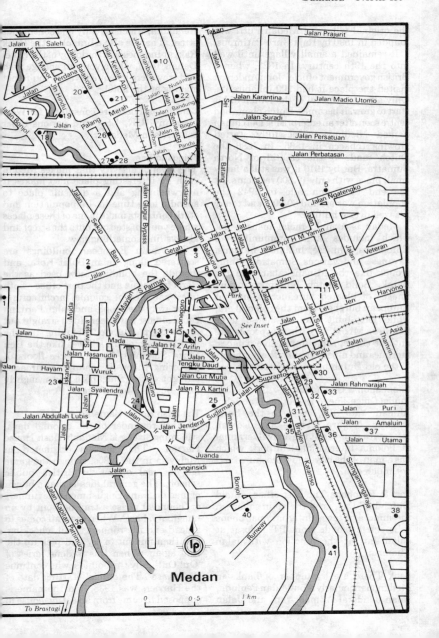

Medan

0   0.5   1 km

To Brastagi

the original village of Medan Putri was founded in 1590 by Raja Guru Patimpus.

It remained a small village until well into the 19th century. In 1823, when a British government official John Anderson visited the place it had 200 inhabitants. Only after the arrival of the Dutch did it start to grow. It became a Dutch plantation centre soon after an enterprising Dutchman named Nienhuys successfully started growing tobacco in 1865. In 1886 the Dutch made it the capital of North Sumatra. But by 1910 it was still a fairly small place with only 17,500 residents. At the end of Dutch rule in 1942 the population was around 80,000, and today it's well over a million.

Medan is a multi-racial melting pot which includes large communities of Europeans, Chinese, Indians, Arabians, Javanese and various Sumatran ethnic groups like the Minangkabau and the Batak. Solid Dutch buildings inspire images of bloated bureaucrats and fat European burghers from the colonial era, while jerry-built lean-tos house large families. Mixed in with the people are antique shops, some impressive palaces, mosques and museums, and the remnants of the old Dutch planter aristocracy.

Information & Orientation

Tourist Office The tourist office is at Jalan Ahmad Yani 107, next to the Bank Dagang Negara. There is also an information centre at the arrival terminal at Polonia International airport, which has a map of the city, a few brochures and not much else.

Post & Telephone The post office, an old Dutch building, is on the main square in the middle of town. International phone calls can be made from PT Indosat at Jalan Jati at the junction with Jalan Thamrin.

Bank There are a number of banks in Medan, particularly along Jalan Pemuda, Jalan Jenderal Ahmad Yani and Jalan Balaikota, which is really one continuous street. There is also a branch of the Bank Rakyat Indonesia in the lobby of the Hotel Danau Toba, where you can change cash and travellers' cheques even if you're not staying at the hotel.

Consulates There are consulates for West Germany, UK, USA and various other countries in Medan.

Things to See

The level of activity that makes Medan such an interesting place also makes it overwhelming and a difficult place to spend a long time in. Its population and stark contrasts make it one of those places where you can step out onto the street and always find something new.

The main European buildings are scattered along Jalan Balai Kota, and include the buildings now used as the Bank Indonesia and the post office – both fine examples of colonial architecture. Clear away the people and Jalan Perdana could almost have been lifted straight out of northern Europe. Breaking up the skyline are modern edifices like the Deli Plaza Shopping Centre, three floors of glittering neon-lit shopping arcades straight out of Singapore and a nightly hang-out for Medan's gays.

The Hash House Harriers

Another reminder of the colonial days, still going strong is Medan's Hash House Harriers. The Harriers originated in Malaysia in the 1930s, though the game has its real origins in British public schools. The general idea is that a bunch of mad dogs and Englishmen (the runners or 'hounds') chase a trail laid out by an imaginary 'hare'. When the trail comes to a dead-end the runners shout 'checking' and then fan out to try and pick up the trail again. When this is done, cries of 'On! On!' rally the hounds, who continue the 'chase'. The official starting date of the Harriers was 1938, and the name is supposed to come from an eating house in

Kuala Lumpur then referred to as the Hash House'. The English would run after work on Monday afternoons – partly for amusement, partly for sport and partly to baffle the locals. The Medan Hash House Harriers run on Thursdays at 5 pm. For instructions on where to meet, collect the Hash Sheet at Lyn's Bar at Jalan Ahmad Yani 98 (next to the Tip Top Restaurant). There's a fee of about 4000 rp and all are welcome. There's a men-only run on Monday nights.

Masjid Raya & Istana Maimoon

The Great Mosque is on Jalan Sisinga-mangaraja while the Maimoon Palace is nearby on Jalan Katamso. The large and lovely mosque dates from 1906 and the palace from 1888. They were both built by the Sultan of Deli.

Museum Bukit Barisan

Diagonally opposite the Danau Toba International Hotel on Jalan H Zainul Arifin 8, this military museum has an extensive collection of weapons and memorabilia from WW II, the War of Independence and the Sumatra Rebellion of 1958.

Other Attractions

The Parisada Hindu Dharma temple is on the corner of Jalan Teuku Umar and Jalan H Zainul Arifin. The amusement park or Taman Ria is on Jalan Binjai and is the site for the Medan Fair each May/June. Medan's zoo, the Taman Margasawata, is a bemo ride further along Jalan Sisingamangaraja. There's a crocodile farm in Medan as well. Belawan is the port for Medan, through which most of the area's exports flow. It's 28 km from the city.

Places to Stay – bottom end

Only a few doors down from the Garuda office the *Sigura Gura* at Jalan Suprapto 2K is rather dull and dismal, though for Medan it's good value with dorm beds for 2000 rp and rooms for 5000 rp.

The *Hotel Irama*, in a little alley at

Jalan Palang Merah 1125, by the junction of Jalan Listrik and very close to the big Hotel Danau Toba International. It's a convenient, friendly and well-kept place with dorm beds for 2000 rp and rooms for 3000/4000 rp.

The *Tapian Nabaru Hotel* (tel 512155) at Jalan Hang Tuah 6, right by the river, has rooms at 2000 rp per person. It's quiet, and somewhat off the beaten track.

Wisma Sibayak is at Jalan Pattimura 627, several km from the city centre on the road towards Brastagi. It's associated with Wisma Sibayak in Brastagi and has dorm beds at 1000 rp, rooms at 3000 rp.

Other cheap places in town include the *Hotel Rion* at Jalan Palang Merah 5b, near the railway lines. Also try the *Hotel Melati* (tel 516021) at Jalan Amaluin 6, close to the bus station on Jalan Sisingamangaraja. It's a larger hotel with rooms at 5000, 12,500 and 15,000 rp.

Places to Stay – middle

There are a string of middle and upper-range hotels along Jalan Sisingamangaraja. The *Hotel Sumatera* (tel 24973) at Jalan Sisingamangaraja 21 has rooms from 10,000 rp, from 15,000 with mandi, and from 20,000 rp with air-con.

The *Hotel Garuda* (tel 22775) at Jalan Singamangaraja 27 is a straight-forward middle-range hotel with rooms from 10,000 rp without bathroom, and 12,000 rp with bathroom. It's a bit lacklustre and glum, and rooms facing the street would be incredibly noisy.

The *Hotel Dhaksina* (tel 324561) on Jalan Singamangaraja has rooms from 10,000 rp with bathroom, and up to 25,000 rp with bathroom, air-con and television. It's a clean, bright place and much better than the Hotel Garuda.

Places to Stay – top end

There are a couple of up-market hotels in Medan. Not to be confused with the *Hotel Garuda* is the *Hotel Garuda Plaza* (tel 326255) at Jalan Sisingamangaraja 188. It

is a fine hotel with rooms from 33,000/
36,000 rp.

In the middle of town is the high-rise
Hotel Dharma Deli (tel 327011) at Jalan
Balai Kota, next to the Deli Dharma
Shopping Complex. Rooms start from
32,000/34,000 rp plus tax and service
charges.

The *Hotel Danau Toba* (tel 327000) at
Jalan Imam Bonjol 17 is a huge edifice in
the middle of town with rooms from
37,000/41,000 rp. Similarly priced is the
Polonia Hotel (tel 325300) at Jalan
Jenderal Sudirman 14. It has rooms from
32,000 rp plus tax and service.

The *Hotel Dirga Surya* (tel 321555) at
Jalan Imam Bonjol 6 has rooms from
50,000 rp. The *Hotel Tiara Medan* (tel
516000) at Jalan Cut Mutiah has rooms
from about 60,000 rp.

Places to Eat

During the day Jalan Semarang is just a
dirty back alley but come nightfall it's
jam-packed with foodstalls which set up
along the street across Jalan Bogor
between Jalan Pandu and Jalan Bandung.
Jalan Semarang is the third block beyond
the railway line. It's got great Chinese
food.

Kampung Keling on Jalan H Zainul
Arifin is an area with lots of small *gangs*
and numerous warungs specialising in
different kinds of food – Chinese, Indian,
Indonesian and European.

The *Tip Top Restaurant* at Jalan
Ahmad Yani 92 has consistently good food
at reasonably cheap prices. They also
do baked goods and ice cream. A few doors
down at 98 is *Lyn's Restaurant*, a
gathering place for Medan business people
and expatriates, with a predominantly
western menu. The *France Modern
Bakery* is at 24 C Jalan Pemuda.

There are several Padang restaurants
near the junction of Jalan Sisingamangaraja
with Jalan Pandu. Or try the *Rumah
Makan Famili* at Salan Sisingamangaraja
21B or the *Rumah Makan Gembira* by the
railway line.

Medan Bakers just beyond the Hindu
temple at Jalan H Zainul Arifin 150 has
excellent baked goods. Turn the corner at
Jalan Cik Ditiro and again at Jalan Kediri
to the *Indian Restaurant* at 96. They have
a variety of north Indian dishes, including
biriyanis as well as yoghurt and lassis.

Things to Buy

Medan has a number of interesting arts
and crafts shops, particularly along Jalan
Ahmad Yani. Try Toko Asli at 62, Toko
Rufino at 64 and Toko Bali Arts at 68.
There is a good selection of antique
weaving, Dutch pottery, carvings and
other pieces in all of these shops. Other
good ones include Rufino at Jalan Ahmad
Yani 64 which has a wide range of artefacts
from Nias and northern Sumatra. The
Toko Buku Deli at Jalan Ahmad Yani 48
has many books on Indonesia in English.

Getting There & Away

Medan is the major travel centre in
Sumatra and an important arrival or
departure point for overseas.

Air There are international flights from
Medan to Singapore, Kuala Lumpur and
Penang. For details see the Getting There
section at the start of the Sumatra
chapter.

MAS (tel 519333) is in the Hotel Danau
Toba International at Jalan Imam Bonjol
17. Garuda (tel 25700) is at Jalan
Suprapto 2 and they also have an office in
the Dharma Deli Hotel, opposite the post
office. Singapore Airlines (tel 51811) is in
the Polonia Hotel on Jalan Jenderal
Sudirman. Merpati (tel 514102) is at
Jalan Katamso 41 J. Mandala (tel 513309)
is at Jalan Katamso 37 E. SMAC (tel
516617) is at Jalan Imam Bonjol 59.

Garuda has flights from Medan to
many destinations in Sumatra and other
parts of Indonesia. In Sumatra these
include daily flights to Banda Aceh, Batu
Besar (Batam Island), Padang and
Palembang. There are also daily flights to
Jakarta, Denpasar and Ujung Pandang.

Mandala has daily flights from Medan to Jakarta. SMAC has daily flights from Medan to Gunung Sitoli on Nias Island.

Bus Medan is the major crossroads for bus travel in North Sumatra. See the relevant sections for more detailed information. Prapat is the number one destination from Medan and buses depart very regularly. The trip takes about four hours and costs 2000 rp. Touts may besiege you for this bus but you can safely ignore them. The buses depart along Jalan Sisingamangaraja.

There are a number of bus stations in Medan for various destinations. See the map for locations. The trip to Brastagi takes less than two hours and costs 750 rp. Other fares include Bukittinggi or Padang at 9000 to 10,000 rp or Banda Aceh for 12,000 rp.

Boat See the introductory Sumatra transport section for information on the ferry service between Penang and Medan. The Medan agent for the *Gadis Langkasuka* is Eka Sukma Wisata Tour at Jalan Brigadir Jenderal Katamso 62A. Pelni ships connect Medan with Jakarta and on to other ports in Indonesia. The *Lawit* operates a service from port to port along the Sumatran east coast. The Pelni office in Medan is at Jalan Sugiono, a block back from Jalan Pemuda and close to the tourist office and Garuda office.

Taxi There are several long-distance taxi operators from Medan. Inda Taxi (tel 510036) is at Jalan Brigadir Jenderal Katamso 60, near the Merpati office and the Penang ferry office. They have taxis to Prapat for 7500 rp, to Sibolga for 9000 rp and to Pekanbaru for 25,000 rp. Bidadari Taxi (21435) is just around the corner.

Getting Around

Airport Transport The standard taxi fares from the airport depend on your destination in the city, but count on around 4000 rp. Becaks are not allowed right into the airport area, so you have to walk the last couple of hundred metres. However, if you walk out of the terminal, becak drivers will instantly materialise. The fare into town is 1000 to 1500 rp.

The domestic terminal has a restaurant, snack bar, magazine stand and is much better than the international terminal. There's a tourist office outside the international terminal.

Local Transport There are plenty of oplets around town at a standard 150 rp. You can get out to the port of Belawan for 250 rp.

Medan also has plenty of motorised and human-powered becaks. Fares are from 500 to 1000 rp for most destinations around town by motorised becak, but you need to bargain.

BUKIT LAWANG

Eighty km from Medan at Bukit Lawang is the Orangutan Rehabilitation Station where these fascinating creatures are retrained to survive in the wild after a period of captivity. Apart from the attraction of the apes, the country around here is wild and enchanting with dense jungle and clear, fast-flowing rivers. There is a large rubber plantation on the edge of the reserve and it may be possible to visit the processing plant.

The Orang-utans

The reserve is bordered by the Bohorok River, and the PHPA have set up a viewing point over the river, a half an hour walk uphill into the jungle. You need a permit to visit the reserve. These are available from the PHPA office in Bukit Lawang. The permit is valid for three days and costs 3000 rp. The orang-utan feeding times – once in the morning and once in the afternoon – are posted in the PHPA office. These are the only times you're allowed to visit the reserve, other than with a guide and an organised trek.

As for the orang-utans themselves, you are likely to see about half a dozen during each feeding session. A wooden platform has been built in the jungle and the Indonesian PHPA staff feed the orang-utans milk and bananas. The animals live off this until they have learnt to fend for themselves in the wild, and then wander off on their own accord.

Despite their remarkably human expressions, of all the great apes the orang-utan is considered to be the most distantly related to humans. In contrast to the smaller monkeys, the orang-utan is actually quite a lumbering creature, moving far slower and with less agility than, say, the gibbons. Unlike the gorilla, the orang-utan spends most of its time in the trees, only occasionally walking on the ground. They have very long arms, and use their heavy weight to sway trees back and forth until they can reach the next.

The name *orang hutan* is Malay for 'person of the forest'. Stories were told of how the orang-utan would carry off pretty girls. Others told of how the orang-utan could speak, but refused to do so because it did not want to be made to work. The orang-utan lives solely in Sumatra and Borneo, though fossilised remains have been found in China and Java.

The orang-utan has large jaws and teeth for tearing up tree bark, breaking open hard nuts and grinding up tough vegetation. It eats mostly fruit, the rest of it's diet is mainly leaves and the shoots of plants, although it also eats insects, tree bark, eggs and small mammals.

The orang-utan has a long life-span but tends to breed slowly. Females reach sexual maturity at about the age of ten years. They have few young but care for them well over a long period of time rather than having many young in the hope that a few will survive out of the pack. The females remain fertile until about the age of 30, and on average have only one baby every six years. The infants don't leave their mothers completely until they are about seven to 10 years old. The orang-utan tends to be quite a solitary creature.

Apart from Bukit Lawang and the Gunung Leuser National Park, orang-

utans can also be found in Tanjung Puting and Kutai National Parks and the Gunung Palung and Bukit Raja reserves in Kalimantan, and in neighbouring Sarawak and Sabah.

Places to Stay

Those expecting accommodation in the wilds of Bukit Lawang to consist of a bamboo hut presided over by a weather-beaten ranger will be disappointed or relieved, depending on your point of view. Whereas once the only accommodation was the PHPA guest house, the tourist trade is now catered for by a row of bungalows and restaurants resembling a slap-up, low-budget Club Med Resort.

The *Wisma Sibayak*, complete with bungalows, restaurant and concrete mock-up giraffes, is by the river on the edge of the reserve. Bungalows are 4000 rp. A few minutes walk downstream is the *Wisma Bukit Lawang* with bungalows for the same price.

On the whole, both places are pretty much the same, though the *Bukit Lawang* is probably cleaner. Food is pretty limited so don't expect too much, although the Sibyaak does toss together the biggest fruit salads you have probably ever laid eyes on. There are a few warungs on the other side of the river which cater to the Indonesian tourist trade – the Sunday deluge is amazing to behold.

Getting There & Away

The Orangutan Rehabilitation Station is part of the Taman Nasional Gunung Leuser (Gunung Leuser National Park). Bukit Lawang is the name of the settlement on the edge of the reserve, where the tourist camp and PHPA camp are situated. The small township near Bukit Lawang is called Bohorok, and you pass through it on your way up from Medan.

It takes two steps to get from Medan to Bukit Lawang. First you take a bus from Jalan Gatot Subrato (near the Tamanria Park) in Medan to Binjei. The fare is 200 rp and the trip takes 45 minutes. The bus will drop you off on the street in Binjei where you catch another bus to Bukit Lawang. This costs 750 rp and takes two to three hours. You should allow five hours to get from Medan to Bukit Lawang.

There are, reportedly, one or two direct buses daily from Medan to Bukit Lawang. There is a daily bus direct from Bukit Lawang to Brastagi.

PRAPAT

Almost sliding into the crater of Lake Toba is Prapat, pleasure spot of the Medan wealthy set. The main centre in the area, Prapat is described glowingly in local tourist literature as the 'most beautiful mountain and lake resort in Indonesia' although, in fact, it's quite ordinary. For travellers it's mainly a jumping-off point for Samosir Island. Most travellers head straight to the island nine km away, unless they arrive after dark or at an inconvenient time to catch a boat.

Information & Orientation

Prapat is essentially in two parts, the line of restaurants and shops up on the Trans-Sumatran Highway, which buses bound to or from Medan or Bukittinggi pass by, and the part down by the lakeside from where ferries to Samosir Island depart. It's about one km between these two areas. Just where Jalan Pulau Samosir turns off from the Trans-Sumatran Highway there's a small tourist office with some limited information about Prapat and the lake.

Prapat travel agents are notorious for bungling bus bookings, neglecting to make flight reservations from Medan (after you've paid) and other problems. Andilo Travel, with a main office up on the main road and a smaller one by the ferry dock, generally seem to be quite good and will also change money (at 5% less than the bank rate). Bolok Silau are another agency by the dock, and operate a weekly tourist bus between Prapat and Brastagi.

Things to See

Look in at the expensive Prapat Hotel, they sometimes put on performances of Batak singing or other local culture for tour groups. Prapat is also a good place to get Batak handicrafts like lime containers, leather, batik or wood carvings.

Cultural Performances

At Jalan Josep Sinaga 19 there is a Batak Cultural Centre where performances of dance and music are held on Saturday nights. Admission is 1000 rp. Batak dances, music and theatre are also performed at the Prapat Hotel, usually for tour groups. The week-long Danau Toba Festival is held every year in June. Canoe races are a highlight of the festival but there are also Batak cultural performances.

Labuhan Garaga

The village of Labuhan Garaga, 25 km from Prapat, is well worth a visit if you are interested in buying Batak blankets (kain kulos). The colour and patterns vary a bit from tribe to tribe but the majority of weavings have vertical stripes on a background of ink blue with rust red and white the predominant colours. They're not cheap, but they are attractive and practical buys. The price range is from 25,000 rp to 60,000 rp or more for good quality cloth.

Places to Stay – bottom end

Prapat has plenty of places to stay, some of them quite pleasant, but the places over on Samosir Island are such a bargain that Prapat ends up looking very expensive. You've got a choice of either staying up on the main road which is handy for buses but rather noisy, or down by the lake which is handy for the Samosir ferry. The expensive hotels, popular with weekend visitors from Medan or local holiday-makers, are mainly along the road from the Trans-Sumatran Highway to the ferry dock.

At Jalan Sisingamangaraja 41, *Andilo Travel* has a small losmen and restaurant

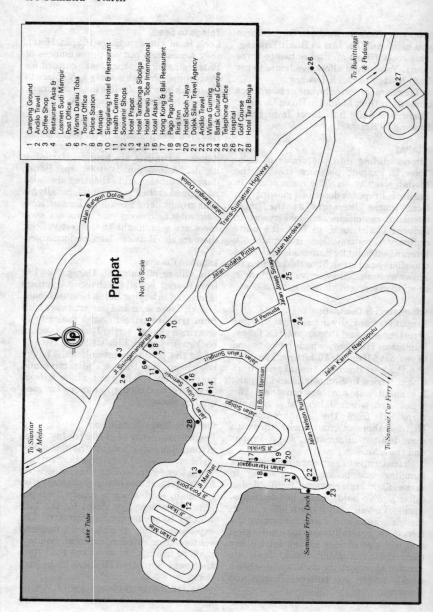

Prapat

Not To Scale

1 Camping Ground
2 Andilo Travel
3 Coffee Shop
4 Restaurant Asia &
   Losmen Sudi Mampir
5 Post Office
6 Wisma Danau Toba
7 Tourist Office
8 Police Station
9 Mosque
10 Singgalang Hotel & Restaurant
11 Health Centre
12 Souvenir Shops
13 Hotel Prapat
14 Hotel Tarabunga Sibolga
15 Hotel Danau Toba International
16 Hotel Atsari
17 Hong Kong & Bali Restaurant
18 Pago Pago Inn
19 Riris Inn
20 Hotel Soloh Jaya
21 Dolok Silau Travel Agency
22 Andilo Travel
23 Wisma Gurning
24 Batak Cultural Centre
25 Telephone Office
26 Hospital
27 Golf Course
28 Hotel Tara Bunga

Lake Toba

To Siantar & Medan

To Bukittinggi & Padang

Samosir Ferry Dock

To Samosir Car Ferry

Jalan Bangun Dolok
Trans-Sumatran Highway
Jalan Sisingamangaraja
Jalan Pulu Samosir
Jalan Siddaha Pintu
Jalan Merdeka
Jalan Josep Sinaga
Jl Pemuda
Jalan Talun Sungkit
Jalan Bukit Barisan
Jalan Sibigo
Jl Sirikki
Jalan Haranggaol
Jalan Nelson Purba
Jalan Karmel Napitupulu
Jl Marhat
Jl Pora-pora
Jl Ikan
Jl Ikan Mas

behind their travel agency with rooms at 3000 and 4000 rp. Although it's right on the road the rooms at this very popular place are at the back, by the lake, and are quieter. At 84, directly opposite the lakeside turn-off, is the small and rather basic *Sudi Mampir* with rooms at 3000 rp. Continue further along and at 109 the *Singgalang Hotel* has rooms at 3000/6000 rp for singles/doubles.

Down at the lakeside there are several places along Jalan Haranggaol, including the popular *Pago Pago Inn* close to the harbour at 50. It's airy, has clean but simple rooms with shared toilet facilities at 4000/5000 rp and there are fine views across the lake. Just down from it at 47, the *Hotel Soloh Jaya* is also a modern place, but some of the rooms are just little boxes, even windowless, at 5000 and 6000 rp. Better rooms with mandi are 10,000 and 12,500 rp.

Go right down to the ferry dock at the end of the road, turn the corner and *Wisma Gurning* is by the lakeside. It is a simple place with twin rooms with mandi for 5000 rp.

Places to Stay – middle

The *Hotel Atsari* has rooms from 27,000/30,000 rp. The *Wisma Danau Toba* (not to be confused with the Hotel Danau Toba) has rooms from 18,000/21,000 rp. There are several other hotels along Jalan Pulau Samosir.

The *Riris Inn* (tel 41392) at Jalan Haranggaol 39, is a modern place with straightforward, well-kept rooms with mandis at 10,000/15,000 rp.

Places to Stay – top end

The *Hotel Prapat* (tel 41012 at Jalan Marihat 1 is the best of the up-market hotels with rooms from 47,000 rp. It's a very salubrious hotel on a spacious block of land overlooking the lake.

The *Hotel Danua Toba* (tel 41583) at Jalan Pulau Samosir 17 has rooms from 32,000/37,500 rp. Despite it's rather mundane appearance, it's actually quite a comfortable place.

The *Hotel Tarabunga* (tel 41700) at Jalan Pulau Samosir 20, has rooms from 24,000/36,000 rp. The rooms are comfortable, and there is a restaurant overlooking the lake. The similarly named *Hotel Tarabunga Sibolga* (tel 41800) has rooms from 24,000/29,000 rp but it's a rather cavernous and sterile building.

Places to Eat

There are many cheap restaurants along Jalan Haranggaol, including some good Padang places. Padang and Chinese restaurants can also be found along Jalan Sisingamangaraja, as you come into Prapat from Medan. Down towards the lake there are several restaurants along Jalan Haranggaol, including the side-by-side *Restaurant Hong Kong* at 9 and 11 and the *Restaurant Bali* at 13. They have very similar Chinese menus which are not cheap, but chicken with lychees at the Bali for 4500 rp is delicious.

Getting There & Away

Bus Buses to or from Medan run very regularly and cost 2000 rp. The trip takes about four hours. If you want to travel via Brastagi you have to change buses at Siantar and Kabanjahe and it takes quite a time. See the Brastagi section for details and for information on the weekly tourist bus.

Buses on to Bukittinggi take about 15 hours (although it can take much longer) and cost around 9000 rp. There's a weekly tourist minibus which costs 12,500 rp and is supposed to make the trip in 12 or 13 hours. See the Lake Toba section for details of ferries to Samosir Island.

Typical bus fares from Prapat are: Brastagi 2000 rp, Medan 2000 rp, Sibolga 3000 rp, Bukittingi 8000 rp, Padang 9000 rp, Pekanbaru 11,000 rp, Palembang 23,000 rp, and Jakarta 33,000 rp.

Tours There are various agencies operating tours of the surrounding area. Try PT

Dolok Silau at the ferry dock. They have a tourist coach once or twice a week which includes tours to coffee, tea, ginger, clove and cinnamon farms, as well as other places of interest.

Getting Around

Oplets around Prapat, including from the main road down to the harbour, cost 150 rp.

SIBOLGA

Sibolga is north of Bukittinggi, where the road turns inland to Prapat and Lake Toba. The descent into Sibolga, approaching from Prapat, is very beautiful, particularly at sunset. The harbour itself is attractive and there are some good beaches nearby. While there's no real attraction to bring you to this little port, Sibolga is by no means an unpleasant place, although it's largely just an overnight stop between Bukittinggi and Prapat or a jumping-off point for Nias.

Orientation

The main streets in the centre of town are Jalan Suprapto, Jalan Diponegoro and Jalan S Raja. There are two harbours. One is at the end of Jalan Horas. The other is at Jalan Pelabuhan. The centre of town is about mid-way between these two harbours, both only a short becak ride away.

Places to Stay

The only sore point regarding Sibolga is a lack of decent hotels. Most are drab, gloomy and depressing. Many hotels are on Jalan Suprapto, Jalan Horas and Jalan Diponegoro.

The best in town, and an exception to the rule, is the *Hotel Hidap Baru* (tel 21957) at Jalan Suprapto 123. This is a clean, quiet, modern hotel. Simple rooms start from 5000 rp. Rooms with bathroom and air-con start from 8000 rp.

Also try the reasonable *Hotel Indah Sari* which has air-con rooms with bathrooms. In the north of town is the *Hotel Taman Nauli* which is quite nice with rooms with balcony and bathroom.

The *Losmen Anwar* at Jalan Suprapto 103 is very dingy and depressing with grimy bathrooms. Rooms, and the term may be used loosely, start from 3300 rp.

Other cheap places include the *Losmen Subur* at Jalan Diponegoro 19, the *Hotel Sudi Mampir* and the *Hotel Murni Indah*. All of these have rooms for around 4000 rp. The *Maturi*, opposite the *Hotel Indah Sari*, is dirt cheap.

There are a number of cheap hotels and losmen along Jalan Horas near the port. Try the *Penginapan Karya Samudra*.

Getting There & Away

Bus The main bus station is on Jalan Sisingamangaraja, but a number of bus companies have their own offices and terminals around town.

Buses ALS on Jalan Sisingamangaraja have buses to Medan and to Padang, Bukittingi and onwards to Jakarta. PT PMTT at Jalan Diponegoro 62 also has buses to these destinations. PO Terang at Jalan Diponegoro 50 has buses to Padang.

Typical fares and journey times from Sibolga are: Bukittingi 6000 rp (takes 12 hours), and Medan 8000 rp (takes eight hours).

Boat Pelni's *KM Kerinci* departs Sibolga once every two weeks for Padang, Tanjung Priok, Surabaya and beyond. See the Getting Around chapter for details. Pelni (tel 21193) is at Jalan Pelabuhan 48.

From Sibolga you can take a ferry to Teluk Dalam and/or Gunung Sitoli on the island of Nias.

Karo Batak Highlands

The Karo Bataks inhabit a portion of north Sumatra covering some 5000 square km immediately to the north of Lake Toba. The town of Brastagi is the main centre of the area. The Karo Bataks are bounded by coastal Malays in the east, the Simalungun Bataks to the south, and other ethnic groups to the west. Only Lake Toba prevents any direct contact between the homelands of the Karo Batak and the Toba Bataks,

The Karo are just one of several Batak groups in northern Sumatra, grouped together because of their similar culture and languages. Not much is known about the pre-colonial history of the Karo Bataks, nor for that matter of the other Batak people. Although there is an indigenous Batak script it was never used to record events, and for the most part it seems to have been used only by priests and *dukuns* in divination and to record magic spells.

Batak stories suggest that the Bataks came from somewhere to the east of Sumatra, perhaps from India. The cultivation of wet field rice, the type of houses, chess, cotton and even the type of spinning wheel used by the Bataks has been put down to Indian influence. Indian writing as well as Hindu religious ideas are also supposed to have had a strong influence on the Batak. Much of this may have come to an end as Islam began to take hold in Sumatra.

However, the Karo Batak for the most part never adopted Islam themselves. They were constantly at odds with the Islamic Acehnese to the north, who several times tried to conquer them and convert them to Islam. The Karo were possibly able to resist because they could never be finally defeated in battle. The Karo were never organised as a single political entity and had no centralised authority. If one Karo group was defeated, the enemy always had the next group to contend with.

Interestingly enough, despite long years of resistance to the Acehnese, when the Dutch arrived on the scene the Karo were easily subdued. Poorly armed, the Karo put up little show of resistance against the Dutch who established control of this part of northern Sumatra in 1906. The Karo now came under centralised colonial control. Slavery was abolished, inter-village warfare was brought to a halt, and Christianity began to take root. Kabanjahe developed as the centre of Dutch administration of the region, until the Japanese invasion and occupation in WW II.

Today, the Karo Batak highlands are known primarily in Indonesia as a rich source of fruit and vegetables, much of it sent down to Medan and other cities of eastern Sumatra, or exported to Penang and Singapore. The area is also an important tourist area, rivalling Lake Toba in popularity. In the area around Brastagi you can find many interesting villages with high roofed traditional houses, very different from those built by the Toba Bataks, where it is still possible to see traditional marriage, funeral and other ceremonies. Brastagi is also close to some of north Sumatra's mighty volcanoes, some of which can be climbed.

BRASTAGI (Berastagi)

Centre of the Karo Batak people, Brastagi is a hill town some 1300 metres above sea level and 70 km along the back road from Medan to Lake Toba.

Information & Orientation

Wisma Sibayak and the Hotel Ginsata are both good information sources. Brastagi is essentially one main road, Jalan Veteran, with these two places to stay at opposite ends.

Post The post office is on Jalan Veteran.

Bank The Wisma Sibayak will change US dollar travellers' cheques, as well as cash for various foreign currencies. The Bank Negara Indonesia on Jalan Sakti in Kabanjahe, near Brastagi, will only change US dollar travellers' cheques.

Things to See

Staring down the main street of Brastagi is the cone-shaped volcano Gunung Sibayak. Although it's not visible from

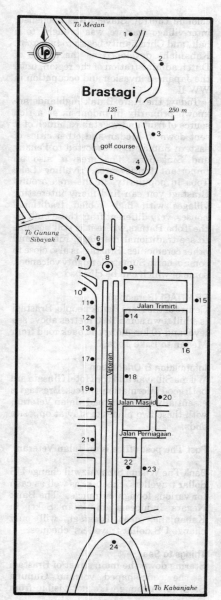

Brastagi

To Medan

To Gunung Sibayak

To Kabanjahe

| 0 | 125 | 250 m |

golf course

Jalan Trimirti

Jalan Masjid

Jalan Perniagaan

1	Peceren Traditional Long House
2	Rose Garden Hotel
3	Rudang Hotel
4	Bukit Kuba Hotel
5	Power Station
6	Petrol Station
7	Fruit Market
8	Memorial
9	Hotel Ginsata
10	Telephone Office
11	Post Office
12	Torong Inn
13	Asia Restaurant
14	Shangri La Seafood Restaurant
15	Losmen Trimurty
16	Losmen Pusat
17	Public Health Centre
18	Rumah Makan Terang
19	Eropah Restaurant
20	Ria Cinema
21	Restaurant Ora et Labora
22	Bus & Oplet Station
23	Market
24	Wisma Sibayak

Brastagi because of the buildings, you can see it on the walk to Lingga or from the bus heading down to Kabanjahe. Although Brastagi has some interesting markets, the main attractions are the villages and volcanoes in the surrounding area.

Places to Stay – bottom end
Brastagi has a very popular travellers' centre and some other good back ups. *Wisma Sibayak*, at the Kabanjahe end of the main street, has dorm beds at 2000 rp and rooms at 3000/4000 rp, all with shared toilet facilities. It's packed with travellers and has a very popular restaurant. A lot of people seem to make lengthy stays here and their guest books are packed with useful and amusing information about sightseeing, festivals, transport, walks, climbs and other things to do in the area. The owner, Mr Pelawi, is a fund of local information.

At the other end of the main street at

Jalan Veteran 79 is the *Ginsata Hotel*. This hotel is clean and quite OK with rooms with mandi for 3000/4000 rp and a nasi Padang restaurant downstairs. The manager, Mr Ginting, is helpful and informative.

There are a number of alternatives in Brastagi, including the modern *Torong Inn* at Jalan Veteran 128 with rooms at 5000 rp. Or just off the main road there's *Losmen Trimurty* and *Losmen Pusat* on Jalan Trimurty.

Places to Stay – top end

There are a couple of expensive hotels on the northern outskirts of the town. The *Rose Garden Hotel* has rooms for 40,000 rp. It's a great place, decorated in a pseudo-Spanish hacienda style with two and three storey buildings built around a central courtyard and swimming pool. Despite its rather ordinary appearance from the street, it's a fine hotel.

The *Rudang Hotel* has bungalow accommodation at 25,000/27,000 rp. It's set in a valley with a large restaurant overlooking a big swimming pool. It's hard to pick between the up-market hotels in Brastagi, but this one is probably the most appealing.

The *Hotel Bukit Kubu* has rooms from 17,000/19,000 rp. This is a fine, chalet-style hotel in the middle of a manicured golf-course – there are even a few tennis courts thrown in.

The *Hotel International Sibayak* is just outside Brastagi on the road to Bukit Gundaling. At the time of writing it was under construction and looks like becoming Brastagi's Number One hotel.

Places to Eat

Restaurants are stretched out like beads on a string along Jalan Veteran, Brastagi's main street. It's probably pointless to mention any one in particular, but one place which really does stand out is the *Rumah Makan Muslimin* at Jalan Veteran 128, just around the corner from the cinema. This place has a great selection of meat (including chicken heads), fish and vegie dishes at remarkably cheap prices.

Other restaurants include the simple Chinese *Rumah Makan Terang* at 369 with straightforward but tasty food. Across the street is the equally bright and cheerful *Eropah Restaurant* at 48G. The *Asia Restaurant* at 9 and 10 is a bigger, more expensive Chinese place. The *Shangri La Sea Food Restaurant* at 93-94 has great Chinese food, especially the seafood.

There are several nasi Padang places, including at the *Ginsata Hotel*, and the food is deservedly popular at the *Wisma Sibayak*. You can buy your own food from the fruit and vegetable market off Jalan Veteran or try the local market further up the road. At night try the delicious cakes made from rice flour, palm sugar and coconut and steamed in bamboo cylinders. Buy them at the stall outside the cinema for 50 rp.

The only places in Indonesia where the sweet *marquisha*, a type of passionfruit, grows are Brastagi and Sulawesi. In Brastagi it's used to make a cool drink which is very popular locally.

Things to Buy

There are a number of interesting antique and souvenir shops along Jalan Veteran. Crispo Antiques has particularly interesting items.

Getting There & Away

Bus Brastagi's bus terminal is on Jalan Veteran. There are frequent buses from Brastagi to Medan. The trip takes two hours and costs 800 rp. There are also frequent buses from Brastagi to Kabanjahe, 12 km away.

There is a daily bus direct from Brastagi to Bukit Lawang, which leaves from in front of the Ora et Labora Restaurant on Jalan Veteran. The fare is 1700 rp.

Otherwise, to get to Bukit Lawang take a bus from Brastagi to the Sei Wampu Terminal in Medan for 750 rp. From there

Mt. Sibayak, Brastagi

Around Brastagi

you take another bus to Binjei for 200 rp, and another bus from Binjei to Bukit Lawang for 750 rp.

To get to Prapat from Brastagi, first take a bus to Kabanjahe for 150 rp. From Kabanjahe, take another bus to Pematang Siantar for 1000 rp. From Pematang Siantar, take a bus to Prapat for 500 rp. From Prapat you can catch the ferry to Pulau Samosir in Lake Toba. It's a rough ride between Pematang Siantar and Kabanjahe and takes three to four hours.

Brastagi is the jumping-off point for visiting Kutacane and the Gunung Leuser National Park. For details, see the section on Kutacane.

AROUND BRASTAGI
Gunung Sibayak
From Brastagi you can climb Gunung Sibayak, a 2094-metre-high volcano, and have a soak in the hot springs on the way back. Wear good walking boots because the path is wet and slippery all year round and start early because the walk takes all day. Bring food and water and a torch (flashlight), just in case it takes more than a day. The guest books at Wisma Sibayak have a lot of useful information about

making this climb and various other walks in the area. The walk takes about six hours there and back and you should be able to get a map at the Ginsata or the Wisma Sibayak. Avoid going on weekends as there are hordes of Medan weekenders on the mountain.

Gunung Sinabung

Taking the bus from Brastagi to Kabanjahe you'll spot the cone-shaped volcano Gunung Sinabung. It's also possible to climb this volcano – six hours up and four hours back down. The trek starts from the village of Mardingding. The trail to the top of the mountain starts near the village; you take the same one down again. The views from the top are very impressive. Take food and water with you, and a torch just in case you end up walking back down in the dark. Gunung Sinabung is some 2450 metres high.

Si Piso-Piso Waterfalls

On the way there from Lake Toba, near the northern end of the lake, are the impressive Si Piso-Piso waterfalls. They're 24 km from Kabanjahe and only about 300 metres from the main road.

Kampung Peceren

This cluster of traditional houses is on the outskirts of Brastagi and has almost been absorbed by the town. The village comprises half a dozen traditional houses – all occupied, except one.

Lingga

If you're interested in architecture, visit the village of Lingga 16 km south of Brastagi.

The design of these houses with their horn-shaped roofs has remained unchanged for centuries. Most of the ones in Lingga are reputed to be well over 250 years old and not a single nail was used in their construction. Whether the houses are that old is not really known. Lingga is an interesting, if rather run-down Karo Batak village with many traditional houses – some in a very poor state of repair. The people, especially the women, do not like being photographed.

To get to Lingga by bus, first go by bus

Kids near Lingga

from Brastagi to Kabanjahe for 150 rp. Then take a bemo to the junction of Jalan Kapten Bangsi Sembiring, Jalan Kapten Pala Bangun and Jalan Veteran, where you catch another bemo to Lingga for 100 rp.

Cingkes

Cingkes is a Karo Batak village in the Simalungun Batak region, about 22 km from Brastagi. You have to take a roundabout way to get there.

The village has about two dozen traditional houses, most in a good state of preservation, as well as a spirit house or *tambak law burawan*. From Cingkes you can head back to Brastagi via the Si Piso-Piso Waterfall.

To get to Cingkes on public bemos, you first have to go from Brastagi to Kabanjahe, then Kabanjahe to Situng-gulung, Situnggulung to Saribudolok, and Saribudolok to Cingkes. You would be better off chartering a bemo from Kabanjahe. If you have a particular interest in Karo Batak architecture, it is worth visiting this village.

Barusjahe

Barusjahe has a number of impressive traditional houses and rice barns, but their dilapidated condition suggests that this form of architecture is gradually dying out. There are several uninhabited houses as you come into Barsujahe, and another cluster of inhabited houses at the other end of the village. Two km from Barusjahe is the village of Sukajulu, which has one remaining traditional house, also in poor condition.

Buses to Barusjahe depart from the bus terminal in Kabanjahe. The trip takes half an hour to cover the 20 km and and costs 400 rp. It stops off at Sukajulu.

Jungle Trekking

The great Sumatran jungle trekking scene is probably the most comical product of the island's mass tourist trade. While there are a few good guides around, the usual thing seems to be for little bands of foreigners to lumber off into the wilds in the company of self-appointed escorts who speak minimal English, can't knock together two facts about a jungle (or if they can, can't explain it) and get lost anyway.

Those people who are really hoping to see the elusive Sumatran tigers, woolly rhino or even a couple of wild orang-utan, would be better off teaming up with David Attenborough the next time he wanders through. Or try the local zoo. Failing that, there are always the locals who actually make their living in the jungle. But contacting them would require a different approach to travel – plus more time, money and effort than most people care to put into it.

On the other hand, if you don't expect too much, then by most accounts the wild and unruly expeditions seem to be fun. Gather together a few hardy Swedes, a couple of lunatic-fringe Australians, stir gently with some wacky Indonesians, add water (usually in the form of great tropical downpours) and you wind up with Tarzan's Sumatran Adventure. The guest books in the Wisma Sibayak at Brastagi are a fine source of comment and opinions regarding the various jungle jaunts around Brastagi and Bukit Lawang. A few interesting extracts include:

If you're looking for a real jungle experience (I really mean a good one) you shouldn't miss out on this trip. We had to fight our way through branches, trees, rocks and other 'jungle stuff'. I would suggest that you take a guide if you want to go into the jungle. They might be expensive but they are worth it.

When... (I was told about plans for) ...bringing a group into 'totally unexplored jungle', my first thought was how many times had it been 'unexplored'. When we were in the middle of it two weeks later, I was sure that I never would see civilisation again... Everybody should go! You're not watching a David Attenborough jungle-special, you're in it!

An incomparable account of jungle trekking is a ribald and bawdy tale which appears in the Wisma Sibayak guest book. This epic journey was presided over by two chain-smoking Indonesian guides – one of whom had high spirits and a wide smile having 'lunged his length into some kraut trollop the night before we left' and who insisted on stripping off his trousers at every available opportunity to reveal a pair of lewd underpants 'the sole construction material of such being nothing more than moth eaten white fish net'. The band of heroic explorers beat a path through the jungle for four days from Bukit Lawang to Brastagi, sheltering under polythene topped lean-tos, dog-paddling across swollen rivers and fighting off cockroaches – the 'titalating tickle of six little Blatodian points scurrying along ones spine, smile or auricle was quite a thrill'.

Lake Toba Region

The Bataks, who live around Prapat, Lake Toba and in the Karo highlands, are one of North Sumatra's most interesting ethnic groups. Kabanjahe, Lingga and Brastagi are the centres of the Karo Batak lands. Samosir Island is in the middle of Lake Toba, and Prapat, on the shores of the lake, is the main jumping-off point for the island.

History

In 1783, Marsden astonished the 'civilised' world with his account of a cannibalistic kingdom in the interior of Sumatra, who nevertheless had a highly developed culture and a system of writing. The Bataks actively avoided direct contact with the outside world for as long as it was possible in several effective ways. Unlike most other early Indonesian states, which began in coastal valleys, the Bataks chose the natural barrier of the mountains as the best site to establish and protect their kingdom. They were among the most warlike tribes of Sumatra, the natives of

Nias were the other, and cannibalism was one of their forms of defence – a permanent deterrent to any stranger who stupidly strayed into Batak territory. Apart from their suspicion of outsiders, they were so mistrustful of each other that they did not build or maintain natural paths between villages, nor construct bridges.

Perhaps part of this can be explained by the fact that the Bataks were pushed unceremoniously from their original homelands. A Proto-Malay people descended from neolithic mountain tribes in northern Thailand and Burma, the Bataks were driven out by the hordes of migrating Mongolian and Siamese tribes. When they arrived in Sumatra they did not linger long at the coast but trekked inland, making their first settlements around Lake Toba and gradually spreading out from there. Batak land extends up to 200 km north and 300 km south of Lake Toba.

The name 'Batak' was certainly in use in the 17th century but its origins are not clear. It could come from a derogatory Malay term for robber or blackmailer, while another suggestion is that it was an abusive nickname coined by Muslims and means 'pig-eater'. Whatever its origins it has been adopted by a number of inter-related ethnic groups including the Karo, Pakpak, Simalungun, Mandailing, Angola and the Toba Batak. The Bataks are primarily an agricultural people although the horses they raise, particularly in the Karo highlands, are famous. In contrast to the matrilineal Minangkabau, the Bataks have the most rigid patrilineal structure in Indonesia. Women not only do all the drudgery around the house but also much of the work in the fields.

Religion & Mythology

Squeezed between two Islamic strongholds, the Acehnese to the north and the Minangkabau to the west, the Bataks were traditionally repressed or ignored. They were virtually isolated until the mid-19th century when Christian missionaries moved in.

Today the northernmost Batak groups are animists, Toba Bataks are Protestant and those further south Muslim, but most Bataks practise a complex mixture of traditional animist belief and ritual combined with aspects of Hinduism, Christianity and Islam. This combination is split into three main divisions: cosmology, *tondi* or concept of the soul, and ancestor and spirit worship.

The Bataks regard the banyan as the tree of life and relate a creation legend of their omnipotent god Ompung:

One day Ompung leant casually against a huge banyan tree and dislodged a decayed bough that plummeted into the sea. From this branch came the fish and all the living creatures of the oceans. Not long afterwards, another bough dropped to the ground and from this issued crickets, caterpillars, centipedes, scorpions and insects. A third branch broke into large chunks which were transformed into tigers, deer, boars, monkeys, birds and all the animals of the jungle. The fourth branch which scattered over the plains became horses, buffalo, goats, pigs and all the domestic animals. Human beings appeared from the eggs produced by a pair of newly-created birds, born at the height of a violent earthquake.

The tondi is described as the spirit, the soul, or a person's individuality. It is believed to develop before the child is born. It exists near the body and from time to time takes its leave, which causes illness. It is essential for Bataks to make sacrifices to their tondi to keep it in good humour.

Customs & Traditions

A purely Batak tradition is the *sigalegale* puppet dance, once performed at funeral ceremonies but now more often a part of wedding ceremonies. The puppet, carved from the wood of a banyan tree, is a life-sized likeness of a Batak youth. It is dressed in the traditional costume of red turban, loose shirt and blue sarong. A red *ulos* (a piece of rectangular cloth traditionally used to wrap round babies or

around the bride and groom to bless them with fertility, unity and harmony) is draped from the shoulders.

One story of the origin of the sigalegale puppet concerns a loving but childless couple who lived on Samosir Island. Bereft and lonely after the death of her husband, the wife made a wooden image of him. Whenever she felt intensely lonely she hired a dalang to make the puppet dance and a dukun to communicate with the soul of her husband through the puppet.

The other story goes that there was once a king who had only one child, a son. When his son passed away the king was grieved because he now had no successor. In memory of his dead son, the king ordered a wooden statue to be made in his likeness, and when he went to see it for the first time invited his people to take part in a dance feast.

The sigalegale are stood up on long, wooden boxes, through which ropes are threaded and operated like pulleys to manipulate the jointed limbs of the puppet. This enables the operator to make the sigalegale dance to gamelan music accompanied by flute and drums. In some super-skilled performances the sigalegale weeps or smokes a cigarette. Its tongue can be made to poke out, and its eyelids to blink. The sigalegale is remarkably similar in appearance to the *tau tau* statues of Tanatoraja in central Sulawesi, however, the tau tau do not move.

Whatever, the sigalegale soon became part of Batak culture and was used at funeral ceremonies to revive the souls of the dead and to communicate with them. Personal possessions of the deceased were used to decorate the puppet and the dukun would invite the deceased's soul to enter the wooden puppet as it danced on top of the grave. At the end of the dance, the villagers would hurl spears and arrows at the puppet while the dukun performed a ceremony to drive away evil spirits. A few days later the dukun would return to perform another ceremony, sometimes lasting 24 hours, to chase away evil spirits again.

Architecture

Traditional Batak houses are built on stilts a metre to two metres from the ground. They are made of wood and roofed with sugar palm fibre or, more often these days, rusting corrugated iron. The roof has a concave, saddleback bend, and each end rises in a sharp point which, from certain angles, look like the buffalo horns they are invariably decorated with. The gables are usually extravagantly embellished with mosaics and carvings of serpents, spirals, lizards and monster heads complete with bulbous eyes.

The space under the main structure is used for rearing domestic animals like cows, pigs and goats. The living quarters, or middle section, is large and open with no internal walls and is often inhabited by up to a dozen families. This area is usually sectioned off by rattan mats which are let down at night to provide partial privacy. It is dark and gloomy, the only opening being a door approached by a wooden ladder.

A traditional village is made up of a number of such houses, similar to the villages of the Toraja people of central Sulawesi. A traditional Toba village (a huta) was always surrounded by a moat and bamboo trees to protect the villagers from enemy attack. The villages had only one gateway because of this. The houses in the village are lined up to the left and right of the king's house. In front of the houses is a line of rice barns, used for storing the harvest. Even today, walking around Samosir, you can still see how the villages were designed with defence in mind.

Arts & Crafts

Traditionally the Bataks are skilled metalworkers and woodcarvers; other materials they use are shells, bark, bone and horns. They decorate their work with fertility symbols, magic signs and animals.

One particularly idiosyncratic form of art developed by the Toba Bataks is the magic augury book called *pustaha*. These books comprise the most significant part of their written history. Usually carved out of bark or bamboo, they are important religious records which explain the established verbal rituals and responses of priests and mourners. Other books, inscribed on bone or bamboo and ornately decorated at each end, document Batak myths.

Music is as important to the Bataks as it is to most societies, but traditionally it was played at religious ceremonies, rather than for everyday pleasure. Today they are famous for their powerful and emotive hymn singing. Most of their musical instruments are similar to those found elsewhere in Indonesia – cloth-covered copper gongs in varying sizes struck with wooden hammers, a small two-stringed violin which makes a pure but harsh sound, and a kind of reedy clarinet.

An interesting artefact commonly sold in souvenir shops around Tomok, Tuk Tuk and Ambarita, are *porhalaan*. These are divining calendars – of 30 days and 12 months – used to determine auspicious days on which to embark on certain activities such as marriage or the planting of the fields.

LAKE TOBA & SAMOSIR ISLAND

Lake Toba is dead centre in North Sumatra, 176 km south of Medan. Lake Toba is high (800 metres above sea level), big (over 1700 square km) and deep (450 metres). The largest lake in South-East Asia, it is completely surrounded by steep mountains and ridges and sandy, pine-sheltered beaches.

The lake is, in fact, a volcanic depression now filled with water. The last volcanic eruptions are said to have occurred some 30,000 to 75,000 years ago. Samosir Island, right in the middle of the Lake Toba, is covered in lake sediment which indicates that at one time it was also submerged.

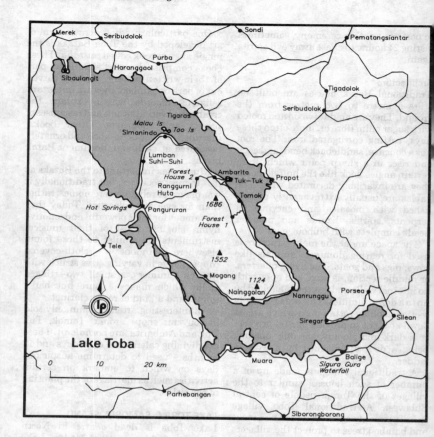

As the legendary birthplace of the mountain-dwelling Bataks, it is the centre of Batak culture and has several villages of historical interest. Tomok, Ambarita and Simanindo are the main ones. Christian tombs and the boat-shaped stone graves of Batak animists are scattered around the fields. Behind the narrow lakeside strip there's a high plateau.

Information & Orientation
The villages of Tomok, Tuk Tuk and Ambarita are the main tourist centres. Tuk Tuk and Ambarita have most of the accommodation, while Tomok and Ambarita are noted for their handicrafts and souvenir markets. From Tomok or Ambarita it is possible to trek over the mountains to the other side of the island. There are many villages along this route, and a number of settlements on the west coast of the island. The largest town is Pangururan on the west coast.

Post The post office is in Ambarita. Several shops in Tuk Tuk sell stamps and have post-boxes and lists of rates for overseas mail.

Bank Change your money before you get to Lake Toba; exchange rates in Prapat or on Samosir are poor. The Bank Rakyat Indonesia is in Ambarita.

Things to See

Samosir Island is much more commercial than it was 10 or 15 years ago. What you get out of the place depends on what you're interested in doing here. Tuk Tuk is a tourist resort on the bulb-shaped peninsula on the east coast. This is where most foreigners stay, although there's nothing to do here. However, if you're recovering from your 19th nervous breakdown it's great. On the other hand, it's fair to say that the peninsula is chronically overrated as a tourist attraction. Anyone with an interest in the Toba Batak will gain more satisfaction from scrambling over the mountain ridge to the villages on the other side of the island. Take Tuk Tuk for what it is – a quiet foreigner's enclave – and you'll probably have a pleasant enough time there, but don't expect to do much more than swim, talk or gaze pensively across the water from the verandah of your hotel or restaurant.

Tomok

The village of Tomok is on the southern coast of Samosir. There are many examples of traditional Batak houses in Tomok and also fine old graves and tombs – carved stone sarcophagi with grotesque three-horned heads and bulging eyes. These creatures are called *singa* and their faces also decorate the facades of Toba Batak houses, at either end of the two big beams which support the main house structure.

If you follow the road away from the lakefront and the souvenir stalls in the village you will come to the grave of King Sidabatu. This powerful Batak animist king not only had his own image carved on his tombstone but also that of his Muslim military commander and bodyguard, Tengku Mohammed Syed, and that of the woman he is said to have loved for many years without fulfilment, Anteng Melila Senega.

One of Tomok's traditional houses is now being used as a museum by the descendants of a Batak king said to have ruled Tomok 500 years ago.

Ambarita

A few km beyond Tuk Tuk is Ambarita, a pretty village. Like Tuk Tuk it's undergone something of a development boom but it's still nowhere near as popular a place to stay as Tuk Tuk. Ambarita has several well-preserved reminders of its gory past. The most important of them is a group of stone chairs and a table, known as the cannibal king's dinner table. It was here that village meetings were held, disputes settled, war declared and wrongdoers tried and judged. It is said that serious offenders were led to a further group of stone furniture in an adjoining courtyard, where they had to kneel down and rest their head on a stone chopping block. Then, watched by a crowd of village men, they were dispatched from this world by the swift application of axe to neck. The villagers revel in telling you how the bodies were carved up and consumed bit by bit, but it's probably just stories for the tourists.

Simanindo

About 16 km from Ambarita on the northern tip of the island is the village of Simanindo. Simanindo has a fine old adat house, that has been meticulously restored and now functions as a museum. Formerly the home of a Batak king, Raja Simalungun, and his 14 wives the roof was originally decorated with 10 buffalo horns which represented the 10 generations of the dynasty. Simalungun was the last in a line of 13 kings, and one story goes that he was assassinated because he collaborated with the Japanese. Other people say the last king died a natural death.

The museum has a fine collection of brass cooking utensils, spears, krises, weapons, Dutch and Chinese crockery, sculptures and other Batak carvings. Batak dances are performed at the museum daily (at least during the tourist season) in the late morning, including a performance using a sigalegale.

Just off the coast near Simanindo, Tao Island has expensive accommodation and a restaurant. You can swim, waterski and rent speedboats at the resort.

Pangururan

Pangururan is the main settlement on the island, and is 16 km beyond Simanindo on the west coast. Stop off at the village of Lumban Suhi-Suhi if you are interested in seeing hand-weaving.

The big attraction at Pangururan is the hot springs. If you cross over the bridge to the mainland and take the first turn right you'll find them about halfway up the hill. Try the small pools near the bottom of the cliffs where the water is cooler, those higher up are scaldingly hot.

From Pangururan a bus goes to Nainggolan on the south coast, but there is no regular transport from there to Tomok. Nainggolan has a few traditional

Samosir Island, Lake Toba

houses and a losmen, and it may be possible to get a boat to Prapat.

Trekking Over the Island

There are two main routes you can take to trek from the Tuk Tuk/Tomok/Ambarita area to the other side of the island. These are the Long Trek and the Short Trek.

Either way, you don't need to take much with you, but raingear may make life more comfortable. The Samosir Bataks are hospitable people and although there are no warungs you can buy cups of coffee at villages along the way and reasonably priced meals can be arranged. All you have to do is ask and someone will volunteer to accommodate you, offer you coffee or prepare you a meal. The going rate for overnight accommodation is about 1500 rp.

If you are interested in ornithology there are many different kinds of birds to observe along the way. The flora is also varied with lots of coffee, cinnamon and clove trees as well as a carnivorous plant known as a monkey cup, which grows profusely on vines and devours insects. Neither walk takes you through jungle or rainforest. In fact, most of Samosir is either pine forest, rubber trees or mixed scrub.

When you reach Pangururan on the other side of the island you can catch a bemo back to Ambarita and Tomok.

The reverse trek, from Pangururan to Tomok or Ambarita, is slightly easier as you avoid the steep climb from the east coast.

The Long Trek The long trek takes you from Tomok to Pangururan. It can be done in two days, or more comfortably in three days: the first day from Tomok to Forest House One, the second day to Forest House Two or Runggurni Huta, and the third day to Pangururan.

From Tomok you walk about two km south and then follow a sealed road up diagonally to the top of the mountain range to Sigarantung and Parmonangan.

After about 13 km you come to what is now a derelict building with a radio tower, called Forest House One (or Pasanggrahan to the locals). The house is reportedly very basic with a 'filthy mandi' although the people here will put you up for the night (for about 1500 rp) and cook food for you.

From Forest House One you walk along a muddy, dirt road 15 km to Forest House Two. The road is overgrown and in some places only a faint trail is visible. There is usually someone around to point the way if you lose the track. Forest House Two is a ruin, although it's OK to shelter in. There's also a Batak village nearby. Better accommodation can be found in Runggurni, about an hour away.

Shortly after Forest House Two the track forks. Take the right fork, which soon afterwards crosses a bridge with a roof over it – one of several such bridges. The track leads to Runggurni, a quiet, friendly village. A few places, such as *Love Happy* homestay, provide accommodation, food and good trekking information.

From here you follow the long and winding road downhill, 16 km to Pangururan. Buses operate between Pangururan and villages along this road, usually in the very early morning.

The Short Trek More popular is the short trek from Ambarita to Pangururan, via Dolok. If you start fairly early in the morning you can do the whole trek in a day, but it's better to stay overnight at Dolok.

This trek takes you straight up the mountain ridge behind Ambarita, a strenuous two to three hour climb. It is almost impossible to describe the starting point for this trek as there are many trails at the foot of the mountain running in many different directions. You have to ask or get people to show you the way initially. Once you have overcome this initial hurdle the rest of the trail is clear. Walking up this hill is hard work and *very* hot – bring lots of water!

The trail takes you over the mountains to a place called Dolok (also known as Partungkoan), where there's a cluster of Batak houses and bungalows belonging to a family who regularly put up people for the night. They charge only 500 rp plus the cost of meals.

From here there are two possibilities. One is to take the easy way down to Pangururan, following a gentle downhill path (which can be traversed easily by vehicle or motorcycle during the dry season), or a longer route via Runggurni and Lake Sidihoni.

Places to Stay

Samosir is a great place to rest up if you've just suffered the rigours of long days travelling on Sumatran buses from Padang or further south. Or to prepare yourself for that trip if you've only just arrived from Medan! Although it's no longer the traffic-free island it once was, Samosir is certainly easy-going and carefree enough to suit most people. This is not a place for frenetic activity, unless you define walking that way.

The standard cheaper losmen cost around 1500 rp for singles, 2500 or 3000 rp for doubles, often in wooden Batak-style buildings with private mandi although overall they're pretty simple and basic. Some places have dorms. You can still find some very basic places at 1000 rp single and 1500 or 2000 rp double but these are extremely spartan.

Above these basic cheapies are the better-equipped rooms in batak-style houses, typically around 5000 rp and usually with a verandah. There are so many places to stay the best advice is to wander around until you find something that suits. Some places are off by themselves, quiet if you like that, isolated if you don't. Nearly all of them are right by the lake.

Tuk Tuk

There are now some larger hotels popping up on Samosir, appealing to wealthy

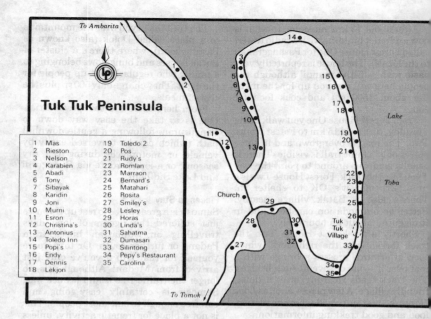

Tuk Tuk Peninsula

To Ambarita

1	Mas	19	Toledo 2
2	Rieston	20	Pos
3	Nelson	21	Rudy's
4	Karabien	22	Romlan
5	Abadi	23	Marraon
6	Tony	24	Bernard's
7	Sibayak	25	Matahari
8	Karidin	26	Rosita
9	Joni	27	Smiley's
10	Murni	28	Lesley
11	Esron	29	Horas
12	Christina's	30	Linda's
13	Antonius	31	Sahatma
14	Toledo Inn	32	Dumasari
15	Popi's	33	Silintong
16	Endy	34	Pepy's Restaurant
17	Dennis	35	Carolina
18	Lekjon		

Lake

Toba

Church

Tuk Tuk Village

To Tomok

North Sumatrans or package tourists from Singapore.

Carolina is still the longest running and most popular up-market place. They have a wide variety of rooms starting from the simplest ones at 5000 and 6000 rp through to 7500, 10,000 and 12,500 rp for the deluxe rooms with bathroom and balcony overlooking the lake. There's a restaurant, bar and even a diving board into the lake.

The famous Pepy has a couple of 2000 rp rooms with her *Pepy's* restaurant, close to Carolina. Continuing round the peninsula from Carolina you come to the big *Silintong Hotel* with rooms at US$10/13 up to US$28/32. Then there's *Bernard's* and *Matahari's* which are two of the longest-running places on Samosir. Both have regular rooms for 3000 rp with bathroom, but they're pretty basic. Better rooms in Batak-style houses are 5000 rp. Others in this area include *Marraon*, *Romlan* and *Rudy's*.

After this cluster of places at Tuk Tuk there are more scattered along the road. These include *Endy's* with rooms at 1500, 2000 rp. Then there's a gap before coming to the *Toledo Inn*, a big package-tour hotel with rooms at 15,000 to 35,000 rp. After another gap there's another tightly packed cluster of places. These include *Abadi's*, *Tony's*, *Kuridin's* and the very basic *Antonius*, all with rooms from 1500 to 3000 rp.

Continue on towards Ambarita and a trail descends down from the road to *Tuktuk Timbul* by the lakeside. This quiet and isolated place has dorm beds for 1500 rp, simple rooms for 2500 rp and nicer rooms for 5000 rp. It's a fine place if you want to get away from it all.

Ambarita

In Ambarita itself, *Rohandy's* is another simple place with rooms at 1000/2000 rp, right on the lake. For those who really want to get away from it all *Gordon's* is a couple of km beyond Ambarita on the way to Simanindo, and is a friendly place with good food. Right next to it is the flashy *Sopotoba* with rooms at 30,000 and 35,000 rp, surrounded by lots of barbed wire.

Tomok

Few people stay back at Tomok these days although there are plenty of restaurants and warungs here for day trippers. If you really want to stay there's *Mongoloi's* and a few other straightforward places like the *Tomok Shoganda Penginapan*.

Pangururan

The best place to stay is the *Hotel Wisata Samosir* (tel 50) at Jalan Kejaksaan 42, on the west coast of Pulau Samosir. This is a new hotel, spotlessly clean, with rooms from 12,000 rp. They also have dorm beds in bright, spacious dorms for 4000 rp per person.

Places to Eat

Once upon a time dining at Samosir was quite an occasion. 'Smorgasbords' were laid out for everybody at the place you stayed and these communal dinners were a nightly highlight of a Samosir stay. These days the food is much like in any other travellers' centre and there are no real surprises although most places still run a book for each guest, with each banana pancake or fruit salad added to a list which can stretch to a surprising length over a week or two.

There are few independent eating places, most are connected with the places to stay. An exception is the famous *Pepy's Restaurant*. Back in the early days the Samosir smorgasbord reached its heights when Pepy was the power in the kitchen at *Bernard's*. Today her restaurant, just outside Carolina's, still turns out good food.

Things to Buy

Day-to-day artefacts include wooden cylinders used to store lime, and old gunpowder flasks and bullet-holders made from buffalo horn. The *topeng* is a wooden mask used in funerary dances, designed to assure the deceased that his descendants will continue to serve him. *Silaon na bolon* are small wooden ancestral figures (usually in male/female pairs) revered as protection against evil. Most motifs on Batak artefacts have some meaning. For example, the land lizard which Batak farmers often encounter when clearing forest for cultivation represents the earth spirit and is thus a symbol of fertility.

Toba Batak musical instruments include the *grantung*, consisting of several pieces of non-resonating slats of wood strung out on a harness, and hit with sticks like a xylophone.

Both the Toba Batak and the Karo Batak employed *datu* – magic men, sorcerers or witch doctors. *Pustaha* are magic books made of accordion-folded bark leaves and wooden covers, and which contain the datu's magic formulae written in Batak script. The *tunggal panaluan* is a magic wand which was used by the datu to predict the future and protect the village.

A Karo Batak variation on this is the *tungkot malehat* which is a magic wand characterised by a carved figure on the top end sitting on a horse which has the head of a *singa*. A singa is a mythical underworld figure which is half buffalo and half snake and which has the power to drive away evil spirits.

A *porhalaan* is a cylinder of bamboo engraved with a calendar of 12 months of 30 days each, and is used as a diving tool to determine auspicious days on which to carry out tasks such as marriage, planting the fields, etc.

There is a great deal of badly produced carving and handicrafts around Tuk Tuk and Ambarita. One person who produces much better wood-carving than almost everything else you'll see is Marlen Manik who has a coffee and cake shop on the road from Tuk Tuk to Ambarita.

Getting There & Away

See the Prapat section for information on bus travel to and from Lake Toba.

Ferries operate between Prapat and Samosir on an irregular but reasonably frequent schedule. Treat departure times with caution and double check them. There are always a host of colourful boats at the Prapat harbour side but most of them are tour boats, the actual ferry is a simpler thing. The trip over costs 500 rp and takes about half an hour if the weather is reasonable.

The ferries will pick you up from various points on the Tuk Tuk Peninsula – such as Carolina's, and Marruon's losmen. They pull into the main ferry dock in Prapat, where buses are usually waiting to gather up passengers for Medan, Sibolga and other destinations.

There's also a car ferry which runs from Ajibata, about two km from Prapat, to Tomok. Passenger fare is 400 rp on this ferry which crosses about five times a day.

For a different way of getting to Samosir, a daily ferry runs from Tigaras, on the mainland, to Simanindo, and there is also a ferry twice a week from Ambarita

to Haranggaol. Boats carrying freight t other towns on Samosir may also tak passengers – ask around Prapat.

There may be a daily bus service from Pangururan to Brastagi, via Tele, but th road is very poor.

Getting Around

It is possible to take bemos from Tomok t Ambarita and as far around the island a Pangururan. A road circles the entir island.

There are now some minibuses regularly running between Tomok and Ambarita and continuing to Simanindo less frequently. There is no specific time schedule but services are more frequent in the morning. Don't count on finding any public transport after 3 pm. Even at the best of times you can wait a long time between minibuses. It's a pleasant one hour, five-km stroll from Tomok to Tuk Tuk. Buses also run several times a week from Runggurni Huta to Pangururan and continue to Simanindo.

You can rent motorcycles in Tuk Tuk for 10,000 to 15,000 rp a day, which is expensive compared to elsewhere in Indonesia.

King's table, Ambarita, Samosir Island

Nias

Off the west coast of Sumatra, along the same latitude as Sibolga, is the large island of Nias. The island is very rugged, consisting mainly of rolling hills and thick tropical jungle. It is said that the first Niassans were six people, some of whom were descended from the gods. Like other people of Sumatra and various parts of Indonesia, the Niassans made use of stone to produce monumental works of art.

Head-hunting and human sacrifice once played a part in their culture, as it did in the culture of the Bataks and the Torajas. Because of this and other cultural connections, the Niassans are thought to be related to the Bataks of Sumatra, the Naga of Assam in India, the aborigines of Taiwan, and various Dayak groups in Kalimantan.

The Niassans developed a life based mainly on agriculture and pig raising. Hunting and fishing, despite the thick jungle and the proximity of many villages to the coast, was only of secondary importance. The Niassans relied on the cultivation of yams, rice, maize and taro. Pigs were both a source of food and of wealth and prestige; the more pigs you had the greater your status in the village. Gold and copper work, as well as wood carving, were important village industries.

The indigenous religion was thought to have been a combination of animism and ancestor worship, together with some Hindu influences. Christianisation of the island did not really get under way until the 1850s, and during the first decades of the 20th century had become tied up with a number of indigenous messianic movements. Islam only gained some converts around the coast, and in townships like Gunung Sitoli.

Villages were presided over by a village chief, heading a council of elders. Beneath the aristocratic upper caste were the common people, and below them the slaves (often used as trade merchandise). Sometimes villages would band together in federations, which were often perpetually at war with other federations. Prior to the Dutch conquest, inter-village warfare was fast and furious, usually spurred on by the desire for revenge, slaves, or human heads. Heads were needed when a new village was built and during the burial ceremony of the chief. In central Nias, heads were reportedly a prerequisite for marriage. Today you can still see samples of the weapons used in these feuds: vests of buffalo hide or crocodile skin; helmets of metal, leather or plaited rattan; spears, swords and shields.

The recorded history of Nias only begins in the last years of the 18th century and the first years of the 19th century, when people like the Englishman Stamford Raffles began to send back reports about the island, and when the Dutch military and German missionaries began to make forays into it. Yet it was not until 1914 that the island came under complete Dutch control.

Getting There & Away

You can reach Nias either by boat from Sibolga or by air from Medan. The southern part of the island is interesting for its traditional villages, unique customs and fine beaches. Roads around Nias are rotten but the most interesting places in the south are fairly close together, connected by roads and jungle tracks.

Teluk Dalam is the port and main town in the south. Gunung Sitoli is the main town in the north.

Air SMAC has daily flights from Medan to Gunung Sitoli. The airport is 20 km from Gunung Sitoli and it's 3000 rp per person into town by SMAC taxi. There has been talk of building another airport at Teluk Dalam, but nothing has come of this.

Boat There are regular ferries from Sibolga to Gunung Sitoli and Teluk Dalam. Most of the places of interest are in the south, so

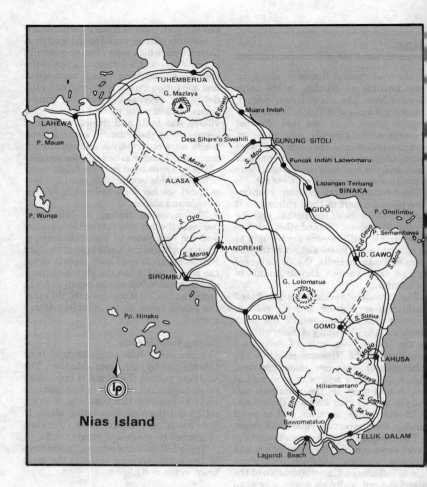

Nias Island

Teluk Dalam is the better destination to head for.

In Sibolga, ask at the shipping office at Jalan Pelabuhan 9 for tickets to Gunung Sitoli. For tickets to Teluk Dalam ask next door at the Sibolga Nauli office. If they're closed, go to the Damai ticket agency on Jalan Horas, near the entrance to Sibolga's other harbour.

Depending on the weather, there are

daily boats (usually except Sunday) from Sibolga to Gunung Sitoli, departing around 10 pm. The fare is 7000 rp and it's an overnight trip taking about nine hours.

There are regular boats from Sibolga to Teluk Dalam. Two boats make the crossing, and the larger, two-deck boat is more comfortable. The smaller one is a cramped cargo boat and passengers tend o be treated like cargo. There are a few abins available with bunk beds. The fare s 6000 rp and the trip takes about 12 ours. There are usually about two or hree departures per week, but schedules re irregular. In Teluk Dalam you can buy ickets at the Sibolga Nauli office on Jalan Ahmad Yani, near the harbour. Coming ack from Teluk Dalam, the ferry arrives n Sibolga in time to catch the buses north o Medan or south to Padang and Bukittingi.

Boats also go every two weeks from Teluk Bayur, the port of Padang. The trip akes about two days, so it's much less rduous to go by land from Padang to Sibolga and take a boat from there.

Getting Around

The only road of any consequence connects Teluk Dalam and Gunung Sitoli, and ven half of that is barely more than a goat rail. The island is a sadly neglected part of Indonesia. Motorised transport is very oor and many villages are only accessible by foot. To get around you can rent icycles, catch some trucks and buses or walk. The locals will give you pillion rides n their motorbikes for a price.

Gunung Sitoli to Teluk Dalam

There are daily buses from Gunung Sitoli to Teluk Dalam. The fare is 5000 rp. Buses leave from the terminal on Jalan Diponegoro.

The trip from Gunung Sitoli to Teluk Dalam takes about six hours, but that depends on the condition of the road. The road from Gunung Sitoli to Teluk Dalam is surfaced for the first half, but deteriorates badly after that. It's amazing the route is not lined by overturned buses and shattered surfboards! Transport is OK in the dry season, but during the wet the roads turn to mud and the flimsy bridges are washed away, in which case buses often form a shuttle service. One bus goes as far as it can, then passengers pile out and clamber over (or under) the obstacle and board another bus on the other side. On the other hand, when one bus tries to make it the whole way this is what (according to one reader) can happen:

The road is... appalling... we hit a section of mud holes which on a conservative estimate would have been one metre deep. Charged in at full speed relying on momentum to get us through – this was not always successful and all western passengers were seconded to dig and push the thing out... so 4000 rp, a broken window, cut feet, a wrecked set of clothes and 11 hours later we got to Teluk Dalam (we also sat for an extra three hours on the bus before it left while they worked on the engine!). Met one couple who took 18 hours! Chartered bus back to Lagundi and collapsed!

Teluk Dalam to Lagundi From Teluk Dalam you catch a truck the last dozen km to Lagundi Beach (Pantai Lagundi) for 300 rp. This stretch of road is surfaced as far as the village of Botohili. Or hire a motorcyclist to take you.

Boat You may be able to catch a small boat from Gunung Sitoli to Teluk Dalam, but this could involve hanging around for several days before one departs.

GUNUNG SITOLI

This is the main town of Nias. It's a fairly innocuous little place with a certain seedy, tropical charm to it.

Things to See

There are several nice walks near town. There are some traditional houses uphill from the village of Hilimbawodesolo, about 14 km from Gunung Sitoli. You get there by bus. There are other traditional houses on the road in from the airport, and on the road to Teluk Dalam.

Information

Post The post office is on Jalan Gomo.

Bank The Bank Negara Indonesia on Jalan Pattimura, will change American and Australian dollar travellers' cheques, but the rate really is very bad. This,

To Pelabuhan Baru
(Ferry To Sibolga)

Pier

1 Bank Rakyat
2 Mosque
3 Pelni & Ticket
  Office For
  Sibolga Ferry
4 Post Office
5 Hotel Gomo
6 Bank Negara
  Indonesia
7 Market
8 Penginapan
  Banuadu
9 Hotel Beringin

Jl Gomo

Jl Sirao

Jl Pattimura

Jl Korpri

Jl Beringin

Gunung Sitoli

To Bus Station

however, is the only place where you can change money on the island.

Places to Stay

The best place to stay is the *Wisma Soliga* which is on the main road into town. It's clean, spacious and they serve up big Chinese meals. Rooms start from around 6000 rp. The disadvantage is that it's two km out of town.

In the centre of town is the *Hotel Gomo* (tel 21926) at Jalan Gomo 148. This used to be a very drab hotel (and there still are a number of very dreary rooms) but it seems to have been done up a bit in recent years and is a fine place to stay. Rooms start from 7500 rp. Rooms with television, bathroom and air-con start from 15,000 rp.

The *Hotel Beringin* on Jalan Beringin is nothing more than a concrete shed divided into thinly-partitioned compartments. It's very dark and depressing and is reminiscent of a two-storey cattle shed. Beds are 2000 rp and rooms are 6000 rp.

Even sadder is the *Penginapan Banuadu* on Jalan Kopri. Box-like rooms are 1000 rp per person, but you will really have had to hit rock-bottom to stay there.

One reader has recommended a place which she dubs the *Hotel Bata* because it used to be a shoe store at one time and the Bata sign is still there. This place is a few minutes walk from the bus station and charges about 750 rp per person. They also have a restaurant.

TELUK DALAM

Teluk Dalam is a non-descript township in the south of Nias. Set on a pretty, palm-fringed bay this is the jumping-off point for Lagundi Beach, about 12 km away. There are also ferries from Teluk Dalam to Sibolga.

Places to Stay

The only hotel in Teluk Dalam seems to be the *Wisma Jamburae*, by the harbour. It's a very simple place, with beds for 2500 rp and rooms from 7500 rp. It's basic but clean.

LAGUNDI BEACH

Lagundi Beach is a perfect horseshoe bay 2 km from Teluk Dalam. This is Indonesia's surfing Mecca, destination for a steady stream of surfing enthusiasts. For those not into surfing it is also an idyllic place to swim and bask in the sun. The far end of the peninsula is still untouched by development, and for the most part the wood and thatch losmen blend in sympathetically with the shoreline. Only in a few places have too many palm trees been cut down to make way for the hotels, and this may be a sad portent of things to come, as more people head for the island.

Places to Stay

There are many losmen, many of them clustered together at the far end of the horseshoe where the waves roll in across the reef. Most cost between 1000 to 2000 rp per person. All the losmen provide food from menus which are almost exactly the same: omelettes, mie goreng, fried rice and vegetables, gado gado, pancakes, chips and so on. People also catch fish and lobster out on the reef, then sell them on the beach – you can buy your dinner straight from the ocean and get the losmen to cook it for you.

It would be pointless, and maybe a bit unfair, to mention any one losmen in particular. They are all pretty much the same, with wooden and bamboo huts of varying size built on stilts by the shore. The losmen on the beach have been taken over by the swimming community, while the peninsula attracts the surfers.

Near the centre of the horseshoe are two more established losmen, the *Limadona* and the *Yanty*. The owner of the *Yanty*, Mr Milyar, is friendly, helpful and speaks good English. He also acts as a guide and knows a lot about the area. Rooms are 1000 rp per person.

The white-washed concrete *Fanayama* (behind the *Yanty*) is a government-run place. It has rooms for 4000/8000 rp with bathroom. While it's less 'primitive' than other accommodation, it's appearance is unsympathetic with the beach.

Other places include the *Losmen Saradodo* towards the far end of the peninsula. It's a small house on stilts with a few rooms, and is run by a friendly family. It's a bit more isolated from the other places and very quiet.

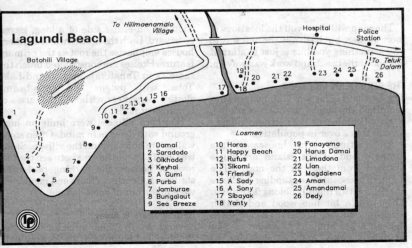

Lagundi Beach

To Hilimaenamalo Village

Hospital

Police Station

To Teluk Dalam

Botohili Village

Losmen		
1 Damai	10 Horas	19 Fanayama
2 Saradodo	11 Happy Beach	20 Harus Damai
3 Oikhoda	12 Rufus	21 Limadona
4 Keyhol	13 Sikomi	22 Llan
5 A Gumi	14 Friendly	23 Magdalena
6 Purba	15 A Sady	24 Aman
7 Jamburae	16 A Sony	25 Amandamai
8 Bungalaut	17 Sibayak	26 Dedy
9 Sea Breeze	18 Yanty	

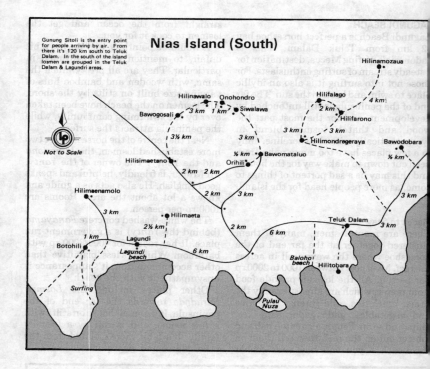

Gunung Sitoli is the entry point for people arriving by air. From there it's 120 km south to Teluk Dalam. In the south of the island losmen are grouped in the Teluk Dalam & Lagundri areas.

Nias Island (South)

Not to Scale

The map will show you the locations of more losmen, but basically the best way to find something you like is just to start at one end of the beach and work your way up.

THE SOUTHERN VILLAGES

The southern villages of Nias have always contained the largest numbers of people, often outnumbering the northern villages several times over in population.

Architecturally the houses at the southern end of the island are quite different from those in the north. The northern houses are free-standing dwellings on stilts, with a roughly oblong floor-plan. They look a bit like wood and thatch mock-ups of flying saucers. The houses in the south are built like London or San Francisco town houses, shoulder to

shoulder on either side of a long, paved courtyard. Both the northern and southern houses emphasise the roof as the primary feature. Houses are constructed much the same as in Tanatoraja and around Lake Toba, with pylons and cross-beams slotted together without the use of bindings or nails.

Southern villages were built on high ground with defence in mind. Often stone walls were built around the village. Stone was used to pave the area between the two rows of houses, the bathing pools and staircases. Benches, chairs and memorials were made out of carved stone.

Getting There & Away

Several south Nias villages, such as Botohili and Hilimaeta, are an easy walk rom Lagundi Beach. Bawamataluo is only 14 km from Lagundi, but the road is very long, winding and mostly uphill. It's a tedious walk, so it's much better to pay someone to take you there on the back of their motorcycle. Occasionally trucks take passengers to some villages, but others are only accessible on foot.

Bawamataluo (Sunhill)

At Bawamataluo you can see high-roofed traditional houses. The village is impressive if only for its size – it's virtually a small town. The focus of interest is the reconstructed 'palace' of the former king, a monumental structure supported by huge pylons made from whole tree trunks. In the paved area between the houses are stone tables where, it is said, dead bodies were once left to decay.

Traditional war dances may be performed at festival time (or at shows staged for tourists) by young, unmarried males, who decorate themselves with feathers. Stone-jumping is also performed. Once a form of war training, the jumpers had to leap over a two-metre-high heap of stones surmounted by pointed sticks. These days the sticks are left off.

Bawamataluo is now very touristy and prices for statues or for watching the stone jumping really are exorbitant by anyone's standards. Many of the villagers will pose for photographs and then demand money for doing it – and sometimes get quite aggressive if you don't pay up.

Orihili

From Bawamataluo a stone staircase and trail leads downhill to the village of Orihili. From Bawamataluo you can see the roof-tops of Orihili in a clearing in the trees.

Hilisimaetano

This larger, newer village is 16 km from Teluk Dalam and has around 140 traditional houses. Stone-jumping is performed here most Saturdays.

Botohili

This is a smaller village on the hillside above the peninsula of Lagundi Beach. It has two rows of traditional houses, with a number of new houses breaking up the skyline. The remains of the original entrance way, stone chairs and paving can still be seen.

Hilimaeta

This village is similar to Botohili. The stone-jumping pylon can still be seen and there are a number of stone monuments, including benches and a four legged stone table. In the middle of the paved area stands a two-metre-high stone penis. A long pathway of stone steps leads uphill to the village.

Hilimaenamolo

This is a small village. It's in particularly poor condition with much of the paving ripped up and many stone monuments either collapsed or dismantled.

Woman & Child, Bawamataluo

Aceh

I am the mighty ruler of the Regions below the wind, who holds sway over the land of Aceh and over the land of Sumatra and over all the lands tributary to Aceh, which stretch from the sunrise to the sunset

This extract from a letter sent by the Sultan of Aceh to Queen Elizabeth I of England in 1585 marked the beginning of a trade agreement between the two powers – Aceh and England – that lasted until the 19th century. It also shows the extent of Aceh's sphere of influence as a trading nation, its sense of independence and its autonomy at that time.

Years before Melaka fell to the Portuguese, Aceh was Melaka's chief competitor for trade. Rivalry between them was intensified by religious hostility as Aceh was one of the earliest centres of Islam in the archipelago. Religious differences and the harsh Portuguese rule spurred many traders of different nationalities – Islamic scholars, Egyptians and Arabians, craftspeople from India and goldsmiths from China – into abandoning Melaka and setting themselves up in Aceh.

The influx of traders and immigrants contributed to Aceh's wealth and influence. Aceh's main exports were pepper and gold; others were ivory, tin, tortoise-shell, camphor, aloe-wood, sandalwood and spices. The city of Greater Aceh was also important as a centre of Islamic learning and as a gateway for Indonesian Muslims making the pilgrimage to Mecca.

Aceh is also interesting because, despite its early and strong allegiance to Islam, there have been four women rulers – although it is possible that real power lay with a council of 12 men. However, such a state of 'grace' could not last and in 1699 a legal recommendation from Mecca condemned rule by women as contrary to Islamic practice. The fourth woman ruler was deposed and replaced by a government headed by religious leaders.

Although Aceh's power began to decline towards the end of the 17th century it was able to remain independent for a long time. Singapore and Aceh were active trading partners with the help of the long standing secret treaty with Britain. All that came to an end in 1871 when the Dutch negotiated a new treaty with the British in which England withdrew all objections to the possibility of a Dutch occupation of Aceh. The Acehnese tried to counteract this blow by negotiating with both the Italian and United States consuls in Singapore. The draft of an American-Acehnese treaty of friendship was sent to Washington. The Dutch, however, forestalled further attempts by declaring war on Aceh in 1873.

The first Dutch expeditionary force of 7000 retreated when its commander, General Kohler, was killed. A new army contingent, twice as large, succeeded in taking the capital, the central mosque and the sultan's palace, but the war went on for 35 years before the last of the sultans, Tuanku Muhamat Dawot, surrendered. Even then no Dutch area was safe from sabotage or guerrilla attack from the Acehnese until the Dutch surrendered to Japan in 1942.

The Japanese were welcomed at first but resistance soon sprang up when local institutions were not respected. During this period the Islamic Party, which had been formed in 1939 under the leadership of Daud Beureuh, gained increasing support. In 1951 the central government dissolved the Province of Aceh and incorporated its territory into the Province of North Sumatra under a governor in Medan. The dissatisfaction of the people was so widespread that Daud Beureuh proclaimed Aceh an Islamic Republic in September 1953. This state lasted until 1961 when the military and religious leaders had a falling out.

The central government resolved the conflict by giving Aceh provincial status again. The military yielded to this decision because it felt its objective had been achieved and the religious leaders, without the support of the military, were forced to surrender. Jakarta later granted special status to the province in the areas of religion, culture and education and in 1967 Aceh was given the title of Special Territory.

People & Religion

The Acehnese are the majority people in this province. Others are the Gayo and Alas in the mountains, the Minangkabau along the west coast, the Kluet in the south and Javanese and Chinese throughout. Aceh is the most staunchly Muslim part of Sumatra and Christians and Buddhists comprise only a small percentage of population.

Nevertheless, animism is also part of the everyday fabric of Acehnese life. There is a prevailing popular belief in the existence of spirits who dwell in old trees, wells, rocks and stones. Ghosts and evil spirits are said to be particularly malicious around dusk when they can wreak havoc on all those they come in contact with. Dukuns are still called in to help solve grievances, cure illnesses and cast spells on enemies.

Offerings and rituals are still observed at significant times of the agricultural year, such as harvest time, and dreams and omens are interpreted. In some parts of Sumatra pilgrimages are made to the tombs of Acehnese scholars and religious leaders.

Music & Dance

Every region in Aceh has its local dances but there are three that are popular throughout the province – the *seudati*, *meusakat* and *ranub lam puan*.

Seudati The seudati is a quick-tempoed dance which involves a complicated pattern of forward, sideward and backward leaps. The songs are led by a dancer (called the *syech*) and two narrators

(*aneuk syahi*), and no instruments are used. The rhythm is accentuated by the variation in the movements of the dancers, who also heighten the tension by snapping their fingers and beating their chests. The pace is hotted up even more when contests are held between performing groups. The traditional seudati has five parts: the *salam* (greeting), *likok* (special movements), *kisah* (story), *dhiek* (poetry) and *syahi* (songs). Recently this dance has been used to disseminate information on government policy and to urge people to become better Muslims.

Meusakat The meusakat, or dance of the thousand hands, originated in the region of Meulaboh and is performed by a group of 13 young girls. It consists of a series of precise hand, head, shoulder and torso movements. Traditionally, the dance was performed to glorify Allah or to offer prayers, but today, like the seudati, it is often used to get across a government message on development policy. Like the seudati, instruments are not used. The songs are led by a girl positioned in the middle of a row of kneeling performers.

Ranub Lam Puan The ranub lam puan is a modern adaptation of various traditional dances from throughout Aceh. It is performed to welcome guests and to convey hospitality, which is symbolised in the offering of betel nut or snacks by the dancers. The *seurene kalee*, a single-reed woodwind, provides the haunting musical accompaniment.

Musical Instruments Other typical Acehnese instruments include a three-stringed zither (called an *arbab*) made of wood from the jackfruit tree with strings of bamboo, rattan or horsetail hair; bamboo flutes (*buloh merindu, bangsi, tritit* and *soeling*); gongs and tambourines (*rapai*). The tambourines are made of goatskin, while the gongs are usually brass (sometimes dried goatskin) and are struck with padded wooden hammers.

They come in three sizes: *gong, canang* and *mong-mong*.

Crafts

Weapons Metallurgy was learned early from Arab and Persian traders and, because of Aceh's continued involvement in wars, weapon-making became a highly developed skill. Acehnese daggers and swords comprise three parts: blade, handle and sheath. The blade can have both edges sharpened or just one, and can be straight, concave or convex. The handles of weapons are usually of buffalo horn, wood or bone, and carved in the form of a crocodile's mouth, a horse's hoof or a duck's tail and embellished with gold or silver. The sheaths are made of rattan, silver or wood and fastened with bands of a mixture of gold, brass and copper called *sousa*. The best example of this art form is the *rencong*, a dagger which has a convex iron, damascened blade with one sharpened edge. Less well-known Acehnese weapons are the *siwah* (knife) and *pedang* (a pointed sword).

Jewellery While there is a long tradition, stemming from the early days of the sultanate, of fine craftsmanship in gold and silver jewellery, there is almost no antique jewellery to be found in Aceh today. Most of it was sold to raise money for the war against the Dutch. Excellent gold and silver jewellery is still produced but there is not much variation in design.

Weaving & Embroidery Despite its long history and high reputation Acehnese weaving is rapidly disappearing.

On the other hand, embroidery is a very vital art form. Areas around Sigli, Meulaboh and Banda Aceh are renowned for embroidery using gold-coloured metallic thread (*soedjoe*) on tapestry, cushions, fans and wall hangings. The main motifs are flowers, foliage and geometric designs and the finished work is also decorated with mirrors, golden pailletes, sequins and beads in an effect known as *ble blot*.

One type of embroidery which is no doing so well is *mendjot beboengo*. Thi kind of hand embroidery originated in th region of Takengon around Gayo and Ala and was done by men only. Stylised motif of geometric flowers in red, white, yellow and green thread were embroidered on black background.

Other Crafts Various domestic items ar made from coconut husks, tree bark water buffalo horns, palm leaves and clay These include spoons, baskets, mats earthenware pots and dishes.

BANDA ACEH

Banda Aceh, capital of Aceh, is a large sprawling city at the northern tip o Sumatra. A city of contrast, it's an odd mix of faded grandeur and economie prosperity. Money is being poured into prestigious buildings and development programmes and the appearance of the city is changing rapidly.

As a result of their history of extensive and mixed immigration, the Acehnese are a curious racial blend of Indonesian, Arab, Tamil, Chinese, and hill tribe. Some of the tallest people in Indonesia live here. Unlike Medan, Banda Aceh is a much more relaxed city and the Acehnese tend on the whole to leave you alone. Foreign prejudices about Aceh being the stronghold of the Sumatran Muslim 'heavies' are more in the imagination of the beholders than they are in those of the believers.

Information & Orientation

The city centre is marked by an imposing five-domed mosque and clustered around it are markets, bus terminals and some hotels. The Krueng Aceh River divides the city in two. On the other side of the river from the mosque is Jalan Ahmad Yani, which has several hotels.

Tourist Office The tourist office (tel 21377) is at Jalan T Nyak Arief 35.

Post & Telephone Long distance telephone calls can be made from PERUMTEL at Jalan Nyak Arief 13. The main post office is on Jalan Kuta Alam, one block from Simpang Tiga.

Bank The Bank Rakyat Indonesia on Jalan Cut Meutia, will change only US dollar travellers' cheques. Also try the Bank Negara Indonesia 1946 on Jalan Merduati.

Central Market
The meat and fish market on Jalan Sisingamangaraja is one of the most striking and lively in Sumatra. At the rear, by the river, you can see the boats off-loading their cargo of shark, tuna and tubs of prawns. Nearby, running off Jalan S M Yamin, is 'Banana Street', an alley full of banana stalls. Opposite is a bundle of huts where two dozen workers shell and pulverise coconuts, grating the flesh with noisy machines. Not only is this a good place for picking through the meat and vegies, it's also a great place for people watching.

Sultanates
Of the old Acehnese Sultanates there is not a great deal left. Just a few peculiar buildings, a gateway, a couple of white-washed tombs attest to a once powerful royal house. For those wishing to forgo the imperial days for a reminder of the colonial days, travelling joggers will be pleased to know that the Banda Aceh Hash House Harriers have a run every second Friday afternoon.

For those with a more spiritual bent, behind the Governor of Aceh's official residence, Pendopo, is a new complex built in 1981 for the National Koran Reading Competition. Two modern buildings surround an open-air performance centre where dances and theatre are staged on special occasions.

The Mosque
With its stark white walls and licorice-black domes, this imposing building rises up in the centre of Banda Aceh. The first section of the mosque was kindly built by the Dutch in 1879 as a conciliatory gesture towards the warring Acehnese after the original one had been burnt down. Two more domes – one on each side of the first – were added by the Dutch in 1936 and another two in 1957 by the Indonesian government. Ask the keeper to let you climb the staircase to one of the minarets so you can get a view of the city.

Gunongan
For a contrast in architectural styles go and see the Gunongan on Jalan Teuku Umar, near the clock tower. This 'stately pleasure dome' was built by Sultan Iskandar Muda (who reigned 1607-1636) as a gift for his wife, a Malayan princess, and was intended as a private playground and bathing place. Its three storeys are each meant to resemble an open leaf or flower. The building itself is a series of frosty peaks with narrow stairways and a walkway leading to hummocks which were supposed to represent the hills of her native land. Basically, it looks like the concoction of a confectioner given carte blanche to create a pop art wedding cake. Whether it actually cheered her up is anyone's guess since it doesn't conjure up much feeling nowadays. Directly across from the Gunongan is a low vaulted-gate in the traditional *Pintu Aceh* style, which gave access to the sultan's palace and was supposed to have been used by royalty only.

Dutch Cemetery (Kerkhof)
Nearby is the last resting place for more than two thousand Dutch and Indonesian soldiers who died fighting the Acehnese. The entrance is about 250 metres from the clock tower on the road to Uleh-leh. Tablets implanted in the walls by the entrance gate are inscribed with the names of the dead soldiers – many of whom include native Dutch, Eurasians, Javanese and Ambonese.

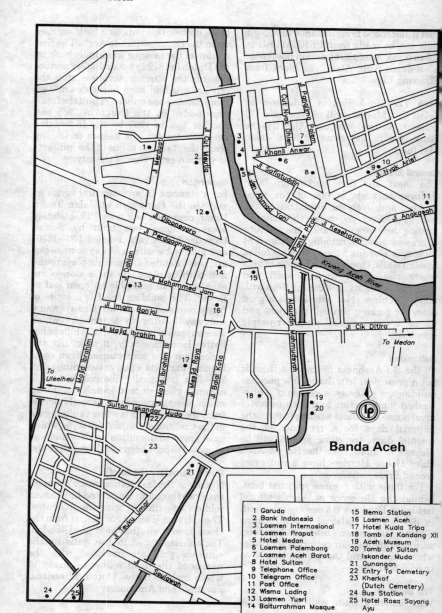

Banda Aceh

To Medan

To Uleelheu

To

1 Garuda
2 Bank Indonesia
3 Losmen Internasional
4 Losmen Prapat
5 Hotel Medan
6 Losmen Palembang
7 Losmen Aceh Barat
8 Hotel Sultan
9 Telephone Office
10 Telegram Office
11 Post Office
12 Wisma Lading
13 Losmen Yusri
14 Baiturrahman Mosque
15 Bemo Station
16 Losmen Aceh
17 Hotel Kuala Tripa
18 Tomb of Kandang XII
19 Aceh Museum
20 Tomb of Sultan
   Iskander Muda
21 Gunongan
22 Entry To Cemetary
23 Kherkof
   (Dutch Cemetery)
24 Bus Station
25 Hotel Rasa Sayang
   Ayu

Jl Merduati
Jl Cut Meutia
Jl Cut Nyak Dhien
Jl Panglima Polen
Jl Khairil Anwar
Jl Safiatuddin
Jl Jen Ahmad Yani
Jl Nyak Arief
Jl Angkasah
Jl Kesehatan
Jl Diponegoro
Jl Perdagangan
Jl Dahlan
Jl Mohammed Jam
Jl Imam Bonjol
Jl Alaudin Mahmudsyah
Jl Cik Ditiro
Jl Majid Ibrahim II
Jl Majid Ibrahim
Jl Majid Ibrahim III
Jl Mesjid Raya
Jl Balai Kota
Jl Sultan Iskandar Muda
Jl Teuku Umar
Jl Seulawah
Krueng Aceh River
Ponte Ishak

Museums

Banda Aceh has a large museum with three floors of exhibits of weapons, household furnishings, ceremonial costumes, everyday clothing, gold jewellery and books. The museum is at Jalan Yakapeh 12, and is open Tuesday to Thursday from 8.30 am to 2 pm, and on Fridays and Saturdays from 8.30 am to 12 noon. In the same compound is the Rumah Aceh – a fine example of traditional Acehnese architecture, built without nails and held together with cord or pegs. It's open Tuesday to Saturday from 4 to 6 pm, and contains more Acehnese artefacts and war memorabilia. In front of the Rumah Aceh is a large cast-iron bell, which is said to have been given to the Acehnese by a Chinese Emperor centuries ago.

Uleh-leh

Five km west of Banda Aceh is the old port of Uleh-leh where you can while away a few interesting hours watching the traders come in from outer islands. There are some attractive villages around Uleh-leh and a not so attractive black-sand beach, stripped of its trees, and complete with sharks and other dangers. In colonial times the Dutch cordoned part of it off with metal netting and came up here for a dip.

Beaches

Against a backdrop of mountains is the beach of Lhok Nga, base for a large expatriate community who work for the company Semen Andalas Indonesia. Lhok Nga is only about 16 km out of Banda Aceh along the East Coast road near the mosque. Its beach is inconsequential and the rocky coast seems far too rough for swimming. It's mainly set up as a weekend picnic spot for the Acehnese, with lots of warungs and shorn grass. Bemos from Jalan Diponegoro in Banda Aceh are 500 rp.

About 15 km along the road to Krueng Raya is Ujung Bate, a black-sand beach rimmed with pines and overlooking the Melaka Straits. It is said that Ujung Bate

is haunted by ghosts, but whether it is or not, it is a good beach to walk along and collect shells. Sabang Island is visible from here.

Lampu'uk is a beautiful white-sand beach on the Indian Ocean. Take the road to Meulaboh and turn left after passing the golf course and left again when you reach the sea. It is not advisable to wear bikinis, or to walk along beaches in Aceh dressed only in a swimsuit. Most local women swim fully clothed.

Places to Stay - bottom end

A decent bottom-end hotel is the *Losmen International* on Jalan Ahmad Yani, opposite the night market. There are small rooms for 4000 rp, and larger rooms with bathroom for 6500 rp. It's very basic but reasonably clean, and rooms at the rear are quiet.

Better than the Losmen International is the *Wisma Lading* (tel 21359) at Jalan Cut Meutia 9. Rooms start from 4000 rp, and there are more expensive rooms with fan for 6000 rp and with air-con for 10,000 rp. All rooms have private bathroom.

The *Losmen Sri Budaya* on Jalan Madjid Ibrahim III, has rooms for 8000 rp, with fan and private bathroom. It's an old Dutch house, with spartan but clean and well-kept rooms.

The *Losmen Yusri* at Jalan Dahlan 74 has musty rooms from 10,000 rp. It's fairly dreary and not recommended. Also try the *Losmen Aceh Barat* on Jalan Kharil Anwar – not to be confused with the Losmen Aceh which is opposite the big mosque. Avoid the *Penginapan Palembang* on Jalan Kharil Anwar, unless you enjoy heavy-metal television.

Places to Stay - middle

The *Hotel Medan* on Jalan Ahmad Yani, has basic but agreeable rooms for 7500 rp with private bathroom, and up to 22,000 rp with air-con. The *Hotel Prapat* on Jalan Ahmad Yani is similar to the Hotel Medan. It has rooms for 8000 rp, and for 12,000 rp with air-con. Like the Hotel

Medan, it may get quite a lot of street noise.

The *Losmen Aceh* on Jalan Mohammed Jam is opposite the big mosque in the centre of town. Rooms are 12,000 rp with air-con. The hotel appears to have once been an old Dutch villa, or perhaps even an army barracks. The appearance and design suggests a certain colonial elegance and detachment gone completely to rack and ruin. It has a certain dilapidated charm.

Places to Stay – top end

The *Sultan Hotel* (tel 23582) is on an alley leading off Jalan Panglima Polem. Rooms start from 20,000 rp and have three-quarter size beds, carpet, television, and air-con. It's a quiet location. Deluxe rooms are 30,000/45,000 rp.

The *Hotel Rasa Sayang Aya* (tel 21379) on Jalan Teuku Umar, has rooms from 20,000/25,000 rp. It's very well kept and the rooms have big double beds, carpet and television. It's a bit far out of town, though it is convenient for the Seutia Bus Terminal diagonally opposite.

The *Kuala Tripa Hotel* (tel 21455) at Jalan Mesjid Raya 24 is similar to the Rasa Sayang, and though its centrally located the rooms are much more expensive at 45,000 rp. It also has a basement swimming pool.

Places to Eat

Jalan Ahmad Yani is a good place to start looking for food. There are many moderately priced Padang-style places along this street, and along nearby Jalan Cut Nyak Dhien and Jalan Panglima. For seafood and kindergarten decor, try the *Restaurant Happy* at Jalan Ahmad Yani 74-76.

The night market at the corner of Jalan Ahmad Yani and Jalan Kharil Anwar is a good place for cheap food, and has a lively atmosphere.

Like other Sumatran cities there are also many bakeries around the middle of town, try *Satyva Modern Bakery* at

Khairil Anwar 3, *Toko Muara* at Jalan K H A Dahlan 17, *Toko Nirwana* facing the mosque on Jalan Balai Kota, and *Toko Setia Baru* across from the Pasar Setui on Jalan Teuku Umar.

Things to Buy

There are several markets in Banda Aceh with a colourful jumble of laden stalls of different foodstuffs. In the large city block area beside the mosque is the vast Pasar Aceh, which is good for buying fresh fruit and vegetables or household goods.

Most of the jewellery shops are in a row along Jalan Perdagangan. Goldsmiths can produce any design you like provided they have something to copy from. If you are interested in antiques there are several shops worth browsing around. Toko Daud on Jalan Perdagangan has a good selection of Acehnese weapons, including traditional knives and swords.

The shop at Jalan Perdagangan 115 specialises in Acehnese antiques, but also has a good selection of old Dutch and Chinese porcelain. The owner has a private collection at his house (not for sale) which you might be able to arrange to see.

Another possible source of souvenirs are the *tukang* (skilled labourers or artisans), who occasionally drop by hotels. They're a bit like travelling souvenir shops with their bundles of artefacts, however, their stuff is often of fine quality.

Try the Pasar Aceh area, on the Jalan Diponengoro side, for utilitarian handicrafts. Close to the police station on Jalan Cut Meutia is a small government shop called Pusat Promosi Industri Kecil, which has a limited selection of handicrafts on display.

Getting There & Away

Air SMAC (tel 21626) is at Jalan Cut Nyak Dhien 93. Garuda (tel 21983) is in the Hotel Rasa Sayang Aya on Jalan Teuku Umar, at the southern edge of town.

Garuda has daily flights from Banda Aceh to Medan, connecting with flights to

Singapore, Jakarta, Ujung Pandang, Yogyakarta, and a number of other Sumatran cities such as Padang, Palembang and Pekanbaru.

Bus The main bus terminal is the Terminal Bus Seuti on Jalan Teuku Umar at the southern end of town. From here you can get buses to Medan.

Several companies have daily buses to Medan. Air-con buses cost 8000, while non air-con buses are 7000 rp. The road is surfaced all the way, but because sections may get washed out in the wet season you should be prepared to wait. Normally the bus trip takes about 14 hours. The road takes you through numerous villages, mountains, rice paddies and rolling country.

You can also get buses to from Banda Aceh to Meulaboh (seven hours along a sealed road) and from Meulaboh to Tapaktuan (four hours, also along a good sealed road).

From Tapaktuan it's a 14-hour ride to Sidikalang. It's a rough trip through virgin jungle and little villages in a very wild and remote area, involving at least three river crossings and a road which is mile after mile of great crater-size potholes.

Bemos to Ulee Lheu, Lhok Nga and Pelabuhan Malahayati leave from Jalan Diponegoro, near the big mosque. Fares to Ulee Lheau are 300 rp, Lhok Nga 600 rp, and Pelabuhan Malahayati 1000 rp.

Boat Pelni (tel 23976) is at Jalan Cut Meutia 51. Pelni's *KM Lawit* departs Banda Aceh about once every two weeks bound for Belawan (the port of Medan), Dumai (from where you can bus to Pekanbaru), Tanjung Priok (the port of Jakarta) and beyond. For more details see the Getting Around chapter at the start of this book.

SABANG

North of Banda Aceh by ferry is the port of Sabang on Pulau Weh. One of the attractions of this small island on the western rim of Indonesia, at least for the Acehnese, is that it's a duty free port. Otherwise it also has lots of attractive, palm-fringed beaches.

Things to See

This is lotus-eating territory. There is not much to do except to lie around basking on a beach and there are plenty of beaches to stretch out on. Ten minutes from Sabang is Pantai Paradiso, a white-sand beach shaded by coconut palms. Not much further away is Pantai Kasih and about 30 minutes from town is Sumur Tiga Beach, popular as a picnic place. Less than two km from town is a serene freshwater lake called Danau Anak Laut. From the nearby hills it is possible to see the port and the whole of Sabang Bay. An hour away by boat is Pulau Rubiah, a densely forested island, surrounded by coral eaches and reefs, great for snorkelling.

Places to Stay & Eat

There are several places to stay in Sabang, none of them cheap. The *Sabang Hill Hotel* has a good view of the bay but unless you have transport it's too far from town. Right in the centre are two cheap losmen, the *Pulau Jaya* and *Raja Wali*. Somewhat pricier are the *Sabang Guest House* and the *Hotel Sabang Marauke*. Sabang has many coffee houses and a number of Chinese and Indonesian restaurants on or in the vicinity of Jalan Perdagangan.

Getting There & Away

Boats from Banda Aceh to Sabang leave from Pelabuhan Malahayati. The voyage takes two hours and costs 3000 rp. Pelabuhan Malahayati is at Krueng Raya 35 km from Banda Aceh. There are regular bemos throughout the day leaving for Pelabuhan Malahayati from Jalan Diponegoro in Banda Aceh. The trip takes one hour and costs 1000 rp.

Getting Around

Sabang is 12 km from the harbour. Get an

oplet there for 500 rp or a taxi for 5000 rp. The taxi station is on Jalan Perdagangan. Ask about renting motorcycles and boats.

PULAU BERAS

It's possible to hire a boat for a day and go out to Pulau Beras or several other islands off the coast of Banda Aceh when the sea and weather are calm. Fishing boats can be rented by the day at Uleh-leh. You may have to get permission from the harbour master before you set off. Pulau Beras is lightly populated but most of the other islands are uninhabited. If you like snorkelling there are some good spots around these islands, so take equipment with you. You will also need food, drink, insect repellent and, if possible, life jackets.

MEULABOH

Almost 250 km west of Banda Aceh is the small, sleepy town of Meulaboh. It's a long, dusty, bumpy ride down the west coast road, which is riddled with potholes and involves five, often time-consuming, river crossings. The beauty of the scenery with its contrasting scenes of wild seas, jungle and rocky shorelines surpasses the agony of the journey.

Meulaboh is the departure point for Simeulue Island but it is also a surfing Mecca. Lhok Bubon, an excellent and safe beach, is 16 km back towards Banda Aceh. The beaches closer to Meulaboh are considered dangerous because of strong, unpredictable currents. Take extreme care if you are swimming at any of them. In the meantime, watch out for the monument honouring Teuku Umar, hero of the Acehnese resistance – it's shaped like a traditional Acehnese hat (*kupiah meukeutop*).

There are a number of unspoiled and tranquil villages nearby which are worth exploring. Articles of clothing and other items embroidered in the traditional style are for sale in some of these villages. Tutut, the site of an old gold mine

which was in operation until 1945, is 60 km north of Meulaboh along a dirt track.

Places to Stay

In Meulaboh stay at either the *Mustika* or the *Mutiara*. They're basic but clean.

Getting There & Away

Meulaboh is theoretically a 12-hour trip by road from Banda Aceh, but as there are five river crossings it may take a lot longer. Merpati flies from Banda Aceh to Meulaboh.

SIMEULUE

Off the west coast of Aceh is the isolated island of Simeulue, known for its clove and coconut plantations. It's a long, hard haul to get there but it could be worth the effort. The island is said to be restful and the people friendly and helpful. There are very few shops on Simeulue and no luxuries but there is plenty of fruit, coffee, rice, noodles and fish to eat.

Getting There & Away

From Meulaboh it's a sardine-packed boat trip to Sinabang on Simeulue. Merpati flies from Meulaboh to Sinabang.

BANDA ACEH TO MEDAN

There are several interesting villages on this road if you want to take it easy and stop off along the way.

Saree

Saree is about 1½ hours from Banda Aceh. It's not as pretty as Sigli but the climate is refreshingly cool and the surrounding area attractive.

You can climb the nearby Seulawah volcano (1000 metres) but it's best to go with a guide – perhaps ask the local police. It takes up to six hours to climb to the top and another three hours to descend at a fairly brisk pace. Take a sweater or jacket as it's cold at the top.

One of Sumatra's last elephant herds lives around Seulawah for part of the year. You may also come across monkeys, deer and tropical birds. Corn, sweet potatoes and a local variety of almonds grow in abundance in this region and are usually available at the market.

Sigli

About three hours from Banda Aceh, Sigli is the source of many traditional regional handicrafts. Gold embroidered cloth and other articles are available from Kampung Garot, eight km from Sigli. Pots and ceramics are available from Kampung Klibeit. It's also the centre for a major irrigation project and has a factory which produces pre-stressed concrete units for bridges.

You can stay here at the air-con *Hotel Riza* and eat at one of the many coffee houses or the local Chinese restaurant. Sigli is well known for its curries.

Lhokseumawe

About halfway between Medan and Banda Aceh is Lhokseumawe, interesting only because it is the port and headquarters for largest liquefied natural gas fields in South-East Asia.

PT Arun has a modern, well-equipped guest house where you may be able to stay. If not, try the *Dewi Plaza* or the *Kuta Karang Hotel*. Both are comfortable, if somewhat expensive, but the environment around the Dewi Plaza has been spoilt because the nearby lake is so polluted.

KUTACANE, KETEMBE & GUNUNG LEUSER NATIONAL PARK

The Ketembe area of the Gunung Leuser National Park is about 30 km north of Kutacane, in the south of Aceh Province. The area is predominantly Muslim, although there's also a large Christian Batak minority. Few foreigners came this way until a few years ago, when the area started to become more popular because of the jungle trekking possibilities offered by the Gunung Leuser National Park.

This park carves out a sizeable chunk of northern Sumatra, and also includes the Orangutan Rehabilitation Centre at Bukit Lawang, Pakembang, which is noted for its birds, and Aras Napal, which has elephants. The Leuser is, in fact, one of the largest national parks in the world encompassing about 800,000 hectares of virgin rainforest. It is spread across both the province of Aceh and southern Sumatra, cut almost in half by the Alas River valley which is a prime agricultural region. The park contains many species of animals, including orang-utan, gibbons, monkeys, elephants, tigers and the elusive Sumatran rhinoceros.

The departure point for the park is the town of Kutacane. The town itself has nothing really to offer, although it's set in the middle of a picturesque valley. However, from Kutacane there are buses to Ketembe which is the tourist area of the Gunung Leuser National Park.

Permits To enter the Leuser National Park you need a permit. You get this from the PHPA (national parks and forests) office in Tanah Merah, about 15 minutes by bemo from Kutacane. Permits are obtained from the Departmen Kehutanan Taman Nasional Gunung Leuser. The permit costs 1000 rp, and you need to provide three photocopies of your passport. You also pay for accommodation at the government guest house in Ketembe.

Things to See

Tigers, rhinos and elephants lure many people to Ketembe, but your chances of seeing them appear fairly slim. People report seeing the tracks of rhinos and big cats, and occasionally hear growling tigers, but actual sightings seem to be few and very far between. Since there are very few animals (perhaps 300 elephants, 500 tigers and 100 rhinos) in a very large area, there's no guarantee that you will get to see them. Areas where there are concentrations of these animals are deeper inside the park, and you have to walk for several days to get there. On the other side of the Alas River from the guest house is a Gibbon research station. Apparently there are

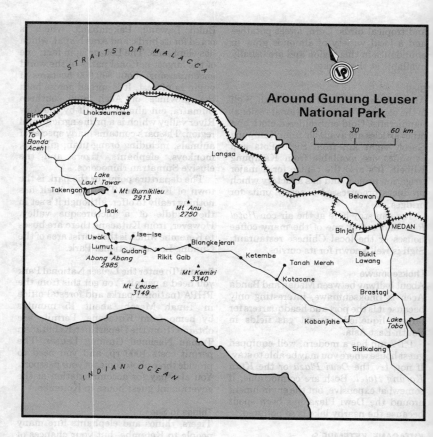

Around Gunung Leuser National Park

STRAITS OF MALACCA

To Banda Aceh

Birven

Lhokseumawe

Langsa

Belawan

Lake Laut Tawar

Takengon

Mt Burniklieu 2913

Isak

Mt Anu 2750

Blnjal

MEDAN

Ise-Ise

Uwak

Blangkejeran

Bukit Lawang

Lumut

Gudang

Rikit Gaib

Ketembe

Tanah Merah

Brastagi

Abong Abong 2985

Mt Kemiri 3340

Kotacane

Lake Toba

Mt Leuser 3149

Kabanjahe

Kaban jahe

Sidikalang

INDIAN OCEAN

0   30   60 km

also giant Rafflesia flowers on this side of the river, but it's very hard to get a permit to be allowed to see them.

Short Walks

There are a couple of walks in the vicinity of the guest house which you can do without a guide, although many of the trails are overgrown and not easy to follow. Even the easy trails can be slippery and muddy and occasionally sections of the trails disappear because of landslides. Of several short walks possible in the area, one popular one is the four-hour round-

trip to the hot springs. The trail starts from immediately behind the guest house. At least three separate sulphurous springs feed directly into the river. Bathing, however, can be dangerous because of sudden changes in temperature. The water from the springs is boiling (100°C) and can cause bad burns.

Long Walks

Most of the other trails are difficult and some involve walking in rivers. Sometimes it's hard to find the starting point and some seem to end up in the middle of nowhere. Longer walks can be undertaken with the help of guides. Guides can be hired in Ketembe. There is no set charge although it's usually around 10,000 rp per day. The guides will construct shelters at night, cook food, carry baggage, cut through the trails (or what's left of them) and, if possible, show you the wildlife.

One possibility is to trek up to the Lawe Mamas, one of the major tributaries of the Alas River that forms the central valley of southern Aceh Province. The Mamas enters the Alas about 15 km north of Kutacane, near the village of Tanjung Muda. For such a trek you will have to hire a PHPA guide (no fixed fee) and they should be able to outfit you with the necessary trekking gear, such as proper tents and sleeping bags (it gets quite cool in the evenings). Gibbons, hornbills, butterflies and the tracks of the elusive rhinos and big cats are all thrown in. The Mamas is a wild, raging river with white-water rapids.

It's also possible to walk to Gunung Leuser, which could possibly be a round-trip of two weeks or more. The fist step is to take a bus to Kuta Panjang, then walk to the village of Panosan. The trek starts from Panosan. Or you can start from the village of Agusang, near Kungke.

Gunung Bendahara is a ten to 14-day round-trip starting either from the Ketembe guest house or from the village of Aunan near Laklak.

Gunung Kapi is a one-week round-trip starting from the village of Marpunga near the Ketembe guest house. The area around Marpunga is supposed to offer the best chance of seeing wild elephants.

Gunung Simpali is a one-week round-trip starting from the village of Engkran and following the valley of the Mamas River. Rhinos live in this area.

Rafting

It is possible to raft the Alas River in an inflatable rubber boat. An expedition would normally take four to five days. You start from a point north of Ketembe and finish down river in Gelombang where the river reaches the lowland areas before entering the sea. Crocodiles inhabit the lower reaches of the river. From Gelombang there are buses to Medan, Lake Toba and Brastagi. For more details try contacting Sobek Expeditions, c/o Pacto Travel Agency, Jalan Palah Merah 29F, Medan.

Places to Stay – in Kutacane

There are a couple of places to stay in Kutacane. Nearly all the accommodation is in the same area, on Jalan Besar, near the bus terminal.

The *Hotel Lawe Mamas* on Jalan Besar is central but quite noisy and not very clean. Rooms are 2500/5000 rp, some with private bathroom. Other places of similar quality and price are the *Penginapan Suryadewi Kutacane* and the *Losmen Kutacane*

The *Wisma Sari Alga* is probably the best value for money. It's on Jalan Besar, about 100 metres from the bus station. It's quite spacious and clean, and the staff are friendly. Rooms are 3000 rp. Dorm beds are 2000 rp.

The *Hotel Bru Dihe* is more expensive, and is on a road which runs parallel to Jalan Besar from the mosque (on Jalan Mesjid, behind the central market). Rooms start from 7500 rp with fan and bathroom, and 15,000 rp with air-con.

Places to Stay – Ketembe

In Ketembe the guest house is by the Alas River. Rooms are 5000 rp a double. There are some coffee shops by the main road where you can eat, though the fare is pretty sparse. There is also a camp ground near the guest house – a jungle clearing with raised concrete slabs used as a base for a tent. The warung owners and some of the rangers may also put you up for a small price.

Getting There & Away

To get to Ketembe from Brastagi, first take a bus to Kabanjahe. There are buses every 10 minutes or so, and the trip takes about 20 minutes and costs 200 rp. Coming from Lake Toba you have to take a bus from Prapat to Pematang Siantar, and another from there to Kabanjahe.

From Kabanjahe, take a bus to Kutacane. The trip takes five to seven hours and the fare is 2200 rp. The road winds its way over the mountains with fine views of Gunung Sinabong, valleys occupied by the Karo Batak people, and the Alas River valley. The winding road allows the drivers to use their favourite toy – the air horn. Every bend, shack and village is an excuse for a triple or quadruple blast.

From Kutacane, take a minibus to the PHPA (national parks) office in nearby Tanah Merah, where you get a permit for the park. Buses from Kutacane to Ketembe take about 1½ hours and costs 500 rp.

BLANGKEJEREN TO TAKENGON

Further north of Kutacane, on the road to Takengon, is Blangkejeren. From Blangkejeren it's a 30-km walk to the village of Gudang, via the village of Rikitgaib (otherwise known as Koneng). From Gudang it's about 30-km walk through beautiful jungle to the village of Ise-Ise. From Ise-Ise it's 20-km walk to Uwak via Lumut. From Lumut or Uwak you can catch a bus to Takengon.

You can buy food and coffee in the villages along the way, and most will put you up for the night for a small price.

It's possible to bus the whole way from Blangkejeren to Takengon, but the frequency of the bemos and buses depends on the will of Allah. From Takengon you can carry on by bus to Bireuen which is on the Medan to Banda Aceh highway, thus completing a loop through northern Sumatra.

TANGSE

Tangse is in a cool valley in the mountains about seven hours from Banda Aceh. It is considered by many people to grow the best rice in Aceh. There are lots of good

walks around here through picturesque rice paddies and forest.

Places to Stay

Tangse is also the site of a Save the Children aid project and it's possible to stay at their guest house by contacting the office.

Getting There & Away

Approaching Tangse from Banda Aceh get off at the 118 km signpost. Tangse is about 70 km along a road branching off to the right from here.

TAKENGON

Takengon is a remote town on the banks of Lake Tawar, surrounded by rice paddies and small coffee plantations and overlooked by mountains and forests. The eerie beauty and rather foreboding atmosphere of the area is increased by stories of the elusive tiger and the dreaded cobra being seen. The town itself is rather ordinary, predominantly Muslim and quite large.

Things to See

This is the place to buy the traditional Gayo/Alas tapestry – made up into embroidered clothes, belts, purses, cushion holders and tapestry. Brightly woven mats can be bought at Isak or at one of the other small villages on the road to Isak. At the market in Takengon it's sometimes possible to buy highly decorative, engraved pottery called *keunire* which is used in wedding ceremonies.

Visit the village of Bintang across the lake by boat. Or visit Angkup or the village of Pondok Baru where the Geuremong and Telong volcanoes dominate the scenery. Hire a guide and climb Telong to see the moss forest with its numerous exotic orchids. It's a four to six hour walk. Or wander up Gunung Tetek for a 360° view of the countryside and sea, a much less energetic climb taking under an hour.

Six km before you get to Takengon is Bukit Menjagan, which also has a wonderful view of the area, but the road up is very steep.

Places to Stay

The best place to stay is the *Wisma Pabrik Kertas*, which is fairly basic, but clean and better than any of the other hotels. Turn left about 250 metres from the service station at the Kantor Camat Bebesan (office) and it's about a km from here to the guest house on the lake. Other places to try are the *Hotel Buntul Kubu* on the hill overlooking the crater lake or the *Hotel Danau Laut Tawar*.

Getting There & Away Takengon is about 100 km off the Trans-Sumatran Highway through hills, forests, coffee plantations and rice paddies. Get off at Bireuen, a junction town, and catch a minibus to Takengon from there.

Nusa Tenggara

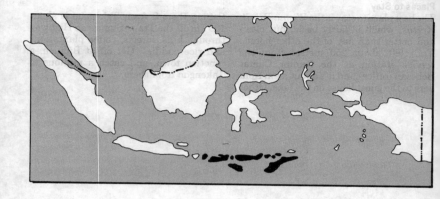

Nusa Tenggara – the name means 'South-East Islands' – is quite different from the rest of Indonesia. As you travel east the climate becomes drier; the land, flora and fauna are more like parts of Australia than tropical Bali; and there is a great variety of cultures and religions.

Each island has its own peculiar sights, some of which rival anything to be seen in Java or Bali. The great stone-slab tombs and traditional villages of Sumba, the intricate *ikat* weaving of Sumba and Flores, the brilliantly coloured volcanic lakes of Keli Mutu and the dragons of Komodo must rate as some of the great attractions of South-East Asia. Though there are few beaches where you can peel off and lie back undisturbed by a crowd of goggling locals, there's fine coral off some of the coasts. Though the region's diverse cultures are less accessible than those of Java or Bali, this is an area where tourism has so far made relatively little impact.

All the islands are underdeveloped from every point of view, including the tourist industry's. While a steady stream of travellers passes through, and numbers have grown since flights between Darwin and Timor began in 1986, there is still nothing like the hordes you find in Bali or Java. Transport in Nusa Tenggara has improved but there are still long, bumpy bus rides and sea crossings in uncomfortable boats. There's accommodation in most towns, but little in the top-end bracket. The lack of tourists is actually an advantage because the local people generally react more naturally. It does create one headache, however, as you are repeatedly the centre of attention. It's no trouble at all to generate an entourage of over 100 children in a small village in Flores and the 'hello misters' fly thick and fast.

HISTORY

Despite Portuguese interest in the 16th century and Dutch interest from the 17th, Nusa Tenggara was never in the mainstream of colonial activity in Indonesia. Since the area offered few economic temptations, the Dutch largely concentrated on Java, Sumatra and the spice islands of Maluku. In Nusa Tenggara they set up trading posts but didn't find it necessary to exercise much authority. Local rulers and their conflicts, and traditional ways of life including animist religions were largely left to run their own course until around 1840, when the Dutch were spurred into action for a variety of reasons: to protect their ships from pirates; because of disputes (like with the Balinese) over the salvaging of shipwrecks; and to protect their possessions from other powers. As the Europeans scrambled for the last available morsels of Asia and Africa in the last quarter of the 19th century, the Dutch began to grab anything that was left in the archipelago.

Piracy and disputes over shipwrecks motivated the first Dutch assault on Bali in 1846. When the indigenous Sasaks of Lombok rebelled against their Balinese overlords in 1891 and appealed to the Dutch for help, the Dutch took the opportunity to send in a military expedition, finish off the Balinese and take control of Lombok themselves. Flores, further east, was another target. A desire to control the slave trade and disputes over the rights to shipwrecks led to two Dutch expeditions against the island in 1838 and 1846, and a local rebellion in 1907 prompted a complete takeover. The Dutch waited until the early 1900s to subdue the tribespeople in the interior of the Nusa Tenggara islands, and the eastern half of Timor never fell into Dutch hands at all (it remained a Portuguese colony until 1975 when Indonesia invaded and took it over).

After Indonesian independence in the 1940s, Nusa Tenggara remained a remote and lonely outpost, kept in order by a handful of Javanese officials and soldiers who considered themselves virtual exiles. The difficulty of the terrain, poor communications and the islands' location on the path to nowhere in particular all helped to deter visitors and maintain this isolation.

Divisions Nusa Tenggara is divided into three provinces: West Nusa Tenggara, comprising Lombok and Sumbawa, with its capital at Mataram in Lombok; East

Nusa Tenggara, comprising Flores, Sumba, Timor and a number of smaller islands, with the capital at Kupang in Timor and East Timor with its capital at Dili.

THE NUSA TENGGARANS

Bold lines on a map, the promotion of *Bahasa Indonesia*, the government in Jakarta and, in recent years, steady improvements in transport are about all that bind these islands together. Only about 2% of the Indonesian population lives in Nusa Tenggara, but there are so many different languages and cultures it's impossible to think of these people as one group.

There are, however, some similarities between these islands which distinguish them from those to the west. Many of the people are now at least nominally Christian; Christians predominate on Flores and Roti, Muslims on Lombok and Sumbawa, and on Timor there's a mixture. But a very strong layer of animism persists, with customs, rituals and festivals stemming from this older tradition still very much a part of life.

One consistent characteristic of the people throughout Nusa Tenggara is their extraordinary, sometimes overwhelming, curiosity and friendliness. One visitor commented that he saw no other white faces for two whole weeks but every window was always filled with the curious faces of warm and friendly people.

ECONOMY

Nusa Tenggara has hardly any modern industry; the export of cattle and horses pays for goods imported from Java, and apart from a little sulphur there are few minerals. East Nusa Tenggara in particular has one of the lowest standards of living in Indonesia and a very high infant mortality rate of 12.5%.

Nusa Tenggara is mostly drier than Bali or Java: most of the crops are planted on dry fields and the slash-and-burn technique is the normal method of clearing fields prior to planting. In some parts of Nusa

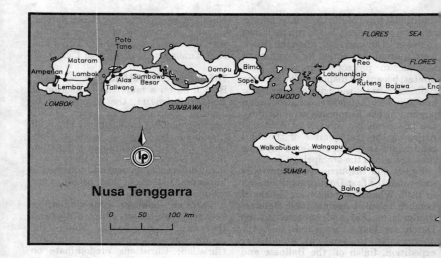

Nusa Tenggarra

Tenggara the raising of livestock – particularly horses and cattle – is most important. Corn and sago are the staple foods for some people – owing to the dry weather and generally poor soil, little rice is grown.

The Wallace Line

Even the wildlife of Nusa Tenggara is different from that of western Indonesia. A 300-metre-deep channel (one of the deepest in the archipelago) runs between Bali and Lombok and extends north between Kalimantan and Sulawesi. The channel marks the 'Wallace Line', named after 19th century naturalist Alfred Russel Wallace, who observed that from Lombok eastwards, the islands are characterised by more arid country, thorny plants, cockatoos, parrots, lizards and marsupials; while from Bali westwards the vegetation is more tropical and the animals include monkeys and tigers. It's actually not as clear cut as Wallace thought, but there definitely is some difference which makes Nusa Tenggara a transition zone between Asian and Australian flora and fauna.

LANGUAGE

A lot of people in Nusa Tenggara know a few phrases of English but rarely more than that. It's essential to learn a little Indonesian if you're going to travel easily through these islands. Otherwise, you might consider one of the tours which operate out of Bali – those to Komodo are fairly regular.

Nusa Tenggara has a high number of distinct local languages – about 50 of them on the tiny island of Alor alone. These are a fascinating subject of study but you won't need to bother with them as a traveller – at least a few people just about everywhere will speak Bahasa Indonesia.

MONEY & COSTS

Nusa Tenggara is marginally more expensive for food, accommodation and transport than Bali and Java, and you don't get such good value for money. But by any standards, costs are still low. Allowing enough cash for a couple of flights not only provides an interesting and time-saving variation on other transport, but could save you backtracking by bus and ferry if you do a round trip.

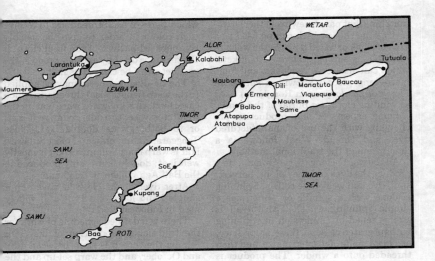

There will generally be at least one bank in each main town that will change major foreign currencies and also travellers' cheques of the larger companies like American Express, Thomas Cook or Bank of America. If in doubt take US dollars – they're the most widely accepted foreign currency throughout Indonesia. Exchange rates are generally the same as in Bali or Java except sometimes in the remoter centres like Bima (Sumbawa) or Maumere (Flores).

IKAT

The Indonesian word *ikat*, which means to tie or bind, is used as the name for intricately patterned cloth whose threads are tie-dyed by a very painstaking and skilful process *before* they are woven together.

Ikat cloth is made in many scattered regions of the archipelago, from Sumatra to Maluku. Outstanding work comes from the Dayaks of Kalimantan and Sarawak; the people of Tenganan on Bali; the Batak, Lampung and Kroe regions of Sumatra; and the Donggala and Rongkong areas of central Sulawesi, but it's in Nusa Tenggara that this ancient art form thrives strongest. Ikat garments are still in daily use in many areas, and there's an incredible diversity of colours and patterns, with villages a few km apart sometimes turning out cloths of utterly different appearance. The spectacular ikat of Sumba and the intricate patterned work of Flores are the best known, but Timor and Lombok and small islands like Roti, Sawu, Ndao and Lembata all have their own varied and high quality traditions.

Making Ikat

Ikat cloth is nearly always made of cotton, still often handspun, though factory-made cotton thread and even some synthetic threads have come into use. Dyes are traditionally handmade from local plants and minerals which give ikat its characteristic earthy brown, red, yellow and orange tones as well as the blue of indigo. Again some factory dyes have come into use, and even some pre-dyed thread.

Ikat comes in a variety of shapes and sizes including *selendang* (shawls); sarongs (which may consist of two matching ikat panels sewn together); two-metre-long tubes which can be used as a kind of cloak or rolled down to the waist to resemble a sarong; *selimut* (blankets) which can also serve as cloaks; and four-metre-long pieces (known as *katipa* in Flores or *parilonjong* in Rongkong) used as winding cloths for burial of the dead.

Some aspects of ikat production are changing with the use of manufactured dyes and thread. What follows is a description of the traditional method.

All the work belongs to the women; they produce the dyes and they plant, harvest, spin, dye and weave the cotton. Spinning is done with a spindle or sometimes a simple spinning wheel. The thread is strengthened by immersion in stiffening baths of grated cassava, fine stamped rice, or a meal made of roasted maize, and then threaded onto a winder. The product is usually thicker and rougher than machine-spun cotton, although thread of amazing fineness and smoothness can also be made this way.

Traditional dyes are made from natural sources. The most complex processes are those concerned with the bright rust colour, known on Sumba as *kombu*, which is produced from the bark and roots of the kombu tree. A few dips of the cotton into the dyes will produce pale colours; many dips are needed to obtain the most valued deep colours. Purple or brown can be produced by dyeing the cloth deep blue and then over-dyeing it with kombu.

Each time the threads are dipped in dye, those sections of them that are not due to receive the colour in question are bound together ('ikatted') beforehand with dye-resistant fibre, so that they do not take up the colour. A separate tying and dyeing process is carried out for each colour that will appear in the finished cloth – and the sequence of dipping has to consider the effect of over-dyeing. This tying-and-dyeing stage is what makes ikat ikat and it requires great skill, since the dyer has to work out – *before* the threads are woven into cloth – exactly

which parts of each thread are to receive each colour in order to give the usually complicated pattern of the final cloth. If the thread is dyed by another process, the product can't be classed as ikat.

The tie-dyeing process may be applied to the warp (lengthwise) threads, in which case the cloth is known as warp ikat; or the weft (crosswise) threads, giving weft ikat; or to both, giving double ikat. Nusa Tenggara, Kalimantan and most Sulawesi ikat is warp ikat; Sumatran ikat is mostly weft ikat; double ikat is only produced in the Bali Aga village of Tenganan.

After dyeing, the cloth is woven on a simple hand loom of a type still widely used in Indonesia today.

There is a defined schedule of work for the traditional production of ikat. On Sumba the thread is spun between July and October, and the warp set up and the patterns bound between September and December. After the rains end in April, the blue and kombu dyeing is carried out (some dyeing may be done in January and February when the indigo plant is plentiful). In August the weaving starts – more than a year after work on the thread began.

Origins & Meaning of Ikat

The ikat technique probably came to Indonesia over 2000 years ago with

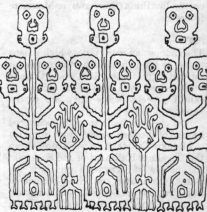

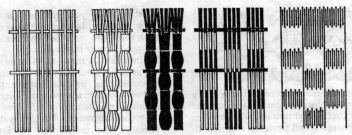

The phases of ikat dyeing

migrants bringing the Dongson Culture from southern China and Vietnam. It has survived in more isolated regions that were by passed by later cultural influences.

Ikat styles vary according to the village and sex of the wearer, and some types of cloth are reserved for special purposes. The spectacular *pua* cloths of Kalimantan serve as wall hangings at rites of passage like marriages and circumcisions; double ikat *kain geringsing* weavings from Tenganan in Bali are thought to have healing powers and appear at ceremonies all over the island; in parts of Nusa Tenggara high-quality ikat, along with beads or ivory, is part of the 'dowry' that a bride's family must give to the bridegroom's family at a marriage, in return for 'masculine' valuables like gold or livestock. Large collections of such ceremonial cloths are a status symbol. At religious rituals the leaders will sometimes wear ikat garments with potent or significant motifs.

On Sumba, less than 90 years ago only members of the highest clans could own ikat textiles and only they and their personal attendants could make or wear them. Certain motifs were traditionally reserved for noble families (as on Sumba and Roti) or members of a particular tribe or clan (Sawu or among the Atoni of Timor).

In the 20th century particularly, new influences have corrupted the meaning of ikat. Commercial trade in ikat, and outside demand for it, which in Sumba began with the Dutch, have turned it into just another product for sale in some areas. Traditional motifs have become mixed up with new ones, some of European origin, and ikat's function in indicating its wearer's role or rank has declined.

Motifs & Patterns

An incredible range of designs is found on ikat across the archipelago, among the most spectacular being the geometric or ancestor-figure motifs of Kalimantan, which are interlinked to form complex overall patterns, and the extraordinary variety of pictorial designs on Sumba.

Some experts believe that representations of face-on people, animals and birds, such as are found on Sumba, stem from an artistic tradition even older than the Dongson. The main Dongson influence on patterning was in geometric motifs like diamond and key shapes (which often go together), meanders and spirals. Before European contact, Asian traders also influenced design and the fairly common dragon motif probably came from Chinese porcelain.

A particularly strong influence was cloths known as *patola* from Gujarat in India, which (coincidentally it seems) were made by using the double-ikat process on silk. In the 16th and 17th centuries these became highly prized in Indonesia and one characteristic motif of patola cloths was copied by local ikat weavers. It's still a favourite today – a hexagon framing a sort of four-pronged

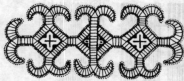

star which is reminiscent of those nasty critters that bleep around Space Invader screens. On the best patola and geometric ikat, repeated small patterns combine to form larger patterns, and the longer you look at it the more patterns you'll see – rather like a mandala.

More recently, European influence has brought motifs such as the Dutch royal coat of arms on Sikka ikat in Flores, figures of Dutch monarchs in Sumba, floral patterns instead of the old clan symbols of Sawu, even tourist-oriented motifs like Keli Mutu volcano in Flores or the whales of Lembata.

Judging Ikat

Not so easy! Books on the subject aren't much help when you're confronted with a market trader telling you that yes, this cloth is at least 100 years old and no, it definitely isn't factory thread and yes, of course the dyes are natural ('Look at that blue – it can only be real indigo...'). Still, *Textiles of Indonesia* (Indonesian Arts Society, Australia) and *Indonesian Ikats* by Suwati Kartiwa (Penerbit Djambatan, Jakarta) are two well-illustrated, informative and affordable introductions. Taking a look at the process in action is

informative too: you can see women weaving in many places, and at the right time of year you may see dye-making, thread-spinning or tie-dyeing.

The best ikat is made from handspun cotton thread, coloured by the traditional tying-and-dyeing process with natural dyes, then woven on a handloom. Factory-spun thread and factory-made dyes can also give pleasing results, but if they don't go through the traditional tie-dyeing process the resulting cloth isn't true ikat.

Mass production techniques include tie-dyeing the same design on to threads for a number of cloths at the same time. These may be woven by hand or machine: they *are* ikat – because the correct hand-dyeing method has been used – but they'll probably be inferior quality, often with sloppy outlines to the patterns. Other cloths, however, appear to be either plain machine-woven fabric which has simply been printed with a design resembling those on genuine ikat, or fabric that is machine-woven from thread which has been pre-dyed with appropriate ikat-like colour schemes. Neither of these last two types is genuine ikat because the proper tie-dyeing method is absent. Cloths made in villages will nearly always be hand-dyed and hand-woven. Machine-produced stuff comes from towns. Here are some tips on distinguishing the traditional product:

Thread Handspun cotton has a less perfect 'twist' to it than factory cotton.

Weave Handwoven cloth, whether made from handspun or factory thread, feels rougher and, when new, stiffer than machine-woven cloth. It will probably have imperfections (perhaps minor) in the weave. On machine-woven cloth you may find specks of colour detached from the motifs that they're supposed to be part of, where the machine hasn't been able to correct for inaccuracies in the dyeing.

Dyes Until you've seen enough ikat to get a feel for whether colours are natural or chemical, you often have to rely on your instincts as to whether they are 'earthy' enough. Sometimes this is obvious, but beware – dye manufacturers are clever at reproducing natural tints. Some cloths contain both natural and artificial dyes.

Dyeing Method The patterns on cloths which have been individually tie-dyed by the authentic method will rarely be perfectly defined, but they're unlikely to have the detached specks of colour that often appear on mass-dyed cloth.

Age Whatever anybody tells you, there are very few antique cloths around: most of what you'll be offered for sale will be new or newly second-hand. A study made in Sumba in the late 1960s noted that as few as 20 examples could be documented as having been made in the 19th century. There are several processes to make cloth *look* old.

Buying Ikat
Price depends on the fineness of the materials, techniques and design used in a cloth, the length of time it took to make it (in the best pieces this will amount to maybe four or five months of solid work spaced out over a year or two), its age – and the bargaining powers of you and the seller. You can buy ikat not only in the villages where it's made and in nearby markets, but from shops and merchants in towns in ikat-making regions and further afield in places like Bali and Jakarta. Buying ikat in its home area is on the whole cheaper, but villagers can bargain just as staunchly as shopkeepers (to whom they may have already sold their best stuff anyway) while shopkeepers often have a bigger range and *might* have to offload some stock.

When bargaining, be ready to *wait* – they show you all the crap first but will eventually bring out the better stuff. Hang in there until you finally see something you like. As a foreigner you must expect to pay more than a local: if

you see something you really want and can get it for a reasonable price then buy it! You won't get it cheaper anywhere else (you may not even get it anywhere else) and you'd be mad to spend the airfare to Indonesia, tramp all the way to some remote region, then go home empty-handed all for the sake of a few rupiah!

While researching this edition Susan and John bought several pieces of ikat in Nusa Tenggara including the following:

Sumba Hinggi (man's sarong) 2½ by one metre, almost certainly handspun thread and natural dyes, mainly in blue and earthy red – 75,000 rp from a Chinese trader in Waingapu, might have got it for 60,000 to 65,000 rp if we had bargained better!

Sumba Shawl 1½ by 1/2 metres, probably natural dyes and factory-spun thread – 20,000 rp from Chinese shopowner in Waingapu, OK price for the place.

Nggela (Flores) Shawl 1-⅔ by 2/3 metres, probably factory-made thread and colours but dyed by the ikat process and handwoven in a complicated patola pattern – 18,000 rp from a part-time merchant in Moni, a reasonable price.

Probably the best piece of ikat that John and Susan saw was offered to them by a losmen owner on Lembata – a burgundy-based sarong with multiple patterning of incredibly fine detail and obvious antiquity. It was of the type used in marriage exchanges and the first asking price was 1.5 million rp!

GETTING THERE & AROUND
The good news is that transport in Nusa Tenggara has improved immensely in the last decade. There are now more surfaced roads, more and more regular ferries and buses, and more flights. Previously a lot of travel in Nusa Tenggara was just plain awful – you'd spend days in dreary ports waiting for boats, hour upon hour shaking your bones loose in trucks attempting to travel on terrible roads. Some of it is still like that, but on the whole if you stick to the main routes you shouldn't have much

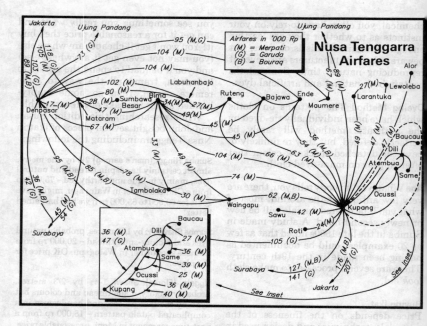

Nusa Tenggarra Airfares

Airfares in '000 Rp
(M) = Merpati
(G) = Garuda
(B) = Bouraq

trouble. The only problems are likely to occur in the rainy season – roughly November to March but shorter and less intense in the eastern and southern parts of the chain. Roads on Flores are often cut by floods or landslides at this time.

Air You can fly direct between Darwin (Australia) and Kupang (Timor) with Merpati which also has a good network of internal flights serving about 20 towns in Nusa Tenggara. Every place on the list gets at least two flights a week, usually many more. Many flights start or finish in Kupang or Bima (Sumbawa), with Ende and Maumere on Flores, Dili (Timor), Waingapu (Sumba) and Mataram (Lombok) the other busiest airports. Some flights come straight through from Bali or even Java, and from Kupang or Maumere you can fly to Ujung Pandang (Sulawesi) and Kalimantan without changing planes. Bouraq also has a

number of flights between Bali and Maumere, Waingapu and Kupang. Garuda flies between Bali and Lombok and Timor.

While it is sometimes possible to get a seat even on the morning of departure, it is wise to book, and essential in the peak August tourist season. The most popular routes are Mataram/Bima/Labuhanbajo and Maumere/Denpasar. If flights from Labuhanbajo or Maumere are full, try Ruteng, which is a less popular departure point. Theoretically, Merpati only sells tickets after booking with the office in the city where the flight originates. In practice, flights are often overbooked or bookings are not radioed through. Make sure your booking has been made when you buy your ticket, and always reconfirm.

Boat Most of the islands are connected by ferries which are regular, if rarely comfortable – daily between Bali and Lombok, and Lombok and Sumbawa;

three times a week between Sumbawa and Flores (one of which stops at the island of Komodo), and Timor and Roti; twice a week between Timor and Flores, and Timor and Alor; and once a week between Timor and Sawu. A welcome recent addition is the Pelni passenger liner *Kelimutu* which makes a circuit every two weeks from Semarang in Java to Kupang (Timor) and back, stopping at Banjarmasin (Kalimantan), Surabaya (Java), Padangbai (Bali), Lembar (Lombok), Ujung Pandang (Sulawesi), Bima (Sumbawa), Waingapu (Sumba) and Ende (Flores) on both the inward and outward voyages. There are several different classes on the *Kelimutu*: the most expensive is usually about two-thirds of the price of an air ticket. Small boats chug daily from Flores to the islands of Adonara, Solor and Lembata.

If you want to do something different you might try finding one of Pelni's other more basic ships, or a freighter working its way through the islands – you can often make quite an interesting trip on the same ship since they usually sail at night and unload during the day, so you have at least a full day in each port. Ask around the harbour, at the office of the harbour master (*syahbandar*) or the shipping offices; someone is bound to know when a ship's due in. Some vessels, like Pelni's *Baruna Eka*, which links Kupang, Sawu, Ende and Waingapu, have fairly regular schedules. Otherwise wait around until one comes by, bargain your fare with the captain, unroll your sleeping bag on the cargo hold and make yourself at home. The food and sanitary facilities are often pretty hopeless, but making friends with the cook can help with the food.

For short hops you can often charter sailing boats or small motorboats. The standard means of getting to Komodo for instance is to charter a motorboat for a round trip from Labuhanbajo on the west coast of Flores – though prices on this particular run have inflated now due to the tourist traffic. Sometimes Bugis

schooners find their way right down into Nusa Tenggara – if you want a really different way of getting to Sulawesi!

Local Transport Many towns in Nusa Tenggara are small enough to walk around and those that aren't have a variety of efficient and cheap local transport systems – ranging from the jingling dokars (horse-buggies) of Lombok and Sumbawa to the bemos of Ende and Kupang which seem to cover every street every couple of minutes.

Motorcycles If you can organise it, motorcycling is a great way to see Nusa Tenggara. There are ferries (on which you can transport your bike) between most of the islands, and the only hazards are those which normally apply to motorcycling in Asia. It's probably best to bring your own bike with you – in Bali at least, it's difficult to rent one if you want to go to other islands. You might be able to find short-term hires in a few Nusa Tenggara towns. Twelve years ago, when researching the original edition of *South-East Asia on a Shoestring*, Tony and Maureen Wheeler rode a motorcycle from one end of Nusa Tenggara to the other.

Bicycles Bicycles are for rent in and around the main centres of Lombok, but so far they are not a very popular form of transport anywhere in Nusa Tenggara except Sumba. Long-distance cycling is a possibility on Sumba, where there's a lot of flat terrain, but the idea of trying it out on hilly Flores or Sumbawa doesn't appeal at all! If you do want to cycle then bring your own bicycle with you, or be prepared to do some maintenance work on one of the local rusty hulks.

Lombok

Lombok has all the lushness of Bali combined with the starkness of outback

Australia. Parts of the island drip with water while pockets are chronically dry, parched and cracked like crocodile skin. Droughts on this small island can last for months, rice crops fail and people starve to death in their thousands. In 1966, 50,000 people died of starvation and many others only survived by eating mice.

The people too reflect these extremes. Many are outgoing and friendly, others shy and withdrawn. There are villages in Lombok where westerners are such a rarity that children run away in fear – in other parts the *orang bulan* (moon person) causes such a sensation that you're surrounded by crowds all wanting to touch your skin.

Lombok also has an intact, largely Balinese Hindu culture – a leftover of the time when Bali controlled Lombok – with the same colourful processions and ceremonies, as well as a number of magnificent though rather neglected temples. Coupled with that are the animist rituals of the indigenous Sasaks, who make up about 80% of the population, and the raucous sound of loudspeakers calling Allah's faithful to prayer.

History

Numerically the Sasaks are the predominant ethnic group on Lombok. Physically and culturally they have much in common with the Javanese, Balinese and the Sumbawanese; they're Malay people, agriculturalists and animists who practised ancestor and spirit worship although the majority are now Muslim. Islam may have been brought to the island from Java but there's really no firm evidence that Java controlled the island. Not much is known about Lombok before the 17th century, at which time it was split into numerous, frequently squabbling, petty states each presided over by a Sasak 'prince' – a disunity which the neighbouring Balinese exploited.

In the early 1600s, the Balinese from the eastern state of Karangasem established colonies and took control of west Lombok.

At the same time the roving Makassarese crossed the straits from their colonies in western Sumbawa and established settlements in east Lombok. This conflict of interests ended with the war of 1677-78 which saw the Makassarese booted off the island, and east Lombok temporarily reverting to the rule of the Sasak princes. Balinese control soon extended east and by 1740 or 1750 the whole island was in their hands. Squabbles over royal succession soon had the Balinese fighting amongst themselves, and Lombok split into four separate kingdoms. It was not until 1838 that the Mataram kingdom subdued the other three, reconquered east Lombok (where Balinese rule had weakened during the years of disunity) and then crossed the Lombok Straits to Bali and overran Karangasem, thus reuniting the 18th-century state of Karangasem-Lombok.

While the Balinese were now the masters of Lombok the basis of their control in west and east Lombok was quite different and this would eventually lead to a Dutch takeover. In west Lombok, where Balinese rule dated from the early 17th century, relations between the Balinese and the Sasaks were relatively harmonious. The Sasak peasants, who adhered to the mystical Wektu Telu religion, easily assimilated Balinese Hinduism. They participated in Balinese religious festivities and worshipped at the same shrines, intermarriage between Balinese and Sasaks was common and they were organised in the same irrigation associations (the *subak*) that the Balinese used for wet-rice agriculture. The traditional Sasak village government, presided over by a chief who was also a member of the Sasak aristocracy, had been done away with and the peasants were ruled directly by the raja or a land-owning Balinese aristocrat.

Things were very different in the east, where the recently defeated Sasak aristocracy hung in limbo. Here the Balinese had to maintain control from garrisoned forts and although the

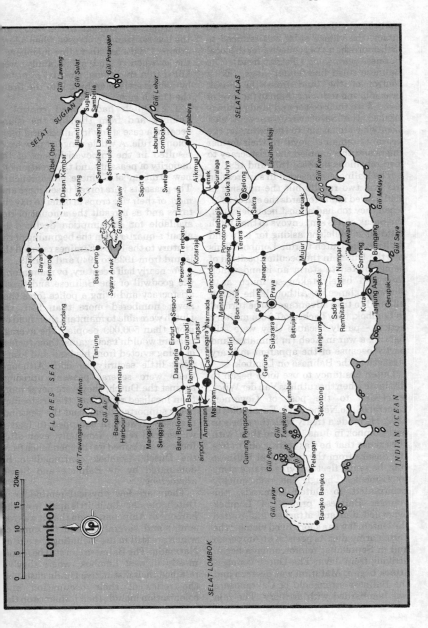

traditional village government remained intact, the village chief was reduced to little more than a tax collector for the local Balinese *punggawa* (district head). The Balinese ruled like feudal kings, taking control of the land from the Sasak peasants and reducing them to the level of serfs. With their power and land holdings slashed the Sasak aristocracy of east Lombok were hostile to the Balinese; the peasants remained loyal to their former rulers and this enabled the aristocracy to lead rebellions in 1855, 1871 and 1891.

The Balinese succeeded in suppressing the first two revolts but the uprising of 1891 proved fatal. Towards the end of 1892, when they too had almost been defeated, the Sasak chiefs sent envoys to the Dutch resident in Buleleng asking for help and inviting the Dutch to rule Lombok. This put the Dutch in the peculiar position of being invited to storm an island which they had barely taken so much as a sideways glance at. Although the Dutch planned to take advantage of the turmoil in Lombok, they backed off from military action – partly because they were still fighting a war in Aceh (in Sumatra) and partly because of the apparent military strength of the Balinese on Lombok.

Dutch hesitancy to use force began to dissipate when the ruthless Van der Wijck succeeded to the post of Governor-General of the Netherlands East Indies in 1892. He made a treaty with the rebels in east Lombok in June 1894 and then, with the excuse that he was setting out to free the Sasaks from the tyrannical Balinese rule, he sent a fleet carrying a large army to Lombok. Though the raja quickly capitulated to Dutch demands, the younger Balinese princes of Lombok overruled him and attacked and routed the Dutch. It was a short-lived victory; the Dutch army dug its heels in at Ampenan and in September reinforcements began arriving from Java. The Dutch counter-attack began, Mataram was overrun and the Balinese stronghold of Cakranegara was bombarded with artillery. The raja

eventually surrendered to the Dutch and the last resistance collapsed when a large group of Balinese, including members of the aristocracy and royal family, were killed in a traditional suicidal *puputan* by deliberately marching into the fire of the Dutch guns.

The Dutch had gained control of Lombok and from then on the island became a case study in callous and inept colonial rule. A whole range of new taxes resulted in the impoverishment of the majority of peasants and the creation of a new stratum of Chinese entrepreneurs. The peasants were forced to sell more and more of their rice crops in order to pay the taxes and as a result the amount of rice available for consumption declined by about a quarter from the beginning of the century to the 1930s. Famines ravaged the island from 1938 to 1940 and in 1949.

For nearly half a century, by maintaining the goodwill of the Balinese and Sasak aristocracy and using a police force that never numbered more than 250, the Dutch were able to maintain their hold on more than 500,000 people! The average peasant wouldn't act against them for fear of being evicted from his land and losing what little security he had. Although there were several peasant uprisings against the Dutch, they were never more than localised rebellions, the aristocracy never supported them, and the peasants themselves were ill-equipped to lead a widespread revolt. Ironically, even after Indonesia attained its independence from the Dutch, Lombok continued to be dominated by its Balinese and Sasak aristocracy.

There are few physical reminders of Dutch rule; they built little apart from the harbour at Ampenan (even then it was too small) and several aqueducts, some of which are still in use including the one at Narmada. The Balinese can still be found mostly in west Lombok, where they've retained their distinctive Hindu customs; the relics of their occupation and colonisation include their influence on the

asak's unique Wektu Telu religion.
ther leftovers of the Balinese presence
iclude the temples they built at
'akranegara, Narmada, Lingsar and
uranadi, as well as the temple processions
nd ceremonies still seen on the island
oday. They hold cremation ceremonies
lentical to those on Bali, and in western
.ombok you can see all the traditional
salinese dances, particular favourites
eing the legong, Arja and Joget Bumbung.

he Sasaks

.ombok has a population of just over two
nillion people, the majority congregated
n and around the main centres of
.mpenan, Cakranegara, Mataram, Praya
nd Selong. Almost 80% of them are
sasak, the remainder mainly Balinese.
There are also minority populations of
Chinese, Javanese, Arabs, Sumbawanese
n the east of the island, and Buginese
long the coast. There may still be some
solated villages of the Bodha, said to be
he aboriginal people of Lombok.

Basically hill people, the Sasaks are
low spread over central and east Lombok,
leavily Islamic and generally much
oorer than the Balinese minority.
)fficially most Sasaks are Muslims, in
ractice they retain many of their ancient
nimist beliefs. Unlike the Balinese they
lave not developed their traditional
lances or religious rituals as tourist
ttractions and to see anything other than
he extraordinary form of combat known
is *Peresehan* or their traditional weaving
echniques would be sheer luck.

There are a number of traditional Sasak
illages scattered over the island; the
easiest to get to that are still completely
inspoilt are the villages of Sukarara,
3ayan and Senaro. Typical Sasak huts
ire square or rectangular, constructed of
vooden frames daubed with lime and
covered with grass. Some sit squat on the
round, but generally they rest on stilts
ind have a high thatched roof. Usually the
village is surrounded and protected by a
iigh paling fence and the houses are built

in long, straight lines. One of Lombok's
most attractive hotels, the Sasaka Beach
Cottages on the coast near Ampenan, was
designed in this traditional style.

Economy & Geography

Lombok is a tiny island, just 80 km east to
west and about the same north to south.
While the south is similar to Bali with rich
alluvial plains, the far south changes to
dry, scrubby, barren hills, bearing a
striking resemblance to parts of outback
Australia. The majority of the population
lives, as it always has, in the long narrow
corridor of fertile land that stretches
between the west coast and the east coast,
bounded by the dry, barren areas to the
south and the mountainous regions to the
north. The central plain is divided into
two distinct parts – a smaller, well-
watered region along the west coast which
is the home of Lombok's Balinese
minority and the somewhat less fertile
East Lombok, the land of the Sasaks.

The rice grown on Lombok is noted for
its excellent quality, but the climate
which is drier than Bali's can only
produce one crop a year. Though rice is
the staple crop there are both small and
large plantations of coconut palms,
coffee, kapok, tobacco and cotton; new
crops such as cloves, vanilla and pepper
have been introduced. Stock breeding on
Lombok is only done on a small scale.
Attempts are being made to promote
Lombok as a tourist resort – money is
being invested in upgrading facilities,
particularly hotels and roads, but Bali is
far ahead as a popular destination.

Religion

Sasak society is intricately woven around
religion. Three religions Islam, Balinese
Hinduism and the indigenous Wektu Telu
predominate on Lombok.

Wektu Telu is unique to Lombok. It's
thought to have originated in the northern
village of Bayan. In the Sasak language
wektu means 'result' and *telu* means
'three'. This probably denotes the complex

mixture of Hindu, Islamic and animist influences that make up this religion and perhaps the concept of a trinity which appears to incorporate not only Allah, Mohammed and Adam, but the sun, moon and stars (representing heaven, earth and water), and the head, body, arms and legs (representing creativity, sensitivity and control). Wektu Telu also involves rituals and feasts based on village adat except in Wektu Lima villages where it's been replaced by the more orthodox beliefs and rituals designated by the written laws of Islam. *Lima* means 'five' and refers to the five pillars of Islam which are considered obligatory for the believer to follow.

The Wektu Telus do not observe Ramadan, the month-long period of abstinence so important in the Islamic faith. Their only concession to it is just three days of fasting and prayer. They also do not follow the practice of praying five times a day as laid down by Islamic law and, although their dead are buried with their heads facing Mecca, it is unheard of for a Wektu Telu follower to make a pilgrimage there. The Wektu Telus believe in praying from the heart whenever and wherever they feel like it so instead of building mosques, all their public buildings are designed with a prayer corner or a small room which faces Mecca. As for eating pork, the Wektu Telus consider everything which comes from Allah to be good.

Burial rituals also vary: the Wektu Telu believe that ancestral spirits affect the living, and rituals are performed at graves as part of a continuing interaction between the living and dead. Wektu Lima maintains the Islamic concept of an afterlife and the belief that the deceased is destined for either heaven or hell depending on his performance during his lifetime. The concept of hell is, however, quite alien to Wektu Telu. In fact the only fundamental tenet of Islam that the Wektu Telu seem to hold is the belief in Allah and that Mohammed is his prophet.

They regard themselves as Muslims although they are not officially accepted by orthodox Muslims as such. Relations between the two groups – at least in the early part of this century after the Dutch invasion upset Balinese control – have not always been good. Part of the problem seems to have been that the native administrators appointed by the Dutch were invariably orthodox Muslims, who were intolerant of Wektu Telu beliefs and customs. Just what percentage of the Sasak population at this time was Wektu Telu is debatable, but it seems that the numbers have gradually declined as more young people turn to orthodox Islam. Possibly 30% of the island's total population – or about 600,000 people now follow Wektu Telu.

Underlying everything is the unwritten code of adat. 'If we do not possess adat we are not more than horses and cows' is saying on Lombok. Adat is all-pervasive regulating marriage, kinship obligations, courting, burial rituals, and circumcision ceremonies. As in Bali and Sumbawa elopement is a traditional form of taking one's bride – an accepted means of overcoming the law that a girl may not marry a man of lower caste, of eluding other competitors for the girl's hand, of avoiding family friction or being confronted with an expensive wedding ceremony. Closely related to adat is the Wektu Telu concept of *maliq* – the word which refers to all acts which are considered breaches of adat. The performance of forbidden acts can be punished during a person's lifetime: illness, madness, poverty and death are all thought to be punishment for maliq. The Wektu Lima equivalent is sin, but that's punished in the afterlife.

Balinese customs have affected Wektu Telu. Like the Balinese Hindus the Wektu Telu have a caste system, another factor which distinguishes them from the orthodox Muslims of Lombok. Traditionally, caste regulates the acquisition of official positions in the village, and particularly marriage – Sasak men can marry women of a lower caste than themselves, but a woman may not marry a man of a lower caste. You are born a Wektu Telu – you cannot become one through conversion, as you can a Muslim. The caste divisions are reflected in the Sasak language, which is closely related to Javanese and Balinese, and has three caste-associated levels of high, middle and low. Sanskrit words appear in the high language – likewise many Arabic words crop up in villages which follow Wektu Lima.

Festivals

Most of the religious festivals of Lombok take place at the beginning of the rainy season from October to December or at harvest time from April to May, with celebrations in villages all over the island. Many of these ceremonies and rituals are annual events but do not fall on specific days. Sasak ceremonies are nowhere near as obvious a part of daily life as the ceremonies in Bali – you can't expect to see them as often.

Festivals are good times for seeing traditional dances and exhibitions of physical prowess – Lombok has its fair share of both. Unlike Bali which encourages, in fact hustles, westerners to go along and see the culture, getting to see any on Lombok depends on word of mouth or pure luck – that is *if* some of the traditional dances or music are still being performed at all! If you see any of the possibilities listed below write and tell us about it.

Dances The *Cupak Gerantang* is a dance popular all over the island and is usually performed at celebrations and festivals. It probably originated in Java in the 15th century and tells the story of Panji, a romantic hero like Arjuna. The *Kayak Sando* is another version of a Panji story but here the dancers wear masks; it's only found in central and east Lombok.

The *Gandrung* is a dance about love and courtship – *gandrung* means being in love or longing. It's a social dance, usually

performed by both the young men and women of the village. Everyone stands around in a circle and then, accompanied by a full gamelan orchestra, a young girl dances by herself for a time before choosing a male partner from the audience to join her. It's seen in Narmada in west Lombok, Suangi and Lenek in east Lombok and Praya in central Lombok.

The *Oncer* is a war dance performed vigorously by men and young boys at festivals in central and east Lombok. The highly skilled and dramatic performance involves the participants playing a variety of musical instruments in time to their movements. The severe black of the costumes is slashed with crimson and gold waist bands, shoulder sashes, socks and caps.

The *Rudat* is another traditional Sasak dance performed by pairs of men dressed in black caps and jackets and black and white check sarongs. They're backed by singers, tambourines and cylindrical drums called *jidur*. This dance and its music, lyrics and costume is a combination of Islamic and Sasak influences.

Music The *Tandak Gerok* is an east Lombok performance which combines dance, theatre and singing to music played on bamboo flutes and the bowed lute called a *rebab*. It's unique feature is that the vocalists imitate the sound of the gamelan instruments. It's usually performed after harvesting or other hard physical labour, but is also put on at traditional ceremonies. The *Genggong* involves seven musicians using a simple set of instruments which includes a bamboo flute, a rebab and knockers; they accompany their music with dance movements and stylised hand gestures. The *Barong Tengkok* is the name given to the procession of musicians who play at weddings or circumcision ceremonies.

Contests If you're inclined to blood sports you'll find the Sasak fascination with physical prowess, heroic trials of strength and battles fought on a one-to-one basis most appealing – the latter are similar to battles found on Bali and Sumbawa.

The *Peresehan* is a favourite all over Lombok. Usually held in the late afternoon in the open air, a huge crowd – all men apart from the occasional curious female traveller – gather together to watch two men bash each other with long rattan staves, protecting themselves only with small rectangular shields made from cow or buffalo hide. The staves are ceremoniously handed around the crowd lined up in a large roped-off area, then returned to the referee. The gamelan starts to play and two men, dressed in exquisite clothing including turbans or head scarves and wide sashes at the waist, feign the movements of the contest about to be fought.

Having shown everyone how it is supposed to be done, the men look around the crowd for possible contestants, who are carefully chosen to match each other as closely as possible in height and strength. Skill is another matter altogether. Anyone can be chosen – some perform several times during the afternoon, others refuse to take part at all. No one cares if somebody doesn't want to join in, but it's clearly status-boosting to do so. Having put on the scarves and waist bands, which are supposed to have magical powers of protection, the challengers take off their shirts and shoes, roll up their trousers, pick up their staves and shields and begin to flay at each other.

The battle is usually refereed by one of the two men who select the contestants. If either of the fighters loses his headscarf or waistband the contest is stopped immediately until he puts it back on. It goes for three rounds – often five with more experienced fighters – or until one of the two is bleeding or surrenders. The referee can also declare the contest over if he thinks things are getting out of hand – which they often do. Although the movements are very stylised, unlike western wrestling matches there's nothing

choreographed or rigged about this – both contestants generally come off with great welts all over them. The crowd gets wildly excited and each fighter has his own groupies cheering him on. At the end of each contest the winner is given a T-shirt or sarong and the loser also gets some token prize.

The *Lanca* is another trial of strength. It originated in Sumbawa and was adopted by the Sasaks who perform it on numerous occasions, particularly when the first rice seedlings are planted. Like the Peresehan it is a contest between two well matched men – this time using their knees as implements of annihilation by striking their opponents with them.

Books
The Village Economies of the Sasak of Lombok: A Comparison of Three Indonesian Peasant Communities by Ruth Krulfeld is a fascinating description of a 20-month study of several Lombok villages in 1960 and 1961. Alfons van der Kraan's *Lombok: Conquest, Colonization and Underdevelopment, 1870-1940* (Heinemann, 1980) describes the economic destitution of the island brought about by the Dutch.

Getting There & Away
Lombok is connected by regular ferries to Bali and Sumbawa, and by air to various parts of Indonesia.

Air
Airline offices are in Ampenan. Garuda and Merpati (a little cheaper) both fly daily between Denpasar and Mataram, the capital of Lombok. Garuda has daily nonstop flights from Mataram to Surabaya and on to Jakarta, Yogyakarta, Solo, Banjarmasin or Ujung Pandang. Merpati goes daily to Sumbawa Besar and Bima on Sumbawa. From Denpasar or Bima there are Merpati connections to Surabaya or to other places in Nusa Tenggara.

oat

ombok-Bali Ferries depart Lembar, about
0 km south of Ampenan, for Padangbai
n Bali at 9 am and 12 noon daily. Buy
our tickets at the office in Mataram-
Ampenan or at the wharf on the day of
eparture – bus and bemo drivers drop
ou off almost directly in front of the
icket office. The ferry fare is about 5000 rp
n 1st class, 3500 in ekonomi, and the trip
akes about five hours, sometimes more in
he afternoon. You can also take vehicles
on board – see the Bali Getting There &
Away section for prices. It's a
ood idea to arrive at Lembar well before
eparture – they sometimes run out of
ickets. You can get drinks and snacks on
oard or at Lembar. There's a canteen
ear the wharf office but don't expect to be
ble to buy any food from people on the
vharf. They're nowhere to be seen. See
Lembar for information on transport
etween there and Ampenan-Mataram.

ombok-Sumbawa There are three ferries
aily from Labuhan Lombok on Lombok's
east coast to Poto Tano on Sumbawa.
Schedules vary slightly but they usually
eave at 8 or 9 am, 11 am or 12 noon, and
5 pm. The crossing takes about 1½ hours
and two services each day are run by
arger, relatively modern boats, the other
– usually the midday one from Lombok –
s by a smaller, probably slower wooden
craft.

The ferries have three passenger classes:
the higher the class, the less crowded the
seats. In ekonomi you pay 2000 rp, in 2nd
class 3100 rp, and in 1st class 4100 rp.
A bicycle will cost you 600 rp, motorbike
2500 rp, jeep 25,000 rp, and a car 33,000 rp.
Passenger tickets can be bought on the
day of departure from the ticket office
near Labuhan Lombok pier.

On board the ferry, guys come round
selling bus tickets to destinations in
Sumbawa: their prices are the same as if
you buy them on shore. In Ampenan some
losmens like the Hotel Zahir can sell you
bus-ferry-bus tickets all the way through

to Sumbawa Besar (6000 rp, about eight
hours) or Bima (11,000 rp, 16 hours).
These cost about 10% more than buying
the three fares separately. See Labuhan
Lombok and Poto Tano for more details on
bus connections.

Other Lembar is on the route of the Pelni
passenger liner *Kelimutu* which makes a
round trip every two weeks from Java to
Kalimantan, Bali, Lombok, Sulawesi, east
Nusa Tenggara and back. See the Nusa
Tenggara introductory Getting Around
section. On Lombok the Pelni office is at
Jalan Kapitan 1, Ampenan (tel 21604).

Getting Around
There are several bemo terminals on
Lombok including one at Cakranegara
and another at Ampenan, but the main
station is at Sweta, a couple of km out of
Cakranegara. Here buses, minibuses,
bemos and colts depart for various points
all over the island. Public transport is
generally restricted to main routes, which
means that if you want to explore places
that are off the beaten track you have to
walk or hire a dokar (horse-drawn cart) or
motorcycle or charter a bemo or colt.

Lombok has an extensive network of
roads, although there are many outlying
villages that are difficult to get to by
public transport. In the flatter areas
between Gunung Rinjani and the southern
highlands, the roads are good and
numerous and it's easy to get around. It's
much more difficult to travel through the
highlands of Rinjani and down the south
coast to the Kuta region where there are
either no roads at all or public transport is
very irregular.

Up in the north-east highlands, the
choice is either motorcycle or your own
feet. If you are exploring these regions
bear two things in mind – often food and
drinking water are scarce so it's a good
idea to carry supplies, and secondly so few
westerners have been in these parts you'll
be regarded as a sensation by any villagers
you come across. During the wet many

roads are flooded or washed away, others are impassable because of fallen rocks and rubble, making it impossible to get to many of the out-of-the-way places. The situation may improve radically if the government's ambitious road improvement scheme, part of a long-term plan for putting Lombok on the tourist map, eventuates.

Motorcycles There are motorcycle hire places in Lombok but there are not as many nor are they as easy to find as in Bali. It's mainly individual owners who rent out their bikes and a couple of specialist places in Ampenan and Mataram. As in Bali, 100 cc is the usual size and rental charges are also similar to Bali's.

Once you get out of the main centres of Lombok there's not much traffic on the roads – just people, dogs and water buffaloes. You'll find yourself on bumpy dirt tracks – no different really from other out-of-the-way parts of Indonesia – having to contend with numerous potholes and unmarked roadworks. It's particularly hazardous at night when you can round a corner and suddenly be confronted by unlit 44-gallon drums of tar. And to entertain you in the mountains there are perilous roads and unprotected edges complete with inviting drops down sheer cliff faces.

There are petrol stations around the larger towns but out in the villages, petrol can be difficult to find. Look for the roadside stalls that sell it by the beer bottle.

AMPENAN, MATARAM, CAKRANEGARA & SWETA

Although they are officially four separate towns Ampenan, Mataram, Cakranegara and Sweta actually run together and it's virtually impossible to tell where one stops and the next starts. Collectively they're the main 'city' on Lombok and you'll have to come here to handle any type of bureaucracy from changing money to buying airline tickets. They also have a

few things to see but once that's out of the way most visitors head off to other places on the island. These days it's not even necessary to stay in the town, Senggigi Beach is easy commuting distance.

Ampenan

Once the main port of Lombok, Ampenan is now not much more than a small fishing harbour, though cattle are still exported from here to Jakarta, Surabaya, Hong Kong and Singapore. It's dirty and dusty and the stench of the open drains pervades the whole township at times. It's inundated with mosques which makes it impossible to get away from the raucous sound of the loudspeakers, calling the faithful to prayer. But it's also full of hustle and bustle and colour and life. The long main road through Ampenan-Mataram-Cakranegara does not actually reach the coast at Ampenan. Somehow it simply fades out, just before it gets to the port's grubby beach.

Ampenan has a curious mixture of people. Apart from the Sasaks and Balinese, there is also a small Arab quarter known as *Kampung Arab*. The Arabs (probably descendants of Arab merchants and Sasak women) living here are devout Muslims; they're inclined to hold themselves aloof from the other people on Lombok. They marry amongst themselves, are well educated and relatively affluent – many follow professions such as teaching and medicine, others are insurance agents or office workers. They're also extremely friendly towards foreigners.

Most of the Chinese living in Lombok today are based in Ampenan or up the road in Cakranegara – almost every shop and every second restaurant in Cakra is run or owned by the Chinese. The Chinese first came to Lombok with the Dutch as a cheap labour force, to work as coolies in the rice paddies. Later, as in other parts of the archipelago, the Dutch fostered them as economic entrepreneurs between the Dutch and Indonesian population.

The Chinese soon became a privileged minority and were allowed to set up and develop their own businesses. When the Dutch were ousted from Indonesia in 1949 the Chinese stayed and continued to expand their business interests. Many of those in eastern Lombok however, were killed in the aftermath of the attempted '65 coup. The massacres were perhaps as much anti-Chinese as anti-Communist.

Mataram

Mataram is the administrative capital of the province of Nusa Tenggara Barat which comprises Lombok and Sumbawa islands. It is surprising how much money has been poured into unexpectedly impressive buildings like the Bank of Indonesia, the new post office and the governor's office and residence. There are also some surprisingly palatial houses around the outskirts of town, the homes of Lombok's elite.

Cakranegara

Now the main commercial centre of Lombok, Cakranegra is usually referred to as Cakra. Formerly the old capital of Lombok under the Balinese rajas, Cakra today is a cacophony of bemos and motorbikes and people trying to keep their heads above the exhaust fumes. It has a thriving community of Chinese as well as many Balinese residents. It's also a centre for craftwork and is particularly well known for its basketware and weaving. Check out the bazaar and watch the silver and goldsmiths at work. You may also be able to find some of the idiosyncratic clay animal figures and ceramics produced on Lombok.

Sweta

Seven km from Ampenan and only about 2½ km beyond Cakra is Sweta – the central transport terminal of Lombok. This is where you catch bemos, buses and minibuses to other parts of the island. There are several warungs here and numerous food, tobacco and drink vendors. Stretching along one side of the terminal is a vast covered market, the largest on Lombok. Wander through its dim alleys where stalls spill over with coffee beans, eggs, rice, fish, fabrics, fruit and hardware. There's also a bird market.

Information & Orientation

The division is effectively Ampenan the port, Mataram the administrative centre, Cakranegara the trading centre, and Sweta the transport centre. There's one main road running east from the port all the way to Sweta and it's one way until you get through Cakranegara. The road starts as Jalan Pabean in Ampenan but quickly becomes Jalan Yos Sudarso then changes to Jalan Langko, Jalan Pejanggik and Jalan Selaparang. Just as it's difficult to tell where one town merges into the next it's also difficult to tell where the road changes names. Indeed it seems that they actually overlap since some places appear to have more than one address.

A second one-way street, Jalan Sriwi Jaya which turns into Jalan Mahapahit, brings traffic back in the other direction and bemos run a shuttle service between the bemo station in Ampenan and the big terminus in Sweta about seven km away. Getting back and forth is, therefore, dead easy. You can stay in Ampenan, Mataram or Cakra since there are hotels and restaurants in all three locales. Most budget travellers tend to head towards Ampenan, however, because it has a handy little enclave of cheap hotels and a choice of good places to eat.

The Mataram government buildings are chiefly found along Jalan Pejanggik. The main square, Lampangan Mataram, is bounded by Jalan Pejanggik and Jalan Cempaka. Art exhibitions, theatre, dance and wayang kulit performances are held in the square but it's by word of mouth that you'll find out about these shows. Alternatively swarms of police and military personnel are the most obvious sign of such an occasion.

Mataram has a small 'centre' near the

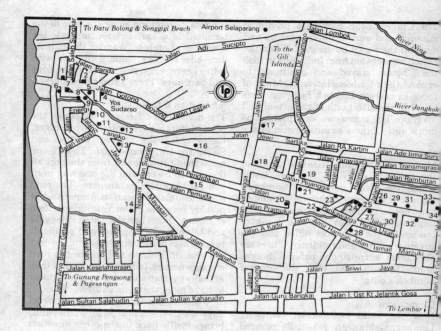

river and a larger shopping area across the crossroads of Jalan Selaparang-Jalan Hasanuddin, where Cakra begins and where you will also find the market.

Tourist Office The main tourist office on Lombok, the Kantor Dinas Pariwisata Daerah (tel 21866, 21730), is in Ampenan on Jalan Langko 70 on the left side heading towards Mataram, almost diagonally opposite the post office. The people at the office are helpful and reasonably well informed. They have a good map of Ampenan-Mataram-Cakranegara and of Lombok and a few other pamphlets and brochures in English with information on sights, customs, addresses and so on.

Banks There are a number of banks along the main drag through Mataram and into Cakra, all of them in impressively large buildings. Most appear to change travellers' cheques without any difficulty. The Bank

Export-Import seems to be open longer hours than some of the others – weekdays 7.30 am to 12 noon and 1 to 2 pm, Saturdays 7.30 to 11.30 am.

Remember that there are only minimal banking facilities elsewhere on the island so make sure you have enough cash with you. In particular there is nowhere to change foreign currency on the Gili Islands. In more remote parts of Lombok changing large denominations can be difficult so break down big notes.

Post The Ampenan post office is conveniently central on Jalan Langko but the imposing Mataram post office is on the outskirts of town on Jalan Ismail Marzuki, and is the only branch in Lombok to have a post restante service. Getting there is not easy since it's not on the regular bemo routes, but you can charter a bemo or dokar in Mataram. Mail sent from Lombok goes to Bali first for

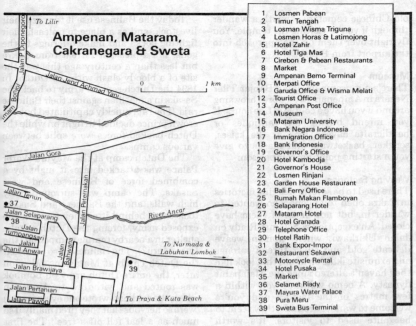

Ampenan, Mataram, Cakranegara & Sweta

To Lilir

Jalan Jend Achmad Yani

Jalan Gora

Jalan Tenun

Jalan Selaparang

Jalan Tumpangsari

Jalan Chanil Anwar

Jalan Brawijaya

Jalan Pertanian

Jalan Pawon

Jalan Peternakan

Jalan Bahwana

River Ancar

To Narmada & Labuhan Lombok

To Praya & Kuta Beach

0   1 km

• 37
• 38
• 39

1	Losmen Pabean
2	Timur Tengah
3	Losmen Wisma Triguna
4	Losmen Horas & Latimojong
5	Hotel Zahir
6	Hotel Tiga Mas
7	Cirebon & Pabean Restaurants
8	Market
9	Ampenan Bemo Terminal
10	Merpati Office
11	Garuda Office & Wisma Melati
12	Tourist Office
13	Ampenan Post Office
14	Museum
15	Mataram University
16	Bank Negara Indonesia
17	Immigration Office
18	Bank Indonesia
19	Governor's Office
20	Hotel Kambodja
21	Governor's House
22	Losmen Rinjani
23	Garden House Restaurant
24	Bali Ferry Office
25	Rumah Makan Flamboyan
26	Selaparang Hotel
27	Mataram Hotel
28	Hotel Granada
29	Telephone Office
30	Hotel Ratih
31	Bank Expor-Impor
32	Restaurant Sekawan
33	Motorcycle Rental
34	Hotel Pusaka
35	Market
36	Selamet Riady
37	Mayura Water Palace
38	Pura Meru
39	Sweta Bus Terminal

sorting so it can take some time to get through.

Telephone The telephone office is at Jalan Pejanggik 24 in Mataram, right beside the Bank Umum. It's in a very anonymous building so look for the bank as a landmark. The office is surprisingly efficient and you can get through to overseas in a matter of minutes.

Immigration Lombok's Kantor Imigrasi is on Jalan Udayana, the road out to the airport. The staff are friendly and co-operative.

Bookshops There are several bookshops on Jalan Pabean in Ampenan including Toko Buku Titian opposite the Ampenan bemo station. It has maps of Lombok for 750 and 900 rp. The *Jakarta Post*, also sold here, is only a day out of date. Apart from that it's virtually impossible to pick up anything

in English apart from English/Indonesian dictionaries. There is no Sasak/English dictionary.

Entry Charges Unlike in Bali, entry charges are not so common apart from in a few places like Narmada. Usually the charge will be 100 or 200 rp. If there is no set charge those are good figures to work with!

Pura Segara – Sea Temple
This Balinese temple complex is on the beach a few km north of Ampenan. Along the beach you can watch the coming and going of the fishing boats. Nearby are the remnants of a Muslim cemetery and an

old Chinese cemetery – worth a wander through if you're visiting the temple. You fly right over them on the approach into the airport from Bali.

Museum

There's a museum on Jalan Banjar Tiler Negara in Ampenan – well worth browsing around if you have a couple of free hours. If you intend buying any antiques or handicrafts have a look at the krises, songket, basketware and masks to give you a starting point for comparison.

Weaving Factories

There used to be several weaving factories in Cakra open to anyone who wanted to wander in, but now most of them have closed. An exception is Selamet Riady on Jalan Ukirkawi, where women weave delicate gold and silver thread sarongs and exquisite ikats on looms that look like they haven't altered since the Majapahit dynasty. A bemo will drop you within a few metres of the factory and you're welcome to wander around – they seem to be quite used to visitors. It's worth checking out the prices in the shop but you're not obliged to buy anything – you can try to bargain but they won't lower prices by much. The factory is open from 7.30 am.

Mayura Water Palace

Just beyond the market, on the main road through Cakra, stands the Mayura Water Palace. It was built in 1744 and was once part of the Royal Court of the Balinese kingdom in Lombok. The centrepiece is the large artificial lake covered in water lilies. In the centre of the lake is an open-sided hall connected to the shoreline by a raised footpath. The hall or floating pavilion (*bale kampung*), was used both as a court of justice and a meeting place for the Hindu lords. There are other shrines and fountains dotted around the surrounding park. Entrances to the walled enclosure of the palace are on the north and west sides.

Today the Balinese use it to graze their livestock, and as a place to unleash their fighting cocks and make offerings to the gods. It's a pleasant retreat from Cakra but less than a century ago this was the site of a bloody clash with the Dutch. In 1894 the Dutch sent an army to back the Sasaks in a rebellion against their Balinese raja. The raja quickly capitulated but the crown prince decided to fight on while the Dutch-backed forces were split between various camps.

The Dutch camp at the Mayura Water Palace was attacked late at night by a combined force of Balinese and west Sasaks. The camp was surrounded by high walls, and the Balinese and Sasaks took cover behind it as they fired on the exposed army, forcing the Dutch to take shelter in a nearby temple compound (the Pura Meru?). The Balinese also attacked the Dutch camp at Mataram and, soon after, the entire Dutch army on Lombok was routed and withdrew to Ampenan where the soldiers (wrote one eye-witness) 'were so nervous that they fired madly if so much as a leaf fell off a tree'. The first battles had resulted in enormous losses of both men and arms for the Dutch.

While the Balinese had won the battle they had just begun to lose the war. Now they would not only have to continue to fight the east Sasaks but also the Dutch, who were quickly supplied with reinforcements from Java. The Dutch attacked Mataram a month after their initial defeat, fighting street to street not only against Balinese and west Sasak soldiers but also the local population. The Balinese crown prince was killed in the battle for the palace and the Balinese retreated to Cakranegara, where they were well-armed and where the complex of walls provided good defence against infantry. Cakra was attacked by a combined force of Dutch and east Sasaks, and (as in Mataram) Balinese men, women and children staged repeated suicidal lance attacks, only to be cut down by rifle and artillery fire. The Raja and a small group of *punggawas* fled to the village of Sasari in the vicinity of the pleasure gardens at Lingsar. A day or two later he surrendered to the Dutch – but even the capture of the raja did not lead the Balinese to surrender.

In late November the Dutch attacked Sasari and a large number of Balinese committed the traditional suicidal *puputan*. With the downfall of the dynasty the local population abandoned the struggle against the Dutch. The conquest of Lombok, thought about for decades, had taken the Dutch barely three months. The old raja died in exile in Batavia in 1895.

Pura Meru

Directly opposite the water palace and just off the main road, is the Pura Meru – the largest temple on Lombok. It was built in 1720 under the patronage of the Balinese prince, Anak Agung Made Karang of the Singosari kingdom, as an attempt to unite all the small kingdoms on Lombok. Though now rather neglected looking, it was built as a symbol of the universe and is dedicated to the Hindu trinity of Brahma, Vishnu and Shiva.

The temple has three separate courtyards. The outer courtyard has a hall housing the wooden drums that are beaten to call believers to festivals and special ceremonies. In the middle court are two buildings with large raised platforms for offerings. The inner court has one large and 33 small shrines, as well as three meru (the Balinese multi-roofed shrines). Each shrine is looked after by members of the Balinese community. The three meru are in a line, the central one of 11 tiers is Shiva's house, the one in the north with nine tiers is Vishnu's and the seven-tiered one to the south is Brahma's. In June each year a festival is held here.

Gunung Pengsong

This Balinese temple is built – as the name suggests – on top of a hill, nine km from Cakra and has great views overlooking the town below. Try to get there early in the morning before the clouds envelop Mt Rinjani. Once a year, generally in March or April, a buffalo is taken up the steep 100-metre slope and sacrificed to celebrate a good harvest. The *Bersih Desa* festival also occurs at harvest time – houses and gardens are cleaned, fences white-washed, roads and paths repaired. Once part of a ritual to rid the village of evil spirits, it is now held in honour of the rice goddess Dewi Sri.

Places to Stay – bottom end

The most popular cheap places to stay are in Ampenan. There is no shortage of choice elsewhere but few travellers bother to go further afield unless they intend to head straight out to beautiful Senggigi Beach, just 10 km to the north. From there it's easy to commute into town if there's any business to be done.

Losmen Pabean (tel 21758) at Jalan Pabean 146 is close to the centre of Ampenan and has reasonably clean and pleasant rooms – some with attached mandi – for 2500/3500 rp. It's almost directly opposite several of the popular rumah makans. Beware of the street name confusion in this area, Jalan Pabean is also known as Jalan Yos Sudarso at certain points.

Nearby and just south of Jalan Pabean (or Jalan Yos Sudarso if you prefer) is *Hotel Tiga Mas* (tel 23211) in the Kampung Melayu Tengah. It's basic and a bit grubby with singles/doubles at 1500/2500 rp. It's also next door to a mosque so be prepared for noise.

At the first junction from Jalan Pabean/Jalan Yos Sudarso, Jalan Koperasi branches off to the north-east and if you continue far enough it takes you all the way to the airport. The other Ampenan cheapies are found along this road. A hop, skip and a jump from the town centre at Jalan Koperasi 12 is the very popular *Hotel Zahir* (tel 22403) with singles/doubles including breakfast for 3000/4000 rp or at 3500/4500 rp with attached mandi. The rooms each have a small verandah and are built around a central courtyard. The Zahir is run by friendly and helpful people.

Continue along the road to Jalan Koperasi 65 where Losmen Horas (tel 21695) is very clean and well kept and has rooms at 2500/3500 rp with spotlessly clean bathrooms. Virtually next door is the Latimojong at No 64. It's dirt cheap at 1000/1500 rp but this is a strictly bottom end place and very basic.

Continue along Jalan Koperasi and you reach the Losmen Wisma Triguna (tel 21705), about a km out from the centre of Ampenan. The Wisma Triguna is owned by the same helpful people as the Horas and it's quiet and pleasantly relaxed. The spacious rooms have attached mandis and open out on to the bright verandah. You can organise Rinjani climbs at the Horas or the Wisma Triguna.

There are other cheap places in Mataram and Cakra but there's really no pressing reason to search further afield than Ampenan. At Jalan Supratman 10 in Mataram the pleasant and cheap Hotel Kambodja (tel 22211) has rooms at 5000 rp. Nearby at Jalan Panca Usaha 18 the Losmen Rinjani (tel 21633) is slightly cheaper with rooms at 4500 rp. Hotel Tenang is also nearby but it's hidden away on Jalan Rumah Sakit Islam. Rooms are 7000/12,500 rp for singles/doubles and the arrival of a western visitor is a rare occurrence.

On the Mataram/Cakra border there's the Hotel Pusaka (tel 23119) at Jalan Sultan Hasanuddin 23. They have a wide variety of rooms at 4000/5000 rp, 5000/6500 rp, 6500/8000 rp and 8000/10,000 rp. Close by at No 17 is the more basic Losmen Merpati with rooms at 1500/2500 rp, 3000/4000 rp and 4000/6000 rp.

Places to Stay – top end

There is a plentiful choice of more expensive hotels as well. Hotel Granada (tel 22275) is on Jalan Bung Karno, a little south of the centre in Mataram. Rooms here all have air-con, include breakfast and with discount cost 21,000, 25,000 or 35,000 rp. There's a swimming pool and the cheapest rooms are right beside it and excellent value. With its quiet location and pleasant gardens this is probably the best hotel in Ampenan-Mataram-Cakra. The only catch is the caged animals and birds dotted around the gardens. The Granada is undoubtedly the most heavily advertised hotel in Lombok, there are Hotel Granada signs everywhere you go from Kuta Beach to the Gili Islands.

At Jalan Yos Sudarso 4, right next to the Garuda airline office, the Wisma Melati (tel 23780) is a pleasant, well kept hotel with rooms ranging from 22,000 to 45,000 rp, all with air-conditioning. There's a restaurant and bar and all the rooms have a telephone and television.

Continue along the main road into Mataram and at Jalan Pejanggik 40-42 the Selaparang Hotel (tel 22670) has rooms ranging from 12,000/15,000 rp up to 22,000/25,000 rp with air-con. Across the road at No 105 there's the Mataram Hotel (tel 23411) with rooms starting at 12,500/15,000 rp and going up to 26,000/28,000 with air-con, hot water and other mod cons. Both these hotels have pleasant little restaurants but note that this is another area where the road mysteriously changes names, the street may also be called Jalan Selaparang.

Hotel Kertayoga (tel 21775) at Jalan Selaparang 82 is very pleasant with singles/doubles at 9000/12,000 rp. These middle priced hotels are all comfortable and well kept with quiet courtyard gardens, they're typical of losmen style at its very best. The street names continue to jump back and forth so the next place is back at Jalan Pejanggik 127 where the Hotel Ratih (tel 21096) has rooms from 4000/6500 rp climbing slowly up to 12,500/17,500 rp with air-con. There's a pleasant garden area and breakfast is included, the scale and scope of the breakfast grows with each room price increment!

Top: Coast of Komodo Island, Nusa Tenggara (JN)
Bottom: Komodo dragon at Banu Nggulung, Komodo Island, Nusa Tenggara (JN)

Top: Rain clouds gather over rice paddy, Lombok, Nusa Tenggara (HF)
Left: Stone tomb at Anakalang, Sumba, Nusa Tenggara (AS)
Right: Waterfront at Labuhanbajo, Flores, Nusa Tenggara (AS)

Places to Eat

Ampenan has several Indonesian and Chinese restaurants including the very popular *Cirebon* at Jalan Pabean 113. It has a standard Indonesian/Chinese menu with most dishes at 1000 to 2000 rp. Next door at No 111 the *Pabean* has very similar food and is run by the same family. You can get a cold beer at these places and the Cirebon menu even has steak & chips for 2000 rp. Meatball soup for 500 rp is very filling and the crab and asparagus soup has been recommended. The whole fish in sweet & sour sauce makes a good splurge.

Closer to the Ampenan bemo station is the *Rumah Makan Arafat* at No 64 with good, cheap Indonesian food. Other alternatives are the *Setia* at Jalan Pabean 129, the *Depot Mina* at Jalan Yos Sudarso 102 and the *Timur Tengah* at Jalan Koperasi 22, right across from the Hotel Zahir. There are lots of snack possibilities to be found in Ampenan market and there are also a couple of bakeries around town.

The Mataram shopping centre beside the river off Jalan Pejanggik, several hundred metres down the road from the governor's residence has a couple of interesting restaurants. The *Garden House Restaurant* is a pleasant open-air place with nasi campur, nasi goreng and similar standard Indonesian dishes at 1000 to 1500 rp or others at 1500 to 3000 rp. They also have a variety of ice cream dishes from 300 to 400 rp, or casatta and tutti-frutti for 750 rp. Nearby the *Taliwan* offers local dishes.

Continue further along the main road towards Cakra and you come to the *Rumah Makan Flamboyan*, a pleasant place with seafood and regular Indonesian dishes.

In Cakra the *Sekawan Depot Es* has cold drinks downstairs and a seafood and Chinese restaurant upstairs. Round the corner at Jalan Hasanuddin 20 is the shiny clean *Rumah Makan Madya 2* with Indonesian food. The older looking

Rumah Makan Madya is right across the road. There are a number of other restaurants in this area, a handful of bakeries and, of course, plenty of other food opportunities at the market.

Things to Buy

There are a surprising number of antique and handicrafts shops in Lombok. Toko Sudirman in Ampenan is at Jalan Pabean 16A, across from the bemo station. They sell some excellent woodcarvings, baskets and traditional Lombok weavings, songket and so on.

Musdah at Dayan Penen, Jalan Sape 16 also has an interesting collection of masks, baskets, krises and carving. Describing how to get to this shop-in-a-home is virtually impossible but a series of signs leads you there from the Hotel Zahir or other places on Jalan Koperasi.

It's more difficult to bargain in Lombok than it is in Bali; you need to take your time – don't rush or be rushed. It's also harder to make an accurate evaluation of things, particularly antiques. You'll hear a lot of talk about special Lombok prices – these are supposed to be much cheaper than Bali prices – but unless you know what you're doing you can pay as much, if not more. Be very sure you want to buy before making an offer. Try to get the dealer to put a price on the object before starting to bargain. Always bargain for what you buy – particularly for items like cloth, basketware or antiques. If you manage to get the price down to half of the asking price then you're doing very well; it's more likely that you will end up paying about two-thirds of the starting price or only get a nominal amount knocked off.

If you want to mail things from Lombok you have to get customs clearance before they can be sent. You may need forms CP2 and five copies of form C2 and CP3 from the post office. Don't write on the form that anything you're sending is an antique. From the post office the maximum parcel size is three kg, but you can send 10 kg from the main post office.

Getting There & Away

Air See the Lombok Getting There & Away section for details of the flights to and from Lombok. The Garuda office (tel 23762) is at Jalan Yos Sudarso 6 in Ampenan. There's a Merpati office (tel 21037) a little closer to the centre of Ampenan at Jalan Yos Sudarso 22 and a second Merpati office (tel 22670 & 23235) at the Hotel Selaparang at Jalan Pejanggik 40-42 in Mataram.

Bus The Sweta bus terminal is at the inland end of the Ampenan-Mataram-Cakra-Sweta development and is the main bus terminus for the entire island. It's also the eastern bemo terminus, bemos shuttle back and forth between Ampenan at one end and Sweta at the other. Check fares on the notice board at the office in the middle of the bus paddock before you're hustled on board one of the vehicles. Some distances and approximate bemo fares from Sweta to other parts of Lombok include:

East Direction (Jurusan Timor) Sweta to Narmada (6 km) 150 rp; Mantang 350 rp; Kopang (25 km) 400 rp; Terara 550 rp; Sikur 600 rp; Masbagek 700 rp; Selong (47 km) 700 rp; Aikmel 800 rp; Apitaik 900 rp; Pringgabaya (60 km) 900 rp; Labuhan Lombok (69 km) 1000 rp; Sambelia (89 km) 1200 rp; Tetebatu (46 km) 700 rp; Sesaot (15 km) 300 rp.

South & Central Direction (Jurusan Selatan dan Tenggara) Sweta to Kediri 150 rp; Gerung 300 rp; Lembar (22 km) 400 rp; Praya (27 km) 400 rp; Mujur 550 rp; Keruak 1000 rp; Tjoluar 800 rp; Rambang 900 rp; Labuhan Haji 1000 rp; Kuta (52 km) 900 rp; Tetebatu (46 km) 700 rp.

North Direction (Jurusan Utara) Sweta to Pemeneng (31 km) 500 rp; Tanjung 600 rp; Gondang 700 rp; Amor-Amor 900 rp; Desa Anyar 1200 rp; Bayan (79 km) 1200 rp.

Boat See the Lombok Getting There & Away, Lembar and Labuhan Lombok sections for ferry info to/from Bali and Sumbawa. Some losmens can arrange buses to these ferries or even through-

tickets to places like Bima. The SP ferry office is at Jalan Pejanggik 49 in Mataram

Getting Around

Airport Transport Lombok's Selaparang Airport is only a couple of km from Ampenan or Mataram, it costs about 3000 rp for a taxi. Alternatively walk out of the car park to the main road and No 7 bemos come by frequently and run straight to the Ampenan bemo terminal for 125 rp. It's not even necessary to go into town from the airport if you want to head out to Senggigi Beach or to the Gili Islands. See those sections for more details.

Local Transport Ampenan-Mataram-Cakra-Sweta is surprisingly sprawling, don't plan to walk from place to place. Bemos shuttle back and forth along the main route between the Ampenan terminal at one end and the Sweta terminal at the other. The fare is a standard 125 rp regardless of the distance. There are plenty of dokars to rent for shorter trips around town.

Bicycle, Motorcycle & Bemo Rental You can rent bicycles for 1500 rp a day from the Losmen Horas or Wisma Triguna in Ampenan.

Motorcycles can be rented in Mataram from Jalan Gelantik, off Jalan Selaparang near the junction with Jalan Sultan Hasanuddin (at the Cakranegara end of Mataram). There are a bunch of motorcycle owners hanging around there with bikes to rent at 6000 to 10,000 rp a day. As usual the more you pay the better you get and it's wise to check a bike over carefully before saying yes. See the introductory Getting Around Lombok chapter for more details.

Chartering a bemo in Lombok is easy, count on about 25,000 rp a day but check the bemo over carefully as some of them are in decidedly poor condition. The introductory Getting Around Lombok chapter has more details. The bemo station in Ampenan is a good place to charter a bemo.

SENGGIGI BEACH

On a superb sweeping bay about 10 km north of Ampenan, Senggigi Beach has become *the* place to stay on Lombok and these days many travellers don't bother staying in town at all. Promotional work for the big Senggigi Beach Hotel has focused much more interest on Senggigi and Lombok as a whole.

Senggigi has a fine beach although it slopes off very steeply. There's some snorkelling off the point and in the sheltered bay across the headland. There are amazing views from Senggigi across Lombok Strait to Bali, dominated by mighty Gunung Agung. The sunsets are particularly wonderful.

Information

There's no place to change money or travellers' cheques at Senggigi although the Senggigi Beach Hotel will change for their guests. Eating there will probably qualify you as a guest, particularly if you don't have enough Indonesian currency to pay the bill!

Batu Bolong – Hollow Rock

This temple is about a km before Senggigi Beach, about eight km from Ampenan. While not terribly interesting in itself, the site of this large rock with a hole in it offers a fantastic view across Lombok Strait to Bali and Gunung Agung – and particularly good sunsets. Periodically the local people make offerings here and legend has it that beautiful virgins were once chucked into the sea from the top of the rock (virgins always get a rough deal). Locals like to claim that this is why the temple was built and why there are so many sharks in the water near Batu Bolong.

Places to Stay & Eat

The most popular travellers' centre at Senggigi is the *Pondok Senggigi* with rooms at 3000/4500 rp including attached

mandi and toilet. The rooms run off a long verandah with a pleasant garden area in front. Along the other side of the garden there are comfortable individual bungalows at 7500 rp. Pondok Senggigi has an open air restaurant which is deservedly popular from breakfast time until late at night.

On the beach side, between the Pondok Senggigi and the Senggigi Beach Hotel, is the *Senggigi Holiday Inn* with rooms with a small mezzanine at 12,500/17,500 rp, two beds on each floor. Right next door *Mascot Bungalows* are pleasant individual cottages at 7500/10,000 rp. The Holiday Inn has a restaurant but it's not very busy.

Senggigi's one big 'international standard' hotel is right on the headland. Operated by Garuda Airlines the *Senggigi Beach Hotel* (tel 23430) has rooms at US$45/75, a beautiful setting, a swimming pool and other mod cons.

In the opposite direction the small *Pondok Melati Dua* is next door to the Pondok Senggigi and has rooms at 12,500 rp. Further along on the beach side of the road *Batu Bolong Cottages* is a brand new development. There will undoubtedly be more places springing up as Senggigi becomes increasingly popular.

Continuing towards Ampenan you eventually come to the *Sasaka Beach Cottages*, about midway between Ampenan and Senggigi, close to the turn-off to Lendang Bajur. This up-market development never caught on and is now run down and neglected, the pool is empty and nobody stays there. If you really wanted to you can get a room for 10,000 rp.

Pondok Senggigi is far and away the number one dining attraction but you can also eat for a much higher cost, at the *Senggigi Beach Hotel* where main courses cost around 8000 rp plus 21% service and tax. Or there's the small *Warung Nasi Sederhana*, it was right next to Pondok Senggigi but may have moved further down the road. It makes a real effort to cater for visitors with an English menu.

A new restaurant is also planned for across the road from the Pondok Senggigi.

Getting There & Away

Take a bemo from the Ampenan bemo terminal to Lendang Bajur, just north of the airport on the road to Pemenang and the Gili Islands. From there you can catch a bus to Senggigi, total fare about 400 rp. The direct road along the coast between Ampenan and Senggigi is actually quicker but there's no regular transport that way. Nevertheless there will often be bemos taking that route, again for about 400 rp, or you can charter one.

NARMADA

Laid out as a miniature replica of the summit of Mt Rinjani and its crater Lake Segara Anak, Narmada is a hill about 10 km east of Cakra, on the main east-west road crossing Lombok. It takes its name from a sacred river in India and the temple here, Pura Kalasa, is still used. The Balinese *Pujawali* celebration is held here every year in honour of the god, Batara, who dwells on Gunung Rinjani. At the same time the faithful who have made the trek up the mountain and down to Lake Segara Anak, hold a ritual called *Pekelan* in which they dispose of their gold trinkets and artefacts by ceremonially throwing them into the lake.

Narmada was constructed by the king of Mataram in 1805, when he was no longer able to climb Rinjani to make his offerings to the gods. Having set his conscience at rest by placing offerings in the temple he spent at least some of his time in a concealed spot on the hill lusting over the young girls bathing in the artificial lake.

It's a beautiful place to spend a few hours, though the gardens are neglected. *Don't* go there on weekends since it's overrun with the hordes. Apart from the lake there are two other pools in these grounds. One is an Olympic-size pool with changing rooms – admission is 200 rp for adults, 100 rp for children. Entry fee to Narmada itself is 100 rp (children 50 rp).

Along one side of the pool is the remains of a vast aqueduct built by the Dutch and still in use. When land tax was tied to the productivity of the land, the Dutch were keenly interested in increasing agricultural output. They did this by extending irrigation systems to increase the area under cultivation. The Balinese had already built extensive irrigation networks, particularly in the west.

The construction of roads and bridges was also given high priority, since from both a political and economic point of view it was in the Dutch interests to establish a good communication system. A large number of roads and tracks were constructed – like the aqueducts they were built and maintained with the unpaid labour of Lombok peasants.

Places to Eat

Right at the Narmada bemo terminal is the local market which is sells mainly food and clothing and is well worth a look. There are a number of warungs scattered around offering soto ayam and other dishes.

Getting There & Away

There are frequent bemos from Sweta to Narmada, costing around 125 to 200 rp. When you get off at the bemo terminal at Narmada, the gardens are directly across the road. Walk 100 metres or so along a side road to the entrance gate. There are parking fees for bicycles, motorcycles and cars.

LINGSAR

This large temple complex, just a few km north of Narmada, is said to have been built in 1714. The temple combines the Bali-Hindu and Islam-Wektu Telu religions in one complex. Designed in two separate sections and built on two different levels, the Hindu pura on the north is higher than the Wektu Telu temple on the south.

The Hindu temple has four shrines. The one on the left, Hyang Tunggal, looks towards Gunung Agung which is the seat of the gods in Bali – the shrine faces north-west rather than north-east as it would in Bali. On the right is a shrine devoted to Mt Rinjani, the seat of the gods in Lombok. Between these two shrines is a double shrine symbolising the union between the two islands. The left hand side of this shrine is named in honour of the might of Lombok. The right hand side of the shrine is dedicated to a king's daughter, Ayu Nyoman Winton, whom legend decrees gave birth to a god.

The Wektu Telu temple is noted for its small enclosed pond devoted to Lord Vishnu. It has a number of holy eels that can be enticed from their hiding places along the water ducts by persistent tapping of the walls and the use of hard-boiled eggs as bait. Apart from their outstanding size, they're rather unprepossessing – like huge swimming slugs. The stalls outside the temple complex sell boiled eggs – expect to pay around 200 rp or so. Next to the eel pond is another enclosure with a kind of large altar or offering place, bedecked in white and yellow cloth and mirrors. The mirrors were offered by Chinese business people asking for good luck and success. Many local farmers come here also with offerings or to feed eggs to the holy eels.

On the right as you enter the temple, running almost its entire length and hidden behind a wall, is a women's washing place. It's mainly a series of individual fountains squirting holy water and once again there are holy eels here. There's a men's mandi at the back. You can bathe here but Narmada is probably a better place to swim.

Once a year at the beginning of the rainy season – somewhere between October and December – the Hindus and the Wektu Telus make offerings and pray in their own temples. Then they come out into the communal compound and pelt each other with ketupat – rice wrapped in banana leaves. No-one quite knows what this ceremony is for – some say it's to bring the rain, others to give thanks for the rain. Be prepared to get attacked with ketupat from both sides if you visit Lingsar at this time.

Getting There & Away

There are frequent bemos from Sweta to Narmada for 125 to 200 rp. At Narmada catch another bemo to Lingsar for the same price and walk the short distance from here to the temple complex. Watch for the school on the main road, it's easy to

Kids in the rain, Lingsar

miss the temple which is set back off the road.

There is a large square in front of the temple complex, with a couple of warungs to the right before you enter the main area and a small stall closer to the temple where you can buy snacks and hard-boiled eggs for the holy eels. If the temple is locked ask at one of the warungs for a key.

SURANADI

A few km east of Lingsar, Suranadi has one of the holiest temples on Lombok. This small temple, set in pleasant gardens, is noted for its bubbling, icy cold springwater and restored baths with ornate Balinese carvings. The eels here have also been sanctified. Drop a hard-boiled egg into the water and watch the eels swim out of the conduits for a feed.

You can also swim here so bring your swimsuit. It is polite to ask permission before jumping in.

Places to Stay & Eat

The *Suranadi Hotel* (tel 23686) has rooms at a wide variety of prices starting from 9000/11,000 rp and going up to 24,000/30,000 rp, plus 21% tax and service. There's a swimming pool, as well as a tennis court, restaurant and bar. People not staying at the hotel can use the swimming pool and tennis court for 500 rp (children 250 rp).

Apart from the restaurant in the hotel, there are also a few warungs in the main street.

SESAOT

About five km from Suranadi and worth a visit is Sesaot, a small quiet market town on the edge of a forest where wood-felling is the main industry. There's regular transport from Suranadi to Sesaot and you can eat at the warung on the main street which has simple but tasty food. By the bridge are separate bathing places for men and women.

LEMBAR

One of the two main ports of Lombok, this is where the ferries from Bali dock. Situated in a protected bay with palm-covered hills sweeping down to the edge of the harbour, Lembar is about 30 km south of Ampenan. Several small islands dot the narrow channel leading into the harbour.

Places to Eat

There's a canteen at the ferry wharf where you can buy snacks and drinks while waiting to catch the ferry. Lembar has no overnight accommodation, nor does it have any rumah makan.

Getting There & Away

See the introductory Getting There & Away section for Lombok for information on the Bali-Lombok ferry service.

Regular buses and bemos from Sweta cost 400 rp during the day. If you arrive in Lembar on the afternoon ferry from Bali, buy a bemo ticket on the journey over. While you'll be paying more than the normal price, this will guarantee you transport to Ampenan, Mataram or Cakranegara. A minibus from the Zahir Hotel in Ampenan often meets the ferry.

Bemo drivers meeting travellers off this ferry often jack their prices up to over 1000 rp after dark. The ferry office is directly in front of where the bemo or bus puts you down.

SUKARARA

Twenty-five km south of Mataram on the Kediri-Puyung road is the small village of Sukarara. On the way to this traditional weaving centre you pass picturesque thatched-roof villages surrounded by rice fields. More unusual are the houses built from local stone found in Sukarara. Look out for Sasak women in their traditional black costumes around this area.

Lombok is renowned for its traditional weaving, the techniques for which have been handed down from mother to daughter for generations. Each piece of cloth is woven on a handloom in established patterns and colours. Some fabrics are woven in as many as four directions, interwoven with gold thread and can be so complicated that they take one person three months to complete. Many incorporate flower and animal motifs including buffaloes, dragons, lizards, crocodiles and snakes. Several villages specialise in this craft including Sukarara and Pringgasela.

Nearly every house in Sukarara has an old wooden handloom and along the main street you'll see displays of sarongs hanging in bright bands outside the houses. You can stop at one, watch the women weaving and buy direct. Another place worth trying is the Taufik Weaving Company on Jalan Tenun. The manager's name is Widasih and he has sarongs, songkets, Sasak belts, tablecloths and numerous other pieces.

Before you go to Sukarara it may be a good idea to check prices in the Selamat Riady weaving factory in Cakranegara and get some idea of how much to pay and where to start bargaining. If you're accompanied to Sukarara it will inevitably cost you more through commissions. Although the village is a regular stop for tour groups the people are very friendly and if you eat or drink at the warung you'll be surrounded by locals.

Places to Stay
Stay with the kepala desa or make a day trip. You could also check with the woman who runs the warung – she sometimes puts people up for the night and has a fine selection of cloth for sale.

Getting There & Away
Bemos from Sweta to Puyung cost 350 rp. From Puyung take a dokar to Sukarara, the two-km ride will cost 200 rp.

REMBITAN & OTHER VILLAGES
From Sengkol down to Kuta Beach is a centre of traditional Sasak culture, and there are many relatively unchanged Sasak villages where the people still live in customary houses and engage in indigenous crafts.

Only a couple of km south of Sengkol is Rembitan, the best known village with a population of about 750. The Masjid Kuno, an old thatched roof mosque, tops the hill around which the village houses cluster. A short distance further south is Sade, a smaller and more traditional village with each house fronted by a rice barn. Dotted on the hills all around are other Sasak villages.

KUTA BEACH
Lombok's Kuta Beach is a magnificent stretch of sand with impressive hills rising around it but it's much less touristed than the better known version in Bali. At the annual nyale fishing celebration, people flock to Kuta but otherwise the small village is very quiet. Stinging seaweed makes swimming unpleasant at times but Kuta is also good for surfing and wind surfing.

The bay is flanked by a mountain chain to the west and an enormous rock about four km from the village to the east. If you climb this early in the morning you get superb views across the countryside.

Kuta isn't just one beach but a series of bays punctuated by headlands. Travelling east from Kuta the main centres are Segara Beach and Tanjung Aan. It's five km to Tanjung Aan where there's a market on Wednesday and Thursday. Gerupak is a fishing village about eight km from Kuta where there's a market on Tuesday. From there you can cross by boat to Bumgang. An alternative excursion from Kuta turns north just before Tanjung Aan but beyond Serneng the road deteriorates and you can get as far as Awang only with a motorcycle or on foot.

Information
Once a year a special Sasak celebration is held in Kuta for the opening of the nyale fishing season. On the 19th day of the 10th month in the Sasak calendar – generally February or March – hundreds of Sasaks

gather on the beach and when night falls fires are built and the young people sit around competing with each other in rhyming couplets called *pantun*. At dawn the next morning, the first nyale are caught, after which it is time for the Sasak teenagers to have fun. In a colourful procession boys and girls put out to sea – in different boats – and chase one another with lots of noise and laughter.

Kuta has a market twice a week on Sundays and Wednesdays.

Places to Stay & Eat

At the point where the road from the north meets the coast, a road turns off east and a short distance along you'll find Pondok Sekar Kuning and Warung Anda side by side. *Pondok Sekar Kuning* or 'Yellow Flower Cottage' has double rooms from 5000 rp and a nice view from the upstairs rooms. Next door *Warung Anda* has very plain rooms for 4000 rp and a menu featuring nasi campur, nasi goreng and other straightforward Indonesian dishes.

A bit further along are the *Mandalika Seaview Cottages* or Mascot Cottages with rooms at 4000 rp, bungalows at 5000 rp and a pleasant grassy area beside the road. There's another place to stay at Tanjung Aan, they might decide to call it the *Tanjung Aan Hotel*. Accommodation is decidedly low-key at Kuta, and at present there isn't much of it.

Getting There & Away

Although Kuta is just 45 km from Cakra, getting there by public transport is not easy. It's no trouble getting to Praya but beyond there it's a matter of waiting for transport to Sengkol and then again down to Kuta. Market day in Sengkol is Thursday when there may be more transport. The final five km to Kuta is a steep and winding descent which suddenly leaves the hills to arrive at the coast.

KOTARAJA

Basketware from Lombok has such a fine reputation in the archipelago that many Balinese make special buying trips to Lombok, selling it in Bali at inflated prices to foreigners. Kotaraja and Loyok villages in eastern Lombok used to be noted for their craftwork, particularly their basketware and plaited mats but it all seems to have disappeared today. Exquisitely intricate jewellery, vases, caskets and other decorative objects also used to come from Kotaraja.

'Kotaraja' actually means 'City of Kings' although no kings ruled from here. Apparently when the Sasak kingdom of Langko, located at Kopang in central Lombok, fell to the Balinese invaders the rulers of Langko fled to Loyok, the village to the south of Kotaraja. After the royal compound in that village was also destroyed two brothers, sons of the ruler of

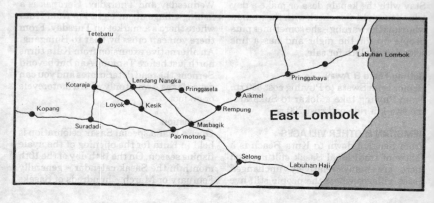

Langko, went to live in Kotaraja. The aristocracy of Kotaraja can trace their ancestry back to these brothers although the highest caste title of raden has now petered out through intermarriage.

Places to Stay
If you want to spend the night in the area, stay with the kepala desa in Kotaraja. Otherwise it's a day trip from Ampenan, Mataram, Cakranegara or Sweta.

Getting There & Away
Kotaraja is 32 km from Sweta. If you go by bemo you have to change a couple of times. From Sweta you take a bemo to Narmada for 150 rp, and from there another bemo to Pomotong (also spelt Pao' Motong) for 400 rp. From Pomotong you can either get a dokar to Kotaraja or wait for another bemo (cheaper than dokars, but not as plentiful). There is a direct bus from Sweta to Pomotong but you may have to wait around for a while and it may actually be quicker and easier to take the bemos.

LOYOK
Loyok is a tiny village just a few km from Kotaraja and is noted for its fine handicrafts although it is very much off the trampled track. Most of the crafts-people work out of their homes and if you ask the dokar driver he will take you to where the basket weavers work although it's hard to find anything to buy.

Getting There & Away
To get to Loyok, you can get a bemo from Pomotong to take you as far as the turn-off to the village and then either walk the rest of the way or get a dokar for 150 rp per person. If you're setting out from Kotaraja for Loyok you've got the same options – either take a dokar or walk. Its a pretty drive with traditional thatched Sasak huts and lush rice terraces along the way.

TETEBATU
A mountain retreat at the foot of Gunung Rinjani, Tetebatu is 50 km from Mataram and about seven km north of Kotaraja. Like Loyok it was originally an offshoot settlement of Kotaraja. You can climb part way up Rinjani from here but the formerly magnificent stands of mahogany trees have virtually all disappeared. There are still lots of jet black monkeys to shriek at you.

Places to Stay & Eat
Wisma Sudjono is the only place to stay here – a couple of two-storey bungalows with separate living and sleeping areas, western-style toilets, and showers with hot and cold water. They charge around 10,000 rp for a bungalow, though there may be some cheaper rooms. Food here is excellent, but costs extra – they'll even pack lunch for you if you want to spend the day out walking. In fact everything here costs extra, they charge you to park a motorcycle while you have lunch! There are several warungs in Tetebatu.

Getting There & Away
Getting to Tetebatu involves a number of changes if you haven't got your own wheels. From Sweta take a bemo to Narmada for 200 rp, and then another to Pomotong for 400 rp. There are direct buses from Sweta to Pomotong but you may have to wait around for a while and in the long run it's probably quicker and easier to go by bemo. From Pomotong take a bemo or a dokar to Kotaraja, though a bemo is cheaper at 200 rp.

From Kotaraja there is a dirt road most of the way to Tetebatu – smoother than the old rocky road. Take a bemo from Kotaraja to Tetebatu for 150 rp – or alternatively a dokar for around 2500 rp for four people.

If you're not in a hurry and aren't carrying much of a load, it's a nice walk from Pomotong to Tetebatu through attractive country patched with rice fields. It will take you an easy 2½ to three hours.

LENDANG NANGKA

Lendang Nangka is a small village seven km from Tetebatu. Radiah, a local primary school teacher, will put you up at his house. He speaks excellent English and is a mine of information on the surrounding countryside and customs. He enjoys acting as guide and will drive you around to nearby villages and sights on his motorcycle.

Since the first edition of the *Bali & Lombok* guide Pak Radiah has written to us encouraging people to stay in Lendang Nangka, which he says is a traditional Sasak village and has similar surroundings to Tetebatu. He has a map for local walks. In the village and surrounding area you can see blacksmiths who still make knives, hoes and other tools using indigenous techniques. Jojang, the biggest spring in Lombok, is a few km away or you can walk to a waterfall with beautiful views or see the black monkeys in a nearby forest.

In August, at Lendang Nangka, you should be able to see the traditional Sasak form of boxing – a violent affair with leather-covered shields and bamboo poles. Local dances are a possibility at Batu Empas, one km away. At the village of Pringgasela the girls weave Sasak cloths, blankets and sarongs – it's only two km from Lendang Nangka – take a dokar or walk.

Places to Stay

Staying with Pak Radiah will cost you about 5000 rp per person, including three excellent meals per day of local Sasak food, and tea or coffee. You will get customary Sasak cake and fruit for breakfast, it's not cheap but highly recommended. His house is fairly easy to find (see the map) and has seven bedrooms for guests, each with attached bathroom and toilet. He and his family are very friendly and helpful.

Getting There & Away

Take a bemo from Sweta to Masbagik (42 km, 700 rp) and then take a dokar to Lendang Nangka (about four km, 250 rp). Lendang Nangka is about 4½ km from Pomotong and connected by a surfaced road – take a dokar for 250 rp (300 rp if you have a heavy load).

LABUHAN LOMBOK

There are fantastic views of mighty Rinjani from the east coast port of Labuhan Lombok. Ferries run from here to Sumbawa Island. It's a friendly, sleepy little place, a mixed bag of concrete houses, thatch shacks and stilt bungalows. You can climb the hill on the right-hand side of the harbour and watch the boats plying between here and Sumbawa.

If you walk about four km north from Labuhan Lombok towards Sembalia there is a reservoir and fishing village – the children either run away in fear or surround you and touch your white skin to see if it feels the same as brown skin.

South of Labuhan Lombok on the coast is Labuhan Haji which is supposed to have a good beach and is accessible by bemo and dokar.

Places to Stay

If you're just passing through Labuhan Lombok on your way to Sumbawa there's no need to stay overnight at all. You can catch an early bus from Sweta (5.30 am at the latest) and get to the port in time for the Sumbawa ferry. The Ampenan

Lendang Nangka

Radiah's House
Mosque
To Masbagik
To Kotaraja
Monument
Market
To Bagek Bontong

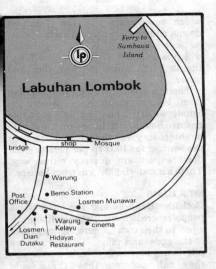

losmen are quite used to getting their guests on the road by that time.

If, however, you do want to stay for a day or two Labuhan Lombok has gone through an accommodation upheaval with the old Sudimampir finally closing down. New overnight options include the basic *Losmen Dian Dutaku* with rooms at 2000/3000 rp. Or on Jalan Khayangan there's *Losmen Munawar*, also pretty simple and basic, with rooms at 2500/5000 rp. Neither are anything to write home about but they're both quite habitable for a short stay.

Places to Eat

There are a couple of warungs around the bemo station, but they all feature a restricted menu and the food is not that good. You can always buy a fish at the market and get it cooked at a warung. The *Hidayat Restaurant*, across the road from the bemo station, is a friendly place. Alternatively there's the fairly clean *Warung Kelayu* next door.

Getting There & Away

Bus There are regular bemos and colts from Sweta, the 69 km trip costs 1000 rp

and should take a bit less than two hours. It's possible to leave Ampenan early enough in the morning to get to Labuhan Lombok in time for the ferry departure to Sumbawa. The popular Ampenan travellers' losmen will organise this dawn departure for you. If you're zipping straight across Lombok bound for Bali you can take a bus via Sweta to Lembar for 1500 rp, a 97 km trip. Pancor, 37 km away, costs 600 rp.

Boat The ferry to Labuhan Alas on Sumbawa departs from a pier about a km from the bemo station. It's not far to walk if you've got little to carry – alternatively a dokar will cost you about 100 rp per person. The ferry departs around 7 to 8 am and the fare is 2100 rp. You can also transport motorcycles for about 2500 rp. The ticket office is by the pier and the trip takes about 3½ to four hours. See the Lombok introductory Getting Around section for more details.

There are a couple of stalls at the pier where you can buy biscuits or bananas and there are one or two warungs serving nasi campur. Guys come on board the boat selling fried rice wrapped in banana leaves and hard-boiled eggs. Take a water bottle with you – it's a bloody hot ride! The ferry is a floating pile of closely compacted humanity – could be a good idea to get down to the dock early to get a seat – or bring a hat for sun protection and stretch out on the roof.

BAYAN

Midway between Desa Anyar and Senaro, Bayan is the birthplace of the Wektu Telu religion. Bayan is still an isolated village but the main road now extends to it. Traditional Hindu dances are still performed in Bayan, but getting to see them is a case of stumbling in at the right time, or asking around to find out when they're on. Bayan is also one of the main starting points for the climb up Mt Rinjani.

Places to Stay & Eat

Stay with the kepala desa here for around 2500 rp per person per night, including two meals. There are a couple of warungs in Bayan, one on the road to Senaro just off to the right. You can get fried chicken and rice here for 1500 rp.

Getting There & Away

Lombok's main north-south road ends at Bayan. There are several buses daily from Sweta to Bayan, the first leaving around 9 am. The fare is around 1200 to 1400 rp and it takes about three hours. The last bus back to Sweta departs Bayan around 6 pm.

SENARO

Perched high up in the foothills of Rinjani about nine km from Bayan, this small traditional village seems utterly unchanged from the time it evolved. It exudes a feeling of untainted prehistory that is quite unnerving. In fact it was less than 20 years ago that the villagers of Senaro saw their first westerners, and not many years before that that they began to have regular contact with people from the surrounding area. Until then they lived completely isolated from the rest of the world and are still very timid, making no attempt to communicate with strangers and showing none of the overt curiosity that occurs in most parts of Lombok.

The village itself is surrounded by a high wooden paling fence and comprises about 20 thatched wooden huts in straight lines, some on stilts, others low to the ground. On the left, just before you come to the village, is a small coffee plantation. Unless accompanied by a local person it's polite to ask permission before entering Senaro. Nobody here speaks a word of English.

Many of the men from this village work in the nearby forests as woodcutters. Part of the ritual of climbing Rinjani is that guides usually stop at Senaro to stock up on betel nut. Young boys in the village thresh rice with long wooden mallets

which reverberate like the sound of drums, adding to the primitive atmosphere. A large percentage of the population, which is less than 500, have goitre due to the lack of iodine in their diet and water.

There is a truck that picks up timber from Senaro regularly – usually on Sundays – so you may be able to get a ride down to Bayan on it. In Senaro you should be able to stay with the schoolmaster or at the warung for 1000 rp per person – but don't expect any privacy either way. There's a waterfall 2½ km from Senaro.

MT RINJANI

Both the Balinese and the local Sasak people revere Rinjani. To the Balinese it is equal to their own Gunung Agung, a seat of the gods, and many Balinese make a pilgrimage here each year. In a ceremony they call pekelan they throw gold jewellery into the lake and make offerings to the spirit of the mountain. As for the Sasaks some make several pilgrimages a year – full moon is the favourite time for them to pay their respects to the mountain and cure their ailments by bathing in its hot springs.

Rinjani is the highest mountain in Lombok, the second highest in Indonesia outside of Irian Jaya. At 3726 metres it soars above the island and dominates the landscape. Early in the morning it can be seen from anywhere on the island, but by mid-morning on most days the summit is shrouded in cloud. The mountain is actually an active volcano – though the last eruption was in 1901 – with a huge half-moon crater, a large slime-green lake and an extensive network of steaming hot springs said to have remarkable healing powers, particularly for skin diseases. The large caldera drops 200 metres below the rim and there's a new cone in the centre, beside the lake.

You should not tackle this climb during the wet season as it's far too dangerous. You need three clear days to do it and probably at least another day to recover.

Don't go up during the full moon because it will be very crowded. There are at least two ways of getting up Mt Rinjani. The first and apparently easier route is via Bayan, Batu Koq and Senaro in the north. The other route starts at Sapit in the east.

Guides & Equipment

You can do the trek without a guide, but in some places there's a confusion of trails branching off and you could get lost. The other advantage of guides is that they're informative, good company, and also act as porters, cooks and water collectors. When you're doing this walk with a guide make sure you set your own pace – some of them climb Rinjani as many as 20 or 30 times a year and positively gallop up the slopes!

It's worthwhile talking to Mr Batu Bara, at the Losmen Wisma Triguna, in Ampenan. For US$75(!) he will organise the complete trip for you – food, tent, sleeping bag and a guide. But if you don't want to come at that he will tell you how to go about it on your own. He'll explain what food to take, and will rent you a two or three person tent for 10,000 rp and a sleeping bag for 7500 rp – steep prices but a sleeping bag and tent are absolutely essential.

He will also write a letter to the school teacher in Batu Koq, Raden Kertabakti (known locally as Guru Bakti). He is a very nice man who will not only arrange a guide but feed you, put you up on the first night and more than likely on the evening you get down from the mountain. To stay here overnight costs around 2500 rp per person. The food is good and there's plenty of it. There are two rooms, in one of the school buildings, that have double beds with ground sheets and pillows. There are no toilets here, but the children will show you where to go.

Food & Supplies

You need to take enough food to last three days – including food for your guide. It's better to buy most of it in Ampenan,

Mataram or Cakra as there's more choice available. Take rice, instant noodles, sugar, coffee, eggs (lots – if you stay at Mr Batu Bara's losmen he will lend you a container to carry the eggs in), tea, biscuits or bread, some tins of fish or meat, onions, fruit and anything else that keeps your engine running.

It's also a good idea to take plenty of matches, a torch (flashlight), a water container and some cigarettes. The teacher and guide will provide water and containers for you, but it's good to be able to have some handy. Even if you don't smoke, the guides really appreciate being given cigarettes. If you have any food left over, leave it at the school.

Getting There & Away

Ampenan to Bayan If you're setting off from Ampenan get to the bus terminal at Sweta before 9 am – there's a bus that leaves for Bayan around then. The 70-km journey to Bayan costs 1200 rp, takes approximately three hours and goes through some spectacular country – it's the same road to Pemenang for the Gili Islands – so get a window seat up front if possible. The new coast road may be even more picturesque.

Bayan to Batu Koq When you get to Bayan you either have to walk the four or five km up the road to Batu Koq where the school teacher lives or take a truck. The latter is a far better alternative as you will probably arrive here in the middle of the day and it's a hot, dusty walk – there's not much shade along this road and you'll could be carrying a fair amount of junk as well as food for three days. Trucks go up and down here with regular irregularity. There are a couple of warungs near where the bus stops and the odd shop where you can buy last minute bits and pieces if necessary. Once you get to Batu Koq numerous children will rush out shouting their 'Hello Misters' and take you to the school teacher. Westerners are still seven-day-wonders here.

Make sure you go to the magnificent

waterfall near Batu Koq – it can be heard from far away. It's a pleasant hour's walk partially through forest, and along the side of an irrigated water course for much of the way. Watch for the sleek, black monkeys swinging through the trees. Splash around near the waterfall – the water cascades down the mountain slope so hard and so fast that it's strong enough to knock the wind out of you.

Ascending the Mountain

Day 1 Depart Batu Koq about 8 am for base camp. The climb takes about six hours and is relatively easy going through dappled forest, the quiet only broken (*shattered*) by the occasional bird, animal, bell or woodchopper. At base camp pitch the tent, collect wood and water and if you have enough energy left climb up to the clearing and watch the sunset. The ground is rock hard at base camp and it's very cold so bring thick woollen socks, a sweater and a ground sheet with you. If a flock of 30-odd Lombokians arrives unexpectedly out of the gloom the chances of seeing the lake and the hot springs at their solo-in-the-wilderness best are gloomy indeed. Go somewhere else and try again another day.

Day 2 Set off at about 8 am again and after approximately 1½ hours you will arrive at the rim of the volcano, an altitude of 3025 metres.

Rinjani is covered in dense forest up to 2000 metres, but at around this height the vegetation changes from thick stands of mahogany and teak trees to the odd stand of pine. As you get closer to the rim the pines become sparser and and the soil rubbly and barren. The locals cut down the mahogany and teak trees with handaxes (no chainsaws yet) and then carry the huge logs down the steep slopes, by hand! Monkeys, wild pigs, deer and the occasional snake inhabits the forest. Once you get above the forest and up to the clearing the going is hot as there's not much shade – the land here is harsh and

inhospitable – but you have superb views across to Bali and Sumbawa.

From the rim of the crater it takes between five and six hours to get down to Lake Segara Anak and around to the hot springs. The descent from the rim into the crater is quite dangerous – for most of the way the path down to the lake clings to the side of the cliffs and is narrow and meandering. Watch out for rubble – in certain spots it's very hard to keep your footing. Close to the lake a thick forest sweeps down to the shore. There are several places to camp along this lake, but if you head for the hot springs there are many more alternatives. The track along the lake is also narrow and very slippery – be careful and take it slowly. There are a number of different kinds of small waterbirds on the lake – but no fish in it.

After setting up camp at the lake it's time to soak your weary body in the springs and recuperate. It's not as cold here as it is at base camp, but it is damp and misty from the steaming springs. Despite the hundreds of local people around it can still be an eerie place. Watch your step on the paths – although this is a holy place the locals have few inhibitions or qualms about relieving themselves when and wherever they need to – they don't even bother to move off the main paths.

Day 3 Departure time is approximately 8 am once again, and you walk more or less all day, arriving at Batu Koq in the late afternoon. It's a hard eight to 10 hour walk.

Day 4 If you get back to Batu Koq late in the afternoon, it's preferable to stay overnight with the school teacher. Even if you can get a lift down to Bayan by truck, the last bus from there to Cakra departs around 6 pm and there's a good chance you'll miss it. This means that you'll be stuck in Bayan until the following morning without anywhere to stay after a tiring trip, unless you can find the kepala desa. If you do stay overnight at Batu Koq it's a good idea to leave early in the morning before the sun gets too hot. You may have to walk down to Bayan but there's a bus to Cakra from here at about 8.30 am. If you miss this one there are frequent other buses during the day.

A Solo Climb

It's easy enough to do the climb without a guide although we thought the climb to the rim from the north and not bothering with the actual peak was just as good value and easy to do. But a traverse across the mountain is also perfectly feasible. Sign the book in Senaro and collect water since it's scarce along the track. Hundreds of paths lead uphill from Senaro so if you get lost ask *several* locals and take the most logical advice. One guy pointed back to Bayan when I asked him which was the path to Gunung Rinjani!

The track is erratically numbered from 0 to 200 (200 is the crater rim). You can camp at about 65-75, 110, 170 and 185. The last is an excellent spot above the bushline with fabulous views and only half an hour from the rim for sunrise the next morning. Water is only available at 114 and 185.

From the crater rim to Lake Segara is steeply downhill. From here across the top and down to Sapit takes two to three days. A tent and sleeping bag are essential.

Mark Austin, New Zealand

To the Very Top

The first two days were pretty much as described but on the third day we warmed up in the springs before making a three-hour climb to a shelter by the path just before the junction with the summit route. This shelter is just a hollow scooped out of the ground and lined with dry grass. A few old sheets of iron serve as a roof. It fits three people, or maybe an intimate four.

There is wood that can be used for a fire – useful, as the shelter must be at 3000 metres or more and as soon as the sun goes down it gets very cold.

The next morning we watched the sun rise over Sumbawa from the junction of the paths, before starting the final ascent. The view from the rim is great, but it's nothing compared to the view from the very top! From the top, you look down into the crater which fills up with 'cotton wool' cloud streaming through the gap in the crater wall at the hot springs. In the distance, you look over Bali in one direction and Sumbawa in the other.

It's a difficult three-hour climb from the shelter; the air gets thinner and the terrain is horrible to walk on. It's powdery to start with, then you find loose stones on a steep slope (offering little support for your weight). It's a case of climbing one step up, then sliding two-thirds of a step back down, and the peak always looks closer than it is! Climbing without strong-toed shoes or boots would be masochistic.

Richard Tucker, England

SEMBULAN BUMBUNG & SEMBULAN LAWANG

High up on the eastern slopes of Mt Rinjani is the cold but beautiful Sembulan Valley. The inhabitants of the valley claim descent from the Hindu-Javanese and a relative of one of the Majapahit rulers is said to be buried here. Whilst it seems unlikely that Java ever controlled Lombok directly, similarities in music, dance and language have suggested that Lombok may have come under some long-lasting Javanese influence several hundred years ago.

In the valley, five km apart, are the traditional Sasak villages of Sembulan Bumbung and Sembulan Lawang. It's only a 45 minute walk from one village to the other and there are many pleasant walks in the surrounding area. From Sembulan Bumbung there is a steep 1½ hour climb to a saddle with a beautiful view all round. Five hours' walk from Sembulan Bumbung, first through rainforest, later coffee, paw paw, rice and vegetable fields, you arrive at a small village close to the village of Sapit. From there you can take a bemo to Pringgabaya and on to Labuhan Lombok.

You can reach the summit of Rinjani direct from either Sembulan Bumbung or Sembulan Lawang, but you must come prepared with sleeping bag, tent, food and other supplies – or walk the five hours from Sembulan Lawang to Sapit and trek to the summit from there. You can walk from Senaro to Sembulan Lawang but you have to start early; it's a long way and would take around 12 hours. Sometimes there are trucks between Bayan and Sembulan Lawang – walking takes a day.

Places to Stay

Stay with the kepala desa in Sembulan Lawang – expect to pay about 2500 rp per person, possibly more. Accommodation with the kepala desa in Sembulan Bumbung is more basic but will probably cost less than in Sembulan Lawang.

THE GILI ISLANDS

Off the north-west coast of Lombok are three small coral-fringed islands – Gili Air, Gili Meno and Gili Trawangan – with superb, white sandy beaches, clear water, coral reefs, brilliantly coloured fish – and the best snorkelling on Lombok. It's a toss up which you prefer and they're so close together it's quite easy to try each in turn. Although they're still relatively untouched these delightful dots on the map are rapidly becoming a major attraction.

Apart from Gili Trawangan's hill all three islands are pancake flat. Fishing, raising cattle and goats and growing corn, tapioca and peanuts are the main economic activities. Along with the growing number of tourists.

There are few facilities on these islands although some of the places to stay have their own electricity generators and there are small shops with a bare minimum of supplies. You may want to bring a few basic supplies with you like toilet paper, matches, a packet of biscuits or whatever. You can usually get a cool to cold beer at most places. There is no place to change money on the islands, in fact the nearest place to change money is back at Ampenan-Mataram. If possible bring your own snorkelling equipment although these days most of the losmen have some to lend.

Places to Stay & Eat

Most places on all three islands come out of the standard mould – you get a plain little bungalow, raised off the ground on stilts, with a small verandah out front. Inside there will be one or two beds with mosquito nets, the verandah will probably have a table and a couple of chairs. Mandi and toilet facilities are shared. The nightly costs are typically 7000/10,000 rp for singles/doubles and that includes breakfast, lunch and dinner plus tea or coffee on call. The food is simple but healthy and fresh, you live well here and

Bungalow, Gili Trawangan

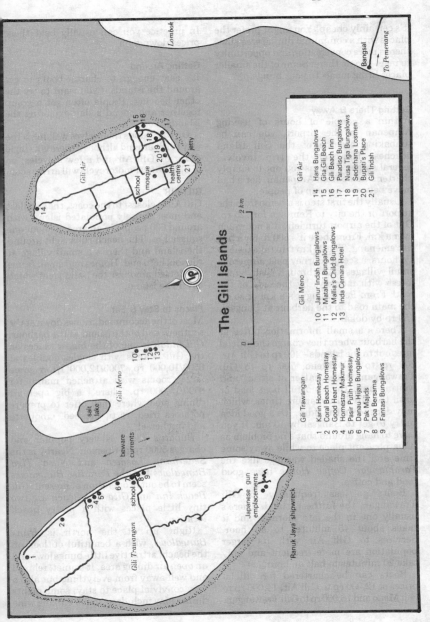

The Gili Islands

Gili Trawangan
1 Karin Homestay
2 Coral Beach Homestay
3 Good Heart Homestay
4 Homestay Makmur
5 Pasir Putih Homestay
6 Danau Hijau Bungalows
7 Pak Majids
8 Doa Bersama
9 Fantasi Bungalows

Gili Meno
10 Janur Indah Bungalows
11 Matahari Bungalows
12 Mallia's Child Bungalows
13 Inda Cemara Hotel

Gili Air
14 Hans Bungalows
15 Gita Gili Beach
16 Gili Beach Inn
17 Paradiso Bungalows
18 Nusa Tiga Bungalows
19 Sederhana Losmen
20 Bupati's Place
21 Gili Indah

Lombok

Bangsal

To Pemenang

Gili Air

Gili Meno

salt lake

beware currents

Gili Trawangan

Ranuk Jaya shipwreck

Japanese gun emplacements

school

mosque

health centre

jetty

2 km

it's certainly cheap! You might prefer the places with a communal dining area since there's more conversation and opportunity to meet people there. Some of the smaller places bring meals to your bungalow.

Getting There & Away

Within a couple of hours of leaving Ampenan or the airport, you can be sunbaking on one of the Gili Island beaches. However the trip involves several stages – unless you opt to simply charter a bemo from Ampenan, not a bad move between a group of people.

Usually the first step is a bemo from the airport or the city to Rembiga for 125 rp. Out of the airport turn left, it's not much over a km. From there it's 500 rp for a bus to Pemenang. The 25 km trip takes one to 1½ hours, a scenic journey past numerous small villages and through lush, green forest with monkeys by the side of the road. From Pemenang it's a km or so off the main road to the harbour at Bangsal, 150 rp by dokar.

There's a small information office at the harbour where they charge the official fares out to the islands – 400 rp to Gili Air, 600 rp to Gili Meno, 700 rp to Gili Trawangan. It's a matter of sitting and waiting until there's a full boat load or until the official departure times, which may depend on the tides. It's a good idea to try to get to Bangsal by 10 am. If you have to hang around that's no problem as it's a pleasant place to while away some time and the shaded warungs like the *Parahiangan Coffee House* have good food and coffee.

Boats go less frequently to Gili Trawangan, the furthest island. There's usually one in the late morning and it takes about 45 minutes to an hour. Services to Gili Air with its larger population are more frequent and only take 20 minutes to half an hour.

Boats can be chartered for official prices of 12,000 rp to Gili Air, 14,000 rp to Gili Meno and 16,000 rp to Gili Trawangan.

In practice you can usually beat those prices down a bit.

Getting Around

It's easy enough to charter boats to get around the islands if you want to try the other beaches. People often get a group together and spend a day exploring the islands.

On the islands themselves walking is the way to get around although there is a single dokar on Gili Air and a few bicycles; no doubt the first motorcycle will arrive soon.

GILI AIR

Gili Air is closest to the coast, the smallest and most densely populated island with around 600 people in an area of about one square km. The beach runs right around the island and there's a small village at the southern end. Homes and small farms are dotted amongst the palm trees which cover the island.

Places to Stay & Eat

Most of the accommodation is down at the southern end of the island at the harbour. *Gili Indah* is one of the bigger places on the Gili Islands with singles/doubles at 6500/10,000 rp, 7000/12,000 rp or some larger rooms with attached mandi for 8500/15,000 rp. There's a big open-air dining area where they offer to prepare potatoes fried, rösti, mashed, croquette and duchesse!

Bupati's Place is very popular and charges 5000 rp per person. Nearby is the *Sederhana Losmen* and *Nusa Tiga Bungalows* but the *Paradiso Bungalows* seem to be out of operation at present. *Gili Beach Inn* and *Gita Gili Beach* are two tiny little places with a pretty beach location.

Right up at the north is *Hans Bungalows*, with a beautiful outlook on the beach, attractive little bungalows and an open air dining area. It's quiet, relaxed and well away from everything but also a very convivial place to stay; some nights dinner may include as much banana wine as you can drink, and still stand up! Costs are 7000/10,000 rp for singles/doubles including all meals. You can arrange to be dropped off right at Hans, to save the walk from the harbour.

GILI MENO

Gili Meno is the middle island in size and location but has the smallest population, around 300. There's a salt lake in the middle of the island where salt is produced when it dries up in the dry season. It's said to cause mosquito problems at some times of year. Otherwise the island is much like the others with lots of palm trees and some fine snorkelling just off the beach.

Places to Stay & Eat

The accommodation here is all on the east beach and it's more varied than on the other islands. At the southern end there's the brand new *Inda Cemara*; planned to be the largest and most expensive hotel on the Gili Islands it's run by the Gazebo Hotel at Sanur, Bali. This is an indication that big time tourism has noticed what's happening here.

Next up is *Mallia's Child Bungalows* with straightforward rooms at 5000/10,000 rp or larger rooms at 7500/12,000/18,000 rp for a single/double/triple. One bungalow has rooms upstairs on a common verandah, ideal for a family. Then there's *Matahari Bungalows* and the *Janur Indah Bungalows* at similar prices to Mallia's Child. Again the bungalows here are a bit bigger than usual and Janur Indah also has triples. One km north from Janur Indah, past the planned Matan Bay development, is the quiet *Blue Coral* with only three bungalows.

GILI TRAWANGAN

Gili Trawangan is the largest island, with a population of about 400 and an area of about 3½ square km. It can be very dusty and dry at some times of the year but the snorkelling off the east coast here is simply superb. You just step out of your room, stroll across the beach and into the water, swim a few strokes out from the shore and there are fish everywhere. There's a nice little drop-off not far from the shore with lots of coral.

Beware of the rip which runs between Gili Trawangan and Gili Meno at the change of tide. The locals have got so used to foolish *orang turis* getting caught in it that they seem to have an outrigger ready and waiting to go and save their guests when necessary! On the other hand strong swimmers sometimes swim across to Gili Meno.

Like the other islands most of Gili Trawangan is very flat and much of the island has far fewer trees than Gili Air or Gili Meno. However, Gili Trawangan also has a hill rising abruptly at the south of the island. On the western flanks of the hill you can find traces of a couple of Japanese WW II gun emplacements. Down below on the reef is the wreck of the *Ranuk Jaya*, a Bugis schooner which went aground in 1985. In a few more years it will probably be totally demolished. It's quite easy to walk right around the island in a few hours.

Gili Trawangan has recently become the favourite island for travellers and new developments are springing up, including a bar that has opened near Coral Beach Homestay.

Places to Stay & Eat

The accommodation on Gili Trawangan is also along the east coast of the island, fronted by that wonderful beach. Starting at the south again there's *Fantasi Bungalows* and *Doa Bersama*, both in the standard format at the standard price of 7000/10,000 rp. *Pak Majid* is the original Gili Trawangan losmen and still deservedly popular. Pak's Javanese wife Suparmi cooks up a storm and it's a friendly place to stay with lots of fellow travellers to chat to. As well as the bungalows there are some cheaper and plainer rooms.

Continuing north other places are *Danau Hijau Bungalows, Pasir Putih Homestay, Homestay Makmur, Good*

Heart Homestay, Coral Beach Homestay and away at the northern tip of the island *Karin Homestay*. Homestay Makmur is another of the early places and over the years a number of people have written to recommend it as being a friendly place. As with most places on the Gilis, the food is wholesome but plain and can get very tiresome after a few days.

Sumbawa

Between Lombok and Flores and separated from them by narrow straits is the rugged land mass of Sumbawa. Larger than Bali and Lombok combined, Sumbawa is a sprawling island of twisted and jutting peninsulas, with a coast fringed by precipitous hills and angular bights, and a mountain line of weathered volcanic stumps stretching along its length.

Sumbawa is the most predominantly Muslim island anywhere east of Java or south of Sulawesi, and few places in Indonesia adhere to Islam in a more orthodox fashion. Christian missionaries never even bothered to try here. The people, particularly in the western half of the island, are curious about foreigners and on the whole pretty friendly – though they're more reserved around Bima in the east. Women travellers find life easier if they cover most of their bodies.

Islam seems to have obliterated much of Sumbawa's indigenous traditions, but it's a scenic island with plenty of scope for exploring off the beaten track. The mountain and coastal regions in the south – not converted to Islam until around the turn of the 20th century – and the Tambora peninsula in the north are rarely visited by outsiders. The villages will probably prove to be more interesting than the towns and if you're in the right place at the right time (on holidays and festivals) you might see traditional Sumbawan fighting, a sort of bare-fist boxing called *berempah*. Horse and water buffalo races are held before the rice is planted.

Towards the east end of the island, the narrow Bima Bay cuts deep into the north coast forming one of Indonesia's best natural harbours. It's surrounded by fertile lowlands which reach west into the rich interior Dompu plains.

History

For centuries Sumbawa has been divided between two linguistically – and to some extent ethnically – distinct peoples: the Sumbawanese speakers who probably reached the west of the island from Lombok, and the Bimanese speakers who independently occupied the east and the Tambora peninsula. The squatter, darker-skinned Bimanese are more closely related to the people of Flores, whilst the western Sumbawans are closer to the Sasaks of Lombok. Both their languages have considerable variation in dialect, but the spread of Bahasa Indonesia has made communication easier in the last couple of decades.

Sumbawa, with its rich timber resources in the west, was probably an early trading call for Javanese merchants on the way to or from the spice islands in Maluku. Bima and parts of western Sumbawa are said to have been under the control of the Javanese Majapahit empire, although it's more likely they simply sent tribute.

Along the western coastal lowlands the local population expanded and petty kingdoms developed along the entire length of the island. In eastern Sumbawa the region around Bima Bay, and probably later the Dompu plains, became the leading centres for the Bimanese-speaking population. Before 1600 these were probably animist kingdoms. By that time the domestic horse was being used and irrigated rice agriculture, possibly introduced by Javanese traders, was well established. There appears to have been some intermarriage between the Balinese and western Sumbawanese aristocracy

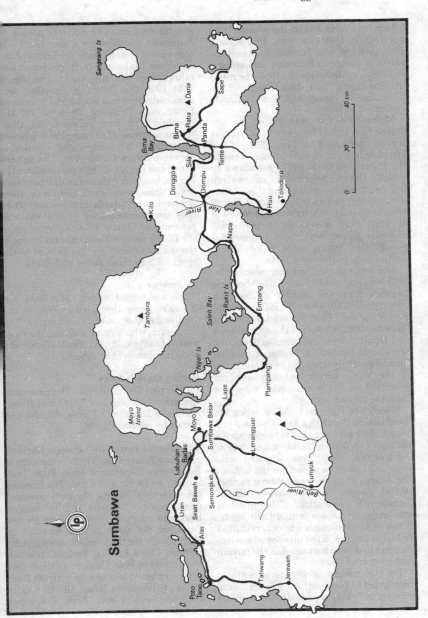

which may have linked the islands from the 15th or 16th centuries. In the early 17th century, the Islamic Makassarese states of southern Sulawesi undertook a military expansion and by 1625, the rulers of Sumbawa had been reduced to Makassarese vassals and had nominally converted to Islam.

Makassar's rise was halted by the Dutch East India Company (VOC) whose forces occupied it in 1669. Soon afterwards treaties were made between the Dutch and the rulers of Sumbawa by which Dutch hegemony in eastern Indonesia was recognised and these rulers were obliged to pay tribute to the Dutch who maintained only a distant supervision of what they considered a politically unstable island with poor commercial possibilities, taking more or less direct control only in the early 1900s.

The western Sumbawans, meanwhile, held nominal control over neighbouring Lombok from the middle of the 17th century till 1750, when the Balinese took it over instead. Then followed 30 years of sporadic warfare between the Sumbawans and the Balinese, including at least one large-scale Balinese invasion of western Sumbawa. Only through the intervention of the VOC, which was interested in maintaining the status quo, were the Balinese turned back.

Barely had the wars finished, when Mt Tambora on Sumbawa exploded in April 1815 killing perhaps 10,000 people with a shower of choking ash and molten debris. Agricultural land was wrecked and livestock and crops wiped out throughout the island. It's estimated that a further 66,000 people, nearly two-thirds of Sumbawa's population, either died of starvation or disease or fled their lands. Some went to other islands, others shifted to higher ground in the interior where less damage had been sustained or the terrain had recovered faster.

By the middle of the 19th century, immigrants from other islands were brought in to help repopulate the blighted

coastal regions. The 850,000 people o Sumbawa are therefore a diverse lot – i the coastal regions there are traces of the Javanese, Makassarese, Bugis, Sasak an other groups who migrated to the island

In 1908 the Dutch government sen administrators and soldiers to Sumbawa Besar and Taliwang to head off the possibility of war between the three separate states that comprised wester Sumbawa. This inaugurated a period o far more direct Dutch rule. The sultan kept a fair degree of their power under the Dutch, but after Indonesian independence their titles were abolished; now their descendants hold official power only when they are functionaries of the nationa government. Little evidence remains o the Dutch presence and the only traces o the old sultanates are the palaces in the towns of Sumbawa Besar and Bima.

Information

There's no tourist office on Sumbawa, but if you're going through Lombok on the way, call at the one at Jalan Langko 70 in Ampenan, which deals with Sumbawa as well as Lombok. It has some leaflets and a good relief map of Sumbawa.

Getting There & Away

Air Merpati flies daily from Denpasar and Mataram to Sumbawa Besar and Bima, and links Bima with Flores, Sumba and Timor by regular flights.

Boat Ferries run daily between Lombok and Poto Tano on the north-western tip of Sumbawa. Departures from Poto Tano are at 7 and 8 am and 1 pm. The crossing takes about 1½ hours: the early morning one is made in an older, smaller wooden boat, the others in more modern ferries. Fares are the same as from Lombok to Poto Tano – see the Lombok introductory Getting There & Away section. You can buy tickets at Poto Tano, or alternatively get a combined bus and ferry ticket from Bima or Sumbawa Besar all the way to Lombok, Bali or even Java. Combined ickets work out a little dearer but make things a bit easier. A three times weekly erry links Sape on the eastern end of Sumbawa with Labuhanbajo on Flores, topping at Komodo once a week. For its imetable and fares see the Sape ection.

Pelni's *Kelimutu* stops at Bima every week as it shuttles around Nusa Tenggara, Sulawesi, Bali, Kalimantan and Java. You nay be able to pick up other irregular boats rom Bima or smaller ports on Sumbawa.

Getting Around

Sumbawa's single main road runs all the way from Taliwang near the west coast through Sumbawa Besar, Dompu and Bima, to Sape on the east coast. It's surfaced all the way. Fleets of buses, many of them new and comfortable by Nusa Tenggara standards, link all the towns on this road. Particularly in the east of the island, watch out for brats who try to pinch things – including your person – through bus windows. Off the main drag, the roads are mostly dirt but older buses or trucks still head out to most of the distant towns and villages. There are no longer any flights between Sumbawa Besar and Bima.

In towns there are some bemos, but for short trips Sumbawa must be the dokar capital of Indonesia: these rattling horse buggies with their jingling bells are fun, cheap and reach surprising speeds!

POTO TANO

The port for ferries to and from Lombok is a shabby little straggle of stilt houses beside a mangrove-lined bay. It's a few km of dirt track away from Sumbawa's single main road.

Getting There & Away

Buses drop you or await you in a raucous yard beside the ferry ticket office at the entrance to the pier. There's quite a melee when ferries arrive from Lombok as bus conductors try to fill up all the waiting buses quickly. Save a bit of hassle by buying a bus ticket from the guys who come round selling them on the ferry – their prices are the same as you pay on dry land. Fares and journey times: Taliwang 1500 rp, one hour; Alas 1000 rp, one hour; Sumbawa Besar 2000 rp, 2½ hours; Bima 6500 rp, 10 hours.

Buses to Poto Tano from elsewhere on Sumbawa connect with the ferry departures.

TALIWANG

During the 19th century Taliwang was one of the 'vassal states' of the kingdom of Sumbawa based in Sumbawa Besar. Today it's a sleepy, oversized village, with people who can be friendly and curious almost to the point of being overpowering. It lies close to the west coast of Sumbawa, 30 km from Poto Tano along a narrow road winding through the hills. By the road into Taliwang, coming from the north, is Lake Taliwang.

Potobatu, six km from Taliwang, is a local sea resort with many caves, and a decent white-sand beach. Trucks from Taliwang cost 100 rp. Labuhanbalat is a fishing community of just eight houses, seven km from Taliwang – take a truck or dokar there.

Places to Stay & Eat

Taliwang's market is next to the bus station. Behind the market is the lemon-coloured *Losmen Ashar*, with spartan but clean rooms for 1500 rp per person. There's another losmen in front of the cinema in the opposite direction from the bus station, and a tiny rumah makan at the bus station.

Getting There & Away

Direct buses from the ferry at Poto Tano to Taliwang are expensive at 1500 rp. Regular buses between Alas and Taliwang cost just 1000 rp for a 1½-hour trip. There are some direct buses from Taliwang to Sumbawa Besar (2000 rp), but you'll most likely have to change at Alas.

Local transport in Taliwang

ALAS

'Alas' is Javanese for 'forest' and may have received its name from Javanese timber traders. It's an ordinary little town on the north coast road between Poto Tano and Sumbawa Besar, with the usual very interested people.

Labuhan Alas

The little port just off the Sumbawa Besar road about three km east of Alas was, until 1988, the terminal for ferries from Lombok. It's set in a pretty little bay and is not much more than a dock and a few houses. A Sulawesi fishing village clusters offshore on stilts, with television antennae jutting up from its roofs. Dokars (100 rp) run to and from Alas.

Places to Stay & Eat

Losmen Selamat (tel 26) at Jalan Pahlawan 7 in Alas has good clean rooms for 1750 rp per person, or 2000 rp with private mandi. It's a one-minute walk in the Sumbawa Besar direction from the bus/bemo/dokar station. A further 700 metres up the same road the *Losmen Anda* has rooms with small patios round a

garden for 2500 rp per person. The *Rumah Makan Sebra* beside the bus station serves reasonable food – fish, sambal and *lodeh* (a vegetable dish with jackfruit, beans and beanshoots) for 1000 rp. You can buy fruit at the bus station.

Getting There & Away

Buses go to Sumbawa Besar (1000 rp, about 1¾ hours), to Poto Tano (1000 rp, one hour) for the ferries and to Taliwang (1000 rp, 1½ hours).

SUMBAWA BESAR

At one time the name 'Sumbawa' only applied to the western half of the island – the region over which the Sultan of the state of Sumbawa held sway; the eastern half of the island was known as Bima. Almost all that remains of the old western sultanate is the wooden palace in Sumbawa Besar – the showpiece of the town.

Sumbawa Besar is the chief town in the western half of the island; a friendly place of concrete block houses, thatch-roofed and woven-walled stilt bungalows, shacks clinging to hillsides and footpaths of small oulders connecting them with dirt roads. The people are very interested in oreigners – even the women will come and practise their few words of English – and he place has quite an 'Asian' feel to it, with dokars rattling round the streets and Muslim men flooding out of the mosques after mid-day prayer. The town itself has no 'attractions' except the old palace, but rips out to villages or Moyo Island might prove rewarding.

If you want to do someone a favour introduce yourself to Mr Muhammad Yusuf at SMA 1 (high school). He's a Florinese who teaches English and is only too glad to get conversation practice. He'll show you around and take you to his tiny bungalow perched on the side of a hill to meet his wife and kids. Try and leave him an English book if you have one spare.

Information

Bank The Bank Negara Indonesia (tel 21936) is at Jalan Kartini 10. It's open Monday to Saturday from 7.30 am to 1 pm. They'll change major foreign currencies and travellers' cheques from larger companies like Thomas Cook, American Express, and Bank of America, so long as they're in US or Australian dollars.

Post For poste restante, go to the main post office which is out past the airport on Jalan Garuda (fairly regular bemos 150 rp). For stamps, there's also a sub-post office near the town centre on Jalan Yos Sudarso. Both are open Monday to Thursday from 8 am to 2 pm, plus Friday until 11 am and Saturday until 12.30 pm.

PHPA The national parks people (tel 21358) are in the Direktorat Jenderal Kehutanan office at Jalan Garuda 12. See them about trips to Moyo Island. The office is open until 2 pm Monday to Thursday, 11 am Friday and 12 noon Saturday.

Maps There are large maps of Sumbawa

Island in the Hotel Tambora restaurant and the Tirtasari reception.

Sultan's Palace (Dalam Loka)

Back in the early '60s Helen and Frank Schreider passed through Sumbawa Besar in their amphibious jeep, and later described the remnants of this palace in their book *The Drums of Tonkin*:

Sumbawa Besar... had a sultan. A small man with tortoise-shell glasses and a quiet, friendly dignity... his old palace, now deserted except for a few distant relatives, was a long barn-like structure of unpainted wood that seemed on the point of collapsing. Beneath the ramshackle entrance, a rusted cannon from the days of the Dutch East India Company lay half-buried in the ground... Mothers and fathers and naked little children made the palace shake as they followed us up the ramp into a great empty room that was once the audience chamber... Only when the few remaining court costumes, the faded silver brocade kains, the gold-handled krises and the long gold fingernails that were a sign of royalty's exemption from labour were modelled for us did we have any idea of the extravagance of this past era. By government decree, the sultans are no longer in power.

The palace was restored in the early 1980s – only a few of the original pillars and carved beams remain. It's an interesting wooden building, set on stilts, with a sloping walkway leading up to the 1st floor. Boys will show you round and tell you (in Indonesian) what each room was used for – though there's little in them except a couple of old palanquins. Then they'll ask you to make a donation towards the cost of turning the place into a museum.

New Palace

The imposing building with the bell tower at its gate on Jalan Merdeka is the HQ of the *bupati* (head government official) of west Sumbawa. It's built in imitation of the style of the old sultan's palace – a reminder that the national government now holds the power that was once the sultan's.

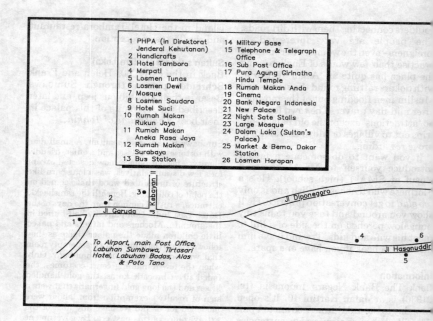

1 PHPA (in Direktorat Jenderal Kehutanan)
2 Handicrafts
3 Hotel Tambora
4 Merpati
5 Losmen Tunas
6 Losmen Dewi
7 Mosque
8 Losmen Saudara
9 Hotel Suci
10 Rumah Makan Rukun Jaya
11 Rumah Makan Aneka Rasa Jaya
12 Rumah Makan Surabaya
13 Bus Station
14 Military Base
15 Telephone & Telegraph Office
16 Sub Post Office
17 Pura Agung Girinatha Hindu Temple
18 Rumah Makan Anda
19 Cinema
20 Bank Negara Indonesia
21 New Palace
22 Night Sate Stalls
23 Large Mosque
24 Dalam Loka (Sultan's Palace)
25 Market & Bemo, Dokar Station
26 Losmen Harapan

Jl Diponegoro

Kebayan II

Jl Garuda

To Airport, main Post Office, Labuhan Sumbawa, Tirtasari Hotel, Labuhan Badas, Alas & Poto Tano

Jl Hasanuddir

Pura Agung Girinatha

This Balinese Hindu temple is on Jalan Yos Sudarso near the corner of Jalan Setiabudi. It's small and usually locked. Next door is a *banjar*, a Balinese community hall.

Handicrafts

The Kantor Departemen Perindustrian (Small Industries Department), on Jalan Garuda near the PHPA office, has a display of Sumbawan handicrafts (most for sale) and, if you speak a bit of Indonesian, can tell you where and how they're made and what they're used for. The most interesting items are *songket* ceremonial sarongs and shawls. You won't find much songket anywhere east of Sumbawa in Nusa Tenggara: it's an almost exclusively Muslim craft.

The Hotel Tambora near this office has a shop selling fabric from Sumbawa and other parts of Nusa Tenggara.

Places to Stay

Four losmen are lined up along Jalan Hasanuddin, a five-minute walk from the bus station. All are also in easy range of the 5 am wake-up call from the mosque! *Hotel Suci* (tel 21589) is probably the best of this group. The shabby but clean rooms surround a courtyard and garden which keep out much of the traffic noise. Singles/doubles are 3500/4500 rp without fan, or 6000/7700 rp with air-con. All have private mandi and toilet and a snack breakfast is included. On the same side of the road the *Losmen Tunas* (tel 21212) is friendly and reasonably clean at 2200/3500 rp with attached mandi.

Losmen Saudara (tel 21528), opposite the Suci, has lots of traffic noise and is grubby. Singles/doubles are 3300/5600 rp with private mandi, 2000/3000 rp without, but they'll ask for more. *Losmen Dewi* (tel 21170) is no cleaner but the layout of the building holds much of the traffic noise at

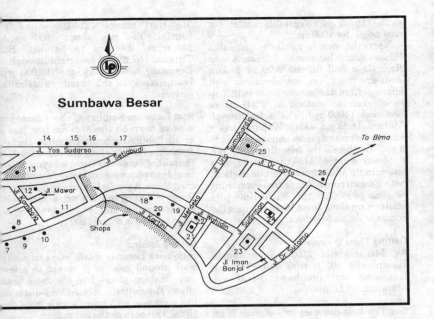

Sumbawa Besar

To Bima

JL Yos Sudarso

Jl Setiabudi

Jl Mawar

Jl Kamboja

Shops

Jl Kartini

Jl Merdeka

Jl Urip

Jl Dr Cipto

Jl Sumbawa

Jl Wahidin

Jl Sudirman

Jl Dr Sutomo

Jl Iman Bonjol

bay. Rooms with attached mandi and toilet are 3000/4500 rp.

A good alternative to Jalan Hasanuddin is the *Losmen Harapan* on Jalan Dr Cipto, where clean rooms with private mandi and an endless supply of tea cost 2500/3500 rp.

Easily the best place in the town itself is the *Hotel Tambora* (tel 21555), just off Jalan Garuda on Jalan Kebayan II, a 15-minute walk from the bus terminal (or take a dokar for 100 rp per person). Singles/doubles are 4000/5000 rp with a mandi; 6000/8000 rp with a fan; 15,000/20,000 rp with all mod cons including bathtub, shower, air-con and TV. The hotel has its own restaurant and is helpful to travellers.

The most attractive hotel of all – if you don't mind a 10-minute bemo ride from town – is *Tirtasari* (tel 21987), by the beachfront 5½ km west of Sumbawa Besar on the road to Alas. It has a good restaurant and is set in a garden; there's also a swimming pool but don't rely on it containing water. Clean economy rooms with private mandi are 5500 rp single or double; standard rooms for 11,000 rp have verandahs facing the sea and are airy and comfortable with a semi-open-air shower and toilet; there are also VIP rooms for 16,500 rp, even a 'sweet room' at 33,000 rp. In all except economy, a breakfast of egg with toast and coffee is part of the price. Buses from the west can drop you at Tirtasari on the way into Sumbawa Besar.

Places to Eat

The restaurants in the Hotel Tambora and Tirtasari are probably the best. The Tambora has a long menu with items ranging from stir-fried vegetables at 1000 rp to chicken, crab, prawn or squid for 2500 to 3500 rp. The Tirtasari is similar: the prawns fried in butter (*mentega*) are good at 2500 rp, or get a vegetable omelette or nasi pecel for 1000 rp.

Near the centre of town on Jalan Hasanuddin, the *Rumah Makan Aneka Rasa Jaya* and *Rumah Makan Rukun Jaya* are two clean, newish places with offerings from *nasi goreng biasa* at 1250 rp to chicken or seafood at 2500 rp or beefsteak (4000 rp). The older *Rumah Makan Anda* on Jalan Wahidin has a similar menu and prices and stays open to 9 pm. Or there's the friendly, cheap but flyblown *Rumah Makan Surabaya*, a one-minute walk from the bus station, with a menu consisting of nasi everything or gado-gado (750 rp). Night-time sate stalls set up along Jalan Wahidin, near the corner of Jalan Merdeka.

Getting There & Away
Air Merpati (tel 21026) is at Jalan Hasanuddin 80. It flies daily between Denpasar and Sumbawa Besar via Mataram on Lombok.

Bus The long-distance bus station is on Jalan Diponegoro. Fares, distances and approximate journey times from Sumbawa Besar include:

Dompu	190 km	3500 rp	5½ hours
Bima	250 km	4500 rp	7½ hours
Alas	69 km	1000 rp	1¾ hours
Poto Tano		2000 rp	2½ hours

Buses leave for Poto Tano at 4 and 9 am to catch the 8 am and 1 pm ferries to Lombok. Buses start for Bima hourly from 7 to 10 am, but after that you have to hope for a seat on a bus coming through from the ferries at Poto Tano.

You can buy combined bus and ferry services from Sumbawa Besar through to Lombok or Bali. The Langsung Jaya bus leaving at 9 am daily will have you in Mataram, Lombok, about 5 pm and the same company has a service through to Lembar where you board the Lombok-Bali ferry. Get tickets from Toko Titian Mas (tel 21686) at Jalan Kartini 89, or

Toko Hari Terang (tel 21403) also on Jala Kartini. You pay about 7000 rp t Mataram, 9000 rp to Lembar. Bu Tirtasari (tel 21079) goes right through t Denpasar every day for 16,000 rp Losmens may be able to tell you of simila services.

Boat Labuhan Sumbawa, about three km west of town on the Alas road, is just small fishing harbour. Labuhan Badas seven km further along the same road, i the port of Sumbawa Besar and you *migh* be able to pick up a coastal or inter-island craft there. A public bemo from Sumbawa Besar is 200 rp but it's not a very well trodden route and you may have t charter one for about 1500 rp.

Getting Around
Sumbawa Besar is small; you can easily walk around most of it except to a few more distant places like the main post office. The centrally located long-distance bus station is a 15-minute walk from the Hotel Tambora or the old palace.

The local bemo and dokar station is at the corner of Jalan Setiabudi and Jalan Urip Sumohardjo but if you want a bemo out west to, say, the Hotel Tambora, the airport, the main post office, Labuhan Sumbawa or the Tirtasari it's simpler to flag one down on Jalan Hasanuddin. Dokars are 100 rp per person just about anywhere round town. Bemos are 150 rp, even as far as the Tirtasari which is 5½ km out.

For trips to villages, etc, around Sumbawa Besar, there should be public buses or bemos but alternatively you could charter a bemo for maybe 10,000 to 15,000 rp a day. The Tirtasari rents motorbikes for 550 rp an hour or 5000 rp a day plus petrol.

AROUND SUMBAWA BESAR
Moyo Island
Two-thirds of Moyo Island, off the coast just north of Sumbawa Besar, is a nature reserve. There are good coral reefs with

lots of fish at the southern rim of the island – but watch out for currents and sharks – and a number of villages in the north. Moyo rises to 648 metres and its centre is composed mainly of savannah with stands of forest. The reserve is inhabited by wild domestic cattle, deer, wild pigs, and several varieties of birds.

Getting There & Away

Make arrangements with the PHPA in Sumbawa Besar, which has a good map of Moyo. The PHPA can help you find a ride on a motorbike to Aik Bari on the coast half an hour north of Sumbawa Besar. From there hire a fishing boat for the three-km crossing to the south coast of the island. You must negotiate your own prices: about 2000 to 5000 rp per person each way for the motorbike, 10,000 rp each way for the boat, including all petrol. There are four PHPA guard posts on Moyo – one at the south end, the others in villages – where you can stay overnight for 2500 rp per person, but take your own food and water. It's about an eight-hour walk from the south to the centre of the island, and about six hours across the middle from east to west.

The PHPA may have a snorkel to lend but don't count on it. You might be able to get a boat independently from Labuhan Sumbawa to Moyo for about 25,000 rp return. The Tirtasari hotel has a boat on which you can do a Moyo day trip for 45,000 rp.

Other Attractions

Look out for 'horse racing' – in reality boys on ponies but still a big local event – around Sumbawa Besar from August to October. Some of the best songket sarongs are made in the village of Poto 12 km east of Sumbawa Besar (500 rp by bus or bemo) and two km from the small town of Moyo. At Semongkat, about 15 km up the road which leads south-west from Sumbawa Besar into the hills, there's an old Dutch swimming pool fed by a mountain river. A stretch of the south coast near Lunyuk,

about 60 km from Sumbawa Besar, is said to be a nesting ground for giant turtles. Liang Petang and Liang Bukal are caves near Batu Tering village which locals say are worth a visit. Take a torch. Batu Tering is about 25 km from Sumbawa Besar: you turn off the Bima road after about 10 km. There should be buses to all these places – ask.

CENTRAL SUMBAWA

It's a beautiful ride from Sumbawa Besar to Bima. After Empang you start moving up into the hills through rolling green countryside, thickly forested with the occasional spray of palm trees along the shoreline.

Mt Tambora

Dominating the peninsula which juts north in central Sumbawa is the 2820-metre volcano, Tambora. Apparently it can be climbed from the western side; the huge crater contains a two-coloured lake and there are views as far as Mt Rinjani on Lombok. The usual base for ascents is the small logging town of Cilacai, which is eight hours by truck from Dompu, or an hour by speedboat from Sumbawa Besar. The climb is said to take three days.

Tambora's peak was obliterated in the explosion of April 1815 (see Sumbawa History), but since then all has been quiet. The eruption wiped out the entire populations (perhaps 8000 people) of Tambora and Pekat, two small states at the base of the mountain, as well as devastating much of the rest of Sumbawa.

Dompu

The seat of one of Sumbawa's former independent small states, Dompu is now the third biggest town on the island but if you're travelling between Sumbawa Besar and Bima you don't get to see it: buses detour via the lonely Ginte bus station on a hill two km out of Dompu. From there bemos run into town if you need one. There are a few cheapish losmens in Dompu, which is about two hours (1000 rp) by bus from Bima, 5½ hours (3500 rp) from Sumbawa Besar.

Huu

On the coast south of Dompu, this is where surfers head for on Sumbawa. Special surf camps set up by Australian companies are nearby. You can daytrip from Dompu or stay with the Huu kepala desa for maybe 2000 rp a night. Take your own food and water.

Donggo

Buses run to the village of Donggo from Sila on the Dompu-Bima road (500 rp by bus from Dompu or Bima to Sila). You should be able to stay with the kepala desa in Donggo, on the flank of the mountainous west side of Bima Bay. The Dou Donggo ('mountain people') living in these highlands speak an archaic form of the Bima language, and may be descended from the original inhabitants of Sumbawa. Numbering about 20,000 they've adopted Islam and Christianity instead of their traditional animism over the past few decades with varying degrees of enthusiasm; they're being absorbed into Bimanese culture and will probably eventually disappear as a distinct group. The most traditional village is Mbawa where, at least until a few years ago, people still wore distinctive black clothes. A few *uma leme*, traditional houses whose design was intimately connected with the traditional religion, were still standing.

BIMA & RABA

The conurbation of Bima and Raba is the major town in the eastern half of Sumbawa. Bima, Sumbawa's chief port, is the main centre; Raba, a few km east, is the departure point for buses east to Sape where you get the ferry to Komodo or Flores.

Bima is one of the most orthodox Muslim areas in Indonesia: girls play volleyball in full headscarves and body-coverings. Bimanese are distinctly cooler to outsiders than are the people of western Sumbawa. The Bima region has been known since the 14th century for its sturdy horses, which even then were being exported to Java. Local tradition claims that before the 17th century, when Bima fell to the Makassarese and its ruler was converted to Islam, it had some sort of political control over Timor, Sumba and parts of western Flores.

Today, the former sultan's palace apart, the town is a collection of ramshackle buildings that look like they're either in the middle of being built or in the middle of being demolished. Apart from the usual 'Hello Misters' some of the kids have learnt to say 'I love you'. The Jalan Flores night market is worth a wander. Mick Jagger and President Suharto rub shoulders among the posters on sale there.

Information

Bank The Bank Negara Indonesia 1946 on Jalan Sultan Hasanuddin will change major travellers' cheques in US and Australian dollars, as well as cash provided it's in major currencies. The bank is open from 7.30 am to 1.30 pm Monday to Friday and from 7.30 am to 12 noon Saturday.

Post The post office is on Jalan Kampung Salama, out in the eastern suburbs past the palace. A dokar from the centre costs 100 rp. Approximate opening hours are Monday to Thursday from 8 am to 2 pm, Friday 8 to 11 am, Saturday 8 am to 12 noon.

Sultan's Palace

The former home of Bima's rulers – until they were put out of a job after Indonesian independence – is now partly a museum. The building itself is less impressive than its counterpart at Sumbawa Besar but the exhibits inside – chainmail shirts, sedan chairs, battle flags, weapons, a chart comparing the alphabets of Indonesian languages with our Latin alphabet – hold some interest. The palace had fallen into

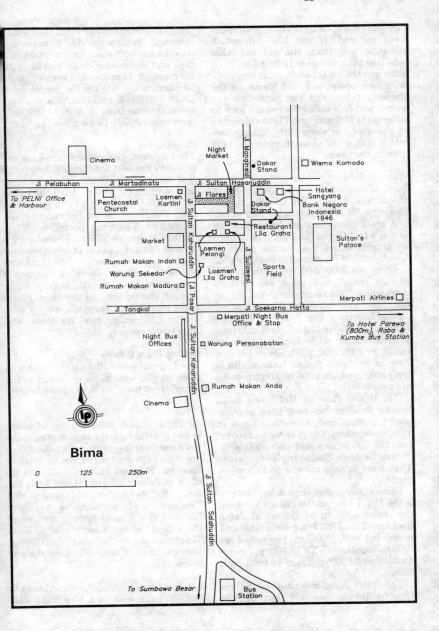

Bima

0   125   250m

To PELNI Office
& Harbour

To Sumbawa Besar

To Hotel Parewa
(800m), Raba &
Kumbe Bus Station

Cinema

Jl Pelabuhan

Jl Martadinata

Pentecostal
Church

Losmen
Kartini

Night
Market

Dokar
Stand

Jl Mangisidi

Wisma Komodo

Jl Sultan Hasanuddin

Jl Flores

Hotel
Sangyang

Jl Sultan Kaharuddin

Dokar
Stand

Bank Negara
Indonesia
1946

Market

Losmen
Pelangi

Restaurant
Lila Graha

Sultan's
Palace

Rumah Makan Indah

Warung Sekedar

Rumah Makan Madura

Losmen
Lila Graha

Jl Pasar

Jl Sulawesi

Sports
Field

Merpati Airlines

Jl Tongkol

Jl Soekarno Hatta

Merpati Night Bus
Office & Stop

Night Bus
Offices

Warung Persanabatan

Jl Sultan Kaharuddin

Rumah Makan Anda

Cinema

Jl Sultan Salahuddin

Bus
Station

complete disrepair by the late '50s but has been restored. If you look interested, someone will fetch the old caretaker who'll explain things in Indonesian. He'll show you the royal bedchamber complete with four-poster bed and Koran on the dressing table, and can rattle off the names and dates of all the sultans back to at least the 17th century. There are photos of the tombs of some early Bima rulers which still stand somewhere in the hills outside the town.

Places to Stay

Bima is compact and most losmen are in the middle of town. You usually have to bargain a bit to get the right room price.

A good place to start looking is the *Losmen Lila Graha* (tel 740), a 10-minute walk from Bima bus station at Jalan Lombok 20. With shared mandi, singles/doubles are 3500/5500 rp; doubles with private mandi and toilet are 6600 rp downstairs, 7700 rp upstairs. You get an egg, toast and coffee breakfast. Also on Jalan Lombok, the friendly *Losmen Pelangi* (tel 878) has small, dark but clean singles/doubles with fan and private mandi for 4500/5500 rp. The dingy *Losmen Kartini* on Jalan Sultan Kaharuddin is truly spartan from 2500/5000 rp; mandis are communal.

The *Wisma Komodo* (tel 70) on Jalan Sultan Ibrahim has long been popular with travellers and, at certain times of year, mosquitoes. Large three-bed rooms face the old palace and cost 4000/5000/6000 rp for single/double/triple occupancy. They have private mandis and there's a garden.

Bima's only vaguely upmarket hostelry is the *Hotel Parewa* (tel 652), a km from the centre (100 rp by dokar) at Jalan Soekarno Hatta 40. It's comfortable and roomy but dull. Standard fan rooms are 7000 rp double, with TV 12,100 rp; air-con doubles are 24,000 rp. There's a restaurant here.

The *Hotel Sangyang* on Jalan Sultan Hasanuddin was obviously designed to be the top place in town but is usually echoingly empty – could be something to do with its reputation for waterless baths, taps and distressing drain smells. Still the manager's friendly and keen – it might be worth a try. He can be bargained to about 5500/8000 rp in 'standard' rooms (with antique fans) or 8000/11,000 rp in large comfortable-looking 'fan' rooms.

Places to Eat

The brightest, cleanest surroundings and probably the best food are at the central *Restaurant Lila Graha*. Gado-gado or nasi campur are 1000 rp, fried chicken or prawns 2500 rp, and you can get a beer here. The Hotel Parewa restaurant is OK too with its nasi goreng special for 1250 rp, chicken or prawns 3000 rp. Elsewhere the *Rumah Makan Anda* out towards the bus station is a little cheaper, less clean and the food's ordinary. There's a selection of even more basic rumah makan along Jalan Kaharuddin, and the Jalan Flores night market has foodstalls serving sate, curry, gado-gado, rice creations and interesting snacks.

Getting There & Away

Heading eastwards Bima is the last major town on the way to Sape, which is the jumping-off point for Komodo and Flores Islands.

Air Bima airport is 16 km out of town: bemos (300 rp) from the airport gates to the town can be infrequent, taxis ask 6000 rp but can be bargained down to 1000 or 2000 rp. Merpati (tel 197/382) has its office at Jalan Soekarno Hatta 30. It has daily flights to/from Mataram and Denpasar with connections to Java. Merpati also flies at least every two or three days to/from other places in Nusa Tenggara including Labuhanbajo, Ruteng, Bajawa, Ende, Kupang, Tambolaka and Waingapu.

Bus Bima bus station, for most buses to and from the west, is a 10-minute walk

Top: Pelabuhan Sape, Sumbawa, Nusa Tenggara (AS)
Bottom: 'Smiles all around' Larantuka, Flores, Nusa Tenggara (AS)

Top: Brahmin bulls, Sumba, Nusa Tenggara (AS)
Left: Stone tomb at Prai Bokul, Sumba, Nusa Tenggara (AS)
Right: Effigy on tomb at Rende, Sumba, Nusa Tenggara (AS)

from the centre of town (100 rp by dokar). In addition to daytime buses, there are night buses on which you can get tickets to Lombok, Bali or Java with ferry fares included. Bus ticket offices are mostly near the corner of Jalan Sultan Kaharuddin and Jalan Soekarno Hatta in the town. For night buses it's advisable to get a ticket in advance – some of them leave from the town instead of the bus station.

Regular fares from Bima include Dompu 1000 rp (two hours) and Sumbawa Besar 4500 rp (7½ hours). Night buses leave about 7 or 8 pm and are a bit more expensive. The most comfortable is the Merpati night bus (tel 825) which departs from its office at Jalan Soekarno Hatta 33. Fares include Sumbawa Besar 5500 rp, Mataram 13,000 rp (arriving about 12 noon), Denpasar 23,500 rp, Surabaya 32,500 rp. Other night buses such as Damai Indah or Surya Kencana tend to be about 10% cheaper.

Buses east to Sape go from Kumbe bus station in Raba, a 20-minute bemo ride (150 rp) east of Bima. Catch the bemo from Jalan Sultan Hasanuddin or Jalan Soekarno Hatta in Bima. Buses leave Kumbe for Sape from about 7.30 am till late afternoon. The trip takes 1½ to two hours and costs 750 rp. Don't rely on these buses for getting to Sape in the early morning in time for the ferry to Komodo or Flores. Losmens in Bima, however, usually sell tickets for a special 1500 rp bus to Sape that picks up in Bima itself in the early morning in time to get you to the ferry.

Boat Pelni (tel 203) is in the port of Bima at Jalan Pelabuhan 103; take a dokar there for 100 rp. The *Kelimutu* calls at Bima every second Friday on the way to Waingapu, Ende and Kupang; and on Tuesdays in intervening weeks en route for Ujung Pandang, Lombok, Bali, Java and Kalimantan.

Fares in 1st class/2nd class/economy to Sumba and Sulawesi are: Waingapu (12 hours) 34,000/26,900/14,700 rp; and Ujung Pandang (17 hours) 38,400/30,300/15,600 rp.

There are other irregular ships from Bima to various destinations – ask around the port to see if any cargo boats will take passengers.

SAPE

Sape is a pleasant little town with amiable people and immense numbers of dokars, which the locals call Ben Hurs from their faint resemblance to the vehicles made famous by the movie of that name. These jingling little buggies with their skinny pompommed horses don't look much like Roman chariots, but the drivers obviously think they're Charlton Heston as they race each other along the main street after dark.

If you have to wait for the ferry to Komodo or Flores then it's as well to wait here as in Bima (as long as you aren't run down by an express dokar). The ferry leaves from Pelabuhan Sape which is about three km down the road from Sape.

Information

There's a PHPA office, a two-minute walk down the road from the Losmen Give, but it can't tell you anything about Komodo. That job belongs to a second PHPA office a further 1½ km down the road towards Pelabuhan Sape, which has some interesting-looking maps and charts but doesn't seem to open till just before the ferry leaves. Go the previous day before 2 pm if you want to talk to the people there.

Places to Stay

A new losmen is being built beside the bus station on the road to Pelabuhan Sape which may be an improvement on the existing options, which are the *Losmen Friendship* and the *Losmen Give*, about 100 metres apart. The Friendship is the better choice. It charges 2500 rp per person, is basic but friendly and the rooms and shared mandis are clean. You can get a reasonable meal for 1000 rp. The Give costs 2500/3500 rp for singles/doubles

Fishing boats at Sape

but the owner has a knack of trying to put extra people into your room and/or wanting to up the price after you've agreed it. There's also a persistent tale that someone was murdered there not very long ago.

Places to Eat

If you're not eating in your losmen, two rumah makan between the market and the bridge specialise in nasi campur suitable for convicts and concentration camp inmates. The *Rumah Makan Pusaka*, if you can find it, reportedly does a good *soto kambing* plus rice and tea for 1000 rp. Or stock up in the market and shops.

Getting There & Away

Bus For points west, you must go to Bima then take another bus from there. Sape bus station is on the Pelabuhan Sape side of town but most buses also hang around a while just past the bridge on the way out towards Bima. The fare to Bima is 750 rp.

Some buses may meet ferries arriving at Pelabuhan Sape.

Boat The ferry to Labuhanbajo on Flores leaves three times a week from Pelabuhan Sape, the port about three km down the road from Sape. Once a week the ferry calls in at Komodo Island which is about two-thirds of the way to Labuhanbajo. But to visit Komodo, it can be better to go all the way to Labuhanbajo then come back to Komodo – see the Komodo Getting There & Away section.

Pelabuhan Sape is just one street leading down to the dock, lined by the stilt houses of Bugis people from Sulawesi whose chief hobby is building anything from canoes to galleons beside their houses. The ferry schedule is:

Pelabuhan Sape-Komodo-Labuhanbajo departs Pelabuhan Sape at 8 am every Saturday.

Pelabuhan Sape-Labuhanbajo departs

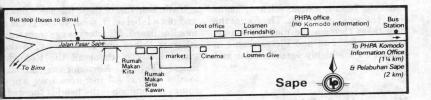

Pelabuhan Sape at 9 am every Monday and Wednesday.

Labuhanbajo-Komodo-Pelabuhan Sape departs Labuhanbajo at 8 am every Tuesday.

Labuhanbajo-Pelabuhan Sape departs Labuhanbajo at 9 am every Thursday and Sunday.

You can buy tickets at the Pelabuhan Sape harbour office on the morning of departure, after paying 100 rp port entry charge. Sape-Labuhanbajo and Sape-Komodo fares are both 6700 rp. Between Komodo

and Labuhanbajo only, it's 2100 rp. You can take a bicycle from Sape to Labuhanbajo for 1300 rp, a motorcycle for 5700 rp, a jeep for 50,000 rp, a car for 60,000 rp. The duration of the crossing varies with tides and weather but allow five to seven hours from Sape to Komodo, seven to 10 hours to Labuhanbajo. You can buy drinks and the odd light snack on the ferry but it's advisable to bring a few supplies with you – unless of course the wind's up, in which case you'll probably be more concerned with things coming out of your stomach than with putting things in it.

On the way out from Pelabuhan Sape,

Fishing boats at Sape

Sangeang Island, a huge volcano, looms out of the ocean on the left. The course the ferry takes through the maze of islands between Sumbawa and Flores seems to depend on the highly variable tides and winds.

Komodo & Rinca

A hilly, desolate island sandwiched between Flores and Sumbawa, Komodo's big attraction is lizards – three metre, 130 kg monsters, appropriately known as Komodo dragons. The island is surrounded by some of the most tempestuous waters in Indonesia, fraught with rip tides and whirlpools. From the sea it looks far more fitting for a monstrous lizard than for the few hundred people who live in its lone village.

Komodo gets a constant stream of visitors these days, but to understand how far off the beaten track it used to be, read *Zoo Quest for a Dragon* by naturalist-adventurer-TV personality David Attenborough who filmed the dragons in 1956. Dragons also inhabit the nearby islands of Rinca and Padar and coastal west Flores. Some people now prefer to visit Rinca rather than Komodo since it's closer to the Flores coast, has fewer other visitors and dragon-spotting is less organised – if less certain of success.

Komodo Dragons
There were rumours of these awesome creatures long before their existence was confirmed in the west. Fishermen and pearl divers working in the area had brought back tales of ferocious lizards with enormous claws, fearsome teeth and a fiery yellow tongues. One theory holds that the Chinese dragon is based on the Komodo lizard. The first Dutch expedition to the island was in 1910; two of the dragons were shot and their skins taken to Java, resulting in the first published description.

If you hold one of these monsters down and pin a label on it, what you've got is a monitor lizard. Monitors range from tiny 20 gram things just 20 cm long, to the grand-daddy of them all the Komodo dragon (*Varanus Komodoensis*), known locally as *ora*. All monitors have some things in common – the head is tapered, the ear-openings are visible, the neck is long and slender, the eyes have eyelids and round pupils, and the jaws are powerful. The body is usually massive with four powerful legs, each bearing five clawed toes. The tail is long and thick and functions as a rudder, and can also be used for grasping and as a potent weapon. The body is covered in small, non-overlapping scales – some may be spiny, or raised and bony.

Monitors are sun-worshippers – they reach their peak of activity when the sun is up and their habitat has been warmed. Some use their claws as tools to dig out dens. Their powerful legs allow them to sprint short distances and when they run they lift their tails up. Many species stay in or near water and can swim quite well, with an undulating movement of the trunk and tail. When threatened they'll take refuge in their normal resting places – holes, trees (for the smaller monitors) or water. They *are* dangerous if driven into a corner, and will then attack a much larger opponent. They threaten by opening the mouth, inflating the neck and hissing. The ribs may spread, thus flattening the top of the body, or the body may expand slightly making the monitor look larger. It often rises up on its hind legs just before attacking and the tail can deliver well-aimed blows that will knock down a weaker adversary.

Their best weapons are their sharp teeth and dagger-sharp claws which can inflict severe wounds. All monitors feed on other animals – small ones on insects, larger ones on frogs and birds, and the Komodo on deer and wild pig which inhabit the island. The Komodo eats rotting carcasses and also hunts – lying in

Komodo Dragon

wait beside frequently used tracks and grabbing a leg of a passing victim or knocking it over with a swing of the tail then ripping out its intestines. Once they've caught their prey they don't readily let go! The dragons will also eat their own dead. They can expand their mouth cavity considerably, enabling them to swallow large prey – the Komodo can push practically a whole goat into its throat.

Being such a large reptile the Komodo rarely moves until thoroughly warmed by the sun, though in fact the villagers complain of night-time dragon raids for goats or fish kept under their houses. The dragons *seem* to be absolutely stone deaf – you could fire a cannon three metres from them and they wouldn't bat an eyelid. But they have a very keen sense of smell which makes rotting meat such good dragon bait. Of all the monitors the Komodo lays the largest eggs. They are up to 12 cm long and weigh as much as 200 grams.

Monitors are *not* relics of the dinosaur age – they're a remarkably versatile, hardy modern lizard. As long as they can find enough warmth they can live in practically any habitat. Nevertheless the Komodo variety is only found on and around Komodo Island. Why the dragons exist here and nowhere else remains a mystery. Today there are 1000-plus dragons on each of Komodo and Rinca, fewer in the other locations.

The villagers never hunted them because they weren't as good to eat as the numerous wild pigs that inhabit the island and, in any case, the dragons are considered dangerous. Today the dragons are a protected species. Another curious animal inhabiting this group of islands is the megapode or bush turkey – it collects a mound of rotting vegetation and buries its eggs in them, the temperature acting as an incubator. Dragons, pigs and human beings all dig them up, but some survive and the chick emerges from the shell fully clawed and feathered and flies away.

Information & Orientation

Komodo The only village is Kampung Komodo, a fishing village in a bay on the east coast. On the same bay a half-hour

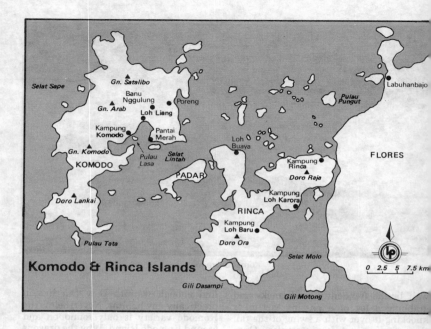

Komodo & Rinca Islands

walk north of the village is Loh Liang, the tourist accommodation camp run by the PHPA – the Indonesian government body responsible for managing nature reserves and national parks. You pay a 1000 rp park entry fee when you arrive on Komodo.

The PHPA warn you not to walk outside the camp without one of their guides, who cost 2500 rp for up to three hours, plus 1000 rp for each extra hour. A lot of emphasis is put on 'danger'. This includes encounters with Komodo dragons that can snap your leg as fast as they'll cut through a goat's throat, or treading on poisonous snakes. Signs around the camp warn you to wear trousers and shoes and to watch for snakes. The PHPA guys will probably get the blame if you have to be shipped home in a crate. Several years ago an elderly European did wander off alone and was never found – Dragons 1, Foreigners 0. In any case, many trails

around the island are overgrown and you could get lost. No one's likely to stop you if you do head off without a guide – but they're not really expensive, especially between a group, and they're friendly fellows who are full of interesting information if you can speak a bit of Indonesian.

Rinca There's a PHPA tourist camp at Loh Buaya and a few more villages. The park entrance fee here is also 1000 rp; PHPA guides are 1000 rp an hour.

Dragon Spotting
Komodo You're likely to see dragons any time of year at Banu Nggulung, a dried up river bed about a half-hour walk from Loh Liang. The beasts get fairly regular feeds here from those tourists who provide them with goats, so they don't need to stray far in search of food. Poreng Valley, 5½ km from Loh Liang, is a second favourite

dragon haunt and has a more out-in-the-wild feeling than Banu Nggulung. Elsewhere on the island May to September, the driest part of the year, holds the best chance of seeing dragons as it's hot and there are more of them out looking for food. From December to February is the wettest season and the dragons don't like rain. Komodo's hot most of the year: take water if you're going further afield than Banu Nggulung.

Unlike days of yore when you had to trek into the interior, string out the bait, hide behind a bush and hope something would happen, these days lizard hunting at Banu Nggulung is almost like going to the theatre. On the way there you pass a helipad built for President Suharto in 1988. A little 'grandstand' – where presumably the great man sat – overlooks the river bed. A pulley is strung over the river bed for presenting dragons with dead goat, their preferred diet. You don't need a goat just to see the dragons, but if you take one you're likely to see more activity from them. The PHPA will provide a goat, slit its throat and string it up for 30,000 rp,

plus 2500 rp for a porter to take it to the execution spot. You *might* be able to get one cheaper in Kampung Komodo or even Labuhanbajo. But taking a goat can be more harassment than it's worth, for you as well as it:

I went without a goat... but on the way back to the camp I met some other tourists and, following 50 yards behind, a porter with a thoroughly exhausted goat which had been dragged and kicked all the way from the village... Later they said the goat had had its throat cut with a blunt knife used in a sawing action, which took about 30 seconds to kill it. When the sole reason for having a goat is to satisfy the tourists' desire to see an 'active' dragon, then it's really not on. Especially when in the village there are children with bloated bellies (not bloated from overeating as the dragons' bellies are).

If you buy a goat in Flores, have it tied inside the prahu.

However bizarre you might think this set-up is, the sight of the dragons makes it worthwhile. Susan and John saw at least

eight ranging from relatively lively youngsters to lumbering three-metre monsters, clambering over each other to get at the last legs of a goat provided by an earlier party of visitors. The only sound from the river bed was an occasional deep exhalation from some of the larger beasts. The guides may let you go down to the river bed for a close-up look if there aren't too many of you. You need the sun overhead to get good photographs.

Rinca There are no established dragon-feeding places on Rinca so spotting them is more a matter of luck and your guide's knowledge. But other wildlife seems to be more abundant than on Komodo – there are monkeys, water buffalo, deer and wild horses.

Around Komodo Island

Kampung Komodo is a half-hour walk from the tourist camp. It's a fishing village of stilt houses, infested with goats, chickens and children – the fishing boats go out with the latter piled high. The inhabitants are all descendants of convicts who were exiled to the island last century by one of the sultans on Sumbawa. You can climb up the hills at the rear of Kampung Komodo or Loh Liang for sweeping views across the islands in the region.

If you go trekking around the island, to climb Mt Ara (about a six-hour round trip), to Poreng Valley, or anywhere else, be warned that this place can be bloody hot! The PHPA guides perform like mountain goats, marching up and down the hilly terrain in the fierce heat. Sights around the island include wild deer and large, poisonous (though not deadly) spiders.

There's good coral just off Pantai Merah east of Loh Liang and the small island of Pulau Lasa near Kampung Komodo – the PHPA guys say there's little danger from sea snakes or sharks. If you want to snorkel bring your own equipment, although the PHPA may have a snorkel

and mask for hire. The PHPA has fixed prices for boat charters from Loh Liang: Kampung Komodo 1000 rp, Pulau Lasa 10,000 rp, Pantai Merah 12,000 rp, both plus Pulau Kalong (which has a large fruit bat colony) 15,000 rp.

Wild pigs are often seen close to the camp or on the beach in front of it early in the morning. The Komodo dragons occasionally wander into the camp, but they normally avoid the kampung because there are too many people. Whales and dolphins are quite common in the seas between Komodo and Flores.

Places to Stay & Eat

The PHPA camp at Loh Liang is a collection of large, spacious, clean wooden cabins on stilts. Each cabin has four or five rooms, a sitting area and two mandis (with toilet). You pay 3000 rp per person in a room with two single beds, 8000 rp per couple in a room with a double bed. You can pitch a tent for 500 rp. Electricity, produced by a noisy generator near the camp office, operates from 6 to 10 pm. Once that goes off there's almost total silence.

There's a restaurant at the camp too but the menu is limited to very average nasi goreng or mie goreng at 1000 rp each, plus some expensive drinks including beer and mineral water. Bring other food yourself – the PHPA guys may cook it for you – or try in Kampung Komodo. You should be able to buy fish or eggs there or perhaps get them to kill and cook a chicken for around 2000 rp. Accommodation at the PHPA camp at Loh Buaya on Rinca Island is similar to Komodo's, at the same prices.

Getting There & Away

Komodo You can reach Komodo on the regular ferry from Labuhanbajo in Flores or Pelabuhan Sape on Sumbawa, or by chartering a boat from either place.

The ferry costs 6700 rp from Sape or 2100 rp from Labuhanbajo, plus 1000 rp per person for a small boat to transfer you between ferry and shore at Komodo. (The latter operation can be quite an adventure as a score or more people try to squeeze off the ferry and on to a tiny deck – on one occasion in 1989 too many people stood on one side of the small boat and it tipped over, depositing numerous travellers and their backpacks in the sea. Fortunately no one was hurt.)

The ferry only calls at Komodo twice a week, once in each direction – see under Sape, Sumbawa for the timetable. If you don't want to wait for the ferry, you must find another boat to get on or off the island. This costs around 40,000 rp per boat one way – though boat owners have been known to insist on as much as 100,000 rp for big groups who were in a hurry to get off Komodo. It's generally easier to find a boat from Labuhanbajo to Komodo than vice versa, but you rarely have to wait more than a day at either place unless the seas are too rough. To get off the island, look for a charter from a Komodo villager (one may be hanging around the PHPA camp), or maybe a Labuhanbajo boat that has just dropped tourists on Komodo. You may be able to get a lift with tourists who are making a round trip from Labuhanbajo.

To make things easier, many people opt to charter a boat from Labuhanbajo to Komodo and back. You can fix this through losmens, the PHPA, or by asking around the waterfront. An ordinary motorboat costs 40,000 to 60,000 rp for a day trip, or 60,000 to 75,000 rp for a two-day trip with an overnight stay; bigger better faster boats go up to 125,000 rp. Additional nights will cost more. Make any agreement with the boatmen very clear, particularly if you might recruit extra passengers. Labuhanbajo to Komodo takes three to four hours in an ordinary boat, which gives you maybe four hours on the island if you're making a day trip – enough to see the dragons and have a swim and a meal.

Boat charters to Komodo from Pelabuhan Sape on Sumbawa are possible, but more expensive because it's a longer trip.

Rinca It's only about two hours by motorboat from Labuhanbajo to Loh Buaya, the PHPA camp on Rinca, but the PHPA in Labuhanbajo still asks 60,000 rp per boat for a day trip there, or 75,000 rp for two days and one night. Most other boats will take you for less – the Waecicu Beach losmen runs day trips for 30,000 rp. If you want to stay at Loh Buaya, make sure your boatman drops you in the right place – otherwise you could be faced with a 30-km walk to Loh Buaya.

In A Hurry Labuhanbajo has an airport with Merpati flights from Denpasar, Mataram and elsewhere in Nusa Tenggara. You *could* be back in Denpasar 50 hours after leaving it, having visited Komodo in the meantime. There are also a few Komodo tours run from Bali: look around the travel agents there. The prices for these trips decrease the more people there are on the tour: one three-day, four-night tour costs US$420 per person if there are just two of you, but $365 each if there are three or four people.

Flores

One of the biggest, most rugged and most beautiful islands in Nusa Tenggara, Flores also has some of the most interesting cultures, with a strong layer of animism beneath the prevalent Catholicism.

Geographically, a turbulent volcanic past has left Flores with a complicated relief of V-shaped valleys, knife-edged ridges and a collection of active and extinct volcanoes. One of the finest of the latter is the caldera of Keli Mutu in central Flores with its three coloured lakes. There are 14 active volcanoes in Flores – only Java and Sumatra have more. The central mountains slope more gently to the north coast, but along the south coast the spurs of the volcanoes plunge steeply into the sea. The island is part of one of the world's most unstable

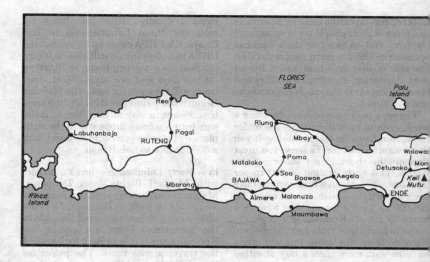

fracture zones and earthquakes and tremors hit every year. The rugged terrain makes road construction very difficult; although Flores is about 375 km long, its end-to-end road winds and twists for nearly 700 km, and heavy wet season rains as well as the frequent earthquakes and tremors mean that it has to be repaired year round.

Difficulties of communication have also contributed to the diversity of Flores' cultures. In some remoter areas you'll find older people who don't speak a word of Bahasa Indonesia and whose parents grew up in purely animist societies.

Physically the people of the western end of Flores are more 'Malay' whilst the other inhabitants are more Melanesian. The island's 1.4 million population is divided into five main language and cultural groups: from west to east the Manggarai (main town Ruteng), the Ngada (Bajawa), the closely related Ende and Lio peoples (Ende), the Sikkanese (Maumere) and the Lamaholot (Larantuka). Around 85% of the people are Catholic (Muslims tend to congregate in the coastal towns) but, in rural areas particularly, Christianity is welded on to traditional beliefs in which a big part is still played by animist rituals for a variety of occasions from birth, marriage and death to the building of a new house or important points in the agricultural cycle. Even educated, English-speaking Florinese still admit to sacrificing a chicken, pig or buffalo to keep their ancestors happy when rice is planted or a new field opened up. In former times, it seems, it took more than just animal blood to keep the gods and spirits friendly: there are persistent tales of children or virgin girls being sacrificed.

Flores has a thriving ikat-weaving tradition, with almost as many different styles as there are weaving villages, plus the beginnings of a beach spot at Labuhanbajo and some fine snorkelling off some parts of its coast. It has attracted an increasing flow of travellers in recent years, but there's nothing resembling the tourist scene of Bali or even Lombok.

The rainy season (from November to March) is much more intense in western Flores, which receives the brunt of the north-west monsoon and has the highest mountains. Ruteng, near Flores'

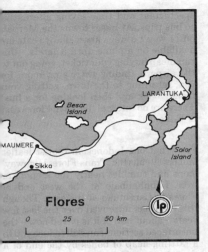

highest peak, the 2400-metre Renaka, gets an average 3350 mm of rain a year, but Ende has only 1140 mm and Larantuka just 770 mm.

HISTORY

Flores owes its name to the Portuguese who named its easternmost cape *Cabo das Flores* or 'Cape of Flowers'. The island's diverse cultures have enough similarities to suggest that they developed from a common type, differentiated by geographical isolation and the varying influence of outsiders. Long before Europeans arrived in the 16th century, much of at least coastal Flores was firmly in the hands of the Makassarese and Bugis from southern Sulawesi. The Bugis even established their own ports as part of a trading network throughout the archipelago. They brought gold, coarse porcelain, elephant tusks (used as money), a sort of machete known as a *parang*, linen and copperware, and left with rubber, sea cucumber (much of it fished from the bay of Maumere), shark fins, sandalwood, wild cinnamon, coconut oil, cotton and fabric from Ende. Bugis and Makassarese slave raids on the coasts of Flores were a common problem, forcing people to retreat inland.

Fourteenth century Javanese chronicles place Flores (probably rather imaginatively) within the Majapahit realm. In the 15th and 16th centuries most of west and central Flores is thought to have become a colony of the Makassarese kingdom of Gowa in south Sulawesi, while east Flores came under the sway of Ternate in Maluku.

As early as 1512, Flores was sighted by the Portuguese navigator Antonio de Abreu and Europeans had probably landed by 1550. The Portuguese, involved in the lucrative sandalwood trade with Timor, built fortresses on Solor off eastern Flores and at Ende on Flores, and in 1561 Dominican priests established a mission on Solor. From here the Portuguese Dominicans extended their work to eastern Flores, founding over 20 missions by 1575. Despite attacks by pirates, local Islamic rulers and raids from Gowa, the missionaries converted – it is claimed – tens of thousands of Florinese. The fortress at Ende was overrun in 1637 by Muslims and the mission was abandoned, as eventually were all the other missions on southern Flores, but the growth of Christianity continued. Today the church is the centrepiece of almost every village.

In the 17th century the Dutch East India Company (VOC) kicked the Portuguese out of most of their possessions on and near Flores, and concentrated on monopolising the trade in sappan wood (used to make a red dye) and wild cinnamon. The slave trade was also strong; a treaty with Ende outlawed it in 1839 but it was reported to exist into the first years of the 20th century.

Though Ternate and Gowa ceded all their rights on Solor, Flores and east Sumbawa to the Dutch in the 17th century, Flores was too complex and isolated for the Dutch to gain real control. Around 1850 the Dutch bought out

Portugal's remaining enclaves in the area including Larantuka, Sikka and Paga on Flores. Dutch Jesuits then took over missionary work on Flores and founded new bases in Maumere and Sikka – still their centres on Flores today.

Even into the first decade of this century, the Dutch were constantly confronted with rebellions and inter-tribal wars. Finally in 1907 a major military campaign brought most of the tribes of central and western Flores under firm control. Missionaries moved into the isolated western hills in the 1920s.

Getting There & Away
Air Merpati flies every day into Ende from Kupang and Bima, and into Maumere from Kupang and Ujung Pandang. It also flies four times weekly between Surabaya, Denpasar and Maumere, and Bouraq goes with the same frequency from both Kupang and Denpasar to Maumere. Larantuka at the far eastern end of Flores has two flights a week to/from Kupang and Lewoleba on Lembata island. Labuhanbajo, Ruteng and Bajawa in the western half of Flores all have at least four Merpati flights a week to/from Bima.

Boat There are regular ferries between Sape (Sumbawa) and Labuhanbajo (calling at Komodo once a week), and between Kupang (Timor) and Larantuka. In addition the Pelni passenger ship *Kelimutu* calls at Ende twice a fortnight on its route back and forth between Kupang and Semarang (Java) via several islands of Nusa Tenggara, Sulawesi, Bali and Kalimantan. Other boats of varying regularity ply between Flores and the rest of Nusa Tenggara and islands further afield. Ende, Larantuka, Maumere, Reo and Labuhanbajo are the best places to look.

Getting Around
Air Merpati's flights between Ende and Bima stop at Labuhanbajo, Ruteng or Bajawa, so it's possible to make short hops by air in western Flores. These can make a spectacular and time-saving alternative to bus trips. At lesser towns the Merpati office won't always know if any seats are available on a plane until it lands – this can mean buying your ticket, going out to the airport, finding there's no room for you, returning to the town, getting your money back and then looking for a bus! There are no internal flights in Flores east of Ende.

Bus What one Indonesian tourist leaflet laughably calls the 'Trans-Flores Highway' loops and tumbles nearly 700 scenic km from Labuhanbajo at the west end of Flores to Larantuka at the east. Though this road has improved over the last few years – about half of it is paved now – the unsurfaced sections can still reduce you to a rattling heap of bones by the end of a three-hour session. In the rainy season sections of it become clogged with mud or, worse, are washed away by floods or landslides. The latter event leaves you with the choice between a long muddy walk, or trying to get on to a suddenly very popular aeroplane, or resorting to boats – long the traditional transport between Flores' coastal settlements.

Still, the bus system has improved a lot and you no longer have to ride in the open back of a truck to get from one main town to the next. Buses link all the towns on the main road daily – of course they get bogged like anyone else when the roads are muddy, and a trip that might take four hours in the dry season can take half a day or more. The Labuhanbajo-Ruteng stretch is notorious for this. To get to the outlying towns you have to rely mainly on bemos or trucks.

Boat A variety of craft, often small and crowded, chug with varying frequency along most of the coasts of Flores, some of them providing transport even cheaper than the buses. These can make an interesting variant on bus travel and also come in handy when the roads are cut.

Labuhanbajo-Reo and Ende-Nggela are two useful routes.

Other Walking is an excellent way to see parts of Flores. Travellers who take to their feet rarely have any problem finding accommodation – village hospitality is tremendous. The same goes for cycling – if you don't mind hills!

LABUHANBAJO

A little Muslim/Christian fishing town at the extreme western end of Flores, this is the jumping-off point for Komodo, Rinca and Sumbawa. If you've got a few days to while away then Labuhanbajo ain't a bad place to do it. The harbour is littered with outrigger fishing boats and is sheltered by several small islands which give the impression that you're standing on the shore of a large lake. Prices for boat trips from Labuhanbajo have inflated recently as locals cash in on the tourist tide, but accommodation is still reasonably priced.

Information

Money The Bank Rakyat Indonesia changes major brand travellers' cheques (American Express, Bank America, Thomas Cook), but the rate is poor.

PHPA The PHPA office is a two-minute walk from the Bajo Beach and Mutiara losmens and is open till 2 pm. They're quite helpful with information on Komodo, Rinca and the Labuhanbajo area, and have a few displays and a list of fixed fees for transport to Komodo and Rinca.

Things to See & Do

Apart from visiting Komodo or Rinca, you can hire a boat for a snorkelling or diving trip or just to drop you on an uninhabited island in the morning and collect you in the afternoon. Ask at losmens or the waterfront or maybe the PHPA. A half-day trip to Pulau Bidadari, where there's lots of coral and clear water, costs around 15,000 rp. If you have your own snorkelling

gear, local boys might take you to nearby islands for less, or even nothing, in exchange for borrowing your gear. For divers, there's good coral between the islands of Sabolo Besar and Sabolo Kecil. Nusa Dua Bali Tours, almost opposite Losmen Bajo Beach, will rent diving gear and take you out for two dives and lunch, for between US$55 and US$75.

Waecicu Beach near Labuhanbajo is that rarity in Nusa Tenggara, an easily-accessible beach where (except sometimes at weekends) you can relax without a crowd of curious onlookers. At low tide

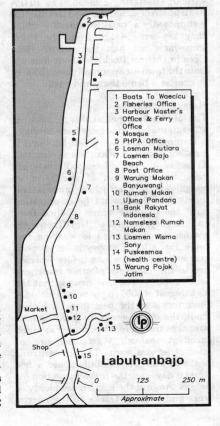

1 Boats To Waecicu
2 Fisheries Office
3 Harbour Master's Office & Ferry Office
4 Mosque
5 PHPA Office
6 Losman Mutiara
7 Losmen Bajo Beach
8 Post Office
9 Warung Makan Banyuwangi
10 Rumah Makan Ujung Pandang
11 Bank Rakyat Indonesia
12 Nameless Rumah Makan
13 Losmen Wisma Sony
14 Puskesmas (health centre)
15 Warung Pojok Jatim

Market

Shop

Labuhanbajo

0   125   250 m
Approximate

you can walk there in 1½ hours along the coast from the north end of Labuhanbajo, but it's simpler to take a 20-minute ride in the boat run by the Waecicu losmen. The boat usually leaves from near the fisheries office at about 9 am and once or twice later in the day too. The return trip is 2000 rp but is free if you stay at the losmen. The beach at Waecicu is clean and there's reasonable coral off a small island opposite. You can walk to the island at low tide.

A couple of natural features in the Labuhanbajo area may be worth tracking down – but no one seems willing to say where they are, for fear that you'll go there without chartering a bemo. The PHPA has a photo of some fossilised tree stumps – supposedly a 'petrified forest' – which they say are 18 km from the town, somewhere out past the airport. Batu Cermin (Mirror Rock) is about four km from the town – it apparently costs 5000 rp to charter a bemo there and back.

Places to Stay & Eat

The laid-back losmen at *Waecicu Beach*, a 20-minute boat ride from Labuhanbajo, is inspired by Lombok's Gili Isles and is great for a spell of relaxation. Accommodation is still fairly basic but there are mosquito nets. Most of the 20 or so bungalows have attached mandis and toilets, but these won't be in operation until the planned water pipeline from Labuhanbajo is installed. Until then there are just bush toilets and, for washing, two wells. But a lot of money is being spent here and it won't be long before Waecicu has all the 'comforts' of other travellers' beach centres. The best news is that the nightly cost of 5000 rp per person includes three meals of the best food on Flores. Rudi, the cook, serves up great banana pancakes and for lunch or dinner as much excellent seafood, vegetables, rice or noodles as you want. The losmen runs boats to and from Labuhanbajo a few times a day – see the previous section for details. Around the losmen are plenty of trees and walking tracks to the nearby monkey-inhabited jungle. The losmen also does Komodo day trips for 12,000 rp per person (for a minimum of five) as well as Rinca trips.

In the town, the best place to stay is the *Losmen Bajo Beach* which has a range of very clean rooms costing 4500/6000/9000 rp for singles/doubles/triples, or 7500/10,000/12,500 rp with private mandi and toilet. Sometimes you have to pay more for a fan, sometimes you don't. There's a pleasant open-air sitting-eating area with decent food from a small omelette at 250 rp to a plate of vegetables at 1000 rp or chicken at 3250 rp. Don't be put off by having to sign your name six times when you check in or by the local resentment towards this place because it's run by Chinese.

Across the road the *Losmen Mutiara* is cheaper and more basic than the Bajo Beach and more popular with rats. For 3000/5000 rp you can choose between upstairs with a breeze but shared mandi, and downstairs with a private mandi but no breeze. Meals are 1000 to 1250 rp – are ordinary. The third option in town is the *Wisma Sony*, five minutes' walk up the hill towards the airport. Small rooms with mosquito nets and private mandi cost 3000/6000 rp. Meals are 1000 to 1500 rp.

Labuhanbajo's cheapest meals are at the handful of little rumah makan towards the southern end of town. Choice of food is limited here, and quality variable, but the *Banyuwangi* does a respectable 750-rp *nasi goreng* and the *Ujung Pandang*'s chicken soup contains recognisable pieces of chicken.

Getting There & Away

If you're heading west in a real hurry and don't want to take to the air, it's possible – fluctuating tides and timetables permitting – to get from Labuhanbajo to Bali in 1½ days as one letter relates:

Ferry to Sape 8 am arriving at 5 pm. Horse cart to bus to Kumbe to Bima where we caught a night bus across Sumbawa arriving in time for 8 am ferry to Lombok. Then bus across Lombok to reach Lembar and the Padangbai Bali ferry. Were sitting at Poppies at dinner 7 pm...

Some people really know how to move.

Air Merpati flies four times a week to and from Bima and Ende, with connections elsewhere from those places. Some Labuhanbajo-Ende flights also stop at Ruteng. In the wet, flying can be a good alternative to the questionable Ruteng road. The airfield is a 15-minute drive from the town and losmens can arrange a bemo (1000 rp) to get you there. The Merpati office is a 10-minute walk up the hill towards the airport from the town.

Boat Information on trips to Komodo and Rinca islands is given in the Komodo and Rinca section. The ferry to/from Sape on Sumbawa runs three times a week, stopping at Komodo once weekly in each direction. See under Sape for times and prices. In Labuhanbajo it docks at the north end of the main street. Get tickets from the harbour master's office (*Direktorat Jenderal Perhubungan Darat*) near the pier there.

If there are some really bad hold-ups on the Labuhanbajo-Ruteng road or if you just fancy an unusual route, you can try getting a boat to Reo on the north coast then a bus from Reo to Ruteng. Ask at the harbour master's office or the fisheries office (*Kantor Perikanan*), both at the north end of Labuhanbajo's main street. Something sails to Reo every few days. The boat fare is 2000 rp and the voyage takes eight to 10 hours if no stops are made. Alan took this route while researching the first edition of this book:

My boat was due to leave 'any time after 3 pm' and finally departed, with 10 passengers, at 7 pm. It moored offshore from the fishing village of Bari around midnight, got going again around 11 am and pulled into Reo around 2.30 pm. Bring a hat and sunglasses for the day and warm clothes or a blanket for the night – it gets bloody cold regardless of the oven Flores can be

during the day! Bari is a pretty sight in the early morning. Kids wearing T-shirts with motifs like 'Spinetingling Tang Food' or 'Singapore Buddhist Lodge' paddle up to the boat in canoes to sell bananas and fish.

There are also occasional boats from Labuhanbajo to Maumere or Bima (both about 5000 rp), or even Ende.

Bus & Truck The 137-km road to Ruteng, formerly one of the horrors of Indonesian travel, is finally in the process of being paved. But until the job is finished, long stretches remain more like a river bed than a road – notably the first 30 km or so climbing out of Labuhanbajo. In the dry, buses take four hours to Ruteng, in the wet they can take 10 hours or even longer. Three or four buses leave Labuhanbajo daily around 7 am – a few more depart up till early afternoon, and there's usually an evening bus when the ferry arrives from Sape. The fare to Ruteng is 3500 rp – you can buy advance tickets from losmens or from buses which hang around town displaying signs like *Besok Ke Ruteng*. If you get an advance ticket, the bus will pick you up from your losmen.

Passenger trucks also ply the route to Ruteng. They have harder, more cramped seats, are open to the weather and, bizarrely, cost the same 3500 rp. The only possible advantage is that you may see more of the country than from a bus. If you do find yourself on a truck, it's imperative to get a seat in front of the rear axle; positions behind it are good approximations of ejector seats.

If you do get stuck along the way you'll find the people in the villages are extraordinarily hospitable, but bring some food.

REO

Set on an estuary a little distance from the sea, Reo's focal point is the large Catholic church compound in the middle of the town. From the port of Kedindi, five km from Reo, 3000 buffalo per year are

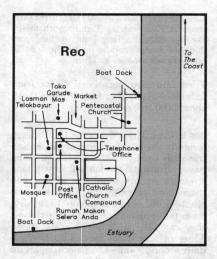

shipped to Surabaya. If you want to make a boat trip between Reo and Labuhanbajo, it's probably better to do it from Labuhanbajo than from Reo, so that if you have to wait days for a boat, you do so in a more agreeable place.

Places to Stay & Eat

The *Losmen Telukbayur* at Jalan Mesjit 8 has rooms at 3000/6000 rp. The toilets and mandis are Indonesian versions of Australian backyard dunnies and about as clean as you would expect. The top floor rooms are probably best for avoiding the crowds of staring children. This losmen has its own warung. One reader reported that a place called something like *Penginapan Nisangnai* (maybe *Nusawangi*?), on Jalan Pelabuhan a little way out of town towards Kedindi, was better and cleaner for the same price. The *Rumah Makan Selera Anda* is a five-minute walk from the Telukbayur near the Catholic church.

Getting There & Away

There are fairly frequent buses, trucks and bemos (more in the morning than later) between Reo and Ruteng, taking three hours and costing 750 rp. The whole road is surfaced now. They circle Reo picking up passengers before heading off to Ruteng – the best place to catch one is the main street where the market and all the shops are. You may be able to catch one at the dock when the boats from Labuhanbajo pull in.

Look around the river for small boats to Labuhanbajo – these go irregularly and the fare is 2000 rp per person. Locals may tell you there aren't any and try to get you to charter a boat for 100,000 rp: you should be able to bargain them down to 50,000 rp at most. For boats to Sape, Bima, Maumere or further afield you may have to go to Kedindi. It will cost 5000 to 10,000 rp to these places.

RUTENG

A market town and meeting point for the hill-people of western Flores, Ruteng is the heart of the Manggarai country, the region extending to the west coast from a line drawn north from Aimere. The town is surrounded by rice fields on gentle slopes beneath a line of volcanic hills, and is cooler and less humid than the coast – though still hot when the sun shines. Take water if you go hiking.

The Manggarai hill people are everything you'd expect hill-people to be: scruffy, shy, curious. You'll see them in their distinctive black sarongs trailing droopy-stomached black-haired pigs into market, or herding beautiful miniature horses. There are also prolific numbers of Chinese who play their traditional role as the retailers and businessmen.

The Manggarai language is unintelligible to the other people on Flores. Makassarese from Sulawesi have mixed with the coastal Manggarai for well over a century and the Bimanese dominated some coastal regions for at least 300 years until early this century, when the Dutch finally took over all of Flores.

Christianity now predominates among the upland Manggarai and Ruteng has several large Christian schools and churches. Traditional animistic practices linger but are less evident than among the Ngada people further east. Traditionally the Manggarai would carry out an annual cycle of ceremonies – some involving buffalo or pig sacrifices – to ask favour from ancestor and nature spirits and the supreme being, Mori. In some villages you can still find the *compang*, a ring of flat stones on which offerings are placed, or you may be shown ritual paraphernalia such as drums which are beaten to accompany sacrifices.

Trials of strength and courage known as *caci* were once a frequent accompaniment to ceremonies. They still take place in Ruteng during the national Independence Day celebrations on 17 August. The two combatants wear wooden masks like up-tilted welders' helmets – one carries a rawhide oval shield and a metre-long whip; the other a short, springy stick and a thick cloth wrapped around his forearm. The two combatants circle each other, loudly proclaiming their own bravery while musicians beat an accompaniment on gongs and wooden drums. The combatant with the whip lashes at his opponent who tries to deflect the blow with his stick. A blow to the body is a signal for the two to change weapons for the next round.

The Manggarai traditionally practised slash-and-burn agriculture. They were introduced to rice cultivation around 1920 by the Dutch, but only in the last two or three decades has the area devoted to permanent rice terraces, both irrigated and non-irrigated, begun to increase substantially. Maize (sweet corn) is the other main crop though other crops (like coffee and onions) are grown for export. The Manggarai also herd animals and raise fine horses and large water buffalo, the latter primarily for export.

Information

Bank The Bank Rakyat Indonesia on Jalan Yos Sudarso will change major travellers' cheques so long as they're in US

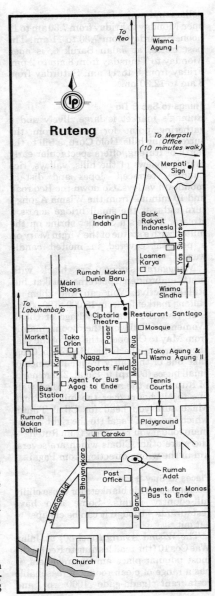

dollars and major foreign currencies. It's open Monday to Friday from 7.30 am to 12 noon, Saturday from 7.30 to 11 am. The post office, at Jalan Baruk 6, is open Monday to Thursday from 8 am to 2 pm, Friday from 8 to 11 am, Saturday from 8 am to 12.30 pm.

Things to See & Do

Ruteng's market is large, lively and a gathering point for people from the surrounding hills. Golo Curu, a hill to the north of Ruteng, offers spectacular early morning views of the hills, valleys, rice paddies, terraced slopes and distant mountain valleys. Go down the Reo road and 10 minutes from the Wisma Agung I turn right at the small bridge across a stream. There's a derelict shrine on the hilltop with a statue of the Virgin Mary on a pedestal covered in melted candle wax.

Manggarai sarongs are black with pretty embroidered patterns, not ikat, but still attractive. You can find them in Ruteng market for from 15,000 to 20,000 rp – or visit the weaving village of Cibal. Women at Cibal work their looms mainly from May to October – the rest of the year they work in the fields. To reach Cibal take one of the fairly frequent bemos or small buses (500 rp) to Pagal, 21 km north of Ruteng on the road to Reo, then walk one to 1½ hours over the hill to Cibal. Make sure you head for Cibal Timur, which is east of Pagal (to the right off the main road if you're coming from Ruteng) – there are other Cibals which are several km in the wrong direction from Pagal.

Places to Stay & Eat

Losmens provide blankets for those chilly hill-country nights. Some also have restaurants – though it can be cheaper to eat out.

The *Wisma Agung I* (tel 80) at Jalan Wae Cos 10 (the road leading to Reo) is the most popular place among travellers; it has a range of clean rooms, a reasonable restaurant (gado-gado 1000 rp) and

helpful management. Class I rooms, with private mandi, are 6000/8000 rp; class I rooms, a bit smaller with shared mandis are 4000/6000 rp. The Agung I is about 15-minute walk from the town centre *Wisma Agung II*, behind Toko Agung on Jalan Motang Rua, is more central but darker, shabbier and dearer at 10,000 13,000 rp for class I, 6600/8000 for class II The *Rumah Makan Agung* next door ha standard Chinese food at around 1500 rp for most dishes.

On a par with the Agung I, the more central *Wisma Sindha* on Jalan Yo Sudarso has a helpful owner but no restaurant. Officially rooms are from 7000 to 18,000 rp but you can usually get the cheapest (with shared mandi) for 5000 rp double, or good clean ones at the back with private mandi for around 9000 rp double Room standards are similar at the newe *Wisma Dahlia* (tel 377) on Jalan Kartini economy rooms with shared mandi are 5000/7500 rp, rooms with private mandi 10,000/12,500 rp and up. Some have hot water. Try bargaining. There's a restaurant here too with noodle dishes 1500 rp, soups from 2000 to 3000 rp, also chicken and steak.

The *Losmen Karya* is a decent little place near the town centre but it's often 'full'. Some foreigners get in though – it seems to help if you're Dutch. Singles, doubles are 3500/7000 rp.

For meals out, try the central *Rumah Makan Dunia Baru*, with good Chinese food at from 1200 to 2000 rp, or the *Rumah Makan Beringin* for Padang food. There are a few other places in the town and a handful of warungs at the market, some of which may serve buffalo soup (soto kerbau). The market has fresh fruit.

Getting There & Away

Air The Merpati office (tel 147) is out in the rice paddies, about a 10-minute walk from the centre (see map). There are flights most days to/from Bima and Kupang; some of the Bima flights call at Labuhanbajo. The airport is a half-hour walk from the town if you don't want to charter a bemo.

Bus Most buses will drop you at losmens on arrival in Ruteng. Buses to Labuhanbajo (3500 rp), Bajawa (3000 rp) and Ende (6500 rp) leave in the early morning about 7 am. There may be occasional afternoon buses to Bajawa or Labuhanbajo, but don't rely on them. You can buy tickets for the morning buses at the bus station or agents in shops the afternoon before – most losmens will also get them for you, sometimes for a commission. If you have a ticket, buses will pick you up from wherever you want. Then they circle Ruteng's rutted back streets collecting other passengers.

In the dry, it takes about four hours to Labuhanbajo, six hours to Bajawa, 13 hours to Ende. In the wet, it can take 10 hours to Labuhanbajo but the road west from Ruteng is better – though still subject to slower going and hold-ups on the unpaved stretches. Trucks cover the same routes but at no saving on cost.

Buses, trucks and bemos to Reo leave fairly often until about midday, costing 750 rp for the 60-km, three-hour journey. Pick them up at the bus station or as they circle the streets.

RUTENG TO BAJAWA

This trip is 133 km. From Ruteng the road descends, unpaved and bumpy, to Borong on the south coast, where buses usually stop for a meal-break and there's one losmen; then goes inland and over a small range before heading down towards the coast again where bitumen mercifully takes over; and finally winds its way up to Bajawa. The last section is spectacular as the coast stretches out behind and you climb up into the volcanoes dominating the Bajawa region.

BAJAWA

The small hill town of Bajawa, with a

Komodo dragon sculpture, Ruteng

population of about 10,000, is the centre of the Ngada people, one of the least modernised groups on Flores. The town is 1100 metres high and surrounded by volcanic hills with the 2245-metre Mt Inerie to the south predominant. Bajawa is cool, spacious and low-key - an excellent base for trips out to Ngada villages and the surrounding country.

The Ngada

The 60,000 Ngada people inhabit both the upland Bajawa plateau and the slopes around Mt Inerie stretching down to the south coast. They were subdued by the Dutch in 1907 and Christian missionaries arrived about 1920. Older animistic beliefs remain strong and the religion of many Ngada, to a greater extent than in most of Flores, is a fusion of animism and Christianity.

The most evident symbols of continuing Ngada tradition are the pairs of *ngadhu* and *bhaga*. The ngadhu is a parasol-like structure about three metres high consisting of a carved wooden pole and thatched 'roof', and the bhaga is like a miniature thatch-roofed house. You'll see groups of them standing in most Ngada villages, though in the less traditional ones some of the bhaga have disappeared.

The functions and meanings of ngadhu and bhaga are multiple, but basically they symbolise the continuing presence of ancestors. The ngadhu is 'male' and the bhaga 'female' and each pair is associated with a particular family group within a village. Though the carved trunks of ngadhu often feel like solid stone, their tops are usually dilapidated - some are said to have been built to commemorate people killed in long-past battles over land disputes, and may be over 100 years old. Periodically, on instruction from ancestors in dreams, a pair of ngadhu and bhaga is remade according to a fixed pattern, accompanied by ceremonies which may involve buffalo sacrifices.

The main post of a ngadhu, known as *Sebu*, should come from a tree which is

dug up complete with its main root then 'planted' in the appropriate place in the village. Each part of the post has specific designs carved on it on different days: an axe and a cassava on the top part, a dragonhead in the form of a flower in the middle, and a geometric design around the bottom. The three parts are also said to represent the three classes of traditional Ngada society: from top to bottom, the *gae*, *gae kisa* and *hoo*. A crossbeam with two hands holding an arrow and a sword links the top of the pole to the roof. The walls of the bhaga must be cut from seven pieces of wood. Near the ngadhu there's usually a small stone post which is the 'gate-keeper', and the bases of both ngadhu and bhaga are often surrounded by circles of stones, said to symbolise meeting places.

The traditional Ngada village layout - of which there are still a few examples left - is two rows of high-roofed houses on low stilts. These face each other across an open space which contains ngadhu and bhaga and groups of man-high stone slivers surrounding horizontal slabs. The latter, which appear to be graves of important ancestors, have led to some exotic theories about the Ngada's origins.

Traditionally the Ngada believe themselves to have come from Java and they may have settled here three centuries ago. But stone structures which are in varying degrees similar to these 'graves' crop up in other remote parts of Indonesia - among them Nias Island, Sumatra's Batak highlands, parts of Sulawesi, Sumba and Tanimbar - as well as in Malaysia and Laos. The common thread is thought to be the Dongson culture, which arose in southern China and north Vietnam about 2700 years ago then migrated into Indonesia bringing, among other things, the practice of erecting large monumental stones (megaliths). This practice, it's thought, survived only in isolated areas which were not in contact with later cultural changes.

Some writers also claim to have

recognised Hindu, Semitic, even Caucasian elements in Ngada culture – and one theory, seeking to explain apparent similarities between Indonesian and Balkan culture, suggests that the Dongson Culture originated in south-east Europe!

What makes the Ngada unusual today is their preservation of animistic beliefs and practices. 'Straight' Christianity has made less inroads in the villages than in Bajawa itself. Apart from ngadhu and bhaga and the ancestor worship which goes with them, agricultural fertility rites continue (sometimes involving very gory buffalo sacrifices) as well as ceremonies marking birth, marriage, death or house building. The major annual festival is the six-day *Reba* ceremony at Bena, 19 km from Bajawa, held around late December/ early January, which includes dancing, singing, buffalo sacrifices and the wearing of special black ikat costumes. The highest god in traditional Ngada belief is Gae Dewa who unites Dewa Zeta (the heavens) and Nitu Sale (the earth).

Orientation & Information

Bajawa is three km north of the Ruteng-Ende road. It's a small town and everything is within walking distance of the bus station and market. The post office, on Jalan Boulevard, is open Monday to Thursday from 8 am to 2 pm, Friday from 8 to 11 am, Saturday from 8 am to 12.30 pm. There's nowhere to change foreign money or travellers' cheques.

Things to See

Bajawa market is busy with lots of Ngada women wearing ikat cloth some of which is on sale, both from the Ngada area and further afield. The better local stuff is black with white motifs, often of horses or people. A sarong should cost 15,000 to 20,000 rp. There's a ngadhu at the end of Jalan Satsuitubu.

Places to Stay

The *Losmen Kambera* on Jalan Slamet Riyadi gets more travellers than anywhere

else – partly because the owner seems to have some deal with bus drivers who often offer to drop you there. The rooms – at 3000/6000 rp, or 3500/7000 rp for slightly bigger, brighter ones – are clean enough but nothing special and none has a private mandi. But this losmen is quite helpful with information – and the family cooks up good meals: a feast of fried potatoes, gado-gado, fish, egg and rice will cost about 2500 rp, though you can also eat (and pay) more sparingly! Local students sometimes hang around the losmen to practise their English, and may offer to show you round nearby villages for free in order to get a day's English conversation!

At the other lower-end places you can sometimes bargain prices down a bit. The *Wisma Johny* on Jalan Yani is bare, but decent with assorted rooms (some with attached mandi) mostly at around 3000/ 5000 rp. You can get meals here. Also cheap is the basic, but clean and friendly *Wisma Mawar* where you pay 3000 rp per person in a room with mandi or 2000 rp without mandi. Prices include a bite of breakfast – other meals are 750 to 2500 rp. The *Losmen Dam* has clean little rooms at 3500/6000 rp or larger ones with mandi and toilet for 5500/9000 rp, but no food.

The more up-market *Losmen Kembang* at Jalan Diponegoro 18 has very clean rooms facing a small garden, at 12,500 rp with private mandi and breakfast included.

Places to Eat

Meals, cheaper than those in most losmens, can be found in a few other places scattered around town. The *Rumah Makan Komodo Jaya* on Jalan K H Dewantara, near the Losmen Kambera, has tasty, quite big portions from a pretty standard menu with most dishes at 500 to 1000 rp. The friendly *Rumah Makan Kasih Bahagia*, on Jalan Yani almost opposite the bus station, has cold beer and will do you a multi-egg omelette for 600 rp, or nasi campur, cap cai, chicken, etc. The *Rumah Makan Beringin* on Jalan Basuki Rahmat has a fairly limited range of

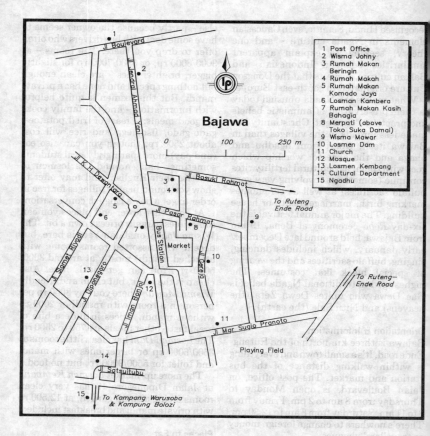

Bajawa

0   100   250 m

1 Post Office
2 Wisma Johny
3 Rumah Makan Beringin
4 Rumah Makah
5 Rumah Makan Komodo Jaya
6 Losman Kambera
7 Rumah Makan Kasih Bahagia
8 Merpati (above Toko Suka Damai)
9 Wisma Mawar
10 Losmen Dam
11 Church
12 Mosque
13 Losmen Kembang
14 Cultural Department
15 Ngadhu

Jl Boulevard
Jl Jenderal Ahmad Yani
Jl K H Dewan Toro
Jl Basuki Rahmat
Jl Pasar Rahmat
Jl Sumat Riwu
Jl Bayu Muda
Jl Diponegoro
Jl Imam Bonjol
Jl Gereja
Jl Mgr Sugio Pranoto
Jl Satsultubu

Bus Station
Market
Playing Field

To Ruteng Ende Road
To Ruteng– Ende Road
To Kampang Warusoba & Kampung Bolozi

Padang food – fried fish, rice and green leaves would add up to 750 rp, *nasi telur campur* costs the same. The market usually offers a good range of fruit: avocados 50 rp, a comb of bananas 250 rp.

Getting There & Away

Air Merpati's four flights a week to and from each of Bima, Ende and Kupang use a sloping grass strip about seven km out of town on the way to Ende. Tickets can be bought from the agent above Toko Suka Damai, just off Jalan Pasar Baru. To get to the airstrip you can either charter a bemo or try to get on a regular bemo or bus going to somewhere not too far beyond the airstrip such as Mangulewa, Mataloko or maybe Boawae. Ende buses won't usually take people just for a short hop.

Bus Most buses to Ende and Ruteng leave at about 7 or 8 am, though there are usually a few more through the morning and sometimes an early afternoon departure. It takes about six hours and costs 3000 rp to either place. Small buses and bemos also run from Bajawa to other places on the main road like Mataloko and Boawae in the Ende direction or Aimere in the Ruteng direction. The 125-km Bajawa-Ende road isn't badly surfaced. It twists around a vast panorama of hills and valleys and passes Mt Alaboba, a huge barren volcano scarred by lava flows.

AROUND BAJAWA
Kampung Bolozi
Only a 30 to 45-minute walk along a dirt track from Bajawa, Kampung Bolozi has some ngadhu, an old tomb and a few traditional houses. See the map for directions – if in doubt, ask for Kampung Warusoba which is on the way to Kampung Bolozi.

Langa
There are 10 ngadhu and bhaga and several steep-roofed houses in Langa, seven km from Bajawa. From Bajawa bus station you might find a bemo going all the way, otherwise take one to Watujaji on the main Ruteng-Ende road and walk the remaining four km, or walk the whole way. It's probably a good idea to ask the kepala desa or some other responsible looking person before taking photos. You might be offered special ceremonial sarongs for sale here. They're worth 100,000 to 150,000 rp depending on the thickness of the material. Locals sometimes exchange a ceremonial sarong for a horse. Three km from Langa is another traditional village, Borado.

Bena
Right underneath the Inerie volcano, 19 km from Bajawa, Bena is one of the most traditional Ngada villages and its stone monuments are a protected site. High thatched houses line up in two rows on a ridge, the space between them filled with ngadhu, bhaga and strange megalithic tomb-like structures. Once, all Ngada villages followed this design. Some of the 'tombs' are said to contain hoards of treasure. The house of the leading family in each part of the village has a little model-house on top of its roof. There's a

small Christian shrine on a mound at the top end of the village, showing that Christianity and animism coexist here. Bena is the scene of the important six-day *Reba* ceremony every December to January.

On arrival, try to chat to the villagers and at least ask before wandering round or taking photos. You may be asked to sign a visitors' book and give up to 5000 rp per person: this seems to be a matter for negotiation. Taking a small gift like cigarettes or betel nut, or offering maybe 500 or 1000 rp before you're asked, will probably start you off on a friendlier, less commercial footing. If you want to stay with the kepala desa – which it's possible to do – you could offer to pay 2000 or 3000 rp for the accommodation instead of paying the 'visitor's fee'. In the daytime most of the men and some women are usually out in the fields – only the elderly and a few mothers and ragged children remain in

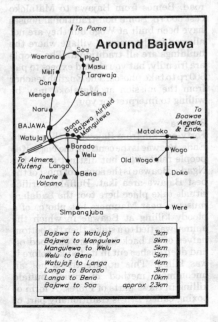

Around Bajawa

To Poma
Soa
Waerana · Piga
Meli · Masu
Gon · Tarawaja
Menge · Surisina
Naru
BAJAWA · Bena Bajawa Airfield · Mangulewa
Watujaji · Matatoko
To Aimere, Ruteng · Borado · Welu · Old Wogo · Wogo
Langa · Inerie Volcano · Bena · Doka
Simpangjuba · Were

To Boawae Aegela, & Ende.

Bajawa to Watujaji	3km
Bajawa to Mangulewa	9km
Mangulewa to Welu	5km
Welu to Bena	5km
Watujaji to Langa	4km
Langa to Borado	3km
Langa to Bena	10km
Bajawa to Soa	approx 23km

the village, pounding rice or doing other chores. Once you have got past any uneasy money matters, the people will probably be happy to talk.

Bena is 10 km from Langa – occasional vehicles go from Langa to Bena but more often you have to walk. An easier way from Bajawa is to take a bemo (200 rp) to Mangulewa on the Ende road, then walk the 10 km from Mangulewa to Bena – downhill all the way. Occasionally bemos go from Bajawa to Welu (300 rp), half way between Mangulewa and Bena. Take water and as much food as you'll need. From Bena you can apparently climb Mt Inerie in about three or four hours. If it's clear, Sumba and the north coast of Flores will be visible.

Wogo

There are beautiful houses and eight or nine sets of ngadhu and bhaga at Wogo, a 10-minute walk from Mataloko, which is about 20 km from Bajawa on the Ende road. Bemos from Bajawa to Mataloko cost 300 rp. Some non-traditional houses have been built at Wogo but they are not allowed in the original village where the buildings are all traditional. The people are friendly, but you should expect to pay 500 rp to take photos. The English teacher from the mission at Mataloko may be willing to interpret for you.

Boawae

Forty-one km from Bajawa on the road to Ende, Boawae is the centre of the Nage-Keo people related to, but distinct from, the Ngada. Boawae is the source of most of the best Bajawa-area ikat. Buffalo-sacrifice rituals take place here too: the Ladalero museum near Maumere has photos of a bloody killing at Boawae in which the animal was tied to a stake, then the bottom halves of its back legs were chopped off and deep gashes cut in its flanks before it was killed. This apparently is not an uncommon method of ritual buffalo killing in these parts of Flores. A form of boxing called *Etu* is traditionally part of the May to August post-harvest festivities among the Nage-Keo: the boxers wear garments made from tree bark and painted with animal blood, and their gloves may be studded with broken glass!

Soa

About an hour's truck ride (700 rp) north of Bajawa, Soa's attraction is the weekly market which brings in villagers from a very wide area. It starts on Sunday afternoon and seems to go on most of the night and well into Monday. Villagers tramp into Soa with sacks of rice or lone melons perched on their heads. There are also some hot springs (*air panas*) in a river about 1½ km walk from a village six km beyond Soa. Trucks from Soa to the village are 200 rp.

Riung

There are giant iguanas on an island off the north coast near the village of Riung. The beasts are more brightly coloured than Komodo dragons and some readers reported seeing one four metres long – as long as a very long Komodo. There's also some excellent snorkelling over the coral around the iguana island and several others nearby. In Riung you can stay with the PHPA or the kepala desa or at *Romah Pacamat*, which also provides food. A PHPA guide will take you to the iguana island or to Tanjung Lima Belay a viewpoint with a great outlook over the islands.

Trucks (3000 rp) leave Bajawa a few times a week in the early morning for Riung. The route is a spectacular but roundabout 160 km or so via Boawae and Aegela on the Ende road, then north-west along rough roads through Mbay. Or you could take a truck to Soa then walk about 60 km. From Ende you can get a bus to Mbay, or to Aesesa which is also on the Aegela-Riung road and has a small losmen, and wait for the truck from Bajawa – or walk. Aegela is the last place where you can stock up on food.

ENDE

The Endenese are the people gathered in south central Flores in and around the port town of Ende. Like their neighbours, they have a mix of Malay and Melanesian features. The aristocratic families of Ende link their ancestors, through mythical exploits and magical events, with the Hindu Majapahit kingdom of Java. Today most of the 55,000 people living in Ende are Christian, but there's also many Muslims.

It's a drab town running down to a revolting beach, but is surrounded by fine mountain scenery. The perfect cone of Gunung Meja rises almost beside the airport and the larger Gunung Iya occupies a promontory south of Gunung Meja.

Ende is mainly a stopover on the way to or from the attractions of eastern Flores, but trips to some nearby villages may be worthwhile, and you can at least look at some interesting ikat weaving here.

Orientation & Information

Ende is at the neck of a peninsula jutting south into the sea. The port of Ende and most of the shops and offices are on the western side of the neck. Another port, Pelabuhan Ipi, is on the eastern side; north of Pelabuhan Ipi is the airport.

Bank The Bank Rakyat Indonesia on Jalan Sudirman will change US and Australian dollar travellers' cheques from major companies. It will also change some foreign cash. It's open from 8 am to 12.30 pm Monday to Friday and from 8 am to 11.30 am Saturday.

Post & Communications The main post office, where you must go for poste restante, is out in the north-west of town on Jalan Gajah Mada. It's open Monday to Thursday from 8 am to 2 pm, from Friday 8 am to 11 am, and Saturday from 8 am to 1 pm. For stamps, there's a sub-post office a short walk from the centre of town opposite Wisma Dwi Putra. The

Telephone & Telegraph Office is on Jalan Kelimutu, about a 15-minute walk from the waterfront, or take a bemo.

Markets There's a market beside the town bemo station on Jalan Pasar, and lots of shops on and around this street. The Pasar Potulando, with fruit, vegetables and fish, is on Jalan Kelimutu, out towards the airport.

Things to See & Do

In 1933, the Dutch exiled Sukarno to Ende – his house on Jalan K H Dewantara is now a museum. It's a well-cared for, cream building with red trim behind a high fence with a big sign outside and is open Monday to Saturday from 8 am to 2 pm.

The Ende area has its own style of ikat weaving. Owing to the Koran's ban on representations of living creatures, the mainly Muslim weavers here stick to abstract motifs but rather indistinct patterns, and Ende ikat is generally not as fine as that from the Nggela and Maumere regions further east. Mainly commercial dyes are used – beware of poor factory-printed copies. People come round to some losmens selling these as well as better ikat from other areas; you'll see some in shops around Jalan Pasar and in the market next to the town bemo station. Some of the best comes from the village of Ndona, eight km east of Ende. It's 175 rp by bemo from Ende to Ndona, but sometimes quicker to go Wolowona four km out (150 rp), then take another bemo from Wolowona to Ndona (75 rp). Or walk from Wolowona. A large new good-quality Ndona *selendang* (shawl) might cost about 30,000 rp.

Wolotopo, about eight km east of Ende, also produces reasonable ikat. From Wolowona, walk almost to the black-sand beach of Nanga Nesa then follow a well-defined path for about 45 minutes along the coast to Wolotopo. There are some traditional houses here and you might be asked for a 500 rp 'administrative fee' to enter the village.

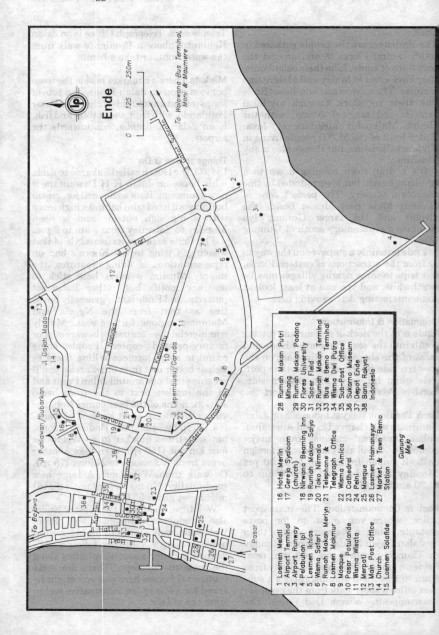

Ende

0   125   250m

To Wolowona Bus Terminal,
Moni & Maumere

Gunung
Meja

Jl Pasar

1 Losmen Melati
2 Airport Terminal
3 Airport Runway
4 Pelabuhan Ipi
5 Losmen Ikhlas
6 Wisma Safari
7 Rumah Makan Merlin
8 Losmen Mokmur
9 Mosque
10 Pasar Potulande
11 Wisma Wisata
12 Merpati
13 Main Post Office
14 Church
15 Losmen Solafide
16 Hotel Merlin
17 Gereja Syaloom
   (church)
18 Nirwana Beaming Inn
19 Rumah Makan Sayo
20 Toko Nirmala
21 Telephone &
   Telegraph Office
22 Wisma Amica
23 Cathedral
24 Pelni
25 Mosque
26 Losmen Hamansyur
27 Market & Town Bemo
   Station
28 Rumah Makan Putri
   Minang
29 Rumah Makan Padang
30 Flores University
31 Socer Field
32 Rumah Makan Terminal
33 Bus & Bemo Terminal
34 Wisma Dwi Putra
35 Sub-Post Office
36 Sukarno Museum
37 Depot Ende
38 Bank Rakyat
   Indonesia

To Bajawa

Places to Stay

Ende is a spread-out town but the frequent bemos make it easy to get around. Accommodation is in three areas: near the town centre, near the airport and in between.

Central These places are all 20 minutes' walk or less from the centre. The *Wisma Dwi Putra* (tel 223) on Jalan K H Dewantara is one of the best places in town. Clean, bright singles/doubles with fan and mandi are 8500/12,500 rp, or with air-con 20,000/25,000 rp. Breakfast is included.

The cheaper *Wisma Amica* (tel 283), at Jalan Garuda 15, is 3500 rp per person (5000 rp with meals) but they'll come down to 5500 rp double if not they're not busy. Tea/coffee is free all day. All rooms have mandis. It's a decent, clean place whose owner speaks good English and might rent you his car for 30,000 rp for a Keli Mutu day trip.

The *Nirwana Beaming Inn* (tel 199) at Jalan Pahlawan 29 has big, bright and clean rooms with mandi for 5000/7000 rp downstairs, 6000/8000 rp upstairs with fans. You have to bargain a little to get these prices, which include breakfast. It looks as if they ran out of money half way through building this place.

Close by, the *Losmen Solafide* at Jalan One Kore 2 is dingy and damp but in a quiet part of town. Rooms, some with attached mandi and toilet, cost from 3300 to 6600 rp. Next door, the *Hotel Merlin* (tel 465) is friendly but unhygienic. Small rooms without mandi cost 4500/6500 rp, with private mandi and fan 5500/8500 rp and it's 12,500 rp for a triple. The helpful owner plans to open a new, probably better, 25-room losmen *Merlin II* at Jalan Ahmad Yani, near the new eastern bus terminal at Wolowona, 5 km from the centre of Ende.

Airport area *Losmen Ikhlas*, on Jalan Ahmad Yani about 400 metres from the airport, is in a 'khlas' of its own among the cheaper places in Ende – friendly and on the ball with information for travellers. Clean rooms cost 2500/4000 rp without mandi, 4000/7000 rp with mandi. Food is available – nasi goreng or nasi campur 1000 rp, lunch or dinner 1600 rp.

Next door, the good and clean *Wisma Safari* (tel 499) at Jalan Ahmad Yani 3 costs 7500/10,000 rp; all rooms have mandis and the price includes a light breakfast. *Losmen Melati* at Jalan Gatot Subroto just around the corner from the airport has OK rooms with mandi for 5500/9900 rp and with western-style toilet for 6600/12000 rp, again including light breakfast. The Wisma Safari is probably better.

In Between At Jalan Ahmad Yani 17, the *Losmen Makmur* is basic, but OK, although it's right next to a mosque. The mandis and toilets could be cleaner but the beds have mosquito nets. Rooms cost 2500 rp per person.

The not-very-busy *Wisma Wisata* (tel 368) at Jalan Kelimutu 68 is swish with a lobby and TV lounge but no restaurant. The cheapest uncarpeted rooms are 4000/6000 rp. Carpeted ones with fan, attached mandi and toilet and small verandah are 8000/10,000 rp, with air-con from 15,000/17,500 rp. A 10% tax is added to these prices.

Places to Eat

Around the bus station on Jalan Hatta warungs offer sate, rice, goat soup and vegetables at night. Otherwise it's the usual Chinese places with bare rooms and fierce neon lights – or a few Padang places.

The *Depot Ende* at Jalan Sudirman 6 has good food and a clean kitchen. Its Chinese and Indonesian dishes are around 1250 rp, more for chicken or fish. Try the fresh marquisa juice, in season from August to December for 500 rp. Ice cream and beer are also available.

Right next to the Jalan Hatta bus station, the *Rumah Makan Terminal* has seemingly reasonable food but travellers have been known to get sick after eating here. On Jalan Pasar, the *Rumah Makan Putri Minang* is friendly and has cheap Padang food.

Near the Hotel Merlin and Nirwana Beaming Inn, the *Rumah Makan Saiyo* on Jalan Banteng serves Padang food and is clean. A smallish fish in a mild spicy sauce, plus green leaves (sayur hijau), rice and a banana costs 1100 rp.

The *Rumah Makan Merlyn* on Jalan Kelimutu, about 300 metres from the airport, looks a decent little place with a longish menu of Chinese and Javanese dishes mostly around 1250 rp. Also in the airport area, over the road from the Losmen Melati, the *Rumah Makan Dewi* has cheap Indonesian food.

Getting There & Away

For details on reaching Keli Mutu and the Wolowaru-Nggela area weaving villages, see the separate sections on those places.

Air Merpati flies to and from Bima and Kupang daily, and to/from Bajawa and Labuhanbajo four times a week. There are no regular flights further east in Flores from Ende. Merpati (tel 355) is on Jalan Nangka, a 15-minute walk from the airport. The airport staff also usually know about schedules and seat availability.

Bus The terminal for buses to and from the east is Wolowona, four km east of Ende centre. Bemos between Ende and Wolowona are 150 rp. Many of the buses to the east also call at the downtown terminal if they are not full. You may be able to buy tickets from losmens or agents in Ende, saving an advance trip out to the terminal. Buses to Moni depart at 7 and 10 am, and occasionally around noon; trucks run throughout the day on Tuesdays (Moni's market day). Buses to Wolowaru and Maumere depart at 8 am, 4 and 5 pm. If you want an afternoon bus to Moni, you can take the Maumere bus but you have to pay the full fare to Maumere.

Buses to and from the west still use the downtown terminal on Jalan Hatta. Buses leave for Bajawa at 8 am, 2 and 3 pm, and direct Ruteng buses leave at 8 am.

Distance, fares and journey times are:

East

Moni	52 km	1000 rp	2½ hrs
Wolowaru	65 km	1250 rp	3 hrs
Maumere	148 km	3000 rp	6½ hrs

West

Bajawa	125 km	3000 rp	5 hrs
Ruteng	258 km	6250 rp	10 hrs

You can charter bemos in Ende for 4500 rp an hour. This might be an option if you want to do a Keli Mutu day trip from Ende.

Boat The *Kelimutu* sails every second Saturday from Ende to Kupang and two days later from Ende to Waingapu, during its fortnightly loop round Nusa Tenggara, Sulawesi, Bali, Kalimantan and Java. It puts in at the port of Ende in front of the town centre. The Pelni office (tel 43) is a five-minute walk from the pier, on the corner of Jalan Pabean and Jalan Sukarno. From Ende, *Kelimutu* 1st class/2nd class/economy fares are Kupang (10 hrs) 32,300/26,000/14,800 rp, Waingapu (7 hrs) 24,900/20,600/12,400 rp, Bima (22 hrs) 39,000/32,100/19,200 rp, Ujung Pandang (46 hrs) 80,100/65,800/34,100 rp.

Other boats sail irregularly to these and other destinations – ask at the harbour masters' offices at Ende and Pelabuhan Ipi.

Small boats also chug regularly along the south coast of Flores. To Nggela, about 55 km east of Ende, the regular fare is 500 rp in a slow, stopping boat, 750 rp in a quicker, more direct one. You may struggle to pay the same price as the locals. When the Ende-Moni road was out of action in late 1988, one boat owner started up a semi-direct 'ferry service' from Pelabuhan Ipi to Paga 90 km east, where the Moni-Maumere road meets the past. Somehow, outsiders found themselves paying 4000 rp for this trip, while locals were charged only 2000 rp – and the normal fare for the journey was 750 rp! There are usually boats several days a week to Nggela from Pelabuhan Ipi, leaving at about 6.30 am. Boats to the west are more likely to leave from Ende harbour.

Getting Around

Ende is hot and a walk of more than 15 minutes can be exhausting. Fortunately bemos run very frequently just about everywhere in the town for a flat fare of 50 rp, even out to the airport or Pelabuhan Ipi. You can often get one to where you want simply by hailing the first couple of bemos that pass where you are – most of their routes seem to cover the whole town. If not, the main terminals are the bus/bemo station on Jalan Hatta and the town bemo station at the Jalan Pasar market.

For Pelabuhan Ipi, you might have to change bemos at the corner of Jalan Ahmad Yani and Jalan Ipi. To catch a bemo from the airport, walk 100 metres to the roundabout on Jalan Ahmad Yani.

DETUSOKO & CAMAT

Between the villages of Detusoko and Camat, 35 km from Ende and 113 km from Maumere, *Wisma Santo Fransiskus* is quiet and peaceful. It's presided over by Sister Maria Graciana who has the distinction of producing a book with 100 recipes for tapioca roots! The nightly price of 3500 rp includes good meals. It's a popular retreat from the towns. Three km from the Wisma is a statue to which the locals pay homage and there are other walks in the area. It should even be possible to walk along foot trails all the way to Keli Mutu.

KELI MUTU

Of all the sights in Nusa Tenggara, the coloured lakes of Keli Mutu are the most fantastic. The three lakes, set in deep craters at a height of 1600 metres near the

Keli Mutu

pine-forested summit of the Keli Mutu volcano (in this region 'Keli' means 'mountain') have a habit of changing colour from time to time. Most recently the largest was a light turquoise, the one next to it olive green and the third black. Only a few years ago the colours were blue, maroon and black, while back in the '30s the colour scheme was similar to today's, and in the '60s the lakes had changed to blue, red-brown and cafe-au-lait.

No one has managed to explain the cause of the colours (except to suppose that different minerals are dissolved in each lake) or why they change. The moonscape effect of the craters gives the whole summit area a distinctly otherworldly atmosphere. There is a story among the local people that the souls of the dead go to these lakes: young people's souls to the warmth of the green lake, old people's to the cold of the milky-turquoise one, and those of thieves and murderers to the black lake. How a soul knows which lake to hop into when the colours keep changing, no one explains!

Keli Mutu has attracted sightseers since Dutch times and today there's a

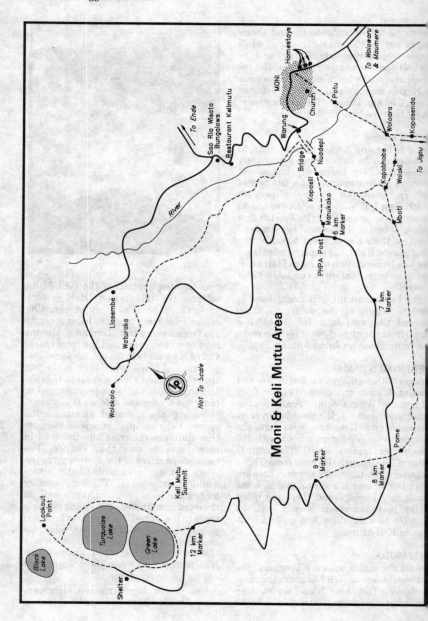

Moni & Keli Mutu Area

Not to Scale

To Ende

To Wolowaru & Maumere

To Japu

MONI

Homestays

Church

Warung

Potu

Woloara

Koposenda

Nuadepi

Bridge

Koposili

Kopohobe

Woloki

Mboti

Manukako

6 km Marker

PHPA Post

7 km Marker

Liasembe

Waturaka

Wolokolo

Lookout Point

Keli Mutu Summit

Black Lake

Turquoise Lake

Green Lake

Shelter

12 km Marker

9 km Marker

8 km Marker

Pome

River

Sao Ria Wisata Bungalows

Restaurant Kelimutu

½-km road, nearly all paved, up to the kes from near the village of Moni at the ase of the mountain. You even get an ccasional busload of tourists up there.

gravelled clearing between two of the kes was constructed in 1980 for a vice-residential visit. The staircase up to the ighest lookout point, from which you can e all three lakes, was refurbished but the oncrete platform at the top is covered in raffiti and looks monstrously out of lace.

Fortunately it's no problem to get away om any intruders – there's a wonderfully pacious feeling up here and you can cramble round the perimeters of two of ae lake-craters or walk in the surrounding ine forests. Hope for a sunny day – the irquoise lake is a stunning colour but it nly reaches its full brilliance in the inlight when wisps of yellow-green swirl round in it. You also need strong sunlight o bring out the colours in the green and aaroon lakes. The best time to see Keli Iutu is in the early morning before clouds ettle down later on. If you get a bad day, ome back the next day because it really is orth seeing!

You could camp up here, but bring ater as there's none available. The earest losmens are in Moni.

etting There & Away

'he easiest and best way of seeing Keli Iutu is to base yourself in Moni, 52 km ast of Ende on the Maumere road. taying in Moni enables you not only to et up to the lakes early but also to assess ne weather on the mountain before going p. You can walk, ride a horse or notorbike, or rent a bemo. The Keli Mutu pad forks off the Ende-Moni road about ½ km before Moni. It's 13½ km winding phill, but not steep, to the lakes. After bout six km there's a PHPA post where ou have to pay 200 rp per person – plus nore for any vehicles – to continue into he protected summit area. Beware of alse 'PHPA posts' which have been nown to set up lower down the road and

extract 1000 rp or more from unsuspecting visitors!

Usually the best time to be up at the lakes is sunrise and the two or three hours afterwards. Later, clouds often roll over and blot out the view. The sun rises earlier at the top than down in the valley below, so check the time it starts getting light the previous day and aim to be at the lakes soon after that hour. Walking up by the road takes most people three or four hours, so leave Moni well before dawn.

There is a short cut (*jalan potong*) which leaves the Moni-Ende road beside a small warung about 3/4 km from the centre of Moni, and comes out on the Keli Mutu road beside the PHPA post: this cuts about six km off the journey, but is easier to follow in daylight, so a lot of people only use it on the way down (unless they have checked it out in daylight the previous day). It's a good idea to take a torch in any case. A second short cut branches off the first one at Koposili, before the PHPA post, and reaches the Keli Mutu road 5½ km from the summit – but this one really is almost impossible to find in the dark!

If you don't want to walk, ask in Moni about the other options: for a horse the standard up-and-down charge is 7500 rp with a saddle, 5000 rp without, but most of the animals are weary creatures who go little faster than human walking pace, and leave you with a sore bum into the bargain. You might be offered a similarly decrepit motorbike for a similar price. One unlucky customer's bike broke down, so he not only failed to see the lakes but the bike's owner, far from offering a refund, tried to charge him for the repairs! Easiest and most expensive is to charter a bemo, jeep or truck for around 20,000 rp – maybe more if there are more than two or three of you, or if you want to spend more than an hour or so at the top.

From Ende You can charter bemos from Ende for 4500 rp an hour. It takes about 2½ hours from Ende to the top of Keli Mutu, so if you want three hours up there, a round trip should cost 36,000 rp. You'll probably have to bargain to get the right price. The disadvantage of going straight to Keli Mutu from Ende is that you have no idea of the weather on the mountain before you set off – so you could wind up spending a heap of money for a panorama of fog.

A regular bus from Ende can drop you at the Keli Mutu turn-off 1½ km before Moni. The walk to the top will take about three hours from here. If you don't want to carry your baggage to the top, you could probably leave it at the Sao Ria Wisata Bungalows a short distance towards Moni from the Keli Mutu turn-off. This way, you won't reach the lakes till around midday – by which time they may well be obscured by cloud even if it has been clear earlier on. Nor can you rely on finding a bus back to Ende in the afternoon. The same drawbacks apply to going direct from Maumere, which is even more expensive than from Ende.

MONI (Mone)

This village strung along the Ende-Maumere road at the base of Keli Mutu is in the heart of the Lio region, which extends from just east of Ende to beyond Wolowaru. Lio people speak a dialect of the Ende language and are renowned for their fine ikat weaving, which reaches its height in the coastal village of Nggela. A colourful hill-country market spreads over the playing field in front of Moni's large church every Tuesday morning. People start arriving in Moni on Monday afternoon for the market. The local Moni/Keli Mutu area ikat is quite attractive with bands of blue and rusty-red, but you'll see cloth from the Nggela and Maumere regions too.

In the church an image of Christ stands inside a model rumah adat – a revealing symbol of how Christianity has been fused with traditional beliefs. In the kampung behind the Moni homestays there's a genuine high-thatched *rumah adat*, still

inhabited, with some carved woodwork. You may be asked 500 rp to enter.

Apart from the trek up Keli Mutu, you can do several shorter walks from Moni. From the warung at the beginning of the short cut to Keli Mutu, 3/4 km along the Ende road from the middle of Moni, paths lead down to a 10-metre waterfall, with a pool big enough for swimming in, and a couple of hot springs (*mandi panas*). Locals sometimes use these for washing their clothes and themselves. Another short walk is out past the church to the villages of Potu and Woloara (about 1½ km from Moni). From Woloara you could continue to Jopu, about five km further.

Orientation

The road from Ende winds downhill into Moni, passing the Keli Mutu turn-off and Sao Ria Wisata bungalows about 1½ km before the centre of the village, which focuses on the market and playing field beside the main road. Homestays are across the road from the market; the church and Wisma Kelimutu are behind the playing field.

Places to Stay & Eat

Several new places have opened in Moni and competition between them can be keen: one homestay owner sometimes even ventures out to Wolowaru to catch travellers from Maumere before they reach Moni. Cheapest are the *Homestay Daniel*, *Homestay Amina Moe* and *Homestay John* along the main road opposite the market. All three charge 2000 rp per person with shared mandi. The Amina Moe and the Daniel are both friendly and clean and serve decent meals (breakfast 500 rp, evening meal 1000 rp) but the Amina Moe is particularly welcoming. You don't have to be staying at these places to eat there, if you order in advance. The John doesn't do meals and ain't so clean.

The *Wisma Kelimutu* is run by the church next door and has bigger rooms than the homestays at 4500 rp per person again with shared mandi). The accommodation's fine but the food (1000 rp a meal) is ordinary. The other option is *Sao Ria Wisata*, a set of small bungalows with private mandi 1½ km out of Moni close to the Ende road – near the Keli Mutu turn-off. The cost here is 4000 rp per person and here's a dining room with evening meals around 1500 rp. *Restaurant Kelimutu* is a popular tourist-oriented restaurant 200 metres down the road from Sao Ria Wisata.

Getting There & Away

Moni is 52 km from Ende and 96 km from Maumere. The first bus for Moni usually leaves Ende at 7 am. The fare is 1000 rp for the 2½-hour trip. From Moni to Ende, there may be an early morning bus – if not, wait for a bus from Maumere at about 11 am or 12 noon. There are also usually others coming through from Maumere at about 7 or 8 pm. On Tuesday, market day, trucks go to Ende and Wolowaru throughout the day.

From Maumere to Moni, you probably need to take an Ende bus. These start leaving about 7.30 or 8 am. Maumere to Moni costs 2000 rp and takes about four hours including a half-hour break for lunch in Wolowaru, just 13 km before Moni. In the opposite direction, the first buses to Maumere start coming through Moni around 9 or 10 am. Buses through Moni from Ende or Maumere are usually pretty crowded: sometimes you'll have to stand, or you may even have to wait for the next bus. From Moni to Wolowaru costs 250 rp.

WOLOWARU

The village of Wolowaru, straggling along the Maumere road 13 km east of Moni, is a convenient base for visiting the ikat-weaving villages of Jopu, Wolojita and Nggela. The road to these villages branches south from the main road in Wolowaru. Wolowaru itself also has quite a few weavers: people may approach you with ikat to sell, or you may be invited into houses. Otherwise look at the daily market – it winds down about 9 am except on Saturday, the main market day. As you

come into Wolowaru from Ende you'll see a group of five traditional houses distinguished by their high sloping roofs.

Places to Stay & Eat

Wolowaru has three losmen, all friendly. The new *Losmen Kelimutu*, beside the Rumah Makan Jawa Timur where most buses stop, has helpful staff and decent clean rooms for 5000 rp a double with shared mandi and 7000 rp with private mandi. Prices include breakfast. *Losmen Setia*, down near the market, is older but still clean. Doubles with shared mandi are 5000 rp, with private mandi 6000 rp, again including breakfast. A good big evening meal is 1000 rp. The basic *Losmen Hidaya*, behind the Rumah Makan Selara Kita on the main road, has no sign, smaller rooms, and is not as clean – but it's cheaper at 3000 rp double with shared mandi (breakfast not included). Meals range from 500 rp (*mie goreng*) to 1000 rp.

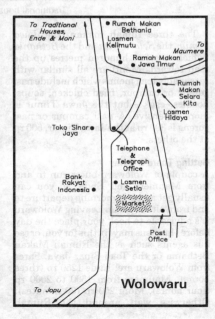

Traditional house at Wolowaru

The three rumah makan, the *Jawa Timur*, the *Selara Kita* and the *Bethania* (which is a few hundred metres up the road towards Moni) are all similar with reasonably long menus which include nasi goreng or campur, fried chicken, soups, noodles, eggs – but the Jawa Timur is more expensive. A nasi campur or nasi goreng is 800 rp at the Jawa Timur, 500 rp at the others.

Getting There & Away

A couple of Wolowaru-buses run to and from Maumere and Ende, so you can usually get an early morning departure to and from either place. Leaving Wolowaru it's advisable to book your place the day before –losmens may fix this for you, or see bus agents such as the Rumah Makan Bethania or the Toko Sinar Jaya. Fares from Wolowaru are: Ende 1250 rp (three hours), Maumere from 1500 to 2000 rp (four hours), Moni 250 rp (30 minutes). Otherwise wait around the Rumah Makan Jawa Timur for a bus heading in your direction; you should be able to get one to Maumere or Ende around 10 am to midday – and there may be more at about 7 or 8 pm. As in Moni, it's first come, first served for seats if you're hopping on a bus in mid-route.

NGGELA, WOLOJITA & JOPU

Beautiful *ikat* sarongs and shawls can be found in these and other small villages between Wolowaru and the south coast.

Though also worth a visit for its fine hilltop position above the coast, the chief attraction of Nggela is its stunning weaving; it's hand done and still uses many natural dyes and often handspun cotton. This is among the finest weaving in Flores and you'll be able to see women weaving it as well as the final products. In former times the size, colour and pattern of the ikat shawls of this region indicated the status of the wearer. Patterns range from intricate patola designs to more ecent representations of animals, people, ships, and nowadays even Keli Mutu. Nggela ikat is typically black or dark-brown based with patterns in earthy reds, browns or orange.

You have to bargain hard if you want to buy; for a sarong the starting price might be 100,000 rp, whereas 30,000 or 35,000 rp is more realistic. A *selendang* (shawl) should cost from around 15,000 to 20,000 rp. As always, watch out for synthetic dyes – though these are a lot less common in Nggela than in many other weaving centres. Nggela ikat is also sold in Ende, Wolowaru and Moni. In the village there are a number of traditional houses as well as a large church and Christian graves. You can stay with the kepala desa or maybe another family for around 3000 rp including a couple of meals.

Wolojita, about 3½ km inland from Nggela, has similar quality weavings but doesn't have Nggela's fine location. At Jopu, a further four km inland and the same distance from Wolowaru, weaving has taken a plunge in the last few years. They no longer seem to use natural dyes, and the designs are not as intricate – once you used to get soft pastel oranges and yellows, but now it's bright yellows with garish red splotches or borders. Still, you might pick up a reasonably good sarong for from 10,000 to 15,000 rp or a poor one for 3000 rp. Old weaving could be worth looking at – there might still be examples of cloth using natural dyes and the patterns may be more intricate. Jopu has a very big church and a market on Thursday.

Getting There & Away

A rough road branches off the Ende-Maumere road at Wolowaru to Jopu (four km), Wolojita (eight km) and Nggela (11½ km). Occasionally a bus or truck goes down it in the morning, but usually you have to walk from Wolowaru. It's only two or three km further to walk from Moni, so you could almost as easily start from there. An alternative is the

small boat which chugs most days from Pelabuhan Ipi at Ende to Nggela and back. It leaves Pelabuhan Ipi at around 6.30 am and takes about 3½ hours to Nggela if it doesn't make too many stops and isn't too overloaded. The cost is from 500 to 750 rp. Going from Nggela to Ende, the boat usually leaves about 12 noon. You board or disembark at Nggela by canoe from a rocky cove about 1½ km below the village.

It's an interesting walk from Wolowaru, so long as you avoid the heat of the day. The volcano-studded skyline is beautiful,

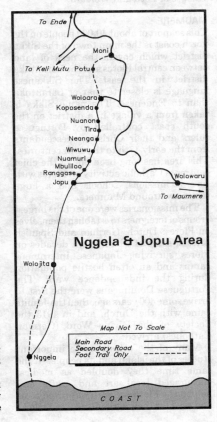

Nggela & Jopu Area

To Ende

Moni

To Keli Mutu — Potu

Woloara

Koposenda

Nuanon

Tira

Neanga

Wiwuwu

Nuamuri

Mbuliloo

Ranggase

Jopu

Wolowaru

To Maumere

Wolojita

Nggela

Map Not To Scale

Main Road
Secondary Road
Foot Trail Only

COAST

particularly near Nggela. From Wolowaru it's about an hour's walk to Jopu, then about an hour from Jopu to Wolojita. From Wolojita to Nggela you can either follow the 'road' or take a short cut (ask for the *jalan potong ke Nggela*). Allow about an hour down to Nggela, a bit more going back uphill. You can easily get from Wolowaru to Nggela and back in a day, even if you have to walk both stretches and allow plenty of time for rests. You might be offered drinks in villages on the way, but take your own too. From Moni, it's a six or seven km walk to Jopu via the villages of Potu and Woloara.

MAUMERE

This seaport of about 40,000 people on the north coast is the main town of the Sikka district which covers the neck of land between central Flores and the Larantuka district in the east. The Sikkanese language is closer to that of Larantuka than to Endenese. The name Sikka is taken from a village in a district on the south coast controlled by Portuguese rulers and their Christian descendants from the early 17th to the 20th centuries. This area has long been one of the chief centres of Catholic activity on Flores with several missions, schools and a large seminary around Maumere.

The missionaries were one of the largest groups of foreigners to establish themselves on Flores: Dutch, German and Spanish priests, some of whom spent decades on Flores surviving Japanese internment camps and an often hostile population during the independence wars. The Portuguese Dominicans were the first to arrive some 400 years ago, then the Jesuits came with the Dutch, and in 1913 the Society of the Divine Word (German Catholics) arrived.

Many of the priests made important studies of the island and its people. At the same time they doubled as medics, encouraged local art and crafts and helped the Florinese with improved tools and seed for their agriculture – as little as two decades ago many Florinese were still tilling the soil with sharpened sticks, and moving slash-and-burn farming is still pretty common. The missions were once real oases and visitors were often dependent on them for transport and, in pre-Bahasa Indonesia days, for their understanding of the local language. Today the European priests are slowly being replaced by Florinese.

To prove that God isn't always white, the interior of Maumere's cathedral on Jalan Slamet Riyadi is adorned with a series of paintings of the crucifixion of a very Indonesian-looking Jesus. Behind the cathedral is a cemetery full of tombstone-monuments to the western impact on Indonesia.

There's a strong ikat-weaving tradition in the Maumere region, and a few interesting trips can be made out of the town. Maumere itself is a rather functional place, though the market is interesting – look for heavy ikat blankets. A shop on Jalan Pasar Baru Timur, beside the market, has the most comprehensive collection of ikat (from Flores and other islands) that you'll find anywhere in Nusa Tenggara except Sumba.

Orientation & Information

Maumere is a rather spread-out town but most of what you're likely to need is within walking distance of the central market – apart from the bus station (1½ km south-west of the centre), the airport (three km east) and a couple of losmens on the way out to them.

Bank & Post The post office is on Jalan Pos next to the soccer field – hours are Monday to Thursday from 8 am to 2 pm, Friday from 8 to 11 am and Saturday from 8 am to 12.30 pm. The Bank Rakyat Indonesia on Jalan Soekarno Hatta will change cash and major travellers' cheques in several currencies, but rates are below average for anything other than US dollars.

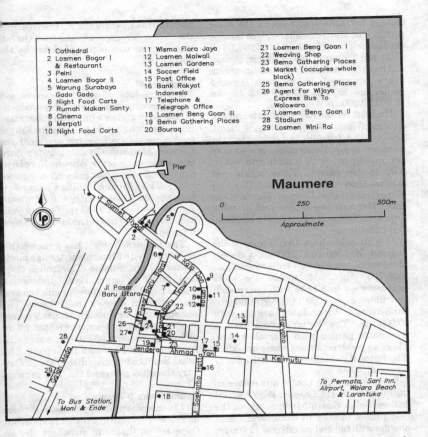

1 Cathedral	11 Wisma Flora Jaya	21 Losmen Beng Goan I
2 Losmen Bogor I & Restaurant	12 Losmen Maiwali	22 Weaving Shop
3 Pelni	13 Losmen Gardena	23 Bemo Gathering Places
4 Losmen Bogor II	14 Soccer Field	24 Market (occupies whole block)
5 Warung Surabaya Gado Gado	15 Post Office	25 Bemo Gathering Places
6 Night Food Carts	16 Bank Rakyat Indonesia	26 Agent For Wijaya Express Bus To Wolowara
7 Rumah Makan Santy	17 Telephone & Telegraph Office	27 Losmen Beng Goan II
8 Cinema	18 Losmen Beng Goan III	28 Stadium
9 Merpati	19 Bemo Gathering Places	29 Losmen Wini Rai
10 Night Food Carts	20 Bourag	

Maumere

Pier

J. Slamet Riyadi

Jl Raja Don Tomas

Jl Pasar Baru Utara

Jl Pasar Baru Barat

Jl Moa Toda

Jl Jenderal Ahmad Yani

Jl Kelimutu

Jl Soekarno Hatta

Jl Gajah Mada

To Bus Station, Moni & Ende

To Permata, Sari Inn, Airport, Waiara Beach & Larantuka

0   250   500m
Approximate

It's open from 8 am to 12 noon Monday to Friday, and from 8 to 11 am Saturday.

Places to Stay

Most places in Maumere offer a range of comfort and price – if not in the same building then in sister-establishments a short walk away. The best of the cheaper central places is the *Losmen Bogor II* (tel 271) at Jalan Slamet Riyadi 1-4 where comfortable rooms with fan, toilet and shower start at 6000/8,500 rp, including breakfast. It could get a bit hot here since

most of the rooms are along a single corridor. Its cheaper relative across the road, *Losmen Bogor I*, is friendly but dingy with rooms at 5500 rp and shared mandis.

The *Losmen Beng Goan I* (tel 247), across the road from the market on Jalan Pasar Baru, is clean enough and relatively quiet. Basic singles/doubles are 4500/8000 rp, or with fan, attached mandi and toilet 7000/12,500 rp. Beds have mosquito nets and there's an outdoor sitting area. *Losmen Beng Goan II*, on Jalan Pasar Baru Barat, entered through a shop, is cleaner but airless with much the same prices. The third member of this family, the *Losmen Beng Goan III* (tel 284/532) on Jalan K S Tubun, is newer, bigger, cleaner and more expensive but with an atmosphere like a graveyard. Rooms with fan and mandi are 7500/13,500 rp, with air-con 15,000/20,000 rp.

The little *Wisma Flora Jaya*, also central on Jalan Raja Don Thomas, is clean, homely and friendly but rooms at the front are noisy. Basic rooms are 4000 rp per person or, with mandi and toilet, 5000 rp per person. Three meals cost another 5000 rp per person or 2000 rp for dinner only. The *Losmen Gardena* on Jalan Haryono two blocks east of Jalan Raja Don Tomas is supposed to be cheap and friendly too.

Also on Jalan Raja Don Tomas is the *Losmen Maiwali* (tel 220/180), a decent place which has a few no-frills rooms from 3500/7000 rp. Most rooms are more expensive – a small one with fan, mandi and toilet costs 8000/14,000 rp and air-conditioned bungalows are 16,000/30,000 rp. The better rooms face a reasonable garden with a small aviary. There's a good restaurant where breakfast is included if you take a room with a fan or air-conditioner.

Further from the centre but nearer to the bus station, the *Losmen Wini Rai* (tel 388) on Jalan Gajah Mada is one of the best places to stay in Maumere. Clean doubles with fan and mandi cost 12,000 rp, but the management will probably come down to 10,000 rp. There are also cheaper standard rooms and dearer air-con rooms. The service is good with free tea and snacks.

Another good place, on the opposite edge of town, is the *Permata Sari Inn* (tel 171/249) at Jalan Jenderal Sudirman 1, opposite the airport turn-off. Clean rooms with fan and mandi start at 7500/12,000 rp, with air-con from 17,500/22,500 rp. It's friendly and has a restaurant facing the sea. To get here, take a bemo (100 rp) heading east. The hotel is about two km from the town centre and 800 metres from the airport. Transport to and from the bus station or airport is provided free by the hotel.

Places to Eat

There are lots of small cheap rumah makan serving Padang food or specialising in goat soup and sate on Jalan Pasar Baru Barat near the market. Numerous night food carts set up here too and near the *Losmen Maiwali*. On Jalan Pasar Baru nearer the water is the *Warung Surabaya Gado Gado* for – you guessed it – gado gado. The *Rumah Makan Santy* is spacious and clean with a long menu; simple dishes cost 1250 rp. Or buy your own fish and try to get the losmen to cook it for you.

The *Losmen Bogor I* has a reasonable restaurant with a long menu though many dishes are unavailable. The food is tasty and portions large. Basic Indonesian dishes cost 1250 rp, more for chicken and seafood, and there's cold beer. The restaurant at the *Losmen Maiwali* is very good with a more tourist-oriented menu including burgers (2000 rp), spaghetti, fruit juices (500 rp) and fresh fruit. The usual basic Indonesian dishes are 1250 rp – try the gado-gado and the fried prawns.

Getting There & Away

Air Maumere is probably the easiest place on Flores to fly into from other islands, but there are no flights to anywhere else on Flores. Merpati (tel 242), with its office on Jalan Raja Don Tomas, has daily flights to/from Kupang and Ujung Pandang, and four a week to/from Denpasar and Surabaya. You can connect in Ujung Pandang for a number of places in Kalimantan, in Denpasar for Mataram, or in Surabaya for other places in Java. Bouraq (tel 165) is on Jalan Pasar Baru Timur and has four flights a week to/from Denpasar (with connections for Java and Banjarmasin) and Kupang.

Bus & Bemo Long-distance buses leave

from the main bus station 1½ km from the centre on the Ende road, though losmens may be able to organise them to come and pick you up. Buses go east to Larantuka (3500 rp, about 5½ hours) and west to Ende (3000 rp, 6½ hours). To Larantuka they leave about hourly from 8 am to 12 noon and at about 4 and 5 pm. Ende buses go earlier – about 7 or 8 am – but there may also be late afternoon buses. There are also usually some morning buses just to Wolowaru (1500 to 2000 rp). For Moni, take an Ende bus.

Bemos and small buses leave frequently all through the day to places in the Maumere district like Lela, Sikka, Ladalero and Watublapi. Some go from around the main market but, if you get no joy there take one for 100 rp to the main bus station and find another to where you want.

Boat The Pelni office is on Jalan Slamet Riyadi, across the road from the Losmen Bogor. There are no regular passenger craft but you may be able to find something to Reo, Labuhanbajo, Bima, Ujung Pandang or even Surabaya. PT Ujung Tana on Jalan Masjid is an agent for an irregular boat to Ujung Pandang. Also ask around the harbour.

Getting Around

Maumere's Wai Oti airport is three km out of town, 800 metres off the Maumere-Larantuka road. A taxi to/from town is 2000 rp per person, but you might be able to charter a bemo for less. Otherwise walk from the airport down to the Maumere-Larantuka road and pick up a public bemo (100 rp) into town. Bemos also run between the main bus station and the town centre for 100 rp. Maumere bemo folk are heavily into trying to overcharge tourists as you might expect from the names painted on their vehicles, such as 'Gangland Boss' and 'Zero Zero Seven'.

AROUND MAUMERE
Ladalero & Nita

Many Florinese priests studied at the Roman Catholic seminary in Ladalero, 10 km from Maumere on the Ende road. The chief attraction is the museum run by Father Piet Petu, a Florinese. This has been going for around 20 years, originally with a collection of prehistoric stone implements, but over the past few years Piet Petu has built up a collection of Florinese ikat (some of it for sale) – you'll see examples of design and natural dyes that are either rare or extinct, including softly textured, pastel-coloured old Jopu sarongs. There are also many photo albums showing Florinese rituals and artefacts. All in all, despite its somewhat haphazard layout, the museum is an excellent place to try to piece together the jigsaw of Florinese culture.

It also has an interesting collection of artefacts from elsewhere in Indonesia. Father Petu speaks English and is most helpful, but if he's not there, other attendants speaking varying amounts of English can answer questions. The best way to repay him is to make a donation to the museum! It's closed on Sunday.

Nita, two km beyond Ladalero on the main road, has a Thursday market. There are bemos to Ladalero and Nita from Maumere bus station for 200 rp.

Sikka

On the south coast, 27 km from Maumere, Sikka was one of the earliest Portuguese settlements in Flores dating from the early 17th century; it remained in Portuguese control till the mid-19th century. Its rulers dominated the Maumere region until this century. Today it's interesting mainly as the chief home of the distinctive Sikkanese ikat. A lot of Sikka weaving is predominantly in maroons, blues and browns, and designs have been heavily influenced by the Dutch – you see the Dutch royal coat of arms and even pairs of baby cherubim probably copied from Dutch porcelain. Prices for the stuff, however, seem to be no lower in the village than in Maumere.

You may be able to stay with the Dutch

priest in Sikka. The road to Sikka leaves the Ende road 20 km from Maumere. Take a bemo from Maumere to Sikka – 500 rp, about one hour. About four km before Sikka, Lela is also a Catholic and weaving centre and boasts a large hospital and a few colonial buildings. There's a long, rocky black-sand beach here.

Watublapi

In the hills south-east of Maumere is the large Catholic Mission of Watublapi. From here, you can walk to Ohe and other villages where you can see both coasts of Flores.

Waiara Beach

Thirteen km east of Maumere, just off the Larantuka road, Waiara is the jumping-off point for the Maumere 'sea gardens'. There's coral inshore here, but in the wet season the water can get so murky you'll hardly see the end of your nose. To get the best out of snorkelling here you may need to rent a boat – the coral round the offshore islands of Pulau Besar, Pulau Kambing and Pulau Pemana is supposed to be particularly good. Apparently there are some enormous drop-offs.

Two establishments at Waiara provide accommodation, food and equipment for divers and snorkellers. The newer, more luxurious *Sao Wisata* offers a diving package with two dives a day for between US$65 and US$115 per person a day, depending on the room and how many people share it. Just to stay there, without the diving, costs from US$30 to US$70 including meals and transport to/from Maumere airport. The Merpati office in Maumere acts as an agent for Sao Wisata.

The more dilapidated *Sea World Club*, also called *Waiara Cottages*, charges $US25 a day for bungalow (for one or two people) and breakfast; lunch is $US4 per person, dinner $US5. It also has boats and diving and snorkelling gear for hire. Snorkelling gear costs 3000 rp a day. You can eat and take a dip at Sea World's

semi-private beach without staying there, if you just want a day out from Maumere though, the beach is nothing special.

Renting a boat alone from one of these establishments would probably cost 30,000 rp or more. Try bargaining – or look for a fisherman to take you out (and bargain again). Whoever takes you, make sure they know where the good snorkelling spots are!

Getting There & Away By public transport, take a Talibura bus from Maumere to Waiara (300 rp), or a bemo to Geliting (250 rp) then walk 1½ km along the Larantuka road. A sign points to Sea World Club/Waiara Cottages, which is about 300 metres off the road. The turn-off to Sao Wisata is a further 500 metres along the road towards Larantuka.

LARANTUKA

This little port of about 25,000 people nestles round the base of the Ili Mandiri volcano at the eastern end of Flores, separated by a narrow strait from the islands of Solor and Adonara. Larantuka is the departure point for boats to the Solor Archipelago east of Flores and for a twice-weekly ferry to Kupang.

The Larantuka area has long had closer links with the islands of the Solor Archipelago – Adonara, Solor and Lembata – than with the rest of Flores. It shares a language, Lamaholot, with the islands and the whole area – particularly outside the towns – fascinates anthropologists because of a complex social and ritual structure which in some parts survives pretty well intact. There's a web of myths about the origins of the Lamaholot people: one version has them descended from the offspring of Watowele, the extremely hairy female god of Ili Mandiri, and a character called Patigolo who was washed ashore, got Watowele drunk, cut her hair (thus simultaneously removing her magic powers and discovering that she was female) and made her pregnant. Alternatively, locals believe their forebears came from *Sina Jawa* ('China Java'), Seram or India – take your pick.

At some stage, probably before the 16th century, the Lamaholot area became divided between two groups known as the Demon and the Paji. The Demon, associated with the 'Raja' of Larantuka, were mainly grouped in east Flores and the western parts of Adonara, Solor and Lembata; the Paji, with allegiance to the 'Raja' of Adonara, were centred in the eastern parts of the three islands. Anthropologists tend to believe that the conflict between the two groups was mainly a ritual affair – as one writer puts it, 'two groups representing the two halves of the universe engaged in regular combat to produce human sacrifices for the securing of fertility and health'. Such a pattern is not uncommon in eastern Indonesia. Today people still know who is Paji and who Demon, but ritual warfare seems to have subsided. Other animist rites survive, including those for birth, name-giving, marriage, the building of a new house, the opening of new fields in *ladang* (slash-and-burn) agriculture, and the planting and harvesting of crops.

This corner of Indonesia, though always isolated, was one of the first parts of the archipelago to attract European interest. Lying on sea routes used by Portuguese seeking sandalwood from Timor, the Larantuka-Solor area saw Portuguese forts and over 20 Dominican missions being built by 1575. Portugal even maintained a few enclaves until the mid-19th century – among them Larantuka which was the centre of a community of *Topasses* (from *tupassi*, a south Indian word for 'interpreter'), the descendants of Portuguese men and local women. The Topasses are still a significant group in Larantuka today.

Portuguese-style Catholicism also flourishes in Larantuka. There's a large cathedral, and the smaller Holy Mary Chapel (*Kepala Tuan Maria*) contains Portuguese bronze and silver known as *ornamento*. On Saturdays in this chapel women say the rosary in Portuguese, and on Good Friday an image of the Virgin from the chapel is carried in procession around the town to the accompaniment of songs in Latin.

The market in Larantuka has weaving – look for ikat from Lembata, Adonara and Solor. A half-hour walk up the hills at the back of town as far as the tree line gives a fine view of Adonara and beyond.

Orientation & Information

The losmens, main pier, shipping offices and main bus stop are in the compact southern part of town shown on the map. Further north are the homes, mosques and fishing boats of the Muslim population – and the post office and airport.

There's some kind of tourist office, Bapparda, at Batuata, near the post office which is on Jalan Pasar, a few km north of the centre, past the main market. Take a bemo from the centre of town opposite the main pier. Hours are Monday to Thursday from 8 am to 2 pm, Friday from 8 to 11 am and Saturday from 8 am to 12.30 pm. You can't change foreign money or travellers' cheques at Larantuka's bank.

Places to Stay & Eat

The friendly, spotless and spacious *Penginapan Rulies Inn* is highly recommended with rooms at 4000 rp per person. Breakfast is 1000 rp, other meals cost 2500 rp. Next door the *Hotel Tresna* looks better from outside than it is. It's clean but basic, rooms with shared mandi are 4500 rp per person or 6500 rp with fan and private mandi. Meals are also available. A few minutes' walk down Jalan Niaga and right in the middle of town the seedy-looking *Losmen Kartika* would be OK if Rulies or the Tresna are full or you want something cheaper. Asking price for singles/doubles is 3000/6000 rp.

An unnamed warung on Jalan Niaga just along from the Losmen Kartika has *nasi ikan* or *nasi telur* at 600 rp, *nasi ayam* at 1200 rp. There's also a clutch of rumah makan/warungs on the right as you go

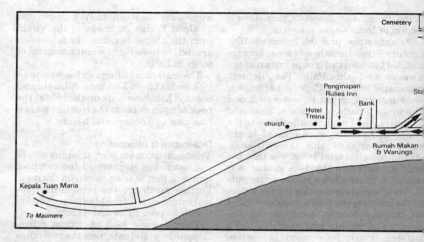

down to the pier. Buy fruit and vegetables from the pasar or from the street market just past the unnamed warung.

Getting There & Away

Air Merpati flies from Kupang to Larantuka, then on to Lewoleba on Lembata and back to Kupang, twice a week. Its office is house No 64, diagonally opposite the cathedral.

Bus Buses to/from Maumere cost 3500 rp and take about 5½ hours. It's a 137-km journey and the section between about 10 and 40 km out of Larantuka is pretty rough – but the scenery crossing this little-populated part of Flores makes up for it. If you're coming in by boat from the Solor or Alor archipelagos there'll probably be buses waiting to load passengers and take them to Maumere, maybe even Ende.

Boat The Kupang ferry leaves on Tuesday and Friday afternoons. You can buy tickets at the office at the pier entrance the same day. The price for the 14-hour voyage is 8350 rp, plus 7700 rp for a motorbike or 75,000 rp for a car. There are some seats on board but they get pretty crowded: it's better to find some deck

space and rent a sleeping mat on board for 500 rp – the earlier you board the better, since the under-cover deck space fills up pretty fast. Take your own food and drink as there's none available once the ferry has sailed. Occasionally this ferry goes via Adonara or Lembata.

Smaller boats to Adonara, Solor and Lembata leave virtually daily, often several times a day, from the same pier – see the Solor & Alor archipelagos section. For information on these and other boats out of Larantuka ask around the pier or go to the Pelni and harbour master's offices on Jalan Niaga. Unlikely possibilities occasionally crop up – boats taking Florinese workers to Sabah, cargo ships to Surabaya and Ujung Pandang. The mission ship *Ratu Rosario* is still doing its regular three-week run from Kupang to Surabaya through other ports in Nusa Tenggara, and will take passengers. Its fare to Surabaya is 60,800 rp.

Getting Around

Bemos run up and down Jalan Niaga and Jalan Pasar and to outlying villages. Catch them from Jalan Niaga opposite the pier. From the centre of town to the pasar is 50 rp, to the post office 100 rp.

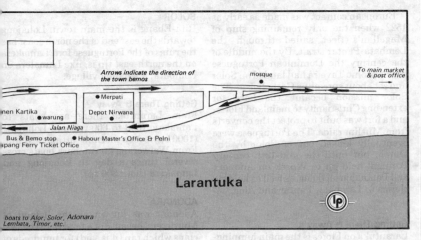

Arrows indicate the direction of
the town bemos

mosque

To main market
& post office

• Merpati

Depot Nirwana

nen Kartika

• warung

Jalan Niaga

Bus & Bemo stop   • Habour Master's Office & Pelni
pang Ferry Ticket Office

Larantuka

boats to Alor, Solor, Adonara
Lembata, Timor, etc.

Chartering a bemo to the airport costs
2500 rp per person.

AROUND LARANTUKA

Six km north of Larantuka there's a nice
beach at Weru, accessible by bemo, but
beware of stone-throwing children.
Waibarung, about four km out of
Larantuka along the Maumere road, is
said to be a weaving village. Lewoloba
(Leloba) and Lehowala are apparently
traditional villages where you might see
rumah adat, weaving, or ceremonies of
various kinds. People in Larantuka may
know of coming village festivities.
Lewoloba and Lehowala are both reportedly
near the village of Oka (150 rp by bemo).
In Oka ask the kepala desa for someone to
show you the short walk to Lewoloba.

The Solor &
Alor Archipelagos

A chain of small islands stretches out from
the eastern end of Flores: volcanic,
mountainous specks separated by swift,
narrow straits. Adonara is directly

opposite Larantuka; south of Adonara is
Solor where the Portuguese first established
themselves in the 16th century; further
east is Lembata (formerly Lomblen), with
the fishing village of Lamalera where
whales are still hunted with small boats
and harpoons and beyond that the islands
of Pantar and Alor whose people were still
head-hunting just 30 years ago. The Solor
Archipelago – Solor, Adonara and
Lembata – has close cultural links with
the Larantuka area on Flores and together
these people are known as the Lamaholot.
Pantar and Alor are the main islands of
the Alor Archipelago.

Travel in these remote regions involves
sea crossings in small, crowded boats and
stays in very basic accommodation. On
land, be prepared to walk – roads are few
and rough. Apart from in Lembata and
Alor, which now see steady trickles of
travellers, people here are not used to
westerners: children will run away or
follow you in large excited bunches. The
scenery is spectacular, all the islands
(notably Lembata) produce distinctive
ikat weaving, and there are some very
traditional, almost purely animist villages,
despite the spread of Christianity and
(less so) Islam.

European contact was made as early as 1522 when the only remaining ship of Magellan's fleet sailed through the Lembata-Pantar strait. By the middle of the century the Dominican Portuguese friar Antonio Taveira had landed on Solor and set about spreading Catholicism. The Solor mission became the base for extending Christianity to mainland Flores, and a fort was built to protect the converts from Muslim raids. The Portuguese were eventually kicked out of Solor by the Dutch, but until the mid-19th century Portugal held on to Wurek on Adonara and Pamakajo on Solor, as well as holding claims to Lembata, Pantar and Alor.

Getting There & Away
Larantuka on Flores is the main jumping-off point for these islands, with small boats sailing virtually every day to Solor, Adonara and Lembata, plus less frequent bigger ones which may go on to Pantar and Alor. Merpati flies from Kupang (Timor) and Larantuka to Lembata, and from Kupang to Alor. There's also a twice-weekly ferry between Kupang and Alor. The Larantuka-Kupang ferry sometimes calls at Adonara, Solor or Lembata. Departure times and frequency of boats depend on the season and day of the week – ask around the pier and shipping offices in Larantuka.

SOLOR
Rita-Ebang is the main town. Lohajong towards the east end of the north coast has the ruins of the Portuguese fort. Lamakera on the north-east tip is, like Lamalera on Lembata, a whaling village.

Getting There & Away
From Larantuka there are boats to Pamakajo (500 to 600 rp) and Lohajong (1000 rp) every morning at about 8 am. From Waiwerang on Adonara boats cross several times a day to Lohajong and Lamakera (both 300 rp).

ADONARA
Adonara was known as the 'Island of Murderers' because of a feud between two clans which ran (it is said) for hundreds of years with people in the hills being killed and houses burned year in, year out – very likely a case of ritual conflict between the Demon and Paji groups (see Larantuka). Though such extremes of animism seem to have died out, there are still villages in the hinterland where Christianity has only the loosest of footholds. One traveller reported placing her hands on a sacred rock above one village and being unable to remove them! The chief settlements are Wailebe on the west coast and Waiwerang on the south. A few bemos link the main villages.

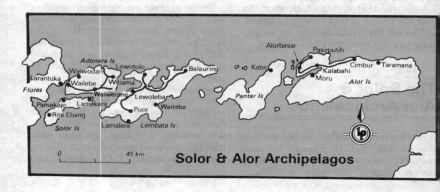

Solor & Alor Archipelagos

Waiwerang

There's an uninspiring market every Monday and Thursday – follow the streets about 400 metres in the Lembata direction from the pier. The *Losmen Taufiq*, run by a stern but friendly Muslim woman, is on the main street a minute's walk from the pier. Rooms are 2500 rp per person, an evening meal costs 2000 rp. The *Losmen Tresna* is supposedly a little cheaper. A few rumah makan dot the main street and there's another opposite the market.

Getting There & Away

Boats to Waiwerang depart Larantuka every day around 8 or 9 am and 12 noon. The two-hour trip costs 1000 rp. To Wailebe (400 rp) and Waiwodan (750 rp, further up the west coast) boats usually leave Larantuka about 11 am. At Waiwerang you can pick up boats to Solor any day, to Lewoleba on Lembata most days, to Lamalera on Lembata usually once a week, to Pantar/Alor maybe three times a week.

LEMBATA (Lomblen)

Lembata is famous for the whale-hunting village of Lamalera on the south coast. As in the rest of the Lamaholot region, many Lembata inhabitants still use the slash-and-burn method of clearing land – a technique relatively low on labour but high on soil depletion and erosion and which forces the field to lie fallow for several years between crops. Corn, bananas, papayas, and coconuts are grown and most rice is imported.

Lewoleba

Despite Ili Api volcano's smoking ominously in the background, Lewoleba is a relaxed little place and the chief settlement on Lembata. Boats unload you at a pier about a 20-minute walk west of the town; a similar distance from the pier, away from the town, are some fine, empty beaches. Between pier and town is a Bugis stilt village built out over the sea – some of its people are pearl divers and you can arrange to go out with them on diving trips and/or buy pearls at absurdly low prices. Locals will also take you out to a sandbank off Lewoleba for swimming or snorkelling; 1000 rp would be a good price for a trip of a few hours.

The centre of Lewoleba is its market place, which comes alive every Monday afternoon and evening with buyers and sellers from around Lembata and other islands. The post office and Merpati agent are in the streets surrounding the market.

The nuns in charge of Lewoleba's two hospitals are friendly and will show you round and maybe invite you to eat or stay. At the Rumah Sakit Lepra (Leper Hospital), Sister Isabella speaks German; at the Rumah Sakit Bukit, Sister Anna speaks Dutch.

Places to Stay & Eat

The pleasant little *Wisma Rejeki* is in the centre of town opposite the market. Singles/doubles cost 4000/8000 rp and have mosquito nets; mandis are shared but clean. The food's reasonable too – 1500 rp for a big evening meal. There's a large map of the island on the losmen wall. The manager can fix you up with things like motorbike rental, pearl-diving trips or a hiking guide if you want one, and will look after your baggage while you're away. He also sells some very fine Lembata ikat, including old and new ceremonial sarongs which are given in marriage exchanges. Handspun cotton and vegetable dyes are still used in the good cloths. His asking prices range from 40,000 to 1.5 million rp!

The very basic *Penginapan Rachmat* is at the end of Jalan Aulolon (the street down to the left from the far end of the market as you come from the pier). A bed is 2500 rp per person, and there's no food. There's a row of warungs behind the market. One of them does a decent gado gado with rice for 1000 rp.

Getting There & Away

Boats ply daily both ways between Larantuka and Lewoleba (except, it seems, from Lewoleba to Larantuka on Mondays). They normally leave between 7 and 9 am, cost 2000 rp, and take four hours (longer if they call at Waiwerang). See the Alor & Pantar section for boats to/from those islands. Merpati flies Kupang-Larantuka-Lewoleba-Kupang twice a week.

Around Lewoleba

Most of Lembata's finest ikat – recognisable by its burgundy-coloured base and highly detailed patterning – comes from villages on the slopes of Ili Api 15 or 20 km from Lewoleba. Kotagede is one such village – but locals seem reluctant to show, let alone part with, their best work.

Jontona village is near the west side of Teluk Waienga, the deep inlet in Lembata's north coast. Trucks go there about three times a week – or rent a motor bike in Lewoleba for maybe 10,000 rp a day. An hour's walk towards Ili Api from Jontona is the *kampung lama* (old village) with at least 50 traditional houses. These contain many sacred and prized objects including a huge number of elephant tusks, but are occupied by the villagers only for ceremonies such as the *kacang* (bean) festival in late September/early October. You'll probably be able to stay with villagers in Jontona.

Balauring

A port on the peninsula jutting off the eastern end of Lembata; apparently there is one small losmen here. Buses or trucks leave Lewoleba for Balauring about four days a week, and the trip takes about three hours. There are also two or three boats a week from Lewoleba to Balauring, probably via the village of Lewotolo at the foot of Ili Api. Boats between Lewoleba and Alor call at Balauring once or twice a week: from Balauring to Kalabahi on Alor takes about eight hours for about 7500 rp.

Lamalera

Like characters out of *Moby Dick*, the people who live in this village on the south coast of Lembata still hunt whales using small boats. There's the added drama of a harpooner who leaps from the boat on to the back of the whale and plunges his harpoon deep into its flesh. The whaling season is limited to those months of the year from about May to October when the seas aren't too rough. Even then, the whales are infrequent and unpredictable, though curiously enough they appear in the wake of south-easterly winds.

Only a few whales a year are caught now, perhaps 20 or 25, since there aren't so many around any more. Declining whale numbers have also meant that quite a few young men have left the village to seek work elsewhere, and there's a possibility that the whale-hunting skills will decline. Most whales caught are sperm whales though occasionally smaller pilot whales are taken. When whales are scarce the villagers harpoon sharks, manta rays and dolphins, which are available all year round. Using nets is alien to these people and fishing rods are used only for sharks.

The whaling boats are made entirely of wood with wooden pegs instead of nails. Each vessel carries a mast and a sail made of palm leaves, but these are lowered during the hunt when the men row furiously to overtake the whale. There's usually a crew of about 15 and as the gap between the boat and the whale narrows, the harpooner takes the three-metre long harpoon, which is attached by a long coil of rope to the frame of the boat, leaps on to the back of the whale and plunges in the harpoon. An injured whale will try to dive, dragging the boat with it, but cannot escape since it has to resurface to breathe.

The whale meat is shared out by traditional dictates. The heads go to two families of original landowners – a custom observed, it is said, since the 15th century. Later settlers from Maluku and Sulawesi were allowed to stay and hunt whales only on condition that the head of each whale be given to the two families. The crew, the boatbuilder, the harpoon maker and the rope keeper all take a share of the catch with the boat owner and harpooner being especially rewarded. Most of the whale meat is dried in the sun. The blubber is melted to make fuel for oil lamps. Not all the meat is used in the village – some is traded with the mountain villages for fruit and vegetables.

In Lamalera you may be able to stay with the padre, otherwise ask the kepala desa for somewhere to stay.

Getting There & Away

The easiest way to get to Lamalera is on the boat from Lewoleba, which usually leaves each Monday night after the Lewoleba market. The return trip is made a few days later. There's also a weekly boat between Lamalera and Waiwerang on Adonara – its days seem to vary.

Alternatively walk from Lewoleba to Lamalera. There are two roads – long and short. For the short one, head out of Lewoleba and ask directions for the nearby village of Namaweke. If you simply ask for the road to Lamalera you could end up being directed along the road that takes a wide circular route around the island. It takes about seven to 10 hours to walk to Lamalera from Lewoleba along the short route – basically it's uphill for the first half, then downhill from shortly before Udek. Keep asking directions as you go. If you really want a guide, ask at the Wisma Rejeki.

You really need a proper backpack with a frame if you're going to walk. Bring some food but even more importantly bring *lots* of water with you – any activity more strenuous than breathing will have you thirsting! Another possibility is to take a truck from Lewoleba to Puor, about three-quarters of the way to Lamalera by the long route. There are about three trucks a week, then you might be able to hire a

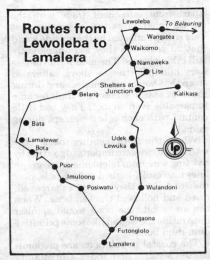

Routes from Lewoleba to Lamalera

horse in Puor or find a motorcycle in Lewoleba.

If you're worried about the reaction of village people on distant islands, the wariness works both ways; if you've ever been greeted by a machete-carrying kepala desa you'll realise that a large, hairy foreigner isn't the most daunting creature that could wander into an Indonesian village. You'll endear yourself to them if you cultivate that dehydrated, heat-stroked, couldn't-lift-a-finger-to-harm-a-gecko appearance – you'll soon be in someone's house gulping down water, surrounded by dozens of wide-eyed children.

ALOR & PANTAR

East of the Solor group are the islands of Alor and Pantar. Alor in particular is so rugged, and travel there so difficult, that its roughly 100,000 people are divided into some 50 tribes, with about as many different languages. There are seven major language groups on Alor alone, and five on Pantar.

Although the Dutch installed local rajas along the coastal regions after 1908, they had little control over the interior.

Apart from infrequent trade with the coastal inhabitants the interior peoples were so little affected by the outside world that 30 years ago they were apparently still taking heads! The mountain villages were hilltop fortresses above valleys so steep that horses were useless and during the rainy season some of the trails became impassable even on foot. They had little contact with each other – except during raids.

When the 20th century came, the warriors put western imports to good use by twisting wire from telephone or telegraph lines into multi-barbed arrowheads, over the tip of which they pressed a sharpened, dried and hollowed chicken bone. When the arrow hit, the bone would splinter deep inside the wound like some primitive dum-dum bullet.

The coastal populations are predominantly Muslim and today Christianity has made some inroads into the interior, but indigenous animist cultures survive, mainly because travel remains very difficult. Roads are few and boat is a commoner form of transport.

Alor's chief fame in the outside world lies in its mysterious *mokos* – bronze drums (perhaps more accurately 'gongs') about half a metre high and a third of a metre in diameter, tapered in the middle like an hour-glass and with four ear-shaped handles around the circumference. They're closed at the end with a sheet of bronze that sounds like a bongo when thumped with the hand. There are thousands on the island – the Alorese apparently found them buried in the ground and believed them to be gifts from the gods.

Most mokos have decoration similar to that on bronze utensils made in Java in the 13th and 14th century Majapahit era, but others resemble earlier South-East Asian designs and may be connected with the Dongson culture which developed in Vietnam and China around 700 BC and then pushed its influence south into Indonesia. Later mokos even have Dutch or English-influenced decoration.

Theories of the mokos' origins usually suggest they were brought to Alor from further west by Indian, Chinese or Makassarese traders. This fails to explain why old bronze drums found on Java, Bali, Sumatra and Borneo are larger and display finer workcraft than those on Alor – or why the mokos were found in the ground. It's possible that groups of mokos reached Alor at different periods, perhaps with the better examples being bought up earlier on the traders' routes. Maybe the Alorese buried theirs in now-forgotten times, as an offering to spirits at a time of plague, or to hide them during attacks.

Today the mokos have acquired enormous value among the Alorese and men devote great energy and time to amassing collections of them, along with pigs and land. Such wealth is the only avenue to obtaining a bride in traditional Alorese society. The value of a moko depends mainly on its age: the newest, cheapest ones apparently go for 200,000 rp-plus. In former times, whole villages would sometimes go to war in an attempt to win possession of a prized moko.

Kalabahi & Around

Kalabahi is the chief town on Alor, at the end of a long, narrow, palm-fringed bay on the west coast. Losmens include the *Adi Dharma* at Jalan Martadinata 12, the *Marlina* on Jalan El Tari, and the *Melati* at Jalan Dr Sutomo 1. Most travellers head for the Adi Dharma, where the owners can advise you on where to go on the island and how to get there. They'll also rent you a vehicle for 30,000 rp a day to reach indigenous villages like Antimerang or Alor Kecil.

Getting There & Away

Merpati flies from Kupang to Kalabahi and back six days a week. Kalabahi airport is 28 km from the town. The Perum ASPP ferry from Tenau, the port of Kupang, leaves for Kalabahi on Tuesday and Saturday around 12 noon, costing 10,500 rp for the 17-hour voyage. It departs on Wednesday and Sunday afternoons for the return trip. The Pelni ship *Elang* calls at Kalabahi every week or two on its circuits round various ports in Timor, Flores and southern Maluku.

Most weeks at least one Kalabahi-based boat makes a trip to Lewoleba on Lembata and back, usually reaching Lewoleba in time for its Monday market and leaving there early on Tuesday morning. They'll stop at one or more of Kabir (Pantar), Balauring (eastern Lembata), Waiwerang (Adonara) or Larantuka on the round trip. Boats to look for include the *Karya Dua Lima* and the *Safari*. The fare from Lewoleba to Kalabahi is about 10,000 rp for a roughly 12-hour trip.

Timor

If you arrive in Timor from Darwin, it will hit you with all the shock of Asia. Kupang, the main city, is very Indonesian with its buzzing streets, honking horns, third world smells and sights. Timor's culture however seems rather bland by comparison with that of Sumba or Flores. Away from Kupang, it's little-touristed – a fairly scenic island with a number of destinations that are interesting or agreeable without being unmissable. New interest was added in 1989 when East Timor, a former Portuguese colony, was opened up to foreign tourists for the first time since Indonesia invaded and took it over in 1975.

Timor's landscape is unique with its spiky lontar palms, rocky soils and central mountains dotted with villages of beehive-shaped huts. The island has some fantastic coastline but no tourist-type beach spots as yet, though you can take trips from Kupang to nearby islands for swimming and snorkelling. East Timor's beaches which attracted travellers before 1975 are again accessible.

Thanks to Merpati's twice-weekly

flights between Kupang and Darwin since 1986, and to improved transport in Nusa Tenggara, more travellers to or from Australia are now passing through Timor. Some Darwinites are also choosing Timor instead of Bali for holidays because it's infinitely less developed and cheaper to reach.

Apart from Kupang, which is probably the most prosperous town in Nusa Tenggara, Timor is poor, especially the eastern half. West Timor has a population of 1.2 million and East Timor about 650,000. Christianity – both Protestant and Catholic – is widespread, though still fairly superficial in some areas: the old animistic cultures have not been completely eradicated. In the hills of the centre and the east, country folk still defer to their traditional chiefs – though major damage seems to have been done to traditional East Timorese society by the Indonesian takeover.

The dark-skinned and lightly built Timorese resemble the Bataks of Sumatra and the Torajans of Sulawesi. About 14 languages are spoken on the island, both Malay and Papuan types, although *Tetum* (the language of a people who are thought to have first settled in Timor in the 14th century) is understood in most parts.

HISTORY

The Tetum of central Timor are one of the largest ethnic groups on the island. Before the Portuguese and Dutch colonisation they were fragmented into dozens of small states. Skirmishes between them were frequent and headhunting was a popular activity, although when peace returned the captured heads were kindly returned to the kingdom from which they came.

Another major group, the Atoni, are thought to be the earliest inhabitants of Timor and one theory is that they were pushed westward by the Tetum. The Atoni form the predominant population of west Timor and like the Tetum were divided into numerous small kingdoms before the arrival of Europeans. It's

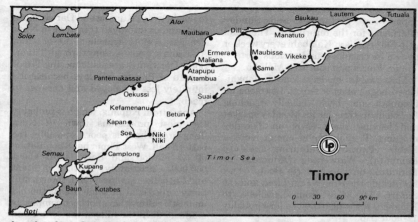

Timor

thought that their traditional political and religious customs were strongly influenced by Hinduism, possibly as a result of visits by Javanese traders, but like the Tetum they held to a strong belief in spirits, including ancestor spirits.

The first Europeans in Timor were the Portuguese, perhaps as early as 1512, the year after they captured Melaka. Like Chinese and western Indonesian traders before them, the Portuguese found the island a plentiful source of sandalwood (prized in Europe for its aroma and the medicinal santalol made from the oil). In the mid-17th century the Dutch occupied Kupang, Timor's best harbour, beginning a long conflict for control of the sandalwood trade. In the mid-18th century the Portuguese withdrew to the eastern half of Timor. The division of the island between the two colonial powers, worked out in agreements between 1859 and 1913, gave Portugal the eastern half plus the enclave of Oekussi on the north coast of the western half, while Holland got the rest of the west. Today's Indonesian province of East Timor has the same boundaries as former Portuguese Timor.

Neither European power penetrated far into the interior until the second decade of this century and the island's political structure was left largely intact, both colonisers ruling through the native kings. Right through to the end of Portuguese rule in East Timor many ostensibly Christian villagers continued to subscribe to animist beliefs. When Indonesia won independence in 1949 the Dutch cleared out of West Timor, but the Portuguese still held East Timor – setting the stage for the tragedy that would take place during the 1970s and '80s.

East Timor

Until the end of the 19th century, Portuguese authority over their half of the island was never very strong. Their control was often effectively opposed by the *liurai*, the native Timorese rulers, and by the *mestico*, the influential descendants of Portuguese men and local women. The Dominican missionaries were also involved in revolts or opposition to the government. Eventually a series of rebellions between 1894 and 1912 led to bloody and conclusive 'pacification'.

The colony had been on the decline much earlier as the sandalwood trade fizzled out, and as Portugal fell into a depression after WW I, East Timor drifted into economic torpor. Neglected by Portugal, it was notable only for its modest production of high-quality coffee and as a distant place of exile for opponents of the Portuguese regime. The ordinary Timorese were subsistence farmers using the destructive *ladang* or slash-and-burn system, with maize (sweet corn) the main crop.

In WW II, though Portugal and her overseas territories were neutral, the Allies assumed that the Japanese would use Timor as a base to attack Australia. Several hundred Australian troops were landed in East Timor and until their evacuation in January 1943 they carried out a guerrilla war which tied down 20,000 Japanese troops, of whom 1500 were killed, on the island. The Australian success was largely due to the support they got from the East Timorese, for whom the cost was phenomenal. The Japanese razed whole villages, seized food supplies and killed Timorese in areas where the Australians were operating. Farms were abandoned in the war zones, resulting in starvation, while other Timorese were killed by Allied bombing. By the end of the war, between 40,000 and 60,000 East Timorese had died.

After the war the Portuguese resumed control. Dili was rebuilt, the plantations were put back in shape, and the production of livestock and grain increased. Even into the '70s, however, there was little industry, no sign of valuable mineral resources and scant improvement in education.

The turning point came on 25 April 1974 when a military coup in Portugal overthrew the Salazar dictatorship. The new government sought to discard the remnants of the Portuguese empire as quickly as possible. With the real possibility of East Timor becoming an independent state, three major political groups quickly formed in the colony:

UDT The original members of the Timorese Democratic Union were mostly officials and small property holders and, although they started out in favour of continued association with Portugal, within a few weeks they were advocating independence.

ASDT From the start the Association of Timorese Social Democrats advocated complete independence for East Timor. Later known as Fretilin (Revolutionary Front for an Independent East Timor), it gained the edge over the UDT, perhaps partly because of its more radical social policies.

Apodeti This party advocated integration with Indonesia. Its membership probably never exceeded a few hundred, and it probably would not have survived if the Indonesians had not given it financial and moral support, eventually turning it into a front for their own goals.

Indonesian leaders had had their beady eyes on East Timor since the 1940s, though before the '70s they were too involved with separatist rebellions, campaigns in Irian Jaya and *Konfrontasi* with Malaysia to do much about it. Fretilin, however, was regarded by many of them as Communist and there were fears that an independent East Timor might inspire separatism in Indonesia. The Australian government also expressed a preference for integration of East Timor into Indonesia.

In East Timor the rumours flew thick and fast and suspicions grew. On 11 August 1975, the UDT staged a coup in Dili which led to a brief civil war between it and Fretilin. Military superiority lay from the outset with Fretilin which was supported by 2000 or so Timorese soldiers in the colony – only a few Portuguese soldiers remained. The bulk of the fighting was over by the end of August and the UDT remnants withdrew to Indonesian Timor.

Fretilin proved surprisingly effective in getting things almost back to normal, but by the end of September Indonesia had decided on a takeover. In October Indonesian troops staged trial attacks just within the East Timor border. East Timor and Fretilin now faced Indonesia alone; the Portuguese were certainly not coming back. On 7 December 1975 the Indonesians launched their invasion of East Timor with an assault on Dili, coincidentally less than 24 hours after 'Sideshow' Kissinger had left Jakarta.

From the start the invasion met strong resistance from Fretilin troops who quickly proved their worth as guerilla fighters. Though East Timor was officially declared Indonesia's 27th province on 16 July 1976, Fretilin kept up regular attacks on the Indonesians, even on targets very close to Dili, until at least 1977. But gradually Indonesia's military strength and Fretilin's internal divisions and lack of outside support took their effect. By 1989, Fretilin appeared to have been pushed back to just a few hideouts in the far east of the island. Indonesia was confident enough to open up East Timor to foreign tourists in 1989. But the remaining 'low-intensity' security problem seems to warrant the continued presence of 15,000 Indonesian troops (including local militia).

The cost of the takeover to the East Timorese people has been huge. International humanitarian organisations estimate that about 100,000 people may have died in the hostilities and from disease and famine that followed. It's also estimated that 90% of the population has been relocated since 1975 for 'security reasons' with only 20% of villages now occupying ancestral sites, although some people are being moved back.

There are still complaints about indiscriminate arrests, restrictions of movement and human rights abuses. East Timor is the poorest province in Indonesia with an average income of US$200 a year against the national average of US$500 (official figures), but relatively large amounts of money are being spent by the Indonesian government in an effort to improve roads, electricity and water supplies, and social welfare. Despite this, health care is poor with 123 doctors for the population of 650,000. Technical skills are lacking and malaria is a problem.

Compounding the problems is the alleged predominance of the military in economic life. The military deny this, yet private companies are unwilling to get involved. East Timor's most valuable export is high quality coffee, of which it produces 9000 tonnes a year. Most of this is collected and exported through Surabaya by PT Denok, a company run by Indonesian-Chinese businessmen but apparently set up by a group of Indonesian generals with a view to controlling all industry and commerce in East Timor, including the sandalwood trade. Coffee growers say they receive less for their product than growers in West Timor.

Some readers' letters have reported that the police question locals who have been talking to foreigners. After long isolation, the East Timorese are intrigued by westerners. As of April 1989, no permit was required for foreigners to travel to East Timor and even though four districts were officially closed, in practice travellers were getting right through to Tutuala, East Timor's most easterly point. The situation is not expected to change unless there is an unforeseen increase in Fretilin activity.

Books

Probably the best account of events surrounding the Indonesian invasion of East Timor is John Dunn's *Timor – A People Betrayed* (Jacaranda Press, Brisbane, Australia, 1984). Dunn was Australian consul in East Timor from 1962 to 1964; he was also part of an Australian government fact-finding mission to East Timor in June to July 1974 and returned in 1975, just after the Fretilin-UDT war, to lead an Australian relief effort. *Timor, The Stillborn Nation* by Bill Nicol (Widescope International, Melbourne, Australia, 1978) provides something of a balance to Dunn's book: Nicol tends to criticise Fretilin leaders and places much more of the blame on the Portuguese who, he says, provoked the UDT-Fretilin civil war and invited

Indonesian military intervention by their attempts to rid themselves of East Timor as fast as possible.

For the inside story from a Fretilin point of view, read *Funu: The Unfinished Saga of East Timor* by Jose Ramos Horta (Red Sea Press, New Jersey, USA, 1987). Horta was a Fretilin leader in 1975 and has since been its UN representative. Also sympathetic to Fretilin is *The War Against East Timor* by Carmel Budiardjo and Liem Soei Liong, (Pluto Press, Leichhardt, Australia, 1984).

GEOGRAPHY

Timor is 60% mountainous with high plateaux, deep valleys and rocky soils. Its rugged central backbone has many peaks over 2500 metres; the highest, Tata Mai, stands at about 3000 metres, half way along the range.

Most of the narrow south coast plain is covered in tropical vegetation giving way to bushland dominated by eucalypts and acacias on the slopes. Along the north coast the mountains slope right into the sea. The numerous streams become torrents in the wet season and frequently sever the roads, but in the dry season they are just dry beds. For much of the year, the north coast is arid with clumps of gnarled and stunted trees, but the wet season turns it green.

Aggravated by dry winds from northern Australia, the dry season is distinct and results in hunger and water shortages. To remedy the water problem, at least in the west around Soe, there is an intensive programme of small earth-dam building.

The slash-and-burn method of agriculture is still used to clear fields and the Timorese have never accepted the plough. Teams of seven or eight buffalo will be driven across the fields to turn them into squishy mud for planting. Maize is the staple crop, but dry rice is also important and some irrigated rice is grown in the river valleys.

KUPANG

Kupang is virtually a booming metropolis compared with the overgrown villages that pass for towns in other parts of Nusa Tenggara. It's the capital of East Nusa Tenggara (NTT) province which covers West Timor, Roti, Sawu, the Solor and Alor Archipelagos, Sumba, Flores and Komodo. As such it comes fully equipped with footpaths and brightly decorated bemos with sophisticated sound systems.

The centre is busy, noisy and untidy while the wealthier residential areas are in the suburbs. There's a lot of building going on, particularly on the eastern edge of town.

Merpati's regular Darwin/Kupang flights are attracting many short-term Australian visitors from the Northern Territory. One unpleasant outcome of increased tourism is local youths calling out obscenities (in English) to tourists as they pass you on their motorbikes. This

apart, it's not a bad place to hang around for a few days – Captain Bligh did when he arrived here after his *Bounty* misadventures.

History

The Dutch East India Company occupied Kupang in the middle of the 17th century, mainly in an attempt to gain control of the sandalwood trade. The Portuguese had built a fort at Kupang but abandoned it before the Dutch arrived, leaving the Portuguese-speaking Christian mixed-blood *mestico* population (or the 'black Portuguese' as they were known) to oppose the Dutch. It was not until 1749, after an attack by the mestico on Kupang had been decisively defeated, that the Dutch went more or less unchallenged in west Timor.

Timor was however very much a side-show for the Dutch. Supplies of sandalwood had already dwindled severely by 1700, and by the late 18th century Kupang was little more than a symbol of the Dutch presence in Nusa Tenggara. Not until the 20th century did they pay much attention to the interior of the island.

The original inhabitants of the Kupang area were the Helong who, squeezed by the Atoni, had by the 17th century been limited to a small coastal strip at the western tip of the island. Later, partly because of the Dutch-supported migration of people from the nearby island of Roti to Kupang, most of the Helong migrated to the small island of Semau off Kupang. By the mid-20th century they were confined to just one village near Tenau (the port of Kupang) and several villages on Semau.

Orientation

Kupang is hilly. Its downtown area hugs the waterfront with the main streets – Siliwangi, Garuda, Sumatera, Sumba, Yani, Sumohardjo and Soekarno – forming a large loop which takes in most of the shops. Hotels and losmen are scattered throughout the town. One focal point is the junction of Jalan Siliwangi and Jalan Soekarno, where the central bus and bemo station – known simply as the *Terminal* – is located. Most of the restaurants are around here. Kupang's El Tari airport is 15 km east of town and Tenau Harbour is eight km west.

Information

Tourist Office The tourist office is on Jalan Soekarno near the Terminal. Usually someone speaks good English. They have leaflets and displays with lots of ideas for places to go – including Roti, Sawu and the rest of East Nusa Tenggara. The office is open Monday to Thursday from 7.30 am to 2 pm, Friday from 7.30 am to 1 pm and Saturday from 7.30 am to 12.30 pm.

Communications The main post office, with the poste restante, is at Jalan Palapa 1. It's open Monday to Thursday from 8 am to 2 pm, Friday from 8 to 11 am and Saturday from 8 am to 1 pm. To get there, take a five-lamp bemo from downtown. There's a sub-post office on Jalan Soekarno, a short walk from the Terminal. The Telephone & Telegraph office is on Jalan Urip Sumohardjo.

Money The Bank Dagang Indonesia near the Terminal on Jalan Soekarno will change major currency notes and major US and Australian dollar travellers' cheques. It's open Monday to Friday from 7 am to 12 noon and from 1 to 2.30 pm and Saturday from 7 to 11 am. Bank Negara Indonesia 1946 on Jalan Sumatera, next to *Wisma Maliana*, changes major US and Australian dollar travellers' cheques and some cash. Service is fast here. It's open from 7.30 am to 2.30 pm Monday to Friday and from 7.30 am to 11.30 am on Saturday. Pitoby Travel at Jalan Siliwangi 75 gives about 100 rp less for the US dollar but it's open on Sundays. A money changing office opens at Kupang airport when flights from Darwin come in. It gives same the rate as the banks.

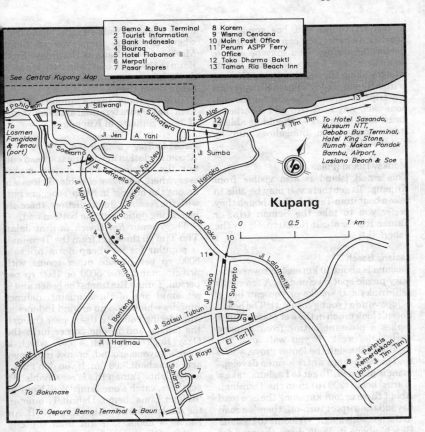

1	Bemo & Bus Terminal	8	Korem
2	Tourist Information	9	Wisma Cendana
3	Bank Indonesia	10	Main Post Office
4	Bouraq	11	Perum ASPP Ferry
5	Hotel Flobamor II		Office
6	Merpati	12	Toko Dharma Bakti
7	Pasar Inpres	13	Taman Ria Beach Inn

See Central Kupang Map

Kupang

0   0.5   1 km

Markets

The main market is the rambling Pasar Inpres off Jalan Suharto in the south of city. To get there, you can take an 'Oepura' bemo down Jalan Suharto and walk the short distance to the market from Jalan Suharto. There's a lesser market on the seafront off Jalan Garuda.

Museum NTT

The interesting East Nusa Tenggara Museum is on Jalan Perintis Kemerdekaan on the eastern edge of the city. It has exhibits of arts, crafts and artefacts from all over the province. There are helpful English-speaking guides and most of the labels are in Indonesian and English. This is a good place to get an introduction to Nusa Tenggara if you've just arrived, or to pull together what you've seen if you're leaving. To get there, take a 'Walikota' bemo from the Terminal. It's open Monday, Thursday and Saturday from 9 am to 12 noon. Entry is free, but give a donation when you leave.

Semau Island

Semau, visible from Kupang, is interesting

to wander round and has some good beaches (where you can snorkel) and freshwater springs. You may be able to organise a boat from one of the fishing villages along the beach outside Kupang or from Tenau. Teddy's Bar in Kupang runs day trips to Semau. The cost for the one-hour each way boat trip and a barbecue lunch is 15,000 rp. You should be able to stay overnight in bungalows run by Teddy's Bar.

Monkey Island (Pulau Kera)

This small island is also visible from Kupang. To get there you may be able to take a boat from Teddy's Bar, though they prefer you to take the Semau trip, or Taman Ria for about 10,000 rp. Or try the fisherfolk!

Lasiana Beach

Lasiana is about 10 km east of town and a busy picnic spot on Sunday. A few stalls sell drinks and snacks or you can buy a *kelapa muda* (young coconut). The beach doesn't look much in the wet season, but it makes a pleasant outing from Kupang during the week. If you walk over the headland through the lontar grove, you'll find more beaches where losmen development is planned. To get to Lasiana, take a 'Tarus' bemo (200 rp) from the Terminal. About three or four km along the Soe road beyond the airport turn-off, there's a road to the left with a sign 'Welcome to Lasiana Beach' above it. Walk down the road for about one km.

Baun

A small, quiet village 25 km south of Kupang in the hilly Amarasi district, Baun is a centre of ikat weaving and has a few Dutch buildings. You can visit the *rumah raja*, the last raja's house, now occupied by his widow. She loves to chat with foreigners and will show you some of her interesting weavings and her rose garden. If your Indonesian is good enough, you can learn a lot about the area's history from her, particularly about WW II. The

house is a short walk straight ahead from where the bemo drops you in Baun. Market day in Baun is Saturday. From Baun to the south coast and back is a good day's hike – apparently there's a surf beach down there.

To get to Baun, take a minibus (350 rp) from the Oepura terminal at the south end of Jalan Suharto in Kupang.

Places to Stay – bottom end

Accommodation in Kupang is spread out, but the efficient bemo system makes everywhere easily accessible. Prices are among the highest in Nusa Tenggara but, with the recent influx of visitors, there are increasing options at the bottom end.

The *Taman Ria Beach Inn*, at Jalan Tim Tim 69 three km from the Terminal, is popular for its cheap dorm prices – 3000 rp per person; other rooms with private mandi cost 5000 or 7500 rp per person. Taman Ria fronts the beach and is set amid one of those quaint, defunct funfairs which crop up around Indonesia. Mouldering concrete tigers peer through the foliage and in one corner lurks the Ozzy Rock Cafe with a bar, which if there's anyone around, cranks into noisy action at about 9.30 pm. If you don't need early nights Taman Ria is reasonable. To get there, catch a one-lamp 'Wali Kota' or 'Kelapa Lima' bemo. Definitely quieter, the *Backpackers* at Jalan Kancil 37B, Air Nona, is about four km from the city centre. It's part of the International Network Group which has hostels in Darwin, Sydney, Los Angeles and elsewhere. The cost is 5000 rp per person in doubles or small dorms. It's a friendly place but rooms are dark and cramped, mosquitoes are active and the shared mandis could be cleaner. You have to eat out – there's a cheap gado-gado warung where Jalan Kancil meets the main road. To get to the hostel, catch a three-lamp bemo from the terminal.

Losmen Rahmat, the signless green and white building next to the mosque on Jalan Lakaan, is more central, and reputedly

1 Dutch Graveyard
2 Pelni
3 Teddy's Bar
4 Pantai Laut Restaurant
5 Toko Sinar Baru
6 Bank Dagang Negara
7 Night Warungs
8 Sub Post Office
9 Tourist Information
10 Restaurant 5 Jaya Raya
11 Bemo & Bus Terminal
12 Toko Columbia
13 Restaurant Karang Mas
14 Pitoby Travel
15 Paris Indah Bus Agent
16 Wisma Setia
17 Church
18 Departemen Pendidikan & Kebudayaan
19 Bank Indonesia
20 Kupang Indah Inn
21 Laguna Inn
22 Bemo Interchange
23 Telephone & Telegraph Office
24 Losmen Rahmat
25 Mosque
26 Garuda
27 Cinema
28 Beach Market
29 Night Warungs
30 Rumah Makan Beringin Jaya
31 Wisma Susi
32 Wisma Maliana
33 Bank Negara Indonesia 1946

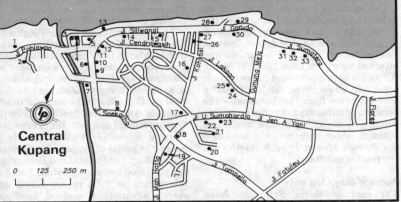

friendly, but tatty. Singles/doubles with shared mandi are 3500/5000 rp.

Places to Stay – middle

Many of these places have a range of prices so the middle and top end overlap to some extent. Facing out to sea at Jalan Sumatera 37, the good and fairly central *Wisma Susi* (tel 22172) has a wide range of prices starting with downstairs rooms at 7000 rp single or 8500/12,500 rp for singles/doubles with fan. Upstairs rooms with fan and mandi are 10,000/15,000 rp, more with air-con. Prices include tax. You can buy breakfast for 1500 rp – good enough when it arrives, but something is always missing.

Teddy's Bar (tel 21142), at Jalan Ikan Tongkol 1-3 opposite the seafront close to the Terminal, has rooms with fan and shared bathrooms for 7500/10,000 rp. It's popular with Darwinites.

Losmen Eli Fangidae at Jalan Pahlawan 65, next door to a church about 1½ km from the centre of town towards Tenau, is a quiet, homely place run by a preacher. It costs 6500 rp per person including breakfast. They do your laundry for free.

The *Laguna Inn* (tel 21559, 21384) on Jalan Kelimutu in a quiet, fairly central part of town is busy and popular with Indonesians. Small basic singles are around 5000 rp. Doubles with fan, mandi and a small verandah are 10,000 or 12,000 rp. It's clean and bare but adequate; there's also a restaurant. On the same street the *Kupang Indah Inn* (tel 226382) at Jalan Kelimutu 25A has a range of rooms with fans from 6000/7500 to 8000/10,000 rp, plus more expensive air-con rooms.

The *Wisma Cendana* (tel 21541) is at Jalan Raya El Tari 15, about four km from the centre. To get there, take a five-lamp bemo with a green or red board to Jalan

Raya El Tari. Apparently it's clean and friendly and English is spoken. All rooms have attached mandi and toilet. An economy room with breakfast is 6000 rp single. Singles/doubles with fan and three good Indonesian meals cost 13,500/22,000 rp, with air-con and three meals 18,500/33,000 rp. There's an extra 10% tax.

Out of town towards the airport on Jalan Tim Tim, the *Hotel King Stone* (tel 21148, 22014) has good, clean rooms. Singles with shared mandi cost 7500 rp, singles/doubles with fan or air-con and attached mandi and toilet 12,500/17,500 rp. All rooms have a patio and prices include breakfast. To get there, catch a 'Tarus' or 'Penfui' bemo from the Terminal – the bemos tend to be very full at dusk and stop running at 8 pm. The beach is a pleasant, short walk from the hotel and the *Rumah Makan Pondok Bambu* out the front is excellent.

Places to Stay – top end

The central *Wisma Setia* on Jalan Kohsasi is 40,000 rp double, including three meals – they won't negotiate a no meals price. The rooms are very clean and the decor tasteful. A bit further out, the *Wisma Maliana* (tel 21879) at Jalan Sumatera 35, next door to the Wisma Susi, has rooms with big double beds, air-con and TV for 20,000/25,000 rp.

The *Hotel Flobamor II* (tel 21346) at Jalan Sudirman 21 next to the Merpati office, has good air-con rooms at 25,000/30,000 rp. It's frequented by Timor's expatriate population.

Kupang's ritziest accommodation is in the *Sasando International Hotel* (tel 22224) on Jalan Perintis Kemerdekaan. It's on a windy hilltop to the south of the main road to the airport. Rooms are air-conditioned and they start at 31,000/36,000 rp.

Places to Eat

Kupang is no gourmet's delight but there are several reasonable places to eat. The best is probably the *Restaurant Lima Jaya Raya* at Jalan Soekarno 15, near the Terminal. It has a long menu of Chinese and Indonesian dishes including sea cucumber, frogs' legs and hens' feet. Gado-gado at 1000 rp is ordinary but the chicken dishes at 2500 rp are quite good. Various seafood meals cost around 3000 rp. The restaurant has air-con and the Chinese owner likes to entertain by playing an old lute-like instrument.

Teddy's Bar at Jalan Ikan Tongkol 1-3 has good food including a few western dishes. A large, tasty cap cai is 2000 rp and good beef, chicken and prawn sates are 2000/2500 rp. Fish, chips and salad is 2500 rp, barbecued meats and seafood 4000 rp. This place is the centre of tourist nightlife with a few hostess-like types floating around and sometimes crowds of Kupang schoolkids lurking outside to watch the antics of drunken Darwinites.

Next door, the *Pantai Laut Restaurant* has good food and amiable staff. Nasi and mie goreng at 1500 rp are filling and there's a variety of seafood, beef and chicken dishes from 3000 rp. The *Restaurant Karang Mas* at Jalan Siliwangi 88, a short walk from the Terminal, is on the seafront but more interesting for its look-at-the-sunset location than its food. It's a bit of a travellers' hang-out, a good place for a cold beer and a snack. Tomato omelettes are 1250 rp, fried prawns from 2000 to 2500 rp and steaks 3000 rp.

On Jalan Garuda, the eastward continuation of Jalan Siliwangi, the *Rumah Makan Beringin Jaya* has good Padang food at reasonable prices and air-con.

Several km further out, along Jalan Tim Tim towards the airport, the *Rumah Makan Pondok Bambu* is worth the effort of getting to. Take a Penfui or Tarus bemo from the Terminal, but don't make the return journey too late as bemos stop about 8 pm. The fare includes a big range of seafood dishes at around 3000 rp, excellent gado-gado at 750 rp and fruit juices at 1000 rp.

Night warungs crop up around town,

particularly along the street leading down to the bridge off Jalan Soekarno, just a short walk from the Terminal. Try *bubur kacang* (mung beans and black rice in coconut milk) for only 250 rp. Gado-gado is 500 rp and there are also sate stalls. Similar stalls set up off Jalan Garuda almost opposite the Rumah Makan Beringin Jaya. On Jalan Ikan Paus, there's an excellent cake shop, the *Toko Nirwana*.

It's quite difficult to get fruit in Kupang. Try the seafront market, the roadside stalls near the *Taman Ria* or make a trip to Pasar Inpres, the main market.

Things to Buy

Timorese ikat is colourful with a huge variety of designs, and there are lots of other embroidered textiles. Purists will be disappointed that natural dyes have all but disappeared from Timor, though you may have some luck in Soe, Kefamenanu, Baun or other rural towns and villages or at Kupang's market – Pasar Inpres – where country people often bring weavings to sell.

Several shops in Kupang sell ikat, handicrafts, old silver jewellery, ornamented bamboo sirih boxes and more – bizarrely shaped lontar leaf hats from Roti make a fun purchase. These shops also have ikat from other parts of East Nusa Tenggara including Sawu and Roti. Prices are quite high and bargaining won't bring them down dramatically, but it's still cheaper to buy the Timorese stuff in Timor than in Bali or elsewhere. Try *Dharma Bakti*, at Jalan Sumba 32, out towards Jalan Tim Tim. *Toko Sinar Baru* on Jalan Siliwangi opposite the Terminal has interesting stock, but is hard to shift at prices. Expect to pay around 100,000 rp for a large Sawu blanket, around 20,000 rp for a *selendang* (shawl) – Sawu designs are distinctive and elegant but natural dyes are rarely used. You can watch ikat weavers at work in Kupang at Ibu Bunga's Sentra Tenun Ikat on Jalan Tifa, about one km south-west of the Terminal. Locals will give you directions. Cloths, shoes and bags are on sale here. Sometimes the shop at Kupang airport has handicrafts for sale at cheaper prices than the city shops.

Outside Kupang, the asking price for woven sarongs may be as little as 25,000 rp but always check the work carefully. Close inspection may reveal flaws such as the two halves not lining up exactly.

Getting There & Away

Kupang is the transport hub of Timor, with buses and flights to and from the rest of the island, plus planes and regular passenger boats to the rest of Nusa Tenggara and beyond.

Permits You should be able to travel freely anywhere in Timor, but if permits are reintroduced for parts of the island you'll probably need to go to Korem (Komando Resor Militer). It's out in the east of the city on Jalan Lalamentik, 2½ km beyond the main post office. To get there, take an 'Oebufi' bemo. It may be advisable to take someone from the tourist office or some other helpful person with you.

Air Merpati flies to and from Darwin twice a week (see the introductory Getting There chapter) and Kupang is well connected to other parts of Indonesia.

Merpati operates most of the flights from Kupang to other parts of Timor including Dili (daily), Oekussi and Atambua. Garuda flies daily to Dili but it's more expensive.

Merpati also runs the bulk of the flights between Kupang and other destinations in Nusa Tenggara. Useful connections – some daily, others a few times a week – include Roti; Sawu; Waingapu and Tambolaka (Waikabubak) on Sumba; Larantuka, Maumere, Ende, Bajawa, Ruteng and Labuhanbajo on Flores. Bouraq also flies to Maumere and Waingapu.

Merpati and Bouraq fly to Denpasar, as

does Garuda for a higher fare. There are a number of flights further afield - for example to Jakarta with all three airlines or to Ujung Pandang and Balikpapan with Merpati.

Merpati (tel 21121, 21961) is at Jalan Sudirman 21 on a three-lamp bemo route, next to the Hotel Flobamor II. It's open Monday to Saturday from 8 am to 4 pm, Sunday and holidays from 9 am to 3 pm. Bouraq (tel 21421) is almost opposite at Jalan Sudirman 20. Garuda (tel 21205) is more central at Jalan Kohsasi 13. There are also numerous air ticket agents around town, including Pitoby Travel (tel 21222) at Jalan Siliwangi 75, which is open Sunday.

Bus Not too long ago, roads in Timor were really rotten. It was a pretty close thing whether the Portuguese half was more or less neglected than the Indonesian half prior to the invasion. But if the war in East Timor has benefited anyone other than arms manufacturers, it's you. The road from Kupang to Atambua via Soe and Kefamenanu is now well-surfaced all the way - so well in fact that some drivers put their feet down and speed manically. Most roads in East Timor are still pretty rough with only a few sealed stretches, the better ones being between Dili and Baukau (now the chief military air-base), Dili and Maliana, and Dili and Same. (The latter two pass through the main coffee growing districts.)

Kupang's main bus and bemo terminal, known simply as *Terminal*, is near the waterfront where Jalan Soekarno and Jalan Siliwangi meet. Leaving Kupang for the east, daytime buses start at the Terminal and subject you to a tedious sightseeing tour of Kupang as they search out more passengers and finally get going an hour or two after you hop in. The later in the morning a bus sets off, the longer it spends *keliling* (driving round in circles). Buses to Soe (three hours) cost 2000 rp, to Kefamenanu (five hours) 3000 rp and to

Atambua (eight hours) 4500 rp (day), 6000 rp (night) - times include *keliling*.

From Kupang to Dili, if you're a glutton for punishment, you may be able to go straight through but most people overnight in Atambua. For more details, see the Dili section.

There's an agent for the Paris Indah night bus to Kefamenanu and Atambua on Jalan Siliwangi. A few yards towards Jalan Siliwangi from the town centre Terminal, Toko Columbia is an agent for three daily buses to Atambua and Dili (16,000 rp) at 7 am, 3 pm and 7 pm. Toko Sinar Baru across the road is an agent for the Tunas Mekar night bus leaving at 7 pm to Atambua and Dili.

Coming back to Kupang from the east, some buses stop at the Oebobo terminal on Jalan Perintis Kemerdekaan on the eastern edge of Kupang, close to the Museum NTT. There are frequent bemos into town from there.

Boat Regular ships to Flores, Sawu, Roti, Alor, Sumba and further afield leave from the port of Tenau, eight km west of Kupang. From the Kupang bemo Terminal a 'Tenau' bemo (250 rp) will take you straight to Tenau harbour and drop you right outside the harbour master's office (tel 21790) at Jalan Yos Soedarso 23.

Pelni and the ferry company Perum ASPP both have ticket offices in Kupang. Pelni is at Jalan Pahlawan 3 within walking distance of the Terminal. The *Kelimutu* leaves Kupang every second Sunday, reaching Semarang on Java a week later then returning by the same route in reverse. From Kupang the *Kelimutu* stops at Ende, Waingapu, Bima, Ujung Pandang, Lembar, Padangbai, Surabaya, Banjarmasin, and Semarang.

First class/2nd class/economy fares on the *Kelimutu* include: Ende (11 hrs) 31,600/25,100/14,100 rp, Waingapu (21 hrs) 45,000/36,700/18,400 rp, Bima (36 hrs) 72,800/60,000/31,600 rp, and Ujung Pandang (60 hrs) 86,000/66,700/34,900 rp.

Pelni also runs the KM *Elang* which oops every 10 days or so round Timor and he small islands to the north. A typical oute is Kupang, Larantuka, Kalabahi, Kupang again, Oekussi, Atapupu, Dili, Kisar in southern Maluku, Kalabahi, Kupang.

Pelni's *Baruna Eka* and/or *Baruna Fajar* do about one circuit a week round Kupang, Sawu, Ende, Waingapu, Sawu, Kupang, sometimes with extra stops such as Maumbawa in Flores, south of Bajawa. The ships usually spend the day in port and sail overnight. From Kupang to Sawu is overnight and costs 7550 rp. Kupang to Ende takes two nights and one day for 10,150 rp. Kupang to Waingapu is three nights and two days for 12,150 rp.

The Perum ASPP ferry office (tel 21140) at Jalan Cak Doko 20, sells tickets the day before departure for the ferries *Kerapu I*, *Kerapu II* and *Madidihang* to Larantuka (Flores), Kalabahi (Alor), Sawu and Roti. The office is open from 8 am to 4 pm, and a five-lamp bemo from downtown gets you there. The Larantuka ferry leaves Tenau on Monday and Thursday afternoons. The fare is 8250 rp per person, 7700 rp for a motorbike and 75,000 rp for a car. It's a 14-hour overnight trip, sometimes via Lembata or Adonara. See under Larantuka for more on this ferry.

The Kalabahi ferry leaves Tenau on Tuesday and Saturday around midday. It's about a 12-hour trip and the fare is 10,500 rp. The Sawu ferry leaves on Thursday afternoons and costs 8250 rp. There are ferries to Roti on Monday, Wednesday and Saturday mornings. The four-hour trip costs 3200 rp.

The mission ship *Ratu Rosario*, which plies the Kupang-Surabaya route, makes a loop every three weeks which takes her to many of the islands of Nusa Tenggara. She will take passengers.

Other You can rent cars or motorcycles or fix up tours to places like Semau island, Soe, the surf beach near Baun, or Roti at Teddy's Bar.

Getting Around

Kupang's El Tari airport is 15 km east of the city centre. To get a bemo from the airport, walk out of the gates and about 200 metres down the road to a junction where the bemos wait. The fare to town is 200 rp. A taxi from the airport into the city is a fixed 5000 rp. The airport has a reasonable restaurant. From the city centre, 'Penfui' and 'Baumata' bemos go to the airport.

Kupang is too spread out to do much walking – you need the bemos. The bemo system is efficient if very noisy. Music is played full blast and is heavy on the bass – Kupangites like their music loud! The hub of the bemo system is the Terminal, at the junction of Jalan Soekarno and Jalan Siliwangi. From here bemos zoom up and down the main streets. Many do a loop round Siliwangi, Garuda, Sumatera, Sumba, Yani and Sumohardjo before heading out to the suburbs.

You can identify bemos both by what's written on their route-board, and by the number of lamps (*lampu*) on top of the route-board. For example, all three-lamp bemos go to the suburb of Air Nona. All bemos within town cost 150 rp.

CAMPLONG

Camplong, 41 km from Kupang on the Soe road, has some caves, a small forest and an artificial lake. The Camplong convent runs a reasonable penginapan. Rooms with attached mandi are 6000 rp single, including breakfast and dinner.

SOE

Soe, with its backdrop of hills and cooler temperatures, makes a pleasant change from Kupang. The road from Kupang passes through beautiful countryside, reminiscent of Australia's bush. Soe is a sprawl of wooden and iron-roofed houses, but there's a large market where you'll see people in their traditional garb.

Like most of rural Timor, Soe district is very poor: in 1985 the average annual income here was the equivalent of about

US$140, against US$210 for East Nusa Tenggara province as a whole, and it's a poor province. Apples used to provide the area with a steady income, but in 1988 a bug killed all the trees.

A number of Australian expatriates live in Soe and Kefamenanu, around 100 km further east. Australian aid projects include building small dams around Soe to cope with dry season water shortages. Health education projects are also planned.

Lopo, the local beehive-shaped houses, give the region a distinctive character but they have been banned by the authorities who consider them unhealthy as they're small and smoky. The locals, however, believe that their new houses are equally unhealthy as they're cold – so they construct new lopos behind the approved houses. Another smaller type of lopo, which acts as a meeting place, has no walls and a toadstool-like roof.

Orientation

Soe's bus and bemo terminal is on the far side of Soe if you're coming from Kupang. Accommodation is on and near Jalan Diponegoro in the town centre, a km or so back from the terminal. The market is a km in the opposite direction from the terminal. To get to the losmens, turn left out of the bus station and walk uphill past the post office, then turn right at the first junction.

Around Soe

There are village markets worth visiting from Soe. Niki Niki, 34 km to the east along the main road, is the site of some old royal graves. Its busy market is on Wednesdays when people come in from miles around – it's supposed to be a good place to buy weavings. One reader's letter reported visiting Ayotupas which has a 'great' market. To get there, hop on a truck in Niki Niki. The uncomfortable trip on a shocking road is apparently worth it. Oenlasi is 58 km north-east of Soe, high up in the rugged mountains.

Buses or trucks go there from Soe, at least on Tuesdays for the weekly market.

Kapan, 21 km north of Soe, has its interesting market on Thursdays when the roads are blocked with stalls. The village is situated on steep slopes from where you can see Gunung Mutis (2470 metres).

Fatumenasi

This town, 20 km beyond Kapan on the slopes of Gunung Mutis, doesn't have a market but has great views of the surrounding rocky, alpine landscape. Some trucks run between Kapan and Fatumenasi, or charter a jeep from Kapan for 20,000 rp – try the Chinese shopowner there.

Weaving

There are good weavings to be had in Soe itself. The shop attached to the *Wisma Bahagia* has an excellent but expensive collection. Bargaining in Bahasa Indonesia will drop the price a little. Locals come around to the losmens to show you weavings which are much cheaper, but sometimes poor in quality. You can watch women weaving in the kampungs on the edge of the town – you're likely to be invited there.

Places to Stay & Eat

The best and most expensive place to stay is the *Wisma Bahagia* (tel 15) at Jalan Diponegoro 72. Clean singles/doubles with shared mandi are 8000/10,000 rp, with attached mandi from 9000/12,500 rp. Its restaurant is good with basic Indonesian dishes at 1500 rp, fried chicken and other meat dishes at around 3000 to 4000 rp.

Around the corner on Jalan Kartini, the brightly-decorated *Losmen Anda* has a talkative English/Dutch/German-speaking owner from Roti who used to work with Save the Children on Java. Basic rooms without private mandi cost 3000 rp per person, 3500 rp with private mandi. They cook reasonable meals for around 1000 rp and throw in the occasional snack. The

Wisma Cahaya TTS next door is 3000 rp per person.

There are a few warungs and rumah makan near the market. Try the *Restaurant Karya*. Keep your eyes open for mandarins and avocados which sometimes appear at the bus station. As fruit is scarce in Timor, these are a treat.

Getting There & Away

Buses from Kupang cost 2000 rp and the 110-km journey takes three to four hours, including *keliling* in Kupang. It's best to set off early and get a 6.30 or 7 am bus as the chances are your bus will fill up quickly and leave sooner. If you ask, your bus may drop you off at a losmen in Soe before going on to the bus terminal.

Leaving Soe, many buses circle the town on the way so you will probably be able to pick up one at your losmen. Buses to Kupang leave regularly between sunrise and sunset. Buses to Kefamenanu (1500 rp) leave early in the morning and around 12 noon.

In Soe, bemos run around town and to nearby villages. The fare to both Niki Niki and Kapan is 500 rp.

KEFAMENANU

Kefamenanu, 217 km from Kupang, is cool and quiet but apart from some lovely walks to surrounding hills, there's little to hold you. The town had a reputation in the past as a place to buy fine rugs. Locals bring around reasonable ikats to the losmens and you could strike a bargain. Oelolok, a weaving village 26 km from 'Kefa' by bus and a further three km by bemo, has a Tuesday market.

Places to Stay & Eat

Best value is the *Losmen Ariesta* on Jalan Basuki Rachmat. It has big, clean doubles with attached mandi and patio at 11,000 rp; smaller singles/doubles with shared mandi are 3300/6600 rp. There's a garden with a brightly painted dragon and a fish pond. The restaurant here serves good food, but you need to let them know early what you want.

The *Losmen Setangkai* is on Jalan Sonbay close to the central intersection near the market. Run by a friendly family, the clean rooms cost 4400 rp per person. Next door and directly opposite the market is the *Rumah Makan Surabaya* with cheap Indonesian food. About 300 metres south of the market, the *Losmen Soko Windu* on Jalan Kartini has basic rooms at 3850/7700 rp, including breakfast.

Getting There & Away

The market doubles as the bus and bemo station. Buses between Kupang and Kefa cost 3000 rp. Buses leave Kupang early in the morning. From Kefa to Kupang there are several buses in the morning and two at night. The journey takes five hours if there's no stop in Soe. To or from Soe costs 1500 rp and takes two hours. There are regular buses to Atambua (2000 rp, three hours).

OEKUSSI

This former Portuguese coastal enclave north-west of Kefamenanu is part of East Timor province. When East Timor was re-opened to tourists in January 1989, travellers were only permitted to visit Oekussi on condition that they passed straight through. The situation should have eased by now.

ATAMBUA & BELU

Atambua is the major town at the eastern end of West Timor. It's a pleasant enough place with amiable people. Overland travellers to East Timor usually break the long bus journey between Kupang and Dili by overnighting here.

Atambua is the capital of Belu (formerly Tetun) province which borders East Timor. Formerly you needed a permit, which was rarely given, to enter Belu. The district is mainly dry-farmed using traditional time-consuming methods though there are some wet padi lands on the south coast. Belu has some beautiful scenery and unspoilt villages.

Some readers have reported getting as far as Betun, 60 km south of Atambua, where there are a couple of losmens and rumah makan. The nearby villages of Kletek, Kamanasa and Bolan are apparently worth visiting – you can see flying foxes and the sun set over the mountains at Kletek.

Places to Stay & Eat
Losmen Nusantara is the best value in Atambua at 6000 to 7500 rp per person, including breakfast. The clean rooms have attached mandis and the people are friendly. *Wisma Sahabat* at Jalan Merdeka 7 has been going a longtime and standards have slipped. It costs 4000 rp per person including breakfast.

Eat at the *Rumah Makan Sinar Kasih* which is a five-minute walk from the Wisma Sahabat. It has quite a long menu and decent-sized helpings at decent prices. There are also a couple of warungs in the vicinity of the Wisma Sahabat.

Getting There & Away
For details of buses to Atambua from Kupang, see the Kupang section. In Atambua the Pitoby Express Bus 'Horus' (a night bus to Kupang) can be booked at the Restoran Roda Baru at Jalan Merdeka 73.

Buses from Atambua to Dili cost 10,000 rp and leave early in the morning, reaching Dili around 3 or 4 pm. Your losmen should help with the booking. The journey may not be straightforward in the wet season – see the Atambua to Dili section for details.

Merpati has some flights between Atambua and Kupang.

ATAMBUA TO DILI
Atapupu, 25 km from Atambua, is a major port for the export of cattle to other parts of Indonesia and to Hong Kong and Singapore. You might find boats to other islands here.

During the wet season, you may have to get out of your bus and wade across the River Loes, about 20 km east of Atapupu. If it's running high, dinghies are used to ferry passengers across. Another bus collects you on the other side.

In early 1989 Stephen Meredith from Darwin experienced the river crossing like this:

The operation took over two hours as there was only one dinghy which took about eight people at a time, and there were three busloads of 20 passengers each plus truckloads of people livestock and freight to be ferried across. . . . A packed lunch and drink were provided by the bus company before we started the crossing This is an experience not to be missed. . .

Maliana is the first town inside East Timor. The *Losmen Purwosari Indah* costs 12,500 rp per person. Ermera, about 2½ hours south-west of Dili, is next and has no accommodation. This was the main coffee town of Portuguese Timor. Following the Indonesian invasion the plantations and former Portuguese state holdings were taken over by the PT Denok company. The improvement of East Timor's roads by the Indonesians has been done not only for military purposes but also to assist PT Denok's exploitation of the former colony.

Maubara on the coast west of Dili has an old European-built fort. This was the centre of one of the most important old kingdoms in Portuguese Timor and it was here in 1893 that the first of a series of revolts took place, eventually leading to bloody pacification of the island by the Portuguese.

DILI
Dili was once the capital of Portuguese Timor. When the English scientist Alfred Russel Wallace spent several months here in 1861, he noted Dili as:

. . .a most miserable place compared with even

Top: Near Ruteng, Flores, Nusa Tenggara (AS)
Left: Near Ruteng, Flores, Nusa Tenggara (AS)
Right: Between Ruteng and Bajawa, Nusa Tenggara (AS)

Top: Kids, Moni, Flores, Nusa Tenggara (JN)
Bottom: Boat under construction, Pelabuhan Sape, Sumbawa, Nusa Tenggara (AS)

Mercado Municipal, Dili

the poorest of the Dutch towns. . . . After three hundred years of occupation there has not been a mile of road made beyond the town, and there is not a solitary European resident anywhere in the interior. All the government officials oppress and rob the natives as much as they can, and yet there is no care taken to render the town defensible should the Timorese attempt to attack it.

In fact, it probably wasn't all that different to Dutch Timor, where until the beginning of this century little effort was put into development and few officials went outside Kupang.

When he became Australian consul in Dili in 1962, James Dunn noted:

The rusty hulks of Japanese vessels still lined the harbour foreshore, while bomb-damaged buildings were to be seen in several parts of the town. There were no sealed streets or roads and it was only later in that year that the citizens of the capital were to enjoy the luxury of a town electricity supply . . . . It was not until 1965 that the wharf at Dili was in use for shipping. Hitherto the. . . unloading of vessels [had been] carried out by landing barges or, in the case of fuel, by the intriguing technique of rolling

drums into the harbour current, which would slowly carry them on to the beach!

In the early 1970s, before the Indonesian invasion, Dili was a pleasant, lazy place. Today it appears relatively prosperous with lots of new public buildings including a stadium and office blocks. Few women wear sarongs, unlike in west Timor where they are common. Visitors to Dili in 1989 reported that police kept a close eye on foreigners, even to the extent of checking up on locals who were seen talking to westerners.

Places to Stay

Dili accommodation is expensive. The *Wisma Basmeri* on Jalan Kaikoli, opposite the University of Timor Timur, is the cheapest at 7500 rp per person in bare rooms with attached mandi and fan. It's hot and the mandis could be cleaner, but the people are friendly.

Best value is the *Hotel Dili* on the beachfront Jalan Avenida Marechal Carmona, a short walk east of the town centre. It has good singles/doubles with

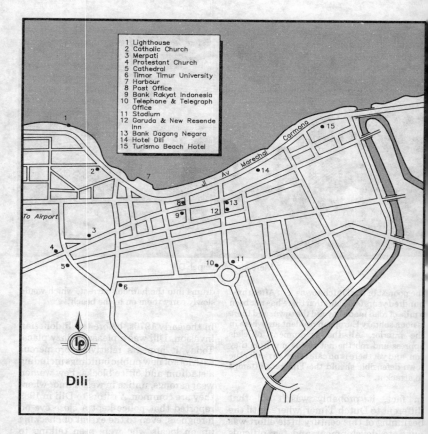

1 Lighthouse
2 Catholic Church
3 Merpati
4 Protestant Church
5 Cathedral
6 Timor Timur University
7 Harbour
8 Post Office
9 Bank Rakyat Indonesia
10 Telephone & Telegraph Office
11 Stadium
12 Garuda & New Resende Inn
13 Bank Dagang Negara
14 Hotel Dili
15 Turismo Beach Hotel

To Airport

Dili

attached mandi at 10,000/15,000 rp and rooms with four bunks for 15,000 rp, economical if there are more than two of you.

A short walk further away from the centre, also on Jalan Avenida Marechal Carmona, the *Turismo Beach Hotel* (tel 22029) is more expensive but has had a few rave reviews. Rooms with a balcony seaview, private mandi and breakfast start at 18,000/22,000 rp (16,000/19,000 rp without the seaview), all plus 10% tax.

The *Wisma Cendana* on Jalan Ameriko Thomas is spotlessly clean with rooms for 25,000 rp. At Jalan Avenida Bispo Medeiros 5, the *New Resende Inn* has very expensive air-con rooms from 39,000 rp.

Places to Eat

For some reason, East Timor can import directly from overseas without goods going through Jakarta, so you can buy Singapore Tiger beer and even Portuguese wines like Mateus.

There are a few restaurants serving the usual Indonesian fare scattered around town, but nowhere memorable. Many warungs set up at the east end of town – one serves good fish.

As Stephen Meredith discovered when he was one of the first travellers to visit Dili in 1989, the *Turismo Beach Hotel* has two restaurants:

. . an 'Indonesian' restaurant with an English-language menu including not only nasi goreng but also pizza Bolognese and minestrone, and a 'Portuguese' restaurant with a Bahasa Indonesia menu that seemed to consist mainly of Indonesian dishes! Both serve good food at reasonable prices in a beautiful garden setting.

Getting There & Away

Air Garuda and Merpati both fly daily both ways between Kupang and Dili. You could fly to Kupang from Darwin with Merpati then on to Dili with Garuda the same day. Your passport will probably be checked at both airports. Merpati also has flights linking Dili with Oekussi, Atambua and Suai on the south coast of East Timor. Garuda flights from Dili go on to Denpasar after Kupang. Merpati connects at Kupang for several places. Garuda's Dili office (tel 2403) is in the New Resende Inn on Jalan Avenida Bispo Medeiros. Merpati (tel 2477) is at Jalan Da Calmera 8.

Bus You can buy through tickets from Kupang to Dili for 20,000 rp, but most people break the long bus journey between Kupang and Dili and overnight in Atambua. For details of Kupang-Atambua buses see the Kupang section. Buses from Atambua to Dili cost 10,000 rp, leave around 7 am and reach Dili around 3 pm. You'll probably have your passport checked on both sides of the East Timor border and your details recorded in a book. You may also be asked your profession.

Buses connect Dili with Baukau (four hours, 3000 rp), Ermera (2½ hours, 1500 rp) and other major towns. They depart from Dili's central Mercado bus station. Long-distance buses will pick you up at your hotel.

Boat Pelni's KM *Elang* loops every 10 days or so round Timor and the small islands to the north. One route is Kupang, Oekussi, Atapupu, Dili, Kisar in southern Maluku, Kalabahi, Kupang. There should be other possibilities. Ask at the harbour!

Getting Around

Dili airport is five km west of the town centre and a taxi to your accommodation costs 3500 rp. There are three bus stations with buses and bemos running between them, though these are fewer than in Kupang. The best way to get around is by taxis which cost a flat 500 rp within the town.

SAME

A spectacular route runs through the rugged interior to Same south of Dili. This was a centre of late 19th and early 20th century revolts led by Boaventura, the liurai of Same.

BAUKAU

The second largest centre of what was Portuguese Timor, the charmingly run-down colonial town of Baukau (formerly Baucau) had an international airport eight km west of the centre, now used by the Indonesian military. The altitude makes Baukau pleasantly cool and the beaches, five km sharply downhill from the town, are breathtakingly beautiful. To get to the beaches you can walk down and take the risk of having to walk back up – or charter a bemo for around 5000 rp for a couple of hours.

Dili to Baukau is a four-hour bus trip (3000 rp) along the coast. The bus stops at Manatuto where the warung has good Padang food. You may be asked by the police to show your passport there. The road is unsealed and pretty rough all the way from Manatuto to Lautem, beyond Baukau.

Places to Stay & Eat

The Portuguese-built *Hotel Flamboyant* is the only hotel. It may have been good 15 years ago but now nothing seems to work although the beds are fine and the views beautiful. Singles/doubles are 5000/10,000 rp. There is no food available. If you want to stay a couple of nights it may be worthwhile talking with the kepala desa or government officials as private accommodation is available. There's one restaurant in town.

BAUKAU TO TUTUALA

There's an old Portuguese fort at Laga, on the coast about 20 km beyond Baukau. Lautem, a further 35 km, is the next town. From Lautem the road improves dramatically for 15 km until it reaches Lospalos. Lospalos to Tutuala, on the eastern tip of Timor, is about 30 km and you should be able to get a bemo if it's not too late in the day. Tutuala has interesting houses built on stilts, plus spectacular views out to sea. While Timorese houses are usually built out of timber, bamboo and palm leaves the design varies greatly from region to region. The following is part of an account of a whirlwind trip from Lospalos to Tutuala in 1989 by Joakim Boes of Sweden and Martin Dufty of England, the first western tourists in the area for 13½ years:

We managed to borrow a bemo to go to Tutuala. It was in the afternoon and no one wanted to drive us down there at night. The army are scared of Fretilin ambushes and the people are not allowed to move around at night . . . So we had to drive ourselves – but we had no idea that the road was more suited to a four-wheel drive vehicle than a bemo. We got stuck once and spent half an hour digging in the mud to get on the road again . . . Eventually we reached Tutuala and stayed overnight in the police station. The police were friendly and brought us food. Driving back in the morning was fantastic. Sunrise, people on the way to the fields, misty and. . . well, it was just beautiful. The funny thing was that people in the villages were used to seeing our bemo (number 555) and waved and stopped us to get a ride to Lospalos. It's hard to describe their faces when they saw two white people sitting in the front seat . . .

There are no losmens in the area but we were offered accommodation by the padre in the Catholic church. The priests in the area are extremely friendly and helpful.

VIKEKE

A road heads south over the mountains from Baukau to Vikeke which is close to the south coast. There were reports of Fretilin activity around Vikeke in early 1989 so it's possible that travellers may not be allowed in the area.

Roti & Sawu

Between Timor and Sumba the small dry islands of Roti and Sawu (also spelt Savu or Sabu) are little visited but, with their successful economies based on the lontar palm, have played a significant role in Nusa Tenggara's history and now preserve some interesting cultures.

The Lontar Economy

The traditional Rotinese and Sawunese economies have for centuries centred on the lontar palm. The wood from this multi-purpose tree can be used to make houses, furniture, musical instruments, mats, baskets and even cigarette papers. Its juice can be tapped and drunk fresh, or boiled into a syrup and diluted with water – and this syrup formed the staple diet. The juice can be further boiled into palm sugar and the froth from the boiling juice can be fed to pigs and goats kept in small coral-walled enclosures (doing away with the time-consuming fencing of fields required for cattle). The lontar palm is also drought and fire resistant and there was no annual period of hunger on Roti or Sawu as there was on the other islands of Nusa Tenggara. Meanwhile vegetables could be grown in dry fields or in small garden plots, kept fertilised with animal manure or lontar leaves.

Since the lontar palm only required two or three months of work each year, and since the women were the gardeners and handicrafts people, the men had plenty of time for other activities. Thus the Rotinese and Sawunese became the entrepreneurs of Nusa Tenggara, especially on Sumba and Timor to which many of them emigrated with Dutch encouragement. By the 20th century, the Rotinese dominated both the civil service *and* the local anti-colonial movements on these islands.

ROTI

Off the west end of Timor, Roti is the southernmost island in Indonesia. The lightly built Rotinese speak a language similar to the Tetum of Timor. Traditionally Roti is divided into 18 domains. In 1681 a bloody Dutch campaign placed their local allies in control of the island, and Roti became a source of slaves and supplies for the Dutch base at Kupang. In the 18th century, the Rotinese started taking advantage of the Dutch presence, gradually adopted Christianity and, with Dutch support, established a school system which, with the time left available for education by the lontar economy, eventually turned them into the region's educated elite.

The Rotinese openness to change is the main reason their old culture is no longer so strong as Sawu's – though animistic beliefs and rites linger behind their Protestantism. At some festivals, families reportedly cut separate chunks out of a live buffalo then take them away to eat.

Ikat weaving on Roti today uses mainly black, red and yellow chemical dyes but the designs can still be complex: typical are floral and patola motifs, and/or a wide central black stripe with several patterned and coloured stripes either side of it. In former times the motifs were different for each of Roti's 18 domains, and patola motifs were status symbols. One tradition which hasn't disappeared is the wearing of wide-brimmed lontar leaf hats with a curious spike sticking up near the front – perhaps representing a lontar palm, an old Portuguese helmet or a mast. Rotinese also love music and dancing.

The tiny island of Ndao off west Roti is another lontar-tapping and ikat-weaving centre. In the dry season, Ndao men take off for other islands to sell ikat and work as gold and silversmiths.

Baa

Roti's main town is on the north coast. The main street is close to the ocean and a couple of churches stand beside the central square. *Losmen Ricki* on the square near the new mosque is adequate with rooms at 5000 rp per person but there's no food – and crowds of kids peer in at the windows! You might be better off finding a room with a family. There are some coral beaches near Baa. Some houses have boat-shaped thatched roofs with carvings (connected with traditional ancestor cults) at the ends. There's plenty of good fresh fish to be bought if someone will cook it for you!

Getting There & Around

Perum ASPP ferries leave Tenau, the port of Kupang, for Roti on Monday, Wednesday and Saturday mornings and return the same day. The four-hour one-way trip costs 3200 rp. The ferries dock about an hour's bemo ride (1000 rp) from Baa. Smaller boats also make the crossing. Merpati has three flights a week to/from Kupang.

There are only a few buses or bemos on Roti, but you might be able to rent a motorbike for around 5000 rp a day in Baa.

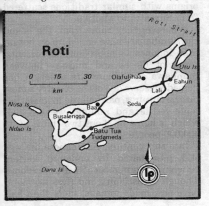

SAWU

Mid-way between Roti and Sumba, but
with closer linguistic links to Sumba, the
low, bare little island of Sawu is still a
stronghold of animistic beliefs, collectively
known as *jingitiu*. These persist even
though Portuguese missionaries first
arrived before 1600 and the Dutch
continued their work.

Sawu's roughly 40,000 people are
divided into five traditional domains and
the main settlement, Seba on the north-
west coast, was the centre of the leading
domain in Dutch times. Sawunese society
is divided into clans named after their
male founders, but also into two 'noble'
and 'common' halves determined by a
person's mother's lineage: the halves are
called *hubi ae* (greater flower stalk) and
hubi iki (lesser flower stalk). Sawunese
women have a thriving ikat-weaving
tradition – their cloth typically has stripes
of black or dark blue interspersed by
stripes with floral motifs, clan or hubi
emblems.

There's one losmen in Seba, but some
families will also put you up – ask in
Kupang or Waingapu for contacts before
you go. Seba has a market and a handful of
trucks provides the island's public
transport. A group of stones at Namata
near Seba is a ritual site: animal
sacrifices, with a whole community
sharing the meat, take place around
August to October. Another festival in the
second quarter of the year sees a boat
pushed out to sea as an offering – in Timu
in the east, it may carry a buffalo.

Getting There & Away

A Perum ASPP ferry to Sawu leaves
Tenau, Kupang, on Thursday afternoons,
returning on Friday. The one-way fare is
8250 rp. One of the Pelni ships *Baruna
Eka* or *Baruna Fajar* makes a loop about
once a week from Kupang to Sawu to
Ende to Waingapu to Sawu to Kupang.
From Kupang to Sawu it's 7500 rp, from
Waingapu 7000 rp – both trips are

overnight. Merpati flies Kupang to Sawu
and back twice a week.

Sumba

A great ladder once connected heaven and
earth. By it, the first people came down to
earth; they found their way to Sumba and
settled at Cape Sasar on the northern tip
of the island – or so the myth goes.
Another Sumbanese tale recounts how
Umbu Walu Sasar, one of their two
ancestors, was driven away from Java by
the wars. Transported to Sumba by the
powers of heaven he came to live at Cape
Sasar. The other ancestor, Umbu Walu
Mandoko, arrived by boat, travelled to
the east and settled at the mouth of the
Kambaniru River.

Such myths may come as near the truth
as any version of the origins of a people
who are physically of Malay stock with a
tinge of Melanesian; whose language falls
into the same bag that holds the Bimanese
of east Sumbawa, the Manggarai and
Ngada of west Flores and the Sawunese of
Sawu; whose death and burial ceremonies
are strongly reminiscent of Torajaland in
Sulawesi; and whose brilliant *ikat*
textiles, fine carved stone tombs and high,
thatched clan houses suggest common
origins with similar traditions scattered
from Sumatra to Maluku.

Wherever they came from, the island
the Sumbanese have ended up on lies far
from Indonesia's main cultural currents,
south of Flores and midway between
Sumbawa and Timor. Its isolation has
helped preserve one of the country's most
bizarre cultures, particularly in its wetter,
more fertile and remoter western half
which is home to about two-thirds of its
400,000 people.

Into this century, Sumbanese life was
still punctuated by endemic warfare
between a huge number of rival princedoms.
Though Christianity and (less so) Islam
have now made inroads, more than half

the people in the west and about a third in the east still adhere to the animist *marapu* religion, and old conflicts are recalled every year at west Sumba's often violent Pasola festivals – semi-mock battles between teams of mounted horsemen. Many Sumbanese men still carry long-bladed knives in wooden sheaths tucked into their waistbands; they wear scarves as turbans and wrap their brightly coloured sarongs so that they expose the lower two-thirds of their legs and have a long piece of cloth hanging down in front.

The last 20 years have seen an increasing flow of visitors to Sumba, attracted chiefly by the ikat cloth of east Sumba. The ikat made in west Sumba, while still interesting, isn't nearly as exciting. Other Sumbanese traditions are generally stronger in the west – though you'll find traditional villages, with their exotic houses, tombs and ceremonies, in both parts. The tombs are a constant reminder that, for the Sumbanese, death is the most important event in life. Against this background the most recent attraction of Sumba – surfing – hardly seems to fit. Every year, however, a few more western surfies come in search of different waves.

Despite their warlike past, the Sumbanese are friendly, and more reserved than many other peoples in Nusa Tenggara. 'Hello Mister' is not yet common – don't encourage it! Bahasa Indonesia apart, East and West Sumbanese speak different dialects of one language. The eastern one is called Kambera.

HISTORY

Fourteenth-century Javanese chronicles place Sumba under the control of the Majapahits. After that empire declined the island is supposed to have come under the rule of Bima in Sumbawa, then of Gowa in southern Sulawesi. But Sumbanese history is mostly a saga of internal wars, mainly over land and trading rights, between a great number of petty princedoms. A ruler's authority rested on his descent from the legendary hero-founder of the princedom together with the prestige and wealth of his clan. The most powerful clans claimed direct descent from the legendary original settlers, Sasar and Mandoku. The traditional social order was legitimised in lengthy all-night recitations. Despite their mutual hostility, princedoms often depended on each other economically. The inland regions produced horses, lumber, betel nuts, rice, fruit and dyewoods, while the much-valued ikat cloth was made on the coast, where the drier climate was suitable for cotton growing. The coastal people also controlled trade with other islands.

The Dutch at first paid little attention to Sumba because, like the rest of Nusa Tenggara, it lacked commercial possibilities. The sandalwood trade conducted in the 18th century was constantly interrupted by wars amongst the Sumbanese. Only in the mid-19th century did the Dutch arrange a treaty permitting one of their representatives to live in Waingapu, buy horses and collect taxes. Towards the end of the century Sumba's trade with other islands through Waingapu led to extensive internal wars as various princes tried to dominate it – and in the early 20th century the Dutch finally decided to secure their own interests by invading and placing the island under direct military rule. That lasted until 1913 when a civilian administration was set up, although the Sumbanese nobility continued to reign and the Dutch ruled through them. When the Indonesian republic ceased to recognise the authority of the native rulers, many of them became government officials, so their families continued to exert influence.

Climate has also played a part in Sumbanese history. The island is dry by Indonesian standards, especially in the east which is much more like Timor and Australia than the lush islands to the north. Its extensive grasslands made it

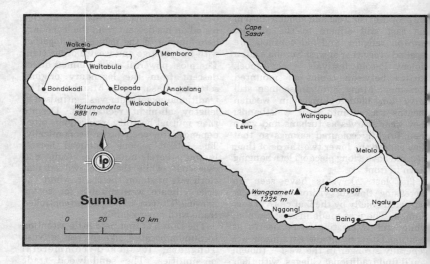

Sumba

into one of the leading horse-breeding islands in Indonesia. Horses are still used as transport in the more rugged regions; they are a symbol of wealth and social status and have traditionally been used as part of the bride-price. Brahmin bulls, first brought to Sumba in the 1920s, are also bred.

CULTURE

Old beliefs fade, customs die and rituals change: the Sumbanese still make textiles, but no longer hunt heads; 20 years ago the bride-price may have been coloured beads and two buffaloes, today it might include a bicycle. Churches are now a fairly common sight and in some areas the following traditions are dying – but in others, particularly in the west, they thrive.

Religion

The basis of traditional Sumbanese religion is *marapu* – a collective term for all spiritual forces including gods, spirits, and ancestors. The most important event in a person's life is death, when he joins the invisible world of the marapu, from

where he can influence the world of the living. *Marapu mameti* is the collective name for dead people. The living can appeal to them for help, especially to their own relatives – but they can also be harmful if irritated. The *marapu maluri* have always been marapu (unlike human beings who become marapu when they die). Their power is sometimes concentrated on certain places or objects, much like the Javanese idea of *semangat*.

Death Ceremonies

On the day of burial horses or buffaloes are killed to provide the deceased with food for their journey to the land of the marapu. Ornaments and a *sirih* (betel nut) bag are also buried with the body. The living must bury their dead as richly as possible to avoid being reprimanded by the marapu mameti. Without a complete and honourable ceremony the dead cannot enter the invisible world, and roam about menacing the living. It was said the dead travel to Cape Sasar to climb the ladder to the invisible world above. One Sumbanese custom – which parallels the Torajan customs of central

Sulawesi – is the deliberate destruction of wealth. Traditionally a major goal of the family is the accumulation of wealth: buffaloes, horses, textiles and jewellery. A family would gain prestige by sponsoring religious festivals at which this wealth would be displayed and many buffaloes slaughtered. Funerals may be delayed for several years until enough wealth has been accumulated for a second burial accompanied by the traditional rites and the erection of a massive stone slab tomb. In such cases the dragging of the tombstone from outside the village is an important part of the procedure. Everyone takes part – sometimes hundreds are needed to move the block of stone – and the family of the deceased feeds them. A *ratu* (priest) sings for the pullers, urging them on with songs which are often answered in chorus by the group. The song functions as an invocation to the stone. Once upon a time, important people's slaves would be buried with them.

When the Indonesian republic was founded, the government tried to stop the destruction of livestock by introducing a slaughter tax, as in Toraja. This reduced the number of animals killed but didn't alter basic attitudes. The Sumbanese, like the Torajans, believe you *can* take it with you!

Villages

A traditional village usually consists of two more or less parallel rows of houses facing each other, with a square between. In the middle of the square is a stone with another flat stone on top of it, on which are made offerings to the village's protective marapu. These structures, spirit stones or *kateda* can also be found at the main entrance to the village, keeping out the angry spirits of evil and disease, and other outside marapu. Kateda are also found in the gardens and rice fields and mark the places where people call on the agricultural marapu, and bring them offerings when planting, weeding and harvesting.

The village square also contains the large stone-slab tombs of important ancestors, often finely carved, though nowadays often made of cement.

In former times the heads of slain

Sumba huts

enemies would be hung on a dead tree in the village square while ceremonies and feasts took place. This skull-tree is called *andung* which means 'monument' and it's often pictured on east Sumbanese textiles. The andung represents the war marapu and the ceremony of hanging the heads is a celebration of victory.

A traditional Sumbanese dwelling is a large rectangular structure raised on piles; it houses an extended family. The thatched – nowadays often corrugated iron – roof slopes gently upwards from all four sides, then rises sharply toward the centre, and is supported on four central pillar posts. Along the front of the house is a verandah at least a metre wide and about one to 1½ metres above the ground.

Inside the house, a cooking hearth is set in the middle of the floor between the four main roof pillars. Above it in a kind of loft are placed objects representing the marapu maluri. Rituals accompanying the building of a house include an offering, at the time of planting the first pillar, to find out whether or not the marapu agree with the location; one method is to slaughter a chicken and examine its liver. On every important occasion a Sumbanese attempts to cultivate good relations with the invisible world to ensure a secure and peaceful life. If this harmony is disturbed, sickness, drought and bad harvests might follow. Many houses are decked with buffalo horns or strings of pig-jaws from past sacrifices.

Visiting Villages An awkward situation can arise when you visit traditional villages in Sumba or elsewhere in Indonesia. If the villagers ask you to pay to take photos, or even just to visit, should you?

Some Sumbanese villages are completely unaccustomed to tourists, and even those that get a steady stream seem to have difficulty knowing how to handle them. This is hardly surprising for a society which has little understanding of the westerner's desire simply to observe and dip into strange cultures.

If you're interested in their weavings or other artefacts, the villagers can probably put you down as a potential trader. If all you want to do is chat a bit and look around they may be puzzled why you've come, and if you simply turn up with a camera, little of the local language and less time, they're not only likely to think you're nuts but may be offended too.

On Sumba, giving betel nut (*sirih*) is the traditional way of greeting guests or hosts, and if you have time to get friendly with villagers it's a great idea to take some with you. Offer it to the kepala desa or the other most 'senior' looking person around. You can buy it at Waingapu and Waikabubak markets among other places. It gives you a mild buzz and a bright red mouth. Some villages have grown used to foreigners arriving without sirih and without any apparently sensible purpose. In such places a gift of 500 rp has become a usually acceptable substitute; in return you should be able to take pictures and may be offered a drink. (In off-the-beaten-track kampungs 500 rp is also OK, especially if you make clear that you're offering it because you don't have any sirih.) This way you still conform to the give-and-take principle. Some places have seen so many fleeting visits by people they can't converse with that they have lost interest and hospitality will be thin; just a few have become decidedly commercial and will ask you for as many rupiah as they can get.

Some villages are under a kind of government supervision as protected monuments. In these places there'll usually be a kiosk or at least a semi-official person who will ask you for a fee of 500 or 1000 rp. Where the money goes is anybody's guess.

Whatever the circumstances, taking time to chat with the villagers and establish some kind of warmth with them, helps them to treat you more as a human being and guest than as a customer or alien. The more time you have to spend in each place, rather than just dashing lens-in-hand from one kampung to the next, the better.

Ikat

The ikat woven by the women of the eastern coastal regions of Sumba is probably the most dramatic in Indonesia. Not only are the colours predominantly bright – indigo blue and earthy kombu orange-red – but unlike the more abstract patterns on Flores, the Sumba motifs are pictorial history, reminders of tribal wars and an age which ended with the coming of the Dutch – the skulls of vanquished enemies dangle off trees, mounted riders wield spears.

Traditionally ikat cloth was used only on special occasions: at rituals accompanying the harvest and the reception of visitors, as gifts to other families, as offerings to the sponsors of a festival and as clothing for leaders, their relatives and attendants. Less than 90 years ago, only members of Sumba's highest clans and their personal attendants could make or wear it. Death was threatened for those who violated the class monopoly. The most impressive use of the cloth was at important funerals where dancers and the guards of the corpse were dressed in richly decorated costumes and glittering headdresses. The corpse itself was dressed in the finest textiles and then bound with so many of them that it resembled a huge mound. The first missionary on Sumba, D K Wielenga, described a funeral he witnessed in 1925:

The brilliant examples of decorated cloths were carefully kept till the day of burial. The prominent chief took 40 to 50 to the grave with him and the raja was put to rest with no less than 100 or 200. When they appeared in the hereafter among their ancestors, then they must appear in full splendour. And so the most attractive cloths went into the earth.

The Dutch conquest broke the Sumbanese nobility's monopoly on the production and use of ikat, and opened up a large external market for it. Collected by Dutch ethnographers and museums since the late 19th century (the Rotterdam and Basel museums have fine collections), the large cloths became popular in Java and Holland. To cater for the new market, production expanded. Furthermore the trade in horses and, later, in beef cattle brought increased riches to some of the Sumbanese nobility whose demand for textiles consequently increased. By the 1920s, visitors were already noting a fall in standards and the introduction of non-traditional design elements – rampant lions from the Dutch coat of arms, fluttering flags, bicycles and steamships.

A Sumbanese woman's ikat sarong is known as a lau; a hinggi is a large rectangular cloth used by men as a sarong or shawl.

Motifs The skull tree is the most readily identifiable of the amazing range of motifs that appear on Sumba ikat today. Figures of skull trees on the textiles usually also include its stone base and the horns of sacrificed buffaloes attached to the tree.

Deer – whose antlers were exported in large quantities from Sumba in the early 20th century – and the dogs and horsemen that hunted them are also found on textiles. Snakes often appear as nagas – the crowned snake-dragon with large teeth, wings and legs. Turtle motifs also appear – turtles were caught on Sumba's southern beaches and used for food while the shell was exported or used for making combs.

Sumba's famous horses often appear with riders holding long spears. Oddly enough buffaloes, which have been equally important with possibly hundreds slaughtered at the burial of a Sumbanese raja, have rarely been depicted on ikat.

Humans, both male and female, adult and child are included. Sometimes male figures wear the gold forehead decoration known as a lamba, which may represent a boat. On Sumba the lamba was a preserve of the royal class. Boat motifs also appear: although the Sumbanese aren't a seagoing people, many coastal families trace their ancestry from a founder who arrived on a boat. Other motifs which have appeared on Sumba ikat include trees, shrimps, squid, fish, seahorses, scorpions, beetles, centipedes, spiders, horseflies, lizards, crocodiles, apes, chickens, fighting cocks, hawks and eagles. Dragons have also been depicted, possibly inspired by motifs taken from Chinese porcelain long before Europeans arrived. Even elephants have appeared on Sumba ikat!

GETTING THERE & AROUND

You can fly into Waingapu (east Sumba) from Jakarta, Surabaya, Denpasar, Kupang and Bima and into Tambolaka (west Sumba, near Waikabubak) from Kupang and Bima. Regular passenger ships link Waingapu with Kupang, Ende, Bima and Sawu, and occasional boats call at Waikelo in north-west Sumba. There are flights and buses between Waingapu and Waikabubak, plus buses from these two main centres to other destinations on the island.

WAINGAPU

Now the largest town on Sumba, with 25,000 people, Waingapu became the administrative centre after the Dutch took over the island in 1906. It had long been the centre of the trade controlled by the coastal princedoms, with textiles and metal goods being brought in by traders from Makassar, Bima and Ende, and the much-prized Sumba horses, dyewoods and lumber being exported.

Waingapu is the main entry point to Sumba but the island's chief attractions lie elsewhere, in the west and south-east. The town does, however, have a large group of ikat traders who run stores or hang around outside losmens. If you're interested in buying ikat have a look at what they offer before heading out to the villages. You can get an idea of the range of quality, design and price – and if you don't find what you want in the villages, come back to Waingapu. Prices in the town are generally higher than in the actual weaving centres – but not that much higher, and there's more to choose from. Bargaining's equally tough anywhere. The Hotel Sandle Wood has a good range of ikat for sale, and the owner's son has a separate, well-stocked shop out the back of the hotel, on Jalan Metawai.

Prailiu, two km out of Waingapu and just to the right off the road south to Melolo, is an ikat-weaving centre. Kawangu, 10 km from Waingapu and about 300 metres to the right off the same road, has some stone-slab tombs. Traditional houses may be seen at Maru, on the coast heading north-west from Waingapu. Apparently Maru sits below a now-deserted village which was once the fortified hilltop capital of a princedom.

Orientation & Information

Waingapu has two centres, about a km apart: the northern one focuses on the harbour, the southern one on the bus station. Both have markets, and places to stay; banks and offices are divided between the two. The Bank Rakyat Indonesia on Jalan Yani will change major travellers' cheques (it's the only bank on the island that will) – as well as some foreign currencies. It's open from 8 am to 12 noon Monday to Thursday and Saturday, and from 7 to 11 am on Friday. The post office on Jalan Hasanuddin is open from 7 am to 2 pm Monday to Thursday, to 11 am Friday and to 1 pm Saturday.

Places to Stay

There are two cheaper places and two more expensive ones which also have some cheapish rooms. The Hotel Lima Saudara (tel 83), in the northern part of town at Jalan Wanggameti 2, is tatty but friendly; they ask 3000 rp per person in doubles or a small dormitory, all with private mandi, but will usually come down to 2500 rp.

Other accommodation is in the southern

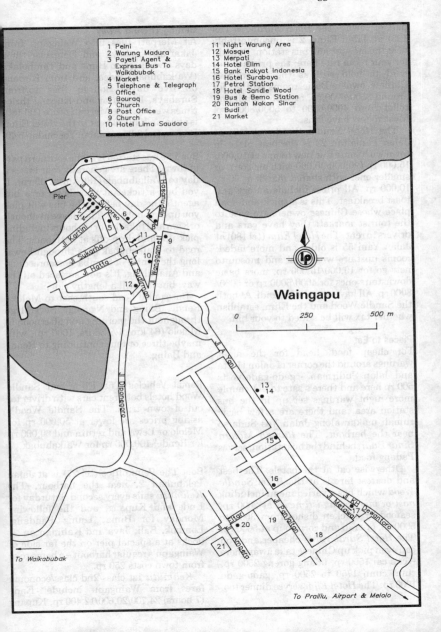

1 Peini
2 Warung Madura
3 Payeti Agent & Express Bus To Waikabubak
4 Market
5 Telephone & Telegraph Office
6 Bouraq
7 Church
8 Post Office
9 Church
10 Hotel Lima Saudara
11 Night Warung Area
12 Mosque
13 Merpati
14 Hotel Elim
15 Bank Rakyat Indonesia
16 Hotel Surabaya
17 Petrol Station
18 Hotel Sandle Wood
19 Bus & Bemo Station
20 Rumah Makan Sinar Budi
21 Market

Pier

Jl. Yos Sudarso

Jl. Kartini

Jl. Sukarno

Jl. Hatta

Jl. Sudirman

Jl. Wanggameti

Jl. Hasanuddin

Jl. Cut Nyak Dien

Waingapu

0   250   500 m

Jl. Yani

Jl. Diponegoro

Jl. Tjitarum

Jl. Ambero

Jl. Panjaitan

Jl. KH Dewantoro

Jl. Matawai

To Waikabubak

To Prailiu, Airport & Melolo

part of town – the *Hotel Surabaya* (tel 125) at Jalan Eltari 2 is uncomfortably near the mosque and bus station. Bargain for your room rate here; the prices are as hard to hold still as the hyperactive Chinese owner. Basic rooms will go for around 3500/6000 rp, or with mandi and toilet from 4000/6500 to 5000/8000 rp. Most rooms have fans.

The *Hotel Sandle Wood* (tel 117) at Jalan Panjaitan 23 is the best place in town with some fine new rooms at 10,000/15,000 rp (20,000/30,000 with air-con), or smaller ones with shared mandi at 6000/10,000 rp. All prices include an egg and toast breakfast. This is a spick-and-span place whose Chinese owners are wise to the tourist market: they have cars and drivers to rent. The *Hotel Elim* (tel 180) at Jalan Yani 55 is older and more faded: rooms upstairs with fans and mosquito nets go for 10,000/15,000 rp, more basic downstairs ones for 4000/6000 rp or 5000/8000 rp. All have attached mandi. At both the Sandle Wood and the Elim, establish whether tax will be added to your bill.

Places to Eat

For cheap food, head for the night warungs around the corner of Jalan Hatta and Jalan Sudirman – gado-gado costs 500 rp here and there's sate too. A couple more night warungs set up in the bus station area, and there are a few basic rumah makan along Jalan Yos Sudarso near the harbour. The *Rumah Makan Sinar Budi*, behind the bus station, serves Padang food.

Otherwise eat at the hotels. The best and dearest fare is at the *Hotel Sandle Wood* which has a varied menu including *nasi* or *mie goreng istimewa* at 2000 rp, seafood or chicken dishes from 3000 to 5000 rp, or crab and corn soup at 5000 rp. The *Hotel Surabaya* is cheaper and you can even pick up Chinese take aways here – cap cai 1500 rp, udang goreng 2500 rp, cumi cumi 1750 to 2500 rp, gado-gado 1000 rp. The *Hotel Elim* serves dinner too.

Getting There & Away

Air Merpati flies into Waingapu from Jakarta, Surabaya and Denpasar three days a week, from Bima and Tambolaka (Waikabubak) twice, and from Kupang on five days. Bouraq flies to/from Surabaya, Denpasar and Kupang thrice times weekly. The Merpati office (tel 180) is at Jalan Yani 73 next to the Hotel Elim. Bouraq (tel 36) is at Jalan Yos Sudarso 49.

Bus The bus station is in the southern part of town. There are generally four buses a day to Waikabubak (136 km, 2500 rp). If you buy a ticket at your hotel or a bus agent's the day before, the bus will pick you up at your hotel. They leave at about 7 or 8 am and take five or six hours including pick-ups and drop-offs at both ends. The road to Waikabubak goes through Lewa, long the centre of Sumba horsebreeding, and Anakalang. It's now surfaced all the way, but it's still a lengthy ride.

Buses also head south-east to Melolo, Rende, Baing and Nggongi. Several go throughout the morning and afternoon to Melolo (64 km, 1½ hours, 1000 rp), with maybe three or four continuing to Rende and Baing.

Rental Vehicles The Elim and Sandle Wood hotels both rent cars with driver for out-of-town trips. The Sandle Wood's asking prices are lower at 50,000 rp for Melolo or Lewa and return and 60,000 rp for Rende, 100,000 rp for Waikabubak.

Boat The Pelni office (tel 27) is at Jalan Pelabuhan 2, near the harbour. The *Kelimutu* sails every second Saturday for Ende and Kupang, and the following Monday for Bima, Ujung Pandang, Lombok, Bali, Java and Kalimantan. It docks at a special pier on the far side of Waingapu's regular harbour – a bemo to or from town costs 250 rp.

Kelimutu 1st class/2nd class/economy fares from Waingapu include: Ende (7 hours) 24,700/20,600/12,400 rp, Kupang

(21 hours) 45,700/37,400/19,100 rp, Bima (12 hours) 34,300/27,200/15,100 rp, Ujung Pandang (36 hours) 64,400/52,900/27,400 rp.

Pelni also operates the *Baruna Eka* and *Baruna Fajar*, one of which loops round Waingapu, Sawu, Kupang, Sawu, Ende, Waingapu roughly each week. From Waingapu to Sawu is 7000 rp (one night), to Kupang 12,400 rp (one day, two nights).

For other, less regular boats ask around the harbour.

Getting Around

Bemos around town are 100 rp. The airport is six km south of town on the Melolo road and a bemo is 250 rp. Vehicles from the hotels Elim and Sandle Wood usually meet incoming flights and will give you a free ride if you stay with them. Going out to the airport, bemos can be infrequent. A chartered bemo costs about 2500 rp.

SOUTH-EAST SUMBA

Some of the villages of south-east Sumba have splendid stone tombs (as well as less exciting concrete ones) and produce some of the island's best weaving, but the traditional way of life is not as strong as it is in the west of the island. You can buy weavings in the villages, but take plenty of patience with you if you want prices below those of the Waingapu merchants.

Melolo

If you don't want to visit the south-east in a day trip from Waingapu, the small town of Melolo, 62 km from Waingapu and close to some of the more interesting villages, has accommodation possibilities. On Thursday afternoon and Friday morning there's a market at Lumbukori, on a hilltop about three km out of Melolo.

Places to Stay & Eat *L D Gah Homestead*, owned by the same people as the Taman

Ria Beach Inn in Kupang, has a couple of rooms at 2500 rp per person. Bus drivers can drop you here and the losmen can arrange for you to rent a motorbike or pushbike to get out to the villages. Basic meals are available at 1500 rp – or try the *Rumah Makan Anda* for goat and rice. There's also a family somewhere in Melolo which takes in travellers on a semi-regular basis.

Getting There & Away Buses to Melolo from Waingapu run about hourly until around 4 pm; it's 1000 rp for the 1½-hour trip. The road is paved and crosses mainly flat grasslands. From Melolo the road continues south to Baing. Another road from Melolo crosses the mountains to Nggongi – trucks run along this road except in the rainy season.

Rende

Seven km towards Baing from Melolo, Rende has an impressive line-up of big stone-slab tombs and makes some of Sumba's best ikat. You may be asked 500 or 1000 rp as a sort of admission/ hospitality fee and photo-licence. If you sit and chat with the villagers rather than just stride in and start pointing your camera, they might not ask you for anything – but you might want to make a small gift anyway! Plenty of good ikat weaving goes on here and the people are usually happy to explain their methods to you. Though Rende still has a 'raja', other traditions are declining owing to the cost of ceremonies and the breakdown of the marapu religion here.

The largest tomb at Rende is for a former chief and consists of four stone pillars two metres high, supporting a rectangular slab of stone about five metres long, 2½ metres wide and a metre thick. Two stone tablets stand atop the main slab and are carved with human, buffalo, deer, lobster, fish, crocodile and turtle figures. A number of traditional-style Sumbanese houses face the tombs.

Getting There & Away Three or four buses a day go from Waingapu to Rende, starting around 7 am each morning. The trip takes about two hours and costs 1200 rp. Or take a bus to Melolo and then walk, hitch a lift or find a vehicle in Melolo. If you walk, take water as there's no shade.

Umabara & Pau

Like Rende, these two villages near Melolo have traditional Sumbanese houses, impressive tombs and weavings. At Umabara the largest tombs are those of relatives of the present 'raja' – who speaks some English and is quite friendly. Apart from serving you coffee he may also offer you betel nut. The moment a Sumbanese opens his or her mouth you'll see that the custom of betel nut chewing is alive and well! Again, expect to pay 500 rp if you're looking for hospitality and/or want to take photos. Apart from ikat you may also be shown *hikung* cloths in which decorative patterns are woven – not dyed – into the cloth.

Getting There & Away Leave Melolo by the main road in the Waingapu direction, and soon after crossing the river on the edge of town, turn left along a dirt road. About a 20-minute walk up here is a horse statue, where you fork right for Umabara or left for Pau, both just a few minutes further. A trail also links the two villages. From Waingapu, ask the bus driver to drop you off at the turning from the main road.

Mangili

This village 38 km from Melolo, a 20-minute walk off the road to Baing, is another high-quality ikat weaving centre, though its people don't seem very interested in bargaining with travellers. About three buses a day from Waingapu and Melolo pass the Mangili turn-off with the first leaving Waingapu at about 7 am and passing through Melolo from 8.30 to 9 am. Altogether it takes around two hours from Melolo to Mangili and the fare is 500 rp. If you take the first morning bus

down to Mangili, you should be able to spend about two hours there before taking the same bus back.

Baing

There's good surf in the first few months of the year near this village at the end of the road south. The same buses as for Mangili carry on to Baing, about 24 km and one hour further, and usually return the same day.

WAIKABUBAK

At the greener western end of Sumba, where the tropical trees and rice paddies contrast with the dry grasslands around Waingapu, is the neat little town of Waikabubak. More a collection of kampungs with the gaps between them filled in, it has clusters of traditional clan houses and small graveyards of old stone-slab tombs carved with buffalo horn motifs. About 600 metres high and cooler than the east, it's a good base for exploring the traditional villages of west Sumba.

Information

The Bank Rakyat Indonesia on Jalan Gajah Mada will change US and Australian cash – but *not* travellers' cheques. It's open from 8 am to 12 noon Monday to Thursday and Saturday, and from 7 to 11 am Friday. The post and Telephone & Telegraph offices are open from 7 am to 2 pm Monday to Thursday, until 11 am Friday and 1 pm Saturday.

Tombs & Traditional Kampungs

Large stone-slab tombs are dotted around Waikabubak and several traditional kampungs occupy ridge or hilltop positions around the town. Kampung Tarung, reached by a path off Jalan Maadaelu marked by a large number of tombs at the junction, is the scene of an important month-long ritual sequence, the Wula Podhu, each November. This is an austere period and even weeping for the dead is forbidden. Rites mainly consist of offerings to the spirits, drum and gong beating and some dancing. The day before it ends,

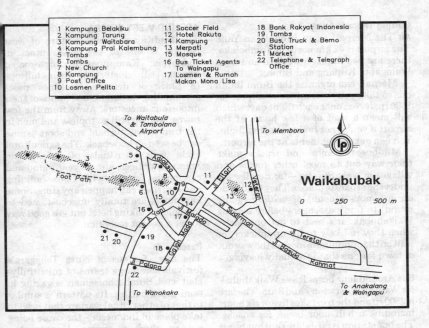

1 Kampung Belakiku	11 Soccer Field	18 Bank Rakyat Indonesia
2 Kampung Tarung	12 Hotel Rakuta	19 Tombs
3 Kampung Waitabara	14 Kampung	20 Bus, Truck & Bemo
4 Kampung Prai Kalembung	13 Merpati	Station
5 Tombs	15 Mosque	21 Market
6 Tombs	16 Bus Ticket Agents	22 Telephone & Telegraph
7 New Church	To Waingapu	Office
8 Kampung	17 Losmen & Rumah	
9 Post Office	Makan Mona Lisa	
10 Losmen Pelita		

Waikabubak

hundreds of chickens are sacrificed and on the final day people sing and dance day-long. Tarung has some fine tombs and its monuments are under official protection. You're usually asked to give 500 or 1000 rp.

Places to Stay & Eat

The cheapest accommodation is the simple little *Losmen Pelita* (tel 104) on Jalan Yani. It's basic, but clean at 3000 rp per person, and includes a light breakfast. Mandis are shared.

The *Losmen Mona Lisa* (tel 24) on Jalan Gajah Mada is more comfortable, serves up some of the better food in town and is the best place for information on trips out of the town. The friendly owner, a locally-born Chinese, has a detailed knowledge and friendly contacts all over the region. He can help you fix transport and cheap places to stay in some out-of-the-way villages and also offers trips in his own jeep. Singles/doubles are 5000/7500 rp

with shared mandi, 7000/10,000 rp or 8000/12,500 rp with breakfast and private mandi. Tax and service charges may be extra. The cheaper private-mandi rooms are outside and probably quieter. You can eat at the Mona Lisa even if you're not staying there; main dishes, mostly of the noodle, rice, cap cai and chicken varieties, range from 1250 to 2000 rp.

The *Hotel Rakuta* on Jalan Veteran has rooms, beds and mandis that are vast by Nusa Tenggara's standards, but the place is musty and little-cared for. Officially rooms cost 10,000 rp per person including three meals or 6000 rp without meals, but since the place is usually empty you can bargain them down. There are lots of basic rumah makan along Jalan Yani and some warungs set up here at night. One on Jalan Eltari next to the soccer field does good goat sate and rice for 750 rp. The market has some fresh fruit and vegetables.

Getting There & Away

Air The Merpati agent is on Jalan Yani. The airport is 42 km north at Tambolaka: there are two flights a week to and from Waingapu, Kupang and Bima.

Merpati can organise the Bumi Indah bus to take you to Tambolaka airport for 1500 rp. It goes once each flight day, which will mean a wait of a few hours at the airport if you're not taking the first flight. You can get refreshments at the airport.

Minibuses, bemos and trucks make their way out to most other towns and villages in west Sumba – for details, see under the separate places. They tend to do an enormous amount of *keliling* (going round) to find passengers before leaving Waikabubak. It's best to get one early, when they're likely to fill up quicker, or wait on the appropriate road on the way out of town for one that is actually leaving.

Bus Around four buses leave Waikabubak for Waingapu between 7 and 8 am. The fare is 2500 rp and the trip takes five or six hours including a half hour break for snacks. The bus station is off Jalan Yani but buses will drop or pick you up wherever you want in Waikabubak. When leaving for Waingapu, it's best to book your ticket the day before: losmens may help or visit the bus ticket agents around the corner of Jalan Yani and Jalan Maadaelu.

Getting Around

The Losmen Mona Lisa rents motorbikes for around 7500 rp a day (plus petrol) and offers a variety of jeep trips out to west Sumba kampungs and the coast for 50,000 to 75,000 rp. There's room for five passengers in the vehicle. While the prices might seem high, you can bargain them down a bit and going with someone who knows the villagers can make a shortish visit more interesting and more friendly, avoiding haggling over village entrance fees and the like. You could probably find other people in town who'd be willing to take you out on a motorbike for maybe 10,000 rp a day.

AROUND WEST SUMBA

The traditional village culture of west Sumba is one of the most intact in Indonesia. Kampungs of high-roofed houses still cluster on their hilltops (a place of defence in times past) surrounding the large stone tombs of their important ancestors. Away from the few towns, women still go topless and men in the traditional 'turban' and short sarong can be seen on horseback. The agricultural cycle turns up rituals, often involving animal sacrifices, almost year round and ceremonies for events like house building and marriage can happen any time. Some kampungs are totally unaccustomed to foreigners – taking betel nut is a good way to get a decent reception.

Pasola

The most famous of Nusa Tenggara's festivals sees large teams of colourfully-clad west Sumba horsemen engaging in semi-mock battles. Its pattern is similar to that of other ritual warfare that used to take place in Indonesia – the cause being not so much a quarrel between the opposing forces but the need for human blood to be spilt to keep the spirits happy and bring a good harvest. Despite the blunt spears that the horsemen now use and efforts at supervision by the Indonesian authorities, few holds are barred; injuries and sometimes deaths still occur.

The Pasola is part of a series of rituals connected with the beginning of the planting season. It takes place in four different areas in February or March each year and its exact timing is determined by the arrival on nearby coasts of a certain type of seaworm called *nyale*. Priests examine the nyale at dawn and from their behaviour predict how good the year's harvest will be. Then the pasola can begin: it's usually fought first on the beach then, later the same day, further inland. The opposing 'armies' are drawn from coastal and inland dwellers.

The nyale are usually found on the eighth or ninth day after a full moon. In

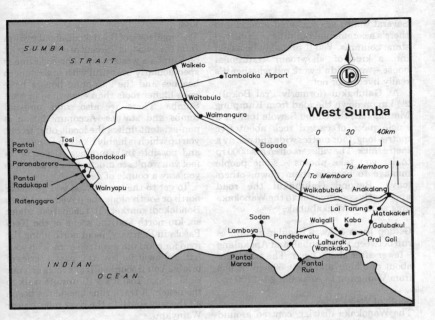

February Pasola is celebrated in the Kodi area (centred on Kampung Tosi) and the Lamboya area (Kampung Sodan); in March it's the turn of the Wanokaka area (Kampung Waigalli) and the remote Gaura area west of Lamboya (Kampung Ubu Olehka).

Anakalang & Around

Kampung Pasunga, beside the Waingapu road at Anakalang, 22 km from Waikabubak, boasts one of the Sumba's most impressive tomb line-ups. The grave of particular interest consists of a horizontal stone slab with a vertical slab in front of it. The vertical slab took six months to carve with figures of a man and a woman. The tomb was constructed in 1926; five people are buried here and 150 buffalo were sacrificed during its construction. There seems to be a standard charge of 1000 rp for a close look at these tombs and/or photos but you can see them fairly well from the road.

Anakalang has a market on Wednesday and Saturday and is the scene of the *Purung Takadonga*, a mass marriage festival held every two years. The exact date is determined by the full moon. At Kampung Matakakeri, a 15-minute walk down the road past Anakalang market, are more traditional houses and tombs. Check in at the *Departemen Kebudayaan* (Cultural Department) hut at the entrance to the kampung: there seems to be no 'fee' here but you'll probably get a guide who'll ask for a tip. One of the Matakakeri tombs is Sumba's heaviest, weighing in at 70 tonnes. The construction of this one apparently took three years, 250 sacrificed buffaloes, and 2000 workers who chiselled it out of a hillside and dragged it to the site. It commemorates a 19th-century raja with the snappy name of Umbusapipateduk. Lai Tarung, the hilltop ancestral village of 12 local clans, now almost deserted but partly renovated with government money is a 15-minute side-trip from Matakakeri.

Several tombs are scattered around and there's a ceremonial building with carved stone columns. You'll probably be asked into a kind of 'showroom' traditional house – we couldn't work out whether it's really lived in or not.

At Galubakul (formerly Prai Bokul), 2½ km on down the road from Kampung Matakakeri, the Umbu Sawola tomb is a single piece of carved rock about five metres long, four metres wide and nearly a metre thick. The villagers often ask 5000 rp to let you take photos – some people manage to bargain them down, others leave. Beyond Galubakul the road apparently continues on to the Wanokaka area south of Waikabubak.

Getting There & Away Regular minibuses run between Waikabubak and Anakalang – fewer after about 1 pm. The trip takes about one hour and costs 500 rp. A bus from Waingapu to Anakalang is 2100 rp.

South of Waikabubak

The Wanokaka district, centred around Laihurak, about 18 km south of Waikabubak towards the coast, has numerous traditional kampungs and is the scene of one of the March Pasolas. The Watu Kajiwa tomb in Prai Goli is said to be the oldest in the area. Kampung Sodan, centre for the Lamboya Pasola further west, was burnt down in 1988 (accidentally, it seems) but will probably be rebuilt. Pantai Rua, a three-km walk south of Pandedewatu, apparently has a beach with swimming spots and there's surf at Pantai Marosi near Lamboya.

Getting There & Away Trucks and bemos rattle irregularly down the rough roads to Wanokaka (500 rp) and to Lamboya (500 rp) via Pandedewatu. Be at Waikabubak bus station as early as you can (eg 6 am) if you want to catch one. Better, start asking the day before – otherwise walk, hitch, or rent a vehicle.

Kodi

The small town of Bondokodi, about two km from the coast, is the centre of this district on Sumba's western tip. The coastline is spectacularly beautiful with some superb beaches and the kampung houses have even higher roofs than elsewhere in west Sumba. There are also some unusual tombs and statues. Accommodation is non-existent unless the locals offer to put you up which is highly likely in Bondokodi and possible in kampungs. If you're on foot you won't see much of the area unless you stay a couple of days.

To get to the kampungs, you go either north or south along the paved road from Bondokodi market. To reach Tosi, about six km north and the scene of the Kodi Pasola in February, head north along the road for a km until you see a track on your left. Follow it for five km, past a series of tombs. You'll soon see Tosi's roofs on your right. From Tosi it's a 10-minute walk to the beach. A track runs beside the beach all the way south to the river mouth near Wainyapu.

If you head south from Bondokodi market for a km, you'll see a dirt track on your right. Take this and keep forking to the right, and you'll reach Paronabaroro after about two km. This kampung is more interesting than Tosi with even higher roofs, stone statues and an elaborate house complete with pig jaws hanging from its verandah, numerous buffalo horns, separate rooms and even a door with a lock! Pantai Radukapal, a beach with white sand, clear water and strong currents, is about a km from Paronabaroro.

From Pantai Radukapal it's roughly two km south along the coast to Wainyapu, on the far side of a river mouth. A dirt track runs along beside the beach to the river mouth. The view here will take your breath away. The seas glisten, coconut palms fringe the shoreline and Wainyapu's tall roofs peep above the treeline. On the near side of the river mouth are some unusual stone tombs and the kampung of Ratenggaro. You can wade across the river mouth to Wainyapu. You can also reach Wainyapu by inland tracks from Paronabaroro or by following the paved road south from Bondokodi and turning off somewhere beyond the Paronabaroro turning.

Getting There & Away From Waikabubak take a bus to Waitabula (1½ hours, 800 rp).

These run until at least 12 noon. From Waitabula there are two or three minibuses each day down the rough dirt road to Bondokodi.

Waikelo

Occasional boats go to Sumbawa, Flores or even further afield from this small port north of Waitabula.

Sulawesi

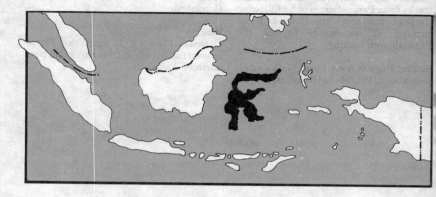

The strangely contorted island of Sulawesi sprawls across the sea between Borneo and Maluku. Three great gulfs between the narrow, mountainous peninsulas – Bone, Tolo and Tomini – give the island its characteristic mutilated-octopus shape. When the Portuguese first came by in the early 16th century they sighted so many narrow points of land they presumed they were passing by an archipelago.

Protected by mountains and, for the most part, walled in by thick jungle, the interior of the island has provided a refuge for some of Indonesia's earliest inhabitants, some of whom have managed to preserve elements of their idiosyncratic cultures well into the 20th century. The Muslim Makassarese and Bugis of the south-west peninsula and the Christian Minahasans of the far north are the dominant groups of Sulawesi. They have also had the most contact with the west, but it's the Christian-animist Toraja, of the Tanatoraja district of the central highlands, who attract large numbers of visitors every year.

Strange cultures are not the only thing that makes Sulawesi so interesting; the landscape is strikingly beautiful and the island, a transition zone between Asian and Australian fauna, is home to some peculiar animals. The *babirusa*, or 'pig-deer', has long legs and tusks which curve upwards like horns, while the rare *anoa* is a metre-high dwarf buffalo.

Few visitors get further than the Ujung Pandang-Tanatoraja area; travel to other parts of the island is still difficult or time consuming. Nevertheless, the Minahasa area of the northern peninsula is interesting and there are stunning coral reefs off the coast of Manado, the chief city of the region. Huge areas of central Sulawesi are almost untouched by tourism.

GETTING THERE

Right in the middle of Indonesia, Sulawesi has for centuries been a transit point between the spice islands of Maluku and the trading ports of Java and the Malay peninsula. The capital, Ujung Pandang, on the tip of the south-western peninsula, is still a transport and communications hub and is the chief entry point to Sulawesi.

Further north, Palu and Pare Pare are departure points for ships to the east coast of Kalimantan. In the far north, Manado

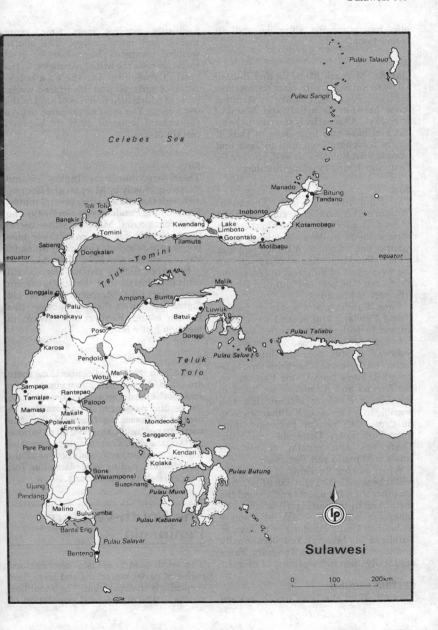

Sulawesi

also has numerous shipping and air connections.

Air

Garuda, Merpati, Mandala and Bouraq all fly to Sulawesi, with most connections via Ujung Pandang. The city is a stepping stone between Java/Bali and Maluku/Irian Jaya. Alternatively you can make an out and back trip from Java or Bali. If you're travelling from Bali to Java and want to visit Sulawesi as well, you can fly Denpasar-Ujung Pandang-Surabaya.

Boat

The Pelni liners *Kerinci*, *Kambuna*, *Rinjani* and *Umsini* do regular loops out of Java. Depending on the ship there are various stops in Java, Sulawesi, Kalimantan and Sumatra. All ships pull into Ujung Pandang. Some carry on up the west coast of Sulawesi to places like Pantoloan (the port of Palu) and Bitung (the port of Manado).

From Surabaya it's a day or two to Ujung Pandang and several days more around to Bitung, with several stops in between. Because road transport in Sulawesi is still poor the intra-island sectors on these and other ships tend to be crowded. Fares from Ujung Pandang on the *Kerinci* and *Kambuna* are listed in the Ujung Pandang section. It's also possible to get across to Kalimantan from Sulawesi with regular passenger ships from Pare Pare, Donggala and Palu. There are also regular connections between Manado and Ternate.

When looking for ships in any of the ports check with the Pelni office first, then the other shipping agents and around the ports. A really interesting trip would be by Makassar schooner – ask at Paotere harbour in Ujung Pandang or in Java at Surabaya or Jakarta. You occasionally find them going to Nusa Tenggara. Fares are totally open to bargaining of course.

GETTING AROUND

Travel beyond the 'easy' south-western peninsula requires more time, more money and more energy. The south-western peninsula has relatively good roads, as does the Minahasa region in the north. Between the two there's a hotch-potch of surfaced and unsurfaced roads, some of which turn to rivers of mud in the wet season. You must be prepared to take the coastal ships or even fly between certain places.

Air

There are numerous flights around Sulawesi, chiefly by Merpati and Bouraq, although Garuda also flies several routes. From Ujung Pandang you can fly Bouraq to Gorontalo and Manado. Other useful flights which get you over those bus-bogging roads include Gorontalo-Manado, Palu-Gorontalo and Palu-Manado.

For other flights, particularly around central Sulawesi and the south-eastern peninsula, take Merpati. They've got flights to out-of-the-way places like Butung Island, Kendari and Luwuk, to mention just a few.

Boat

Apart from the coastal connections there are other ships which allow you to skirt some of the harder sections. These include the regular passenger ships from Poso in central Sulawesi to Gorontalo on the northern peninsula, stopping off at various ports on the way. There are ships along the western and northern coasts between Palu and Manado, calling in at places like Toli Toli, Paleleh and Kwandang.

The South-Western Peninsula

The south-west is a lush, mountainous region of caves, waterfalls and large (but surprisingly shallow) lakes. The 6½ million people – 60% of the total population of

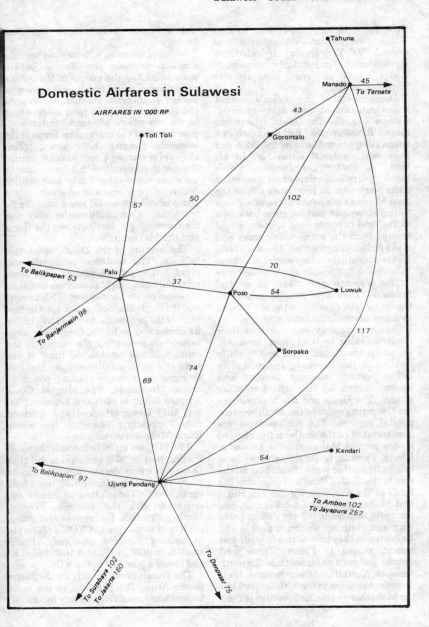

Domestic Airfares in Sulawesi

AIRFARES IN '000 RP

Tahuna

Manado — 45
To Ternate

43

Gorontalo

Toli Toli

102

50

57

To Balikpapan 53

Palu

70

37

54

Luwuk

To Banjarmasin 98

Poso

117

Soroako

74

69

To Balikpapan 97

Ujung Pandang

54

Kendari

To Ambon 102
To Jayapura 257

To Surabaya 102
To Jakarta 160

To Denpasar 75

Sulawesi – include about four million Bugis, two million Makassarese and around 500,000 Toraja. Irrigated-rice agriculture is particularly important. Coffee, cotton and sugar cane are also important crops.

Descendants of the region's earliest tribes still existed until fairly recently. Groups like the the Toala (the name means 'forest people') had dwindled to a single village near Maros by the 1930s and have now vanished altogether. In his book, *A Pattern of Peoples*, Robin Hanbury-Tenison relates how poisonous darts were shot at prospectors from the Inco Mining Company. More often men toting blowpipes and wearing bark loin cloths, and bare-breasted women, would emerge from the surrounding cover and make friendly approaches. Tenison's book also relates other curious stories of strange tribes including people who lived on boats in the swamps and rivers in central Sulawesi. They were possibly related to the *orang laut* ('people of the sea') found in many places in Indonesia.

Toraja mythology suggests that their ancestors came by boat from the south, sailed up the Sadan River and initially dwelled in the Enrekang region, before being pushed into the mountainous central regions by the arrival of other groups. The Bugis and the Makassarese are the main groups of the south-western coastal regions. The Makassarese are concentrated in the southern tip, centred on the port of Makassar (now known as Ujung Pandang). Bugis territory was originally further north, extending all the way to the Gulf of Bone and adjoining the lands of the southern Toraja. The Bugis and Makassarese have similar cultures, the main difference between them being language. Both are seafaring people and for centuries they were active in trade and piracy, sailing to Flores, Timor and Sumba and even as far south as the north coast of Australia. Islam became their dominant religion in the 17th century but the Makassarese retained vestiges of their

old animistic beliefs into the 20th century.

Much of Sulawesi's history has been the conflict between the Toraja in the mountains and the people of the coastal region, who were much more open to foreign influences. Pushed northwards, the Toraja people built their villages high in the mountains of central Sulawesi to guard against the marauding Bugis of the lowlands. Despite the constant threat they never formed a united front against the common enemy; each tribe occupied a valley or some other fairly well-defined pocket of territory, and at most only a group of villages would band together for protection. Complicating the story was the continuing rivalry between the Bugis and the Makassarese.

The coming of the Dutch upset this balance. The southern peninsula was divided into petty kingdoms, the most powerful being the Makassarese kingdom of Gowa (centred on the port of Makassar) and the Bugis kingdom of Bone on the east coast of the peninsula. Around 1530, before its conversion to Islam, Gowa started to expand its power. By the middle of the century it had established itself at the head of a loosely united empire and had emerged as a major trading power in eastern Indonesia. The king of Gowa adopted Islam in 1605 and between 1608 and 1611 Gowa attacked and subdued Bone, spreading Islam to the whole Bugis-Makassarese area.

The VOC set up its first south Sulawesi trading post in 1609 but soon found that Gowa was a considerable hindrance to its plans of total domination of the whole archipelago. The Sultan of Gowa co-operated with the English, French, Danish, Spanish, Portuguese and Asian traders in thwarting the VOC's attempts at gaining a spice monopoly. Peace treaties in 1637, 1655 and 1660 failed to end Gowa's hostility to the VOC.

The Dutch found an ally in the Bugis prince Arung Palakka, one of the most famous warriors of 17th-century Indonesia.

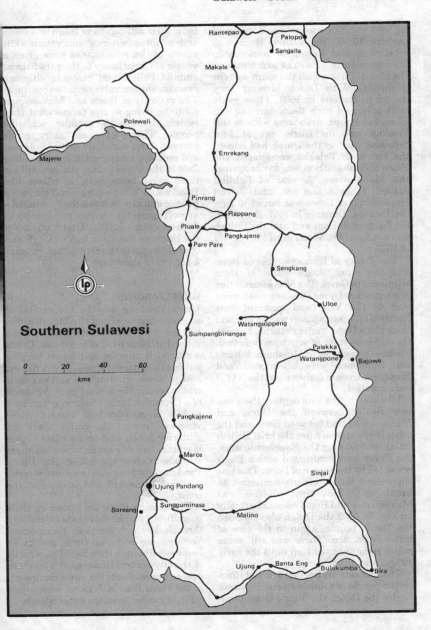

Southern Sulawesi

0   20   40   60
kms

In 1660 Palakka was among a group of perhaps 10,000 Bugis from Bone who rebelled against Gowanese overlordship but were defeated. Palakka took refuge on the island of Butung off the south-eastern peninsula. With Dutch blessing they moved to Batavia in 1663. Three years later a large Dutch fleet, carrying 600 European troops, Ambonese soldiers and Palakka and his Bugis, set sail for Sulawesi. Just as the Dutch had hoped, the return of Palakka encouraged the Bugis of Bone and Soppeng to rise against the Makassarese. A year of fighting ensued on land and sea, and Sultan Hasanuddin of Gowa was forced to sign the Treaty of Bungaya in 1667. Even then the fighting did not end and the Sultan was not finally subdued until the middle of 1669.

The Treaty of Bungaya relieved Bone and the other Bugis states of their allegiance to Gowa. The Makassarese fort at what is now Ujung Pandang was turned over to the VOC and renamed Fort Rotterdam. Gowa's power was broken and in its place Bone, under Palakka, became the supreme state of southern Sulawesi. Makassarese claims to Minahasa, Butung and Sumbawa were abandoned and European traders (other than the VOC) were expelled.

However, by the 18th century there was new rivalry between the Bugis and Makassarese, and between Bone and the other Bugis states. After the brief British interlude following the Napoleonic wars, the Dutch were confronted with a Bugis revolt led by the Queen of Bone. This was suppressed but rebellions continued to break out. Not until 1905-6 was Makassarese and Bugis resistance finally broken. In 1905 the Dutch also subdued the Toraja people, again in the face of bitter resistance. There was still some minor resistance right up until the early 1930s.

The 20th century has had a mixed effect on the people of south-western Sulawesi. Under the Dutch the Toraja came down from their hill-top forts into the valleys and adopted wet-rice cultivation. The efforts of the missionaries have given a veneer of Christianity to their traditional animist beliefs and customs although extravagant funeral ceremonies continue. The majority of Bugis and Makassarese continue living as rice farmers but they remain Indonesia's premier seafaring people. Their schooners carry goods between Java, Kalimantan and Sulawesi and probably comprise the biggest sailing fleet in the world today; you can still see these ships being built in places like Bulukumba. The people are still staunchly Islamic and also independently minded – a revolt against the central government in Java took place in 1957. The reputation of the Bugis as the most *kasar* (rough and coarse) people in the archipelago remains a persistent stereotype.

UJUNG PANDANG

Ujung Pandang may be the capital of southern Sulawesi and the Makassarese, but the images are reminiscent of India more than other parts of Indonesia. This is a city with cripples and lepers begging outside department stores. Becak drivers swoop down on foreigners. Peak-hour traffic needs to be tackled from the inside of a Centurion tank. Cinemas cough up a nightly smorgasbord of western ultra-violence. Around the corner there are glittering hotels and immaculate super-markets alongside canals where labourers struggle to clear the refuse. But Ujung Pandang also has some tree-lined streets, a sunset boulevard and is close to the coast.

The Muslim Bugis are known for their magnificent prahus that trade extensively throughout the Indonesian archipelago. You can see some of these prahus at Paotere harbour, a short becak ride north of the city centre. However, it's nowhere near as impressive as the awesome line-up at the Pasar Ikan in Jakarta, where they off-load timber from the outer islands.

Prahus in Ujung Pandang

The impressive Fort Rotterdam still stands as a reminder of the Dutch occupation, and there are many other Dutch buildings including the Governor's Residence on Jalan Jenderal Sudirman. Ujung Pandang is also the last resting place of Sultan Hasanuddin and of the Javanese prince, Diponegoro. In the surrounding countryside is the palace of the Gowanese kings, waterfalls where the naturalist Alfred Wallace collected butterflies, and cave-paintings left by the first inhabitants of Sulawesi perhaps 5000 years ago.

History

Once known as Makassar, this great city-port of 800,000 people on the south-western limb of Sulawesi has for centuries been the gateway to eastern Indonesia and the spice islands of Maluku. From Makassar the Dutch could control much of the shipping that passed between western and eastern Indonesia. Although

the weaker kingdoms of southern Sulawesi occasionally rose in revolt and the pirates were a constant nuisance, the amount of direct territorial control required to maintain this hegemony was very small. Well into the 19th century the borders of the sultanate of Gowa were just a few km from the port of Makassar, and the only other parts of Sulawesi under direct Dutch control were a few ports on the Gulf of Tomini and the Minahasa region in the northern peninsula.

Early accounts of Makassar describe it as a fine town. An American visitor in the late 1700s noted that the town was:

...pleasant, healthy, and of some size and strength. It contains about 250 whites, and 10,000 blacks, of which 2000 are capable of bearing arms. It has a respectable fort built of stone, and trenched around. The climate is very warm but healthy...

In the mid-1800s the naturalist Alfred Wallace found Makassar 'prettier and

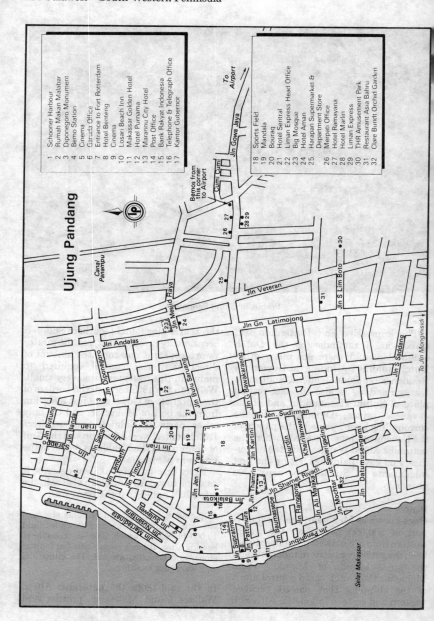

Ujung Pandang

1 Schooner Harbour
2 Rumah Makan Malabar
3 Diponegoro Monument
4 Bemo Station
5 Cinema
6 Garuda Office
7 Entrance to Fort Rotterdam
8 Hotel Benteng
9 Cinema
10 Losari Beach Inn
11 Makassar Golden Hotel
12 Hotel Purnama
13 Marannu City Hotel
14 Post Office
15 Bank Rakyat Indonesia
16 Telephone & Telegraph Office
17 Kantor Gubernor

18 Sports Field
19 Mandala
20 Bouraq
21 Hotel Sentral
22 Liman Express Head Office
23 Big Mosque
24 Hotel Aman
25 Harapan Supermarket &
   Department Store
26 Merpati Office
27 Hotel Ramayana
28 Hotel Marlin
29 Liman Express
30 THR Amusement Park
31 Restaurant Asia Bahru
32 Clare Bundt Orchid Garden

Bemos from this corner to Airport

To Airport

Canal Panampu

Selat Makasar

'cleaner' than any of the towns he had previously seen in the east:

The Dutch have some admirable local regulations. All European houses must be kept well white-washed, and every person must, at 4 in the afternoon water the road in front of his house. The streets are kept clear of refuse, and covered drains carry away all impurities into large open sewers. . . carrying all the sewage into the sea. The town consists chiefly of one long narrow street, along the seaside, devoted to business, and principally occupied by the Dutch and Chinese merchants' offices and warehouses and the native shops and bazaars. This extends northwards for more than a mile, gradually merging into native houses, often of a most miserable description, but made to have a neat appearance by being built up exactly to the straight line of the street, and being generally backed by fruit trees. . .

Orientation

Ujung Pandang is a busy port with its harbour in the north-west corner of the city. The streets immediately back from the harbour – like Jalan Nusantara – are where you'll find Pelni and many of the shipping offices. Heading due south along Jalan Nusantara brings you to Fort Rotterdam, which is pretty much the centre of town. Nearby are several important places like the main post office, bank and Garuda.

Immediately north-east of the fort are streets with a number of cheapish hotels, restaurants, and the main bus and bemo station. There are more hotels and restaurants south of the fort and along the waterfront. Other hotels, restaurants, offices and some of the tourist attractions are more widely dispersed.

The other main streets are those leading off from the vicinity of the fort: Jalan Ahmad Yani, which merges into Jalan Bulu Saruang and then runs past the city's main mosque; and Jalan Thamrin, which goes through a number of name changes before heading off to the airport.

Information

Tourist Office The tourist office (tel 21142)

is on Jalan Andi Pangerang Petta Rani, which is a long way out of town and leads off the airport road. Get there by bemo. There is also a tourist information office at the airport.

Bank The Bank Rakyat Indonesia is on Jalan Slamet Riyadi on the eastern side of the fort. The Bank Negara Indonesia office in the airport terminal changes cash and travellers' cheques. In town the Bank Negara Indonesia is on Jalan Nusantara.

Post & Communications The post office is on the corner of Jalan Supratman and Jalan Slamet Riyadi, south-east of the fort. Telephone & telex offices are at Jalan Balkaikota 2 and Jalan Jenderal Sudirman, opposite the new military hospital.

Fort Rotterdam

One of the best-preserved examples of Dutch architecture in Indonesia, Fort Rotterdam continues to guard the harbour of Ujung Pandang. A Gowanese fort dating back to 1545 once stood here, but that failed to keep out the Dutch. The original fort was rebuilt in Dutch style after the Treaty of Bungaya in 1667. Parts of the crumbling wall have been left pretty much as they were, an interesting comparison to the restored buildings. The fort now bears the rather more nationalistic title of Benteng (Fort) Ujung Pandang.

Of the two museums in the fort the larger, more interesting one is open Tuesday to Thursday from 8 am to 1.30 pm, Friday from 8 to 10.30 am, Saturday and Sunday from 8 am to 12.30 pm, and is closed on Mondays and holidays. It has an assortment of exhibits including rice bowls from Tanatoraja, kitchen tools from south Sulawesi, musical instruments from Manado and various traditional marital costumes.

Also within the walls of the fort are the National Archives, the Historical & Archeological Institute and the Conservatory of Dance & Music.

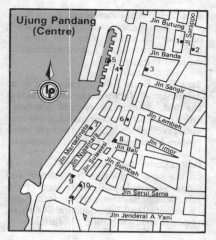

1	Hotel Nusantara
2	Hotel Murah
3	Rumah Makan Malabar
4	Rumah Makan Empang
5	Schooner Dock
6	Chinese Temple
7	Pelni
8	Chinese Temple
9	Chinese Temple
10	Chinese Temple
11	Cinema (Theatre DKM)

Tomb of Sultan Hasanuddin (Makam Hasanuddin)

On the outskirts of Ujung Pandang is the tomb of Sultan Hasanuddin (1629-1670), ruler of the southern Sulawesi kingdom of Gowa in the middle of the 17th century. Hasanuddin is a revered figure amongst the Makassarese because of his struggle against the Dutch colonialists, and today the university and airport of Ujung Pandang are named after him.

Outside the tomb compound is the Tomanurung Stone, on which the kings of Gowa were crowned. Legend has it that the Gowa kings were descended from a heavenly ancestor who first set foot on earth on this stone.

Katangka Mosque

About 15 minutes' walk from the tomb of Sultan Hasanuddin is the site of the Katangka Mosque. A mosque was first built here in 1603 and was one of the earliest in the region. A modern building now occupies the site. More interesting is the attached cemetery with its large crypts, each containing several graves.

Diponegoro Tomb & Monument

Prince Diponegoro of Yogyakarta led the Java War of 1825-30 but his career as a rebel leader came to a sudden halt when he was tricked into going to the Dutch headquarters to negotiate peace, taken prisoner and exiled to Sulawesi. He spent the last 26 years of his life imprisoned in Fort Rotterdam. His grave and monument can be seen in a small cemetery on Jalan Diponegoro.

Paotere Harbour

This anchorage is where the Bugis 'Pinisi' sailing ships berth, although the line-up is nowhere near as impressive as that at the Pasar Ikan in Jakarta.

Chinese Temples

Ujung Pandang has a large Chinese population and there are a number of their temples along Jalan Sulawesi. The most ornate of these is the brilliantly coloured building at the corner of Jalan Sulawesi and Jalan Serui Sama.

Clara Bundt Orchid Garden

This world-famous orchid garden and shell collection is hidden away in a compound at Jalan Mochtar Lufti 15. It's a little oasis in the middle of Ujung Pandang. There's a huge collection of shells including dozens of giant clams, and a small plantation of orchids grown in pots and trays. Admission is free; just knock on the door and someone will let you in. Some of the shells and orchids are for sale.

Top: Beach near Donggala, Sulawesi (AS)
Bottom: A 'duba duba', Tanatoraja, Sulawesi (AS)

Top: Tau tau, wooden effigies of the dead, Lemo, Sulawesi (AS)
Bottom: Becak riders, Ujung Pandang, Sulawesi (AS)

Places to Stay – bottom end

Ujung Pandang is none too cheap. Some of the cheaper places are pretty dismal, and don't take foreigners anyway.

Just south of the fort is the *Hotel Purnama* (tel 3830) at Jalan Pattimura 3-3A. Rooms start at 7500/10,000 rp but the place is rather run-down and depressing, although some people think it's OK. The nearby *Benteng Hotel* (tel 22172) at Jalan Ujung Pandang 8 is a grubby place with rooms for 10,000 rp.

There are one or two cheap places in the streets immediately north-east of the fort. The *Hotel Nusantara* at Jalan Sarappo 103 has rooms at 3000/4500 rp. The rooms are hot, noisy little sweat-boxes with masonite-thin walls. Since there's not much to get dirty the rooms themselves are clean, although the bathrooms are mouldy. The similarly priced *Hotel Murah* across the road is of much the same standard.

Heading east from the waterfront the *Hotel Sentral* at Jalan Bulusaraung 7 is pretty run-down with rooms for 5000/10,000 rp. Further on is the *Hotel Aman* on Jalan Mesjid Raya, across the road from the large mosque. The rooms cost 4000/8000 rp and are cell-like with little cot beds. The bathrooms are scungy and virtually unuseable, and the front rooms are noisy.

Places to Stay – middle

Probably the best place, and also very popular with travellers, is the *Hotel Ramayana* (tel 22165) on Jalan Gunung Bawakaraeng, where rooms start from 9000 rp. It's clean, conveniently located and is generally a pleasant place to stay, although it's starting to look a bit tattered around the edges. Rooms for 15,000/20,000 rp have air-con.

The *Hotel Marlin* at Jalan Gunung Bawakaraeng 120 is diagonally opposite the Hotel Ramayana. Rooms start from 7500/10,000 rp; more expensive rooms have air-con.

On the waterfront there's the *Losari*

Beach Inn (tel 4363) on Jalan Pasar Ikan. It's a three-storey building with good views from the upper floors, though the 'beach' it backs onto is quite ugly. Rooms are 24,000/27,000 rp, and have comfy double beds, carpet, television and sparkling clean bathrooms.

The *Hotel Afriat* is a 10-minute walk from the airport terminal, facing the main road into Ujung Pandang. It's similar to the Hotel Ramayana. Rooms are 7500/11,000 rp, or 10,000/14,500 rp with air-con.

Places to Stay – top end

The *Makassar Golden Hotel* (tel 22208) at Jalan Pasar Ikan 50 is an enormous five-star hotel. Rooms start from US$45/52 plus tax and service charge. It's chief competitor is the *Marannu City Hotel* (tel 21470) at Jalan Sultan Hasanuddin 3, which has rooms from US$30/35.

Places to Eat

Home to two of Indonesia's foremost sea-faring peoples, this place has good seafood in abundance. *Ikan bakar* (barbecued fish) and *cumi cumi bakar* (barbecued octopus) are especially popular. Because of the sizeable Chinese population Ujung Pandang is also a good place for Chinese food. Other options include *soto makassar*, which is a soup made from buffalo innards and sold in the warungs.

There are good, cheap rumah makan along Jalan Sulawesi. The *Rumah Makan Malabar* at Jalan Sulawesi 290 is a specialist in Indian food and serves simple curries and crispy martabak.

The *Asia Bahru Restaurant*, near the corner of Jalan Latimojong and Jalan G Sala, specialises in seafood and when you order a big fish you get a very big fish! A seafood alternative is the *Rumah Makan Empang* at Jalan Siau 7 by the harbour, which serves very good dishes and is excellent value.

The *Rumah Makan Ujung Pandang* at Jalan Irian 42 is an air-con restaurant with a mixed Chinese and Indonesian menu, and very large servings – sates come piled high on the plate.

Try the dozens of evening food trolleys that stretch along the waterfront south of the Makassar Golden Hotel, or the warungs around the THR Amusement Park for a slab of ikan bakar with cucumber, peanut sauce and rice.

The great food hunt continues at the Central Market on Jalan Andalas near the Diponegoro Tomb. There's another food market alongside the putrid Panampu Canal, immediately north of Jalan G Bawakaraeng. *Kentucky Fried Chicken* has a branch diagonally opposite the Marannu City Hotel.

Things to Buy

Jalan Sombu Opu, which is a street to the south of the fort and one block east of the waterfront, has a great collection of jewellery shops. Toko Kerajinam at 20 is good for touristy souvenirs. CV Kanebo, on the corner with Jalan Pattimura, has crafts from all over Indonesia.

Ujung Pandang is supposed to be a good place for buying Kendiri filigree silver jewellery. This is made in Ujung Pandang, not in Kendari on the south-eastern peninsula of Sulawesi as the name would suggest.

Other possible buys include Toraja handicrafts, Chinese pottery, Makassarese brasswork, silk-weaving and mounted butterflies from Bantimurung.

Getting There & Away

Ujung Pandang is the gateway to southern Sulawesi and is connected to many other parts of Indonesia by air and sea. There are numerous buses to various destinations on the south-western peninsula, although for most people the next stop is the Tanatoraja district in the central highlands.

Air Garuda (tel 22705) is at Jalan Selamat Riyadi 6; Merpati (tel 4114) is at Jalan Gunung Bawakaraeng 109; Bouraq (tel 22253) is at Jalan Cokroaminoto 7; and Mandala (tel 21289) is at Jalan Irian 2F (this address is also given as Jalan Dr Wahidin Sudirohusodo 14).

Garuda has daily flights from Ujung Pandang to Manado, Jakarta, Jayapura, Ambon, Denpasar and Surabaya. Mandala has daily flights to Jakarta, Surabaya and Ambon.

Bouraq has daily flights from Ujung Pandang to Gorontalo, Manado and Palu. They also have daily flights to Balikpapan, Samarinda and Tarakan on the east coast of Kalimantan.

Merpati has a number of flights out of Ujung Pandang, but the one of most interest to visitors is the flight to Makale in Tanatoraja. There are flights three times a week and the fare is about 45,000 rp.

Bus The long-distance bus terminal is a few km out of Ujung Pandang, on the road to the airport. Get there by bemo.

From Ujung Pandang most people head direct for Rantepao, the centre of the Tanatoraja region. The road from Ujung Pandang to Rantepao is surfaced all the way. Liman Express, at Jalan Laiya 25 near the market, is probably the best of the companies running daily colts and buses there. This company also has another ticket office diagonally opposite the Hotel Ramayana. There are daily buses to Rantepao via Pare Pare. The trip takes 10 to 12 hours and costs 5000 rp. Take the day-bus to Tanatoraja because the scenery as you enter Tanatoraja from the lowlands is spectacular.

Liman also has buses from Ujung Pandang to Palopo and Malili. A number of other companies run buses, minibuses or colts to Tanatoraja and other parts of south-western Sulawesi.

There are alternative paths to Rantepao. You could head south along the coast to Banta Eng and Bulukumba, turn north to Watampone (Bone), and head north to Palopo, which is a three-hour bus ride from Rantepao. Stop off along the way at Sengkang and Soppeng. Such a route takes you through some of the larger Bugis and Makassarese towns. Or take the direct route along the west coast and stop off at the large port of Pare Pare.

Shared taxis to places like Pare Pare leave from Jalan Sarappo, in the same block as the Hotel Nusantara. There are also shared taxis to other places in the vicinity of Ujung Pandang.

As in other parts of Indonesia there is a great love of abbreviation. TATOR means Tanatoraja, POLMAS is Polewali-Mamasa Regency and SULSEL is Sulawesi Selatan (Sulawesi South).

Boat Pelni (tel 7961) is at Jalan Martadinata 38 on the waterfront. Their passenger ships, including the modern *Kambuna* and *Kerinci*, make regular stops in Ujung Pandang on their various loops out of Java around Sulawesi, Kalimantan and Sumatra. More details about these ships are in the Getting Around chapter.

Typical Economy and 1st-class fares from Ujung Pandang are given in the table. Second, 3rd and 4th-class fares range between these two extremes.

to	1st class	economy class
Belawan	186,000	65,000
Padang	163,000	55,000
Tanjung Priok	109,000	37,000
Surabaya	65,000	23,000
Balikpapan	56,000	20,000
Pantoloan	60,000	24,000
Bitung	103,000	37,000
Ambon	82,000	27,000

Other possibilities include the cargo ships which leave Ujung Pandang for various destinations around Indonesia and in other South-East Asian countries. For inter-island shipping try PT PPSS at Jalan Martadinata 57. If they're not helpful, find out what ships are in port and where they're going, and bargain directly with the captain of the ship.

For foreign ports like Singapore try PT Samudera Indonesia at Jalan Pasar Ikan 1, PT Trikora Lloyd at Jalan Martadinata 26 and PT PRI at Jalan Nusantara 32.

There are other agencies along Jalan Nusantara but note that Ujung Pandang is not an official Indonesian entry/exit port.

Getting Around

Airport Transport Bemos to Ujung Pandang's Hasanuddin airport (22 km out of town) leave from the main bemo station on Jalan Cokroaminoto. If you're staying at the Ramayana Hotel they run past the large intersection just east of the hotel. A taxi from the airport to the city centre is 6000 rp, or take a becak or walk a few hundred metres to the main road and catch a bemo to the city for 500 rp.

Bemo & Becak Ujung Pandang is too big to do much walking and if you stay in hotels on the outskirts, like the Ramayana, or want to visit places like the THR Amusement Park, you'll need the becaks and bemos. The main bemo station is on Jalan Cokroaminoto. Bemos will get you to places like Paotere Harbour, the tourist office, airport, and some of the sights on the outskirts of the city such as the Hasanuddin Tombs and the old palace at Sungguminasa.

Becaks drivers are hard bargainers and it seems almost impossible to get those legs moving for under 500 rp! They're fearless drivers with your life in the frontline – getting into the traffic or cutting across streets during peak hour is a truly horrendous experience!

AROUND UJUNG PANDANG
Sungguminasa

Once the seat of the Sultan of Gowa, Sungguminasa is 11 km from Ujung Pandang. The former residence of the sultan is now the Museum Ballalompoa and houses a collection of artefacts similar to those in the Fort Rotterdam museums. Although the royal regalia, which includes a stone-studded gold crown, can be seen on request, it is the palace itself which is the real attraction. It is constructed of wood and raised on stilts; the same architectural style inspired the palaces

A family outing, Ujung Pandang

you see in Sumbawa Besar and Bima on Sumbawa Island, over which the Makassarese once ruled. To get to Sungguminasa take a bemo from the central bemo station. It's a half-hour trip and the palace can be seen from the road.

Bantimurung

About 45 km from Ujung Pandang, the Bantimurung Waterfalls are set amidst lushly vegetated limestone cliffs. Bantimurung is crowded with Indonesian day-trippers on weekends and holidays; at other times it's a wonderful retreat from the congestion of Ujung Pandang. Entrance to the park is 300 rp.

Past the 15-metre waterfall there's a cave at river level. Scramble along the rocks past the waterfall and get onto the track. Bring a torch (flashlight) to look inside the cave.

There are many other caves in these cliffs but apart from the scenery the area is also famous for its beautiful butterflies. The naturalist Alfred Wallace collected specimens here in the mid-1800's and in his eloquent fashion wrote that:

When the sun shone hottest about noon, the moist beach of the pool below the upper fall presented a beautiful sight, being dotted with groups of gay butterflies – orange, yellow, white, blue, and green – which on being disturbed rose into the air by hundreds, forming clouds of variegated colours.

You may not see quite so many in the vicinity of the falls but there are still enough fluttering around to make the trip worthwhile for any butterfly enthusiast.

Getting There & Away To get to Bantimurung take a bemo from Ujung Pandang's central bemo station. The trip takes a bit over an hour. If you can't find a direct bemo then take one to Maros (400 rp, one hour) and another from there the rest of the way (200 rp, half an hour).

Gua Leang Leang (Leang Leang Caves)

A few km before the Bantimurung turn-off is the turn-off for the Leang Leang Caves, noted for their paintings thought to date back at least 5000 years. The paintings are images of human hands made by placing the hand up against the rock wall and spitting a mixture of red ochre and water around them. Take a bemo from Ujung Pandang to Maros, and another from there to the turn-off then walk the last couple of km – or charter a bemo from Maros.

Malino

Malino is a hill town 74 km east of Ujung Pandang on the slopes of Mount Bawakarang; deer hunting on horseback in these parts was once a favoured sport of the Makassarese royalty. The Takapala Waterfall is nearby.

Banta Eng

Traditional boat-building can be seen at Banta Eng (also known as Bontain or Bantaeng) on the south coast 123 km from Ujung Pandang. Boats are also built in the Bugis and Makassarese villages in the region of Bulukumba which is a further 30 km on from Banta Eng.

Soppeng

Soppeng is a silk production and weaving centre 175 km north of Ujung Pandang.

PARE PARE

The second largest city in southern Sulawesi is a smaller, more manageable version of Ujung Pandang. Pare Pare is a seaport through which a good deal of the produce of southern Sulawesi (rice, corn, coffee, etc) is shipped out. It's a pleasant stopover en route between Tanatoraja or Mamasa and Ujung Pandang. There are also frequent ships to the east coast of Kalimantan and to northern Sulawesi from here.

Orientation

Pare Pare is stretched out along the waterfront. Most of what you need (the hotels, restaurants, etc) is located on a

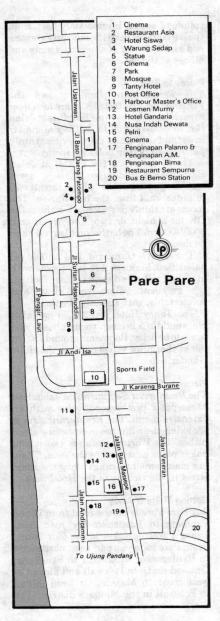

1	Cinema
2	Restaurant Asia
3	Hotel Siswa
4	Warung Sedap
5	Statue
6	Cinema
7	Park
8	Mosque
9	Tanty Hotel
10	Post Office
11	Harbour Master's Office
12	Losmen Murny
13	Hotel Gandaria
14	Nusa Indah Dewata
15	Pelni
16	Cinema
17	Penginapan Palanro & Penginapan A.M.
18	Penginapan Bima
19	Restaurant Sempurna
20	Bus & Bemo Station

Pare Pare

couple of streets immediately back from the harbour between the bus station at one end and a cluster of shipping agents and offices at the other.

Places to Stay

The *Penginapan Palanro* and the *Penginapan A M* (tel 21801) are next door to each other in the same building at Jalan Bau Massepe 154 and 152. They're similar in standard and price with thinly partitioned pigeon holes for rooms.

The *Hotel Siswa* (tel 21374) at Jalan Baso Daeng Patompo 30 is a great rambling run-down place about 20 minutes walk from the bus station. The rooms are thinly partitioned but should be OK for a night or two, and are around 3000/4000 rp. The bathrooms leave a lot to be desired.

The *Hotel Gandaria* (tel 21093) at Jalan Bau Massepe 171 has rooms with attached toilet and shower from 7500 rp. It's excellent value, very clean and comfortable, with friendly people.

The *Tanty Hotel* (tel 21378) on Jalan Hasanuddin 5 is clean though basic, and tends to be noisy. Rooms are around 7500 rp but at that price you should try the Hotel Gandaria first.

Places to Eat

The *Restaurant Sempurna* on Jalan Bau Massepe is pretty good value with an extensive menu. The *Restaurant Asia* is spanking-clean but has overpriced seafood dishes. The *Warung Sedap* is a good ikan bakar place next door to the Asia. There are many small warungs along the main street in the vicinity of the Hotel Siswa.

Getting There & Away

Bus Pare Pare is on the road from Ujung Pandang to Rantepao. By road from Ujung Pandang takes about four hours. From Pare Pare you can head north-west to Rantepao or south-east to Sengkang. Or head north to Polewali and along the west coast to Majene. Or head inland to Polewali in the Mamasa district. The

bus companies have ticket offices at the bus station.

Boat The main reason to come to Pare Pare is to catch a ship to the east coast of Kalimantan. There are daily boats to one port or another. There are also ships once or twice a week from Pare Pare along the coast to Pantoloan (the port of Palu) and to northern Sulawesi. Given the state of the road through central Sulawesi it could be worth back-tracking from Rantepao to Pare Pare in order to get to north Sulawesi.

Pelni (tel 21017) is at Jalan Andicammi 130. The harbour master's office is on the waterfront on Jalan Andicammi, and several shipping companies have their offices here. There are also numerous ticket offices and agents on the main street in the centre of town.

SENGKANG

Inland and south-east of Pare Pare is the Bugis town of Sengkang. There's an interesting market, good for locally made home-woven silk, but very few tourists get down this way.

Places to Stay

Near the market is the very clean *Hotel Al-Salaam* which has doubles for 3000 rp.

Getting There & Away

From Sengkang you can continue south to Watampone, Soppeng or Ujung Pandang, or north to Palopo or Pare Pare.

WATAMPONE (Bone)

Also known as Watangpone, this is a Bugis town and was once the centre of the powerful Bone kingdom. The town lies south-west by road from Sengkang.

Things to See

Not far from town is the Museum Lapawawoi which is run by a prince – well, a former prince – who'll give you an explanation of the collection in Dutch.

Some 34 km north-west is Uloe. Seven km

from Uloe is Gua Mampu, which is the largest cave in south Sulawesi. Legends and stories are told of the many rock formations resembling people and animals.

Getting There & Away

Bus Watampone can be reached by bus from Ujung Pandang, a pretty ride through mountainous country taking about six hours. A number of companies have buses on the route.

Boat You can take a ship to Kolaka on the south-east peninsula of Sulawesi – for details see the Kolaka section.

BULUKUMBA

In the vicinity of Bulukumba you can see traditional boat-building in Bugis and Makassarese villages.

Places to Stay

For cheap accommodation try the quiet *Sinar Jaya* on Jalan Sawerigading 4 or travel on to the losmen in Bira. It's an hour's drive.

Getting There & Away

From Watampone you can also take a colt to Bulukumba on the southern tip of the peninsula (you may have to change buses in Sinjai). From Bulukumba you can bus the 153 km to Ujung Pandang, or take a motorboat to Salayar Island.

SALAYAR ISLAND

This long, narrow island lies off the tip of the south-west peninsula of Sulawesi and is inhabited by Bugis-Makassarese people. Benteng is the chief settlement. South-east of Salayar Island are the Bonerate Islands which are also inhabited by Bugis people.

Getting There & Away

Take a bus from Ujung Pandang to Bulukumba, and a boat from Bulukumba to Benteng. Boats from the port of Bira, east of Bulukumba, go to Pamatata Harbour at the northern end of Salayar Island.

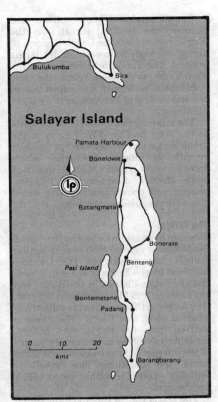

Tanatoraja

Despite their long conflict with their Bugis neighbours to the south, it was only in the early years of this century that the Toraja came into serious contact with the west. It was not until the 1890s that Dutch interest in Sulawesi extended further than the troublesome kingdoms of Makassar and Bone, and westerners first ventured into the central highlands and brought back their accounts of the Toraja people.

The Toraja and their culture had survived the constant threat from the Bugis, but in 1905 the Dutch decided to bring central Sulawesi under their control. The Toraja held out against the Dutch for two years, until the last substantial resistance was wiped out in the mountains of Pangala, north-west of Rantepao.

The missionaries moved in on the heels of the army and by WW II many of the great Toraja ceremonies (except for their remarkable funeral ceremonies which have survived largely intact to this day) were already disappearing. Tourism, mining and transmigration have aided the work the missionaries began.

The Torajas

Despite the isolation caused by the rugged landscape of central Sulawesi, a similar culture has existed in the territory bordered by the Bugis to the south-west, the Gorontalo district in the north, and the Loinang and Mori peoples in the east. The people in this vast area are collectively referred to as the Toraja. The name is derived from the Bugis word *toriaja*, meaning 'men of the mountains' or 'people of the interior' but the connotations of the name are something like 'yokel' or 'hillbilly' – rustic, unsophisticated, oafish highlanders.

The Bugis traded Indian cloth, Dutch coins and porcelain with the Toraja, in return for coffee and slaves. The Bugis are even said to have introduced cock-fighting to the Toraja who incorporated the sport into the death rituals of their noble class. Islam brought a new militancy to the Bugis and under Arung Palakka they attacked the Toraja in 1673 and 1674. However, Islam never spread much further than the southern Toraja areas because, so it is said, of their fondness for pork and *tuak* (palm wine)!

Customarily the Toraja have been split by ethnologists into western, eastern and southern groups. To some extent these divisions represent the varying degrees of influence the old kingdoms of Luwu, Gowa and Bone have had on the Toraja. It *doesn't* reflect any political organisation amongst the Toraja. In the past there has been no organisation beyond the level of the local village or small groups of villages. Sometimes villages would band together in federations to resist the Bugis invaders, and these federations in effect became mini-states. However, there have never been any large Toraja states.

Of all the Toraja peoples the best-known to the western world are the southern Toraja, also known as the Sadan or Saqdan Toraja. These people live in the northern part of south-west Sulawesi, in the mountainous limestone country through which the Sadan River cuts a deep valley. Their main concentration is in the area called Tanatoraja, about 300 km north of Ujung Pandang, where the chief towns are Rantepao and Makale. Tanatoraja has become the chief tourist destination in Sulawesi but, like Bali, the tourist trade is peripheral. The vast majority of the Toraja make a living from farming or raising livestock.

The introduction of wet-rice cultivation after the Dutch conquest has sculpted and terraced the slopes of the steep mountainsides, with streams originating near the hilltops harnessed to flow in a succession of little waterfalls before escaping once more into the natural rivers below. Toraja villages were once built on the summits of hills, sometimes surrounded by fortified walls with the settlement itself reached by tunnels. This was partly for protection, partly because the original clan ancestors were supposed to have arrived from heaven on hilltops. The authority of the village chief rested on his descent from these heavenly beings.

Before the Dutch there were a number of groups of head-hunters in the archipelago, including the Toraja. Their head-hunting was not on any great scale and their raids were basically tests of manhood for the youth of the tribe. Head-hunting was also necessary to find heads for a chief's death-feast to provide slaves for his afterlife. If enough enemies could not be captured in raids then the chief's family would buy slaves and sacrifice them. Under Dutch rule the petty wars and raids came to an end and the Sadan were ordered to build their villages on the plains – a Tanatoraja village now consists of separate farmsteads surrounded by irrigated rice fields.

Before the Dutch the Toraja grew their crops by the slash-and-burn technique, hunting and gathering food in the forests and grazing their buffaloes on bare hillsides. Buffaloes are still a status symbol for the Toraja, and they're of paramount importance in various religious ceremonies. Pigs and chickens are slaughtered at many rituals, the pigs mostly at funerals and at the consecration of new *tongkonan* (traditional houses). Dogs are eaten in some parts of Tanatoraja, occasionally as sacrificial offerings. Coffee (reputedly some of the best produced in Indonesia) is the main cash crop and fish are caught in ponds in the rice fields.

Religion Most of the Toraja are ostensibly Christians, with a few Muslims and so-called 'animists' amongst them. In reality it would be more true to say that Christianity, like Islam in Java, is only a veneer over traditional beliefs and customs.

Physical isolation and the lack of a written language resulted in considerable variations in beliefs, customs and mythology although the ancestor cult has always been very strong. Prior to the arrival of Christianity the Toraja believed in many gods but worshipped one in particular as the special god of their family, clan or tribe. Puang Matua was the nearest the Toraja originally came to the concept of a supreme being and early missionaries began prayers in their churches with his name.

The Toraja have a long and involved creation mythology dividing creation into three worlds, each watched over by its own

god. The Sadan Toraja also had a rigid caste system and a slave class. The Dutch abolished slavery although its effects continued long after. There is also a class of nobles which continues to be important. Christianity undermined some traditional Toraja beliefs.

Although it is one of the five articles of the Pancasila that every Indonesian must believe in *one* god, the Toraja gained official sanction to maintain their animist and polytheistic beliefs, possibly due to the tenuous argument that Toraja beliefs were similar to those of the Balinese for whom an exception had already been made.

Funerals *Tomate* (funeral) literally means 'dead person', and of all Toraja ceremonies the most important are those concerned with sending a dead person to the afterworld. Without proper funeral rights the spirit of the deceased will cause misfortune to its family. The funeral sacrifices, ceremonies and feasts also impress the gods with the importance of the deceased, so that the spirit can intercede effectively on behalf of living relatives. Funerals are sometimes held at the *rante*, funeral sites marked by one or more megaliths. In Tanatoraja there are several arcs or groups of roughly hewn stone slabs, some as high as four metres, usually surrounding a big rock like a sacrificial altar. The origins and purpose of these stone circles are unknown but the efforts to raise even one stone was phenomenal and involved scores of men.

At a funeral, bamboo pavilions for the family and guests are constructed around a field. The dead person is said to preside over the funeral from the high-roofed tower constructed at one end of the field. Like the Balinese, the Toraja generally have two funerals, one immediately after a death and the elaborate second funeral after sufficient time has elapsed to make the preparations and raise the necessary cash. Until the final feast the corpse remains in the house where it died. Food is cooked and offered to the dead person and

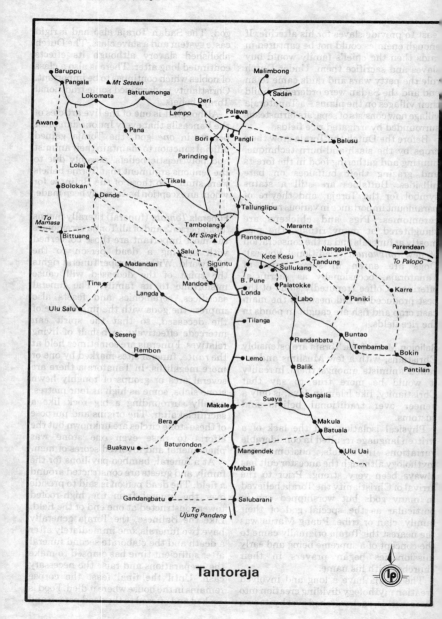

Tantoraja

high-born dead have attendants who stay in their immediate presence from the hour of death to the day of their final progress to the tomb.

The souls of the dead can only go to Puya, the afterworld or realm of the dead, when the entire death ritual has been carried out. A spirit's status in the afterlife is the same as its owner's status in the present life; even the souls of animals follow their masters to the next life – hence the animal sacrifices at funerals. The story also goes that the soul of the deceased will ride the souls of the slaughtered buffaloes and pigs to heaven. The trip to Puya requires a strong buffalo because the long and difficult journey crosses hundreds of mountains and thousands of valleys.

Sons and daughters of the deceased have an equal chance to inherit their parents' property, but their share depends on the number of buffaloes they slaughter at the funeral feast. Buffalo have traditionally been a symbol of wealth and power – even land could be paid for in buffaloes. A modelled buffalo head, fitted with real horns, is the figure-head of traditional Toraja houses, buffalo motifs are carved or painted on the walls of houses, and horns decorate gable poles.

The more important the deceased the more buffaloes that must be sacrificed: one for a commoner, four, eight, 12 or 24 as you move up the social scale. The age of the deceased also determines the number of animals slaughtered; only one pig may be killed for a young child or infant. Pigs are sacrificed at all rituals as pig meat is the food of the dead in the afterlife, as well as for the guests at the funeral ceremony. The Dutch imposed limits on the number of buffaloes which could be slaughtered at a funeral, since the temptation to honour the dead and impress the living by extravagant sacrifices was so great that whole families would be ruined. Today the Indonesian government is also trying to limit the destruction of wealth by taxing each slaughtered animal.

The great funeral ceremonies of today seem to have lost none of their ostentation. In the village of Langda near Rantepao I watched a funeral for a woman which was spread over several days and involved hundreds of guests. The wooden effigy of the woman alone cost about 200,000 rp to make – a year's wages for many Indonesians. The funeral was held in a quadrangle bounded by bamboo pavilions constructed specially for the occasion, with the death tower at one end. After the guests displayed their presents of pigs and buffaloes the traditional Mabadong song and dance was performed. This is a ceremonial re-enactment of the cycle of human life and the life story of the deceased. It also bids farewell to the soul of the deceased and relays the hope that the soul will arrive in the afterworld safely. Cigarettes were circulated, and pork and rice dishes (washed down with alcoholic tuak) were served to the guests by immaculately clad women, their hair tied back in large buns, playing the part of waitresses and squishing barefoot through the thick mud of the compound. The following day, in the early morning, buffalo fights were held.

Funeral ceremonies last from one to seven days, depending on the wealth and social status of the deceased. For the longest and most ostentatious ceremonies months, even years, may be required to accumulate sufficient money, plan the ceremony and to allow time for relatives living far away to make arrangements to return home to take part. Hundreds of buffaloes and pigs might be slaughtered at such a funeral; there would be buffalo fights and *sisemba* kick-fighting, and maybe cock fights at the end of the ceremony. The Mabadong would be performed, and maybe other dances like the Maranding, a war dance performed at the burial service of a patriotic nobleman to remind the people of his heroic deeds. Another dance is the Makatia, which reminds the people of the deceased's generosity and loyalty. Songs may also be sung, and these are meant to console the bereaved family or convey their grief to the other guests at the funeral.

Graves & *Tau Tau* Like the Sumbanese, the Toraja believe you can take it with you and the dead generally go well equipped to their graves. Since this led to grave plundering the Toraja started to hide their dead in caves (of which there are plenty around) or hew niches out of rock faces.

These caves were hollowed out by specialist cave builders who were traditionally paid in buffaloes – and since the building of a cave would cost several buffaloes only the rich could afford it. While the exterior of the cave grave looks small the interior is large enough to entomb an entire family. The coffins would go deep inside the caves and sitting in balconies on the rock face in front of the caves you can see the *tau tau* – life-size, carved wooden effigies of the dead.

Tau tau are only carved for the upper classes. Their expense alone rules out the use of tau tau for poor people. Traditionally the statues only showed the sex of the person, not the likeness, but now they attempt to imitate the likeness of the person's face. The making of tau tau appears to have been a recent innovation, possibly originating in the late 19th century. The type of wood used reflects the status and wealth of the deceased, jackfruit (*nangka*) wood being the most expensive. After the deceased has been entombed and the tau tau placed in front of the grave, offerings are placed in the palm of the tau tau.

Apart from cave graves there are also house graves – houses made of wood in which the coffin is placed when there is no rocky outcrop or cliff face to carve a niche in. Most of the hanging graves in which the wooden coffins were hung from high cliffs have rotted away. Sometimes the coffins may be placed at the foot of a mountain. Babies who died before teething were placed in hollowed-out sections of living trees.

Most tau tau seem to be in a permanent state of disrepair but in a ceremony after harvest time the coffins are supposed to be wrapped in new material and the clothes of the tau tau replaced. Occasionally left lying around the more obscure grave caves is the *duba-duba*, a platform in the shape of a traditional house which is used to carry the coffin and body of a nobleman to the grave.

Houses One of the first things you notice about Tanatoraja is the size and grandeur of the tongkonan, the traditional houses, raised on piles and topped with a massive roof. Throughout Indonesia a house is more than just a home. Each of the scores of Indonesian ethnic groups have their own distinctive form of architecture and the design of a traditional house has a deep symbolic quality. Such houses are

Tau tau – wooden effigies of the dead

called *rumah adat*, which translates as 'traditional house', but actually connotes an emotional tie with a whole range of customs, a social organisation, laws, religion and mythology. The tongkonan houses of Tanatoraja are closely bound up with Toraja traditions; one of their important functions is as a constant reminder of the authority of the original noble families whose descendants alone have the right to build such houses.

In many parts of Indonesia traditional houses are no longer being built and the skills to make them are being lost. More and more traditional houses are being replaced by houses built on the modern Javanese model of brick and cement walls and galvanised iron roofs. Often this is simply because of cost and comfort but they may also be a conscious denial of the traditions of the past and a means of identifying with the dominant Javanese influence in Indonesia.

Whether the tongkonan house will also die out remains to be seen. For the moment the tourist trade has inspired the renovation of some older houses, and even the construction of new ones purely for the benefit of visitors. There are a number of villages in the region still composed entirely of traditional houses but only a small percentage of the Tanatoraja population lives in traditional-style houses. Most of these houses have rice barns, surrounded by several ordinary bungalows on stilts, like the houses of the Bugis and Makassarese.

The roof, rearing up at either end, is the most striking aspect of a tongkonan house and is somewhat similar to the Batak houses of north Sumatra. Some people think that the house represents the head of a buffalo and the rising roof represents the horns. Others suggest that the roof looks more like a boat and that the raised ends represent the bow and the stern. The houses all face to the north – some say because it was from the north that the ancestors of the Toraja came, others because the north (and the east) are

House ceremony, Tanatoraja

regarded as the sphere of life, the realm of the gods.

The high gables are supported by poles and the wall panels are decorated with painted engravings of a geometrical design, of which the stylised buffalo head is the most striking. Other designs may include the entire buffalo, or two buffaloes fighting horns to horns. On these panels red is meant to symbolise human life since red is the colour of blood; white is the colour of flesh and bone and a symbol of purity; yellow represents god's blessing and power; black symbolises death and darkness. Traditionally the colours were all natural – black is the soot from cooking pots, yellow and red is coloured earth, and white is lime. Tuak was used to improve the staying power of the colours. Artisans would decorate the houses, and would be paid in buffaloes. A realistic carving of a buffalo's head decorates the front part of the house. Numerous buffalo horns are attached to the front pole, which supports the gable.

The beams and supports of the Toraja houses are cut so that they all neatly slot or are pegged together; no metal nails are used. The older houses have roofs of overlapping pieces of bamboo but newer houses use corrugated metal sheets. Standing on thick solid piles, the rectangular body of the house is small in contrast to the roof, and consists of two or three dark rooms with low doors and small windows. If necessary the whole house can actually be put on runners and moved to another location.

Toraja houses always face a line-up of rice barns – wealthy owners may have whole fleets of barns. The barns look like miniature houses, and like the living area in a house the rice storage area is surprisingly small considering the overall size of the structure. The barn has a small door at one end and the surface of the walls and the high gables are usually decorated. The rice storage chamber is raised about two metres off the ground on four smooth columns of wood, polished to prevent rats climbing up them. About 60 cm from the ground is a wooden sitting platform stretched between the pillars. The boat-shaped roof shelters an area about twice the size of the rice chamber.

The Toraja have a number of ceremonies connected with the construction of a tongkonan house. Construction is preceded by the sacrificial killing of a chicken, pig or buffalo; its successful completion is celebrated with a large feast in which many pigs and at least one buffalo are killed. At one such feast I saw at Tikala, near Rantepao, the pigs were brought into the compound on *lettoan*, large frameworks of bamboo, decorated with leaves, cloth and even live fish! The pigs were slaughtered outside the compound, and the meat was roasted in bamboo tubes and served to the guests with vegetables and rice. Dancing followed the feasting, with girls wearing long dresses with ceremonial

krises in scabbards tucked into their waist-bands.

Toraja dancing is graceful but less complicated than Balinese or Javanese, and the accompaniment is primarily to the beat of a large drum (or sometimes to taped music). What the dance lacks in complexity is more than made up for by the enthusiasm of members of the audience who dash onto the dance ground and stuff 5000 and 10,000 rp notes into the performers' head-bands. Buskers never had it so good!

Sports As on the islands of Sumbawa and Lombok there's a unique form of man-to-man combat in Tanatoraja, an unarmed contest called sisemba. The aim of the game is to kick your opponent into submission. It's something like Thai boxing except that use of the hands is banned, and you can't kick your opponent when he is down (very sporting). More a feat of strength and endurance now, the original aim of the contest was to instil courage in Toraja children and youth – a useful attribute for a people once hemmed in by their coastal enemies and occasionally at war with each other.

The fights are held at the time of the rice harvest or just after (around June to early August), also the most popular time for funerals and house ceremonies. Fights are held between individuals or teams of two or more and the women look on and cheer their favourites. When the men of one village challenge another anything up to 200 a side is possible.

I once saw one of these fights staged on a harvested rice-paddy near Rantepao. The day's war was progressing in an orderly enough way with pairs of contestants hurling kicks at each other when the whole paddy suddenly erupted into a battlefield with every kid in for the kill. The adults restored order, pairs of combatants went through their paces, then once again the paddy erupted into a furious tangle of arms and legs. Once again order was restored and the fights came to an end when it started to rain.

The Toraja had another contest known as the *sibamba*, in which the contestants used wooden clubs to hit each other, protecting themselves from the blows with a bull-hide shield (very similar to the contests found on Lombok, eastern Bali and Sumbawa) but apparently it was banned during the Dutch rule. A more docile sport is the game known as *takro*, which uses a rattan ball which is kicked and bounced over a bamboo stick about a metre high and fixed parallel to the ground. It's played something like volleyball but uses only two or three players, and only the head and hands can touch the ball.

RANTEPAO

Rantepao is the largest town in Tanatoraja and makes a good base from which to explore the area. The places to see are scattered around the lush green countryside surrounding Rantepao. While there's not much to do in Rantepao itself, there is a large market and a cattle and pig market held every six days.

Orientation

Jalan Pahlawan is the main street and leads south to Makale and north to Pangli, Sadan and Tallunglipu. Jalan Abdul Gani heads east from Jalan Pahlawan to Nanggala and Palopo.

Information

Tourist Office The tourist office is a short walk from the centre of town, on the outskirts of Rantepao on the way to Makale. They're very helpful, have a good map of the area and keep a list of dates and location of the funeral ceremonies.

Bank The Bank Rakyat Indonesia is on Jalan Pahlawan. They change cash and travellers' cheques but rates are lower than in Ujung Pandang. There is a money changer at the intersection of Jalan

Pahlawan and Jalan Abdul Gani, and another at the Hotel Indra.

Post & Communications The post office is on Jalan Pahlawan opposite the Bank Rakyat Indonesia. The telephone & telegraph office is next to the post office.

Books The locally produced *A Guide to Toraja* by A T Marampa is available in some Rantepao shops in English, German and French. It lists dances and ceremonies, some local walks and is quite a useful little book.

Also locally produced is *Toraja – An Introduction to a Unique Culture* by L T Tangdilintin and M Syafei in their own unique and impenetrable style. Much more readable is *Life & Death of the Toraja People* by Stanislaus Sandarupa. These books are sold in the souvenir shops on the main street in Rantepao.

White Stranger – Six Moons in Celebes by Harry Wilcox, was first published in 1949. This British army officer spent six months in the Rantepao district in the late 1940s, after the Dutch had re-occupied the area and included it in their state of East Indonesia. Wilcox lived in the village of Labo to the south-east of Rantepao.

Things to See & Do

The height of the tourist season in Tanatoraja is July and August – the European holiday period – when Rantepao is packed out with foreigners; French, German and Japanese tour groups descend on the place in plague proportions and hotel prices suddenly skyrocket.

The best time to visit Tanatoraja is in the gap between the end of the rainy season and the onset of the tourist season. The rainy season usually begins in December and ends in March – although there can still be a considerable amount of rain after that. Then the rice crops are harvested (from May to August) and the ceremonies begin.

To get the most out of Tanatoraja you

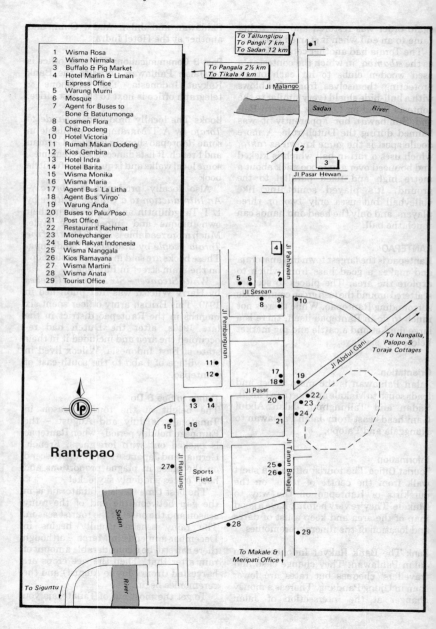

To Tallunglipu
To Pangli 7 km
To Sadan 12 km

To Pangala 2½ km
To Tikala 4 km

Jl Malango

Sadan River

Jl Pasar Hewan

Jl Pahlawan

Jl Sesean

Jl Pembangunan

To Nangalla, Palopo & Toraja Cottages

Jl Abdul Gani

Jl Pasar

Jl Ratulangi

Jl Taman Bahagia

Sports Field

Rantepao

Sadan

To Siguntu

To Makale & Meripati Office

1 Wisma Rosa
2 Wisma Nirmala
3 Buffalo & Pig Market
4 Hotel Marlin & Liman Express Office
5 Warung Murni
6 Mosque
7 Agent for Buses to Bone & Batutumonga
8 Losmen Flora
9 Chez Dodeng
10 Hotel Victoria
11 Rumah Makan Dodeng
12 Kios Gembira
13 Hotel Indra
14 Hotel Barita
15 Wisma Monika
16 Wisma Maria
17 Agent Bus 'La Litha'
18 Agent Bus 'Virgo'
19 Warung Anda
20 Buses to Palu/Poso
21 Post Office
22 Restaurant Rachmat
23 Moneychanger
24 Bank Rakyat Indonesia
25 Wisma Nanggala
26 Kios Ramayana
27 Wisma Martini
28 Wisma Anata
29 Tourist Office

have to be here for the ceremonies. Otherwise what you see is a lot of nicely decorated houses, caves full of coffins and tau tau. It's all a bit like an open-air museum with nothing happening. May, June and early July are good times to be here. Forget about going in the rainy season – apart from being pissed on day in and day out, most of the roads turn into long trails of sludge that mercilessly suck down bemos. You can still get to the main spots like Londa and Kete Kesu easily enough, but there's a lot more to be seen that's only accessible by the beaten tracks.

Some of the locals in Rantepao will take you to the ceremonies for a bargainable price – if they speak enough English or if you speak enough Indonesian you can get some explanation of what's happening. Ask around in the hotels and restaurants; you won't have to search too hard. Some people might tell you that such and such a ceremony is being held the following day and ask you to come along, but then they 'forget' the name of the place and what's happening unless you pay.

If you go to a ceremony don't sit in the pavilions or areas which are designated for the guests and family unless someone invites you to. Take as many photos as you want – with restraint and some degree of decorum; Indonesians like having their photo taken but ask first, the women can be very shy. Dress respectfully; remember this is a funeral, ask yourself how you'd expect someone to act at a funeral in the west. Bring some cigarettes to offer around. There may be certain ceremonies or certain times when outsiders are not wanted – otherwise they usually seem to be open to spectators.

Places to Stay - bottom end
Rantepao has a good selection of cheap hotels – a surprise after the fairly dismal state of affairs in Ujung Pandang. There are lots of places around and our listing is just a sample of what's available. Don't be surprised if prices rise in the tourist season.

One of the more favoured places amongst low-budget travellers is the *Wisma Monika* on Jalan Sam Ratulangi with rooms with private bathroom for 5000 rp. It's an older place run by friendly people and is quiet.

The *Wisma Martini* on Jalan Sam Ratulangi, opposite the sports field, has doubles for 5000 rp. It's actually an ordinary house with some rooms put aside for guests – a very pleasant and friendly place.

The *Losmen Flora* (tel 28) at Jalan Sesean 25 near the market has friendly people and is basic but clean and cheap; rooms cost around 2000/4000 rp. The only disadvantage is the early morning wake-up call from the mosque across the road and the noisy street out front. Near the Losmen Flora the *Hotel Victoria* at the corner of Jalan Sesean and Jalan Pahlawan is good value.

The *Wisma Nanggala* (tel 91) at Jalan Taman Bahagia 81 is a pleasant little place with rooms for 5000 rp.

There are several other hotels on the road north from the junction of Jalan Sesean and Jalan Pahlawan. The *Wisma Nirmala* has rooms for 5000/7500 rp and is clean and tidy with friendly people, though it can be noisy. Worth trying is the *Wisma Rosa* which is on the outskirts of town and has rooms with bathroom for 4000/6000 rp. The *Hotel Marlin* has rooms from 2500/3500 and 7500 rp with bathroom; it's not bad though you may find the rooms dark and a bit like cells.

Places to Stay - middle
The *Hotel Indra* (tel 97) at Jalan Pasar 63, just two blocks west of Jalan Pahlawan, is very pleasant with a central courtyard garden. Rooms cost from 7500/10,000 rp. There is a moneychanger here, and a very good restaurant. Almost next door at number 55, the *Hotel Barita* is a bunker-style concrete block but has good carpeted rooms at 7500/10,000 rp with bathroom.

It's clean and entirely habitable but lacks the pleasant garden that distinguishes some of the other hotels in this town.

Around the corner at Jalan Ratulangi the *Wisma Maria 1* is a comfortable place with a collection of Torajan artefacts in the foyer. Rooms cost from 5000/8000 rp. It has a pleasant, quiet garden and is very popular.

The *Wisma Irama* at Jalan Abdul Gani 16 has been recommended. It's a clean hotel in nice, quiet surroundings. Rooms with bathroom cost 9000 rp.

Places to Stay – top end

The *Misiliana* is on the road from Rantepao to Makale and has rooms for US$25/30. There are actually two hotels with this name, on the same road and not far from each other. The older one, which is closer to Rantepao, is probably the better of the two though the new one has a swimming pool.

Rantepao's main tourist hotel is the *Toraja Cottages* on Jalan Abdul Gani, three km out of town, with rooms slightly more expensive than the Misiliana's.

Places to Eat

There are various restaurants, rumah makan and warungs around Rantepao, some of them catering mostly to the tourist trade, others to the locals. For cheap eats the *Kios Gembira* at Jalan Pembangunan 44 does big nasi campurs. Try the *Warung Murni* on Jalan Sasean, or the shop diagonally opposite Losmen Flora which has a cheap warung inside. The *Warung Makan Rima* is on the main road a little way north of the main block of shops and has friendly people serving up excellent cheap meals.

There are a couple of places with the 'Dodeng' title but the original one is the *Chez Dodeng* near the corner of Jalan Sesean and Jalan Pahlawan. It's run by a friendly guy named Bitty who speaks some English and serves up some excellent food and drinks including a sort of ginger punch called *sarraba*. It has

much the same effect as being hit on the head with a buffalo.

The *Restaurant Rachmat* on Jalan Abdul Gani at the traffic circle caters mainly to the tourist groups. There's good food but it's a deadly dull place – a big bare room with overhead neon tubes and quite expensive food although servings are usually quite large.

Tuak & Other Things in the Market

Rantepao market has local food and there is a whole section devoted to the sale of the alcoholic drink known as tuak. Although known as 'palm wine', tuak is actually sap from the sugar palm, which the Torajas call *induk*. Every few months the palm, with its huge, dark metallic-green fronds and untidy black-haired trunk, produces a great cluster of round, dark fruit. The stem is pierced close to the fruit and if sugary sap flows from the wound the fruit cluster is cut off and a receptacle is hung to catch the juice dripping from the amputated stump.

The sap can be boiled down to produce crystalline sugar or it can be left to ferment to produce tuak, which is also known as *toddy* in India. Buy it by the bamboo-tube full in the market or drink it by the glassful at night in the warungs outside. Tuak is carried into town in long bamboo containers frothing at the top, is left to ferment all day and then consumed at night. It comes in a variety of strengths from lemonade coloured to the stronger orange or red.

Southern Sulawesi grows the most extraordinary variety of bananas: from tiny, sweet specimens grown in Nanggala to the goliaths found on the lowlands and which you'll see sold in warungs on the way up from Ujung Pandang. Tanatoraja is also noted for its fine quality coffee; there are several plantations here and you also see the plants growing wild.

The kids demanding candy ('gula gula mister') can be very persistent. If you tire of that then then indulge your own sweet tooth around Rantepao market. Try *wadi bandung*, a sweet rice-and-grated-coconut confection wrapped in paper; or *kajang goreng*, an almost over-sweet concoction of peanuts and treacle (hard) wrapped in a dry palm leaf; or a *baje*, a sticky rice and molasses mixture rolled in a dry palm leaf like a Christmas cracker. Going to the ceremonies is a good chance to try black rice cooked in coconut milk, and vegetables with pork and buffalo meat cooked in bamboo tubes over an open fire.

Things to Buy

Woodcarving, weaving and basketry are the main crafts of Tanatoraja – some villages are noted for particular specialities. Wood carvings include panels carved like the decorations on traditional houses and painted in the four traditional colours – black, white, yellow and brown. Bamboo containers with designs carved and burnt on them are decorative as well as functional – ideal for keeping spaghetti. All these things can be bought either in the villages or in the shops in Rantepao.

Other artefacts sold in the souvenir shops include mini replicas of Toraja houses with incredibly exaggerated overhanging roofs. Other interesting pieces include hand-spun Toraja weaving and necklaces made of plant seeds.

Getting There & Away

When visiting Rantepao you should try to bus in one way and fly out the other. Huge, rocky cliffs rise out of a sea of green rice paddies and forest studded with Toraja houses. On the way up to Rantepao by road from Ujung Pandang you see pine, clove, grapefruit, papaya, coconut and cassava (tapioca) trees, as well as Bugis stilt-houses.

Air There is an airport at Makale, just south of Rantepao. Merpati has three flights a week between Ujung Pandang and Makale. The fare is about 45,000 rp. The Merpati ticket office (tel 38) is in Rantepao at Jalan Pongtiku 11, on the way to Makale.

Children at the bus station—Tanatoraja

Bus There are regular buses between Ujung Pandang and Rantepao. In Rantepao the offices of the bus companies are around Jalan Pahlawan in the centre of town. The trip to Ujung Pandang takes nine to 10 hours and costs 5000 rp. Rantepao to Pare Pare takes five hours and costs 2500 rp.

Colts head north from Rantepao through central Sulawesi to Poso and Palu. Ticket agents are at the intersection of Jalan Pasar and Jalan Taman Bahagia in the centre of town. The fare from Rantepao to Poso is 20,000 rp, and to Palu 25,000 rp. Do not embark on this trip without first reading the description of the road in the Central Sulawesi section.

There are buses from Rantepao to Soroako on Lake Matana and the road is surfaced all the way. The trip takes about 10 hours and the fare is around 6000 rp.

Tours Travel agents in Bali organise brief tours to Tanatoraja. A typical four-day trip costs around US$250 per person plus air fare. In Bali try the travel agencies at the larger tourist hotels in Kuta, Legian and Sanur Beach. Trekking tours to Tanatoraja and Mamasa can also be organised.

Getting Around

Central Rantepao is small and easy to walk around. Becaks hang around the intersection of Jalan Pahlawan and Jalan Pasar, but you probably won't have much use for them.

Colts and bemos run from Rantepao to various destinations in the surrounding region. Bemos run almost continuously from Rantepao to Makale and you can get off at the signs for Londa or Lemo and walk. There are also frequent bemos towards Palopo for the sights in that direction.

Fares from Rantepao are: Nanggala 300 rp, Londa turn-off 200 rp, Tilanga turn-off 200 rp, Lemo turn-off 200 rp, Makale 300 rp, Sadan 500 rp and Palopo 2000 rp.

Apart from the roads to Makale, Palopo, Sadan, Kete Kesu and a few other places, most of the roads around Rantepao are terrible. Some are constructed out of compacted boulders – you don't get stuck but your joints get rattled loose. Walking is a nice way of getting around! Bring good footwear to negotiate the mud and the rocks. Take a water bottle, something to eat, a torch (flashlight) in case you end up walking at night, and an umbrella or raincoat. Even in the dry season it's likely to rain in the afternoon.

It should be possible to rent a motorcycle in Rantepao – ask around in the restaurants and hotels. Allow two days recovery after one day of riding! It might be cheaper for a group to charter a bemo or a jeep.

AROUND RANTEPAO

The following places (distance in km from Rantepao) are all within fairly easy reach on day trips, but you can make longer trips staying overnight in villages or camping out. If you stay in villages don't exploit the Toraja hospitality – make sure you pay your way. Guides are useful if you have a common language, but in some ways it's better without a guide. The Toraja are friendly and used to tourists so they rarely bother you and it's great to get out on your own into the beautiful countryside around Rantepao. If you're really short on time you could hire a bemo and whip round the main sites in a day or two – but that's not the way to see this place!

Karasbik (1 km)

On the outskirts of Rantepao, just off the road leading to Makale, the traditional-style houses here are arranged in a horseshoe around a cluster of megaliths. Apparently the complex of houses was erected some years ago for a single funeral ceremony. Some of the houses are now inhabited. In the past, temporary houses would be built around a rante for use at a funeral and when the funeral was finished these would be demolished or burnt.

Traditional style houses, Karasbik

Kete Kesu (6 km)

Just off the main road south of Rantepao, the village of Kete Kesu has a reputation for wood carving.

On the cliff face behind the village are some grave caves and there are also some very old hanging graves. The rotting coffins are suspended on wooden beams under an overhang. Others, full of bones and skulls, lie rotting on the ground. If you continue along the vague trail heading uphill you'll come to another grave cave. There are no tau tau, just coffins and bones, similarly neglected. One of the houses in the village has several tau tau on display.

The houses at Kete Kesu are decorated with enough handicrafts to fill a souvenir floor at Harrods; the village is a tourist museum, no one seems to live here anymore and there are surfaced paths to the main caves, but it's still an interesting site.

Take a bemo from Rantepao to Kete Kesu. From Kete Kesu you can continue walking to Sullukang and then along the track to Palatokke.

Buntu Pune

On the way to Kete Kesu, stop by at Buntu Pune where there are two tongkonan houses and six rice barns. The story goes that one of the two houses was built by a nobleman named Pong Marambaq at the beginning of this century. During the Dutch rule he was appointed head of the local district, but planned to rebel and was subsequently exiled to Ambon where he died. His corpse was brought back to

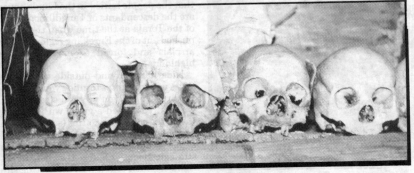

Skulls – Kete Kesu

Toraja and buried at the hill to the north of this village.

Sullukang

Just past Kete Kesu and off to the side of the main road is the village of Sullukang. There is a rante here, marked by a number of large, rough-hewn megaliths.

Palatokke (9 km)

In this beautiful area of lush rice paddies and traditional houses there is an enormous cliff face containing several grave caves and hanging graves. Access to the caves is difficult but the scenery alone makes it worthwhile.

There is a story amongst the Toraja that Palatokke is the name of a person who was able to climb the rock face, his palms being like that of a gecko which could cling easily to the wall. When he died it is said his corpse was put into an *erong* (wooden coffin) and hung on these cliffs. In another

Tau tau in a house grave at Sullukang

part of Tanatoraja there is a story that Palatokke in fact refers to a group of people who were able to climb the rock face like geckos. These people are said to have been a special class of workers whose job it was to hang the erong of the nobleman on the cliff face – climbing the cliff without using ladders!

From Palatokke you could walk to Labo and on to Randanbatu, where there are supposed to be more graves, then continue to Balik, Sangalla, Suaya and Makale.

Londa (6 km)

Two km off the Rantepao-Makale road is this very extensive burial cave at the base of a massive cliff face. A bemo from Rantepao heading towards Makale will drop you at the turn-off to Londa, from where it's a short walk.

The entrance to the cave is guarded by a balcony of tau tau. Inside the cave is a collection of coffins, many of them rotted away, with the bones either scattered or thrown into piles. Other coffins hold the bones of several family members – it's an old Toraja custom that all people who have lived together in one family house should also be buried together in a family grave. There are other cave graves in Tanatoraja where no coffin is used at all – the body is wrapped in cloth, placed in a niche in the rock face and then the door of the niche tightly closed. A local myth says that the people buried in the Londa caves are the descendants of Tangdilinoq, chief of the Toraja at the time when they were pushed out of the Enrekang region by new arrivals and forced to move into the highlands.

Kids hang around outside the Londa caves with oil lamps to guide you around – 1000 rp. Unless you've got a strong torch you really *do* need a guide with a lamp. Inside the caves, the coffins (some of them liberally decorated with graffiti) and skulls seem to have been placed in strategic locations for the benefit of sightseers. It's still it's an interesting site and a beautiful location.

Close to the Londa graves is Pabaisenan (Liang Pia) where the coffins of babies can be found hanging from a tree.

Lemo (11 km)

This is probably the most interesting burial area in Tanatoraja. The sheer rock face has a whole series of balconies for the tau tau. The biggest balcony has a dozen figures – white eyes and black pupils, outstretched arms – like spectators at a sports event. One tall figure stands on a slightly depressed section of floor so it can fit in.

There is a story that the graves are for descendants of a Toraja chief who, hundreds of years ago, reigned over the surrounding district and built his house on top of the cliff into which the graves are now cut. Since the mountain was part of his property only his descendants could use it, although the chief himself was buried elsewhere since the art of cutting grave caves had not then been developed.

It's a good idea to go early in the morning so you get the sun on the rows of figures – by 9 am their heads are in the shadows. A bemo from Rantepao will drop you off at the road to Lemo. From there it's a 15-minute walk to the tau tau.

Suaya & Tampangallo (25 km)

Apart from those at Lemo, it is becoming increasingly difficult to see many tau tau in Rantepao. This is because so many of them have been stolen by grave robbers that the Toraja have taken to keeping the remaining ones in their own homes.

One place where you can still see substantial numbers of tau tau is at Tampangallo, due east of Makale and very close to Suaya. About a km before you get to Suaya, coming in on the road from Sangalla, there is a signpost. You turn off the road and walk about 500 metres through the rice paddies to a place where there are over 40 tau tau.

The local graves belong to the chiefs of Sangalla, descendants of the mythical divine being Tamborolangiq who is believed to have introduced the caste system, the death rituals and techniques of agriculture into Torajan society. The former royal families of Makale, Sangalla and Menkendek all claimed descent from Tamborolangiq who is said to have descended from heaven by a stone staircase.

Tilanga (11 km)

There are several cold and hot springs in the Toraja area and this natural cool-water swimming pool is very pretty. It's an interesting walk along the muddy trails and through the rice paddies from Lemo to Tilanga, but keep asking directions along the way. The natural pool at Tilanga is uphill from a derelict concrete swimming pool and decaying changing rooms. Other natural swimming pools in the Rantepao area include the hot spring at Makula, which is 20 km east of Makale on the road to Sangalla. Another is Sarambu Sikore at the base of a waterfall in Mamullu Mountain.

From Tilanga you can continue to Londa.

Singki (1 km)

This rather steep hill is just west across the river from Rantepao. There's a slippery, somewhat overgrown trail to the summit with its panoramic view across the town and the surrounding countryside. Rantepao looks surprisingly large from high up. From Singki you can continue walking down the dirt road to Siguntu, an interesting walk past the rice fields.

Siguntu (7 km)

This traditional village is on a slight rise to the west of the main road. The path is not obvious so keep asking directions. The walk from Rantepao via Singki and Siguntu to the main road at Alang Alang near the Londa burial site is pleasant. Stop on the way at the traditional village of Mendoe, six km from Rantepao and just off the Siguntu-Alang Alang road. At Alang Alang, seven km from Rantepao where a covered bridge crosses the river, you could head to Londa or back to Rantepao or Makale, or alternatively, remain on the west side of the river and continue walking to the villages of Langda and Madandan.

Marante (6 km)

This very fine traditional village lies close to the road to Palopo. Near Marante there are stone and hanging graves, with several tau tau, skulls on the coffins and a cave with scattered bones.

From Marante you can cross the river on the suspension bridge and walk to the village of Ba'ta, which is set in attractive rice-paddy country.

Nanggala (16 km)

In the same direction but further off the Palopo road, this traditional village has a particularly grandiose traditional house and an impressive fleet of 14 rice barns! The rice barns have a bizarre array of motifs carved into them, including soldiers with guns, western women, and automobiles. Bemos from Rantepao take you straight there for 300 rp.

Paniki & Buntao

From Nanggala you can walk to Paniki and Buntao, a very long walk along a dirt track up and down the Toraja hills. The trail starts next to the rice barns. It's a three-hour walk from Nanggala to the Paniki district, and along the road you'll see coffee-plantation machines grinding and packing coffee into sacks. It's a long, tedious trudge – very hot, so take lots of water. From Paniki it's a two-hour walk to the Buntao turn-off and there are supposed to be some house graves with tau tau there. Alternatively catch a bemo to Rantepao. Buntao is about 15 km from Rantepao. Two or three km beyond Buntao is Tembamba, which has more graves and is noted for its fine scenery.

Sangalla (22 km)

From this junction you can head south-east to Makula, west to the Rantepao-Makale road, or north to Labo and the road to Kete Kesu. There are occasional bemos from Makale and Rantepao to Sangalla. At Makula there is a hot spring and bath-house.

Sadan (13 km)

Sadan is the weaving centre of Tanatoraja and the women have a tourist market where they sell their weaving. All of it is handmade on simple, back-strap looms. You can see the women making the cloth using this technique. There are bemos direct to Sadan along a surfaced road for 500 rp.

Pangli (7 km)

To the north of Rantepao, Pangli has tau tau and house graves. House graves are an interesting innovation used when there are no rock faces available for carving out burial niches. Graves are dug in the earth and a small Toraja-style house is built over the top. Each grave is used for all the members of the family and the bodies are wrapped in cloth and entombed without coffins. Apparently one of the house graves at Pangli has a stone tau tau.

Palawa (9 km)

This traditional village about a km north of Pangli has tongkonan houses and rice barns.

Bori (8 km)

Bori is the site of an impressive rante and a km south is Parinding, which has tongkonan houses and rice barns.

Lempo (25 km)

West of Palawa, Lempo is a traditional village set in an area of stunning paddy fields.

Batutumonga (23 km)

Situated on the slopes of Mt Sesean, this is a good viewpoint from where you can see a large part of Tanatoraja. Occasional bemos from Rantepao (more on market day) take 1½ to two hours along an abominable road.

You can walk from either Lokomata or Batutumonga to Rantepao. One person described it as: 'a beautiful walk and probably one of the highlights of my trip (it is all downhill too). The path is easy to follow as virtually all tracks lead to Rantepao and there are many small villages on the way down, so ask for directions.'

Alternatively, you could take the bemo up from Rantepao to Lokomata, walk back down the same road to the Rantepao-Sadan road, and catch a bemo back to Rantepao. This is a very pleasant downhill walk of about five hours, through some of the finest scenery in Tanatoraja.

Places to Stay There is a losmen at Batutumonga called the *Batutumonga Guest House*, which has very basic accommodation for 6000 rp per person per night, including breakfast and dinner. It's more or less dormitory accommodation. There are spectacular views overlooking Rantepao, and it's often very cold at night. This would be an excellent base for exploring other villages in the area.

Lokomata (26 km)
A few km past Batutumonga there are cave graves in one large rocky outcrop, and more beautiful scenery. To the south-east of Lokomata is Pana, where there are very old graves amidst bamboo.

Pangala (35 km)
This traditional village is noted for its fine dancers.

Bittuang
Connected by road to Makale, this village is the starting point for the 58-km trek west to Mamasa; the shortest route takes about three days. From Mamasa you can take a vehicle south to Polewali and onwards to Pare Pare and Ujung Pandang.

MAKALE
Some people stay here just to be away from more heavily visited Rantepao. Makale is built around an artificial lake, or as one Indonesian guidebook puts it: 'a round big pool of crystal-clear water welcomes jovially to the town'. The town is set amidst cloud-shrouded hills and makes a good base. The old part of town has many Dutch houses. There's also an interesting market with large food and household utensils sections.

Places to Stay
There are a couple of simple but clean places near the town centre. The *Losmen Indra* (tel 43) is a nice place with friendly people, and basic accommodation. Upstairs rooms with balconies are particularly good, and are 7500 rp. The *Losmen Merry* is similar with rooms for 3500/7500 rp.

The *Losmen Litha* has rooms for 3000/6000 rp. The rooms are small, and there's a balcony with comfy chairs overlooking the street. It can be a bit noisy but otherwise is an OK place.

The *Wisma Bungin* at Jalan Pongtiku 5 is a new hotel with rooms for 4000/8000 rp with bathroom. It's quite simple and a bit bare. On the same street, but further out, is the *Losmen Martha* which is a decent, cheap place with friendly people.

Places to Eat
One of the disadvantages of Makale is the lack of restaurants. There's not much and what there is is cheap but forgettable. There are several cheap noodle shops on Jalan Merdeka near the mosque.

Getting There & Away
Air Merpati has flights three times a week from Makale to Ujung Pandang; the fare is around 45,000 rp.

Bus There are colts all through the day from Rantepao and the trip takes 30 to 45 minutes. From Makale you can get buses to the same places (and for the same prices) as you can from Rantepao. The

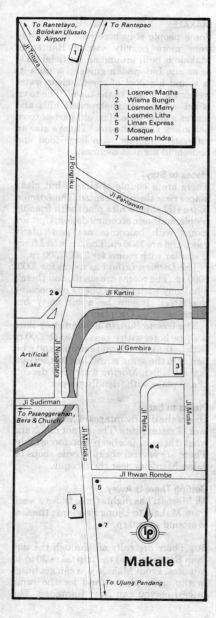

Map legend:
1 Losmen Martha
2 Wisma Bungin
3 Losmen Merry
4 Losmen Litha
5 Liman Express
6 Mosque
7 Losmen Indra

Makale

To Rantetayo, Bolokan Ulusalo & Airport
To Rantepao
Jl Tritura
Jl Pongtiku
Jl Pahlawan
Jl Kartini
Jl Nusantara
Jl Gembira
Artificial Lake
Jl Sudirman
To Pasanggerahan, Bera & Church
Jl Merdeka
Jl Pelita
Jl Musa
Jl Ihwan Rombe
To Ujung Pandang

offices and agents for the buses are all in the middle of town. Liman Express is at Jalan Ihwan Rombe 3. Buses Merry is at the Losmen Merry. Buses Litha is at the Losmen Litha.

PALOPO

This Muslim port town is the administrative capital of the Luwu district. Before the Dutch this was once the centre of the old and powerful Luwu kingdom and the former palace is now the Museum Batara Guru. It is at Jalan Andi Jemma 1 and contains relics of the royal era.

On the waterfront is a Bugis village and a long pier where you can get a closer look at the fishing boats. The bus ride from Rantepao to Palopo takes you high over the mountains, giving some idea of just how isolated the Toraja people were from the coast.

Places to Stay

The *Palopo Hotel* (tel 209) at Jalan Kelapa 11 is opposite the bus station. Rooms with bathroom start from 4000/8000 rp. It's a large hotel, though the rooms are quite simple.

The *Hotel Bumi Sawerigading* is a great rambling place with rooms with bathroom for 6000 rp. It's about a 15-minute walk from the bus station, or take a becak. On the same street at number 10 is the *Hotel Rio Rita* with rooms from around 3000/6000 rp.

Getting There & Away

The frequent colts from Rantepao are a real drag! Allow three hours to cover the distance; the fare is 2000 rp.

There are buses and colts from the Pasar Sentral direct to Pare Pare and Ujung Pandang, Soroako and Malili, Poso and Palu, and to Sengkang and Watampone. Before embarking on the journey to Poso and Palu, read the description of the road in the Central Sulawesi section.

From Rantepao you could take a bus to Palopo and then head down the east coast back to Ujung Pandang, via Sengkang

Independence monument, Palopo

Palopo

and Watampone (Bone). Palopo to Sengkang is 2500 rp; Palopo to Watampone is 4000 rp and takes six hours. The road to Watampone is very good for the first half but deteriorates very badly after that.

South-Eastern Peninsula

The south-eastern peninsula, along with the Buton Island group off its southern tip, is for the most part inhabited by people who look very Torajan, and some of them once practised customs similar to the Toraja. Islamic influence from the Bugis kingdom of Bone was also strong and Islam now predominates on the peninsula.

The peninsula is rich in nickel and there are large Canadian mining developments at Soroako in the neck of the peninsula, and a Japanese venture at Kendari. Soroako is on Lake Matana, the deepest non-volcanic lake in Indonesia.

MALILI & SOROAKO

Any town as distant, isolated and forgotten as Malili is hardly a candidate for a short colourful history, but that's what it has. The Dutch built a thriving settlement here but that was largely destroyed by the Japanese during WW II. Malili was one of the chief rebel strongholds in the Sulawesi rebellion of the 1950s and was repeatedly razed and burnt.

Southern Sulawesi rebelled in 1950 under the leadership of Kahar Muzakar. He was a native of the Luwu region of south Sulawesi and had played a founding role in one of the Sulawesi youth organisations fighting the Dutch on Java after WW II. Sent to Sulawesi in June 1950, Muzakar teamed up with some of the Sulawesi guerrillas who had been fighting the Dutch and led them in a rebellion against the central government. His reasons seem to have been mixed: a combination of personal ambition for the control of his native southern Sulawesi coupled with a general opposition to Javanese and Minahasan domination of the civil and military services. There also seems to have been some link between his movement and the West Javanese Darul Islam rebellion. Whatever, by 1956 Kahar Muzakar's guerrillas controlled most of the southern Sulawesi countryside and the rebellion continued until Muzakar was killed by government troops in 1966.

Next came the mining company PT Inco which officially opened their US$850 million nickel mining and smelting project at Soroako in 1977. The project mines and converts low-grade ore (a nickel content of only 1.6%) into a high-grade product with a nickel content of 75%. The company not only built a smelting plant, but also a town at Malili for its western employees with schools, a hospital, an airport (at Soroako), administration buildings, a road to connect Soroako and Malili with the Bay of Bone, a wharf, and a satellite station to link Soroako directly with its offices in Ujung Pandang and Jakarta.

Getting There & Away

One benefit of the mine as far as central Sulawesi-bound travellers are concerned is the brilliant road between Palopo and Soroako via Malili. There are colts and buses from Rantepao to Malili and Soroako. There is an airport at Soroako and flights with Merpati to several destinations around Sulawesi, but these are irregular.

KOLAKA

A port town on the west coast of the south eastern peninsula, Kolaka is easily accessible from Watampone (Bone).

Getting There & Away

To get there take a bemo from Watampone south-east to the harbour at Bajowe. The ferry leaves nightly and the trip to Kolaka takes about 12 hours. From the harbour in Kolaka there are hordes of minibuses eager to take you to Kendari.

KENDARI

This is a mining town on the east coast of the south-eastern peninsula. Desa Mata, about five km away, has an OK beach.

Places to Stay & Eat

There are a couple of fairly cheap losmens and a few more expensive places. *Wisma Maiwali* is on the road into town from Kolaka. On the main road are *Wisma Mutiara*, *Wisma Nirwana* and *Penginapan Noer Indah*. By the harbour, near the cinema, are more losmen including the *Penginapan Kendari* and the expensive *Wisma Andika*.

There's good food at the night-time foodstalls at the waterfront, about a km from the harbour. There are also a lot of dingy places near the market.

Getting There & Away

Air Since it's a mining town Kendari is well connected by air to other parts of Indonesia. Merpati (tel 109, 360) is at Jalan Sudirman 29; Garuda (tel 21729) is at Jalan Diponegoro 59. Garuda flights include daily connections to Denpasar, Jakarta and Ujung Pandang. Merpati also has numerous connections to other parts of Sulawesi and Indonesia; their fares are somewhat cheaper than Garuda's.

Bus A minibus from Kolaka to Kendari takes you to a place 13 km before Kendari. From there you have to take two different bemos to get into town.

Boat From Kendari you can get ships to Surabaya – try the Meratus shipping company. They have about two ships per month on this route. The trip takes about four days and nights and the crew members on the ships will rent out their cabins. There are also daily boats between Kendari and Baubau on Buton Island.

BUTON (BUTUNG) ISLAND
Baubau
This is the main settlement on Buton and is on the south-west coast. It was once a fortified town, the seat of the former sultanate of Wolio which reigned over the scattered settlements on Buton and the neighbouring islands of Muna, Kabaena, Wowini and Tukangbesi, as well as the adjacent mainland, until they came under direct Dutch rule around 1908 to 1910.

The people of this island group are all closely related culturally and speak similar languages. Like in the south-eastern peninsula of Sulawesi, most of the cultural influences seem to have come from the Bugis; the Butonese are Muslims and they were noted sailors and traders who emigrated widely, especially to Maluku. The island group was also once a pirate bastion and a centre of the slave trade.

Getting There & Away
There are daily boats from Kendari to Baubau. Ships between Ambon and Ujung Pandang sometimes stop at Baubau.

Central Sulawesi

The inhabitants of the interior of the eastern peninsula of central Sulawesi are traditionally known to the coastal dwellers as the Loinang – the term is somewhat derogatory. The highlanders are a mixed bunch, some more akin to the inhabitants of central Sulawesi, while others appear to have mixed with later immigrants from Ternate.

History
Both Christianity and Islam started planting roots in the eastern peninsula in the early 1900s when the Dutch took over the area. However, the town of Palu is known to have been settled – and Islamised – over 200 years ago. One of the earliest western visitors to this region was the unfortunate Bostonian Captain David Woodard. In the early 1790s Woodard, along with four other sailors, became separated from their ship and were taken prisoner by the inhabitants of the coast just to the south of what is now Donggala, a town near Palu. They spent 2½ years in captivity before escaping to Makassar, and the story is recorded in the book *The Narrative of Captain David Woodard & Four Seamen* published in 1805. Woodard was held in Palu (Parlow) for eight months and described it as:

a fine town, containing perhaps five hundred houses. . . Round and near the town are rice-fields, which are occasionally overflowed with water from the river, by means of canals... The inhabitants smoke opium, which they purchase from the Dutch.

Woodard also noted their Muslim aversion to pork, the great distances over which their trading prahus voyaged and events from the bloody war between Palu and Donggala to the north.

Prior to the Dutch intrusion, the sultanate of Ternate held some sway over these areas, as it did in other parts of eastern Sulawesi. Off the tip of the eastern archipelago are the Banggai Islands, whose inhabitants also seem to be a diverse mixture. At one time a royal dynasty of Javanese origin ruled here subject to the sultanate of Ternate. After the Dutch took over in 1908 native rulers were set up to run the islands.

Although the period of Dutch rule was brief, the first Europeans settled in central Sulawesi some 200 years ago. At this time the Dutch had established two settlements on the Bay of Tomini: the northern coast settlement of Gorontalo and another on the south coast called Priggia or Priggy, up country from the coast near what is now Poso. Along with Makassar and Gowa these were the principle Dutch settlements of the time. The rest of the island was controlled by the native tribes, although in the late 1780s or early 1790s the Dutch also attempted to take Toli Toli (because of its fine harbour) but without success.

Getting Around

A road runs east from Rantepao to Soroako on the shores of Lake Matana in central Sulawesi. Mid-way along this road is the village of Wotu. Here a road splits from the Rantepao-Soroako road and cuts its way due north to Pendolo on the southern bank of Lake Poso.

The original track to Pendolo was cut during WW II by the Japanese using Indonesian labour. There is a monument to the Indonesians at the top of the mountain pass at Perbatasan. Further roadwork has turned the track into a road of sorts and it is now possible to go all the way from Rantepao to Pendolo by colt. Most of the Wotu to Pendolo road is pushed through thick jungle and it's

Through Central Sulawesi

absolutely impassable two paces off the side.

Most of the road is abominable: it's constructed of rocks, gravel, mud, holes and more mud. Colts have to be pushed out of metre-deep trenches, piles of matchsticks masquerade as bridges, and cliff ledges are substitutes for roads. As a consolation prize the road from Tentena, the town on the northern side of the lake, to Poso is very nicely surfaced. Work is underway to surface the entire road, but it is not expected to be completed for some time.

Some people actually walk from Wotu to Pendolo: 'Don't let anyone talk you into it,' wrote one traveller, 'unless you're crazy or run up and down a volcano every day before breakfast.' If you do walk it then get good, solid, high walking boots that give plenty of support to the ankles; running shoes are a mistake. Carry a light pack as the road becomes a river after a shower. The sun is blisteringly hot and the air is humid and steamy. When it rains it really rains. You sleep with 15-cm spiders that run away after you've stood on them and plenty of 10-cm-long cockroaches. At night the jungle comes alive and the noise is indescribable – whatever's out there is out there in large numbers! One consolation are the butterflies in this region; some are as big as your hand and they'll flutter down and land on your finger.

MANGKUTANA

On the road from Palopo to Wotu, Mangkutana was established by the Dutch as a transmigration colony for Javanese. Partly because of that this little township has a distinctive feel to it very different from that of other small towns in Sulawesi. It is also home to a whole range of people from other parts of Sulawesi, including Bugis, Makassarese, Gorontalos and others.

Places to Stay

There are a couple of losmen. The *Wisma Sumber Urip* on the main road, at the beginning of the township, is a good place. Rooms are 3500 rp with private bathroom. It's clean and has a restaurant.

Getting There & Away

There is a very good road from Palopo to Mangkutana. The trip takes about three hours and costs 2000 rp. From Mangkutana it should be possible to find a land cruiser heading north through central Sulawesi; the fare to Pendolo is around 12,500 rp. Whether this will speed up the trip is anyone's guess, since even jeeps get bogged on the road through central Sulawesi.

PENDOLO & TENTENA

The two main settlements in central Sulawesi are Pendolo and Tentena. Pendolo is an overgrown village on the southern shores of Lake Poso. Tentena is situated on the northern shore of the lake, and is a larger version of Pendolo.

Things to See

From Tentena there are bemos to the nearby village of Taripa. Across the big covered bridge are some interesting caves near the missionary airstrip. Another possibility is to head to the village of Bada, about 50 km west of Tentena. There is a rough road between the two places.

Getting There & Away

Bus There is a good, surfaced road from Tentena north to Poso and colts make the journey regularly.

Boat It is possible to cross the lake between Pendolo and Tentena by outrigger motor boat.

POSO

Poso is the main town and port on the northern coast of central Sulawesi. It's really nothing more than a rest stop and transit point. From Poso you can head west to Palu and continue on to northern Sulawesi, or take a ship across the Bay of Tomini to Gorontalo on the northern

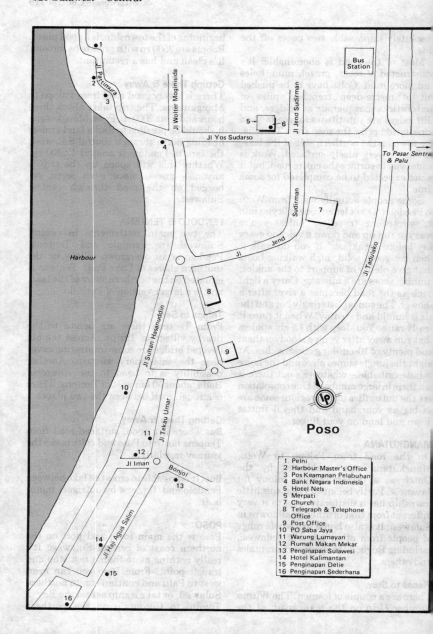

Poso

1 Pelni
2 Harbour Master's Office
3 Pos Keamanan Pelabuhan
4 Bank Negara Indonesia
5 Hotel Nels
6 Merpati
7 Church
8 Telegraph & Telephone Office
9 Post Office
10 PO Saba Jaya
11 Warung Lumayan
12 Rumah Makan Mekar
13 Penginapan Sulawesi
14 Hotel Kalimantan
15 Penginapan Delie
16 Penginapan Sederhana

Jl Pattimura
Jl Wolter Moginsida
Jl Yos Sudarso
Jl Jend Sudirman
Jl Jend Sudirman
Jl Tadulako
Jl Sultan Hasanuddin
Jl Tekau Umar
Jl Iman
Bonjol
Jl Haji Agus Salim

Harbour

Bus Station

To Pasar Sentral & Palu

peninsula. Another alternative is to head out to the peninsula that juts eastwards out of central Sulawesi into the Maluku Sea.

Orientation

Poso is quite spread out but most of what you'll want is close to the waterfront. The harbour and shipping offices are at the northern end of town, the shopping district in the centre, and the large Pasar Sentral in the eastern part of town across the river. Bemos ply the streets but just about everything is within easy walking distance. Most of the hotels are at the southern end of town; you can walk from the Penginapan Sulawesi to the harbour in just 15 to 20 minutes.

Places to Stay

There are a couple of cheap places although none are particularly memorable. The *Hotel Nels* on Jalan Yos Sudarso is probably overpriced with rooms for 3500/7000 rp.

At the southern end of town the *Hotel Kalimantan* on Jalan Haji Agus Salim is a decent place with singles/doubles for 3500/4500 rp.

A few minutes walk up the road at the corner of Jalan Haji Agus Salim and Jalan Imam Bonjol is the *Penginapan Sulawesi* which has singles for 2000 rp. The rooms are basic little boxes but the place is clean and the people who work here are friendly.

Other hotels are the *Penginapan Delie* and the *Penginapan Sederhana*, both on Jalan Haji Agus Salim. At the *Penginapan Antariksa* you can get a big double room with private mandi for around 6000 rp.

Getting There & Away

Air Merpati (tel 368) is on Jalan Yos Sudarso. There are flights from Poso to Luwok and Toli Toli, but these are unlikely to be of much interest to visitors. The airport is 13 km from Poso at Kasiguncu.

Bus There are regular buses from Poso to Tentena on the northern shore of Lake Poso. You can cross Lake Poso on an outrigger motorboat to Pendolo. From Pendolo you can continue by road to Rantepao in southern Sulawesi. Apart from the Poso-Tentena section, roads are abominable and transport is difficult. For details about the trip see the Getting Around section for Central Sulawesi. Buses from Palu bound for Rantepao and Palopo come through Poso, but don't count on being able to get on board.

Or you can head westwards from Poso to Palu. There are regular colts and the fare is 6000 rp. The trip takes around eight to 10 hours, provided that bridges have not been washed away; otherwise the road is good. Several bus companies have their offices in the centre of town and at the bus terminal. Look out for the transmigrated Balinese villages, complete with gamelan orchestras and stone temples, along this route.

There are also buses from Poso to Ampana (5500 rp, six hours) and Kolondale (11,000 rp). Heavy rains may flood these roads and hold up traffic – be prepared to wait a long time.

Boat Ships depart Poso for Gorontalo, on the northern peninsula, at least once a week. The trip takes about two days. Buy your ticket at Pos Keamanan Pelabuhan at the port. The ships usually stop at various ports along the coast or in the Togian Islands – including Ampana, Wakui, Dolong and Pagimana. On these ships you can sometimes rent a cabin or a bunk from the crew.

There are occasional ships to Ujung Pandang, Bitung (the port of Manado) and Surabaya. Enquire at the harbour master's office (tel 444) at Jalan Pattimura 3, and at the Pelni office which is nearby on the same street.

PALU

The capital of Central Sulawesi Province, Palu is a Bugis town and major port at the end of Palu Bay, on the west coast of

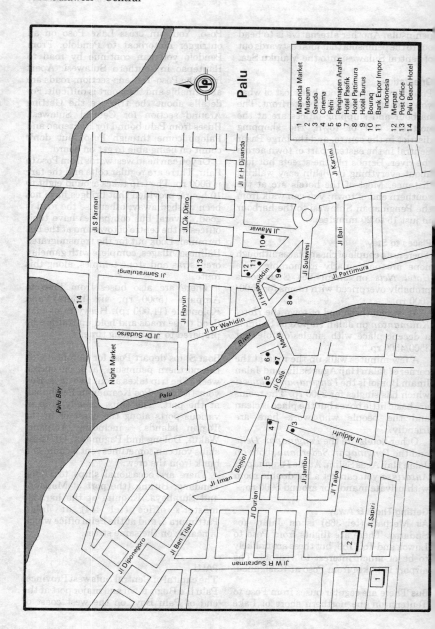

Palu

1 Manonda Market
2 Museum
3 Garuda
4 Cinema
5 Pelni
6 Penginapan Arafah
7 Hotel Pasifik
8 Hotel Pattimura
9 Hotel Taurus
10 Bouraq
11 Bank Expor Impor
     Indonesia
12 Merpati
13 Post Office
14 Palu Beach Hotel

Sulawesi. It's a larger, noisier version of Poso.

There's a large museum on Jalan Sapiri which houses a collection of books in Dutch, Indonesian and English on the anthropology and archaeology of central Sulawesi.

Orientation

Like Poso, Palu is spread out but most of the hotels and shops are centrally located along or in the vicinity of the main streets Jalan Imam Bonjol, Jalan Gajah Mada and Jalan Hasanuddin, and northwards along Jalan Sudirman. The street names constantly change. The large market and the museum are further out in the south-west corner of town. The airport is on the south-eastern outskirts. The town is split neatly in two by the Palu River.

Places to Stay – bottom end

There's quite a range of hotel prices and standards in Palu. One of the cheapest places around is the *Penginapan Arafah* near the Hotel Pasifik, on a street running off Jalan Gajah Mada near the bridge over the river. The rooms are thinly partitioned little boxes for 2500/5000 rp but are reasonably clean.

One of the better places is the *Hotel Pasifik* at Jalan Gajah Mada 130 which has rooms from 7500 rp with bathroom. It can, however, be very noisy – particularly from the heavy-metal music that fills the corridors.

Places to Stay – middle

On the other side of the river the *Hotel Taurus* (tel 21567) on Jalan Hasanuddin has small rooms at 5500/8500 rp. It's a fairly ordinary, nondescript hotel.

The nearby *Hotel Pattimura* (tel 222-311) on Jalan Pattimura is OK, but the bathrooms could do with a clean and the front rooms suffer from traffic noise. Rooms are 6500/10,000 rp, and there are also more expensive air-con rooms.

Places to Stay – top end

The *Palu Beach Hotel* (tel 21126), Palu's top hotel, is on a 'beach' and is worth a visit for the air-con in the coffee lounge. Rooms start at 25,000/28,000 rp. The hotel is a 15-minute walk up Jalan Wahiden and Jalan Dr Sudarso from Jalan Hasanuddin. There is, by the way, no beach worth speaking of.

Places to Eat

There is a string of rumah makans and warungs north along Jalan Wahiden. In the early evening there are martabak trolleys set up on Jalan Hasanuddin near the bridge. There is a large night market on the western extension of Jalan S Parman, in the northern part of town near the Palu Beach Hotel.

Getting There & Away

From Palu (or the nearby ports of Pantoloan, Wani or Donggala) you can take a ship to the east coast of Kalimantan, to northern Sulawesi or Pare Pare in southern Sulawesi. Palu is connected by road to Poso in central Sulawesi and to Gorontalo in northern Sulawesi.

Air Merpati, Garuda and Bouraq have all sorts of flight connections between Palu and other parts of Sulawesi and the other islands of Indonesia.

Garuda (tel 21095) is on Jalan Said Idus Aldjufrie, south of the intersection with Jalan Gajah Mada, and has daily flights to Ujung Pandang.

Bouraq (tel 21195) is at Jalan Mawar 5. This is probably the most useful airline flying out of Palu. They fly to northern Sulawesi, as well as to Kalimantan, Java and Maluku. Destinations include Gorontalo, Manado, Banjarmasin, Samarinda, Ternate, Jakarta, Ujung Pandang and Yogyakarta (all daily flights).

Merpati (tel 21295) is at Jalan Hasanuddin 33. They're particularly useful for flights from Palu to other parts of Sulawesi including Ujung Pandang, Luwok and Toli Toli.

Bus Buses to Poso, Palopo, Rantepao, Gorontalo and Manado all leave from the Terminal Masomba. All the bus companies have their offices at this terminal.

Palu to Manado is around 25,000 rp. Palu to Poso is 5500 rp, and takes about eight hours. Palu to Rantepao is around 25,000 rp and goes via Poso, Tentena and Pendolo through central Sulawesi.

Boat There are three ports near Palu. Larger vessels dock at Donggala which is north-west of Palu, and at Pantoloan which is north-east of Palu. Smaller ships dock at Wani, two km past Pantoloan.

In Palu, the Pelni office (tel 528) is upstairs at Jalan Gajah Mada 86. They also have an office at Pantoloan, opposite the road to the wharf. The offices of the other shipping companies are at the various ports. Pelni ships dock at Pantoloan.

You can avoid the long and winding road through central Sulawesi by taking a ship from Palu to Pare Pare, a port on the south-western limb of Sulawesi. Ships to Pare Pare usually depart from Wani, from where there are also ships northwards to Toli Toli, Leok, Paleleh, Kwandang and Manado. There should be one or two ships a week on this run.

Typical fares from Pantoloan are: Pare Pare 22,000 rp; Toli Toli 15,000 rp; and Manado 33,500 rp.

The timetable of the coastal *KM Mauru* will give you some idea of travelling time:

Wani	dep Fri	8 pm
Toli Toli	arr Sat	10 am
	dep Sat	12 midnight
Leok	arr Sun	7 am
	dep Sun	11 am
Paleleh	arr Sun	3 pm
	dep Sun	12 midnight
Kwandang	arr Mon	7 am
	dep Mon	6 pm
Manado	arr Tue	8 am

Getting Around
Airport Transport Palu's Mutiara airport is seven km from town. Probably the best way to get out there is to charter a bemo. A taxi costs 4000 rp.

Around Town Transport round town is by bemo – 200 rp gets you anywhere. There are also many tongas. The best place to catch a bemo is along Jalan Gajah Mada.

To Pantoloan & Wani There are colts from Palu to Pantoloan and Wani, which take about 30 to 45 minutes. They leave from the Terminal Masomba, which is next to the Pasar Masomba. To get to Terminal Masomba, take a bemo from Jalan Gaja Mada. Palu to Pantoloan or Wani is 1000 rp; Pantoloan to Wani is 300 rp.

DONGGALA
Donggala was once the most important town and port in central Sulawesi – the administrative centre under the Dutch. That all came to an end as the harbour silted up; the ships switched to the harbours on the other side of the bay and Palu became the regional capital.

Today Donggala is a peaceful though dull little place. The only real reason to come here is to catch a ship to northern or southern Sulawesi. There are some pretty stretches of coastline in the surrounding regions and it's not a bad town to hang around.

Things to See
An hour's walk from Donggala are seaside villages and some pretty, palm-fringed white-sand beaches in the vicinity of Tanjung Karang. The villages of Bonoge and Towale (take a bemo from Donggala) have been suggested as day trips.

Places to Stay
Stay at the *Wisma Makmur*, a decent little place with rooms at 3000/6000 rp, although it's very basic.

Getting There & Away

There are shared taxis (1000 rp per person) and bemos (750 rp per person) from Palu to Donggala. A taxi takes 30 minutes and the road is surfaced.

Getting Around

Bemos and taxis for Donggala leave from the Terminal Induk Manonda in Palu. To get to the terminal take a bemo from the town centre (there are also bemos connecting Terminal Induk Manonda with Terminal Masomba). The bemos take you to a terminal just outside Donggala, from where you have to catch a dokkar or another bemo into town.

North Sulawesi

The Dutch have had a more enduring influence on this isolated northern peninsula than anywhere else in the archipelago. This influence was established while the Bugis and Makassarese were trying to repel the Dutch from the south-western peninsula. The greatest economic development in Sulawesi has also taken place in the north.

Unlike the more insular kingdoms of Java and Bali and the isolated hill-peoples of central Sulawesi, northern Sulawesi was once strongly oriented to the sea and had a long history of trade and contact with the outside world. Together with the Sangir-Talaud Islands, it also formed a natural bridge to the Philippines, providing a causeway for the movement of peoples and cultures back and forth between Indonesia and the Philippines. Languages and physical features related to the Philippines can be found in north Sulawesi amongst the Minahasans at the tip of the peninsula, and the inhabitants of the Sangir Islands.

The three largest distinct groups of people in north Sulawesi are the Minahasans, the Gorontalese and the Sangirese. Like much of Indonesia, north Sulawesi was once divided into numerous petty kingdoms and Toraja-type customs may once have predominated, although the institutions and rituals of the royalty seem to have been imported from Islamic Ternate in Maluku, or from Mindanao in the Philippines.

History

At the time of the first contact with Europeans the sultanate of Ternate held some sway over north Sulawesi, and the area was often visited by seafaring Bugis traders from south Sulawesi. The Spanish and the Portuguese, the first Europeans to arrive, landed in north Sulawesi in the 16th century. The main Portuguese trade route rounded south Sulawesi at the port of Makassar, but they also sailed by way of the Sulu Islands (off the north coast of Borneo) and the port of Manado (at the tip of north Sulawesi). The Spanish set themselves up in the Philippines. While they had sporadic contacts with north Sulawesi, Spanish and Portuguese influence was limited by the power of Ternate.

The Portuguese left reminders of their presence in the north in subtle ways. Portuguese surnames and various Portuguese words not found elsewhere in Indonesia, like *garrida* for an enticing woman and *buraco* for a bad man, can still be found in Minahasa. In the 1560s the Portuguese Franciscan missionaries made some converts in Minahasa, and the Jesuit priest Mascarenhas had great success in the Sangir-Talaud Islands. At the same time, however, Islam was arriving from Ternate.

By the early 17th century the Dutch had toppled the Ternate sultanate, and with that out of the way they set about eclipsing the Spanish and Portuguese. As was the usual pattern in the 1640s and '50s the Dutch teamed up with the local population to throw out their European competitors. In 1677 Sangir Island was occupied by the Dutch, followed two years

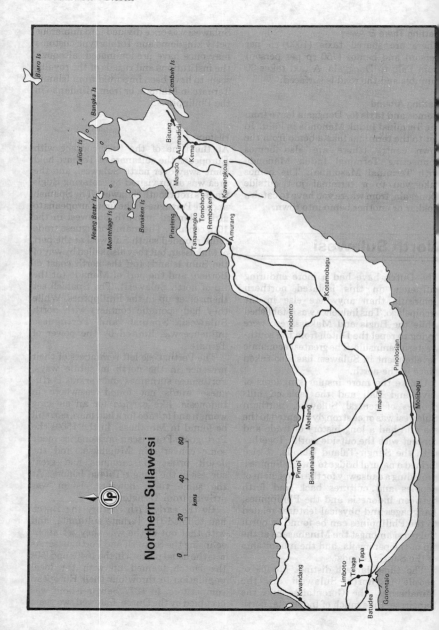

Northern Sulawesi

Biaro Is

Bangka Is

Lembeh Is

Talisei Is

Bitung
Airmadidi
Manado
Kema
Kawangkoan

Neang Besar Is

Mantehage Is

Bunaken Is

Pineleng
Tanawangko
Tomohon
Remboken
Amurang

Kotamobagu

Inobonto

Pinolosian

Imandi

Maelang

Molibagu

Pimpi

Bintanalama

Kwandang

Limboto
Telaga
Tapa

Batudea
Gorontalo

kms

0   20   40   60

later by a visit of the Dutch governor of Maluku, Robert Padtbrugge, to Manado at the tip of the northern peninsula. Out of this visit came a treaty (some say a forced one) with the local Minahasan chiefs, which resulted in domination by the Dutch for the next 300 years. Although relations with the Dutch were often less than cordial (a war was fought around Tondano between 1807 and 1809) and the region did not actually come under direct Dutch rule until 1870, the Dutch and Minahasans eventually came to be so close that the north was often referred to as 'the 12th province of the Netherlands'. For the most part the history of northern Sulawesi is the history of the Minahasans, who have dominated events on the peninsula for the last century.

Portuguese activity apart, the Christianisation of the region really began in the early 1820s when a Calvinist group, the Netherlands Missionary Society, turned from an almost exclusive interest in Maluku to the Minahasa area. The wholesale conversion of the Minahasans was almost complete by 1860. Hand in hand with the missionaries went the mission schools, which meant that, as in Ambon and Roti, western education in Minahasa started much earlier than in other parts of Indonesia. The Dutch government eventually took over some of these schools and also set up others. Since the schools taught in Dutch the Minahasans had an early advantage in the competition for government jobs and places in the Dutch East Indies Army.

The men of Minahasa fought with the Dutch in subduing rebellions in other parts of the archipelago, notably in the Java War of 1825-30, and the tradition of Minahasans serving in the Dutch East Indies Army was maintained right up until WW II. The Minahasans seemed to gain a special role in the Dutch scheme of things. Their loyalty to the Dutch as soldiers, their Christian religion and their geographic isolation from the rest of Indonesia all led to a sense of being 'different' from the other ethnic groups of the archipelago.

The Minahasan sense of being different quickly became a problem for the central government after independence. As in Sumatra there was a general feeling that central government was inefficient, development was stagnating, money was being plugged into Java at the expense of the outer provinces and that these circumstances favoured the spread of Communism.

In March 1957 the military leaders of both southern and northern Sulawesi launched a confrontation with the central government with demands for greater regional autonomy, more local development, a fairer share of revenue, help in suppressing the Kahar Muzakar rebellion in southern Sulawesi, and that the cabinet of the central government be led jointly by Sukarno and Hatta. At least initially the 'Permesta' rebellion was not a separatist movement.

Negotiations between the central government and the Sulawesi military leaders prevented violence in southern Sulawesi, but the Minahasan leaders were dissatisfied with the agreements and the movement split. Inspired, perhaps, by fears of domination by the south the Minahasa leaders declared their own autonomous state of North Sulawesi in June 1957. By this time the central government had the situation in southern Sulawesi pretty much under control but in the north they had no strong local figure to rely upon and there were rumours that the USA, suspected of supplying arms to rebels in Sumatra, was also in contact with the Minahasa rebels.

The possibility of foreign intervention finally drove the central government to seek a military solution to the rebellion. In February 1958 Manado was bombed, coinciding with the bombing of Padang in Sumatra. By May the Minahasans had given up on getting any military support from southern Sulawesi. Permesta forces were driven out of central Sulawesi,

Gorontalo, the Sangir Islands and from Morotai in the Maluku Islands (from whose airfield the rebels had hoped to fly bombing raids on Jakarta). The rebels' few planes (supplied by the US and flown by American, Filipino and Taiwanese pilots) were destroyed. Hopes for further US aid crumbled as American policy shifted, and in June 1958 central government troops landed in Minahasa. The Permesta rebels withdrew into the mountains and the rebellion was finally put down in mid-1961.

The effect of both the Sumatran and Sulawesi rebellions was to strengthen just those trends which they hoped to weaken: central authority was enhanced at the expense of local autonomy, radical nationalism gained over pragmatic moderation, the power of the Communists and Sukarno increased while that of Hatta waned, and the rebellions also enabled Sukarno to establish 'Guided Democracy' in 1959.

Agriculture

Today, around three million people live in the province of Northern Sulawesi. Cloves are one of the main crops, and are used in the production of kretek cigarettes. However, what really holds body and soul together here is coconuts. Much of northern Sulawesi is covered by a solid canopy of coconut trees. The palm tree is one of the most important plants in the tropical economy, not only producing edible fruit but also oil, waxes, fibres and other products.

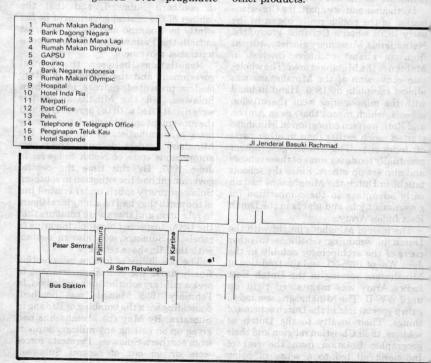

1	Rumah Makan Padang
2	Bank Dagong Negara
3	Rumah Makan Mana Lagi
4	Rumah Makan Dirgahayu
5	GAPSU
6	Bouraq
7	Bank Negara Indonesia
8	Rumah Makan Olympic
9	Hospital
10	Hotel Inda Ria
11	Merpati
12	Post Office
13	Pelni
14	Telephone & Telegraph Office
15	Penginapan Teluk Kau
16	Hotel Saronde

The coconut 'meat' is enclosed in a light-coloured inner shell which eventually turns into the hard, dark shell of the ripe nut which you see in the west. It takes a year for the nut to reach maturity, at which point the hard-shelled nut within the fibrous husk is about 12 cm in diameter and full of sweet liquid and hard, white flesh. Copra is the dried flesh and the second most important export product of northern Sulawesi. Coir is the fibre from the husk of the coconut.

Like bamboo the uses of the coconut tree are manifold. You can eat the meat, drink the juice, dry the meat for export as copra, burn the dried husks as fuel, build your house with coconut timber, use the fronds to thatch the roof or make mats and baskets, burn the oil to provide lighting at night or put it in your hair to keep it moist and glossy, use the leaf as a sieve to strain the sago flour that is the staple of the Maluku Islands, make rope and mats with the fibre, use the thin centre spine of the young coconut leaf to weave hats, or bag your mid-day meal of rice in a palm leaf.

Coconut oil, made from copra, is used instead of cooking fat, and is also used in the manufacture of soaps, perfumes, face creams, hair dressings, and even nitro-glycerine.

GORONTALO

The Gorontalese include the people of the city of Gorontalo as well as a large slice of the surrounding region, including Kwandang to the north and Toli Toli to

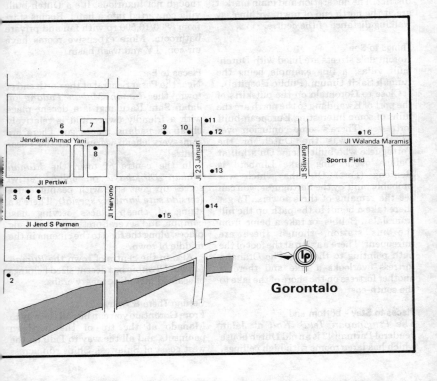

Gorontalo

the west. Perhaps 500,000 people live in the Gorontalo district, the vast majority of them Muslims.

Islam probably arrived here when the Ternate sultanate held sway over the tribes of the Gorontalo region before the Dutch took over. Gorontalo is the chief town of the Gorontalo district and the second largest in north Sulawesi. It's a port on the west shore of Gorontalo Bay and to the south of Lake Limboto, a fertile rice-growing region.

Orientation

Gorontalo Bay forms a narrow estuary; the town is on the west side and the harbour on the east. Although rather spread out, most of the hotels, shops and offices are concentrated in a small central district. The bus station and main market are at the north end of town, within easy walking distance of the centre.

Things to See

Gorontalo's streets are lined with Dutch-built villas, a fine example being the Rumah Sakit Umum (Public Hospital).

Close to Gorontalo on the outskirts of the port of Kwandang to the north are the ruins of some interesting European-built fortresses. There's some confusion over whether it was the Dutch or the Portuguese who built them. On a hill at Dembe overlooking Lake Limboto is Benteng (Fort) Otanaha which was probably built by the Portuguese; you can see the remains of three towers. To get there take a bendi to the path up the hill from Jalan Belibis, or take a bemo from the bus station, though these are infrequent. There's a sign at the foot of the path pointing to the fort. The Otanaha fortress overlooks a lake and there is another fortress on the shore of the lake to the south-east.

Places to Stay – bottom end

The *Penginapan Teluk Kau* at Jalan Jenderal Parman 42 is an old Dutch house which has large rooms with high ceilings,

big double beds and prices of 4000/8000 rp for singles/doubles. It used to be one of the best places to stay in Gorontalo, but it's now run-down and incredibly noisy.

Places to Stay – middle

The *Hotel Inda Ria* (tel 0435) at Jalan Jenderal A Yani, has rooms for 12,500 rp with fan, and for 20,000 rp with air-con. It's a very congenial place and better than the slightly more expensive Hotel Saronde.

Also worth a try is the *Hotel Wisata* at Jalan 23 Januari 19. Rooms start from 8000/12,000 rp. More expensive rooms have air-con.

Places to Stay – top end

The *Hotel Saronde* (tel 21735) at Jalan Walanda Maramis 17 is comfortable though not luxurious. It's a Dutch-built villa converted into a hotel. Rooms start from 8800/16,500 rp with fan and private bathroom. More expensive rooms have air-con, TV and wash basin.

Places to Eat

Near the Pasar Sentral at the north end of town, the *Rumah Makan Padang* on Jalan Sam Ratulangi is a decent place with a friendly owner and is relatively cheap as padang places go. There are some very cheap warungs in the Pasar Sentral.

In the centre of town the *Rumah Makan Dirgahayu* on Jalan Pertiwi serves up goat sate with peanut sauce (*tersida sate kambing spesial*). There's a string of cheap places serving nasi campur, and several pretty good padang places, along the road to the cinema in the middle of town.

Also in the centre of town the *Rumah Makan Olympic* has decent sized helpings of seafood including meaty crabs.

Getting There & Away

From Gorontalo you can bus all the way to Manado at the tip of the northern peninsula and all the way to Palu on the west coast of Sulawesi. Ships run across the Bay of Tomini to Poso; or take a bus to Kwandang and then take a ship along the coast to Manado or to Palu, stopping off at various ports on the way. Gorontalo is also connected by air to various parts of Sulawesi and the other islands of Indonesia.

Air The Merpati office (tel 21736) is in the Hotel Wisata at Jalan 23 Januari 19; Bouraq (tel 21070) is at Jalan Ahmad Yani 34 next to the Bank Negara Indonesia.

There are daily flights from Gorontalo to Ujung Pandang, Manado and Palu with Merpati and Bouraq. Other connections include daily flights with Bouraq to the east coast of Kalimantan and to Java.

The shared Merpati and Bouraq bus will transport you from town to the airport 32 km away. It's an half-hour drive and costs 3000 rp per person.

Bus There are regular buses to Manado. If the road is dry it takes only 12 hours; if it's wet then you could take 24 hours or more. Ask around at the bus station. Also ask about direct buses to Palu and Poso in central Sulawesi.

Boat Pelni (tel 20-419) is at Jalan 23 Januari 31, and there's also an office at the port in Kwandang. Another shipping line, Gapsu (tel 88-173), has an office at Jalan Pertiwi 55 in central Gorontalo, and also at Gorontalo harbour on Jalan Mayor Dullah, (tel 198).

Ships to Manado, Toli Toli, Donggala and other ports on the west and north coasts leave from the port of Kwandang which is two hours by bus from Gorontalo (1000 rp), along a surfaced road. Ships to Poso and Bitung, usually with various stops along the way, depart from Gorontalo harbour.

There are two or three ships a week to Poso. The trip takes about two days and costs 15,000 to 17,500 rp deck class (there are no other classes available). These ships usually stop at various ports along the way including Dolong in the Togian

Islands and Ampana on the eastern peninsula of Sulawesi. They leave from Gorontalo harbour.

Getting Around
Gorontalo is rather spread out and except for the central region you really need the bendis. These are little pony carts rather like a miniature dokar and 100 rp will get you almost anywhere. For longer routes take bemos from the bus station across the road from the Pasar Central. Bemos to Gorontalo harbour are 200 rp and take 15 minutes.

KWANDANG
Kwandang is a port on the north coast of the peninsula, not far from Gorontalo. On the outskirts of Kwandang are the remains of two interesting fortresses, possibly Portuguese built. While the town itself is nothing, the fortresses are worth checking out. Both are just off the Gorontalo-Kwandang road as you enter Kwandang.

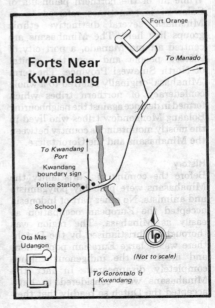

Benteng Ota Mas Udangan

This fortress stands on flat ground and at first glance appears to be ill-placed to defend anything. One suggestion is that the ocean once came right up to the fort, but has since receded. All that remains of the fort are the ruins of a tower alongside the road, a gateway further back, and traces of the walls, though it was evidently a sizeable place.

Benteng Oranje

Benteng Oranje lies on a hill some distance back from the sea and just a short walk from the Gorontalo-Kwandang road. It's been partly restored though Benteng Ota Mas Udangan is probably the more interesting of the two.

Getting There & Away

To get to Kwandang, take a bus from Gorontalo bus station (two hours, 1000 rp).

MANADO

While all of the northern peninsula of Sulawesi is sometimes referred to as Minahasa, several distinctive ethnic groups live here. The Minahasans are centred around Manado, a port city of 250,000 people and now the capital of North Sulawesi Province. The term 'Minahasa' originally referred to a whole confederacy of northern tribes which formed in defence against the neighbouring Bolaang Mongondow tribes who lived in the mostly mountainous country between the Minahasans and the Gorontalese.

History

Before the coming of Christianity the Minahasans were probably polygamists and animists. No other part of Indonesia accepted the European occupation as easily as Minahasa. The region was thoroughly Christianised by the Dutch, there was a large Eurasian population, and much of the indigenous culture completely disappeared. In fact the Minahasans were considered to have accepted the Dutch so readily that they became known to other Indonesians as the Anjing Belanda, or 'Dutch dogs', and they had a reputation as willing collaborators with the colonialists.

Though cloves and copra became the main agricultural products of northern Sulawesi, coffee was the first cash-crop to be introduced by the Dutch in the early 1800s. The chiefs of the villages were induced to undertake its cultivation and to sell it to the Dutch government for a fixed price. In time, roads were built from Manado to the coffee-growing highlands, missionaries settled in the more populous areas and Chinese traders brought in consumer goods.

When the naturalist Alfred Wallace came here in 1859 he described the town as 'one of the prettiest in the East' and the people as 'remarkably quiet and gentle' although he added that they appeared to have only recently given up head-hunting and cannibalism.

Today Manado conveys such an impression of prosperity that it *feels* like you're in the capital of another country. Even the little towns around Manado appear to be well off and the large wooden houses of the inhabitants are arranged in tidy rows, many with front yards and fences in the best tradition of western suburbia.

Manado has a culture all its own. Girls wear T-shirts with motifs like 'Bullshit' and 'For Sale'. Disco versions of rock songs boom out from speakers in the bemos. At the Pelni office a large banner proclaims the 'Royal English Course Royal Computer College'. The cinemas are plastered with posters of gun-toting Rambos, while on the streets law and order is kept by wiry little policemen who look like they could break up a riot single-handed. Even Manado's flashy Suzuki bemos carry names like Sweet Steven, White Dragon, Apostleship and even Rommel Jr.

Orientation

Manado is like an octopus. The heart is

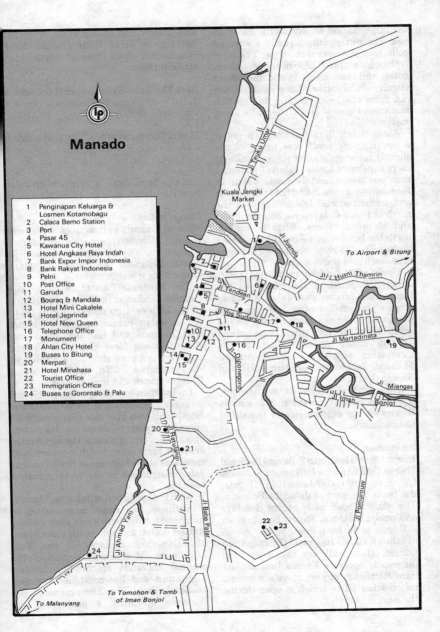

Manado

1 Penginapan Keluarga &
  Losmen Kotamobagu
2 Calaca Bemo Station
3 Port
4 Pasar 45
5 Kawanua City Hotel
6 Hotel Angkasa Raya Indah
7 Bank Expor Impor Indonesia
8 Bank Rakyat Indonesia
9 Pelni
10 Post Office
11 Garuda
12 Bouraq & Mandala
13 Hotel Mini Cakalele
14 Hotel Jeprinda
15 Hotel New Queen
16 Telephone Office
17 Monument
18 Ahlan City Hotel
19 Buses to Bitung
20 Merpati
21 Hotel Minahasa
22 Tourist Office
23 Immigration Office
24 Buses to Gorontalo & Palu

Kuala Jengki Market

To Airport & Bitung

To Tomohon & Tomb of Iman Bonjol

To Malalayang

the large market known as the Pasar 45 near the waterfront, actually a covered collection of permanent shops. The head is the concentrated blob of shops, offices, hotels and restaurants in the immediate vicinity of the market. Long roads stretch out from the head, groping inland like tentacles. Pasar 45 is also the major bemo station.

Along Jalan Sam Ratulangi, a major artery running south, are many of the slightly more up-market restaurants and more expensive hotels. Jalan Diponegoro runs south-east and becomes Jalan 14 Februari, where you'll find the immigration and tourist offices. Immediately to the north of Pasar 45 is the harbour terminal and shipping offices. Slightly further north the large Kuala Jengki fish market backs on to the river which cuts Manado into north and south halves.

Two major bridges cross this river; Jalan Sisingamangaraja runs over the larger arm, further east Jalan Katamso crosses the smaller one. Jalan Sisinga-mangaraja becomes Jalan Singkil on the north side of the river, where there are one or two cheap hotels. Most of the interesting sights are found around Manado, in places like Airmadidi and Kawangkoan.

Although Manado has its own harbour, the main port of northern Sulawesi is Bitung on the eastern side of the tip of the peninsula.

Information

Tourist Office The North Sulawesi Regional Tourist Office (*Dinas Pariwisata Sulawesi Utara*; tel 4299) is off Jalan Eddy Gogola, not far to the west of Jalan 14 Februari. The office is open daily except Sundays and public holidays. To get there take an E Gogola bemo from Pasar 45 and get off at the Kantor Imigrasi (Immigration Office), then walk up the little road diagonally opposite Kantor Imigrasi. At Sam Ratulangi airport there's a tourist information office which is open during the day.

Immigration The immigration office (tel 3491) is on Jalan Eddy Gogola. An E Gogola bemo from Pasar 45 will take you straight there.

Bank The Bank Expor Impor Indonesia on Jalan Yos Sudarso 29, changes money and travellers' cheques.

Post & Communications The post office is on Jalan Sam Ratulangi. The telephone & telegraph office is at Jalan W R Supratman. International phone calls can also be made from Perumtel on Jalan Sam Ratulangi, near the Hotel Kawanua.

Things to See

Most of Manado's attractions are outside the city, although there are a few things in the centre. The Provincial Museum of North Sulawesi on Jalan Ki Hajar Dewantara is worth a visit.

The Kienteng Ban Hian Kiong is a Chinese Confucian temple originally built in the 19th century and rebuilt in 1974 – it's on Jalan Panjaitan and is adorned with dragons and burning joss sticks. After Chinese New Year, mid to late-February is a good time to be around for the festivities, with performances of Chinese dance and martial arts.

On Independence Day (August 17) and on every anniversary of the foundation of North Sulawesi Province (September 23) there are various celebrations. Ask around about other performances throughout the year; see horse races, bendi races and bull-cart races at the Ranomuut Race Track on Jalan Ranomuut in the eastern part of Manado.

With the exception of Jakarta, Manado is perhaps the most monumental of Indonesian cities with some eye-catching statues dotted around. At the eastern end of Jalan Yos Sudarso is the Toar Lumimuut Monument, depicting the original ancestors of the Minahasans, Lumimuut and her combined son and husband Taor. The Monument of Ibu Walanda Maramis, a pioneer of the

Indonesian women's movement, is also on Jalan Yos Sudarso and her tomb is in the village of Maumbi in the Airmadidi district. The Monument to the Worang Battalion commemorates an army battalion which fought against the Dutch during the independence wars; it's on Jalan Sam Ratulangi near the Pasar 45. The Sam Ratulangi Monument honours the first governor of Sulawesi under the republican government. The Monument of the Allied Forces is on Jalan Sarapung, beside the Central Protestant Church of Manado, and commemorates the allied victory over Japan in WW II.

Places to Stay – bottom end

The one drawback of Manado is the lack of good, cheap accommodation. At the bottom of the barrel both in price and standards is the *Penginapan Keluarga* on Jalan Singkil near the bridge. It's a large shed with thinly partitioned little boxes, ants in the mandi, spiders in the toilets, and late night soccer broadcasts punching through the floorboards. Rooms – and I use the term loosely – are 1500/3000 rp.

Places to Stay – middle

The *Ahlan City Hotel* (tel 3454) is at Jalan Sudirman 103. It's basic but clean with rooms from 8000/11,000 rp. The *Hotel Minahasa* (tel 2059) at Jalan Sam Ratulangi 199 is a good place, and is run by an English-speaking man from Sulawesi. Singles/doubles are from 13,300/17,500 rp.

The *Hotel Mini Cakalele* (tel 52942) is at Jalan Korengkeng 40, a street running off Jalan Sam Ratulangi south of the main post office. Rooms are 14,000 rp with fan and 19,000 rp with air-con. It's clean and reasonably comfortable, but definitely overpriced.

Hotel Jeprinda (tel 4049) at Jalan Sam Ratulangi 37 is good though also somewhat overpriced at 16,000/19,000 rp. It's comfortable but probably quite noisy. The *Hotel New Queen* (tel 52979) at Jalan Wakeke 12-14 is one of the best mid-range

places in Manado. It's on a quiet side street and is very comfortable. Rooms start from 16,500/23,000 rp plus tax and service charge.

The *Hotel Angkasa Raya Indah* (tel 2039) at Jalan Sugiono 12A has rooms from 15,000 rp. The hotel is quite basic but the rooms are very big, with big double beds and bathroom. It's in a good, central location.

Places to Stay – top end

The big *Kawanua City Hotel* (tel 52222) at Jalan Sam Ratulangi 1 is Manado's number one establishment. Room prices start at 28,000/32,000 rp.

Places to Eat

Some traditional Minahasan delights include *rintek wuuk* – spicy dog meat, *gulei anjing* in Bahasa Indonesia, or just plain RW for short. For second course there's *kawaok* which is fried forest rat, or *tikus utan goreng*. Top it off with some *lawa pangang* or stewed bat. Then wash it down with *tinutuan* or vegetable porridge. Exactly where you can get such delicacies is a mystery but there are a couple of restaurants around Manado and in the small towns nearby which are supposed to specialise in this idiosyncratic cuisine.

Otherwise there's a string of eating houses all the way along Jalan Sam Ratulangi serving up a mixed bag of Chinese and Indonesian food. They're all pretty good and relatively cheap. There are many cheapish nasi goreng and nasi campur places around the northern boundary of Pasar 45. There are also some cheap warungs and rumah makan on Jalan Dr Sutono. There's a whole string of places along Jalan Yos Sudarso serving Indonesian and Chinese food, though none are worth a specific mention.

Getting There & Away

From Manado you can go by road to Gorontalo and all the way to Palu on the west coast of Sulawesi. You can take a ship along the north and west coasts of the island, or head east to Ternate in the Maluku Islands. There are also numerous flight connections with other parts of Sulawesi and the other islands of Indonesia. You can enter and exit Indonesia via Manado without an Indonesian visa.

Air Garuda is at Jalan Sudirman 2; Bouraq (tel 2757) is at Jalan Sarapung 27; Mandala (tel 51324) is at Jalan Sarapung 17; and Merpati (tel 4027) is at Jalan Sam Ratulangi 138.

Bouraq has some of the more useful flights including daily flights to Gorontalo, Palu, Ujung Pandang, Jakarta and Yogyakarta and to the east coast of Kalimantan. There are flights four days a week to Ternate in Maluku Province.

Garuda has daily flights from Manado to Ujung Pandang, Denpasar and Jakarta. There are twice-weekly flights to Biak and Jayapura.

Merpati has daily flights to Gorontalo, Ternate, Ambon and to the Sangir-Talaud Islands to the north. Mandala has flights three days a week to Jakarta and Surabaya.

Bus From Manado's Gorontalo bus station there are daily buses to Gorontalo. The fare is 9000 rp and the trip normally takes about 12 hours, but that depends entirely on the weather. The vehicles have to ford two rivers which sometimes flood. Don't be surprised if it takes 24 hours or longer to get between the two cities. There are also daily buses to Palu, which take two days and one night and cost 25,000 rp.

Boat Pelni (tel 2844) is at Jalan Sam Ratulangi 3. They have a number of ships calling into Bitung or Manado, but the most important is the modern liner *KM Kambuna* which pulls into Bitung once every two weeks or so on its loop out of Java around Sulawesi, Kalimantan and Sumatra. Deck and 1st-class fares from Manado to other parts of Indonesia are shown here; fares in 2nd, 3rd and 4th class range between these extremes.

to	1st class	deck class
Balikpapan	82,000	33,000
Ujung Pandang	103,000	37,000
Surabaya	167,000	56,000
Jakarta	204,000	67,000

If the Pelni office in Manado can't give you a place on the ship, ask at their office in Bitung.

From Manado it's easy to get ships along the coast of Sulawesi to as far south as Pantoloan (the port of Palu) and Pare Pare. These ships stop off at various ports on the way including Kwandang, Paleleh, Leok and Toli Toli. There are regular ships on this run, including the *KM Mauru*, whose Manado office is at the entrance to the harbour terminal.

For other ships along the northern peninsula and also for ships to Tahulandang, Siau and Sangir Islands enquire at the shipping offices near the port in Manado.

From Manado or Bitung there are ships to Ternate in the Maluku Islands. The fare is around 12,500 rp and there are departures about every 10 days. There are also weekly ships from Bitung to Poso, in central Sulawesi, via Gorontalo, Pagimana and Ampana.

Getting Around

Airport Transport Bemos to Sam Ratulangi airport depart from the Calaca bemo station which is just north of Pasar 45. Take a Lapangan bemo (225 rp, 20 minutes). The airport is 13 km from Manado. A taxi costs 5000 rp.

Bus & Bemo Transport around town is by bemo, for a flat fare of 150 rp. Destinations are shown on a card in the front windscreen, *not* on the side of the van. There are various bus stations around town for destinations outside of Manado. Mercifully the vehicles do not do endless picking-up rounds!

There are several bus/bemo stations from which you get bemos and colts to destinations around town and to other parts of Minahasa and northern Sulawesi. Pasar 45 is the central bemo station. The other important stations are:

Calaca Bemo Station, on Jalan Veteran, which is north of Pasar 45. This street is a bit hard to find – ask directions.

Gorontalo Bus Station for buses to Gorontalo. Take a Sario bemo from Pasar 45, and tell the driver that you want to go to the bus station since the bemo has to make a detour to do this.

Pasar Paal2 (Paal Paal), the station for colts to Bitung and Airmadidi. To get to Pasar Paal2 take a Paal2 bemo from Pasar 45. Paal2 is sometimes written as Pal2.

Pasar Karombasan, the station for colts to Tomohon, Tondano and Kawangkoan. To get to Pasar Karombasan take a Wanea bemo from Pasar 45. There are also colts from Pasar Karombasan to Langowan, Kotamanbagu, Inobonto, Amurang, Belang and Remboken.

The Wanea and Sario bemos from Pasar 45 will take you straight down Jalan Sam Ratulangi, which is useful for the Merpati office, PT Pola Pelita, and the restaurants and hotels along this road.

Sario bemos can also be caught at the southern end of the large bridge over which Jalan Sisingamangaraja runs. Banjer and Paal2 bemos usually pass here from Pasar 45.

The E Gogola bemos from Pasar 45 take you to Jalan Eddy Gogola which is the location of the immigration office, and the tourist office is close by. These bemos go out along Jalan Diponegoro so they're also useful for getting to the telephone office and to Garuda as well.

There are no becaks in Manado. There are some bendis in the city (most are found in the small towns in the surrounding region) but they're not terribly numerous and not very convenient for long distances around the city.

AROUND MANADO
Bunaken Island
Manado's main attractions are the stunning coral reefs off nearby Bunaken Island. You can hop across on one of the regular motorboats although you need your own boat to see the reefs at their best.

To get a boat to Bunaken go to the Toko Samudera Jaya in the Kuala Jengki market; the shop is hidden behind the stalls so ask directions. The shop backs on to the river and steps lead down to water level; outboard-powered outrigger long-boats zip back and forth all through the day, take half an hour and cost 500 rp.

You may be able to hire a boat in Bunaken village to take you out to the reefs, or else walk from the village to the long pier which you'll see as you arrive. Climb down the steps at the end of the pier and you're right on the reef.

The other alternative is to hire your own boat to get further out. If you hire a boat in Manado you can go back whenever you want. It's probably easiest to charter a boat at the Toko Samudera; it costs about 20,000 rp for them to take you out to the reef in the morning, paddle around for a few hours and back to Manado in the afternoon. It's worth every last rupiah!

There are no losmens or penginapans on Bunaken, though you could ask the kepala desa if there's anything available, or you could probably camp. At Liang around the other side of the island from the village there are huts where the tour groups pull in for lunch. There's another beautiful stretch of reef diagonally opposite Liang, with a sudden and quite spectacular drop, but it's so far out you need a boat to get to it.

The travel agency PT Polita Express (tel 52231, 52768) at Jalan Sam Ratulangi 74 organises trips and scuba diving tours to Bunaken Island. Another possibility is to contact the Nusantara Diving Club and see if you can arrange a trip with them to the islands.

Snorkels and masks (and perhaps fins)

can be bought from Toko Akbar Ali on the western boundary of the Pasar 45.

Other Reefs

There are other coral reefs around the Minahasan peninsula. Manado Tua, or 'Old Manado', is a dormant volcano you can see off the coast. The Portuguese and Spanish once based themselves here to trade between northern Sulawesi and Maluku. Nowadays, like Bunaken Island, it's the coral reefs that pull in visitors. Other coral reefs lie off Mantehage Island and Bitung. The boatmen *say* there are no sharks in the waters around Bunaken, but sharks have been reported at the neighbouring islands of Manado Tua and Mantehage, and at Bitung.

Airmadidi

'Airmadidi' means 'boiling water'. Legend has it that there was a bathing place here and nine angels flew down from heaven on nights of the full moon to bathe and frolic in it. One night a mortal man succeeded in stealing a dress belonging to one of them – unable to return to heaven she was forced to remain on earth.

That has nothing to do with the real attraction of the place: the odd little pre-Christian tombs known as *warugas*. They look like small Chinese temples and the corpses were placed in a squatting position with household articles, gold and porcelain – most have been plundered. There's a group of these tombs at Airmadidi Bawah, a 15-minute walk from Airmadidi bemo station. Many are decorated with odd animal and human motifs.

Colts go to Airmadidi from Manado's Paal2 terminal (300 rp). From Airmadidi you can also take a bemo to Tondano (450 rp, 45 minutes) or to Bitung (400 rp, 40 minutes). You can see more warugas at Sawangan, Likupang, and at Kema on the south coast near Bitung.

Kawangkoan

Northern Sulawesi did not escape WW II.

The region was occupied by the Japanese between January 1942 and August 1945, and in 1945 the Allied advance into Indonesia resulted in the bombing of the main towns in northern Sulawesi, including Manado where there was considerable damage. During the occupation the Japanese dug caves into the hills surrounding Manado to act as air-raid shelters, and storage space for ammunition, food, weapons and medical supplies.

One such cave is located three km out of Kawangkoan on the road to Kiawa. There are colts to Kawangkoan from Pasar Karombasan (the Wanea terminal) in Manado.

Tondano

Some of the most impressive Japanese caves are just outside Tondano on the road to Airmadidi. A bus from Airmadidi to Tondano will get you to the caves in 45 minutes. From the caves you can hitch or walk (one hour) to Tondano bemo station and get a colt back to Pasar Karombasan in Manado. Bemos from Tondano to Tomohon take half an hour. Tondano Lake is 30 km south-west of Manado and is 600 metres above sea level.

Tomohon

Several km out of the hill town of Tomohon on the road to Tara Tara are more Japanese caves. Take a colt from Pasar Karombasan (Wanea terminal) to Tomohon and another colt towards Tara Tara. There are also bemos between Tomohon and Tondano, and between Kawangkoan and Tomohon. Tomohon is the site of a Christian college and a centre for the study of Christian theology in Minahasa. The market is worth investigating.

Batu Pinabetengan

This stone, scratched with the vague outline of human figures, is said to be the place where Minahasan chiefs held meetings. It is said that it was at this site that the chiefs divided up the land between the different tribes. The locals sometimes pronounce 'Batu Pinabetengan' as 'Watu Pinawetengan' – 'watu' means 'stone' and 'weteng' means 'divide', meaning this was the place where the division of land was carried out. 'Mina-Esa' (from which the name Minahasa is derived) means to 'become one' or 'united'.

The scratchings on the stone have never been deciphered (it is only presumed they each have a particular meaning) though it is thought that they may record agreements concerning the division of land amongst the tribes, and the political unification of Minahasa in the early meetings between the chiefs.

The stone is close to Pinabetengan village, about 40 km from Manado and five km from Kawangkoan. Take a bemo to Kawangkoan from Manado's Wanea terminal, then a bendi from Kawangkoan to Desa Pinabetengan. The bendi will take you as far as the turn-off road that leads to Batu Pinabetengan and then you have to walk the last half hour.

Tara Tara

About 30 km south of Manado and eight km from Tomohon, Tara Tara is one of the centres of Minahasa art.

BITUNG

Sheltered by Lembah Island, Bitung is the chief port of Minahasa and lies on the southern side of the tip of the peninsula, to the east of Manado. Many ships dock at Bitung rather than at Manado. The Pelni office (tel 21167) is on Jalan Jakarta, within the harbour compound.

Places to Stay & Eat

Stay at the *Penginapan Beringin* near the main market; it has rooms for 6500 rp and a downstairs restaurant. There are several cheap places to eat along the same street. The nearby *Penginapan Minang* is basic but clean, with rooms with fan and attached mandi for 5000 rp.

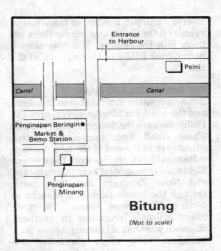

Bitung
(Not to scale)

Getting There & Away

Bitung is 40 km from Manado and is connected by a surfaced racetrack along which kamikaze colt drivers break land, water and air speed records all at once. There are regular departures from Manado's Paal2 terminal; the fare is 800 rp and the trip takes about an hour. The colt drops you off at the Mapalus terminal just outside Bitung, where you catch another bemo into town (200 rp, 10 minutes).

AROUND BITUNG
Kema

Just a few km south of Bitung, Kema was formerly a Portuguese and Spanish seaport. There's supposed to be a Portuguese fortress here but if so it's been well camouflaged against assaults by tourists.

Tangkoko Batuangas Nature Reserve

This nature reserve is 30 km from the port of Bitung and is a home of the black ape, anoa, babirusa and maleo bird (a bird which looks like a huge hen and lays eggs five times hen-size). The reserve also includes the coastline and coral gardens offshore. From Bitung hire a boat to take you to the village of Batuputih on the reserve's western border; or from Kasua village on the south-east border there are trails into the reserve. You may need a permit from PHPA in Manado to visit the reserve.

THE SANGIR-TALAUD ISLANDS

Strewn across the straits between Indonesia and the southern Mindanao region of the Philippines are the Sangir-Talaud Islands. These small and volcanically active islands are at the end of the long chain of volcanoes that stretches from the western highlands of Sumatra, east through Java and Nusa Tenggara and then north through the Banda Islands of Maluku to north-east Sulawesi. One of the more recent volcanic eruptions in northern Sulawesi was that of Gunung Api on Siau Island in 1974, which compelled the temporary evacuation of the entire population of the island (then 40,000 people) to Minahasa.

The main islands in the Sangir group are Sangir Besar, Siau, Tahulandang and Biaro. The Talaud group consists of Karakelong, Salibabu, Kabaruan, Karatung, Nanusa and Miangas. Despite their tiny size, around 300,000 people live on these islands! The capital of the Sangir-Talaud group is Tahuna on Sangir Besar.

History

Once upon a time these islands were subject to strong Islamic influence from the Ternate sultanate to the east. That was checked by the Christian missionaries who followed in the wake of the Dutch takeover in 1677. Most of the population was eventually converted to Christianity, although for many years older religious beliefs persisted. Prior to the arrival of the missionaries, ancestral spirits were important, and some women (and occasionally men) became possessed by spirits and would thus serve as inter-

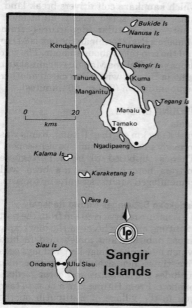

mediaries with the supernatural. Human sacrifice at some ceremonies was also reported.

Not only did the Dutch bring a new religion but they also encouraged the local population to raise coconuts (for copra) and nutmeg. Thus the island economy came to rely heavily on trade in these products, chiefly carried on with Ternate and Manado. Today the main industries are copra and cloves.

Getting There & Away
Air Merpati has almost daily flights to Naha which is the airfield 20 km from Tahuna.

Boat For ships to these islands ask at the shipping offices near the entrance to the harbour terminal in Manado.

There are usually about three ships a week between Manado and Siau and Tahuna. Some of these ships go to Siau and Tahuna and then to the ports along the northern peninsula of Sulawesi. Also ask about ships to Beo and Lirung on Karakelong Island. Fares from Manado are approximately: Siau 7000 rp; Tahuna 10,000 rp; Beo and Lirung 14,500 rp.

Maluku (The Moluccas)

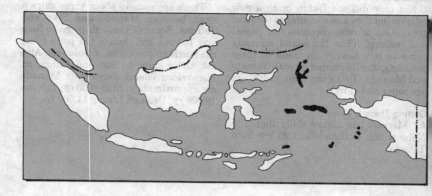

From Halmahera in the north to Wetar off the north-east end of Timor are the thousand islands of Maluku. Sprawled across a vast area of ocean but making up only a tiny proportion of Indonesia's land area, what they lack in size they more than make up for in historical significance. These were the fabled 'spice islands' to which Indian, Chinese, Arab and later European traders came in search of the cloves, nutmeg and mace which grew here and nowhere else; and it was these islands which bore the brunt of the first European attempts to wrest control of the Indonesian archipelago and the lucrative spice trade.

The destinations of most visitors to the region are Ambon, the capital of Maluku province and just south of the large island of Seram; the cluster of islands south-east of Ambon known as the Bandas and the two adjacent northern islands of Ternate and Tidore off the west coast of Halmahera. While spices are still produced in these islands it's the fine tropical scenery, the relics of the early European invasion, some excellent snorkelling and diving, plus some enticing beaches which draw visitors today. Maluku is one of Indonesia's remotest provinces and its lesser known islands offer infinite scope for getting right off the tourist trail.

HISTORY

Before the arrival of the Europeans, the sultanate of Ternate held tenuous sway over some of the islands and parts of neighbouring Sulawesi and Irian Jaya, but there was little political unity – when the Portuguese reached the Indonesian archipelago Maluku was known to them as the 'land of many kings'.

The spice trade, however, goes back a lot further than the Portuguese and Dutch. The Roman encyclopedist Pliny described trade in cinnamon and other spices from Indonesia to Madagascar and East Africa and from there to Rome. By the 1st century AD Indonesian trade was firmly established with other parts of Asia, including India and China, and spices also reached Europe via the caravan routes from India and the Persian Gulf.

Apart from Marco Polo and a few wandering missionaries, Portuguese sailors were the first Europeans to set foot on Indonesian soil. Their first small fleet and

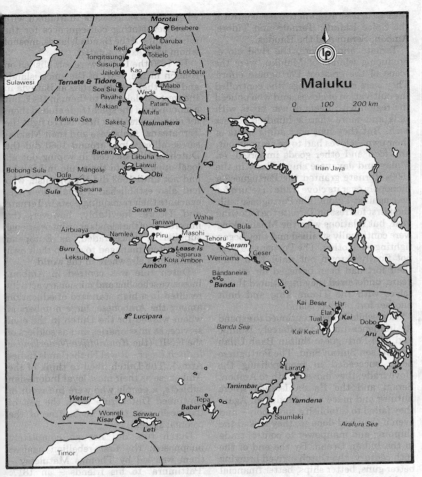

its 'white Bengalis' (as the local inhabitants called them) arrived in Melaka in 1509; their prime objective was the spice islands. For a hundred years previously the Portuguese had been pushing down the west African coast and when Vasco de Gama's ships rounded southern Africa and reached Calicut in India in 1498 the Portuguese suddenly got a whiff of the enormous profits to be made from the Asian trade. Since the trade was almost exclusively in the hands of Muslims they had the added satisfaction (and excuse) that any blow against their commercial rivals was a blow against the infidels. A master plan was devised to bring all the important Indian Ocean trading ports under Portuguese control. The capture of Melaka in 1511, following the capture of Goa on the west Indian coast, preceded the Portuguese attempt to wrest control of the Spice Islands: Ternate and Tidore, Ambon, Seram and the Bandas.

Ternate and Tidore, the rival clove-producing islands of Maluku, were the scene of the greatest Portuguese effort. They were ruled by kings who controlled the cultivation of cloves, and who policed the region with fleets of war boats with sails and more than a hundred rowers each. But they had no trading boats of their own – cloves had to be shipped out, and food and other goods imported, on Malay and Javanese ships. Early in the 1500s Ternate granted the Portuguese a monopoly over its clove trade in return for help against Tidore. The Portuguese built their first fortress on Ternate the following year, but relations with the Muslim king were continually strained and they began fighting each other. The Portuguese were not finally thrown out until 1575 after their fort had been besieged for several years, undeterred they ingratiated themselves with the Tidore king and built another fort on that island.

Meanwhile Ternate continued to expand its influence under the fiercely Islamic and anti-Portuguese Sultan Baab Ullah and his son Sultan Said. The Portuguese never succeeded in monopolising the clove trade; they moved south to Ambon, Seram and the Banda Islands where nutmeg and mace were produced. Again they failed to establish a monopoly – and even if they had done so, they lacked the shipping and manpower to control trade in the Indian Ocean. By the end of the 16th century, the Dutch arrived bringing better guns, better ships, better financial backing and an even more severe combination of courage and brutality. The first Dutch fleet to Indonesia, under the command of Jacob van Neck, reached Maluku in March 1599 and returned to the Netherlands with enough spices to produce a massive profit. More ships followed and the various Dutch companies eventually merged in 1602 to form the Dutch East India Company – the VOC –

whose ships sailed back to Maluku with some devastating consequences for the inhabitants of the Banda Islands, most of whom were exterminated.

By 1630 the Dutch were established on Ambon in the heart of the spice islands and had their headquarters at Batavia in the west. Melaka fell to them in 1641, but a monopoly of the spice trade eluded them for many years; they first had to fight the Ternateans, Ambonese and their Makassarese allies. Only around 1660 did the Dutch finally succeed in wiping out all local opposition to their rule in Maluku and not until 1663 did the Spanish, who had also established a small presence, evacuate their remaining posts in Ternate and Tidore. Inevitably, however, the importance of the islands as an international supplier of spice faded, as European competitors managed to set up their own plantations elsewhere in the world.

Dutch rule was centred in Ambon. Intensive schooling and missionary activity resulted in a high standard of education among the Ambonese, large numbers of whom worked for the Dutch in the civil service, as missionaries and as soldiers of the KNIL (the *Koninklijke Nederlandse Indisch Leger* – Royal Netherlands Indies Army). The Dutch liked to think of the Ambonese as their most loyal Indonesian subjects, a people who were in favour of continued Dutch rule when the rest of Indonesia was trying to be free of the colonial system.

Dutch rule did not go completely unopposed; the first rebellion against them was led by Thomas Matulessy – 'Pattimura' to his friends – in 1817. Pattimura is regarded as one of Indonesia's national heroes – Ambon's university is called Pattimura, and so is the army unit based on Ambon and one of the city's main streets. In the middle of the city stands a giant 1972 statue depicting Pattimura as a warrior of superhuman proportions. He came from Saparua, a small island just east of Ambon, was a professed Christian (Calvinist) and had been a sergeant-major in the British militia when the British occupied Ambon during the Napoleonic Wars. He led the revolt against the Dutch when they re-established themselves after the British left. The uprising lasted only a few months and ended with the capture and execution of Pattimura.

There were several other revolts in Maluku over the next 50 years and not until the 1890s did the Dutch manage to recruit the Ambonese as soldiers in any great numbers – indeed many fought against the Dutch in the Indonesian independence wars.

Further problems arose on Ambon in 1949, when the Dutch finally quit Indonesia, but what really happened is obscured in the smog of history. There are numerous theories: some say Ambonese soldiers revolted against Indonesian rule because they preferred continued Dutch control to Javanese domination, others suggest these soldiers were deliberately sent back (armed) to Ambon by Dutch officers opposed to independence for Indonesia, but others believe the mass of the Ambonese population wanted no part of the independence struggle.

Whatever happened, in April 1950 an independent Republic of the South Moluccas (the RMS, *Republik Maluku Selatan*) was proclaimed in Ambon supported, it appears, by most of the 2000 or so Ambonese KNIL troops on the island. In July, Indonesian government troops occupied Buru and parts of Seram and at the end of September the first landings on Ambon took place, by the middle of November most resistance on Ambon had been put down and in early December the RMS government fled to the Seram jungles (where many RMS troops had already gone).

At this time there were still several camps of Ambonese KNIL soldiers and their families in Java. Initially the Dutch intended to demobilise them and send them back to Ambon, but it was feared this would virtually be sending them to

their deaths. Instead the Dutch government moved them (about 12,000 people) to the Netherlands. It was hoped that once the RMS was suppressed they could be sent back to Indonesia. Meanwhile they were treated as political refugees, dumped in a camp, and demobilised from the KNIL. They and their descendants (now over 40,000) have been in Holland ever since.

On Seram the remainder of the RMS forces clashed every now and then with Indonesian troops. In 1952 the RMS president and a number of ministers of the RMS government were captured; they were tried in Jakarta in 1955 and given relatively mild sentences ranging from three to 10 years imprisonment (perhaps a gesture of reconciliation on Sukarno's part). The fighting on Seram continued into the mid-1960s, but the idea of an independent 'South Moluccas' hung around even longer among the Malukans in the Netherlands. One of their more memorable actions was a headline-grabbing train hijack in the mid-1970s.

Today Maluku is politically stable and Indonesianised though, with its slightly Polynesian feel, it remains different from other parts of Indonesia. Despite its location in Indonesia's remote outer provinces, Ambon has as cosmopolitan an air as anywhere east of Denpasar, and its people maintain a sense of their own distinctness from other Indonesians. Maluku's distance from the centres of national activity prompted the Suharto government to pick Buru Island, west of Ambon, as the site of a stark internment camp for most of the 1970s for the 10,000-plus survivors of its 'anti-Communist' purges.

Spices are still grown on many Maluku islands but they are no longer the mainstay of the economy. Large-scale fishing, logging and mining, controlled jointly by foreign companies and the Indonesian government, are growth industries – but show scant regard for the environment. Agriculture is important with coffee, rice, sago, fruit, sugarcane, maize and copra the major products. Tourism is slowly increasing but, despite obvious potential, it's not yet a big money-earner.

CLIMATE

Timing a visit to Maluku is a bit different from going to the rest of Indonesia. The dry season in Maluku is generally from September to March with average temperatures from 34 to 38°C. The wet season is from April to August, with average temperatures from 18 to 20°C. There's not much point visiting the region in the wet season; the rain *pounds* down endlessly and since the seas are rough, there's less inter-island sea transport.

In some parts, local variations complicate the picture. On Seram, for example, the south coast follows the general Maluku pattern with its wet season from April to August, with particularly rough seas in July and August – but the north coast has its wet season from September to March and associated strong winds blow from January to March. Aru in far south-east Maluku has its wet season from September to April, in tune with most of the rest of Indonesia, but not with Maluku.

STAPLES & SPICES

Sago

The staple food of much of Maluku and other parts of eastern Indonesia is sago, from the sago palm. After 15 years the sago palm produces a flower spike, if the flower is allowed to mature, the fruit will feed off the starchy core of the trunk leaving it a hollow shell. When the palm is cultivated, the tree is cut down when the flower spike forms and the starchy pith of the trunk is scooped out, strained and washed to remove the fibres from the starch.

There's enough starch from one trunk to feed a whole family for months. Sago bread is commonly sold in Maluku in the form of thick wafers. *Papeda*, a unique native dish, is made by pulverising and straining the pulp from the sago palm and then boiling it up to make a glutinous porridge-like mass which is eaten hot. You can also use sago combined with brown sugar to make a sort of fudge; sago wafers and fried fish make a filling meal.

Every scrap of the sago palm is used for making something, the bark for the outer walls of houses, the leaves for roofs and the wood for house frames.

Cassava

Also known as mandioca, tapioca, manioc or yuca, cassava is another tropical staple, particularly among the poor in areas where cereals and potatoes won't grow. It's extracted from the tuberous roots of a South American plant which was brought to Indonesia by the Portuguese.

These roots grow well in poor soils: they are easy to plant, harvest and store, they can be planted at different times of the year to ensure a year-round crop, the yield of starch per hectare is more than from any other crop, and it is not susceptible to many diseases. The drawback is that most of the root is starch, with only a tiny amount of protein and fat, although the leaves have a high protein content. The *tapioca* pellets familiar to westerners are actually cassava starch pellets forced through a mesh then heated while being shaken or stirred on a plate.

Spices

Nutmeg and mace are both produced from the fruit of the nutmeg tree. The fleshy, yellow-brown fruit resembles an apricot and splits in half when it's ripe, exposing a scarlet seed covering which is dried to produce mace. Nutmeg is made from the seed itself. Although both contain much the same type of chemicals, differences in the quantity of these chemicals account for their different tastes. A 17th-century Spanish historian wrote that these spices:

correct stinking Breath, clear the Eyes, comfort the Stomach, Liver, and Spleen, and digest Meat. They are a Remedy against many other

Distempers, and serve to add outward Lustre to the Face...

Cloves come from a tree also native to the spice islands; today they are mainly used as food flavouring, but clove oil can also be used as an anaesthetic (try applying some to your gums). The word 'clove' comes from the French word *clou* which means 'nail' and refers to the dry, unexpanded, nail-shaped flower bud. The buds are picked just before the flower bud opens. Once the flower bud opens its value as a spice is lost, because the composition of its oils changes.

FLORA & FAUNA

Maluku is a transition zone between Asia and Australia/New Guinea and there are some flora and fauna unique to the province. Vegetation is luxuriant and includes some Australian species, such as *kayu putih* or eucalypts, as well as the usual tropical Asiatic species. Maluku hardwoods are prized by timber companies. Clove and nutmeg trees are spread throughout central Maluku, sago and coconut trees through the entire province. Ambon and Tanimbar are famous for their wild orchids while Ternate has some of the most brilliantly coloured bougainvillea you'll ever see.

Maluku's seas teem with life, including dugongs, turtles, trepang, sharks and all manner of tropical and shell fish. On land there are few Asiatic-type mammals such as monkeys but there are small marsupials such as the cuscus and bandicoot. Miniature tree kangaroos, wallabies, crocodiles and monitor lizards are found on the south-eastern island groups of Aru and Kai. Wild pig and deer are common, but they have been introduced. Insect life abounds and butterflies are particularly brilliant.

Maluku is well known for its exotic birdlife, particularly Seram's whose colourful birds are being smuggled out at an alarming rate – you can see some of them in the Ambon pasar. In Maluku there are 22 different varieties of parrots, numerous lories, black cockatoos, kingfishers, varieties of pigeons, the huge flightless cassowary and, on Aru, a couple of varieties of the famous birds of paradise, including the greater bird of paradise and bower birds.

Birds of Paradise

The first exotic bird of paradise specimens reached Europe in 1522 aboard the last surviving ship of Magellan's round-the-world fleet. The skins of these birds had been presented to the sailors by the King of Bacan, an island in Maluku off south-west Halmahera – and were said by the king to have come from a 'terrestrial paradise'. These specimens, like others which came to Europe in later years, had had their legs and wings removed by the native skinners to emphasise the plumes; hence the belief that the birds never alighted on the ground but stayed airborne (despite the lack of wings). It was not until the 18th century that this and other myths were disproved but the romantic aura was never quite dispelled and the first specimen's scientific name, *paradisea apoda*, even indicates its legless form! Of the more than 50 species now known, most live in Papua New Guinea and Irian Jaya although a few are found in outlying Maluku islands like Aru.

BOOKS

The 19th-century naturalist Alfred Russel Wallace spent six years, much of it in Maluku. roaming the Indonesian archipelago. His record of the journey *The Malay Archipelago* still makes fascinating reading. Another Victorian writer, Anna Forbes, in her *Unbeaten Tracks in Islands of the Far East*, presents a lively account of her time in Indonesia, much of it spent on Ambon and Tanimbar. Marika Hanbury-Tenison's *A Slice of Spice* details a visit to Ambon and the wilds of Seram in the early 1970s. Lawrence and Lorne Blair's exciting *Ring of Fire* (Bantam Press, 1988) has chapters on the Bandas and Aru. For an accurate picture of the tourist scene in Banda today, read the relevant chapter of Annabel Sutton's *The Islands In Between* (Impact Books, London, 1989). In his novel *Gifts of*

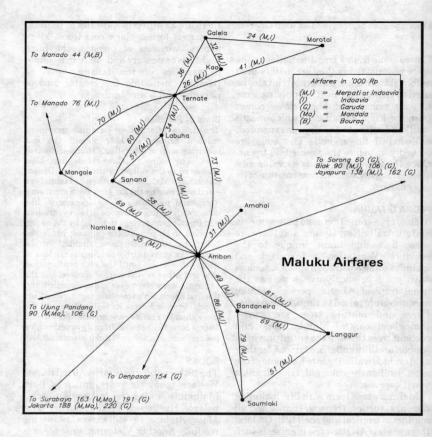

Maluku Airfares

Airfares in '000 Rp.

(M,I) = Merpati or Indoavia
(I) = Indoavia
(G) = Garuda
(Ma) = Mandala
(B) = Bouraq

Galela — 24 (M,I) — Morotai
To Manado 44 (M,B)
36 (M,I)
32 (M,I)
Kao
26 (M,I) — 41 (M,I)
Ternate
To Manado 76 (M,I)
70 (M,I)
60 (M,I)
34 (M,I)
Labuha
51 (M,I)
73 (M,I)
Mangole
Sanana
70 (M,I)
To Sorong 60 (G)
Biak 90 (M,I), 106 (G)
Jayapura 138 (M,I), 162 (G)
69 (M,I)
58 (M,I)
Amahai
Namlea
35 (M,I)
31 (M,I)
Ambon
To Ujung Pandang
90 (M,Ma), 106 (G)
49 (M,I)
81 (M,I)
86 (M,I)
Bandaneira
69 (M,I)
Langgur
79 (M,I)
To Denpasar 154 (G)
51 (M,I)
To Surabaya 163 (M,Ma), 191 (G)
Jakarta 188 (M,Ma), 220 (G)
Saumlaki

Unknown Things (Hodder & Stoughton, London, 1983), Lyall Watson has used a fictitious island in Maluku as the setting for some intriguing, mystical events. See the introductory Facts for The Visitor chapter for more on some of these books.

Shirley Deane's *Ambon, Island of Spices* (John Murray, London) touches on the Lease Islands, Seram, the Bandas, Kai and Aru but mainly deals with Ambon where she lived and worked for a couple of years in the 1970s. She found that many adat customs, including the *pela* law – the traditional Ambonese bond

between two or more villages for mutual protection and help in crises – were adhered to and that magic and witchcraft were still alive. She also observed that adat marriages were often carried out in conjunction with Christian and/or civil marriages.

Dieter Bartel's fascinating book *Guarding the Invisible Mountain*, based on research in central Maluku in 1974 and 1975, also discusses the key role of the pela alliances.

GETTING THERE & AWAY

The main gateway to Maluku is the island of Ambon, virtually at the centre of Maluku, which is well served by Merpati, Garuda and Mandala airlines, with flights to both Irian Jaya and western Indonesia. There are also regular flights from Sulawesi to Ternate in northern Maluku.

The Pelni passenger liners *Rinjani* and *Umsini* call at Ambon and Ternate respectively on their fortnightly runs between western Indonesia, Sulawesi and Irian Jaya. Other irregular ships also link these ports with the rest of the Indonesian archipelago.

The authorities in smaller towns in Maluku are concerned to have all arriving foreigners registered with immigration (in Ternate) or with police (elsewhere).

GETTING AROUND

If you're planning to do a lot of travel in

Flying to Ambon

Maluku, you need either time or money – preferably both! Merpati and its subsidiary, Indoavia, have a number of flights out of Ambon and Ternate to various destinations around Maluku.

Transport by sea between adjacent islands is generally fairly easy. There are regular passenger ferries between Ambon, Saparua and Seram, and frequent motorboats every day making the short hop between Ternate and Tidore, as well as regular passenger ships from Ternate to various places on Halmahera.

Long distance sea transport around the islands becomes more of a problem. There are semi-regular boats from Ambon to Banda and others like the *KM Niaga XVIII* doing loops round northern and southern Maluku from Ambon. Mostly conditions on these are fairly primitive, and how long it takes to reach a particular port depends on which route the ship takes and how many calls it makes on the way. See the relevant island sections for more details.

Ambon

Barely a dot on a map of Indonesia, Ambon Island is the hub of Maluku. Its landscape is dramatic and mountainous with little flat land for cultivation or roads. There are a few good beaches, coral reefs and plenty of opportunities for hiking and exploring Ambon's abundant insect, bird and plant life and its culture. Don't be deceived by its largely Christian and increasingly modern veneer – adat customs and practices plus magic and superstition still exist. To appreciate the island, you need to get out into the villages, where there's a definite Polynesian feel. Ambon reeks with history: visit the old European fort at Hila on the north coast!

The island is just 48 km by 22 km, with a larger northern portion known as Leihitu and a smaller arrow-head shaped southern

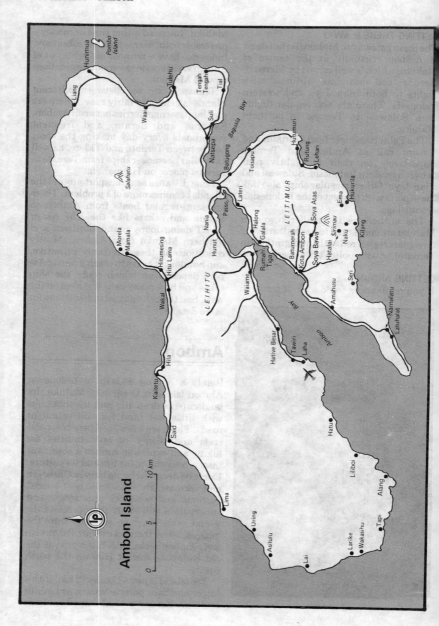

Ambon Island

0   5   10 km

portion known as the Leitimur Peninsula. They're separated for most of their length by Ambon Bay and are connected only by a narrow isthmus at Passo. Kota Ambon, the capital, lies on the Leitimur Peninsula, on the southern side of Ambon Bay.

Although Ambon is in the 'Ring of Fire' there are no active volcanoes. The majority of Ambonese still live in villages strung along the coasts. There are no rice paddies, but many sago and spice plantations (rice is grown on neighbouring Seram). Village craftsmen stitch clove twigs into stick-figure men and large intricate mounted ships. Others pound the trunks of spiky sago palms to extract the sludgy pulp, which forms the staple Maluku diet, while the leaves are woven into baskets.

You may get to see the *bulu gila* or crazy bamboo dance, a feature of Ambonese magic (but not adat), where men in a trance are somehow taken over by the bamboo that they are holding. *Arumbae* or gondola races between traditional carved boats with their sailors decked out in colourful costumes are fairly common on Ambon Bay.

History

Ambon had the misfortune to be located almost at the dead centre of the spice islands. As early as the 14th century, central Maluku found the rest of the world thrust upon it because of the demand for its spices.

The original trade intermediary between central Maluku and western Indonesia was the sultanate of Ternate, which brought Islam to central Maluku and also seems to have had some influence in reducing the incidence of head-hunting. Other colonisers settled along the coasts of these islands – like the Javanese who set up a base at Hitu on the north coast of Ambon. At this time, though Ambon grew no spices, it was an important way-station between Ternate and the nutmeg-producing Bandas.

The Ternateans were displaced on Ambon by the Portuguese; they stayed until 1605 when the Ambonese teamed up instead with the newly-arrived Dutch. When the Portuguese fort (in what is now Kota Ambon) was about to be attacked, the Portuguese appear simply to have surrendered and sailed away; the Dutch occupied the fort, renamed it Victoria and made Ambon their spice-island base.

While the Portuguese probably didn't have much effect on the political fortunes of the Maluku kingdoms, nor on the overall structure of trade, there was one man among them who initiated what would be a permanent change in eastern Indonesia. This was the Spaniard Francis Xavier (later canonised) who co-founded the Jesuit order. In 1546 and 1547 Xavier worked as a missionary in Ambon, Ternate and Morotai and laid the foundations for permanent missions there. After his departure from Maluku others continued his work and by the 1560s there were perhaps 10,000 Catholics in the area, mostly on Ambon. By the 1590s there were said to be 50,000 to 60,000, and these Christian communities survived through the succeeding centuries.

The Portuguese left other signs of their presence: the romantic *keroncong* ballads sung to the guitar are of Portuguese origin. A considerable number of Indonesian words are from Portuguese and many family names still found on Ambon are Portuguese. But overall, given the grandeur of their original designs to conquer the trade of Asia, the Portuguese legacy in Maluku was insignificant: though they had introduced Christianity into the region, it was the Dutch who nurtured it and made Ambon the centre of administration and missionary work for all Maluku.

The Dutch influence is still obvious today – notice the demure blouses that women wear with their pink and white-checked sarongs and the considerable numbers of Dutch and Dutch/Moluccan tourists; if you speak Dutch, you're sure to be invited into some local homes.

In WW II Kota Ambon was bombed and the island was attacked by the Japanese. Australian forces helped to defend Ambon but were defeated. Those who survived were interned in Japanese prisoner of war camps where many of them died of starvation and disease. Australians are liked on Ambon and the maintenance of the Australian War Cemetery in Kota Ambon is funded by the Australian government.

KOTA AMBON

The post-independence RMS rebellion having faded into history, Ambon today is a much more peaceful place. The only substantial urban area on the island is the city of Ambon (Kota Ambon), the capital of Maluku, built around a natural harbour where the Portuguese established Fort Victoria some 400 years ago. It was once, so the descriptions read, a charming coastal port with tree-lined shady promenades, but it was bombed heavily during WW II and battles were fought here during the RMS rebellion.

Today, although it's recovered from the devastation, the city is mostly a drab collection of concrete blocks crowded into a few square km between Ambon Bay and the Leitimur mountains but the setting is beautiful, particularly if viewed from the hills behind. Its port bustles with activity and the bay is full of boats of all kinds.

Kota Ambon may be noisy and smelly but it's not without its oddities. A church on Jalan Anthoni Rhebok exhibits one of those massive murals for which Ambon is memorable; a huge painting on the rear wall depicts the cross as a bridge for hordes of people to walk from earth to heaven.

Becaks add colour and quiet to certain parts of the city. Tuesdays and Fridays see white becaks in action, Mondays and Thursdays yellow, while red is the colour for Wednesdays and Saturdays. Becaks of all three colours operate on Sundays. Many of the pedallers are from Sulawesi and some have becaks of all three colour to get round the restrictions. You hea quite a lot of rock music in Ambon; th Ambonese are well known for their love of music.

Information & Orientation

On the south side of Ambon Bay, Kota Ambon is hemmed in by the hills to the south and stretches along the waterfron for several km. The main street for shops and offices is Jalan A Y Patty and many places to stay are two or three blocks back (south) from here. The bemo and bus terminal and main market – the latter especially busy and colourful early in the morning – are in a new complex on reclaimed coastal land about half a km east. Other markets spread out from the north end of Jalan Pala in the city centre. The main harbour is at the end of Jalan Yos Sudarso, a short walk from Jalan A Y Patty.

The airport is on the far side of Ambon Bay at Laha; a road via Passo connects Kota Ambon to the airport, but a vehicle ferry also crosses the bay between Galala and Rumah Tiga.

Tourist Office The tourist office is on the ground floor of the governor's office (Kantor Gubernor). It's open Monday to Thursday from 8 am to 2.30 pm, Friday from 8 am to 11.30 am and Saturday from 8 am to 1 pm. One of the guys speaks good English and is friendly and helpful. Reasonable maps of the island are sold here and you can rent snorkelling gear for 2500 rp per day.

Immigration You may be asked to register with either immigration or the police at the airport on arrival or departure. Should you need to visit the city immigration office (tel 42128), it's at Jalan Batu Capeo 57/5, way out in the south-west of Kota Ambon. Bemos from the bemo/bus terminal near the new main market will take you straight there.

Top: On the beach, Ai Island, Banda Islands, Maluku (JN)
Bottom: Waterfront, Bandaneira, Banda Islands, Maluku (JN)

Top: 'Just hanging around' Kalimantan (AS)
Bottom: River boat activity, Pontianak, Kalimantan (AS)

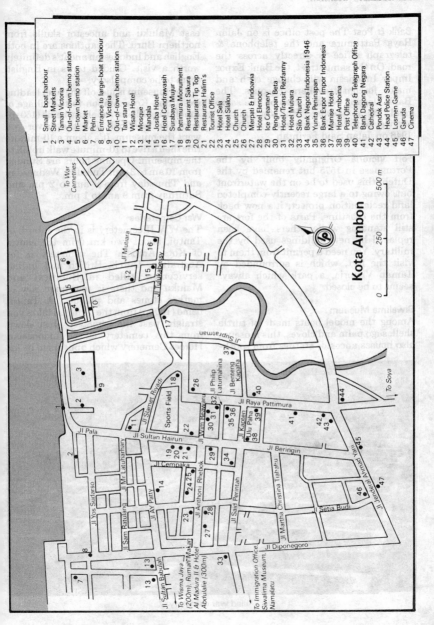

1 Small – boat harbour
2 Street Markets
3 Taman Victoria
4 Out-of-town bemo station
5 In-town bemo station
6 Market
7 Pelni
8 Entrance to large-boat harbour
9 Fort Victoria
10 Out-of-town bemo station
11 Taxi stand
12 Wisata Hotel
13 Mosque
14 Mandala
15 Josiba Hotel
16 Hotel Cendrawasih
17 Pattimura Monument
18 Surabaya Mujur
19 Restaurant Sakura
20 Restaurant Tip Top
21 Restaurant Halim's
22 Tourist Office
23 Hotel Sela
24 Hotel Silalou
25 Church
26 Church
27 Merpati & Indoavia
28 Hotel Elenoor
29 Ice Creamery
30 Penginapan Beta
31 Hotel/Transit Rezfanny
32 Hotel Mutiara
33 Silo Church
34 Bank Negora Indonesia 1946
35 Yunita Peninapan
36 Bank Expor Impor Indonesia
37 Manise Hotel
38 Hotel Amboina
39 Post Office
40 Telephone & Telegraph Office
41 Bank Dagong Negara
42 Cathedral
43 Pondok Asri
44 Head Police Station
45 Losmen Game
46 Garuda
47 Cinema

Kota Ambon

Bank & Post The post office is on Jalan Raya Pattimura and the telephone & telegraph office is directly across the road. On the same street, the Bank Expor Impor Indonesia will change cash and major foreign travellers' cheques. The Bank Dagang Negara, also on the same road, does likewise. But for quicker service, go to the Bank Negara Indonesia 1946 on Jalan Said Perintah.

Fort Victoria Originally built by the Portuguese in 1575 but renamed by the Dutch, this used to be on the waterfront but, owing to a large recently-completed land reclamation project, it's now back from the coastline. Parts of the fort are still standing while others have been replaced by new buildings used by the military. You need a permit from them to visit the fort, which is surrounded by Taman Victoria, a park which always seems to be closed.

Siwalima Museum

Among the model boats made of turtle shell, sago palm and cloves, this museum also houses ancestor statues from south-east Maluku and ancestor skulls from northern Buru. The captions are in both English and Indonesian and it's definitely worth a visit. Guided tours in English seem to be compulsory.

The museum is just off the road leading west from Kota Ambon to the village of Amahusu. Take an Amahusu bemo (150 rp) from the terminal. Tell the driver you want the museum. It's about a 10-minute ride then a five to 10-minute walk uphill to the museum. Opening hours are Sunday from 10 am to 3 pm; Tuesday, Wednesday and Thursday from 9 am to 2 pm and Saturday from 9 am to 1 pm.

War Cemeteries

The WW II cemetery is in the suburb of Tantui, about two km from the centre of Kota Ambon. The cemetery is for Australian, Dutch, British and Indian servicemen killed in Sulawesi and Maluku and there is row upon row of marker stones and plaques. A Tantui bemo (100 rp) from the terminal takes you straight past the cemetery. Just down from this cemetery is the Indonesian Heroes Cemetery which appears to be for

Allied war cemetery

Indonesian servicemen killed fighting the Maluku rebels during the 1950s and 1960s.

Other Attractions The Pattimura Monument stands at one end of the sports field. Pattimura is said to have been betrayed by one of the village chiefs on Saparua who took him prisoner and delivered him to the Dutch on Ambon. The monument stands on the site where he and his followers were hanged.

On a hill overlooking Kota Ambon is the memorial to another revered Maluku freedom fighter, the Martha Christina Tiahahu Memorial. Tiahahu's father supported Pattimura against the Dutch and the story goes that after they were both captured, her father was executed on Nusa Laut Island and she was put onto a ship to be sent to Java; grieved by her father's execution she starved herself to death and her remains were buried at sea.

Nearby is the Karang Panjang tourist village where you may see 'traditional' ceremonies and watch sago being processed. The village is surrounded by gardens of varieties of coconut trees, orchids, bamboo species and fruit trees. To get there, catch a Karang Panjang bemo (125 rp) from the bemo/bus terminal.

Places to Stay – bottom end
Accommodation in Kota Ambon is expensive. If you get a single room for 8000 rp you're doing well.

The best-value rooms are upstairs at the *Penginapan Beta* (tel 3463), Jalan Wim Reawaru 114, in the quieter, more leafy part of town. This place has verandahs, a hint of tropical foliage and some possibility of a cool breeze. Rooms with mandi and fan start at 13,000 rp a double on the ground floor and get slightly cheaper as you go upstairs. Singles/doubles on the uppermost of the three floors are 8000/11,000 rp. There are also some enclosed ground-floor rooms with shared mandis at 9000/13,000 a rp double/triple. Prices don't include a 10% tax. The

Beta is often full so it's a good idea to book if you can.

Next door at Jalan Wim Reawaru 115, the *Hotel/Transit Rezfanny* (tel 41692) has singles/doubles with shared mandi at 8,000/10,000 rp plus more expensive rooms. It's clean but nothing special.

Nearby, the *Hotel Silalou* (tel 3197) at Jalan Sedap Malam 4 is clean and has friendly staff. Singles/doubles at 7000/15,000 rp include breakfast. The rooms are small and a little dark, but adequate. Around the corner on Jalan Anthony Rhebok, the *Hotel Sela* (tel 2422) is a clean, decent place with rooms for 9000/17,000 rp.

Other 'cheapies' are in the western, more-Muslim section of town beyond the mosques on Jalan Sultan Babulah. The *Wisma Jaya* at 13 is actually on a quiet gang just off Jalan Sultan Babulah, about 200 metres beyond the mosques. Its cheaper upstairs rooms cost 8800/13,750 rp and are clean and light.

Close by, on Jalan Sultan Babulah, the *Hotel Abdulaile* (tel 42422) has rooms at 7200/11,000 rp in its dingy, old section. Across the road on the top floor of its bigger, flashier part, brighter rooms with fan and mandi are 8200/14,000 rp. These rooms have a sea view, a rarity for Kota Ambon, but they're quite a climb up.

Places to Stay – top end
The *Hotel Elenoor* (tel 2834) at Jalan Anthony Rhebok 30 has singles/doubles from 11,000 to 17,000 rp including breakfast. It's a nice place with friendly people, but it's really quite over-priced even by Ambon's standards.

On the corner of Jalan Kapten Ulu Paha and Jalan Sultan Hairun, the *Hotel Amboina* (tel 41961) has several storeys of comfortable air-con rooms from 20,400 to 27,600 rp. Rooms here are typical of the top end in Ambon – clean, large, good on the frills, but with no view and no outdoor sitting area. Prices in this range usually don't include a hefty 20% tax.

The *Hotel Mutiara* (tel 3075, 3076) at

Jalan Raya Pattimura 90 has comfortable rooms from 30,000 rp double. Close by, at Jalan Supratman 1, the *Manise Hotel* (tel 42905, 41445) is Ambon's newest and ritziest, starting at 35,000/40,000 rp.

There's a group of expensive hotels along, or just off, Jalan Tulukabessy. The *Josiba Hotel* (tel 41280) at No 19 has singles/doubles from 15,000 to 25,000 rp. The *Wisata Hotel* (tel 3599) at Jalan Halong Mardika 3/15, tucked in behind Jalan Mutiara, has singles/doubles from 27,500 to 35,000 rp – here the 20% tax is included. The friendly *Hotel Cendrawasih* (tel 2487), on Jalan Tulukabessy, has rooms from 18,000 to 25,000 rp.

Places to Eat

Theoretically, Ambon has its own distinctive cuisine based on the staple Maluku diet of sago, along with cassava, sweet potatoes and other root dishes. *Colo colo* is a type of sweet and sour sauce which is used on baked fish, *kohu kohu* is fish salad and *laor* is a sea-worm which is harvested at full moon at end of March. There are also supposed to be several types of bananas available in Ambon which grow only in Maluku. Salaks grown in the mountain village of Soya are also supposed to have a very distinctive flavour.

In practice, if you want to try any of these you'd better head for the villages because the 'local' cuisine is hard to find in the city. Restaurants tend to be expensive and serve Indonesian and Chinese food.

Among the better places is *Halim's*, one of three Chinese places with outdoor tables on Jalan Sultan Hairun. You pay more than 4000 rp for most dishes but the quality is good. Next door *Tip Top Restaurant* has cheaper food with mains around 2500 rp. On the wall inside there's a menu with even cheaper dishes.

Most of the big hotels have restaurants. The excellent Hotel Mutiara restaurant is similarly priced to Halim's. They do a continental breakfast for 3500 rp – tea/ coffee, fruit platter, eggs and toast – and even offer porridge and fruit juices. The gado-gado and homemade sambal are excellent.

There are several reasonable mid-range but less tourist-oriented places such as the *Pondok Asri* on Jalan A Yani, the *Ice-Creamery* (which is also a restaurant) on Jalan Sultan Hairun, the *Surabaya Mujur* at Jalan Tulukabessy 3 and the *Rumah Makan Al Madura II* right by the Hotel Abdulalie on Jalan Sultan Babulah.

Other less spick and span places are dotted along Jalan Pala and Jalan Mr Latuharhary. There are some cheap rumah makan around the bus station and evening food stalls crop up all over the place, particularly along the waterfront. Off the end of Jalan Pala beside the food market, there are some sit-down warungs.

Things To Buy

Model sailing ships made entirely out of cloves can be bought in Kota Ambon. Try the shops along Jalan A Y Patty. Also take a look at the 'flower arrangements' made out of mother of pearl. Turtles are exploited to make turtle-shell fans and kitsch turtle-shell ashtrays and lamp-shades. Also look around for handwoven clothes from south-eastern Maluku. Ambon is a supplier of good eucalyptus oil and there are some interesting animist carvings from South Maluku, available at the hotel shops and from hawkers. You'll see Ambonese women carrying loads in chocolate-brown coloured baskets. These are finely woven and worth buying if you're into baskets. Try the villages or just make an offer when you spot one in use.

Getting There & Away

Kota Ambon is the gateway to Maluku, connected by air and sea to western and eastern Indonesia and the other islands of Maluku.

Air Like Ujung Pandang, Ambon is a crossroads between western and eastern Indonesia. Garuda flies to and from

Sorong, Biak, Timika and Jayapura most days, and has daily flights to and from Ujung Pandang and via Ujung Pandang to Denpasar, Jakarta and elsewhere. The Garuda office (tel 2481) is on Jalan Jenderal Ahmad Yani.

Merpati has a couple of flights a week each way between Jayapura or Biak and Jakarta, stopping at Ambon, Ujung Pandang and Surabaya. Along with its subsidiary Indoavia, Merpati runs the main network of flights around Maluku. Main routes include Merpati to and from Ternate and Manado daily (this service is rather unreliable), Indoavia to and from Langgur (Kai Islands) daily, and to and from Banda twice weekly. Merpati (tel 3480) is at Jalan Anthony Rhebok 28, Indoavia is next door. Office hours are Monday to Saturday from 9am to 3 pm and Sunday from 10 am to 2 pm.

Mandala, with its office (tel 2444) on Jalan A Y Patty, flies to and from Jakarta, Surabaya and Ujung Pandang most days. Merpati and Mandala flights are cheaper than Garuda's.

Boat The Pelni office (tel 3161, 2049) is in the main harbour complex entered from the west end of Jalan Yos Sudarso. Pelni's passenger liner *Rinjani* calls here every second Sunday en route for Sorong and the following Tuesday en route to Baubau on Buton Island off south-east Sulawesi, Ujung Pandang, Surabaya and Jakarta. It follows the same route in reverse to reach Ambon. See the table for fares from Ambon.

Other distinctly less comfortable Pelni ships, some taking cargo as well as passengers on deck (you may be able to rent a small cabin from a crew member), circle various parts of Maluku with irregular schedules from Kota Ambon. The people in the Pelni office are helpful

and there's usually someone who speaks reasonable English. See the relevant island sections for more info. From the same main harbour, other boats also leave for places like Sorong, Bali, Banjarmasin, even Port Moresby or Japan.

Smaller boats to destinations around Maluku leave from a second harbour near the end of Jalan Pala. Common destinations include the north coast of Seram, Buru, Bacan and Obi. A board at the harbour entrance shows what's going where and when. There are fewer small boats in the monsoon (roughly from June to September for much of Maluku). Boats to the south coast of Seram leave from the east coast of Ambon; see the Seram section for details.

Getting Around

Kota Ambon's bus and bemo terminal spreads over a square and two or three streets near the new market at the east end of the city waterfront.

Airport Transport Ambon airport is 48 km out of the city. There is a taxi counter at the airport; a taxi to the city is 12,500 rp or a public bemo, 750 rp per person. Beware of rip-offs – drivers may ask for much more. If you take a public bemo from the bus/bemo terminal to the airport allow lots of time: it's normally about an hour's drive but allow for the usual Indonesian procrastinations. Alternatively charter a bemo or hire a taxi. There's a taxi stand on the corner of Jalan Pala and Jalan Slamet Riyadi, and you can charter vehicles from the terminal, but you're less likely to be ripped off if you get your losmen or hotel to organise it. You can also reach the airport on the Mandala bus (usually once daily, at variable times) for 3500 rp if it coincides with your flight. The bus leaves from the Mandala office on Jalan A Y Patty. The

Rinjani fares	1st class	3rd class	Ekonomi
Sorong (17 hrs)	44,600 rp	26,500 rp	17,400 rp
Ujung Pandang (38 hrs)	81,500 rp	45,500 rp	26,400 rp
Surabaya (64 hrs)	129,900 rp	72,800 rp	42,600 rp

airport restaurant is expensive – 2500 rp for a very average nasi goreng.

Around Town Getting around town is fairly easy. Walking will do for the compact central area; it's about a 10-minute walk from the Penginapan Beta to the terminal. Otherwise there are becaks: try your luck but you usually don't get away with paying less than 300 rp.

For places at the edge of the town, like the Museum Siwalima or the war cemeteries, you need the city bemos. Catch these either on the street or from the terminal (easier). If you try to catch one on the street, you may find yourself waiting around in the sun for ages as vehicles don't usually leave the terminal until they're full.

For travel further afield around the island, bemos and buses depart from the terminal. There are frequent departures for Soya (250 rp), Latuhalat (375 rp), Natsepa (400 rp), Waai (600 rp) and Liang (from 800 to 900 rp). There's a taxi stand at the corner of Jalan Pala and Jalan Slamet Riyadi.

A vehicle and passenger ferry crosses Ambon Bay at Galala village, cutting short the circuitous road route. Bemos and taxis sometimes use it as a short cut to the airport. The fare is 125 rp per person and 800 rp for bemos and cars. The ferry runs every day.

Much of Ambon Island is hilly and inaccessible except on foot so there are plenty of opportunities for hiking. As yet, there's nowhere organised to rent motorbikes or bicycles.

AROUND AMBON
Leitimur Peninsula Villages
Paths connect the villages in the hills on the Leitimur peninsula to each other or to Kota Ambon. Try walking from the city to Soya on Mt Sirimau or catch a bemo from the terminal, a 20 minute (250 rp) ride in clapped-out vehicles. The bemos drop you at Soya Atas and then it's a one-km walk up to Mt Sirimau – the last section is quite

steep. There are great views from the top over Kota Ambon in one direction, over Passo and the east coast in another. On the way up there are also good views down to the south coast. The villages of Hatalai, Ema and Naku on the southern slopes of the mountain may also be worth investigating

Coast & Beaches
Latuhalat & Namalatu These south coast beaches have good scuba diving and snorkelling on the coral reefs offshore. To get there take a bemo from the Kota Ambon terminal (about 45 minutes, 375 rp) Namalatu has a lovely beach and there are secluded coves between it and Latuhalat Even on a Sunday, the busiest day Namalatu is relaxed and pleasant. There are a few rooms available for 10,000 rp in the old governor's house – extensions are planned. Ask for directions. The beachside warung at Namalatu is only open during the day.

Natsepa This beach, on the east coast 14 km from Kota Ambon, is littered with concrete tables and cigarette advertising but it's OK for a swim – avoid Sundays when it gets really crowded. Take a bemo from the terminal; it takes about 45 minutes and costs 400 rp. On weekends there's an entrance fee of about 200 rp to the beach. There are a few basic rooms where you can stay almost on the beach, right next door to the cafe. Rooms with mandi cost from 10,000 to 15,000 rp. There's no food available at night, but during the day there are plenty of snack stalls, some selling *rujak*, an Ambonese favourite consisting of sliced fruit, chilli, palm sugar and peanut sauce – delicious and cheap at 400 rp.

Waai North of Natsepa, 31 km from Kota Ambon, this beach has an underwater cave beneath a mountain spring which is the home of sacred eels and sacred carp. The villagers flick the water surface to draw the creatures from their underground cave, enticing them with eggs. There are also some good murals in the church at Waai.

Toisapau This small beach, 18 km from Kota Ambon, is on the opposite side of Baguala Bay from Natsepa and within reach of outriggers and motorboats from the village of Passo.

Halong On the south side of Ambon Bay, this is the finishing point for the annual Darwin-Ambon yacht race, which takes about five days, each July. The usual prostitute population is moved out of Halong for three weeks when the yachts arrive. Kota Ambon is now Darwin's twin city.

Hila

This village on the north coast 42 km from Kota Ambon is the site of a fortress that was originally Portuguese and an old Christian church. Bemos from the city terminal cost 1000 rp and take from 1½ to two hours.

The fortress was built right on the coast to guard the straits between Ambon and Seram, which are at their narrowest here. It was originally built of wooden palisades by the Portuguese at the end of the 16th century, and was later rebuilt by the Dutch and renamed Fort Amsterdam. The main tower and fragments of the wall remain (the cannons have gone) and the interior of the tower has been taken over by enormous tree roots which have wrapped themselves all over the walls from top to bottom. There are more forts west along the coast from here.

The church is just a few minutes walk from the fort, built in 1780 it is the oldest in Ambon, though it has virtually been rebuilt over the years from the stumps up. There's a Dutch-inscribed plaque on the outside wall. Although it is not the oldest church in Maluku, it is the oldest that is still standing and in use.

Wapauwe is an old mosque near Hila – the original mosque dated back to the early 15th century and, according to folktales, is said to have been dragged down from the hills. It's still an active place of worship.

Hila has a twin village called Kaitetu.

Liang

There's a very Muslim village on the coast here, 32 km from Kota Ambon. The round trip by bemo costs 2000 rp. If you're adventurous you can walk west along the coast, or into the hills where there's some primary rainforest with many butterfly and orchid species. Wear adequate footwear as there are snakes and lizards. The last bemo returns to the city at 4 pm; if you get stuck, walk south and pick up a bemo at the turnoff to Hunimua – one of the departure points for ferries to Seram.

Pulau Pombo

The coral around this tiny, attractive island off north-east Ambon is nowhere near as good as the coral gardens off Manado in northern Sulawesi but it could make for a pleasant few hours. Take care, the water over the reef is very shallow.

To get there take a bemo from the Kota Ambon terminal to the village of Tulehu (one hour, 600 rp). The bemo will drop you at the wharf from where you can hire a speedboat to Pulau Pombo. The ride takes 20 minutes and is expensive at 40,000 rp for the round trip. There's a small beach on Pulau Pombo, sheltered by the reef. You could have the boat drop you off in the morning and pick you up in the afternoon or the next day. There's a small derelict shelter on the island, but but bring your own food and water. You might also be able to get a boat from Waai to take you out to the island. If you're offered a local fishing boat check it out carefully – one traveller almost drowned en route to Pombo because his guide had forgotten to bring a bailer, the need for which only became apparent some distance from the shore.

THE LEASE ISLANDS

Formerly the Uliassers, this small group

east of Ambon consists of Haruku, Saparua, Nusa Laut and Molana, Saparua being the largest and most populated. Saparua is very hilly and is a centre of nutmeg and clove production. Its main claim to fame is that it was the source of the revolt against the Dutch led by Pattimura who was later betrayed, handed over to the Dutch and hanged in Ambon. Visitors to Saparua can view Pattimura's battledress at Haria.

Saparua is also the name of the island's main town midway along the south coast. It has a large twice-weekly market. Nearby is the well-restored Fort Duurstede which Pattimura captured shortly before his betrayal; there are more forts in much poorer condition on other parts of the coast.

The island has good beaches and coral – try Waisisil Beach. At Mahui, there's an expensive hotel geared to people on diving holidays. It costs 35,000 rp per person with meals. Distinctive local pottery can be seen in the village of Ouw, east of Saparua town. The pretty village of Bool on the coast west of Saparua specialises in bricklayers. As on the other Lease Islands, there are hot springs on Saparua. The few roads inland are poor.

Boats to Saparua (1250 rp) depart daily from Tulehu on the east coast of Ambon and dock at Porto from where you can take a bemo into Saparua town and on to Ouw. The boats often stop at Haruku en route to Saparua and may continue to south Seram. Bigger boats from Hurnala, just north of Tulehu, stop off at Saparua en route to southern Seram. There's a ferry to Amahai on Seram from a village near Mahui.

Seram

Maluku's second largest island (17,151 sq km), Seram is wild, mountainous, heavily forested and well watered. The Malukans call it *Nusa Ina* or mother island as it's believed that this is where the ancestors of central Maluku came from. Most of the island is untouched due to its rugged terrain, but logging has now begun with a vengeance and Seram's famed birdlife is being smuggled out in huge numbers. There's also a large oil centre at Bulu on the north-east coast.

Much of the centre has difficult access and is home to the indigenous Alfuro peoples, some of whom have only relatively recently given up head-hunting. One tribe, the Bati of the southern mountains, can fly, so the story goes. They number 2000 and are supposed to have piercing eyes with the power to dominate and whisk a victim into the skies. Apparently, such is their power, the victim is quite happy to accompany them. Their flying is seasonal, but there's always one active group. Most Ambonese and Seramese believe in the powers of the Bati. The south and west coasts are populated by Malays and there are transmigrants from Java and Sulawesi. Both the Dutch and Indonesian governments resettled numbers of the native people on the coast.

A large chunk of the island's centre is marked off as Manusela National Park and supposedly protected, but the park management has to contend with locals who want to use the area for purposes other than conservation. The park comprises a wide lowland plain in the north, a central enclave with the small villages of Manusela, Solumena and Kanikeh in an isolated inner valley at about 700 metres and a giant mountain range in the south. Mt Manusela, at 3000 metres, on the park's eastern border is Seram's highest. There are some beautiful white, sandy beaches and excellent coral off the north coast. The island receives very few visitors and a trek through its interior or a shorter walk along parts of the north or south coasts is a real 'off-the-beaten track' experience. You may need a permit from the PHPA before trekking in Seram. There are PHPA offices at Air Besar near Wahai on Seram and on

Ambon at Balai KSPA VIII, Jalan Laksdya Leo Wattimena, Passo.

Seram is a birdwatcher's paradise, though other wildlife is restricted to cuscus and bandicoots plus introduced deer and pigs. Butterfly species are particularly bright in colour. The birdlife includes lories, parrots, cockatoos, kingfishers, pigeons, cassowaries, hornbills, friar birds and other honeyeaters, megapodes and white eyes.

Seram receives a lot of rain throughout the year but while the centre is always wet, the north has a wetter season from around October to March, and the south from March to October. Boat schedules become erratic during the rough monsoon seas.

History

Before the 15th century Seram had commercial links with the Javanese Hindu kingdoms. In 1480, Ternatean influence and Islam reached Seram and the matrilineal system of succession was replaced by the patrilineal. Portuguese missionaries arrived in the 16th century and then, in the early 17th century, the Dutch established four coastal trading posts. The Dutch controlled Seram, though they didn't bother with the wild interior, from about 1650 until it was occupied by the Japanese in 1942 and used as an air base.

Today Seram is becoming Indonesianised, with oil and timber both being exploited. Copra, rice, spices and a few other crops are grown for export. During the clove season, from October to January on the south coast, it seems the whole population is busy collecting, drying and shipping the spice. The indigenous peoples of the interior still do some hunting and gather forest products such as wild sago.

South Coast

The south coast is heavily populated by Maluku standards. Masohi is the main centre and accommodation is available but expensive. Try the *Wisma Lestari* with good rooms at 15,000 rp per person including meals. There are also the *Penginapan Maharani* and the *Penginapan Ole-Sioh*. Amahai is a smaller place between Masohi and the kampung of Soahuku where the ferry arrives from Tulehu on Ambon. It has one losmen, a few houses, a school and a post office. Bemos from the harbour to Masohi cost 200 rp, 2000 rp if you charter.

Bemos and minibuses run short distances east and west from Masohi and are useful for getting you part of the way to indigenous villages or maybe the beaches. Janeero and Bonara are 'traditional' villages of the Nuaulu people in the Masohi area, but on the surface they're nothing special.

Bemos heading east terminate at Tamilu, 36 km from Amahai's port. To get to Piliani, the slightly inland southern entry point to Manusela National Park, or to villages on the coast beyond Tamilu, you have to walk or catch a boat – motorboats go from Amahai to Tehoru and on to Saunulu and Hatemete at least three times a week. Some start their journeys at Tulehu on Ambon. You could arrange for local boats to take you where you want.

The ferry from Hunimua on Ambon docks at Waipirit, the port for Kairatu, a sizeable town towards the west end of the south coast, but there don't appear to be any roads between Kairatu and Masohi.

Manusela National Park

Walking across Seram to or from Wahai on the north coast through the park is tough going, but is the highlight of a trip to the island – it's less visited than the Balim Valley in Irian Jaya. There are no facilities at all in the park and villagers have little spare food so you must be self-sufficient. It's recommended that you take a guide (for maybe 5000 rp per day, plus food). Good maps of the park are difficult to find but some can be obtained from the

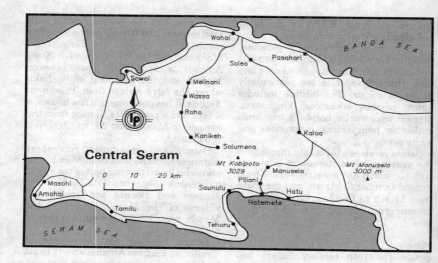

Central Seram

Botanical Gardens Office at Bogor in Java. Keep asking directions as you go.

From the south coast you can walk into the park from Hatu or from Saunulu via Piliani; it's about 1½ hours' walk from Saunulu. This locally-named 'route of sorrow' rises to 2500 metres en route to Manusela village in the inner valley, one to three days' walk away – depending how fit you are. From Manusela it's another three or four days to Wahai. The villages in the interior are virtually untouched apart from churches and schools. Check in with the head of the village, the 'bapak raja', who usually has room for guests – what you pay is up to you.

Wahai is the starting point into the park from the north. The PHPA park office is an half-hour walk along the road east of Wahai, past Air Besar, near the schools. There are three routes of varying difficulty into Manusela. One is via Solea village, 15 km from Wahai – take the path near the park office. From there you walk upriver and over Mt Kobipoto (1500 metres) via Solumena in the inner valley and out via Manusela to the south coast. Reaching Solumena takes from three days

to a week. Or walk south-west from Wahai through Melinani, Wassa and Roho to Kanikeh in the inner valley, and out via Manusela to the south coast – this is another hard route taking from three to six days as far as Kanikeh. Easiest is to take a truck east from Wahai to Pasahari then a logging truck south to Kaloa from where it's a one-day walk to Manusela.

North Coast

Wahai With a population of 1500, this is the main town on the north coast. Roads extend short distances east to Kalisonta and west to Rumah Sokat – catch trucks. You can stay in rooms at Mr Tan Tok Hong's shop on Jalan Sinar Indok, where doubles cost 10,000 rp including an excellent seafood dinner. Pak Leo's place, next to the post office and opposite a church, is 7500 rp, including food.

Sawai West of Wahai, this is a friendly Muslim village with a small offshore island also called Sawai. You can paddle out there or hire a motorised dugout for around 2000 rp per person one way. Locals use the island for making coconut oil and fishing and have built small houses, which you can rent for about 1500 rp per person per day. There is no fresh water on the island.

There's stunning snorkelling off the north coast and amazing beaches – try Asele, one hour east of Wahai!

Getting There & Away

Air Theoretically Indoavia flies from Ambon to Amahai once a week, but the flights have a knack of being cancelled.

Boat

The main boats serving Seram's north coast leave from Kota Ambon – check both the small and large boat harbours there. Boats include the *Wahai Star*, the *Tiga Berlian* and the *Taman Pelita*. Boats stop in at small villages on the way go ashore by dugout – and usually at Sawai, Wahai and then go on to Bula, the eastern oilfield, but not always. Expect to pay around 15,000 rp from Ambon to Wahai – it's about a 30-hour trip.

Boats to Amahai on the south coast go from Tulehu and Hurnala on Ambon, usually via Saparua. Some continue to Tehoru, Saunulu and Hatemete. To Amahai takes about four hours and costs 3600 rp and to Tehoru is about eight hours for 6500 rp. From Hunimua on Ambon, a ferry goes three times daily to Waipirit, the port of Kairatu (1125 rp).

The Banda Islands

To the south-east of Ambon lies the tiny cluster of islands known as the Bandas. The group consists of about a dozen small islands of which the seven main ones are Neira, Gunung Api, Banda Besar (Lonthor), Hatta (Rozengain), Sjahrir (Pisang), Ai and Run. Bandaneira on the island of Neira is the chief township.

One of the most beautiful clusters of islands in Indonesia, the Bandas are littered with deserted forts and deteriorating Dutch villas. The locals are friendly; there's a single cinema and only a handful of motor vehicles. Superb deserted beaches and excellent snorkelling and diving around the numerous coral reefs (the best coral's off the islands of Karaka, Sjahrir and Ai) are major pluses. It's a long way to go, but well worth it; no tourist bungalows line the beaches, there's virtually no pollution and no touts hassle you to buy anything! The atmosphere is possibly the most laid-back and relaxed in all of Indonesia, and certainly in Maluku.

For centuries the Bandas were the centre for the production of nutmeg and mace, and from the 16th century onwards the Portuguese, Dutch and the English all vied for their control. Today with the centre of production moved to other parts of the world, the Bandas have fallen into obscurity, though they're slowly being rediscovered by a steady trickle of tourists.

History

By the time Europeans arrived the native Bandanese had adopted Islam and lived in little coastal communities, virtually village republics. Each one was presided over by its *orang kaya* – a term which signified leading citizens, chiefs or village elders.

The ordinary people earned their livelihood by gathering the ripe fruit of the nutmeg tree and processing it into commercial nutmeg (from the seed of the fruit) and mace (the fibre around the seed). These spices were sold on the spot to resident or visiting Malay, Chinese and Arab traders who traded them on through Asia to Europe. The value of the goods doubled every time they changed hands.

Portuguese ships landed in Banda in 1512 and stayed for a month. Meanwhile, the rival sultans of Ternate and Tidore heard of the impressive Portuguese firepower and sent emissaries to encourage them to travel north and join an alliance. Ternate won the race, and thus by chance it was Ternate (the centre of clove

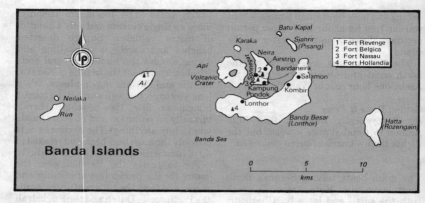

Banda Islands

1	Fort Revenge
2	Fort Belgica
3	Fort Nassau
4	Fort Hollandia

production), and not Banda, which became the first foothold of the Portuguese in Maluku.

For almost 90 years the Portuguese had Maluku to themselves until a Dutch fleet sailed in in 1599, with orders to seek out spices at their source and circumvent the Portuguese monopoly. Part of the fleet sailed to Banda, loaded a cargo of spices, alarmed the Portuguese and sailed back to Holland. Soon afterwards the Dutch forced the Portuguese out of the spice trade but they still had other rivals: in 1601 the English East India Company had set up a fort on Run Island in the Bandas and in 1606 the Spanish got into the act by taking Ternate and Tidore.

From 1605 to 1616, the history of the Bandas is largely one of the successive arrivals of intimidating Dutch fleets, while the English interlopers appear to have had better relations with the Bandanese, helping them to fight off Dutch attacks and frustrating the Dutch desire for a spice trade monopoly.

The turning point came in 1619. Jan Pieterszoon Coen, the new VOC governor-general, envisaged a Dutch commercial empire in the east the would-be grandeur of which would match the extent of his violent ruthlessness. Coen intended to control all trade in the region from India to Japan, his first step was to shift the centre of Dutch activity to Batavia in Java. Next he seized control of the Bandas, got rid of the unhelpful Bandanese and started producing nutmeg using imported slaves and labourers, with Dutch overseers.

In early 1621, Coen sailed from Batavia to Banda with 13 large ships, about 1900 soldiers, 100 Japanese mercenaries and 300 Javanese convicts to serve as rowers and porters. He attacked Lonthor Island, the most important of the group, and almost totally wiped out the native Bandanese population. Coen now returned to Batavia and announced that the VOC would accept applications for land grants in Banda if the applicants would settle permanently in the islands and produce spices exclusively for the company, at fixed prices. The company would import rice and other necessities, provide slaves to work on the plantations and defend the islands against attack.

Relations between the VOC and the licensed planters known as the *perkenier* were often bitter, but by the late 1620s the islands were beginning to produce nutmeg and mace in quantities which soon exceeded those of earlier years. The surviving Bandanese – mostly enslaved – were obediently teaching their skills to imported slaves from a variety of regions. The mixed origins of the people on these tiny islands are still apparent.

The perkeniers and regional traders certainly smuggled out a good deal of the spices but Coen had established something close to the long-sought monopoly of the spice trade. It was not until the Napoleonic Wars, almost 200 years later, that this was finally broken. The Bandas, like other Dutch-held parts of the archipelago, were occupied by the English during the Napoleonic Wars and nutmeg seedlings were shipped off to Sri Lanka, Bengkulu in Sumatra and Penang in Malaysia. By 1860, these areas were almost as important as Banda for producing nutmeg and mace. The invention of refrigeration, however, which allowed meat to be kept without the heavy use of spices, spelt the end of the spice trade.

After the return of Dutch rule to Maluku in the 1820s, their monopolistic slave-based policies were gradually altered but the perkeniers prospered – while they spent most of their time in debt, they also spent most of their money on extravagant houses and lifestyles in Bandaneira.

The islands' economy, so precariously dependent on a single product, declined with the loss of the Dutch spice monopoly and as spices started to be grown in other parts of Indonesia. Today the centres of Indonesian nutmeg production are in Sulawesi and Java. Grenada in the Carribean is the major international centre. The Bandas still produce nutmeg and mace for use in Indonesia, but for the most part the islands have been forgotten by the rest of the world.

Books

While you're in Bandaneira, buy a copy of Willard Hanna's *Indonesian Banda* – it's sold at the Bandaneira museum (15,000 rp). It takes you cannon shot by cannon shot through the history of the islands, from the time the first European ships sailed in until the late 1970s.

BANDANEIRA

Bandaneira on Neira Island is the only town in the Bandas. In its heyday, it was a town of spacious mansions built and rebuilt over the centuries, with floors of polished marble or brightly coloured tiles, and elegant European-style furnishings. The perkeniers spent huge sums of money on their Neira mansions, converting the town into a showpiece enclave of the Netherlands East Indies. When the naturalist Henry Forbes visited Bandaneira in 1881, he was 'charmed with its clean aspect, its green parks with gravelled walks, and pretty dwellings'.

It was a self-indulgent life for the perkeniers, though not a carefree one. Over the centuries, the islands were visited by a series of misfortunes. After the Dutch left, when the marble cracked and the tiles broke, there was no way of repairing them. Today many of the old villas of Bandaneira are steadily crumbling into rubble. Attempts are now being made to preserve what is left (an impressive

Looking down from hills above Bandaneira

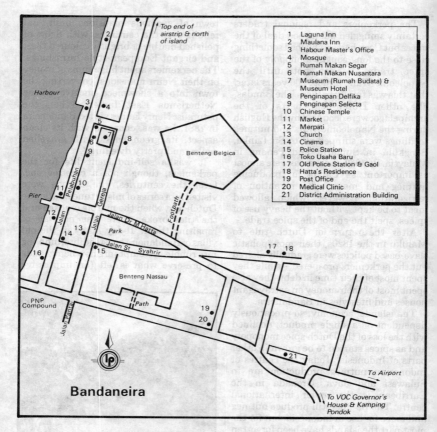

Top end of
airstrip & north
of island

Harbour

Benteng Belgica

Footpath

Benteng Nassau

Pier

PNP
Compound

Path

Jalan Pantai

Jalan St Syahrir

Jalan Dr M Hatta
Park

Jalan Pelabuhan

Jalan Gereja

To Airport

To VOC Governor's
House & Kamping
Pondok

Bandaneira

1	Laguna Inn
2	Maulana Inn
3	Habour Master's Office
4	Mosque
5	Rumah Makan Segar
6	Rumah Makan Nusantara
7	Museum (Rumah Budata) & Museum Hotel
8	Penginapan Delfika
9	Penginapan Selecta
10	Chinese Temple
11	Market
12	Merpati
13	Church
14	Cinema
15	Police Station
16	Toko Usaha Baru
17	Old Police Station & Gaol
18	Hatta's Residence
19	Post Office
20	Medical Clinic
21	District Administration Building

amount) and much of that attempt revolves around the encouragement of the tourist industry.

This is a place for scrambling around old forts, walking in the hills, climbing the volcano or daytripping to other islands' unspoilt beaches and coral reefs. At the north end of Neira itself, Malole is a small beach on the east side. There's coral about 50 metres offshore. Though there are better places to swim and snorkel on other islands, Malole is a pleasant hour's stroll from Bandaneira along a shady path.

Bandaneira has no bank so bring plenty

of cash with you. If you're staying at the *Laguna*, *Maulana* or *Museum* hotels, you can change cash and travellers' cheques.

Museum

Notable buildings in Bandaneira include the Museum (Rumah Budaya). It's an old Dutch villa which also doubles as a hotel and houses a small collection of cannon, muskets, helmets, old coins, maps, china and paintings – including one depicting the massacre of Bandanese by the Dutch in 1621.

Next door to the museum is a restored

house claiming to be the *Rumah Pengasingan* (Exile House) of Sutan Sjahrir, the Indonesian independence hero. It has a few Sjahrir memorabilia – mainly photos – but it *wasn't* where he lodged during his exile to Banda by the Dutch in the 1930s.

Dutch Church

The fine Dutch Church on Jalan Gereja dates from 1852 when it replaced an earlier stone building which was destroyed by an earthquake. There's a whole crowd of people buried beneath the floor. The church's clock no longer works; its hands are stuck where they were at the moment of the Japanese invasion of 1942.

Fort Nassau

On low ground in front of the massive Fort Belgica, the original stone foundations of Fort Nassau were built by the Portuguese around 1529 when they sent troops from their base in Ternate to make a show of force in Banda. The fort, however, wasn't completed and the foundations were abandoned. In 1608 a powerful Dutch fleet under Admiral Pieterszoon Verhoeven arrived with orders to annex the Bandas. When negotiations stalled Verhoeven simply confronted the Bandanese with a *fait accompli* by landing soldiers on Neira Island and constructing a fort on the old Portuguese foundations.

Fort Nassau was restored for use as a warehouse in the early 19th century but eventually lapsed into ruins. Both it and Fort Belgica were restored superficially in the early 20th century by colonial officials more conscious of their picturesque aspects than their military history. Today the area around the fort is much overgrown – only three walls and a gateway remain and an old cannon lies on the ground.

Fort Belgica

The construction of this fort began in 1611 under the direction of Pieter Both who had been appointed governor-general of the region with the assignment of creating a monopoly, and kicking out the English. Both sailed to Maluku with 11 ships and 500 soldiers and after pausing at Ambon continued to Banda. With the prospect of a Banda-English alliance, his men erected the imposing Fort Belgica on the ridge overlooking Fort Nassau. Belgica was maintained as a military headquarters until around 1860.

Fort Belgica is pentagonal with towers at each corner, rather forlorn looking cannons which point out to sea from the battlements, and walls which are disfigured by graffiti. It has been cleaned up a little over recent years. With Gunung Api towering in the distance, the fort's setting is quite beautiful.

Hatta & Sjahrir's Residence

In the later 1930s the Bandas achieved a dim sort of reflected glory as the place of exile for two of Indonesia's top young nationalist leaders, whose political passions the Dutch hoped would be calmed by the serenity of the islands. Mohammed Hatta and Sutan Sjahrir were moved here from Boven Digul, an infamous detention camp in New Guinea. They took up residence in the very spacious house – now restored – next to the prison.

Hatta was a Sumatran, born in 1902. After independence he became vice-president but resigned in 1956 because of conflicts with Sukarno. He continued to be respected, but for a decade after 1956 took no active part in government. An economist educated in Holland, he was attracted to slow and careful national development, based on hard work and thriftiness. Despite being a Muslim, and influenced by Marxism, he was still considered pro-western and a moderate.

Sjahrir was also a Sumatran, born in 1909, and of much the same intellectual and rationalist bent as Hatta. He formed the PSI (*Partai Socialis Indonesia*) in 1945, but it lacked mass appeal and was eventually banned by Sukarno for its involvement with the Sumatran rebellion of the late 1950s. Sjahrir was imprisoned.

VOC Governor's House

The old VOC governor's residence is just back from the waterfront on the way down to Kampung Pondok on the eastern edge of Bandaneira. It's an imposing building but now seemingly disused.

OTHER ISLANDS

Gunung Api

Jutting out of the sea directly in front of Bandaneira harbour, this volcano has been a constant threat to Banda. For three centuries from the first Dutch visit to Banda in 1599, it seemed recurrently on the point of blowing itself apart much as Krakatoa would have in the 19th century. Hot ash from eruptions set fire to thatch-roofed Dutch houses so the Dutch learnt the hard way to use stone, plaster and tile. In Neira stone shelters were erected in case the main buildings were destroyed. Sulphurous fumes sometimes settled over Neira and were held responsible for illness and the high mortality rate.

In one awful hour in April 1778, there occurred simultaneously an especially destructive volcanic eruption, an earthquake, a tidal wave and a hurricane – resulting in great destruction of the nutmeg trees and a massive drop in production.

Since then Gunung Api has erupted twice in the 19th century, in 1901 and again in May 1988 when two people were killed; over 300 houses on its north and south flanks and 120,000 coconut trees were destroyed. On this most recent occasion its caldera grew from 50 to 400 metres wide and is now 200 metres deep. All but a few brave or crazy souls were evacuated to Ambon until the danger of further eruptions subsided.

It's only a short paddle across to Gunung Api from Neira in a canoe. You can climb to the top of the volcano.

Karaka Island

Off the north end of Gunung Api, Karaka only has a small beach but there are some fine coral reefs in shallow water near the shore. It's close enough to paddle from Bandaneira in a dugout canoe and takes about an hour in a two-person canoe.

Taman Laut – the Sea Garden

Between Neira and Lonthor islands, only about 150 metres out from the VOC governor's house and close enough to paddle out to in a canoe, the coral here is nowhere near as good as at Karaka Island.

Banda Besar (Lonthor Island)

There's a good beach (but smaller than the one on Pisang Island) with coral offshore on the south side of Banda Besar behind Fort Hollandia. Fort Hollandia was erected after Jan Pieterszoon Coen's capture of Lonthor Island, now Banda Besar, in 1621. The fort is placed high on the central ridge of the island, commanding the surrounding seas. It was once enormous, but an earthquake wrecked it in 1743 and what little remains is derelict and overgrown. A long flight of steps leads up to it.

Pisang Island (Sjahrir Island)

Pulau Pisang is so called because it's banana-shaped. About 45 minutes by motorboat (5000 rp return) from Bandaneira, it has a good sandy beach and some pretty coral (with a big drop-off) with colourful fish. You can wander uphill to the small village behind the beach.

Ai Island

Ai is a good two hours by boat from Neira but definitely worth visiting. It has an overgrown fort near the village on the north-east side. Facing Gunung Api, about one km east of the fort, there's a long sandy beach with wonderful snorkelling.

Run Island

Beyond Ai, Run was once the centre of English activity in the Bandas. In early

House on Lonthor Island

1615, John Jourdain, the English East India Company's leader in Banten, Java, having set up a post at Makassar, ordered several ships to Maluku to harass the Dutch. In late 1616 the English built a stone fort on a spit of half-exposed coral rock on Neilakka Island which lies off Run Island. Both islands lacked fresh water other than rainwater and any food except fish, so they were vulnerable to prolonged blockade.

When Coen seized Run the English continued to hold out on Neilakka – but Coen had the nutmeg plantations on Run destroyed to make sure that the English could not continue trading. The English stayed for almost a decade. Unable to make a profit, virtually forgotten and fearing for their lives after the 'Ambon massacre' of 1623 (in which the English merchants in Ambon were seized, tortured and executed or expelled by the Dutch for allegedly plotting to take over the town),

they packed up in 1628 and withdrew to Banten.

Under the Treaty of Breda in 1667, the British abandoned their claim to Banda while the Dutch relinquished none other than the small island of Manhattan in what would one day be the USA.

Places to Stay – bottom end

All accommodation is in Bandaneira. The *Penginapan Delfika*, *Penginapan Selecta* and *Museum Hotel* all cost 15,000 rp per person including three meals but they'll come down to 12,500 rp, possibly less (especially in the case of the Selecta) if they're not full. You may also be able to get rates with fewer or no meals if you want. Prices usually don't include 10% tax so it's best to check. The Defika and the Selecta may now be only operating as restaurants.

The Delfika, an old Dutch house painted green, purple and white and run by a friendly family, is the cleanest. It has good home cooking – tuna is the mainstay of the diet in Banda and it's amazing how many different ways it can be dished up. The Delfika has a pleasant garden and a verandah facing the street. Snorkelling gear can be rented for 2500 per day even if you're not staying there.

The Penginapan Selecta also has good food but is a bit dingy. The Museum Hotel's mandis could be cleaner. Food here is brought in from one of the owner's other hotels. The manager is talkative and can be fun.

You can stay with a family for 12,000 rp including food – the local justice department will arrange this.

Places to Stay - top end

The two top-end hotels, the *Laguna Inn* and the *Maulana Inn*, plus the Museum Hotel, are owned by Des Alwi, a Bandanese of Arab descent who became a protege of Mohammed Hatta during Hatta's exile in Banda and was educated in Europe. Alwi has put a lot of effort into developing tourism in the Bandas – including getting the airport built – but at the same time his power over the local economy has attracted some resentment.

The Laguna Inn is on the waterfront and has air-con. There's one nice big room upstairs. They ask 30,000 rp a double plus US$10 per person for food but can be bargained down. One person reportedly paid 12,500 rp a single with breakfast only.

The *Maulana Inn* is even more expensive with singles/doubles from US$30/40 plus US$12 per person for meals. Both hotels apparently rent compressed air tanks, snorkels, masks and fins, and speedboats. They can arrange cruises, visits to nutmeg plantations and take you deep-sea fishing.

The 10% tax, common throughout Malaku, is added to most prices.

Places to Eat

The Bandaneira market has a good range of fruit and salad vegetables, but bargain hard – they're getting used to tourists. Many of the shops bake their own bread rolls which you can buy straight from the oven in the mornings. The food at losmens is mainly good and filling but, if you want more, there are a couple of little restaurants like the *Rumah Makan Nusantara* which has basic Indonesian fare.

Getting There & Away

Air Merpati's subsidiary, Indoavia, flies Ambon to Banda twice a week. It's usually necessary to book ahead. The approach to Banda is spectacular – you fly right over Gunung Api. A shop on Jalan Pelabuhan is the agent for Indoavia in Bandaneira.

Boat Various semi-regular boats – perhaps one every five days or so – make the overnight trip from Ambon to Banda. On Pelni's *Dhuta Nusantara* the deck fare is 5000 rp. The boat may continue to Saumlaki in Tanimbar before returning to Ambon. Pelni's *Niaga VIII* and *Nasuna* also take in Banda (the fare from Ambon is 5000 rp) on loops of southern Maluku. All Pelni boats leave from Ambon's big-boat harbour. The *Putra Indonesia* leaves from the small-boat harbour for Banda about every 10 days. It's a slightly more comfortable trip than the other options, but is still grubby and crowded. The cost is 7500 or 8000 rp, more for a cabin.

Getting Around

Bandaneira is very small; it's a five-minute walk from the museum to the PT Perkebunan Pala Banda, formerly the government nutmeg factory (PNP), and 10 minutes further to the District Admin-istration Building (Kantor Kecamatan) – see the map. The only road on Neira leads to the airport. Walking trails connect other places on this and on the other islands.

By the road it's a 45 minute walk from the town to the airport. You can take a short cut by heading north from the Museum Hotel. The road turns into a dirt trail and takes you to the top end of the airstrip – it's a 20-minute walk.

Motorboats from the pasar and Kampung Pondok, a 10-minute walk east of the town, go fairly regularly to Lonthor Island (500 rp for locals). There aren't any regular boats to the other islands. Ask at the losmens, Bandaneira harbour or Kampung Pondok about renting boats. Prices depend on bargaining. A dugout with a man to paddle it costs around 5000 rp per day. You might be able to take one out yourself but you can only reach places near Neira such as Taman Laut, Lonthor, Gunung Api and Karaka. Pisang Island is too far to paddle to.

If you hire a canoe to go out alone and snorkel it's easy enough to get out of the canoe and into the water, but virtually impossible to get back in without capsizing the canoe. The people insist there are no sharks in the waters immediately around Neira, but watch out around some of the outlying islands.

Motorised fishing boats (kapal motor) to Karaka Island cost around 7500 rp for a half-day. (One person got a full day for 10,000 rp through someone at the Laguna Inn). To Pisang Island costs 15,000 rp for the day, probably more for a group, perhaps 25,000 rp for eight. To Ai Island will cost maybe 40,000 rp for a small group (we paid 60,000 rp for eight people) to Run Island about 60,000 rp.

The Delfika offers a day trip round Karaka, Malole, Pisang, and Taman Laut for 50,000 rp for the boat. The owner of the Selecta ran one guy around by kapal motor for 5000 rp for the day – a really cheap deal.

Speedboats, available from Des Alwi's hotels, cost US$110 per day.

Southern Maluku

Probably the most forgotten islands in Indonesia, the islands of southern Maluku are dispersed across the sea between Timor and Irian Jaya. The three main groups, all south-east of Banda, are Kai, Aru and Tanimbar. West of Tanimbar, two arcs of smaller islands stretch across to Timor – a southern, less fertile arc consisting of the Babar and Leti groups, Kisar and Wetar and a northern arc of volcanic, wooded islands (Serua, Nila, Teun, Damar and Romang).

Southern Maluku is mostly inhabited by people of mixed Malay and Papuan stock with the Papuan features more noticeable on the islands closer to Irian Jaya. The Makassarese and the Bugis traded in this region, and the Dutch came here in the 17th century in the interests of maintaining their spice monopoly, but the islanders were long noted for their hostility to outsiders and propensity for head-hunting, even cannibalism in some instances. Christian missionaries helped to pacify the area and Islam has also established itself in many parts. More recently, there's been logging and fishing by all and sundry. Trepang and pearls, once plentiful are becoming scarce.

Southern Maluku has some deserted white sandy beaches, good snorkelling and diving, colourful and exotic birdlife, unique flora and fauna (all at risk), and traditional cultures quite unaffected by tourism. Its peoples are known for their boatbuilding, woodcarving, ikat weavings and shell artifacts.

ARU

The closest of the island groups to Irian Jaya, Aru is best known as home to the threatened birds of paradise, a species whose males display their full plumage during their courting season from May to December. There are also other fantastic birds, small kangaroos, wallabies, cuscus and crocodiles. Sea life includes dugongs and turtles. The south-eastern part of the group is a marine reserve. Many parts of the islands are swampy. The main town is Dobo on the small, northern island of Wamar; as yet there isn't an airport – Langgur on Kai is the closest one. Unlike some of the other southern Maluku islanders, the people of Aru have the reputation of being peaceful. Despite the influence of Islam and Christian missionaries, animism persists; Aru is supposed to have more *suanggi*, witches, than anywhere else in Maluku.

KAI

Like Aru, the beautiful Kai Islands are uplifted coral reefs which are mountainous and heavily forested. The two main islands are Kai Kecil and Kai Besar. Tual on Dullah Island is the main town, but the airport is five km away at Langgur on Kai Kecil. Birds and butterflies are prolific. The islanders have a reputation for being happy, talkative and excitable. They are also excellent boatbuilders and decorate their boats with woodcarvings, shells and cassowary 'hair'. Apparently there are rock paintings on some of the coastal cliffs and good coral off Dullah Island. The religious break-up is one third Islam, one third Christian and one third animist. Malaria and cholera are widespread.

TANIMBAR

The Tanimbar group, the most southerly of Maluku, consists of 66 islands. The main town is Saumlaki on Yamdena Island, the biggest of the group. The island's interior is uninhabited. In the past, the islanders had a reputation for being ferocious. Though Catholicism is the major religion today, much of the original culture is maintained. Woodcarvings, common decorations on boats and houses, are related to ancestor worship. You'll probably also see smaller woodcarvings of human figures with thin, graceful limbs. Rituals and dances remain an integral part of planting and harvest, weddings and funerals.

At Sanglia Dol, on the east coast of Yamdena, a 30-metre-high stone staircase leads up from the beach to a large boat-shaped carved stone platform 18 metres long – such structures were once a feature of many Tanimbar villages and may link

these islands with other megalithic ('big stone') cultures in Indonesia such as on Nias and Sumba islands.

Tanimbar and the islands west to Timor produce Maluku's best ikat weavings with traditional symbols and motifs predominating. Tanimbar's gold and silversmiths were highly skilled: melting down, recasting and beating gold jewellery and coins into elaborate headpieces. There are at least five separate languages: one related to Tetum which is spoken on Timor. There's said to be good diving off Nustabun Island. A road is being built along the east coast of Yamdena but most travel is by boat.

THE SOUTH-WEST ISLANDS

These islands between Tanimbar and Timor are lightly populated with Kisar, Leti and Babar having the most people. Now largely Christianised, except for Islamic Kisar, the people here were head-hunters and warlike with a phallic, animist religion.

Kisar produces excellent ikat weavings. The island has never had extensive cultural dominance from elsewhere so the traditional motifs on its ikat are very old and probably unique. They include human, animal, and bird-and-rider motifs. Today, commercial and natural cotton and dyes are used together. *Kain sinun* is a special Kisar textile with the tree of life motif and the figure of a man with arms raised. Sinun is usually black or dark blue while other ceremonial ikat fabrics usually have bright colours in stripes.

Animistic woodcarvings are produced on Dawera (in the Babar group), Moa and Lakor (both in the Leti group), and Wetar.

PLACES TO STAY

There are losmens in Tual and Saumlaki. Expect to pay between 10,000 and 15,000 rp, including meals, for an average room. In Dobo you can stay at the mission for a small fee. Tepa on Babar has the new *Hotel Sumber Jaya* with full board at

7500 rp per person. Away from the main towns, check in with the kepala desa.

GETTING THERE & AWAY

These islands are probably the last place anyone thinks of when Indonesia comes to mind. Ambon is the main jumping-off point for flights and boats to southern Maluku. Indoavia flies daily to Langgur (Kai) and three times weekly to Saumlaki (Tanimbar). Some flights take in both places so you can hop from one to the other. There are no flights anywhere else.

Pelni's *Niaga VIII*, *Dhuta Nusantara* and *Nasuna* are among the ships covering southern Maluku from Ambon. Sometimes they just go Ambon, Banda, Tual (Kai), Banda, Ambon; other times they make longer round trips of from 11 to 18 days. Ambon to Kai via Banda takes about 2½ days. Other possible ports of call include Dobo; Saumlaki; Tepa, Lelang, Kroing and Masela (Babar Group); Damar; Romang; Wetar; Kisar; and Leti, Moa and Lakor (Leti Group). Deck fare from Ambon to Saumlaki is from 14,000 to 19,000 rp depending on the boat and the route.

From Timor, Pelni's *KM Elang* sometimes includes Kisar on its loops out of Kupang, often also calling at Dili and Kalabahi (Alor).

Transport around the islands is mostly on foot or by boat.

Northern Maluku

The main town and communications hub of the scattered islands of northern Maluku is Ternate on the small island of the same name, one of a chain of volcanic peaks poking out of the ocean off the west coast of the large island of Halmahera. Apart from Ternate and neighbouring Tidore, northern Maluku is little-visited

Playing volleyball, Ternate

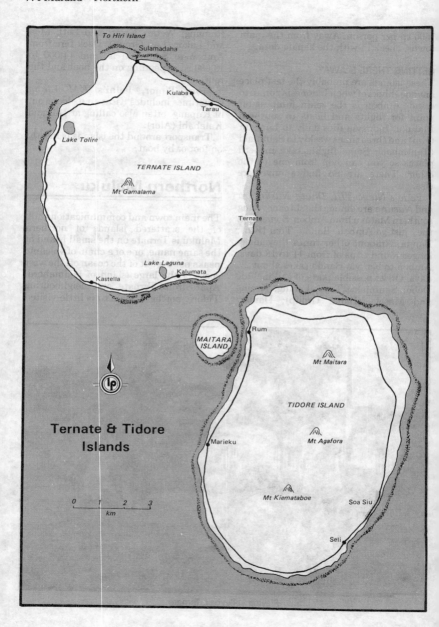

To Hiri Island

Sulamadaha

Kulaba

Tarau

Lake Tolire

TERNATE ISLAND

Mt Gamalama

Ternate

Lake Laguna

Kalumata

Kastella

MAITARA ISLAND

Rum

Mt Maitara

TIDORE ISLAND

Mt Agafora

Marieku

Ternate & Tidore Islands

Mt Kiemataboe

Soa Siu

Seli

0   1   2   3
km

but certainly offers scope for adventurous travellers.

TERNATE

For centuries the sultanate of this little island was one of the most important in Maluku with influence south as far as Ambon, west to Sulawesi and east to Irian Jaya. Islam was probably brought here in the middle of the 15th century by Javanese merchants. Ternate's prosperity came from its abundant production of cloves, which allowed it to become a powerful regional military force. Rivalry with the neighbouring sultanate of Tidore resulted in frequent wars and only in 1814 was peace finally established.

Ternate was one of the first places where the Portuguese and Dutch established themselves in Maluku and it's dotted with the ruins of old European fortifications. Even the Spanish got into the act as the chief foreign power in Ternate and Tidore for much of the 17th century.

Today the town of Ternate is, in contrast to Ambon, a relaxed place only occasionally alarmed by rumblings from the huge volcano, Gamalama, to which it clings. The population is strongly Muslim but surprisingly liberal: women and girls wear snappy modern fashions here in the middle of nowhere, at odds with the usual Islamic code of female dress. Calls to Allah from the numerous mosques compete, on Saturday nights, with amplified Muslim pop music as someone up on the hillside celebrates something into the early hours. There are even a couple of supermarkets in Ternate, something even Ambon doesn't have.

Information & Orientation

The town of Ternate stretches several km along the east coast of the island. The former Sultan's palace is at the northern end of town and beyond that is the airport. The huge Benteng Oranye (Fort Orange) is near the main bemo station and market. The harbour (Complex Pelabuhan) is at the southern end of town and between the harbour and the fort you'll find the hotels, offices and shops. Further south is another port, Bastiong, from where boats go to Tidore. The other attractions, like the old forts, lie at various points around the island, mostly on or just off the ring-road. If you're in a hurry you can do a loop around the island, taking in all the sights, in just a few hours.

There's a tourist information office beside the Kantor Bupati on Jalan Pahlawan Revolusi; you may be able to borrow snorkelling gear here.

Banks & Post The Bank Expor Impor Indonesia, on the waterfront on Jalan Pahlawan Revolusi, changes travellers' cheques including American Express and Thomas Cook in US, Australian and Canadian dollars and sterling, plus cash in most main currencies. It's open Monday to Friday from 8 to 11 am, and Saturday from 8 to 10 am. The main post office is also on Jalan Pahlawan Revolusi, near the Bank Negara Indonesia.

Kedaton (Palace) of the Sultan of Ternate

This interesting creation, looking more like a European country mansion than a palace, lies just back from Jalan Sultan Babulah, the road to the airport. The ill-kept building now houses a museum with little to see – just a few Portuguese cannons, Dutch helmets and armour. To get there take a bemo for 125 rp from the bemo station on Jalan Pahlawan Revolusi.

Fort Orange (Benteng Oranye)

Continuing clockwise from the sultan's palace this fort dates from 1637 and is a Dutch construction. It's right in the middle of Ternate, opposite the bemo station. It has forlorn looking cannons and sadly crumbling walls overgrown with weeds, but you'll get some idea of its importance from its great size; this is quite an interesting building to walk around.

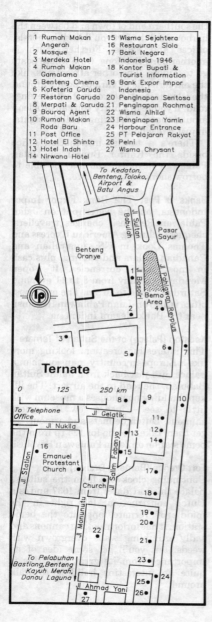

1 Rumah Makan Angerah	15 Wisma Sejahtera
2 Mosque	16 Restaurant Siola
3 Merdeka Hotel	17 Bank Negara Indonesia 1946
4 Rumah Makan Gamalama	18 Kantor Bupati & Tourist Information
5 Benteng Cinema	19 Bank Expor Impor Indonesia
6 Kafeteria Garuda	
7 Restoran Garuda	20 Penginapan Sentosa
8 Merpati & Garuda	21 Penginapan Rachmat
9 Bouraq Agent	22 Wisma Alhilal
10 Rumah Makan Roda Baru	23 Penginapan Yamin
11 Post Office	24 Harbour Entrance
12 Hotel El Shinta	25 PT Pelajaran Rakyat
13 Hotel Indah	26 Pelni
14 Nirwana Hotel	27 Wisma Chrysant

Ternate

Ruins of a European fort, Ternate

Benteng Kayuh Merah

At the southern end of Ternate, a km beyond Pelabuhan Bastiong (where you catch motorboats to Tidore) and just before Desa Kayuh Merah, is the small fort of Benteng Kayuh Merah. Constructed in 1510, it's right on the beach with waves splashing its walls.

Danau Laguna

Take a bemo (200 rp) if you want to visit this volcanic lake just past Ngade. Much of the spring-fed lake is covered in lotuses. A big white-washed wall surrounds part of it and it appears to be some sort of official park. If the main entrance is closed there's a dirt track which leads down to the lake from the start of the wall as you come from Ternate. Just past the main entrance to the lake is Taman Eva (entry fee 300 rp), a popular spot on Sundays with its pleasant gardens and splendid views across the bay to Tidore. You can scramble down to the rocks below and dive into the sea.

Benteng Kastella

Continuing clockwise round the island from Danau Laguna, the road cuts straight through what's left of this fort, which is covered in moss and undergrowth and grazed over by goats. Tree roots have wrapped themselves around the ruins of the main tower. A bemo from Ternate to Kastella will cost you 300 rp. There's a sandy beach but it's not attractive.

Danau Tolire

This volcanic crater on the north-western side of the island is larger than Danau Laguna and filled with deep, green-coloured water. It's less than a 10-minute walk off the road in the vicinity of Takome, but bemos are rare.

Sulamadaha

Sulamadaha, near Ternate's northern tip, has a black sandy beach with big waves and a strong current – take care! It's a popular Sunday picnic spot but is almost deserted, except for a few waifs, during the week. On Sundays it costs 200 rp to go onto the beach; there are a few drinks and snacks stalls. Walk to the left for 15 minutes, over the rocks and headland to a tiny coral beach where the water is calm and safe for swimming – it may be worth snorkelling out from this beach. Boats leave here several times daily for the small island of Hiri, off the northern tip of Ternate (250 rp). Bemos from Ternate to Sulamadaha are 250 rp.

Just before the main beach as you come from Ternate, on the left, is the friendly *Penginapan Pantai Indah* with clean rooms at 13,000 rp per person including three good meals. Get someone to take you to the nearby hot water well for a cliff-top mandi – it's a delicious experience. The track to the well is about 100 metres on the left, back towards Ternate from the penginapan.

Batu Angus (Burnt Rocks)

North of Ternate, Batu Angus is a volcanic lava flow caused by an 18th-century eruption of Gamalama. A massive river of jagged volcanic rocks like a landscape on another planet pushes right into the sea. Take a bemo to just past Tarau village to see this.

Benteng Toloko

This small fort is in better condition than the others. A path leads off the airport road (north of the sultan's palace but south of the airport) down to Dufa Dufa and the Benteng Toloko which lies on a rocky hill above the beach.

Gunung Api Gamalama

This active volcano is, in fact, the entire island of Ternate. The most recent eruptions were in 1980 and 1983. Take a bemo up the mountainside as far as possible and then walk. There are good views over the town and nearby islands. You'll need a guide (villagers from Marikrobo will volunteer) to find the impressively large 350-year-old clove tree, *Cengkeh Afo*, on the slopes. The tree is now dead after having been split by lightning. It is possible and worthwhile to climb right up to the crater.

Places to Stay – bottom end

Many places work on a room-plus-meals basis, a good idea since the choice of eating places in the town is limited. The *Wisma Alhilal* (tel 21404), at Jalan Monunutu 2/32, is plain but run by a friendly family. Rooms with fan and attached mandi and toilet are 5000 rp per person including a small breakfast; dinner is 2500 rp per person. The excellent meals are mainly barbecued fish or fried chicken with noodles and rice and a more than liberal dose of chilli.

The pleasant *Wisma Sejahtera* (tel 21139), on Jalan Salim Fabanyo, has singles/doubles with fan for 5500/11,000 rp or 10,000/20,000 rp with meals.

On Jalan Pahlawan Revolusi, opposite

the entrance to the harbour, the basic *Peningapan Yamin* has rooms at 4000/8000 rp. The penginapans *Sentosa* and *Rachmat* further up the same road are also cheap.

Places to Stay – top end

There's nothing really top-end in Ternate. The *Wisma Chrysant* (tel 21580), at Jalan Yani 131, is possibly the best value but it's nothing flash. Singles/doubles with fan and mandi are 10,000/15,000 rp, with air-con 20,000/30,000 rp. It may be worth bargaining. The 10% tax and 10% service charge are extra. The *Hotel Indah* (tel 21334), at Jalan Bosoiri 3, costs 16,500 rp per person including meals; it's comfortable and often full of government people.

The *Hotel Nirwana* (tel 21787), at Jalan Pahlawan Revolusi 58, is decent enough and central. Singles/doubles with fan and without meals are 5000/10,000 rp, with fan and meals 10,000/20,000 rp and more with air-con. The *Hotel El Shinta* almost next door to the Nirwana, costs 20,500/30,000 rp, including three meals

and tax. It's really overpriced since the rooms do not have attached mandis and it's already getting that dilapidated look.

The *Hotel Merdeka* on Jalan Monunutu costs 12,500 rp per person including three meals. It looks like it must have been Dutch-built.

Places to Eat

About a 10-minute walk west of the centre, the *Restaurant Siola* has probably the best food in Ternate in definitely the most salubrious surroundings. Seafood is a speciality and even the asparagus (4000 rp) and corn (*jagung*, 3500 rp) soups swim with crabmeat. With a bowl of rice, these soups are a meal in themselves. Nasi and mie goreng are 2000 rp, prawns or chicken 4000 rp.

The best place to eat in the centre of town is the *Restoran Garuda* on Jalan Pahlawan Revolusi. A decent cap cai is 2000 rp, fried prawns 2500 rp, fried chicken 2500 rp and crab 7500 rp. They have cold beer. Across the road from the Garuda is its less clean sibling *Kafetaria*

Garuda with cheap and pretty ordinary food. Don't bother with the rujak which is a disappointment if you've sampled the equivalent at Natsepa on Ambon.

The *Gamalama Restaurant*, on Jalan Pahlawan Revolusi, is a good cheap place with gado-gado for 750 rp and udang goreng for 850 rp. The *Rumah Makan Roda Baru* further down Jalan Pahlawan Revolusi is fairly cheap as Padang places go.

There are more cheap eats at the *Rumah Makan Anugerah* on Jalan Bosoiri, across the road from the bemo station. The pasar is generally well-stocked with fruit, but has little else that looks appetising. The savoury martabaks sold from the night stalls that set up around the Merpati office are worth trying.

Getting There & Away

Air Merpati's supposedly daily flights to and from Ambon and Manado are notoriously unreliable – even if you have a reservation for a certain flight, you may have to wait one or two days. Nor do the flights to Manado connect with flights to elsewhere in Sulawesi. More useful are Bouraq's thrice weekly flights between Ternate and Manado, Gorontalo, Palu and Ujung Pandang. From Sulawesi you can fly to Kalimantan.

Ternate is the jumping-off point for flights by Merpati and its subsidiary Indoavia to other places in northern Maluku such as Galela and Kao, both on the north-east coast of Halmahera, Morotai off the north-east of Halmahera, Labuha on Bacan and Sanana on Sula.

The Merpati office (tel 314) is at Jalan Bosoiri 81 and there's a Garuda agent in the same building, though Garuda doesn't fly to Ternate. For Indoavia, book through Merpati. The office is open daily, including Sunday from 9 am to 12 noon.

Bouraq (tel 21042) is at Jalan Sultan Babulah 96 and is open every day from 8 am to 7 pm. There's a more central Bouraq agent on Jalan Bosoiri, opposite Merpati.

Boat The harbour master's office (tel 21129) and the Pelni office (tel 21276) are just inside the Complex Pelabuhan on the corner of Jalan Ahmad Yani and Jalan Pahlawan Revolusi.

Pelni's passenger ship the *Umsini* calls at Ternate every second Tuesday en route to Irian Jaya and each following Sunday on its return journey to Jakarta. Ports of call between Jakarta and Jayapura are Surabaya, Ujung Pandang, Kwandang, Bitung (Manado), Ternate and Sorong. The same route is followed in reverse on the return journey.

Pelni boats from Ambon to northern Maluku include the *Baruna Dwipa*. Ambon to Ternate costs from 16,000 to 18,000 rp and takes about 32 hours if there are no stops. There are also boats which visit various other places in northern Maluku between Ambon and Ternate. Possible calls include Labuha, Laiwui, Falabisahaya, Dofa, Bobong, Sanana, Namlea and Aerbuaya.

Other shipping offices inside the harbour entrance include *PT Perusahaan Peliaran Lokal*, with boats to Daruba on Morotai and Tobelo on Halmahera, and *PT Peramut* with boats to Morotai, Galela on Halmahera and Bitung on Sulawesi. Boats depart daily for Jailolo on Halmahera (1500 rp, 1½ hours) and most days for Dodinga, south of Jailolo (2000 rp, 2½ hours).

Other possibilities out of Ternate include ships to Surabaya, Sorong in Irian Jaya or even Singapore. Enquire at the harbour master's and Pelni offices.

Umsini fares	1st class	3rd class	Ekonomi
Jayapura (51 hrs)	116,200 rp	68,100 rp	44,300 rp
Bitung (7 hrs)	36,500 rp	20,700 rp	12,600 rp
Ujung Pandang (53 hrs)	110,200 rp	62,500 rp	38,000 rp

Getting Around

Airport Transport The airport is at Tarau, north of Ternate township. Charter a bemo for from 1500 to 2000 rp per person or 2500 rp for the vehicle. Or walk a km down to the main road from the airport terminal and pick up a public bemo for 175 rp.

Around Town & Island Ternate town is small and you can walk from the Wisma Alhilal to the bemo station opposite Benteng Oranye in 15 minutes. To more distant places you need the bemos. These cost 125 rp (flat rate) to anywhere around town or to Bastiong, the sultan's palace, or the airport. A surfaced road rings the island and public bemos cover it – though less frequently in the more distant reaches. They also climb part-way up Gamalama from Ternate town. One way of seeing the sights quickly would be to charter a bemo, as the ring-road links Ternate township with Batu Angus, Sulamadaha, Danau Tolire, Benteng Kastella, and Benteng Kayuh Merah. It takes a bit less than two hours to do a non-stop circle around the island – a charter would cost from 20,000 to 25,000 rp.

TIDORE

Tidore has had very similar influences from the outside world to Ternate. Islam arrived in the middle of the 15th century and at the end of that century, the first ruler to take the title of 'sultan' assumed command. Tidore once claimed parts of Halmahera and a number of islands off the west coast of Irian Jaya and for a couple of centuries rivalled Ternate for control of the spice trade. Today Soa Siu is the main township on the island; Rum is the harbour for boats from Ternate.

Things to See

There's a fort above the road as you enter Soa Siu, but you need a local to show you the vague track leading up to it. The jungle has almost gobbled it up and you'd really have to be an enthusiast to come here. There is another fort near Rum.

Soa Siu – the main township on the island of Tidore

Getting There & Away

To get to Tidore from Ternate, take a bemo from Ternate township to Pelabuhan Bastiong (100 rp). Boats powered by outboard motor depart frequently from the Pasar Impris at Pelabuhan Bastiong for Rum on Tidore; they take about half an hour and cost 500 rp. From Rum, take a bemo for 500 rp to the main town of Soa Siu (a 45-minute ride).

HALMAHERA

Looking something like a mini version of Sulawesi, Halmahera was once under the sway of the old Ternate and Tidore sultanates who split the island between them. The inhabitants are a curious mixture. The mainly Muslim coastal people are, like the people of Ternate and Tidore, a mix of Portuguese, Gujarati (from western India), Arab, Malay and Dutch – a result of the long contact with oreign traders who came to this area in search of spices. There are still some indigenous tribes in the interior of Halmahera's northern peninsula and on the east coast. Much of their traditional culture remains intact. Strangely, the native languages spoken by north Halmaherans, Ternatans and Tidorese seem to have more in common with those of Australian Aborigines and the people of inland Irian Jaya and the Andaman Islands in the Indian Ocean, than with the other languages of Indonesia and the Philippines.

Halmahera is little-developed though its seas and forests are starting to be plundered like those in the rest of Maluku with the profits largely leaving the area. There are a number of plywood mills, but these provide employment for Javanese rather than locals. The northern peninsula seems the most populated and developed part, but it has mountains, volcanoes and untouched jungle as well as some coconut plantations on the coast. Tobelo, the main town on the island, only got electricity in 1985 and television in 1987. There is almost no tourism in this area of beautiful, white sandy beaches, excellent coral and clear waters (especially on and around the small islands in Kao Bay and Morotai Island off north-east Halmahera). There's also diving to WW II wrecks off Morotai.

Places to Stay

In Tobelo, the *Pantai Indah* on the seafront costs 15,000 rp per person including excellent meals. Rooms have attached mandi and a balcony with a sea view. Downstairs rooms are cheaper. There are a couple of other places to stay in the town; the *Penginapan Dirgahaya* in Kao costs 10,000 rp per person including meals and the owner is very helpful.

On Morotai, there's a penginapan at Daruba. It also costs 10,000 rp per person including meals.

Getting There & Away

Air Merpati flies between Ternate and Galela four days a week, Ternate and Kao twice a week and Ternate and Morotai once a week.

Ship From Ternate harbour there are boats daily to Jailolo and most days to Dodinga on the west coast of Halmahera – see the Ternate section for details. From Dodinga, you can take a minibus across the narrow waist of Halmahera to Bubane-igo on the east coast and get another boat north to Kao. There are also boats thrice time weekly from Ternate to Tobelo via Daruba on Morotai. These leave Ternate at around 6 pm taking around 12 hours to reach Daruba (8800 rp). Ask about other boats for Halmahera at the shipping offices at Ternate harbour and at Pelabuhan Bastiong.

Getting Around

Tobelo, the biggest town, is about an hour by bus (1500 rp) from Galela. There are only roads around the main towns, so elsewhere you have to walk or take boats along the coast. It's fairly easy to get from the west to the east coast of the northern peninsula.

Kalimantan

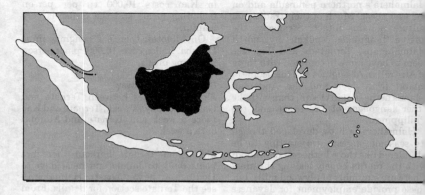

Some people go to Kalimantan expecting to see half naked, heavily tattooed Dayak savages striding down the streets of Balikpapan, Samarinda or Pontianak. Sorry to disappoint you but the parts of Kalimantan near harbours and airports have been impaled on a drill bit and carved up with chainsaws and first impressions are likely to be of oil refineries and timber mills. Tourism is just taking off and most westerners work for foreign companies like Union or Standard Oil.

To see the pre-colonial, pre-Javanised, pre-multinational Kalimantan requires travelling well into the interior. The Bugis, Javanese, Banjarmasis and Chinese dominate the coast while about a million Dayaks – the island's original inhabitants and former head-hunters – live in the vast, jungle covered hinterland along the island's many rivers.

HISTORY

Kalimantan is the southern two-thirds of the island of Borneo. Northern Borneo consists of the Malaysian states of Sarawak and Sabah and the independent sultanate of Brunei. Of the seven million people on Borneo, 5½ million live in

Kalimantan, mostly in settlements and cities along its river banks. The mountain stretching across Borneo's interior feed it rivers which carry immense quantities c silt to the coast. Heavy rainfall and poo drainage produce a broad rim of dense inhospitable swamps along much of the island's shores.

Like Sumatra and Java, Kalimantan was once a cultural crossroads. Hinduism reached Kalimantan by about 400 AD and Hindu temple remains have been unearthed in southern Kalimantan near Amuntai and Negara on the Negara River. There are Sanskrit tablets in the museum at Tenggarong in East Kalimantan.

Kalimantan was a stopover point on the trade routes between China, the Philippines and Java and Chinese settlements were established on the island long before Europeans ever came to the Indonesian archipelago. The coastal ports were Islamic by around the 15th or 16th centuries, and some of the sultanates such as Kutai and Banjarmasin became major trading centres.

In the early 17th century Kalimantan became a scene of conflict between the

British and the Dutch. Much to the annoyance of the Dutch, the British set up bases in Java, Sumatra and in south-west Kalimantan. Banjarmasin was reputed to be a great source of pepper so the British turned their attention there, since the Dutch had control over the spice islands further east. Trade with Banjarmasin seemed promising but when the British stationed a guard ship at the mouth of the Barito River and recruited Bugis mercenaries to guard their warehouses, the Banjarmasin rulers felt threatened. War with the British erupted in 1701. The Banjarmasis were defeated and tolerated the British presence until 1707 when the British were finally ejected.

By the 19th century British and Dutch interests in Borneo had changed markedly. The British interest was mainly strategic as the north and west coasts flanked the sailing routes between China and India. The Dutch interest was mainly colonial.

To the north of the Java Sea, Borneo was a hide-out for pirates and although the interior was unknown and presumed to have little commercial value, the Dutch had some interest in controlling the south and west coasts. By the late 1820s and 1830s the Dutch had concluded treaties with various small west coast states. Parts of the Banjarmasi sultanate were signed over to the Dutch in the early part of the 1800s but the Dutch didn't establish garrisons or administrative offices.

In 1838 the Dutch were jolted by the arrival of Englishman, James Brooke. Brooke, a self-styled adventurer, arrived in Borneo with an armed sloop to find the Brunei aristocracy facing rebellion from the inland tribes. Brooke quelled the rebellion and in gratitude, or so the story goes, was given power over Kuching (in what is now Sarawak) in 1841. Brooke put down the inland tribes, suppressed their head-hunting, eliminated the dreaded Borneo pirates that infested the coast and founded a personal dynasty of white rajas (you could do this sort of thing in

the 19th century) that lasted until the Japanese invasion in WW II.

With Brooke's arrival the spectre of intervention by other European powers suddenly became a reality for the Dutch. In the 1840s and 1850s the Dutch put down several internal disputes and established new treaties with local rulers. From 1846 they opened coal mines in South and East Kalimantan and gradually the island became more commercially important. War broke out between the Dutch and the Banjarmasis in 1859, but after four years the Banjarmasis were defeated and the Dutch instituted direct rule, although some fighting continued until 1905.

The current division of Borneo between Indonesia and Malaysia originates from the British-Dutch rivalry. After WW II the Brooke family handed Sarawak over to the British government, putting Britain in the curious position of acquiring a new colony at the time it was shedding others. Sarawak remained under British control when Malaya (the part of Malaysia formed by the Malay Peninsula) gained independence in 1957.

Sabah was another story. Once part of the Brunei sultanate, Sabah came under the influence of the British North Borneo Company after being avoided for centuries because of its unpleasant pirates. Eventually in 1888 north Borneo's coast became a British protectorate although fighting did not end until the death of the Sabah rebel leader, Mat Salleh, in 1900. After WW II, the administration of Sabah was handed to the British government. Finally in 1963 Sarawak and Sabah joined with the Malay Peninsula and, temporarily, Singapore to form the nation of Malaysia.

The border between Sarawak, Sabah and Kalimantan became the scene of fighting during Indonesia's Confrontation with Malaysia under Sukarno. Even after Confrontation was abandoned anti-Malaysian Chinese guerrillas of the Sarawak People's Guerrilla Troops, originally trained and armed by Indonesia, remained in Kalimantan until the early 1970s. A joint Malaysian-Indonesian military operation suppressed them although it is said Dayak tribesmen played a key role guarding the border and removing support the guerrillas may have had in the villages.

Towards the end of the 19th century the outer islands, rather than Java, became the focus of Dutch commercial exploitation of the archipelago. Rubber and oil became increasingly important and products like pepper, copra, tin and coffee were developed in the outer islands. The existence of oil deposits in north Sumatra's Langkat area had been known since the 1860s and they were commercially exploited by the Dutch by the 1880s. By early this century oil was also being drilled in Kalimantan.

To finance drilling in East Kalimantan, a British company was set up in London: Shell Transport & Trading Company. In 1907 Shell merged with the Royal Dutch Company for the Exploitation of Petroleum Sources in the Netherlands Indies (the first company to start drilling in Sumatra) to form Royal Dutch Shell – giving the Dutch the greater share. Shell expanded rapidly and soon oil was produced everywhere from California to Russia. The Russian properties were confiscated in 1917 but by 1930 Shell was producing 85% of Indonesia's oil. Today the countries in which Shell operates read like a United Nations' roll-call. In the 1920s US companies began taking up major oil concessions in Indonesia followed by the Japanese in 1930.

Economic value aside, East Kalimantan is set to become one of Indonesia's prime transmigration targets. Although Kalimantan is Indonesia's second biggest province and covers an area 30% greater than Java, its population is minute by comparison. Until now the Samarinda and Balikpapan areas have accounted for most of the East Kalimantan transmigration, still less than 5% of the national total. The figure is expected to grow and new immigrants will have to settle further away from the cities. The plan is to send new settlers to the forest districts north of Samarinda and, after ripping down the natural forest, to develop these areas as rubber producers

It's arguable that such transmigration projects indicate a shift away from the idea of reducing the population crush on Java and Bali, and that transmigration is now directed at the economic development of the outer islands. So far most major outer island developments have occurred independently of government-sponsored transmigration. Transmigration tied to estate crop development such as rubber is perhaps the first attempt to link the programme to regional development.

Not everyone goes to Kalimantan on government sponsored transmigration schemes. A major group in East Kalimantan are the Bugis of southern Sulawesi, continuing a transmigration tradition 400 years old, although most have settled since independence. The Kahar Muzakar rebellion in 1951 spurred Bugis movement from Sulawesi and after the rebellion was suppressed, another wave of Bugis transmigrants tempted by the prospect of a better life, joined their relatives in Kalimantan. Some returned to Sulawesi after the disastrous fire which swept East Kalimantan and Sabah in 1982-83.

If you're heading back from Sulawesi to Java then a detour to the east or south coasts of Kalimantan can be worthwhile, particularly to Banjarmasin and Samarinda.

FLORA & FAUNA

The strangest inhabitants of Kalimantan are the orang-utan (originally hutan), 'the man of the forest' whose almost human appearance and disposition puzzled both Dayaks and early European visitors. The English Captain Daniel Beeckman visited Borneo in the early 18th century and in his book *A Voyage to & from the Island of Borneo* wrote:

Top: Market, Martapura, Kalimantan (AS)
Left: A river-side house, Banjarmasin, Kalimantan (AS)
Right: Sunset, almost on the equator, Pontianak, Kalimantan (AS)

Top: Panning for gold, Cempeka, Kalimantan (AS)
Bottom: Prahu moored in Banjarmasin, Kalimantan (AS)

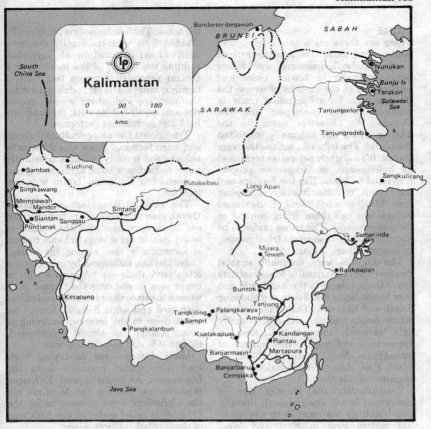

They grow up to be six foot high; they walk upright, have longer arms than men, tolerable good faces (handsomer I am sure than some Hottentots that I have seen) large teeth, no tails nor hair, but on those parts where it grows on human bodies; they are very nimble footed and mighty strong; they throw great stones, sticks and billets at those persons that offend them. The natives do really believe that these were formerly men, but metamorphosed into beasts for their blasphemy. They told me many strange stories of them. . . .

The orang-utan is not the only strange creature inhabiting the interior of this vast but increasingly less mysterious island. The deep waters of the Mahakam River are home to fresh-water dolphin, there are gibbons in the jungles, proboscis monkeys and crab eating macaques in the mangrove swamps, crocodiles, clouded leopards, giant butterflies and hornbills, including the legendary black hornbill. The Dayaks traditionally believe that the black hornbill carries the human soul but because of its feathers and huge beak it was almost hunted into extinction.

PEOPLE

There are three main ethnic groups in Kalimantan today: the recently arrived coastal Malay/Indonesians who follow Islam and live in towns, cities and settlements at the mouths of rivers; the Chinese who have controlled trade in Kalimantan for centuries; and the Dayaks, the collective name for the interior tribes who originally inhabited the island. The tribes do not use the term Dayak. It's a slightly pejorative term used by Indonesians, or indigenous peoples converted to Islam, like the Banjars and the Kutais, to differentiate non-Muslim from Muslim inhabitants. Enlightened Indonesians call them *orang gunung* or mountain people. The tribes prefer to be identified by their separate tribal names, eg Kenyah, Iban, Punan, etc.

The Dayaks were originally coastal dwellers until the arrival of Malay settlers drove them inland to the highlands and river banks. Some also live in neighbouring Sabah and Sarawak. They have definite ethnic commonalities and are generally light skinned, somewhat Chinese in appearance and may be descendants of immigrants from southern China or South-East Asia. Tribal dialects show linguistic similarities.

Traditionally the Dayaks live in communal *lamin* (longhouses), literally long buildings one room deep and up to 300 metres long in East and West Kalimantan. In South Kalimantan, communal houses are called *balai* and in Central Kalimantan *betang*, and may be a shorter, wider rectangle or large square shape. Both are still called longhouses in English.

A group of small longhouses or one large longhouse make up the traditional village. Longhouses are built on wooden piles up to three metres high, as protection against wild animals, flooding and in the past, enemies. Stairs of notched logs leading to the house can be pulled in as needed. Domestic animals, usually pigs or chickens, are kept below the house. The longhouses are traditionally divided into separate family quarters, with either a communal verandah running the length of the building or a central verandah between two rows of family quarters. The verandah is the main thoroughfare and where women pound rice and repair fishing nets, meetings are held and ceremonies performed.

Traditional Dayak agriculture is slash-and-burn farming. Since this drastically reduces soil fertility, villages constantly move to find new land, dismantling and reassembling the entire lamin in a new location.

The most striking feature of many Dayak men and women are their pierced ear lobes stretched with the weight of heavy gold or brass rings but this custom is increasingly rare among the young. Older Dayaks, influenced by missionaries, often trim their ear lobes as a sign of conversion. It was once the custom of all women to tattoo their forearms and calves with bird and spirit designs. Except for tribes deep in the interior, tattooing of young women has almost disappeared, though it is still seen among men.

Many Dayaks are modifying their traditions under pressure from the Indonesian government and European missionaries. Neither the Muslims nor the Christians seem content to let the indigenous belief systems, the backbone of these tribal cultures, alone.

Not all Dayaks live in villages. The Punan are nomadic hunter/gatherers who still move through the jungles although some stay in longhouses at the height of the rainy season and many have settled in permanent riverside villages. The word punan is common to many inland dialects and means upriver or headwaters. To other Dayaks, the Punan are the ultimate jungle dwellers but as logging and ethno-religious evangelism push them deeper into the interior, they can be difficult to find. Over the border in East Malaysia they are known as the Penan, and actively protest against the destruction of their forest homes by government-backed lumber interests.

BOOKS

Two recent publications are highly recommended reading for those planning extensive travel in Kalimantan. *Stranger in the Forest* (Houghton Mifflin Co, Boston; and Century Hutchinson, London, 1988) is an inspiring account of Eric Hansen's six month journey by boat and on foot across Borneo in 1982. The hilarious *Into the Heart of Borneo* (Vintage Departures, New York, 1987) by Redmond O'Hanlon recounts the almost slapstick adventures of the author, a British naturalist, and the English poet James Fenton, as they make their way to Mt Batu in Kalimantan via Sarawak. Both books give a good feel for interior travel in Borneo.

GETTING THERE FROM OUTSIDE INDONESIA

To enter or exit Indonesia via Kalimantan by air, sea or land you'll need an Indonesian visa as Kalimantan's entry and exit points don't seem subject to the no visa rule. Theoretically, Pontianak is a visa-free entry point but don't expect the immigration office in Pontianak to know this. Even with a visa, arrival or departure via Kalimantan is not certain, although Tarakan, Pontianak and Balikpapan seem to accept all new arrivals as long as they have advance tourist visas.

To/from Singapore

Garuda has three flights a week from Singapore to Pontianak, Banjarmasin and Balikpapan. In the reverse direction, Garuda flies daily from Banjarmasin and Balikpapan, weekly from Pontianak. Union Oil has an office at Balikpapan's airport and charters direct flights to Singapore.

The cheapest fare between Singapore and Kalimantan is via Pontianak for 183,000 rp.

To/from Malaysia

Merpati flies weekly between Pontianak and Kuching in Sarawak for 100,000 rp. Pontianak to Kuching by bus is 25,000 rp or, in the reverse direction, about M$40.

Bouraq flies from Tarakan to Tawau in Sabah three times a week for 51,000 rp. There are longboats from Tarakan to Nunukan (12 hours, 8500 rp), and from Nunukan, speedboats to Tawau (4 hours, 15,000 rp). Buy tickets from CV Tam Bersaudara on Jalan Pasar Lingkas in Tarakan. The boats usually depart daily between 7 and 8 am, although they may not run on Sunday.

Rules about crossing the border between Malaysia and Kalimantan seem to change constantly. Some people get through, some don't. Sometimes it's OK if you fly, but not if you go by boat. Experiences vary widely, as letters we've received indicate:

In Manila the Indonesian Embassy would not give us a visa to cross via Kalimantan. We had a mileage ticket which goes Sandarkan, Tawau, Tarakan, Samarinda, etc. We had to change our flight ticket to come in via Jakarta or Denpasar before they would give us a visa. However we met a Danish couple who crossed the border with no problems. They said the Indonesian consul in Tawau was very nice and there were no hassles. . .

Despite the weekly flight on Merpati to Pontianak tourists cannot stay in Pontianak and must continue to Jakarta on a connecting flight. The total cost is probably the same as flying from Kuching to Johore Bahru and boating from Singapore. Travel overland from Sarawak or Sabah to Kalimantan is, we are told, not possible. There is a very helpful Indonesian Consul in Kuching.

Still aren't allowed to overland from Tawau to Tarakan but we flew on Bouraq Indonesian Airlines, a 68-mile puddle jump in an eight-passenger Britten Norman Islander with 'Bali Air' markings. We used our Osaka-Bali mileage ticket, which meant the flight cost us about US$10. In Tawau they quoted M$150, in Tarakan the fare for flying back to Tawau would have been about M$100. Who knows what it would cost from Bouraq in Singapore? Anyway it operates four times a week and is often full – so book ahead.

We tried to get our visas in Kota Kinabalu but were told they didn't do them and that we should get them in Tawau. In Tawau, which is just a branch of the KK consulate, we were asked why we didn't get visas in KK! Fortunately we had a letter from the KK office telling them to give us visas. They issued them in five hours: they cost M$35 each and required two photos.

Supposedly to get airline tickets for Kalimantan-Sarawak or Kalimantan-Sabah flights you need a passport which is still valid six months after your arrival date, a special visa for east Malaysia, a return ticket from Sarawak and US$1000. One slight problem: the Malaysian embassy in Jakarta might not give you the special visa! The Malaysian consulate in Pontianak say you can pick up your visa in Pontianak, however. To be absolutely safe, get the east Malaysia visa in your own country first.

If you want to exit Indonesia by sea via Nunukan in East Kalimantan (to Tawau, Sabah), you'll need an exit permit from the immigration office in Jakarta if you entered Indonesia at a visa-free port. The exit permit isn't necessary if you entered Indonesia on a one month advance (paid) visa. At this writing most people seem able to cross between Kalimantan and Sabah or Sarawak as long as their paperwork is in order. Advance visas for Indonesia are now reportedly available in Kuching and Kota Kinabalu.

At this writing the Malaysian side of the border between Pontianak and Kuching, is definitely open to foreigners who want to cross by land. The Indonesians also plan to open their side by January 1989. The Malaysian Consulate and the Indonesian immigration office in Pontianak report that flying between Pontianak and Kuching is allowed if you have in advance, the east Malaysia visa (going north) or the Indonesian tourist visa (going south). If you want to cross by land check with the

Indonesian immigration office and the Malaysian Consulate in Pontianak first.

To/from Philippines

Presuming you can make it from Tarakan to Tawau, there are on-again and off-again flights between Tawau and Zamboanga in the southern Philippines. Check with Sabre Air Services in Tawau and don't count on anything. Bouraq no longer operates flights from Tarakan to Zamboanga in the Philippines.

GETTING THERE FROM INSIDE INDONESIA

If you don't intend heading inland, Kalimantan is probably best seen as a detour between Java and Sulawesi; the East and South Kalimantan cities of Samarinda and Banjarmasin are particularly worth seeing.

On the other hand, if you plan to spend some time exploring the interior, Banjarmasin or Pontianak are probably your best entry points since they can be reached quickly from Singapore or Jakarta, thus eating up less of your visa time.

Air

Bouraq, Merpati and Garuda all fly into Kalimantan and there are lots of flights from other parts of Indonesia. Garuda flights include Jakarta-Banjarmasin, Jakarta-Pontianak, Jakarta-Balikpapan and Ujung Pandang-Banjarmasin.

Merpati flights are usually cheaper. Check available flights with Merpati and Garuda; there are also connections from Kalimantan to Yogyakarta and Surabaya. Garuda will even fly you from Kupang (in Timor) to Tarakan on the east coast of Kalimantan on the same day.

Some of the most useful flights between Kalimantan and Sulawesi are with Bouraq. They fly from Ternate (in Maluku) to Balikpapan via Gorontalo and Manado in northern Sulawesi, and Palu in central Sulawesi. They also fly from Ujung Pandang to Balikpapan and

Banjarmasin – slightly cheaper than Garuda. There are also connections from Ujung Pandang to Pontianak, Samarinda and Tarakan.

Boat

There are shipping connections with Java and Sulawesi, both with Pelni and other shipping companies.

The Pelni ships *KM Kelimutu*, *KM Kerinci* and *KM Kambuna* pull into various ports on the South and East Kalimantan coast on their loops out of Java around Kalimantan and Sulawesi. Pelni fares are quite low. For example, economy class fares on the *KM Kerinci* from Balikpapan are Toli Toli 20,000 rp, Tarakan 22,200 rp, Ujung Pandang 19,300 rp, Surabaya 28,500 rp. Add about 10,000 rp each time you move up to classes IV, III, II and I (except for *KM Kelimutu*, which only has economy, II and I).

There are also regular passenger-carrying cargo ships between the ports on the east coast of Kalimantan to Pare Pare and Palu in Sulawesi – see the relevant sections for details. Pelni also has regular passenger ships between Surabaya and Banjarmasin – see the Banjarmasin section for details. For details of ships from Jakarta to Pontianak see the Pontianak section. Apart from Pelni, Mahakam Shipping, Jalan Kali Besar Timur 111 in Jakarta, may be worth trying for more information on other ships to Kalimantan.

GETTING AROUND

Although Kalimantan's area is huge, the population is sparse and the dense jungle and rough terrain make communications and travel difficult. Life in Kalimantan centres on the rivers which are the most important roads on the island.

If there are no navigable rivers travel is, in most cases, impossible except by air. All you see from the air is endless jungle cut by winding rivers. Small outboard motorboats, speedboats, longboats and some sizable ferries now cruise the rivers but dugouts paddled by a lone boatman are still a common sight. Thick vegetation cloaks both sides of the rivers, broken only by the occasional village, small riverside town or timber concession.

Apart from the area around Pontianak and the stretch from Samarinda to Banjarmasin there are few real roads and the boats and ferries that ply the numerous rivers and waterways are the most popular forms of long-distance transport. Each of Kalimantan's four provinces has at least one major river into the interior that serves as a slow-moving highway: in East Kalimantan there are the Mahakam and Kayan rivers; in South Kalimantan, the Barito; in Central Kalimantan, the Barito and the Kahayan; in West Kalimantan, the Kapuas and the Melawai.

There are also plenty of flight connections to inland and coastal destinations and some shipping along the eastern coast.

Going upriver into some of the Dayak regions is now relatively easy from Pontianak and Samarinda, but the further you go off the beaten canal the more time you'll need. For serious forays into the interior, even along the main rivers, you must allow about two weeks minimum per province.

Air

There are flights around the coastal cities and into the interior of Kalimantan with the regular airline companies. Merpati carries the bulk of traffic although there are many flights with DAS (Dirgantara Air Service), Bouraq and Deraya Air Taxi. Other possibilities include planes run by the oil companies and the missionaries. If you're in the right place at the right time and ask the right person, and they don't mind the look of you, you may be able to pick up a ride.

DAS's small prop-aircraft fly to all sorts of places with daily flights from Pontianak to inland West Kalimantan towns like Sintang or south-east to the coastal town of Ketapang. They also have flights between Palangkaraya and Banjarmasin or Buntok. Deraya Air Taxi flies in and out of Pangkalan Bun in Central Kalimantan to Pontianak, Palangkaraya and Banjarmasin. In East Kalimantan, Merpati has the best interior routes.

Boat

There are small boats, speedboats, ferries and houseboats plying the rivers between some of the major towns and cities – like the daily ferries and speedboats between Banjarmasin and Palangkaraya or the longboats between Tarakan and Berau or Nunukan.

There are a number of variations on the river ferry theme. The *feri sunggai* (river ferry/cargo boat, also known as a *kapal biasa*), carries both cargo and passengers; the *taxi sunggai* (river taxi) carries cargo downstairs and has an upper level with

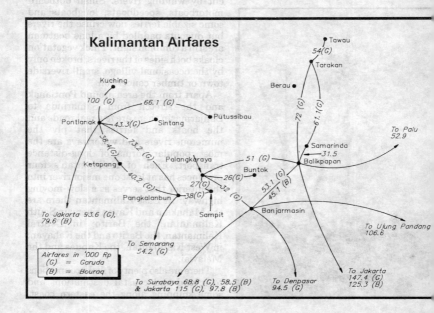

Kalimantan Airfares

Kuching
100 (G)
66.1 (G)
Pontianak
43.3(G) — Sintang
Putussibau
36.4(G)
73.2 (G)
Ketapang
Palangkaraya
40.2 (G)
27(G)
Pangkalanbun
38(G)
32 (G)
Sampit
To Jakarta 93.6 (G),
79.6 (B)
To Semarang
54.2 (G)
To Surabaya 68.8 (G), 58.5 (B)
& Jakarta 115 (G), 97.8 (B)

Tawau
54(G)
Tarakan
Berau
72 (G)
61.1(G)
Samarinda
31.5
Balikpapan
To Palu
52.9
51 (G)
26(G)
Buntok
53.1 (G)
45.1 (B)
Banjarmasin
To Ujung Pandang
106.6
To Denpasar
94.5 (G)
To Jakarta
147.4 (G)
125.3 (B)

Airfares in '000 Rp
(G) = Garuda
(B) = Bouraq

rows of wooden bunks (sometimes with mattresses and pillows); and the *bis air* (water bus) which has rows of seats.

Along the Kapuas River in Pontianak are the *bandung*, large cargo-cum-houseboats that take up to a month to move upriver to Putussibau. A bis air does the same distance in about four days. A *longbot*, as the nan..e indicates, is a long boat – a narrow vessel with two or three large outboard motors at the rear and bench seats in a covered passenger cabin. You commonly see these carrying passengers on the major waterways of Kalimantan.

Speedboats (*speed* or *speedbot*) commonly ply the Barito, Kapuas, Kahayan and Kayan rivers and seem to be appearing elsewhere. Don't get too hung up on the terminology, as what may be called a bis air in one province may be a taxi sunggai in another.

East Kalimantan

Kalimantan Timur, or Kal-Tim for short, is the most populated and developed province in Kalimantan. Lumber, oil, mining, and, to a small extent, tourism, have wrought irreversible changes upon the coastal areas and far into the interior. The Mahakam and Kayan rivers are the main aquatic thoroughfares. In the interior, once thriving Dayak cultures, including Punan, Banuaq, Iban and Kenyah, are fast transforming in the face of logging, oil exploration and missionary activity. Still, with time and effort you can reach places that rarely see a foreign face.

BALIKPAPAN

Apart from the clean, comfortable and highly insulated Pertamina, Union Oil and Total residential areas, Balikpapan is mostly grubby and decayed back streets, ravaged footpaths and rampaging Hondas and Yamahas. The area bounded by Jalan Randan Utara and Jalan Pandanwanyi north of the oil refinery is a suburb built on stilts over the muddy isthmus, with uneven, lurching wooden walkways between the houses.

The huge oil refinery dominates the city and flying in you'll see stray tankers and offshore oil rigs. This is the centre of Kalimantan's oil business and the chief city of the province. There are four Garuda flights from Jakarta to Balikpapan every day; a five star hotel which could easily be ranked as one of the hundred best in the world; and nearly as many American, Australian and European voices as there are Japanese motorcycles. Since the oil glut of the early '80s, Balikpapan's economy has taken a serious downturn and the number of ex-pats working on fat oil-company contracts has declined.

Information & Orientation

A good landmark is the enormous Hotel Benakutai on Jalan Pengeran Antasari near the shorefront. Heading east from Jalan Pengeran Antasari along the shorefront is the airport road; heading west is Kelandasan which runs into Jalan Ahmad Yani. Heading north Jalan Pengeran Antasari merges into Jalan Sutuyo, Jalan Parman and Jalan Panjaitan, at the end of which is the Rapak bus terminal. Most of the hotels and offices can be found along these streets.

The immigration office is on the corner of Jalan Ahmad Yani and Jalan Sudirman. The shop in the foyer of the Benakutai Hotel sells Indonesian and English-language newspapers and foreign news magazines.

Post The post office on Jalan Ahmad Yani is open Monday to Friday 8 am to 6 pm and on Saturday, Sunday and holidays 8 am to 5 pm. The airport post office is open Monday to Thursday 8 am to 2 pm, Friday 8 to 11 am, Saturday 8 am to 1 pm, and Sunday and holidays 8 am to 12 noon. Another post office is on Jalan Suprapto,

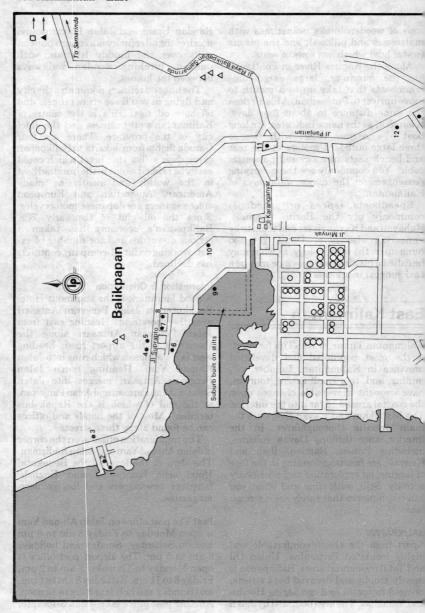

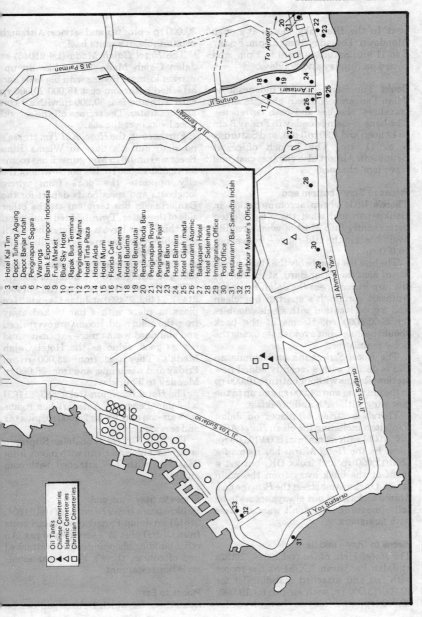

3   Hotel Kal Tim
4   Depot Tuhung Agung
5   Depot Banjar Indah
6   Penginapan Segara
7   Warungs
8   Bank Expor Impor Indonesia
9   Fruit Market
10 Blue Sky Hotel
11 Rapak Bus Terminal
13 Hotel Tirta Plaza
14 Hotel Aida
15 Hotel Murni
16 Florida Cafe
17 Antasari Cinema
18 Hotel Budima
19 Hotel Benakutai
20 Restaurant Roda Baru
21 Penginapan Royal
22 Penginapan Mama
23 Pasar Baru
24 Hotel Bantera
25 Hotel Gajah mada
26 Restaurant Atomic
27 Balikpapan Hotel
28 Hotel Sederhana
29 Immigration Office
30 Post Office
31 Restaurant/Bar Samudra Indah
32 Pelni
33 Harbour Master's Office

Oil Tanks
Chinese Cemeteries
Islamic Cemeteries
Christian Cemeteries

next to the Blue Sky Hotel; it's open Monday to Thursday 8 am to 2 pm, Friday 8 to 11 am, Saturday 8 am to 1 pm, and closed on Sunday and holidays.

Banks The Bank Negara Indonesia on Jalan Pengeran Antasari changes major travellers' cheques and cash currencies. The bank is open Monday to Friday 8 am to 12 noon and 1.30 to 3 pm, and Saturday 8 to 11 am. The branch office at Seppingan Airport also changes cash and travellers' cheques.

Places to Stay – bottom end

There's little cheap accommodation in Balikpapan and what there is, is often permanently full. Most of what's readily available is in the mid-range – from about 10,000 rp.

The best bet is probably the *Penginapan Royal* near the Pasar Baru, at the start of the airport road near the Jalan Pengaran Antasari corner. It's spartan but clean and a good location with singles/doubles for 4000/8000 rp. Rooms at the back should be quiet, but avoid those facing the noisy main street.

The *Hotel Sederhana* on Kelandasan Ulu is decent with a recently added new section. Rooms without bath are 10,000 rp in the old wing and 24,000 rp and up in the new wing with bath and breakfast.

There's a string of places on Jalan Panjaitan including the clean *Hotel Aida* (tel 21006) with rooms from 6000/10,000 rp. Close by the *Hotel Murni* has rooms for 6500/12,000 rp and looks OK, but get a room at the back away from the main street. On the same street the *Penginapan Mama* looks good but always seems to be full – meaning they don't want to mess with foreigners.

Places to Stay – middle

The *Hotel Tirta Plaza* (tel 22324, 22132) at Jalan Panjaitan XX/51-52 has rooms with fan and attached mandi/toilet for 10,000/13,000 rp, with air-con for 19,000/23,000 rp, and air-con bungalows for

30,000 rp – plus tax and service. Although comfortable, it's quite basic.

The *Hotel Gajah Mada* (tel 21046) at Jalan Gajah Mada 108 is like an up-market losmen. Rooms with big beds and attached bathroom cost 18,000/20,000 rp with bath and fan, 30,000 rp with air-con and hot water. The terrace off the second floor looks over the sea.

Further out, the *Hotel Kal Tim* (there's no sign, but it's next to Wisma Bina Bersama) on Jalan Mangunsidi has rooms for 12,500/15,000 rp. It's north-west of the city opposite the dock from where longboats and speedboats depart for the Banjarmasin bus terminal on the other side of the water. Twin-bedded doubles on the third floor have a balcony and you'll probably get coffee and sweet rolls in the morning. Ask for a fan if your room hasn't got one. Colts from the Rapak terminal take you straight to the hotel for 200 rp.

The *Hotel Balikpapan* (tel 21490, 21491, 21492, 21493) at Jalan Garuda 2 is a pleasant place with a bar tucked away from the main road. Rooms are overpriced and standard rooms more expensive and not as good value as the Hotel Gajah Mada's. They cost from 25,000 rp on Friday and weekends, and from 36,000 rp Monday to Thursday.

The *Hotel Budiman* (tel 22583, 21163) on Jalan Pengeran Antasari has rooms with air-con and TV for 25,000 rp, plus tax and service charge.

The *Blue Sky Hotel* on Jalan Suprapto is comfortable and clean with rooms from 28,000 rp with TV, attached bathroom and toilet.

Places to Stay – top end

Balikpapan's *Hotel Benakutai* (tel 21804, 21813) on Jalan Pangeran Antasari costs from US$60 plus 21% service and tax. An office building/shopping centre is attached and of course, there's an international-style bar/restaurant.

Places to Eat

Something for which Balikpapan can be

recommended, are good seafood padang places – although padang food tends to be expensive.

Try the *Restaurant Masakan Padang Simpang Raya* next to the Hotel Murni on Jalan Panjaitan. The *Restaurant Salero Minang* at Jalan Gajah Mada 12B is similarly priced as is the *Restaurant Sinar Minang* on Jalan Pangeran Antasari which serves *udang galah* (giant river prawns) and is marginally better than the Selaro Minang.

Near the Hotel Gajah Mada on the corner of Jalan Ahmad Yani and Jalan Pengeran Antasari is the *Florida Cafe*, which serves western breakfasts and good local seafood at night.

More unusual (for the decor) is the *Restaurant Roda Baru* near the Penginapan Royal – eat underneath a chandelier amidst a rockery with plaster storks. The cheapest eats are at the numerous warungs and food trolleys along Jalan Dondong near the Hotel Benakutai during the evening.

The *Depot Banjar Indah* which serves udang galah and the *Depot Tuhung Agung*, both on Jalan Suprapto, are two cheapies worth visiting if you're staying in the north-west corner of town.

Entertainment

Apart from watching the twinkling lights of the oil refinery at night you could try getting drunk in one of Balikpapan's dwindling number of bars and discos.

Try the *Banua Patra Restaurant & Bar* on Jalan Ahmad Yani. It has a large bar and dance floor; some nights there's a band and other nights, a disco.

Further west, Jalan Ahmad Yani becomes Jalan Yos Sudarso and as it rounds the peninsula you'll come to a couple of smaller bar/disco affairs – there's usually a cover charge and a drink minimum.

Getting There & Away

Air Merpati is near the Pasar Baru on the airport road and open Monday to Thursday 8 am to 3 pm, and Friday to Sunday 8 am to 12 noon. Bouraq (tel 21107, 21087) has an office in the Hotel Benakutai on Jalan Pengeran Antasari. Garuda is diagonally opposite the Hotel Benakutai.

Garuda flies between Jakarta and Balikpapan (two hours) for 149,500 rp; on slower Merpati and Bouraq planes (three hours 20 minutes) it's 128,000 rp. From Surabaya it's 105,100 rp with Garuda (30 minutes) and 95,000 rp with Merpati (one hour 10 minutes).

Garuda flies to and from Singapore via Pontianak three times a week for 109,900 rp.

Union Oil has an office at Balikpapan airport and they charter planes for direct flights from Balikpapan to Singapore (there is a separate Singapore-bound terminal).

Bus From Balikpapan you can head either north to Samarinda or south to Banjarmasin. Buses to Samarinda (1800 rp, two hours) depart from the Rapak terminal. The bus companies have their offices at the terminal.

Buses to Banjarmasin (about 10,000 rp) depart from the Banjarmasin bus terminal on the opposite side of the harbour to the city. To get there take a colt from the Rapak bus station to the pier on Jalan Mangunsidi; from here take a speedboat to the other side – it costs 1000 rp per person or around 3000 rp to charter and takes 10 minutes – the speedboat drivers will mob you. Alternatively a motorised longboat costs 500 rp and takes 25 minutes.

The Banjarmasin bus terminal is immediately behind the speedboat and longboat dock; there are also a couple of warungs here. It may be a good idea to go to the station the day before you want to leave, buy a ticket and find out when the bus departs. The bus trip between Balikpapan and Banjarmasin is a gruelling 12 hours on bad roads and the first six hours are the worst.

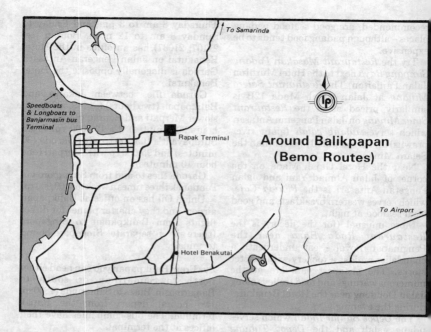

**Around Balikpapan
(Bemo Routes)**

Boat The Pelni ships *KM Kerinci* and *KM Kambuna* call in regularly and connect Balikpapan to Tarakan on the east coast of Kalimantan, Pantoloan, Toli Toli and Ujung Pandang in Sulawesi and to Surabaya and Jakarta. See the table for fares (in rp) from Balikpapan.

In Balikpapan the Pelni office (tel 22187) is on Jalan Yos Sudarso. For regular ships to Surabaya, try PT Ling Jaya Shipping (tel 21577) at Jalan Yos Sudarso 40 and PT Sudi Jaya Agung (tel 21956) at Jalan Pelabuhan 39. Fares are around 30,000 rp.

Also worth considering are the regular

ships to Pare Pare in Sulawesi. Go to the office of PT Nurlina at the pier from where you catch speedboats and longboats to the Banjarmasin bus terminal on the other side of the harbour. Departures for Pare Pare are almost daily and the fare is around 22,500 rp.

Getting Around

Airport Transport Seppingan Airport is about a 15-minute fast drive from Pasar Baru along a surfaced road. A taxi from the airport to town is a standard 4500 rp if you buy your taxi ticket in the terminal.

destination	I	II	III	IV	ekonomi
Jakarta	119,100	87,700	68,000	54,900	44,000
Surabaya	79,000	59,000	45,600	37,100	28,500
Ujung Pandang	55,600	41,000	31,600	25,600	19,300
Pantoloan	34,500	27,200	21,100	17,500	15,400
Toli Toli	50,300	37,700	29,800	24,500	20,000
Tarakan	34,400	42,100	32,600	26,700	22,200

Walk outside and bargain your fare down around 3000 rp.

In town you should be able to charter a bemo to the airport for less – from Pasar Baru for 2500 rp. Chartered bemo or taxi seems to be the only way to the airport. A couple of rumah makan are at the airport.

Bemo Bemos ply the streets; 200 to 300 rp gets you anywhere around town. The chief station is the Rapak bus and bemo terminal at the end of Jalan Panjaitan. From here bemos do a circular route around the main streets. (Guys with motorcyles also hang around the Rapak terminal and will take you anywhere as a pillion passenger).

SAMARINDA

Balikpapan for oil, Samarinda for timber; this is another old trading port on one of Kalimantan's mighty rivers. If you want to look at a timber mill there's a giant one on the road to the town of Tenggarong, not far from Samarinda. This is also the most convenient starting point for trips up the Mahakam River inland to the Dayak areas. The riverbank around Samarinda is pitted with factories and warehouses, and numerous cargo ships ply the water.

Most of the people who have settled Samarinda are Banjars from South Kalimantan, so the main dialect is Banjarese. There are also many Kutais, the indigenous people of this area, most of whom are now Muslims.

On the south side of the Mahakam River in the part of town called Samarinda Seberang (Across from Samarinda), you can visit cottage industries where Samarinda-style sarongs are woven. The traditional East Kalimantan wraparound is woven of *daun doyo*, dried leaves from the doyo tree.

Beside the Mahakam Cinema is an old Chinese temple worth a stroll if you have spare time. About 500 metres north of the Hotel Mesra is a large morning market from 5 to 10 am. Arrive before 7 am to see it at its best.

Information & Orientation

The main part of Samarinda stretches along the north bank of the Mahakam River. The best orientation point is the enormous mosque on the riverfront – Jalan Yos Sudarso runs east and Jalan Gajah Mada west. Most of the offices and hotels are along these two streets or in the streets immediately behind them.

The Hotel Mesra allows day guests to use their large, well-kept pool for 1500 rp per day.

For good information on East Kalimantan trekking and river journeys, contact Jailani, a Kutai guide, through Hotel Rahayu, Jalan K H Abdul Hasan 17, Samarinda.

Banks The Bank Negara Indonesia is on the corner of Jalan Sebatik and Jalan Panglima Batur. It changes only US dollars cash and travellers' cheques and is open Monday to Thursday 8 am to 12.30 pm, Friday 1.30 to 4.30 pm, and Saturday 8 to 11.30 am. The Bank Dagang Negara on Jalan Mulawarman is the only bank in Samarinda that changes travellers' cheques in currencies besides US dollars. It's open the same hours as the BNI.

Post The main post office is on the corner of Jalan Gajah Mada and Jalan Awanglong, opposite the Bank Rakyat Indonesia.

Places to Stay – bottom end

The *Hotel Hidayah* on Jalan K H Kahlid is central and its spartan but clean singles/doubles cost from 5500/8000 rp, more for rooms with mandi. Rooms upstairs are quieter (away from the noisy TV in the foyer) than those at the front. Rates include a small breakfast.

Further up the same street beyond the *Penginapan Siar*, which doesn't accept foreigners, is the similar *Hotel Rahayu*. Rooms here are 6000/10,000 rp including breakfast, 12,000/15,000 rp with mandi.

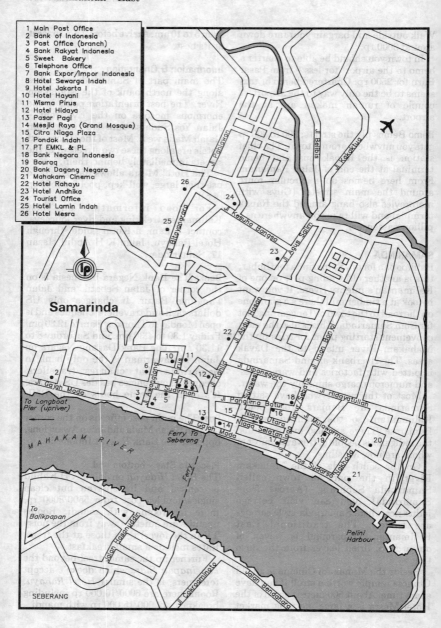

1 Main Post Office
2 Bank of Indonesia
3 Post Office (branch)
4 Bank Rakyat Indonesia
5 Sweet Bakery
6 Telephone Office
7 Bank Expor/Impor Indonesia
8 Hotel Sewarga Indah
9 Hotel Jakarta I
10 Hotel Hayani
11 Wisma Pirus
12 Hotel Hidaya
13 Pasar Pagi
14 Mesjid Raya (Grand Mosque)
15 Citra Niaga Plaza
16 Pondok Indah
17 PT EMKL & PL
18 Bank Negara Indonesia
19 Bouraq
20 Bank Dagang Negara
21 Mahakam Cinema
22 Hotel Rahayu
23 Hotel Andhika
24 Tourist Office
25 Hotel Lamin Indah
26 Hotel Mesra

Samarinda

The *Hotel Andhika* (tel 22358, 23507) at Jalan Haji Agus Salim 37 has been refurbished since the last edition and has clean and quiet economy rooms at 8470/12,100 rp including breakfast, plus more expensive standard and air-con rooms. They have an attached coffee shop/restaurant serving Chinese, European and Indonesian food.

Next door to the Andhika is the cheapest accommodation open to foreigners in Samarinda: *Penginapan Maharani*, with very basic rooms for 4000/6700 rp, no attached mandi.

Two recent discoveries are the pleasant *Wisma Pirus* (tel 21873) and *Hotel Hayani* (tel 22653), both on Jalan Pirus off Jalan Jenderal Sudirman.

The staff at Wisma Pirus are friendly and have information on East Kalimantan travel. Rooms without mandi are 6650/10,890 rp; with mandi they're 10,980/15,730 rp, including tax and service. It's very clean and quiet. The Hayani across the street is also good with singles/doubles for 11,000/14,000 rp, all with mandi.

The *Hotel Jakarta I* is a larger cheapie right on Jalan Jenderal Sudirman between Jalan Veteran and Jalan K H Kahlid. Adequate rooms are 6000/11,000 rp without mandi, 10,000/12,500 rp with. There is a good travel agency in front of this hotel.

An economical choice if you want to stay near Samarinda's airfield is *Hotel Rahmat Abadi* (tel 23462) at Jalan Serindit 215, just across from the mouth of Jalan Pipit which leads to the terminal. Rooms start at 7260/10,164 rp with breakfast.

Down the street toward the town centre is the cheaper *Penginapan Putra Tapin* with basic but clean rooms for 5500 rp.

Places to Stay - top end

The *Hotel Sewarga Indah* on Jalan Jenderal Sudirman has air-con rooms starting at 18,150/21,780 rp, including breakfast and tax/service. It's nothing spectacular, but the cheapest in Samarinda with air-con.

Samarinda's top hotel is the *Hotel Mesra* (tel 21011), complete with a large, clean swimming pool, tennis court, giant chess set and coffee shop. Singles range from a surprisingly low 25,000 rp right up to 65,000 rp. Doubles are from 40,000 to 70,000 rp – plus 21% service and tax. The Mesra is on Jalan Pahlawan on the northwest edge of town in a hilly area that sometimes gets a nice breeze.

South of the Mesra, off the same road but on a higher hill, is the *Hotel Lamin Indah* (tel 23894). Clean rooms with air-con, TV and hot water are a uniform 36,400 rp. There is a restaurant and bar but that's about it.

Places to Eat

Samarinda is a great place if you like eating especially if you like fruit. Along Jalan Mas Tenggarong people sit carving giant nangka into manageable segments. A zurzat will cost you 500 rp and there are pineapples, bananas and salaks aplenty.

Samarinda's chief gastronomic wonder is the udang galah found in the local warungs. The prawns are caught by local fishermen using big rattan baskets. The standard price for udang galah in the markets is 10,000 rp per kg, which should yield roughly seven to 10 giant prawns, depending on the size. Two or three of these suckers are a meal for most individuals. Ask your hotel's kitchen staff to grill them for you.

One of the better places for decent local food at decent prices is the *Citra Niaga* hawkers' centre off Jalan Niaga, east a block or two from the Mesjid Raya. There's an excellent variety of seafood, padang, sate, noodle and rice dishes, *ayam panggang* (roast chicken) and fruit juices as well as beer (usually warm). Ayam panggang is a local specialty and shouldn't be missed. It seems like the kind of place where it might be a good idea to establish prices in advance, though we weren't ever ripped off.

At the Mesra Indah Shopping Centre close to the Hotel Hidayah on Jalan K H Kahlid, are two decent food centres and, upstairs overlooking the street, an ice cream parlour.

If you like pastries for breakfast, try the *Sweet Home Bakery* at Jalan Jenderal Sudirman 8, west of Jalan Pirus on the left. For excellent Chinese breakfasts, your best bet is the spotless *Depot AC*, located behind the Wella Beauty Salon off Jalan Mulawarman – they serve very tasty bubur ayam, nasi bebek, nasi ayam and nasi tahu, all made with top grade Thai rice and quite inexpensive. The Depot AC is open mornings only.

If you prefer Indonesian nasi soto or nasi sop for breakfast, there's the efficient *Warung Aida* on the south side of Jalan Panglima Batur at the Jalan Kalimantan intersection.

Moving upscale, the *Pondok Indah*, next door to the Warung Aida on Jalan Panglima Batur, is a favourite ex-pat hangout, well known for its steak and fries. They also serve very good if pricey Indonesian food.

For a splurge, locals reckon the best hotel restaurants are at the Mesra, Sewarga Indah and the Andhika, in that order. The fanciest restaurant in town is the *Haur Gading Restaurant* off Jalan Sulawesi. They specialise in seafood and the udang galah are 2500 rp each.

The warung across from the airport terminal has good, inexpensive rice dishes, including nasi rawon, nasi pecel and nasi sop. The airport cafeteria is more expensive and limited in variety.

Entertainment

Several bars and discos are tucked away throughout the Kaltim Theatre complex across from the sleazy Sukarni Hotel (always full because it's strictly a brothel). Most are fairly hard-core hostess bars, but the *Blue Pacific* is a slightly upscale discotheque where couples are welcome. Cover charge is 3500 rp which includes a small bottle of beer and peanuts. Take care climbing the metal stairs to the upper floors – they're in advanced decay.

Getting There & Away

Air The Garuda and Merpati offices are on the east side of Jalan Imam Bonjol a couple of blocks north of Bank Negara Indonesia.

Garuda doesn't fly from Samarinda but Merpati has several flights daily to Balikpapan which connect with Garuda flights to other domestic destinations, as well as very useful flights to the upriver villages of Long Lunuk (Data Dawai), Long Ampung and Tanjung Selor. See the section on Visiting The Dayaks for flight details.

Bouraq (tel 21105) is at Jalan Mulawarman 24 and they book daily flights to Tarakan (on small Bali Air planes, 69,600 rp; on Bouraq 75,500 rp), Berau (on Bali Air only, 64,700 rp), Banjarmasin (65,100 rp), Jakarta (138,900 rp) and Surabaya (two flights daily, 103,100 rp).

Bus From Samarinda you can head west to Tenggarong or south to Balikpapan. The long-distance bus station is at Seberang on the south side of the Mahakam River. To get there take a longboat from the pier at Pasar Pagi on Jalan Gajah Mada. The crossing takes a few minutes, costs 200 rp, and there are boats that take motorcycles across. The bus station is immediately behind the boat dock on the other side.

From Seberang there are buses daily to Tenggarong (1000 rp, one hour) and to Balikpapan (1800 rp bus, 2000 minibus, two hours) along well-surfaced roads.

Boat Pelni are at Jalan Yos Sudarso 40/56 or ask at the nearby Terminal Penumpang Kapal Laut Samarinda and the Direktorat Jenderal Perhubungan Laut – both on Jalan Yos Sudarso. However, Balikpapan and Tarakan are the nearest harbours for Pelni passenger ships, which don't operate in or out of Samarinda. Various shipping offices are along the same street, like PT Perusahaan Pelayaran Lokal and PT EMKL.

There are many non-Pelni boats from Samarinda to other ports in East Kalimantan. Possible destinations include Berau, also known as Tanjung Redep, (25,000 rp – about two days and two nights) and Tarakan (30,000 rp – about two days and two nights). If you can't get a ship to Tarakan then take one as far as Berau. From there it's easy to get a boat to Tarakan.

Occasional boats go to Donggala, Palu, Pare Pare and Pantoloan on the west coast of Sulawesi. There should be one or two ships a week to at least one of these places though you may have to hunt around the shipping agencies. The *KM Tanjung Slamat* and the *KM Harapanku III* sail to Pare Pare on Tuesday, Wednesday and Saturday for 25,600 rp per person. Another possibility is to try and catch a Bugis schooner across to Sulawesi.

The *KM Dewi Mutiara* sails to Surabaya twice weekly for 25,600 rp.

Riverboat Boats up the Mahakam River leave from the Sungai Kunjang ferry terminal south-west of the town centre. To get there, take a green city minibus A (called taksi A) west on Jalan Gajah Mada, and ask for 'feri'. The regular fare is 300 rp but if you get in an empty taksi they may try to make you charter. If you don't want to charter, insist on 'harga biasa'.

A riverboat to Tenggarong costs 1000 rp and takes two hours. For other destinations further up the Mahakam River, see the section on Visiting The Dayaks.

Getting Around

Airport Transport The airport is quite literally *in* the suburbs. You might think you're hard up if a freeway gets slapped down over your nature strip, but how many people have Twin Otters landing in their backyards?

A taxi counter is in the terminal. Pay

Getting around by boat, Samarinda

5000 rp into the centre of town or walk a few minutes down Jalan Pipit to Jalan Serindit and catch a public colt (route B) for 500 rp all the way down Jalan Kakaktua to the waterfront.

To the airport you should be able to catch a colt from the corner of Jalan KH Kahlid and Jalan Panglima Batur, but beware of getting into empty colts unless you want to end up chartering them.

Taksi City colts, called taksi, run along several overlapping routes designated A, B and C. Most short runs are 200 rp. It's a standard 300 rp to the ferry pier for boats going upriver and 500 rp to the airfield.

TENGGARONG

On the Mahakam River, 39 km from Samarinda, Tenggarong was once the seat of the sultanate of Kutai. Today it's a little riverside town cut by dirty canals. Like many small towns along the Mahakam,

wooden walkways lead from each house to the toilet shacks built on stilts over the waterways. Both river and canals function as a combined toilet/bath/wash basin/well.

The chief attraction of Tenggarong is the former sultan's palace museum. Some travellers prefer to start long river trips from here, although you'll have more seating choice on boats from Samarinda.

Tourist Office A tourist office next to the sultan's palace has information on river trips and the Kutai Nature Reserve.

Sultan's Palace - Mulawarman Museum

The former sultan's palace is now a museum. It was built by the Dutch in the 1930s in futurist, monolithic, modernist style. It holds a collection of artefacts from the days of the sultan and many Dayak artefacts.

The palace is closed on Monday; open Tuesday to Thursday 8 am to 2 pm,

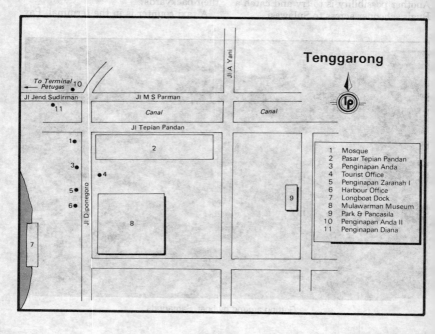

Tenggarong

1 Mosque
2 Pasar Tepian Pandan
3 Penginapan Anda
4 Tourist Office
5 Penginapan Zaranah I
6 Harbour Office
7 Longboat Dock
8 Mulawarman Museum
9 Park & Pancasila
10 Penginapan Anda II
11 Penginapan Diana

Friday 8 to 11 am, Saturday 8 am to 1 pm and Sunday and holidays 8 am to 2 pm. Admission is 200 rp.

Places to Stay

Down on the waterfront are two places right on the boat dock. The *Penginapan Zaranah I* (tel 148) has rooms for 2500/5000 rp. The *Warung & Penginapan Anda* (tel 78) costs 3000/5000 rp.

Up the road and around the corner on Jalan Jenderal Sudirman are the similarly priced *Anda II* and *Penginapan Diana*. The Diana is the pick of the lot, with larger rooms and the restaurant downstairs looks decent.

Places to Eat

A couple of rumah makan and warungs are around the market and the boat dock, but none is memorable. Try the *Rumah Makan Ibunda* in the Pasar Pandan – it's a padang place, so expect to pay a couple of thousand rupiah for a decent meal, but the food is OK.

Getting There & Away

Colts to Tenggarong leave Samarinda's Seberang bus station, across the river from the main part of Samarinda. The one-hour trip costs 1000 rp and the colt pulls into the Petugas Terminal on the outskirts of Tenggarong. From here you have to get a taksi kota, which is another colt into the centre of Tenggarong, for 200 rp.

Guys with motorcycles will also take you into town for 300 rp. The city taxis run between 7 am and 6 pm. It takes about 10 minutes to get from Terminal Petugas to Pasar Tepian Pandan, where you get off for the boat dock, palace and tourist office.

There appear to be no direct buses or colts from Tenggarong to Balikpapan. Boats from Samarinda to Tenggarong leave from the Sunggai Kunjang pier outside of town. The boat costs 1000 rp, takes 2½ hours, and docks at Tenggarong's main pier.

VISITING THE DAYAKS

Probably the best starting point for visits to inland Dayak villages is Samarinda from where longboats ply the Mahakam, Kedang Kapala and Balayan rivers; and Merpati flies to the mouth of the mighty Kayan River.

A good source of information about the Dayak areas is the Kutai guide Jailani in Samarinda. He can be reached through the Rahayu or Hidayah hotels. Jailani speaks good English and is very friendly and helpful (although he does tend to inflate quotes for longboats). His information is free, but he can also serve as a guide at the scheduled government fee of 35,000 rp per day.

Longboats

Longboats trips are a great way to travel into the interior – slow but very relaxing. Generally, you sleep on a covered deck with an unobstructed view of every sunset and sunrise. Every few hours boats without cooking facilities pull in at a village dock and those who haven't brought their own food get off to eat in a warung.

Some boats have warungs onboard and an upstairs sleeping area with mattresses and lockers. Either way it's a good idea to bring snacks and plenty of bottled water. Also, take reading or writing material to help pass the time when you tire of viewing river life – birds, monkeys, fisherfolk, people bathing.

Longboat fares vary according to conditions – when they're just right, the fare is lower; when the water level is too low or too high, the fare is a bit higher. The longboat dock in Samarinda is at the Sungai Kunjang pier outside of town, reached by a taksi kota A for 300 rp.

Tours

Let's face it; not everybody has the time or hardiness to do solo trekking in East Kalimantan. The tourist offices in Samarinda and Tenggarong can arrange official government guides at around

35,000 rp per day, not including food, accommodation, or transport.

It may be less expensive and more organised overall to go with one of the private tour companies based in Samarinda or Balikpapan.

PT Tomaco Tours (tel 21747) in the Hotel Benakutai building, Jalan P Antasari, Balikpapan, has a good reputation for Mahakam and Kedang Kepala river trips. They have three and six-day tours going as far as Rukun Damai on the Mahakam River and Tanjung Manis on the Kedang Kepala River. Rates range from US\$245 to US\$450 per person with ten or more on the tour, and include accommodation, river transport, meals, village performances and transport between Balikpapan and either Loa Janan or Tenggarong, the tours' starting points.

UP THE MAHAKAM RIVER

Regular longboats ply the Mahakam River from Samarinda and Tenggarong all the way to Long Bagun 523 km upriver. If the water is low, you may not be able to get any further than Long Iram, 114 km short of Long Bagun. If the river's too high, the same may apply if the currents are too swift.

Many of the towns and villages along the Mahakam are built over wooden walkways that keep them above water during the rainy season. Often there will be a losmen/penginapan or two or a longhouse where travellers can stay – the standard price everywhere is 2500 rp per person. Alcoholic beverages are very hard to come by upriver, so if you need to, bring along your own supply from Samarinda.

Tanjung Isuy via Muara Muntai

Most people head upriver to Tanjung Isuy on the shores of Lake Jempang in Banuaq Dayak territory. The last families to live in the longhouse moved out in the late 1970s. The provincial government bought the longhouse, renovated it and it's now a tourist attraction.

In nearby **Mancong** there is a longhouse dating from the 1870s. Neither village is particularly scenic, but the local people are friendly and will gladly show you around the longhouses. You can also see Banuaq weaving (*ulap doyo*) in progress. Occasional folk dances are held at the longhouses, for ritual purposes or tourist groups from Balikpapan.

To get to Lake Jempang, you should take a longboat to **Muara Muntai** first and spend the night there before getting a boat on to Tanjung Isuy.

Muara Muntai is a typical Mahakam town, built over wooden walkways parallel to the river. In the evenings, it looks like everybody in town is out for a stroll, the main source of local entertainment. Most of the people living in Muara Muntai are Muslim Kutais.

Places to Stay

There is one losmen in Tanjung Isuy, the *Penginapan Beringan*, which costs 2500 rp per person. The longhouse is also open to guests for the same rate. The couple who run the Beringan also prepare and serve food downstairs.

In Mancong, the only place to stay is the village longhouse, which has an interesting tribal cemetery at the back. Tariff is the usual 2500 rp per person.

Muara Muntai has two losmens along the wooden street near the main pier, the *Penginapan Nitawardana* and the *Penginapan Sri Muntai Indah*. The Nitawardana is the cleanest and has mosquito nets. Both charge 2500 rp per person.

Several warungs are along this street. The best is *Warung Alfian Noor*, which serves good mie/nasi goreng, ikan bakar and nasi campur. You can buy udang galah for 7000 rp a kg from the fish market (it's 10,000 rp a kg in Samarinda).

Muara Muntai seems to have one place in town that serves beer – a boat warung permanently docked at the main pier. These boat warungs are the only places in the vicinity that are open for breakfast

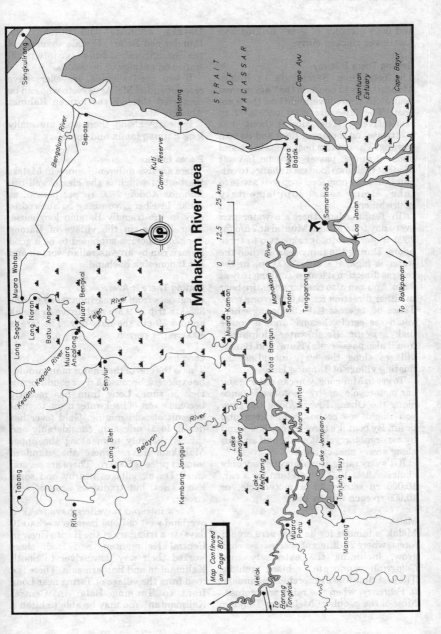

Mahakam River Area

STRAIT OF MACASSAR

0   12.5   25 km

Map Continued on Page 807

and offer a choice of sweet Kalimantan pastries or chicken curry.

Getting There & Away

The boat from Samarinda to Muara Muntai takes 13 hours on the 7 am express boat or 18 hours (overnight) on the 9 am boat. The fares are 3000 and 2000 rp respectively. The slower boat has mattresses on the upper deck and its own warung. The express boat stops in Senoni about 2 pm so passengers who haven't brought their own food get a chance to eat. But that's the only food stop so it's wise to take along some supplementary nourishment.

To Tanjung Isuy there's a water taxi every day from Muara Muntai at 7 am for 2500 rp per person. It takes two to three hours. During the rainy season when the water is high, it's only 2000 rp. In the reverse direction it leaves Tanjung Isuy at 3 am. You can also charter an entire boat in either direction for 10,000 rp one way. These boats cross Lake Jempang where you'll see egrets, herons, and, if you're lucky, *pesut* (fresh-water dolphins). You'll also pass several Kutai and Banjar villages along the way, including the floating village of Tanjung Haur.

To get to Mancong, you can either go by car/motorcycle or by motorised canoe along the Ohong River. Along the river you might see proboscis monkeys and pesut. By boat it's three to four hours and by car or motorcycle it's only half an hour along a very chancy road.

If it's very rainy, canoe may be your only choice. Allow 15,000 rp return for a car, 10,000 rp return for a motorcycle, or 10,000 rp each way by boat.

Melak

Melak is famous for its 5000-acre orchid forest, where 27 different species of orchid grow, including the extremely rare *Cologenia pandurata* or black orchids. The best time to see the orchids is January to February, when the rains are profuse. Most of the people of Melak are Tanjung Dayaks, animists who worship the thunder god Belare. Female shamans of the Tanjung, called *balian*, go into ritual trance on auspicious occasions.

If you need a guide, travellers have recommended Mr. Agus Noto who can be contacted through the losmen Rahmat Abadi in Melak.

In nearby **Eheng**, there is an unusually long Banuaq lamin and cemetery.

Places to Stay

There are five different losmen in Melak, the best of which is the clean, well-run *Rahmat Abadi*, 2500 rp per person, as usual. In Eheng, you may be allowed to stay in the friendly Banuaq longhouse. Near Eheng, in the village of Barong Tongkok, there is supposed to be a good losmen run by an Australian woman and her Indonesian husband.

Getting There & Away

Longboats from Samarinda leave for the 325-km trip at 9 am and arrive in Melak around 10 am the next day. The fare is 4000 rp per person.

Long Iram

This is the end of the line for many would-be explorers, because of river conditions or lack of time. Long Iram has recently become a sort of backwater boom town as a result of gold mining. Gold fever has driven local prices up considerably and this is the only town along the upper Mahakam River where the standard losmen price is 5000 rp. There are several small Dayak villages nearby and some longhouses, but traditions are not very strong.

A few intrepid travellers have trekked overland west of Long Iram (a week to 10 days) to a tributary of the Barito River in Central Kalimantan, and from there worked their way down-river to South Kalimantan and Banjarmasin. There is a road from the village of Tering near Long Iram to Tanjung Balai in Central Kalimantan. You may be able to hitch a ride on a logging truck to Tanjung Balai, and from there to Muara Teweh, where regular longboats ply the Barito all the way to Banjarmasin.

Getting There & Away

Long Iram is 409 km from Samarinda, longboat fare is usually 7500 rp, and the trip takes about 35 hours.

Further Upriver

If conditions allow you to ferry upriver beyond Long Iram, places of interest include **Datah Bilang**, where there are two Bahau Dayak (lamin), one of which is heavily decorated with typical Dayak artwork. A reader has recommended the Dayak village of **Long Hubung**, 45 minutes north of Datah Bilang by motor canoe (5000 rp per person). Yusram, the kepala desa, welcomes visitors to this traditional village.

Between Datah Bilang and Long Bagun is **Rukun Damai**, surrounded by virgin rainforest, and home to the Kenyah Dayak, many of whom still hold fast to their traditions. There are five Kenyah lamin, including one 250 metres long.

Downstream less than 25 km is **Muara Merak**, a Punan Dayak settlement. There is good trekking in this area, especially along the Merak River to the north-east. With a Punan guide hired in Muara Merak, you could trek overland east for three to four days to Tabang and then travel down the Belayan River to

Kotabangun, where you can catch longboat services back to Samarinda.

Long Bagun is the end of the line for regular longboat services from Samarinda along the Mahakam. A longboat from Samarinda to Long Bagun (conditions permitting) takes three days, two nights going up and two days, two nights coming down. The boat docks in Long Iram one night each way while the crew and passengers sleep, since night navigation can be dangerous this far upriver. Fare is 12,000 rp. From here you must charter motorised canoes from village to village or trek through the forests. River conditions must be optimum because of river rapids between Long Bagun and the next major settlement, **Long Pahangai**.

Under normal conditions, it's a one-day canoe trip from Long Bagun to Long Pahangai, then another day to **Long Apari**, where the Mahakam ends as a motor-navigable river. **Long Lunuk**, between Long Pahangai and Long Apari, is a good place from which to visit Kenyah villages.

If you want to start your trip from the top, you can fly to **Data Dawai**, an airstrip near Long Lunuk. Merpati flies every Monday and Thursday for 37,200 rp each way. From there you can work your way down-river back to Samarinda, or trek overland to the Apo Kayan highlands. One way to save a considerable amount of money going downriver is to purchase a canoe and paddle yourself. Price depends

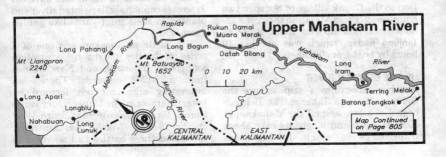

Upper Mahakam River

Mt Liangpran 2240
Long Pahangi
Long Apari
Longblu
Nahabuan
Long Lunuk
Mahakam River
Mt Batuayou 1652
Murung River
Rapids
Long Bagun
Rukun Damai
Muara Merak
Datah Bilang
Mahakam River
Long Iram
Terring Melak
Barong Tongkok
0   10   20 km
CENTRAL KALIMANTAN
EAST KALIMANTAN

Map Continued on Page 805

on the size and condition of the canoe – a decent used canoe runs from 20,000 to 50,000 rp without an engine. If you want an engine it will cost considerably more, as much as double. Besides saving money, having your own canoe means you can stop when and where you want along the way. However, you should absolutely not attempt to navigate the rapids between Long Pahangai and Long Bagun on your own; in fact, it would be best not to start a self-paddled trip above Long Bagun. Downriver from Long Bagun it's a pretty straightforward trip as long as you check in at villages along the way to make sure you haven't taken a tributary of the Mahakam by mistake, as there is the occasional fork.

UP THE KEDANG KEPALA RIVER

There are regular longboat services up the Kedang Kepala River, which branches north off the Mahakam near Muara Kaman, from Samarinda to **Muara Wahau**. This trip takes three days, two nights and goes via the Kenyah and Bahau villages of Tanjung Manis, Long Noran and Long Segar. Longboat fare from from Samarinda to Muara Wahau is 10,000 rp.

In Tarakan, we met an American man and a Swedish woman who had taken a boat north from Muara Wahau to **Miau Baru**, where they stayed with the Dutch-speaking kepala desa and his English-speaking son, Wilson. They then travelled by local school bus to a lumber camp four km north where they hitched a ride on a jeep to the Dayak village of **Marapun** two hours away. From Marapun they got a 12-hour boat ride up the Kelai River to **Tanjung Redep**, which was another 10 hours by boat from Tarakan.

UP THE BELAYAN RIVER

Another adventurous trip is up the Belayan River to Tabang. The Belayan branches north-west off the Mahakam at Kota Bangun and longboats take about three days to reach Tabang from Samarinda. You can also reach Tabang on foot from the town of Muara Merak on the Mahakam River. You can hire a Punan guide in either Tabang or Muara Merak to lead you north of Tabang into extensive virgin rainforests that are nomadic Punan territory.

UP THE KAYAN RIVER

South of Tarakan is **Tanjung Selor** at the mouth of the mighty Kayan River. Merpati flies from Samarinda to Tanjung Selor on Monday and Thursday for 65,000 rp.

There are regular longboat services up the Kayan as far as the Kenyah villages of Mara I and Mara II, but a section of rapids further on prevents boats from reaching the headwaters of the Kayan in the mythic Apo-Kayan highlands.

Fortunately, Merpati flies to **Long Ampung** in the Apo-Kayan area twice weekly for 35,000 rp. There is good trekking in the Apo-Kayan headlands; you could also trek overland to the Mahakam headwaters from here in about a week with a guide from Long Ampung.

TARAKAN

Just a stepping stone to other places, Tarakan is an island town close to the Sabah border and was the site of bloody fighting between Australians and Japanese at the end of WW II. Unless you're really enthused about Japanese blockhouses, or want to try exiting Indonesia to Sabah, there's little of interest. It's not a bad town – just dull. Some of the houses have old Japanese cannon shells painted silver and planted in their front yards like garden gnomes.

The battle at Tarakan was one of a series of battles fought by Australian soldiers in Indonesia and New Guinea from mid-1944 onwards. There's an interesting argument put forward by Peter Charlton in *The Unnecessary War – Island Campaigns of the South-West Pacific 1944-45* (MacMillan, Australia, 1983) that these battles had no value in the defeat of the Japanese. By that time the Japanese in Indonesia were already effectively defeated, reluctant to fight, incapable of being either evacuated or reinforced, had to live off the land and fought only when they were forced to.

The capture of Tarakan (after six weeks of fighting and the deaths of 235 Australians) was carried out to establish an air base which was never used. After the Tarakan operation Indonesia was effectively bypassed, yet in July 1945, an assault was made on Balikpapan. This last large amphibious landing of the war managed to secure a beach, a disused oil refinery, a couple of unnecessary airfields and the deaths of 229 Australians.

Information
The Bank Dagang Negara on Jalan Yos Sudarso will change some travellers' cheques and foreign currency.

Places to Stay
There's a line of cheap and middle-range losmens and hotels along Jalan Jenderal Sudirman (also known as Jalan Kampung Bugis). These include the Losmen Jakarta (tel 21919) at 112 which has little boxes for rooms but is otherwise not bad at 5500/6600 rp for singles/doubles. Experience the local way of life by filling your mandi with a hand-pump.

The Losmen Herlina is basic but habitable at 3000/4500 rp for singles/doubles but avoid the dark, dismal downstairs rooms.

The Barito Hotel (tel 435) on Jalan Jenderal Sudirman 133, has basic but clean rooms for 5500/8800 rp, or 10,000 rp with attached mandi and fan. There are a couple of air-con rooms for 16,500 rp. All rooms include a towel with soap and shampoo and a breakfast of coffee/tea and Chinese rolls, a nice change from the usual slabs of white bread. A laundry is off the second floor on a terrace. Next door the Orchid Hotel has rooms at 5500/10,000 rp but the mandis could be cleaner.

Further along Jalan Jenderal Sudirman near the junction with Jalan Mulawarman the Wisata Hotel (tel 21245) is basic but pleasant with rooms at 8000/11,000 rp. Rooms at the rear will probably be very quiet.

Nearby is the slightly more upscale Hotel Mirama where rooms with air-con, TV and hot water bathrooms are 17,000 rp and up.

Number one in town is the big Hotel Tarakan Plaza on Jalan Yos Sudarso, which comes complete with restaurant and expatriates held up by a bar. Singles are 40,000 rp, doubles 46,000 rp.

Further down Jalan Yos Sudarso towards the Pelni harbour is the Hotel Bunga Muda (tel 21349) at No 78, a newish concrete-block with fairly clean rooms at 7000/9000 rp.

Places to Eat
The Rumah Makan Cahaya on Jalan Jenderal Sudirman (across from the Losmen Jakarta) is pretty good; the menu includes cumi cumi (octopus) goreng at 2000 rp, cap cai goreng at 1500 rp, nasi goreng 1250 rp. The Rumah Makan Sarang Kepeting near Losmen Herlina on the same road has good crab dishes.

At night the happening place is Depot Theola on Jalan Jenderal Sudirman, where they serve the local specialty nasi lalap (batter fried chunks of chicken served with rice and soup). They also have cold beer, ice cream, fruit juices and jamu drinks. There are only one or two tables downstairs, but there's an upstairs area with several more. They'll be glad to play your casettes on their stereo.

Cheap warungs are at the juncture of Jalan Sudirman and Jalan Yos Sudarso and stalls sell reasonably priced imported apples and oranges.

Getting There & Away
Air The easiest way to reach Tarakan is with Bouraq or Merpati flights from Balikpapan or Samarinda. In Tarakan, Merpati is at Jalan Yos Sudarso 10. Bouraq (tel 21248, 21987) is at Jalan Yos

Destination	I	II	III	IV	Ekonomi
Toli Toli	36,000	28,200	22,400	18,400	15,800
Pantoloan	51,700	38,600	30,300	24,700	19,200
Balikpapan	54,700	42,400	32,900	27,000	22,500
Ujung Pandang	106,000	78,000	60,000	47,700	36,000
Surabaya	104,000	80,400	61,500	49,300	40,900
Tanjung Priok (Jakarta)	154,000	112,800	87,100	69,500	54,600

Sudarso 9B, across from the Tarakan Theatre. Bali Air, owned by Bouraq, flies Tarakan-Berau and Tarakan-Samarinda.

Daily flights between Tarakan and Balikpapan on Bouraq are 72,000 rp. Bouraq also flies to Tawau in Sabah three times weekly for 51,000 rp.

Boat The Pelni office is at the port – take a colt almost to the end of Jalan Yos Sudarso. The Pelni ship *KM Kerinci* calls into Tarakan on its regular run around Kalimantan and Sulawesi. See the table for adult fares from Tarakan (in rp).

From Tarakan you can catch longboats to other parts of East Kalimantan. CV Tam Bersaudara, opposite the Pasar Sebengkok, sells tickets for boats from Tarakan to Berau. Departures are at around 6 am daily. Also enquire at the office at the start of the pier just over the bridge from Pasar Sebengkok. Apart from Berau there are longboats to Tanjung Selor (5000 rp), Nunukan (8500 rp) and Pulau Bunju (5000 rp).

For boats to Nunukan and on to Tawau in the east Malaysian state of Sabah, go to the Pelabuhan Tarakan. Longboats leave daily at around 9 am and arrive in Nunukan 12 hours later for 8500 rp per person.

In Nunukan you can catch a speedboat to Tawau for 15,000 rp – it takes about four hours. You can also spend the night at the *Losmen Nunukan* for 5000 rp and get a

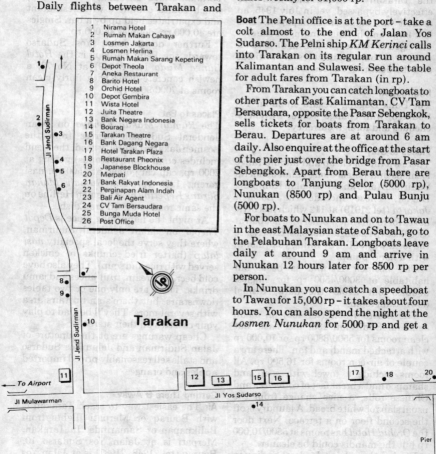

1 Nirama Hotel
2 Rumah Makan Cahaya
3 Losmen Jakarta
4 Losmen Herlina
5 Rumah Makan Sarang Kepeting
6 Depot Theola
7 Aneka Restaurant
8 Barito Hotel
9 Orchid Hotel
10 Depot Gembira
11 Wista Hotel
12 Juita Theatre
13 Bank Negara Indonesia
14 Bouraq
15 Tarakan Theatre
16 Bank Dagang Negara
17 Hotel Tarakan Plaza
18 Restaurant Pheonix
19 Japanese Blockhouse
20 Merpati
21 Bank Rakyat Indonesia
22 Perginapan Alam Indah
23 Bali Air Agent
24 CV Tam Bersaudara
25 Bunga Muda Hotel
26 Post Office

Jl Jend Sudirman

Tarakan

To Airport

Jl Mulawarman

Jl Yos Sudarso

Pier

19

speedboat the next day. Or get a speedboat to Tawau from Tarakan for 35,000 to 40,000 rp, which only takes about five hours.

There is an Indonesian immigration office in Nunukan where you must get your exit stamp. Note that if you got a two month tourist visa on arrival in Indonesia, you will need an exit permit from the immigration office in Jakarta or the Nunukan office won't stamp your passport. If you got a one month tourist visa before coming to Indonesia, they can stamp your passport without an exit permit from Jakarta.

Getting Around
Airport Transport Buy tickets for taxis at the taxi counter in the airport terminal – it's 2500 rp to the city. Or walk down the airport turn-off road to the main road where occasional bemos pass – you should be able to get one going into the city (200 rp, 10 minutes). If you have an early morning flight to catch, expect to charter a bemo. If you're feeling energetic and not carrying much you could even walk into town from the airport.

Colt Transport around town is by colt. A 150 rp flat rate gets you just about anywhere.

South Kalimantan

The province of Kalimantan Selatan, Kal-Sel for short, is an area of about 37,600 square km with a population of approximately 2.5 million. Kalimantan's smallest province, Kal-Sel is an important centre for diamond mining, rattan processing, and of course lumber. It is also the centre of Banjarese culture and a good starting point for treks into Central and East Kalimantan.

Traditional Banjarese clothing is made from *kain sasirangan*, cloth produced by a striking tie-dyeing process that uses motifs reminiscent of Javanese *jumputan* batik. The traditional Banjar-style house is the *bubungan tinggi* or tall roof design and the best examples can be seen in the town of Marabahan, 50 km north of Banjarmasin on the Barito River. A few remaining bubungan tinggi houses are around Banjarmasin and Banjar Baru.

In the mountainous north-eastern interior of South Kalimantan is a group of Dayaks said to be descendants of the original Banjarese race. These original Banjars may have been families from the Barito delta area who fled to the mountains to avoid Muslim conversion in the 15th and 16th centuries. Communal houses (balai) hold up to 30 or more families and serve as a ritual centres for these mountain villages.

BANJARMASIN
This is yet another 'Venice of the East' and the Banjarmasis are indeed up to their floorboards in water. Much of Banjarmasin is planted on swamp land

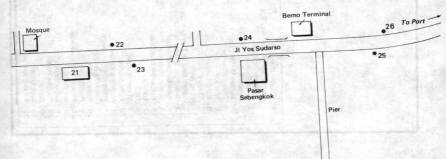

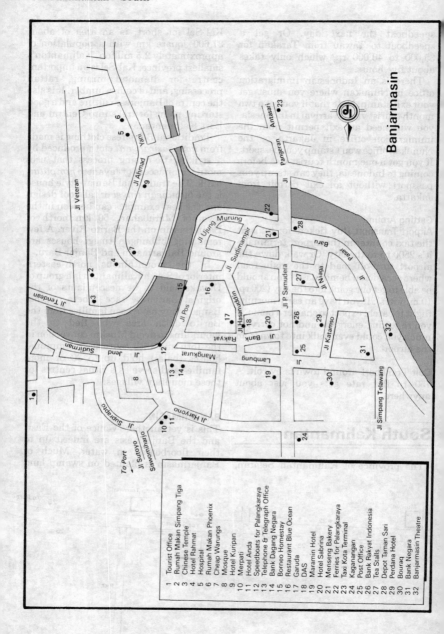

Banjarmasin

1 Tourist Office
2 Rumah Makan Simpang Tiga
3 Chinese Temple
4 Hotel Rahmat
5 Hospital
6 Rumah Makan Phoenix
7 Cheap Warungs
8 Mosque
9 Hotel Kuripan
10 Merpati
11 Hotel Anda
12 Speedboats for Palangkaraya
13 Telephone & Telegraph Office
14 Bank Dagang Negara
15 Borneo Homestay
16 Restaurant Blue Ocean
17 Garuda
18 DAS
19 Maramin Hotel
20 Hotel Sabrina
21 Menseng Bakery
22 Ferries for Palangkaraya
23 Taxi Kota Terminal
24 Kagananan
25 Post Office
26 Bank Rakyat Indonesia
27 Tea Stalls
28 Depot Taman Sari
29 Perdana Hotel
30 Bouraq
31 Bank Negara
32 Banjarmasin Theatre

with the vast number of houses perched on stilts. The city is a short distance up from the mouth of the Barito River at its confluence with the Martapura River and is crisscrossed by numerous smaller rivers and canals lined with stilt houses, even houses built on bundles of floating lashed logs.

Banjarmasin is also an important seaport for the shipping of lumber, rattan and other Kalimantan products. Several harbours are along the Barito River, one for large cargo and passenger ships, one for longboats going up and down the river, one for Buginese and Javanese pinisi, etc.

Information & Orientation

Banjarmasin is big but just about everything you'll need is packed into the city centre around the Pasar Baru, with several cheap hotels along Jalan Ahmad Yani near the banks of the Martapura River. The Barito River lies to the west of the city centre.

Several banks and government offices are along Jalan Lambung Mangkurat. As usual, Bank Dagang Negara has the best rates for travellers' cheques. The office for long-distance phone calls is also on this street and the main post office is further west at the Jalan P Samudera intersection.

Detailed blueprint maps of South and Central Kalimantan are available at Toko Cenderawasih Mas, Jalan Hasanuddin 37, between the Garuda office and Jalan Pos. Across the street a small bookstore sells week-old copies of *Newsweek* and *Asiaweek*.

A good travel agency in Banjarmasin is Adhi Travel (tel 3131), Jalan Hasanuddin 27. Some staff speak English and it's the only agency that accepts credit cards.

Tourist Office The South Kalimantan tourist office is at Jalan D I Panjaitan 3, near the Grand Mosque. The staff are very helpful and generous with information. This is also headquarters for the South Kalimantan Tourist Guide Association,

Grand Mosque, Banjarmasin

which has over 30 members including ten adventure/jungle guides.

Akhmad Arifin (Ifin) speaks fair English and is a knowledgeable guide. Another highly recommended local guide is Johansyah Yasin (Johan). He can be contacted through the tourist office or at the Borneo Homestay at Jalan Pos 123.

The going rate for guides is 10,000 to 15,000 rp per day for local tours (including trips to nearby Pulau Kaget, Martapura, or Cempaka) or 15,000 to 25,000 rp per day for jungle tours (eg to Loksado).

Canal Trips

Banjarmasin should be seen from water level, otherwise it looks just like any Indonesian city. Hire someone to paddle you round the river and the canals in a canoe – 2000 or 2500 rp for an hour or two should be more than enough. Ask around the wharf near the junction of Jalan

Lambung Mangkurat and Jalan Pasar Baru. You could hire a *klotok*, a canoe with a water-pump motor on it (same cost), but don't hire a speedboat – they go too fast to observe or photograph anything.

Everything revolves around the waterways, lined with closely packed stilt houses. Stairs lead from each house to wooden platforms at water level. People squat on these platforms for everything from washing to defecating. Bugis schooners can be seen tied up to the docks or under construction on the riverbanks. River ferries head inland loaded with cargo, motorcycles and people.

Look for *pasar terapung* or floating markets on the river – groups of boats, large and small, to which buyers and sellers paddle in canoes. Trading begins early and is over by 9 or 10 am. At the meeting of the Kuin and Barito rivers is a particularly fine floating market every morning from around 5 to 8 am. There are canoe cafes among the hundreds of boats that converge here, and you can get a nice breakfast of scented tea and Banjarese pastries.

The kampung of Muara Mantuil is a floating village of houses and shops built on logs lashed together. It's on a tributary of the Barito not far from Trisakti harbour.

Pulau Kaget

About 12 km downstream from Banjarmasin is an island reserve inhabited by the comical long-nosed proboscis monkeys. Indonesians call them *kera belanda* or Dutch monkeys because of their long noses, red faces and pot bellies. It's two hours each way – the best time to leave Banjarmasin is 2.30 to 3 pm so you can reach the island around sunset when the monkeys come out to feed. They're very shy creatures so boat pilots usually cut the engines and glide beneath tree perches so the monkeys won't flee.

Speedboats at the pier at the end of Jalan Pos ask 35,000 to 40,000 rp for a round trip, or pay 12,000 to 15,000 rp for a round trip in a klotok.

Pulau Kembang

About 20 minutes from the town centre by boat is another monkey island which is home to a large tribe of long-tailed macaques who congregate at an old Chinese temple near shore. On Sundays when Chinese families give the monkeys huge offerings of eggs, peanuts and bananas, the temple becomes a virtual circus.

There are also long-nose monkeys in the interior of Pulau Kembang, but they're more difficult to approach than on Pulau Kaget because of the dominating macaques.

Mesjid Raya Sabilal Muhtadin

On Jalan Jenderal Sudirman, this is a giant modern art mosque with a copper-coloured flying saucer dome and minarets with lids and spires. The interior is quite striking and visitors must pay a small fee.

Ramadan Cake Fair

During Ramadan, the Muslim fasting month, Banjarmasin is the site for a festive *pasar wadai* or cake fair. Dozens of stalls sell South Kalimantan's famous Banjarese pastries near the city hall or the grand mosque.

Good Muslims, of course, don't eat these delicious pastries till after sundown, but non-believers can gorge themselves all day.

Places to Stay – bottom end

The *Borneo Homestay*, on the Martapura River at Jalan Pos 123, is pleasant and a good information centre. Johan and Lina run the show; Johan speaks very good English and knows South and Central Kalimantan well. A bed in a five-bed room is 2000 rp, a single room is 3000 rp and double 5000 rp.

A couple of acceptable places are on the east side of the river. The *Hotel Rahmat* (tel 4429) on Jalan Ahmad Yani is sizeable with a friendly manager and singles/

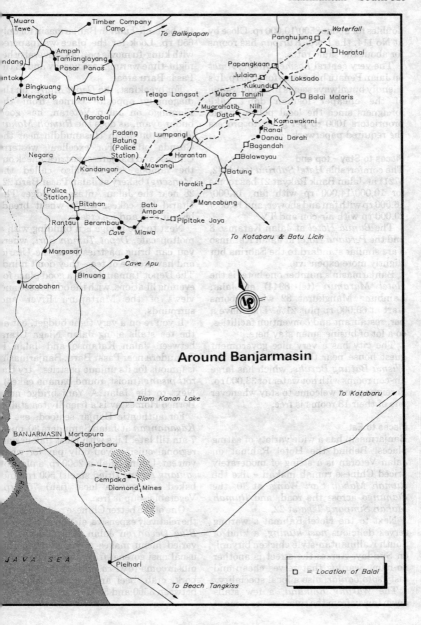

Around Banjarmasin

□ = Location of Balai

doubles for about 8500/10,000 rp. Close by at No 114, the *Hotel Kuripan* has rooms for about the same rates.

The very central *Losmen Abang Amet* on Jalan Penatu has rooms for 4000 rp. It's friendly but always seems to be full. Some of the cheaper losmen don't take foreigners since the local police charge proprietors 1000 rp per guest to process the required paperwork.

Places to Stay – top end

The comfortable *Hotel Sabrina* (tel 4442, 4721) at Jalan Bank Rakyat 21 has rooms for 10,000/14,000 rp with fan, 14,000/16,000 rp with fan and shower, and 16,000/20,000 rp with air-con and TV.

The *Banua Hotel* at Jalan Katamso 8 and the *Perdana Hotel* at Jalan Katamso 3 are similar standard to the Sabrina but slightly more expensive.

Banjarmasin's number one hotel is the *Hotel Maramin* (tel 8944) at Jalan Lambung Mangkurat 32 where rooms start at 60,000 rp plus 21%. They have a bar, restaurant and convention facilities, so a lot of businessmen stay here.

The city has a very nice government guest house near the Mesjid Raya, the *Wisma Batung Batulis*, which has large air-con rooms with hot water for 33,000 rp. Foreigners are welcome to stay whenever one of their 18 rooms is free.

Places to Eat

Banjarmasin has a wide variety of eating places. Behind the Hotel Rahmat on Jalan Veteran is a string of moderately priced Chinese rumah makan – like the *Rumah Makan Sari Wangi* at 70, the *Flamingo* across the road, and *Rumah Makan Simpang Tiga* at 22.

Next to the Hotel Rahmat a warung serves delicious *nasi kuning*, a kind of South Kalimantan-style chicken biryani, on Sunday. Across the street is another no-name warung that serves cheap and tasty *soto banjar*, also a local speciality.

The *Warung Raihana*, a few stalls down (away from the river) serves some of the best *mie kuah* in Banjarmasin for only 650 rp. Look for the place wallpapered with kung-fu movie posters. Several other night-time warungs are nearby and in the Pasar Baru area.

For breakfast, the *Depot Miara*, on the diagonally opposite corner from the Flamingo on Jalan Veteran, has good bubur ayam, as does the *Rumah Makar Jakarta* on Jalan Hasanuddin near the Garuda office. For excellent western Chinese and Banjarese pastries, check out the famous *Utarid* (also called the *Menseng*) bakery at Jalan Pasar Baru 22-28 near the Jalan Antasari bridge. The Utarid has cakes, whole wheat bread biscuit mix and ice cream.

Next to the bridge is a building with a rooftop cafe, *Depot Taman Sari*, where you can bring pastries from the Utarid and have coffee or tea – they don't mind The Depot Taman Sari is a good place for evening libations, with the odd breeze and views of the Martapura River and surrounds.

If you're on a very tight budget, eat at the tea stalls along Jalan Niaga Utara between Jalan Katamso and Jalan P Samudera near Pasar Baru. Banjarmasin is famous for its unique pastries – try the *roti pisang* (moist, round banana cakes). Next to the Jalan A Yani bridge near Borneo Homestay is a friendly tea stall.

For authentic Banjar seafood, eat at *Kaganangan* at Jalan Samudera 30, open 7 am till late. Like with most Indonesian regional cuisine, you only pay for what you eat. Udang galah is 2500 rp, a plate of *saluang goreng* (fried smelt) 500 rp, and baked *papuyu* (a local fish) 750 rp. Vegetable soup is free.

One of the better Chinese restaurants is the relatively expensive, air-con *Restaurant Blue Ocean* on Jalan Hasanuddin. Its varied menu makes a change from the usual nasi goreng: fried chicken ball and mushrooms (*aya ca jamur*) for 3500 rp; pork, crab, beef and pigeon dishes for between 3500 and 5000 rp.

Getting There & Away

Air Banjarmasin is connected by flights to many parts of Kalimantan and several Indonesian provinces. Garuda (tel 4203, 3885) is at Jalan Hasanuddin 31 and open Monday to Thursday 7 am to 4 pm, Friday 7 am to 12 noon and 2 to 4 pm, Saturday 7 am to 1 pm, Sunday and holidays 9 am to 12 noon.

Bouraq (tel 2445, 3285) is at Jalan Lambung Mangkurat 40D. DAS (tel 2902) is across the road from Garuda at Jalan Hasanuddin 6, Blok 4. Merpati (tel 4433, 4307) is on Jalan Haryono near the Jalan Merdeka intersection.

Sample fares ex-Banjarmasin on Bouraq are: Jakarta (two flights daily) 97,800 rp; Balikpapan (three flights daily) 45,100 rp; Samarinda (one flight daily) 63,100 rp; Pangkalan Bun (one flight daily) 61,100 rp; Surabaya (three flights daily) 58,500 rp. Adhi Travel on Jalan Hasanuddin sells discounted Merpati tickets to Surabaya for 54,000 rp (usually 61,000 rp).

DAS flies to Pangkalan Bun in Central Kalimantan daily for 59,100 rp.

Bus Buses and colts depart frequently from the Km 6 Terminal for Martapura and Banjarbaru. Night buses to Balikpapan (10,000 rp) leave daily between 4 and 4.30 pm and arrive in Panajan, just across the river from Balikpapan, about 12 hours later. You have to get a speedboat across the river (1000 rp). The last six hours of the trip are a real bone crusher and it's worse than on Sumatran buses according to several travellers.

Regular day buses go via Rantau, Amuntai and Tanjung and there are buses to other destinations in the south-east corner of the island.

You can break up the trip from Banjarmasin to Balikpapan halfway by spending the night in Tanjung. From Banjarmasin to Tanjung is 4500 rp, five hours and Tanjung to Panajan/Balikpapan is 4500 rp, six hours.

Boat Passenger ships to Surabaya leave about twice a week and the trip takes about 24 hours. They dock at Pelabuhan Trisakti. To get there take a bemo from the taxi kota station on Jalan Samudera for 200 rp. The bemo will take you past the harbour master's and ticket offices.

The harbour master's office (tel 4775) is on Jalan Barito Hilir at Trisakti. Opposite is a line of shops with several agents for boat tickets to Surabaya. The fare from Banjarmasin to Surabaya on Pelni's *KM Kelimutu* is 24,000 rp economy class, 45,300 rp 2nd class and 57,500 rp 1st class. To Semarang, the *Kelimutu* is 26,700 rp economy, 50,400 rp 2nd class and 61,800 rp 1st class.

Another agent for these ships is at the Km 6 bus terminal, and others can be found off Jalan Pasar Baru near the Antasari bridge. The Pasar Baru agents also sell less expensive passenger tickets for cargo boats that leave about every two days – fares are usually 15,000 to 17,500 rp to Surabaya.

Cargo boats to Pangkalan Bun in Central Kalimantan leave about every other day and cost around 20,000 rp. The trip takes a day and a half.

Occasionally cargo ships go to Pontianak on the west coast of the island, but these usually stop in Surabaya and/or Jakarta on the way and are very slow.

A better way between the two cities is a boat from Banjarmasin to Pangkalan Bun in Central Kalimantan (there are usually three or four a week), then another from Pangkalan Bun to Pontianak. Each leg of the trip should cost 17,000 to 20,000 rp. (You'll save a lot of time if you fly.) Occasional ships sail from Banjarmasin to Jakarta but again, don't rely on anything.

Ferry & Speedboat Heading inland, one of the more obvious courses to take is from Banjarmasin to Palangkaraya, a journey of 18 hours in a bis air or about six to seven hours in a speedboat. You go up three rivers – the Barito, Kapuas and the

Kahayan, and through two man-made canals which link them.

Speedboats to Palangkaraya leave from a dock at the end of Jalan Pos near the traffic circle. From Banjarmasin to Palangkaraya is 17,100 rp and there are boats daily. Buy tickets from the office at the dock.

River ferries to Palangkaraya depart from the wharf at the end of Jalan Sudimampir daily and cost 8000 rp. Long distance bis air up the Barito River leave from the Terminal Taksi Sunggai near the Banjar Raya fish market. To get there take a yellow colt (200 rp) to the end of Jalan Jenderal Sutoyo west of the city centre. The end of the route is the town of Muara Teweh in Central Kalimantan, 56 hours away and costing only 10,000 rp.

Getting Around

Airport Transport Banjarmasin's Syamsudin Noor Airport is 26 km out of town on the road to Banjarbaru. To get there take a bemo from Pasar Baru to the Km 6 Terminal. Then catch a Martapura-bound colt, get off at the branch road leading to the airport and walk the short distance to the terminal.

Alternatively a taxi all the way to the airport will cost you 7000 rp. They cluster near the Garuda office and Sabrina Hotel.

From the airport to the city, buy a taxi ticket at the counter in the terminal. Alternatively, walk out of the airport, through the car park, past the post office and the MIG aircraft, turn left and walk down to the Banjarmasin-Martapura highway. From here pick up one of the Banjarmasin-Martapura colts into Banjarmasin.

If you're travelling light you could hire a guy on a motorcycle to pillion passenger you to the airport – these guys hang out at the Km 6 Terminal and at the taxi kota station on Jalan Samudera.

Boat, Bemo & Bajaj You can hire a boatman to navigate the canals. Without a water-pump motor, expect to pay no more than about 2500 rp per hour.

On dry land, the area around Pasar Baru is very small and easy to walk around. You don't need wheels since the hotels, taxi terminal, airline offices, etc are all grouped together. For longer trips there are bemos, becaks, ojek and bajaj – this is one of the few places outside Jakarta where you see bajaj. A bajaj from the centre to Banjar Raya harbour is around 1200 rp; by ojek it would cost 750 rp.

The bemos congregate at the taxi kota station at the junction of Jalan Samudera and Jalan Pasar Baru. They go to various parts of town including the Km 6 Terminal which is the departure point for buses to Banjarbaru, Martapura and Balikpapan. The standard taxi kota fare from Pasar Baru to Km 6 or anywhere in town is 200 rp.

Banjarmasi becak drivers aren't predatory but they do ask hefty prices and are hard to bargain with. The bajaj drivers work the same way.

Guys with taxi motorcycles (ojeks) wait at Pasar Baru and Km 6 and will take you anywhere. If you're travelling light this is a good way to the airport.

BANJARBARU

The chief attraction of this town, on the road from Banjarmasin to Martapura, is its museum collection of Banjar and Dayak artefacts and statues found at the site of Hindu temples in Kalimantan.

Museum

The museum is on the Banjarmasin-Martapura highway. Ask the colt driver to drop you off. It's open to the public on Saturday and Sunday from 8.30 am to 2 pm. If you can't make it on the weekend, go anyway. Someone will probably open the place and show you around. They were also holding dance performances every Sunday at 9 am.

Exhibits include a replica of a traditional Banjar river boat equipment used in traditional Banjar circumcision ceremonies (including an antibiotic leaf and would you believe, a cut-throat razor!); cannons, swords and other artefacts from wars with the Dutch and a small cannon used by British troops in Kalimantan; Dayak and Banjar swords, knives and other pointy things.

Probably the most interesting exhibit are items excavated from the Hindu Laras Temple and Agung Temple in East Kalimantan, including a Nandi bull and a Shiva lingam. The remains of the Laras Temple (Candi Laras) are in Magasari village, near the town of Rantau, 100 km from Banjarmasin. Agung Temple is near Amuntai, 150 km from Banjarmasin. Unless you're a hard core archeology freak, it's not worth going all the way to these villages to view what are mainly heaps of rubble – most of the good stuff is in the museum.

Getting There & Away

There are frequent colts to Banjarbaru from Banjarmasin's Km 6 Terminal.

MARTAPURA

Continuing on from Banjarbaru you come to Martapura. On a good day, the large market is a photographer's paradise, with every type of food on sale and lots of colourfully dressed Banjarmasi women. The Banjarmasis are big people. This is one of the few places in Indonesia where you commonly see fat women.

A section of the market sells uncut gems, silver jewellery and trading beads – the choice, both strung and unstrung, is excellent. Be prepared to bargain diligently for good prices, although the vendors seem honest about the quality and age of their merchandise.

The market is behind the Martapura bus station. A few minutes walk diagonally across the sports field near the bus station is a diamond polishing factory and shop – ask for the *Penggosokan Intan Tradisional Kayu Tangi*.

Places to Stay

Backing on to the market is the *Wisma*

Martapura market

Penginapan Mutiara on Jalan Sukaramai. It's quite decent and pleasant with rooms for 5000/7000 rp.

Getting There & Away

Frequent colts leave from the Km 6 Terminal in Banjarmasin. The fare is 600 rp and it takes about 45 minutes along a good surfaced road.

CEMPAKA

Kalimantan is said to be endowed with fabulous diamond and gold mines. Most of those accessible to the public are small concessions. The big multinationals (mostly Australian) have guarded claims deep in the interior. Cempaka is one place where you can see some of the smaller diamond and gold digs. The mines are, in fact, silt-filled, water-logged holes dug from muddy streams. The diggers spend the day up to their necks in water, diving below and coming up with a pan full of silt which is washed away to separate the gold or diamond specks.

Getting There & Away

The main stream is behind Cempaka village, 43 km from Banjarmasin. Occasional bemos leave from Martapura otherwise charter a bemo from Martapura bus station; it's a 3000 rp round trip with a brief stop at the creek. Ask at the Km 6 Terminal in Banjarmasin for colts direct to Cempaka. The stream is not far off the road from Martapura. If you get a public bemo you can walk from the road to the mine.

NEGARA

The north-western section of South Kalimantan is mostly swamp, but a group of Banjars have made this area their homeland. Negara is typical of many towns and villages built over the swamp and is easily accessible. A visit is a chance to see how the swamp inhabitants have adapted to the local geography.

One amazing local custom is the raising of water buffalo herds on wooden platforms. Besides trading in water buffalo, the locals make a living fishing for serpent fish, a popular freshwater fish eaten throughout South-East Asia. They have a distinctive method to catch them – they use live baby ducks as bait.

To get to Negara from Banjarmasin, you can either catch a bus via Kandangan (2500 rp, 2½ hours to Kandangan; then 1500 rp, one hour to Negara), or you can get one of the twice weekly boats direct from the Banjarmasin river taxi pier for 5000 rp. The boat leaves Banjarmasin around 2 pm and takes a day and a night to reach Negara via the Barito and Negara rivers.

There are no official losmen in Negara, but you can stay with one of the locals for 2500 rp per night.

LOKSADO TREKKING

East of Kandangan in the Muratus Mountains is a collection of villages that are the remnants of an animist Banjar society that may have moved here from the Barito delta to avoid the Islamic tide of the 15th to 16th centuries. About 20 villages are spread over about 2500 square km between Kandangan and Amuntai to the west and the South Kalimantan coast to the east.

Loksado is an important market village in the area and a good base from which to explore. One of the best times to be in Loksado is market day on Wednesday, when villagers from all over the area come to buy and sell.

A 30-minute walk through a bamboo forest south-east of Loksado is the village of **Malaris**, where 32 families or about 150 people live in a large balai.

Before trekking in the Loksado area, you must first check in at the police post in Padang Batung, a town between Kandangan and Mawangi on the road to Loksado. They will ask to see your hotel registration form from Banjarmasin which shows your registration with the South Kalimantan authorities, before giving you a permit for the Loksado area.

Places to Stay

Loksado has basic losmen for 2500 rp per person. Many of the villages in this area – such as Niih, to the south-west of Loksado – will take guests for 1000 to 2000 rp per night.

If you spend the night in Kandangan, you can stay at the *Losmen Sentosa*, near the bus station, for 2500 rp or at the *Loksado Permai Inn* where better rooms are 5000/7000 rp with bath, 3000/5000 rp without.

Getting There & Away

It's a full day's trip to Loksado from Banjarmasin. If you ride on the back of a chartered dirt bike for the Mawangi-Lumpangi leg, you can make Loksado by nightfall. If you plan to walk this section, you should spend the night in Kandangan and start from there.

Buses to Kandangan leave the Km 6 Terminal in Banjarmasin throughout the day. The fare is 2500 rp and the trip takes from 2½ to three hours. In Kandangan you can get a local bus (750 rp) to Mawangi or charter an ojek for 2000 rp and ask to stop at the police post in Padang Batung on the way for your Loksado permit. By bus it's about 30 minutes to Mawangi; by motorcycle it's 15 to 20 minutes.

From Mawangi it's a steep one-hour motorcycle ride to Lumpangi (6000 rp) if the road is dry enough, or a three-hour walk if it's not.

From Lumpangi, you can either hike along the jeep track straight through town or take a path over a bridge to the right. The footpath is about half an hour shorter than the jeep road, has more shade and passes through the villages of Datar Balimbing and Niih. The walk along the jeep track takes four hours to reach Loksado and can be quite hot since there are fewer trees along the way. The main village along this road is Muara Hatib,

which is a bit of a tourist trap since all the 4WD tours from Banjarmasin stop here.

Coming back from Loksado, most trekkers charter a bamboo raft and pole down the Riam Kiwa River to Kandangan. Rafts can be arranged in Loksado and Malaris for about 30,000 rp per raft, or in Niih for about 25,000 rp. If you leave Loksado on market day on Wednesday, you may be able to share a raft with local people for much less. It's an all-day trip and some sections of the river are quite rough – be sure to put things you want to keep dry in a watertight bag.

Another interesting route in or out of Loksado, if you have time, is to follow a trail between Malaris and Rantau through twelve villages that are conveniently spaced about an hour apart – allow about four days to reach Rantau comfortably. Several of these villages have balai where you can spend the night.

UP THE BARITO RIVER TO CENTRAL OR EAST KALIMANTAN

From Banjarmasin, you can travel by riverboat up the Barito River all the way to Muara Teweh in Central Kalimantan and then by speedboat to the Dayak village of Puruk Cahu. From Puruk Cahu a logging road leads to Long Iram in East Kalimantan.

A bis air from Banjarmasin to Muara Teweh costs 10,000 rp and takes about 56 hours. There are several losmen in Muara Teweh where you can stay for about 5000 rp. You can charter a speedboat to Puruk Cahu for 15,000 rp one way which takes about 2½ hours. You can stay in longhouses in Puruk Cahu.

Central Kalimantan

Geographically speaking, Kalimantan Tengah is Kalimantan's largest province. It is also the least populated. The northern part is quite mountainous while the southern part is mostly swamp and mangrove forests. In between is thick, almost uninterrupted rainforest.

The main attractions in Kal-Teng are the mountains north of Muara Teweh and Tanjung Puting National Park in the south near Pangkalan Bun. Every few years a major inter-tribal Dayak festival called Teweh takes place in the mountains of Central Kalimantan, in which the bones of ancestors who have been waiting in state or in temporary graves are finally buried. This translates into a month of feasting, drinking and ritual dancing.

The major river thoroughfares in Kal-Teng are the Barito, the Kahayan, the Arot and the Sampit.

PALANGKARAYA

The story goes that Palangkaraya, a surprisingly large inland town on the Kahayan River surrounded by an extraordinarily pancake flat expanse of jungle, was mooted during the Sukarno period for development as Kalimantan's capital city.

The town's chief attraction is the road connecting it to the nearby village of Tangkiling. Built by the Russians during the Sukarno period, this surfaced road leads 35 km to nowhere and appears to have no use whatsoever to justify the extravagance of building it.

Places to Stay

There's a cluster of cheap hotels by the dock where the longboats, river ferries and speedboats depart for Banjarmasin.

The *Losmen Putir Sinta* at Jalan Nias 2 has good clean rooms with fan for 3000 rp. Across the road the *Losmen Mahkota* at No 5 has rooms from about 4000 rp though they may ask considerably more.

The overpriced *Hotel Virgo* on Jalan Ahmad Yani has singles/doubles for 19,500/22,000 rp. Top hotel in Palangkaraya is *Adidas Hotel* (formerly Andas) (tel 21770) at Jalan Ahmad Yani 90, where decent air-con rooms are 24,000/27,500 rp.

Places to Eat

Lots of cheap rumah makan and warungs are around the dock and near the hotels. Back from the river, Jalan Halmahera and Jalan Jawa turn into night markets with many food trolleys. Several rumah makan are along Jalan Ahmad Yani, some of which serve udang galah.

Getting There & Away

Air Merpati has an office on Jalan Ahmad Yani. DAS and Bouraq have several agents in the main block of shops along the same street. A number of flights leave Palangkaraya, eg Bouraq flies to Banjarmasin and Sampit twice daily and to Pangkalan Bun daily.

Palangkaraya

Boat For details on getting from Banjarmasin to Palangkaraya see the Banjarmasin section. Boats out of Palangkaraya leave from the dock near the hotel cluster. From here speedboats to Banjarmasin cost 17,000 rp and take five hours. Buy your ticket from the little office at the pier.

The river ferries take about 18 hours to Banjarmasin but they're considerably cheaper – about 8000 rp. Buy your ticket from the larger office at the dock.

Getting Around

Airport Transport You practically need a plane to get from the town to the airport. No transport seems to be out this way and you'll probably have to charter a bemo from the city – expect to pay about 5000 rp. The airport has a taxi counter and a taxi between five people will cost 1500 rp each.

Becaks & Bemos Becak drivers congregate around the dock and along Jalan Halmahera at the night market. There are Suzuki bemos for longer stretches. Palangkaraya is rather spread out and the walk from the dock to the centre takes about 20 minutes.

The station for bemos to Tangkiling is *way* past the western boundary of

Palangkaraya. It's a long way and you seem to wait for ages to catch a bemo. There are frequent bemos for the 25-minute trip from the terminal to Tangkiling.

MUARA TEWEH

Muara Teweh is the last longboat stop on the Barito River. Beyond Muara Teweh, travel by speedboat to Puruk Cahu in the foothills of the Muller Range. Hire Dayak guides for treks into the mountains in Puruk Cahu. Near Mt Pancungapung, at the border of Central and East Kalimantan, a cement pillar marks the geographical centre of Borneo.

From Muara Teweh, trek overland to Long Iram in East Kalimantan, then catch a longboat down the Mahakam River to Samarinda. The trek takes up to two weeks and can be done on your own following logging roads or along more interesting footpaths if you hire a guide in Banjarmasin or Muara Teweh.

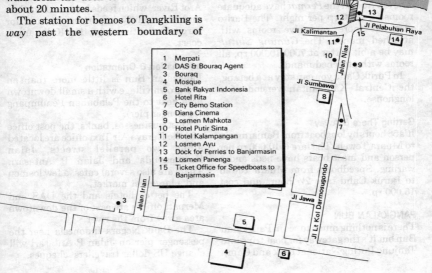

1	Merpati
2	DAS & Bouraq Agent
3	Bouraq
4	Mosque
5	Bank Rakyat Indonesia
6	Hotel Rita
7	City Bemo Station
8	Diana Cinema
9	Losmen Mahkota
10	Hotel Putir Sinta
11	Hotel Kalampangan
12	Losmen Ayu
13	Dock for Ferries to Banjarmasin
14	Losmen Panenga
15	Ticket Office for Speedboats to Banjarmasin

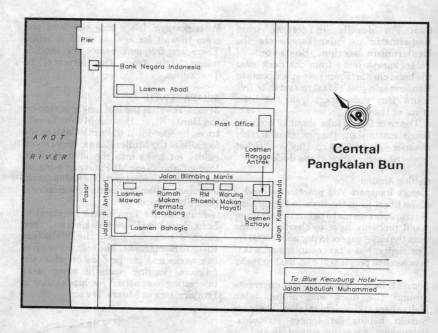

Central Pangkalan Bun

Places to Stay

The *Barito* and the *Permai* have adequate rooms for 5000 rp per night. The Barito also has more expensive rooms with attached mandi. The *Gunung Sintuk* may be a bit better at 7500/10,000 rp, all rooms with attached mandi.

In Puruk Cahu you can stay at a betang, the Central Kalimantan version of a longhouse.

Getting There & Away

It's 56 hours by longboat from Banjarmasin to Muara Teweh. The fare is 10,000 rp per person and most boats have beds and a warung. Speedboats from Muara Teweh to Puruk Cahu take 2½ hours and cost 15,000 rp.

PANGKALAN BUN

There is nothing much to see in Pangkalan Bun but it's the gateway for boat trips into Tanjung Puting National Park and Camp Leakey. The town is on the banks of the Arot River, which feeds into the Java Sea, and it's a fairly important harbour for cargo boats that ply the Kalimantan coast.

Information & Orientation

Pangkalan Bun is little more than an overgrown village with a small downtown area next to the Pelabuhan Penumpang (passenger pier).

Most businesses, banks, the post office and the Deraya Air Taxi office are located along two parallel streets, Jalan Kasumayuda and Jalan P Antasari. There are also several cafes, a few losmen and a large wet market.

The better hotels and the DAS and Merpati offices are east of the downtown area away from the river.

The Bank Negara Indonesia near the passenger pier on Jalan P Antasari will change US dollar travellers' cheques.

Places to Stay – bottom end

The *Losmen Rahayu* and the *Losmen Rangga Antrek* are both on Jalan Kasumayuda not far from the post office. The Rahayu is the cheapest with adequate rooms at 3500/6000 rp. The Rangga Antrek is larger and more of a local hangout – rooms with mandi are 5000/7500 rp.

Over on Jalan P Antasari are the *Abadi* and the *Bahagia* losmens. Both are 3000/4000 rp for basic rooms without mandi, 7500 rp with bath and fan. The Bahagia is the cleanest.

Connecting these two main roads is Jalan Blimbing Manis, where you'll find several good warungs and the *Losmen Mawar*. The Mawar has small, basic rooms for 3500 rp without mandi, 6000 rp with.

East of the centre about 1.5 km are several other choices, only one of which fits bottom-end budgets. Toward the end of Jalan Domba, not far from the up-market Blue Kecubung Hotel, is *Losmen Anda* with clean rooms for only 3500 rp. None have attached mandi.

Muklis Usman, at Jalan Hasanuddin 2, puts up travellers in his home but the price varies according to how much he thinks you can pay – should be no more than 4000 rp a night including breakfast.

Places to Stay – top end

The *Blue Kecubung* on Jalan Domba has well-kept rooms with fan, attached mandi and breakfast for 18,150 rp or with TV and air-con for 30,250 rp. It's a little overpriced and a school across the street plays loud march music at 6 am on schooldays for morning callisthenics. Further along the same road is the smaller *Wisma Sampurga* where rooms with mandi are 7500 rp. They also have more expensive air-con rooms.

Best value in the upper end is *Wisma Andika* around the corner from Losmen Anda on Jalan Hasanuddin to the west. It's very clean, the staff are helpful and the restaurant good. Rooms are 12,500 rp with attached bath, or 25,000 rp air-con.

Places to Eat

On Jalan Blimbing Manis there's a very good Chinese warung, the *Rumah Makan Phoenix*. Close by on the same side of the street away from the river is the inexpensive, friendly and clean *Warung Makan Hayati*, which specialises in South and Central Kalimantan cuisine. They serve nasi kuning – a kind of roast chicken curry with yellow rice – and *soto banjar*, as well as nasi campur and gado-gado. *Warung Permata Kecubung*, on the same street towards Jalan P Antasari, has a similar menu but is slightly more expensive.

Near the Losmen Abadi on Jalan P Antasari is *Warung Pahala*, a tea stall with good ice drinks including the local speciality *es kolak*, a kind of pineapple/coconut smoothie.

If you're staying in the Jalan Domba area away from the centre, you can get good nasi kuning in the morning at Jalan Hasanuddin 2, near the Merpati office. The Wisma Andika hotel has a good and reasonably priced restaurant in front.

Getting There & Away

Air Bouraq flies to Pangkalan Bun from Banjarmasin (61,100 rp), Sampit (39,800 rp), Palangkaraya (50,000 rp) and Surabaya (120,100 rp). DAS flies to/from Palangkaraya (48,400 rp) or Banjarmasin (59,100 rp).

Deraya Air Taxi and Merpati are the only services that fly from West Kalimantan or Java. Deraya has daily flights to/from Semarang for 54,550 rp and three flights weekly to/from Ketapang (40,500 rp) and Pontianak (73,550 rp). On Merpati it's Semarang (65,100 rp), Ketapang (46,100 rp), Bandung (65,100 rp) and Jakarta (121,000 rp), via Bandung.

The Merpati and DAS offices are on Jalan Hasanuddin in Pangkalan Bun, near Wisma Andika. The Deraya Air Taxi office is at Jalan P Antasari 51 near the wet market.

You can book flights at the Blue Kecubung and Wisma Andika hotels as well. You pay cash rupiah for your tickets wherever you book them.

Boat There are no regular passenger ships in or out of Pangkalan Bun but many cargo boats have a few berths or at least deck space. Passage can be booked at the Pelabuhan Penumpang.

At least once every two days there's a boat to Banjarmasin or Pontianak and occasionally to Semarang. A typical fare to Pontianak is 25,000 rp including meals – the trip takes three days, two nights. For an added 10,000 rp you can usually get a bed in a crew cabin, otherwise you sleep on the deck. To Banjarmasin, it's around 20,000 rp and takes two days.

TANJUNG PUTING NATIONAL PARK
Tanjung Puting National Park is 305,000 hectares of tropical rainforest, mangrove forest and swamp. It is home to a vast variety of flora and fauna, including crocodiles, hornbills, wild pigs, bear cats,

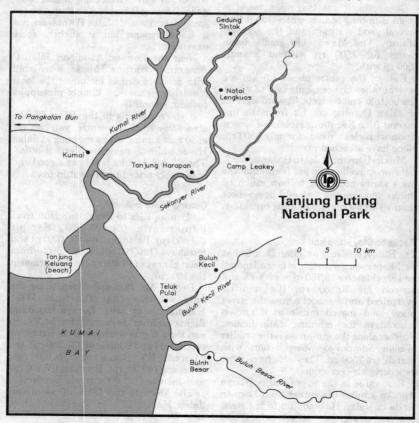

crab-eating macaques, orang-utan, proboscis monkeys, pythons, dolphins and mudskippers, a kind of fish that can walk and breathe on land. This is also a habitat for the dragon fish, an aquarium fish worth 500,000 rp and highly valued by Chinese collectors throughout South-East Asia. Both the dragon fish and the crocodiles are unfortunate prey for the occasional poacher.

A trip into the park begins in the town of Kumai, on the banks of the Kumai River about 25 km south-east of Pangkalan Bun. You must apply for a permit to enter the park at the PHPA office in Kumai. If you're not planning to spend the night in the park, it's best to collect your permit a day in advance, as the whole procedure takes at least an hour. The permit costs 1500 rp and you must show a police report from Pangkalan Bun – the registration form from your hotel or losmen will do – and your passport or a copy of the photo page of your passport.

The only way to see Tanjung Puting is by chartered longboat. This can be arranged at several piers in Kumai. If you decide to have the boat drop you off somewhere in the park (say the Camp Leakey area), you can usually arrange for a boat back from Tanjung Harapan. You can also arrange to have food brought aboard or bring your own from Pangkalan Bun.

The PHPA may try to talk you into hiring a guide or two but they're really not necessary, as the boatmen know where to go. However, some PHPA guides speak some English and will also cook on overnight trips. The official PHPA guide rate nationwide is a bargain 5000 rp per day but they may ask more. Use your discretion.

Most people head directly up the Sekonyer River to visit the orang-utan project in Camp Leakey, but another idea is to follow the Kumai River south into Kumai Bay to visit the deserted beach of Tanjung Keluang.

CAMP LEAKEY

The Orang-utan Research and Conservation Project at Camp Leakey, near the centre of Tanjung Puting National Park, was founded by Canadian Dr Birute Galdikas nearly 20 years ago. Its main function is rehabilitating ex-captive orang-utans to their natural habitat.

It's illegal in Indonesia to own an orang-utan, but many Indonesians in Sumatra and Kalimantan capture baby orang-utans and try to raise them as pets. At this writing there are two rehabilitation camps in the park, one at Camp Leakey and one at Natai Lengkuas two hours north by boat on the Sekonyer River. Another will soon open in Tanjung Harapan, two hours to the south.

There are about 100 orang-utans in the forests around Camp Leakey, half of which are wild, and the others ex-captives. The best time to visit is late afternoon when the orang-utans come down from the trees for feeding. Or bring some peanuts and walk through the rehabilitation area and they'll find you. Other jungle primates seen in the Camp Leakey-Natai Lengkuas areas include crab-eating macaques and the elusive proboscis monkeys.

Camp Leakey is not open to overnight visitors without prior permission. To apply, write to Dr Galdikas c/o Orang-utan Research & Conservation Project, Tanjung Puting National Park, Central Kalimantan.

By late 1989, there are plans to open a losmen for visitors to Camp Leakey at the nearby village of Tanjung Harapan. The room rate is projected to be about 10,000 rp per night. Once this losmen is open, the best plan might be to have a boat from Kumai drop you at Tanjung Harapan, rather than hiring it all day.

Dugout canoes with crew can be hired in Tanjung Harapan for 5000 to 10,000 rp per day. This is a better way around the Sekonyer River and its little tributaries, as some sections are very narrow. The canoes are also much quieter so you're likely to see more wildlife. It's not unusual to see a three to four metre crocodile in this area – keep your hands in the boat.

Getting There & Away

Kumai is about half an hour away from Pangkalan Bun by colt. You can catch colts to Kumai (600 rp) near the market by the Arot River in Pangkalan Bun, or on the road to Kumai, which skirts the north end of Pangkalan Bun. This is the same road that goes to the airport.

Longboats from Kumai take about two hours to reach Tanjung Harapan, four hours to Camp Leakey, or six hours to Natai Lengkuas. Hire rates vary with the size and condition of boats but should cost between 25,000 and 40,000 rp a day including crew. Most boats can take up to 20 people easily. It's wise to get a longboat with a roof to keep off sun and rain. It's the same rate one way and return. A boat to Tanjung Keluang alone should be about 15,000 rp.

West Kalimantan

Kalimantan Barat's major distinction is that it is home to Indonesia's longest waterway, the Kapuas River (1,143 km). Kal-Bar is Kalimantan's third least populated province and yet has the highest concentration of Chinese of any province in Indonesia. It's two largest towns, Pontianak and Singkawang, are 35% and 70% Chinese respectively.

Whether it's a result of the industriousness of the Chinese, as the locals claim, or the relative proximity of prosperous Kuching in Sarawak to the north, West Kalimantan is the business and educational centre of Indonesian Borneo.

In spite of all the activity on the coast, Kal-Bar's interior is relatively unexplored. There are many Punan, Iban and Kenyah Dayak villages in the mountainous eastern part of the province.

PONTIANAK

Situated right on the equator, Pontianak lies astride the confluence of the Landak and Kapuas Kecil rivers. The city was founded in 1771 by Syarif Abdul Rahman Al-Kadri of Saudi Arabia. The economic hub of Kalimantan, Pontianak is surprisingly large, with a giant indoor sports stadium, a sizeable university and a couple of big girder bridges spanning the Landak River.

Like Banjarmasin, it really needs to be seen from the canals, which crisscross the city. Walk over the bridge from Jalan Gajah Mada for a sweeping view of the river and houses and brilliant orange sunsets that make Bali sunsets look pathetic!

As the city has a large proportion of Chinese, there are many Chinese shops selling porcelain, Chinese vases and amphoras, gold and jewellery.

From Pontianak you can take a trip north along the coast to Pasir Panjang, a

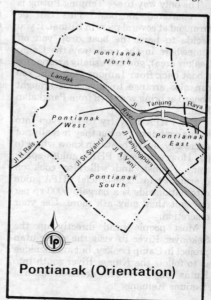

Pontianak (Orientation)

lovely stretch of beach with clean, white sand and calm water, just back from the Pontianak-Singkawang road. The Mandor Nature Reserve is to the north-east.

This is also the starting point for boat trips up the Kapuas River, which terminate in Putussibau in the north-eastern corner of the province.

Information & Orientation

The main part of the city is on the southern side of the Kapuas Kecil River where it meets the Landak. Here you'll find several markets, the main bemo terminal, several hotels, the airline and Pelni offices, banks, etc.

A short distance from the Kapuas Indah terminal there are many small motor boats and a vehicle ferry to Pasar Lintang on the opposite side of the river, which is the site of Terminal Sintian, the main long-distance bus station.

The Pontianak immigration office (tel 4512) is at Jalan L Sutoyo, off Jalan A Yani.

The Malaysian Consulate, at Jalan A Yani 42, issues tourist visas for east Malaysia (Sarawak and Sabah) for 10,000 rp per application. This allows you to fly from Pontianak to Kuching, Sarawak without restrictions. Consulate hours are from 7 am to 3 pm Monday to Saturday, closed 11 am to 1.30 pm Friday.

To cross by land you'll need the East Malaysian visa and an exit permit from the Pontianak immigration office or the Jakarta immigration office .

Tourist Office The West Kalimantan tourist office is at Jalan Achmad Sood 25. They have a good provincial map and provide official guides for river and jungle trips.

Post The post office is on Jalan Rahadi Usman near the Hotel Kartika and open 8 am to 7 pm Monday through Friday (but closed 11 am to 2 pm Friday), 8 am to 1 pm Saturday and 9 am to 2 pm Sunday.

Mesjid Abdurrakhman

This was the royal mosque of Syarif Abdul Rahman (in Indonesian, Abdurrakhman) who reigned as Sultan of Pontianak from 1771 until his death in 1808. It's a very large mosque in the Malay or Sumatran style with a square tiered roof, and made entirely of wood. Beautiful inside and out, it's worth the short canoe trip across the Landak River from the pinisi harbour. Charter a boat for 500 rp or wait for a canoe taxi which is only 100 rp per person.

Istana Kadriyah

About 100 metres behind the sultan's mosque is his former palace, now an interesting museum displaying the personal effects of the sultan's family. Eight sultans reigned following the death of the first in 1808; the last died in 1978.

The palace caretaker is the gracious Syarif Yusuf Alkadri, a descendant of the sultan's family. His features are very Arabic and he is proud to pose for photos. Visiting hours are 8.30 am to 6 pm daily. There is no admission fee to the istana, but a donation is encouraged.

Pinisi Harbour

If you follow Jalan S Muhammad south along the Kapuas Kecil River you eventually come to the pinisi harbour, where you can see East Javanese and Sulawesi-style sailing schooners.

Also docked in this area are the large houseboats peculiar to West Kalimantan, called *bandung*. Bandungs function as floating general stores that ply their way up and down the Kapuas River, trading at villages along the way. Their family owners live onboard. A typical run up the Kapuas might last as long as a month.

Musium Negeri Pontianak (Pontianak National Museum)

Located near Tanjungpura University, south of the city centre on Jalan Ahmad Yani, this recently built museum has a collection of *tempayan*, South-East Asian ceramics (mostly water jugs) from

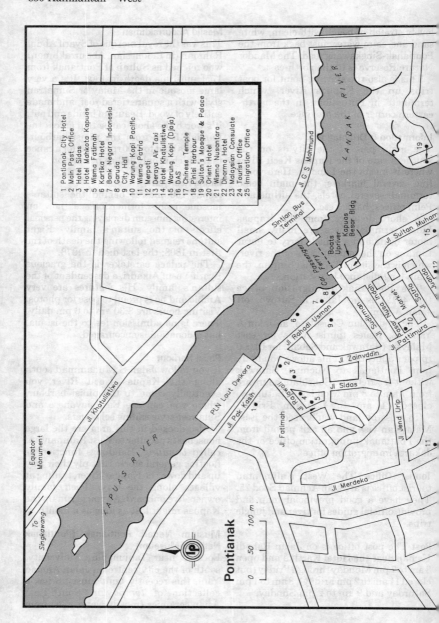

Pontianak

1 Pontianak City Hotel
2 Main Post Office
3 Hotel Sidas
4 Hotel Mahkota Kapuas
5 Wisma Fatimah
6 Kartika Hotel
7 Bank Negara Indonesia
8 Garuda
9 City Hall
10 Warung Kopi Pacific
11 Wisma Patria
12 Merpati
13 Deraya Air Taxi
14 Hotel Khatulistiwa
15 Warung Kopi (Djoja)
16 DAS
17 Chinese Temple
18 Pinisi Harbour
19 Sultan's Mosque & Palace
20 Orient Hotel
21 Wisma Nusantara
22 Dharma Hotel
23 Malaysian Consulate
24 Tourist Office
25 Immigration Office

LANDAK RIVER

KAPUAS RIVER

Jl G S Mahmund

Sintian Bus Terminal

Boats Upriver

Car Passenger Ferry

Kapuas Besar Bldg

Jl Sultan Muhamm

Jl Rahadi Usman

Jl Sudirman

Jl Nusa Indah

Pasar Market

Jl Sadng

Pasar Nusa Indah

Jl Tanjung

Jl Zainvddin

Jl Pattimura

Jl Sidas

Jl Rajawali

Jl Fatimah

Jl Merdeka

Jl Jend Urip

PLN Lout Dwikora

Jl Pak Kasih

Jl Khatulistiwa

Equator Monument

To Singkawang

TAPUAS RIVER

0   50   100 m

Thailand, China and Borneo. The jugs displayed vary from tiny to tank-like and date from the 16th to the 20th century.

Tribal exhibits include dioramic displays of the clothing, musical instruments, tools and crafts of the Dayak cultures of West Kalimantan. All the labels are in Bahasa Indonesian, but if you plan a trip to the interior of the province, this might be a good place to bone up on the different Dayak groups in advance.

Tugu Khatulistiwa Pontianak (Equator Monument)

If you're really stuck for things to do, visit the official monument marking the equator. It was originally erected in 1928 as a simple obelisk mounted with a metallic arrow. In 1930 a circle was welded to the arrow, in 1938 another circle was added in the other direction and it now looks like a big gyroscope on a pillar. On the 23 March and 23 September the sun is supposed to be directly overhead.

At the Kantor Walikotamadya (City Hall), on Jalan Rahadi Usman across from the Hotel Kartika, get a signed proclamation documenting that you crossed the equator in Pontianak. The certificate is printed in Indonesian and English and is free.

Places to Stay – bottom end

Budget accommodation in Pontianak has always been expensive and there are only two places with rooms under 10,000 rp per night.

Backing onto the river opposite the Kapuas Indah ferry terminal is the *Hotel Wijaya Kusuma* (tel 2547) at Jalan Musi 51-53 with rooms from 7500 rp. It has largish, clean rooms with fans and sweeping views across the river. It's a gambling and prostitution centre like most large hotels in this price range, but this is kept fairly discreet. Avoid rooms facing the noisy street and get as far away as possible from the booming TV set. There's a Chinese nightclub downstairs,

open every night until midnight, featuring Chinese and Indonesian pop singers.

Not far away is the pleasant though basic *Wisma Fatimah* (tel 2250) at Jalan Fatimah 5. Singles are 7500 rp, doubles 12,000 rp and rooms have a small attached mandi and toilet. Rates include breakfast. Take a Gajah Mada bemo to get there.

Places to Stay – middle

The *Hotel Khatulistiwa*, Jalan Diponegoro 151, is the only hotel in Pontianak with any atmosphere and one of the few wooden buildings left. Very clean rooms on the 3rd floor of the old wing cost 10,000 rp with fan and mandi, 11,000 rp on the 2nd floor, 12,500 rp on the first floor. There are also a few air-con rooms on the 1st floor with TV for 15,000 rp. VIP rooms in another building attached to a noisy billiard parlour are 15,000 rp with air-con and TV or 20,000 rp with air-con , TV and hot water. Hotel Khatulistiwa also has an entrance at Jalan Sisingamangaraja 126.

The *New Equator Guest House* (tel 2092) is on Jalan Tanjungpura just before the Kapuas Bridge at No 91. Clean, fairly modern rooms are 10,125 rp without mandi, 15,000 rp with. Across the street at No 45 is the better value *Orient Hotel* (tel 2650), a friendly, family-run place where rooms with fan/video/bath are 12,000 rp, with air-con 15,000 rp, or with hot water 27,000 rp.

Another friendly place is *Wisma Patria* (tel 6063) at Jalan Cokroaminoto (also called Merdeka Timur) 497. The rooms are very nice and the atmosphere congenial. Single/doubles are 10,000/ 12,000 rp with fan and mandi, 16,000/ 18,000 rp with air-con. A good buffet cafeteria is downstairs.

Places to Stay – top end

A short distance west of the centre along the river is the *Pontianak City Hotel* (tel 2495) at Jalan Pak Kasih 44 which has air-con rooms from 20,500/22,500 rp. There's a large map of Pontianak in the foyer.

The *Kartika Hotel* (tel 29256) on the

Markets in Indonesia
Top: Martapura, Kalimantan (AS)
Left: Floating market, Banjarmasin, Kalimantan (JC)
Right: Kuta, Lombok (HF)

river across from City Hall is an up-market version of the Hotel Wijaya Kusuma – a recreational hotel for businessmen. Rooms start at 40,000 rp for a single and go as high as 53,000 rp for a double with a river view or 75,000 rp for an executive suite. The rooms are nice enough but the service is very inept.

The *Dharma Hotel* (tel 4759, 2860) on Jalan Imam Bonjol has rooms for 25,000 rp (with air-con, fridge, phone, colour TV, bath tub, hot and cold water, wall-to-wall carpet) or less luxurious rooms for 15,000 rp – plus a service charge and tax. Bemos from the Kapuas terminal run straight past the hotel.

The two top hotels in Pontianak are the *Hotel Mahkota Kapuas* and the *Kapuas Permai Hotel*. The Mahkota, the newest and best, is well located in the centre of town. Comfortable, nicely decorated rooms with air-con and hot water bath and shower start at 42,000 rp for a studio with a double bed, or 48,000/54,000 rp for a single/double standard. Suites are 96,000 rp and the two bedroom Presidential Suite with built-in wet bar is 250,000 rp. The Mahkota has a couple of bars, two restaurants (one on the ninth floor with a view of the city), a fitness centre and a discotheque. They plan to add a swimming pool in the future.

The *Kapuas Permai Hotel* (tel 6122) is further down Jalan Imam Bonjol past the Dharma Hotel towards the airport. It's on sprawling grounds with a little shopping mall that includes a travel agency. They have an amazing 100-metre swimming pool that's well tended. There are three kinds of accommodation: rooms in the main building for 45,000/51,000 rp, cottages for 30,000 rp and drive-in apartments with their own carports for 46,000 rp. The cottage and drive-in apartment areas get very swampy when it rains and mosquitoes are a problem. Rooms smell musty. If you want to do some serious lap swimming, it might be your best choice in Kalimantan; otherwise, the Mahkota is better top-end value.

Places to Eat

The best places to eat are the countless warungs. Good ones in the Kapuas Indah ferry terminal area offer udang galah, ayam goreng, mixed vegetables and nasi putih for around 2500 rp. Try the night warungs and gerobak makanan on Jalan Pasar Sudirman for *sate kambing* (goat sate) and steaming plates of rice noodles, *kepiting* (crab), udang, ikan, vegetables – all fried up in a wok for 1500 rp.

More foodstalls are along Jalan Asahan. For pastries and thick fruit juices, try the *New Holland Bakery* next door to the Hotel Wijaya Kusuma near the Kapuas Indah terminal.

The clean little *Somay Bandung* in the Pontianak Theatre complex on Jalan Sisingamangaraja has delicious Chinese-style bubur ayam for 500 rp and the house specialty *somay*, a tasty concoction of potatoes, tofu, hard-boiled egg and peanut sauce for 800 rp. They also serve good ice drinks.

West Kalimantan grows good coffee and there are great *warung kopi* in Pontianak. The *Warung Kopi Pacific* on the corner of Jalan Nusa Indah II and Jalan Pattimura opens early in the morning and is quite popular. They offer cakes, pies, egg rolls, curry puffs and of course kopi in several styles. A food trolley parked in front has good bubur ayam garnished with peanuts and dried anchovies in the Indonesian style.

Another good one is the *Warung Kopi Djaja (Jaya)* at Jalan Tanjungpura 23. The coffee is particularly good here – they roast their own beans. They have delicious Indonesian pastries, including some of the best pisang goreng in Indonesia, served with a special custard sauce. You can buy bags of freshly ground Djaja coffee here, or with a day's notice they'll sell you a heat-sealed bag of whole roasted beans for 5500 rp per kg.

Along Jalan Diponegoro are several more formal restaurants and a good Chinese night market. Padang food fans shouldn't miss *Rumah Makan Beringin* at No 115. There is also an *American Fried Chicken* and a *Pioneer Fried Chicken* on this street as well as the large *Haramani* supermarket.

Ex-pats claim the best Chinese food in town is at the *Restoran Bambu Kuning* near the Dharma Hotel on Jalan Tanjungpura. Ask for the *ikan jelawat*, a local fresh water fish. Another good choice for Chinese is the *Restoran Hawaii* on Jalan Satria near Pasar Nusa Indah. Also on Jalan Satria is the *Italian Ice Cream Parlor & Steakhouse* where you can get a variety of Western food.

On the road to the car ferry to Pasar Lintang is Pontianak's night-time martabak headquarters with numerous food trolleys dedicated to the pursuit of the perfect stuffed crepe.

Getting There & Away

Air Garuda (tel 21026) is at Jalan Rahadi Usman 8A and open Monday to Friday 8 am to 4 pm, Saturday 8 am to 1 pm, Sunday and holidays 9 am to 12 noon. DAS (tel 583) is at Jalan Gajah Mada 67; Merpati (tel 2332) is at Jalan Ir H Juanda 50A; and Bouraq (tel 2371) is at Jalan Tanjungpura 253.

Flights between Pontianak and Jakarta are 95,700 rp on Garuda, 77,500 rp on Bouraq and 72,500 rp on Sempati. All three airlines have daily flights. The afternoon Garuda flight to Jakarta will only take 50 passengers (normal capacity is 80) when the runway is wet – something to do with the size of the plane versus the size of the runway – so show up early for boarding if it looks like rain.

Garuda flies to/from Singapore four days a week for 183,800 rp. The flight takes an hour. To/from Kuching is 100,000 rp on Garuda.

Deraya Air Taxi flies thrice weekly from Pontianak to Sintang (43,300 rp) and Putussibau (66,100 rp). DAS flies daily to Sintang (51,600 rp) and Putussibau (77,500 rp), and thrice weekly to Nangapinoh (68,400 rp).

Bus From Pontianak you can bus north along the coast to Singkawang (about 3½ hours, 2500 rp). Colts depart every hour from about 6 am from the Sintian Terminal. Colts also leave here further north to Sambas or north-east to Mandor (1½ hours, 1500 rp).

Daily buses head inland to Sintang. These leave the ferry pier on the city side of the river around 8 am, take 10 hours to reach Sintang, and the fare is usually 6000 rp. When the roads are wet, the fare may increase as high as 8500 rp. You can also fly or ferry on the Kapuas River to Sintang. See the section on Kapuas River Trips for more information on travel to Sintang.

To reach Kuching in Sarawak by bus you have to change twice, first at Siantan at the border, than again in Serian (Sarawak) for the final leg to Kuching. Total fare from Pontianak to Kuching is 25,000 rp or M$38. Once the land crossing is open to foreigners on the Indonesian side, a through service to Kuching will probably develop.

Boat Pelni is on Jalan Pak Kasih on the southern bank of the river at the Pelabuhan Laut Dwikora. For other ships ask at the entrance to the port adjacent to the Pelni office.

Pelni's *KM Lawit* does the two-day, two-night Pontianak-Jakarta trip every 10 days. Economy class is 28,800 rp including food; 1st and 2nd class are 70,400 rp and 55,600 rp respectively. At least two non-Pelni cargo ships also take passengers on this run daily. Average fare is 17,000 rp but you may have to sleep on deck.

There may be occasional cargo ships but there are no regular passenger ships on the Pontianak-Singapore route. There are no Pontianak-Banjarmasin ships – you have to go to Pangkalan Bun or Surabaya first and get ships from there to Banjarmasin. Pontianak-Pangkalan Bun-Banjarmasin is about 40,000 rp by cargo boat.

Riverboat

See the Kapuas River Trips section for details on trips into the interior of West Kalimantan by riverboat. Most riverboats leave from the Kapuas Indah ferry terminal (Lalulinta Sunggai dan Feri) near the Hotel Wijaya Kusuma. Some, like the houseboat bandungs, leave from the pinisi harbour near the end of Jalan Sultan Muhammed. Bandungs don't usually take passengers, but they may make exceptions for curious foreigners.

Getting Around

Airport Transport A counter at the airport sells tickets for taxis into town for 5000 rp. Or walk down the road in front of the terminal building bringing you to the main road in Pontianak and from here you should be able to get a colt. From the airport to the Kapuas terminal is an half-hour drive.

Bemo, Taxi & Motorboat The two main bemo stations are in the middle of the city: the Kapuas terminal near the waterfront, and the other on Jalan Sisingamangaraja. There are taxis for hire next to the Garuda office and becaks aplenty – the drivers overcharge but they're not too difficult to bargain with.

Outboard motorboats depart from piers next to the Kapuas Indah building on the river. They cross the river to the Pasar Lintang and Terminal Sintian for 100 rp per person. A car and passenger ferry just north of here will take you to Pasar Lintang at the same cost.

Car Rental

Although renting a car in Pontianak is relatively expensive, it's a way to see coastal West Kalimantan at your own pace. Most roads are in good condition and traffic is relatively light. At Citra Tours & Travel (tel 4248) at Jalan Pak Kasih 6, you can rent an L300 minibus or Kijang (Indonesian jeep) for 80,000 rp per day with a driver. The L300s can hold up to 10 people.

KAPUAS RIVER TRIPS

Pontianak is the launching point for riverboat services along Indonesia's longest river. Boats of all sizes and shapes journey the Kapuas, but the standard is a double-decker with beds on the upper deck. A riverboat to Sintang (about 700 km from Pontianak) costs 12,000 rp per person and takes two days, one night. This includes basic meals and there are warungs aboard most boats.

An interesting side trip off the Kapuas River is from Sintang along the Melawai River to Nangapinoh. There are a couple of losmen in Nangapinoh for 3000 to 5000 rp. From Nangapinoh catch boats further south on the Sayan River to the villages of Kota Bahru and Nangasokan. The journey entails riding sections of thrilling rapids and nights spent in Dayak villages. Boat fares from Nangapinoh to Nangasokan should be about 10,000 rp. Allow a week to do the trip from Sintang; you can fly back to Pontianak from Nangpinoh.

The terminus of all riverboat services, over 1000 km up the Kapuas, is Putussibau. From here you can travel overland to East Kalimantan and the headwaters of the Mahakam River, then catch a series of riverboats all the way to Samarinda on the east coast. The fare to Putussibau is 25,000 rp and the trip takes four days, three nights. Meals are included but you're well advised to supplement the meagre fish and rice diet with food from Pontianak.

Once you arrive in Putussibau visit the office of the bupati (lord mayor) and register your presence. He can also give you a letter of introduction for trekking beyond this point. Near Putussibau in the village of Melapi is a traditional Iban longhouse.

Putussibau to Long Apari The hardy and intrepid can begin a river and jungle trek east across the West/East Kalimantan borders through the Muller Range to Long Apari at the headwaters of the Mahakam River. If you make it all the way to

West Kalimantan

Samarinda, you'll become one of the very few westerners to have accomplished a true trans-Kalimantan journey from west to east. But the journey is arduous and expenses can be considerable.

The first step is to arrange a knowledge-able guide or two in Putussibau – the bupati can assist. If guides cannot be found in Putussibau, you can postpone this until you reach the village of Tanjung Lokan, where guides may be easier to locate. Do not attempt the trip beyond Tanjung Lokan alone, as the trails are not well marked.

While still in Putussibau, you'll have to stock up on provisions for yourselves and your guide(s) – allow about 50,000 rp for the essentials: rice, sugar, coffee and canned fish. Then charter a longboat or motor canoe for around 200,000 rp to make the one-day trip further upriver to Nangabungan. From Nangabungan you must charter a smaller canoe (prahu) for 50,000 rp for another day's travel to Tanjung Lokan.

In Tanjung Lokan, find a guide or guides to lead you through the jungle into East Kalimantan. The walk takes about six days and guides will ask for around 40,000 rp each. Once you reach the logging camp west of Long Apari, the guides will turn around and head back to Tanjung Lokan and you must offer them a substantial amount of rice for their return journey.

From the logging camp it's a four-hour walk plus a three-hour boat ride to the village of Long Apari. You should be able to charter a prahu for the trip for about 20,000 rp. From Long Apari, it's a short boat ride down the Mahakam to Long Lunuk where there's an airstrip with regular flights to Samarinda, or spend a leisurely week gliding downriver to Long Bagun and Samarinda via the regular public riverboat service.

SINGKAWANG

A predominantly Chinese town, Singkawang is known as the Hong Kong of Indonesia. If you've travelled along the west coast of West Malaysia, the atmosphere and colonnaded shop architecture will seem familiar. If nothing else,

it's probably the cleanest town in Indonesia. It's a day trip from Pontianak and the drive is quite beautiful with lush palm trees most of the way.

The main attraction of Singkawang is nearby Pasir Panjang beach, a two to three km stretch of clean, white sand and calm water with few people. At the south end, whisky-coloured river flows into the sea. Pasir Panjang is a 20-minute drive out of Singkawang just off the Singkawang-Pontianak road. There's a little warung on the beach serving bottled drinks and nasi gedug.

On the road to Singkawang you could stop at Pulau Kijing, a seaside picnic spot just before the town of Sungaiduri (also called Seiduri for short – several towns along here shorten Sunggai to Sei).

East of Singkawang 12 km is Gunung Puting, Nipple Mountain (once you see it, you'll know how it got its name), which is a minor hill resort complete with neo-colonial hotel. The largest flower in the world, the Rafflesia, grows wild on these slopes.

The bank next door to the Hotel

Pasir Panjang Beach, Singkawang

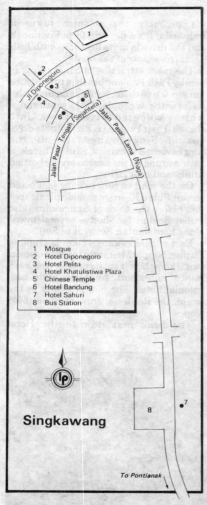

1 Mosque
2 Hotel Diponegoro
3 Hotel Pelita
4 Hotel Khatulistiwa Plaza
5 Chinese Temple
6 Hotel Bandung
7 Hotel Sahuri
8 Bus Station

Singkawang

To Pontianak

Diponegoro will cash US dollar travellers' cheques.

Places to Stay

In Singkawang the *Hotel Bandung* on Jalan Sejahtera (Pasar Tengah), a 10-minute walk from the bus station, is basic but generally clean although you could get a lot of street noise. Singles/doubles are 3500/5000 rp with shared mandi/toilet.

A block or two away is the *Hotel Khatulistiwa Plaza* (tel 21697) at Jalan Selamat Karman 17 with fairly nice rooms from 6600 rp with attached mandi/toilet. Across the road the *Hotel Pelita* has run-down overpriced rooms with small attached mandi/toilet for 6000 rp – and the staff are surly.

The best hotel in this price range is the scrupulously clean *Hotel Diponegoro* (tel 21430) at Jalan Diponegoro 32, on the diagonally opposite corner to the Hotel Khatulistiwa Plaza. The 6600 rp rooms are a little small but all have fans and spotless mandis. Slightly larger rooms are 8800 rp and for 17,600 rp you get air-con. Downstairs an airy restaurant serves good sate.

Cheapest losmen in town is *Losmen Singkawang* on a lane off Jalan Sejahtera south of the centre. Dingy rooms are 3000 rp with shared mandis only. Nearby in the Kal-Bar Theatre complex is the *Hotel Kal-Bar* which is strictly a brothel and gambling venue, no foreigners allowed.

South of town in a quiet residential area is Singkawang's top accommodation, the *Hotel Palapa*. It's a pleasant, clean place, if a little isolated, with standard rooms for 12,500 rp, air-con for 18,000 rp.

At the Pasir Panjang beach, 12 km south of Singkawang, there's a very shabby losmen with rooms for an outrageous 10,000 rp. At the north end of the beach is a recreational park called Taman Pasir Panjang Indah where there's another *Hotel Palapa*. Adequate rooms are 15,000/30,000 rp weekdays, 20,000/40,000 rp weekends. You can also camp among the casuarina trees that line the beach.

Places to Eat

Since this is the Hong Kong of Indonesia, Chinese food is your best bet. The *Rumah Makan Tio Ciu Akho* at Jalan Diponegoro 106 serves some of the best *kwetiaw goreng* in all of Indonesia, loaded with shrimp, squid, wheat gluten and freshly made fishballs. Most of their dishes are prepared in the savory Chiu Chao (Chao Zhou, Tae Jiu) style and the beer is ice-cold. Look for the giant wood stove in front, reminiscent of the Chinese warungs of Ipoh, West Malaysia.

Also on Jalan Diponegoro are the *Bakso 68* and *Bakso 40* noodle shops, serving variations on bakso (Chinese meatballs) with mie (wheat noodles), bakmi (egg noodles) and kwetiaw (rice noodles). The *Rumah Makan Indonesia* on the same street serves, what else, Indonesian (mostly Javanese) food, a rarity in this town.

Along Jalan Johan Godang at the Jalan Diponegoro intersection is a string of good Chinese warung kopi, all with Bentoel International signboards – the *Mexico, Malang, Asoka* and *Tahiti*. The Mexico has the best selection of pastries.

Along Jalan Niaga (Pasar Lama) you'll find three or four decent padang-style places serving Banjarese and Sumatran

food. On Jalan Budi Utomo (Pasar Hilir) in front of the cinema is a Chinese night market.

Getting There & Away
Colts to Singkawang leave Pontianak's Sintian Terminal (2500 rp, 3½ hours). It's a nicely surfaced road plied by lunatic colt drivers trying to break land, water and air speed records all at once.

From Singkawang, it's 500 rp as far as Pasir Panjang and takes about 15 to 20 minutes. To Gunung Poteng catch a Bengkayang bus east for the 12-km trip (500 rp). Let the driver know where you're going and he'll let you off at the foot of the hill. Or offer the driver a little extra fare to take you up the hill to Wisma Gunung Poteng, the only hotel.

You can also get colts north-east to Sanggau (4000 rp), south to Pontianak (2500 rp), north to Pemangkat (500 rp) and Sambas (1500 rp) or east to Mandor (1500 rp).

Irian Jaya

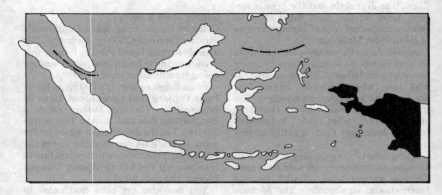

Irian Jaya is being 'discovered' and brutally dragged into the sphere of influence of the technocrats – strange people everywhere; self-seeking people, who have no feeling for this country apart from what they can get from it; mechanical, emotionless people, mouthing cliches as they tear the place apart: very sad and disturbing. There is going to be a great turmoil here very shortly. . .

Robert Mitton, 1974, from *The Lost World of Irian Jaya*

It's a different place from Indonesia with a different people. Culturally and ethnically most of the people of Irian Jaya are classed as 'Papuan' – related to the people of neighbouring Papua New Guinea and similar to the Melanesians of the south Pacific. The terms 'Melanesian' and 'Papuan' are often used interchangeably. Although there does seem to be some distinction between the lighter-skinned coastal dwellers and the darker-skinned highland dwellers, the dividing line is a hazy one.

The people *are* far removed from the Malayan people of the Indonesian islands to the west; the Papuans are dark skinned, woolly haired, the men heavily bearded,

their facial features reminiscent of the Australian Aborigines. They live in some of the most rugged terrain on earth, an island of soaring snow-capped mountains, almost impenetrable jungle, mangrove swamps, and broad river valleys. Communications have always been so difficult that the different tribes have lived – for the most part – in isolation from each other, resulting in a diversity of cultures and languages that defies any attempt at neat pigeon-holing. The Papuans have no connection in appearance, culture or language with the predominantly Malay Indonesians – their sole historical link being that their homeland once formed part of the Dutch East Indies, and even then the interior was mostly just a huge blank on a map.

For visitors, Irian Jaya presents spectacular mountains and jungle, wonderful birdlife, intriguing and little-known peoples who have had minimal contact with the outside world, and some great trekking opportunities. What you're not likely to see much of – because the authorities only allow you to enter a few parts of the province – are the effects of Indonesian colonisation on the land and

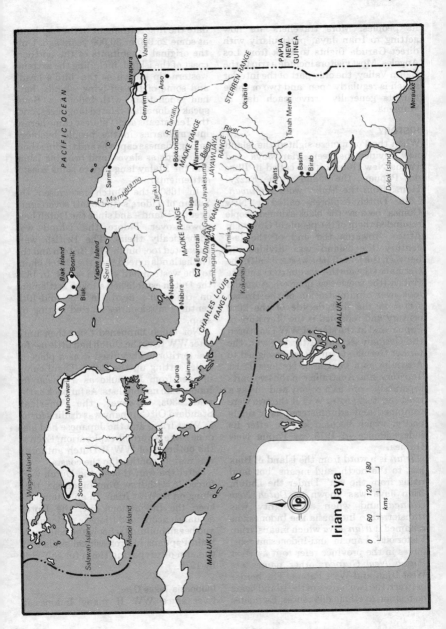

Irian Jaya

its peoples. More travellers are now getting to Irian Jaya, particularly with direct Garuda flights to Biak from Los Angeles. Most visitors include a trip to the Balim Valley, the only part of the interior which is regularly open, and two or three tourists generally arrive each day in Wamena.

HISTORY

When the Portuguese sighted the island now divided between Irian Jaya and Papua New Guinea, they called it 'Ilhas dos Papuas', the Island of the Fuzzy-Hairs, from the Malay word *Papuwah*. Later Dutch explorers called it 'New Guinea' because the black-skinned people reminded them of the people of Guinea in Africa. Towards the end of the last century the island was divided up between the Dutch (the western half), the Germans (the north-east quarter) and the British (the south-east quarter). Australia took over administration of the British sector in the first decade of the 20th century and renamed it the 'Territory of Papua' and at the start of WW I captured the German section. After the war, the former German territory was assigned to Australia as a League of Nations Trust Territory, and Australia ran the two parts separately – one as a colony and one as a trust territory. After WW II the two were combined and administered as a single entity, which became known, after its independence in 1975, as Papua New Guinea.

Irian is a word from the island of Biak just to the north, and means 'hot land rising from the sea'. Under the Dutch, Irian Jaya was known as *Dutch New Guinea* and when sovereignty was transferred to Indonesia the Indonesians renamed it *Irian Jaya* which means 'Irian Victorious'. Papuan anti-Indonesian rebel forces in the province refer to it as *West Papua New Guinea*; other names are West Irian and West Papua. The border between the two halves of the island bears no relation to ethnic differences. Estimates

date the first settlement in the highlands at some 25,000 or 30,000 years ago. Only the original inhabitants of the northern coast of the island, including the extreme western tip known as the 'bird's head', and some of the off-lying islands, have had much to do with Indonesia. Some speak Indonesian-related languages; once the Ternateans and Tidorese came here as intermediaries in the people business, taking Irianese captives and trading them westwards as slaves, and bringing Islam and the Malay language to some coastal settlements.

In 1660, the Dutch recognised the Sultan of Tidore's (fictional) sovereignty over the island – and since the Dutch held power over Tidore the island was theoretically theirs. The British were interested too, but in 1824 Britain and the Netherlands agreed that the Dutch claim to the western half should stand. In 1828 the Dutch established a token settlement on the bird's head. In the mid-19th century, missionaries started setting up shop.

Not much happened from then until after WW II, as the Dutch had little use for the territory. They used it as a place of exile, setting up the Boven-Digul camp upriver from Merauke as a prison for Indonesian nationalists. As far back as the mid-1930s, however, the American Standard Oil Company was drilling for oil in West Irian, and the Japanese had also done some covert oil-exploration. Even at the outbreak of WW II Dutch authority was mainly confined to the coasts.

After the war, though the Dutch were forced to withdraw from Indonesia, they clung on to West Irian. In an attempt to keep the Indonesians out, the Dutch actually encouraged Irianese nationalism and began building schools and colleges to train Papuans in professional skills with the aim of preparing them for self-rule by 1970.

Indonesia Takes Over

Ever since WW II many Indonesian

factions – whether Communists, Sukarnoists or Suhartoists – had claimed the western side of the island as their own. Their argument was that all the former Dutch East Indies should be included in the new Indonesian republic.

It was Sukarno who managed to wrest Dutch New Guinea from its European masters. With the rebellions in Sumatra and Sulawesi mostly put down, early in 1962 Suharto, Sukarno's eventual successor as president, was given command of the campaign in West Irian. Throughout 1962 Indonesian forces infiltrated the area, but with little success. The Papuan population failed to welcome them as liberators, and either attacked them or handed them over to the Dutch. It was US pressure which forced the Dutch to capitulate abruptly in August 1962. The Americans feared the Soviet Union would back the Indonesian military operation and agreed to an Indonesian takeover of West Irian the following year.

A vaguely worded 1962 agreement under United Nations auspices essentially required that Indonesia allow the Papuans of West Irian to determine, by the end of 1969, whether they wanted independence or to remain within the Indonesian republic. This 'Act of Free Choice' (or 'Act Free of Choice' as it became known) was held in 1969, 'supervised' by the UN. The Indonesian government announced that it would use the procedure of *musyawarah* under which a consensus of 'elders' is reached. While it was claimed that this accorded with the traditions of the nation it was also easy to hand-pick and pressurise the assemblies of elders. In July 1969 the Indonesian government announced that the assemblies in Merauke, Jayawijaya and Paniai districts, in which the greater part of the West Irian population lives, had unanimously decided to become part of Indonesia.

Papuan Opposition

Even before the act, the Indonesians faced violent opposition from the Papuans. In

1967 aircraft were used to bomb and strafe Arfak tribesmen threatening Manokwari town on the bird's head but the fighting continued into 1969. In the same year rebellions broke out on the island of Biak and at Enarotali in the highlands. In 1977 there was serious conflict in the highlands around the Balim Valley and Tembagapura, site of the US-run Freeport copper mine. Bombs damaged Freeport installations and cut the pipeline which takes copper concentrates to the coast. In 1981 there was heavy fighting in the Enarotali region, and in early 1984 the consequences of an attempted uprising centred on Jayapura sent thousands of Irianese fleeing into PNG. These were not the only uprisings, nor the last: the pattern is mainly one of intermittent incidents, depending mainly on the levels of resentment against the Indonesians and of organisation of the resistance forces. In 1988 somewhere between 15 and 40 transmigrants from Sulawesi were killed in an attack at Arso, south-east of Jayapura.

The Irianese are provoked by a number of factors, among them the taking of their land for logging, mining or other commercial purposes (often done in a superficially legal way, accompanied by pressure and threats); transmigration, which is bringing large numbers of western Indonesians to Irian Jaya, to live in close proximity to the people whose former land they occupy and whose potential jobs they take in the towns ; the typical Indonesian attitude to the Irianese, which is at best patronising; attempts to 'Indonesianise' the locals by schooling, propaganda, and even some efforts to make them forsake their traditional attire and wear 'proper clothes'; extremely brutal Indonesian responses to conflict, protest or even uncooperativeness (reportedly including mass reprisals, strafing villages from the air, torture and arbitrary killings) and total intolerance of political dissent.

The chief anti-Indonesian guerrilla force

is known as the OPM (Organisasi Papua Merdeka – Free Papua Movement). It appears to have been set up just after West Irian was handed over to the Indonesians, but there seems to be neither a single leader nor a unified command. Numbers of active members go up and down: in the late '80s there were perhaps 500, mainly in the north-east of Irian Jaya. Sometimes there appears to be rivalry between different OPM factions. They have limited weapons other than spears, machetes, bows and arrows. In the mid-'80s an OPM group managed to 'occupy' a 10-km wide strip of territory on the Indonesian side of the PNG border near Mindip Tanah, south of the highlands, but activity there has since waned. Incidents that do occur nevertheless still generate tales of courage, glory and unity, feeding the 'war of independence' mentality of many Papuans.

Refugees

Because the PNG-Indonesia boundary straddles tribal territories, some people in the centre of the island have always wandered back and forth across it. But since the Indonesian takeover many more have crossed as a result of Indonesian (or sometimes OPM) violence or the fear of it. The biggest exodus came in 1984 when over 10,000 people fled to PNG after the abortive OPM uprising that year. Many of these were from Jayapura and included intellectuals, public servants, police, army deserters, students and their families.

Most of these refugees have ended up in camps not very far inside PNG territory – camps whose connections with the OPM provoke tension between the PNG and Indonesian governments. Indonesia complains about the camps harbouring OPM activists; PNG complains about Indonesian armed incursions into its territory in pursuit of the OPM. There have been attempts by both sides to get refugees to go back to Irian Jaya – some have even been forced to do so by PNG –

but most are reluctant for fear of what will happen to them. In 1987 there were an estimated 11,000 Irianese in camps in PNG. The following year, after the Arso attack mentioned above, about 1000 were airlifted from the South Blackwater camp near Vanimo on PNG's north coast to the East Awin camp, south of the highlands and further from the border, where they had to mix with 2000 refugees from southern Irian Jaya who had already been at East Awin since 1987. East Awin has poor soil and a shortage of fresh water. Conditions in the camps are generally poor and there have been reports of starvation. The problem is too large to be solved by the PNG government, which has to tread warily with its powerful neighbour and receives little help on the issue from outside.

When PNG protested in October 1988 at three incursions over the border by Indonesian troops, which apparently culminated in their taking five villagers hostage but later releasing them, Indonesia's response was that such events might continue as long as Melanesian separatists operated in the border area.

Transmigration & Environment

The Indonesian policies which provoke Papuan unrest continue. In 1988, according to official figures, 113,634 of Irian Jaya's 1.2 million people had arrived on government transmigration schemes. Another 180,000 or so western Indonesians had come as independent settlers. So far the transmigrants are mostly grouped near main towns like Jayapura, Merauke, Manokwari, Nabire and Sorong, but there are others up towards the border north of Merauke and in the Fak-fak area. Also there are reports of plans to open up the Central Highlands and the Mappi area, on the swampy west coast south of Agats, to transmigrants.

The government has grandiose plans for moving far larger numbers in – the target (not reached) for 1984 to 1989 was about 600,000. Some reports even talk of an ultimate target of four million. A number of observers, noting the poor locations and lack of planning for many existing settlements, have concluded that the main thrust of transmigration to Irian Jaya is less for the benefit of the transmigrants than to make the province truly Indonesian, by populating it with Indonesians and turning the Irianese into a minority in their own land.

The environment is being exploited at a lightning pace and land concessions to western Indonesian and/or foreign companies threaten the survival of some tribes. The forests of the Asmat district on the west coast are being clear-felled by three companies, using the Asmat people – under conditions which have often been tantamount to slavery – to fell and strip the trees and float them downstream for the concessionaires to collect. There is no reforestation. Erosion and flooding of the low-lying land is expected to increase, eventually destroying the sago palms on which the Asmat depend for food. In the Digul River area, south of the Central Highlands, the American Scott Paper Company and its Indonesian partner Astra, which in 1987 were granted forest concessions 1½ times the size of Bali, plan to produce 1000 tonnes of woodchip and 4000 tonnes of wood pulp a day.

GEOGRAPHY

The landscape is part of what a visit to Irian Jaya is about. One of the last wildernesses, it has a rugged, varied and dramatic geography. Flying across the bird's head from Ambon to Biak over wide, snaking rivers surrounded by thick vegetation gives you a taste of the treats ahead. Approaching Jayapura airport, you see stunningly beautiful lakes girdled by hills. Equally exciting is the view, from the plane en route to the Balim Valley, of the Taritatu River, a tributary of the giant Mamboramo.

A central east-west mountain range is the backbone of Irian Jaya and Papua New Guinea. It reaches its maximum altitude in the west with Gunung Jayakesuma the highest peak at 5030 metres. This and other Irian Jaya peaks such as Puncak Mandala have permanent snowfields and small glaciers. Alpine grasslands, jagged bare peaks, montane forests which include pines, foothill rainforests, ferocious rivers, gentle streams, stunning rock faces and gorges add to the varying landscape of the highlands. The most heavily populated and cultivated areas of the Irian highlands are the Paniai Lakes district and the Balim Valley to the east.

South of the mountains is a coastal plain, widest in the east at the border with Papua New Guinea; there are sago swamps and low-lying alluvial plains (of fine-grained fertile soil consisting of mud, silt and sand deposited by flowing water), though it gets drier and more savannah-like in the far eastern section around Merauke. The northern coastal plain is much narrower and less swampy with larger-than-life tropical vegetation – real jungle! There are coconut-fringed white sandy beaches on the north coast and the offshore islands of Biak, Yapen and Waigeo.

CLIMATE

The coastal climate is hot, humid and rainy most of the year. The highlands have warm to hot days and cool to very cold evenings depending on the altitude. Plenty of rain falls in the highlands too but it's often confined to the evenings. Wetter and drier seasons vary from valley to valley in the highlands. In the Balim Valley from May to July is the driest time and from September to November, the wettest and windiest. From January to March is a good time for trekking as it's neither too muddy nor too hot. The south coast has a distinct dry season from July to October, and the north coast tends to have slightly less rain at this time too.

FLORA & FAUNA

Irian Jaya's flora is as varied as its

geography. Much of the land is covered in impenetrable tropical rainforest with the usual luxurious collection of Asiatic species and some endemic to the island, which is in the transition zone between Asia and Australia. The south coast's vegetation includes mangroves and sago palms plus eucalypts, paperbarks and acacias in the drier eastern section. Highland vegetation ranges from alpine grasslands and heaths to pine forests, bush and scrub that is unique.

Land animals are largely confined to marsupials, some indigenous, others also found in Australia. These include marsupial 'mice' and 'cats', bandicoots, ring-tailed possums, pygmy flying phalangers, big cuscuses, tree kangaroos and, in the south, wallabies. Apparently tree kangaroos can be seen on Salawati Island, off Sorong. Reptiles include snakes, frill-necked and monitor lizards and crocodiles. The spiny anteater is also found. Insects are abundant, particularly the colourful butterflies. Despite large-scale plunder, Irian Jaya's exquisite birdlife is still most famous . There are more than 600 species including numerous bird of paradise species, bowerbirds, cockatoos, parrots and lorikeets, kingfishers, crowned pigeons and cassowaries.

Yapen Island is supposed to be one good place to see birds of paradise. The males are renowned for their ostentatious plumage and long, brightly coloured tail feathers which are employed in energetic dances with the objective of enamouring a mate. Dances can be individual or in groups – they are a fascinating sight but difficult to come across. The best time is early in the morning from May to December. The females' plumage is dull, fortunate for the species as they have been left alone to continue their breeding while the males, though now 'protected', have been hunted to near extinction.

Cendrawasih Bay, between Biak and the mainland, is one of the richest marine life areas in Indonesia. It's a feeding ground for sea turtles and dugongs and its coral islands are nesting sites for many seabirds.

BOOKS

Irian Jaya's unique landscape, flora and fauna and intriguing peoples (particularly the Dani of the Balim Valley) have inspired several excellent books. One is Peter Matthiessen's *Under the Mountain Wall* (Collins Harvill, London, 1989), based on his long visit to the Balim in 1961. In beautifully written semi-fiction he chronicles daily life among the Kurulu tribe including work, relaxation, war, feasts and funerals, somehow capturing the magic of the area before it was swamped by change. *Gardens Of War* by R Gardner and K Heider (Andre Deutsch, London, 1969) also covers the same area at a similar time.

Robert Mitton's *The Lost World of Irian Jaya* (Oxford University Press, Melbourne, 1983) looks like a coffee-table book and is priced like one but is probably *the* classic book on the province. Mitton spent six years, on and off, in Irian Jaya in the '70s, studying and exploring while working for a mining company. The book was compiled from his letters, diaries, maps and photographs after his sudden death from leukaemia in 1976. The book bitterly criticises the reckless way in which the Irianese have been shoved into the modern world.

Indonesia's Secret War: The Guerilla Struggle In Irian Jaya by Robin Osborne (Allen & Unwin, 1985) is an excellently documented account of events up to 1984, and *West Papua: the Obliteration of a People* by Carmel Budiardjo and Liem Soei Liong (TAPOL, London, 1988) is also worth reading. George Monbiot's *Poisoned Arrows* (Michael Joseph, London, 1989) details a remarkable journey by the 24-year-old author to the wilds of Irian Jaya with the objective of uncovering the truth about transmigration, the plight of the refugees and the true nature of the OPM resistance. He travelled without permits to restricted areas and even ventured into

Asmat territory through its backdoor via an overland and river route from Wamena.

Another interesting book is *The Asmat* (Museum of Primitive Art, New York, 1967) which is a collection of photographs of the Asmat people (who live on the south coast of Irian Jaya) and their art, taken by Michael Rockefeller in 1961. Rockefeller disappeared on his second trip to Irian Jaya after his boat overturned at the mouth of the Eilanden (Betsj) River. His body was never found and there are various accounts of what became of him, the usual story being that he was eaten by natives.

Ring of Fire by Lawrence and Lorne Blair devotes a chapter to two visits to the Asmat and also tackles the Rockefeller mystery.

VISAS & PERMITS

The paperwork you need to visit Irian Jaya, and the places you can go to once you get there, fluctuate according to a number of variables including the level of conflict between the native people and the Indonesian colonists and between Indonesia and Papua New Guinea. Other recent visitors to Irian Jaya are the most reliable source of information, but with luck the relatively relaxed situation of recent years – at least as far as entering Irian Jaya is concerned – will continue, and may even improve if PNG and Indonesia open consulates at Jayapura and Vanimo or Wewak, as they planned.

Entering Irian Jaya

If you arrive at Biak airport – most likely on a Garuda flight from the USA – you get the regular two-month tourist pass stamped in your passport. To enter by sea or at any other airport – for example, flying in to Jayapura from PNG – you'll need an Indonesian visa. You can get this from Indonesian consulates and embassies in other countries and it is usually good for 30 days – though it's worth asking for more. The visa *might* be extendable at an *imigrasi* office in Indonesia.

At the time of writing, the only place you could get an Indonesian visa in PNG was the embassy in Port Moresby. It will probably take a few days, a few Kina and a couple of passport photos; you may have to show an onward ticket from Jayapura and a ticket out of Indonesia. At least once, the Indonesians have stopped issuing visas at Port Moresby so it would be worth getting yours before you arrive in PNG, if you can. There are both tourist and visitor visas (both have at different times excluded visits to the highlands); which type is better or easier to get seems to depend on which way the wind is blowing. Your visa might come with a two-day Jayapura transit pass, which means you should report to the Jayapura police within two days of arriving.

From Indonesia Some people take the precaution of getting a *surat jalan* (travel permit), for the parts of Irian Jaya that they plan to visit, from the Jakarta police chief but at the time of writing there didn't seem to be any restrictions on going to Irian Jaya at least by regular means like with Garuda, Merpati or Pelni passenger liners – you'll still have to get another surat jalan in Irian Jaya itself in order to go outside the main coastal towns.

Travel Permits – around Irian Jaya

Unless some political upheaval alters the picture, you can travel to the main coastal cities – Jayapura, Biak, Sorong and probably Merauke – without any permit, but to go elsewhere you need a surat jalan. This you obtain from a head police station – supposedly in either Jayapura, Biak, Sorong or Merauke, but Jayapura is the HQ for Irian Jaya and is less likely to suffer from any 'must contact our superiors' delays (though if you don't get what you want there, you just might get it somewhere else).

The surat jalan is free and takes maybe half an hour to issue. You must provide four passport photos and state where you want to go and for how long. Questions you're likely to be asked include your religion (say you're a Christian) and profession (don't be a journalist). There appears to be no limit on how long you can stay in the areas you're allowed to visit, so long as you don't overstay your Indonesian visa or tourist pass.

Many parts of Irian Jaya are off limits to foreign tourists and you won't get a permit for them. The situation is fluid (presumably depending on the level of tension or OPM activity, or other things Indonesia wants to hide in any given area): head police stations will tell you where you can and can't go. In 1989 Jayapura police were giving permission to go to Wamena and Nabire, but not Agats.

It's worth taking a few photocopies of your surat jalan: it may save you a few hours sitting in small police stations later while dozy cops write your details into their books. Once you arrive in the town you have a permit for, you're supposed to report within 24 hours to the police, who will stamp your surat jalan and probably tell you where, officially, you can go within their area. In the Wamena area (which stretches east to the PNG border) Gunung Trikora, Pass Valley, Lake Archbold, Oksibil, Okbibab and Kiwirok were among the out-of-bounds places in 1989. From Nabire, Enarotali was likewise off-limits. You may also be told to report again to the police each time you enter a new district within the area – such as the Jiwika district in the Wamena area. Some travellers manage to stray beyond official boundaries and visit places they 'shouldn't', because police are pleasantly thin on the ground away from the main centres.

Leaving Jayapura for PNG
Though PNG issues visas on arrival to tourists entering at Port Moresby, it doesn't at Vanimo – which is where you fly into from Jayapura. So you need to get your PNG visa in advance. Until PNG opens a consulate in Jayapura, the only place you can do this in Indonesia is at the PNG embassy in Jakarta.

Since Jayapura is not an officially designated Indonesian exit/entry point, you should strictly speaking have entered Indonesia on a visa, rather than the regular two-month tourist pass, if you want to leave the country through Jayapura. In the past some Indonesian immigration officials have required the aid of items like US$80 *and* a bottle of whisky to help them iron out this little bureaucratic wrinkle for you, but since 1988 they have seemed to be more human, and you should need few formalities and no bribes to exit from Jayapura to PNG, even if you entered Indonesia on a tourist pass.

MONEY
Make sure you change plenty of money before heading into the interior and stock up on 100 rp notes. Rupiah can usually be obtained in Wewak from the Westpac Bank, although the exchange rate is not as good as in Indonesia. You can get rupiah in banks in Jayapura, Biak, Wamena and probably other main towns and, for a reasonable rate, at the MAF office at Jayapura airport.

GETTING THERE & AWAY
From Other Countries
Garuda's thrice-weekly flights from Los Angeles to Jakarta and vice-versa stop en route at Honolulu, Biak and Denpasar. There's a once-weekly border-hop flight on Wednesday from Vanimo in Papua New Guinea to Jayapura and back, in a tiny plane of the little PNG airline Douglas Airways. The one-way fare is US$47 – book through Merpati in Jayapura. Vanimo is connected to Wewak and Port Moresby by internal PNG flights (usually same-day) and you can book right through between Jayapura and these places. Jayapura-Wewak costs US$13 and Jayapura-Port Moresby, US$269. From Jayapura to Wewak, it

used to be US$40 cheaper, and may still be, to fly first to Vanimo then buy another ticket on to Wewak from there. From Port Moresby a ticket to Jayapura costs around 400 Kina (about US$450).

There are occasional mission flights from Jayapura to PNG, but your chances of getting on one are close to zero. There are also aircraft operated by various mining companies, and both mission and mining planes occasionally fly to Australia.

Officially, there is no land or sea crossing between Irian Jaya and PNG.

From Indonesia

Air Garuda flies five times a week both ways between Denpasar and Jayapura (stopping en route at Ujung Pandang, Ambon, Biak and usually Timika), and twice a week both ways between Manado and Jayapura (stopping at Sorong and Biak). Merpati flies twice weekly between Jakarta and Biak calling at Surabaya, Ujung Pandang and Ambon. Jakarta-Biak with Merpati takes 12 hours and you must overnight in Biak if you're going on to Jayapura.

Boat Two Pelni passenger liners serve Irian Jaya. The *Umsini* does a fortnightly trip from Jakarta to Jayapura and back, calling at Surabaya, Ujung Pandang, Kwandang, Bitung (for Manado), Ternate and Sorong on both the outward and homeward voyages. The *Umsini* leaves Jakarta every second Thursday, reaching Jayapura a week later and setting off homeward the same day. For fares from Jayapura see the table.

The *Rinjani*'s fortnightly round-trip takes her from Belawan in north Sumatra to Sorong and back, stopping at Jakarta, Surabaya, Ujung Pandang, Baubau and Ambon in both directions. Arrival at and departure from Sorong is every second Monday. Fares from Ambon to Sorong (17 hours) include: 1st class 44,600 rp, 3rd class 26,500 rp and Ekonomi 17,400 rp.

Other cheaper, less comfortable ships link Jayapura, Sorong, Biak and possibly other ports with the rest of Indonesia with their customary irregularity. As usual it's a case of hanging around and seeing what's available. Surabaya is a fairly frequent point of departure (every couple of days) for ships to Maluku and Irian Jaya. Ask the harbour master at Jalan Kalimas Baru 194.

GETTING AROUND

Unless you're into mounting full-scale expeditions and are adept at cutting your way through jungle with a machete or like shuffling your way round coasts in slow, dirty boats, then flying is the only way to get around Irian Jaya. There are roads in the immediate vicinity of the urban areas and a good paved one extending westwards along the coast from Jayapura, but other than these few stretches there is – as of yet – nothing. An attempt is being made to build a trans-Irian highway, supposedly from Jayapura to Merauke via Wamena, but few people have any confidence that it will ever be finished, let alone kept in working order if it is.

Air

Airlines If you want to go inland you have to fly; Garuda links Timika, Sorong, Biak and Jayapura several days a week, and flies four-times weekly between Jayapura and Merauke, but Merpati carries the bulk of the traffic from the major centres to other parts of the coast and interior.

Merpati's main destinations include

Rinjani fares	1st class	3rd class	Ekonomi
Sorong (33 hours)	73,100 rp	43,100 rp	28,200 rp
Ternate (54 hours)	116,200 rp	68,100 rp	44,300 rp
Bitung (64 hours)	132,200 rp	78,200 rp	51,600 rp
Ujung Pandang (110 hours)	183,500 rp	108,500 rp	71,600 rp
Jakarta (158 hours)	283,200 rp	158,800 rp	98,800 rp

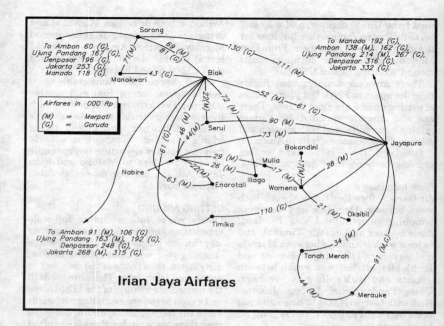

Irian Jaya Airfares

Airfares in 000 Rp

(M) = Merpati
(G) = Garuda

To Ambon 60 (G),
Ujung Pandang 167 (G),
Denpasar 196 (G),
Jakarta 253 (G),
Manado 118 (G)

To Manado 192 (G),
Ambon 138 (M), 162 (G),
Ujung Pandang 214 (M), 267 (G),
Denpasar 316 (G),
Jakarta 332 (G).

To Ambon 91 (M), 106 (G)
Ujung Pandang 163 (M), 192 (G),
Denpassar 248 (G),
Jakarta 268 (M), 315 (G).

Sorong, Manokwari, Biak, Nabire, Timika, Jayapura, Wamena and Merauke. From Biak there are fairly frequent flights to Serui, Manokwari and Nabire. Sorong and Manokwari are the jumping-off points for Merpati flights to places in the bird's head area of north-west Irian Jaya; Nabire is the place for flights to Kaimana, Enarotali and Ilaga. From Jayapura there are Merpati flights daily or several days a week to Biak, Manokwari, Nabire, Serui and Wamena. From Wamena, Merpati flies weekly to Bokondini, Karubaga, Kelila and Oksibil in the highlands and from Merauke to places in the south such as Senggo and Tanah Merah.

Mission Flights For getting to remote parts that even Merpati doesn't reach – or occasionally as a substitute if Merpati is full – you can use flights run by the various missionary groups in Irian Jaya. These cover a truly amazing network of maybe 200-plus airstrips – nearly all grass and many on steep slopes in narrow valleys – all over Irian Jaya with tiny planes and occasionally helicopters, flying where and when the missions need them to.

They *will* accept passengers if they have room, but book as far ahead as possible (at least a week is recommended) though you might be lucky enough to get one sooner. Sometimes they'll try to time their flight to a certain place to coincide with your request if you give them enough notice. They have set rates for carrying passengers which are directly related to distance travelled, but you can also charter planes – at a price.

The two main mission-flight organisations are the Protestant-run Mission Aviation Fellowship (MAF – widely known as the Missionary Air Force) and the Catholic-run Associated Mission Aviation (AMA). Both have offices at Sentani airport, Jayapura, where you can ask about flights and see a price list. Wamena is another main centre where these two organisations also have offices. It's your own responsibility to get any permits you need for places you're visiting in the interior – otherwise you'll probably be flown back at your own expense.

Typical mission flight fares include Jayapura-Wamena (250 km) 82,000 rp, Nabire-Enarotali (120 km) 39,000 rp, Wamena-Pass Valley (40 km) 13,000 rp, Wamena-Bokondini (60 km) 20,000 rp, Wamena-Angguruk (80 km) 26,000 rp, Wamena-Ilaga (160 km) 52,000 rp, Wamena-Oksibil (210 km) 69,000 rp and Merauke-Senggo (330 km) 108,000 rp. Over short distances mission fares are similar to Merpati's, but for longer flights they're considerably dearer. The cheapest charters are small Cessnas for around 250,000 rp an hour – which gives you a 25-minute flight if you're just going one way, since you also have to pay for the plane's turn-round time and its flight back to where you came from.

Boat
Pelni's *Umsini* (see Getting There & Away) will take you between Jayapura and Sorong in comfort if you wish, and other more basic Pelni passenger ships ply the Irian coasts with varying regularity – including the *Dharma Nusantara* whose fares from Jayapura are 8,100 rp to Serui; 12,800 rp to Biak; 14,300 rp to Nabire; 20,900 rp to Manokwari and 25,400 rp to Sorong – all including meals.

Otherwise a selection of small craft makes short-distance hops along parts of the coast and odd freighters call at the main ports.

Ships between Biak and the mainland are notoriously erratic – you might get three in one day then none for two weeks. Apparently there's a Pelni boat sailing from Sorong to Merauke and back every month, stopping at small places on the way.

The North

JAYAPURA & SENTANI
Jayapura is the name now given by the Indonesians to the capital of Irian Jaya. In Dutch times it was known as Hollandia, and was deliberately placed just a few km from the border with German New Guinea to emphasise the Dutch claim to the western half of the island.

Built on hills which slope down to the sea, the city is squeezed on to every available bit of semi-level land. At night it's a pretty sight from above with the lights of fishing boats winking out on the bay but during the day it's heavily polluted and unattractive. There's very little that's Melanesian about the place. It is dominated by Indonesians and looks little different from any other medium-sized Indonesian city. Nearby there are large Indonesian transmigration colonies, like the Genyem settlement just to the south at Nimboran.

Jayapura must be one of the hottest and steamiest places in the world. Everything normally closes down between around 10 am and 3 pm. There's no reason to linger longer than you have to, though you'll almost certainly have to come into the city to get a permit to travel in the interior. Sentani, a small town 36 km from Jayapura, where Jayapura's airport is located, is in many ways a better place to stay – it's quieter, less polluted and for some reason cooler than Jayapura itself.

Information & Orientation
Just about everything you want – most of the hotels, the shops, the head police station, the airline offices – is confined to a very small area near the waterfront. The two main streets are Jalan Ahmad Yani and parallel to it, Jalan Percetakan.

Tourist Office There's a tourist office (tel 411) in the Kantor Gubernor building inconveniently about two km out of the

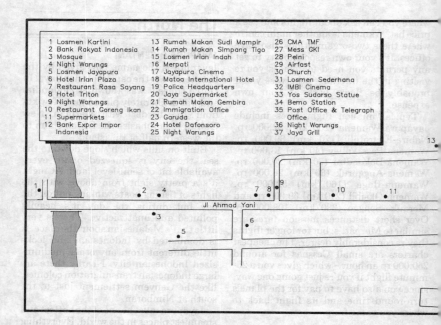

1 Losmen Kartini
2 Bank Rakyat Indonesia
3 Mosque
4 Night Warungs
5 Losmen Jayapura
6 Hotel Irian Plaza
7 Restaurant Rasa Sayang
8 Hotel Triton
9 Night Warungs
10 Restaurant Goreng Ikan
11 Supermarkets
12 Bank Expor Impor Indonesia
13 Rumah Makan Sudi Mampir
14 Rumah Makan Simpang Tigo
15 Losmen Irian Indah
16 Merpati
17 Jayapura Cinema
18 Matoa International Hotel
19 Police Headquarters
20 Jaya Supermarket
21 Rumah Makan Gembira
22 Immigration Office
23 Garuda
24 Hotel Dafonsoro
25 Night Warungs
26 CMA TMF
27 Mess GKI
28 Pelni
29 Airfast
30 Church
31 Losmen Sederhana
32 IMBI Cinema
33 Yos Sudarso Statue
34 Bemo Station
35 Post Office & Telegraph Office
36 Night Warungs
37 Jaya Grill

Jl Ahmad Yani

town centre towards Base G. Take a bemo (250 rp) from the corner of Jalan Percetakan and Jalan Sam Ratulangi. Some of the staff speak English and they may be able to answer your questions.

Bank The Bank Expor Impor Indonesia on Jalan Ahmad Yani and the Hotel Dafonsoro will change US and Australian dollar travellers' cheques and cash – the Dafonsoro's rate is low. The MAF (Mission Aviation Fellowship) office at Sentani airport will probably change small amounts of foreign currency (including PNG Kina) into rupiah at a bit less than the bank rates.

Immigration & Permits The head police station, where you obtain permits for the interior, is on Jalan Ahmad Yani. The immigration office is on Jalan Percetakan in the middle of town. It's open from Monday to Thursday from 7.30 am to

2.30 pm, Friday from 7.30 to 11 am and on Saturday from 7.30 am to 1 pm.

Other The post office is open Monday to Thursday from 8 am to 2 pm, Friday from 8 am to 11 am and Saturday from 8 am to 1 pm. If you want to seek advice or information from missionaries, try the Inter-Mission Business Office at Jalan Sam Ratulangi 11, almost opposite the Mess GKI. The PHPA is at Jalan Tanjung Ria II, Base G. Its postal address is Kotak Pos 545, Jayapura.

Things to See
Apart from relics of WW II there are few sights as such in Jayapura. In April 1944 the Allies stormed ashore up the road at Hamadi and captured the town after only token resistance from the Japanese. It was in Jayapura that General MacArthur assembled his fleet for the invasion of the Philippines.

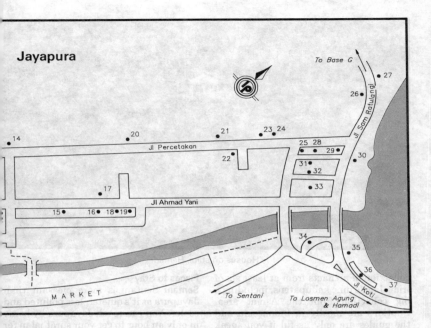

Hamadi

This suburb is about a 15-minute drive from the centre of town. Its market place is stocked with every conceivable variety of fish, including yellow fin tuna, massive 40 kg cod, turtles and sharks.

A nearby beach is the site of the American amphibious landing during WW II, with landing vehicles and tanks rusting away. The first group of landing barges lies opposite a small monument with a plaque which reads 'Allied Forces landed here on April 22 1944'. Further down the beach another landing barge is used for more peaceful purposes – as a toilet and pig pen. A few metres away sits a decaying Sherman tank. To get to the second group you have to walk through a military base – they'll let you in, but you have to leave your passport at the entrance and collect it on leaving. Apparently there are some sunken vessels in the water in front of the beach.

There are bemos all day to and from Hamadi; catch them from the bemo station opposite the post office or on Jalan Koti, the fare is 250 rp.

Base G

If you want to idle away a few hours then try Base G Beach – so named because somewhere around here was MacArthur's headquarters. The beach is a disappointment; although it's mostly deserted and peaceful there is too much broken coral and too many rocks in the water for swimming – and the surf can be strong with real dumpers. Bemos to Base G from the terminal or Jalan Sam Ratulangi drop you about a 15-minute walk from the beach; the fare is 300 rp.

Museum

The Gedung Loka Budaya (museum) is in the grounds of Cendrawasih University at Abepura. It exhibits a fascinating

Houses on stilts, Hamadi

collection of artifacts from at least six of Irian Jaya's nine kabupatens, including a big collection from the Asmat area. Captions are mostly in Indonesian and the guides are only useful if you speak fluent Indonesian. It's open from 7.30 am to 2.30 pm every day, except Sundays. Take an Abepura bemo from the terminal (400 rp).

Lake Sentani & Sentani

This magnificent stretch of water is your introduction to Irian Jaya when you arrive by air and land at Jayapura's Sentani Airport. The lake covers 9630 hectares but as yet is untouched by tourism. You'll see local houses on stilts along its shores and the occasional boat. The Sentani people are known for their woodcarvings and pottery. Ask at your losmen about renting boats on the lake. Sentani town has a lazy feel compared to Jayapura, but there's actually quite a lot of activity particularly with the large numbers of expatriates, mainly missionaries, living here. From the town, you can walk to waterfalls and tropical forests or clamber up hills.

Places to Stay

Sentani Sentani is more pleasant than Jayapura as it's quieter, less polluted and cooler. You can reach Jayapura by bemo in only an hour to get your surat jalan for the interior or to visit the post office. When you arrive at the airport, touts swarm around you like flies.

Probably the best place to stay is *Sentani Inn* on Jalan Raya Sentani at Hawai, about 1½ km in the Jayapura direction from the airport. Singles/doubles with air-con cost 20,000/25,000 rp, without air-con 12,000/20,000 rp. Prices include breakfast. The losmen is set off the road in some fields. The *Losmen Mansapur Rani* is closer to the airport. Turn right just outside the airport and walk about 400 metres. Rooms are basic and clean but without fans. It costs about 7000 per person per night, possibly in shared rooms if they're busy. Breakfast is ordinary at 1000 rp extra.

Losmen Minang Jaya (tel 27143) is just off the main street in the centre of town. Rooms with attached mandi and fan cost 11,000/18,000 rp. It's clean enough and the staff are friendly.

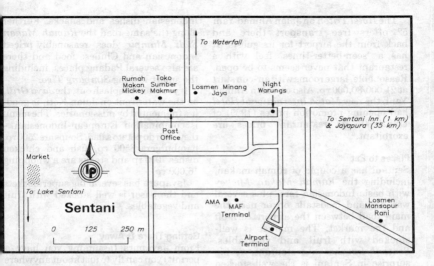

Jayapura - bottom end Hotel prices in Jayapura itself are a black hole for your wallet. Among the cheaper options is the *Losmen Kartini* at the west end of Jalan Ahmad Yani (turn right off Yani just over the bridge). Clean rooms with fan and shared mandi go for 7500/15,000 rp, or 10,000/20,000 rp with fan and private mandi. Tax and breakfast are included. The upstairs rooms and sitting area are quite pleasant.

Losmen Ayu at Jalan Tugu II 101 has good rooms with singles/doubles/triples from 6000/11,500/17,000 rp. Heading away from the centre, Jalan Tugu II is about 500 metres along Jalan Sam Ratulangi from its intersection with Jalan Percetakan.

Jayapura - top end The *Losmen Agung* at Jalan Argapura 37, half way between Jayapura and Hamadi, is a decent friendly place with air-con rooms at 20,000 rp a single or double, including breakfast and tea throughout the day. Upstairs rooms are probably breezier and quieter. A Hamadi bemo will drop you outside.

The *Mess GKI* (tel 21574), pronounced 'Geki', is centrally placed at Jalan Sam Ratulangi 6. The people here are friendly and, while it's a fairly pleasant place, it's expensive at 12,000/24,000 rp for singles/doubles including breakfast and more with three meals. Rooms are small with fans and the shared mandi is outdoors. There's an outdoor sitting area.

Also central is the *Losmen Sederhana* (tel 21291, 22157) at Jalan Halmahera 2. The rooms are clean enough and with fan and shared mandi cost 11,000/19,800 rp, more with meals. There are more expensive rooms with private mandi and air-con from 13,200/24,200 rp. It's right in the hub of the night foodstall area. The *Hotel Irian Plaza* on Jalan Setiapura, off Jalan Ahmad Yani, has rooms with fan at 14,000/21,000 rp, including breakfast. Air-con rooms start at 24,000/30,000 rp.

One of the best bets in the top end is the *Hotel Dafonsoro* (tel 21870, 22285) at Jalan Percetakan 20-24. Air-con rooms are 18,000/28,000 rp, including a big breakfast of eggs, toast and jam and a pot of tea or coffee. It's a busy, friendly place.

The *Hotel Triton* on Jalan Ahmad Yani 52 offers free transport there and back from the airport for its guests. It has a 'seen-better-times' feel with a restaurant that never seems to be open. Reasonable, large rooms with air-con start at 21,000/30,000 rp. Also on Jalan Ahmad Yani, the new *Matoa International Hotel* had opening promotion prices (1989) of US$25/30. Its restaurant prices are exorbitant.

Places to Eat

Sentani has a couple of rumah makan, including the *Rumah Makan Mickey* with basic Indonesian fare, plus several warungs and foodstalls on or near the main road between the airport turn-off and the market. The market is well-stocked with fruit and vegetables. *Sentani Inn* has a restaurant. A big surprise in Sentani is the well-stocked supermarket *Toko Sumber Makmu* with many western foods. You can even buy big sliced loaves of brown bread (*roti tawar*) for 2750 rp.

In Jayapura itself, the best places to eat are the warungs – not just because they're cheaper than the restaurants, but because they serve the best food. Night foodstalls in front of the Pelni office serve up gado-gado or tahu lontong (fried tofu) with hot peanut sauce (both 600 rp), bubur kacang hijau (mung beans in coconut milk broth 300 rp) and other Indonesian dishes. Other stalls here specialise in the tastiest fish you'll eat in eastern Indonesia – juicy charcoal-grilled slabs with rice, coconut sauce, lemon and salad, all for 1500 rp. There are also fruit stalls in the vicinity day and night. More night warungs set up around the mosque on Jalan Ahmad Yani and along the waterfront on Jalan Koti.

On Jalan Percetakan, the *Hotel Dafonsoro* offers fairly expensive but ordinary Indonesian dishes, though the nasi and mie goreng are filling and tasty at 2500 rp. Try *Cafetaria* with its modern decor a few doors away. It offers fruit juices (1000 rp), simple and cheap Indonesian dishes and snacks. Further along the same road the *Rumah Makan Sudi Mampir* does reasonably priced Indonesian and Chinese food and there are also several Padang places, including the smart-looking *Simpang Tigo*.

If you want to splash out, the *Jaya Grill*, on the waterfront on Jalan Koti, is good; it's frequented by missionaries. The menu is combination European-Indonesian – they even do potato salad. Soups are 2500 rp, hamburgers 6500 rp, fish and chicken dishes 7000 rp and steaks are a whopping 16,000 rp.

Jayapura has several big supermarkets and the pasar is well stocked with fruit and vegetables.

Getting There & Away

From Jayapura (assuming you have a permit) you can fly to just about anywhere there's a landing strip in the northern half of Irian Jaya and to many places in the south, as well as to western Indonesia, or east to PNG. The Pelni passenger liner *Umsini* regularly plies between Jakarta and Jayapura. There are also other occasional ships to elsewhere on the coast of Irian Jaya or to western Indonesia. See the Irian Jaya introductory sections for more details.

Air Garuda (tel 21220) has its office next door to the Hotel Dafonsoro at Jalan Percetakan 20-24. It's open Monday to Friday from 8 am to 12.30 pm and 1.30 to 4 pm, Saturday from 8 am to 1 pm and is closed on Sundays.

Merpati (tel 21913, 21810 and 21327) at Jalan Ahmad Yani 15, is open Monday to Thursday from 7 am to 2 pm, Friday from 7 to 11 am, Saturday from 7 am to 2 pm and Sundays and holidays from 10 am to 12 noon.

MAF (Mission Aviation Fellowship) is at Sentani Airport. It's open every day from 5.30 am to 12 noon and from 2 to 4 pm. AMA (Aviation Mission Association) is next to the MAF terminal, open from 5 am to 1 pm Monday to Saturday and closed on Sundays.

Boat The Pelni office (tel 21270) is near the waterfront in the centre of Jayapura, at Jalan Halmahera 1. The closest harbour master's office (tel 21923, 22018) to the city is on Jalan Koti, on the way out towards Hamadi. There's another harbour master's office (tel 21634) further along this road.

Getting Around
Jayapura's Sentani Airport is 36 km out of town. A taxi into town from the airport costs 15,000 rp. Alternatively walk a few minutes down the road directly in front of the terminal to the main road and catch a bemo. From Sentani to the city costs 900 rp: 500 rp to Abepura, where you usually have to change, and 400 rp from Abepura to Jayapura. It takes about an hour in total. Bemos are frequent between Jayapura and Abepura and Abepura and Sentani.

You can walk around downtown Jayapura with ease. For bemos in and around Jayapura, including Abepura, go to the terminal at the start of Jalan Koti, opposite the post office. There are good paved roads in the vicinity of Jayapura. From Jayapura to Hamadi costs 250 rp, to Base G costs 300 rp.

BIAK
Biak is the centre of the large island of the same name, off the north coast of the mainland of Irian Jaya. Like Jayapura it's a more-or-less nothing town, just somewhere on the way to somewhere else, but it's receiving quite a few visitors nowadays, mainly due to direct Garuda flights from Los Angeles.

The most interesting place in town is the central Pasar Panir where lorikeets and cockatoos are sometimes for sale. When a Pelni ship goes through, half the crew seem to buy one to sell later in Java, and at the end of a flight from Biak to Jakarta you can witness the odd spectacle of cages and boxes of live birds rolling out on the luggage conveyer belts.

If you want to make a trip to Biak worthwhile then leave the town and explore the island which feels very Polynesian, especially if you have come from western Indonesia. At Ambroben village, about four km from the town, are some caves that were built by the Japanese during WW II; there are more caves dotted around the island. You can easily make the half-hour bemo trip east to Bosnik which was the former Dutch centre on the island. There are some WW II relics, a reasonable beach and views across to the Owi islands. Korim Beach is on the north coast, about 40 km from town.

Near Bosnik, Parieri Reserve has some original stands of forest. On the northwest tip of the island, Biak Utara Reserve is larger and includes 15 km of beach. It's well-forested with lots of parrots and cockatoos. Separated from Biak Island by only a very narrow channel, Superiori Island is just about all reserve and includes mangrove and montane forests. Apparently its birdlife has been less exploited than Biak's.

Information & Orientation
Biak is a fairly compact town. Jalan Prof M Yamin runs from the airport and connects with Jalan Ahmad Yani which is Biak's main street with many of the hotels, restaurants and offices. The other main street, Jalan Imam Bonjol, cuts at right angles through Jalan Ahmad Yani.

Bank & Post The Bank Expor Impor Indonesia at the corner of Jalan Ahmad Yani and Jalan Imam Bonjol, will change a number of different foreign currency travellers' cheques. It's open Monday to Friday from 8 am to 2 pm, Saturday from 8 to 10 am and is closed Sunday. Get there a good hour before it closes if you want to change money. The post office is on the road coming in from the airport.

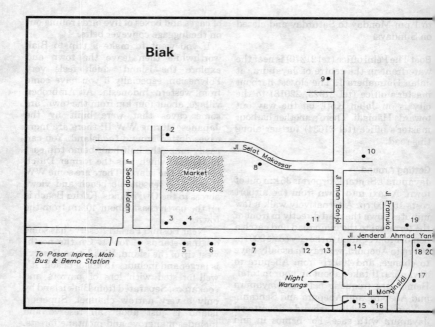

Biak

Jl Selat Makassar

Market

Jl Sedap Malam

Jl Iman Bonjol

Jl Pramuka

Jl Jenderal Ahmad Yani

Jl Monginsidi

Night
Warungs

To Pasar Inpres, Main
Bus & Bemo Station

Police & Immigration The head police
station is on Jalan Selat Makassar
opposite the Pasar Panir. It *should* be
possible to get permits for the interior in
Biak – but don't count on it. The
immigration office is at the corner of Jalan
Ahmad Yani and Jalan Imam Bonjol.

Places to Stay – bottom end
The *Losmen Maju* (tel 21218) on Jalan
Iman Bonjol costs 7700 rp per person
including breakfast and tax. Rooms are
basic, but clean with fan and attached
mandi/toilet. The signless *Losmen Solo* at
Jalan Monginsidi 4, just south of the
junction of Jalan Iman Bonjol and Jalan
Ahmad Yani, has clean rooms for 5500 rp
per person. The food is good and cheap.
Losmen Atmelia (tel 21415), once a good
'cheapie', has been taken over by
telecommunications workers on long-
term contract though it might reopen to
the public some day.

Places to Stay – top end
Hotel Irian (tel 21139, 21839) is straight
across the road from the airport. Singles/
doubles with fan and up to three meals are
19,000/36,000 rp (including tax and
service charge) which is quite expensive
for what you get, though there's a a grassy
seaside garden and the rooms all have
attached mandis. If you fly Merpati from
Jakarta to Jayapura you spend a free
night here. The *Hotel Mapia* (tel 21383,
21961) on Jalan Ahmad Yani is comfortable
and friendly. Rooms with fan and
attached mandi start at 10,000/20,500 rp;
similar rooms with a small sitting area are
15,000/20,500 rp. Rooms with air-con are
more expensive but all prices include a
good breakfast, tax and service charge.
Evening meals cost 4000 rp.

The *Titawaka Hotel* (tel 21835, 21885)
is memorable for the miniature Sulawesi
Toraja-style house built over its foyer –
just a little incongruous in Irian Jaya! It's

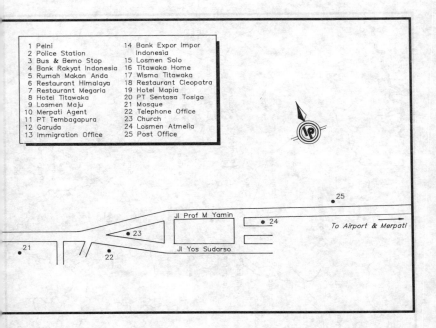

1 Pelni
2 Police Station
3 Bus & Bemo Stop
4 Bank Rakyat Indonesia
5 Rumah Makan Anda
6 Restaurant Himalaya
7 Restaurant Megaria
8 Hotel Titawaka
9 Losmen Maju
10 Merpati Agent
11 PT Tembagapura
12 Garuda
13 Immigration Office
14 Bank Expor Impor
    Indonesia
15 Losmen Solo
16 Titawaka Home
17 Wisma Titawaka
18 Restaurant Cleopatra
19 Hotel Mapia
20 PT Sentosa Tosiga
21 Mosque
22 Telephone Office
23 Church
24 Losmen Atmelia
25 Post Office

Jl Prof M Yamin

Jl Yos Sudarso

To Airport & Merpati

at Jalan Selat Makassar 3 and is comfortable, but really quite basic. Rooms are 18,150/31,460 rp or with air-con 33,880/54,450 rp. Also run by the same friendly family, who speak English and Dutch, the pleasant *Wisma Titawaka* (tel 21658) at Jalan Monginsidi 24, and *Titawaka Home* (tel 21891) at Jalan Monginsidi 14, both cost 43,560/66,550 rp. All rooms have air-con and good bathrooms with showers. The Titawaka Home is on the beach with a view of Yapen Island and has a TV room. All Titawaka prices include meals, tax and service charge, and transport to and from the airport.

Places to Eat
There are a number of places, but few of note. Probably the best are the evening foodstalls on the road leading from the Bank Expor Impor to the sea. There are some cheap places along Jalan Ahmad Yani like the *Rumah Makan Anda*, the *Restaurant Megaria* and the *Restaurant Himalaya*. The *Restoran Cleopatra*, next door to an art shop and opposite the *Hotel Mapia*, has a varied menu with seafood and chicken dishes at 5000 rp, boiled vegetables (*lalapan rebus*) 1000 rp and nasi or mie goreng 2250 rp.

The large *Pasar Inpres* about a km beyond the small, central market has a good range of fruit and vegetables. Just before sunset is a good time to go there.

Getting There & Away
Biak is many people's first stop in Irian Jaya since the flights from the USA and many from western Indonesia land here. There are flights between Biak and some other parts of Irian Jaya, which might save you going to Jayapura if you can get the right permit from Biak police. Biak has shipping connections with western Indonesia, Yapen Island to the south, and mainland Irian Jaya, but these tend to be

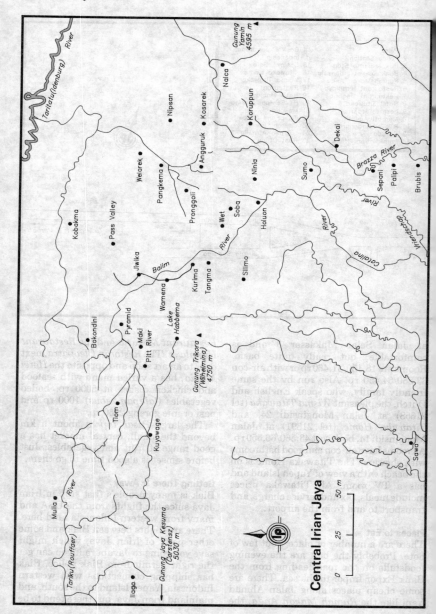

Central Irian Jaya

0   25   50 m

erratic – though you may be able to find fairly frequent small passenger ships to Manokwari on the bird's head. See the Irian Jaya introductory sections for more details.

Air Garuda (tel 21416, 21331) is on Jalan Ahmad Yani near the corner of Jalan Imam Bonjol in the middle of Biak. The Merpati office (tel 21213, 21386) is out of town, across the road from the airport. There's a more convenient Merpati agent in town just off Jalan Imam Bonjol. PT Sentosa Tiga at Jalan Ahmad Yani 36 is also an air ticket agent.

Boat The Pelni office is on Jalan Ahmad Yani, a short distance west of the Garuda office. The harbour entrance is nearby.

Getting Around

Biak is small enough for walking, you can even walk into the city from the airport if you're feeling energetic. It's about a half-hour walk from the airport to the Hotel Mapia. A bemo from the airport to the centre is 250 rp – these run regularly up and down Jalan Ahmad Yani and Jalan Prof M Yamin.

The main bemo and bus terminal is right by the Pasar Inpres. Clearly marked boards indicate where vehicles are heading. Bemos to Bosnik cost 500 rp. Buses go to Korim Beach on the north coast. To charter a bemo costs 10,000 rp for two hours.

For Parieri Reserve, take a bemo to Adibai and then walk. To get to Biak Utara Reserve, it may be more feasible to charter a bemo in Biak but trucks do go to Warsa, about six km from the reserve's eastern boundary. From Warsa, a road continues around the island's northern tip. For Superiori Reserve, boats go from Biak to Sowok on the south-west coast of Superiori Island and take four to five hours – you may be able to make a shorter journey to a village on the south-east coast.

PT Sentosa Tiga at Jalan Ahmad Yani 36, opposite the Hotel Mapia, does a few Biak tours.

The Balim Valley

The first white men chanced upon the Balim Valley in 1938, a discovery which came as one of the last and greatest surprises to a world that had mapped, studied and travelled the mystery out of its remotest corners. Explorer Richard Archbold, who landed on nearby Lake Habbema in a seaplane, wrote:

From the air the gardens and ditches and native-built walls appeared like the farming country of Central Europe. Never in all my experience in New Guinea have I seen anything to compare with it....The agricultural pursuits of natives I saw in other parts of New Guinea were the helter-skelter efforts of children compared with those of the inhabitants of the Grand Valley....they showed an understanding of the basic principles of erosion control and drainage. From the neat stone fences surrounding their carefully weeded fields it was easy to imagine that we were in New England rather than in an isolated valley of the last Stone Age man. . . .

Archbold found that the fencing and irrigation works had all been built by the inhabitants of the valley using stone tools and sharpened sticks. Sweet potatoes were the main crop – taro, spinach, cucumbers and beans were also grown while bananas and tobacco could also be found in the local compounds. The reaction of the valley's inhabitants was friendly:

Whilst temperamental at times, the natives as a whole remained friendly throughout our stay. Some offered themselves as carriers and helped bring supplies down from Lake Habbema in return for small cowrie shells. Others brought bananas, sweet potatoes, and often pigs to trade. As a medium of exchange, steel implements did not interest them so much as shells or mirrors. Apparently they regarded their crude stone instruments as far superior.

One of the natives showed him a steel-headed axe, perhaps having found its way to the highlands along the trade routes from the coast. Archbold found men using spears, bows and arrows and stone axes, and wearing penis gourds, cuscus-fur head-dresses, necklaces of cowrie shells and boar's tusk nose ornaments. He also noted that they were 'ingenious' engineers, capable of building strong suspension bridges of forest vines with split-timber decking which could support large numbers of people.

WW II prevented further exploration and not until 1945 was attention again drawn to the valley when a plane crashed there and the survivors were rescued. The first missionaries arrived in 1954, the Dutch government established a post at Wamena in 1956 and changes to the Balim lifestyle followed. Today the Indonesians have added their own brand of colonialism, bringing schools, police, soldiers and shops and turning Wamena into a town. But local culture has in many ways proved very resilient – helped perhaps by the absence of alcohol – and the Balim Valley remains one of Indonesia's most fascinating and beautiful destinations. The best way to see it is to explore on foot.

Geography

The Balim Valley is one of four densely settled basins in the mountain backbone of Irian Jaya and Papua New Guinea. The others are the Wahgi and Asaro valleys in PNG and the Paniai Lakes region in Irian Jaya.

The Balim River starts from east and west points 120 km apart. The eastern arm rises near the summit of Gunung (Mt) Trikora, not far west of Wamena, and flows west away from Wamena. From the confluence of the east and west arms, near Kuyawage, the river travels east then turns south into what's known as the Balim Grand Valley, 1600 metres above sea level and about 60 km long and 16 km wide, with Wamena roughly at its centre. The valley probably contained a lake at one stage and its flat expanse slows the river and allows sediment to be deposited during floods. From the Grand Valley the river continues south through the massive Balim Gorge – in which it drops 1500 metres in less than 50 km, forming a spectacular series of cataracts – and on down to the Arafura Sea on the south-west coast.

In the Balim Valley a sophisticated system of agriculture using drainage and irrigation systems developed. In other places in the highlands, shifting agriculture has been practised, the land is cultivated for several years and then left to regenerate. By perhaps 5000 years ago, horticulture and pig-raising were established in the highlands. The early inhabitants planted taro and yams, but later arrivals introduced sugar cane and bananas, and much later, the sweet potato.

The People

The tribes of the Balim are usually grouped together under the name 'Dani' – in fact a rather abusive name by which they are known to their neighbours, but it's the one that has stuck. There are a number of other highland groups, distinguished from each other by language, physical appearance, dress and social customs.

The Dani are farmers, skilfully working their fertile land, digging long ditches for irrigation and drainage, and leaving the land fallow between crops. The clearing of the land and the tilling of the soil for the first crop is traditionally men's work; the planting, weeding and harvesting is women's.

The sweet potato or *erom* is the staple diet of the highlands and, if the Danis' physique is anything to go by, they thrive on it. They recognise 70 different types – some varieties can only be eaten by a particular group such as pregnant women or old men; ancestor spirits get the first potatoes from every field. The leaves, which provide protein, are also eaten.

Tobacco and other garden crops like carrots are grown on a small scale. Pigs are also bred, but are only eaten at feasts.

Traditional Dani kampungs are composed of several self-contained fenced compounds, each with its own cooking house, men's house, women's houses, and pigsties. A typical compound might be home to four men and their families, perhaps 20 people. A traditional Dani house (*honay*) is circular, topped by a thatched dome-shaped roof. Despite the introduction of Indonesian-style houses too, you see a great many honays in the valley.

Like the other men of the highlands, as far west as the Charles Louis Mountains, Dani men wear penis sheaths made of a cultivated gourd. These penis gourds are known locally as *horim*. The Indonesian government's campaign in the early 1970s to end the wearing of penis gourds was mostly a failure.

Many Danis wear pig fat in their hair

and cover their bodies in pig fat and soot for health and warmth. The fat makes their hair look like a cross between a Beatle's mop-top and a Rastafarian's locks. Naked except for their penis gourds, as the evening closes in the men stand with their arms folded across their chests to keep warm. Traditionally, no other clothing is worn apart from ornamentation such as string hair nets, bird-of-paradise feathers, and necklaces of cowrie shells. Some people do now wear (often extremely ragged) western-style clothes due as much to missionary as to Indonesian influence.

Despite missionary pressure, many Dani have maintained their polygamic marriage system – a man may have as many wives as he can afford. Brides have to be paid for in pigs and the man must give four or five pigs – each worth about 250,000 rp today – to the family of the girl; a man's social status is measured by the number of pigs and wives he has.

Dani men and women sleep apart. The men of a compound sleep tightly packed in one hut, the women and children in the other huts. After a birth, sex is taboo for two to five years, apparently to give the child exclusive use of its mother's milk. As a result of this care the average Dani life expectancy is 60 years. The taboo also contributes to both polygamy and a high divorce rate.

If a woman wears a grass skirt it usually indicates that she is unmarried. A married woman traditionally wears a skirt of fibre coils or seeds strung together, hung just below the abdomen, exposing the breasts but keeping the buttocks covered. The women dangle bark string bags from their heads, carrying heavy loads of fruit and vegetables, firewood, even babies and pigs in them.

One of the more bizarre Dani customs is for a woman to have one or two joints of her fingers amputated when a close relative dies; you'll see many of the older women with fingers missing right up to the second joint. Cremation was the traditional method of disposing of the body of the deceased, but sometimes the body would be kept and dried. Several villages in the valley have these smoked 'mummies' which you can pay to see and photograph.

Fighting between villages or districts seems to have been partly a ritual matter to appease the ancestors and attract good luck and partly a matter of revenge and settling scores. In formal combat the fighting is carried out in brief clashes through the day and is not designed to wreak carnage. After a few hours the opposing groups tend to turn to verbal insults instead. The Indonesians and missionaries have done their best to stamp out Dani warfare, but with only partial success: an outbreak between the Wollesi and Hitigima districts in 1988 led to about 15 deaths.

The merits of the changes wrought by these outsiders are at the least debatable. A typical – though not universal – Indonesian attitude to the Dani is a colonialist mixture of fear and contempt, but at least the Indonesians don't appear to have made any systematic attempt to wreck Dani culture. There have been however rumblings of plans to start transmigration to the Balim Valley. Among the missionaries, the Catholics have a reputation for being more tolerant of traditional ways than the Protestants. Quite a number of missionaries in the highlands have been killed in return for their efforts. By and large, they're friendly to travellers and are excellent sources of information if you get talking to them.

The Dani around the Wamena area are generally more traditional than those to the north and north-west, where Christianity has taken firmer root. The western Dani apparently regarded white missionaries as their snake ancestors reincarnated and were suitably impressed by the aeroplanes bringing in amazing loads of goods.

The ugliest year in the Balim's modern history was 1977 when a lot of fighting between the Indonesians and the Dani

Top: Market in Wamena, Balim Valley, Irian Jaya (AS)
Left: Mummy at Akima, Balim Valley, Irian Jaya (AS)
Right: Crossing the river, near Wamena, Balim Valley, Irian Jaya (AS)

Top: River crossing, near Wamena, Balim Valley, Irian Jaya (AS)
Bottom: Dani hut, Balim Valley, Irian Jaya (AS)

took place in and around the north of the Grand Valley. While the Dani were armed with spears, bows and arrows, the Indonesians are said to have bombed and strafed villages from the air, even dropping some chiefs to their deaths from helicopters. The scale of fighting and the number of Dani killed depends on which report you believe; estimates range from 30 to 600 dead. What started it all is also uncertain: possibilities that have been advanced include Dani anger with missionaries, provoked by frustration that Christianity wasn't bringing the material rewards they had expected; Indonesian soldiers trying to stop inter-Dani fighting; Dani resentment at 'Indonesianisation' campaigns and efforts to get them to vote in that year's national elections and OPM activists coming up from the coast to rouse the highlanders. There's still little love lost between the Dani and their rulers today.

If you speak some Indonesian you'll be able to get around OK. The northern and western Dani speak a dialect of Dani distinct from that in the Wamena area. In the Wamena area, a man greeting a man says *nayak*; if greeting more than one man *nayak lak*. When greeting a woman, a man says *la'uk*; if greeting more than one woman *la'uk nya*. Women say *la'uk* if greeting one person, *la'uk nya* if greeting more than one person. *Wam* means pig, *nan* is eat, *i-nan* is drink. At first meeting many Dani are friendly, some are shy and occasionally they seem sullen. Long handshakes, giving each person time to really feel the other's hand, are common. In the Grand Valley they'll usually demand 100 rp if you want to take their photo. The major sequence of festivals in the Grand Valley, including young men's initiation rites, mock battles and multiple marriages, takes place every five years and is next due in 1993.

WAMENA

Wamena is an Indonesian colony – a collection of neat rows of tin-roofed bungalows. The main airfield in the highlands is at one side of the town, and a siren blows to warn people off the runway whenever a plane is about to use it. Wamena has the main market in the valley, so lots of Dani come in from the surrounding villages to trade. Some men may put on the simple savage act to get a few cigarettes from you. Smoking is rampant in the valley, even among the Dani women.

Wamena is peaceful and cool, with a beautiful backdrop of mountains, and it's intriguing to watch the endless stream of tribal people wandering around. Even here in the town, this is a very different world! Accommodation in Wamena is expensive – in fact most things are very expensive compared with in the rest of Indonesia, since they have to be flown up here. Petrol is more than twice as expensive here.

Information

The Bank Rakyat Indonesia near the airstrip is open Monday to Friday from 7.30 am to 12 noon and Saturday from 7.30 to 11 am. The post office is close by and open Monday to Thursday from 8 am to 12 noon, from Friday 8 to 10 am and Saturday from 8 to 11 am.

Your surat jalan from Jayapura will probably be checked at Wamena airport and you'll have to show it to the police at the police station too – they're generally friendly and helpful. A surat jalan for Wamena is also good for most places around Wamena. You usually have to report to the police again each time you come to a new village with a police station. The Wamena police station has a map on its wall of the main Balim Valley and another showing most of the villages in the central highlands, plus a list of where you're not supposed to go.

Places to Stay

The *Losmen Anggrek* on Jalan Ambon near the airport is the most comfortable place to stay. Pleasant downstairs rooms

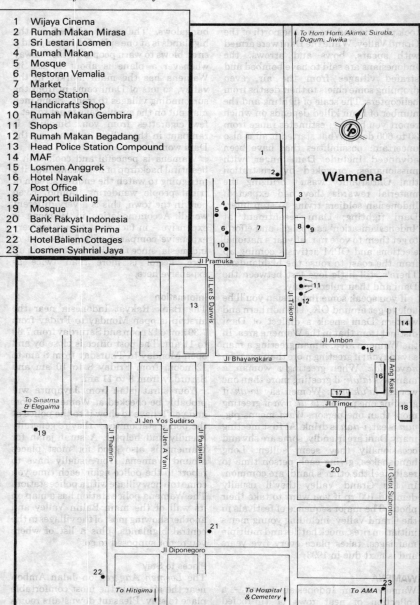

1 Wijaya Cinema
2 Rumah Makan Mirasa
3 Sri Lestari Losmen
4 Rumah Makan
5 Mosque
6 Restoran Vemalia
7 Market
8 Bemo Station
9 Handicrafts Shop
10 Rumah Makan Gembira
11 Shops
12 Rumah Makan Begadang
13 Head Police Station Compound
14 MAF
15 Losmen Anggrek
16 Hotel Nayak
17 Post Office
18 Airport Building
19 Mosque
20 Bank Rakyat Indonesia
21 Cafetaria Sinta Prima
22 Hotel Baliem Cottages
23 Losmen Syahrial Jaya

To Hom Hom, Akima, Suruba, Dugum, Jiwika

Wamena

Jl Pramuka
Jl Let S Darwis
Jl Trikora
Jl Bhayangkara
Jl Ambon
Jl Ang Kasa
Jl Timur
Jl Jen Yos Sudarso
Jl Thamrin
Jl Jen A Yani
Jl Panjaitan
Jl Gatot Subroto
Jl Diponegoro

To Sinatma & Elegaima

To Hitigima

To Hospital & Cemetery

To AMA

with private mandi cost 18,000/30,000 rp; smaller upstairs rooms with shared mandi and toilet are 12,000/20,000 rp.

Losmen Syahrial Jaya (tel 151), at Jalan Gatot Subroto 51 a five-minute walk from the airport, is clean and the staff are friendly and helpful. Rooms with or without mandi cost 10,000 rp per person per night, including a light breakfast and drinks. This place is a bit of a hang-out for locals with nothing better to do, which means you can't sit outside your room without an audience.

The *Nayak Hotel* on Jalan Angkasa, directly opposite the airport terminal, costs 15,600/28,000 rp including breakfast and tax; lunch or dinner is 5000 rp and the restaurant's food can be excellent. The hotel looks like an army barracks from the outside, but the rooms are comfortable, clean and quite large with their own mandi and toilet.

Losmen Sri Lestari (tel 101) is next to the bemo station on Jalan Trikora. It's clean and the people are friendly but the rooms are nothing special. Singles/doubles without private mandi are 15,800/22,500 rp, with private mandi 17,500/26,500 rp. Prices include a light breakfast.

The *Hotel Baliem Cottages*, on Jalan Thamrin a good 10-minute walk from the airport, was one of Wamena's original places to stay; it now looks shabby but it's still taking guests. Singles/doubles are 15,500/30,000 rp including tax, service, breakfast and an afternoon snack. The hotel is made up of dome shaped grass-roofed, concrete-walled bungalows imitating Dani huts. Each has an open-roofed toilet and bathroom attached.

The police may tell you that you can sleep in a house over the road from the police station for less than you'd pay in a losmen – this isn't an attempt to jail you or even extract favours from you!

Places to Eat

There are a couple of good, slightly expensive restaurants serving the local speciality, freshwater crayfish (udang).

The Dani-grown vegetables bought fresh, daily from the market are delicious wherever you eat them. Try the *Cafeteria Nayak* with udang for 4000-6000 rp, chicken dishes for 5000 rp and the other local speciality, fried goldfish (ikan mas goreng) for 4000 rp. The boiled vegetables (sayur lalap) at 2000 rp make a good side dish. They also do cheaper dishes such as nasi and mie goreng for 1800 rp.

Almost on a par, the *Cafetaria Sinta Prima* serves similar fare that's a bit cheaper and whips up good, filling omelettes and sates.

There are several rumah makan behind the market. The *Restoran Vemalia* serves Chinese and Indonesian food including nasi goreng (2000 rp), cap cai (2500 rp) and udang (4000-5500 rp). On Jalan Trikora, the busy *Rumah Makan Begadang* has nasi meals for 1500 rp.

Alternatively you can buy carrots, tomatoes, lettuces, strings of fish, bananas, pineapples, beans and sweet potatoes in the market and fix your own food. Coconuts and papayas, flown up from Jayapura, are expensive. There are several small market kiosks selling doughnuts, pieces of fried potato and fish.

Things to Buy

The Dani are fine craftsmen; traditionally the men are the creators, making stone axes or weaving necklaces of cowrie shells or intricate bracelets. They also make the married women's fibre-coil skirts which circle the body well below the waist and defy gravity by not falling down. Palm and orchid fibres are used, the latter's texture resulting in an almost shimmering effect.

The cost of stone axe blades (*kapak*) depends on the size and amount of labour involved in making it; blue stone is the hardest and considered the finest material and thus more expensive, with black stone a close second. *Sekan* are thin, intricate, handwoven rattan bracelets. *Noken* are bark-string bags; these are made from the inner bark of certain types of trees and shrubs dried, shredded and then rolled into threads; the bags are coloured with vegetable dyes, resulting in a very strong smell.

And of course there are the penis gourds or horim. The gourd is held upright by attaching a thread to the top and looping it around the waist. Incidentally, the Indonesians refer to the penis gourd as *koteka*, from *kotek* meaning 'tail' – it's a derogatory term.

Other handicrafts include head and arm bands of cowrie shells, feathers and bone; containers made of coconuts; four-pronged wooden combs; grass skirts; woven baskets and fossils – you may be approached by people with their own finds for sale. There are two good souvenir shops in Wamena: one next to the bemo station and one in the market, but you can also buy items from the Dani themselves in the market or in villages. Sometimes it's cheaper to buy direct from the Dani people, but they can strike a hard bargain even for a penis gourd so it's best to check out both shop and market prices. Expect to pay around 3000 rp for a medium-sized string bag after bargaining, from 200 to 500 rp for a penis gourd, from 100 rp for sekan, 10,000 rp for grey stone axes, and 50, 000 rp for *asli* (genuine) stone axes.

Asmat woodcarvings, shields and spears are also available in the souvenir shops.

Getting There & Away

Merpati flies daily – often two or three times – between Wamena and Jayapura, with some flights timed so that you can connect at Jayapura for western Indonesia. Merpati also flies weekly from Wamena to Bokondini, Oksibil, Karubaga and Kelila in the highlands, and back. The Merpati desk at Wamena airport opens a few hours before their planes are due to leave.

The MAF and AMA have offices in Wamena and fly to numerous destinations – it's a case of waiting for a flight that has seats to where you want to go. Book as far ahead as you can – even if you're prepared to charter a plane, you might have to wait a week or so before one's available. To reach some places in the interior from Wamena, it's sometimes quicker to fly back to Jayapura and then out again with Merpati. The MAF office is next to the Wamena airport building and usually open Monday to Friday from 5.30 am to 5 pm, closed on Saturday and Sunday. The AMA office is at the southern end of the airstrip.

For more information on Merpati and mission flights, see the Irian Jaya introductory Getting Around section. It's worth asking at the Hotel Baliem Cottages about Hercules freight planes – you might, for instance, be able to get a direct flight to Biak considerably cheaper than going via Jayapura.

AROUND & BEYOND THE BALIM VALLEY

Getting out and wandering the valleys and hills brings you into close contact with the Dani and makes even Wamena seem a distant metropolis! This is great hiking country, but travel light since the trails are muddy and slippery. You have to clamber over stiles, maybe cross rivers by dugout canoe or log raft, traverse creeks or trenches on quaint footbridges or a single rough plank or slippery log.

You can take day or half-day trips out of Wamena, longer treks around the Balim Valley staying in villages as you go, or cross the mountains to remoter areas where you may have to camp some of the time.

Walking in the Balim Valley

Guides You'll almost certainly be approached in Wamena by people offering to guide you on walks. You don't have to have a guide, but taking one usually makes things easier *and* more interesting. They can tell you the options of where to go, facilitate communication with locals, find places to stay and generally keep you informed. In addition you'll get to know a local person.

Young Danis expect around 5000 rp a day, maybe more for distant or strenuous treks. A porter – useful if you have several days' food to take – gets around 3000 rp a day. For this they'll also make fires and cook for you and find places to stay. You provide their food and will probably have to keep them in cigarettes too. If you're happy with them at the end of the trip, a bonus won't go amiss. It's not a bad idea to test out a Dani guide on a short walk or two before hiring him for a longer trip. A few Danis who have become well established in the guiding business manage to get 15,000 rp or even 25,000 rp a day.

In addition, a number of Indonesian travel companies can provide trekking guides for Irian Jaya. The only Wamena-based one is Chandra Tours & Travel (tel 143), run from the Cafetaria Sinta Prima by a friendly Malukan, Sam Chandra, who has been in the Balim Valley since the 1970s. He employs two or three Indonesian guides who are experienced, have good contacts with the Dani and speak good English. But they don't come cheap – the guide alone costs from 25,000 to 35,000 rp a day, then there are extras like porters, food, accommodation. For a five-day walk for two people from Angguruk to Wamena, Sam quoted around US\$460 – including accommodation in Wamena at the start and finish, but *not* counting the airfare from Wamena to Angguruk. The postal address of Chandra Tours & Travel is Tromol Pos 41, Wamena.

What to Take If you need sun block, bring it from Jayapura. You can get most other things you need from Wamena's market and shops: there's no shortage of food and you can buy pots, pans, hats, mosquito coils, umbrellas and blankets. Take a torch if you want to enter any of the caves in the area. Some Grand Valley villages have kiosks selling things like biscuits, bottled drinks, noodles and rice – heading north the last are at Meagaima on the east side and just beyond Pyramid on the west.

Otherwise you can usually get plenty of sweet potatoes, but don't rely on much else except occasional eggs or fruit. It can rain and get cold at night, so bring warm clothes. If you need a tent, bring your own or find a guide who's adept at constructing ad hoc forest shelters (many are).

Places to Stay There are losmens in a few places and in many villages you can get a wooden bed in the house of a teacher or a leading family for usually from 3000 to 5000 rp per person, sometimes including food. Sleeping on the floor of Dani huts is also quite possible – you'll probably be asked to pay 1500 or 3000 rp for this, but make sure you're invited before entering the compound or any particular hut. Missions can put you up in one or two places, but in general you're advised to try elsewhere.

Getting Around You can fly to a large number of places in the highlands and walk back. Merpati goes weekly from Wamena to Bokondini, Kelila and Karubaga. Bokondini also has an MAF flight most days. Other places with airstrips include Angguruk, Danime, Dekai, Holuon, Ibele, Ilaga, Ilugua, Kobakma, Kuyawage, Maki, Ninia, Pass Valley, Pitt River, Pronggoli, Pyramid, Senggo, Soba, Sumo, Tiom and Wolo.

Bemos, known locally as taxis, run to some places around Wamena during daylight hours, more often in the morning, from opposite the market. How far and how often they go depends on the state of the roads and the number of people likely to be travelling the route. You can also charter bemos.

The best road out of Wamena heads north to Homhom, bridges the Balim River at Pikhe, then continues to Akima (500 rp by bemo), Tanah Merah (10 km from Wamena, 700 rp), Jiwika (15 km, 800 rp), Waga Waga (21 km, 1000 rp) and Uwosilimo, where it plunges east into the mountains – it's intended eventually to get to Jayapura from here! Bemos to

Sinatma area, Balim Valley

Jiwika leave roughly hourly – to Waga Waga, usually their furthest limit, they're rarer. The other bemo routes from Wamena are south to Hepuba, Hitigima (1000 rp) and Kurima (in 1989 this road was impassable for bemos south of Hepuba) and west to Sinatma (two km, 200 rp, about every half-hour). Road work north of Sinatma might enable bemos to run to Kimbim before long.

Grand Valley – central & south

Sinatma This is an hour or two's stroll west of Wamena. Walk along Jalan Yos Sudarso to where it turns right at a small shop, where you go straight on past a church over the fields. Near a small hydro power station you can cross the raging Wamena River by a hanging bridge and walk down the far side to Wauma where you meet the main road into Wamena from the south.

Hitigima There are saltwater wells (*air garam*) near the village of Hitigima, an easy two to three hour walk along the main road south from Wamena. To extract the salt, banana stems are beaten dry of fluid

and put in a pool to soak up the brine. The stem is then dried and burned and the ashes collected and used as salt.

The road to Hitigima is a flat stroll past hills with neat chequerboards of cultivated fields enclosed by stone walls. From Wamena walk down Jalan A Yani, over the bridge and straight on, the Balim River making occasional appearances by the roadside as you go. Hitigima is slightly above the road on the west side. The turning is marked by a small green sign saying 'SD Hitigima 500m, Kurima 6 km'. The village has a school and a mission, and the salt wells are a further 45 minutes or so above Hitigima.

Kurima & Hitugi From Hitigima the road continues flat for six km to Kurima, where there's a police post and a hanging bridge over the Balim leading to Hitugi (about three hours away). From Hitugi two trails lead north to Pugima, one nearer the river, the other more mountainous. You'd need two days to do a Wamena, Kurima, Hitugi, Pugima, Wamena circle.

Pugima The village of Pugima lies behind

the first low line of hills as you look east across Wamena airstrip. It's a two to three hour walk from the town. Take the rough road from the southern half of the airstrip past Wesagaput kampung. At the river, turn south along the bank to the Kupelago Manunggal XIII suspension bridge (a half-hour walk from Wamena). The path on the other side of the bridge leads to Pugima.

Akima This nondescript village, about seven km north of Wamena just off the Jiwika road, is also known as Momi after its (in) famous smoked mummy. For the privilege of seeing this former leading citizen you can expect to pay about 6500 rp. It's completely black, decorated with a string mesh cap and cowrie-shell beads, feather and penis gourd. The body is hunched up in a sitting position, head tucked down, arms wrapped around knees, clawed fingers draped over feet. Unfortunately the commercial aspects of looking at it take away much of your curiosity. It's about a two-hour walk from Wamena to Akima along a dreary road – take a bemo.

Suruba & Dugum These two small villages are set beneath rocky outcrops off the Akima-Jiwika road. Life in this part of the valley in the 1960s is described in fascinating detail in Peter Matthiessen's *Under The Mountain Wall* and R Gardner and K Heider's *Gardens of War*. Suruba has nine compounds, Dugum five. Both have friendly people and 'losmens' for visitors – compounds set slightly apart from the villagers' own, with Dani-style huts made of traditional materials, intended specifically for tourists to stay in. For 5000 rp per person you get a floor covered in comfortable dry grass, and there's a separate hut for cooking. You wash in the creek. It's best to go with a guide who can introduce you to the villagers – they'll talk, smoke and drink with you and show you round their own compounds. Waking up here as the sun

Smoked body in Akima, Balim Valley

breaks into the valley's morning mists and the villagers holler to each other in the fields is a magical moment.

To reach Suruba, walk a few minutes east off the Jiwika road at Tanah Merah, 10 km from Wamena. For Dugum continue a km beyond Tanah Merah then do the same. Bemos from Wamena will drop you at the turnings.

Jiwika There's a busy Sunday morning market at the largish village of Jiwika (pronounced 'Yiwika'), 15 km from Wamena. Kurulu, the long-time chief here, was once such a powerful man in the valley that the Indonesians named the whole district surrounding Jiwika after him. The Jiwika mission is Catholic. About an hour's climb up the forested valley east of the village are some salt wells similar to those at Hitigima. At the foot of the path up to them is a kiosk where you're supposed to pay 1000 rp – but it's usually only open in the morning. Jiwika also has a mummy for which the going viewing price is about 3000 rp.

Accommodation options include the basic, but friendly *La'uk Inn* which is run by a locally popular Javanese family. A bed is 7000 rp per person and there are good meals: breakfast costs 2000 rp and lunch or dinner, 3000 rp. This is a fine alternative to Wamena as a base in the valley. There's also *Wijuk Huts* near the police station at 5000 rp per person in Dani-style huts, including breakfast – or you might be able to stay in a Dani compound. A bemo from Jiwika to Waga Waga, if you can get one, is 500 rp.

Grand Valley – north

You can do a loop up one side of the Grand Valley, across the bridge near Pyramid and down the other side, in three days or more, saving a day by taking a bemo between Wamena and Jiwika or Waga Waga, or lengthening the trip with deviations into side valleys of the Balim or across the ranges into other valleys.

Waga Waga to Meagaima At Waga Waga, 21 km from Wamena and the usual furthest point on the east side for bemos, there are some caves whose chambers apparently contain the bones of victims of a past tribal war. You have to pay 1000 rp to enter and aren't likely to see them. The caves at Uwosilimo, two hours' walk along the open, truck-infested road from Waga Waga, are better. You'll need someone to show you the entrance, which is to the right of the 'Jayapura' road just after it turns off east shortly before Uwosilimo. Locals will probably ask you for 500 rp to enter the caves, which are said to be three km long, with a river and a boat somewhere deep inside.

From Uwosilimo it's 1½ hours' walk through wooded country to the tiny village of Meagaima on a rise overlooking the Balim River. Before Meagaima, another track leads down to the Balim River which you can cross by canoe to Pommo, where there's another mummy (6500 rp).

Wolo Valley & Beyond This is one of the most beautiful and spectacular side-valleys of the Balim. From Manda, half an hour north of Meagaima, the gently rising riverside track to Wolo village is about 2½ hours' walk. Wolo, inspired by a strong strain of Evangelical Protestantism, is a non-smoking place with lovely flower gardens. It won the 1988 'Most Progressive Village in Irian Jaya' title for a string of self-initiated projects including fish farming and a mini hydro scheme that provides street lights. Two villagers went to Jakarta to meet Suharto. It's said that in the upheavals of 1977, Indonesian troops and Dani enemies from the Jiwika area came up the valley burning and looting and left not a house standing. The honays have been rebuilt in neat rows, with a dramatically sloping airstrip at one side of the village.

From Wolo there are two-hour walks to a waterfall in the hills to the north, or up the Wolo River to where it emerges from another cave. The main track up the Wolo Valley, however, leads to Ilugua (about 2½ hours). About two-thirds of the way to Ilugua, a side track to the right leads round a huge sinkhole and down to Yogolok cave and Goundal, a tiny kampung on the floor of an awesome canyon. From Goundal you can continue on to Ilugua – a full day's walk from Wolo. To see Goundal from the top of the canyon precipice, take a 10-minute side track to the right off the main Ilugua track about 20 minutes before Ilugua. You need a guide to help you find these side tracks.

The Lake Archbold area, home to the few thousand Gem-speakers, is down around 1000 metres about 1½ days' walk north-east of Ilugua via Babu. Kobakma is about 15 km east of Lake Archbold.

Meagaima to Kimbim It's about 3½ hours flat walking west from Meagaima to the bridge over the Balim just north of Pyramid, through Manda, past Jalengga, through Pilimo (a pretty place beside the Balim) and Munak. Pyramid, a major mission and education centre near a pyramid-shaped hill about 35 km from Wamena, is about 1½ hours south of the bridge. Kimbim, with a police station and a Saturday morning market, another two hours south, is a better place to stay.

Kimbim to Wamena This is a fairly dull stretch down the open west side of the main Balim valley – about eight hours' walk through Holkima, Elegaima and Sinatma. There's a lower-lying, usually muddier, route from Pyramid to Wamena via Miligatnem, Musatfak and Homhom.

North & West of the Grand Valley

The north end of the Grand Valley and the regions around it are more heavily Christianised, mainly by Protestants, than the Wamena area. They were also the centre of conflict and destruction in 1977.

North Directly north of the Grand Valley it's up-and-down walking. From Bolakme,

just north of the bridge near Pyramid, it's about seven hours via Tagime to Kelila, which is at about 1300 metres but you climb to over 2000 metres on the way. Kelila has a police station. From Kelila down to Bokondini, a missionary centre, is about 2½ hours (four or five hours coming back). The information on the following walk round the Bokondini-Karubaga area and back to Pyramid comes from a reader: Bokondini to Wunen, about eight hours with an exhausting ascent; Wunen to Karubaga, seven hours over one moderate mountain (you can stay and eat at *Karubaga Guest House* 4000 rp per person; Karubaga to Wunggilipur (on the way to Kangime), one hour; Wunggilipur to Jugwa, seven hours over a high mountain and Jugwa to Pyramid, 10 hours over mountains.

Western Dani West along the Balim upstream from Pyramid is the country of the western Dani, who call themselves Lani.

There are tracks to Maki, the first main village, from Kimbim, Pyramid and Bolakme. Between Pitt River and Kuyawage the Balim disappears underground for two km. Ilaga is about 60 km west of Kuyawage, beyond the western Balim watershed. West of Pitt River the going is often swampy.

Lake Habbema From Ibele, west of the main Wamena-Pyramid track, it's two days up to Lake Habbema, 3450 metres high below the 4750-metre Gunung Trikora. The 1938 Archbold expedition set up a big camp beside Lake Habbema, ferrying men and supplies in by seaplane. You'll need to camp if you come up here.

Yali Country
East and south of the Dani region are the Yali people, who have rectangular houses and whose men wear 'skirts' of rattan hoops, their penis gourds protruding from underneath. Missionaries are at work here, but the Indonesian presence is

thinner than in the Balim Valley. Bordering the Yali on the east are the Kim-Yal, amongst whom cannibalism was still practised at least in the 1970s.

Reaching Yali country on foot involves plenty of ups and downs on steep trails. Pronggoli, the nearest centre from Wamena as the crow flies, is three days' hard walking by the most direct route, with camping needed en route. From Pronggoli to Angguruk takes a day. Easier, but longer is a southern loop through Kurima, Tangma (where there's a hanging bridge over the Balim), Wet, Soba (the last Dani village, in a side-valley off the Balim Gorge), Ninia, then north to Angguruk. This takes about seven days. Along the way you can stay in teachers' or village houses. In Angguruk and Pronggoli the missions can often put you up.

Pass Valley, a settlement in the north of the Yali area, is 1½ days' walk from Jiwika. A steep four-hour walk past the Jiwika salt wells leads to Watlangu, from where it's a long day to Pass Valley.

South

It's about two weeks' walk from Wamena down to Dekai via Soba, Holuon and Sumo. From Dekai it could be possible to canoe downriver as far as Senggo on the fringes of the Asmat region – though you might need a special surat jalan from Wamena to go that far.

Other Destinations

Almost anywhere in Irian Jaya will probably be of interest, if you're permitted to go there. Despite the exploitation of the land and its people, it remains one of the earth's last wildernesses. The towns may be unappealing but you might find some of the nearby mining sites or transmigration colonies of interest. The nature reserves, while mostly requiring expedition-type efforts to reach, would also be rewarding.

Robert Mitton's *The Lost World of Irian Jaya* is a good source of info on several areas.

MERAUKE

Merauke, at the south-east corner of Irian Jaya, is the last major town in Indonesia – *dari Sabang ke Merauke* is the slogan denoting the spread of Indonesian territory. It has long dry seasons and eucalypts – a more Australian landscape than anywhere else in Irian Jaya. Despite uninviting red soils 30,000 or more transmigrants had been moved to the Merauke area by 1988. Several of the transmigrant centres have faced severe problems resulting in large numbers seeking work in Merauke itself. There are possibilities of river trips from Merauke to elsewhere in southern Irian Jaya. Places to stay include the *Hotel Asmat* and the cheaper *Losmen Abadi* and *Wisma Praja*.

Rawa Biru-Wasur Reserve, 60 km east of Merauke on the southern border with PNG, contains a blue coloured swamp (rawa biru), acacia and eucalypt trees, long grass and giant termite hills. Cockatoos, parrots, crowned imperial pigeons, cassowaries, wallabies, crocodiles and dugongs are among the reserve's wildlife. Get there by jeep from Merauke in the dry season.

TANAH MERAH

Inland, to the far north of Merauke, is Tanah Merah which means 'red earth'. The Dutch called it Boven Digul and this was the site of their prison camp for Indonesian nationalists – both Hatta and Sjahrir spent time here before being sent to the Banda Islands.

AGATS

Agats, on the south-west coast, is a jumping-off point for visiting the Asmat people, once cannibals and head-hunters. The Asmat live in the lowland swamps where the Balim River (known here as the Sirets or Eilanden) reaches the sea as a wide, muddy tidal river. The Indonesian takeover has overturned the Asmat lifestyle; traditionally they were mainly nomadic, living in temporary shelters for a few months then moving on as food in an area was depleted. Now the push is towards permanent settlements with schools, missionary stations and clinics. The area has been sold out to timber companies who use the Asmat to fell their own forests, often by coercion and for no pay – no wonder the area has been off-limits to tourists for several years.

The Asmat are master carvers, famous for their two-to-three-metre tall *Bisj* poles – tree trunks carved with crouching, interlocked phallic figures. They also decorate ceremonial shields, sago bowls, canoe paddles and intricate prows for their dugout canoes. You can buy their fantastic work in Biak, Wamena and Jayapura or, for more exorbitant prices, in Bali and Jakarta.

FREEPORT MINE & PUNCAK JAYA
Tembagapura is the town serving the Freeport Copper Mine at Gunung Bijih (formerly Mt Ertzberg), just a little north-west of Puncak Jayakesuma (Mt Carstensz). At over 5000 metres, Puncak Jaya is the highest peak between the Andes and the Himalaya. The mine's crushing plant is 3700 metres high. The Dutch geologist Dozy in 1936 described Ertzberg as 'a mountain of copper ore' but it was not until the late 1960s that anyone attempted to mine it. At that time the Suharto government's desire for foreign capital led to a reappraisal of even the most remote reserves and an agreement allowing the Freeport Company from the US to mine.

Tembagapura is 10 km south of the mine, about 70 km south-east of Enarotali and 50 km north-east of Timika. The road connecting the mine and the town passes through a 900-metre-long tunnel. The road south from Tembagapura to the coast passes through a second tunnel 1500 metres long.

On snow-capped Puncak Jaya you could stand on a glacier in the tropics and see the sea. The surrounding area is rugged with other peaks and more small glaciers. It's apparently possible to reach the summit by some routes without serious mountaineering gear – but take serious advice before you try. Four climbers who went missing in the area in 1987 were believed to be victims of the OPM. Now it's impossible to get a permit to enter the area, let alone climb the mountain. Ilaga used to be the starting point for assaults on the mountain.

PANIAI LAKES
On the western edge of the central highlands, these lakes surrounded by mountains are legendary for their beauty. The district is home to the Ekagi people who are very short in stature. Enarotali, on the east side of Lake Paniai, is the town.

SORONG
At the tip of the bird's head this is a big Pertamina oil and timber base, but really nothing more than a stopover unless you visit the Raja Ampat Islands Reserves off the coast. By 1987 there were 30,000 transmigrants in the Sorong area. Sorong Airport is 32 km from the town, on another island linked to the mainland by a regular ferry, but there are plans to build another closer to the town.

The *Penginapan Indah*, about 200 metres from the harbour on the main road, has economy rooms for about 6000/9000 rp and newer better rooms for 15,000 rp. The *Hotel Bangaria* has similar prices and is possibly better. There are several other places to stay.

There's an island off the town where you can go for walks – get there by boat from the dock (300 rp). The PHPA office is at Jalan Pemuda 40 (postal address: PO Box 353, Sorong). They can advise you about visiting the Raja Ampat Reserves which take in parts of Waigeo Island, known for its birdlife including two bird of paradise species, Batanta Island and

Salawati Island. Apparently each island has its own endemic species.

MANOKWARI

The Manokwari area, on the north-eastern tip of the bird's head, is mountainous but has fertile lowlands. Some 100,000 people (including many transmigrants) are spread along the coast in and near the town. Sago and cassava are the major crops but soybeans, rice, vegetables and groundnuts are also grown and there are coffee, coconut and oilpalm plantations. The town has a clean beach with white sand and clear water, plus lots of trees, good shops including a bakery, a hospital and a cinema.

Places to stay include the *Hotel Arfak* (tel 21293) at Jalan Brawijaya 8, 12 km from the airport (10,000 rp by taxi). It's an old Dutch building on a hill with a bay view, beside a military camp. Clean doubles with fan, terrace and private mandi cost 17,500 rp, including three good meals and good service.

Glossary

abangan – nominal Muslim, whose beliefs owe more to older, pre-Islamic mysticism

adat – traditional laws and regulations

air – water

air panas – hot springs

Airlangga – an 11th century king of considerable historical and legendary importance in Bali

aling aling – guard wall behind the entrance gate to a Balinese family compound; demons can only travel in straight lines so the aling aling prevents them from coming straight in through the front entrance

alun alun – main public square of a town or village

alus – 'refined', high standards of behaviour and art, characters in Wayang Kulit performances are traditionally alus or kasar

andong – a horse drawn passenger cart

angklung – a musical instrument of differing lengths and thicknesses of bamboo suspended in a frame

anjing – dog

arak – colourless distilled palm-wine firewater

Arja – a particularly refined form of Balinese theatre

Arjuna – a hero of the *Mahabharata* epic and a popular temple gate guardian image

ayam – chicken

Ayodya – Rama's kingdom in the *Ramayana*

Babad – early chronicle of Balinese history

babi – pork

Bahasa Indonesia – Indonesia's national language

bajaj – a motorised three-wheeler taxi found in Jakarta

bakar – barbecued

bakmi – rice-flour noodles

bakso – meatball soup

balai – communal house in South Kalimantan

bale – Balinese pavilion, house or shelter, a meeting place

Bali Aga – the 'original' Balinese, the people who managed to resist the new ways brought in with the Majapahit migration

banjar – the local area of a Balinese village in which community activities are organised

Bapak – father, also a polite form of address to any older man

Baris – warrior dance

Barong – mythical lion-dog creature, star of the Barong dance and a firm champion of the good in the eternal struggle between good and evil

Barong Landung – the enormous puppets known as the 'tall barong'. You can see them at an annual festival on Serangan Island

Barong Tengkok – Lombok name for portable form of gamelan used for wedding processions and circumcision ceremonies

batik – cloth made by coating part of the cloth with wax, then dyeing it and melting the wax out. The waxed part is not coloured and repeated waxings and dyeings build up a pattern.

becak – trishaw

bemo – popular local transport, a bemo is traditionally a small pickup-truck with a bench seat down each side in the back. The traditional bemos are now disappearing in favour of small minibuses

bendi – a two-person *dokar* used in Sulawesi

betang – communal house in Central Kalimantan

blimbing – starfruit

Bouraq – a winged horse-like creature with the head of a woman; also the name of the domestic airline which mostly services the outer islands

Brahma – the creator, one of the trinity of Hindu gods

brem – fermented rice wine

bubur ayam – Indonesian porridge of rice or beans with chicken

bukit – hill

bupati – government official in charge of a regency (kabupaten)

camat – government official in charge of a district (kecamatan)

candi bentar – split gateway entrance to a Balinese temple

candi – shrine of originally Javanese design, also known as prasada

cap cai – fried vegetables, sometimes with meat

cap – a metal stamp used to apply motifs to batik

catur yoga – ancient manuscript on religion and cosmology

Colt – minibus, popular form of public transport

cumi cumi – squid

dalang – the story teller who operates the puppets, tells the story and beats the time in a wayang kulit shadow puppet performance, a man of varied skills and considerable endurance

danau – Lake, as in Danau Toba

delman – a horse-drawn passenger cart

desa – village

Dewi Sri – goddess of rice

dokar – horse cart, still a popular form of local transport in many towns and larger villages

dukun – 'witch doctor' actually a faith healer and herbal doctor or mystic

durian – 'the fruit that smells like hell and tastes like heaven'

fu yung hai – sweet and sour omelette

gado-gado – traditional Indonesian dish of steamed bean sprouts, vegetables and a spicy peanut sauce

Gajah Mada – famous Majapahit prime minister

Gambuh – classical form of Balinese theatre

gamelan – traditional Javanese and Balinese orchestra, usually almost solely percussion with large xylophones and gongs

gang – alley or footpath

Garuda – mythical man-bird, the vehicle of Vishnu and the modern symbol of Indonesia; also the name of Indonesia's international airline

gereja – church

gili – islet or atoll

gringsing – rare double ikat woven cloth of Tenganan

gua – cave

gunung – mountain, as in Gunung Agung or Gunung Merapi

haji – a Muslim who has made the pilgrimage to Mecca. Many Indonesians save all their lives to make the pilgrimage, and a haji commands great respect in the village.

harga biasa – usual price

homestay – a small family run losmen

hutan – forest

huta – Batak village

Ibu – mother, also polite form of address to any older woman

ikan – fish

ikat – cloth where the pattern is produced by dyeing the individual threads before weaving

Jaipongan – a relatively modern, West Javanese dance incorporating elements of *pencak silat* and *Ketuktilu*

jalan – street or road

jalan jalan – to walk

jalan potong – short cut

jam karet – 'rubber time'

jamu – herbal medicine; most tonics go under this name and are supposed to cure everything from menstrual problems to baldness

jembatan – bridge

jeruk – citrus fruit

jidur – large cylindrical drums played widely throughout Lombok

jukung – prahu

Kabupaten – regency

kacang – peanuts

kain – cloth

kamar kecil – toilet, usually the traditional hole in the ground with footrests either side

kantor – office, as in kantor imigrasi (immigration office) or kantor pos (post office)

kasar – rough, coarse, crude; everything that is opposite of *alus* Javanese refinement

Kawi – classical Javanese, the language of poetry

kebaya – Chinese long-sleeved blouse with plunging front and embroidered edges

kebun – garden

kecapi – a Sundanese (West Javanese) lute

kelapa – coconut

kepala desa – village headman

kepeng – old Chinese coins with a hole in the centre, they were the everyday money during the Dutch era and can still be obtained quite readily from shops and antique dealers for just a few cents

kepiting – crab

ketoprak – popular Javanese folk theatre

Ketuktilu – a traditional Sundanese dance in which professional female dancers (sometimes prostitutes) dance for male spectators

klotok – canoe with water-pump motor used in Kalimantan

Konfrontasi – a catch phrase of the early '60s when Sukarno embarked on a confrontational campaign against western imperialism, and expansionist policies in the region, aimed at Malaysia.

kopi – coffee

kraton – a walled city palace and traditionally the centre of Javanese culture. The two most famous and influential kratons are those of Yogyakarta and Solo.

kretek – Indonesian clove cigarette

kris – wavy bladed traditional dagger, often held to have spiritual or magical powers

Kuningan – holy day celebrated throughout Bali 10 days after Galungan

ladang – a non-irrigated field, often using slash-and-burn agriculture, for dry-land crops

langsam – a crowded, peak hour commuter train to the big cities

lesehan – traditional style of dining on straw mats

longbot – a high-speed motorised canoe used on the rivers of Kalimantan

lontar – type of palm tree, traditional books were written on the dried leaves of the lontar palm

losmen – basic accommodation, usually cheaper than hotels and often family-run

lumpia – spring rolls

Mahabharata – one of the great Hindu holy books, tells of the battle between the Pandavas and the Korawas

Majapahit – the last great Hindu dynasty in Java, pushed out of Java into Bali by the rise of Islamic power

mandi – usual Indonesian form of bath, consists of a large water tank from which you ladle water to pour over yourself like a shower

martabak – pancake found at foodstalls everywhere, can be savoury but usually very sweet

Merpati – the major domestic airline

meru – multi-roofed shrines in Balinese temples, takes its name from the Hindu holy mountain Mahameru

mesjid – mosque

mie goreng – fried noodles, usually with vegetables, and sometimes meat

mikrolets – a small taxi, a tiny *oplet*

moko – bronze drum from Alor (Nusa Tenggara)

muezzin – those who call the faithful to the mosque

naga – a mythical snake-like creature

nanas – pineapple

nasi – cooked rice. *Nasi goreng* is the ubiquitous fried rice. *Nasi campur* is rice 'with the lot' – vegetables, meat or fish, peanuts, krupuk. *Nasi gudeg* is cooked jackfruit served with rice, chicken and spices. *Nasi rames* is rice with egg, vegetables, fish or meat. *Nasi rawon* is rice with a spicy hot beef soup.

ngadhu – a parasol-like, thatched roof, ancestor totem of the Ngada people of Flores

nusa – island, as Nusa Penida

Odalan – the temple festival held every 210 days, the Balinese 'year'

ojek – motorcycle becak

oplet – a small intra-city minibus, usually with side benches in the back

opor ayam – chicken cooked in coconut milk

Padang – the city and region of Sumatra which has exported its cuisine to all corners of Indonesia. Padang food consists of spicy curries and rice, and is traditionally eaten with the right hand. In a Padang restaurant a number of dishes are laid out on the table, and only those that are eaten are paid for.

paduraksa – covered gateway to a Balinese temple

Pak – shortened form of bapak

pandanus – palm plant used to make mats

Pantun – ancient Malay poetical verse in rhyming couplets

pasanggrahan – a lodge for government officials where travellers can usually stay

pasar – market

pasar malam – night market

patih – prime minister

patola – an *ikat* motif of a hexagon framing a type of four-pronged star

peci – black Muslim felt cap

pedanda – high priest

pelan pelan – slowly

Pelni – *Pelayaran Nasional Indonesia*; the national shipping line with major passenger ships operating throughout the archipelago

pencak silat – a self-defence dance, originally from Sumatra but now popular throughout Indonesia

penginapan – a simple lodging house

perbekel – government official in charge of a village (desa)

peresehan – popular form of one-to-one physical combat peculiar to Lombok in which two men fight armed with a small hide shield for protection and a long rattan stave as a weapon

Pertamina – the huge state-owned oil company

pinang – betel nut

pinisi – Makassar or Bugis schooner

pisang goreng – fried banana

pondok – a guest house or lodge

prahu – traditional Indonesian outrigger boat

prasada – see candi

Pulaki – the sparsely populated, dry and hilly west end of Bali

pulau – island

pura – temple

puri – palace

pusaka – sacred heirlooms of a royal family

Rafflesia – a gigantic flower found in Sumatra, with blooms spreading up to a metre

raja – lord or prince

Ramadan – Muslim month of fasting, when devout Muslims refrain from eating, drinking and smoking during daylight hours

Ramayana – one of the great Hindu holy books, stories from the *Ramayana* form the keystone of many Balinese & Javanese dances and tales

Rangda – the widow-witch, the evil black magic spirit of Balinese tales and dances

rattan – hardy, pliable vine used for handicrafts, furniture and weapons such as the staves in the spectacular trial of strength ceremony, peresehan, in Lombok

Ratu Adil – the Just Prince, who by Javanese prophecy will return to liberate Indonesia from oppression

rebab – a two stringed bowed lute

rijstaffel – Dutch for 'rice table'; a banquet of Dutch-style Indonesian food

rintek wuuk – spicy dog meat; a Minahasan (Sulawesi) delicacy

roti – bread; usually white and sweet

Rudat – traditional Sasak dance overlaid with Islamic influence

rumah adat – traditional house

rumah makan – lit. eating house – a restaurant or *warung*

rumah sakit – hospital

sambal – chilli sauce

Sanghyang Widi – the Balinese supreme being is never actually worshipped as such; one of the 'three in one' or lesser gods stand in

Sanghyang – trance dance in which the dancers impersonate a local village god

santri – orthodox, devout Muslim

saron – a xylophone-like gamelan instrument, with bronze bars struck with a wooden mallet

sarong – all-purpose cloth, often sewed into a tube, and worn by men, women and children

Sasak – native of Lombok

sate – a classic Indonesian dish; small pieces of charcoal grilled meat on a skewer served with a spicy peanut sauce

sawah – an individual rice field, or the wet-rice method of cultivation

sayur – vegetable

selendang – shawl

selimut – blanket

Sempati – domestic airline which flies to Kalimantan, southern Sumatra and Java

sirih – betel nut, chewed as a mild narcotic

songket – silver or gold threaded cloth, hand woven using floating weft technique

sop – soup

soto – soup

sudra – the lowest or common caste to which the majority of Balinese belong

suling – bamboo flute

syahbandar – harbour master

tahu – soya bean curd

taman – 'garden with a pond', ornamental garden

tari topeng – a type of masked dance peculiar to the Cirebon area

tarling – a musical style of the Cirebon area, featuring guitar, *suling* and voice

tau tau – life-size carved wooden effigies of the dead placed on balconies outside cave graves in Torajaland, Sulawesi

taxi sungai – a river ferry which carries cargo downstairs and has bunks on the upper level

telur – egg

tempe – fermented soya bean cake

Tomate – Toraja funeral ceremony

tongkonan – traditional Toraja house

topeng – a wooden mask used in funerary dances

tuak – an acoholic drink fermented from palm sap or rice

uang – money

udang – prawn

Wali Songo – the nine holy men who brought Islam to Java

Wallace Line – the imaginary line between Bali and Lombok which marks the end of Asian and beginning of Australasian flora and fauna. In reality the line is a fuzzy one.

wantilan – open pavilion used to stage cockfights

waringin – banyan tree, the holy tree found at many temples, a large shady tree which sends out drooping branches which root and can produce new trees. It was under a banyan tree (the bo tree) that the Buddha achieved enlightenment

waruga – pre-Christian Minahasan (Sulawesi) tomb

warung – food stall, a sort of Indonesian equivalent to a combination of corner shop and snack bar

wayang kulit – puppet shadow play

wayang wong – masked drama playing scenes from the *Ramayana*

Wektu Telu – religion peculiar to Lombok which originated in Bayan and combines many tenets of Islam and aspects of other faiths

wisma – a guest house or lodge

Index

884 Index

MAPS

Acknowledgements continued from p4

Chris Barnes (Aus), S & S Barratt (Aus), Maes Bart (B), J & T Bartow (UK), Chris Beale (Aus), Alexandre Beaudet (Can), Claus Becker (Dk), Daphne Bell (NZ), George Bell (USA), Jannine Bennett, Mark Beshara (Aus), Kees Beukelman (Nl), Gerry Bill (Aus), Jim Bird, Machiel Blok (Nl), R F de Bode (Nl), J & M Dufty Boes (Sw), Odd Bolin (Sw), Michael Bonin (UK), Ju Bouven (Nl), Myriam Bouverat (CH), David Bowles (UK), Mark Braddock (NZ), Mariet Brannuijh, Sue Brierly (UK), K Briggs (UK), Eric Bronson (USA), Andrea Broughton (UK), David Brownscombe (Aus), M H Bruce (Aus), Glen Buras, Antonio Calderisi (It), Mary Cameron, M & C Caprio (Jap), Ralph Carabetta (USA), Paul & Leslie Carr (UK), Richard Carroll (Ire), Lee Cass (Aus), Sonja Ceulemans (B), Herbert Chouinard, Campbell Clarke (Aus), Paul Clarke, E A M W de Clercq (Nl), Carolyn Cole (Aus), Carol Cooke (UK), Justin Corrfield (UK), Ineke Crezee (NZ), Peter Croome, Ian Cunningham (Indo), J Curran (Ire), Bruce Cuthbertson (USA), Michael D'Sauza (Aus), Erin Ann Daly (USA), Darlene Davis (Aus), Jaap De Graaf (Nl), Roger Deacon (UK), Mark Denys (B), Alison Dickson (Aus), Achmad Djimar (Indo), Tjeerd Djkstra (Nl), D B Duncan (Aus), Roman Dyer, Dyke (Aus), Alan Ehrlich (USA), Melanie Ellicot (UK), Philip Elliott (Aus), Jell Ellis, F L & M A Ellis (Aus), Mark Errett (C), Victor Esbensen (S), Soren Eskildsen (Dk), John Everard, Jerry Fardell (Aus), Michael Fasman (USA), Sabine Feldwieser (D), Tim Fisher (Aus), Ilana & Raffi Frank (Isr), Maria Frasse, Patrick Freeline (USA), Jennifer Freeman (Aus), J Sjoman & A Frezmanis (Sw), Andrew Fries (Aus), Gloria Frydman (Aus), Michael Fysh QC (UK), Brian Gabriel (USA), Phil Game (Aus), Kristin Gaughan (USA), G Gautier (Afr), Lex Geers, Harry de Gelder (Nl), Anna Gelzer (Swit), Marian Gersen (Nl), Carol Giddings (UK), Anna Gleeson (UK), Yoga Gontama, Barbara Gordon (Can), Jonathon Gorty, Stephen Greig (Aus), Emyr Griffiths (UK), D C Griffiths (Aus), Susanne Groble (CH), Gisela Groticke (D), Ruth Hackh (D), Kathy Haire (Aus), Doug Hamilton (USA), Mike Haylor, Carl J Hefner (USA), Mac vd Helm (Nl), Nick Henderson (UK), Klaus Hensler (D), Jeff Herrick (USA), T E Hesse (D), H Hoffmann (UK), Nils Hogberg (Sw), Miel Hollander (Nl), Jeremy Horner (UK),

Horst, Belinda Howell (UK), Abdullah Husin (Indo), Pippa Hyde (UK), Muhammad Nur Isnaeni (Indo), Henrik Jensen (Dk), Murray & Susan Johnson (C), Ian Johnston (Aus), Malcolm Jones (Aus), Jan Junge (D), Jan Justesen (USA), Bruno Kahn (Fr), Gerhard Karl (Aus), Michael Keith (USA), Michael Kerrisb (I), Carina Killick (Aus), Nancy King (USA), Ray Kitson (Aus), Richard Knights (Aus), Ben Koster (Nl), Suzanne Krakover-Nickel (USA), Annie Kramer (Nl), E J A Kselik (Nl), Victor Kuijper (Nl), J Kullmann (D), Henrik Lanfeldt (N), Ian Lange (Aus), Claire Larrivee (Aus), Dave Lawson (UK), Jan Lensing (Nl), N Z van der Linde-Pulk (Nl), Karen Linden (Sw), David Lindup (Aus), Laurie Living (Aus), Dee Loader-Oliver (UK), Michelle Loretz (Aus), Rowena Love (UK), Adrian Lucas (UK), Poul Lundby (Dk), Sue Macgregor (Aus), Rachael MacHeese (UK), Marc Maes (B), G Maldlakis (Aus), Lex Marinos (Aus), Brigette May, George Mayo (Can), Kate Mc Cafferty (USA), Roslyn McConaghy (Aus), Brenda McDonald (Aus), Rory McDonough (USA), Kathy McPherrin (C), Baul & Barbara Meertens (Aus), Elaine Mendes (USA), Stephen Meredith (Indo), Michael (USA), Erik Michels (Nl), Lee Yew Moon, Kevin & Betta Morgan (Aus), Jeremy Mottershead (Aus), Rusty Muchfree (Indo), Steve Muir (Aus), Susan Murray (UK), Saddia Naizal Narewan, Rachma Natawijaya (Indo), Mike Naylor (Aus), Sue Nuttall (Aus), Susannah O'Ferrall (UK), Brian Oakes (Aus), Emily Owen, Angela Palmer (NZ), Russell Parker (Aus), Arnold Parzer (Fr), James Paterson (Aus), Harry Pearson (NZ), Whitney Peckman, Ian Percy (Aus), Deborah Perry (UK), Th Peters (Nl), Leonie Petersen (UK), M & P Phelan (Aus), Jan Piesse (Aus), Assy Pipecidou (Gr), Mrs Poluan-Lasut (Indo), Adam Pope (UK), Alan Preston (Aus), Larry Price (Aus), S M T Puister, Feddy von Rabenau (Aus), Andrea Radic (It), P Rae (Aus), Hans en Agnes Recourt (Nl), Garry Renshaw (Aus), Vera & Reto (CH), A Rijsdijk (Nl), Ian & Andrew Riseley (Aus), Sue Roberts (PNG), Peter Roberts (Aus), Peter and Susan Robinson (UK), Cristina Rodes (Sp), Stanley F Rose (USA), Laura Rosenfeld (Indo), Julian Ross (UK), Julia Rux (USA), Paul R Ryan (Aus), Paul Ryan (Aus), Amiruddin Saharuna (Indo), Shell Sanders (USA), Peter Schatz (Aus), S Oelnes & M Schawlann (N), Reimer Schefold, Birgit Schindler (D), Barbara

Schirmer (CH), Mike Schwab (D), Gitte Schwartz (Dk), M Y Setty (Indo), Vonny Setty (Indo), R T Shannon (NZ), R & A Sinukoff (C), Colin Skinner (Aus), L A Smith (UK), Pamela Smith (Aus), Katja Smits (Hol), Bent Somrod (DK), Bruce Spinks (Aus), C Sprokel (Nl), S M Stephens (Aus), Carl Stevenage (Aus), Alan Strahan (Aus), Sisi Sukiato (Indo), Ingan Survakti (Indo), Ms U Switucha (C), Frans Tak, Bruce Tamagno (Aus), John Taman (Nl), Belasen Tarigan (Indo), Di Taylor (HK), Robert Thomas (UK), Douglas Thomas (USA), Marion Thruger (Aus), Mieke Timmermans (B), Margaret Traeger (Aus), Ian & Fiona Trimble (UK), Julian Trudinger (Aus), Al Trujillo (USA), Henk Tukker (Nl), Ian Turland (Aus), Adrian & Andrea Turner (UK), Michael Turner (UK), Helene Turner (USA), Vega Vahitalo (Fin), Marianne Van Buick (Nl), Wouter & Andrie Van den Berg (Nl), Mark Van der Haan (Nl), John Van der Stoep (Nl), E P Van Hoarst (Nl), Rineke Van Houten (Nl), Marc Vassart (Fr), William Walker (C), D Wells (Aus), Nick Welman (Nl), Leslie Wener (C), Dieter Wettis (D), Dr J B Wibawa (Nl), Ian Wilson (Aus), Robert F Winans (USA), P M Wink (Nl), Alyson & Nicky Wood (UK), Andrew Wooster (UK), Joyce Wouters (Nl), Arthur Wurgler (CH), Johansyah Yasin (Indo), Dick Zegezs (Nl).

Aus – Australia, C – Canada, CH – Switzerland, D – West Germany, HK – Hong Kong, Indo – Indonesia, It – Italy, N – Norway, NZ – New Zealand, Sw – Sweden, UK – UK, USA – USA Dk – Denmark

In   **cm**
0 — 0

Temperature

To convert °C to °F multiply by 1.8 and add 32

To convert °F to °C subtract 32 and multiply by · 55

Length, Distance & Area

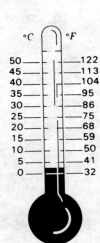

	multiply by
inches to centimetres	2.54
centimetres to inches	0.39
feet to metres	0.30
metres to feet	3.28
yards to metres	0.91
metres to yards	1.09
miles to kilometres	1.61
kilometres to miles	0.62
acres to hectares	0.40
hectares to acres	2.47

Weight

	multiply by
ounces to grams	28.35
grams to ounces	0.035
pounds to kilograms	0.45
kilograms to pounds	2.21
British tons to kilograms	1016
US tons to kilograms	907

A British ton is 2240 lbs, a US ton is 2000 lbs

Volume

	multiply by
Imperial gallons to litres	4.55
litres to imperial gallons	0.22
US gallons to litres	3.79
litres to US gallons	0.26

5 imperial gallons equals 6 US gallons
a litre is slightly more than a US quart, slightly less
than a British one

Metric Con[versions]

Temperature

To convert °C to °F multiply by 1.8 and add 32

To convert °F to °C subtract 32 and multiply by .555

Length, Distance & Area

	multiply by
inches to centimetres	2.54
centimetres to inches	0.39
feet to metres	0.30
metres to feet	3.28
yards to metres	0.91
metres to yards	1.09
miles to kilometres	1.61
kilometres to miles	0.62
acres to hectares	0.40
hectares to acres	2.47

Thermometer scale:

°C	°F
50	122
45	113
40	104
35	95
30	86
25	76
20	68
15	59
10	50
5	41
0	32

Weight

	multiply by
ounces to grams	28.35
grams to ounces	0.035
pounds to kilograms	0.45
kilograms to pounds	2.21
British tons to kilograms	1016
US tons to kilograms	907

A British ton is 2240 lbs a US ton is 2000 lbs

Volume

	multiply by
Imperial gallons to litres	4.55
litres to imperial gallons	0.22
US gallons to litres	3.79
litres to US gallons	0.26

5 imperial gallons is equals 6 US gallons
a litre is slightly more than a US quart, slightly less than a British one

Other Lonely Planet guides to the region

Malaysia, Singapore and Brunei
– a travel survival kit

These three nations offer amazing geographic and cultural variety – from hill stations to beaches, from Dyak longhouses to futuristic cities – that is Asia at its most accessible.

The Philippines – a travel survival kit

The 7000 islands of the Philippines are a paradise for the adventurous traveller. The friendly Filipinos, colourful festivals, superb natural scenery, and frequent travel connections make island hopping addictive.

Thailand – a travel survival kit

Beyond the Buddhist temples and Bangkok bars there is much to see in fascinating Thailand. This extensively researched guide presents an inside look at Thailand's culture, people and language.

Papua New Guinea – a travel survival kit

Papua New Guinea is truly 'the last unknown', the last inhabited place on earth to be explored by Europeans. This guide has the latest information for travellers who want to find just how rewarding a trip to this remote and amazing country can be.

Australia – a travel survival kit

Australia is Lonely Planet's home territory so this guide gives you the complete low-down on Down Under, from the red centre to the coast, from cosmopolitan cities to country towns.

Also Available:
Indonesia phrasebook and Filipino phrasebook

Other Lonely Planet guides to the region

Malaysia, Singapore and Brunei – a travel survival kit
These three nations offer amazing geographic and cultural variety – from hill stations to beaches, from Dyak longhouses to futuristic cities – this is Asia at its most accessible.

The Philippines – a travel survival kit
The 7000 islands of the Philippines are a paradise for the adventurous traveller. The friendly Filipinos, colourful festivals, superb natural scenery, and frequent travel connections make island hopping addictive.

Thailand – a travel survival kit
Beyond the Buddhist temples and Bangkok bars there is much to see in fascinating Thailand. This extensively researched guide presents an inside look at Thailand's culture, people and language.

Papua New Guinea – a travel survival kit
Papua New Guinea is truly 'the last unknown' – the last inhabited place on earth to be explored by Europeans. This guide has the latest information for travellers who want to find just how rewarding a trip to this remote and amazing country can be.

Australia – a travel survival kit
Australia is Lonely Planet's home territory so this guide gives you the complete low-down on Down Under, from the red centre to the coast, from cosmopolitan cities to country towns.

Also Available:
Indonesia phrasebook and *Pilipino phrasebook*

Lonely Planet shoestring guides

South-East Asia on a shoestring
For over 10 years this has been known as the 'yellow bible' to travellers in South-East Asia. It offers detailed travel information on Brunei, Burma, Hong Kong, Indonesia, Macau, Malaysia, Papua New Guinea, the Philippines, Singapore, and Thailand.

North-East Asia on a shoestring
Concise and up-to-date information on six unique states, including one of the largest countries in the world and one of the smallest colonies: China, Hong Kong, Japan, Korea, Macau, Taiwan.

West Asia on a shoestring
A complete guide to the overland trip from Bangladesh to Turkey. Updated information on Bangladesh, Bhutan, India, Iran, Maldives, Nepal, Pakistan, Sri Lanka, Turkey and the Middle East. There's even a section on Afghanistan as it used to be.

South America on a shoestring
This extensively updated edition covers Central and South America from the USA-Mexico border all the way to Tierra del Fuego. There's background information and numerous maps; details on hotels, restaurants, buses, trains, things to do and hassles to avoid.

Africa on a shoestring
From Marrakesh to Kampala, Mozambique to Mauritania, Johannesburg to Cairo – this guidebook gives you all the facts on travelling in Africa. It provides comprehensive information on more than 50 African countries – how to get to them, how to get around, where to stay, where to eat, what to see and what to avoid.

Eastern Europe on a shoestring
With all the facts on beating red tape, and detailed information on the GDR, Poland, Czechoslavakia, Hungary, Romania, Bulgaria, Yugoslavia, Albania and the USSR, this book opens up a whole new world for travellers.

Lonely Planet Guidebooks

Lonely Planet guidebooks cover virtually every accessible part of Asia as well as Australia, the Pacific, Central and South America, Africa, the Middle East and parts of North America. There are four main series: 'travel survival kits', covering a single country for a range of budgets; 'shoestring' guides with compact information for low-budget travel in a major region; trekking guides; and 'phrasebooks'.

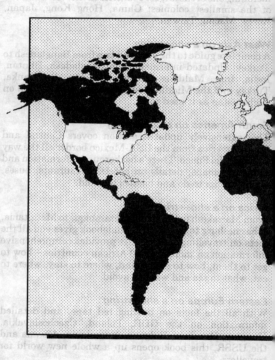

Mail Order

Lonely Planet guidebooks are distributed worldwide and are sold by good bookshops everywhere. They are also available by mail order from Lonely Planet, so if you have difficulty finding a title please write to us. US and Canadian residents should write to Embarcadero West, 112 Linden St, Oakland CA 94607, USA and residents of other countries to PO Box 617, Hawthorn, Victoria 3122, Australia.

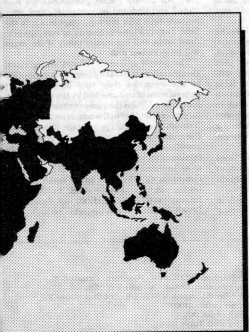

Lonely Planet

Lonely Planet published its first book in 1973. Tony and Maureen Wheeler had made a lengthy overland trip from England to Australia and, in response to numerous 'how do you do it?' questions, Tony wrote and they published *Across Asia on the Cheap*. It became an instant local best-seller and inspired thoughts of a second travel guide. A year and a half in South-East Asia resulted in their second book, *South-East Asia on a Shoestring*, which they put together in a backstreet Chinese hotel in Singapore in 1975. The 'yellow book', as it quickly became known, soon became *the* guide to the region and has gone through five editions, always with its familiar yellow cover.

Soon other writers came to them with ideas for similar books – books that went off the beaten track with an adventurous approach to travel, books that 'assumed you knew how to get your luggage off the carousel,' as one reviewer put it. Lonely Planet grew from a kitchen table operation to a spare room and then to its own office. Its international reputation began to grow as the Lonely Planet logo began to appear in more and more countries. In 1982 *India – a travel survival kit* won the Thomas Cook award for the best guidebook of the year.

These days there are over 70 Lonely Planet titles. Over 40 people work at our office in Melbourne, Australia and another half dozen at our US office in Oakland, California.

At first Lonely Planet specialised in the Asia region but these days we are also developing major ranges of guidebooks to the Pacific region, to South America and to Africa. The list of walking guides is growing and Lonely Planet now has a unique series of phrasebooks to 'unusual' languages. The emphasis continues to be on travel for travellers and Tony and Maureen still manage to fit in a number of trips each year and play a very active part in the writing and updating of Lonely Planet's guides.

Keeping guidebooks up to date is a constant battle which requires an ear to the ground and lots of walking, but technology also plays its part. All Lonely Planet guidebooks are now stored and updated on computer, and some authors even take lap-top computers into the field. Lonely Planet is also using computers to draw maps and eventually many of the maps will be stored on disk.

The people at Lonely Planet strongly feel that travellers can make a positive contribution to the countries they visit both by better appreciation of cultures and by the money they spend. In addition the company tries to make a direct contribution to the countries and regions it covers. Since 1986 a percentage of the income from each book has gone to aid groups and associations. This has included donations to famine relief in Africa, to aid projects in India, to agricultural projects in Central America, to Greenpeace's efforts to halt French nuclear testing in the Pacific and to Amnesty International. In 1989 $41,000 was donated by Lonely Planet to these projects.
